PICKLES TAILS

Also by Brian Crane

Pickles

Pickles, Too

Still Pickled After All These Years

Let's Get Pickled

How Come I Always Get Blamed for the Things I Do?

Oh, Sure! Blame It on the Dog!

Grampa, Will You Tell Me a Story?

PICKLES TAILS

BRIAN CRANE

BAOBAB PRESS

Pickles is syndicated by the Washington Post Writers Group

First Edition

20 21 22   10 9 8 7 6 5 4 3 2 1
ISBN-13: 978-1-936097-25-8
ISBN-10: 1-936097-25-7
Library of Congress Control Number: 2019956444

Layout and Design by
Baobab Press
Reno, Nevada
www.baobabpress.com

Printed and bound in Canada

FOREWORD

Back in the day (and not so very long ago) the only splash of color on our newspapers was confined to the section my dad called the "funny pages." Of course, that was the section I reached for first. Little did I know then that one day I would play a role in syndicating Brian Crane's comic strip *Pickles*. In 1989, I was the sales manager at the *Washington Post* Writers Group, representing some of the best-known editorial page columnists in the country, such as George Will, Ellen Goodman, and David Broder. The syndicate had built a prestigious reputation representing these writers to newspapers around the country. Over the years, the Writers Group had also represented a few comic strips, but the Writers Group wasn't in the business of seeking out new comics. So when Brian Crane's *Pickles* submission came in, it caught our eye. Brian had found a niche that wasn't represented on the comics pages: an older couple, Opal and Earl, navigating their retirement years; their daughter Sylvia; her husband, Dan; and their adorable, curious grandson, Nelson. And their pets . . . Roscoe the dog and Muffin the cat.

When *Pickles* came over the transom at the Writers Group, Brian was working at an advertising agency in Nevada. His wit, gentle humor, and spot-on characterization of the foibles of life in later years combined with crisp, clean art, was refreshingly different. It didn't take long working with Brian to see that he had plenty of ideas for the strip. The relationships between the human characters were nicely crafted, his clean art well- suited to newsprint. Brian was open to suggestions for the strip, and we soon realized that in addition to the people, dopey Roscoe and sneaky Muffin offered even more possibilities for the storyline.

It was a pleasure to help Brian polish *Pickles* and offer it for syndication. The strip was well received when it launched in 1990 and gradually built a solid following. In the fickle world of comics, success is elusive. I don't think Brian or I could have envisioned that thirty years later that Muffin and Roscoe would now be featured in their own compilation or that the strip would continue to resonate with readers, young and old, daily and Sunday. I must admit I've always been more of a "cat person" than a "dog person," although I've enjoyed the company of both over the years. So, enjoy a break from the real world . . . Whether you're a dog person or a cat person, this new collection of *Pickles* will put a smile on your face.

— Jan Harrod
December 2019

DAILIES
(1990-2007)

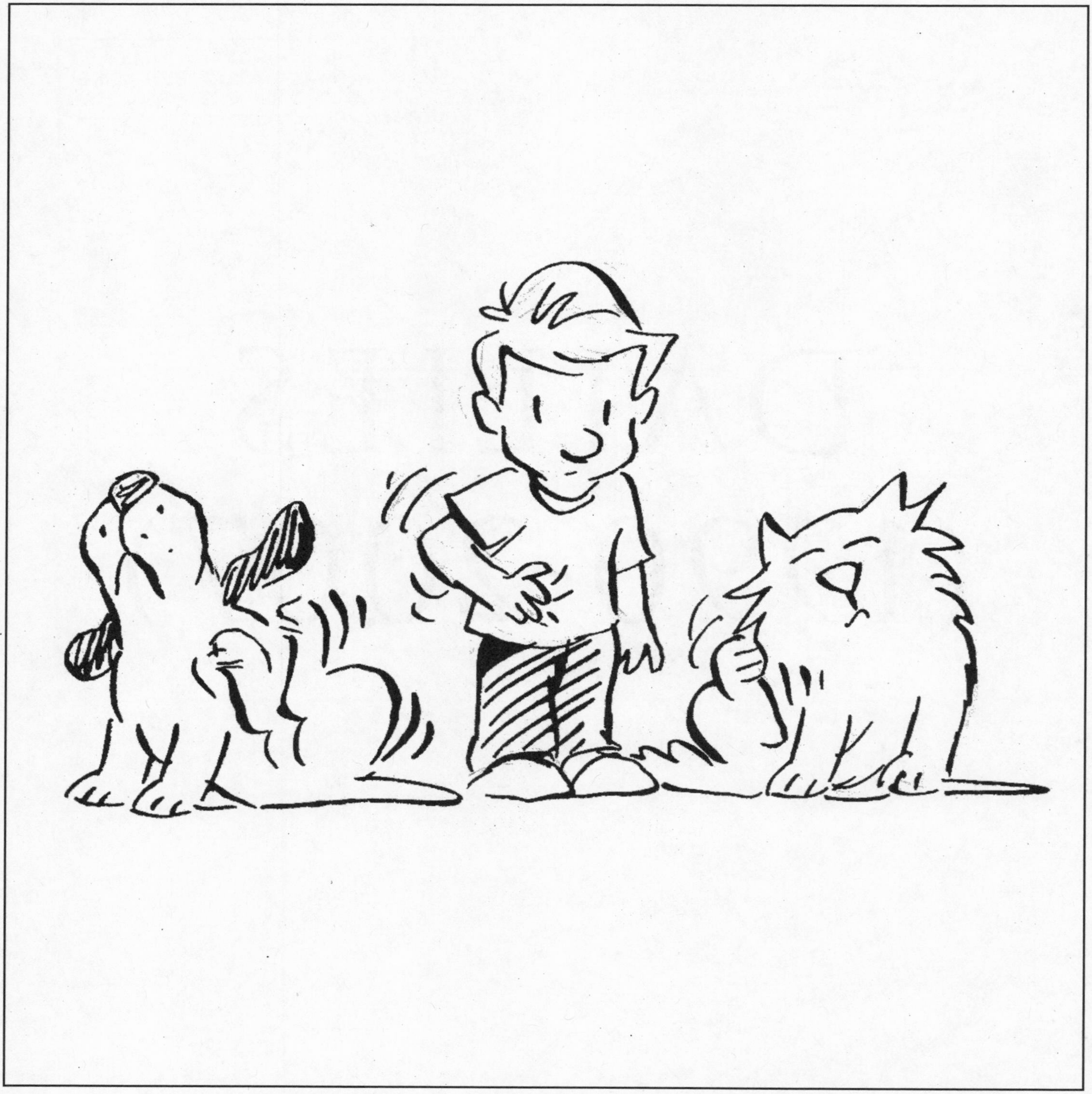

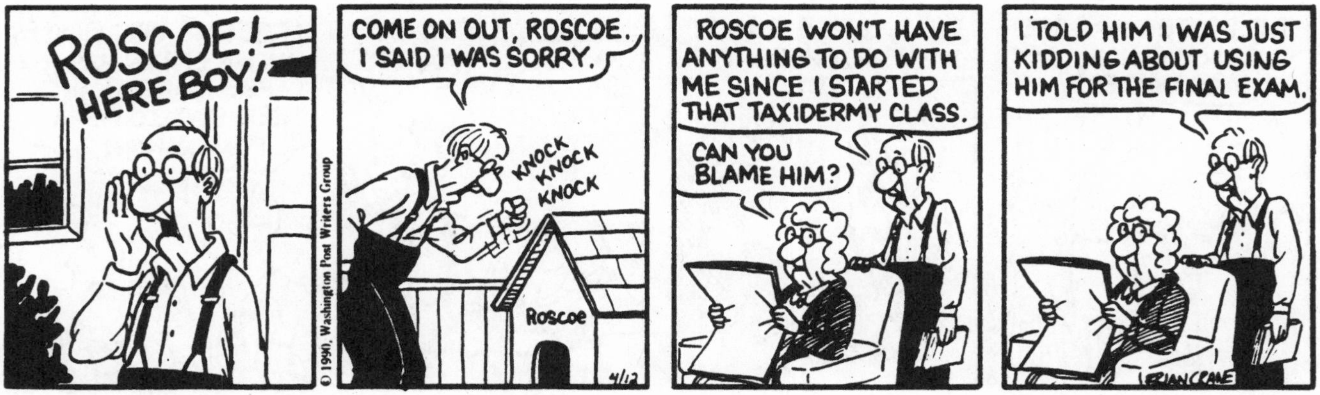
ROSCOE! HERE BOY!
© 1990, Washington Post Writers Group
COME ON OUT, ROSCOE. I SAID I WAS SORRY.
KNOCK KNOCK KNOCK
ROSCOE
ROSCOE WON'T HAVE ANYTHING TO DO WITH ME SINCE I STARTED THAT TAXIDERMY CLASS.
CAN YOU BLAME HIM?
I TOLD HIM I WAS JUST KIDDING ABOUT USING HIM FOR THE FINAL EXAM.
BRIAN CRANE

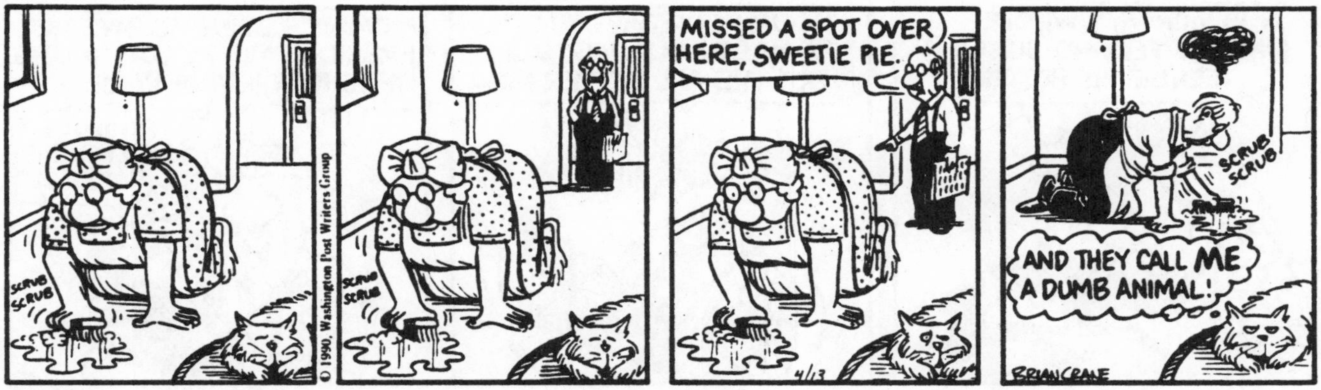
SCRUB SCRUB
© 1990, Washington Post Writers Group
SCRUB SCRUB
MISSED A SPOT OVER HERE, SWEETIE PIE.
SCRUB SCRUB
AND THEY CALL ME A DUMB ANIMAL!
BRIAN CRANE

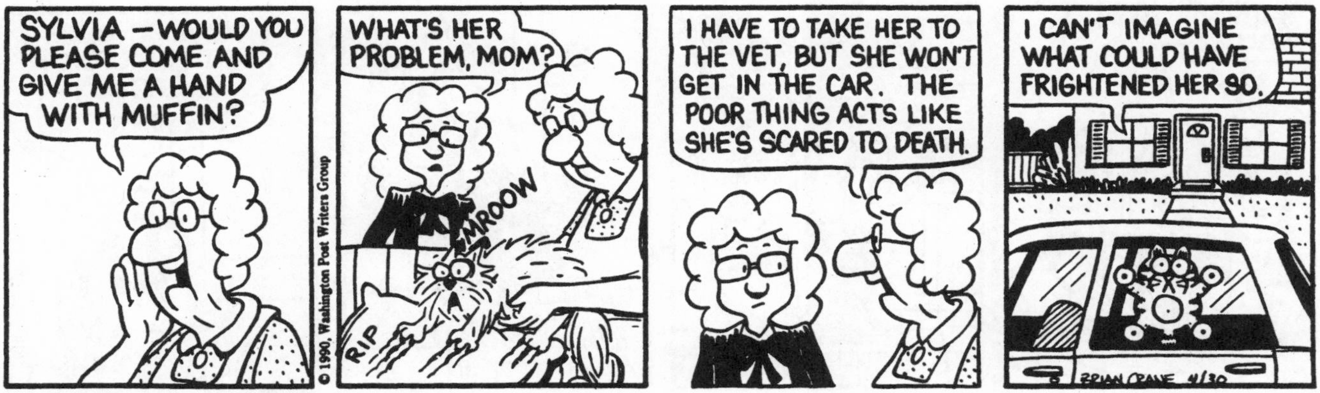
SYLVIA – WOULD YOU PLEASE COME AND GIVE ME A HAND WITH MUFFIN?
© 1990, Washington Post Writers Group
WHAT'S HER PROBLEM, MOM?
MROOW
RIP
I HAVE TO TAKE HER TO THE VET, BUT SHE WON'T GET IN THE CAR. THE POOR THING ACTS LIKE SHE'S SCARED TO DEATH.
I CAN'T IMAGINE WHAT COULD HAVE FRIGHTENED HER SO.
BRIAN CRANE

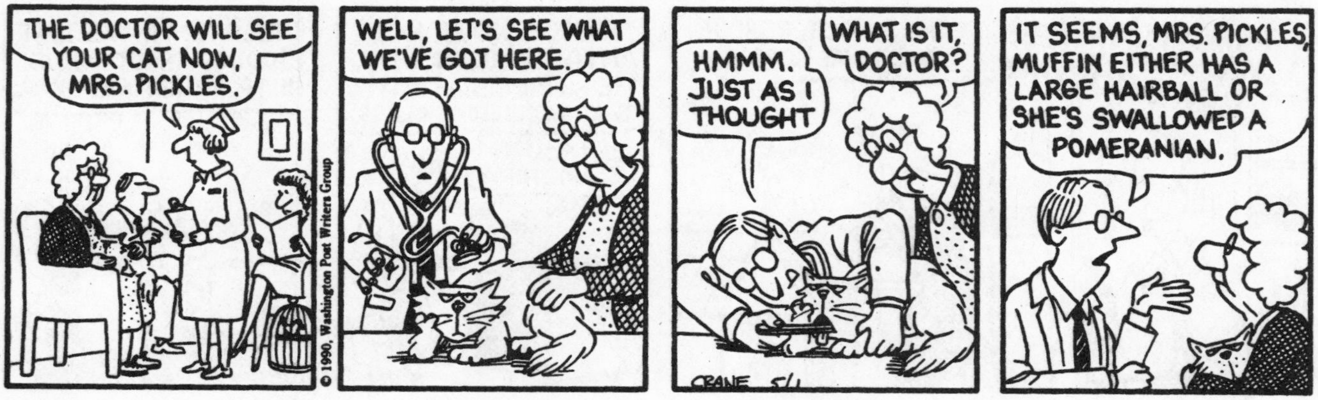
THE DOCTOR WILL SEE YOUR CAT NOW, MRS. PICKLES.
© 1990, Washington Post Writers Group
WELL, LET'S SEE WHAT WE'VE GOT HERE.
HMMM. JUST AS I THOUGHT
WHAT IS IT, DOCTOR?
CRANE 5/1
IT SEEMS, MRS. PICKLES, MUFFIN EITHER HAS A LARGE HAIRBALL OR SHE'S SWALLOWED A POMERANIAN.

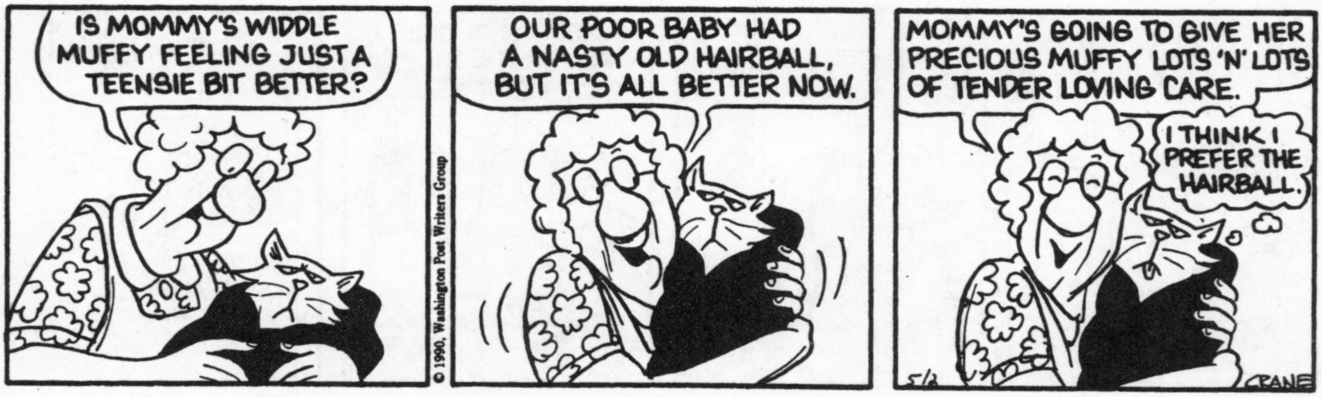
IS MOMMY'S WIDDLE MUFFY FEELING JUST A TEENSIE BIT BETTER?
© 1990, Washington Post Writers Group
OUR POOR BABY HAD A NASTY OLD HAIRBALL, BUT IT'S ALL BETTER NOW.
MOMMY'S GOING TO GIVE HER PRECIOUS MUFFY LOTS 'N' LOTS OF TENDER LOVING CARE.
I THINK I PREFER THE HAIRBALL.
5/2
CRANE

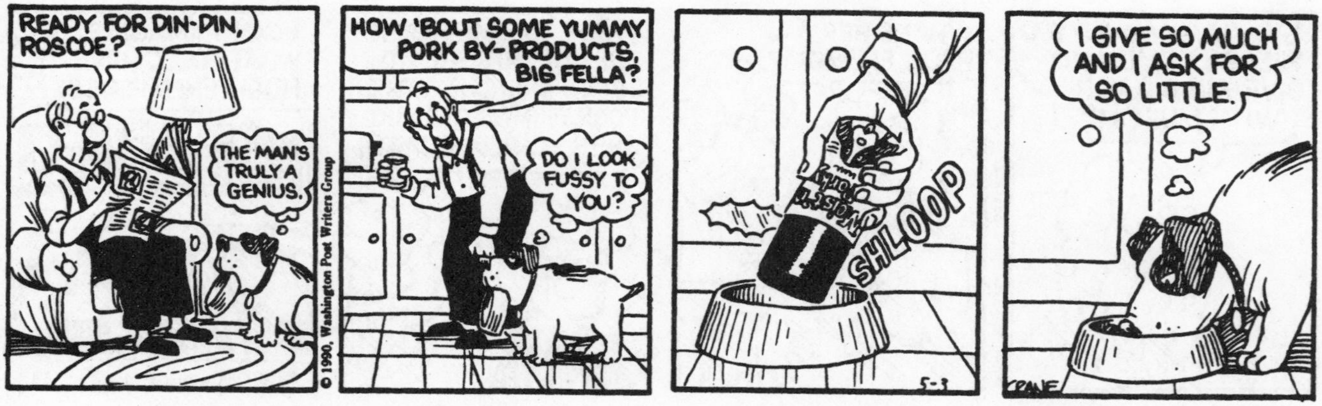
READY FOR DIN-DIN, ROSCOE?
THE MAN'S TRULY A GENIUS.
© 1990, Washington Post Writers Group
HOW 'BOUT SOME YUMMY PORK BY-PRODUCTS, BIG FELLA?
DO I LOOK FUSSY TO YOU?
SHLOOP
5-3
I GIVE SO MUCH AND I ASK FOR SO LITTLE.
CRANE

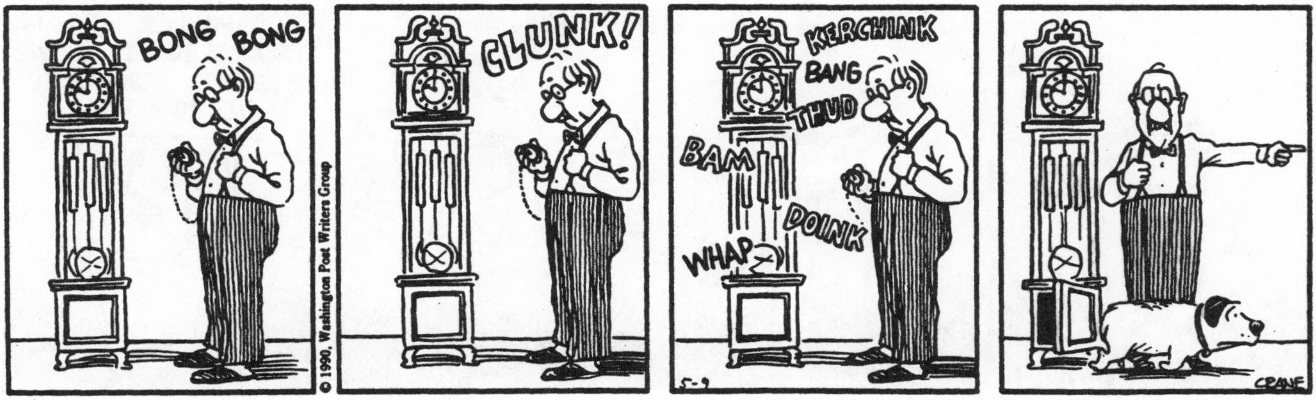
BONG BONG
© 1990, Washington Post Writers Group
CLUNK!
KERCHINK
BANG
THUD
BAM
DOINK
WHAP
5-9
CRANE

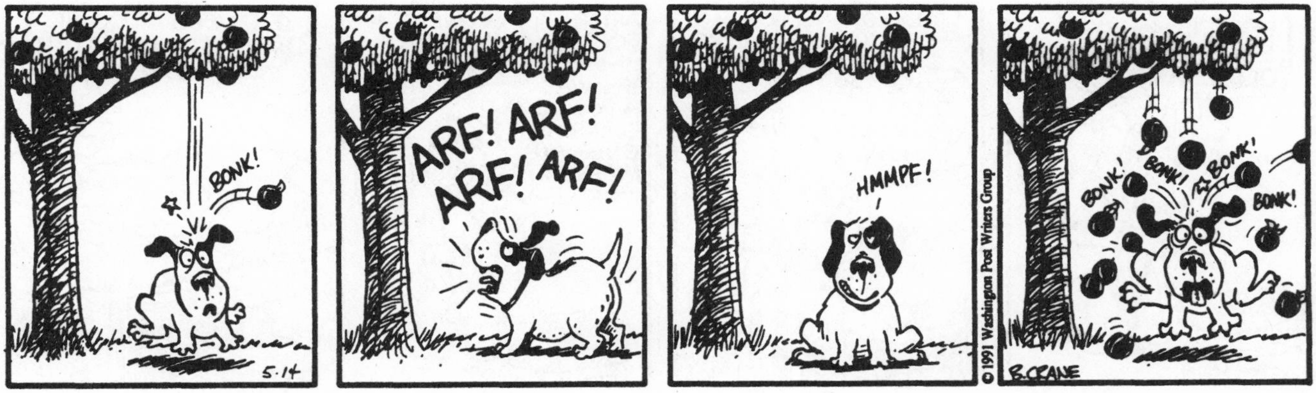
BONK!
5.14
ARF! ARF!
ARF! ARF!
HMMPF!
© 1991 Washington Post Writers Group
BONK!
BONK!
BONK!
BONK!
B. CRANE

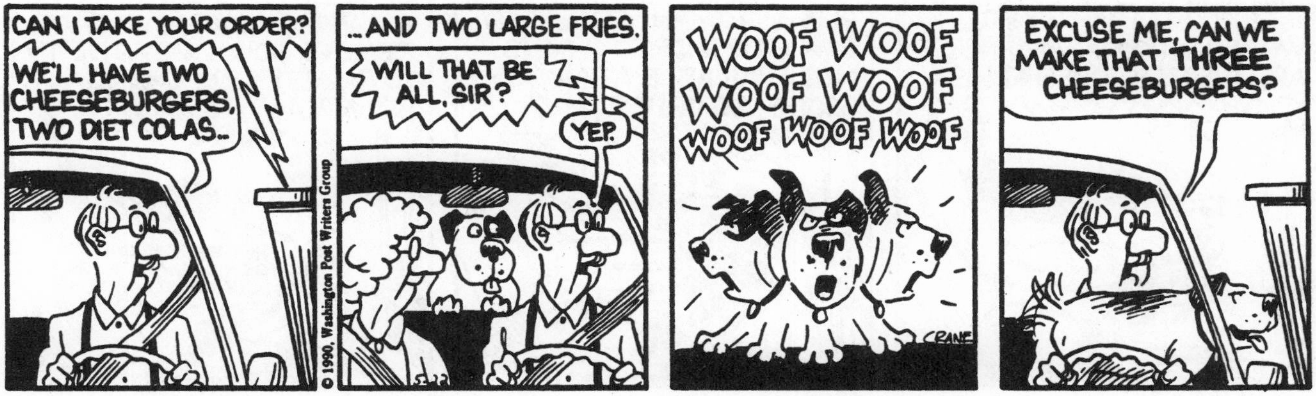
CAN I TAKE YOUR ORDER?
WE'LL HAVE TWO CHEESEBURGERS, TWO DIET COLAS...
© 1990, Washington Post Writers Group
...AND TWO LARGE FRIES.
WILL THAT BE ALL, SIR?
YEP.
WOOF WOOF WOOF WOOF WOOF WOOF WOOF
CRANE
EXCUSE ME, CAN WE MAKE THAT THREE CHEESEBURGERS?

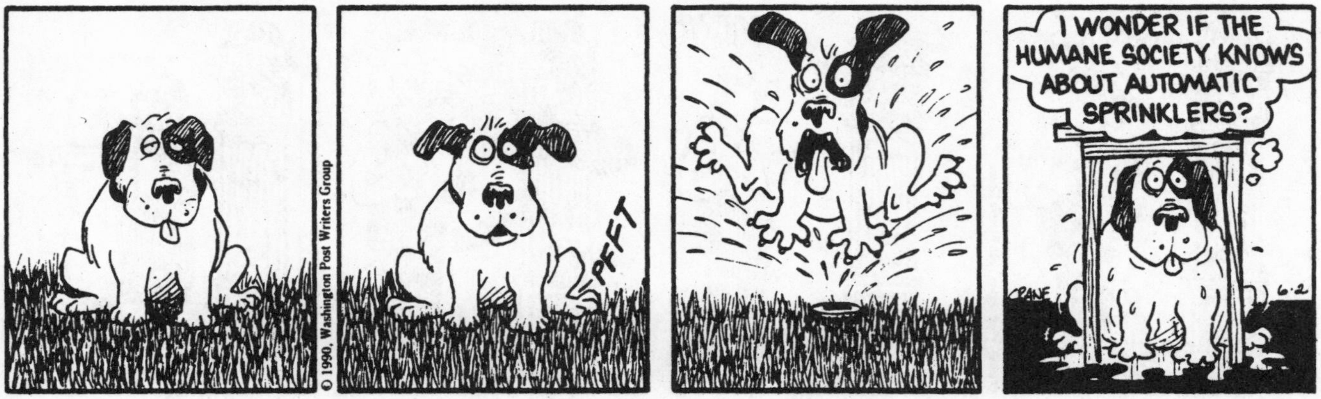
© 1990, Washington Post Writers Group
PFFT
I WONDER IF THE HUMANE SOCIETY KNOWS ABOUT AUTOMATIC SPRINKLERS?
CRANE
6·2

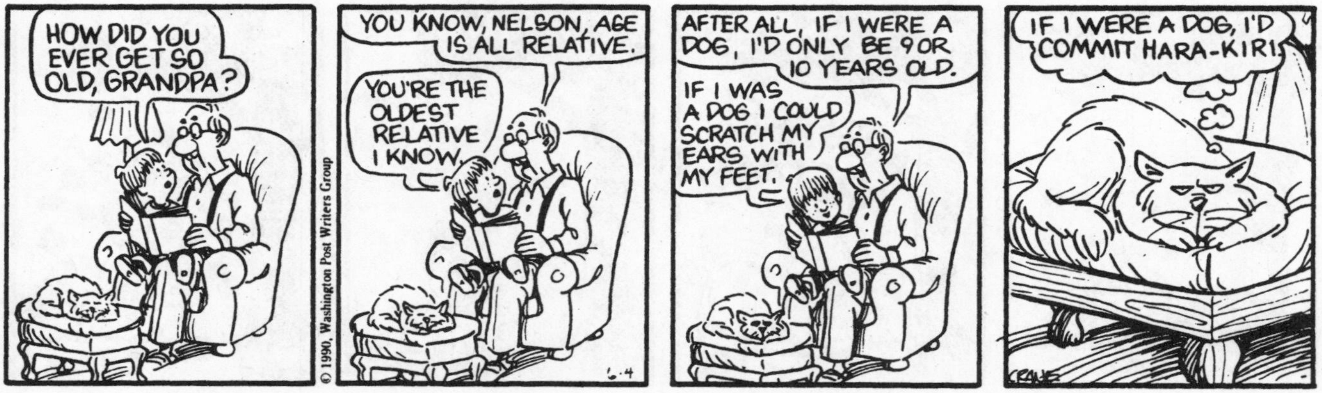
HOW DID YOU EVER GET SO OLD, GRANDPA?
© 1990, Washington Post Writers Group
YOU KNOW, NELSON, AGE IS ALL RELATIVE.
YOU'RE THE OLDEST RELATIVE I KNOW.
6·4
AFTER ALL, IF I WERE A DOG, I'D ONLY BE 9 OR 10 YEARS OLD.
IF I WAS A DOG I COULD SCRATCH MY EARS WITH MY FEET.
IF I WERE A DOG, I'D COMMIT HARA-KIRI.
CRANE

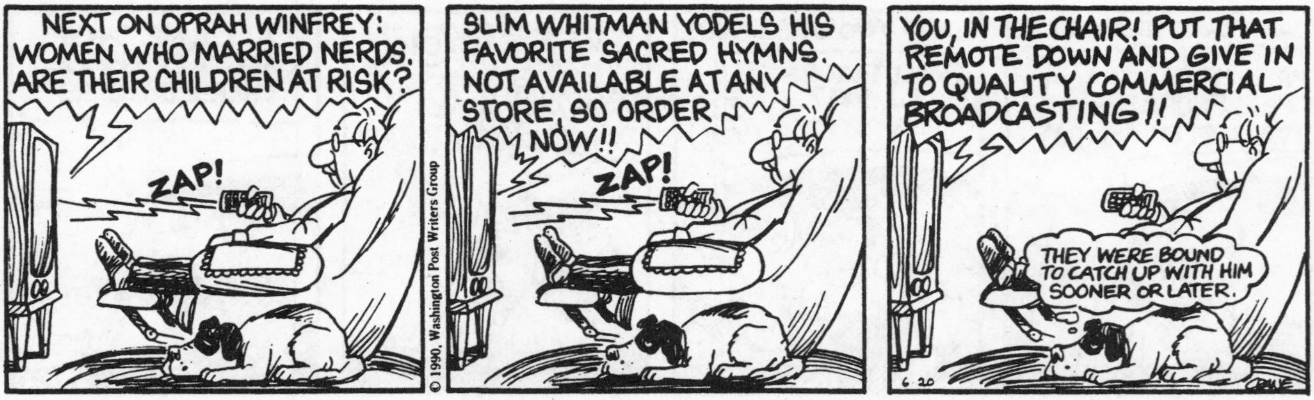
NEXT ON OPRAH WINFREY: WOMEN WHO MARRIED NERDS. ARE THEIR CHILDREN AT RISK?
ZAP!
© 1990, Washington Post Writers Group
SLIM WHITMAN YODELS HIS FAVORITE SACRED HYMNS. NOT AVAILABLE AT ANY STORE, SO ORDER NOW!!
ZAP!
YOU, IN THE CHAIR! PUT THAT REMOTE DOWN AND GIVE IN TO QUALITY COMMERCIAL BROADCASTING!!
THEY WERE BOUND TO CATCH UP WITH HIM SOONER OR LATER.
6·20
CRANE

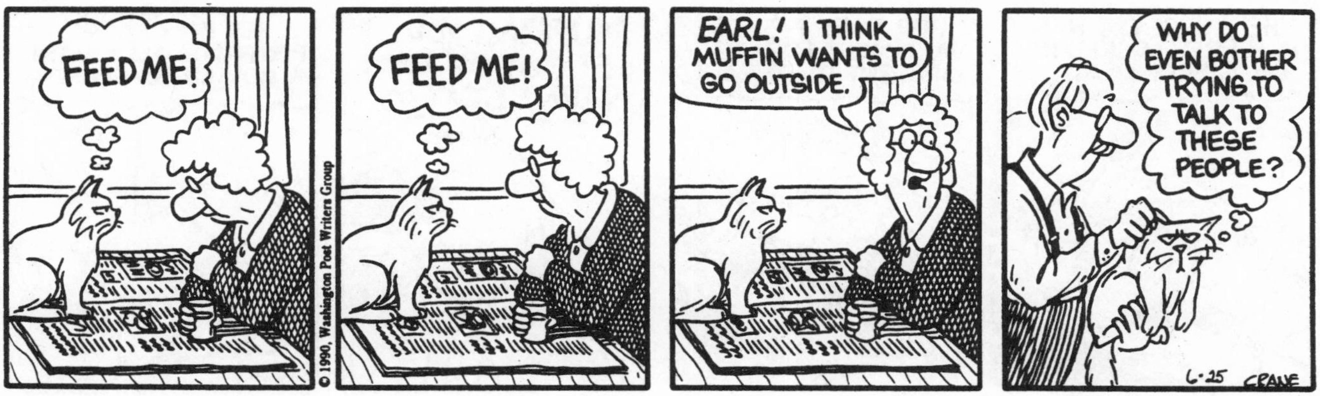
FEED ME!
FEED ME!
EARL! I THINK MUFFIN WANTS TO GO OUTSIDE.
WHY DO I EVEN BOTHER TRYING TO TALK TO THESE PEOPLE?
6-25 CRANE
© 1990, Washington Post Writers Group

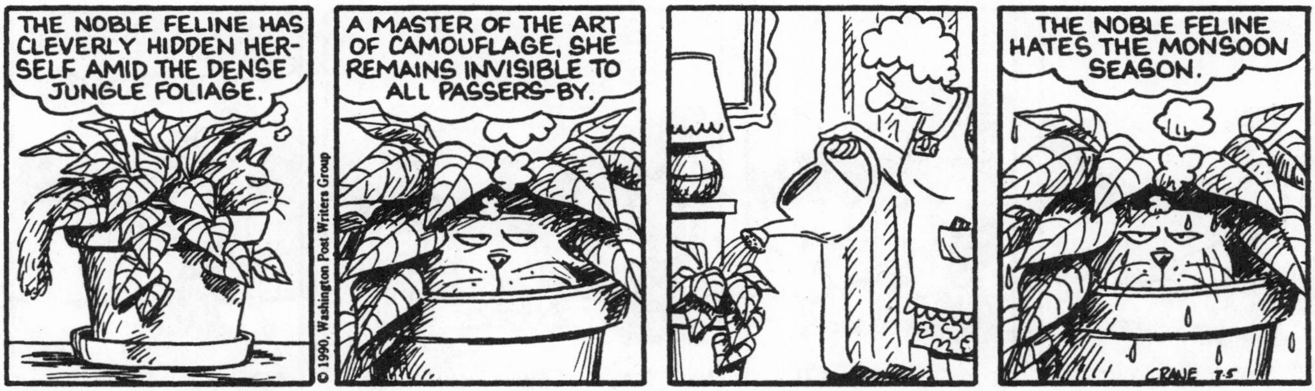
THE NOBLE FELINE HAS CLEVERLY HIDDEN HERSELF AMID THE DENSE JUNGLE FOLIAGE.
A MASTER OF THE ART OF CAMOUFLAGE, SHE REMAINS INVISIBLE TO ALL PASSERS-BY.
THE NOBLE FELINE HATES THE MONSOON SEASON.
CRANE 7-5
© 1990, Washington Post Writers Group

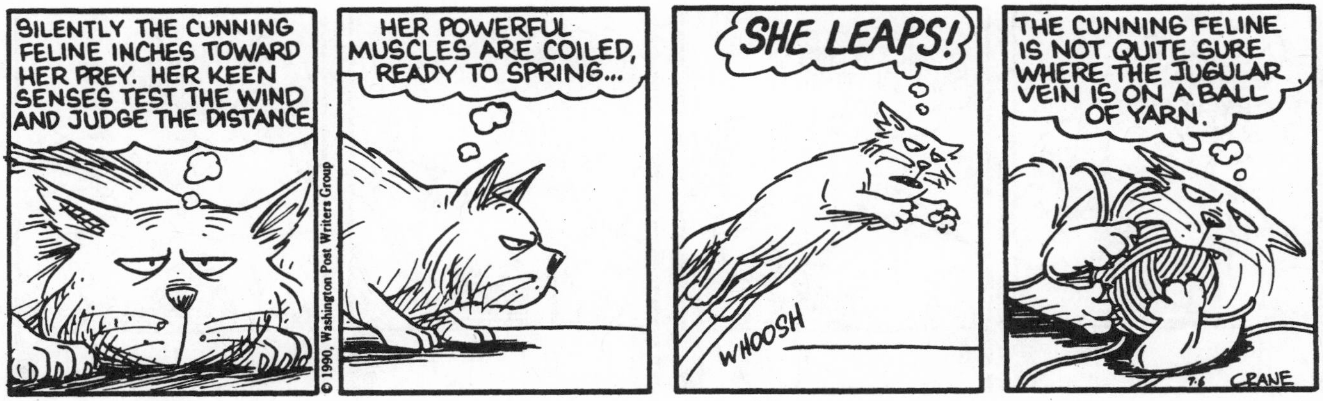
SILENTLY THE CUNNING FELINE INCHES TOWARD HER PREY. HER KEEN SENSES TEST THE WIND AND JUDGE THE DISTANCE.
HER POWERFUL MUSCLES ARE COILED, READY TO SPRING...
SHE LEAPS!
WHOOSH
THE CUNNING FELINE IS NOT QUITE SURE WHERE THE JUGULAR VEIN IS ON A BALL OF YARN.
7-6 CRANE
© 1990, Washington Post Writers Group

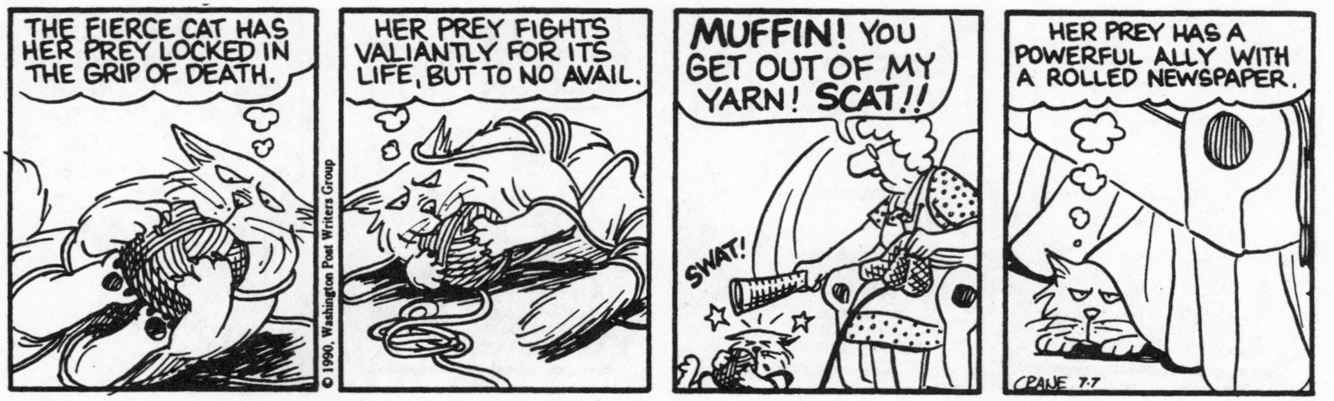
THE FIERCE CAT HAS HER PREY LOCKED IN THE GRIP OF DEATH.
HER PREY FIGHTS VALIANTLY FOR ITS LIFE, BUT TO NO AVAIL.
© 1990, Washington Post Writers Group
MUFFIN! YOU GET OUT OF MY YARN! SCAT!!
SWAT!
HER PREY HAS A POWERFUL ALLY WITH A ROLLED NEWSPAPER.
CRANE 7-7

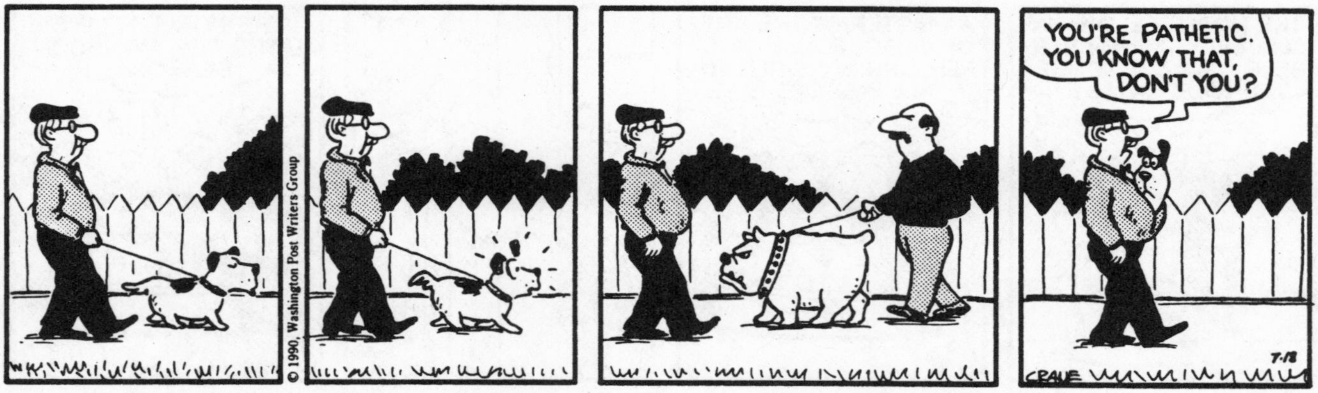
© 1990, Washington Post Writers Group
YOU'RE PATHETIC. YOU KNOW THAT, DON'T YOU?
CRANE 7-13

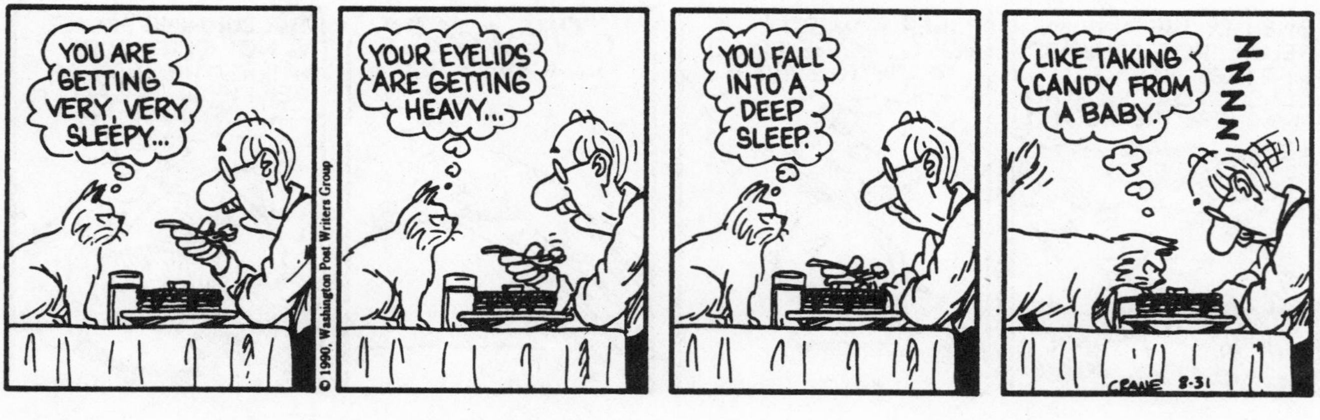
YOU ARE GETTING VERY, VERY SLEEPY...
© 1990, Washington Post Writers Group
YOUR EYELIDS ARE GETTING HEAVY...
YOU FALL INTO A DEEP SLEEP.
LIKE TAKING CANDY FROM A BABY.
ZZZZ
CRANE 8-31

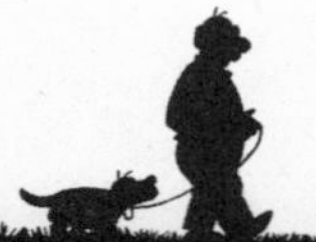

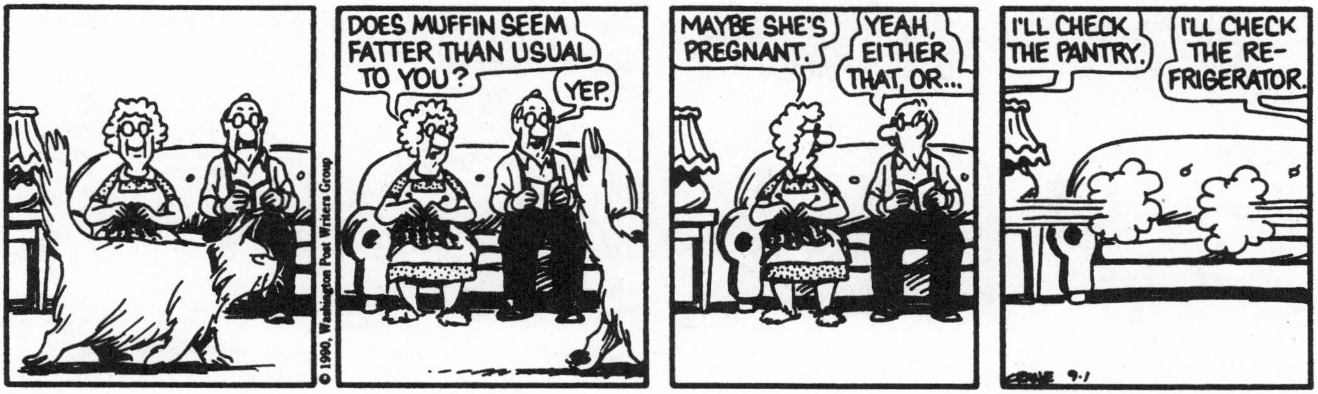
© 1990, Washington Post Writers Group
DOES MUFFIN SEEM FATTER THAN USUAL TO YOU?
YEP.
MAYBE SHE'S PREGNANT.
YEAH, EITHER THAT, OR...
I'LL CHECK THE PANTRY.
I'LL CHECK THE RE-FRIGERATOR.
CRANE 9-1

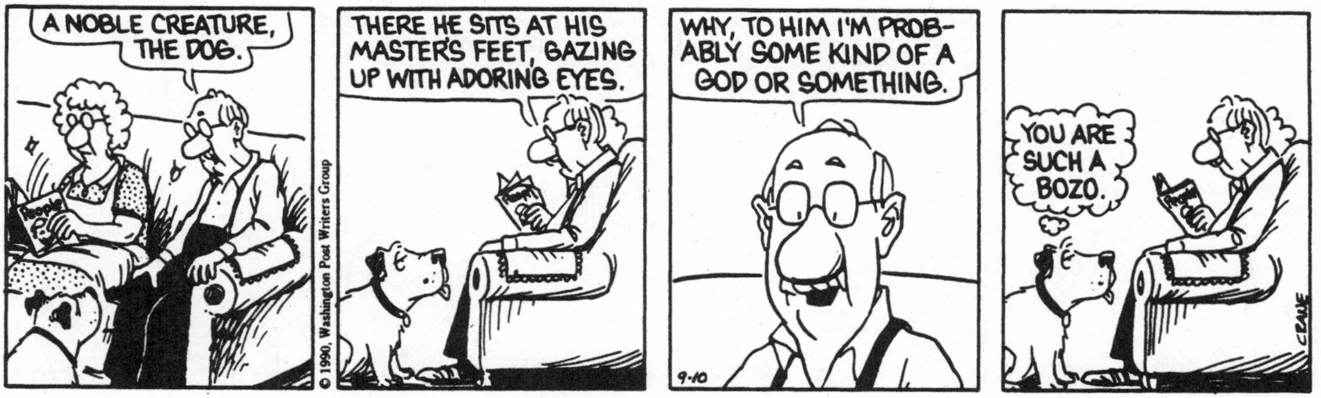
A NOBLE CREATURE, THE DOG.
© 1990, Washington Post Writers Group
THERE HE SITS AT HIS MASTER'S FEET, GAZING UP WITH ADORING EYES.
WHY, TO HIM I'M PROBABLY SOME KIND OF A GOD OR SOMETHING.
9-10
YOU ARE SUCH A BOZO.
CRANE

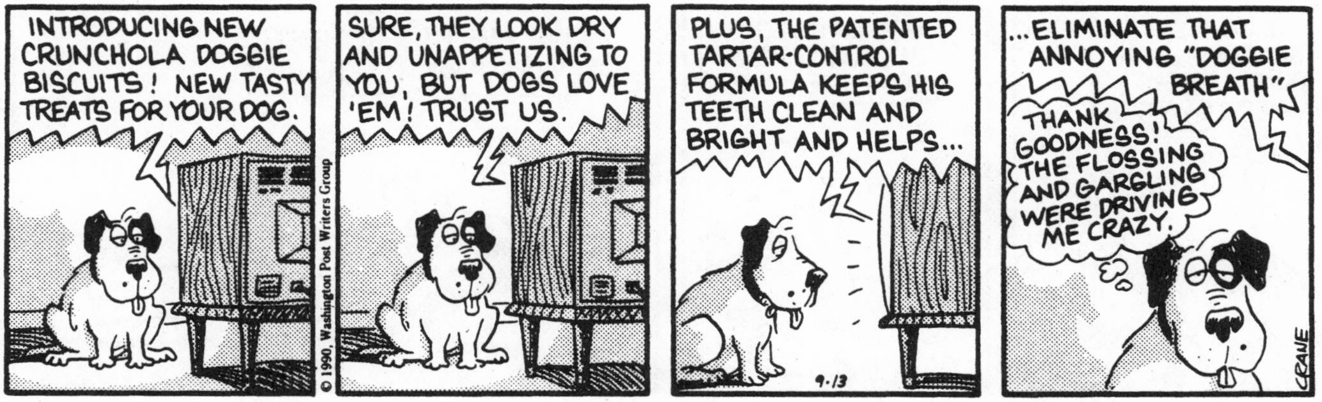
INTRODUCING NEW CRUNCHOLA DOGGIE BISCUITS! NEW TASTY TREATS FOR YOUR DOG.
© 1990, Washington Post Writers Group
SURE, THEY LOOK DRY AND UNAPPETIZING TO YOU, BUT DOGS LOVE 'EM! TRUST US.
PLUS, THE PATENTED TARTAR-CONTROL FORMULA KEEPS HIS TEETH CLEAN AND BRIGHT AND HELPS...
9-13
...ELIMINATE THAT ANNOYING "DOGGIE BREATH"
THANK GOODNESS! THE FLOSSING AND GARGLING WERE DRIVING ME CRAZY.
CRANE

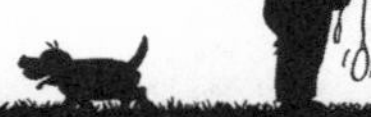

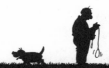

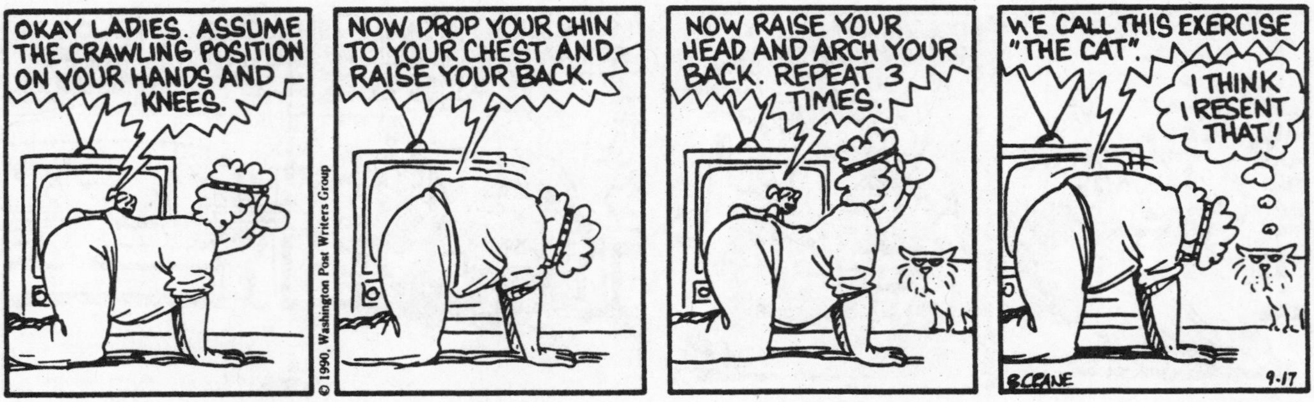
OKAY LADIES. ASSUME THE CRAWLING POSITION ON YOUR HANDS AND KNEES.
© 1990, Washington Post Writers Group
NOW DROP YOUR CHIN TO YOUR CHEST AND RAISE YOUR BACK.
NOW RAISE YOUR HEAD AND ARCH YOUR BACK. REPEAT 3 TIMES.
WE CALL THIS EXERCISE "THE CAT".
I THINK I RESENT THAT!
B. CRANE
9-17

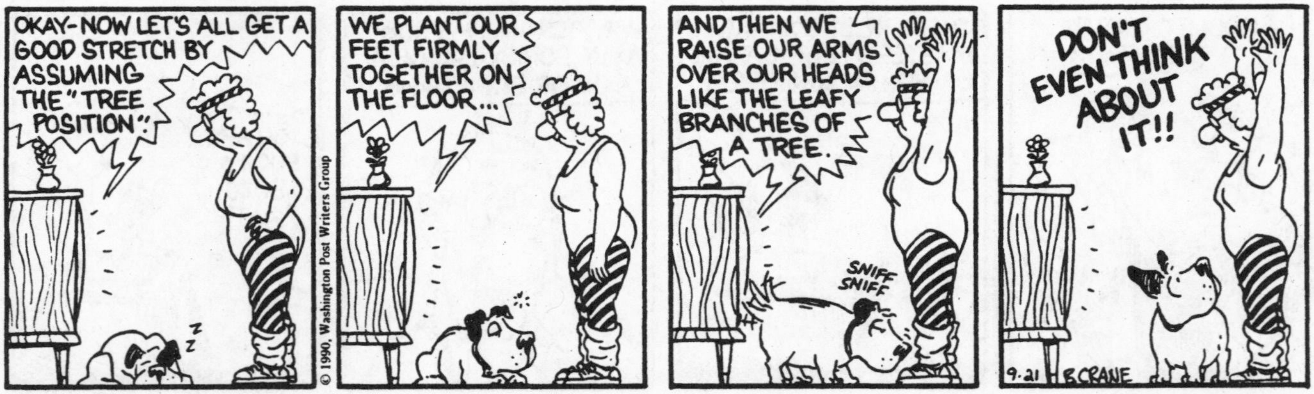
OKAY- NOW LET'S ALL GET A GOOD STRETCH BY ASSUMING THE "TREE POSITION".
Z Z
© 1990, Washington Post Writers Group
WE PLANT OUR FEET FIRMLY TOGETHER ON THE FLOOR...
AND THEN WE RAISE OUR ARMS OVER OUR HEADS LIKE THE LEAFY BRANCHES OF A TREE.
SNIFF SNIFF
DON'T EVEN THINK ABOUT IT!!
9-21
B. CRANE

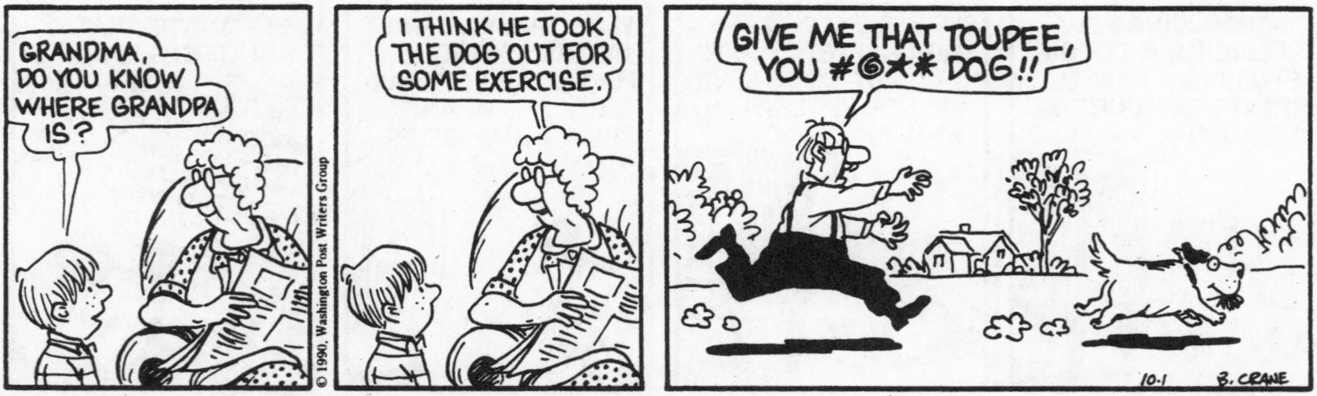
GRANDMA, DO YOU KNOW WHERE GRANDPA IS?
© 1990, Washington Post Writers Group
I THINK HE TOOK THE DOG OUT FOR SOME EXERCISE.
GIVE ME THAT TOUPEE, YOU #@★✱ DOG!!
10-1
B. CRANE

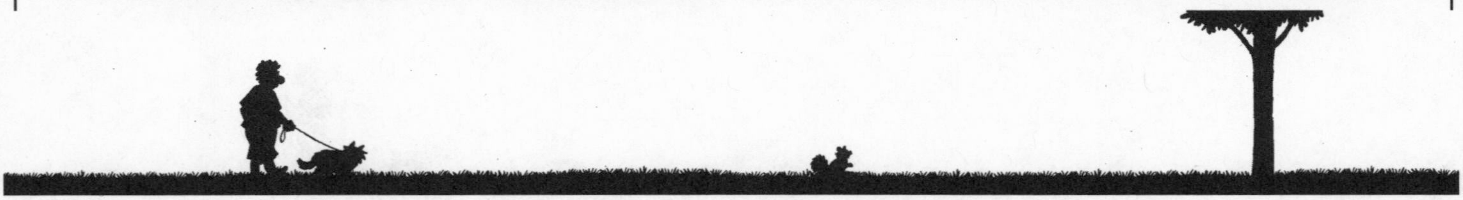

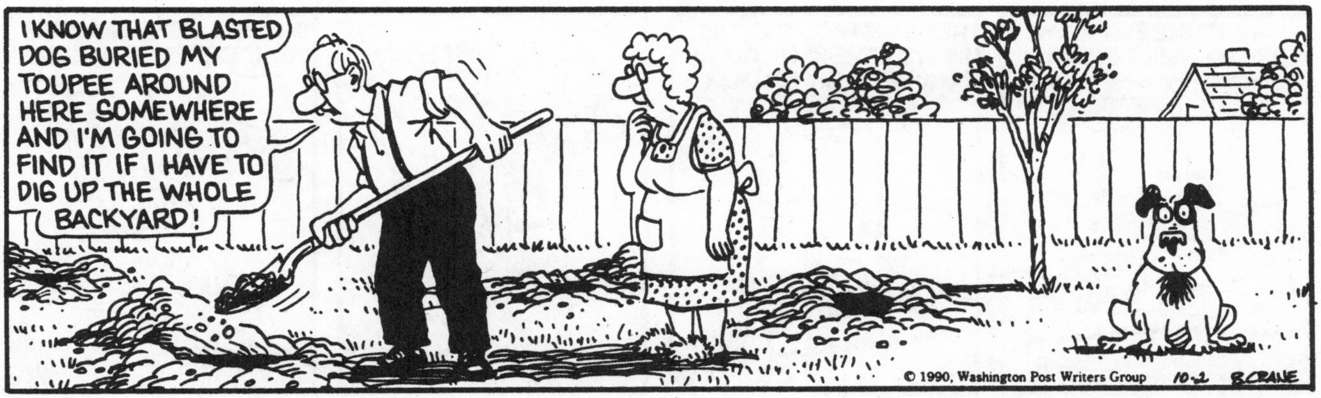
I KNOW THAT BLASTED DOG BURIED MY TOUPEE AROUND HERE SOMEWHERE AND I'M GOING TO FIND IT IF I HAVE TO DIG UP THE WHOLE BACKYARD!
© 1990, Washington Post Writers Group
10-2
B.CRANE

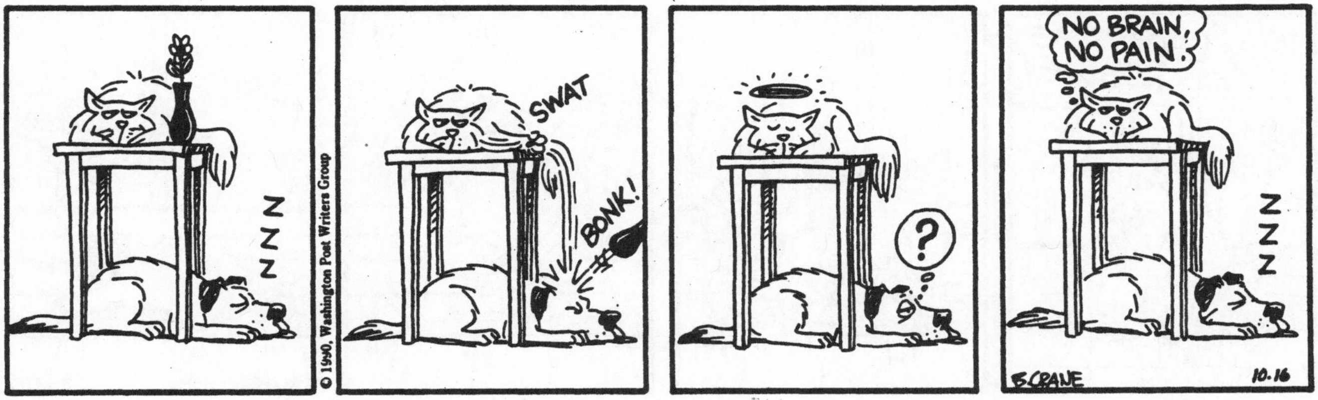
Z Z Z
SWAT
BONK!
?
NO BRAIN, NO PAIN.
Z Z Z
B.CRANE
10.16
© 1990, Washington Post Writers Group

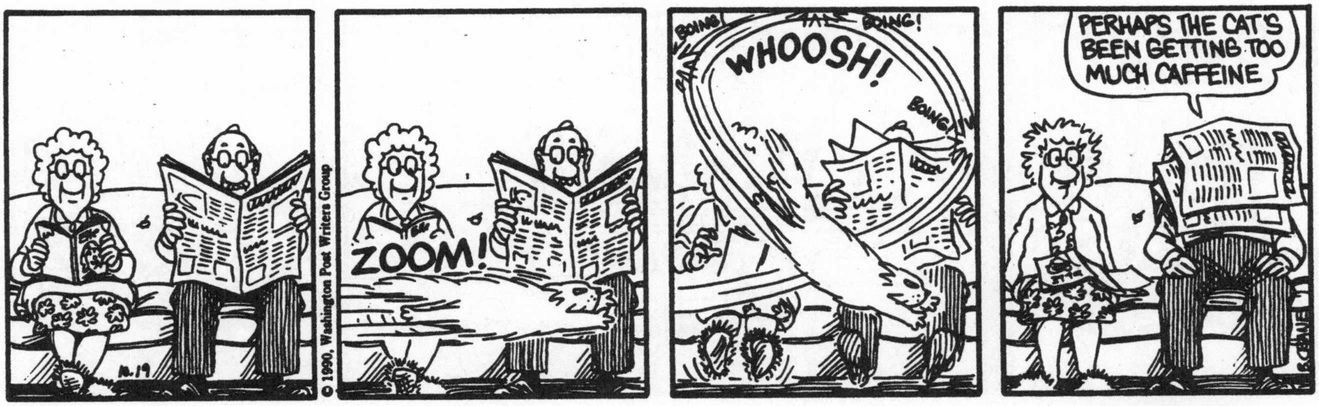
10.19
© 1990, Washington Post Writers Group
ZOOM!
WHOOSH!
BOING!
BOING!
PERHAPS THE CAT'S BEEN GETTING TOO MUCH CAFFEINE
B.CRANE

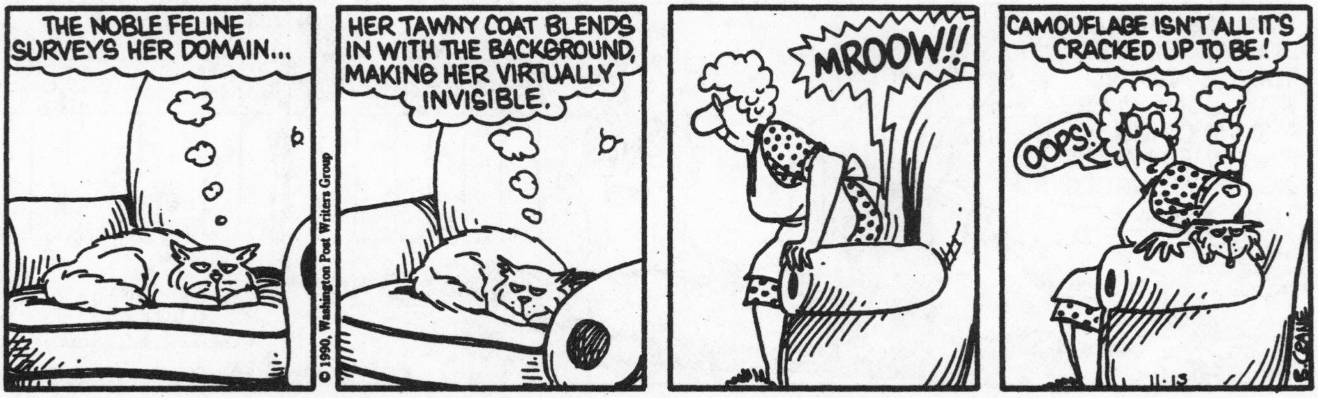
THE NOBLE FELINE SURVEYS HER DOMAIN...
HER TAWNY COAT BLENDS IN WITH THE BACKGROUND, MAKING HER VIRTUALLY INVISIBLE.
© 1990, Washington Post Writers Group
MROOW!!
CAMOUFLAGE ISN'T ALL IT'S CRACKED UP TO BE!
OOPS!
11-15
B. CRANE

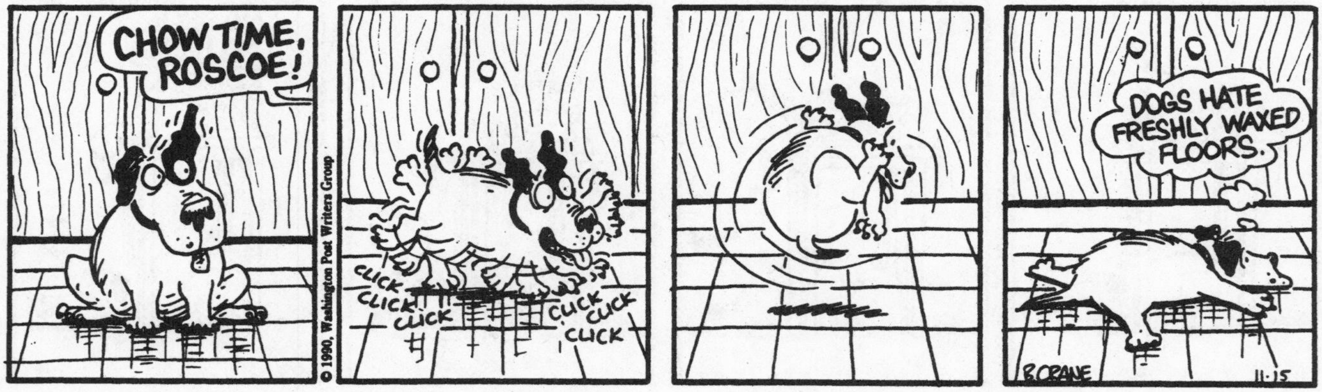
CHOW TIME, ROSCOE!
© 1990, Washington Post Writers Group
CLICK CLICK CLICK CLICK CLICK CLICK
DOGS HATE FRESHLY WAXED FLOORS.
B. CRANE
11-15

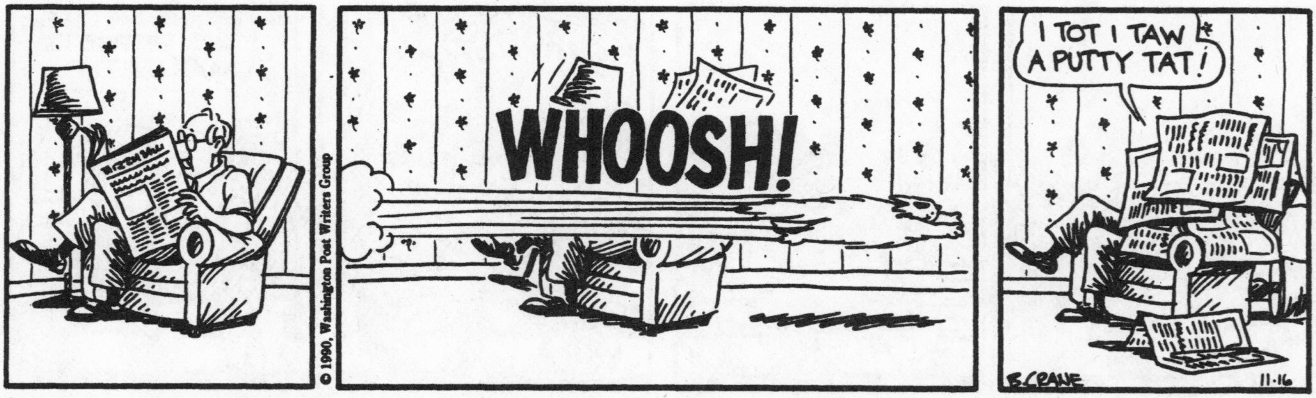
© 1990, Washington Post Writers Group
WHOOSH!
I TOT I TAW A PUTTY TAT!
B. CRANE
11-16

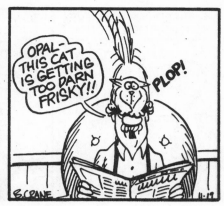

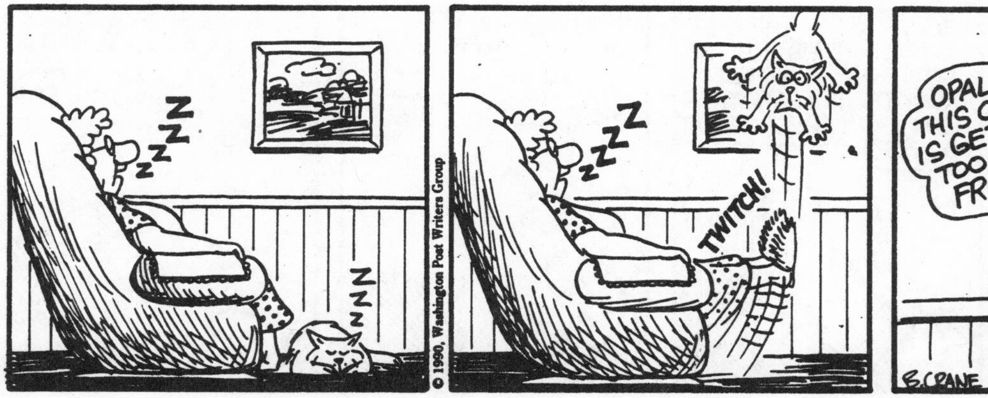
Z Z Z
Z Z Z
© 1990, Washington Post Writers Group
Z Z Z
TWITCH!
OPAL-
THIS CAT
IS GETTING
TOO DARN
FRISKY!!
PLOP!
B.CRANE
11-19

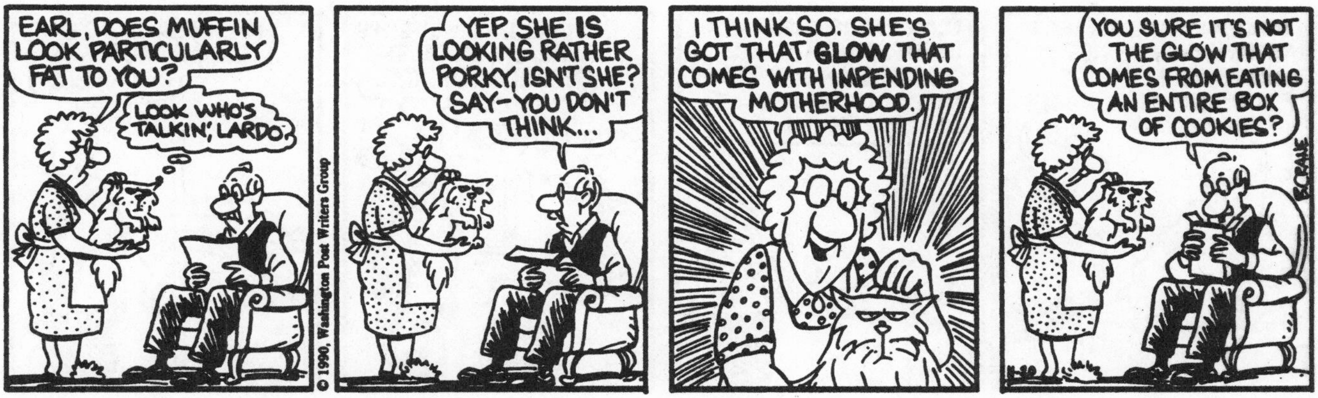
EARL, DOES MUFFIN LOOK PARTICULARLY FAT TO YOU?
LOOK WHO'S TALKIN', LARDO.
© 1990, Washington Post Writers Group
YEP. SHE IS LOOKING RATHER PORKY, ISN'T SHE? SAY- YOU DON'T THINK....
I THINK SO. SHE'S GOT THAT GLOW THAT COMES WITH IMPENDING MOTHERHOOD.
YOU SURE IT'S NOT THE GLOW THAT COMES FROM EATING AN ENTIRE BOX OF COOKIES?
B.CRANE
11-20

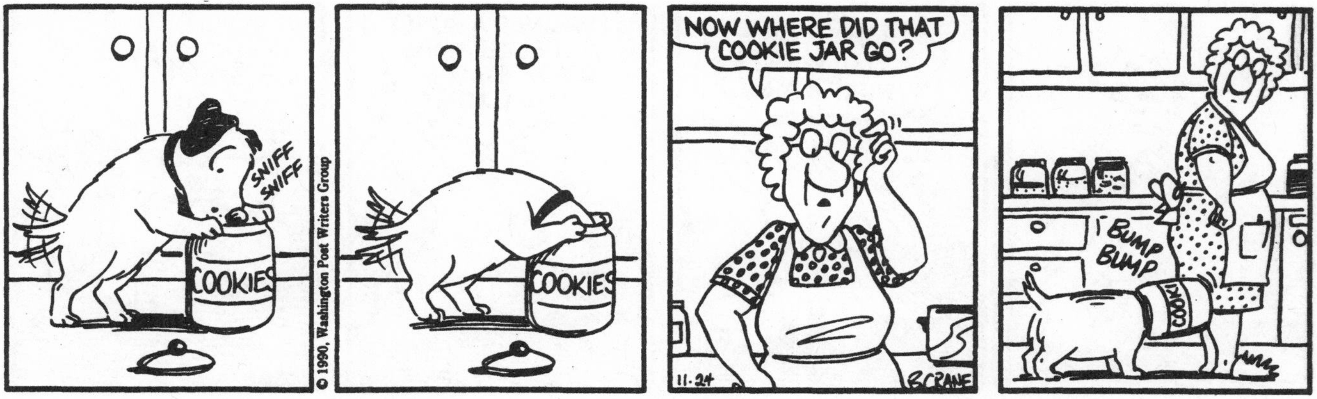
SNIFF SNIFF
COOKIES
© 1990, Washington Post Writers Group
COOKIES
NOW WHERE DID THAT COOKIE JAR GO?
11-24
B.CRANE
BUMP BUMP

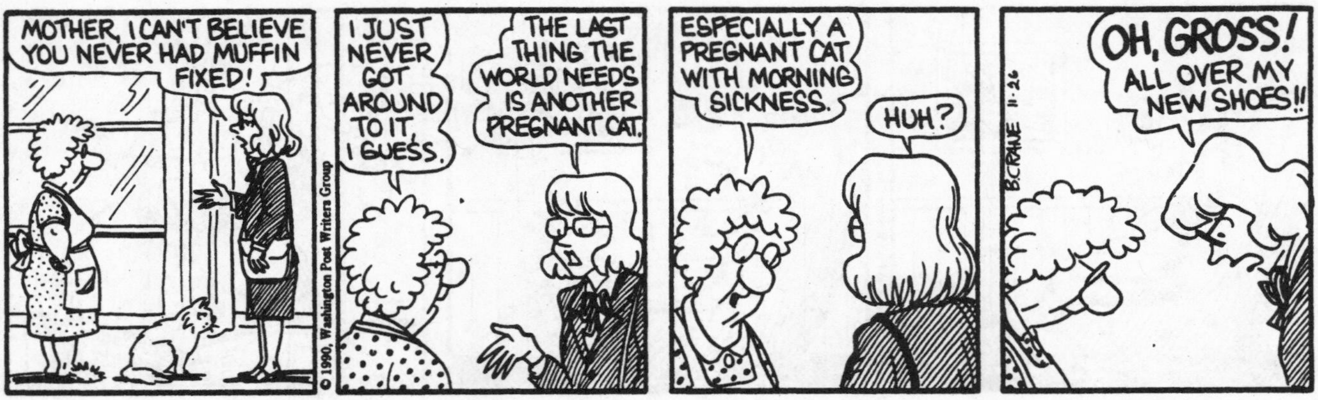
MOTHER, I CAN'T BELIEVE YOU NEVER HAD MUFFIN FIXED!
I JUST NEVER GOT AROUND TO IT, I GUESS.
THE LAST THING THE WORLD NEEDS IS ANOTHER PREGNANT CAT.
ESPECIALLY A PREGNANT CAT WITH MORNING SICKNESS.
HUH?
OH, GROSS! ALL OVER MY NEW SHOES!!
© 1990, Washington Post Writers Group
B.CRANE 11-26

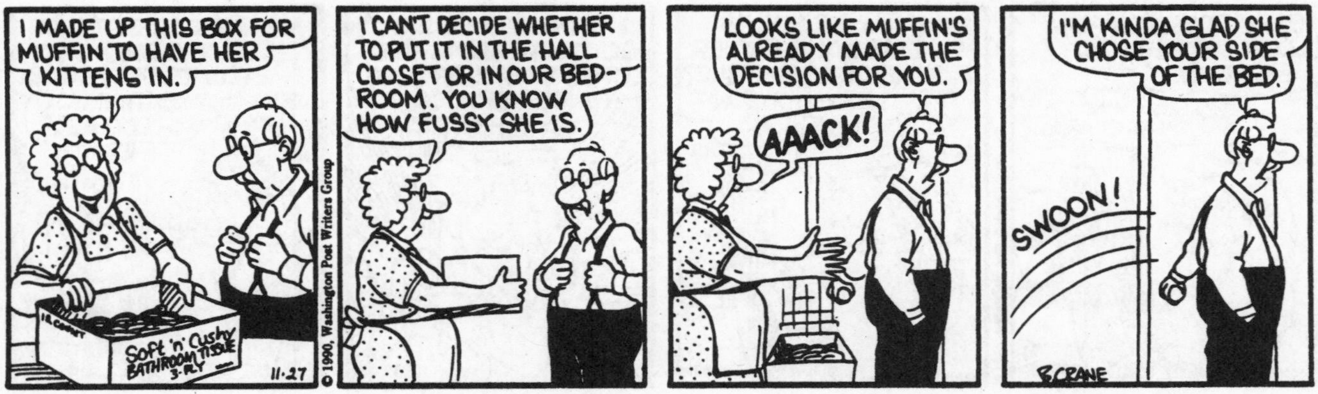
I MADE UP THIS BOX FOR MUFFIN TO HAVE HER KITTENS IN.
Soft 'n' Cushy BATHROOM TISSUE 3-PLY
11-27
I CAN'T DECIDE WHETHER TO PUT IT IN THE HALL CLOSET OR IN OUR BED-ROOM. YOU KNOW HOW FUSSY SHE IS.
LOOKS LIKE MUFFIN'S ALREADY MADE THE DECISION FOR YOU.
AAACK!
I'M KINDA GLAD SHE CHOSE YOUR SIDE OF THE BED.
SWOON!
© 1990, Washington Post Writers Group
B.CRANE

16

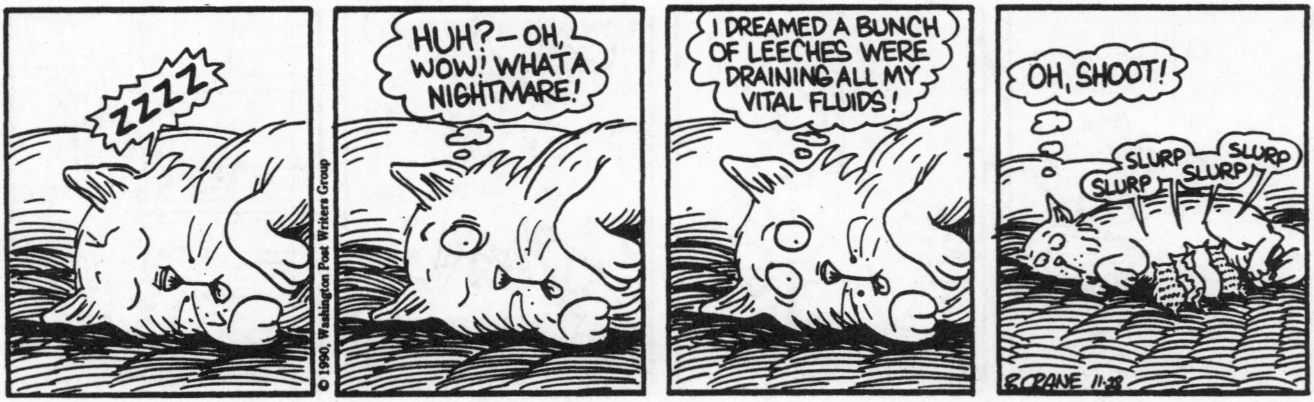
ZZZZ
HUH?—OH, WOW! WHATA NIGHTMARE!
I DREAMED A BUNCH OF LEECHES WERE DRAINING ALL MY VITAL FLUIDS!
OH, SHOOT!
SLURP
SLURP
SLURP
SLURP
© 1990, Washington Post Writers Group
B.CRANE 11-28

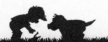

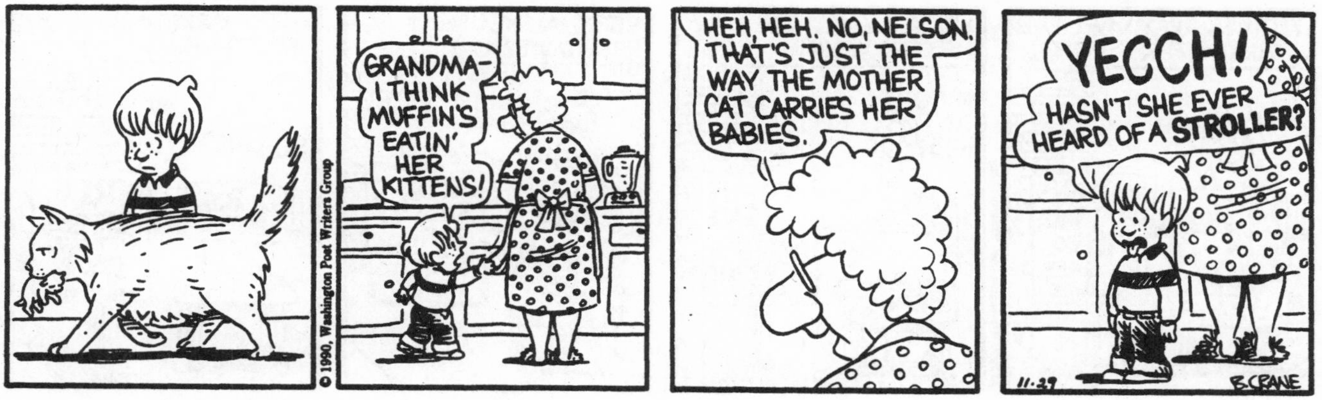
GRANDMA- I THINK MUFFIN'S EATIN' HER KITTENS!
© 1990, Washington Post Writers Group
HEH, HEH. NO, NELSON. THAT'S JUST THE WAY THE MOTHER CAT CARRIES HER BABIES.
YECCH!
HASN'T SHE EVER HEARD OF A STROLLER?
11-29
B.CRANE

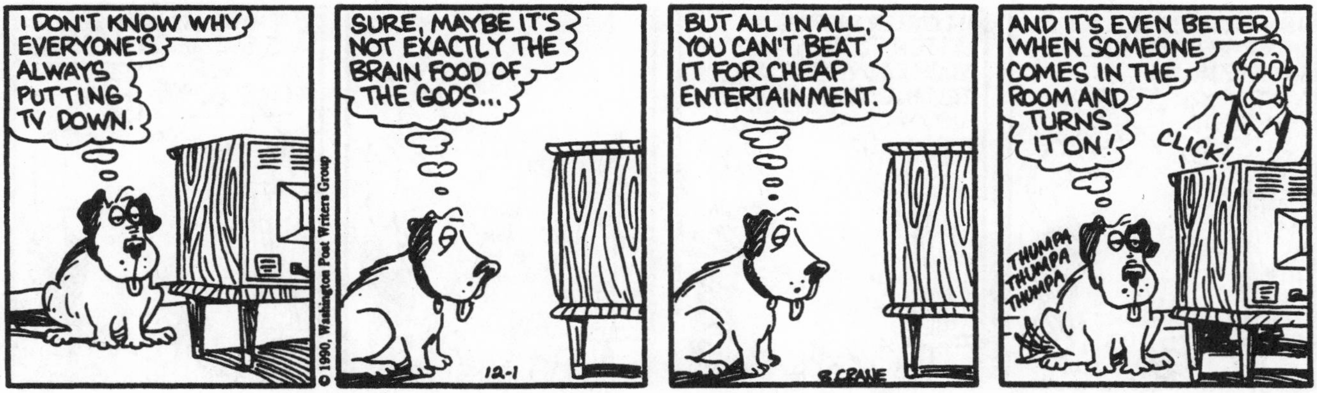
I DON'T KNOW WHY EVERYONE'S ALWAYS PUTTING TV DOWN.
© 1990, Washington Post Writers Group
SURE, MAYBE IT'S NOT EXACTLY THE BRAIN FOOD OF THE GODS...
12-1
BUT ALL IN ALL, YOU CAN'T BEAT IT FOR CHEAP ENTERTAINMENT.
B.CRANE
AND IT'S EVEN BETTER WHEN SOMEONE COMES IN THE ROOM AND TURNS IT ON!
CLICK!
THUMPA THUMPA THUMPA

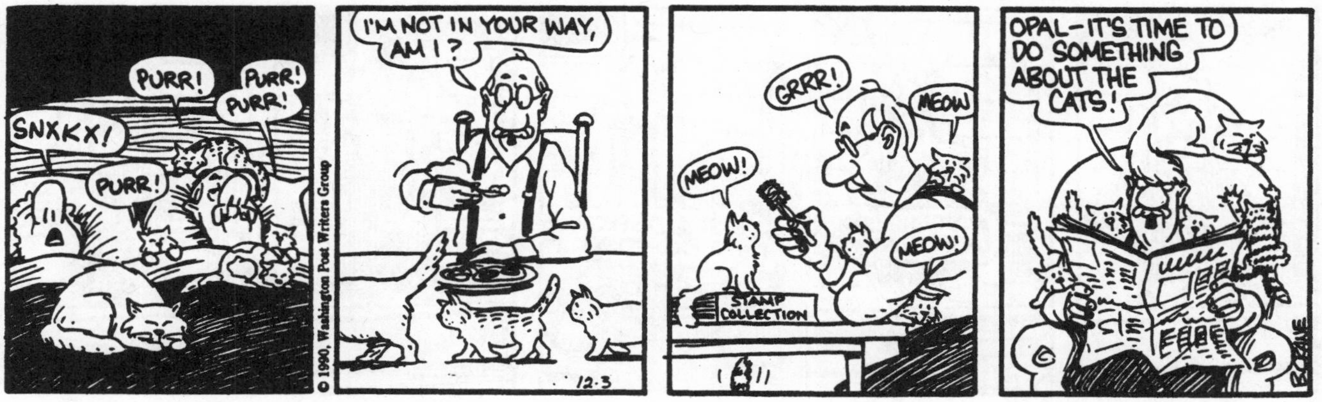
PURR!
PURR! PURR!
SNXKX!
PURR!
© 1990, Washington Post Writers Group
I'M NOT IN YOUR WAY, AM I?
12-3
GRRR!
MEOW
MEOW!
MEOW!
STAMP COLLECTION
OPAL- IT'S TIME TO DO SOMETHING ABOUT THE CATS!
B.CRANE

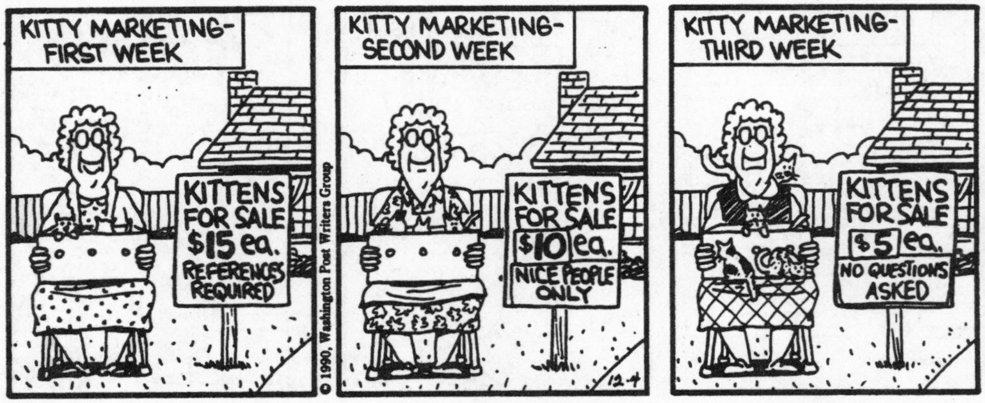
KITTY MARKETING- FIRST WEEK
KITTENS FOR SALE $15 ea. REFERENCES REQUIRED
© 1990, Washington Post Writers Group
KITTY MARKETING- SECOND WEEK
KITTENS FOR SALE $10 ea. NICE PEOPLE ONLY
12-4
KITTY MARKETING- THIRD WEEK
KITTENS FOR SALE $5 ea. NO QUESTIONS ASKED
KITTY MARKETING- FOURTH WEEK
INQUIRE WITHIN
FREE KITTENS SIX MONTH SUPPLY OF CAT FOOD INCLUDED
B. CRANE

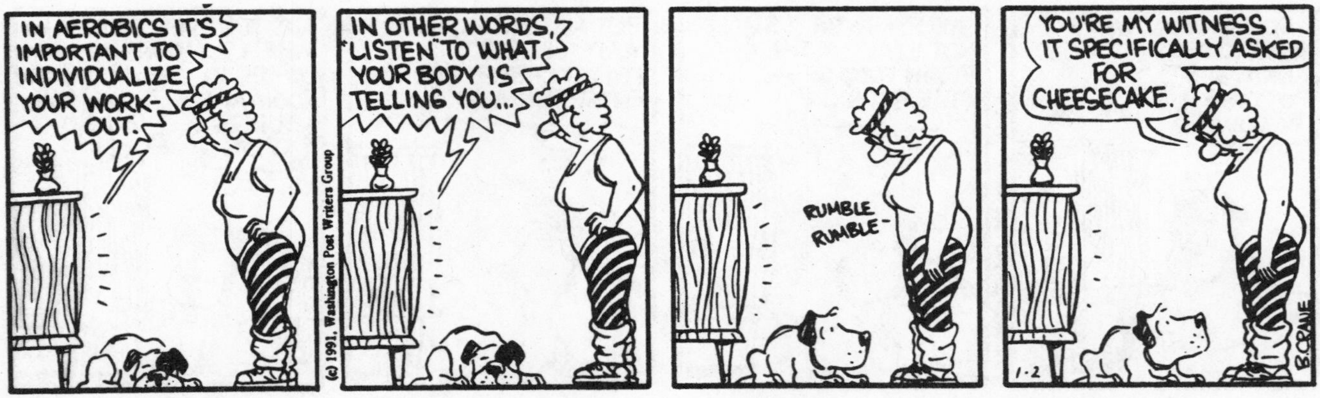
IN AEROBICS IT'S IMPORTANT TO INDIVIDUALIZE YOUR WORK-OUT.
(c) 1991, Washington Post Writers Group
IN OTHER WORDS, "LISTEN" TO WHAT YOUR BODY IS TELLING YOU...
RUMBLE RUMBLE
1-2
YOU'RE MY WITNESS. IT SPECIFICALLY ASKED FOR CHEESECAKE.
B. CRANE

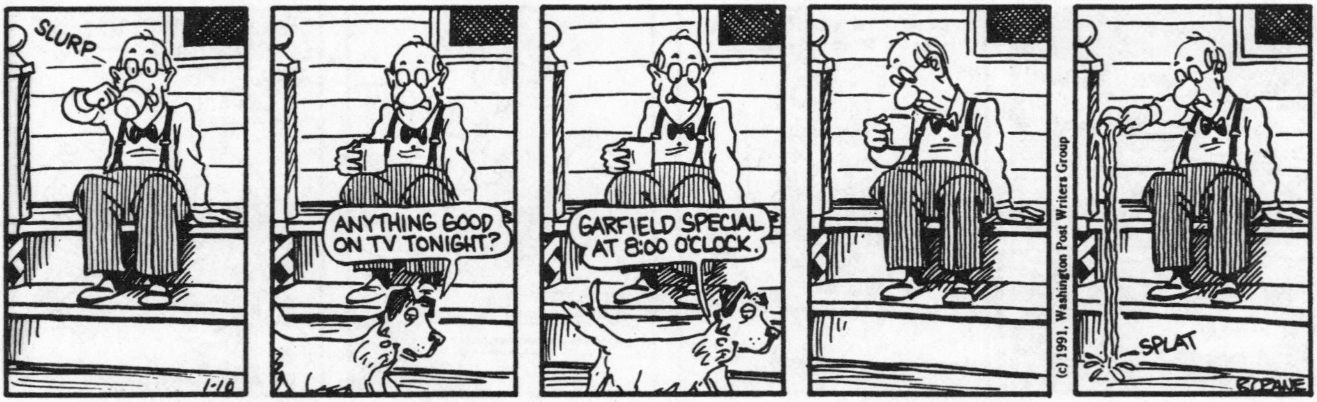
SLURP
1-10
ANYTHING GOOD ON TV TONIGHT?
GARFIELD SPECIAL AT 8:00 O'CLOCK.
(c) 1991, Washington Post Writers Group
SPLAT
B. CRANE

18

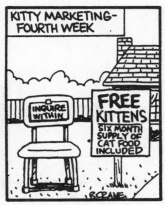

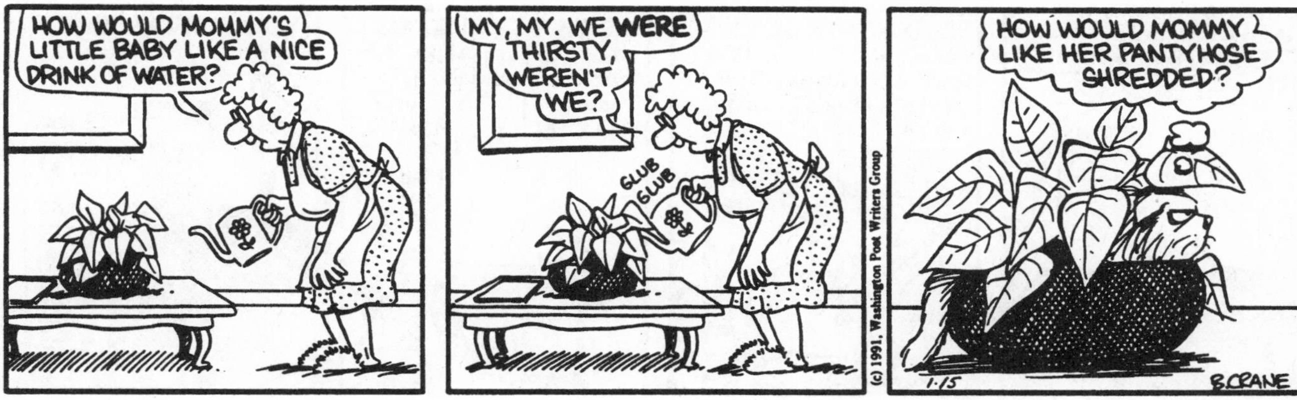
HOW WOULD MOMMY'S LITTLE BABY LIKE A NICE DRINK OF WATER?
MY, MY. WE WERE THIRSTY, WEREN'T WE?
GLUB GLUB
(c) 1991, Washington Post Writers Group
HOW WOULD MOMMY LIKE HER PANTYHOSE SHREDDED?
1·15
B.CRANE

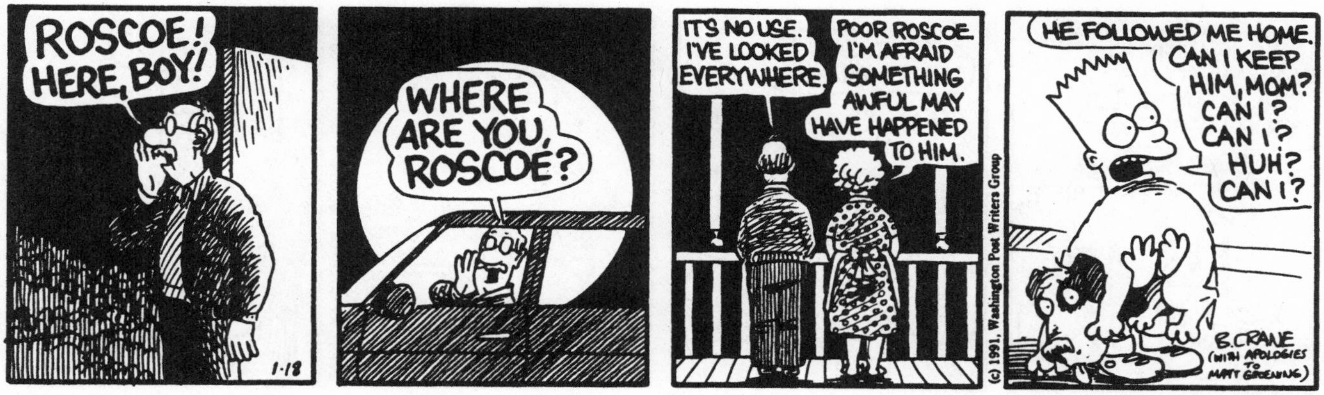
ROSCOE! HERE, BOY!
1·18
WHERE ARE YOU, ROSCOE?
IT'S NO USE. I'VE LOOKED EVERYWHERE.
POOR ROSCOE. I'M AFRAID SOMETHING AWFUL MAY HAVE HAPPENED TO HIM.
(c) 1991, Washington Post Writers Group
HE FOLLOWED ME HOME. CAN I KEEP HIM, MOM? CAN I? CAN I? HUH? CAN I?
B.CRANE
(WITH APOLOGIES TO MATT GROENING)

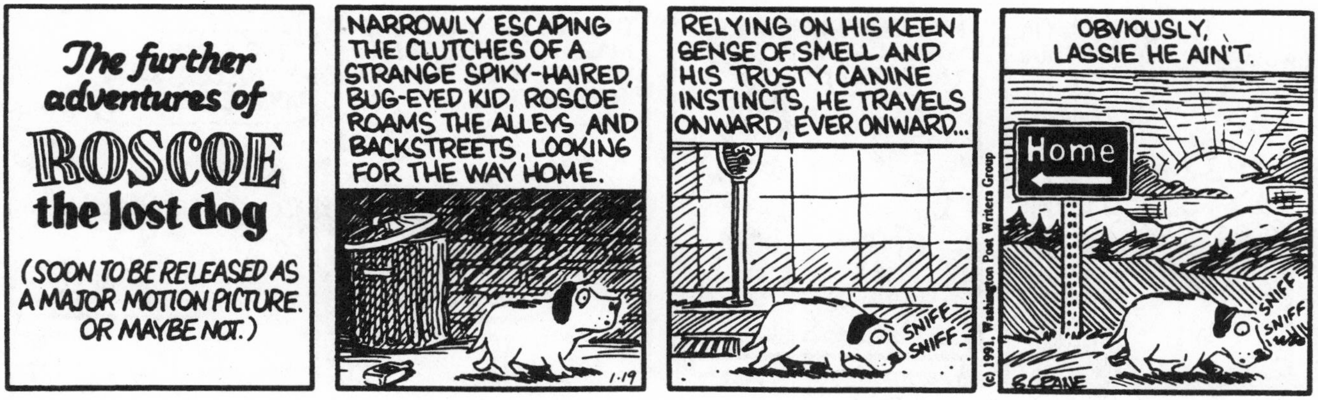
The further adventures of
ROSCOE
the lost dog
(SOON TO BE RELEASED AS A MAJOR MOTION PICTURE. OR MAYBE NOT.)
NARROWLY ESCAPING THE CLUTCHES OF A STRANGE SPIKY-HAIRED, BUG-EYED KID, ROSCOE ROAMS THE ALLEYS AND BACKSTREETS, LOOKING FOR THE WAY HOME.
1·19
RELYING ON HIS KEEN SENSE OF SMELL AND HIS TRUSTY CANINE INSTINCTS, HE TRAVELS ONWARD, EVER ONWARD...
SNIFF SNIFF
(c) 1991, Washington Post Writers Group
OBVIOUSLY, LASSIE HE AIN'T.
Home
SNIFF SNIFF
B.CRANE

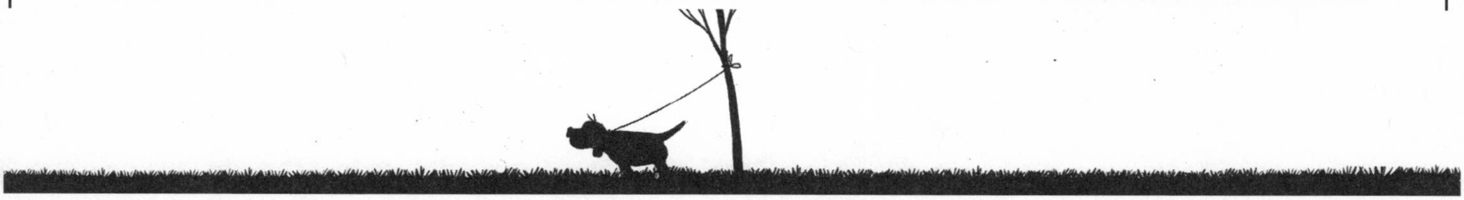

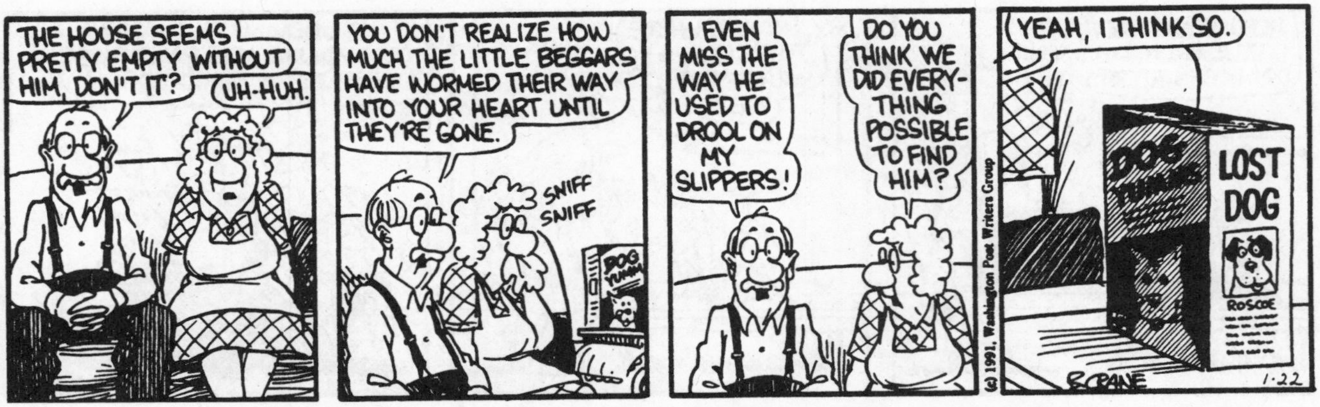
THE HOUSE SEEMS PRETTY EMPTY WITHOUT HIM, DON'T IT?
UH-HUH.
YOU DON'T REALIZE HOW MUCH THE LITTLE BEGGARS HAVE WORMED THEIR WAY INTO YOUR HEART UNTIL THEY'RE GONE.
SNIFF SNIFF
I EVEN MISS THE WAY HE USED TO DROOL ON MY SLIPPERS!
DO YOU THINK WE DID EVERY-THING POSSIBLE TO FIND HIM?
(c) 1991, Washington Post Writers Group
YEAH, I THINK SO.
LOST DOG
ROSCOE
B.CRANE
1-22

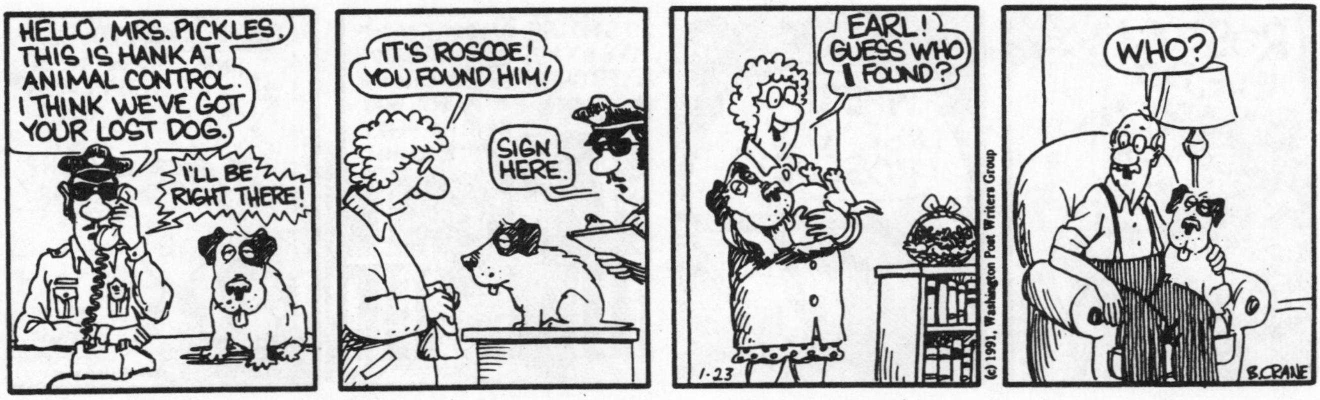
HELLO, MRS. PICKLES. THIS IS HANK AT ANIMAL CONTROL. I THINK WE'VE GOT YOUR LOST DOG.
I'LL BE RIGHT THERE!
IT'S ROSCOE! YOU FOUND HIM!
SIGN HERE.
EARL! GUESS WHO I FOUND?
1-23
(c) 1991, Washington Post Writers Group
WHO?
B.CRANE

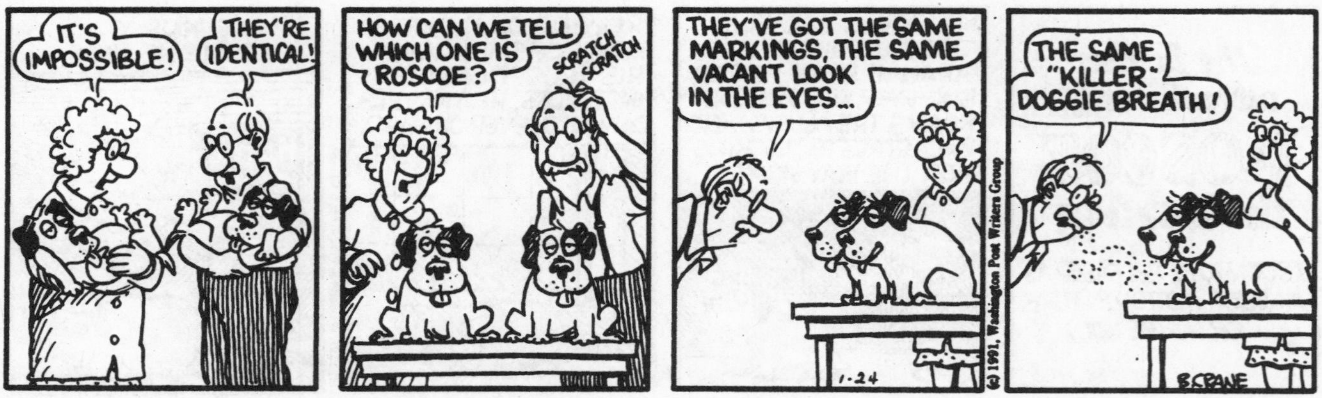
IT'S IMPOSSIBLE!
THEY'RE IDENTICAL!
HOW CAN WE TELL WHICH ONE IS ROSCOE?
SCRATCH SCRATCH
THEY'VE GOT THE SAME MARKINGS, THE SAME VACANT LOOK IN THE EYES...
1-24
(c) 1991, Washington Post Writers Group
THE SAME "KILLER" DOGGIE BREATH!
B.CRANE

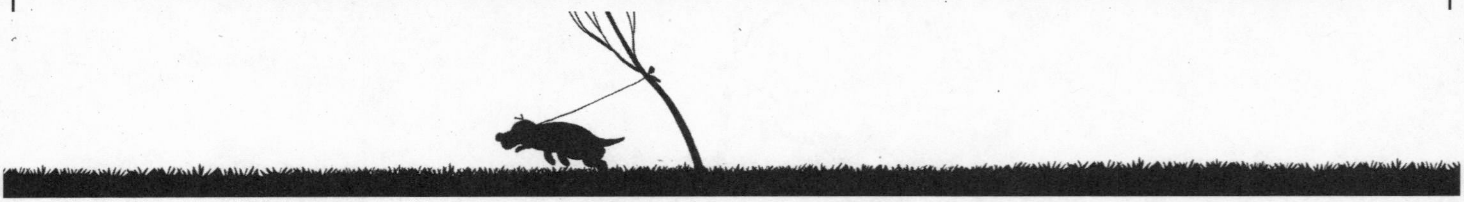

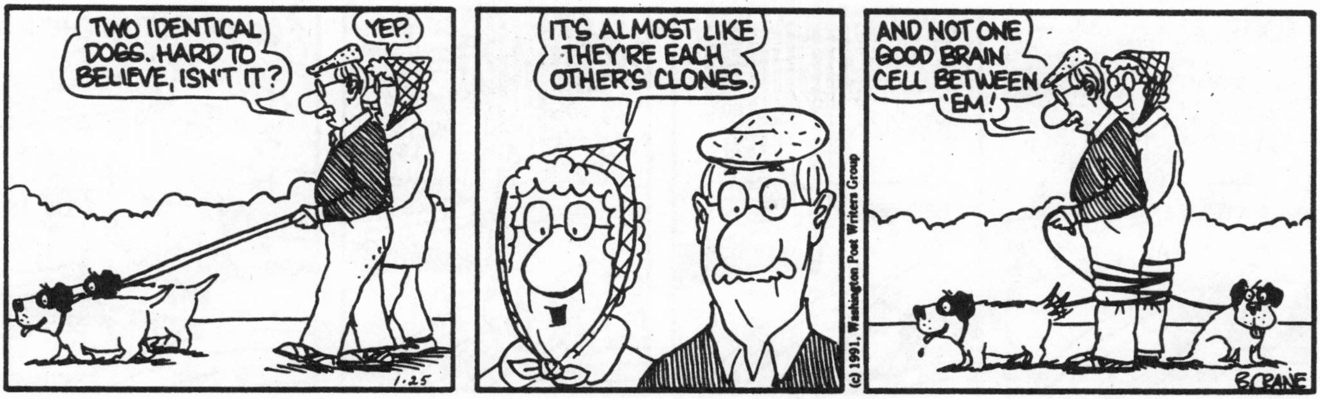
TWO IDENTICAL DOGS. HARD TO BELIEVE, ISN'T IT?
YEP.
IT'S ALMOST LIKE THEY'RE EACH OTHER'S CLONES.
AND NOT ONE GOOD BRAIN CELL BETWEEN 'EM!
1·25
(c) 1991, Washington Post Writers Group
B.CRANE

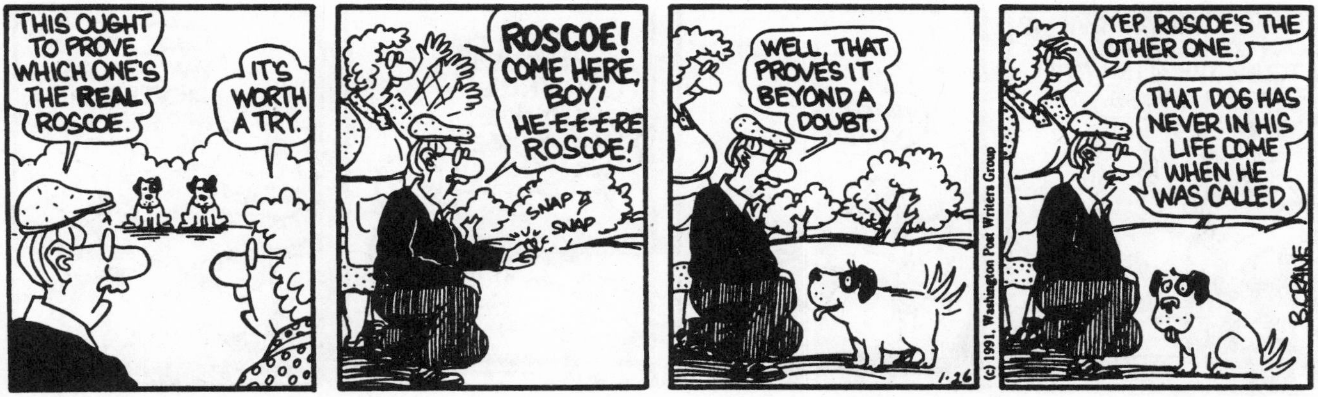
THIS OUGHT TO PROVE WHICH ONE'S THE REAL ROSCOE.
IT'S WORTH A TRY.
ROSCOE! COME HERE, BOY! HE-E-E-E-RE ROSCOE!
SNAP
SNAP
WELL, THAT PROVES IT BEYOND A DOUBT.
1·26
(c) 1991, Washington Post Writers Group
YEP. ROSCOE'S THE OTHER ONE.
THAT DOG HAS NEVER IN HIS LIFE COME WHEN HE WAS CALLED.
B.CRANE

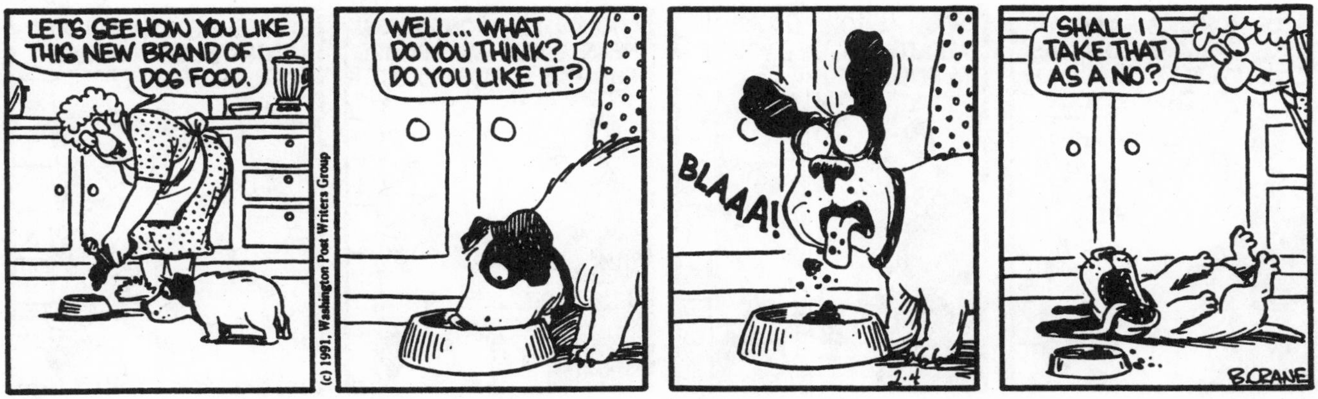
LET'S SEE HOW YOU LIKE THIS NEW BRAND OF DOG FOOD.
(c) 1991, Washington Post Writers Group
WELL... WHAT DO YOU THINK? DO YOU LIKE IT?
BLAAAA!
2·4
SHALL I TAKE THAT AS A NO?
B.CRANE

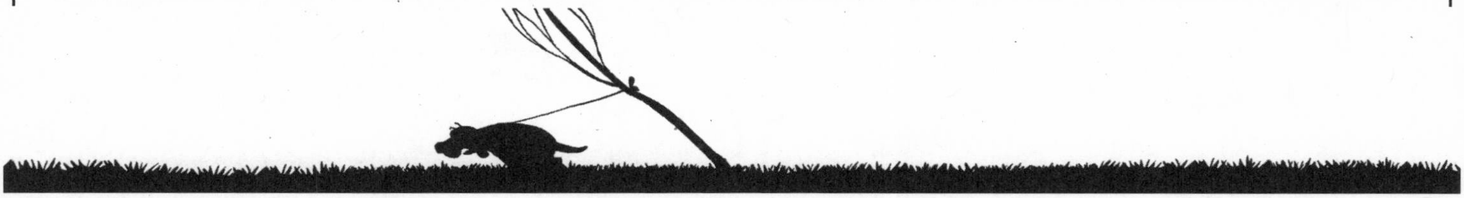

22

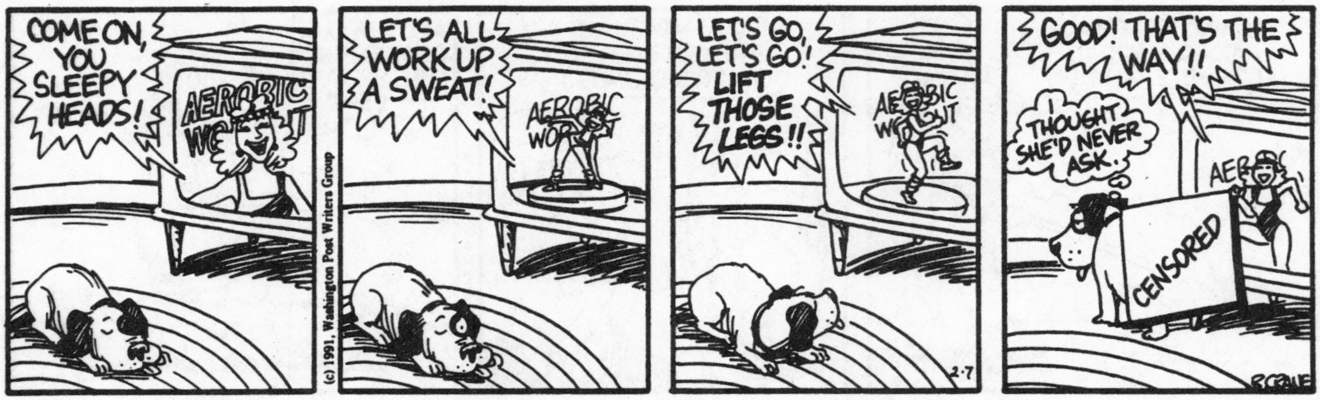
COME ON, YOU SLEEPY HEADS!
AEROBIC
(c) 1991, Washington Post Writers Group
LET'S ALL WORK UP A SWEAT!
AEROBIC
LET'S GO, LET'S GO! LIFT THOSE LEGS!!
2·7
GOOD! THAT'S THE WAY!!
I THOUGHT SHE'D NEVER ASK.
CENSORED
B.CRANE

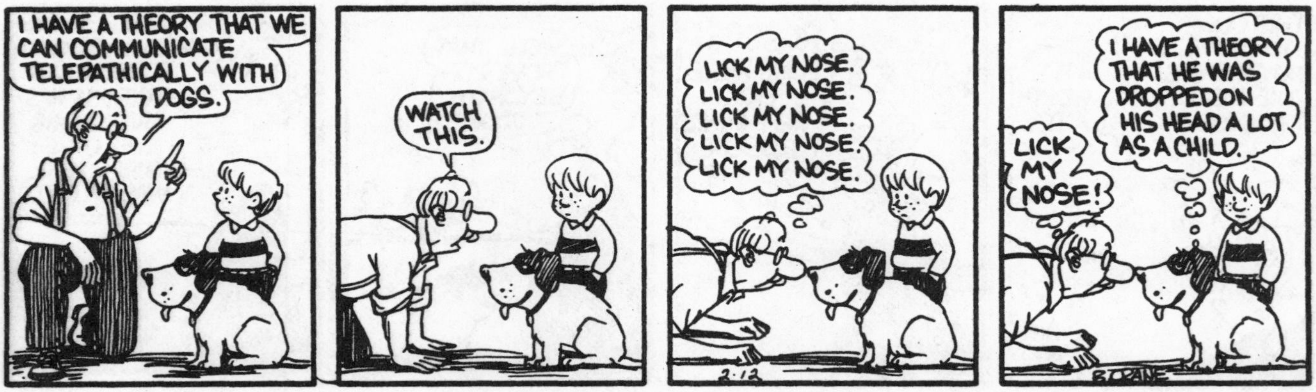
I HAVE A THEORY THAT WE CAN COMMUNICATE TELEPATHICALLY WITH DOGS.
WATCH THIS.
LICK MY NOSE. LICK MY NOSE. LICK MY NOSE. LICK MY NOSE. LICK MY NOSE.
2·12
LICK MY NOSE!
I HAVE A THEORY THAT HE WAS DROPPED ON HIS HEAD A LOT AS A CHILD.
B.CRANE

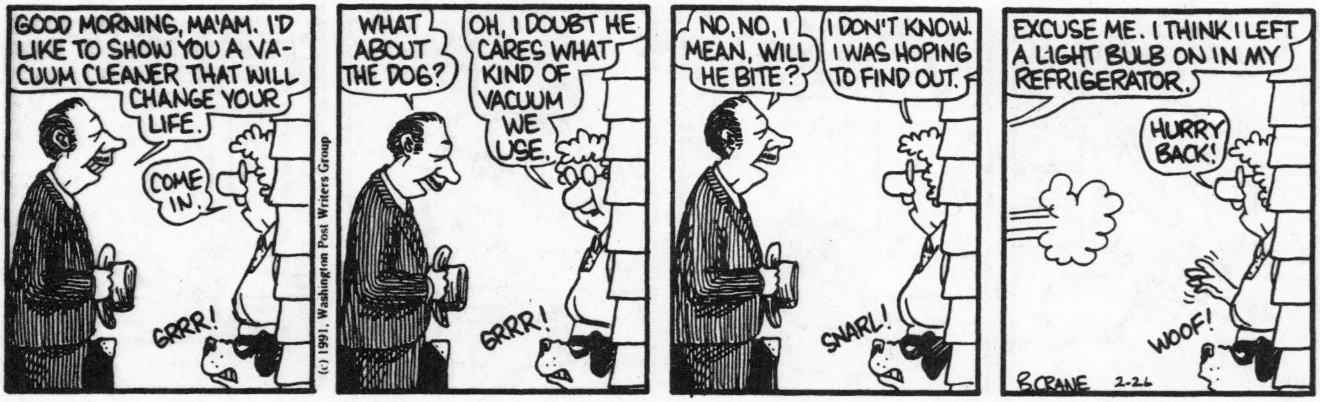
GOOD MORNING, MA'AM. I'D LIKE TO SHOW YOU A VA-CUUM CLEANER THAT WILL CHANGE YOUR LIFE.
COME IN.
GRRR!
(c) 1991, Washington Post Writers Group
WHAT ABOUT THE DOG?
OH, I DOUBT HE CARES WHAT KIND OF VACUUM WE USE.
GRRR!
NO, NO, I MEAN, WILL HE BITE?
I DON'T KNOW. I WAS HOPING TO FIND OUT.
SNARL!
EXCUSE ME. I THINK I LEFT A LIGHT BULB ON IN MY REFRIGERATOR.
HURRY BACK!
WOOF!
B.CRANE 2-26

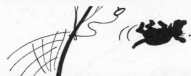

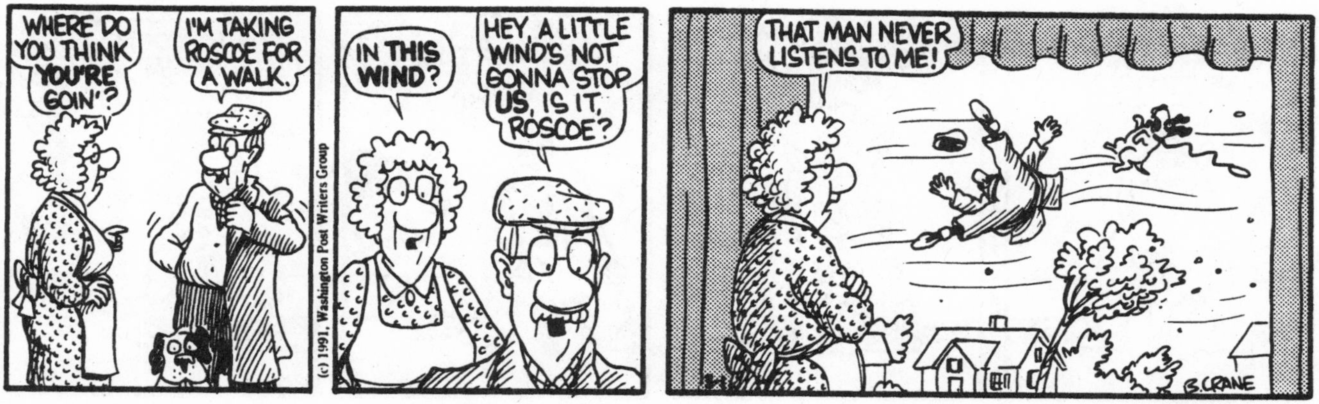
WHERE DO YOU THINK YOU'RE GOIN'?
I'M TAKING ROSCOE FOR A WALK.
(c) 1991, Washington Post Writers Group
IN THIS WIND?
HEY, A LITTLE WIND'S NOT GONNA STOP US, IS IT, ROSCOE?
THAT MAN NEVER LISTENS TO ME!
B.CRANE

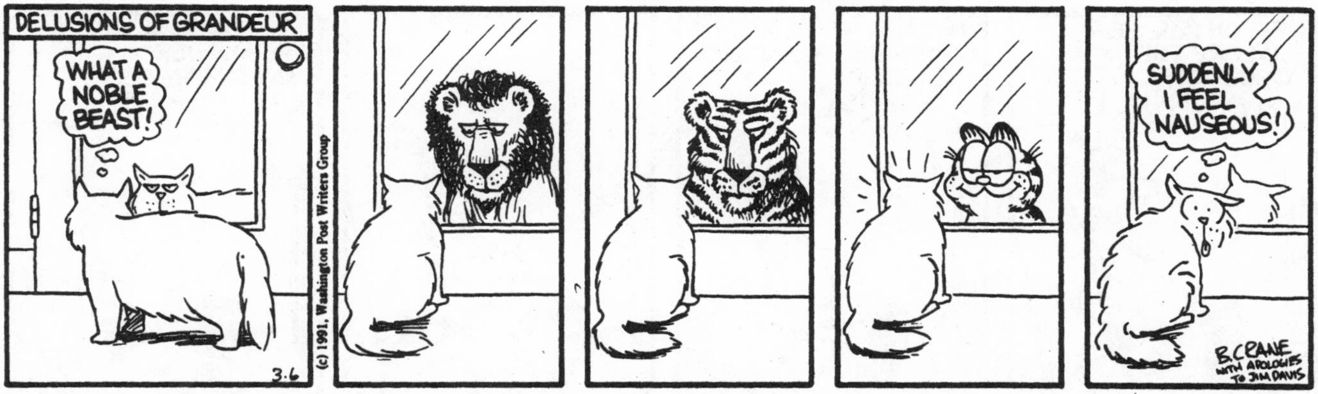
DELUSIONS OF GRANDEUR
WHAT A NOBLE BEAST!
3.6
(c) 1991, Washington Post Writers Group
SUDDENLY I FEEL NAUSEOUS!
B.CRANE
WITH APOLOGIES TO JIM DAVIS

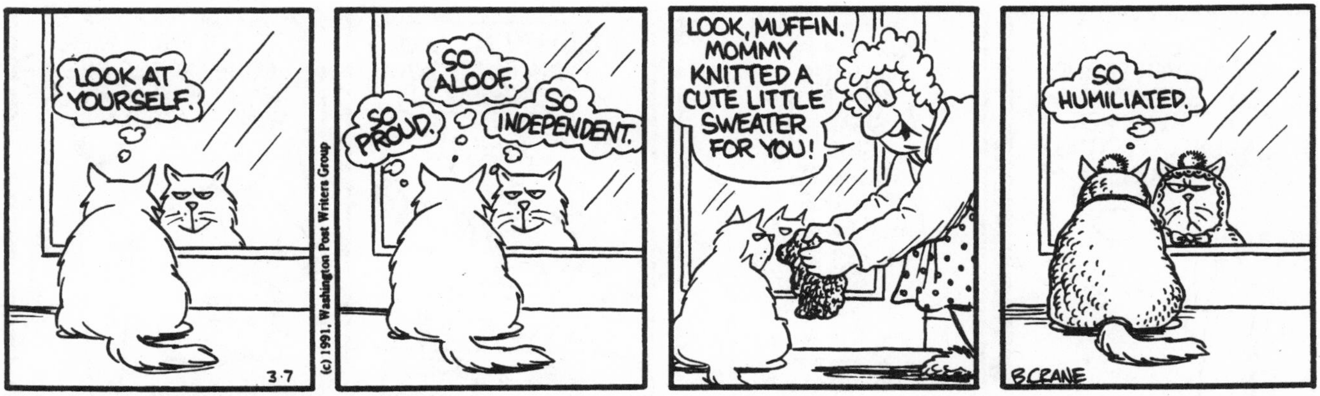
LOOK AT YOURSELF.
3.7
(c) 1991, Washington Post Writers Group
SO PROUD.
SO ALOOF.
SO INDEPENDENT.
LOOK, MUFFIN. MOMMY KNITTED A CUTE LITTLE SWEATER FOR YOU!
SO HUMILIATED.
B.CRANE

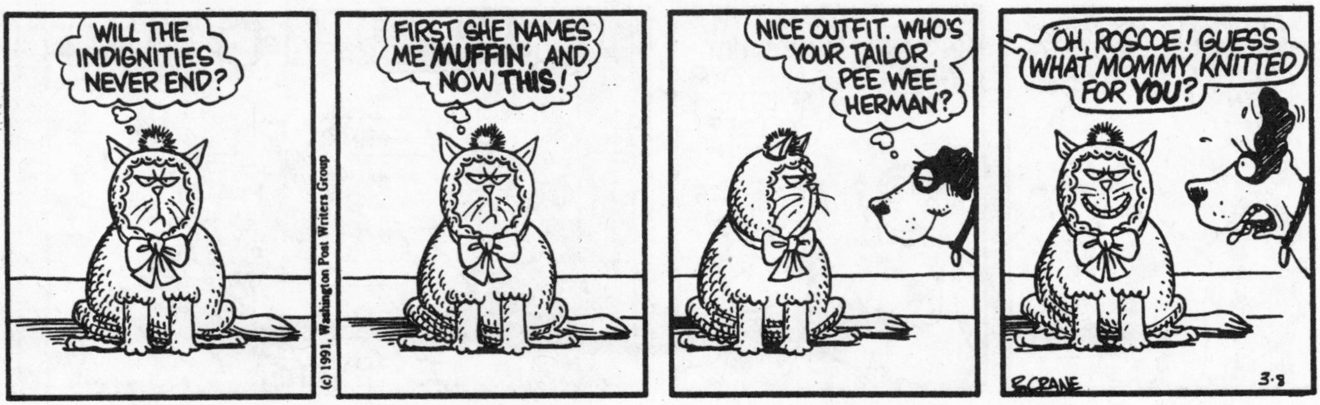
WILL THE INDIGNITIES NEVER END?
FIRST SHE NAMES ME 'MUFFIN', AND NOW THIS!
NICE OUTFIT. WHO'S YOUR TAILOR, PEE WEE HERMAN?
OH, ROSCOE! GUESS WHAT MOMMY KNITTED FOR YOU?
(c) 1991, Washington Post Writers Group
B.CRANE
3-8

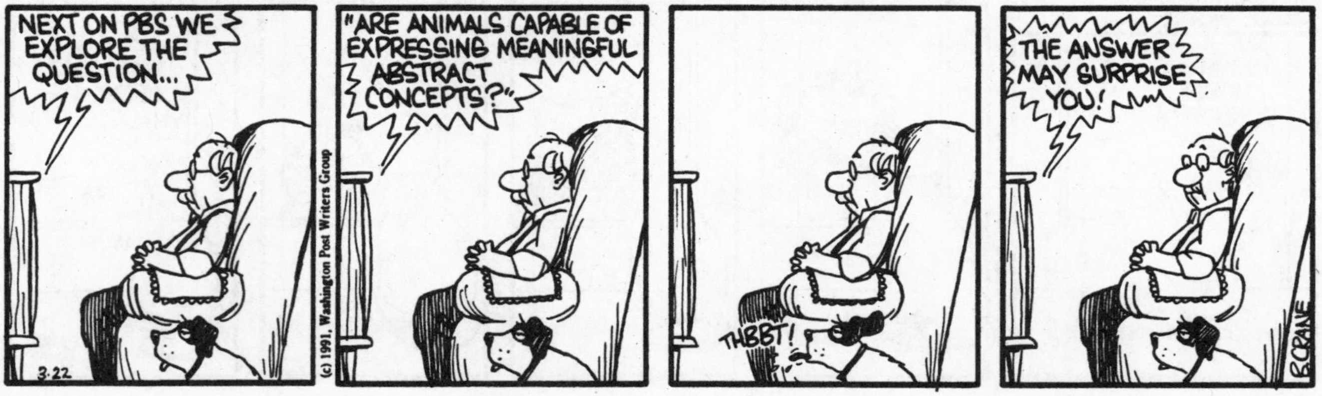
NEXT ON PBS WE EXPLORE THE QUESTION...
"ARE ANIMALS CAPABLE OF EXPRESSING MEANINGFUL ABSTRACT CONCEPTS?"
THBBT!
THE ANSWER MAY SURPRISE YOU!
3-22
(c) 1991, Washington Post Writers Group
B.CRANE

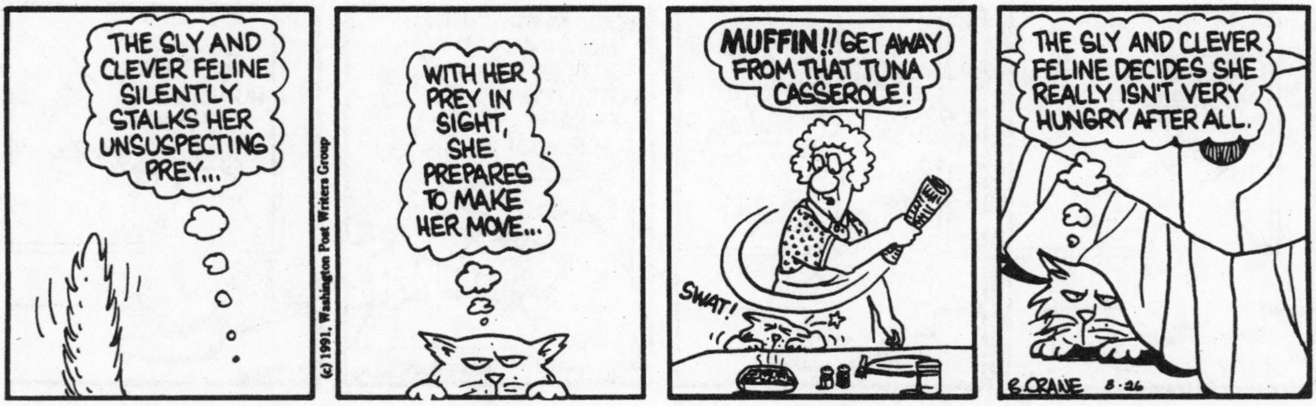
THE SLY AND CLEVER FELINE SILENTLY STALKS HER UNSUSPECTING PREY...
WITH HER PREY IN SIGHT, SHE PREPARES TO MAKE HER MOVE...
MUFFIN!! GET AWAY FROM THAT TUNA CASSEROLE!
SWAT!
THE SLY AND CLEVER FELINE DECIDES SHE REALLY ISN'T VERY HUNGRY AFTER ALL.
(c) 1991, Washington Post Writers Group
B.CRANE
8-26

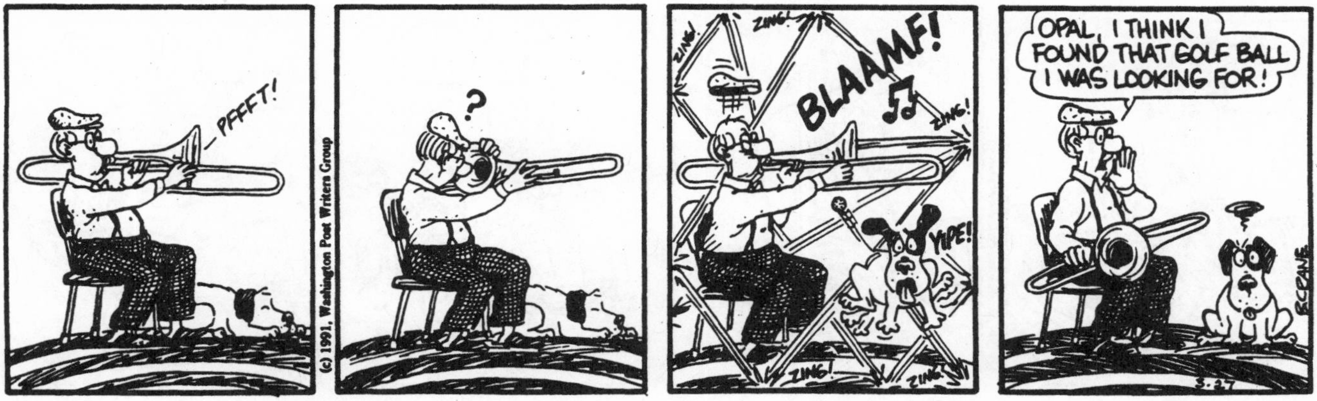
PFFFT!
(c) 1991, Washington Post Writers Group
?
ZING! ZING! BLAAMF! ZING! YIPE! ZING! ZING!
OPAL, I THINK I FOUND THAT GOLF BALL I WAS LOOKING FOR!
B.CRANE
5.27

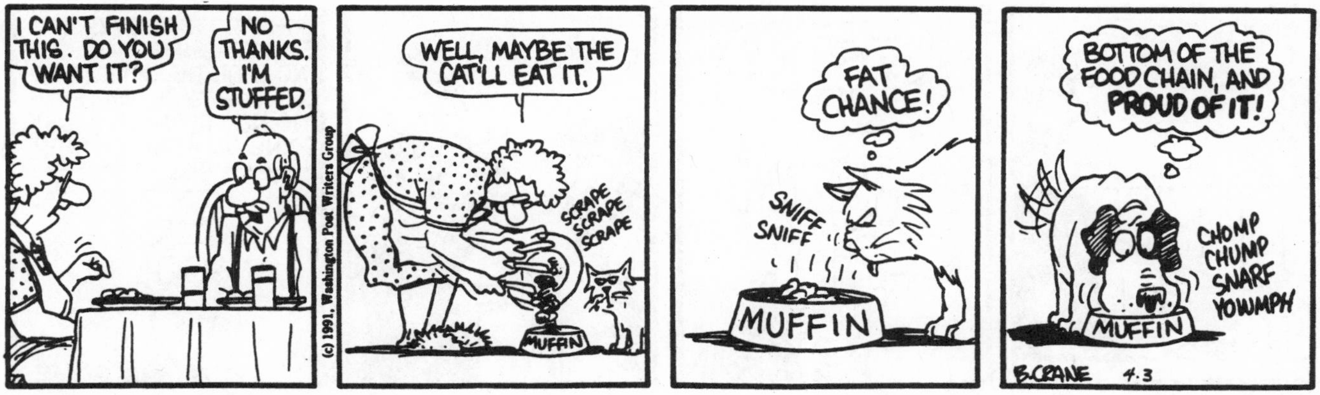
I CAN'T FINISH THIS. DO YOU WANT IT?
NO THANKS. I'M STUFFED.
(c) 1991, Washington Post Writers Group
WELL, MAYBE THE CAT'LL EAT IT.
SCRAPE SCRAPE SCRAPE
MUFFIN
FAT CHANCE!
SNIFF SNIFF
MUFFIN
BOTTOM OF THE FOOD CHAIN, AND PROUD OF IT!
CHOMP CHUMP SNARF YOWMPH
MUFFIN
B.CRANE 4.3

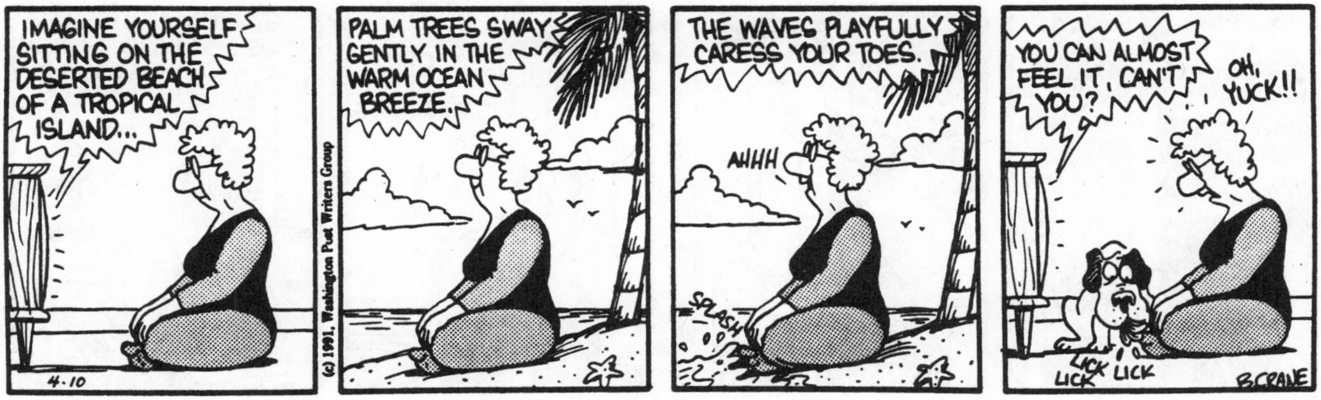
IMAGINE YOURSELF SITTING ON THE DESERTED BEACH OF A TROPICAL ISLAND...
4.10
(c) 1991, Washington Post Writers Group
PALM TREES SWAY GENTLY IN THE WARM OCEAN BREEZE.
THE WAVES PLAYFULLY CARESS YOUR TOES.
AHHH
SPLASH
YOU CAN ALMOST FEEL IT, CAN'T YOU?
OH, YUCK!!
LICK LICK LICK
B.CRANE

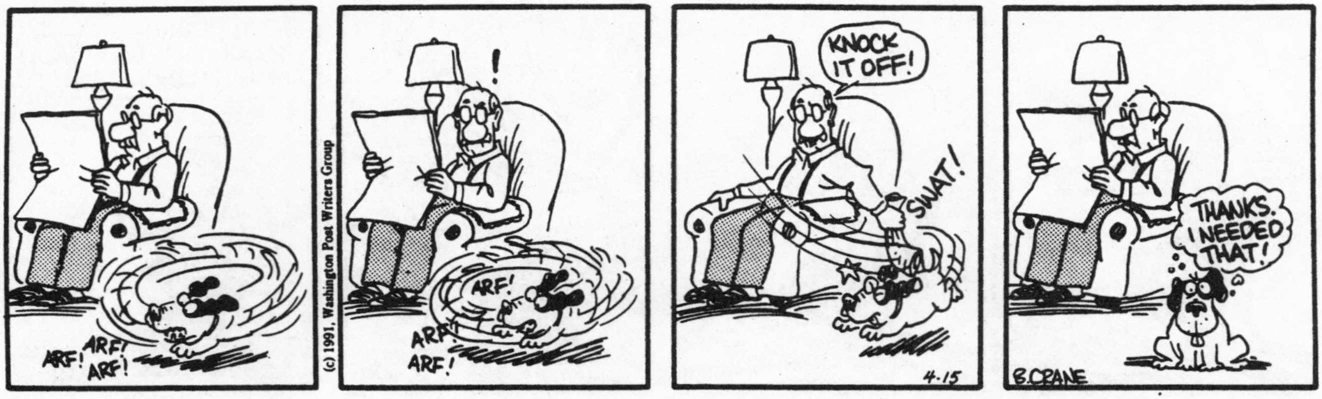
ARF! ARF! ARF!
(c) 1991, Washington Post Writers Group
!
ARF! ARF! ARF!
KNOCK IT OFF!
SWAT!
4-15
THANKS. I NEEDED THAT!
B.CRANE

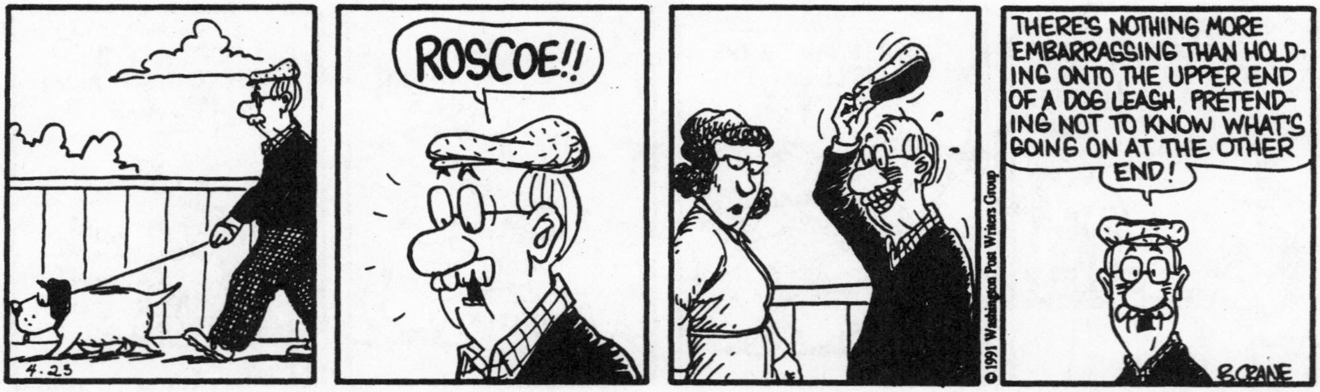
4-23
ROSCOE!!
© 1991 Washington Post Writers Group
THERE'S NOTHING MORE EMBARRASSING THAN HOLDING ONTO THE UPPER END OF A DOG LEASH, PRETENDING NOT TO KNOW WHAT'S GOING ON AT THE OTHER END!
B.CRANE

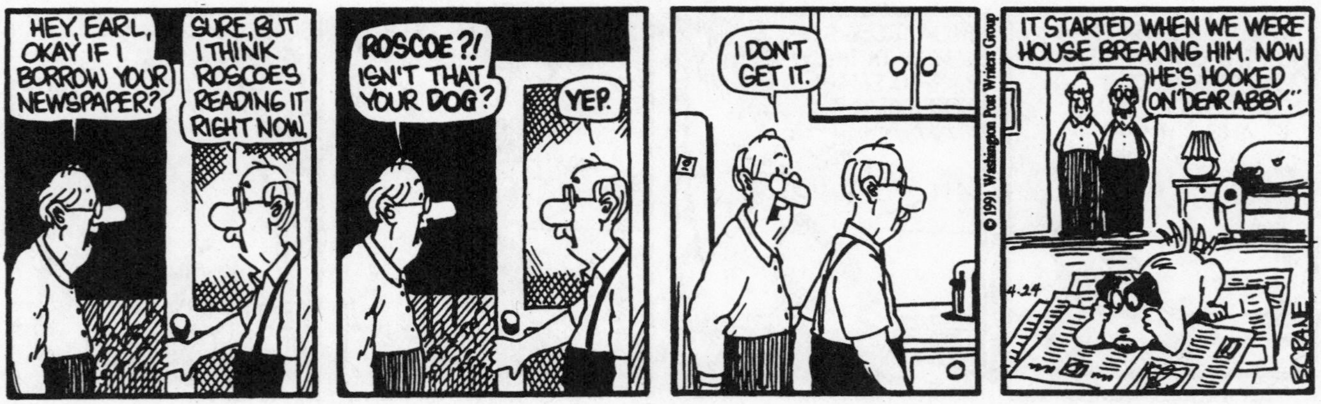
HEY, EARL, OKAY IF I BORROW YOUR NEWSPAPER?
SURE, BUT I THINK ROSCOE'S READING IT RIGHT NOW.
ROSCOE?! ISN'T THAT YOUR DOG?
YEP.
I DON'T GET IT.
© 1991 Washington Post Writers Group
IT STARTED WHEN WE WERE HOUSE BREAKING HIM. NOW HE'S HOOKED ON 'DEAR ABBY.'
4-24
B.CRANE

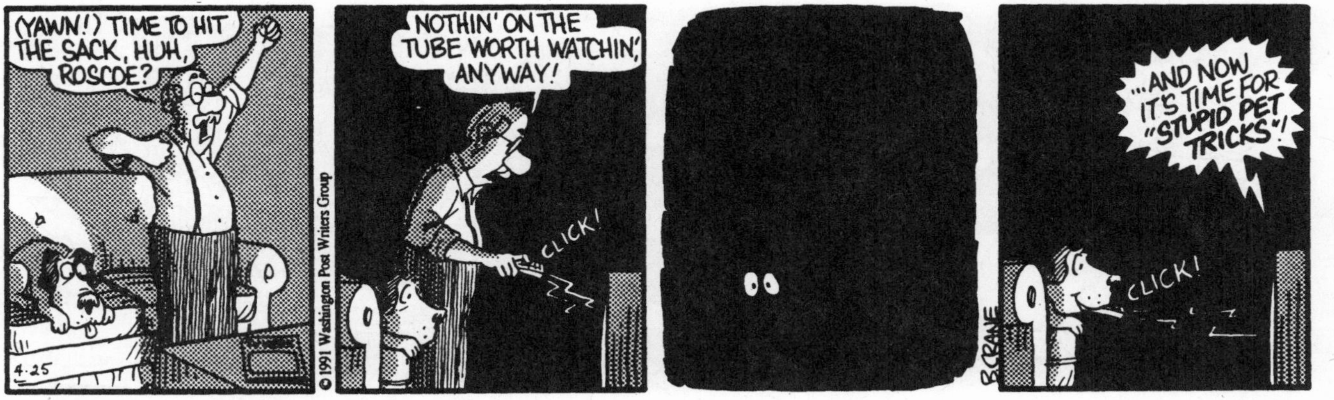
(YAWN!) TIME TO HIT THE SACK, HUH, ROSCOE?
4-25
NOTHIN' ON THE TUBE WORTH WATCHIN', ANYWAY!
CLICK!
© 1991 Washington Post Writers Group
...AND NOW IT'S TIME FOR "STUPID PET TRICKS"!
CLICK!
B.CRANE

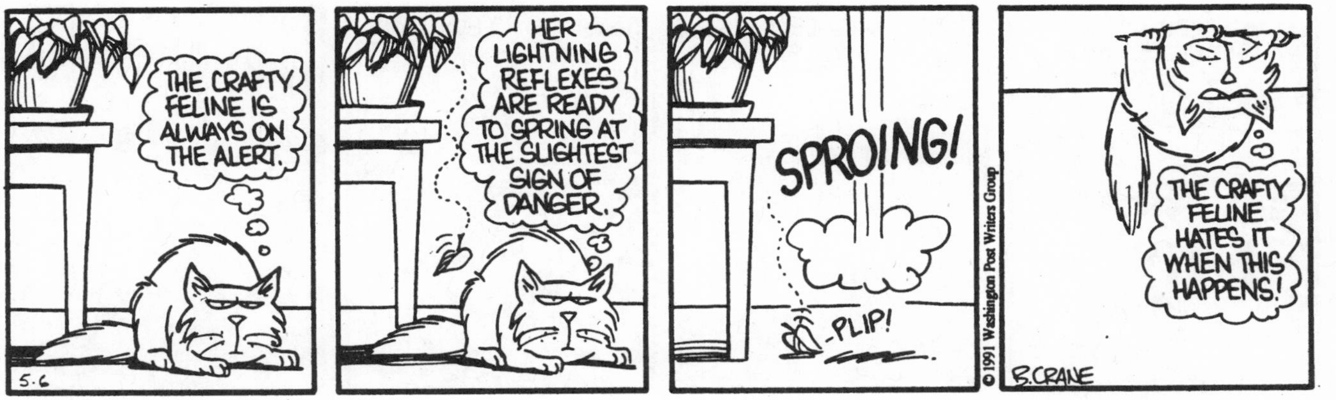
THE CRAFTY FELINE IS ALWAYS ON THE ALERT.
5-6
HER LIGHTNING REFLEXES ARE READY TO SPRING AT THE SLIGHTEST SIGN OF DANGER.
SPROING!
PLIP!
© 1991 Washington Post Writers Group
THE CRAFTY FELINE HATES IT WHEN THIS HAPPENS!
B.CRANE

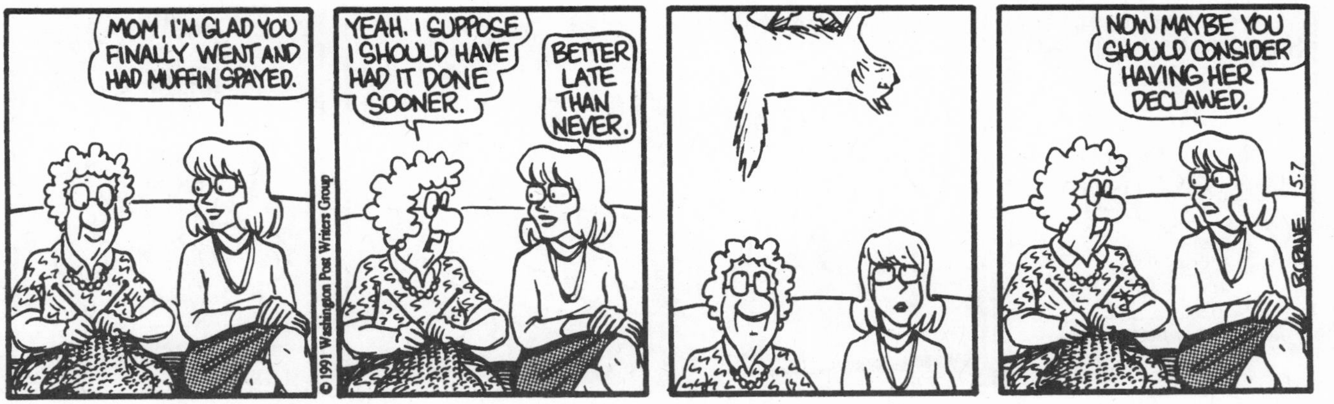
MOM, I'M GLAD YOU FINALLY WENT AND HAD MUFFIN SPAYED.
© 1991 Washington Post Writers Group
YEAH. I SUPPOSE I SHOULD HAVE HAD IT DONE SOONER.
BETTER LATE THAN NEVER.
NOW MAYBE YOU SHOULD CONSIDER HAVING HER DECLAWED.
5-7
B.CRANE

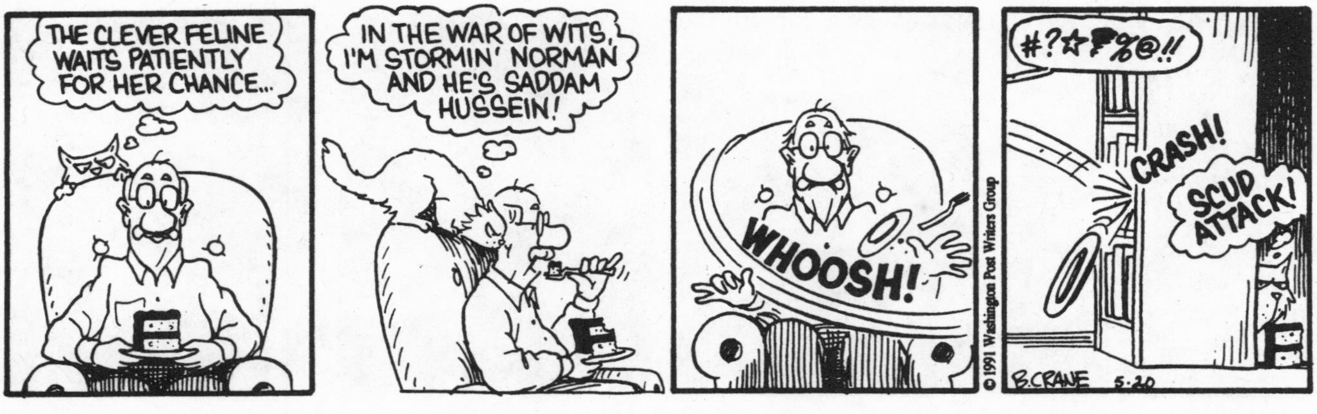
THE CLEVER FELINE WAITS PATIENTLY FOR HER CHANCE...
IN THE WAR OF WITS, I'M STORMIN' NORMAN AND HE'S SADDAM HUSSEIN!
WHOOSH!
#?☆?%@!!
CRASH!
SCUD ATTACK!
© 1991 Washington Post Writers Group
B.CRANE 5-20

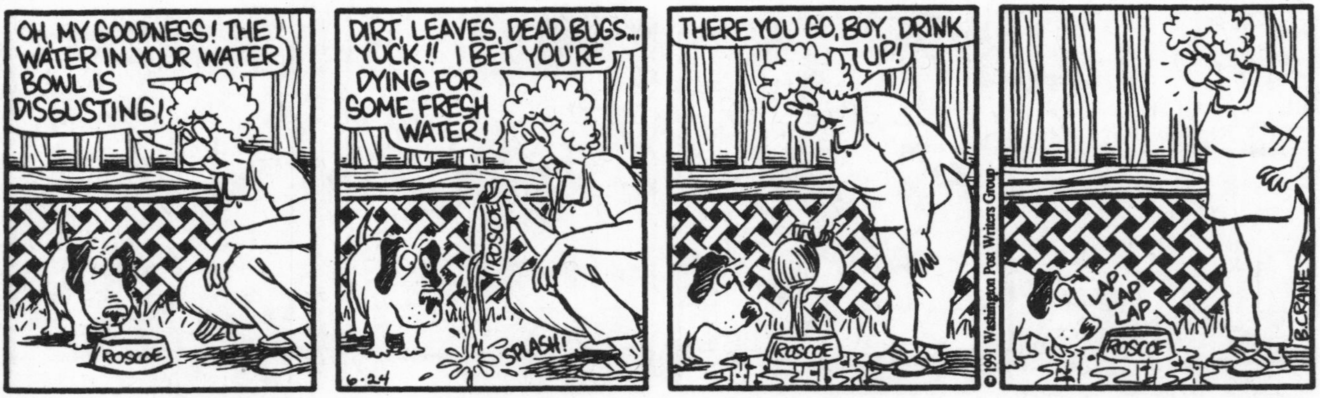
OH, MY GOODNESS! THE WATER IN YOUR WATER BOWL IS DISGUSTING!
ROSCOE
DIRT, LEAVES, DEAD BUGS... YUCK!! I BET YOU'RE DYING FOR SOME FRESH WATER!
ROSCOE
SPLASH!
6-24
THERE YOU GO, BOY. DRINK UP!
ROSCOE
© 1991 Washington Post Writers Group
LAP LAP LAP
ROSCOE
B.CRANE

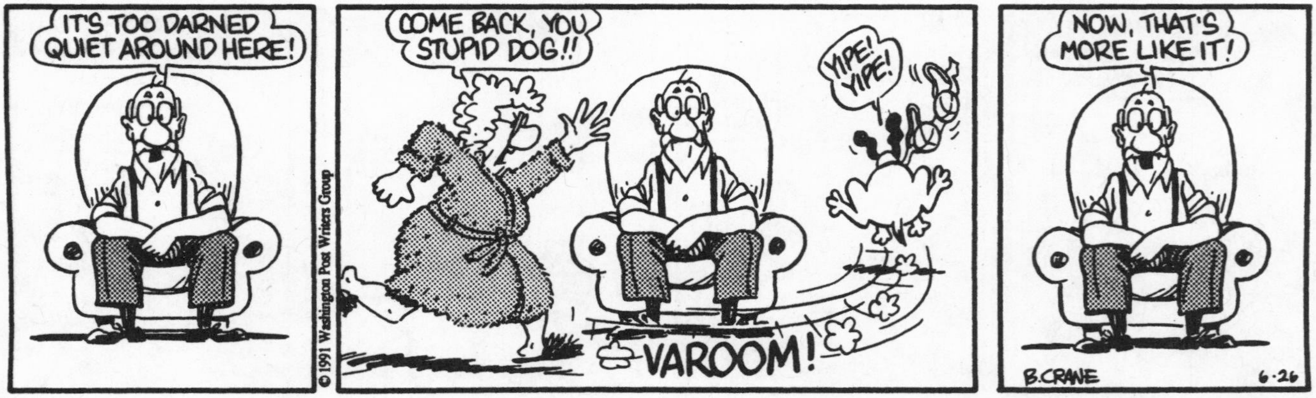
IT'S TOO DARNED QUIET AROUND HERE!
© 1991 Washington Post Writers Group
COME BACK, YOU STUPID DOG!!
YIPE! YIPE!
VAROOM!
NOW, THAT'S MORE LIKE IT!
B.CRANE
6-26

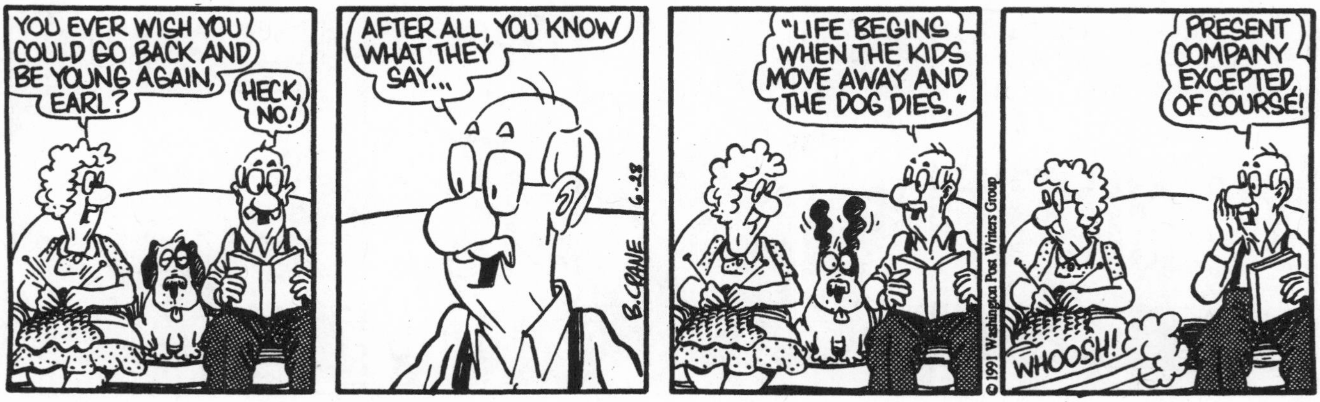
YOU EVER WISH YOU COULD GO BACK AND BE YOUNG AGAIN, EARL?
HECK, NO!
AFTER ALL, YOU KNOW WHAT THEY SAY...
6-28
B.CRANE
"LIFE BEGINS WHEN THE KIDS MOVE AWAY AND THE DOG DIES."
© 1991 Washington Post Writers Group
PRESENT COMPANY EXCEPTED, OF COURSE!
WHOOSH!

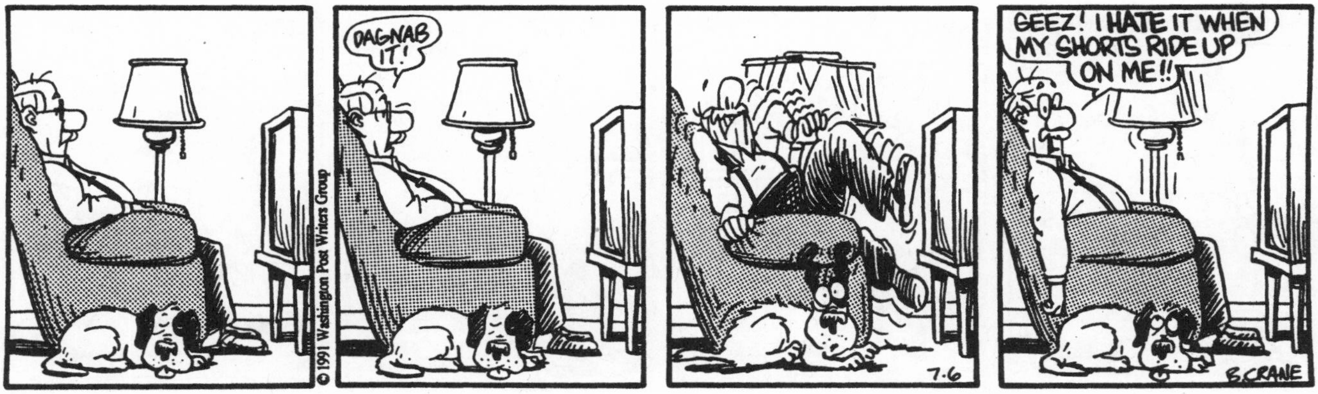
© 1991 Washington Post Writers Group
DAGNAB IT!
7-6
GEEZ! I HATE IT WHEN MY SHORTS RIDE UP ON ME!!
B.CRANE

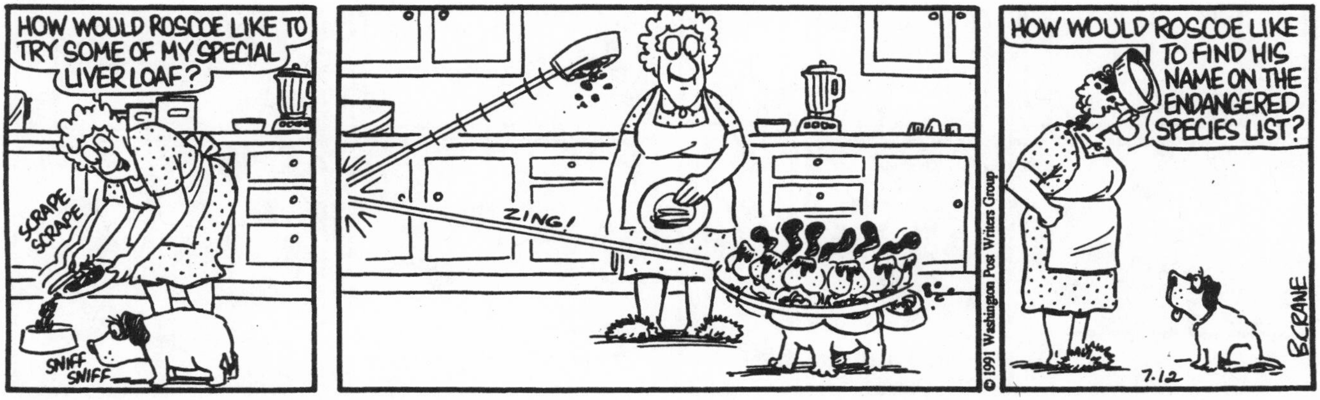
HOW WOULD ROSCOE LIKE TO TRY SOME OF MY SPECIAL LIVER LOAF?
SCRAPE SCRAPE
SNIFF SNIFF
ZING!
© 1991 Washington Post Writers Group
HOW WOULD ROSCOE LIKE TO FIND HIS NAME ON THE ENDANGERED SPECIES LIST?
B.CRANE
7-12

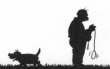

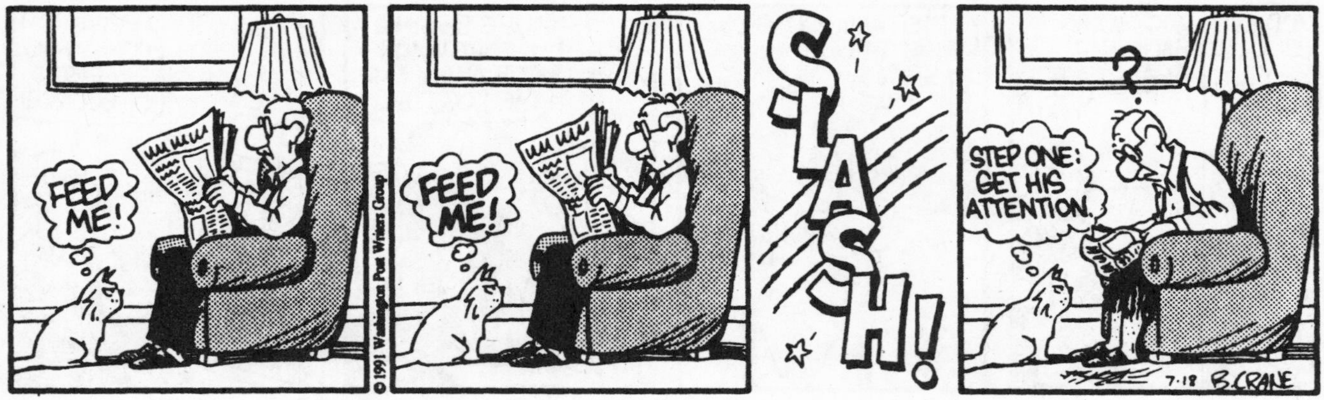
FEED ME!
FEED ME!
SLASH!
STEP ONE: GET HIS ATTENTION.
?
© 1991 Washington Post Writers Group
7·18 B. CRANE

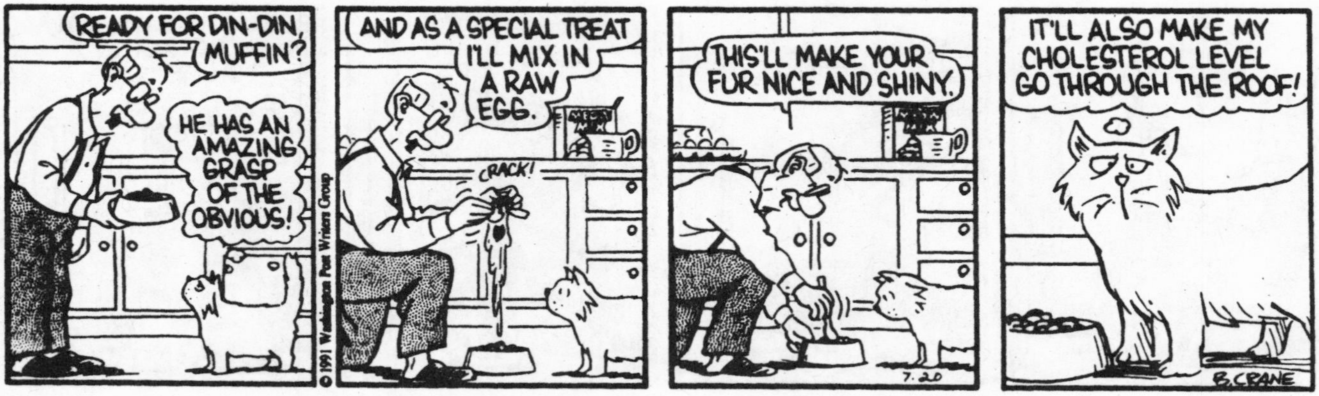
READY FOR DIN-DIN, MUFFIN?
HE HAS AN AMAZING GRASP OF THE OBVIOUS!
AND AS A SPECIAL TREAT I'LL MIX IN A RAW EGG.
CRACK!
THIS'LL MAKE YOUR FUR NICE AND SHINY.
IT'LL ALSO MAKE MY CHOLESTEROL LEVEL GO THROUGH THE ROOF!
© 1991 Washington Post Writers Group
7·20
B. CRANE

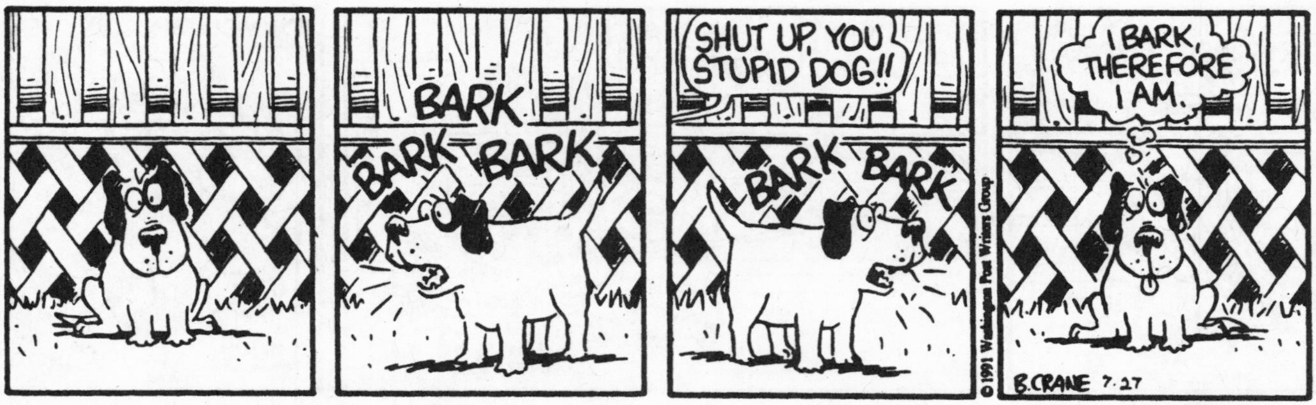
BARK
BARK
BARK
SHUT UP, YOU STUPID DOG!!
BARK
BARK
I BARK, THEREFORE I AM.
© 1991 Washington Post Writers Group
B. CRANE 7·27

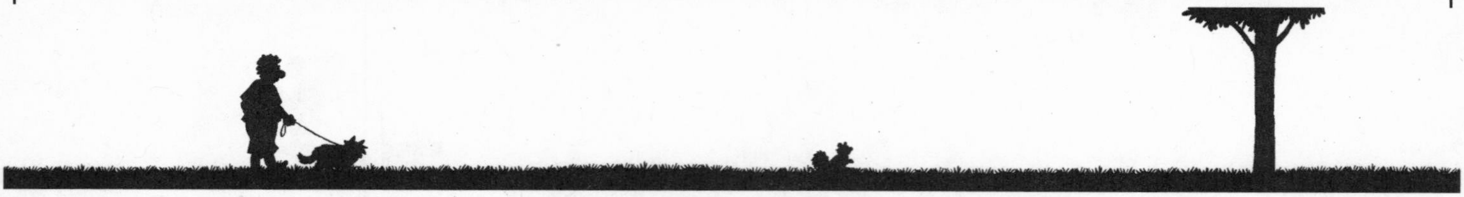

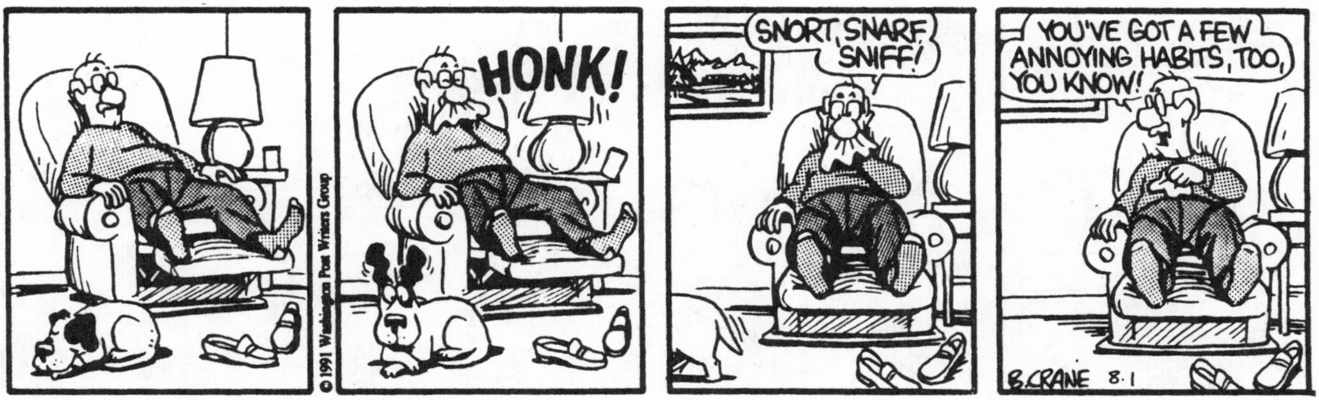
HONK!
SNORT, SNARF, SNIFF!
YOU'VE GOT A FEW ANNOYING HABITS, TOO, YOU KNOW!
© 1991 Washington Post Writers Group
B. CRANE 8.1

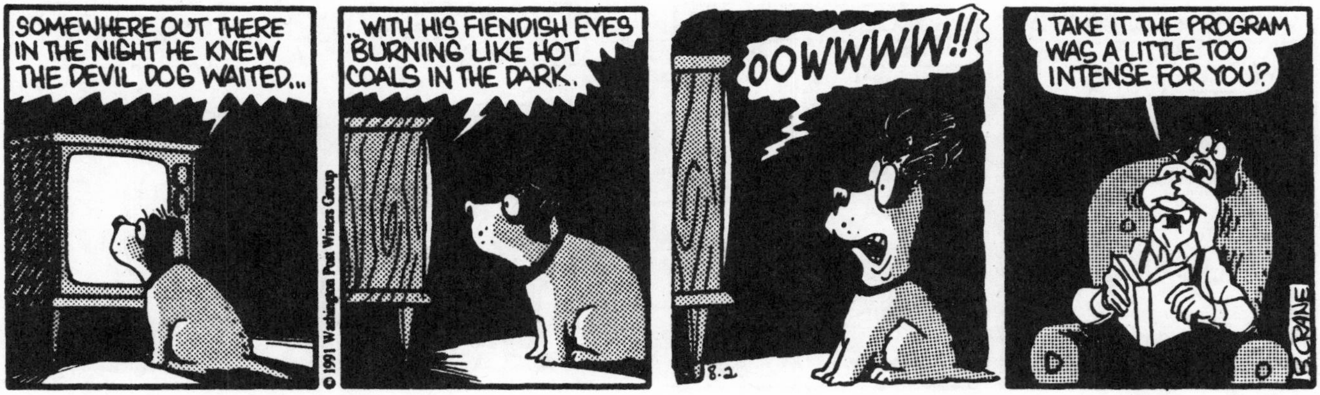
SOMEWHERE OUT THERE IN THE NIGHT HE KNEW THE DEVIL DOG WAITED...
...WITH HIS FIENDISH EYES BURNING LIKE HOT COALS IN THE DARK.
OOWWWW!!
I TAKE IT THE PROGRAM WAS A LITTLE TOO INTENSE FOR YOU?
© 1991 Washington Post Writers Group
8.2
B. CRANE

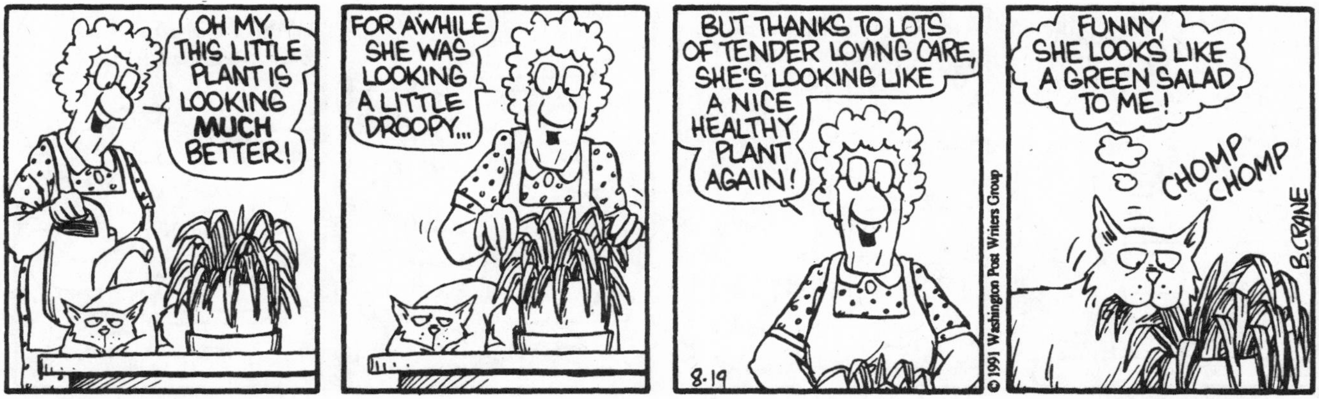
OH MY, THIS LITTLE PLANT IS LOOKING **MUCH** BETTER!
FOR AWHILE SHE WAS LOOKING A LITTLE DROOPY...
BUT THANKS TO LOTS OF TENDER LOVING CARE, SHE'S LOOKING LIKE A NICE HEALTHY PLANT AGAIN!
FUNNY, SHE LOOKS LIKE A GREEN SALAD TO ME!
CHOMP CHOMP
© 1991 Washington Post Writers Group
8.19
B. CRANE

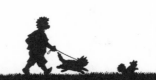

32

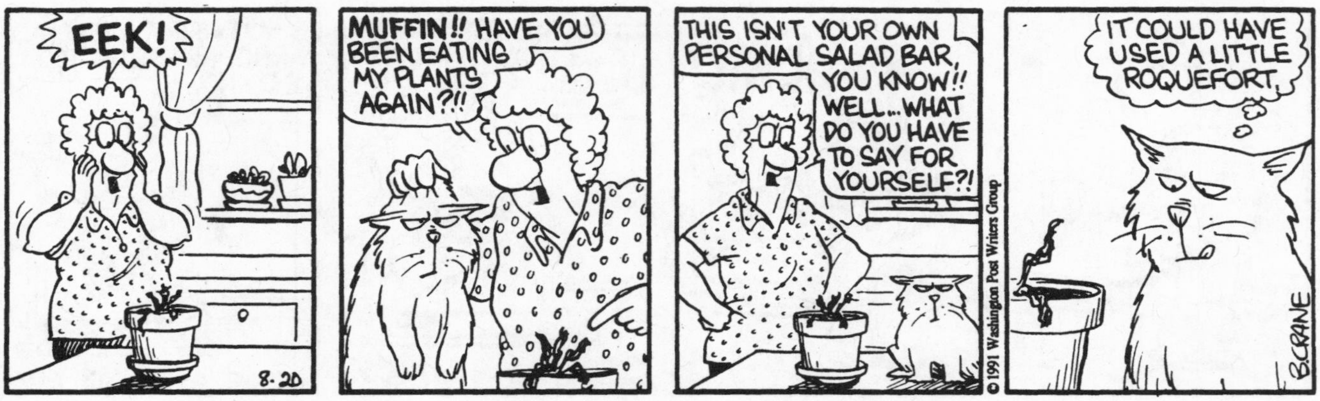
EEK!
8.20
MUFFIN!! HAVE YOU BEEN EATING MY PLANTS AGAIN?!!
THIS ISN'T YOUR OWN PERSONAL SALAD BAR, YOU KNOW!!
WELL...WHAT DO YOU HAVE TO SAY FOR YOURSELF?!
© 1991 Washington Post Writers Group
IT COULD HAVE USED A LITTLE ROQUEFORT.
B.CRANE

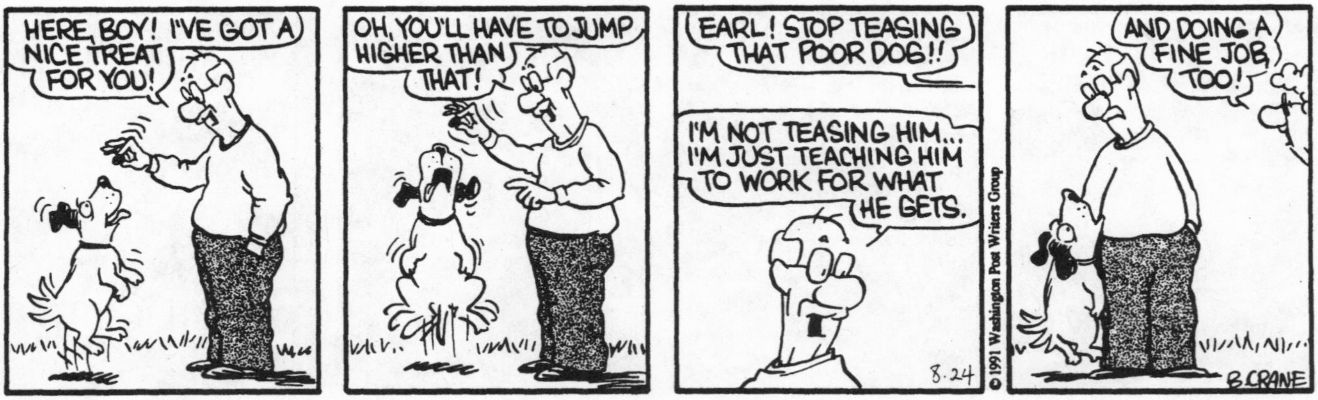
HERE, BOY! I'VE GOT A NICE TREAT FOR YOU!
OH, YOU'LL HAVE TO JUMP HIGHER THAN THAT!
EARL! STOP TEASING THAT POOR DOG!!
I'M NOT TEASING HIM... I'M JUST TEACHING HIM TO WORK FOR WHAT HE GETS.
8.24
© 1991 Washington Post Writers Group
AND DOING A FINE JOB, TOO!
B.CRANE

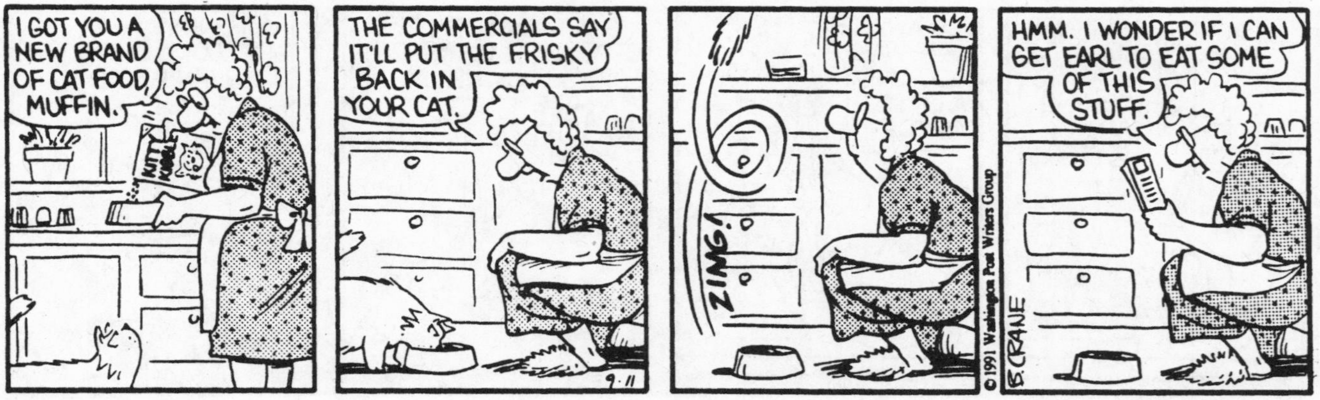
I GOT YOU A NEW BRAND OF CAT FOOD, MUFFIN.
THE COMMERCIALS SAY IT'LL PUT THE FRISKY BACK IN YOUR CAT.
9.11
ZIING!
© 1991 Washington Post Writers Group
B.CRANE
HMM. I WONDER IF I CAN GET EARL TO EAT SOME OF THIS STUFF.

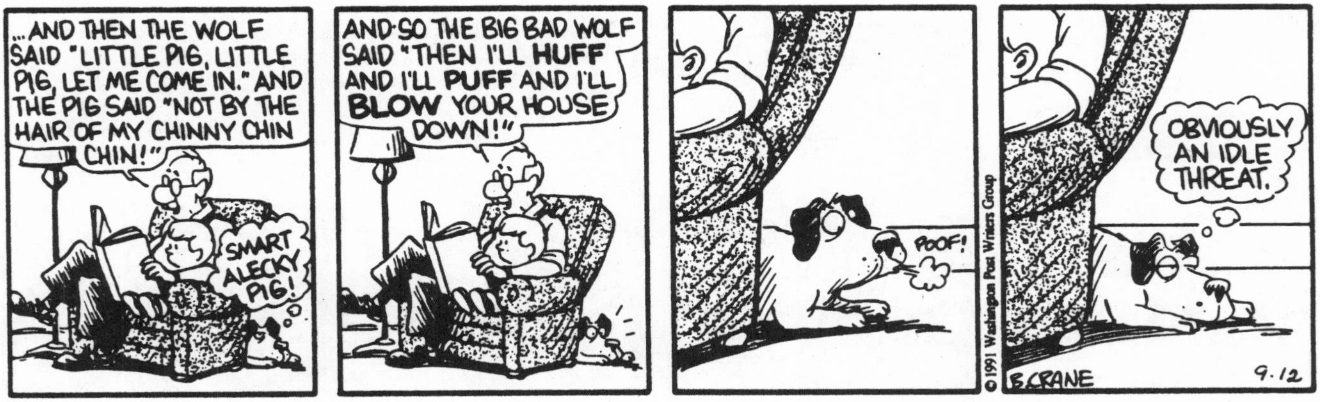
...AND THEN THE WOLF SAID "LITTLE PIG, LITTLE PIG, LET ME COME IN." AND THE PIG SAID "NOT BY THE HAIR OF MY CHINNY CHIN CHIN!"
SMART ALECKY PIG!
AND SO THE BIG BAD WOLF SAID "THEN I'LL HUFF AND I'LL PUFF AND I'LL BLOW YOUR HOUSE DOWN!"
POOF!
© 1991 Washington Post Writers Group
OBVIOUSLY AN IDLE THREAT.
B.CRANE
9.12

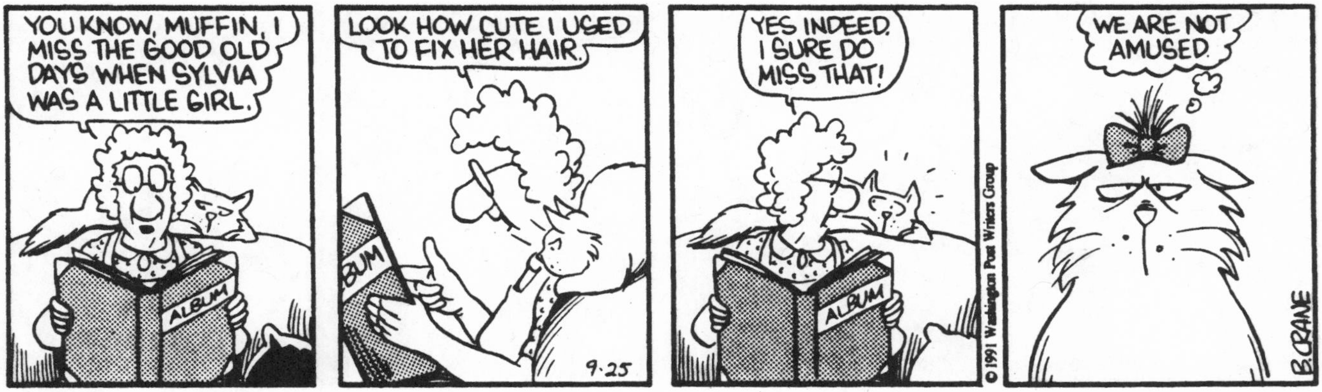
YOU KNOW, MUFFIN, I MISS THE GOOD OLD DAYS WHEN SYLVIA WAS A LITTLE GIRL.
ALBUM
LOOK HOW CUTE I USED TO FIX HER HAIR.
9.25
YES INDEED. I SURE DO MISS THAT!
ALBUM
© 1991 Washington Post Writers Group
WE ARE NOT AMUSED.
B.CRANE

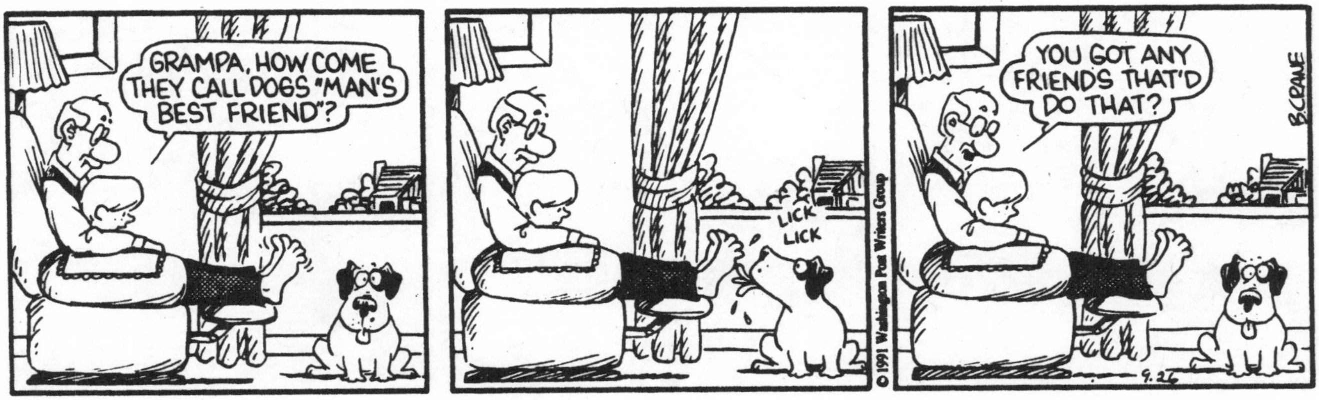
GRAMPA, HOW COME THEY CALL DOGS "MAN'S BEST FRIEND"?
LICK LICK
© 1991 Washington Post Writers Group
YOU GOT ANY FRIENDS THAT'D DO THAT?
B.CRANE

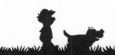

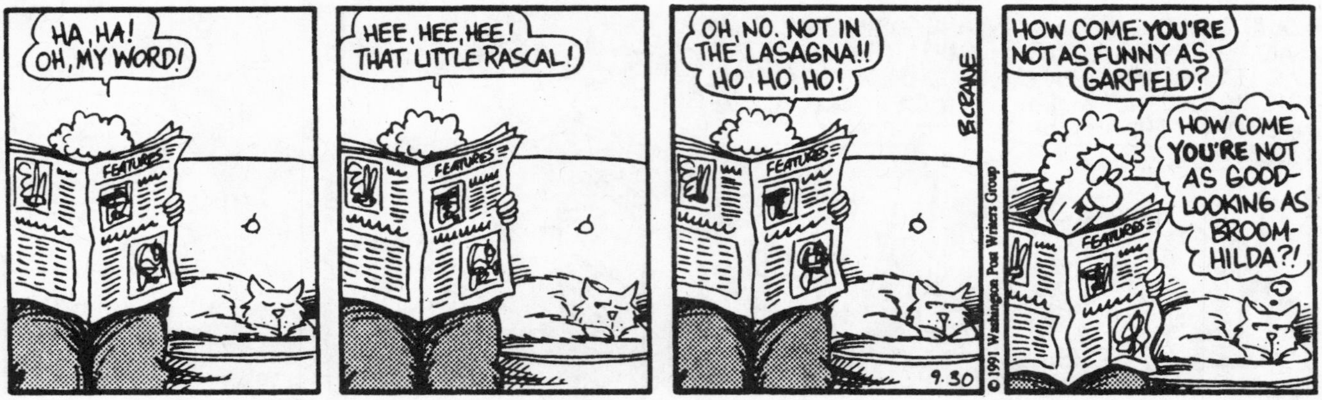
HA, HA! OH, MY WORD!
HEE, HEE, HEE! THAT LITTLE RASCAL!
OH, NO. NOT IN THE LASAGNA!! HO, HO, HO!
B. CRANE
9.30
© 1991 Washington Post Writers Group
HOW COME YOU'RE NOT AS FUNNY AS GARFIELD?
HOW COME YOU'RE NOT AS GOOD-LOOKING AS BROOM-HILDA?!

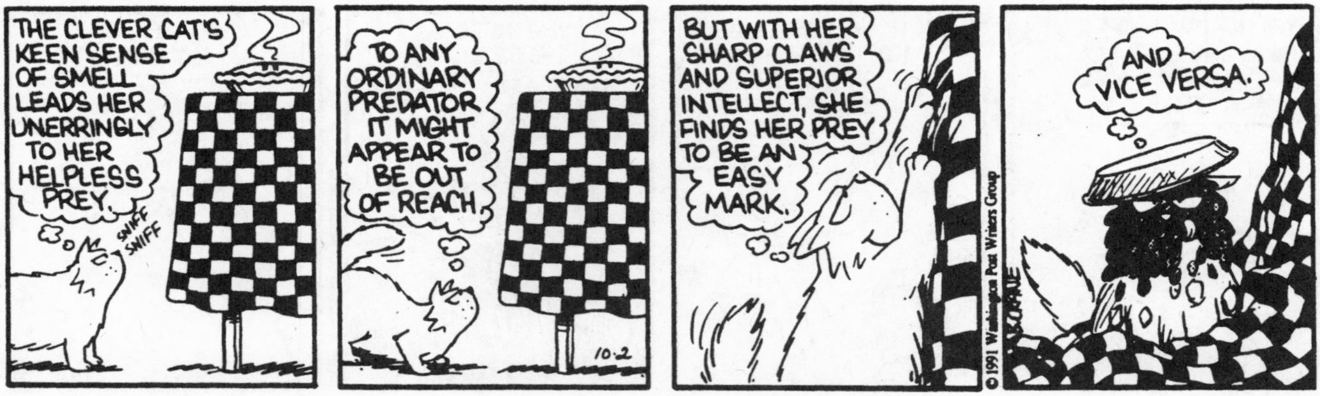
THE CLEVER CAT'S KEEN SENSE OF SMELL LEADS HER UNERRINGLY TO HER HELPLESS PREY.
SNIFF SNIFF
TO ANY ORDINARY PREDATOR IT MIGHT APPEAR TO BE OUT OF REACH.
10.2
BUT WITH HER SHARP CLAWS AND SUPERIOR INTELLECT, SHE FINDS HER PREY TO BE AN EASY MARK.
© 1991 Washington Post Writers Group
AND VICE VERSA.

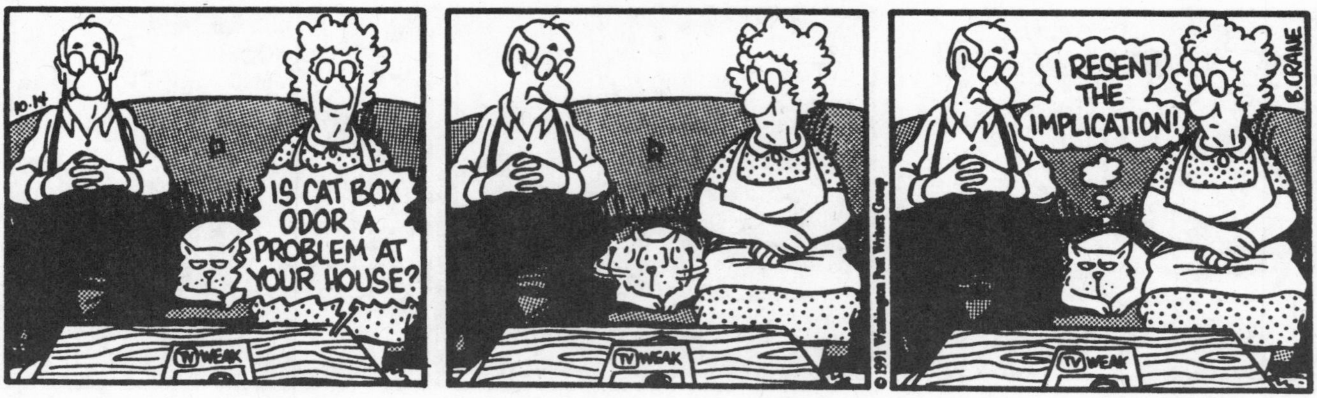
10.14
IS CAT BOX ODOR A PROBLEM AT YOUR HOUSE?
TV WEAK
© 1991 Washington Post Writers Group
I RESENT THE IMPLICATION!
B. CRANE

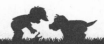

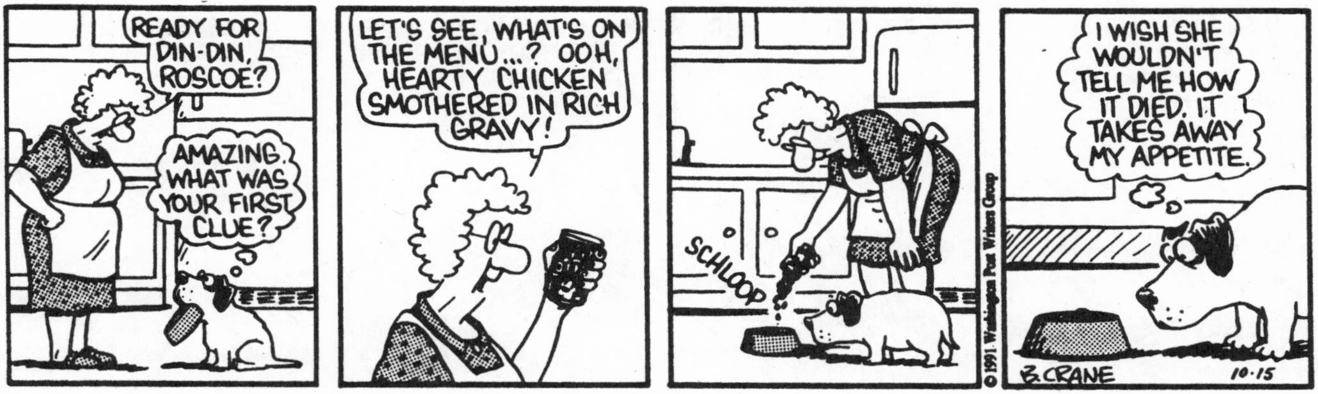
READY FOR DIN-DIN, ROSCOE?
AMAZING. WHAT WAS YOUR FIRST CLUE?
LET'S SEE, WHAT'S ON THE MENU...? OOH, HEARTY CHICKEN SMOTHERED IN RICH GRAVY!
SCHLOOP
© 1991 Washington Post Writers Group
I WISH SHE WOULDN'T TELL ME HOW IT DIED. IT TAKES AWAY MY APPETITE.
B. CRANE
10-15

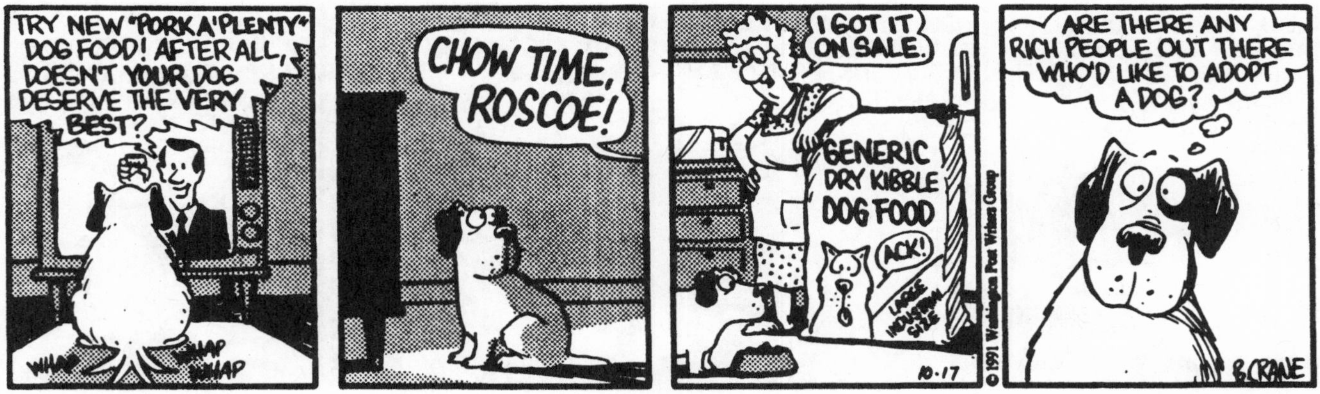
TRY NEW "PORK A'PLENTY" DOG FOOD! AFTER ALL, DOESN'T YOUR DOG DESERVE THE VERY BEST?
WHAP
WHAP
WHAP
CHOW TIME, ROSCOE!
I GOT IT ON SALE.
GENERIC DRY KIBBLE DOG FOOD
ACK!
LARGE INDUSTRIAL SIZE
10-17
© 1991 Washington Post Writers Group
ARE THERE ANY RICH PEOPLE OUT THERE WHO'D LIKE TO ADOPT A DOG?
B. CRANE

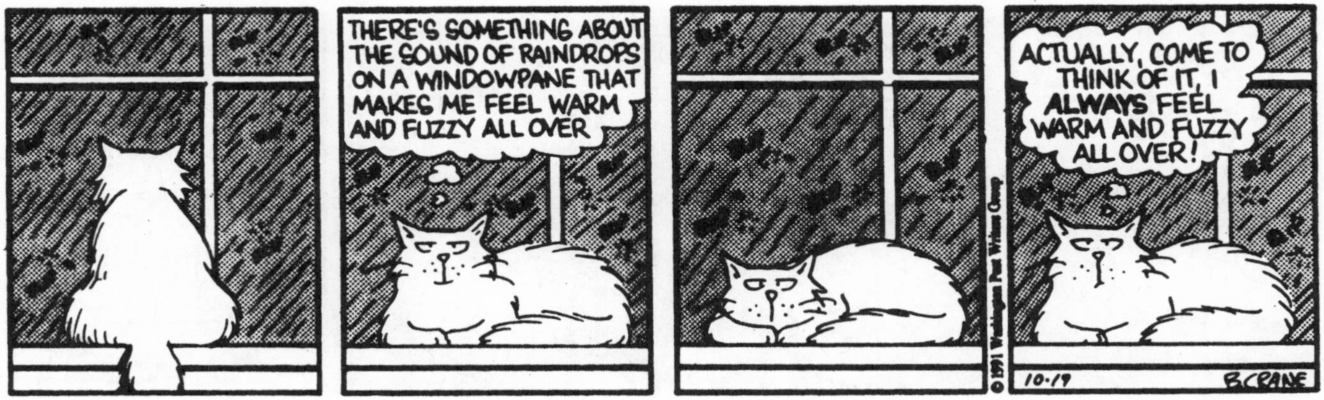
THERE'S SOMETHING ABOUT THE SOUND OF RAINDROPS ON A WINDOWPANE THAT MAKES ME FEEL WARM AND FUZZY ALL OVER
© 1991 Washington Post Writers Group
ACTUALLY, COME TO THINK OF IT, I ALWAYS FEEL WARM AND FUZZY ALL OVER!
10-19
B. CRANE

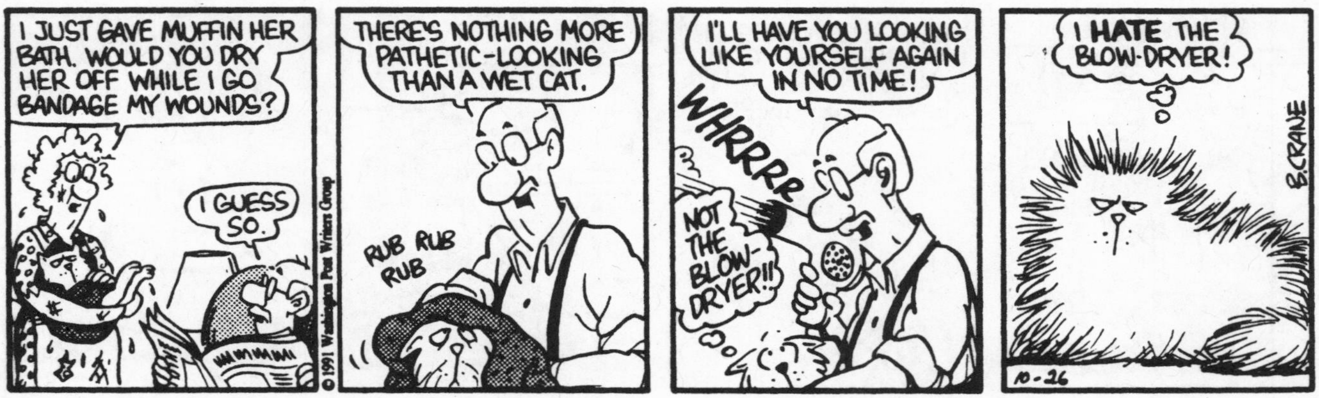
I JUST GAVE MUFFIN HER BATH. WOULD YOU DRY HER OFF WHILE I GO BANDAGE MY WOUNDS?
I GUESS SO.
© 1991 Washington Post Writers Group
THERE'S NOTHING MORE PATHETIC-LOOKING THAN A WET CAT.
RUB RUB RUB
I'LL HAVE YOU LOOKING LIKE YOURSELF AGAIN IN NO TIME!
WHRRRR
NOT THE BLOW-DRYER!!
I HATE THE BLOW-DRYER!
B.CRANE
10-26

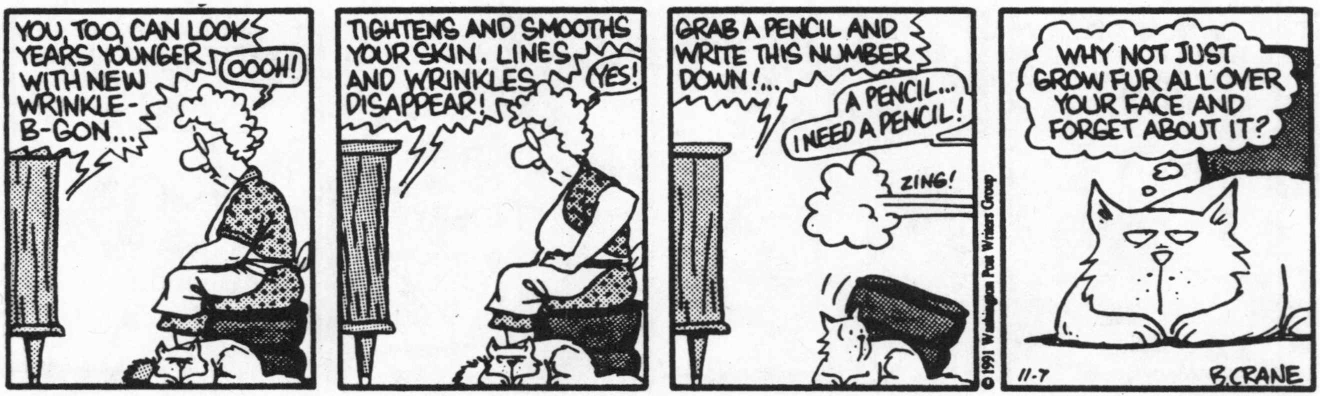
YOU, TOO, CAN LOOK YEARS YOUNGER WITH NEW WRINKLE-B-GON...
OOOH!
TIGHTENS AND SMOOTHS YOUR SKIN. LINES AND WRINKLES DISAPPEAR!
YES!
GRAB A PENCIL AND WRITE THIS NUMBER DOWN!...
A PENCIL... I NEED A PENCIL!
ZING!
© 1991 Washington Post Writers Group
WHY NOT JUST GROW FUR ALL OVER YOUR FACE AND FORGET ABOUT IT?
11-7
B.CRANE

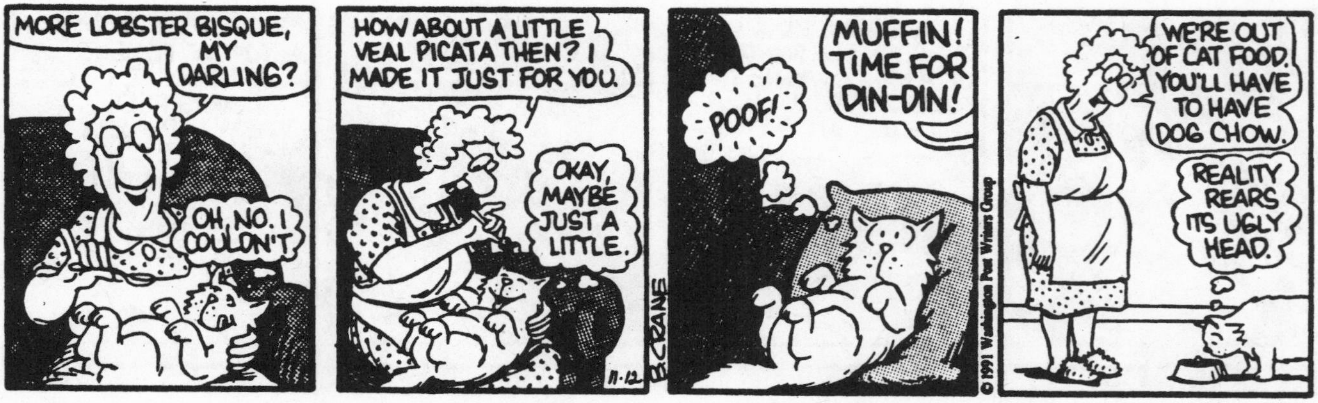
MORE LOBSTER BISQUE, MY DARLING?
OH, NO. I COULDN'T.
HOW ABOUT A LITTLE VEAL PICATA THEN? I MADE IT JUST FOR YOU.
OKAY, MAYBE JUST A LITTLE.
B.CRANE
11-12
POOF!
MUFFIN! TIME FOR DIN-DIN!
© 1991 Washington Post Writers Group
WE'RE OUT OF CAT FOOD. YOU'LL HAVE TO HAVE DOG CHOW.
REALITY REARS ITS UGLY HEAD.

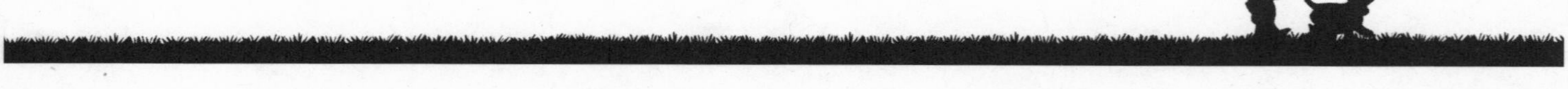

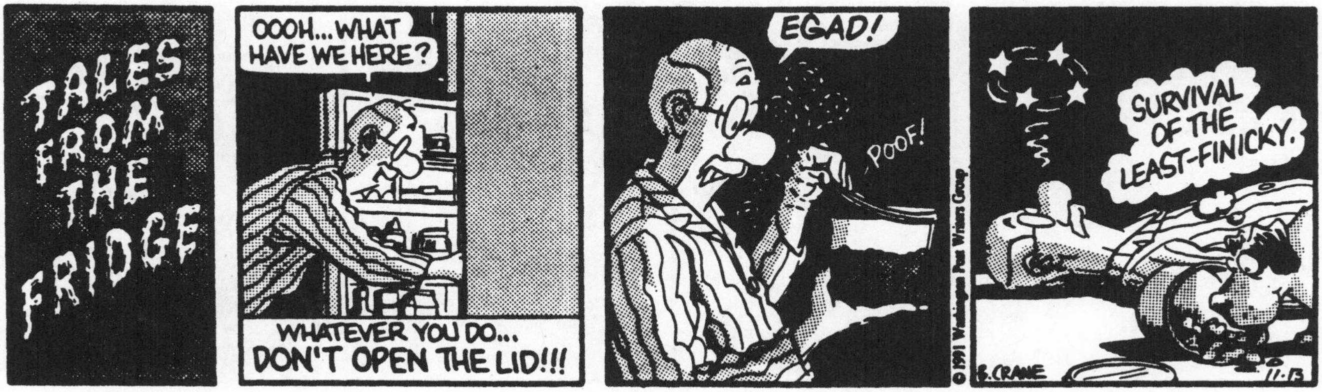
TALES FROM THE FRIDGE
OOOH... WHAT HAVE WE HERE?
WHATEVER YOU DO... DON'T OPEN THE LID!!!
EGAD!
POOF!
SURVIVAL OF THE LEAST-FINICKY.
© 1991 Washington Post Writers Group
B. CRANE
11-13

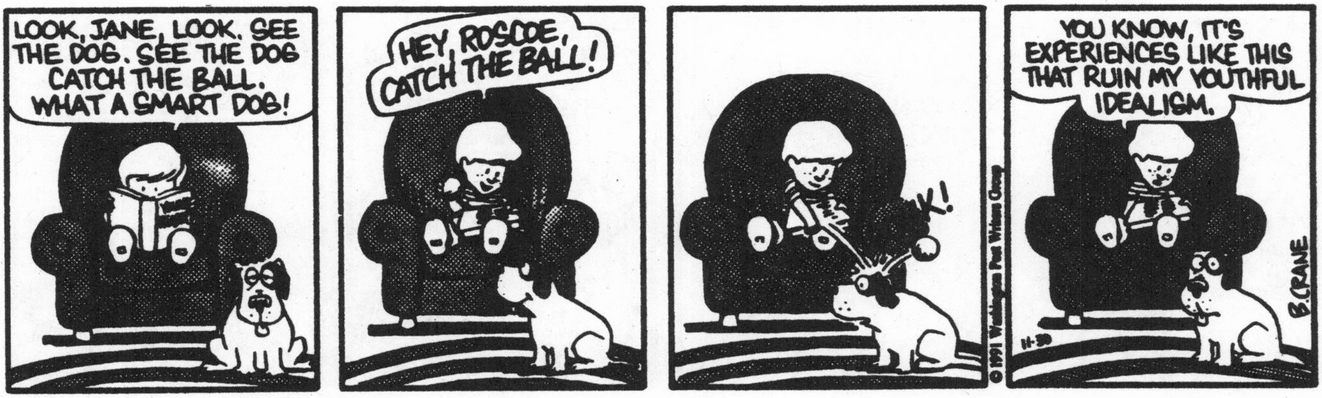
LOOK, JANE, LOOK. SEE THE DOG. SEE THE DOG CATCH THE BALL. WHAT A SMART DOG!
HEY, ROSCOE, CATCH THE BALL!
YOU KNOW, IT'S EXPERIENCES LIKE THIS THAT RUIN MY YOUTHFUL IDEALISM.
© 1991 Washington Post Writers Group
11-30
B. CRANE

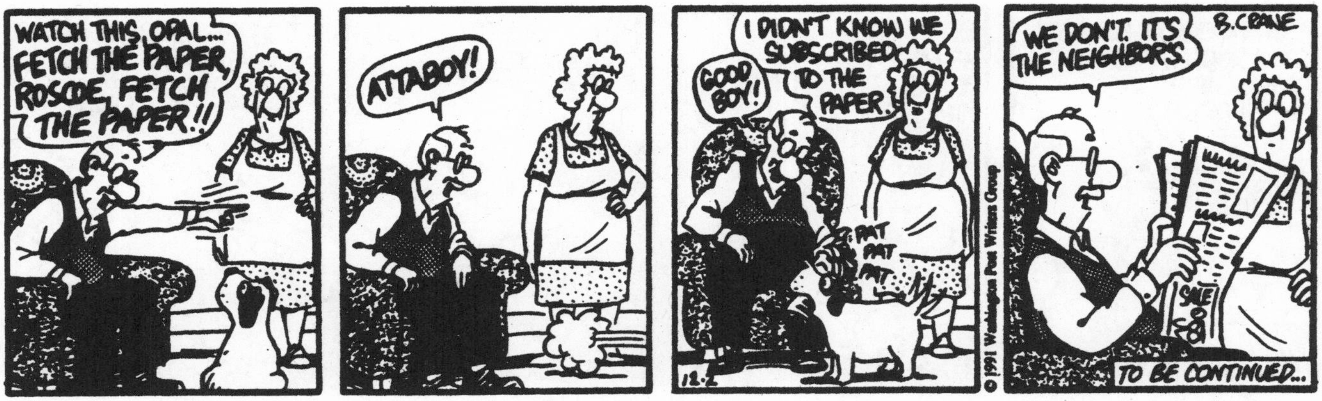
WATCH THIS, OPAL... FETCH THE PAPER, ROSCOE, FETCH THE PAPER!!
ATTABOY!
GOOD BOY!
I DIDN'T KNOW WE SUBSCRIBED TO THE PAPER.
PAT PAT PAT
12-2
© 1991 Washington Post Writers Group
WE DON'T. IT'S THE NEIGHBOR'S.
B. CRANE
SALE
TO BE CONTINUED...

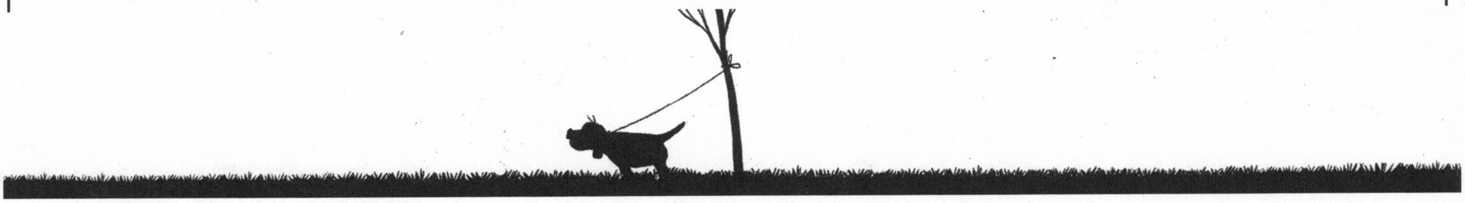

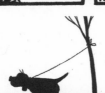

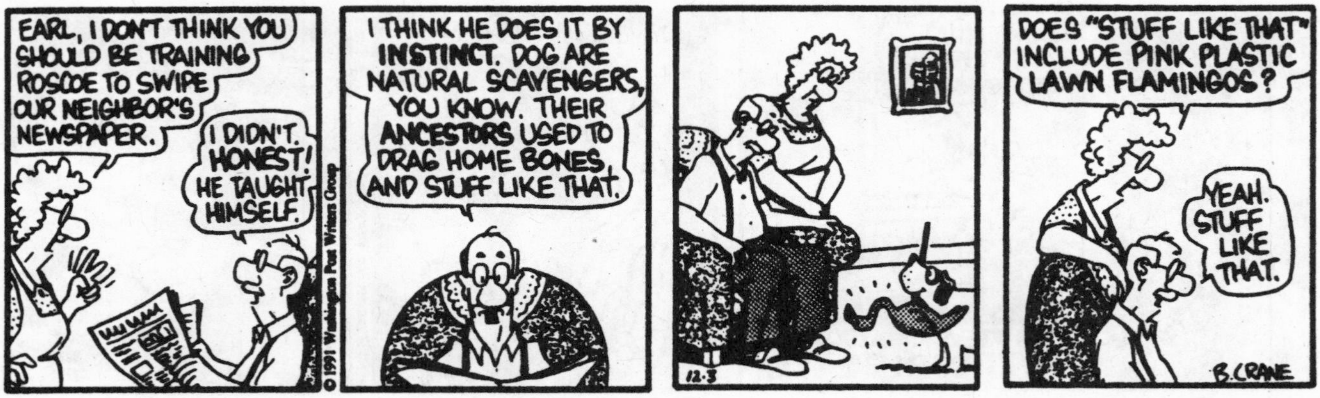
EARL, I DON'T THINK YOU SHOULD BE TRAINING ROSCOE TO SWIPE OUR NEIGHBOR'S NEWSPAPER.
I DIDN'T. HONEST! HE TAUGHT HIMSELF.
I THINK HE DOES IT BY INSTINCT. DOG ARE NATURAL SCAVENGERS, YOU KNOW. THEIR ANCESTORS USED TO DRAG HOME BONES AND STUFF LIKE THAT.
© 1991 Washington Post Writers Group
12-3
DOES "STUFF LIKE THAT" INCLUDE PINK PLASTIC LAWN FLAMINGOS?
YEAH. STUFF LIKE THAT.
B. CRANE

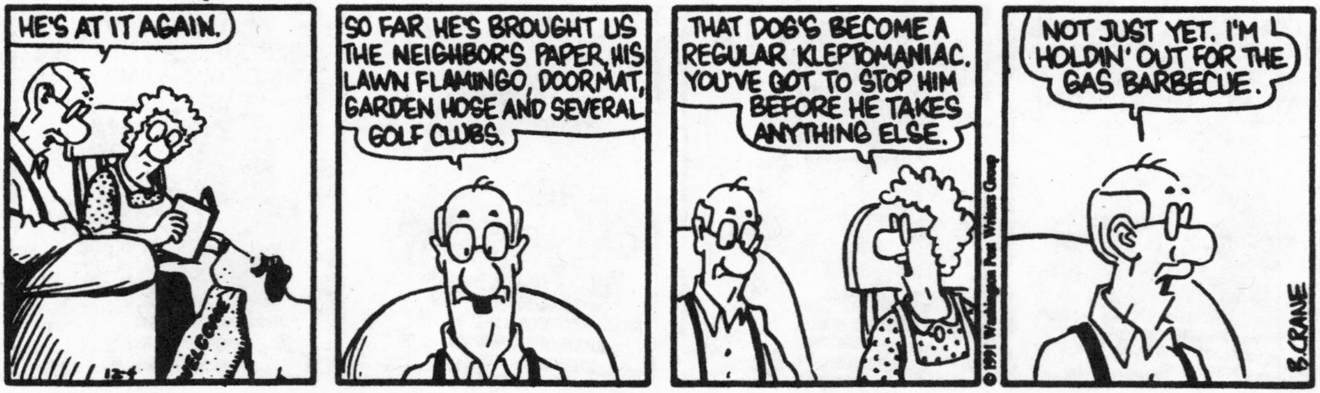
HE'S AT IT AGAIN.
SO FAR HE'S BROUGHT US THE NEIGHBOR'S PAPER, HIS LAWN FLAMINGO, DOORMAT, GARDEN HOSE AND SEVERAL GOLF CLUBS.
THAT DOG'S BECOME A REGULAR KLEPTOMANIAC. YOU'VE GOT TO STOP HIM BEFORE HE TAKES ANYTHING ELSE.
© 1991 Washington Post Writers Group
NOT JUST YET. I'M HOLDIN' OUT FOR THE GAS BARBECUE.
B. CRANE

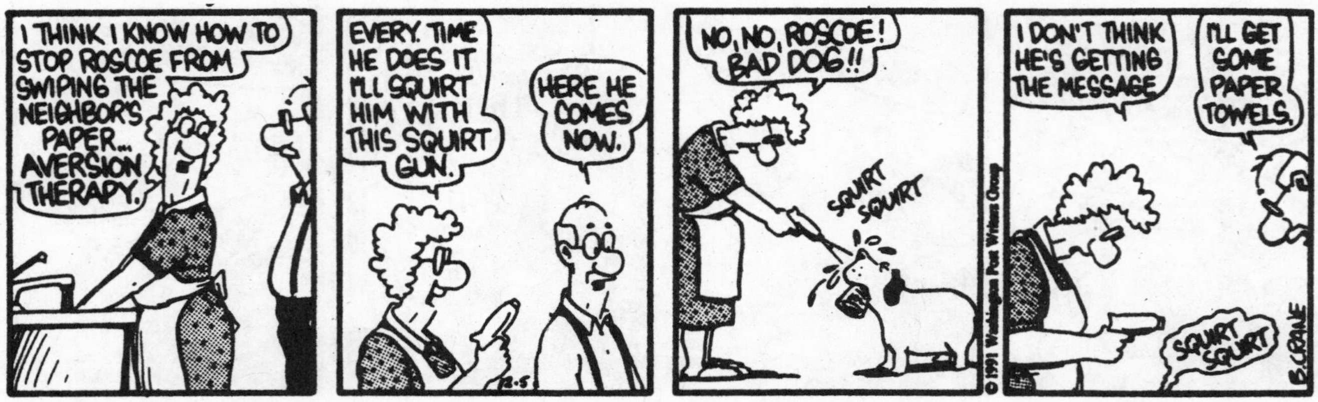
I THINK I KNOW HOW TO STOP ROSCOE FROM SWIPING THE NEIGHBOR'S PAPER... AVERSION THERAPY.
EVERY TIME HE DOES IT I'LL SQUIRT HIM WITH THIS SQUIRT GUN.
HERE HE COMES NOW.
12-5
NO, NO, ROSCOE! BAD DOG!!
SQUIRT SQUIRT
© 1991 Washington Post Writers Group
I DON'T THINK HE'S GETTING THE MESSAGE.
I'LL GET SOME PAPER TOWELS.
SQUIRT SQUIRT
B. CRANE

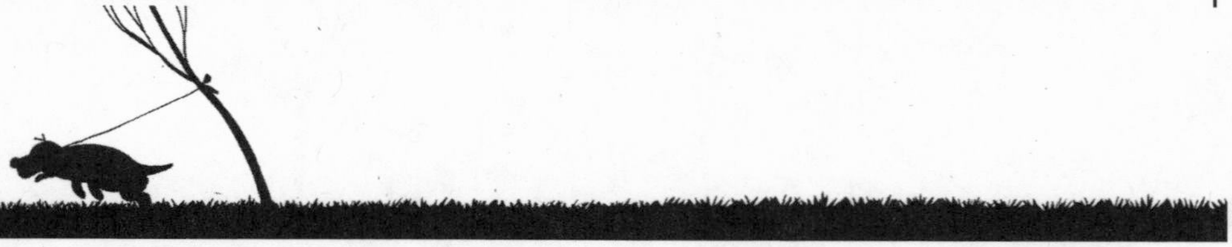

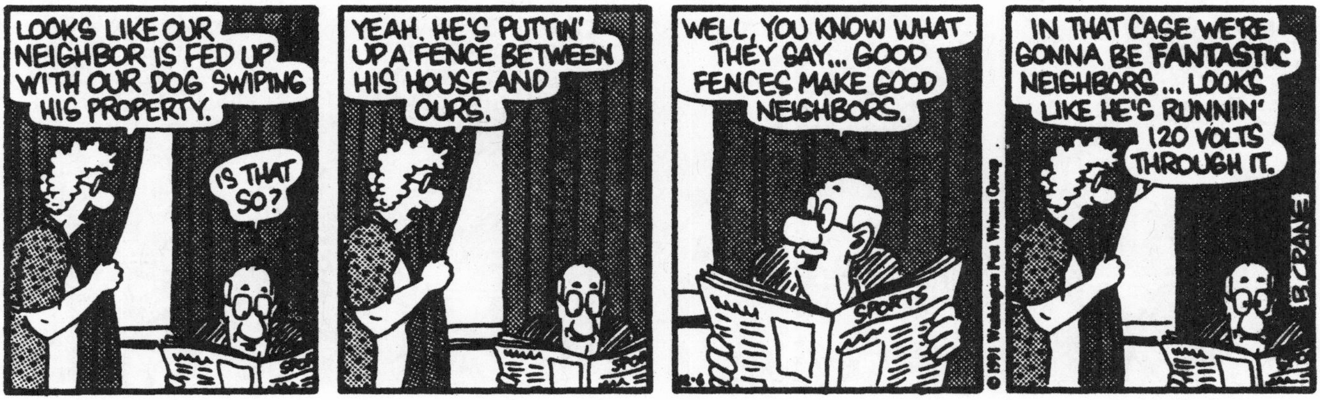
LOOKS LIKE OUR NEIGHBOR IS FED UP WITH OUR DOG SWIPING HIS PROPERTY.
IS THAT SO?
YEAH. HE'S PUTTIN' UP A FENCE BETWEEN HIS HOUSE AND OURS.
WELL, YOU KNOW WHAT THEY SAY... GOOD FENCES MAKE GOOD NEIGHBORS.
SPORTS
© 1991 Washington Post Writers Group
IN THAT CASE WE'RE GONNA BE **FANTASTIC** NEIGHBORS... LOOKS LIKE HE'S RUNNIN' 120 VOLTS THROUGH IT.
B.CRANE

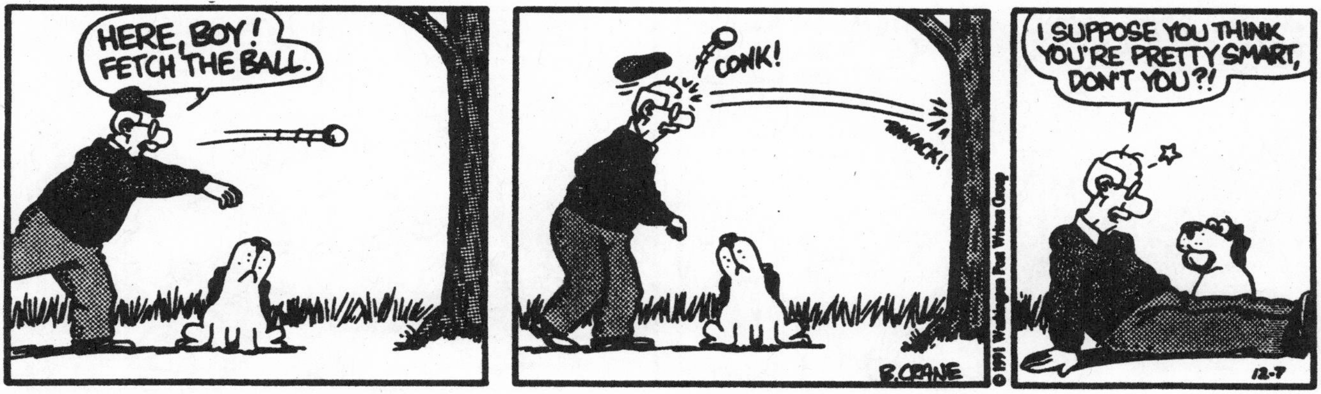
HERE, BOY! FETCH THE BALL.
CONK!
THWACK!
B.CRANE
© 1991 Washington Post Writers Group
I SUPPOSE YOU THINK YOU'RE PRETTY SMART, DON'T YOU?!
12-7

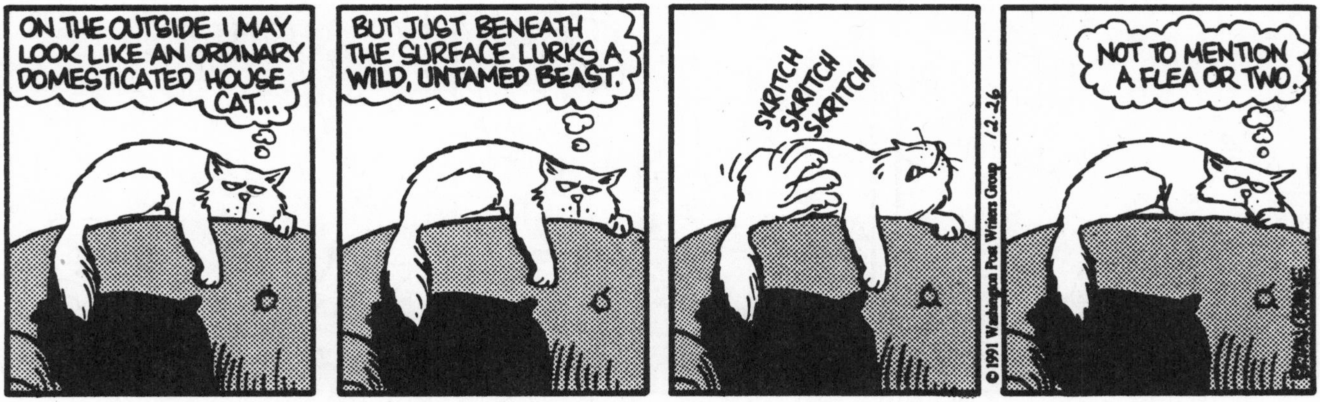
ON THE OUTSIDE I MAY LOOK LIKE AN ORDINARY DOMESTICATED HOUSE CAT...
BUT JUST BENEATH THE SURFACE LURKS A WILD, UNTAMED BEAST.
SKRITCH SKRITCH SKRITCH
12-26
© 1991 Washington Post Writers Group
NOT TO MENTION A FLEA OR TWO.
B.CRANE

39

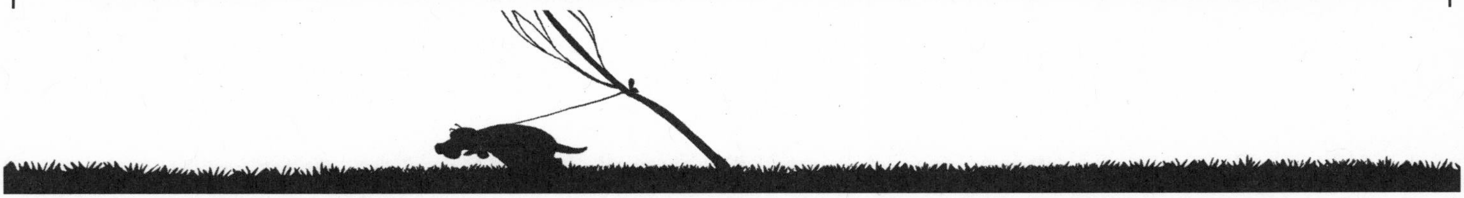

TONIGHT ON THE NATIONAL GEOGRAPHIC SPECIAL...
...WE VISIT THE FASCINATING WORLD OF THE TURKEY BUZZARD...
WATCH AS THE MOTHER BUZZARD REGURGITATES SOME ROADKILL INTO THE HUNGRY MOUTHS OF HER YOUNG ONES.
12-27
© 1991 Washington Post Writers Group
BLECHH! THAT'S THE LAST TIME I WATCH A NATURE PROGRAM WHILE I'M EATING!
SCRAPE
SCRAPE
SCRAPE
BRIAN CRANE

WHATCHA GOT THERE, EARL?
DOG WHISTLE.
IT MAKES A NOISE SO HIGH-PITCHED ONLY DOGS ARE ABLE TO HEAR IT.
BETCHA FIVE BUCKS IT DON'T WORK!
© 1991 Washington Post Writers Group
I STAND CORRECTED.
12-31
BRIAN CRANE

40

DON'T BOTHER ME ROSCOE-I'M DOIN' MY LEG LIFTS.
THERE'S NOTHING LIKE A GOOD LEG LIFT.
© 1992 Washington Post Writers Group
TELL ME ABOUT IT!
11-11
BRIAN CRANE

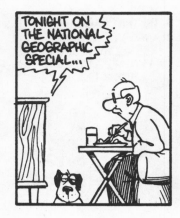

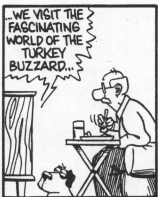

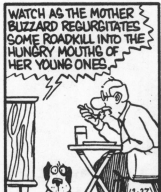

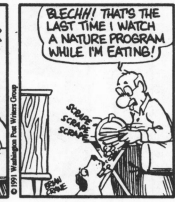

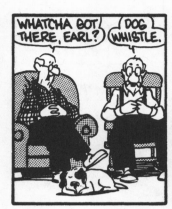

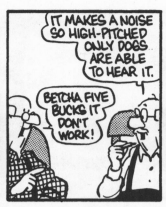

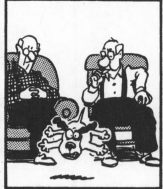

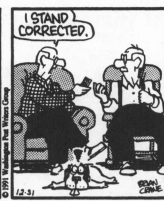

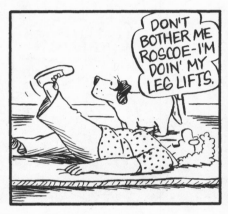

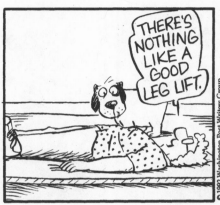

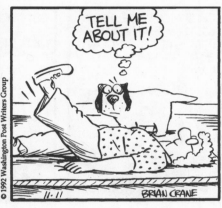

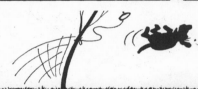

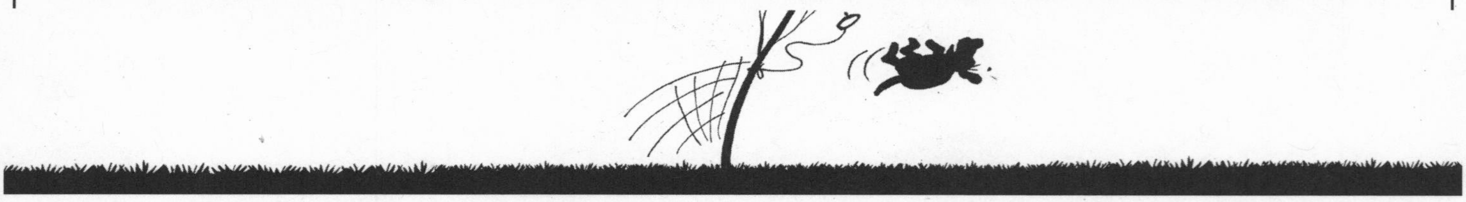

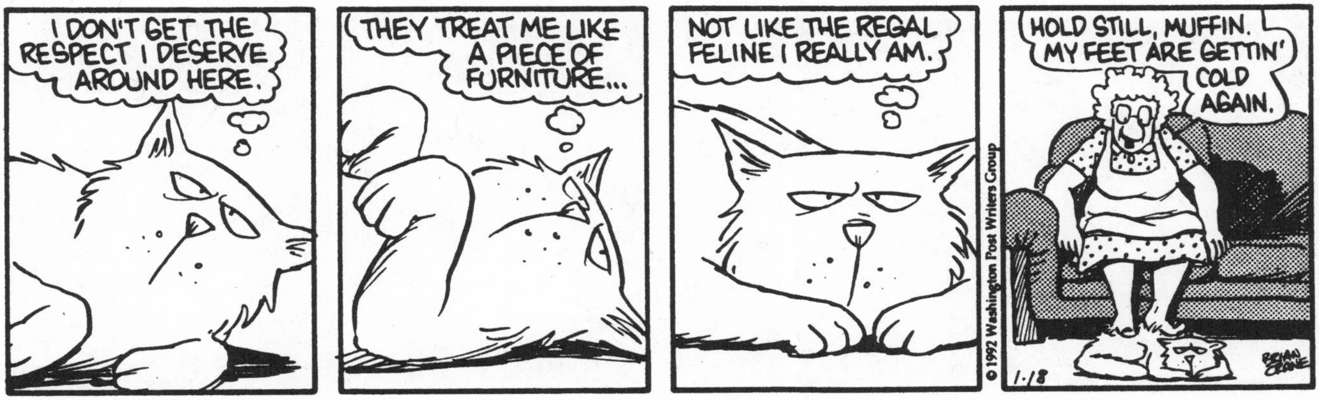
I DON'T GET THE RESPECT I DESERVE AROUND HERE.
THEY TREAT ME LIKE A PIECE OF FURNITURE...
NOT LIKE THE REGAL FELINE I REALLY AM.
© 1992 Washington Post Writers Group
HOLD STILL, MUFFIN. MY FEET ARE GETTIN' COLD AGAIN.
1·18
BRIAN CRANE

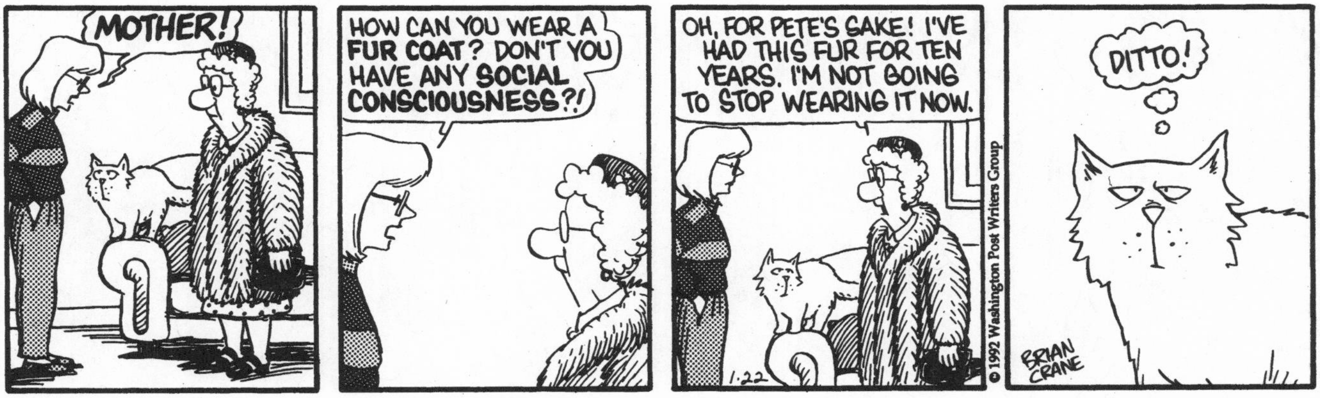
MOTHER!
HOW CAN YOU WEAR A FUR COAT? DON'T YOU HAVE ANY SOCIAL CONSCIOUSNESS?!
OH, FOR PETE'S SAKE! I'VE HAD THIS FUR FOR TEN YEARS. I'M NOT GOING TO STOP WEARING IT NOW.
1·22
© 1992 Washington Post Writers Group
BRIAN CRANE
DITTO!

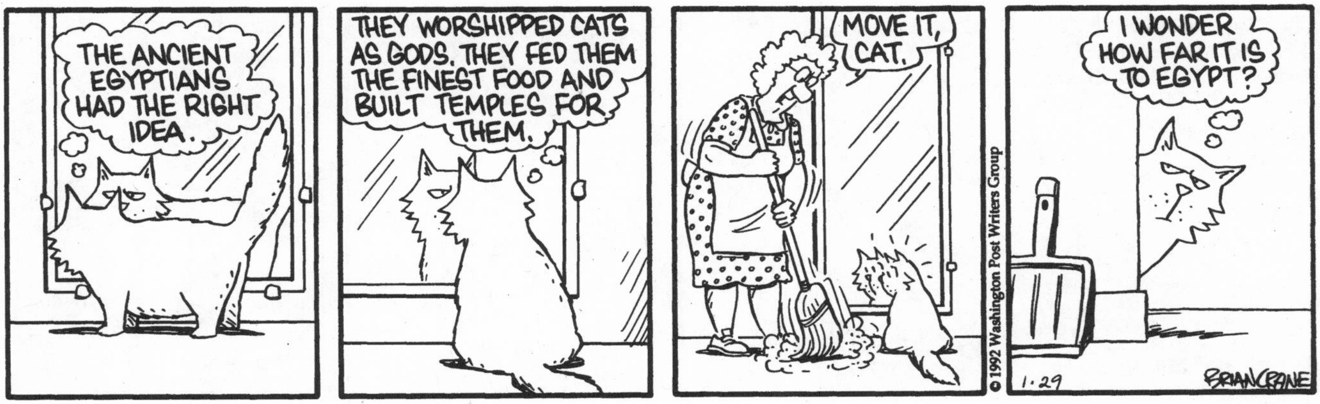
THE ANCIENT EGYPTIANS HAD THE RIGHT IDEA.
THEY WORSHIPPED CATS AS GODS. THEY FED THEM THE FINEST FOOD AND BUILT TEMPLES FOR THEM.
MOVE IT, CAT.
© 1992 Washington Post Writers Group
I WONDER HOW FAR IT IS TO EGYPT?
1·29
BRIAN CRANE

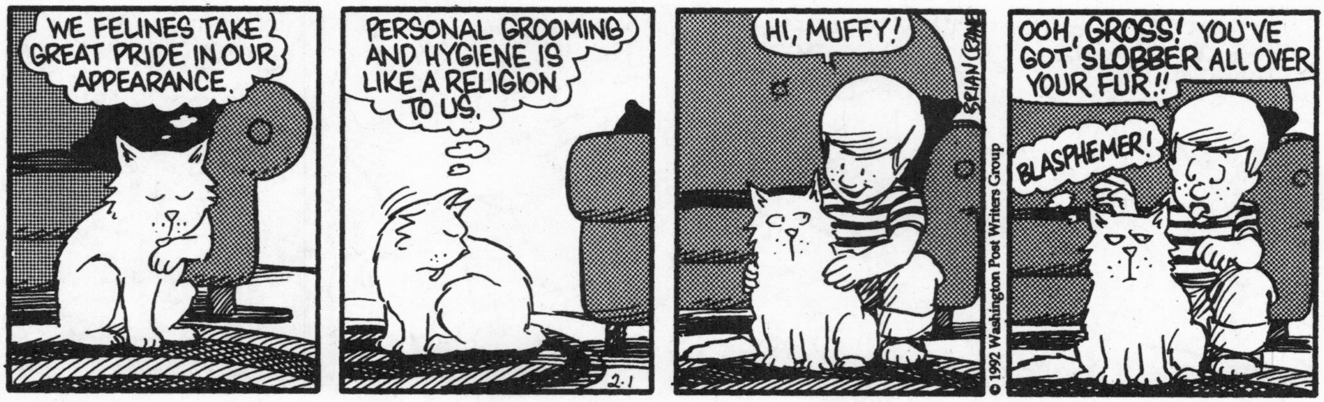
WE FELINES TAKE GREAT PRIDE IN OUR APPEARANCE.
PERSONAL GROOMING AND HYGIENE IS LIKE A RELIGION TO US.
2·1
HI, MUFFY!
BRIAN CRANE
© 1992 Washington Post Writers Group
OOH, GROSS! YOU'VE GOT SLOBBER ALL OVER YOUR FUR!!
BLASPHEMER!

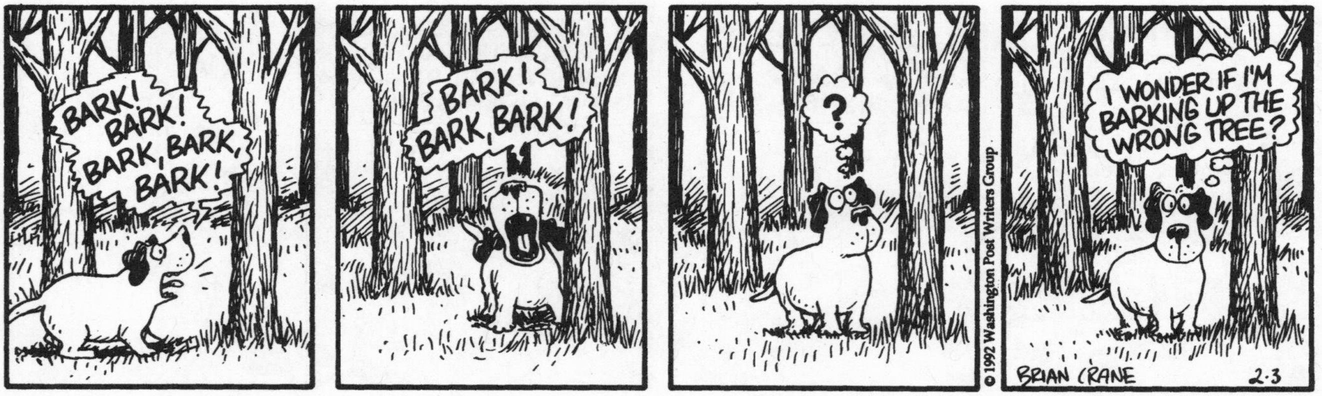
BARK! BARK! BARK, BARK, BARK!
BARK! BARK, BARK!
?
© 1992 Washington Post Writers Group
I WONDER IF I'M BARKING UP THE WRONG TREE?
BRIAN CRANE
2·3

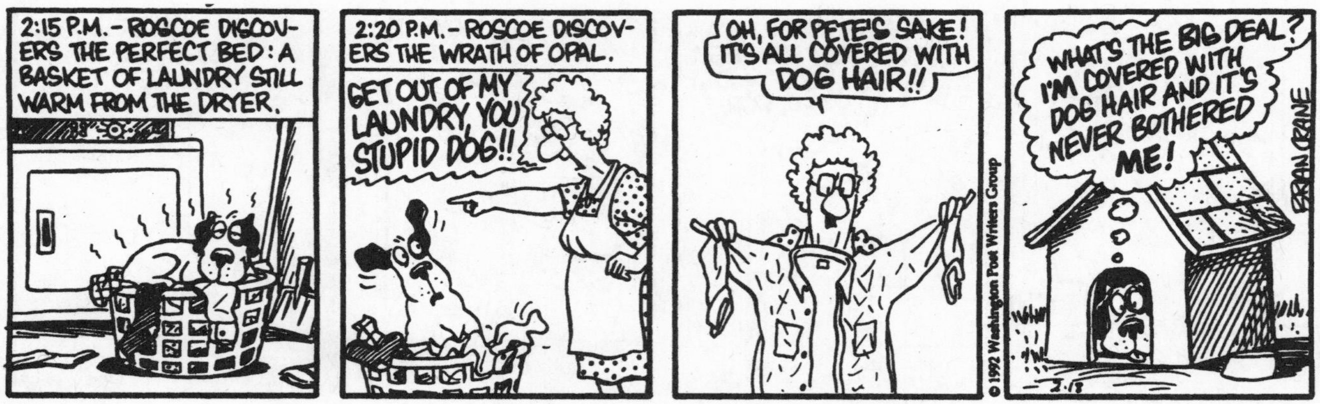
2:15 P.M. - ROSCOE DISCOVERS THE PERFECT BED: A BASKET OF LAUNDRY STILL WARM FROM THE DRYER.
2:20 P.M. - ROSCOE DISCOVERS THE WRATH OF OPAL.
GET OUT OF MY LAUNDRY, YOU STUPID DOG!!
OH, FOR PETE'S SAKE! IT'S ALL COVERED WITH DOG HAIR!!
© 1992 Washington Post Writers Group
WHAT'S THE BIG DEAL? I'M COVERED WITH DOG HAIR AND IT'S NEVER BOTHERED ME!
BRIAN CRANE

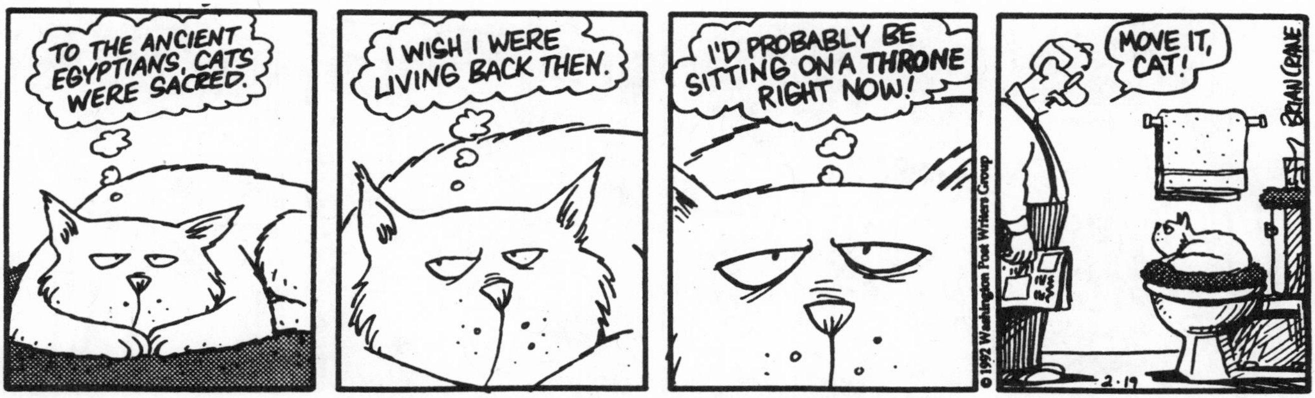
TO THE ANCIENT EGYPTIANS, CATS WERE SACRED.
I WISH I WERE LIVING BACK THEN.
I'D PROBABLY BE SITTING ON A **THRONE** RIGHT NOW!
MOVE IT, CAT!
© 1992 Washington Post Writers Group
BRIAN CRANE
2-19

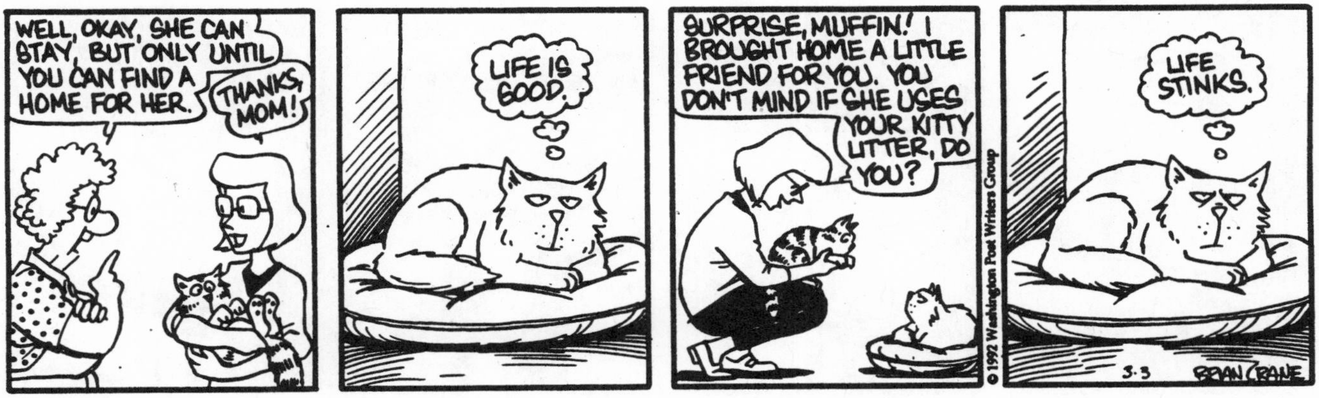
WELL, OKAY, SHE CAN STAY, BUT ONLY UNTIL YOU CAN FIND A HOME FOR HER.
THANKS, MOM!
LIFE IS GOOD.
SURPRISE, MUFFIN! I BROUGHT HOME A LITTLE FRIEND FOR YOU. YOU DON'T MIND IF SHE USES YOUR KITTY LITTER, DO YOU?
© 1992 Washington Post Writers Group
LIFE STINKS.
3-3
BRIAN CRANE

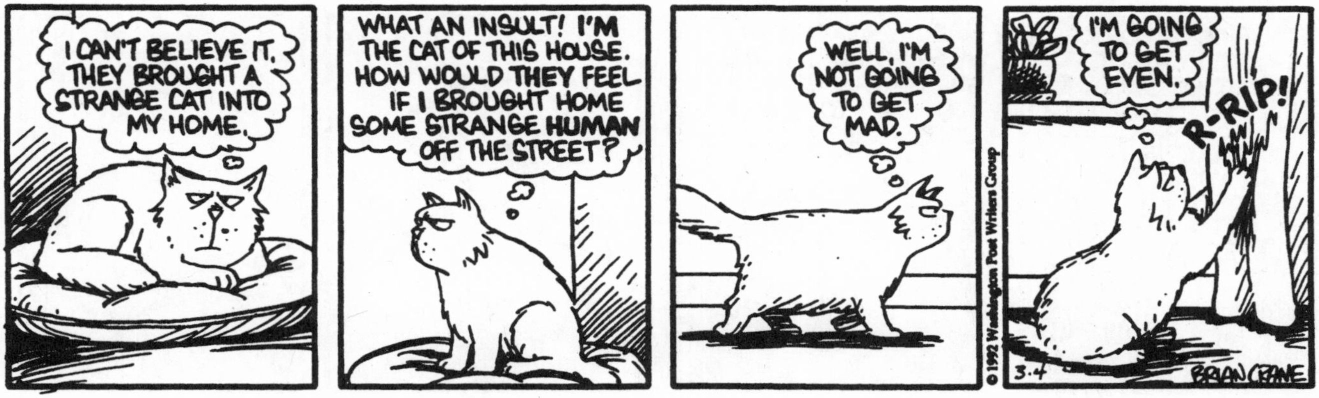
I CAN'T BELIEVE IT. THEY BROUGHT A STRANGE CAT INTO MY HOME.
WHAT AN INSULT! **I'M** THE CAT OF THIS HOUSE. HOW WOULD THEY FEEL IF I BROUGHT HOME SOME STRANGE **HUMAN** OFF THE STREET?
WELL, I'M NOT GOING TO GET MAD.
© 1992 Washington Post Writers Group
I'M GOING TO GET EVEN.
R-RIP!
3-4
BRIAN CRANE

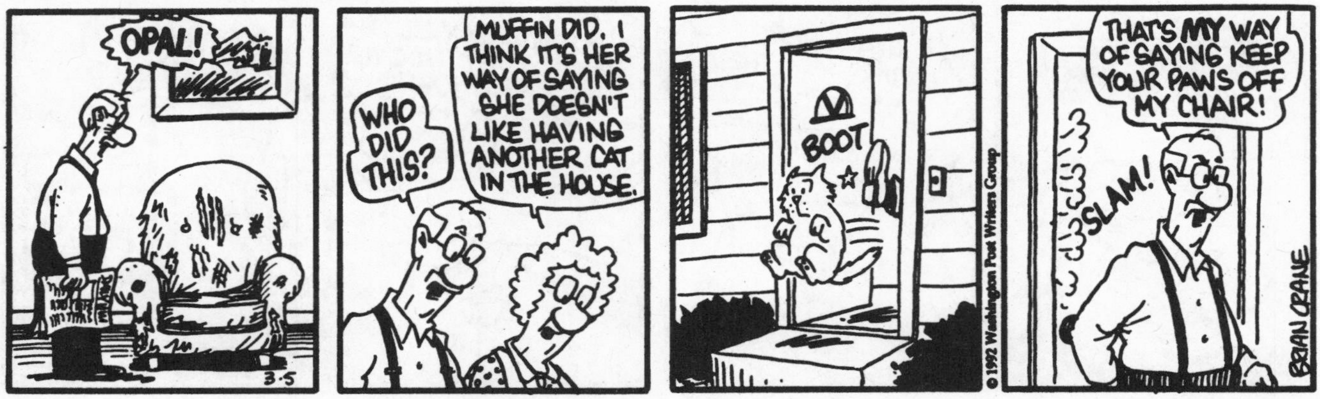
OPAL!
3-5
WHO DID THIS?
MUFFIN DID. I THINK IT'S HER WAY OF SAYING SHE DOESN'T LIKE HAVING ANOTHER CAT IN THE HOUSE.
BOOT
© 1992 Washington Post Writers Group
THAT'S MY WAY OF SAYING KEEP YOUR PAWS OFF MY CHAIR!
SLAM!
BRIAN CRANE

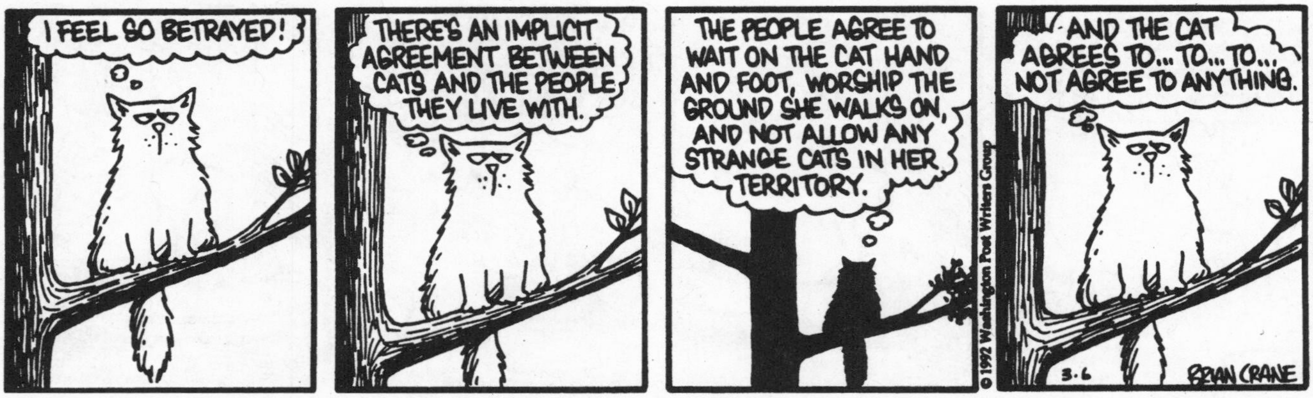
I FEEL SO BETRAYED!
THERE'S AN IMPLICIT AGREEMENT BETWEEN CATS AND THE PEOPLE THEY LIVE WITH.
THE PEOPLE AGREE TO WAIT ON THE CAT HAND AND FOOT, WORSHIP THE GROUND SHE WALKS ON, AND NOT ALLOW ANY STRANGE CATS IN HER TERRITORY.
© 1992 Washington Post Writers Group
AND THE CAT AGREES TO... TO... TO... NOT AGREE TO ANYTHING.
3-6
BRIAN CRANE

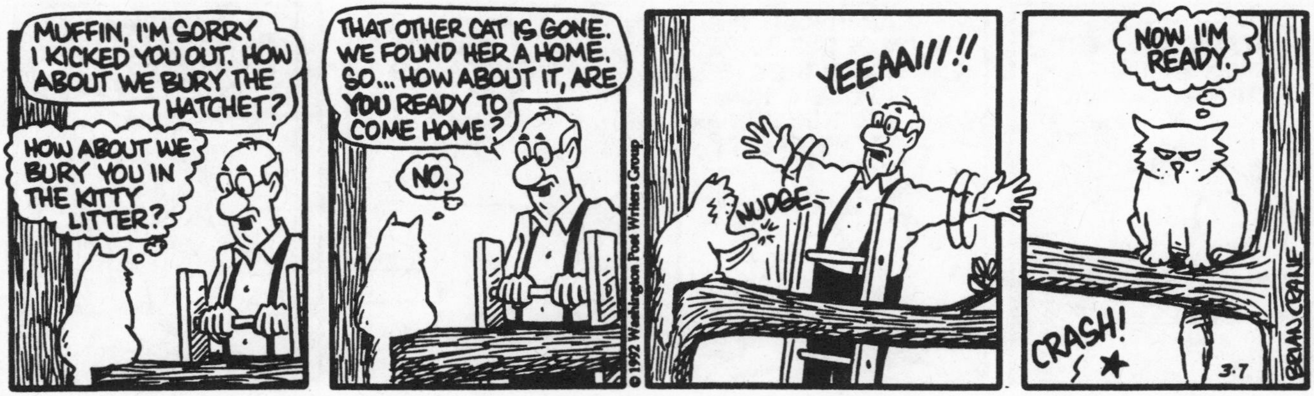
MUFFIN, I'M SORRY I KICKED YOU OUT. HOW ABOUT WE BURY THE HATCHET?
HOW ABOUT WE BURY YOU IN THE KITTY LITTER?
THAT OTHER CAT IS GONE. WE FOUND HER A HOME. SO... HOW ABOUT IT, ARE YOU READY TO COME HOME?
NO.
© 1992 Washington Post Writers Group
YEEAAI!!!!!
NUDGE
NOW I'M READY.
CRASH!
3-7
BRIAN CRANE

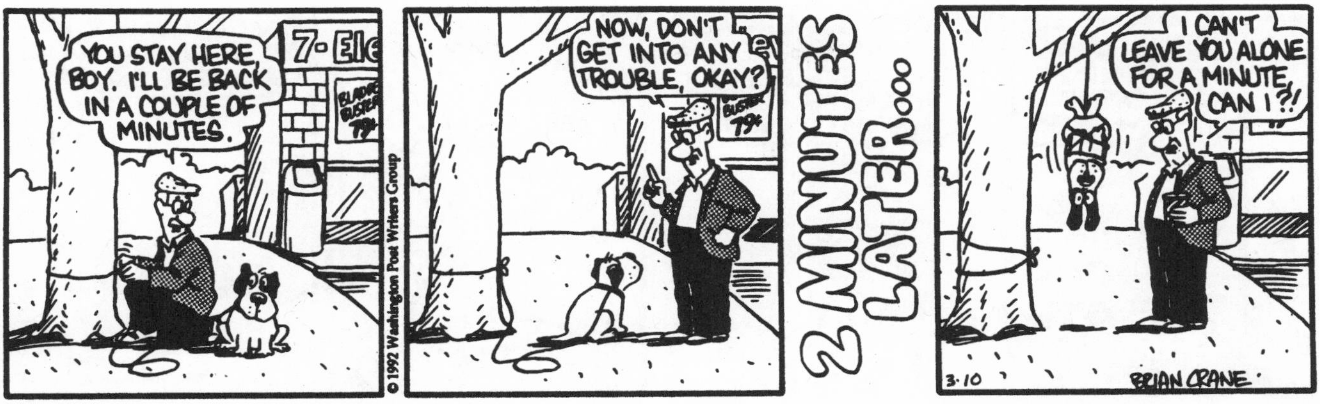
YOU STAY HERE, BOY. I'LL BE BACK IN A COUPLE OF MINUTES.
7-Ele
NOW, DON'T GET INTO ANY TROUBLE, OKAY?
2 MINUTES LATER...
I CAN'T LEAVE YOU ALONE FOR A MINUTE, CAN I?!
© 1992 Washington Post Writers Group
3·10
BRIAN CRANE

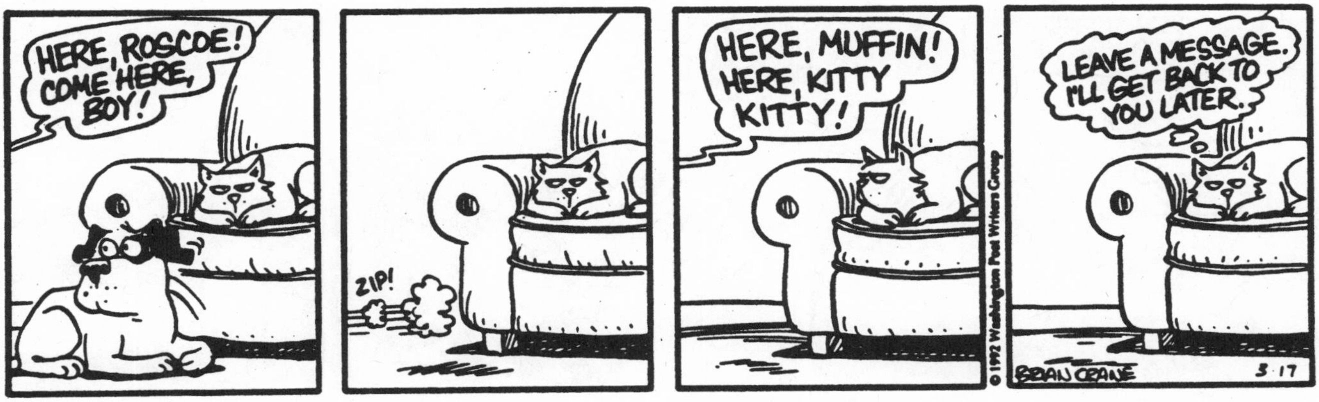
HERE, ROSCOE! COME HERE, BOY!
ZIP!
HERE, MUFFIN! HERE, KITTY KITTY!
LEAVE A MESSAGE. I'LL GET BACK TO YOU LATER.
© 1992 Washington Post Writers Group
BRIAN CRANE
3·17

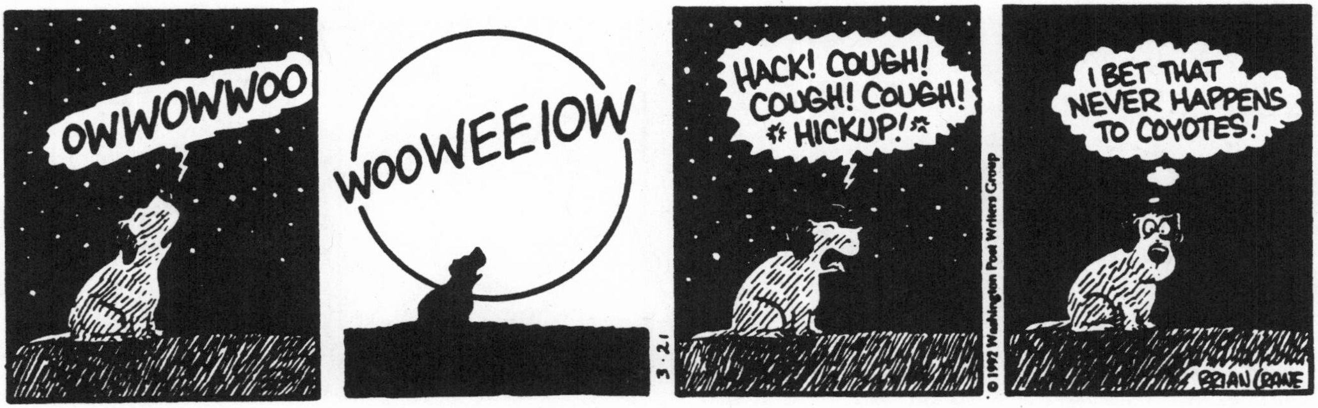
OWWOWWOO
WOOWEEIOW
3·21
HACK! COUGH! COUGH! COUGH! HICKUP!
I BET THAT NEVER HAPPENS TO COYOTES!
© 1992 Washington Post Writers Group
BRIAN CRANE

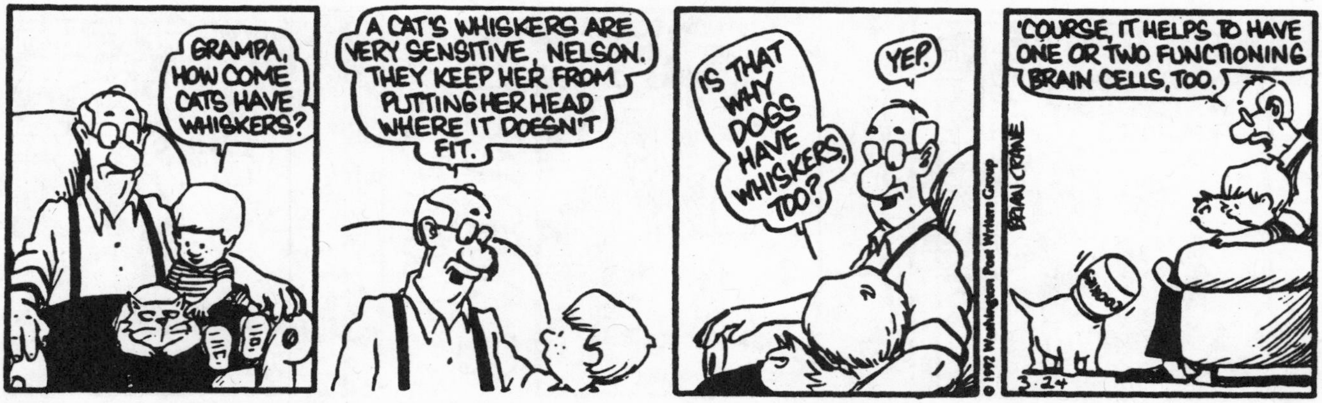
GRAMPA, HOW COME CATS HAVE WHISKERS?
A CAT'S WHISKERS ARE VERY SENSITIVE, NELSON. THEY KEEP HER FROM PUTTING HER HEAD WHERE IT DOESN'T FIT.
IS THAT WHY DOGS HAVE WHISKERS, TOO?
YEP.
'COURSE, IT HELPS TO HAVE ONE OR TWO FUNCTIONING BRAIN CELLS, TOO.
© 1992 Washington Post Writers Group
BRIAN CRANE
3·24

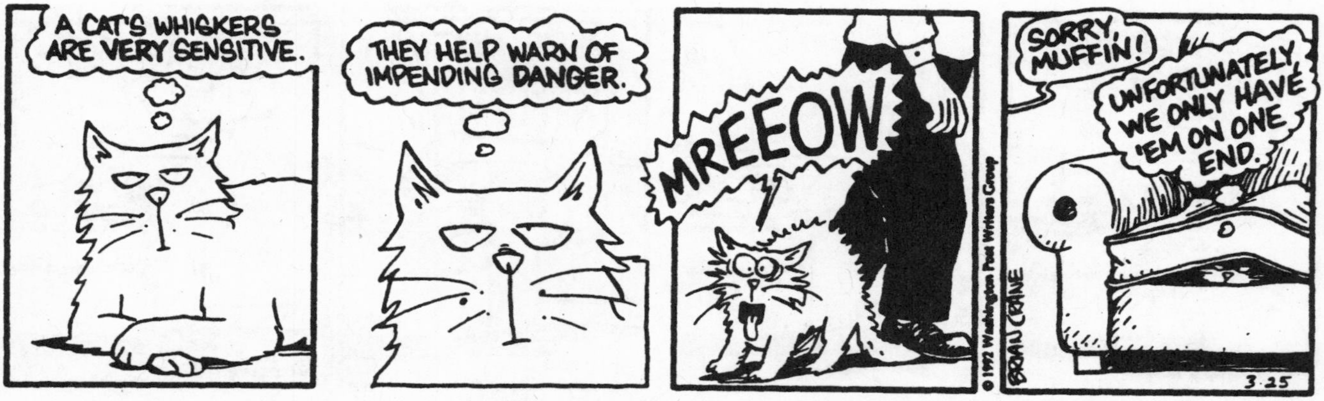
A CAT'S WHISKERS ARE VERY SENSITIVE.
THEY HELP WARN OF IMPENDING DANGER.
MREEOW
© 1992 Washington Post Writers Group
BRIAN CRANE
SORRY, MUFFIN!
UNFORTUNATELY, WE ONLY HAVE 'EM ON ONE END.
3·25

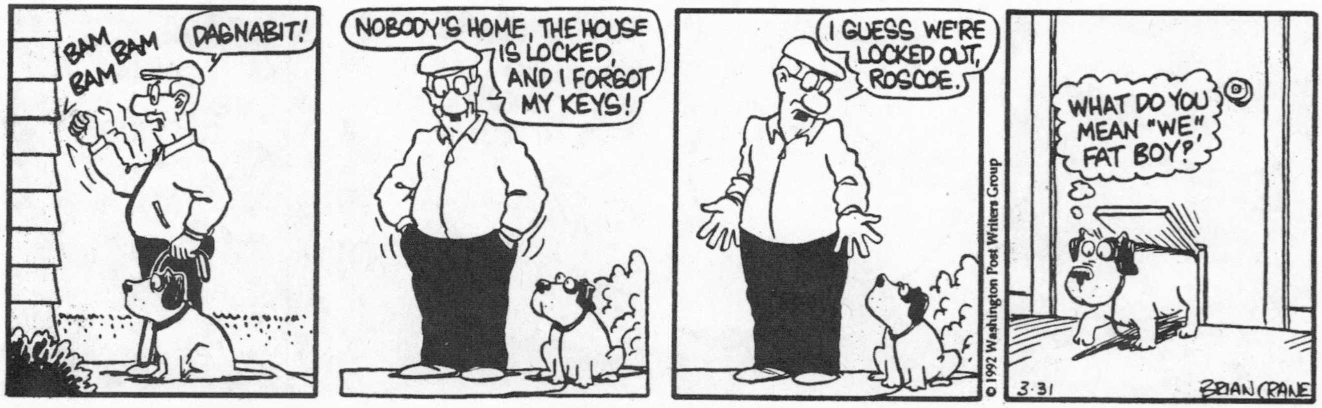
BAM BAM BAM BAM
DAGNABIT!
NOBODY'S HOME, THE HOUSE IS LOCKED, AND I FORGOT MY KEYS!
I GUESS WE'RE LOCKED OUT, ROSCOE.
© 1992 Washington Post Writers Group
WHAT DO YOU MEAN "WE", FAT BOY?
3·31
BRIAN CRANE

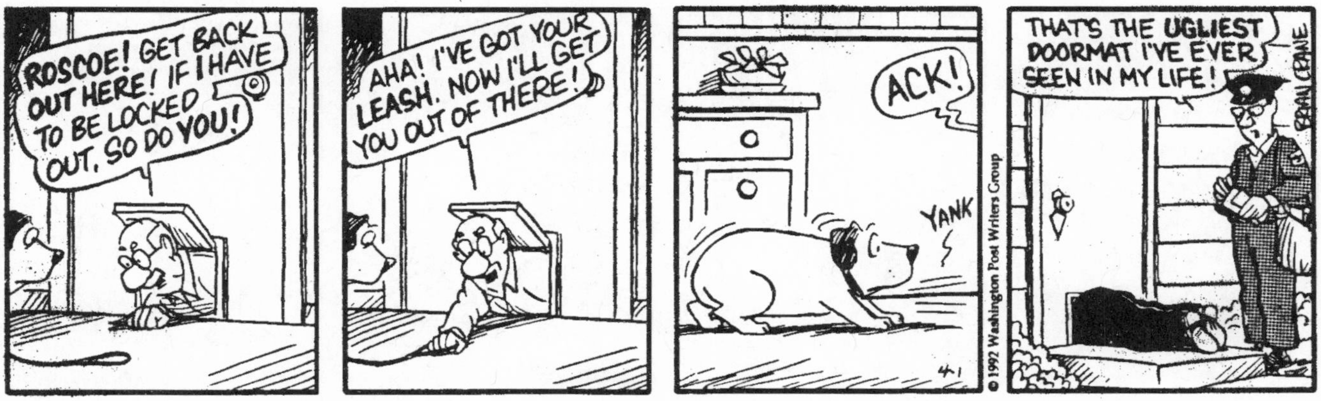
ROSCOE! GET BACK OUT HERE! IF I HAVE TO BE LOCKED OUT, SO DO YOU!
AHA! I'VE GOT YOUR LEASH. NOW I'LL GET YOU OUT OF THERE!
ACK!
YANK
4.1
© 1992 Washington Post Writers Group
THAT'S THE UGLIEST DOORMAT I'VE EVER SEEN IN MY LIFE!
BRIAN CRANE

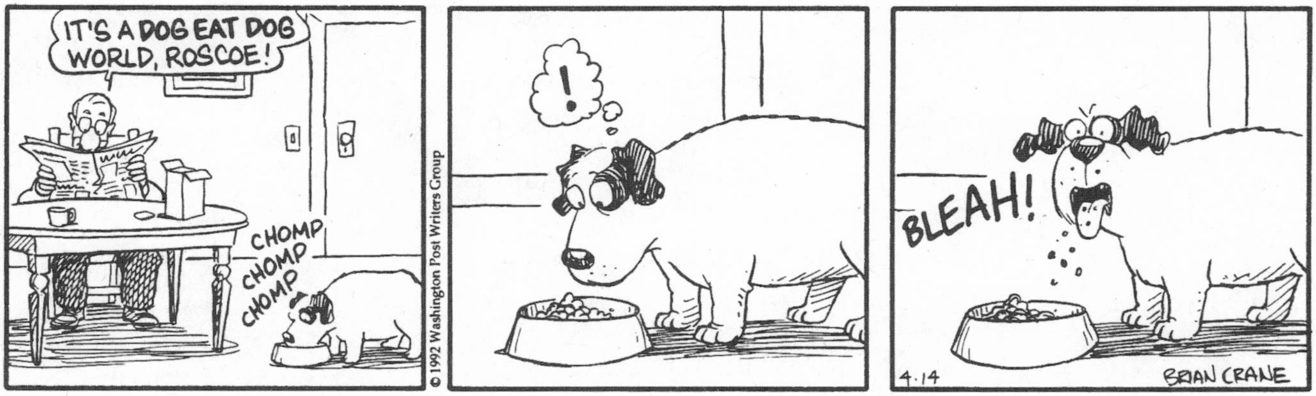
IT'S A DOG EAT DOG WORLD, ROSCOE!
CHOMP CHOMP CHOMP
© 1992 Washington Post Writers Group
!
BLEAH!
4.14
BRIAN CRANE

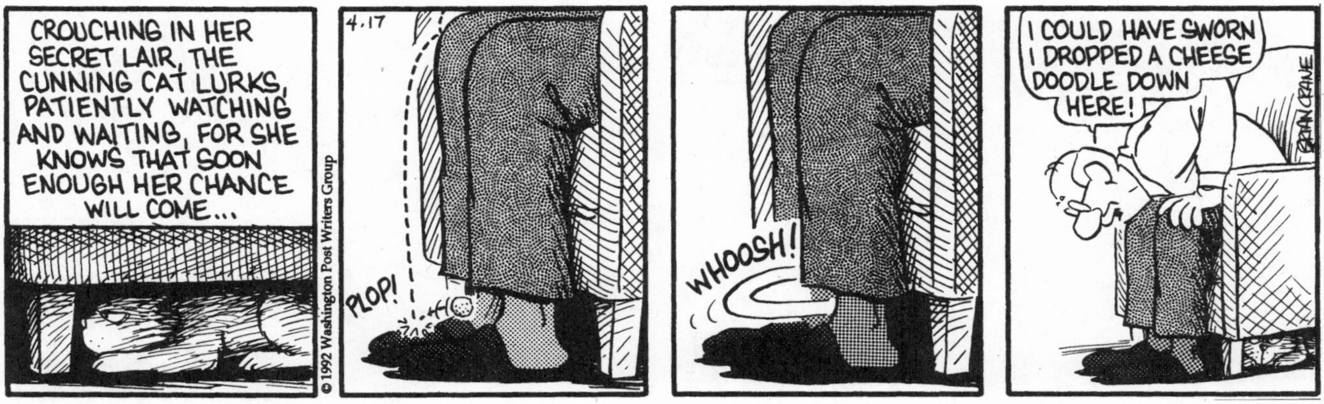
CROUCHING IN HER SECRET LAIR, THE CUNNING CAT LURKS, PATIENTLY WATCHING AND WAITING, FOR SHE KNOWS THAT SOON ENOUGH HER CHANCE WILL COME...
© 1992 Washington Post Writers Group
4.17
PLOP!
WHOOSH!
I COULD HAVE SWORN I DROPPED A CHEESE DOODLE DOWN HERE!
BRIAN CRANE

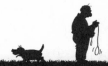

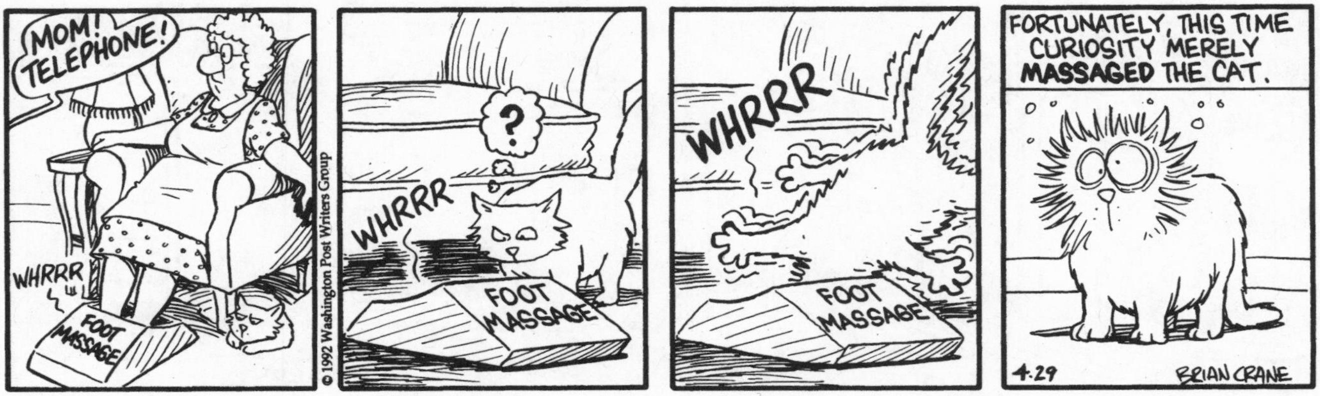
MOM! TELEPHONE!
WHRRR
FOOT MASSAGE
© 1992 Washington Post Writers Group
?
WHRRR
FOOT MASSAGE
WHRRR
FOOT MASSAGE
FORTUNATELY, THIS TIME CURIOSITY MERELY **MASSAGED** THE CAT.
4-29
BRIAN CRANE

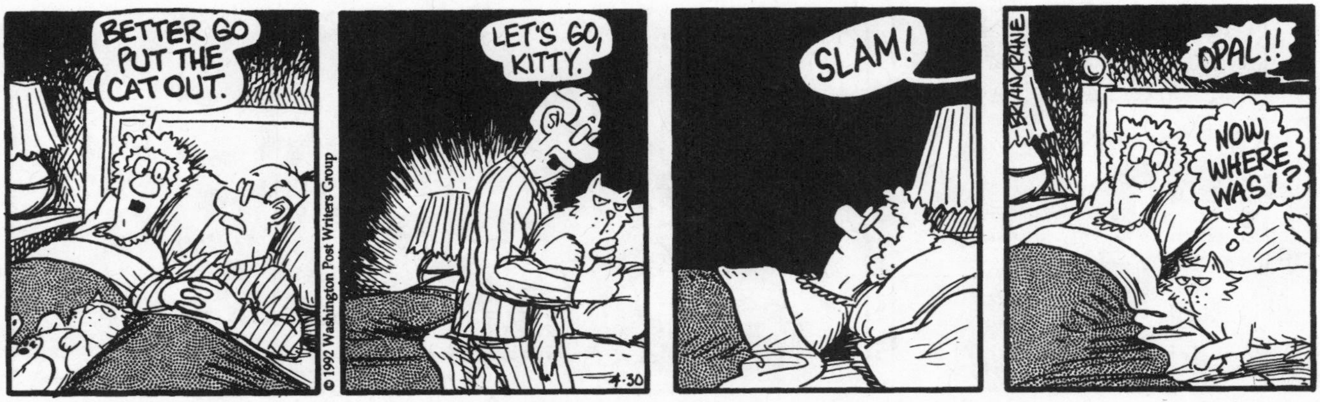
BETTER GO PUT THE CAT OUT.
© 1992 Washington Post Writers Group
LET'S GO, KITTY.
4-30
SLAM!
BRIAN CRANE
OPAL!!
NOW, WHERE WAS I?

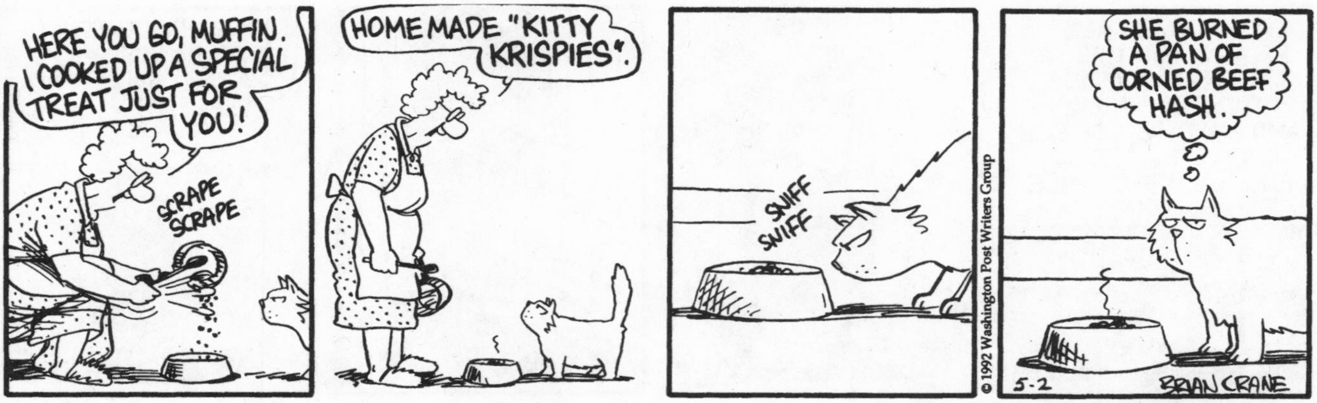
HERE YOU GO, MUFFIN. I COOKED UP A SPECIAL TREAT JUST FOR YOU!
SCRAPE SCRAPE
HOMEMADE "KITTY KRISPIES".
SNIFF SNIFF
© 1992 Washington Post Writers Group
SHE BURNED A PAN OF CORNED BEEF HASH.
5-2
BRIAN CRANE

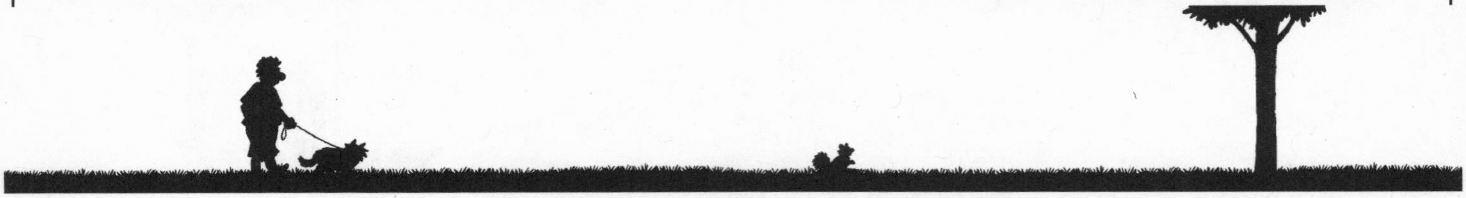

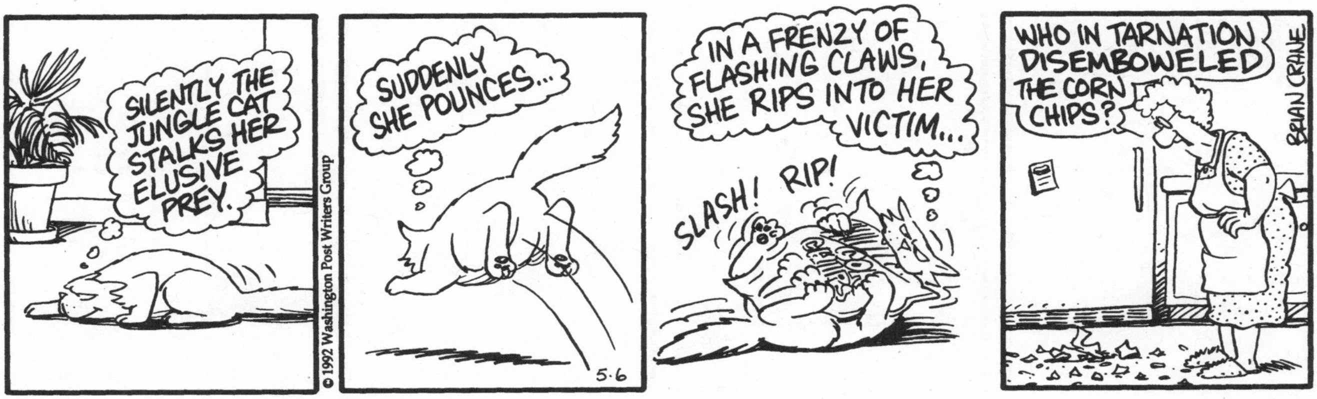
SILENTLY THE JUNGLE CAT STALKS HER ELUSIVE PREY.
© 1992 Washington Post Writers Group
SUDDENLY SHE POUNCES...
5·6
IN A FRENZY OF FLASHING CLAWS, SHE RIPS INTO HER VICTIM...
SLASH! RIP!
WHO IN TARNATION DISEMBOWELED THE CORN CHIPS?
BRIAN CRANE

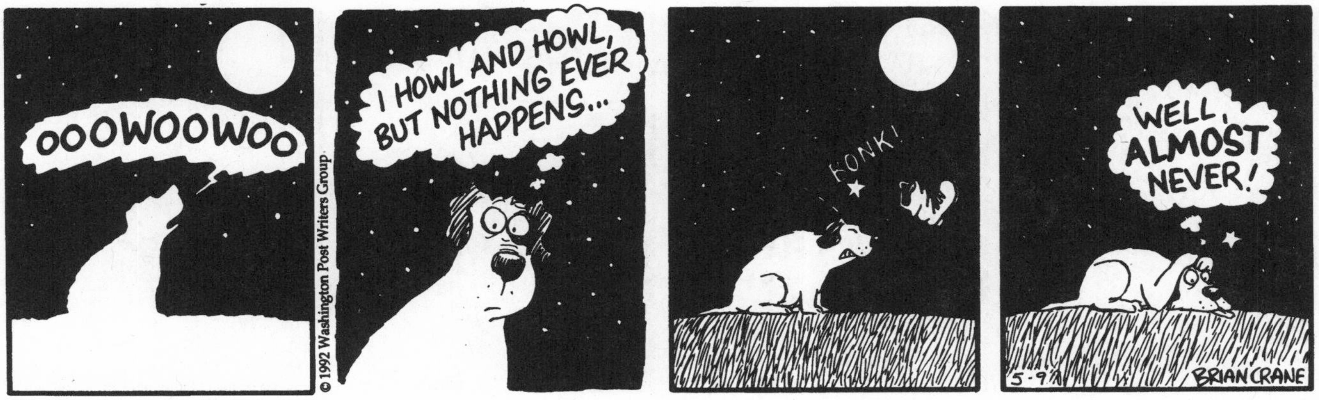
OOOWOOWOO
© 1992 Washington Post Writers Group.
I HOWL AND HOWL, BUT NOTHING EVER HAPPENS...
KONK!
WELL, ALMOST NEVER!
BRIAN CRANE

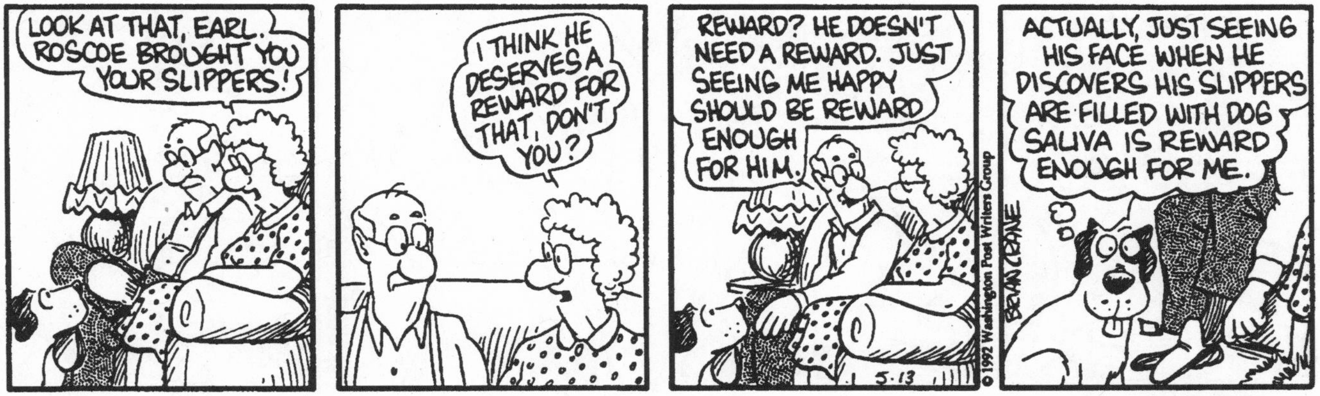
LOOK AT THAT, EARL. ROSCOE BROUGHT YOU YOUR SLIPPERS!
I THINK HE DESERVES A REWARD FOR THAT, DON'T YOU?
REWARD? HE DOESN'T NEED A REWARD. JUST SEEING ME HAPPY SHOULD BE REWARD ENOUGH FOR HIM.
5·13
© 1992 Washington Post Writers Group
BRIAN CRANE
ACTUALLY, JUST SEEING HIS FACE WHEN HE DISCOVERS HIS SLIPPERS ARE FILLED WITH DOG SALIVA IS REWARD ENOUGH FOR ME.

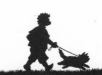

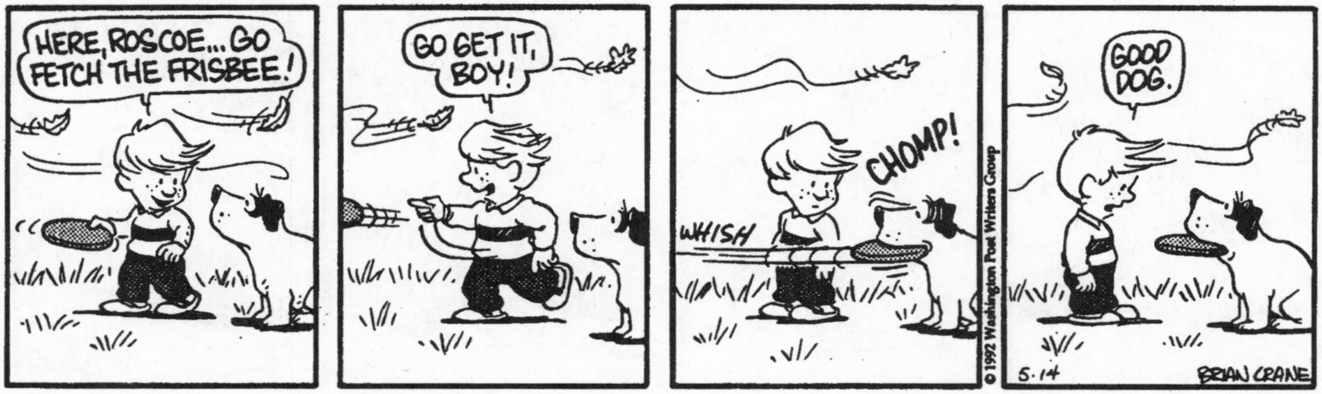
HERE, ROSCOE... GO FETCH THE FRISBEE!
GO GET IT, BOY!
WHISH
CHOMP!
© 1992 Washington Post Writers Group
GOOD DOG.
5.14
BRIAN CRANE

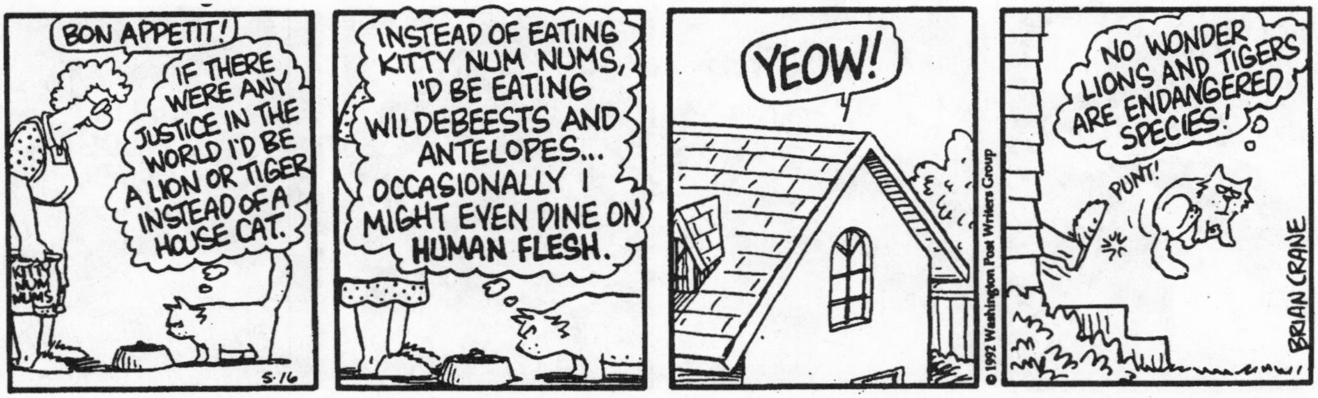
BON APPETIT!
IF THERE WERE ANY JUSTICE IN THE WORLD I'D BE A LION OR TIGER INSTEAD OF A HOUSE CAT.
KITTY NUM NUMS
5.16
INSTEAD OF EATING KITTY NUM NUMS, I'D BE EATING WILDEBEESTS AND ANTELOPES... OCCASIONALLY I MIGHT EVEN DINE ON HUMAN FLESH.
YEOW!
© 1992 Washington Post Writers Group
NO WONDER LIONS AND TIGERS ARE ENDANGERED SPECIES!
PUNT!
BRIAN CRANE

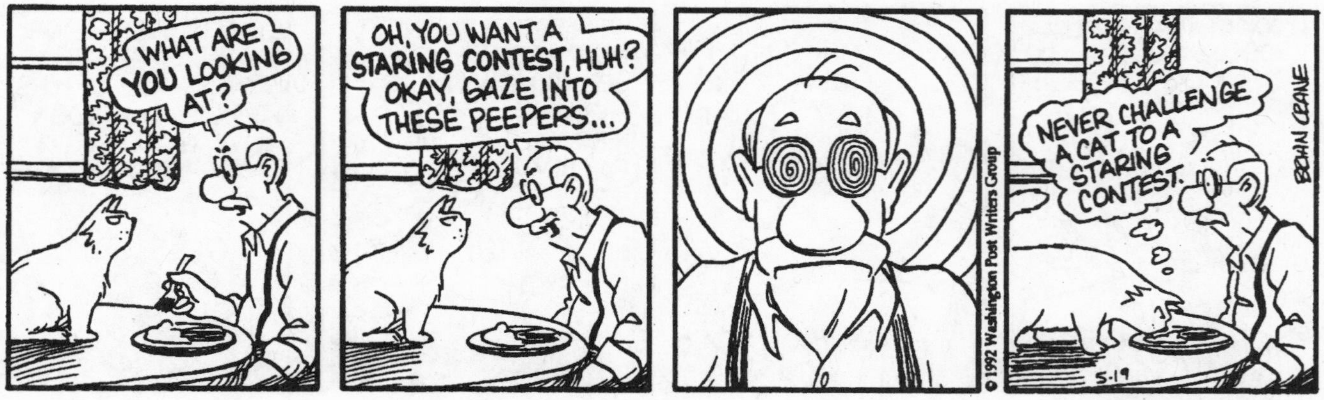
WHAT ARE YOU LOOKING AT?
OH, YOU WANT A STARING CONTEST, HUH? OKAY, GAZE INTO THESE PEEPERS...
© 1992 Washington Post Writers Group
NEVER CHALLENGE A CAT TO A STARING CONTEST.
BRIAN CRANE
5.19

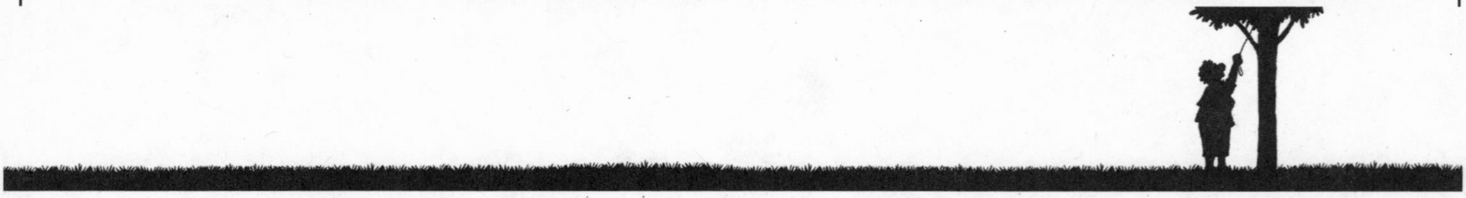

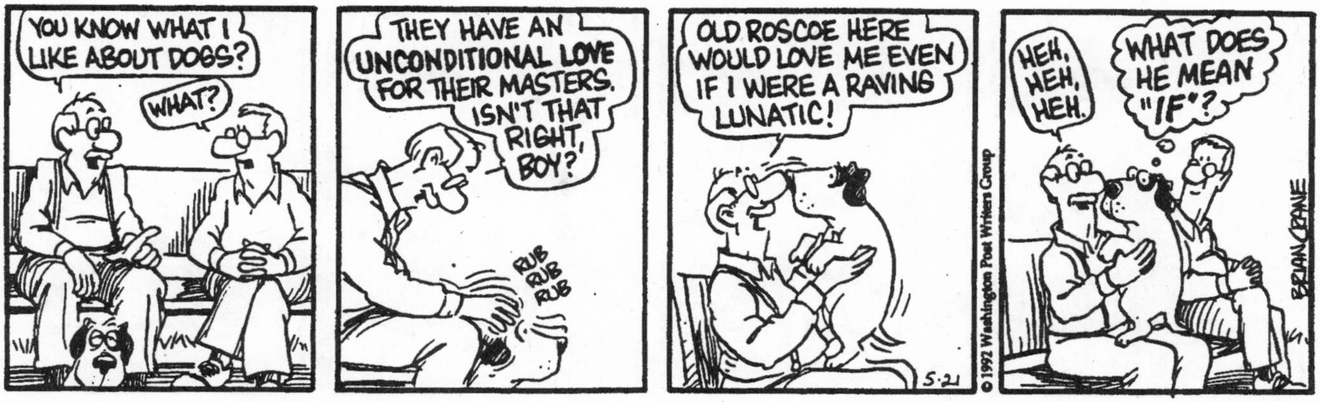
YOU KNOW WHAT I LIKE ABOUT DOGS?
WHAT?
THEY HAVE AN UNCONDITIONAL LOVE FOR THEIR MASTERS.
ISN'T THAT RIGHT, BOY?
RUB RUB RUB
OLD ROSCOE HERE WOULD LOVE ME EVEN IF I WERE A RAVING LUNATIC!
5·21
© 1992 Washington Post Writers Group
HEH, HEH, HEH.
WHAT DOES HE MEAN "IF"?
BRIAN CRANE

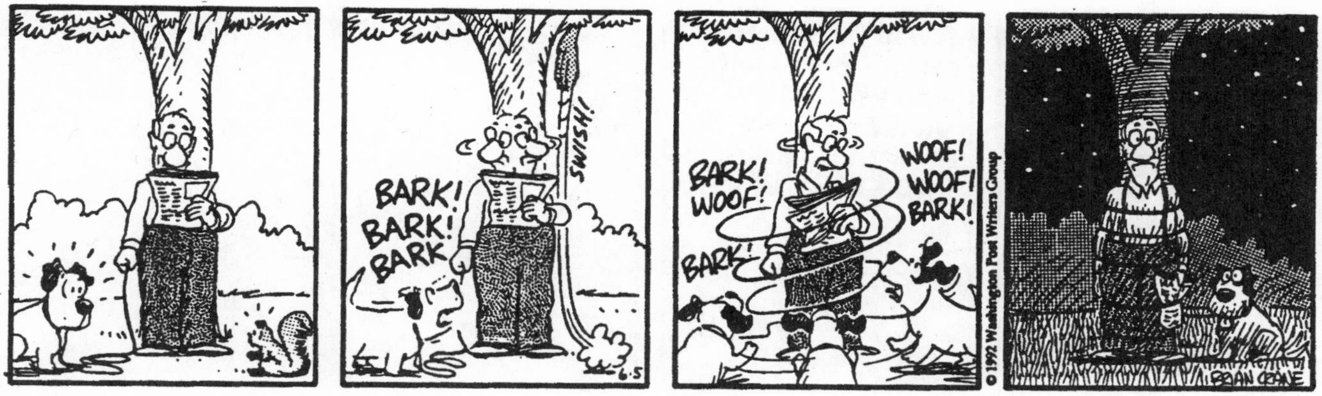
BARK! BARK! BARK
SWISH!
6·5
BARK! WOOF!
WOOF! WOOF! BARK!
BARK!
© 1992 Washington Post Writers Group
BRIAN CRANE

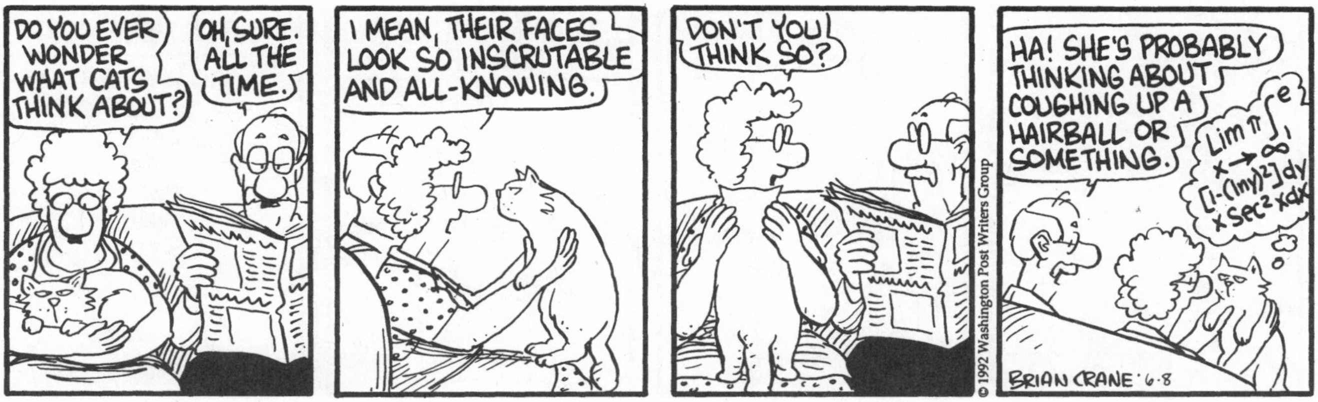
DO YOU EVER WONDER WHAT CATS THINK ABOUT?
OH, SURE. ALL THE TIME.
I MEAN, THEIR FACES LOOK SO INSCRUTABLE AND ALL-KNOWING.
DON'T YOU THINK SO?
© 1992 Washington Post Writers Group
HA! SHE'S PROBABLY THINKING ABOUT COUGHING UP A HAIRBALL OR SOMETHING.
Lim π ∫ e
x→∞ 1
[1-(lny)²] dy
x Sec² xdx
BRIAN CRANE 6·8

52

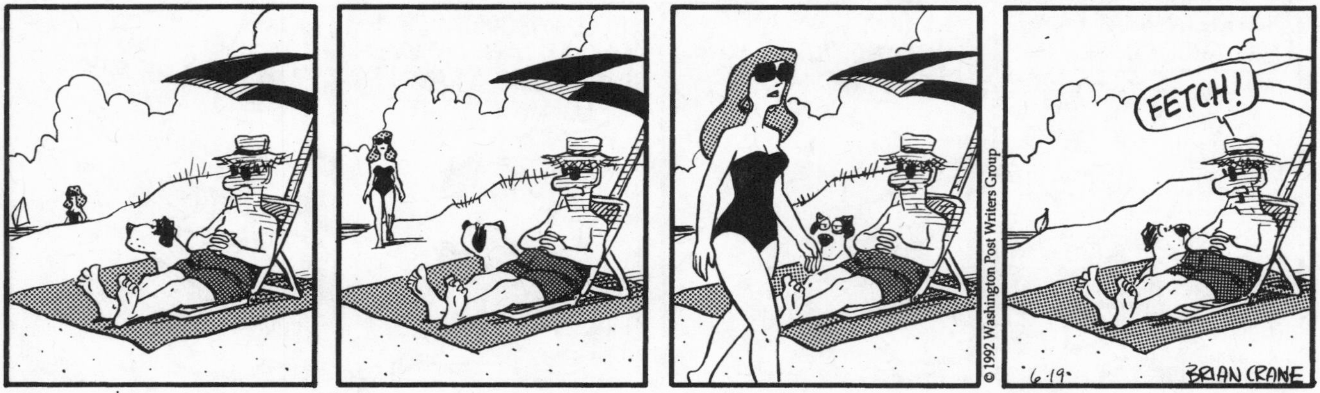
© 1992 Washington Post Writers Group
FETCH!
6·19
BRIAN CRANE

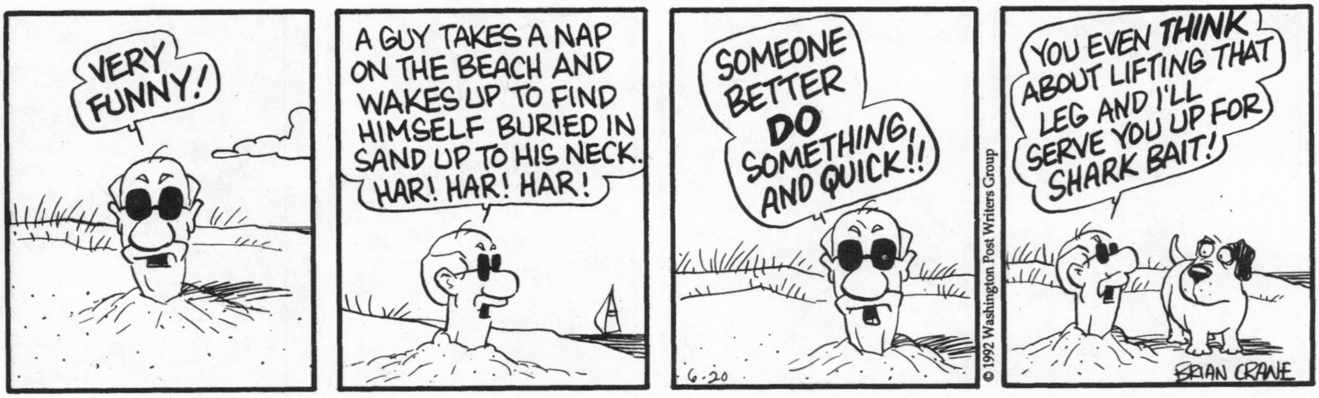
VERY FUNNY!
A GUY TAKES A NAP ON THE BEACH AND WAKES UP TO FIND HIMSELF BURIED IN SAND UP TO HIS NECK. HAR! HAR! HAR!
SOMEONE BETTER DO SOMETHING, AND QUICK!!
6·20
© 1992 Washington Post Writers Group
YOU EVEN THINK ABOUT LIFTING THAT LEG AND I'LL SERVE YOU UP FOR SHARK BAIT!
BRIAN CRANE

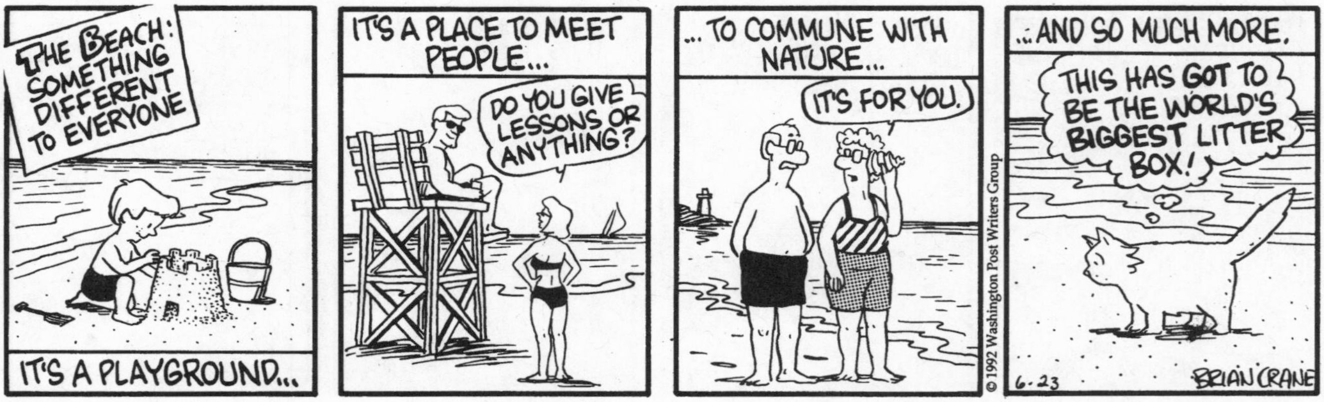
THE BEACH: SOMETHING DIFFERENT TO EVERYONE
IT'S A PLAYGROUND...
IT'S A PLACE TO MEET PEOPLE...
DO YOU GIVE LESSONS OR ANYTHING?
...TO COMMUNE WITH NATURE...
IT'S FOR YOU.
© 1992 Washington Post Writers Group
...AND SO MUCH MORE.
THIS HAS GOT TO BE THE WORLD'S BIGGEST LITTER BOX!
6·23
BRIAN CRANE

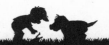

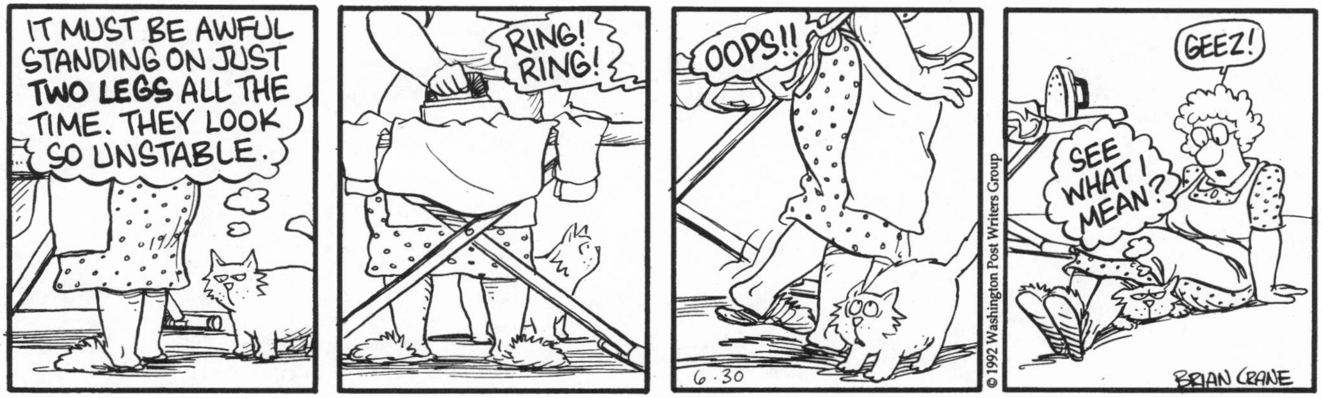
IT MUST BE AWFUL STANDING ON JUST TWO LEGS ALL THE TIME. THEY LOOK SO UNSTABLE.
RING! RING!
OOPS!!
6·30
© 1992 Washington Post Writers Group
GEEZ!
SEE WHAT I MEAN?
BRIAN CRANE

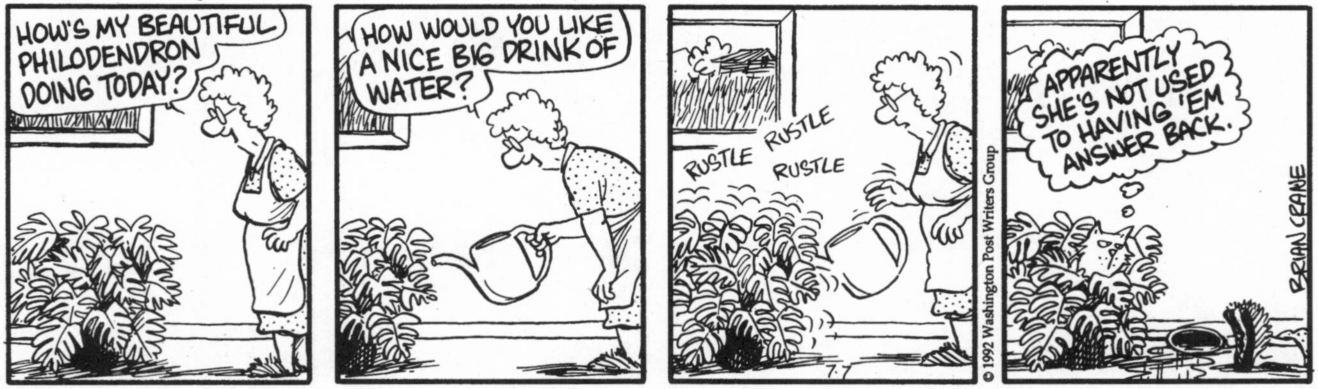
HOW'S MY BEAUTIFUL PHILODENDRON DOING TODAY?
HOW WOULD YOU LIKE A NICE BIG DRINK OF WATER?
RUSTLE RUSTLE
RUSTLE
7·7
© 1992 Washington Post Writers Group
APPARENTLY SHE'S NOT USED TO HAVING 'EM ANSWER BACK.
BRIAN CRANE

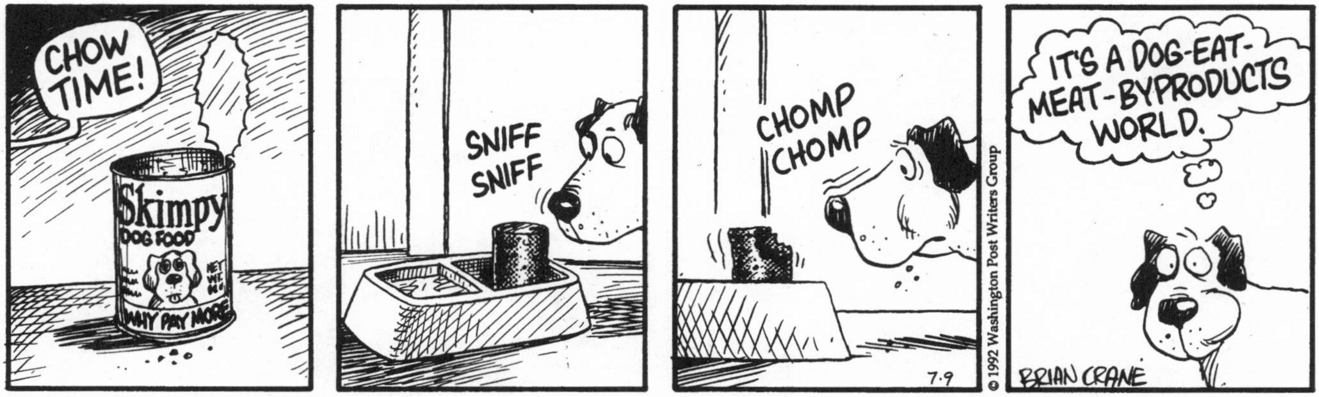
CHOW TIME!
Skimpy
DOG FOOD
WHY PAY MORE
SNIFF SNIFF
CHOMP CHOMP
7·9
© 1992 Washington Post Writers Group
BRIAN CRANE
IT'S A DOG-EAT-MEAT-BYPRODUCTS WORLD.

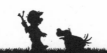

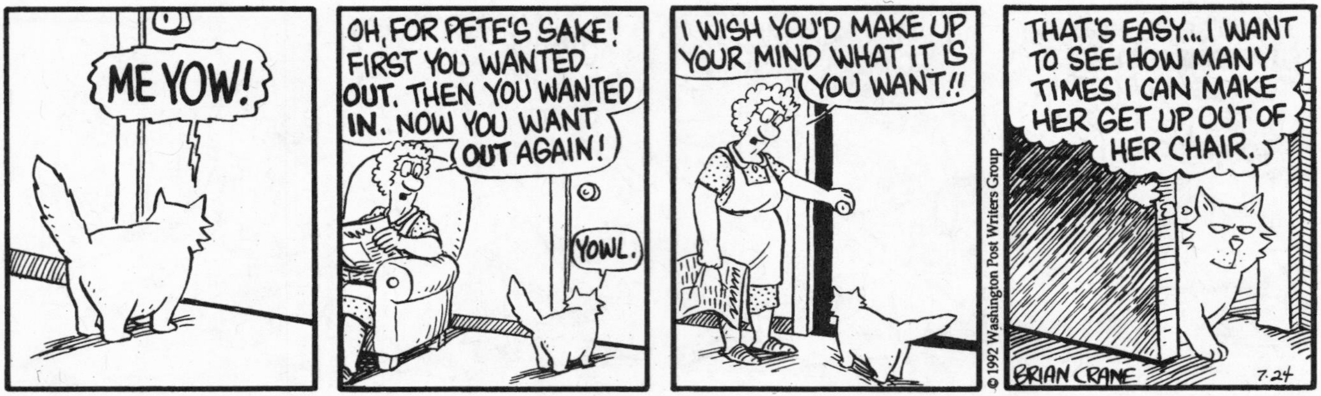
ME YOW!
OH, FOR PETE'S SAKE! FIRST YOU WANTED OUT. THEN YOU WANTED IN. NOW YOU WANT OUT AGAIN!
YOWL.
I WISH YOU'D MAKE UP YOUR MIND WHAT IT IS YOU WANT!!
© 1992 Washington Post Writers Group
THAT'S EASY... I WANT TO SEE HOW MANY TIMES I CAN MAKE HER GET UP OUT OF HER CHAIR.
BRIAN CRANE
7.24

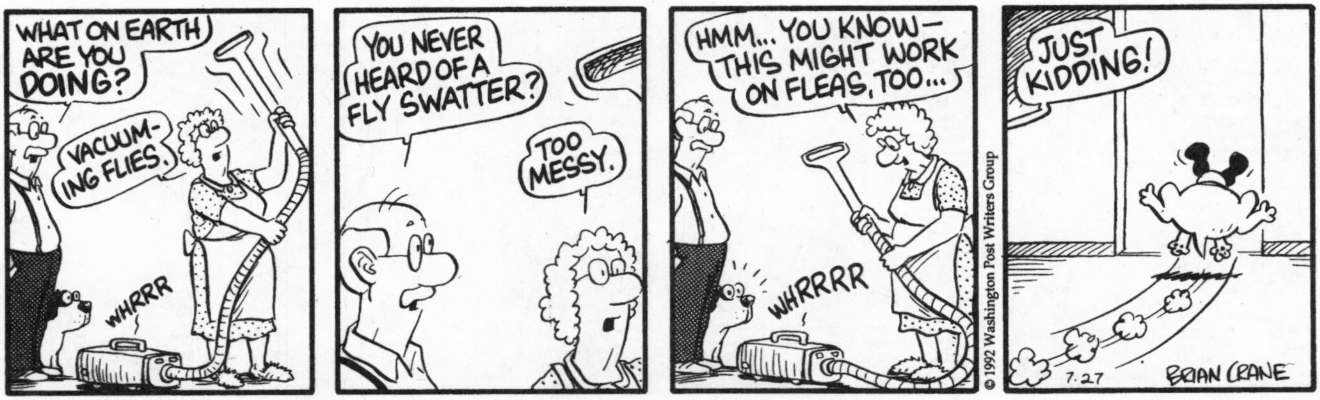
WHAT ON EARTH ARE YOU DOING?
VACUUM-ING FLIES.
WHRRR
YOU NEVER HEARD OF A FLY SWATTER?
TOO MESSY.
HMM... YOU KNOW— THIS MIGHT WORK ON FLEAS, TOO...
WHRRRR
© 1992 Washington Post Writers Group
JUST KIDDING!
7.27
BRIAN CRANE

54

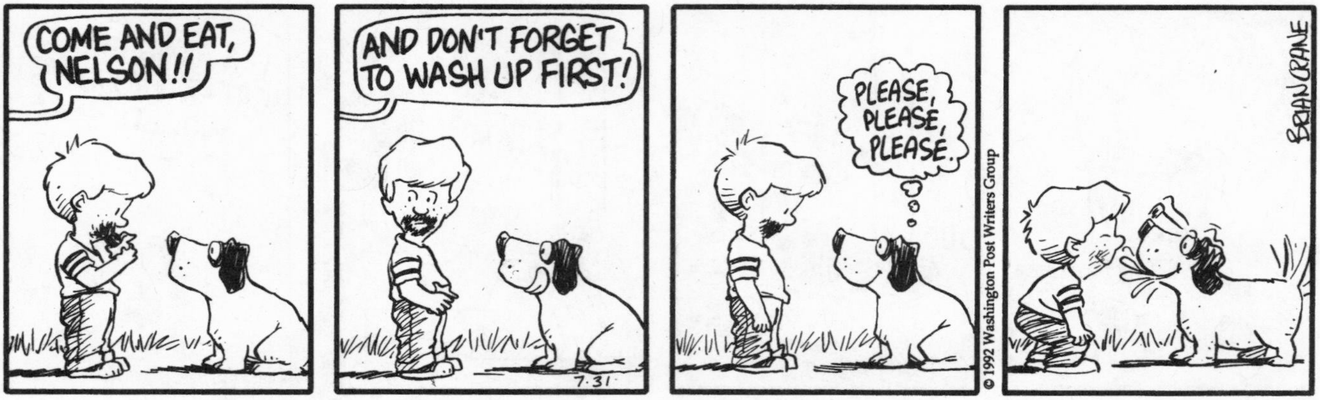
COME AND EAT, NELSON!!
AND DON'T FORGET TO WASH UP FIRST!
7.31
PLEASE, PLEASE, PLEASE.
© 1992 Washington Post Writers Group
BRIAN CRANE

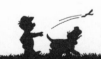

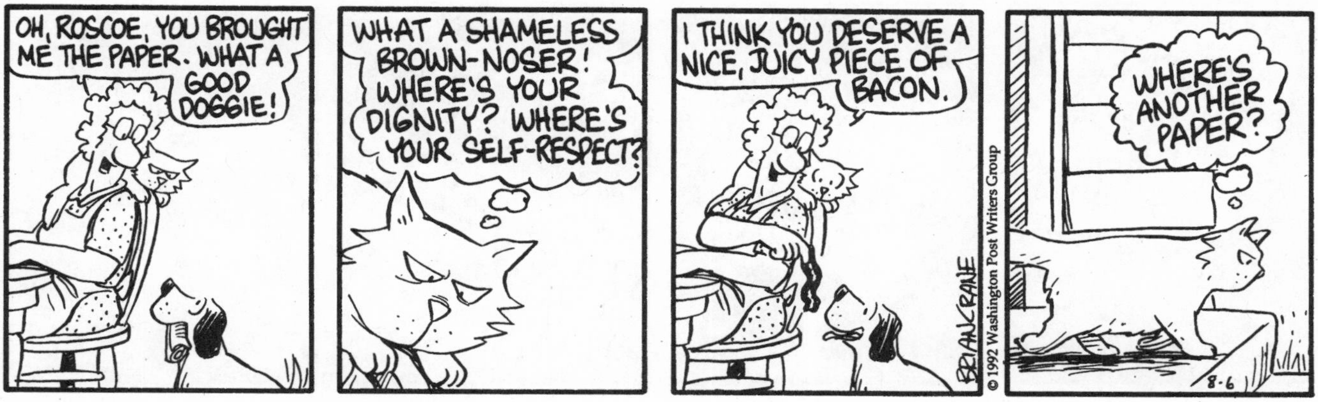
OH, ROSCOE, YOU BROUGHT ME THE PAPER. WHAT A GOOD DOGGIE!
WHAT A SHAMELESS BROWN-NOSER! WHERE'S YOUR DIGNITY? WHERE'S YOUR SELF-RESPECT?
I THINK YOU DESERVE A NICE, JUICY PIECE OF BACON.
BRIAN CRANE
© 1992 Washington Post Writers Group
WHERE'S ANOTHER PAPER?
8-6

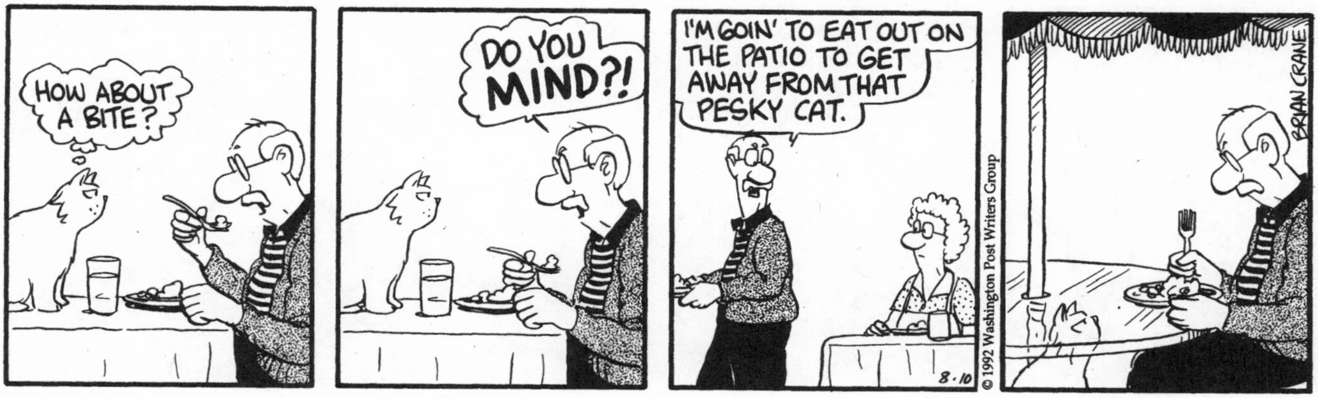
HOW ABOUT A BITE?
DO YOU MIND?!
I'M GOIN' TO EAT OUT ON THE PATIO TO GET AWAY FROM THAT PESKY CAT.
8-10
© 1992 Washington Post Writers Group
BRIAN CRANE

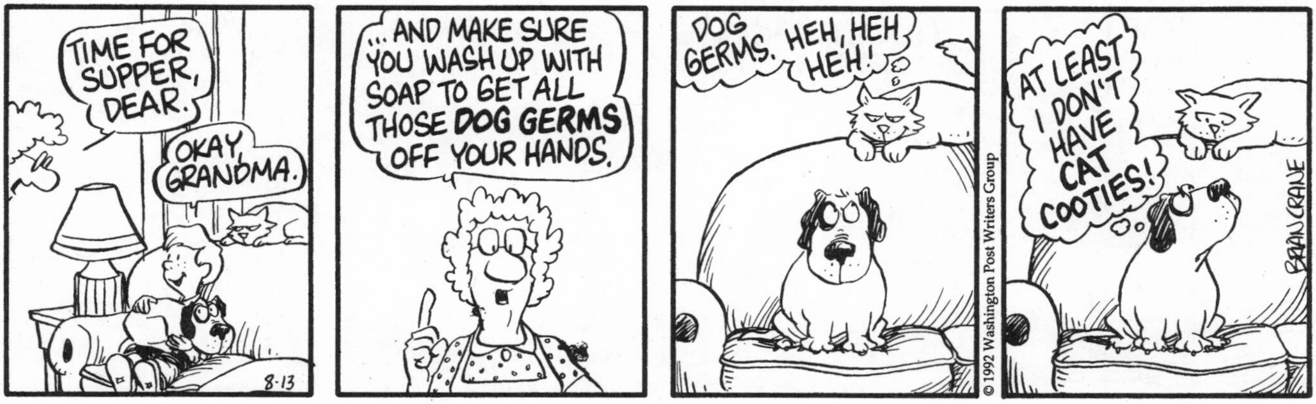
TIME FOR SUPPER, DEAR.
OKAY, GRANDMA.
8-13
...AND MAKE SURE YOU WASH UP WITH SOAP TO GET ALL THOSE DOG GERMS OFF YOUR HANDS.
DOG GERMS. HEH, HEH HEH!
© 1992 Washington Post Writers Group
AT LEAST I DON'T HAVE CAT COOTIES!
BRIAN CRANE

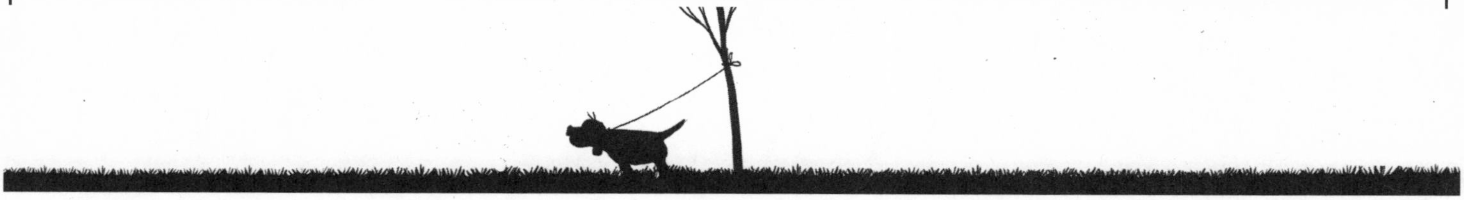

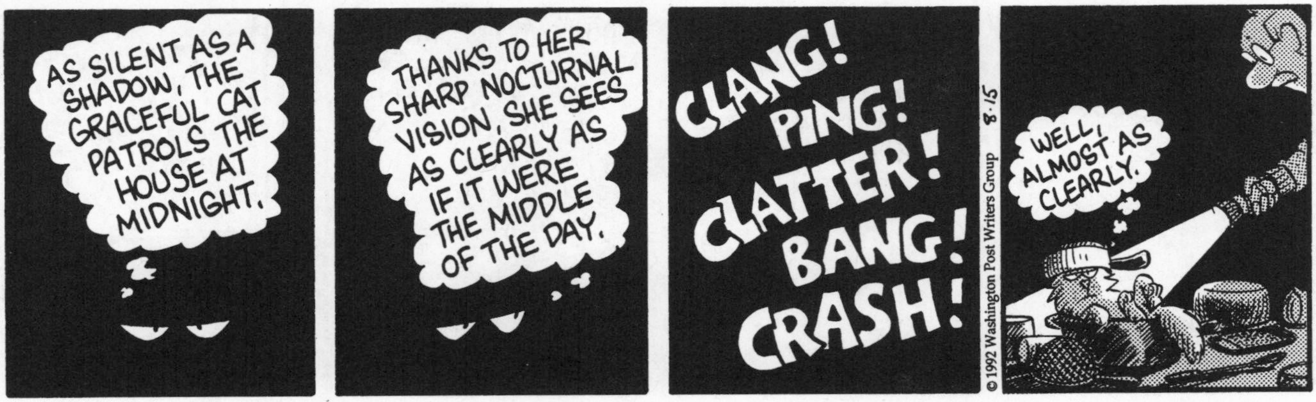
AS SILENT AS A SHADOW, THE GRACEFUL CAT PATROLS THE HOUSE AT MIDNIGHT.
THANKS TO HER SHARP NOCTURNAL VISION, SHE SEES AS CLEARLY AS IF IT WERE THE MIDDLE OF THE DAY.
CLANG! PING! CLATTER! BANG! CRASH!
8-15
© 1992 Washington Post Writers Group
WELL, ALMOST AS CLEARLY.

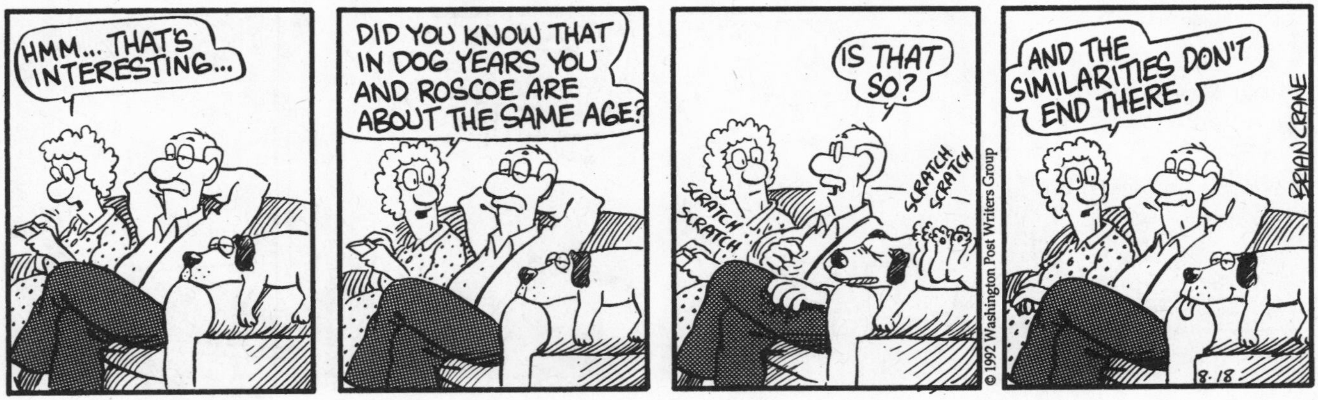
HMM... THAT'S INTERESTING...
DID YOU KNOW THAT IN DOG YEARS YOU AND ROSCOE ARE ABOUT THE SAME AGE?
IS THAT SO?
SCRATCH SCRATCH
SCRATCH SCRATCH
© 1992 Washington Post Writers Group
AND THE SIMILARITIES DON'T END THERE.
BRIAN CRANE
8-18

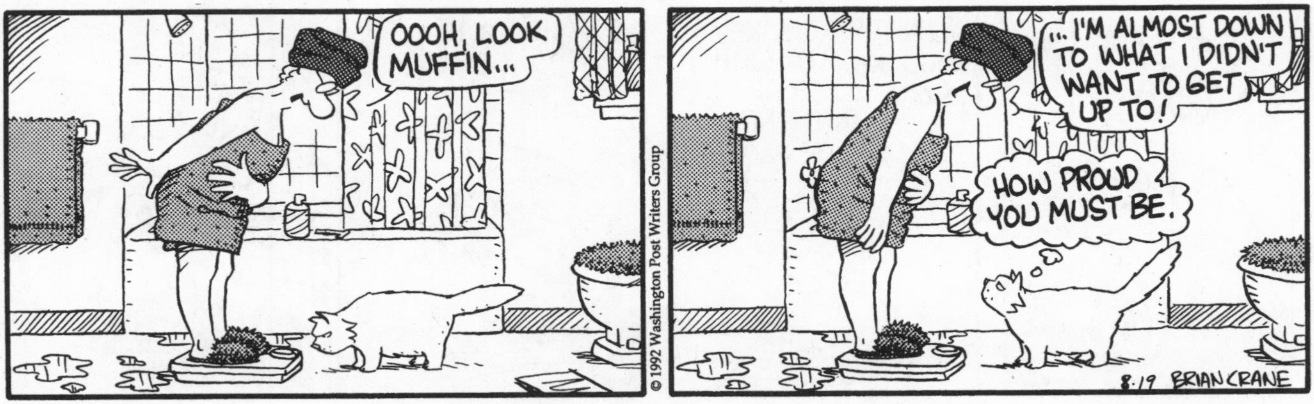
OOOH, LOOK MUFFIN...
© 1992 Washington Post Writers Group
... I'M ALMOST DOWN TO WHAT I DIDN'T WANT TO GET UP TO!
HOW PROUD YOU MUST BE.
8-19 BRIAN CRANE

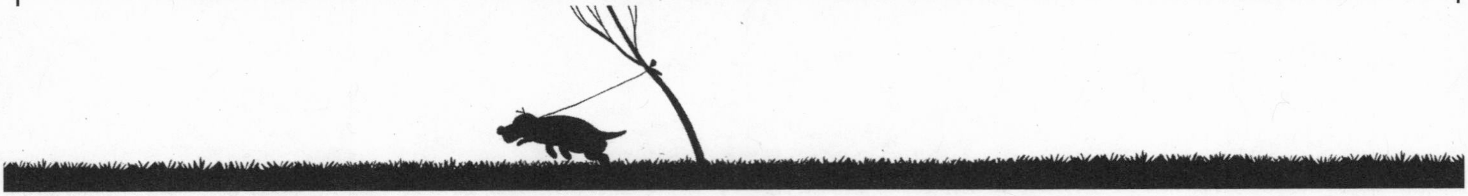

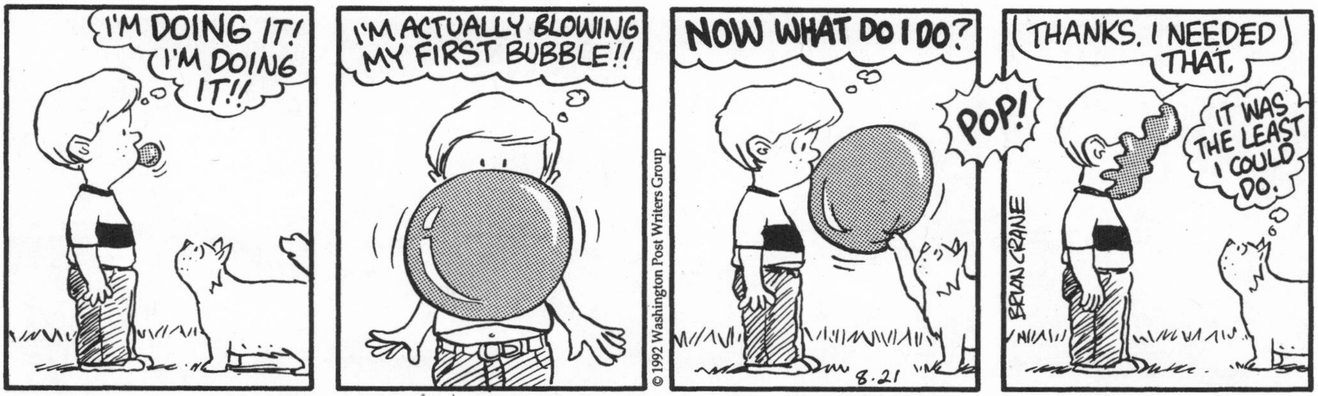
I'M DOING IT! I'M DOING IT!!
I'M ACTUALLY BLOWING MY FIRST BUBBLE!!
© 1992 Washington Post Writers Group
NOW WHAT DO I DO?
POP!
8·21
BRIAN CRANE
THANKS. I NEEDED THAT.
IT WAS THE LEAST I COULD DO.

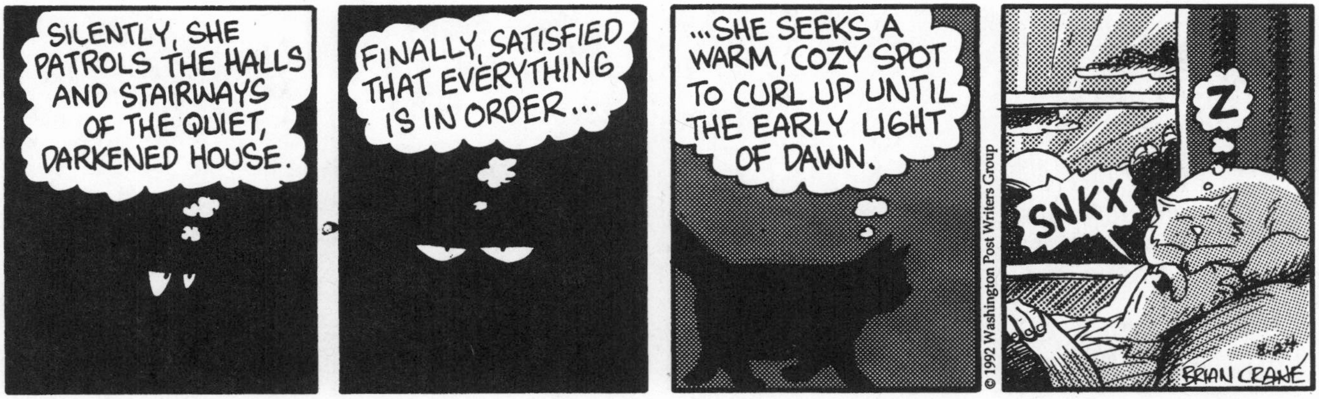
SILENTLY, SHE PATROLS THE HALLS AND STAIRWAYS OF THE QUIET, DARKENED HOUSE.
FINALLY, SATISFIED THAT EVERYTHING IS IN ORDER...
...SHE SEEKS A WARM, COZY SPOT TO CURL UP UNTIL THE EARLY LIGHT OF DAWN.
© 1992 Washington Post Writers Group
Z
SNKX
BRIAN CRANE

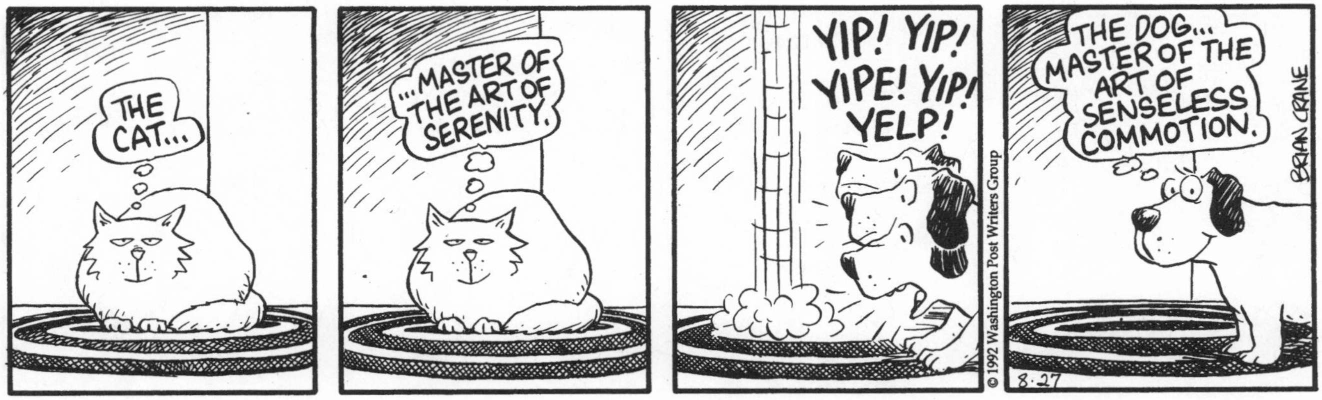
THE CAT...
...MASTER OF THE ART OF SERENITY.
YIP! YIP! YIPE! YIP! YELP!
© 1992 Washington Post Writers Group
8·27
THE DOG... MASTER OF THE ART OF SENSELESS COMMOTION.
BRIAN CRANE

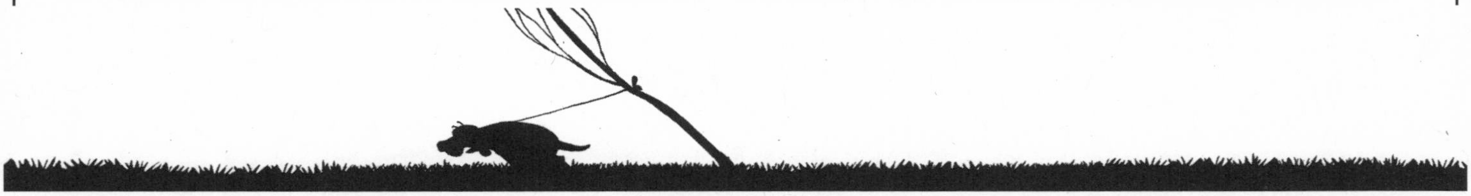

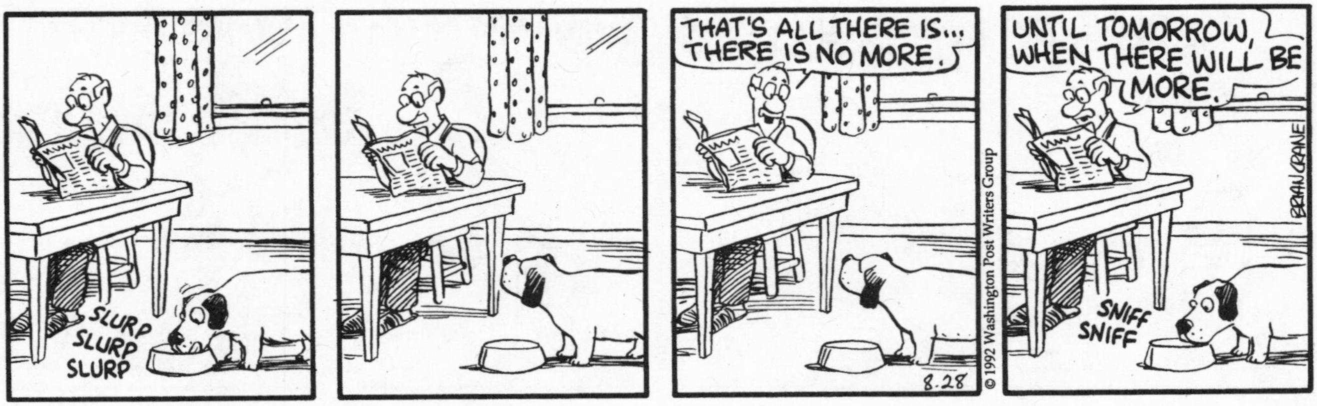
SLURP
SLURP
SLURP
THAT'S ALL THERE IS... THERE IS NO MORE.
8.28
© 1992 Washington Post Writers Group
UNTIL TOMORROW, WHEN THERE WILL BE MORE.
SNIFF
SNIFF
BRIAN CRANE

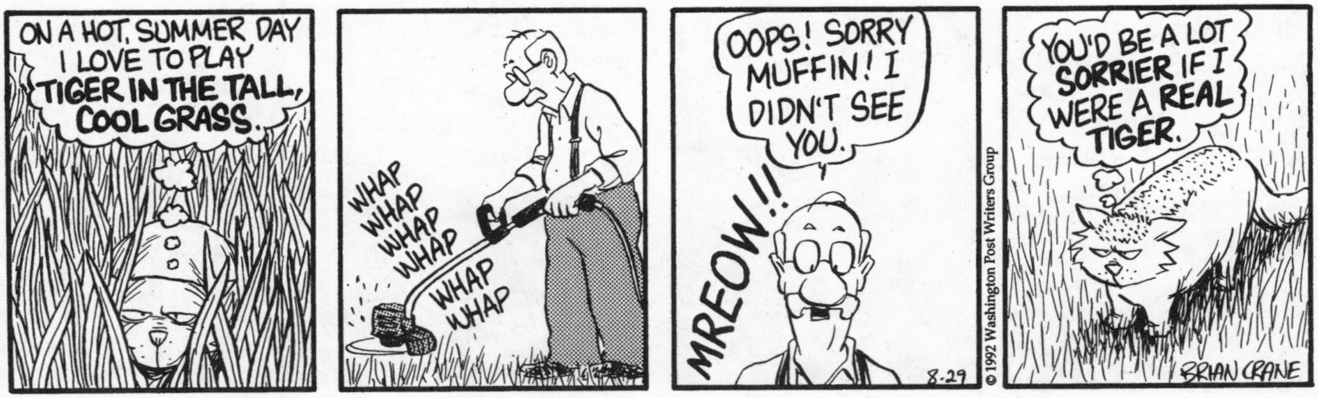
ON A HOT, SUMMER DAY I LOVE TO PLAY TIGER IN THE TALL, COOL GRASS.
WHAP
WHAP
WHAP
WHAP
WHAP
WHAP
OOPS! SORRY MUFFIN! I DIDN'T SEE YOU.
MREOW!!
8.29
© 1992 Washington Post Writers Group
YOU'D BE A LOT SORRIER IF I WERE A REAL TIGER.
BRIAN CRANE

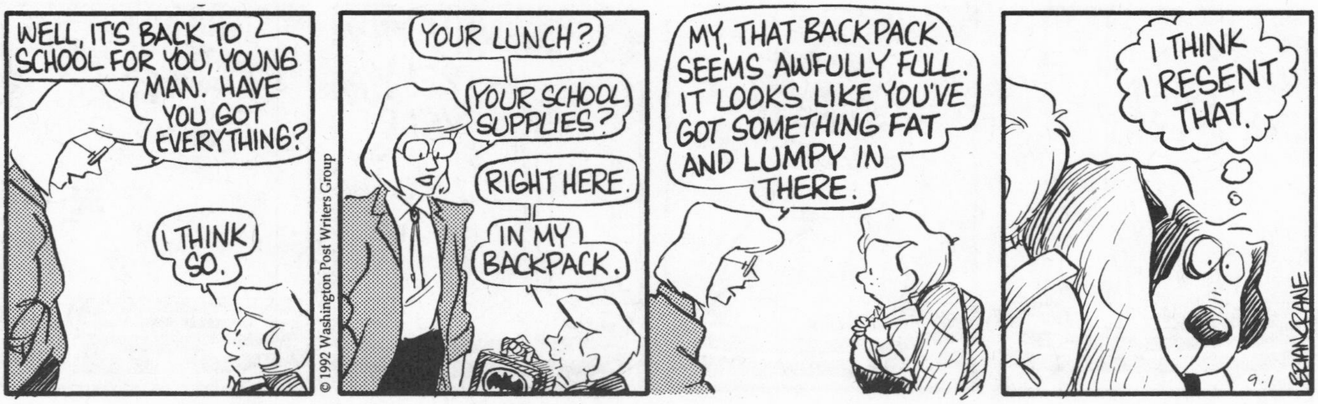
WELL, IT'S BACK TO SCHOOL FOR YOU, YOUNG MAN. HAVE YOU GOT EVERYTHING?
I THINK SO.
© 1992 Washington Post Writers Group
YOUR LUNCH?
YOUR SCHOOL SUPPLIES?
RIGHT HERE.
IN MY BACKPACK.
MY, THAT BACKPACK SEEMS AWFULLY FULL. IT LOOKS LIKE YOU'VE GOT SOMETHING FAT AND LUMPY IN THERE.
I THINK I RESENT THAT.
9.1
BRIAN CRANE

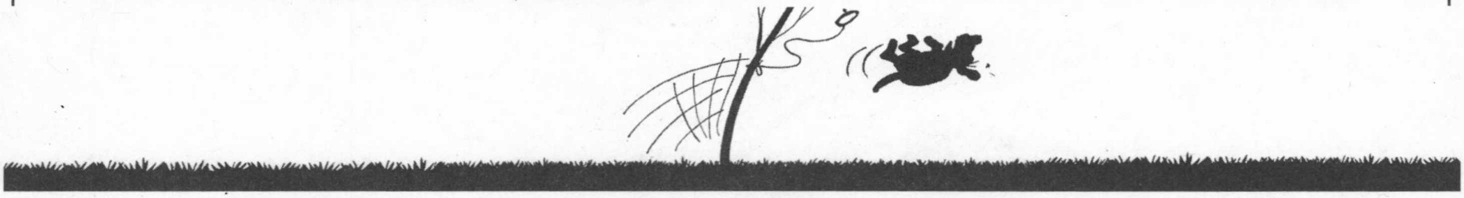

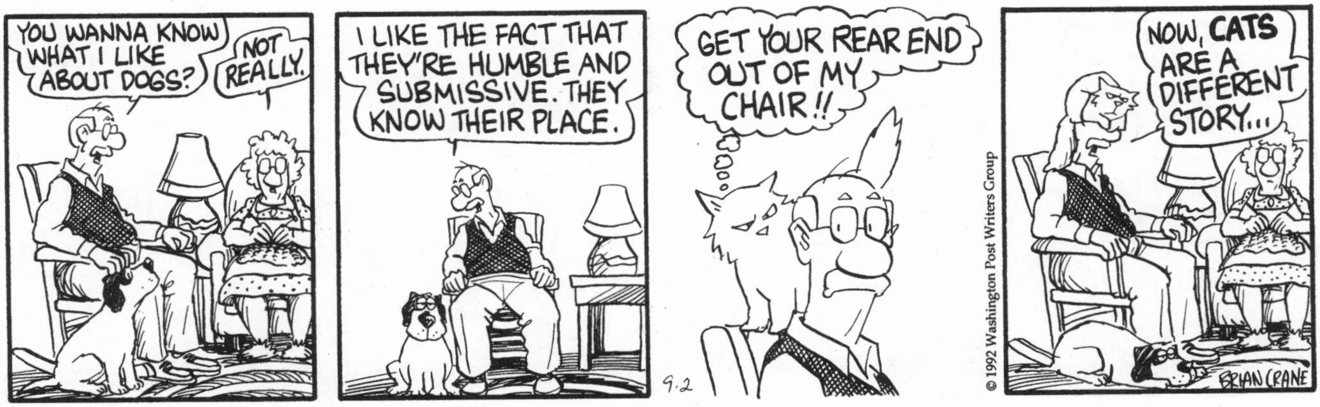
YOU WANNA KNOW WHAT I LIKE ABOUT DOGS?
NOT REALLY.
I LIKE THE FACT THAT THEY'RE HUMBLE AND SUBMISSIVE. THEY KNOW THEIR PLACE.
9.2
GET YOUR REAR END OUT OF MY CHAIR!!
NOW, **CATS** ARE A DIFFERENT STORY...
BRIAN CRANE

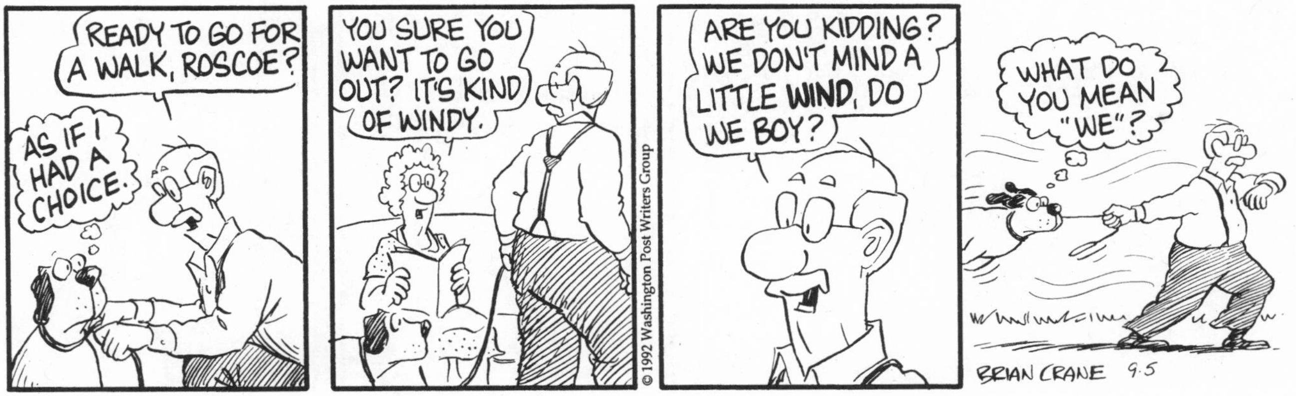
READY TO GO FOR A WALK, ROSCOE?
AS IF I HAD A CHOICE.
YOU SURE YOU WANT TO GO OUT? IT'S KIND OF WINDY.
ARE YOU KIDDING? WE DON'T MIND A LITTLE **WIND**, DO WE BOY?
WHAT DO YOU MEAN "WE"?
BRIAN CRANE 9.5

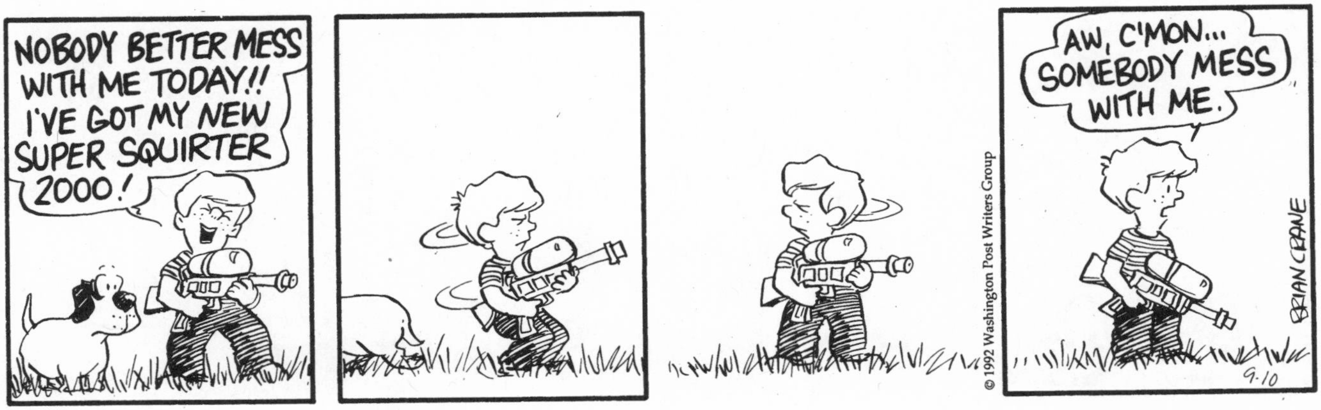
NOBODY BETTER MESS WITH ME TODAY!! I'VE GOT MY NEW SUPER SQUIRTER 2000!
AW, C'MON... SOMEBODY MESS WITH ME.
BRIAN CRANE
9.10

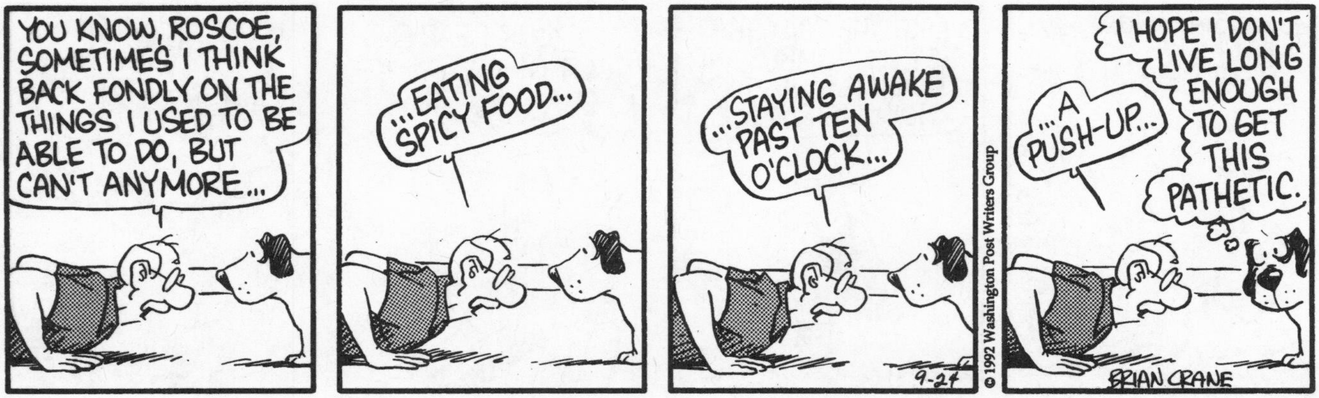
YOU KNOW, ROSCOE, SOMETIMES I THINK BACK FONDLY ON THE THINGS I USED TO BE ABLE TO DO, BUT CAN'T ANYMORE...
...EATING SPICY FOOD...
...STAYING AWAKE PAST TEN O'CLOCK...
...A PUSH-UP...
I HOPE I DON'T LIVE LONG ENOUGH TO GET THIS PATHETIC.
9-24
© 1992 Washington Post Writers Group
BRIAN CRANE

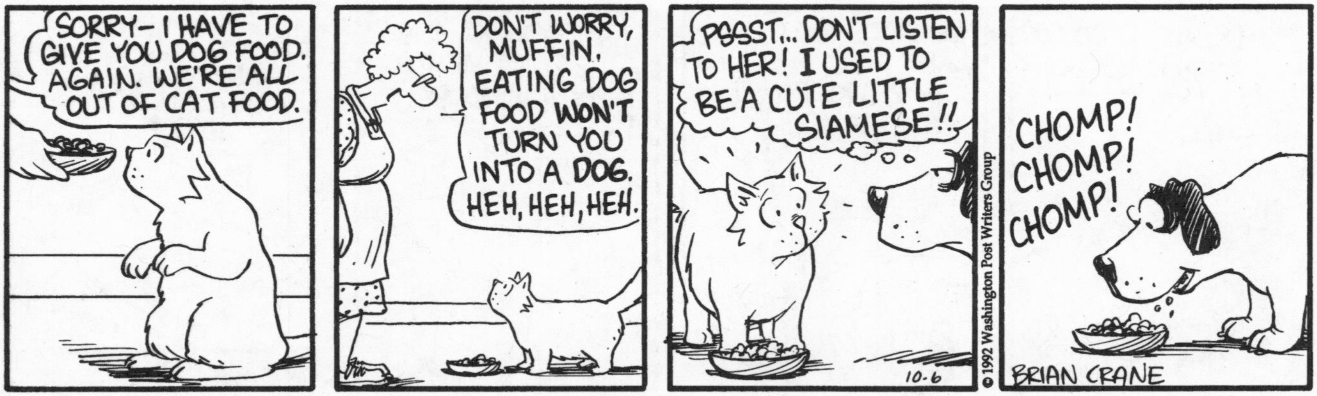
SORRY– I HAVE TO GIVE YOU DOG FOOD AGAIN. WE'RE ALL OUT OF CAT FOOD.
DON'T WORRY, MUFFIN. EATING DOG FOOD WON'T TURN YOU INTO A DOG. HEH, HEH, HEH.
PSSST... DON'T LISTEN TO HER! I USED TO BE A CUTE LITTLE SIAMESE!!
CHOMP! CHOMP! CHOMP!
10-6
© 1992 Washington Post Writers Group
BRIAN CRANE

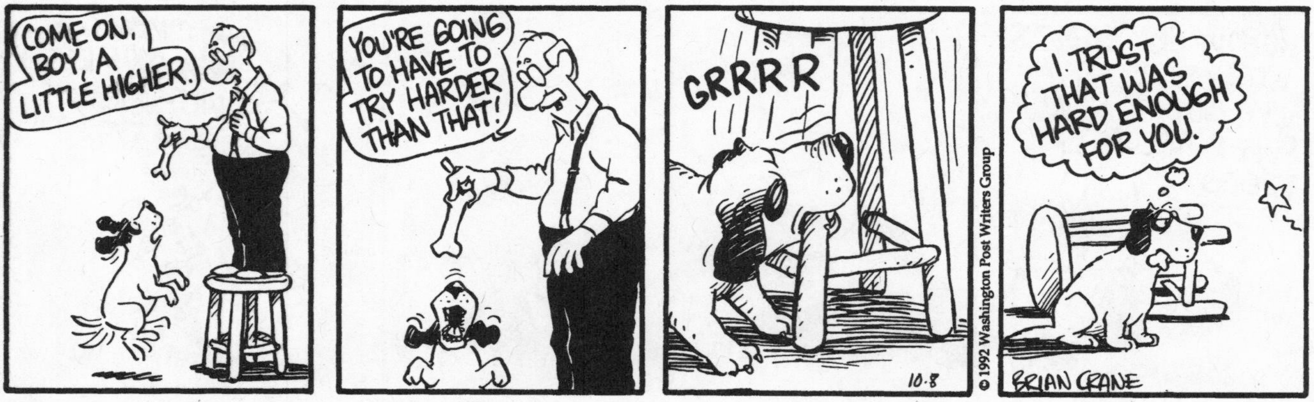
COME ON, BOY, A LITTLE HIGHER.
YOU'RE GOING TO HAVE TO TRY HARDER THAN THAT!
GRRRR
I TRUST THAT WAS HARD ENOUGH FOR YOU.
10-8
© 1992 Washington Post Writers Group
BRIAN CRANE

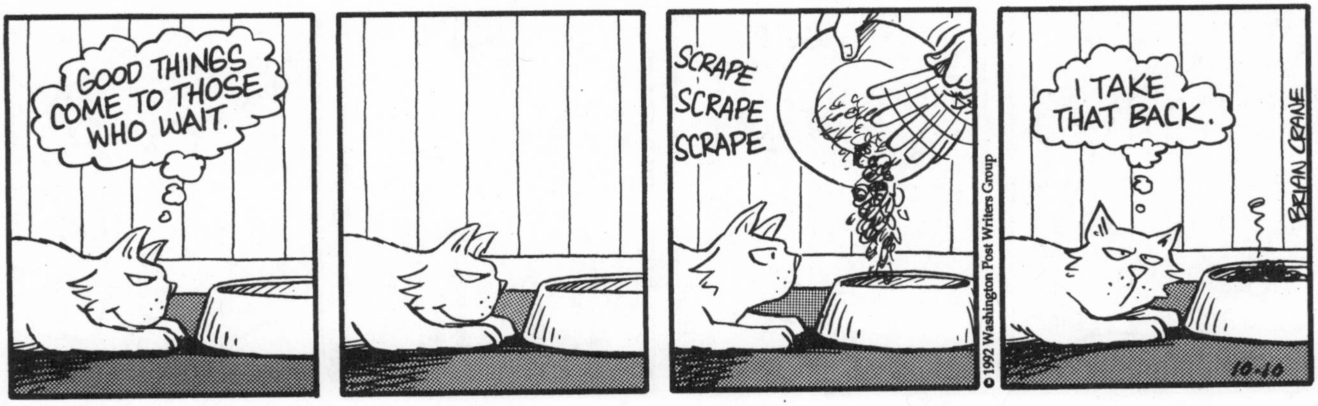
GOOD THINGS COME TO THOSE WHO WAIT.
SCRAPE
SCRAPE
SCRAPE
I TAKE THAT BACK.
© 1992 Washington Post Writers Group
BRIAN CRANE
10-10

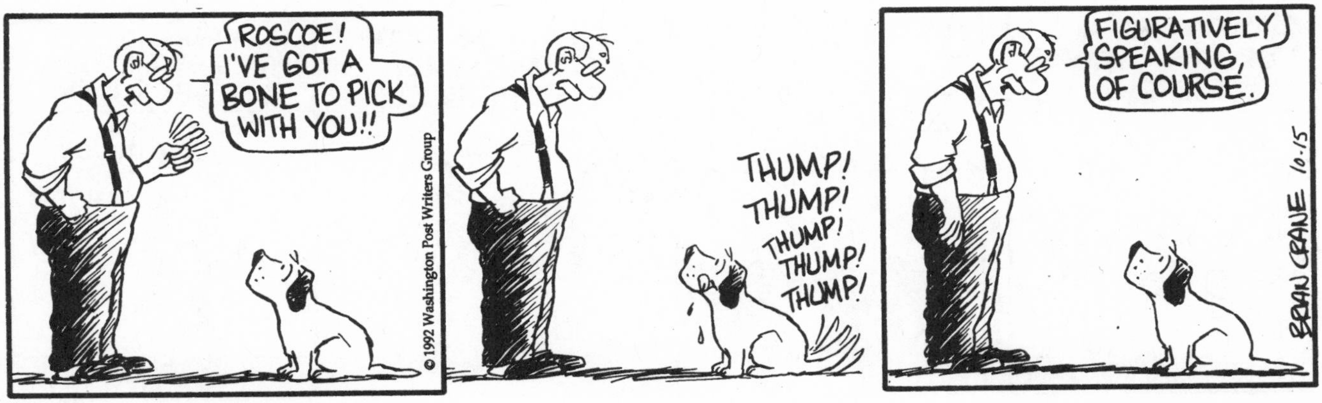
ROSCOE! I'VE GOT A BONE TO PICK WITH YOU!!
© 1992 Washington Post Writers Group
THUMP! THUMP! THUMP! THUMP! THUMP!
FIGURATIVELY SPEAKING, OF COURSE.
BRIAN CRANE 10-15

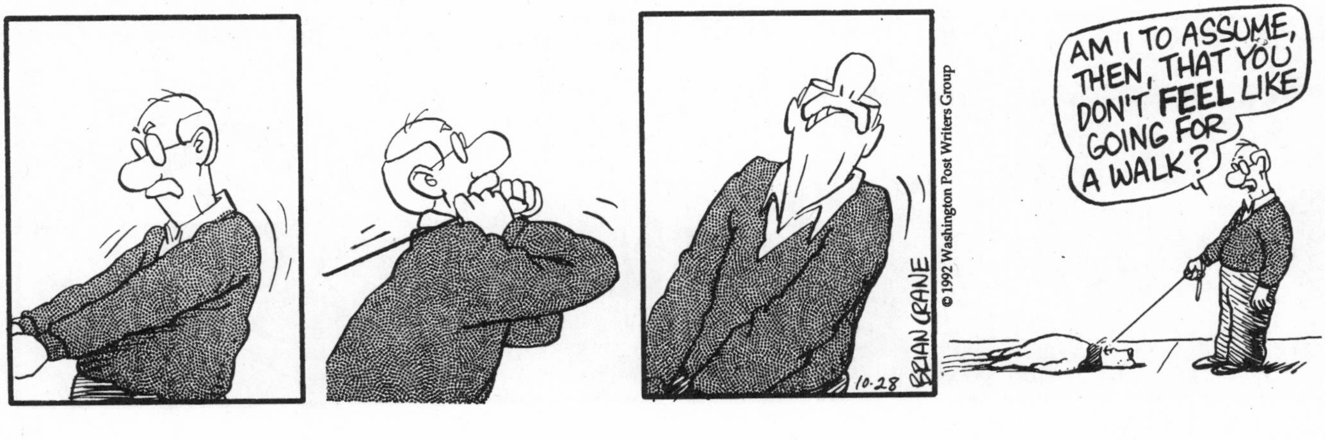
© 1992 Washington Post Writers Group
BRIAN CRANE
10-28
AM I TO ASSUME, THEN, THAT YOU DON'T FEEL LIKE GOING FOR A WALK?

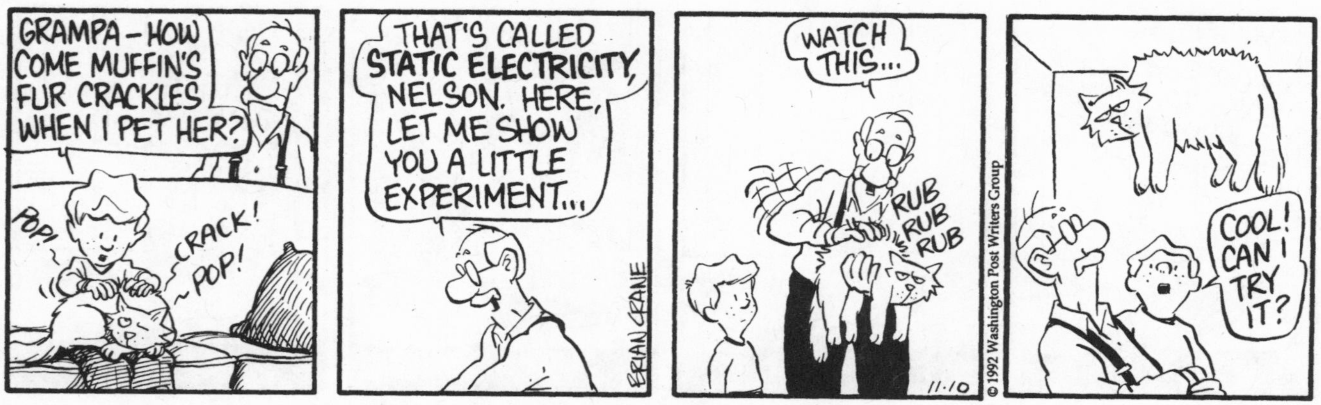
GRAMPA – HOW COME MUFFIN'S FUR CRACKLES WHEN I PET HER?
POP!
CRACK! ~POP!
THAT'S CALLED **STATIC ELECTRICITY**, NELSON. HERE, LET ME SHOW YOU A LITTLE EXPERIMENT...
BRIAN CRANE
WATCH THIS...
RUB RUB RUB
11.10
© 1992 Washington Post Writers Group
COOL! CAN I TRY IT?

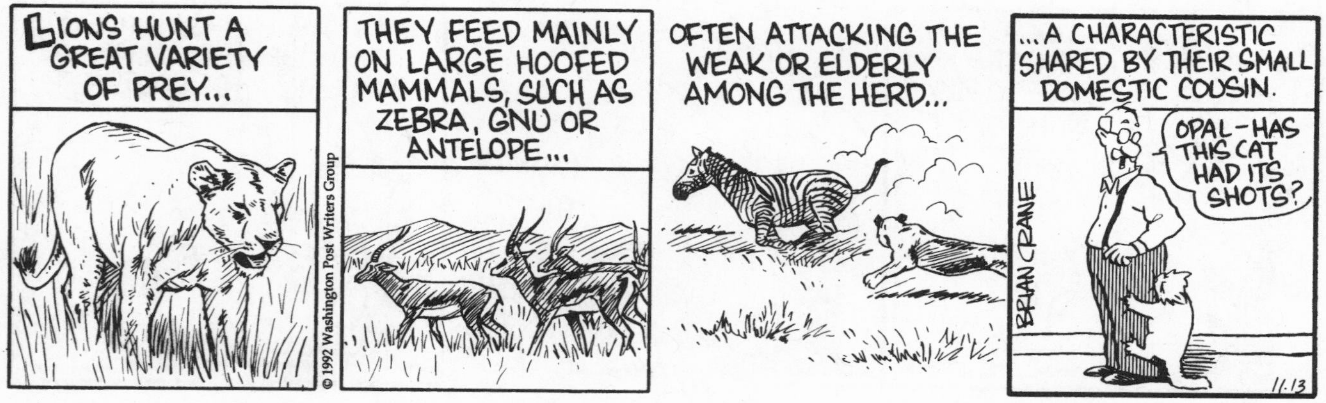
LIONS HUNT A GREAT VARIETY OF PREY...
© 1992 Washington Post Writers Group
THEY FEED MAINLY ON LARGE HOOFED MAMMALS, SUCH AS ZEBRA, GNU OR ANTELOPE...
OFTEN ATTACKING THE WEAK OR ELDERLY AMONG THE HERD...
BRIAN CRANE
...A CHARACTERISTIC SHARED BY THEIR SMALL DOMESTIC COUSIN.
OPAL – HAS THIS CAT HAD ITS SHOTS?
11.13

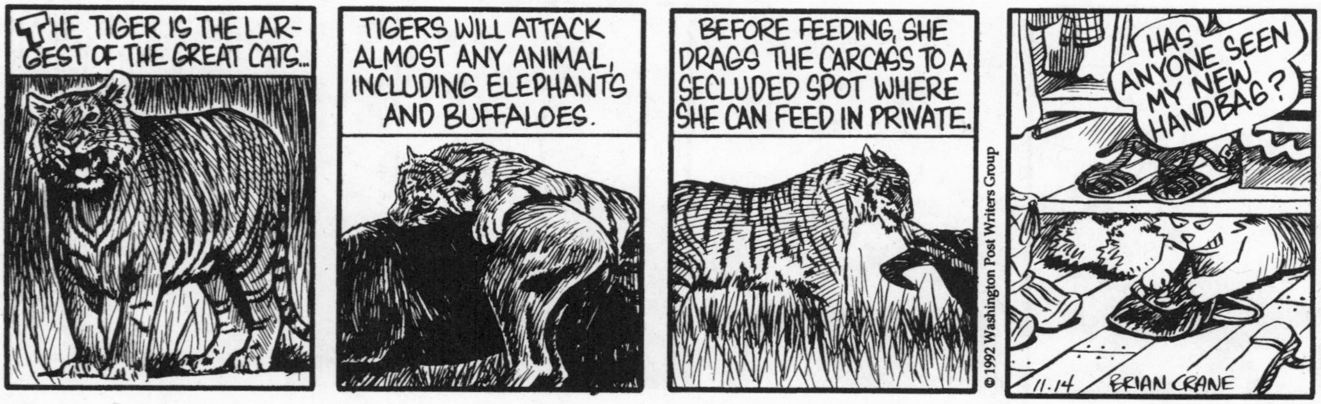
THE TIGER IS THE LARGEST OF THE GREAT CATS...
TIGERS WILL ATTACK ALMOST ANY ANIMAL, INCLUDING ELEPHANTS AND BUFFALOES.
BEFORE FEEDING, SHE DRAGS THE CARCASS TO A SECLUDED SPOT WHERE SHE CAN FEED IN PRIVATE.
© 1992 Washington Post Writers Group
HAS ANYONE SEEN MY NEW HANDBAG?
11.14
BRIAN CRANE

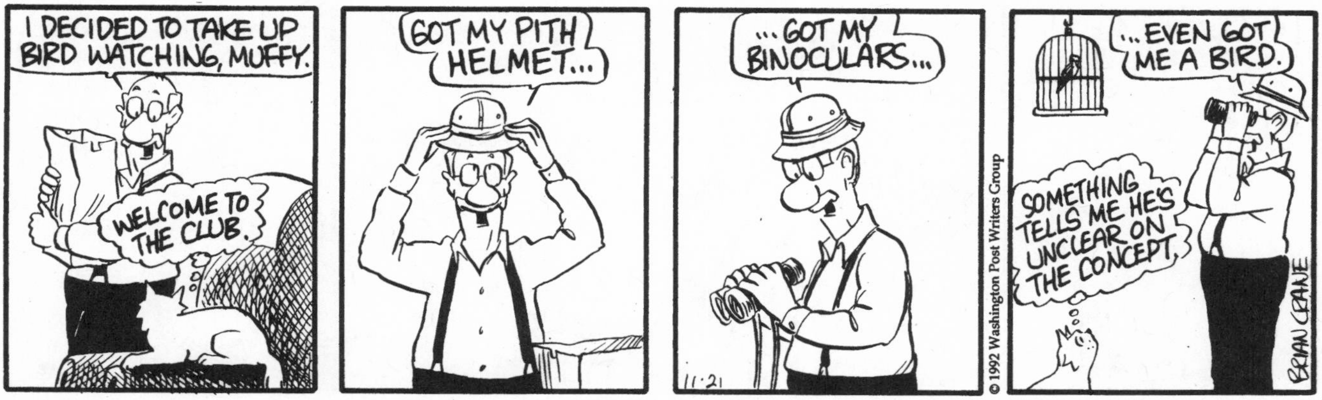
I DECIDED TO TAKE UP BIRD WATCHING, MUFFY.
WELCOME TO THE CLUB.
GOT MY PITH HELMET...
...GOT MY BINOCULARS...
11·21
© 1992 Washington Post Writers Group
...EVEN GOT ME A BIRD.
SOMETHING TELLS ME HE'S UNCLEAR ON THE CONCEPT.
BRIAN CRANE

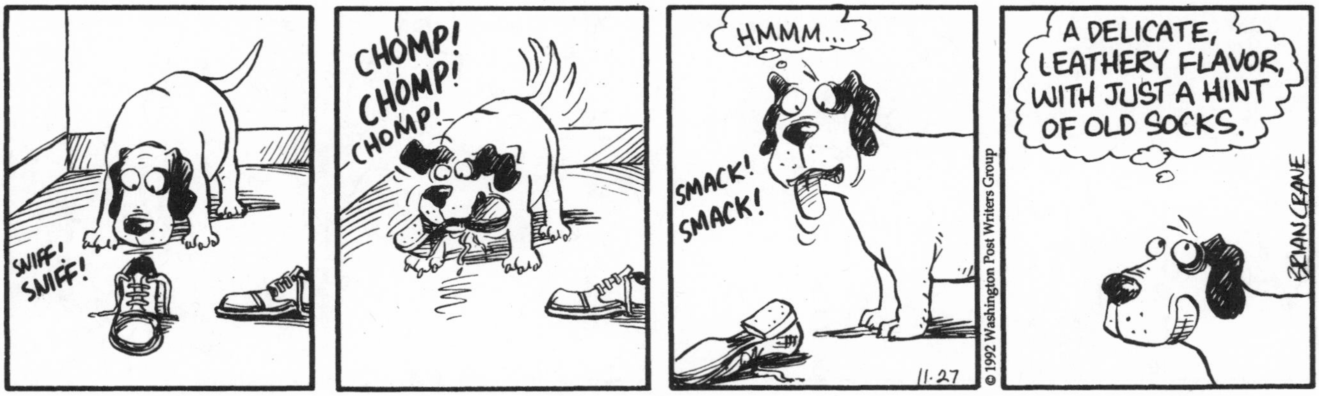
SNIFF! SNIFF!
CHOMP! CHOMP! CHOMP!
HMMM...
SMACK! SMACK!
11·27
© 1992 Washington Post Writers Group
A DELICATE, LEATHERY FLAVOR, WITH JUST A HINT OF OLD SOCKS.
BRIAN CRANE

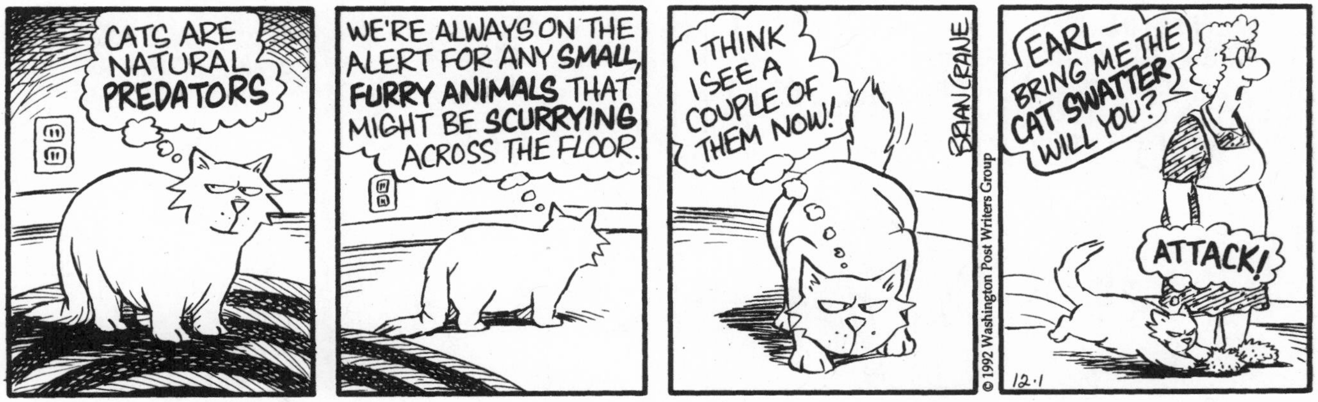
CATS ARE NATURAL PREDATORS
WE'RE ALWAYS ON THE ALERT FOR ANY SMALL, FURRY ANIMALS THAT MIGHT BE SCURRYING ACROSS THE FLOOR.
I THINK I SEE A COUPLE OF THEM NOW!
BRIAN CRANE
© 1992 Washington Post Writers Group
EARL— BRING ME THE CAT SWATTER WILL YOU?
ATTACK!
12·1

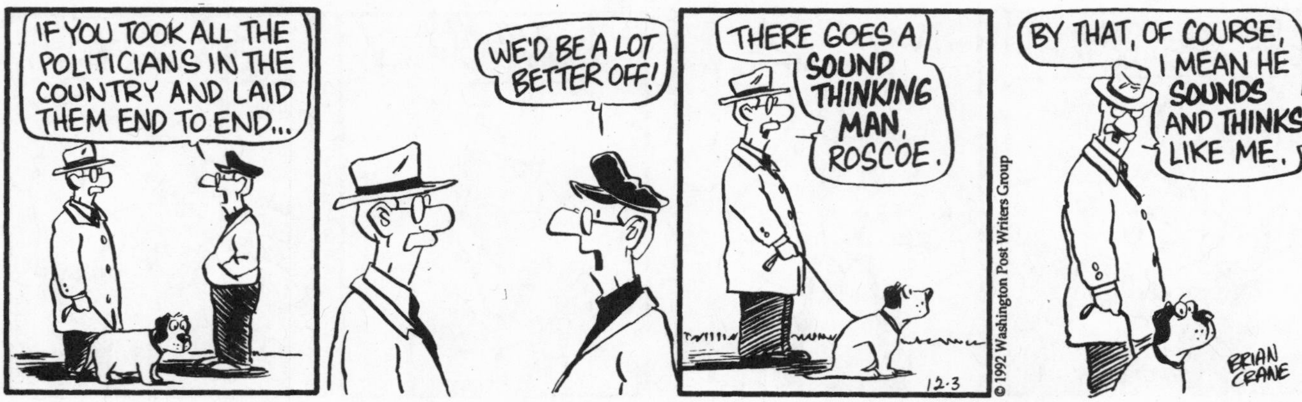
IF YOU TOOK ALL THE POLITICIANS IN THE COUNTRY AND LAID THEM END TO END...
WE'D BE A LOT BETTER OFF!
THERE GOES A **SOUND THINKING MAN**, ROSCOE.
BY THAT, OF COURSE, I MEAN HE **SOUNDS** AND **THINKS** LIKE ME.
BRIAN CRANE
12·3
© 1992 Washington Post Writers Group

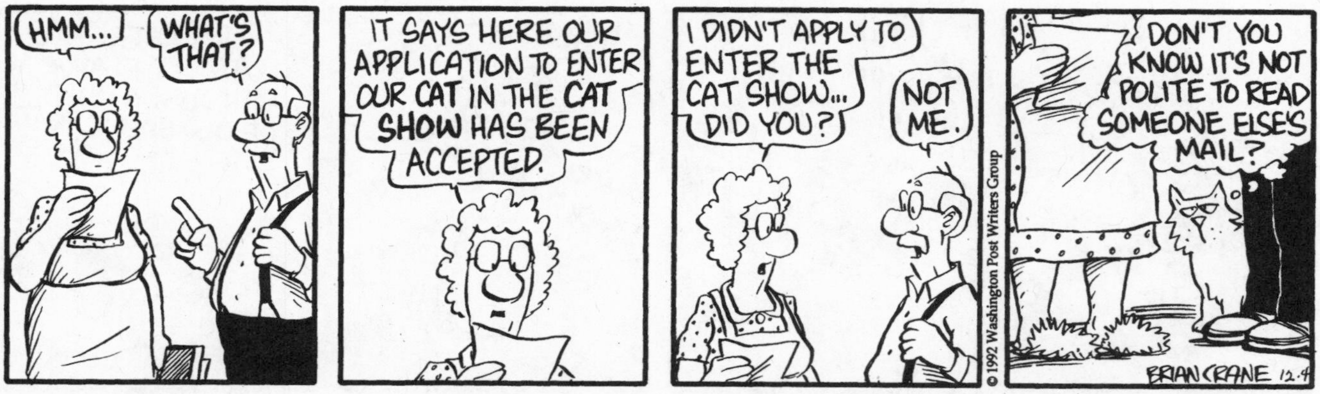
HMM...
WHAT'S THAT?
IT SAYS HERE OUR APPLICATION TO ENTER OUR **CAT** IN THE **CAT SHOW** HAS BEEN ACCEPTED.
I DIDN'T APPLY TO ENTER THE CAT SHOW... DID YOU?
NOT ME.
DON'T YOU KNOW IT'S NOT POLITE TO READ SOMEONE ELSE'S MAIL?
BRIAN CRANE 12·4
© 1992 Washington Post Writers Group

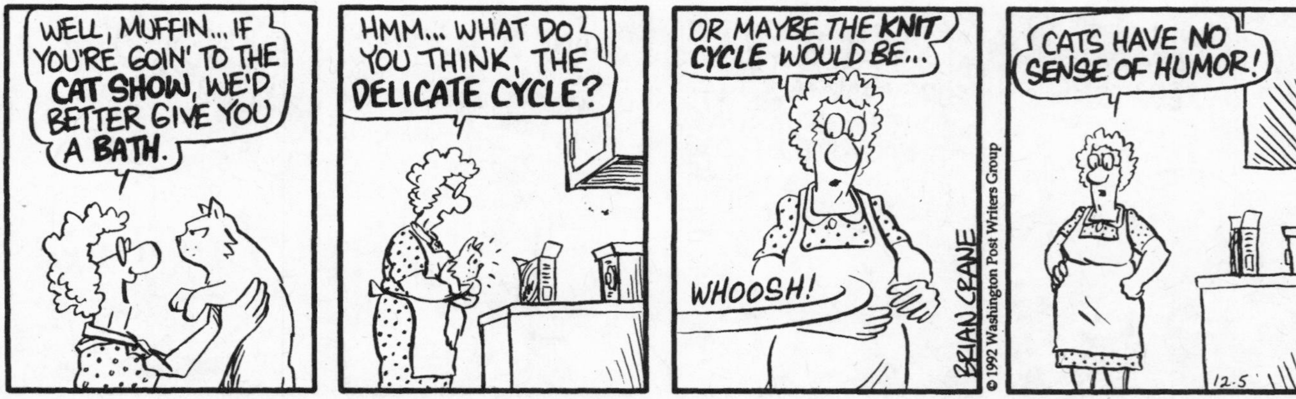
WELL, MUFFIN... IF YOU'RE GOIN' TO THE **CAT SHOW**, WE'D BETTER GIVE YOU A **BATH**.
HMM... WHAT DO YOU THINK, THE **DELICATE CYCLE**?
OR MAYBE THE **KNIT CYCLE** WOULD BE...
WHOOSH!
BRIAN CRANE
CATS HAVE **NO SENSE OF HUMOR**!
12·5
© 1992 Washington Post Writers Group

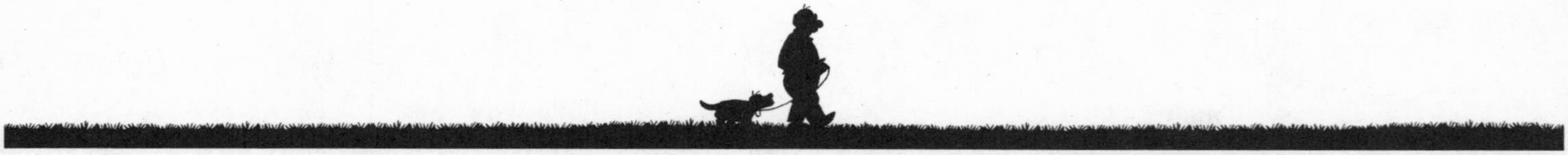

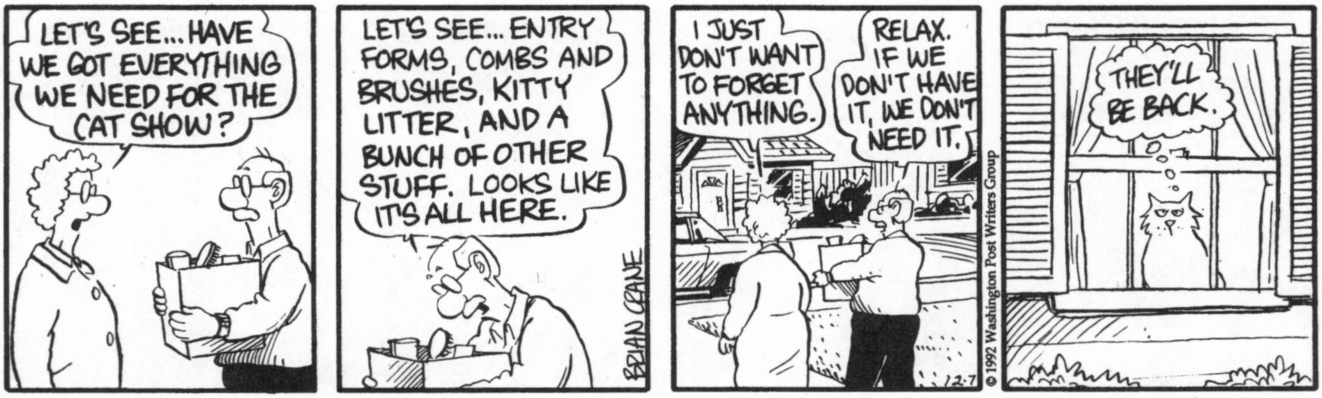
LET'S SEE... HAVE WE GOT EVERYTHING WE NEED FOR THE CAT SHOW?
LET'S SEE... ENTRY FORMS, COMBS AND BRUSHES, KITTY LITTER, AND A BUNCH OF OTHER STUFF. LOOKS LIKE IT'S ALL HERE.
BRIAN CRANE
I JUST DON'T WANT TO FORGET ANYTHING.
RELAX. IF WE DON'T HAVE IT, WE DON'T NEED IT.
12-7
© 1992 Washington Post Writers Group
THEY'LL BE BACK.

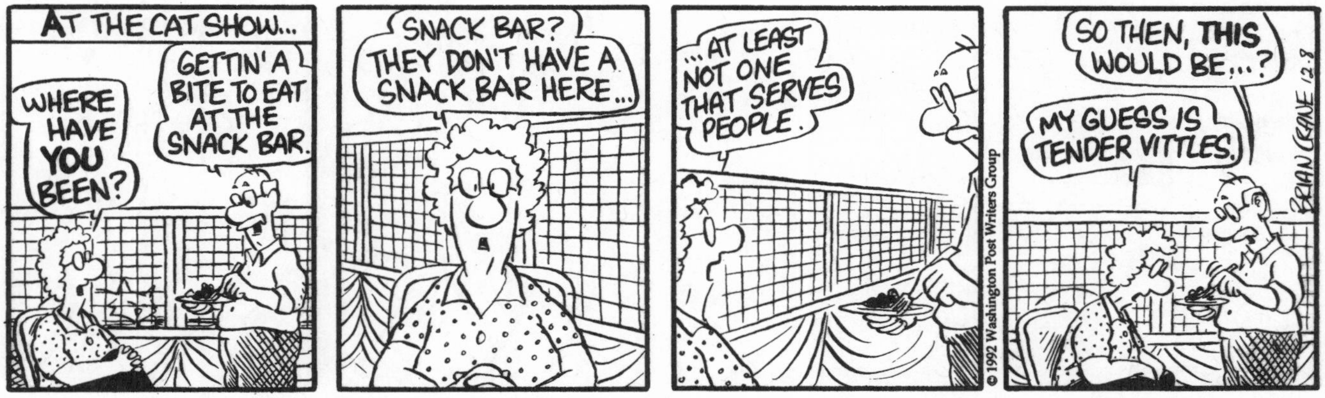
AT THE CAT SHOW...
WHERE HAVE YOU BEEN?
GETTIN' A BITE TO EAT AT THE SNACK BAR.
SNACK BAR? THEY DON'T HAVE A SNACK BAR HERE...
...AT LEAST NOT ONE THAT SERVES PEOPLE.
© 1992 Washington Post Writers Group
SO THEN, THIS WOULD BE...?
MY GUESS IS TENDER VITTLES.
BRIAN CRANE 12-8

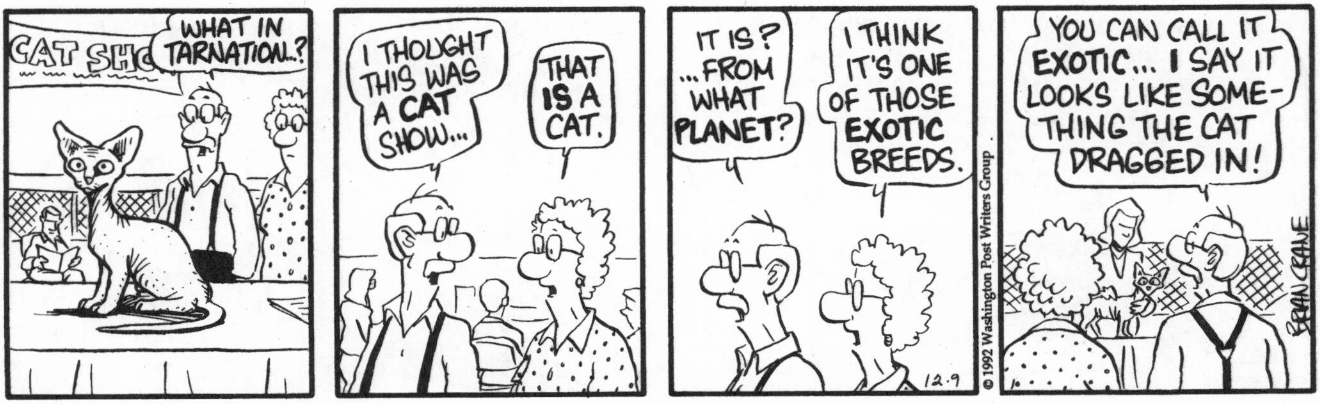
CAT SHO
WHAT IN TARNATION...?
I THOUGHT THIS WAS A CAT SHOW...
THAT IS A CAT.
IT IS? ...FROM WHAT PLANET?
I THINK IT'S ONE OF THOSE EXOTIC BREEDS.
12-9
© 1992 Washington Post Writers Group
YOU CAN CALL IT EXOTIC... I SAY IT LOOKS LIKE SOMETHING THE CAT DRAGGED IN!
BRIAN CRANE

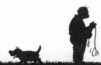

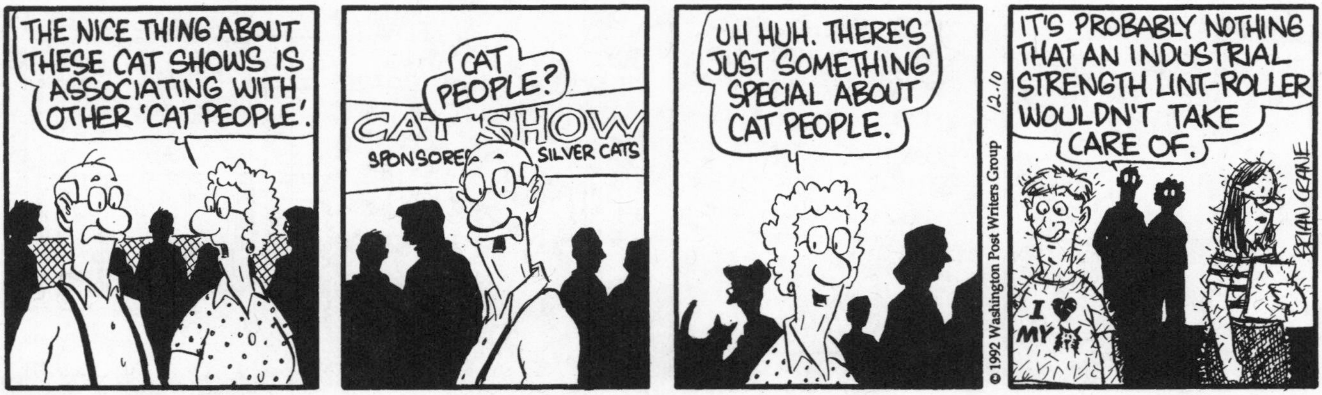
THE NICE THING ABOUT THESE CAT SHOWS IS ASSOCIATING WITH OTHER 'CAT PEOPLE'.
CAT PEOPLE?
CAT SHOW
SPONSORE
SILVER CATS
UH HUH. THERE'S JUST SOMETHING SPECIAL ABOUT CAT PEOPLE.
12-10
© 1992 Washington Post Writers Group
IT'S PROBABLY NOTHING THAT AN INDUSTRIAL STRENGTH LINT-ROLLER WOULDN'T TAKE CARE OF.
I ♥ MY
BRIAN CRANE

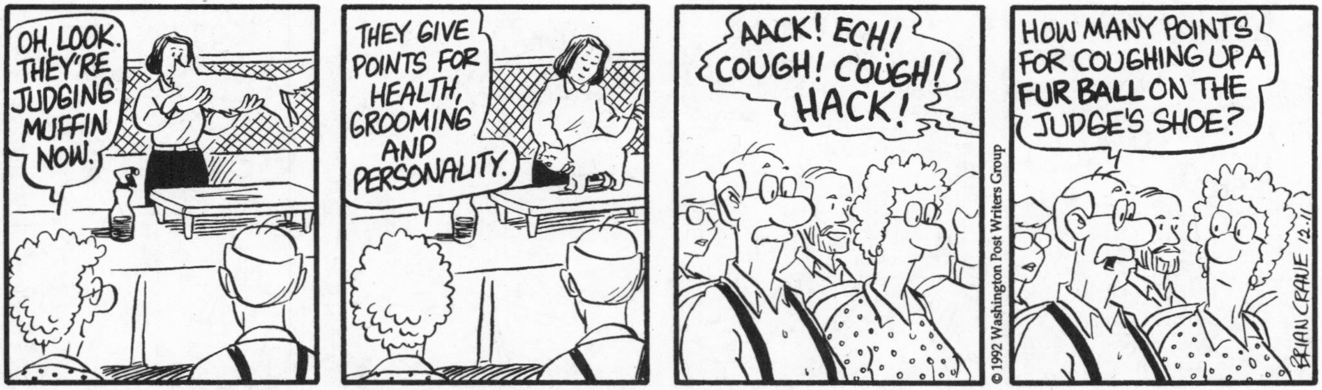
OH, LOOK. THEY'RE JUDGING MUFFIN NOW.
THEY GIVE POINTS FOR HEALTH, GROOMING AND PERSONALITY.
AACK! ECH! COUGH! COUGH! HACK!
© 1992 Washington Post Writers Group
HOW MANY POINTS FOR COUGHING UP A FUR BALL ON THE JUDGE'S SHOE?
BRIAN CRANE 12-11

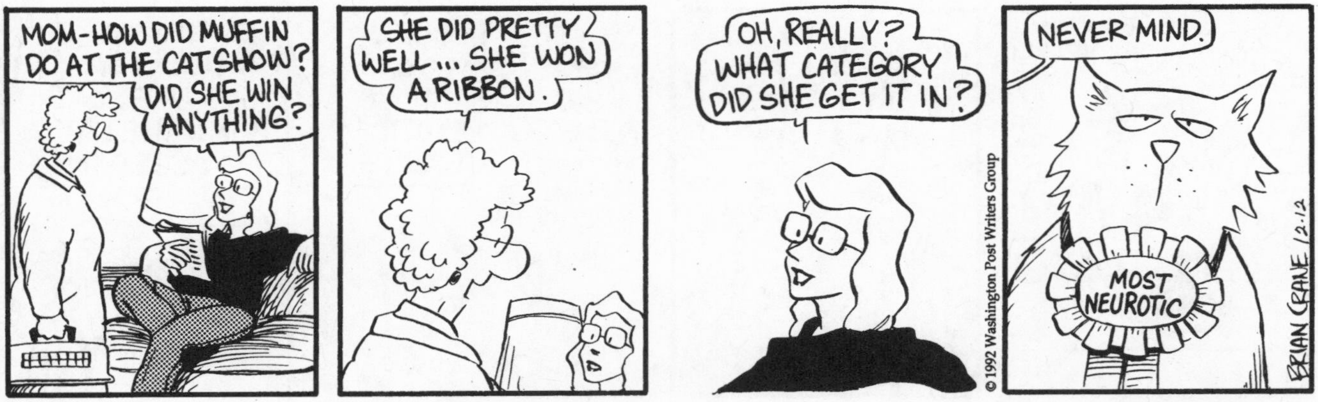
MOM-HOW DID MUFFIN DO AT THE CAT SHOW?
DID SHE WIN ANYTHING?
SHE DID PRETTY WELL... SHE WON A RIBBON.
OH, REALLY? WHAT CATEGORY DID SHE GET IT IN?
© 1992 Washington Post Writers Group
NEVER MIND.
MOST NEUROTIC
BRIAN CRANE 12-12

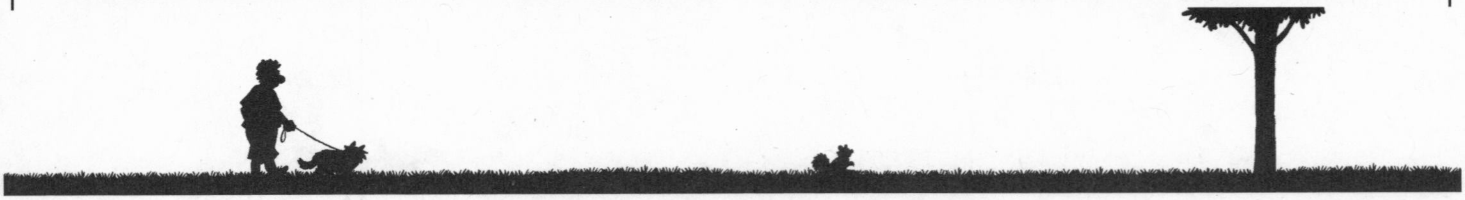

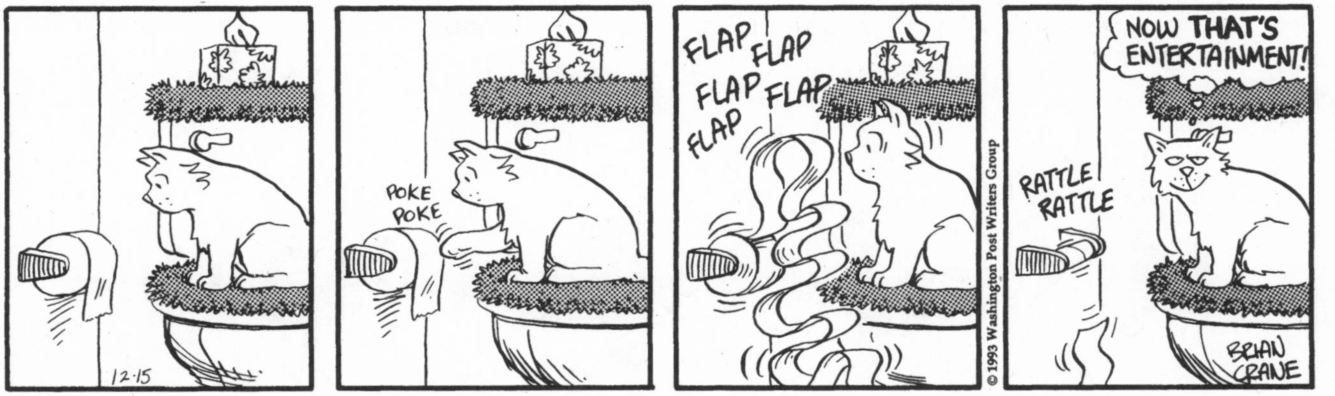

12·15
POKE
POKE
FLAP FLAP
FLAP FLAP
FLAP FLAP
© 1993 Washington Post Writers Group
NOW THAT'S ENTERTAINMENT!
RATTLE
RATTLE
BRIAN CRANE

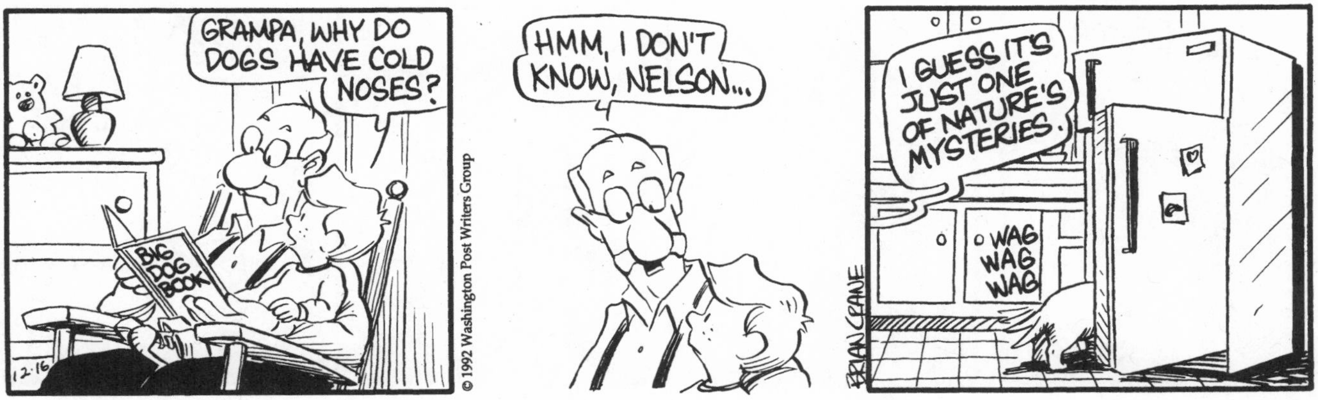

GRAMPA, WHY DO DOGS HAVE COLD NOSES?
BIG DOG BOOK
12·16
© 1992 Washington Post Writers Group
HMM, I DON'T KNOW, NELSON...
BRIAN CRANE
I GUESS IT'S JUST ONE OF NATURE'S MYSTERIES.
WAG
WAG
WAG

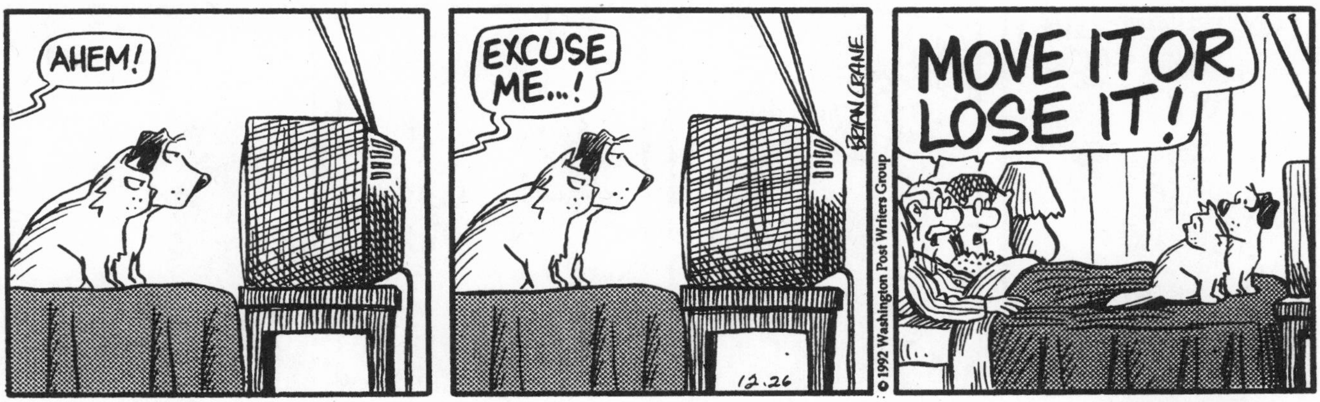

AHEM!
EXCUSE ME...!
12.26
BRIAN CRANE
© 1992 Washington Post Writers Group
MOVE IT OR LOSE IT!

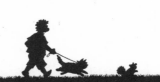

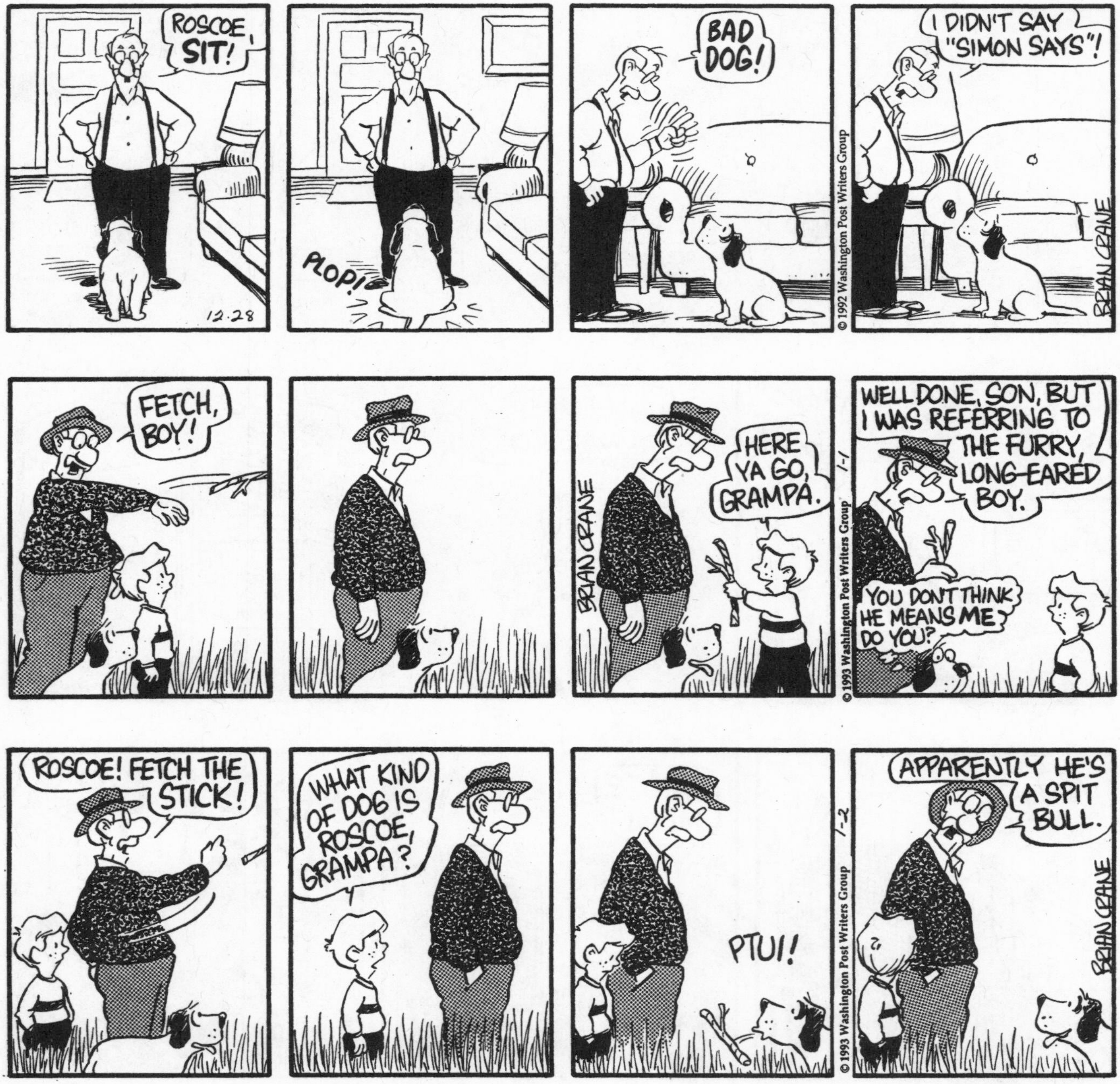
ROSCOE, SIT!
12.28
PLOP!
BAD DOG!
© 1992 Washington Post Writers Group
I DIDN'T SAY "SIMON SAYS"!
BRIAN CRANE
FETCH, BOY!
BRIAN CRANE
HERE YA GO, GRAMPA.
1-1
© 1993 Washington Post Writers Group
WELL DONE, SON, BUT I WAS REFERRING TO THE FURRY, LONG-EARED BOY.
YOU DON'T THINK HE MEANS ME, DO YOU?
ROSCOE! FETCH THE STICK!
WHAT KIND OF DOG IS ROSCOE, GRAMPA?
1-2
PTUI!
© 1993 Washington Post Writers Group
APPARENTLY HE'S A SPIT BULL.
BRIAN CRANE

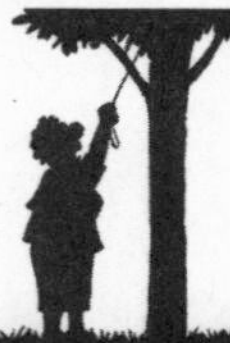

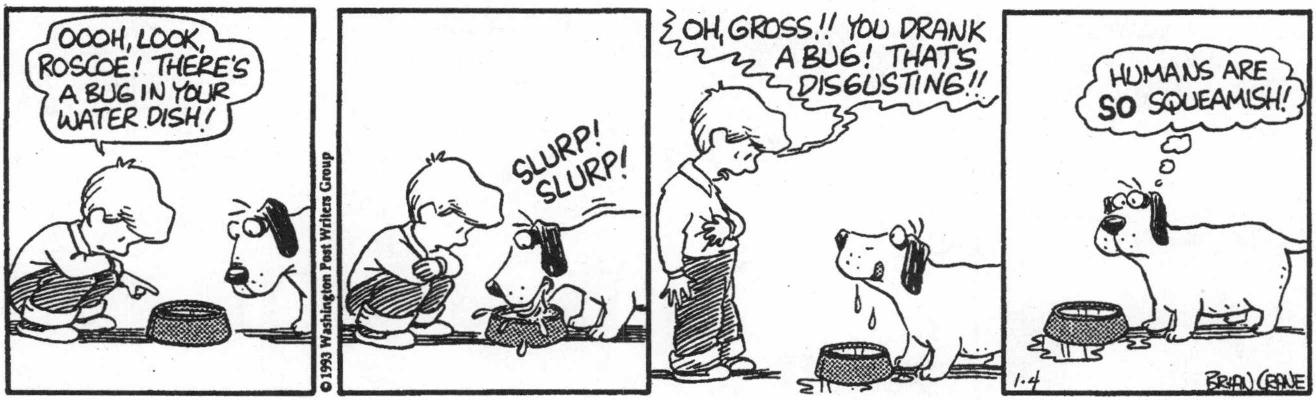
OOOH, LOOK, ROSCOE! THERE'S A BUG IN YOUR WATER DISH!
© 1993 Washington Post Writers Group
SLURP! SLURP!
OH, GROSS!! YOU DRANK A BUG! THAT'S DISGUSTING!!
HUMANS ARE SO SQUEAMISH!
1-4
BRIAN CRANE

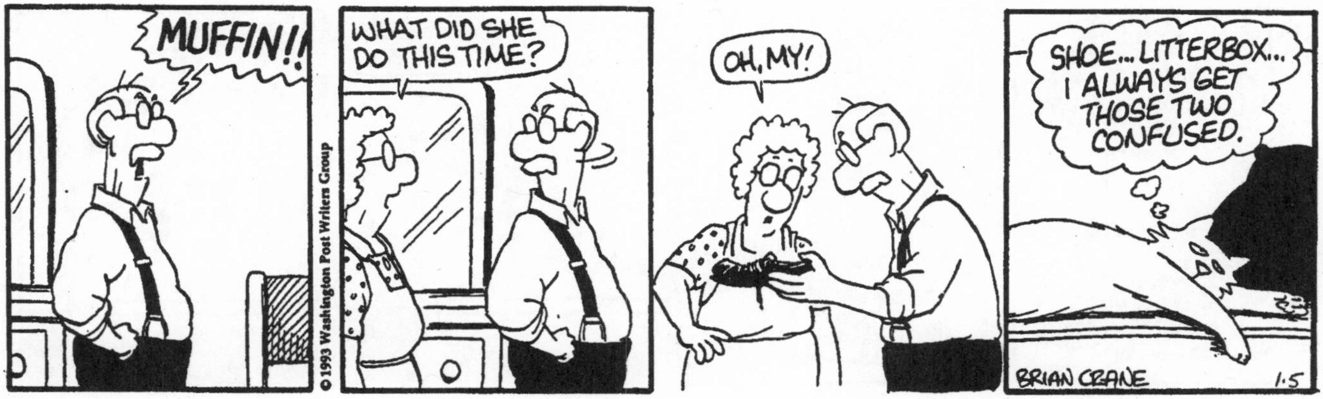
MUFFIN!!
© 1993 Washington Post Writers Group
WHAT DID SHE DO THIS TIME?
OH, MY!
SHOE... LITTERBOX... I ALWAYS GET THOSE TWO CONFUSED.
BRIAN CRANE
1-5

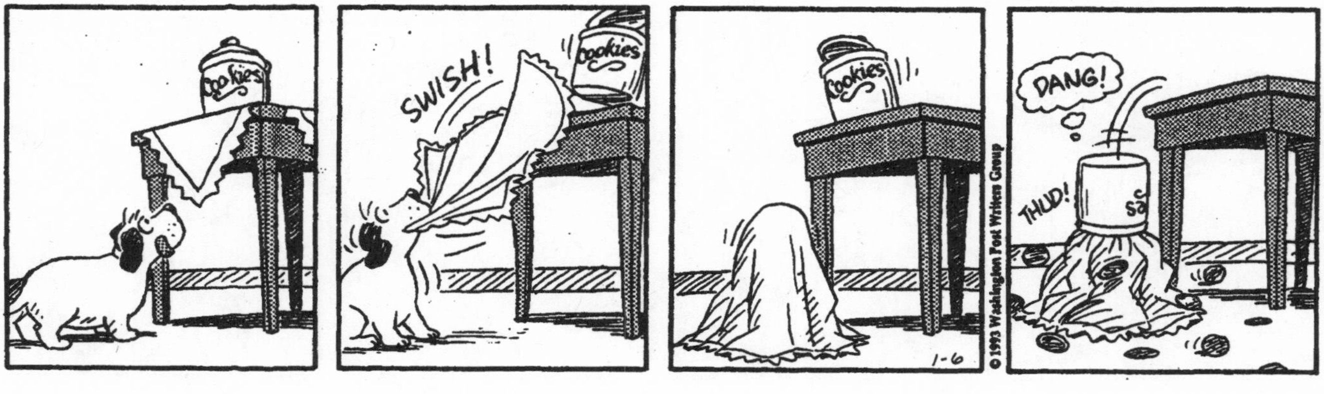
Cookies
SWISH!
Cookies
Cookies
1-6
© 1993 Washington Post Writers Group
DANG!
THUD!

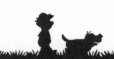

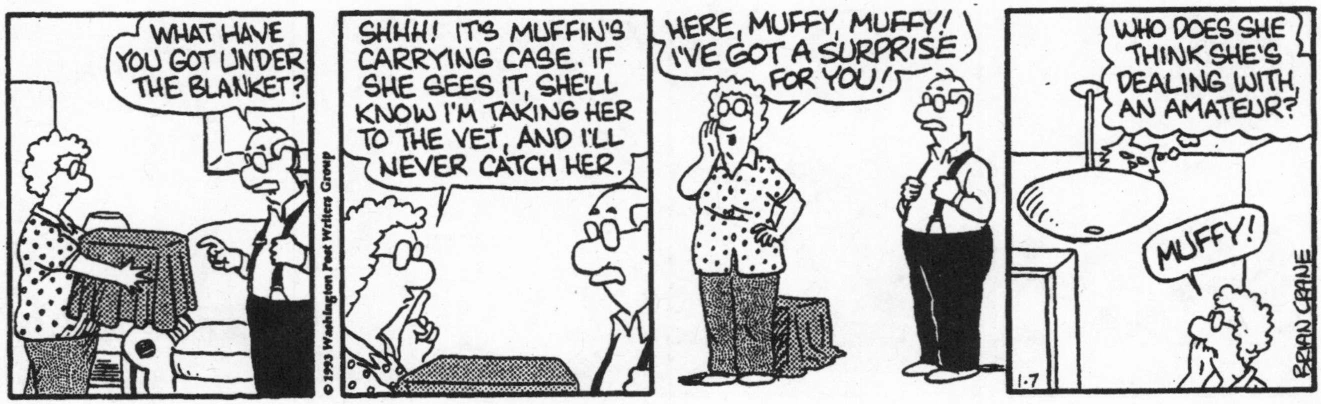
WHAT HAVE YOU GOT UNDER THE BLANKET?
SHHH! IT'S MUFFIN'S CARRYING CASE. IF SHE SEES IT, SHE'LL KNOW I'M TAKING HER TO THE VET, AND I'LL NEVER CATCH HER.
© 1993 Washington Post Writers Group
HERE, MUFFY, MUFFY! I'VE GOT A SURPRISE FOR YOU!
WHO DOES SHE THINK SHE'S DEALING WITH, AN AMATEUR?
MUFFY!
1·7
BRIAN CRANE

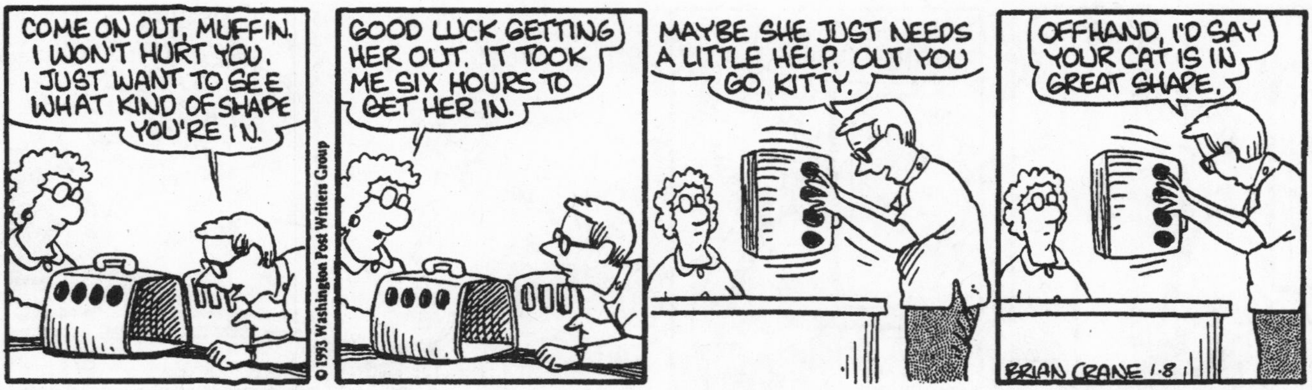
COME ON OUT, MUFFIN. I WON'T HURT YOU. I JUST WANT TO SEE WHAT KIND OF SHAPE YOU'RE IN.
© 1993 Washington Post Writers Group
GOOD LUCK GETTING HER OUT. IT TOOK ME SIX HOURS TO GET HER IN.
MAYBE SHE JUST NEEDS A LITTLE HELP. OUT YOU GO, KITTY.
OFFHAND, I'D SAY YOUR CAT IS IN GREAT SHAPE.
BRIAN CRANE 1·8

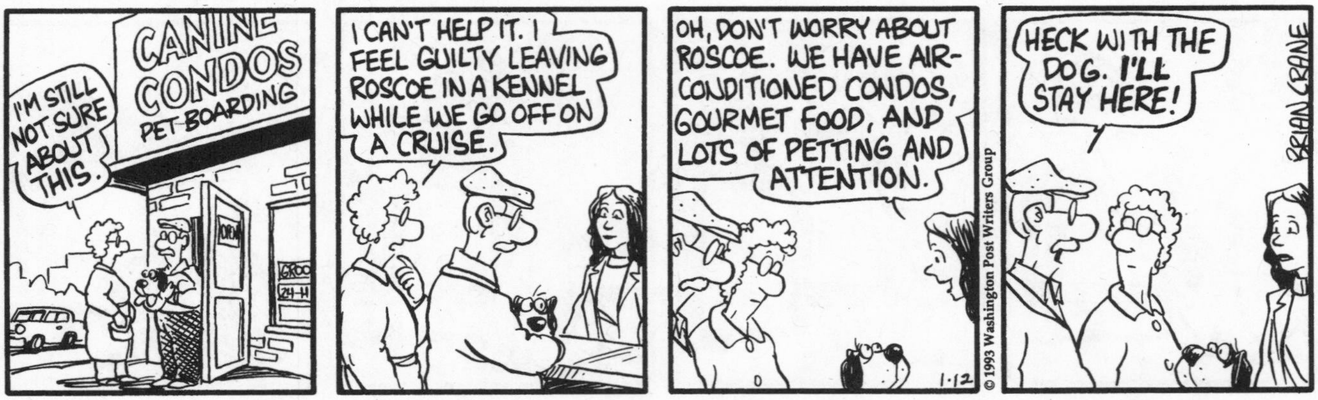
CANINE CONDOS
PET BOARDING
I'M STILL NOT SURE ABOUT THIS.
I CAN'T HELP IT. I FEEL GUILTY LEAVING ROSCOE IN A KENNEL WHILE WE GO OFF ON A CRUISE.
OH, DON'T WORRY ABOUT ROSCOE. WE HAVE AIR-CONDITIONED CONDOS, GOURMET FOOD, AND LOTS OF PETTING AND ATTENTION.
1·12
© 1993 Washington Post Writers Group
HECK WITH THE DOG. **I'LL** STAY HERE!
BRIAN CRANE

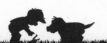

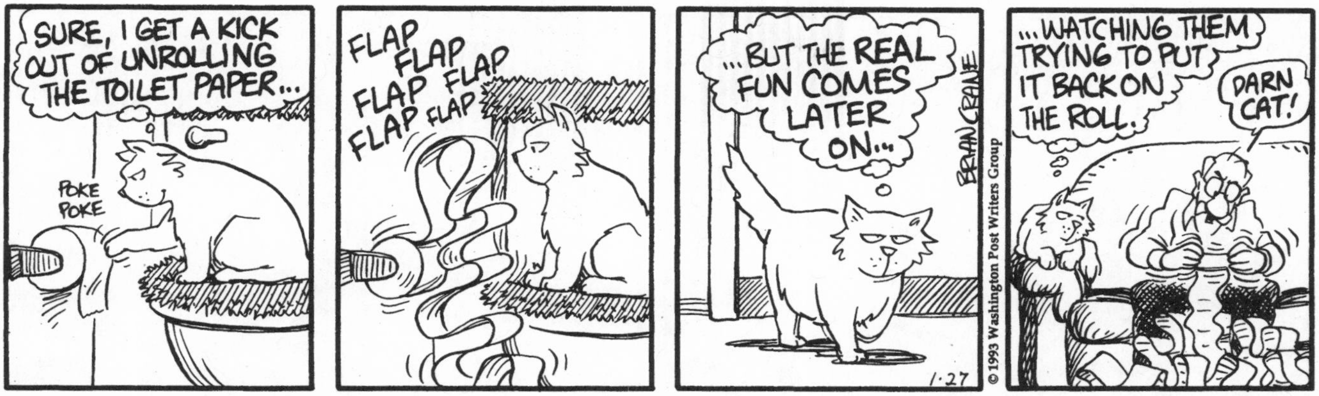
SURE, I GET A KICK OUT OF UNROLLING THE TOILET PAPER...
POKE POKE
FLAP FLAP FLAP FLAP FLAP FLAP
...BUT THE REAL FUN COMES LATER ON...
BRIAN CRANE
1·27
© 1993 Washington Post Writers Group
...WATCHING THEM TRYING TO PUT IT BACK ON THE ROLL.
DARN CAT!

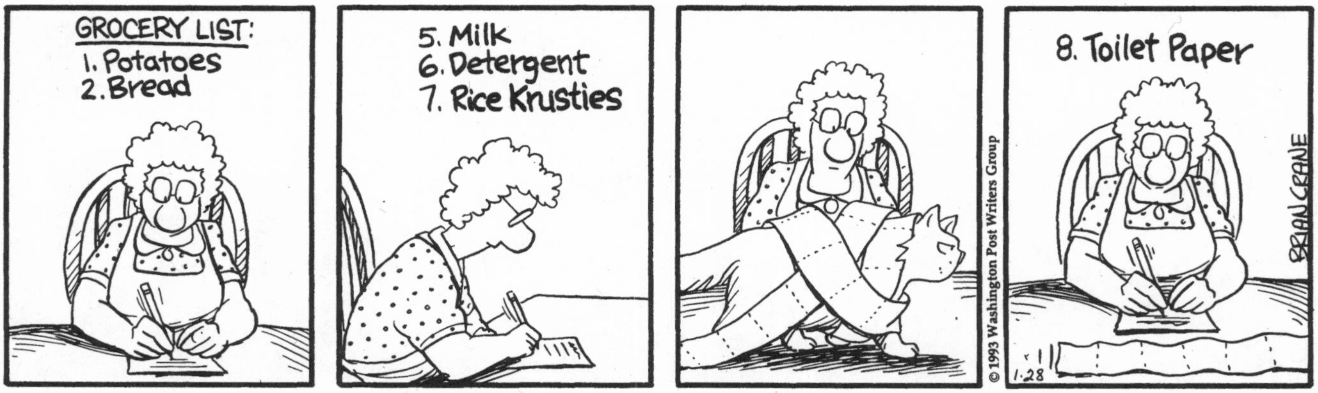
GROCERY LIST:
1. Potatoes
2. Bread
5. Milk
6. Detergent
7. Rice Krusties
© 1993 Washington Post Writers Group
8. Toilet Paper
BRIAN CRANE
1·28

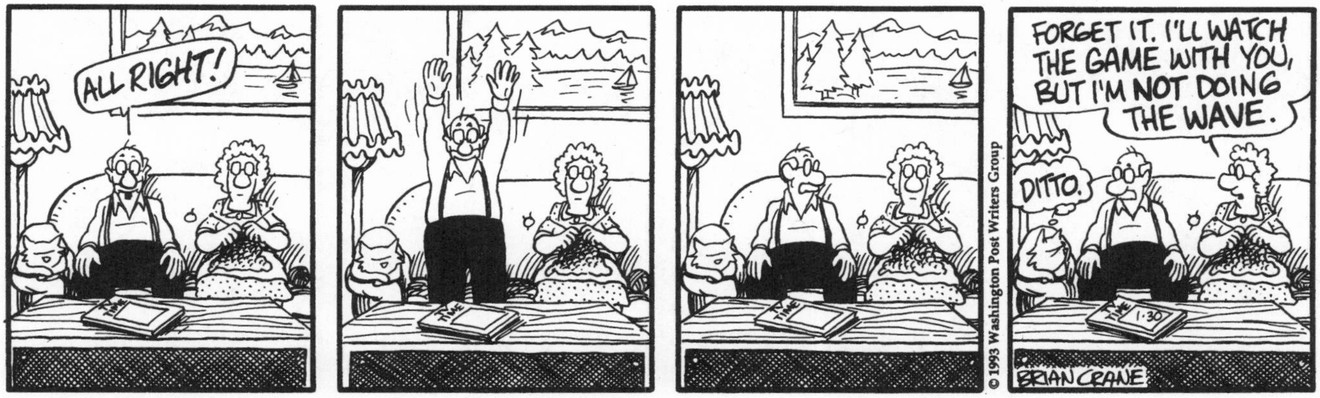
ALL RIGHT!
© 1993 Washington Post Writers Group
FORGET IT. I'LL WATCH THE GAME WITH YOU, BUT I'M NOT DOING THE WAVE.
DITTO.
1·30
BRIAN CRANE

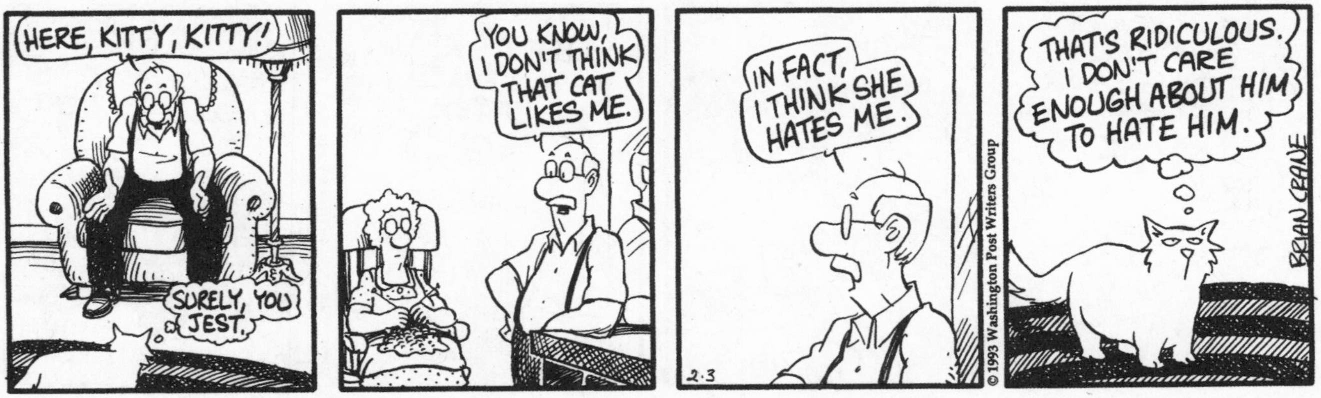
HERE, KITTY, KITTY!
SURELY, YOU JEST.
YOU KNOW, I DON'T THINK THAT CAT LIKES ME.
IN FACT, I THINK SHE HATES ME.
2·3
© 1993 Washington Post Writers Group
THAT'S RIDICULOUS. I DON'T CARE ENOUGH ABOUT HIM TO HATE HIM.
BRIAN CRANE

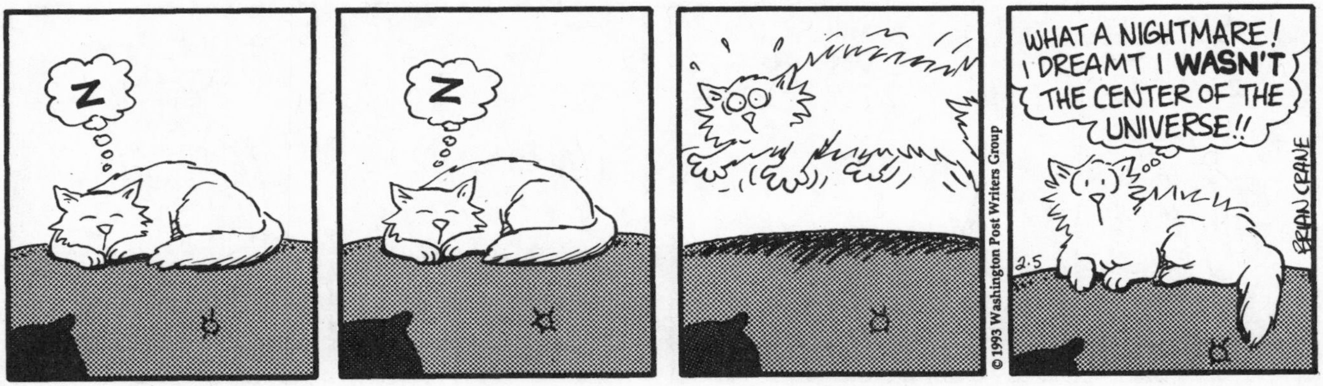
Z
Z
© 1993 Washington Post Writers Group
WHAT A NIGHTMARE! I DREAMT I **WASN'T** THE CENTER OF THE UNIVERSE!!
BRIAN CRANE
2·5

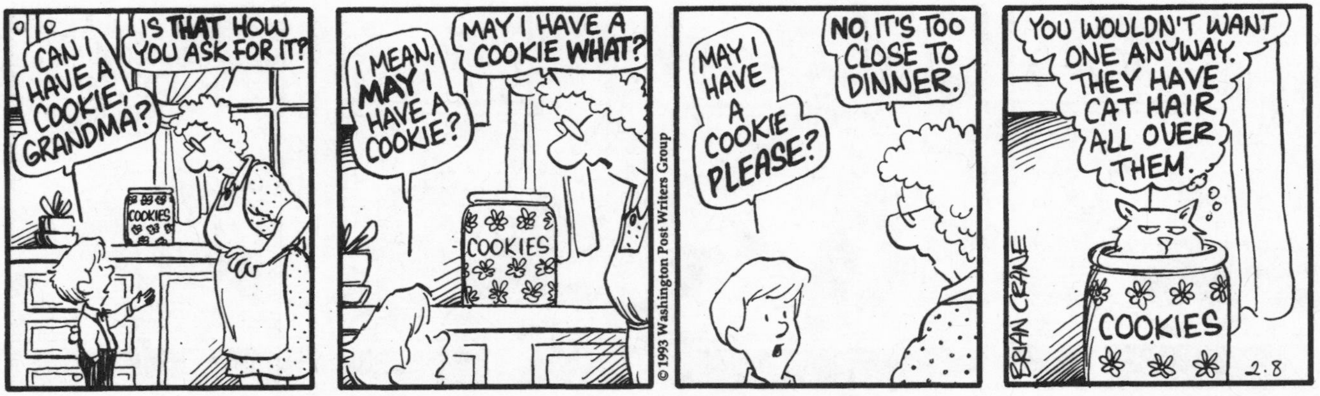
CAN I HAVE A COOKIE, GRANDMA?
IS **THAT** HOW YOU ASK FOR IT?
COOKIES
© 1993 Washington Post Writers Group
I MEAN, **MAY** I HAVE A COOKIE?
MAY I HAVE A COOKIE **WHAT**?
COOKIES
MAY I HAVE A COOKIE **PLEASE**?
NO, IT'S TOO CLOSE TO DINNER.
BRIAN CRANE
YOU WOULDN'T WANT ONE ANYWAY. THEY HAVE CAT HAIR ALL OVER THEM.
COOKIES
2·8

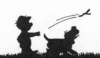

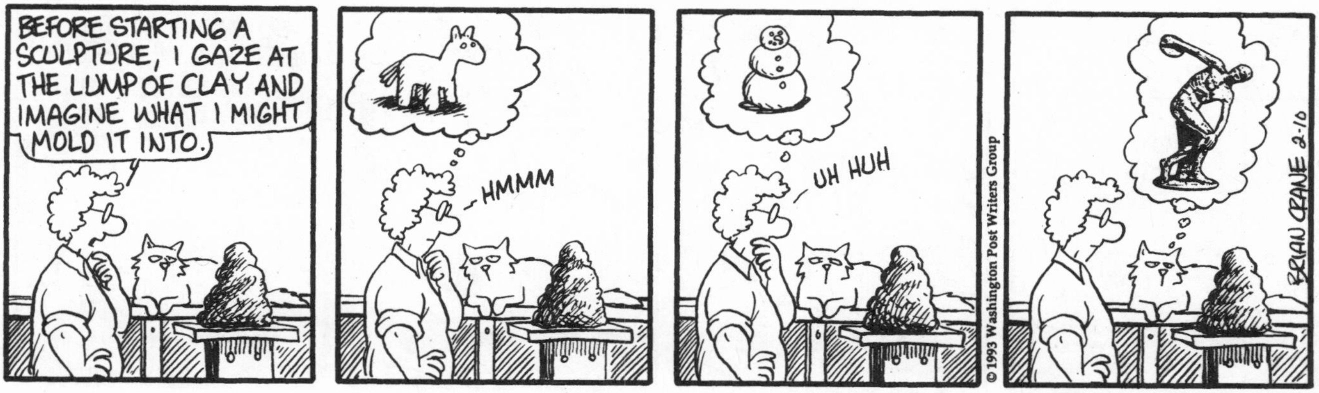
BEFORE STARTING A SCULPTURE, I GAZE AT THE LUMP OF CLAY AND IMAGINE WHAT I MIGHT MOLD IT INTO.
HMMM
UH HUH
© 1993 Washington Post Writers Group
BRIAN CRANE 2-10

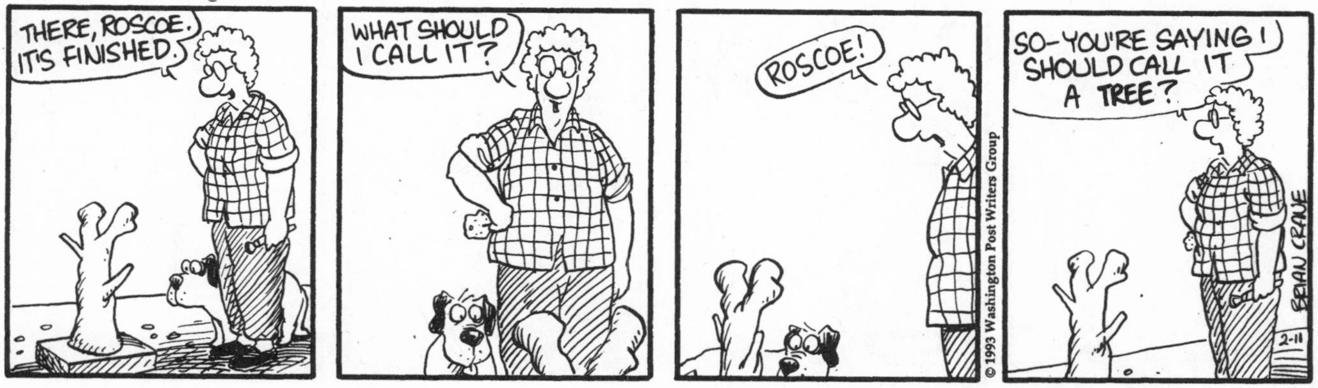
THERE, ROSCOE. IT'S FINISHED.
WHAT SHOULD I CALL IT?
ROSCOE!
© 1993 Washington Post Writers Group
SO- YOU'RE SAYING I SHOULD CALL IT A TREE?
BRIAN CRANE 2-11

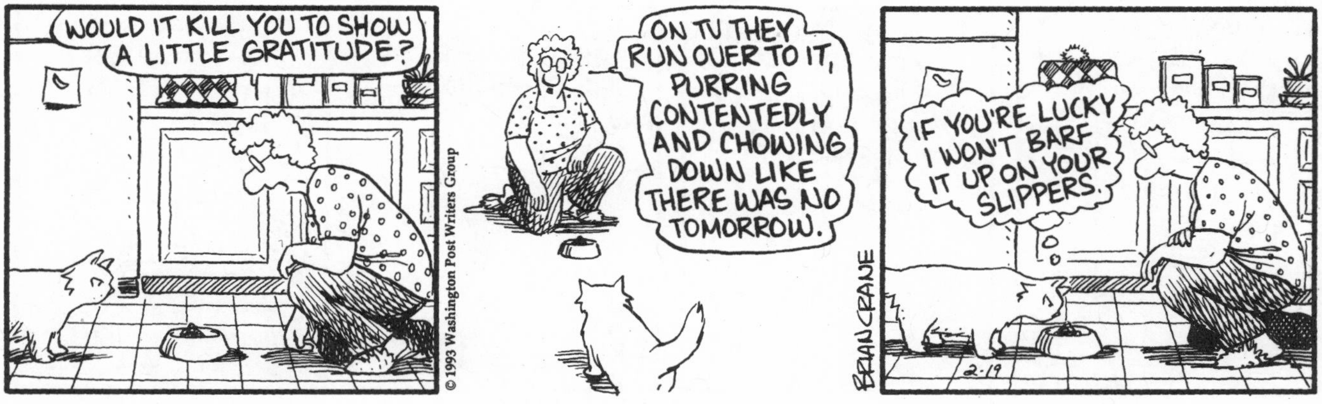
WOULD IT KILL YOU TO SHOW A LITTLE GRATITUDE?
© 1993 Washington Post Writers Group
ON TV THEY RUN OVER TO IT, PURRING CONTENTEDLY AND CHOWING DOWN LIKE THERE WAS NO TOMORROW.
BRIAN CRANE
IF YOU'RE LUCKY I WON'T BARF IT UP ON YOUR SLIPPERS.
2-19

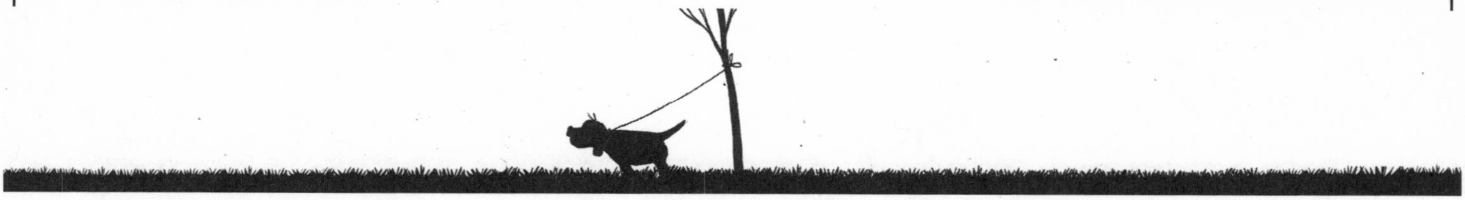

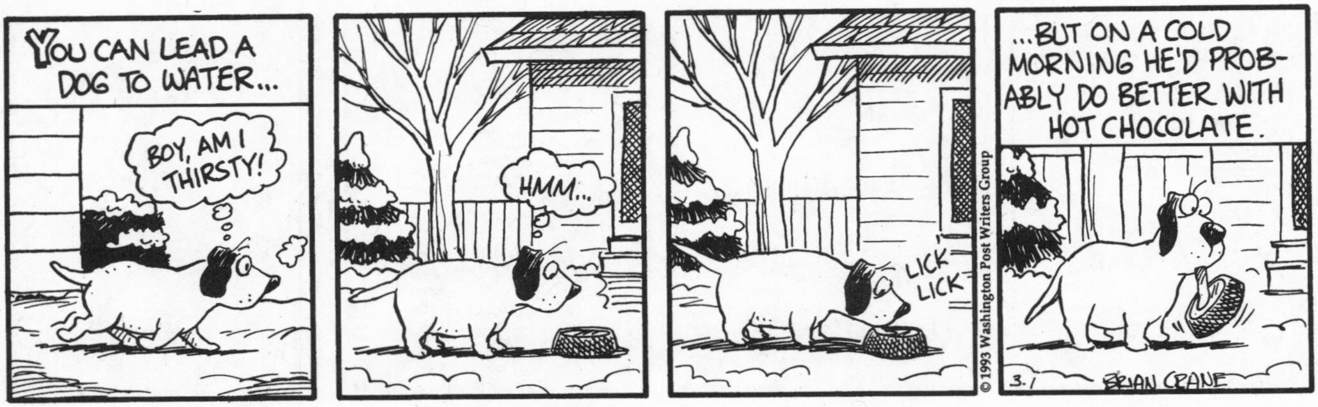
YOU CAN LEAD A DOG TO WATER...
BOY, AM I THIRSTY!
HMM...
LICK LICK
...BUT ON A COLD MORNING HE'D PROBABLY DO BETTER WITH HOT CHOCOLATE.
© 1993 Washington Post Writers Group
3.1
BRIAN CRANE

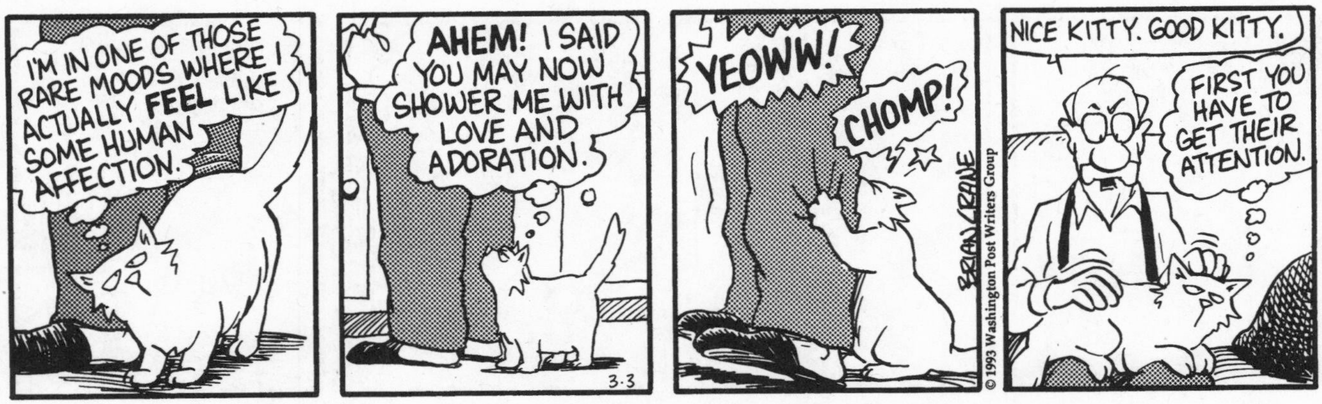
I'M IN ONE OF THOSE RARE MOODS WHERE I ACTUALLY FEEL LIKE SOME HUMAN AFFECTION.
AHEM! I SAID YOU MAY NOW SHOWER ME WITH LOVE AND ADORATION.
3.3
YEOWW!
CHOMP!
BRIAN CRANE
© 1993 Washington Post Writers Group
NICE KITTY. GOOD KITTY.
FIRST YOU HAVE TO GET THEIR ATTENTION.

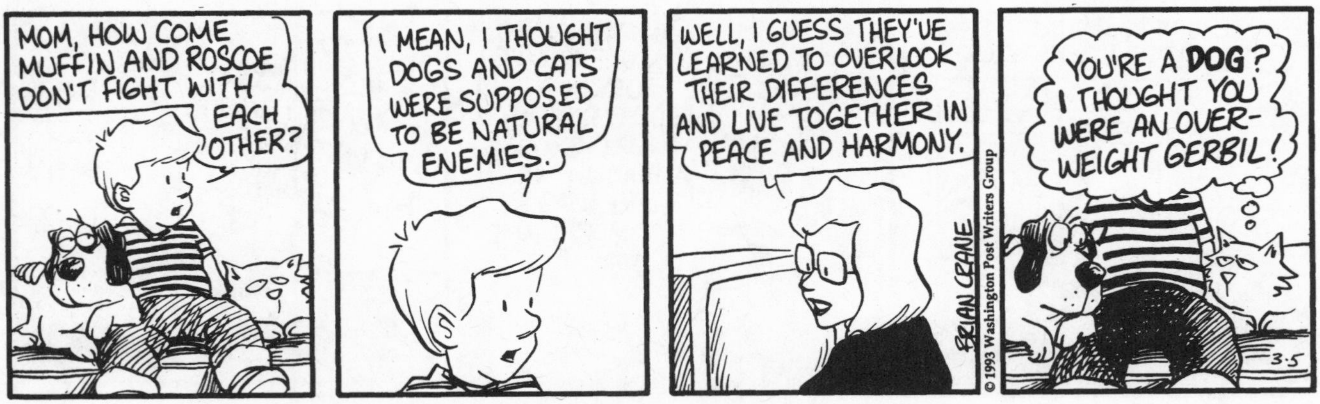
MOM, HOW COME MUFFIN AND ROSCOE DON'T FIGHT WITH EACH OTHER?
I MEAN, I THOUGHT DOGS AND CATS WERE SUPPOSED TO BE NATURAL ENEMIES.
WELL, I GUESS THEY'VE LEARNED TO OVERLOOK THEIR DIFFERENCES AND LIVE TOGETHER IN PEACE AND HARMONY.
BRIAN CRANE
© 1993 Washington Post Writers Group
YOU'RE A DOG? I THOUGHT YOU WERE AN OVERWEIGHT GERBIL!
3.5

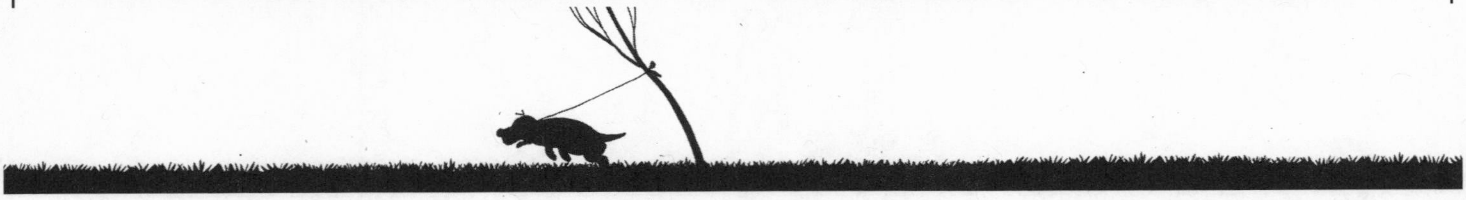

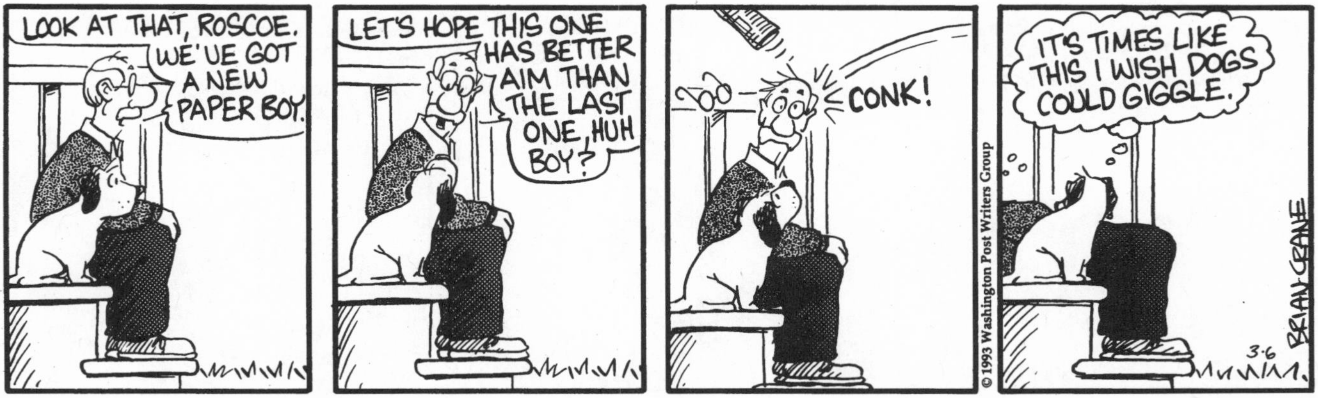
LOOK AT THAT, ROSCOE. WE'VE GOT A NEW PAPER BOY.
LET'S HOPE THIS ONE HAS BETTER AIM THAN THE LAST ONE, HUH BOY?
CONK!
© 1993 Washington Post Writers Group
IT'S TIMES LIKE THIS I WISH DOGS COULD GIGGLE.
3-6
BRIAN CRANE

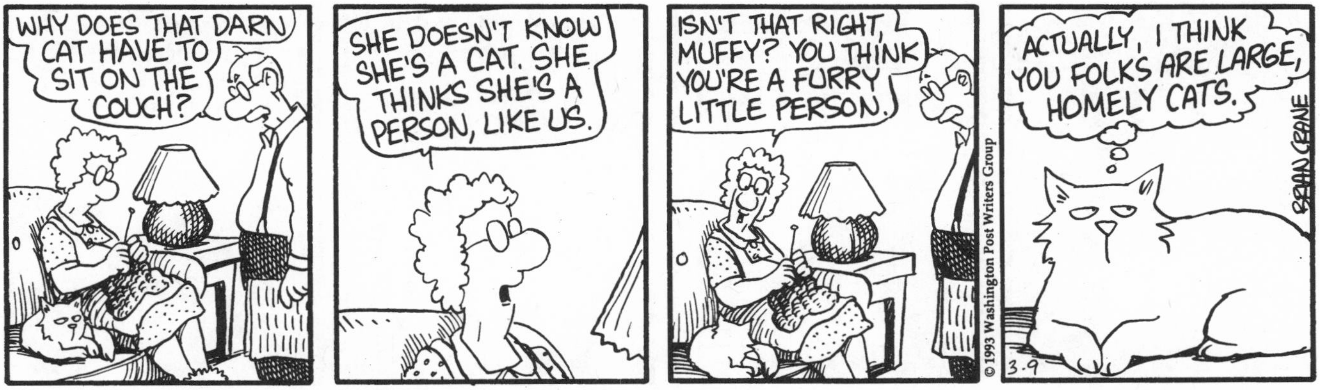
WHY DOES THAT DARN CAT HAVE TO SIT ON THE COUCH?
SHE DOESN'T KNOW SHE'S A CAT. SHE THINKS SHE'S A PERSON, LIKE US.
ISN'T THAT RIGHT, MUFFY? YOU THINK YOU'RE A FURRY LITTLE PERSON.
© 1993 Washington Post Writers Group
ACTUALLY, I THINK YOU FOLKS ARE LARGE, HOMELY CATS.
BRIAN CRANE
3-9

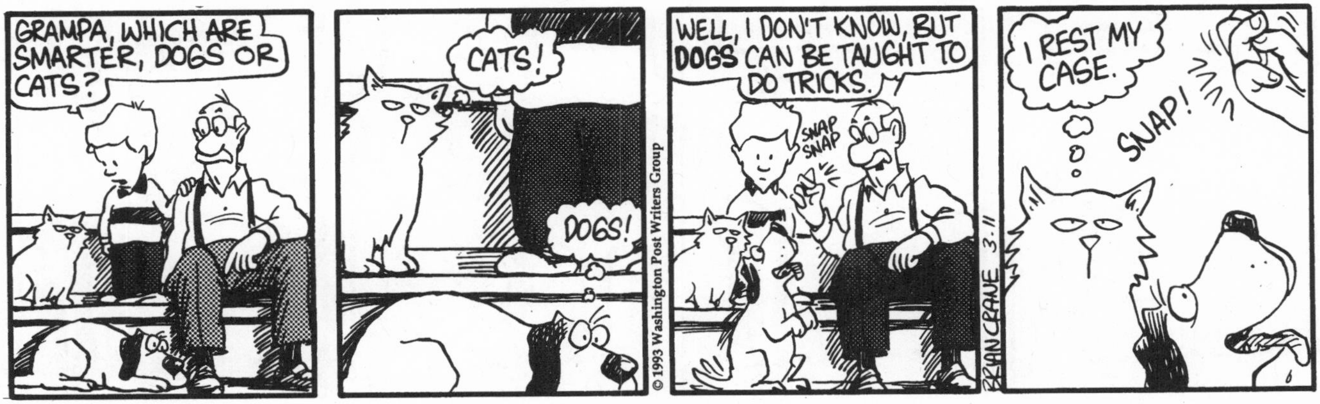
GRAMPA, WHICH ARE SMARTER, DOGS OR CATS?
CATS!
DOGS!
© 1993 Washington Post Writers Group
WELL, I DON'T KNOW, BUT **DOGS** CAN BE TAUGHT TO DO TRICKS.
SNAP SNAP
3-11
BRIAN CRANE
I REST MY CASE.
SNAP!

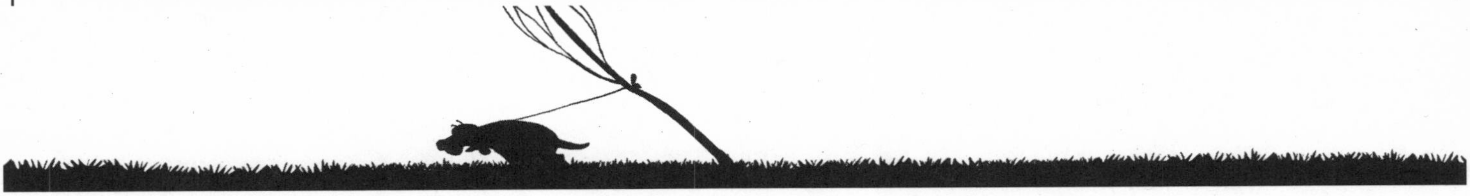

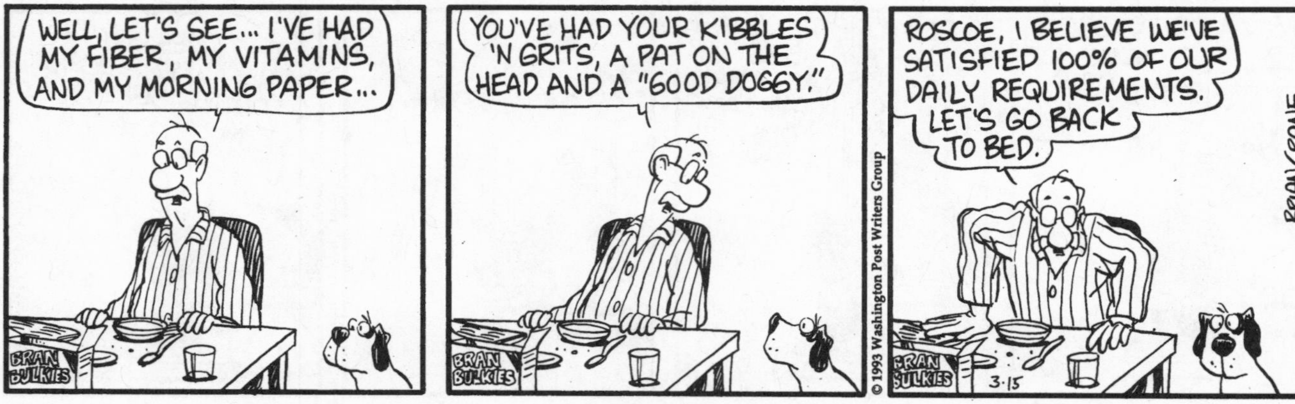
WELL, LET'S SEE... I'VE HAD MY FIBER, MY VITAMINS, AND MY MORNING PAPER...
BRAN BULKIES
YOU'VE HAD YOUR KIBBLES 'N GRITS, A PAT ON THE HEAD AND A "GOOD DOGGY."
BRAN BULKIES
© 1993 Washington Post Writers Group
ROSCOE, I BELIEVE WE'VE SATISFIED 100% OF OUR DAILY REQUIREMENTS. LET'S GO BACK TO BED.
BRAN BULKIES
3·15
BRIAN CRANE

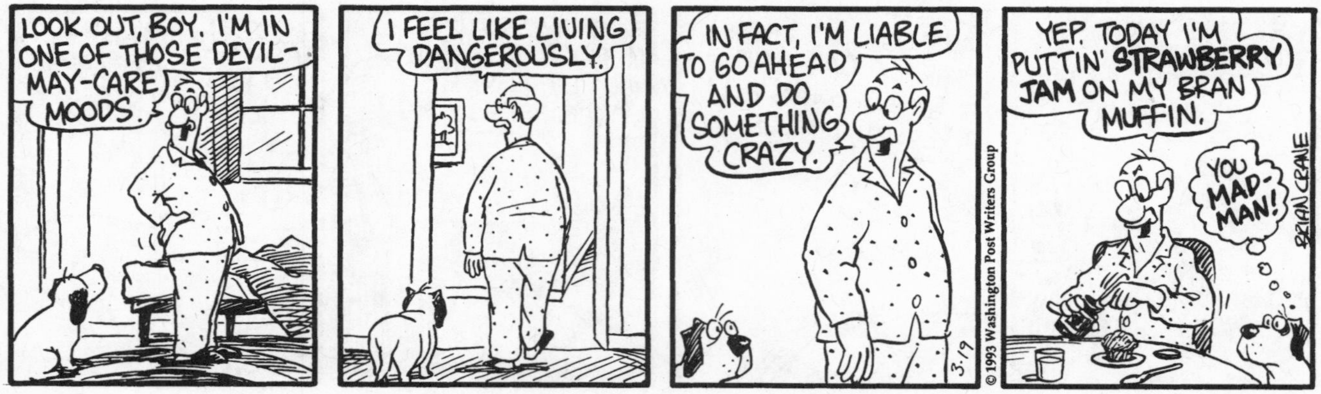
LOOK OUT, BOY. I'M IN ONE OF THOSE DEVIL-MAY-CARE MOODS.
I FEEL LIKE LIVING DANGEROUSLY.
IN FACT, I'M LIABLE TO GO AHEAD AND DO SOMETHING CRAZY.
3·19
© 1993 Washington Post Writers Group
YEP. TODAY I'M PUTTIN' **STRAWBERRY JAM** ON MY BRAN MUFFIN.
YOU MAD-MAN!
BRIAN CRANE

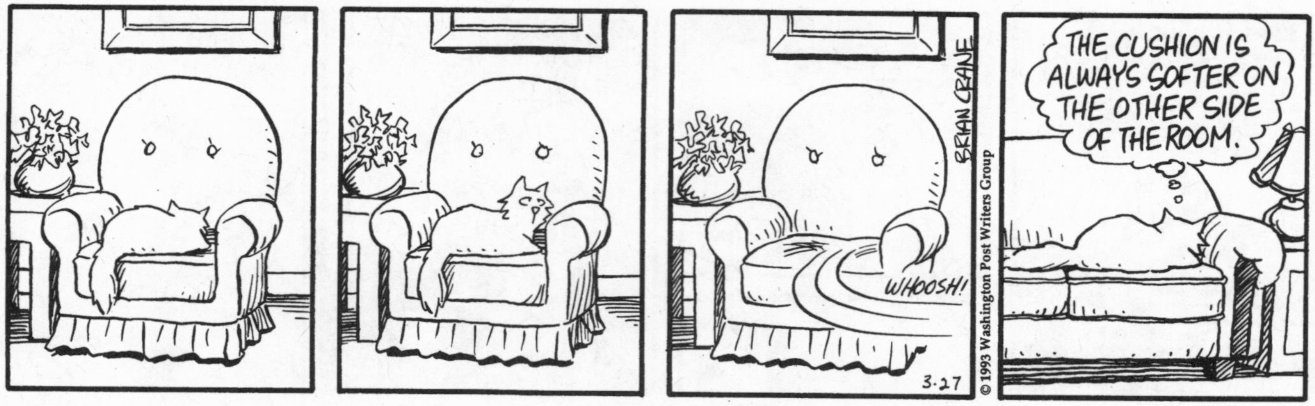
BRIAN CRANE
WHOOSH!
3·27
© 1993 Washington Post Writers Group
THE CUSHION IS ALWAYS SOFTER ON THE OTHER SIDE OF THE ROOM.

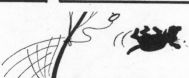

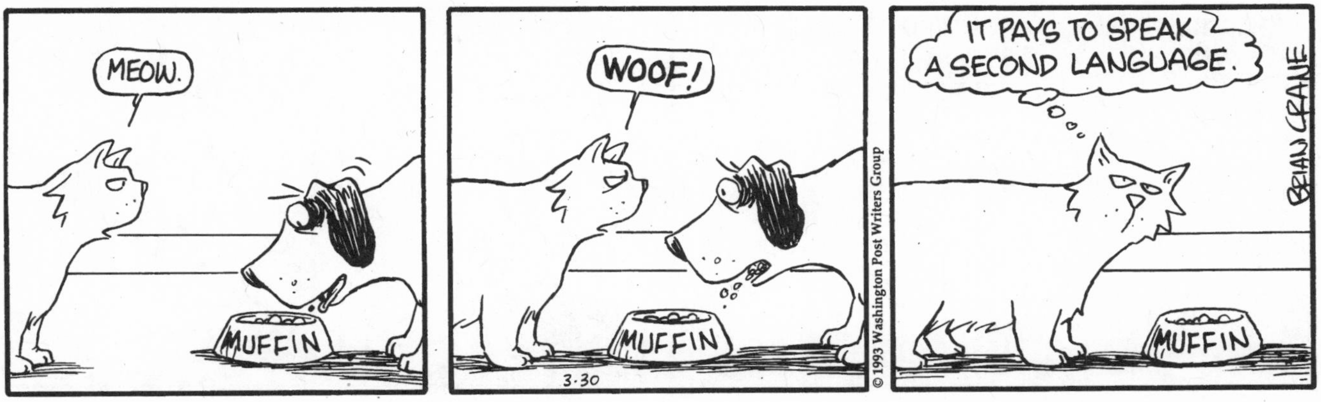
MEOW.
WOOF!
IT PAYS TO SPEAK A SECOND LANGUAGE.
MUFFIN
3·30
© 1993 Washington Post Writers Group
BRIAN CRANE

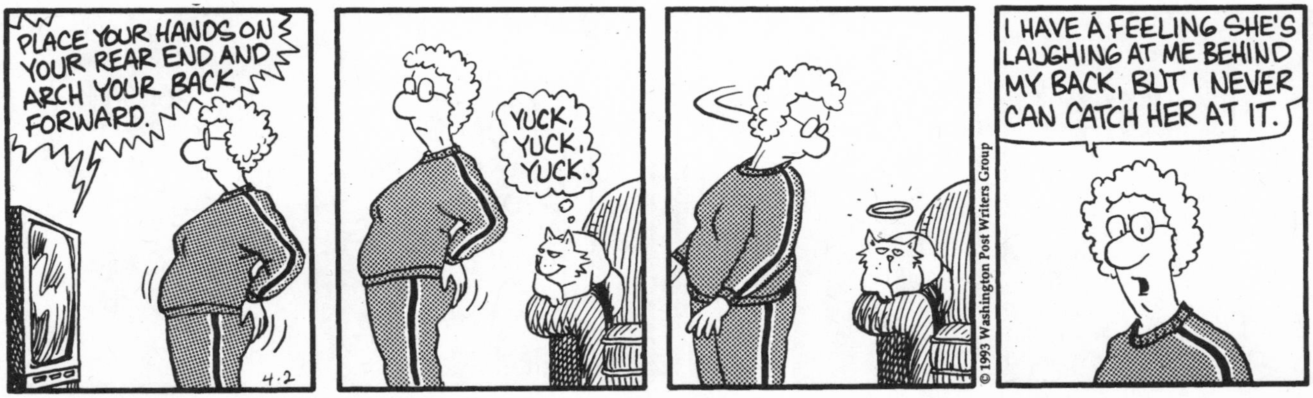
PLACE YOUR HANDS ON YOUR REAR END AND ARCH YOUR BACK FORWARD.
4·2
YUCK, YUCK, YUCK.
© 1993 Washington Post Writers Group
I HAVE A FEELING SHE'S LAUGHING AT ME BEHIND MY BACK, BUT I NEVER CAN CATCH HER AT IT.

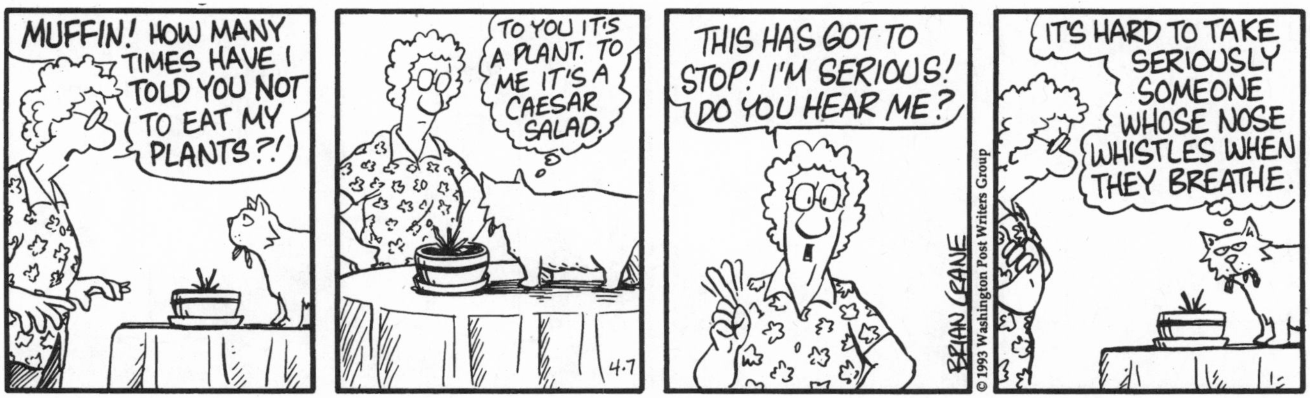
MUFFIN! HOW MANY TIMES HAVE I TOLD YOU NOT TO EAT MY PLANTS?!
TO YOU IT'S A PLANT. TO ME IT'S A CAESAR SALAD.
4·7
THIS HAS GOT TO STOP! I'M SERIOUS! DO YOU HEAR ME?
BRIAN CRANE
© 1993 Washington Post Writers Group
IT'S HARD TO TAKE SERIOUSLY SOMEONE WHOSE NOSE WHISTLES WHEN THEY BREATHE.

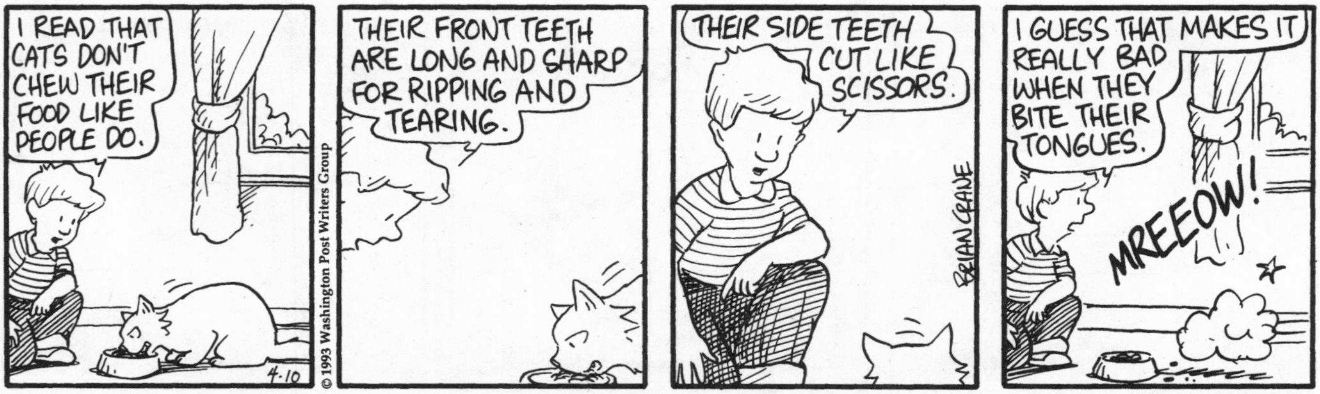
I READ THAT CATS DON'T CHEW THEIR FOOD LIKE PEOPLE DO.
4·10
© 1993 Washington Post Writers Group
THEIR FRONT TEETH ARE LONG AND SHARP FOR RIPPING AND TEARING.
THEIR SIDE TEETH CUT LIKE SCISSORS.
BRIAN CRANE
I GUESS THAT MAKES IT REALLY BAD WHEN THEY BITE THEIR TONGUES.
MREEOW!

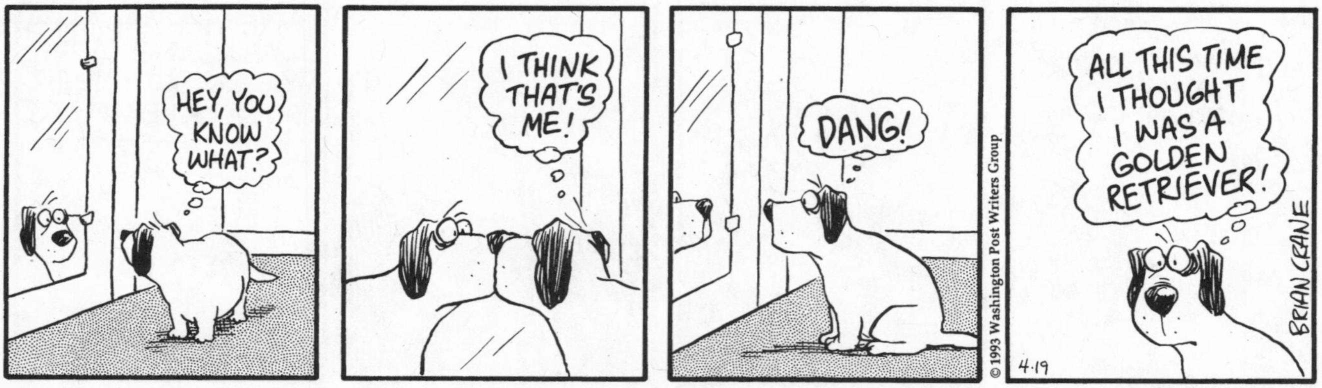
HEY, YOU KNOW WHAT?
I THINK THAT'S ME!
DANG!
© 1993 Washington Post Writers Group
ALL THIS TIME I THOUGHT I WAS A GOLDEN RETRIEVER!
BRIAN CRANE
4·19

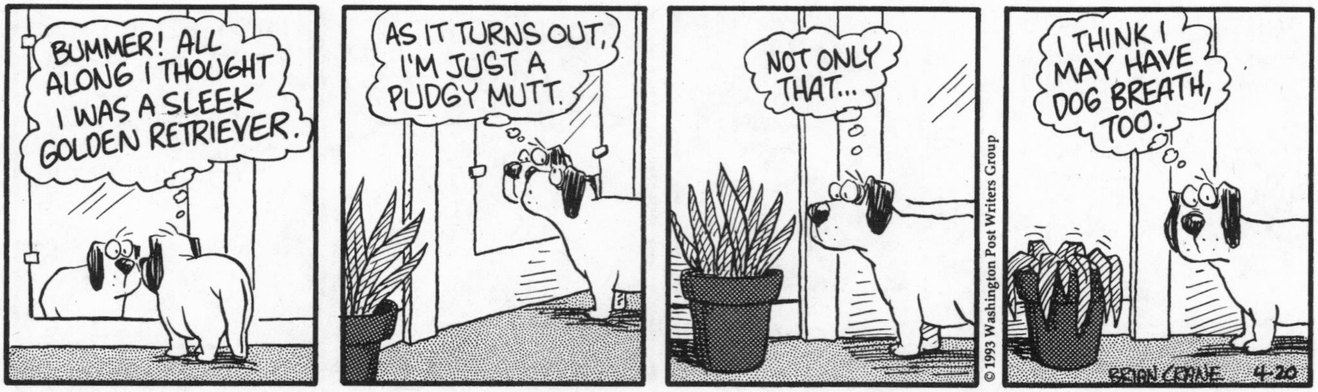
BUMMER! ALL ALONG I THOUGHT I WAS A SLEEK GOLDEN RETRIEVER.
AS IT TURNS OUT, I'M JUST A PUDGY MUTT.
NOT ONLY THAT...
© 1993 Washington Post Writers Group
I THINK I MAY HAVE DOG BREATH, TOO.
BRIAN CRANE
4·20

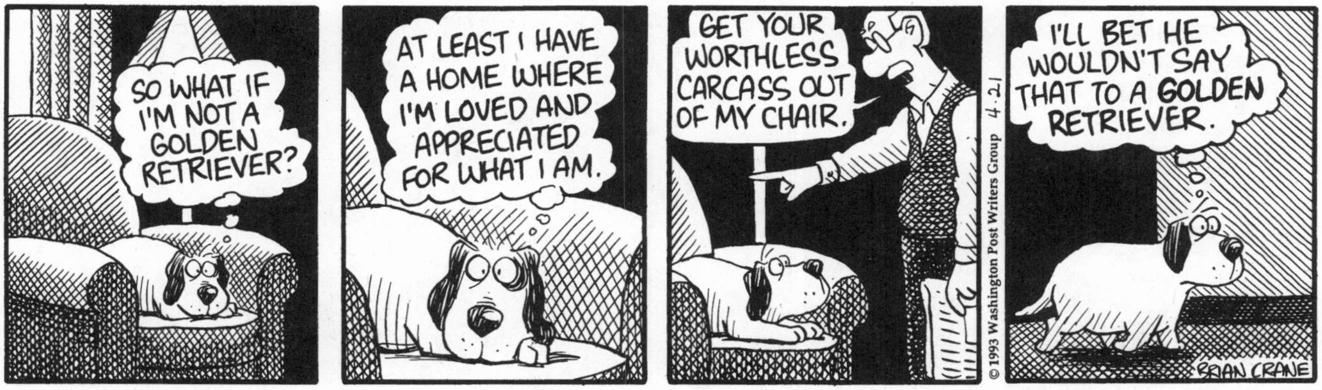
SO WHAT IF I'M NOT A GOLDEN RETRIEVER?
AT LEAST I HAVE A HOME WHERE I'M LOVED AND APPRECIATED FOR WHAT I AM.
GET YOUR WORTHLESS CARCASS OUT OF MY CHAIR.
4·21
© 1993 Washington Post Writers Group
I'LL BET HE WOULDN'T SAY THAT TO A GOLDEN RETRIEVER.
BRIAN CRANE

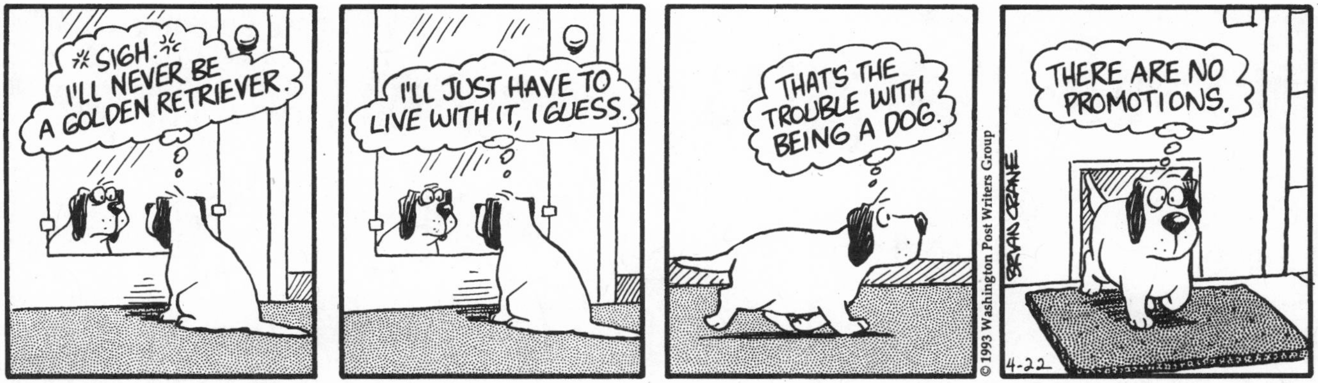
SIGH. I'LL NEVER BE A GOLDEN RETRIEVER.
I'LL JUST HAVE TO LIVE WITH IT, I GUESS.
THAT'S THE TROUBLE WITH BEING A DOG.
© 1993 Washington Post Writers Group
BRIAN CRANE
THERE ARE NO PROMOTIONS.
4-22

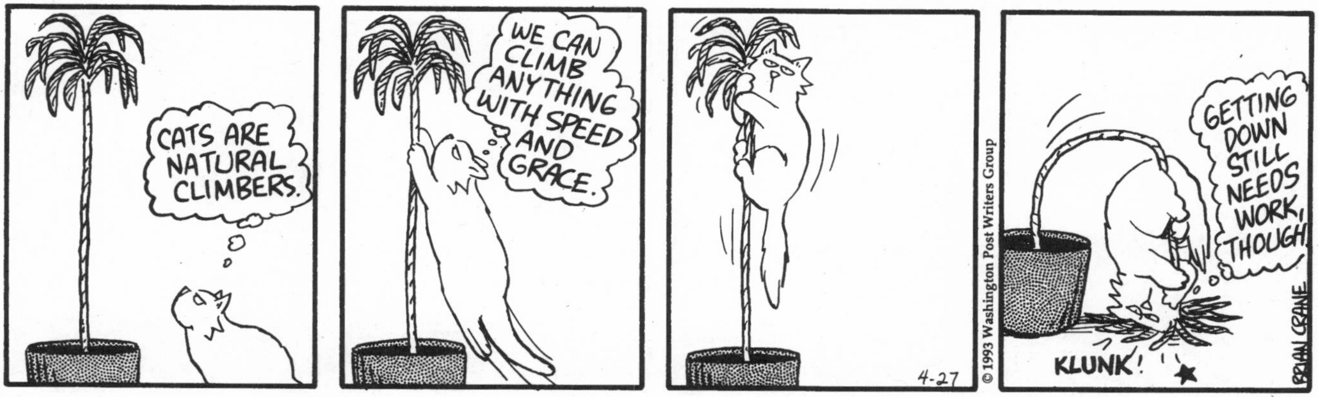
CATS ARE NATURAL CLIMBERS.
WE CAN CLIMB ANYTHING WITH SPEED AND GRACE.
4-27
© 1993 Washington Post Writers Group
GETTING DOWN STILL NEEDS WORK, THOUGH!
KLUNK!
BRIAN CRANE

79

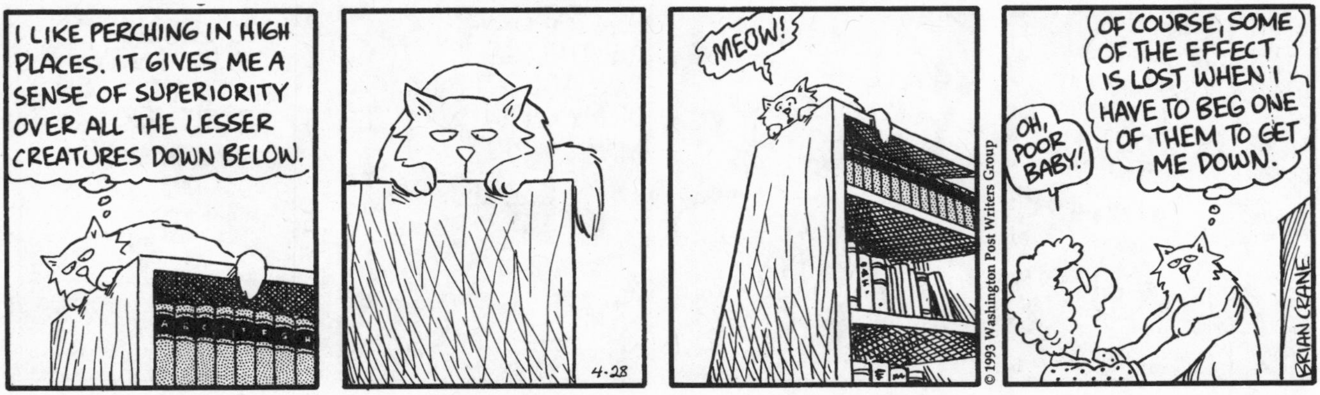
I LIKE PERCHING IN HIGH PLACES. IT GIVES ME A SENSE OF SUPERIORITY OVER ALL THE LESSER CREATURES DOWN BELOW.
4-28
MEOW!
© 1993 Washington Post Writers Group
OH, POOR BABY!
OF COURSE, SOME OF THE EFFECT IS LOST WHEN I HAVE TO BEG ONE OF THEM TO GET ME DOWN.
BRIAN CRANE

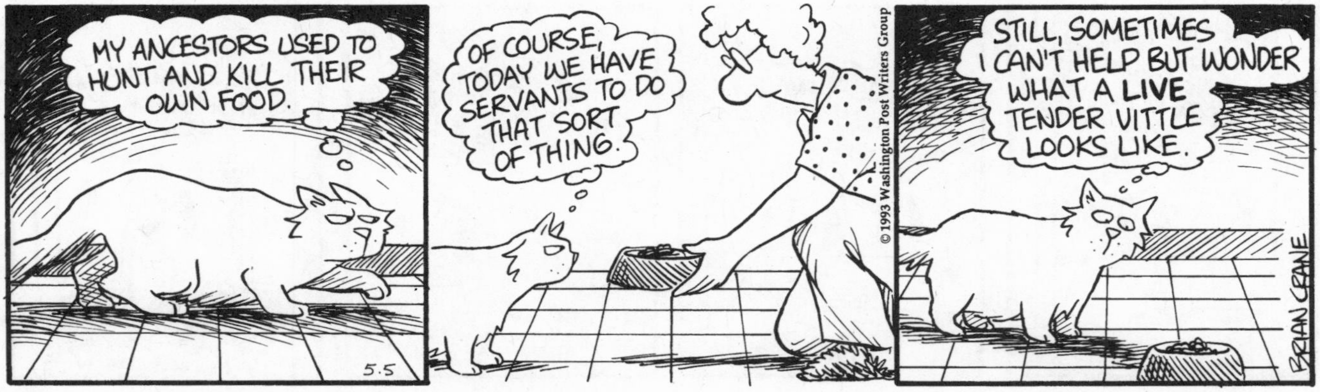
MY ANCESTORS USED TO HUNT AND KILL THEIR OWN FOOD.
5.5
OF COURSE, TODAY WE HAVE SERVANTS TO DO THAT SORT OF THING.
© 1993 Washington Post Writers Group
STILL, SOMETIMES I CAN'T HELP BUT WONDER WHAT A **LIVE** TENDER VITTLE LOOKS LIKE.
BRIAN CRANE

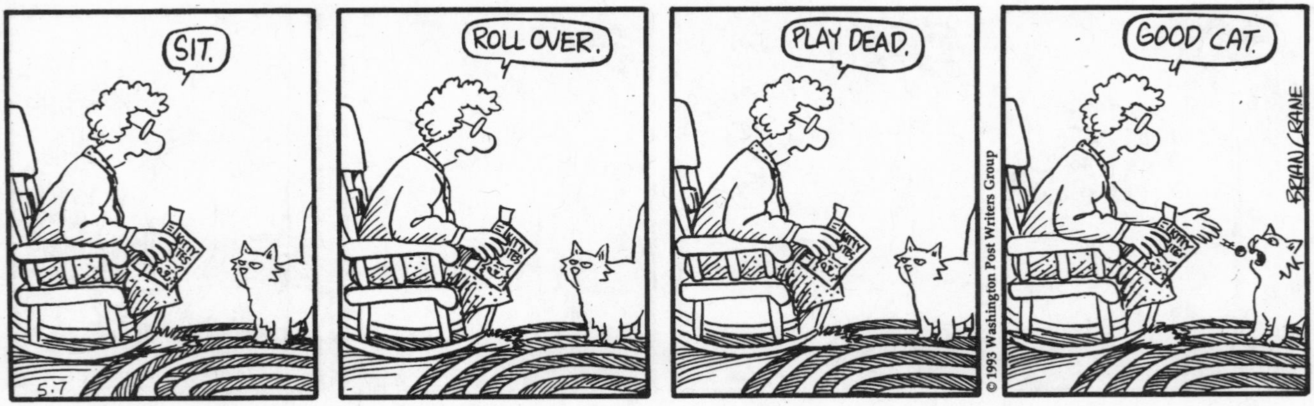
SIT.
5-7
ROLL OVER.
PLAY DEAD.
© 1993 Washington Post Writers Group
GOOD CAT.
BRIAN CRANE

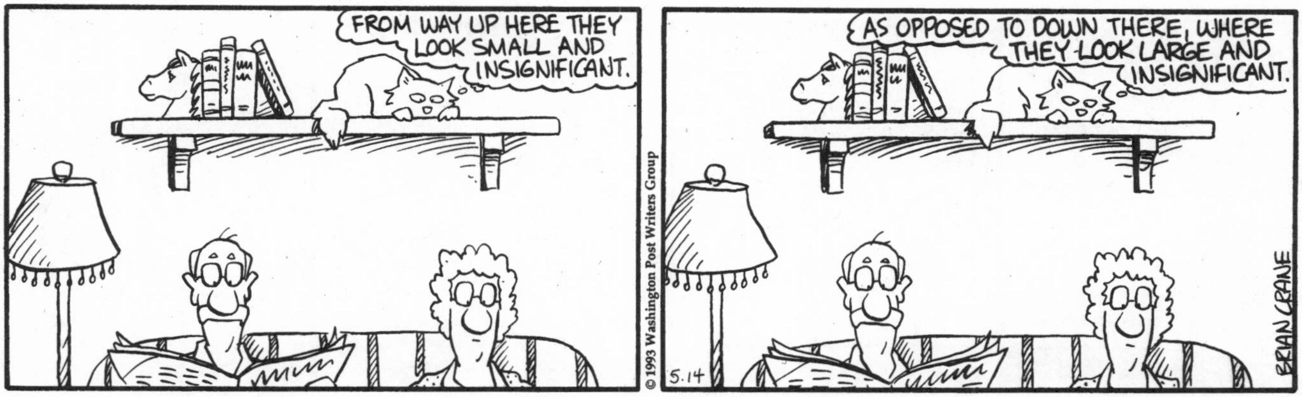
FROM WAY UP HERE THEY LOOK SMALL AND INSIGNIFICANT.
AS OPPOSED TO DOWN THERE, WHERE THEY LOOK LARGE AND INSIGNIFICANT.
© 1993 Washington Post Writers Group
5.14
BRIAN CRANE

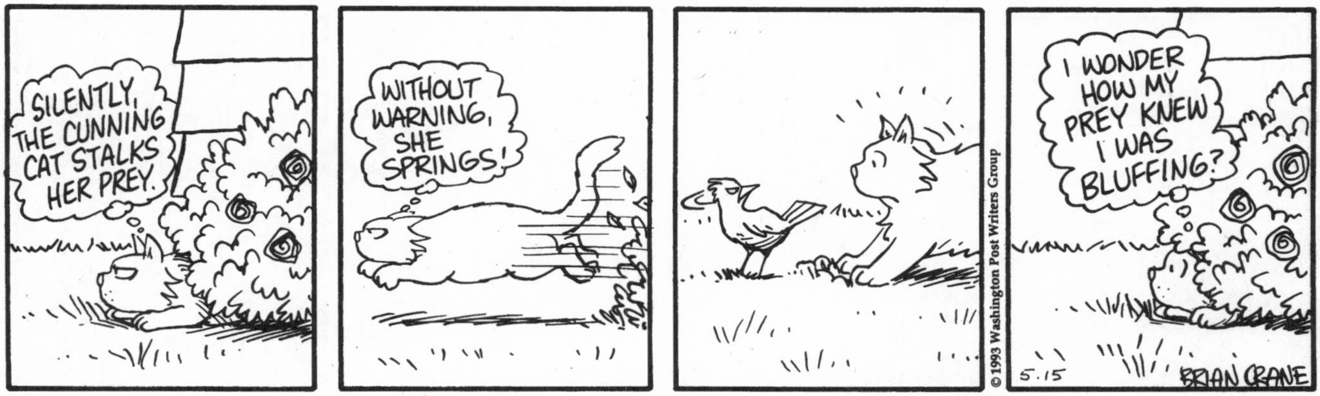
SILENTLY, THE CUNNING CAT STALKS HER PREY.
WITHOUT WARNING, SHE SPRINGS!
I WONDER HOW MY PREY KNEW I WAS BLUFFING?
© 1993 Washington Post Writers Group
5.15
BRIAN CRANE

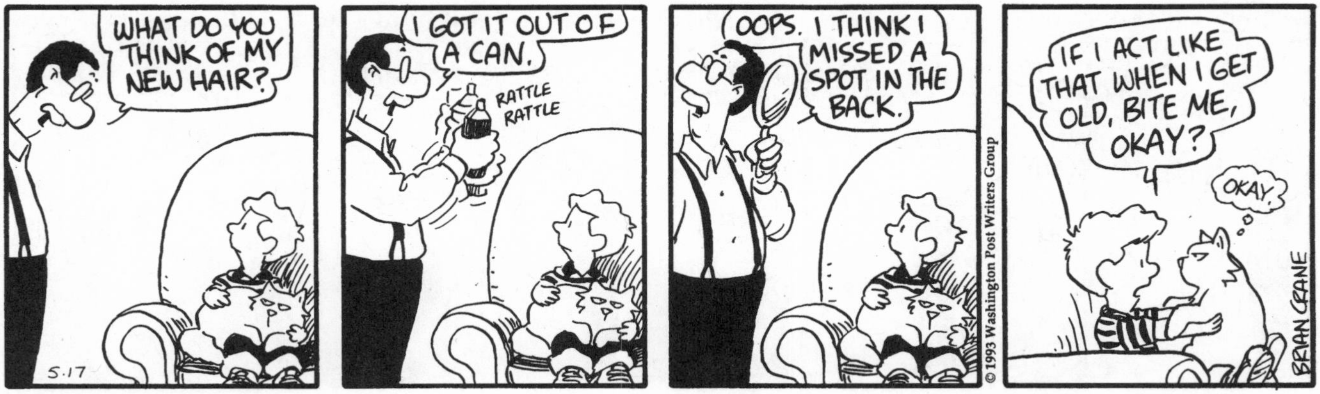
WHAT DO YOU THINK OF MY NEW HAIR?
5.17
I GOT IT OUT OF A CAN.
RATTLE RATTLE
OOPS. I THINK I MISSED A SPOT IN THE BACK.
© 1993 Washington Post Writers Group
IF I ACT LIKE THAT WHEN I GET OLD, BITE ME, OKAY?
OKAY.
BRIAN CRANE

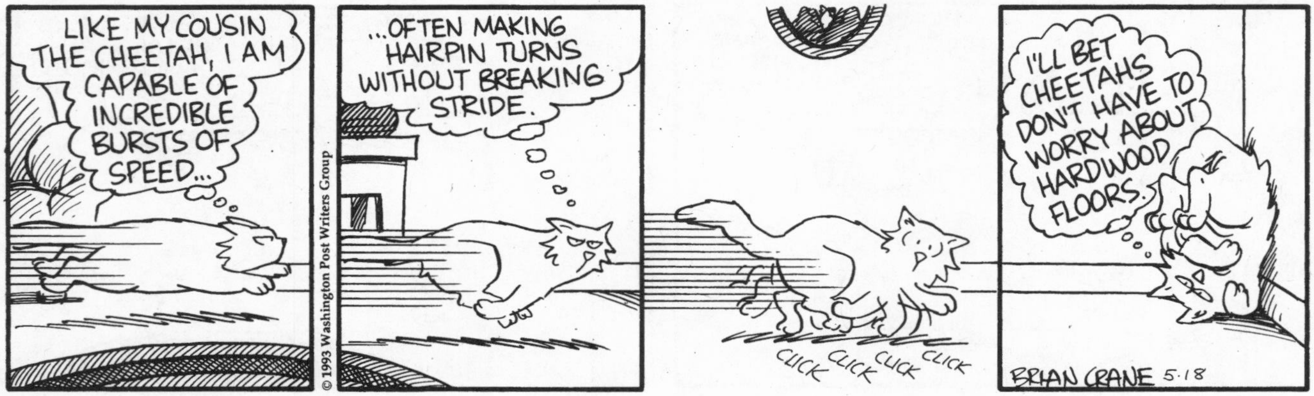
LIKE MY COUSIN THE CHEETAH, I AM CAPABLE OF INCREDIBLE BURSTS OF SPEED...
...OFTEN MAKING HAIRPIN TURNS WITHOUT BREAKING STRIDE.
CLICK CLICK CLICK CLICK
I'LL BET CHEETAHS DON'T HAVE TO WORRY ABOUT HARDWOOD FLOORS.
© 1993 Washington Post Writers Group
BRIAN CRANE 5·18

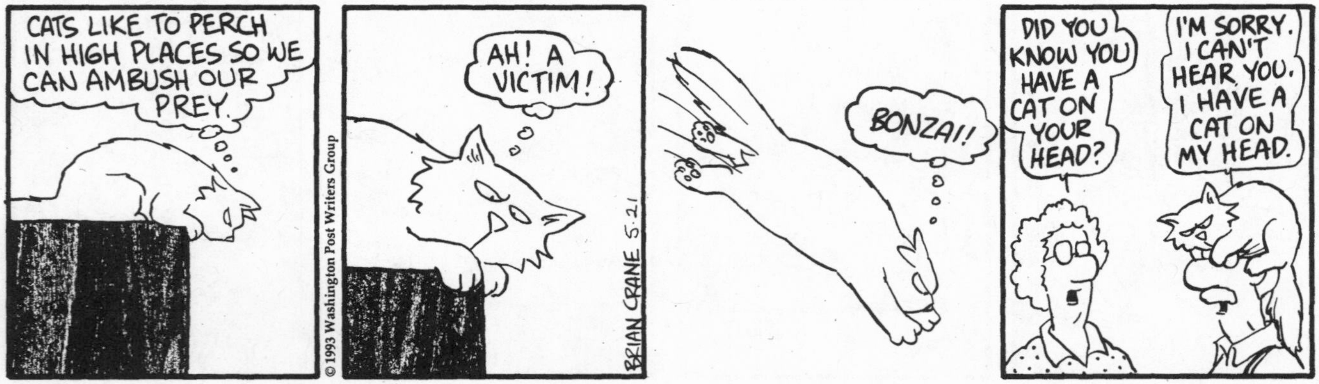
CATS LIKE TO PERCH IN HIGH PLACES SO WE CAN AMBUSH OUR PREY.
AH! A VICTIM!
BONZAI!!
DID YOU KNOW YOU HAVE A CAT ON YOUR HEAD?
I'M SORRY. I CAN'T HEAR YOU. I HAVE A CAT ON MY HEAD.
© 1993 Washington Post Writers Group
BRIAN CRANE 5·21

82

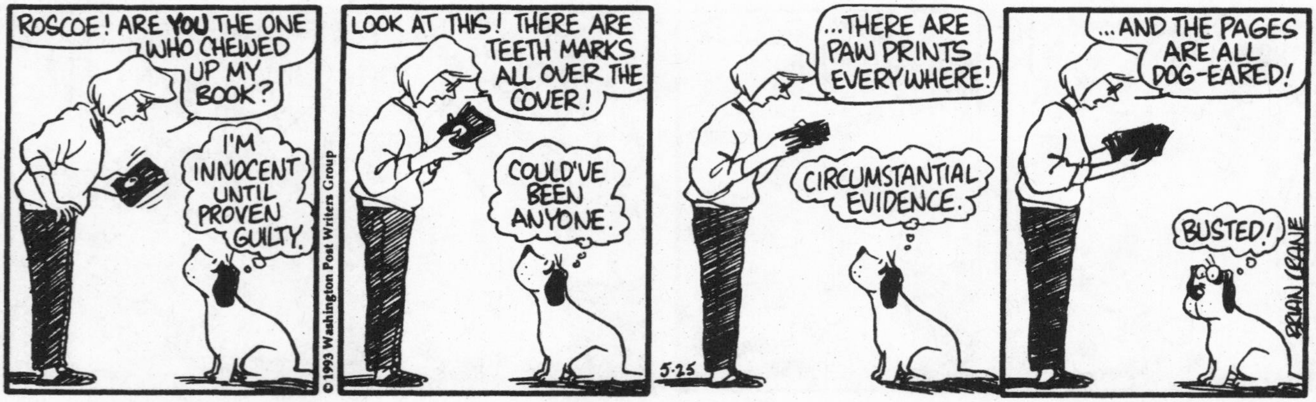
ROSCOE! ARE YOU THE ONE WHO CHEWED UP MY BOOK?
I'M INNOCENT UNTIL PROVEN GUILTY.
LOOK AT THIS! THERE ARE TEETH MARKS ALL OVER THE COVER!
COULD'VE BEEN ANYONE.
...THERE ARE PAW PRINTS EVERYWHERE!
CIRCUMSTANTIAL EVIDENCE.
...AND THE PAGES ARE ALL DOG-EARED!
BUSTED!
© 1993 Washington Post Writers Group
5·25
BRIAN CRANE

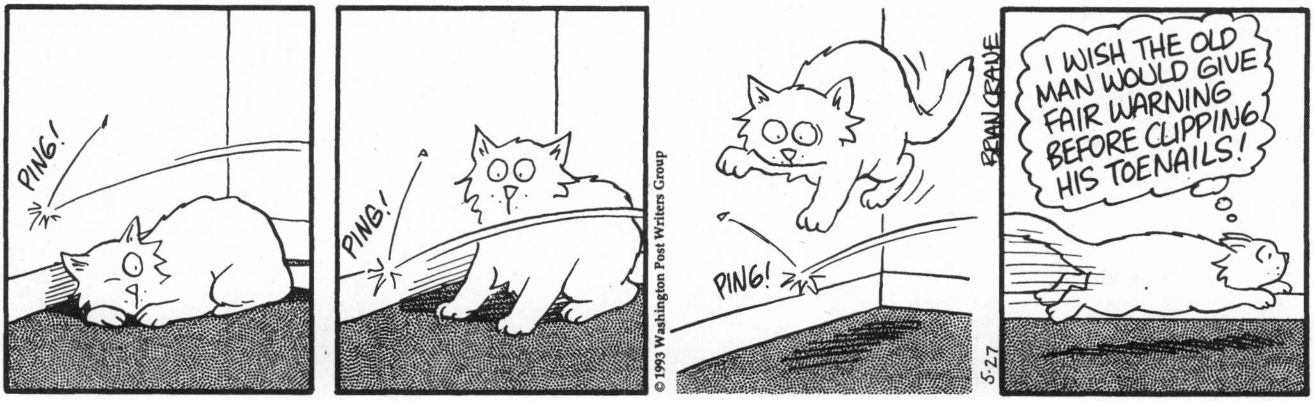
PING!
PING!
PING!
BRIAN CRANE
5-27
I WISH THE OLD MAN WOULD GIVE FAIR WARNING BEFORE CLIPPING HIS TOENAILS!
© 1993 Washington Post Writers Group

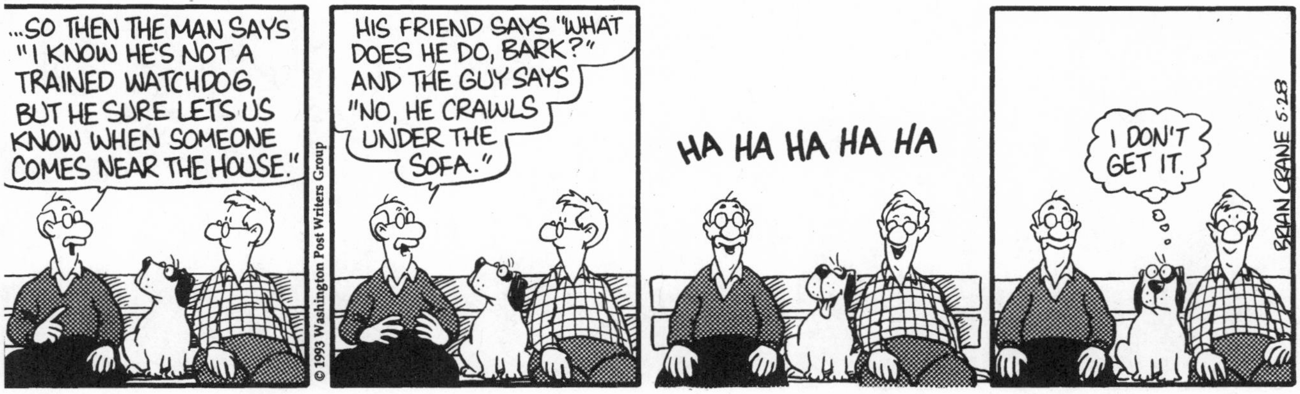
...SO THEN THE MAN SAYS "I KNOW HE'S NOT A TRAINED WATCHDOG, BUT HE SURE LETS US KNOW WHEN SOMEONE COMES NEAR THE HOUSE."
HIS FRIEND SAYS "WHAT DOES HE DO, BARK?" AND THE GUY SAYS "NO, HE CRAWLS UNDER THE SOFA."
HA HA HA HA HA
I DON'T GET IT.
BRIAN CRANE 5-28
© 1993 Washington Post Writers Group

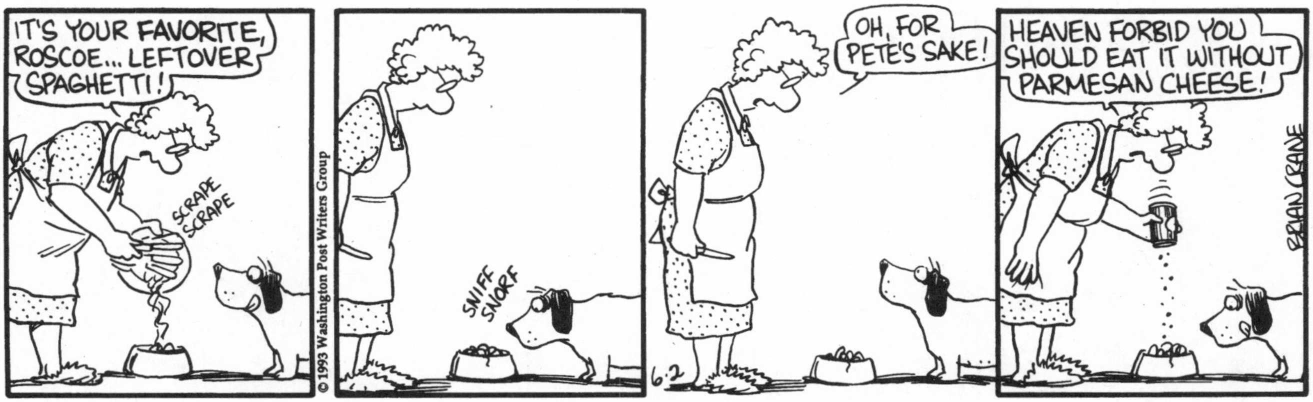
IT'S YOUR FAVORITE, ROSCOE... LEFTOVER SPAGHETTI!
SCRAPE SCRAPE
SNIFF SNORF
6-2
OH, FOR PETE'S SAKE!
HEAVEN FORBID YOU SHOULD EAT IT WITHOUT PARMESAN CHEESE!
BRIAN CRANE
© 1993 Washington Post Writers Group

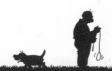

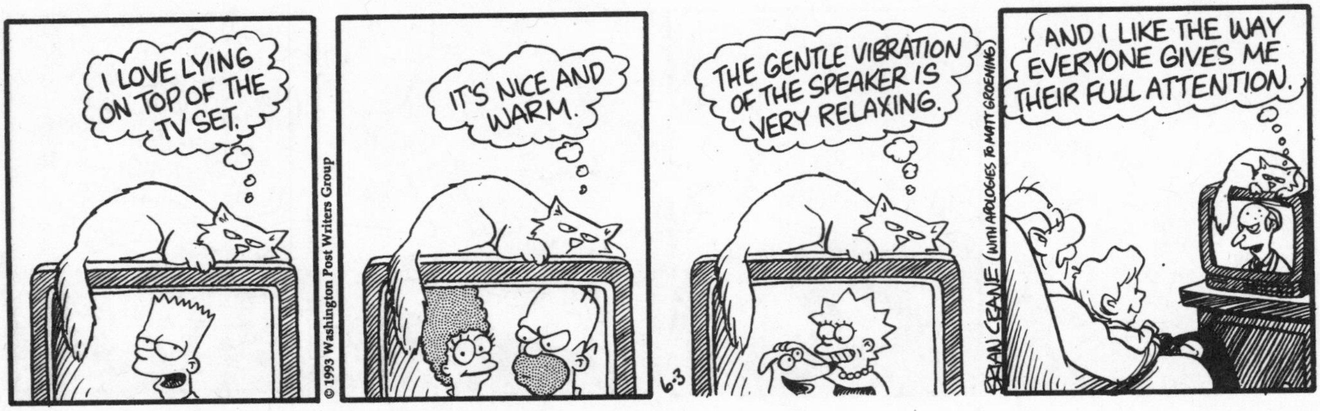
I LOVE LYING ON TOP OF THE TV SET.
© 1993 Washington Post Writers Group
IT'S NICE AND WARM.
THE GENTLE VIBRATION OF THE SPEAKER IS VERY RELAXING.
6·3
BRIAN CRANE (WITH APOLOGIES TO MATT GROENING)
AND I LIKE THE WAY EVERYONE GIVES ME THEIR FULL ATTENTION.

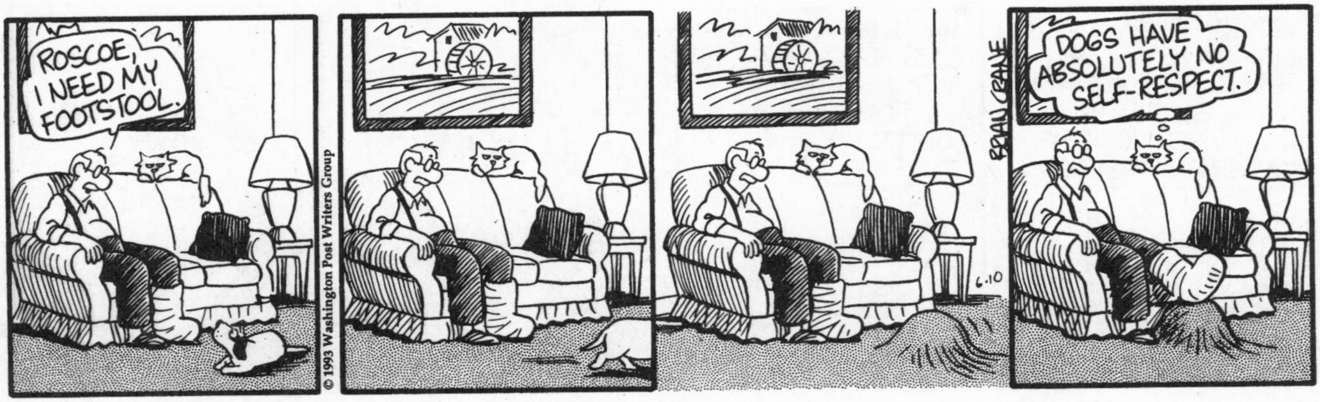
ROSCOE, I NEED MY FOOTSTOOL.
© 1993 Washington Post Writers Group
6·10
BRIAN CRANE
DOGS HAVE ABSOLUTELY NO SELF-RESPECT.

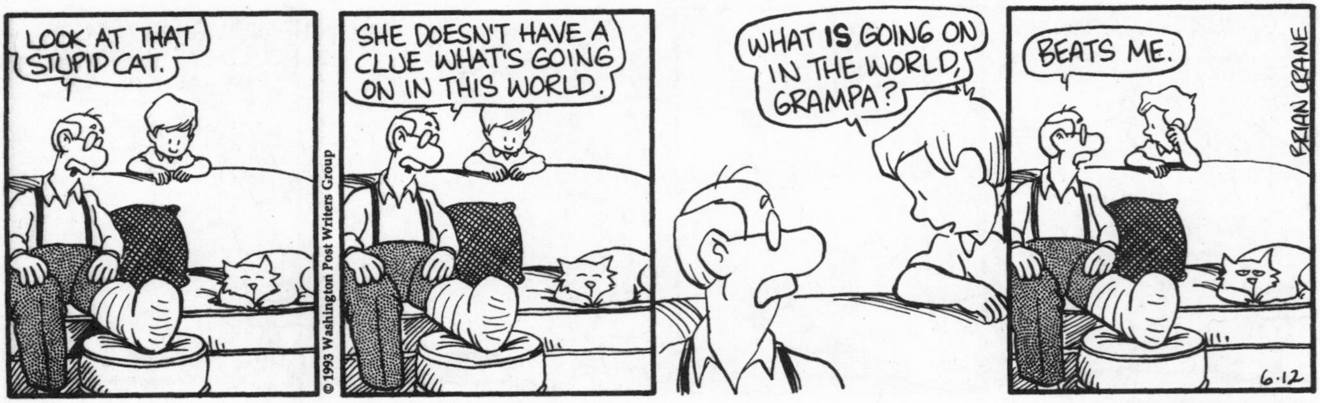
LOOK AT THAT STUPID CAT.
© 1993 Washington Post Writers Group
SHE DOESN'T HAVE A CLUE WHAT'S GOING ON IN THIS WORLD.
WHAT **IS** GOING ON IN THE WORLD, GRAMPA?
BEATS ME.
BRIAN CRANE
6·12

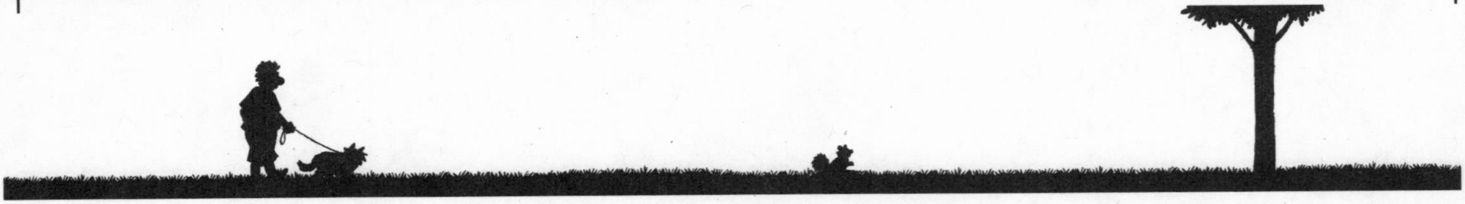

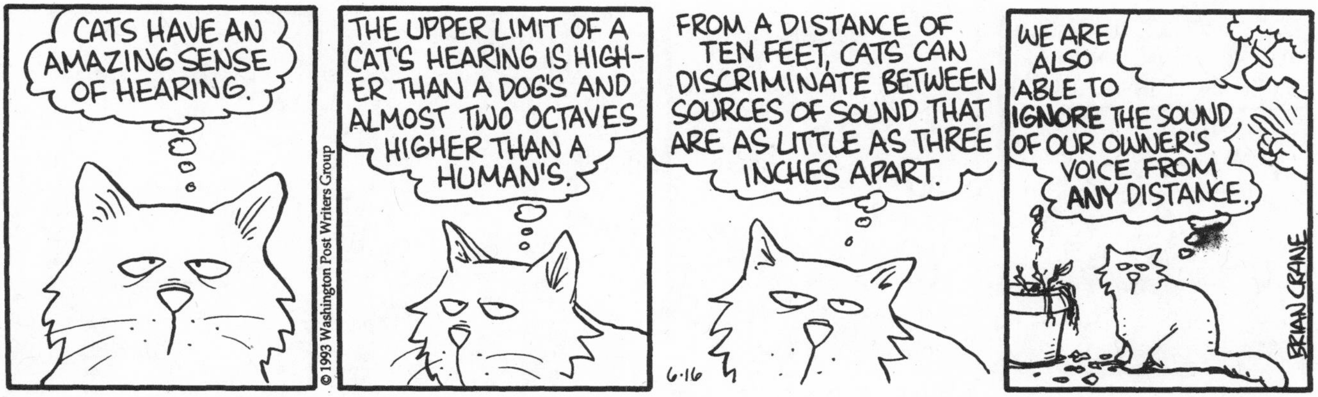
CATS HAVE AN AMAZING SENSE OF HEARING.
THE UPPER LIMIT OF A CAT'S HEARING IS HIGHER THAN A DOG'S AND ALMOST TWO OCTAVES HIGHER THAN A HUMAN'S.
© 1993 Washington Post Writers Group
FROM A DISTANCE OF TEN FEET, CATS CAN DISCRIMINATE BETWEEN SOURCES OF SOUND THAT ARE AS LITTLE AS THREE INCHES APART.
6·16
WE ARE ALSO ABLE TO **IGNORE** THE SOUND OF OUR OWNER'S VOICE FROM **ANY** DISTANCE.
BRIAN CRANE

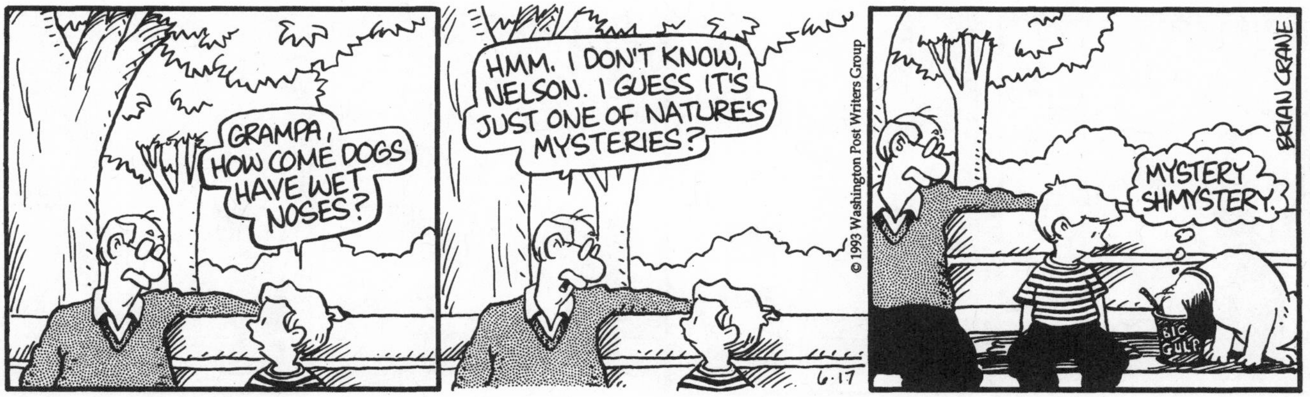
GRAMPA, HOW COME DOGS HAVE WET NOSES?
HMM. I DON'T KNOW, NELSON. I GUESS IT'S JUST ONE OF NATURE'S MYSTERIES?
6·17
© 1993 Washington Post Writers Group
MYSTERY SHMYSTERY.
BIG GULP
BRIAN CRANE

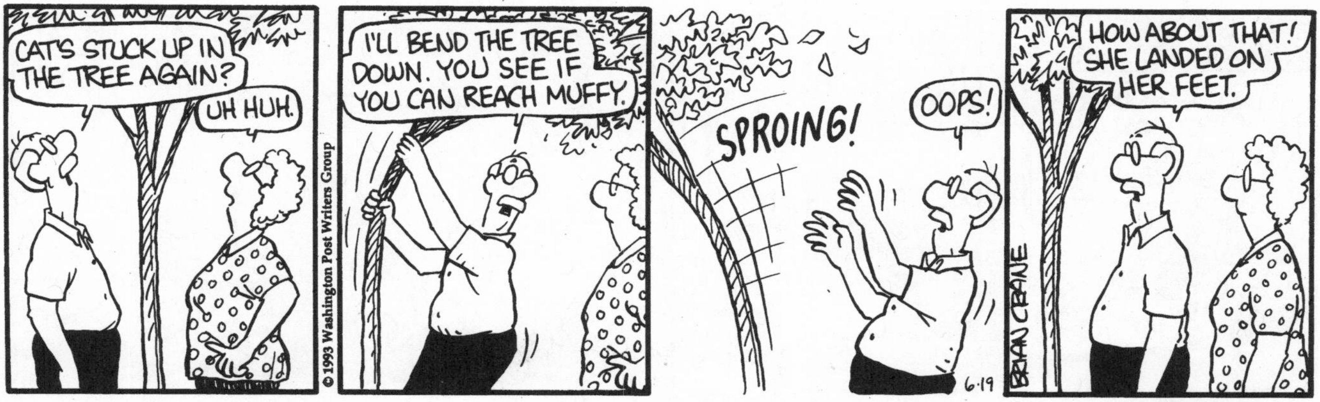
CAT'S STUCK UP IN THE TREE AGAIN?
UH HUH.
© 1993 Washington Post Writers Group
I'LL BEND THE TREE DOWN. YOU SEE IF YOU CAN REACH MUFFY.
SPROING!
OOPS!
BRIAN CRANE
6·19
HOW ABOUT THAT! SHE LANDED ON HER FEET.

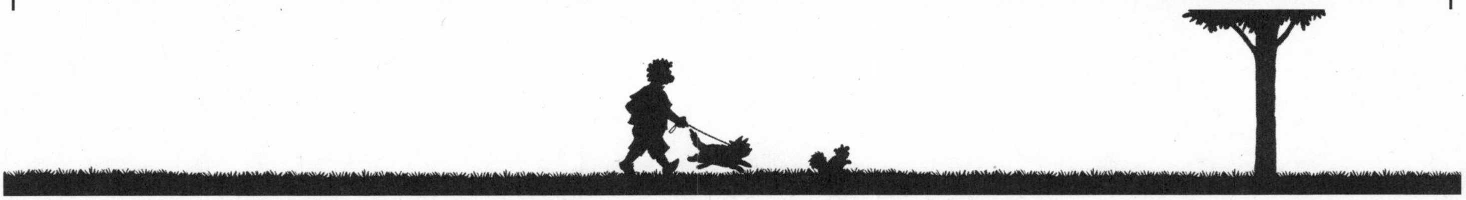

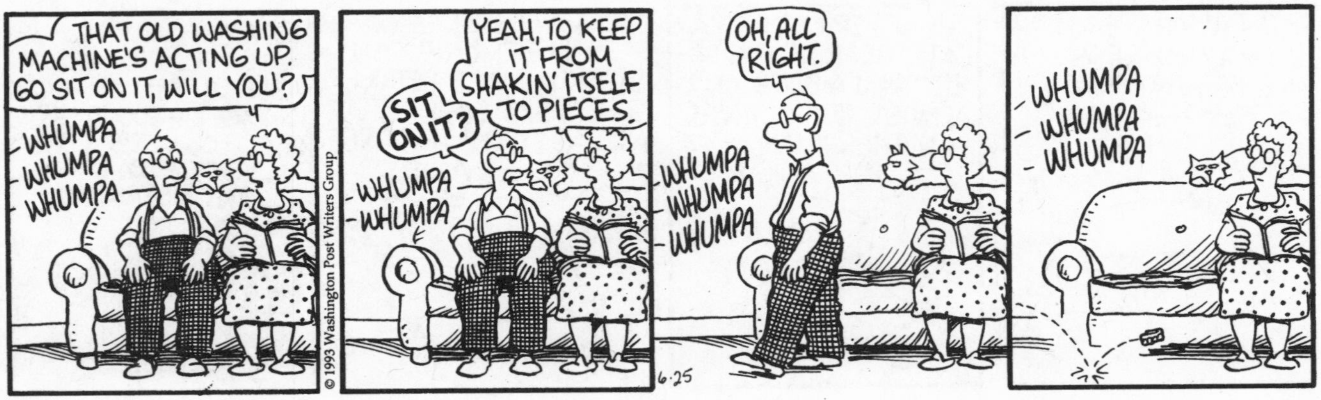
THAT OLD WASHING MACHINE'S ACTING UP. GO SIT ON IT, WILL YOU?
WHUMPA WHUMPA WHUMPA
© 1993 Washington Post Writers Group
SIT ON IT?
YEAH, TO KEEP IT FROM SHAKIN' ITSELF TO PIECES.
WHUMPA WHUMPA
OH, ALL RIGHT.
WHUMPA WHUMPA WHUMPA
6·25
WHUMPA WHUMPA WHUMPA

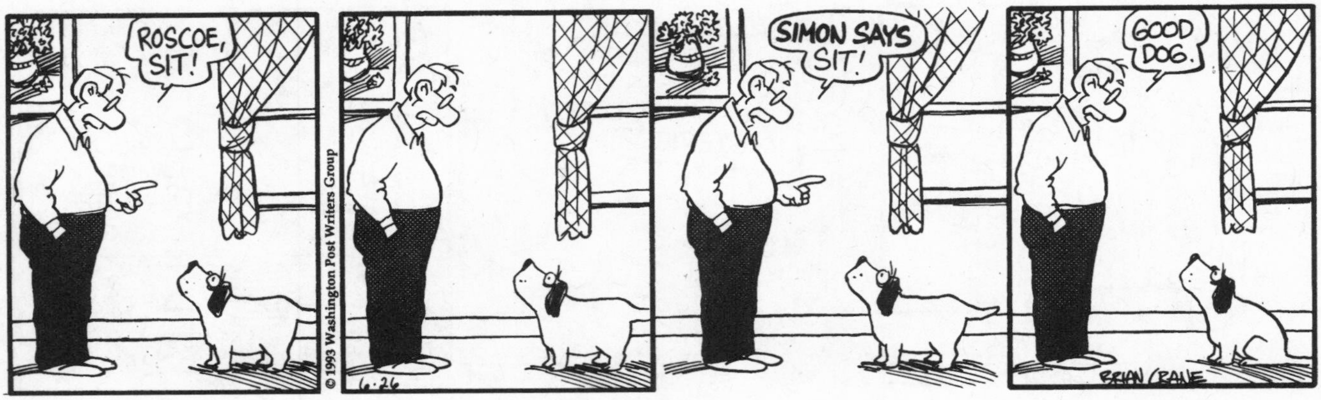
ROSCOE, SIT!
© 1993 Washington Post Writers Group
6·26
SIMON SAYS SIT!
GOOD DOG.
BRIAN CRANE

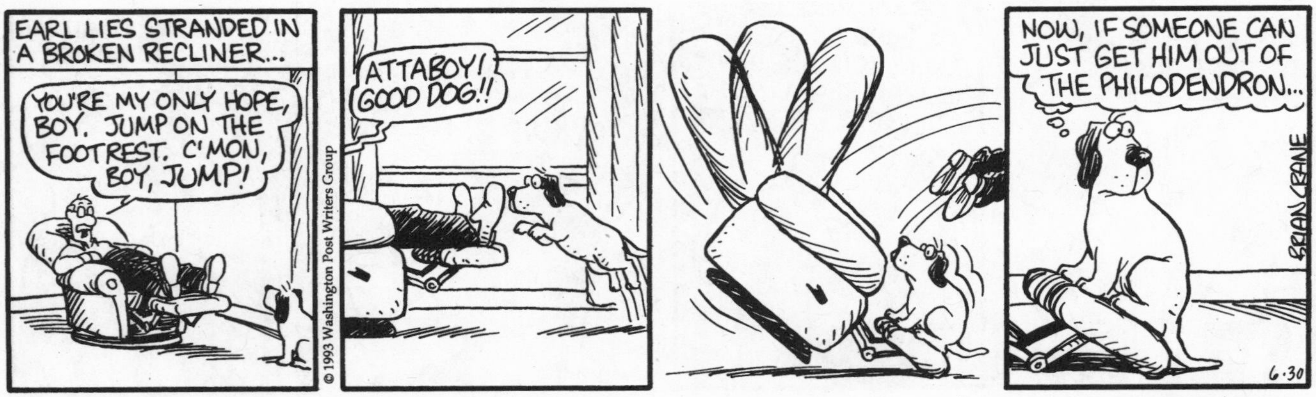
EARL LIES STRANDED IN A BROKEN RECLINER...
YOU'RE MY ONLY HOPE, BOY. JUMP ON THE FOOTREST. C'MON, BOY, JUMP!
© 1993 Washington Post Writers Group
ATTABOY! GOOD DOG!!
NOW, IF SOMEONE CAN JUST GET HIM OUT OF THE PHILODENDRON...
BRIAN CRANE
6·30

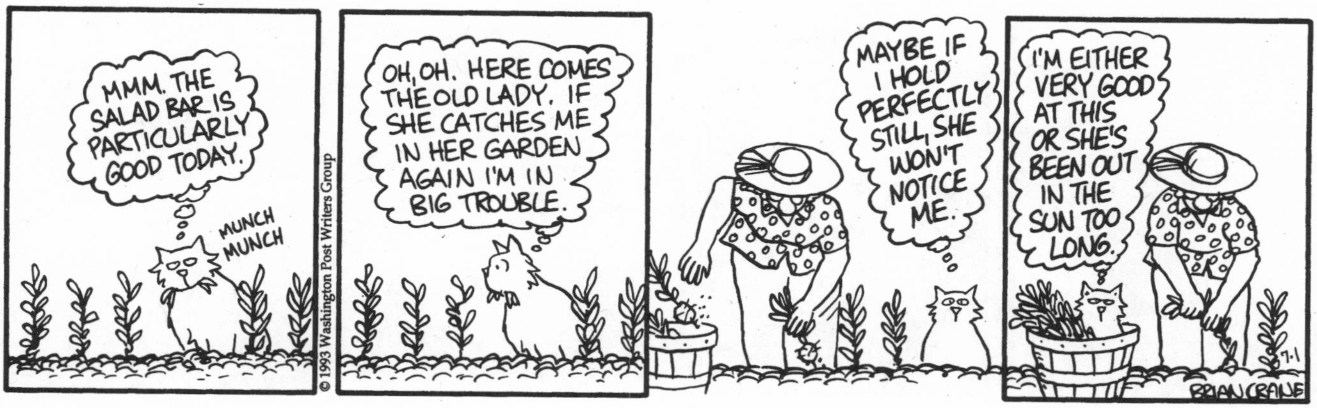
MMM. THE SALAD BAR IS PARTICULARLY GOOD TODAY.
MUNCH MUNCH
© 1993 Washington Post Writers Group
OH, OH. HERE COMES THE OLD LADY. IF SHE CATCHES ME IN HER GARDEN AGAIN I'M IN BIG TROUBLE.
MAYBE IF I HOLD PERFECTLY STILL, SHE WON'T NOTICE ME.
I'M EITHER VERY GOOD AT THIS OR SHE'S BEEN OUT IN THE SUN TOO LONG.
7-1
BRIAN CRANE

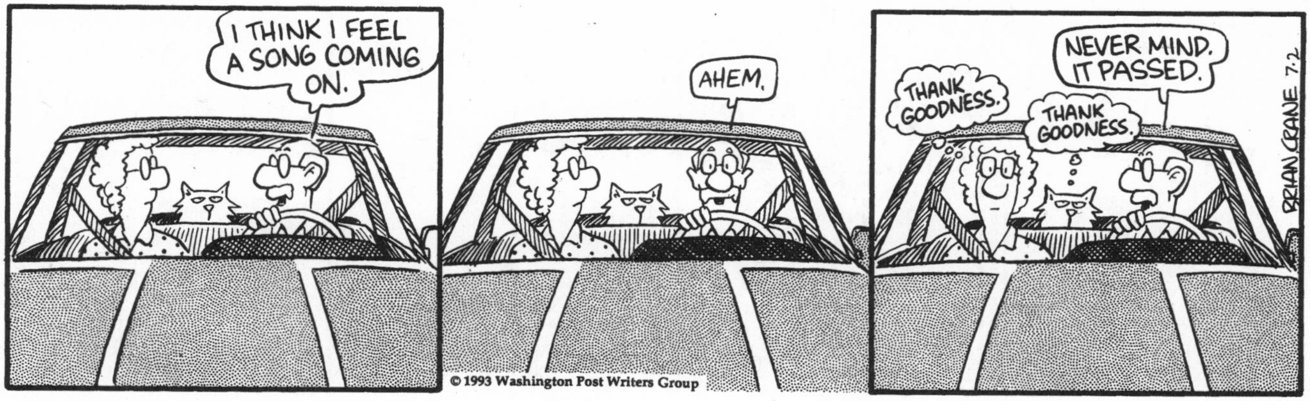
I THINK I FEEL A SONG COMING ON.
AHEM.
© 1993 Washington Post Writers Group
NEVER MIND. IT PASSED.
THANK GOODNESS.
THANK GOODNESS.
BRIAN CRANE 7-2

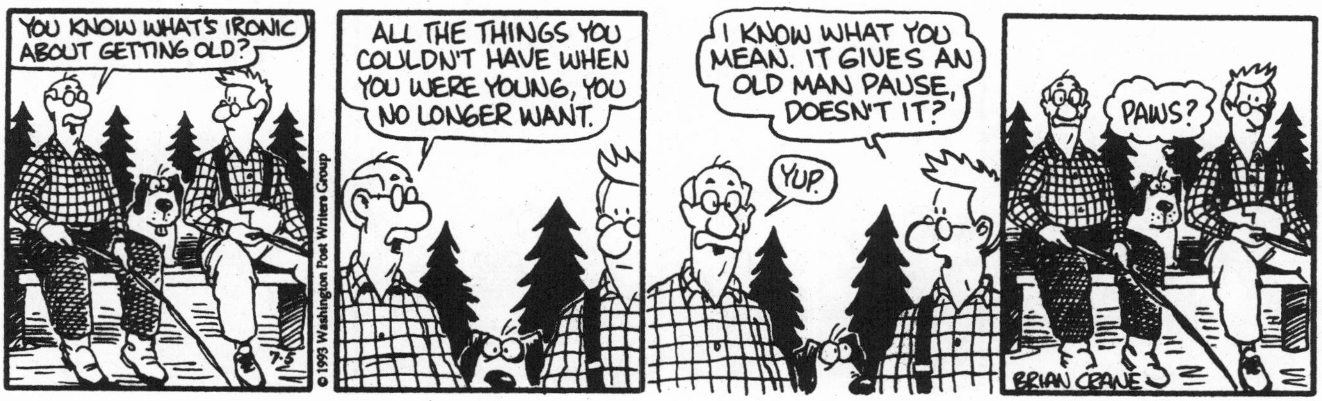
YOU KNOW WHAT'S IRONIC ABOUT GETTING OLD?
7-5
© 1993 Washington Post Writers Group
ALL THE THINGS YOU COULDN'T HAVE WHEN YOU WERE YOUNG, YOU NO LONGER WANT.
I KNOW WHAT YOU MEAN. IT GIVES AN OLD MAN PAUSE, DOESN'T IT?
YUP.
PAWS?
BRIAN CRANE

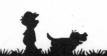

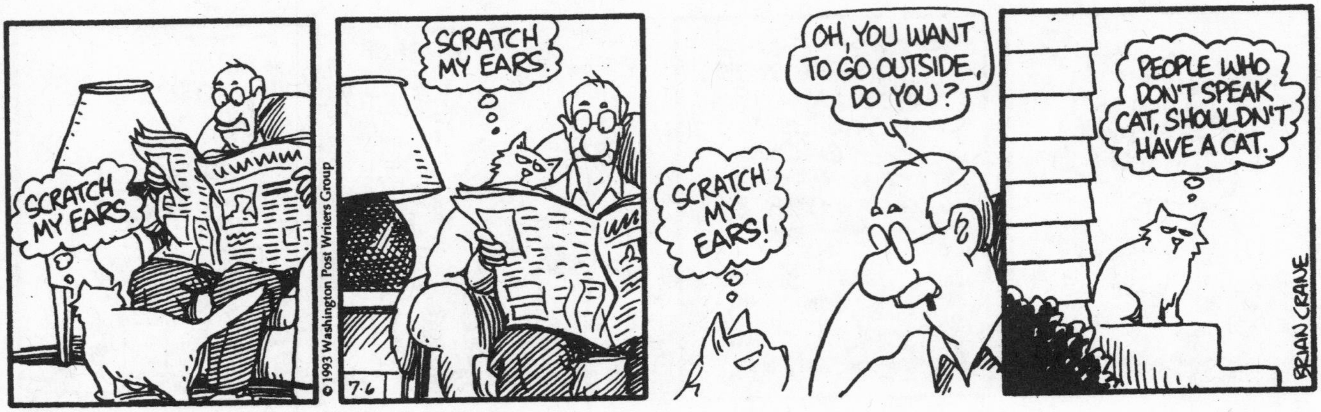
SCRATCH MY EARS.
© 1993 Washington Post Writers Group
SCRATCH MY EARS.
7·6
SCRATCH MY EARS!
OH, YOU WANT TO GO OUTSIDE, DO YOU?
PEOPLE WHO DON'T SPEAK CAT, SHOULDN'T HAVE A CAT.
BRIAN CRANE

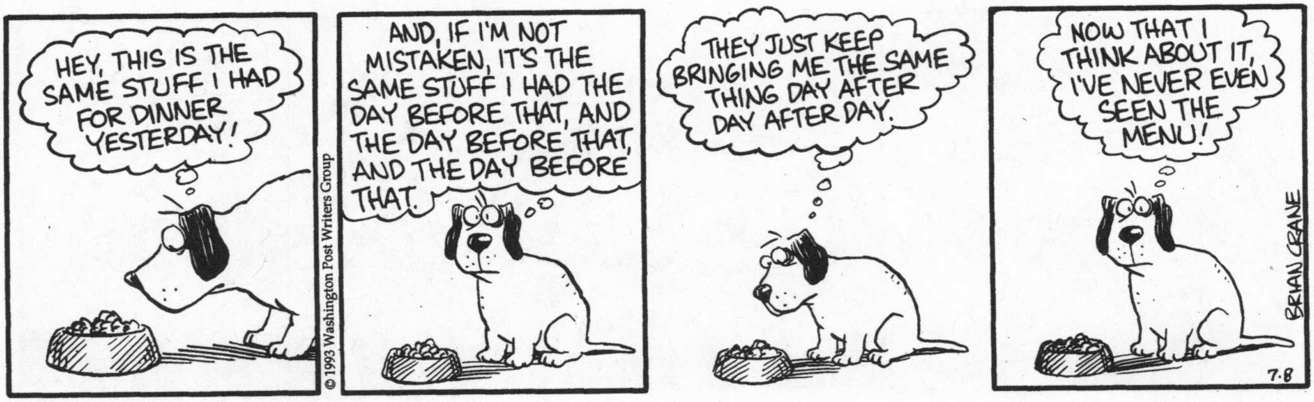
HEY, THIS IS THE SAME STUFF I HAD FOR DINNER YESTERDAY!
© 1993 Washington Post Writers Group
AND, IF I'M NOT MISTAKEN, IT'S THE SAME STUFF I HAD THE DAY BEFORE THAT, AND THE DAY BEFORE THAT, AND THE DAY BEFORE THAT.
THEY JUST KEEP BRINGING ME THE SAME THING DAY AFTER DAY AFTER DAY.
NOW THAT I THINK ABOUT IT, I'VE NEVER EVEN SEEN THE MENU!
BRIAN CRANE
7·8

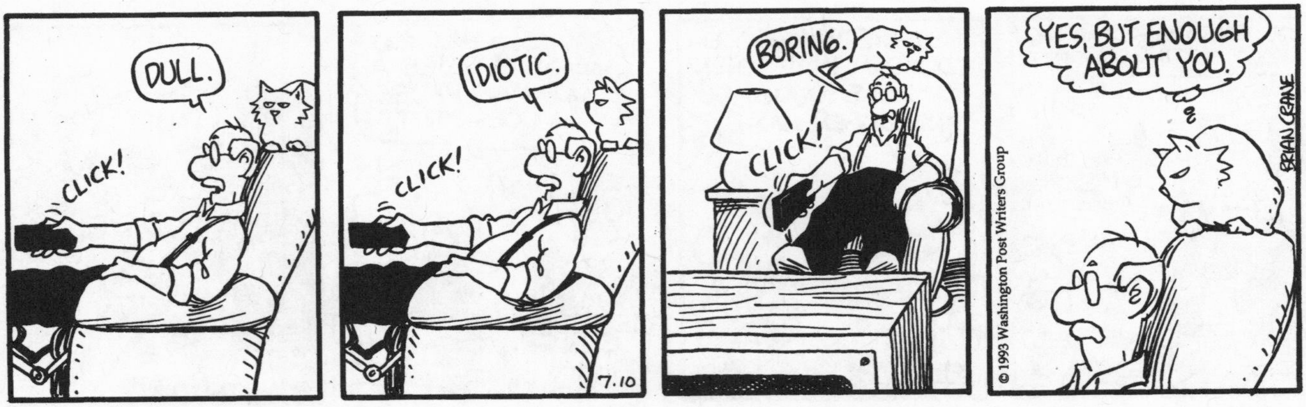
DULL.
CLICK!
IDIOTIC.
CLICK!
7.10
BORING.
CLICK!
© 1993 Washington Post Writers Group
YES, BUT ENOUGH ABOUT YOU.
BRIAN CRANE

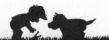

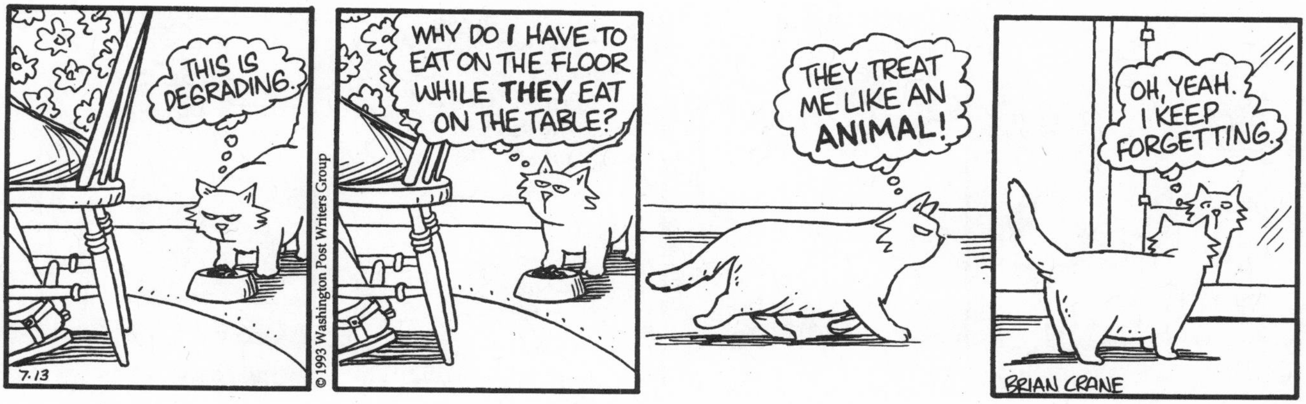
7·13
THIS IS DEGRADING.
© 1993 Washington Post Writers Group
WHY DO I HAVE TO EAT ON THE FLOOR WHILE THEY EAT ON THE TABLE?
THEY TREAT ME LIKE AN ANIMAL!
OH, YEAH. I KEEP FORGETTING.
BRIAN CRANE

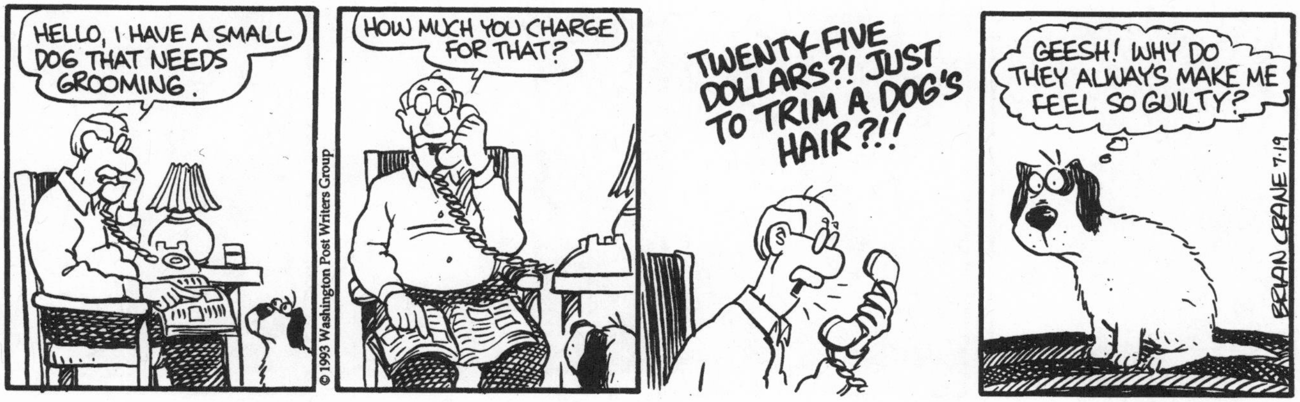
HELLO, I HAVE A SMALL DOG THAT NEEDS GROOMING.
© 1993 Washington Post Writers Group
HOW MUCH YOU CHARGE FOR THAT?
TWENTY-FIVE DOLLARS?! JUST TO TRIM A DOG'S HAIR?!!
GEESH! WHY DO THEY ALWAYS MAKE ME FEEL SO GUILTY?
BRIAN CRANE 7·19

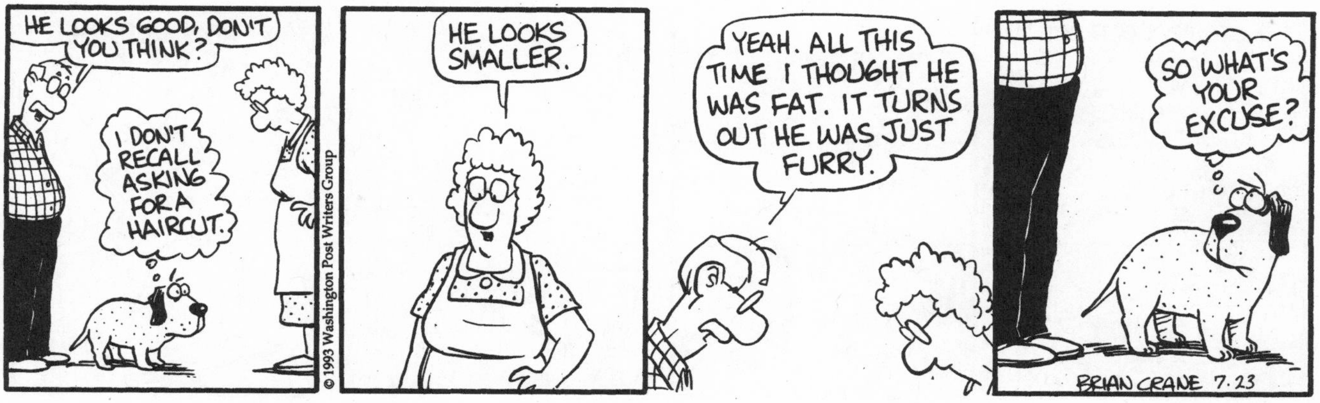
HE LOOKS GOOD, DON'T YOU THINK?
I DON'T RECALL ASKING FOR A HAIRCUT.
© 1993 Washington Post Writers Group
HE LOOKS SMALLER.
YEAH. ALL THIS TIME I THOUGHT HE WAS FAT. IT TURNS OUT HE WAS JUST FURRY.
SO WHAT'S YOUR EXCUSE?
BRIAN CRANE 7·23

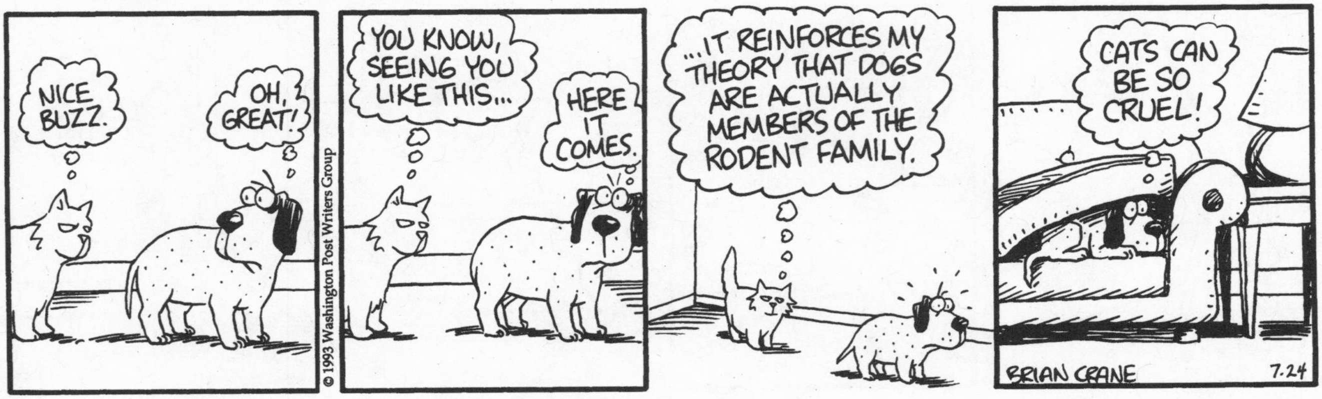
NICE BUZZ.
OH, GREAT!
YOU KNOW, SEEING YOU LIKE THIS...
HERE IT COMES.
...IT REINFORCES MY THEORY THAT DOGS ARE ACTUALLY MEMBERS OF THE RODENT FAMILY.
CATS CAN BE SO CRUEL!
BRIAN CRANE
7.24
© 1993 Washington Post Writers Group

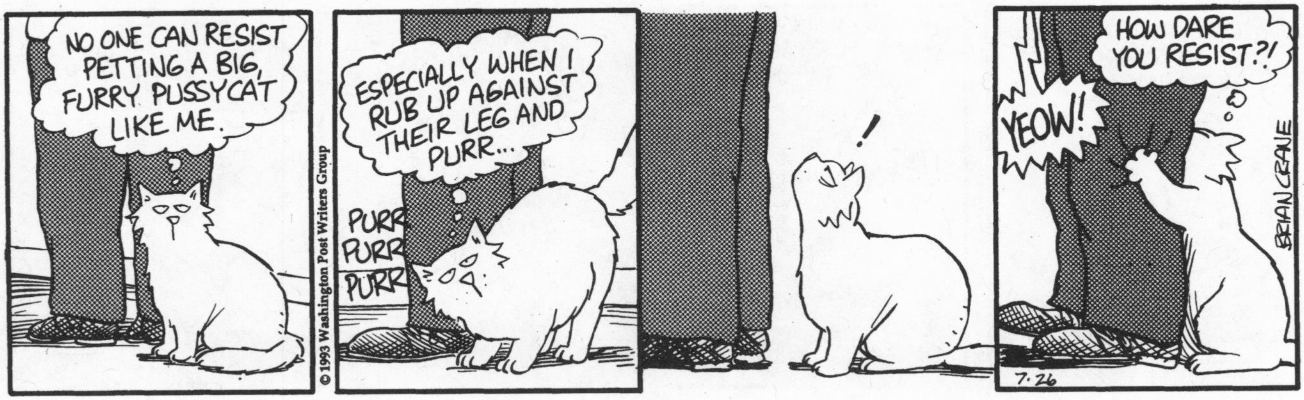
NO ONE CAN RESIST PETTING A BIG, FURRY PUSSYCAT LIKE ME.
ESPECIALLY WHEN I RUB UP AGAINST THEIR LEG AND PURR...
PURR
PURR
PURR
!
HOW DARE YOU RESIST?!
YEOW!
BRIAN CRANE
7.26
© 1993 Washington Post Writers Group

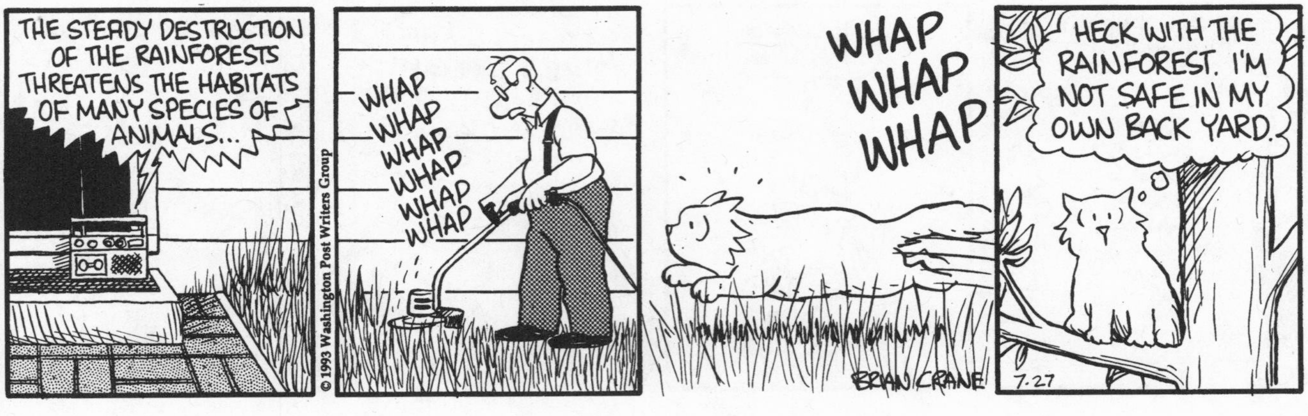
THE STEADY DESTRUCTION OF THE RAINFORESTS THREATENS THE HABITATS OF MANY SPECIES OF ANIMALS...
WHAP
WHAP
WHAP
WHAP
WHAP
WHAP
WHAP
WHAP
WHAP
HECK WITH THE RAINFOREST. I'M NOT SAFE IN MY OWN BACK YARD.
BRIAN CRANE
7.27
© 1993 Washington Post Writers Group

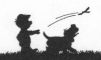

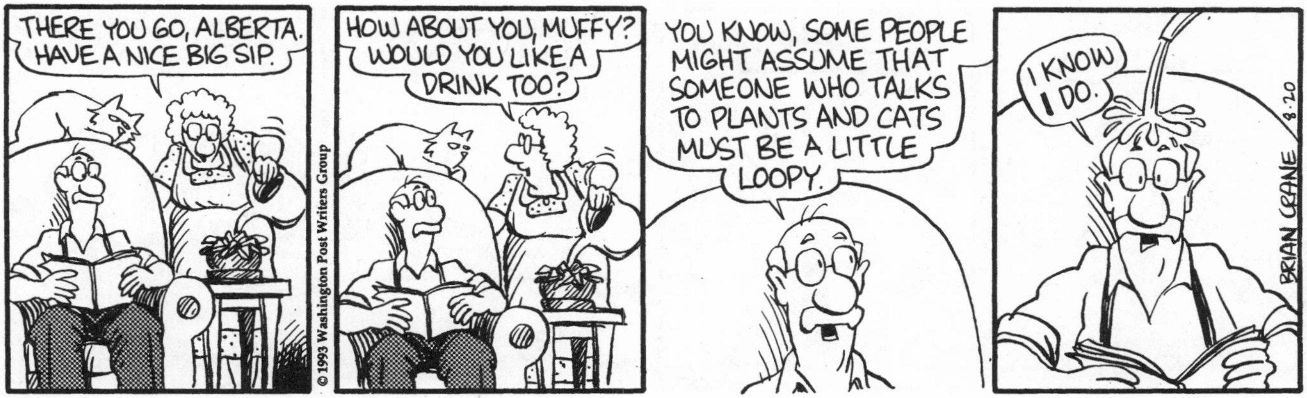
THERE YOU GO, ALBERTA. HAVE A NICE BIG SIP.
© 1993 Washington Post Writers Group
HOW ABOUT YOU, MUFFY? WOULD YOU LIKE A DRINK TOO?
YOU KNOW, SOME PEOPLE MIGHT ASSUME THAT SOMEONE WHO TALKS TO PLANTS AND CATS MUST BE A LITTLE LOOPY.
I KNOW I DO.
BRIAN CRANE 8·20

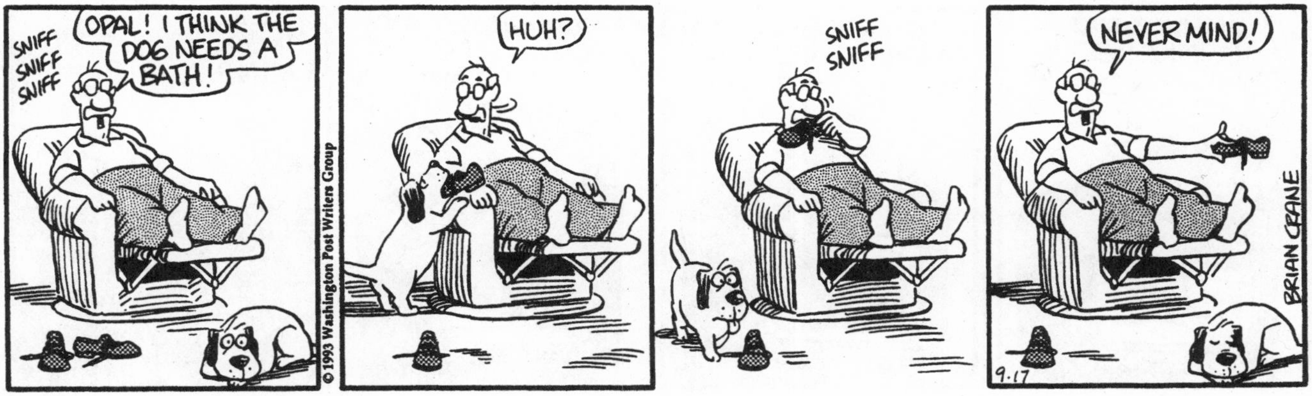
SNIFF SNIFF SNIFF
OPAL! I THINK THE DOG NEEDS A BATH!
© 1993 Washington Post Writers Group
HUH?
SNIFF SNIFF
NEVER MIND!
BRIAN CRANE 9·17

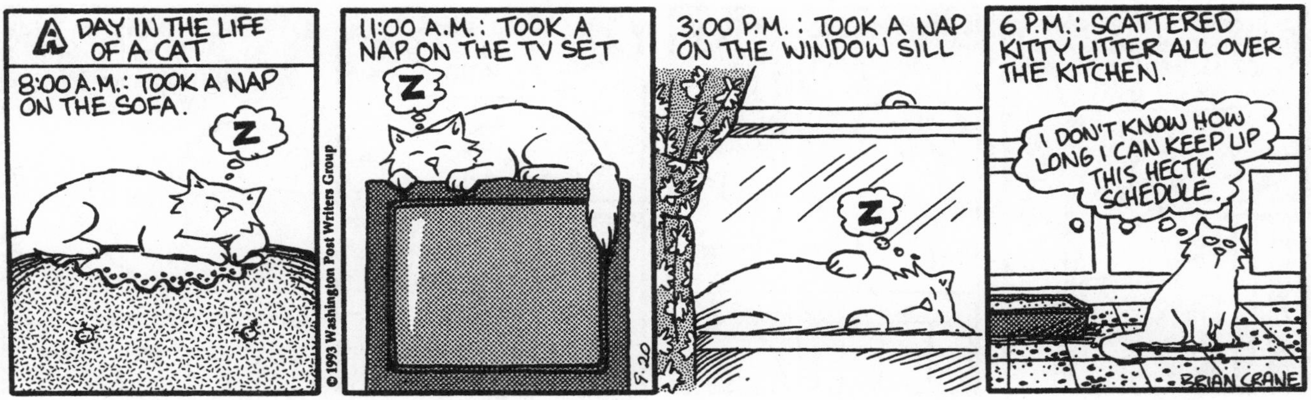
A DAY IN THE LIFE OF A CAT
8:00 A.M.: TOOK A NAP ON THE SOFA.
Z
© 1993 Washington Post Writers Group
11:00 A.M.: TOOK A NAP ON THE TV SET
Z
9·20
3:00 P.M.: TOOK A NAP ON THE WINDOW SILL
Z
6 P.M.: SCATTERED KITTY LITTER ALL OVER THE KITCHEN.
I DON'T KNOW HOW LONG I CAN KEEP UP THIS HECTIC SCHEDULE.
BRIAN CRANE

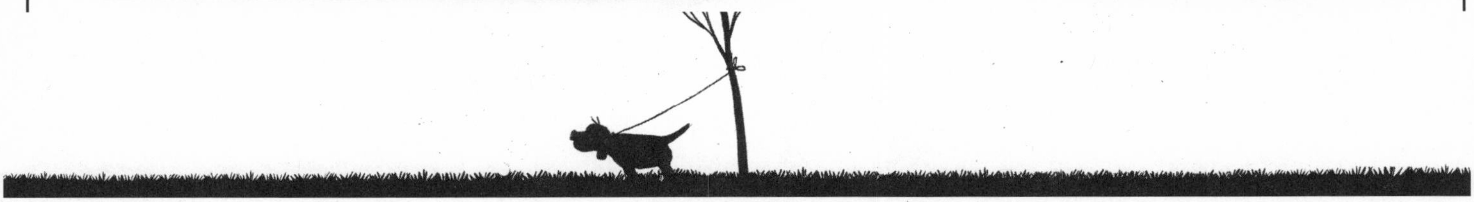

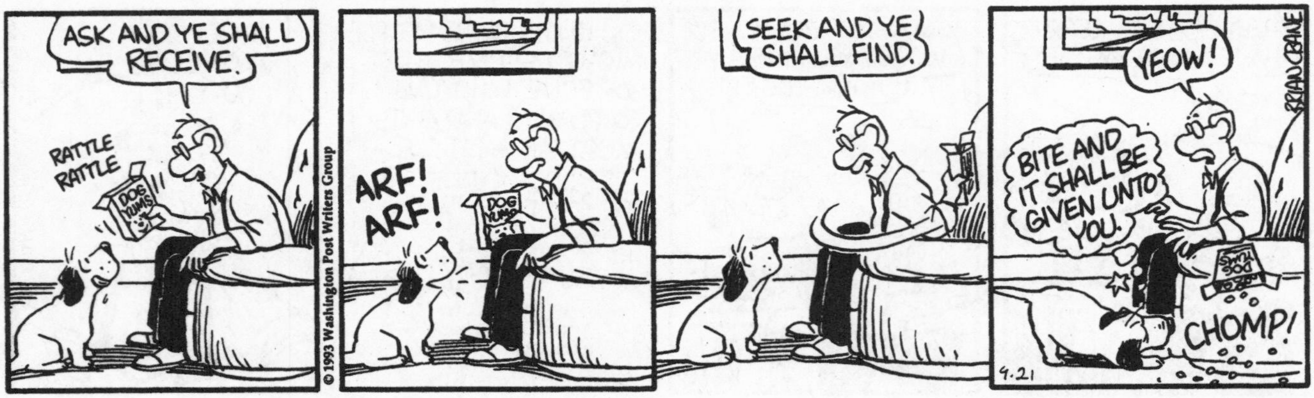
ASK AND YE SHALL RECEIVE.
RATTLE RATTLE
DOG YUMS
© 1993 Washington Post Writers Group
ARF! ARF!
SEEK AND YE SHALL FIND.
YEOW!
BITE AND IT SHALL BE GIVEN UNTO YOU.
CHOMP!
BRIAN CRANE
9.21

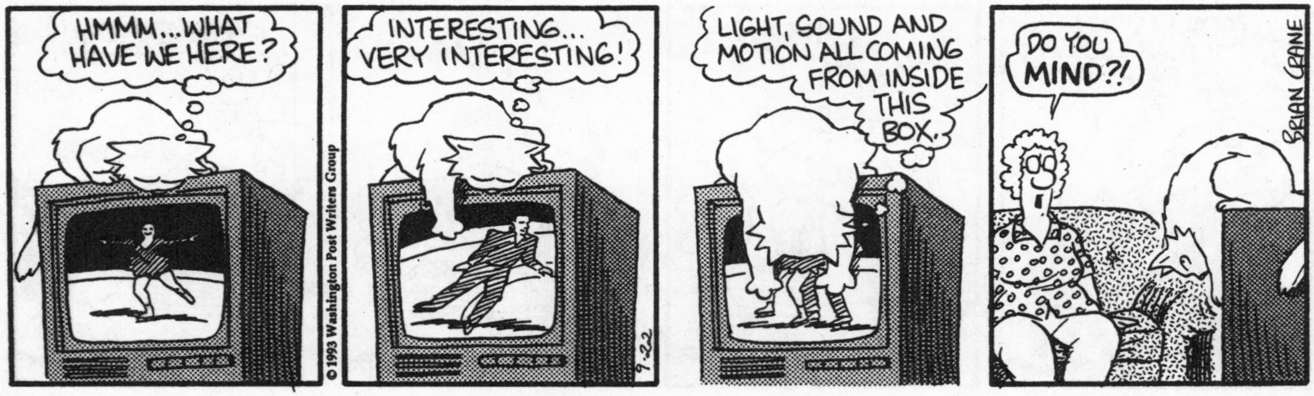
HMMM...WHAT HAVE WE HERE?
© 1993 Washington Post Writers Group
INTERESTING... VERY INTERESTING!
9.22
LIGHT, SOUND AND MOTION ALL COMING FROM INSIDE THIS BOX.
DO YOU MIND?!
BRIAN CRANE

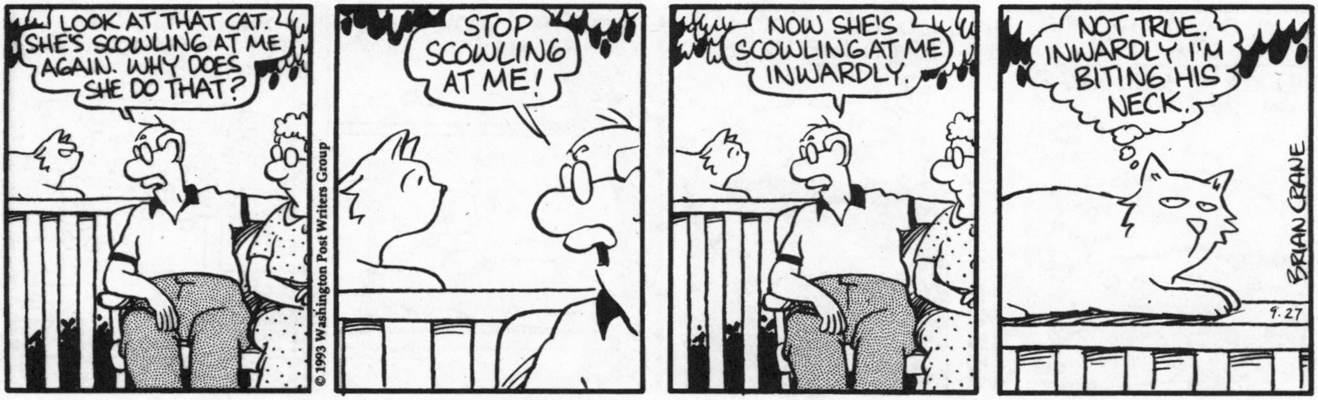
LOOK AT THAT CAT. SHE'S SCOWLING AT ME AGAIN. WHY DOES SHE DO THAT?
© 1993 Washington Post Writers Group
STOP SCOWLING AT ME!
NOW SHE'S SCOWLING AT ME INWARDLY.
NOT TRUE. INWARDLY I'M BITING HIS NECK.
BRIAN CRANE
9.27

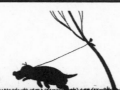

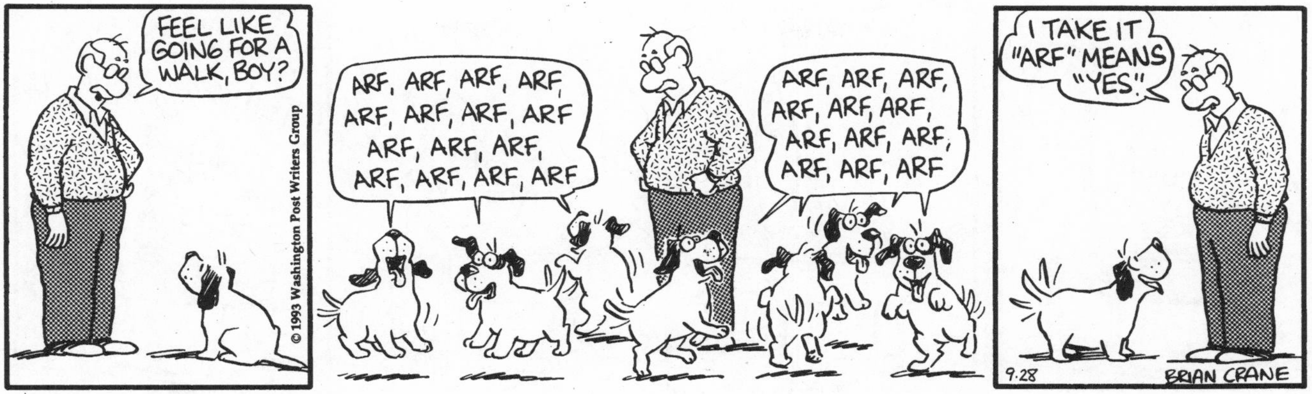
FEEL LIKE GOING FOR A WALK, BOY?
© 1993 Washington Post Writers Group
ARF, ARF, ARF, ARF, ARF, ARF, ARF, ARF ARF, ARF, ARF, ARF, ARF, ARF, ARF
ARF, ARF, ARF, ARF, ARF, ARF, ARF, ARF, ARF, ARF, ARF, ARF
I TAKE IT "ARF" MEANS "YES."
9.28
BRIAN CRANE

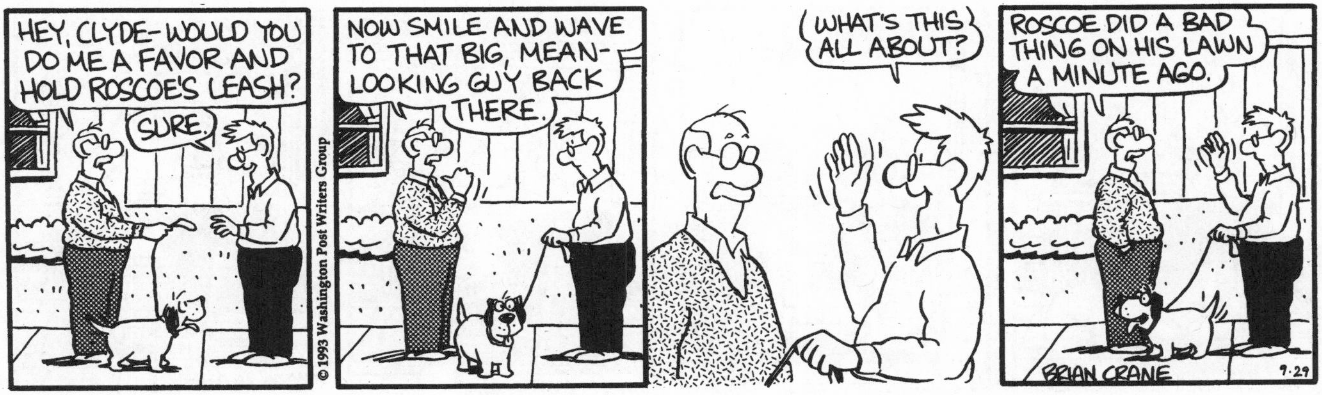
HEY, CLYDE- WOULD YOU DO ME A FAVOR AND HOLD ROSCOE'S LEASH?
SURE.
© 1993 Washington Post Writers Group
NOW SMILE AND WAVE TO THAT BIG, MEAN-LOOKING GUY BACK THERE.
WHAT'S THIS ALL ABOUT?
ROSCOE DID A BAD THING ON HIS LAWN A MINUTE AGO.
BRIAN CRANE
9.29

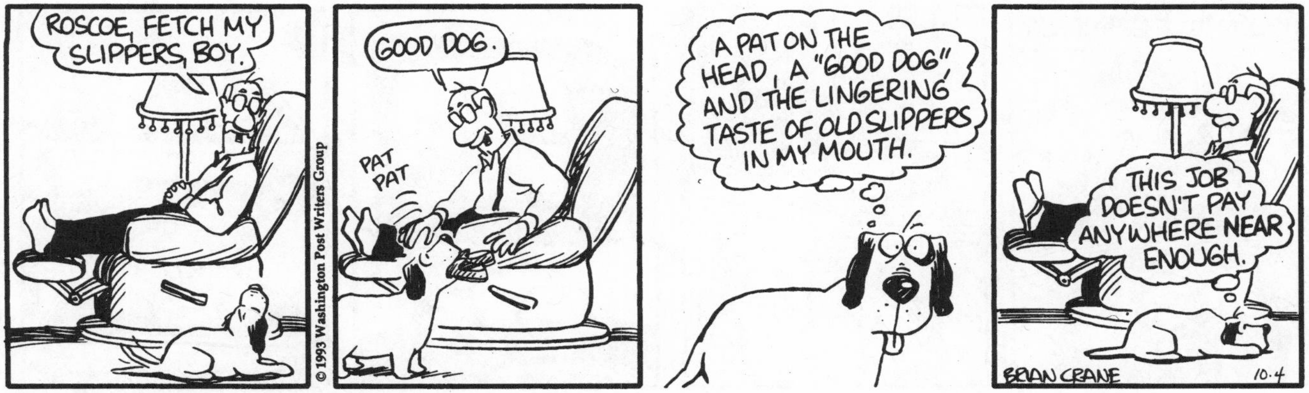
ROSCOE, FETCH MY SLIPPERS, BOY.
© 1993 Washington Post Writers Group
GOOD DOG.
PAT PAT
A PAT ON THE HEAD, A "GOOD DOG" AND THE LINGERING TASTE OF OLD SLIPPERS IN MY MOUTH.
THIS JOB DOESN'T PAY ANYWHERE NEAR ENOUGH.
BRIAN CRANE
10.4

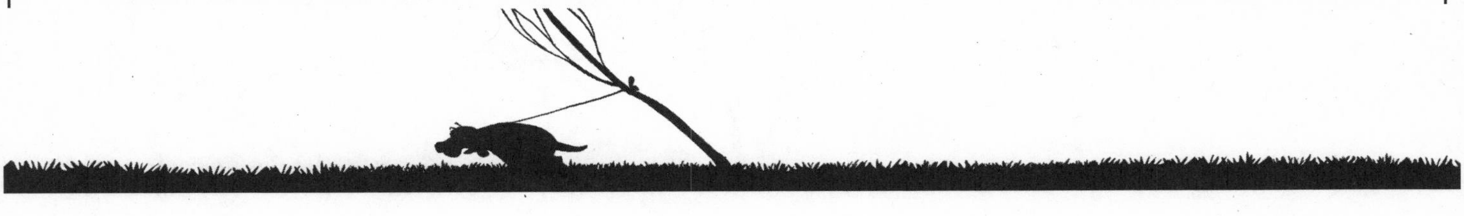

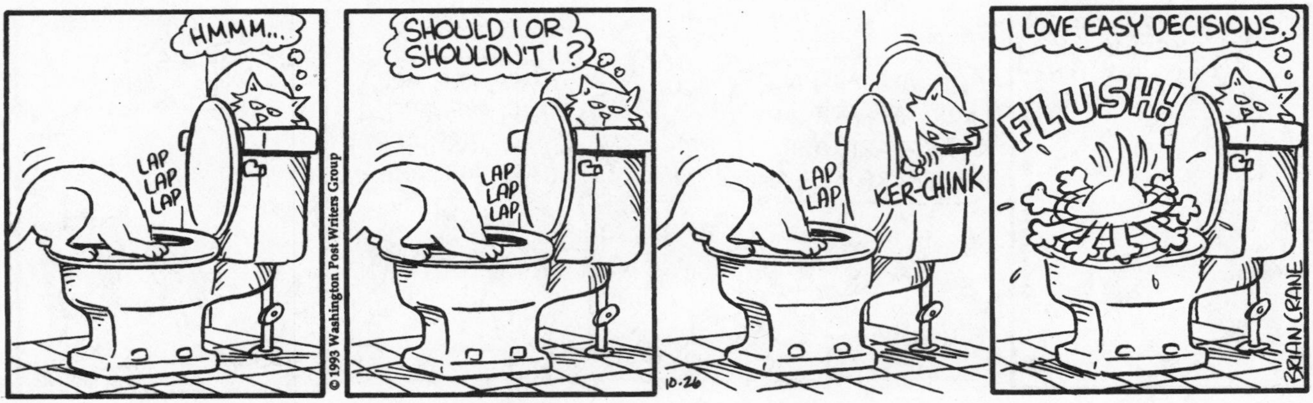
HMMM...
LAP LAP LAP
SHOULD I OR SHOULDN'T I?
LAP LAP LAP
LAP LAP
KER-CHINK
I LOVE EASY DECISIONS.
FLUSH!
© 1993 Washington Post Writers Group
10·26
BRIAN CRANE

94

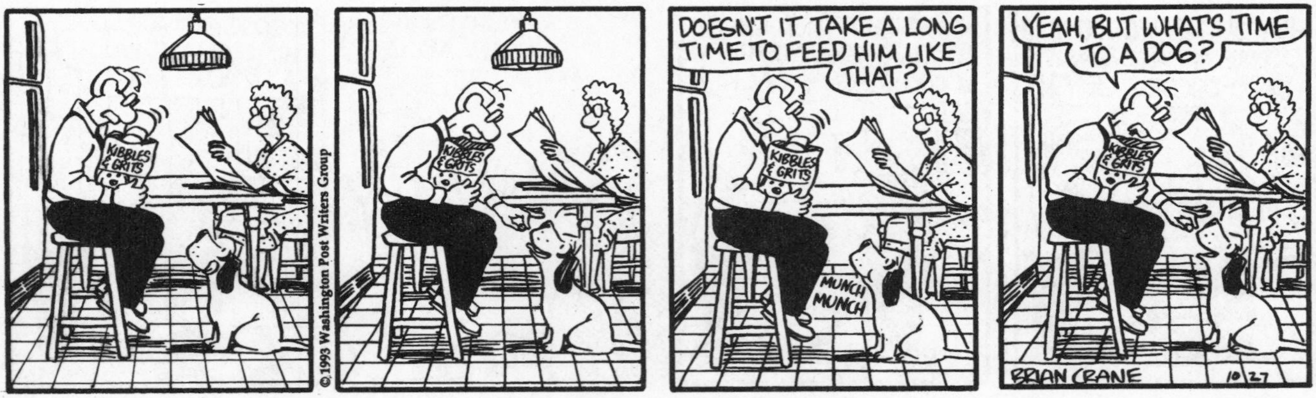
KIBBLES & GRITS
© 1993 Washington Post Writers Group
DOESN'T IT TAKE A LONG TIME TO FEED HIM LIKE THAT?
MUNCH MUNCH
YEAH, BUT WHAT'S TIME TO A DOG?
BRIAN CRANE
10/27

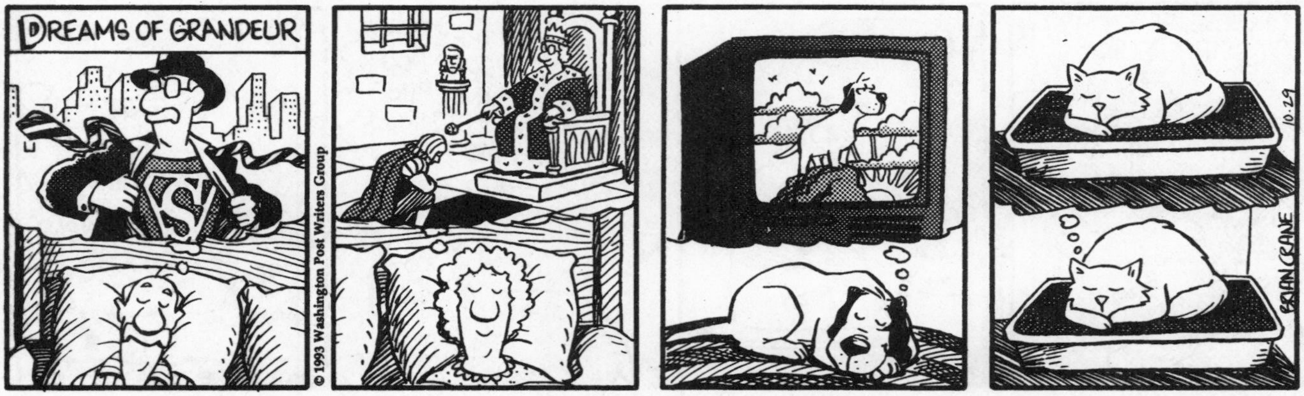
DREAMS OF GRANDEUR
© 1993 Washington Post Writers Group
© 1993 Washington Post Writers Group
10·29
BRIAN CRANE

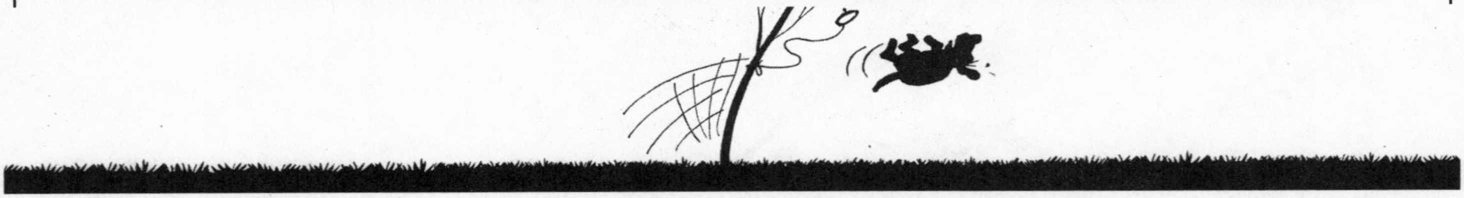

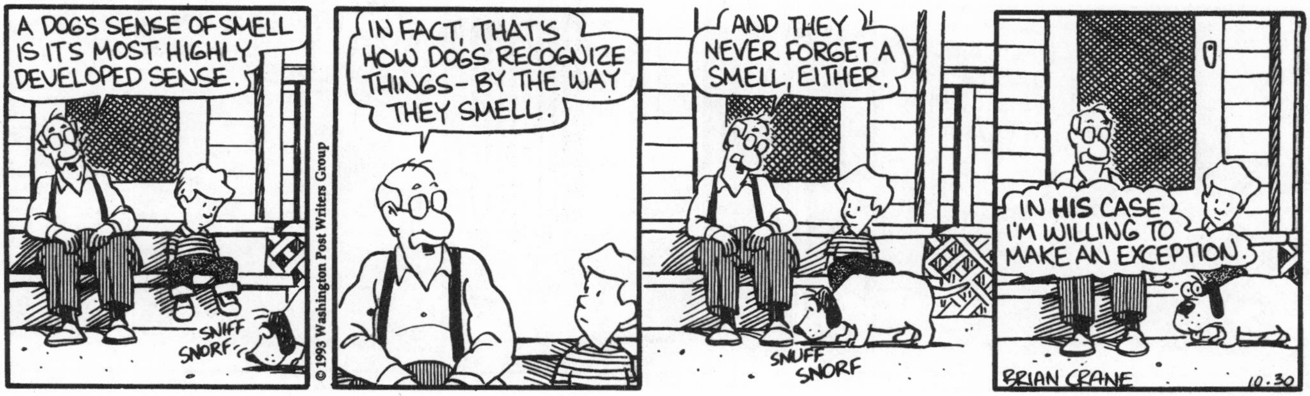
A DOG'S SENSE OF SMELL IS ITS MOST HIGHLY DEVELOPED SENSE.
SNIFF SNORF
© 1993 Washington Post Writers Group
IN FACT, THAT'S HOW DOGS RECOGNIZE THINGS - BY THE WAY THEY SMELL.
AND THEY NEVER FORGET A SMELL, EITHER.
SNUFF SNORF
IN **HIS** CASE I'M WILLING TO MAKE AN EXCEPTION.
BRIAN CRANE
10.30

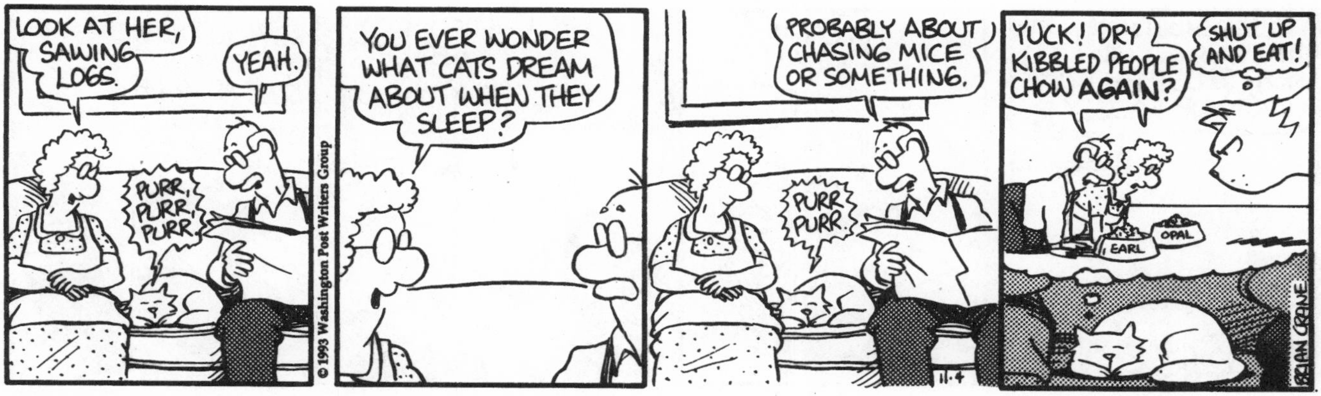
LOOK AT HER, SAWING LOGS.
YEAH.
PURR, PURR, PURR.
© 1993 Washington Post Writers Group
YOU EVER WONDER WHAT CATS DREAM ABOUT WHEN THEY SLEEP?
PROBABLY ABOUT CHASING MICE OR SOMETHING.
PURR PURR
11.4
YUCK! DRY KIBBLED PEOPLE CHOW **AGAIN**?
SHUT UP AND EAT!
EARL
OPAL
BRIAN CRANE

95

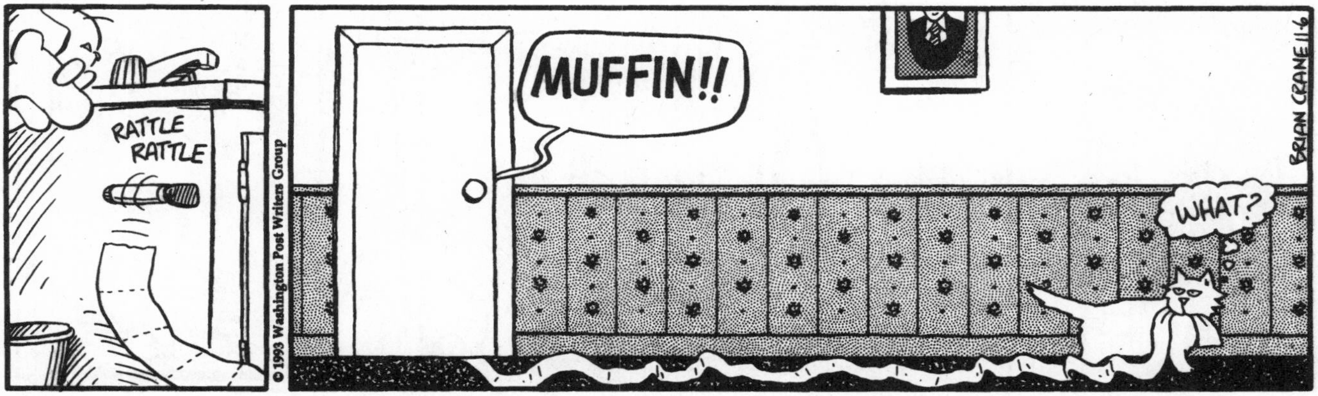
RATTLE RATTLE
© 1993 Washington Post Writers Group
MUFFIN!!
BRIAN CRANE 11.6
WHAT?

96

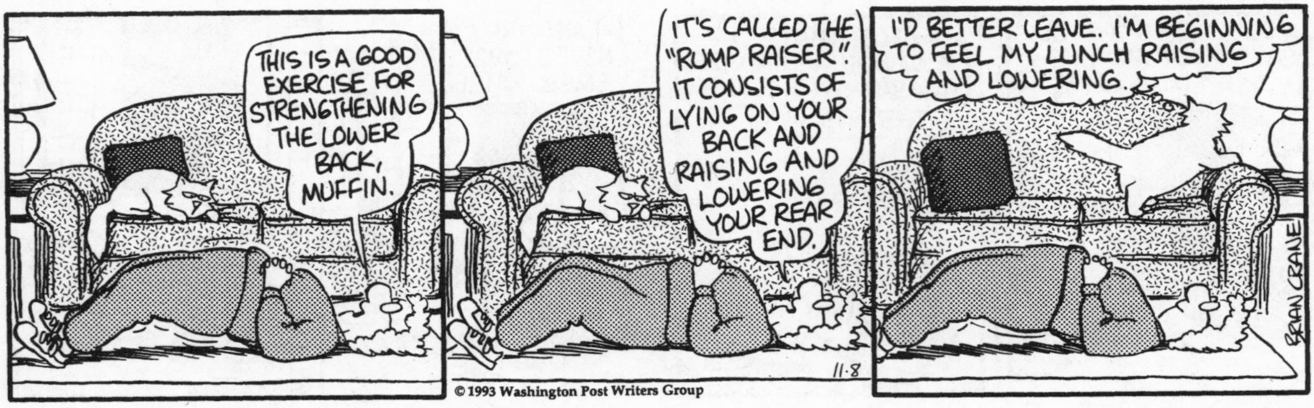
THIS IS A GOOD EXERCISE FOR STRENGTHENING THE LOWER BACK, MUFFIN.
IT'S CALLED THE "RUMP RAISER". IT CONSISTS OF LYING ON YOUR BACK AND RAISING AND LOWERING YOUR REAR END.
I'D BETTER LEAVE. I'M BEGINNING TO FEEL MY LUNCH RAISING AND LOWERING.
BRIAN CRANE
11·8
© 1993 Washington Post Writers Group

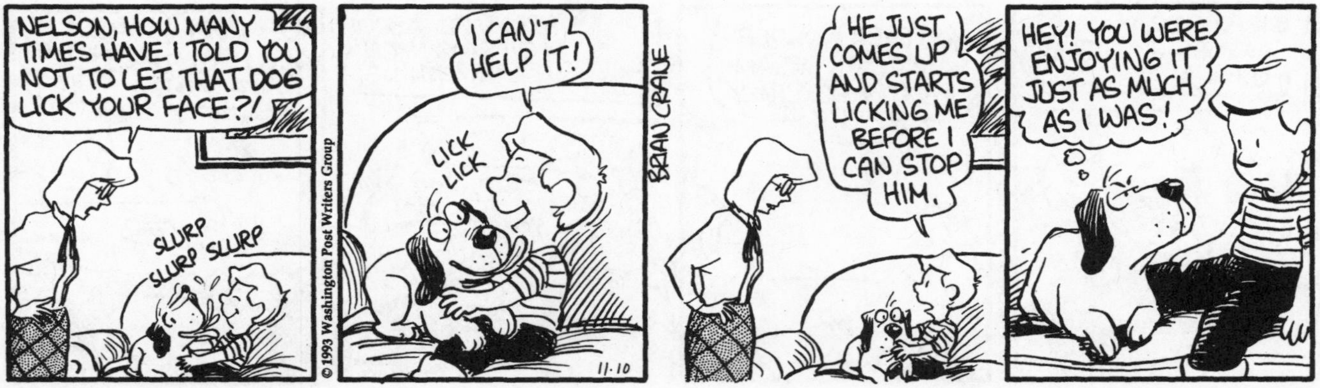
NELSON, HOW MANY TIMES HAVE I TOLD YOU NOT TO LET THAT DOG LICK YOUR FACE?!
SLURP SLURP SLURP
© 1993 Washington Post Writers Group
I CAN'T HELP IT!
LICK LICK
BRIAN CRANE
11·10
HE JUST COMES UP AND STARTS LICKING ME BEFORE I CAN STOP HIM.
HEY! YOU WERE ENJOYING IT JUST AS MUCH AS I WAS!

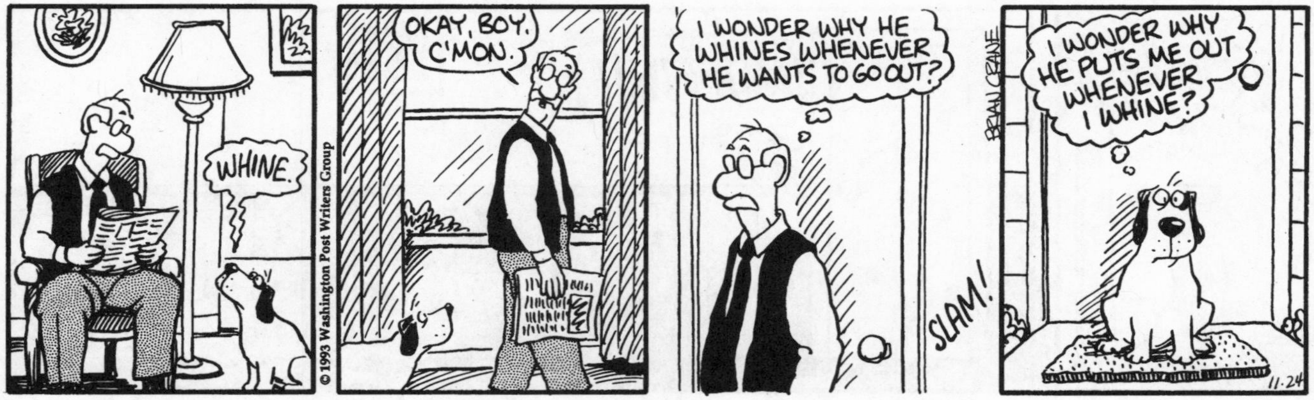
WHINE.
© 1993 Washington Post Writers Group
OKAY, BOY. C'MON.
I WONDER WHY HE WHINES WHENEVER HE WANTS TO GO OUT?
SLAM!
BRIAN CRANE
I WONDER WHY HE PUTS ME OUT WHENEVER I WHINE?
11·24

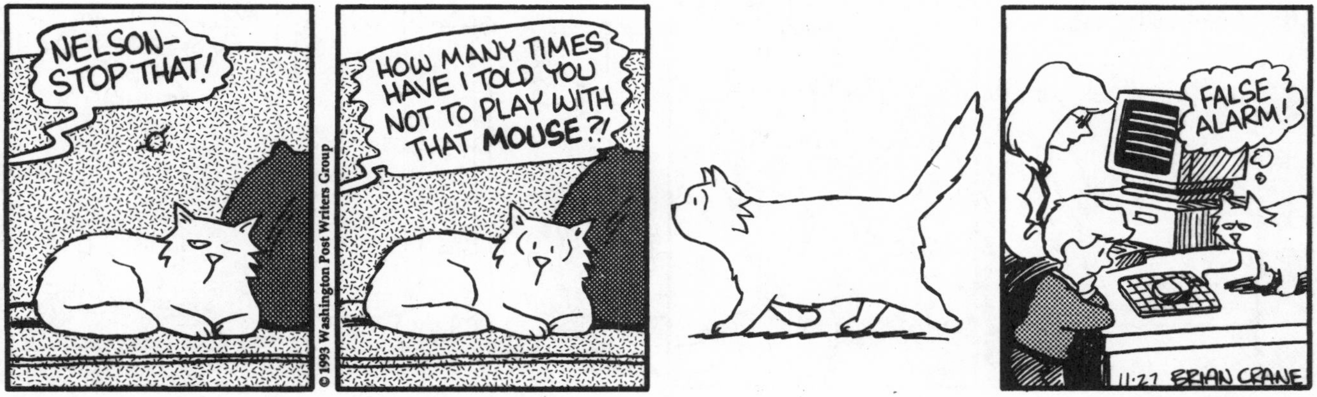
NELSON– STOP THAT!
HOW MANY TIMES HAVE I TOLD YOU NOT TO PLAY WITH THAT MOUSE?!
© 1993 Washington Post Writers Group
FALSE ALARM!
11-27 BRIAN CRANE

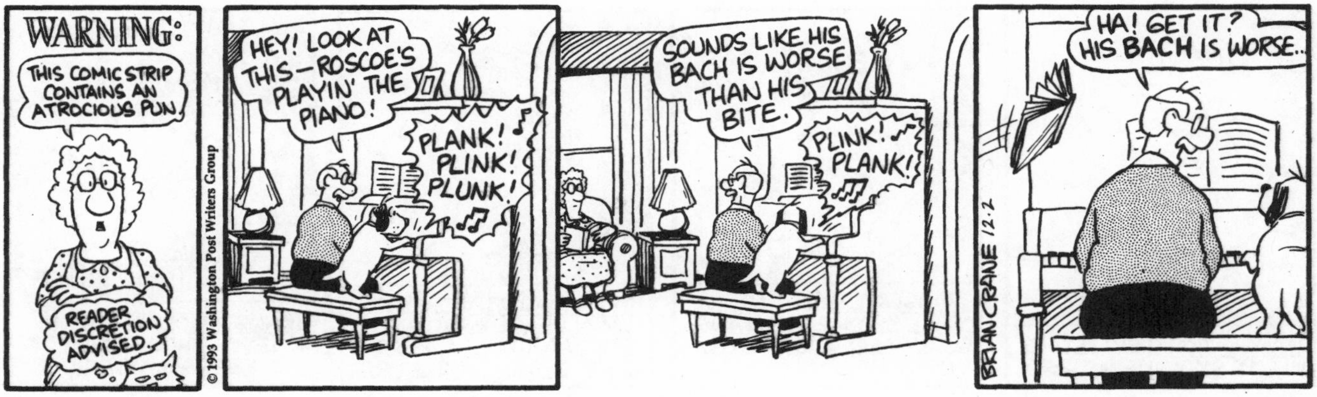
WARNING:
THIS COMIC STRIP CONTAINS AN ATROCIOUS PUN.
READER DISCRETION ADVISED.
© 1993 Washington Post Writers Group
HEY! LOOK AT THIS—ROSCOE'S PLAYIN' THE PIANO!
PLANK! PLINK! PLUNK!
SOUNDS LIKE HIS BACH IS WORSE THAN HIS BITE.
PLINK! PLANK!
BRIAN CRANE 12-2
HA! GET IT? HIS BACH IS WORSE...

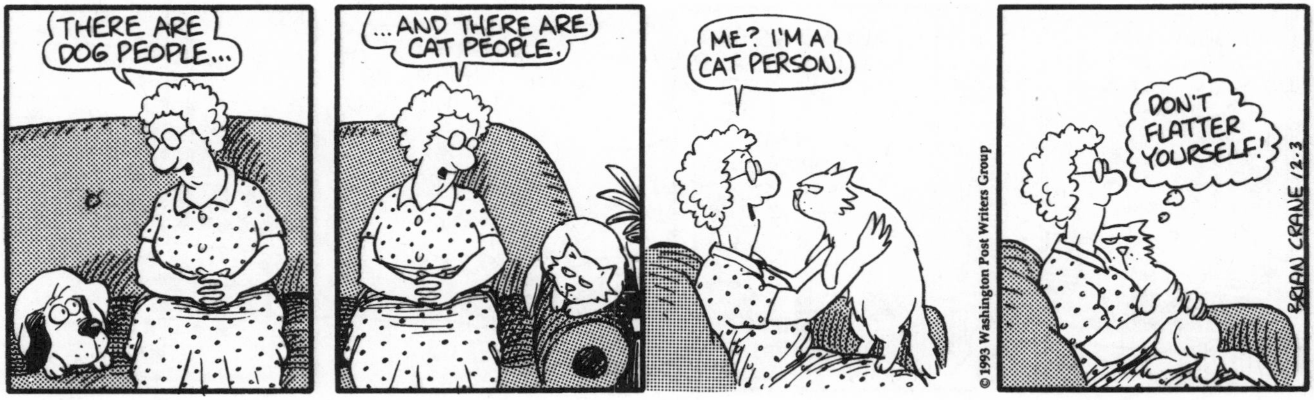
THERE ARE DOG PEOPLE...
...AND THERE ARE CAT PEOPLE.
ME? I'M A CAT PERSON.
© 1993 Washington Post Writers Group
DON'T FLATTER YOURSELF!
BRIAN CRANE 12-3

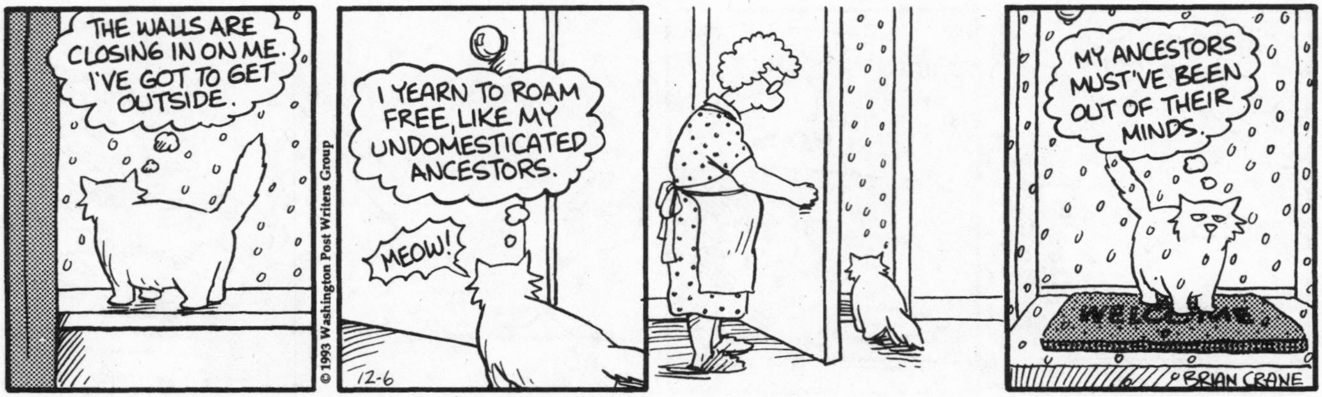
THE WALLS ARE CLOSING IN ON ME. I'VE GOT TO GET OUTSIDE.
I YEARN TO ROAM FREE, LIKE MY UNDOMESTICATED ANCESTORS.
MEOW!
© 1993 Washington Post Writers Group
12-6
MY ANCESTORS MUST'VE BEEN OUT OF THEIR MINDS.
WELCOME
BRIAN CRANE

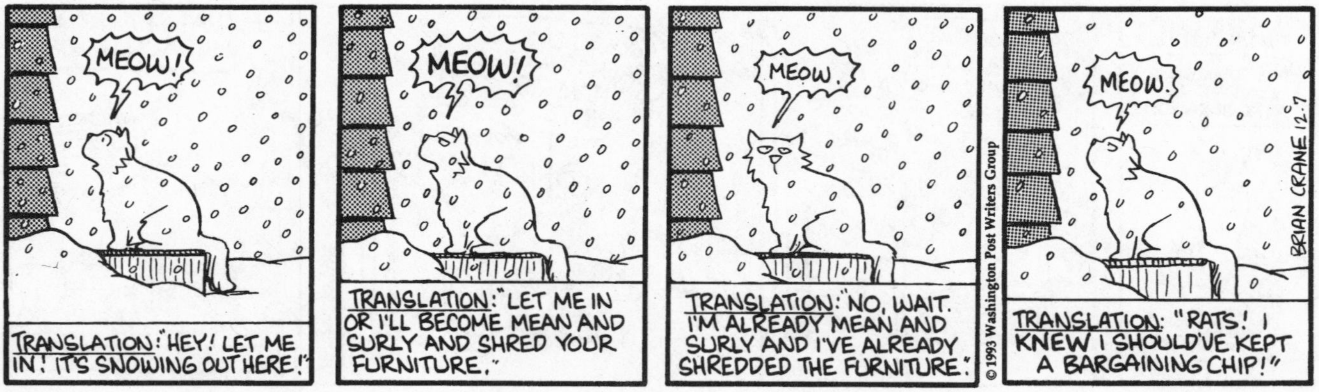
MEOW!
TRANSLATION: "HEY! LET ME IN! IT'S SNOWING OUT HERE!"
MEOW!
TRANSLATION: "LET ME IN OR I'LL BECOME MEAN AND SURLY AND SHRED YOUR FURNITURE."
MEOW.
TRANSLATION: "NO, WAIT. I'M ALREADY MEAN AND SURLY AND I'VE ALREADY SHREDDED THE FURNITURE."
© 1993 Washington Post Writers Group
MEOW.
TRANSLATION: "RATS! I KNEW I SHOULD'VE KEPT A BARGAINING CHIP!"
BRIAN CRANE 12-7

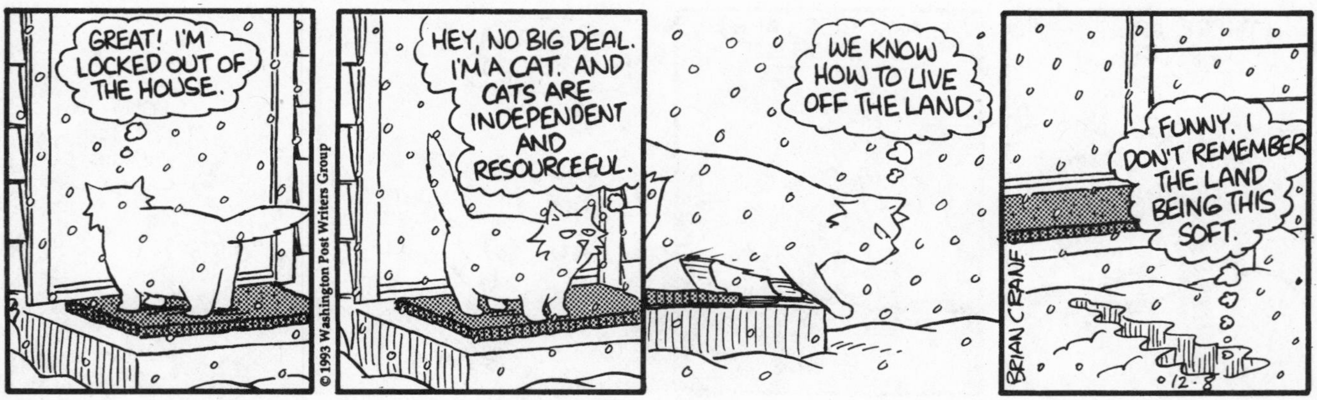
GREAT! I'M LOCKED OUT OF THE HOUSE.
© 1993 Washington Post Writers Group
HEY, NO BIG DEAL. I'M A CAT. AND CATS ARE INDEPENDENT AND RESOURCEFUL.
WE KNOW HOW TO LIVE OFF THE LAND.
FUNNY. I DON'T REMEMBER THE LAND BEING THIS SOFT.
BRIAN CRANE
12-8

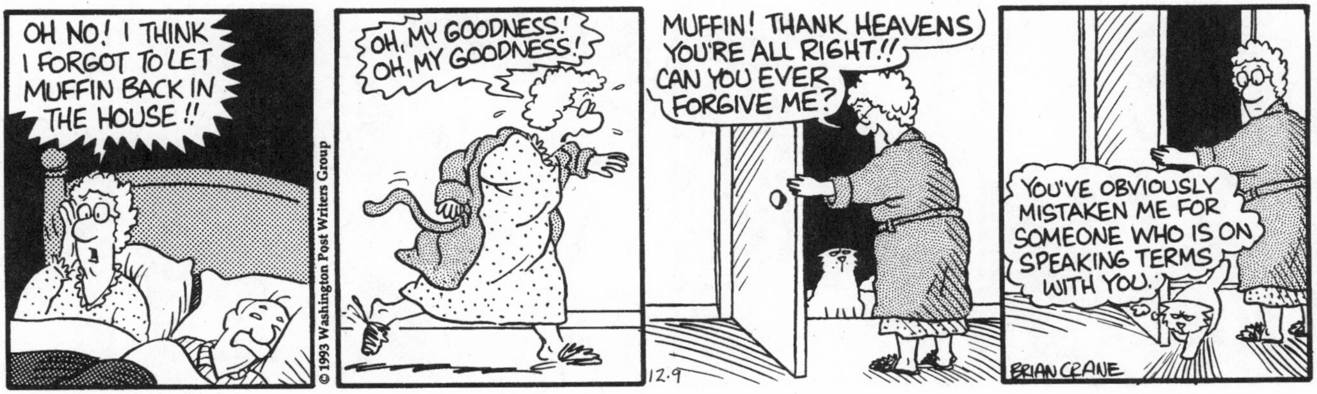
OH NO! I THINK I FORGOT TO LET MUFFIN BACK IN THE HOUSE!!
© 1993 Washington Post Writers Group
OH, MY GOODNESS! OH, MY GOODNESS!
MUFFIN! THANK HEAVENS YOU'RE ALL RIGHT!! CAN YOU EVER FORGIVE ME?
12-9
YOU'VE OBVIOUSLY MISTAKEN ME FOR SOMEONE WHO IS ON SPEAKING TERMS WITH YOU.
BRIAN CRANE

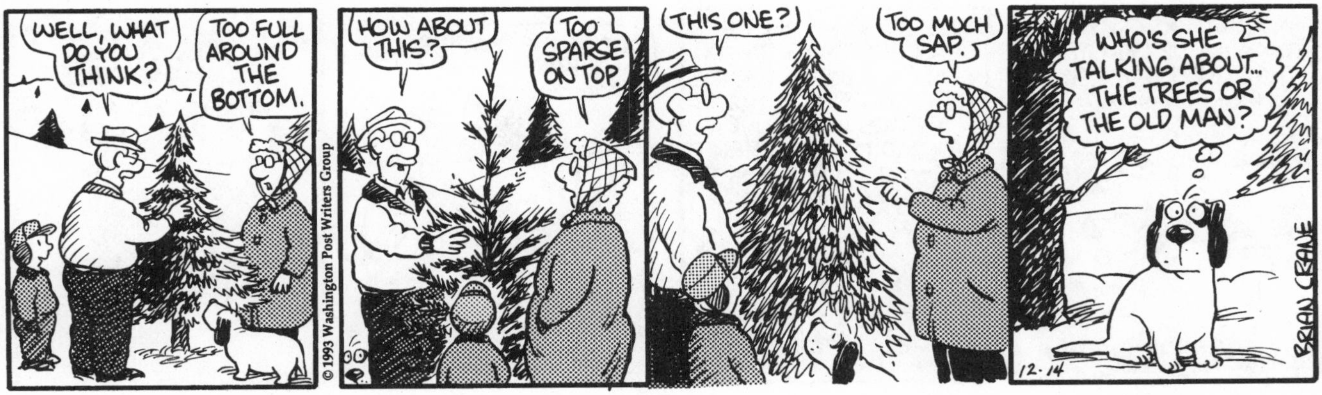
WELL, WHAT DO YOU THINK?
TOO FULL AROUND THE BOTTOM.
© 1993 Washington Post Writers Group
HOW ABOUT THIS?
TOO SPARSE ON TOP.
THIS ONE?
TOO MUCH SAP.
WHO'S SHE TALKING ABOUT... THE TREES OR THE OLD MAN?
12-14
BRIAN CRANE

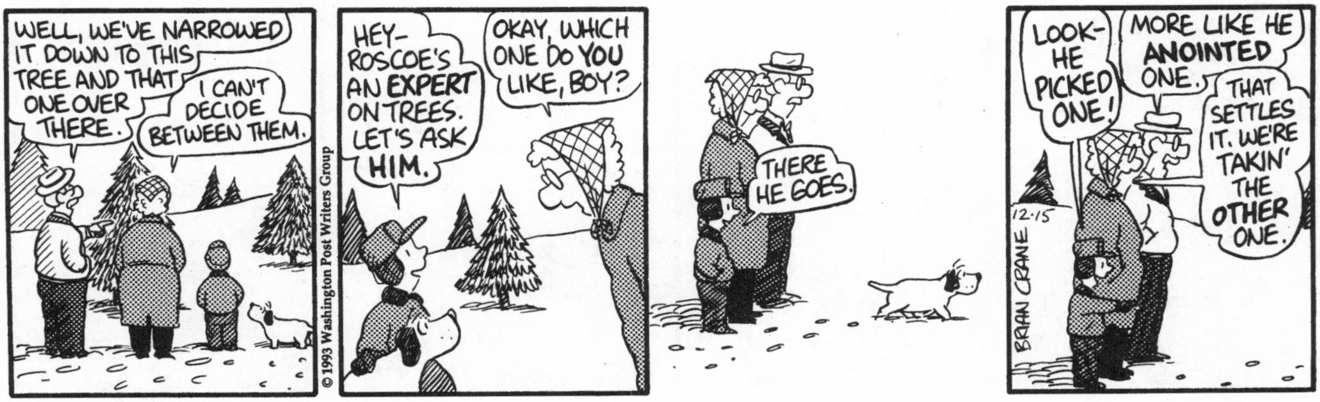
WELL, WE'VE NARROWED IT DOWN TO THIS TREE AND THAT ONE OVER THERE.
I CAN'T DECIDE BETWEEN THEM.
© 1993 Washington Post Writers Group
HEY- ROSCOE'S AN EXPERT ON TREES. LET'S ASK HIM.
OKAY, WHICH ONE DO YOU LIKE, BOY?
THERE HE GOES.
LOOK- HE PICKED ONE!
MORE LIKE HE ANOINTED ONE.
THAT SETTLES IT. WE'RE TAKIN' THE OTHER ONE.
12-15
BRIAN CRANE

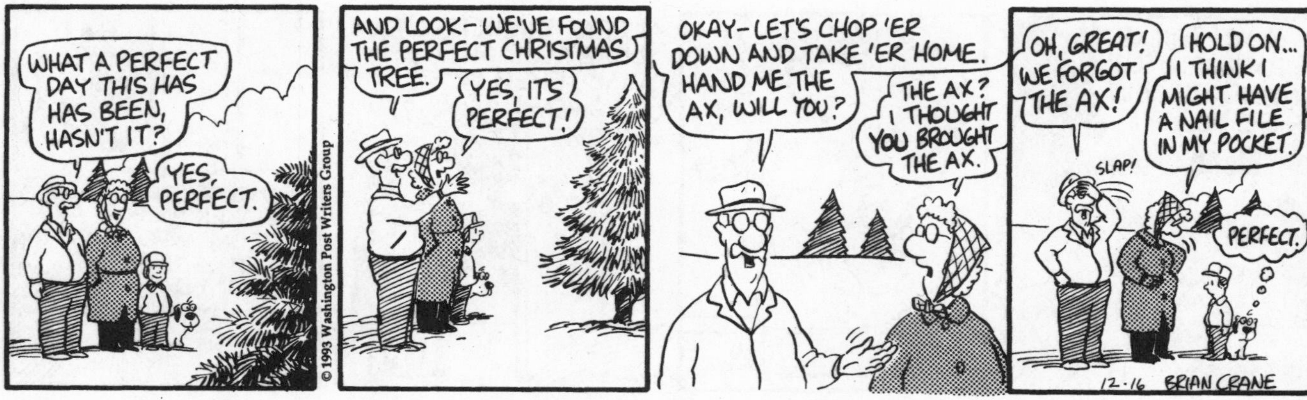
WHAT A PERFECT DAY THIS HAS HAS BEEN, HASN'T IT?
YES, PERFECT.
© 1993 Washington Post Writers Group
AND LOOK- WE'VE FOUND THE PERFECT CHRISTMAS TREE.
YES, IT'S PERFECT!
OKAY- LET'S CHOP 'ER DOWN AND TAKE 'ER HOME. HAND ME THE AX, WILL YOU?
THE AX? I THOUGHT YOU BROUGHT THE AX.
OH, GREAT! WE FORGOT THE AX!
HOLD ON... I THINK I MIGHT HAVE A NAIL FILE IN MY POCKET.
SLAP!
PERFECT.
12·16 BRIAN CRANE

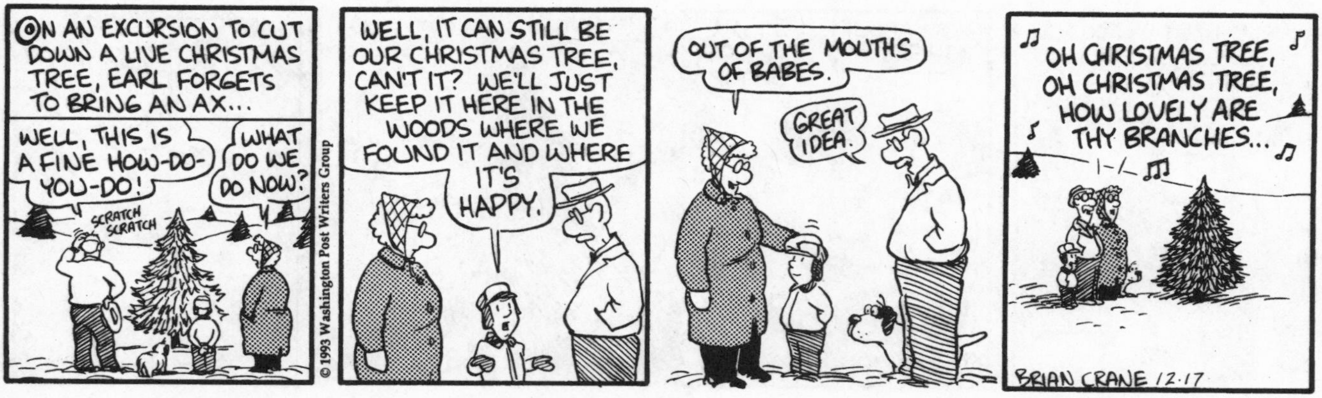
ON AN EXCURSION TO CUT DOWN A LIVE CHRISTMAS TREE, EARL FORGETS TO BRING AN AX...
WELL, THIS IS A FINE HOW-DO-YOU-DO!
WHAT DO WE DO NOW?
SCRATCH SCRATCH
© 1993 Washington Post Writers Group
WELL, IT CAN STILL BE OUR CHRISTMAS TREE, CAN'T IT? WE'LL JUST KEEP IT HERE IN THE WOODS WHERE WE FOUND IT AND WHERE IT'S HAPPY.
OUT OF THE MOUTHS OF BABES.
GREAT IDEA.
OH CHRISTMAS TREE, OH CHRISTMAS TREE, HOW LOVELY ARE THY BRANCHES...
BRIAN CRANE 12·17

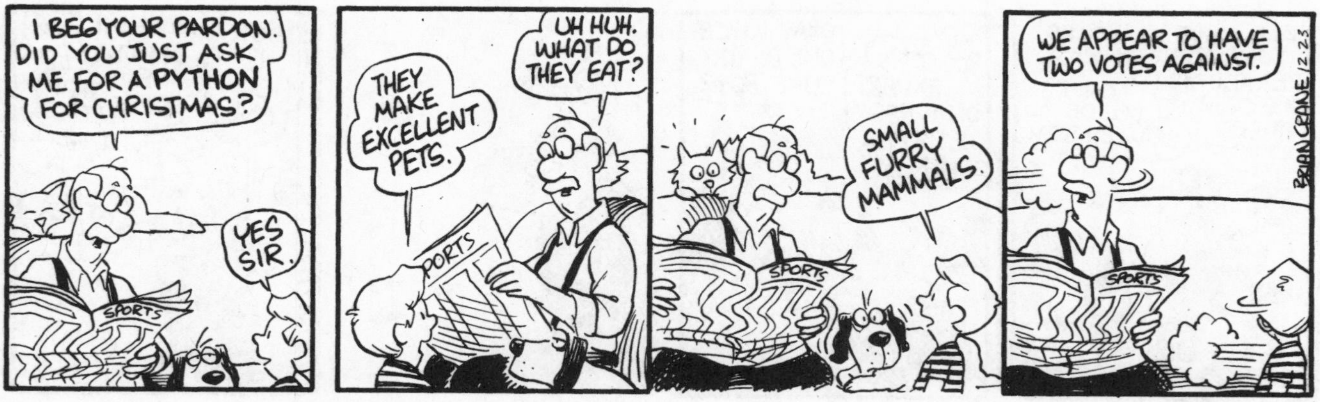
I BEG YOUR PARDON. DID YOU JUST ASK ME FOR A PYTHON FOR CHRISTMAS?
YES SIR.
SPORTS
THEY MAKE EXCELLENT PETS.
UH HUH. WHAT DO THEY EAT?
SMALL FURRY MAMMALS.
WE APPEAR TO HAVE TWO VOTES AGAINST.
BRIAN CRANE 12·23

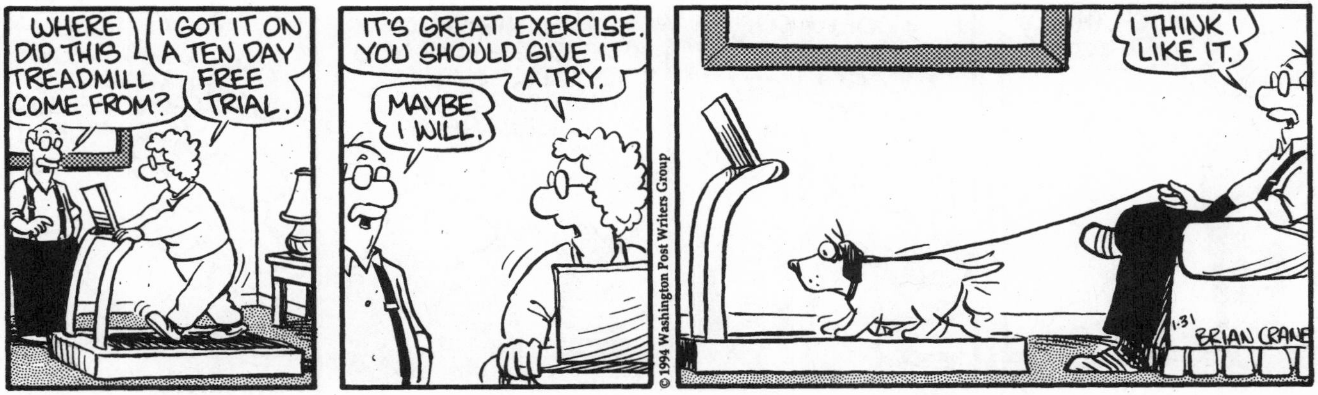
WHERE DID THIS TREADMILL COME FROM?
I GOT IT ON A TEN DAY FREE TRIAL.
IT'S GREAT EXERCISE. YOU SHOULD GIVE IT A TRY.
MAYBE I WILL.
I THINK I LIKE IT.
© 1994 Washington Post Writers Group
1-31
BRIAN CRANE

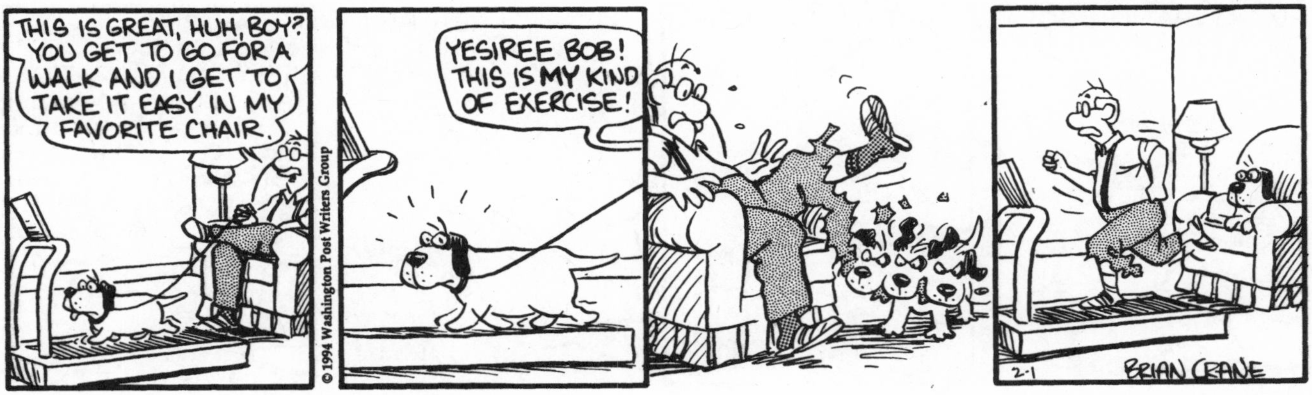
THIS IS GREAT, HUH, BOY? YOU GET TO GO FOR A WALK AND I GET TO TAKE IT EASY IN MY FAVORITE CHAIR.
© 1994 Washington Post Writers Group
YESIREE BOB! THIS IS MY KIND OF EXERCISE!
2-1
BRIAN CRANE

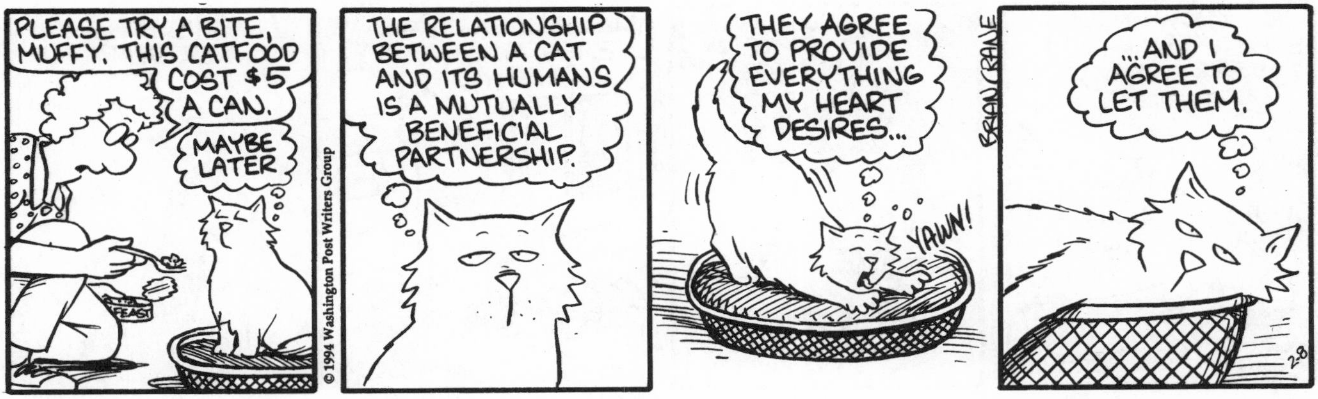
PLEASE TRY A BITE, MUFFY. THIS CATFOOD COST $5 A CAN.
MAYBE LATER
FEAST
© 1994 Washington Post Writers Group
THE RELATIONSHIP BETWEEN A CAT AND ITS HUMANS IS A MUTUALLY BENEFICIAL PARTNERSHIP.
THEY AGREE TO PROVIDE EVERYTHING MY HEART DESIRES...
YAWN!
BRIAN CRANE
...AND I AGREE TO LET THEM.
2-8

101

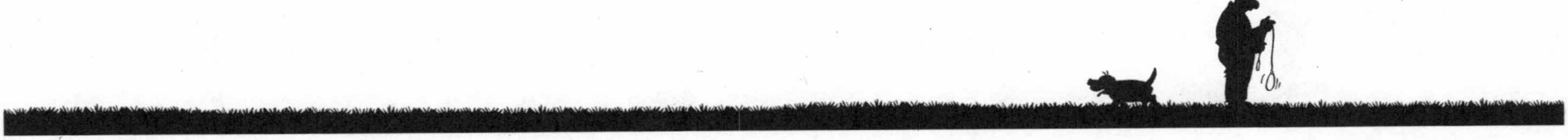

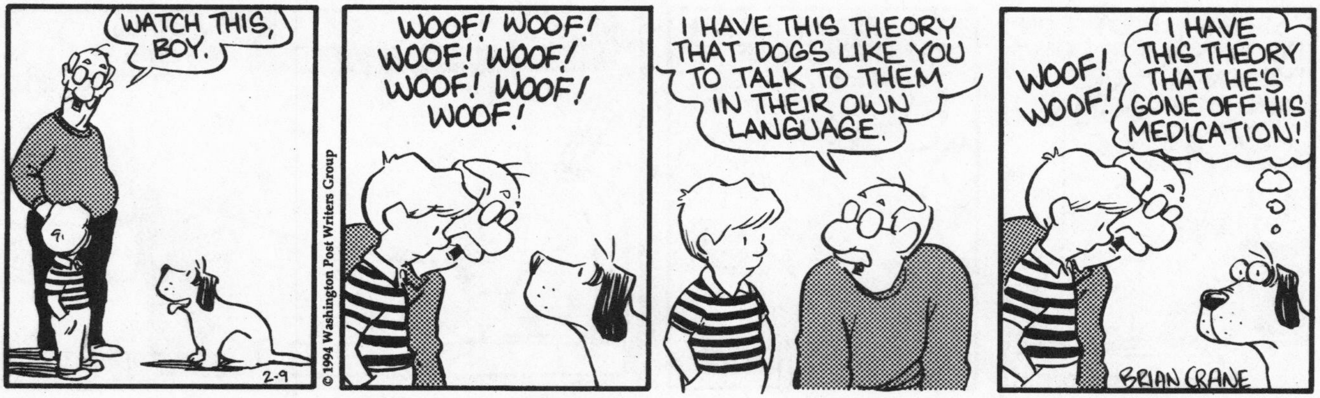
WATCH THIS, BOY.
2-9
© 1994 Washington Post Writers Group
WOOF! WOOF! WOOF! WOOF! WOOF! WOOF! WOOF!
I HAVE THIS THEORY THAT DOGS LIKE YOU TO TALK TO THEM IN THEIR OWN LANGUAGE.
WOOF! WOOF!
I HAVE THIS THEORY THAT HE'S GONE OFF HIS MEDICATION!
BRIAN CRANE

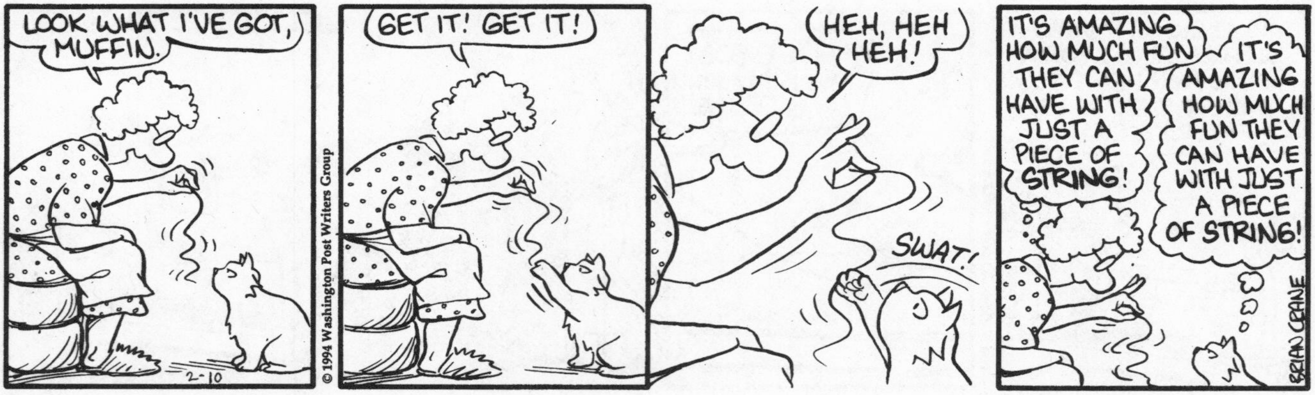
LOOK WHAT I'VE GOT, MUFFIN.
2-10
© 1994 Washington Post Writers Group
GET IT! GET IT!
HEH, HEH HEH!
SWAT!
IT'S AMAZING HOW MUCH FUN THEY CAN HAVE WITH JUST A PIECE OF STRING!
IT'S AMAZING HOW MUCH FUN THEY CAN HAVE WITH JUST A PIECE OF STRING!
BRIAN CRANE

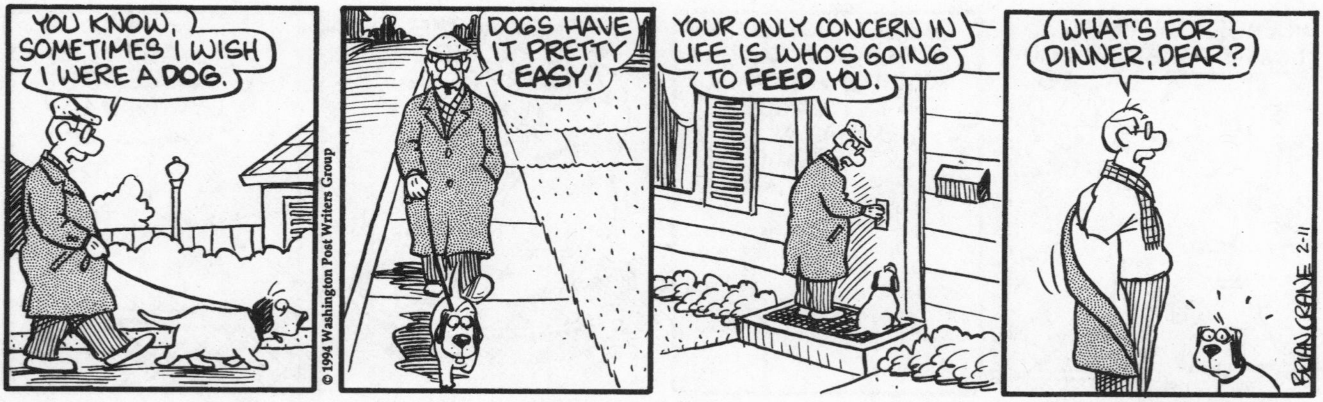
YOU KNOW, SOMETIMES I WISH I WERE A DOG.
© 1994 Washington Post Writers Group
DOGS HAVE IT PRETTY EASY!
YOUR ONLY CONCERN IN LIFE IS WHO'S GOING TO FEED YOU.
WHAT'S FOR DINNER, DEAR?
BRIAN CRANE 2-11

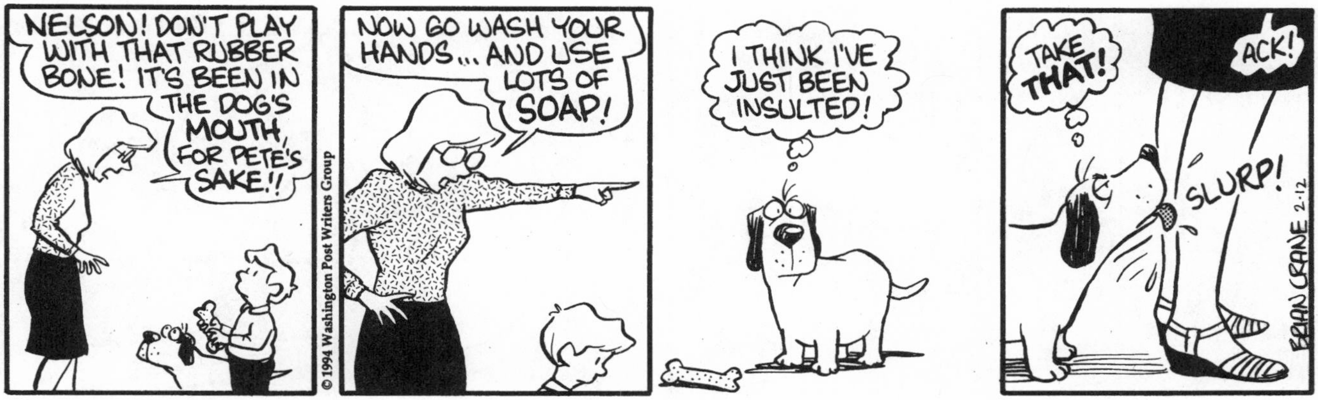
NELSON! DON'T PLAY WITH THAT RUBBER BONE! IT'S BEEN IN THE DOG'S MOUTH, FOR PETE'S SAKE!!
© 1994 Washington Post Writers Group
NOW GO WASH YOUR HANDS... AND USE LOTS OF SOAP!
I THINK I'VE JUST BEEN INSULTED!
TAKE THAT!
ACK!
SLURP!
BRIAN CRANE 2·12

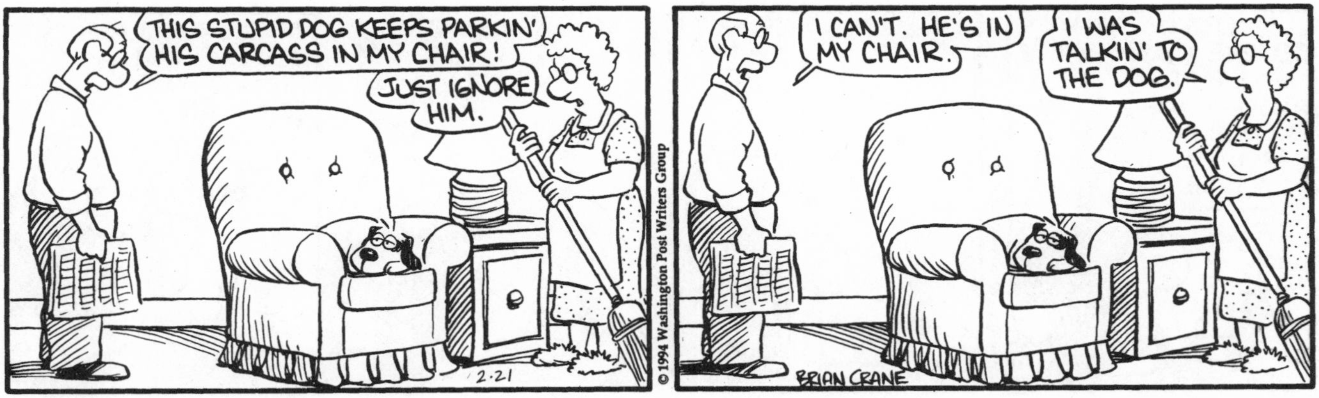
THIS STUPID DOG KEEPS PARKIN' HIS CARCASS IN MY CHAIR!
JUST IGNORE HIM.
2·21
© 1994 Washington Post Writers Group
I CAN'T. HE'S IN MY CHAIR.
I WAS TALKIN' TO THE DOG.
BRIAN CRANE

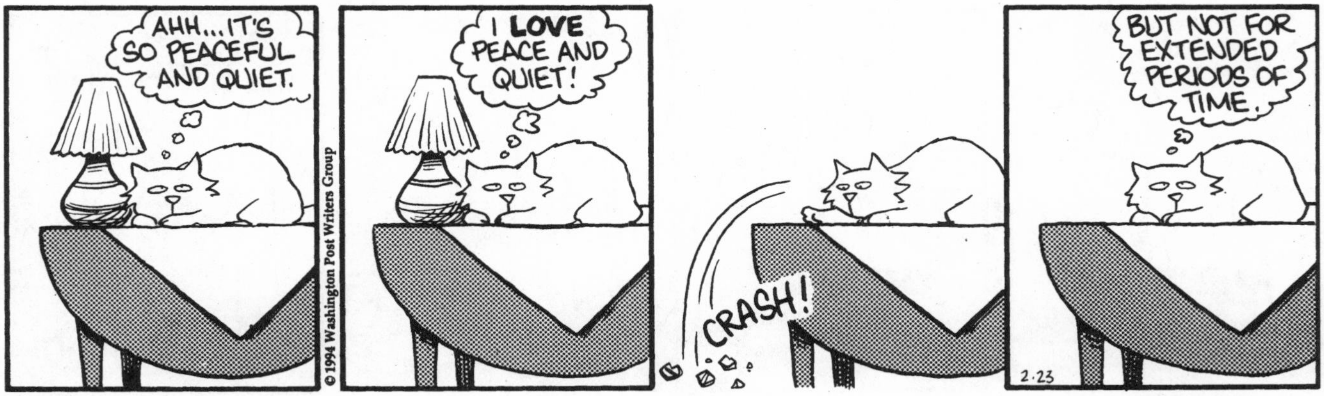
AHH...IT'S SO PEACEFUL AND QUIET.
© 1994 Washington Post Writers Group
I LOVE PEACE AND QUIET!
CRASH!
BUT NOT FOR EXTENDED PERIODS OF TIME.
2·23

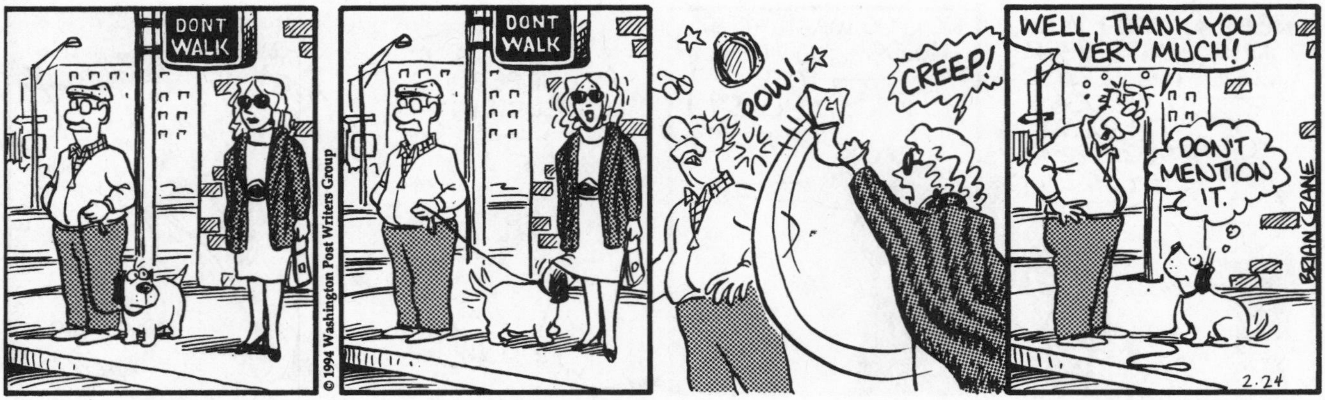
DONT WALK
DONT WALK
POW!
CREEP!
WELL, THANK YOU VERY MUCH!
DON'T MENTION IT.
BRIAN CRANE
2.24
© 1994 Washington Post Writers Group

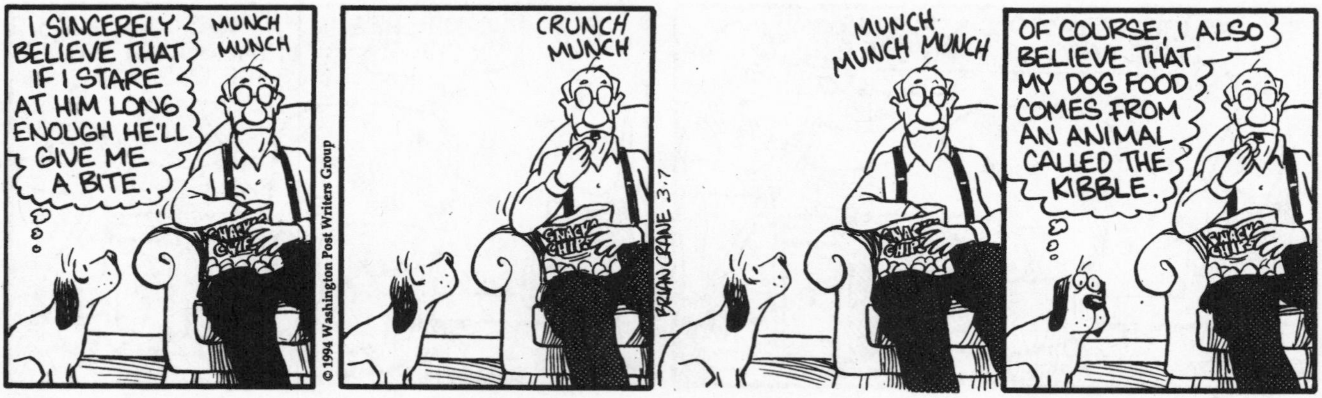
I SINCERELY BELIEVE THAT IF I STARE AT HIM LONG ENOUGH HE'LL GIVE ME A BITE.
MUNCH MUNCH
CRUNCH MUNCH
MUNCH MUNCH MUNCH
OF COURSE, I ALSO BELIEVE THAT MY DOG FOOD COMES FROM AN ANIMAL CALLED THE KIBBLE.
BRIAN CRANE 3.7
© 1994 Washington Post Writers Group

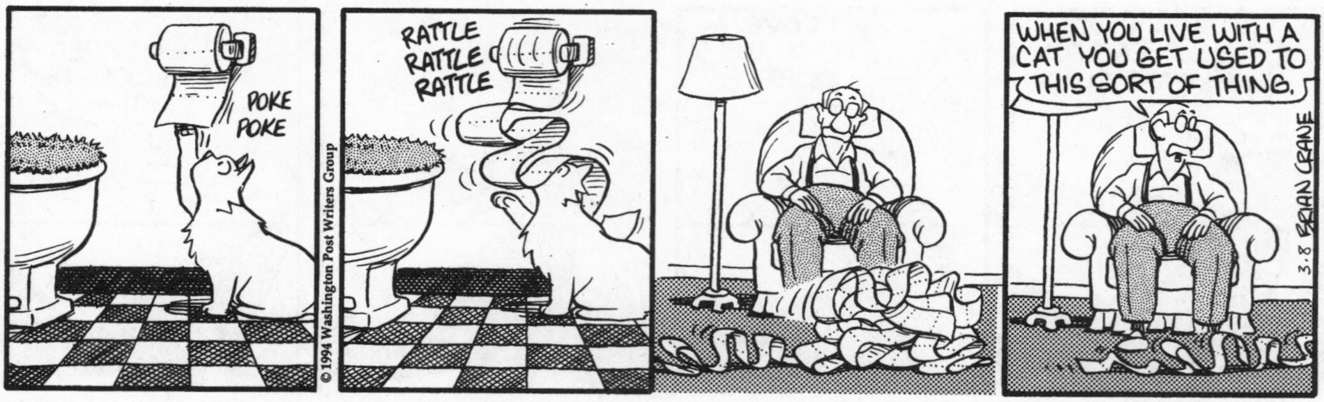
POKE POKE
RATTLE RATTLE RATTLE
WHEN YOU LIVE WITH A CAT YOU GET USED TO THIS SORT OF THING.
3.8 BRIAN CRANE
© 1994 Washington Post Writers Group

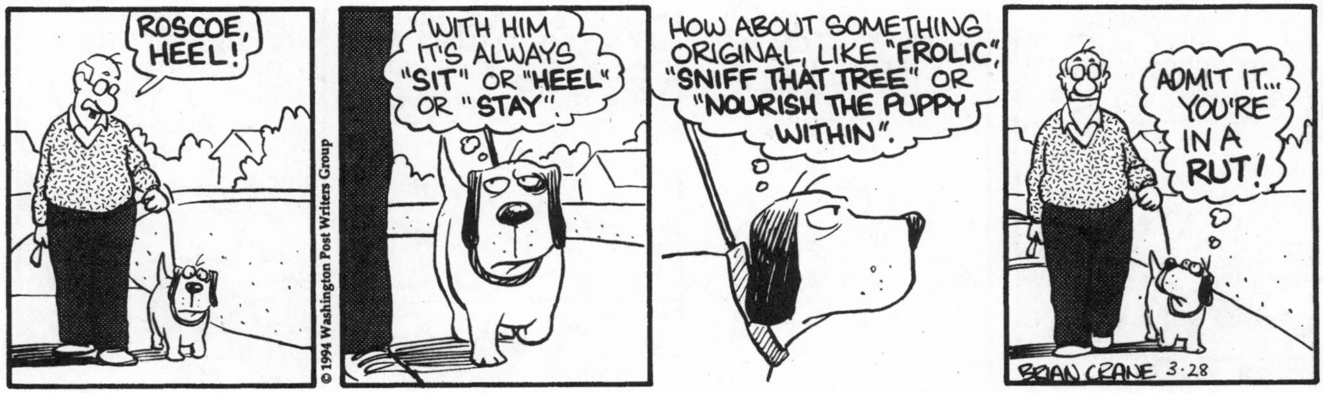
ROSCOE, HEEL!
WITH HIM IT'S ALWAYS "SIT" OR "HEEL" OR "STAY".
HOW ABOUT SOMETHING ORIGINAL, LIKE "FROLIC", "SNIFF THAT TREE" OR "NOURISH THE PUPPY WITHIN".
ADMIT IT... YOU'RE IN A RUT!
BRIAN CRANE 3·28

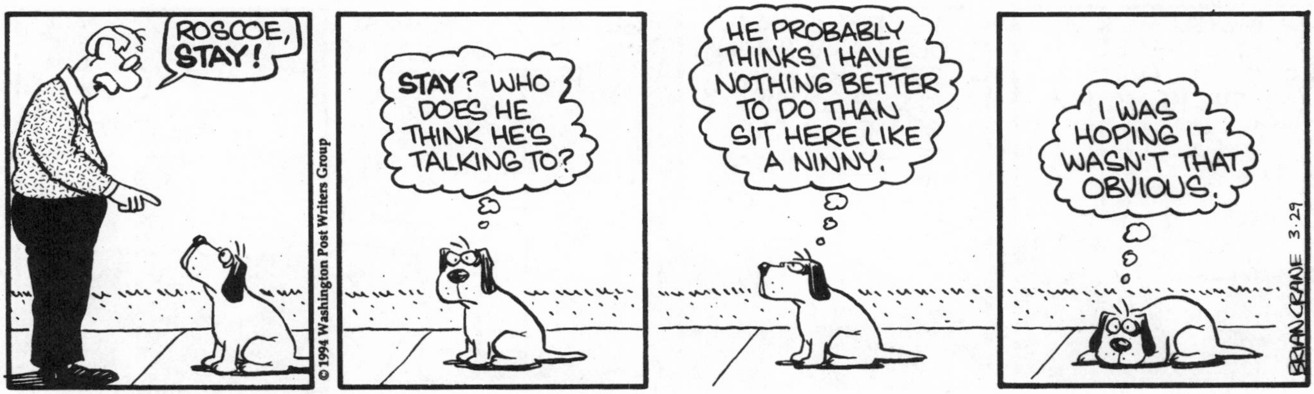
ROSCOE, STAY!
STAY? WHO DOES HE THINK HE'S TALKING TO?
HE PROBABLY THINKS I HAVE NOTHING BETTER TO DO THAN SIT HERE LIKE A NINNY.
I WAS HOPING IT WASN'T THAT OBVIOUS.
BRIAN CRANE 3·29

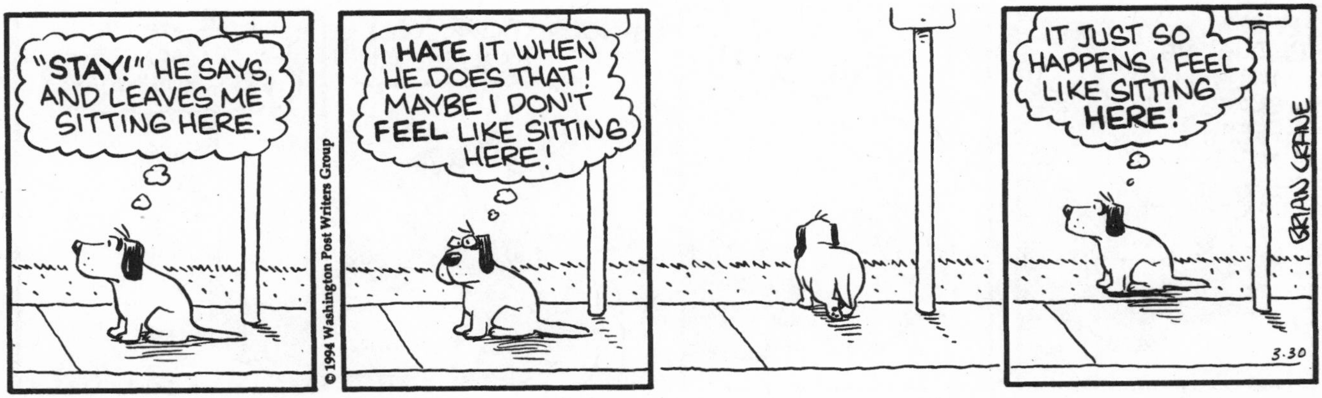
"STAY!" HE SAYS, AND LEAVES ME SITTING HERE.
I HATE IT WHEN HE DOES THAT! MAYBE I DON'T FEEL LIKE SITTING HERE!
IT JUST SO HAPPENS I FEEL LIKE SITTING HERE!
BRIAN CRANE
3·30

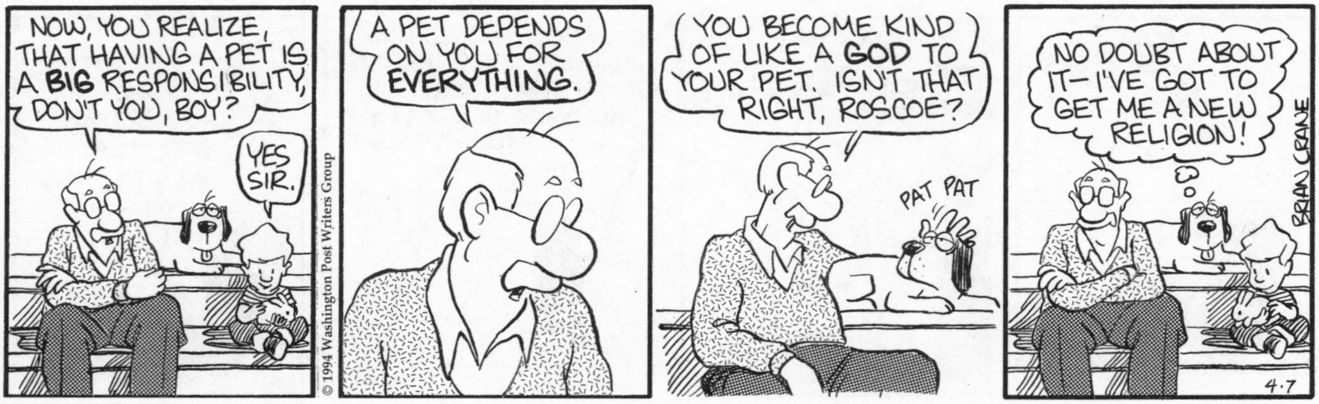
NOW, YOU REALIZE, THAT HAVING A PET IS A BIG RESPONSIBILITY, DON'T YOU, BOY?
YES SIR.
© 1994 Washington Post Writers Group
A PET DEPENDS ON YOU FOR EVERYTHING.
YOU BECOME KIND OF LIKE A GOD TO YOUR PET. ISN'T THAT RIGHT, ROSCOE?
PAT PAT
NO DOUBT ABOUT IT— I'VE GOT TO GET ME A NEW RELIGION!
BRIAN CRANE
4·7

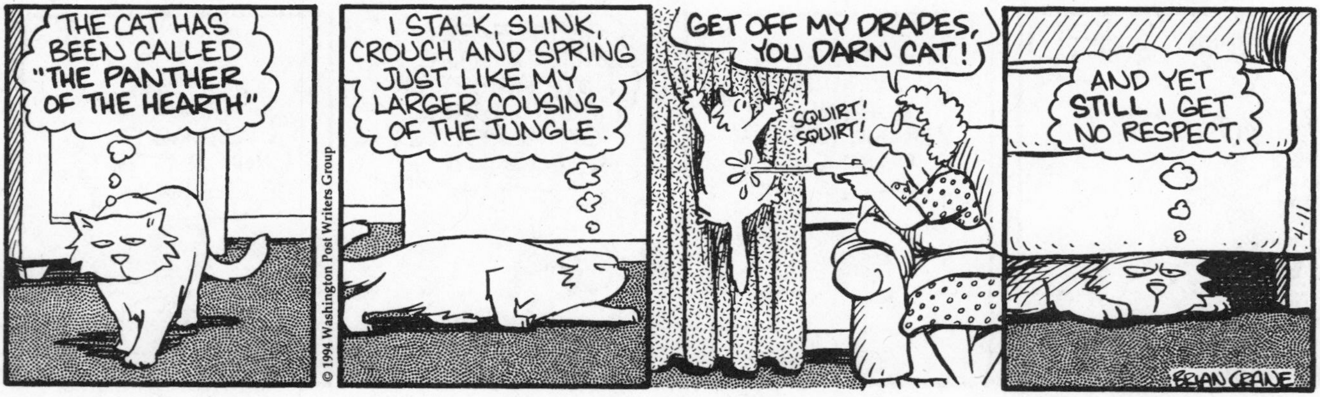
THE CAT HAS BEEN CALLED "THE PANTHER OF THE HEARTH"
© 1994 Washington Post Writers Group
I STALK, SLINK, CROUCH AND SPRING JUST LIKE MY LARGER COUSINS OF THE JUNGLE.
GET OFF MY DRAPES, YOU DARN CAT!
SQUIRT! SQUIRT!
AND YET STILL I GET NO RESPECT.
4·11
BRIAN CRANE

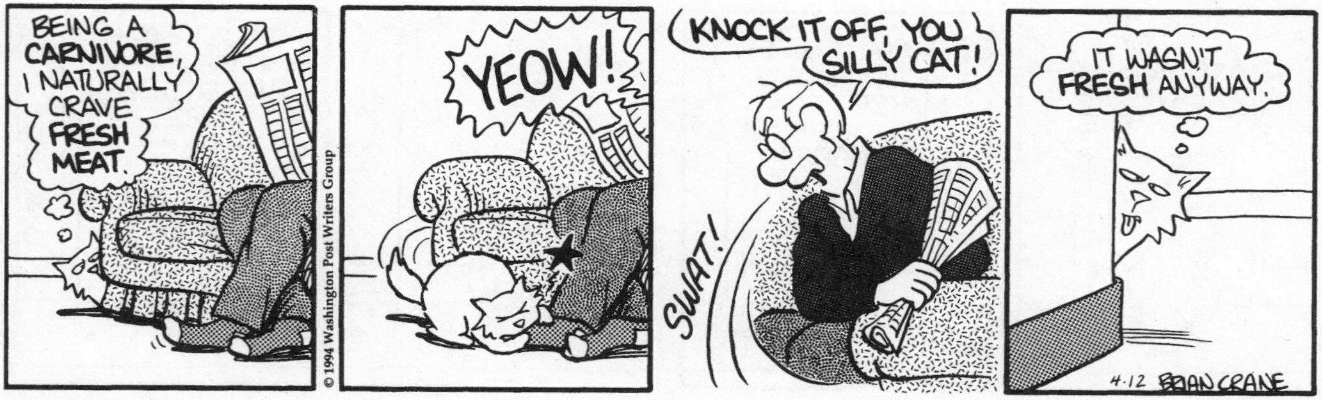
BEING A CARNIVORE, I NATURALLY CRAVE FRESH MEAT.
© 1994 Washington Post Writers Group
YEOW!
KNOCK IT OFF, YOU SILLY CAT!
SWAT!
IT WASN'T FRESH ANYWAY.
4·12 BRIAN CRANE

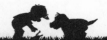

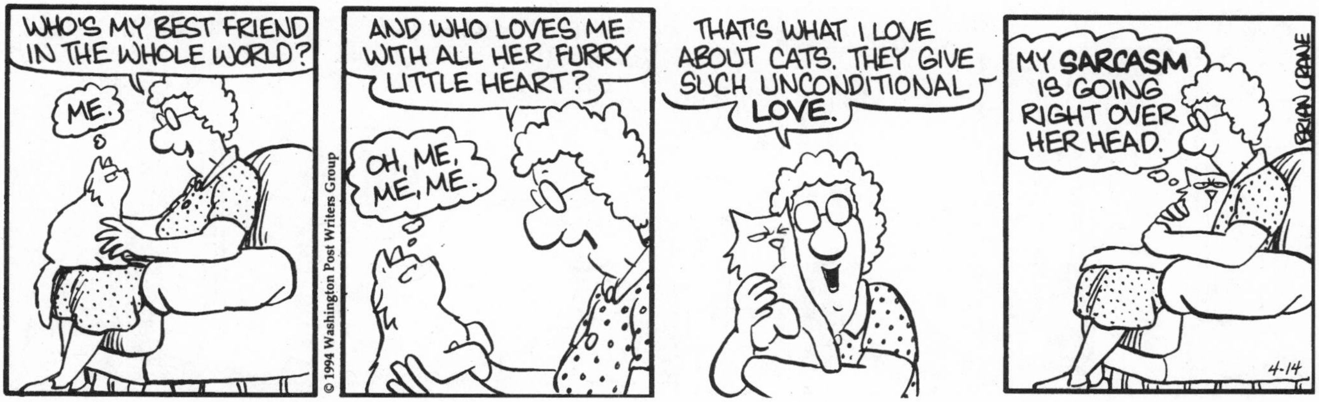
WHO'S MY BEST FRIEND IN THE WHOLE WORLD?
ME.
© 1994 Washington Post Writers Group
AND WHO LOVES ME WITH ALL HER FURRY LITTLE HEART?
OH, ME, ME, ME.
THAT'S WHAT I LOVE ABOUT CATS. THEY GIVE SUCH UNCONDITIONAL **LOVE.**
MY **SARCASM** IS GOING RIGHT OVER HER HEAD.
BRIAN CRANE
4-14

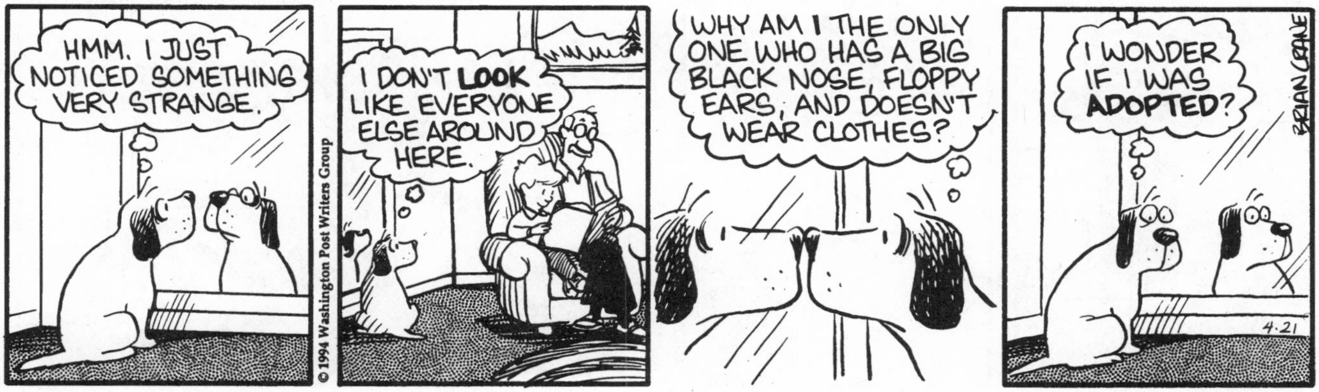
HMM. I JUST NOTICED SOMETHING VERY STRANGE.
© 1994 Washington Post Writers Group
I DON'T **LOOK** LIKE EVERYONE ELSE AROUND HERE.
WHY AM **I** THE ONLY ONE WHO HAS A BIG BLACK NOSE, FLOPPY EARS, AND DOESN'T WEAR CLOTHES?
I WONDER IF I WAS **ADOPTED**?
BRIAN CRANE
4.21

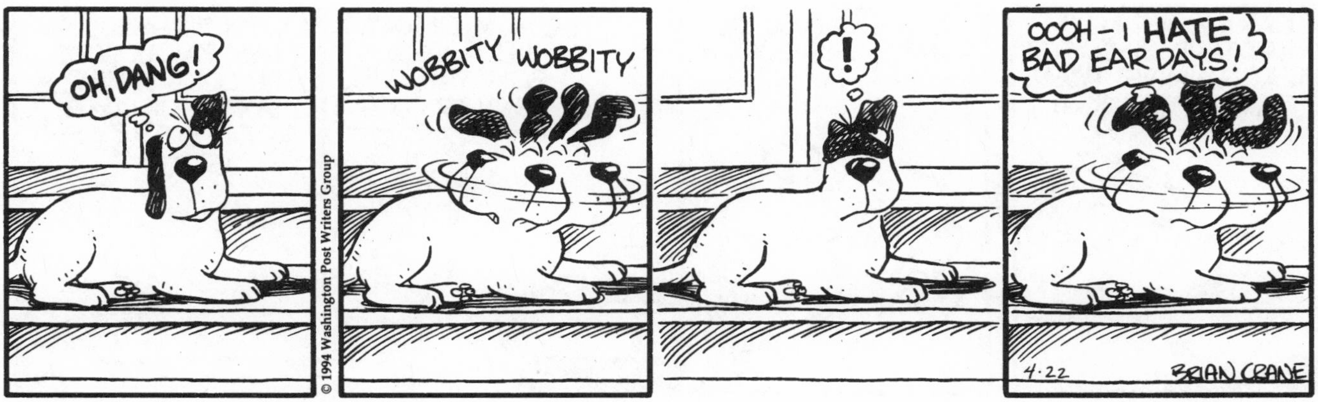
OH, DANG!
© 1994 Washington Post Writers Group
WOBBITY WOBBITY
!
OOOH - I **HATE** BAD EAR DAYS!
4.22
BRIAN CRANE

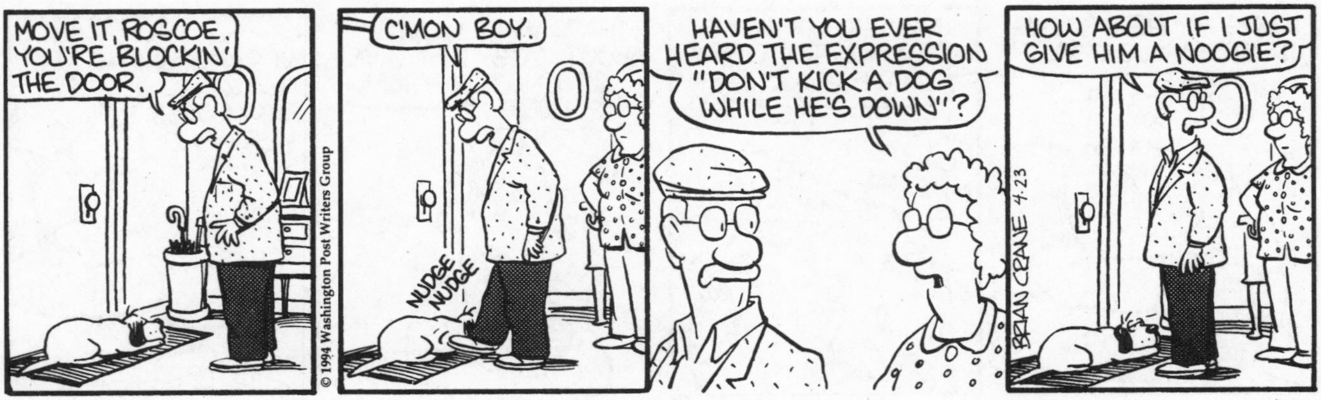
MOVE IT, ROSCOE. YOU'RE BLOCKIN' THE DOOR.
© 1994 Washington Post Writers Group
C'MON BOY.
NUDGE NUDGE
HAVEN'T YOU EVER HEARD THE EXPRESSION "DON'T KICK A DOG WHILE HE'S DOWN"?
BRIAN CRANE 4.23
HOW ABOUT IF I JUST GIVE HIM A NOOGIE?

108

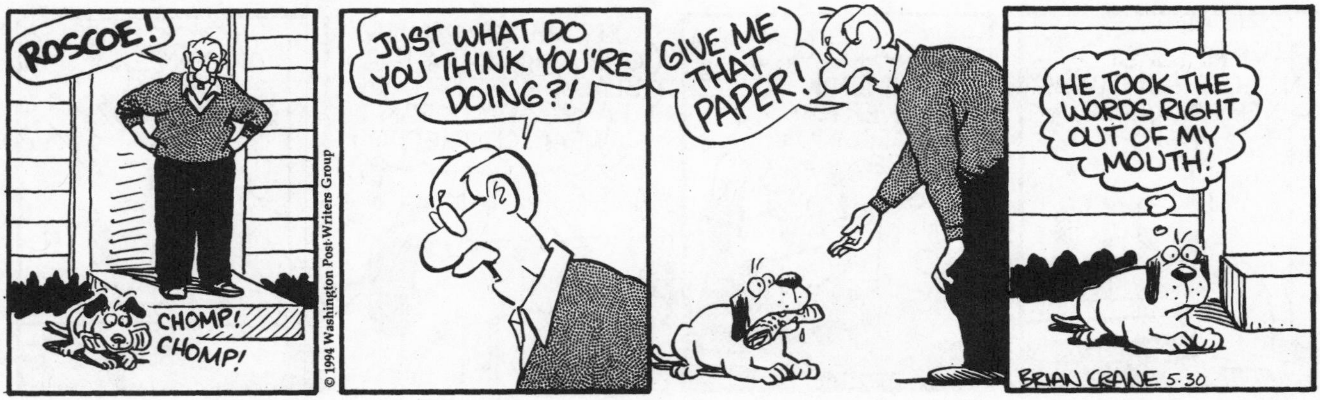
ROSCOE!
CHOMP! CHOMP!
© 1994 Washington Post Writers Group
JUST WHAT DO YOU THINK YOU'RE DOING?!
GIVE ME THAT PAPER!
HE TOOK THE WORDS RIGHT OUT OF MY MOUTH!
BRIAN CRANE 5.30

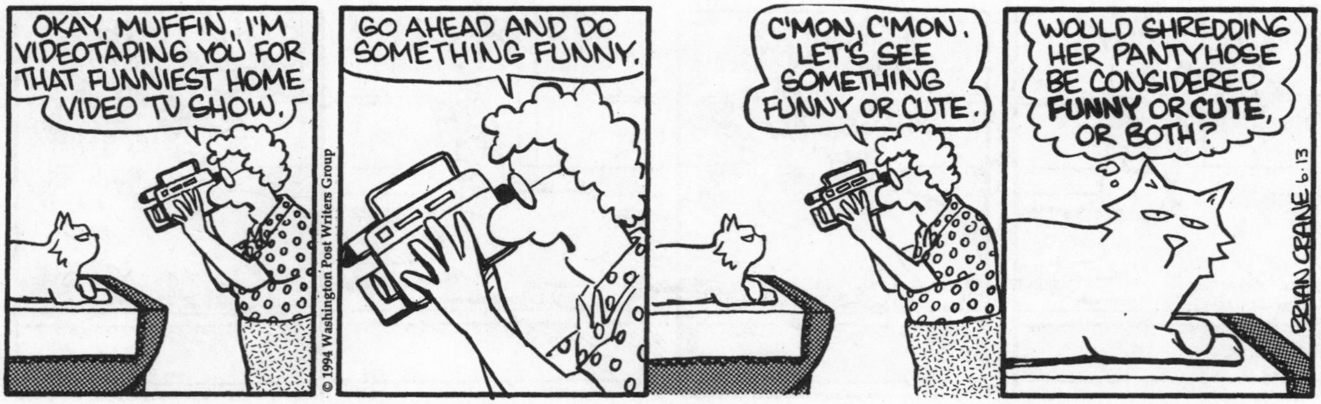
OKAY, MUFFIN, I'M VIDEOTAPING YOU FOR THAT FUNNIEST HOME VIDEO TV SHOW.
© 1994 Washington Post Writers Group
GO AHEAD AND DO SOMETHING FUNNY.
C'MON, C'MON. LET'S SEE SOMETHING FUNNY OR CUTE.
WOULD SHREDDING HER PANTYHOSE BE CONSIDERED **FUNNY** OR **CUTE**, OR BOTH?
BRIAN CRANE 6.13

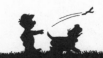

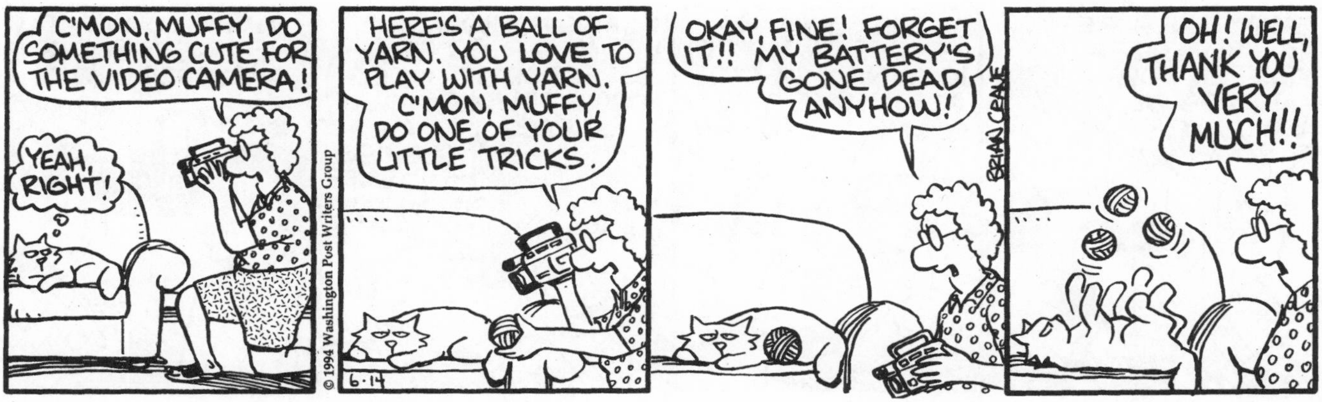
C'MON, MUFFY, DO SOMETHING CUTE FOR THE VIDEO CAMERA!
YEAH, RIGHT!
© 1994 Washington Post Writers Group
6·14
HERE'S A BALL OF YARN. YOU LOVE TO PLAY WITH YARN. C'MON, MUFFY, DO ONE OF YOUR LITTLE TRICKS.
OKAY, FINE! FORGET IT!! MY BATTERY'S GONE DEAD ANYHOW!
BRIAN CRANE
OH! WELL, THANK YOU VERY MUCH!!

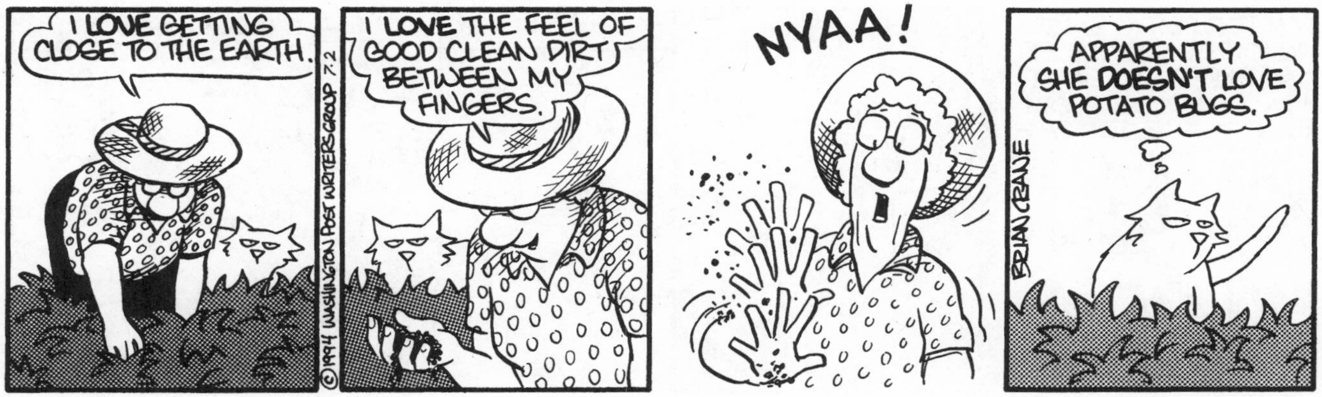
I LOVE GETTING CLOSE TO THE EARTH.
© 1994 WASHINGTON POST WRITERS GROUP 7·2
I LOVE THE FEEL OF GOOD CLEAN DIRT BETWEEN MY FINGERS.
NYAA!
BRIAN CRANE
APPARENTLY SHE DOESN'T LOVE POTATO BUGS.

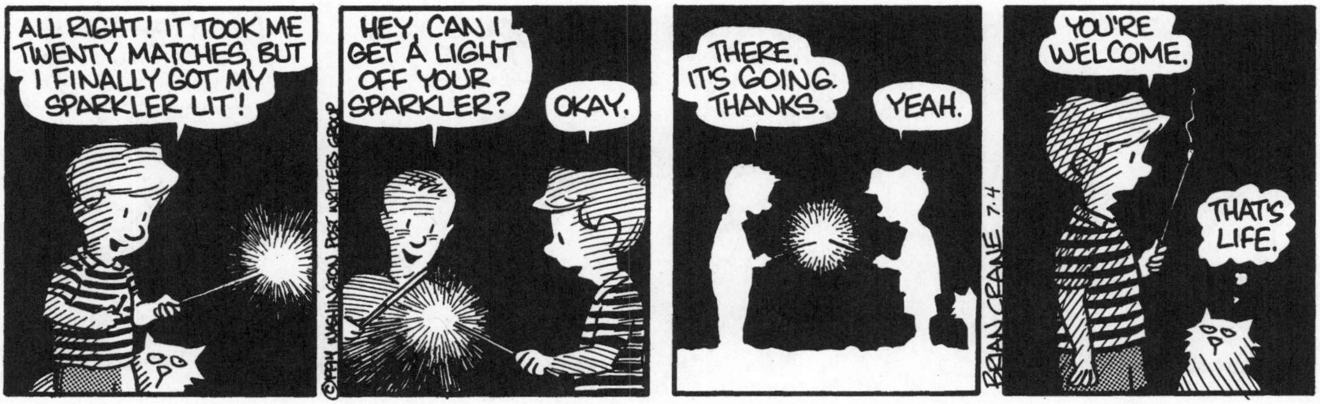
ALL RIGHT! IT TOOK ME TWENTY MATCHES, BUT I FINALLY GOT MY SPARKLER LIT!
© 1994 WASHINGTON POST WRITERS GROUP
HEY, CAN I GET A LIGHT OFF YOUR SPARKLER?
OKAY.
THERE. IT'S GOING. THANKS.
YEAH.
BRIAN CRANE 7·4
YOU'RE WELCOME.
THAT'S LIFE.

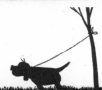

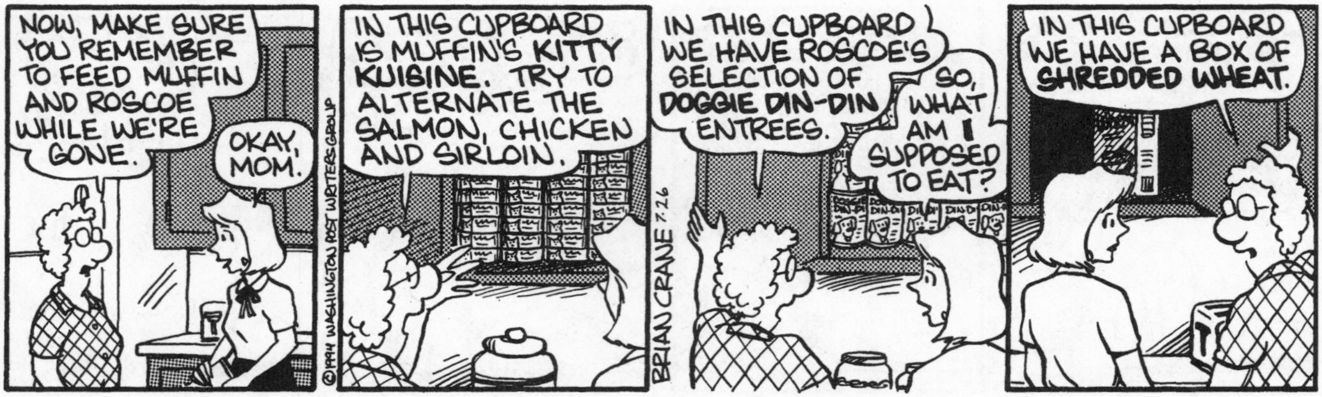
NOW, MAKE SURE YOU REMEMBER TO FEED MUFFIN AND ROSCOE WHILE WE'RE GONE.
OKAY, MOM.
IN THIS CUPBOARD IS MUFFIN'S **KITTY KUISINE**. TRY TO ALTERNATE THE SALMON, CHICKEN AND SIRLOIN.
©1994 WASHINGTON POST WRITERS GROUP
IN THIS CUPBOARD WE HAVE ROSCOE'S SELECTION OF **DOGGIE DIN-DIN** ENTREES.
SO, WHAT AM **I** SUPPOSED TO EAT?
BRIAN CRANE 7.26
IN THIS CUPBOARD WE HAVE A BOX OF **SHREDDED WHEAT**.

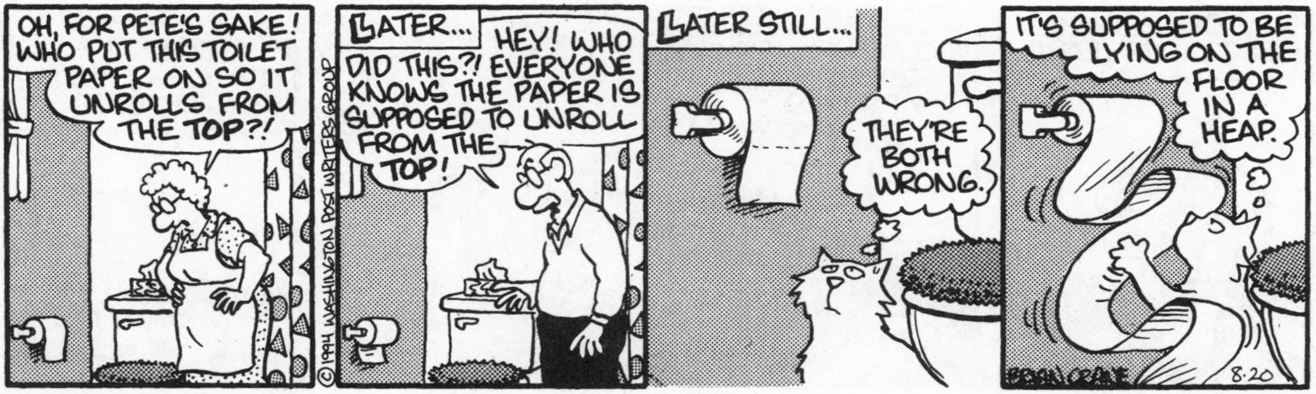
OH, FOR PETE'S SAKE! WHO PUT THIS TOILET PAPER ON SO IT UNROLLS FROM THE **TOP**?!
©1994 WASHINGTON POST WRITERS GROUP
LATER...
HEY! WHO DID THIS?! EVERYONE KNOWS THE PAPER IS SUPPOSED TO UNROLL FROM THE **TOP**!
LATER STILL...
THEY'RE BOTH WRONG.
IT'S SUPPOSED TO BE LYING ON THE FLOOR IN A HEAP.
BRIAN CRANE 8.20

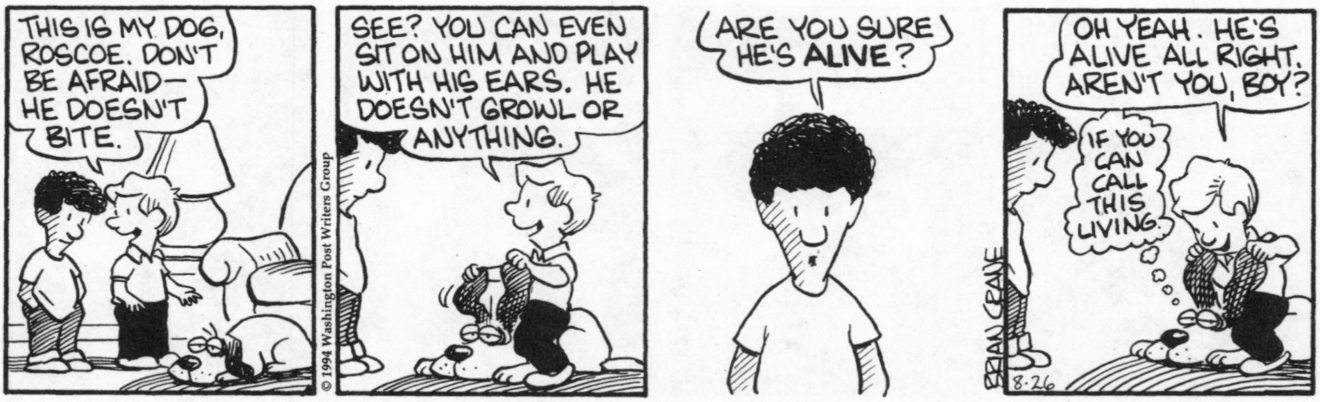
THIS IS MY DOG, ROSCOE. DON'T BE AFRAID— HE DOESN'T BITE.
© 1994 Washington Post Writers Group
SEE? YOU CAN EVEN SIT ON HIM AND PLAY WITH HIS EARS. HE DOESN'T GROWL OR ANYTHING.
ARE YOU SURE HE'S **ALIVE**?
BRIAN CRANE
OH YEAH. HE'S ALIVE ALL RIGHT. AREN'T YOU, BOY?
IF YOU CAN CALL THIS LIVING.
8.26

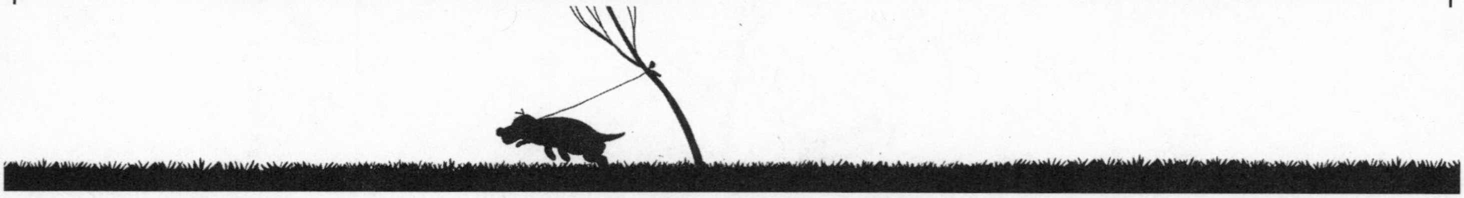

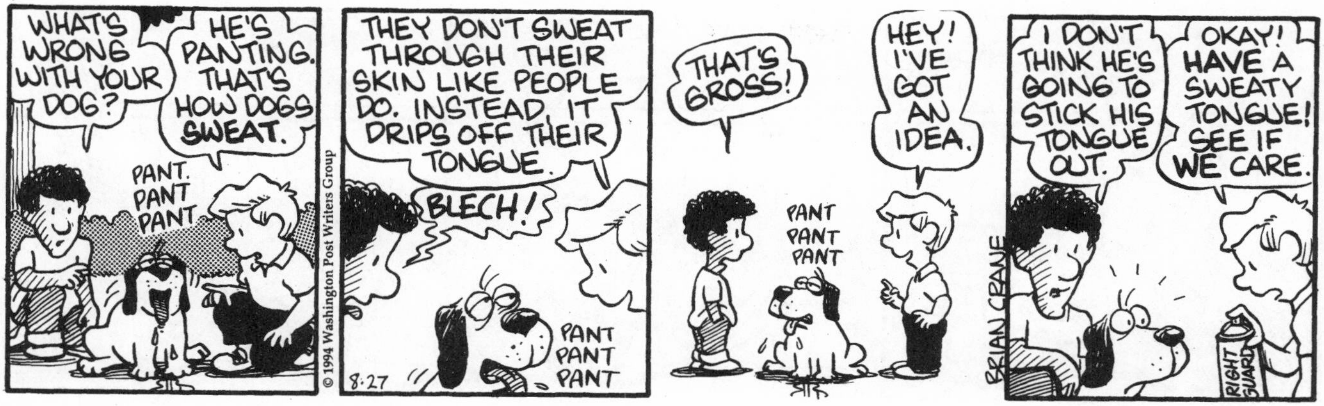
WHAT'S WRONG WITH YOUR DOG?
HE'S PANTING. THAT'S HOW DOGS **SWEAT**.
PANT. PANT PANT
© 1994 Washington Post Writers Group
8·27
THEY DON'T SWEAT THROUGH THEIR SKIN LIKE PEOPLE DO. INSTEAD, IT DRIPS OFF THEIR TONGUE.
BLECH!
PANT PANT PANT
THAT'S GROSS!
PANT PANT PANT
HEY! I'VE GOT AN IDEA.
BRIAN CRANE
I DON'T THINK HE'S GOING TO STICK HIS TONGUE OUT.
OKAY! **HAVE** A SWEATY TONGUE! SEE IF **WE** CARE.
RIGHT GUARD

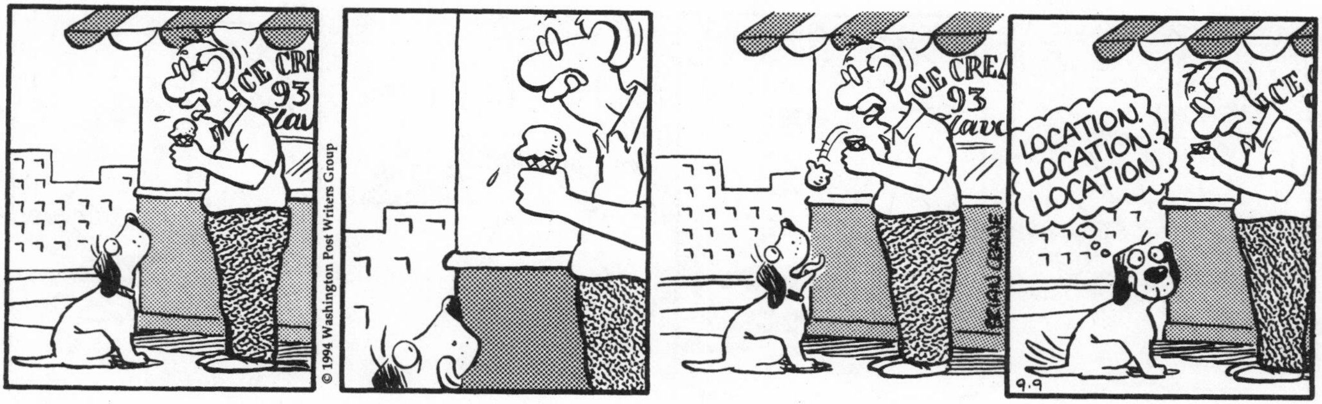
CE CRE 93 Flav
© 1994 Washington Post Writers Group
BRIAN CRANE
LOCATION. LOCATION. LOCATION.
9·9

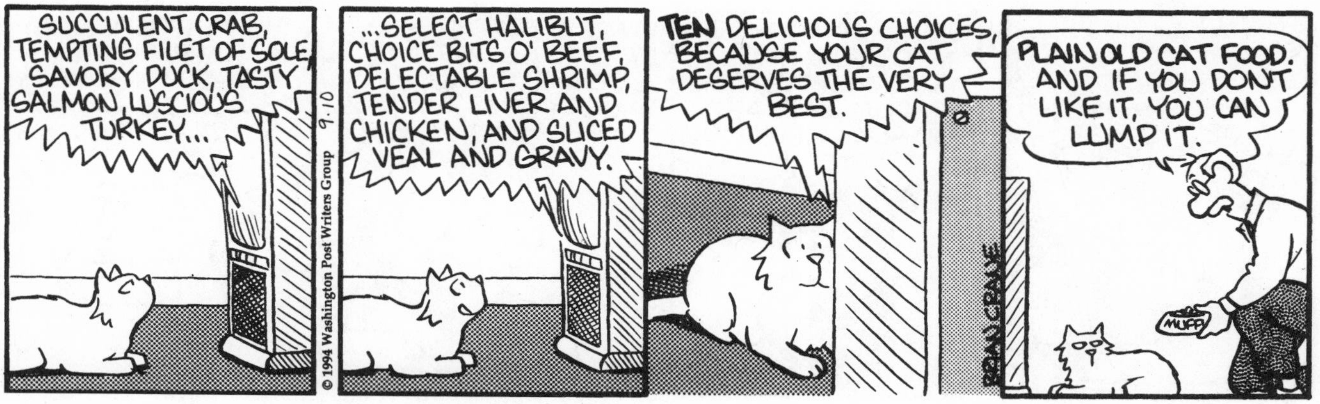
SUCCULENT CRAB, TEMPTING FILET OF SOLE, SAVORY DUCK, TASTY SALMON, LUSCIOUS TURKEY...
9·10
© 1994 Washington Post Writers Group
...SELECT HALIBUT, CHOICE BITS O' BEEF, DELECTABLE SHRIMP, TENDER LIVER AND CHICKEN, AND SLICED VEAL AND GRAVY.
TEN DELICIOUS CHOICES, BECAUSE YOUR CAT DESERVES THE VERY BEST.
BRIAN CRANE
PLAIN OLD CAT FOOD. AND IF YOU DON'T LIKE IT, YOU CAN LUMP IT.
MUFF

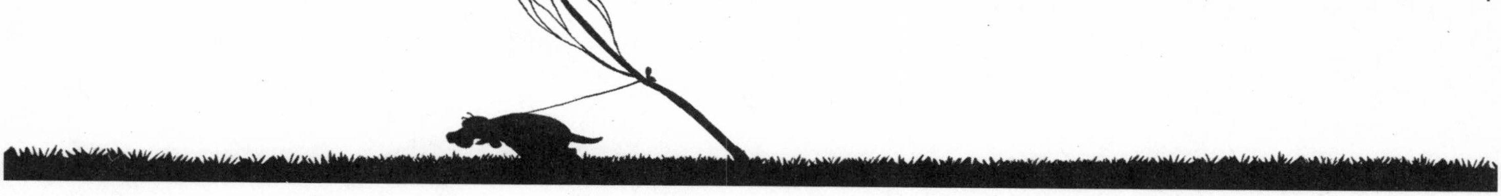

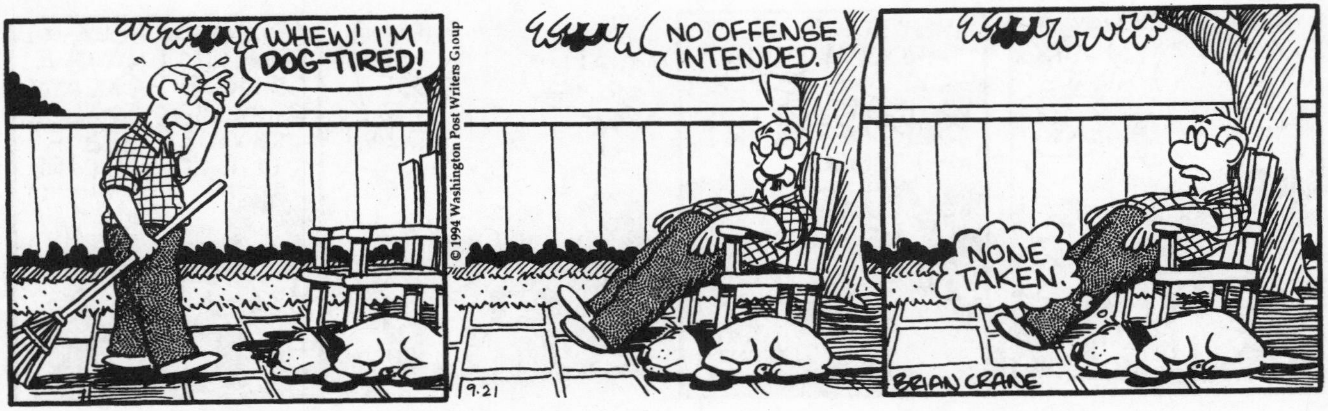
WHEW! I'M DOG-TIRED!
NO OFFENSE INTENDED.
NONE TAKEN.
© 1994 Washington Post Writers Group
9·21
BRIAN CRANE

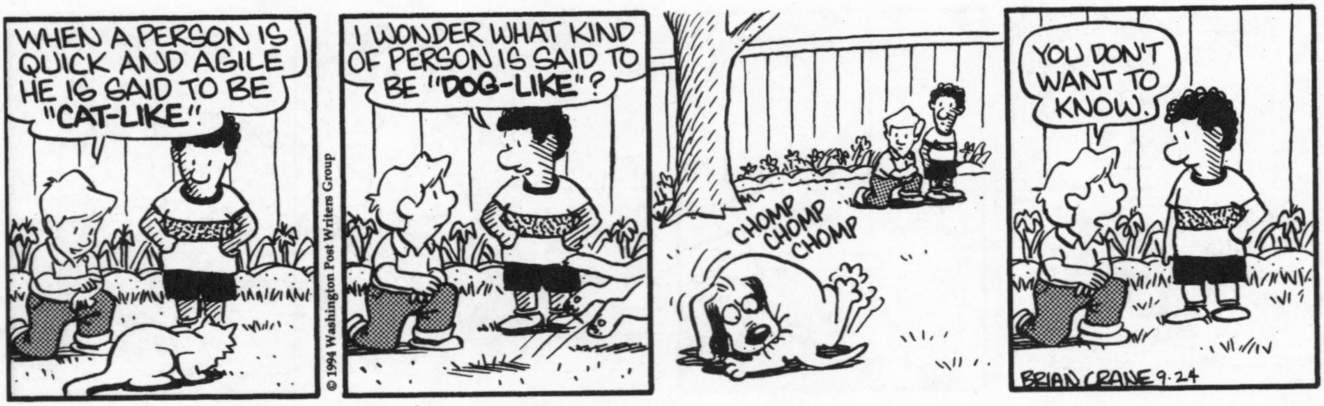
WHEN A PERSON IS QUICK AND AGILE HE IS SAID TO BE "CAT-LIKE".
I WONDER WHAT KIND OF PERSON IS SAID TO BE "DOG-LIKE"?
CHOMP CHOMP CHOMP
YOU DON'T WANT TO KNOW.
© 1994 Washington Post Writers Group
BRIAN CRANE 9·24

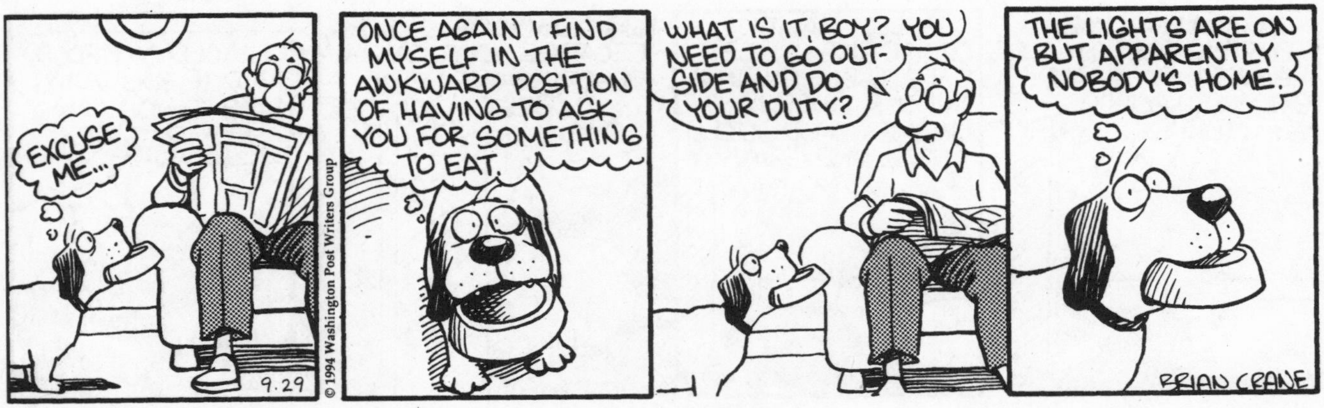
EXCUSE ME...
ONCE AGAIN I FIND MYSELF IN THE AWKWARD POSITION OF HAVING TO ASK YOU FOR SOMETHING TO EAT.
WHAT IS IT, BOY? YOU NEED TO GO OUT-SIDE AND DO YOUR DUTY?
THE LIGHTS ARE ON BUT APPARENTLY NOBODY'S HOME.
© 1994 Washington Post Writers Group
9·29
BRIAN CRANE

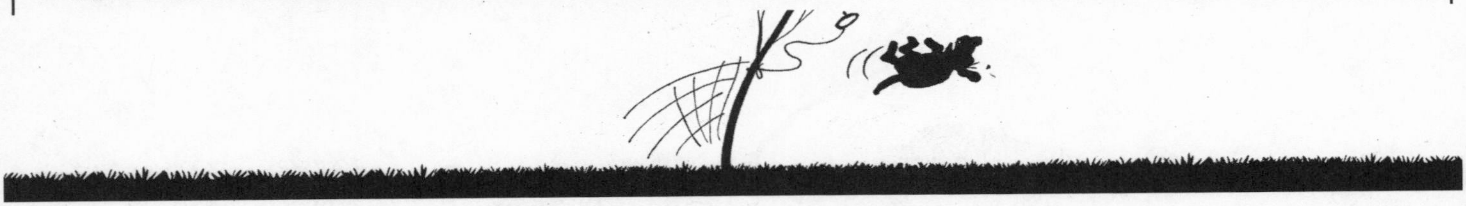

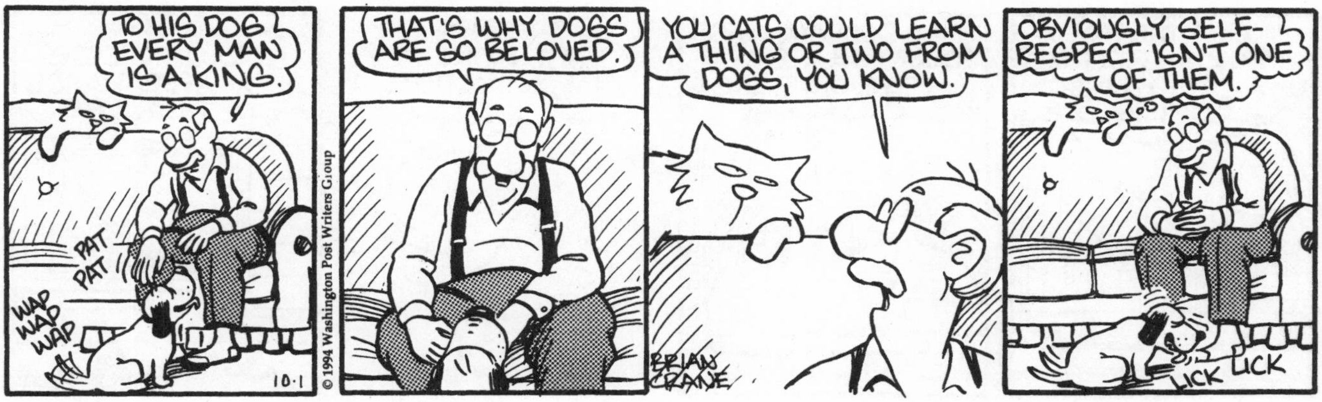
TO HIS DOG EVERY MAN IS A KING.
PAT PAT
WAP WAP WAP
10·1
© 1994 Washington Post Writers Group
THAT'S WHY DOGS ARE SO BELOVED.
YOU CATS COULD LEARN A THING OR TWO FROM DOGS, YOU KNOW.
BRIAN CRANE
OBVIOUSLY, SELF-RESPECT ISN'T ONE OF THEM.
LICK LICK

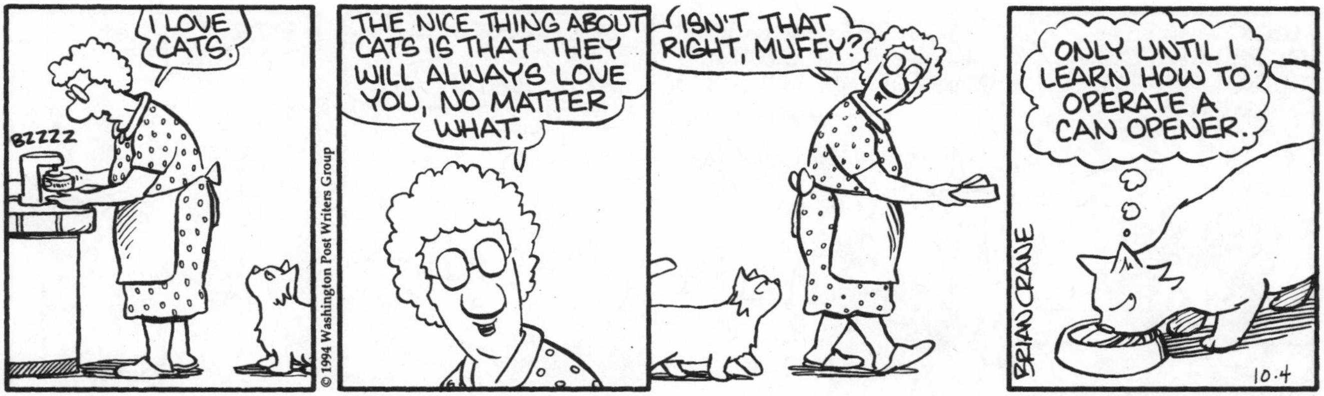
I LOVE CATS.
BZZZZ
© 1994 Washington Post Writers Group
THE NICE THING ABOUT CATS IS THAT THEY WILL ALWAYS LOVE YOU, NO MATTER WHAT.
ISN'T THAT RIGHT, MUFFY?
BRIAN CRANE
ONLY UNTIL I LEARN HOW TO OPERATE A CAN OPENER.
10·4

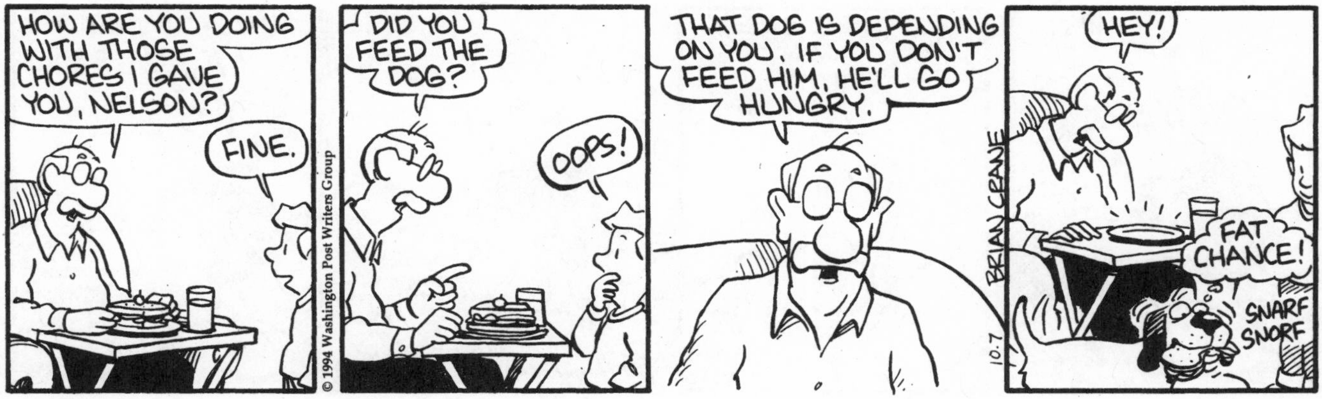
HOW ARE YOU DOING WITH THOSE CHORES I GAVE YOU, NELSON?
FINE.
© 1994 Washington Post Writers Group
DID YOU FEED THE DOG?
OOPS!
THAT DOG IS DEPENDING ON YOU. IF YOU DON'T FEED HIM, HE'LL GO HUNGRY.
BRIAN CRANE
10·7
HEY!
FAT CHANCE!
SNARF SNORF

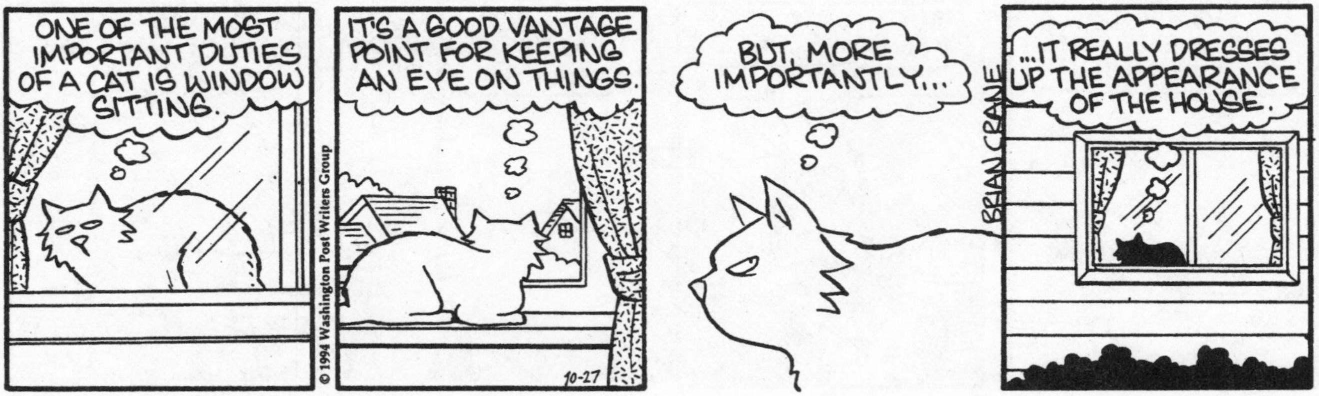
ONE OF THE MOST IMPORTANT DUTIES OF A CAT IS WINDOW SITTING.
IT'S A GOOD VANTAGE POINT FOR KEEPING AN EYE ON THINGS.
© 1994 Washington Post Writers Group
10-27
BUT, MORE IMPORTANTLY,...
BRIAN CRANE
...IT REALLY DRESSES UP THE APPEARANCE OF THE HOUSE.

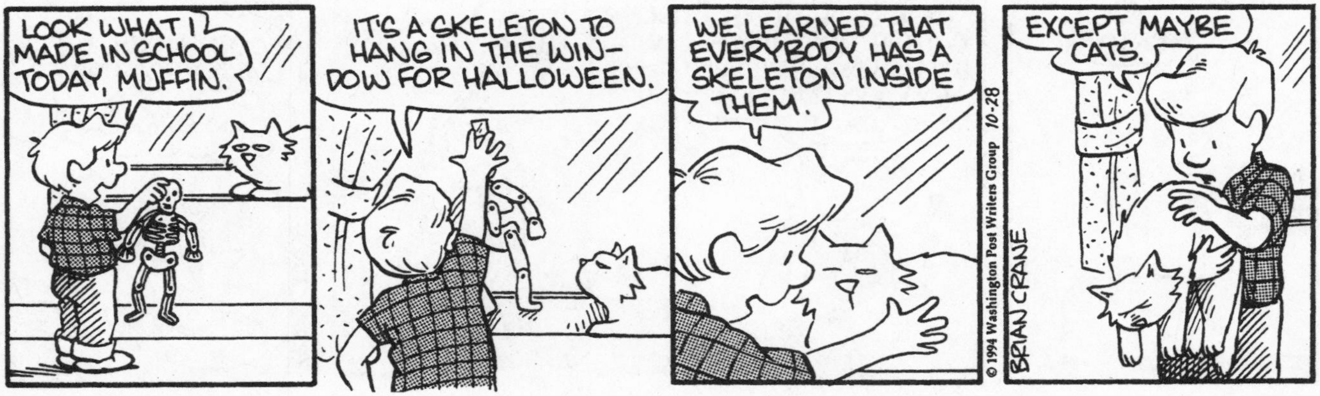
LOOK WHAT I MADE IN SCHOOL TODAY, MUFFIN.
IT'S A SKELETON TO HANG IN THE WINDOW FOR HALLOWEEN.
WE LEARNED THAT EVERYBODY HAS A SKELETON INSIDE THEM.
10-28
© 1994 Washington Post Writers Group
BRIAN CRANE
EXCEPT MAYBE CATS.

114

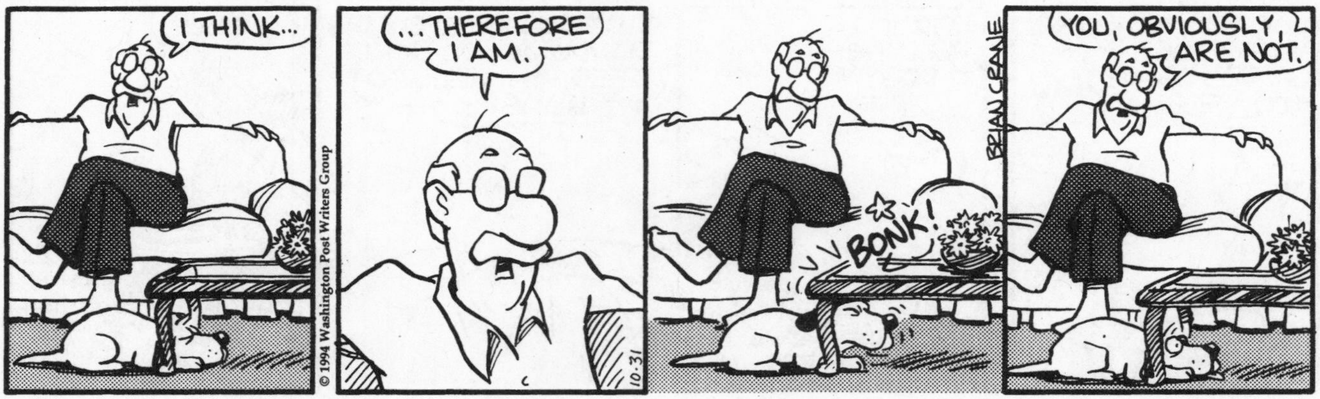
I THINK...
© 1994 Washington Post Writers Group
...THEREFORE I AM.
10-31
BONK!
BRIAN CRANE
YOU, OBVIOUSLY, ARE NOT.

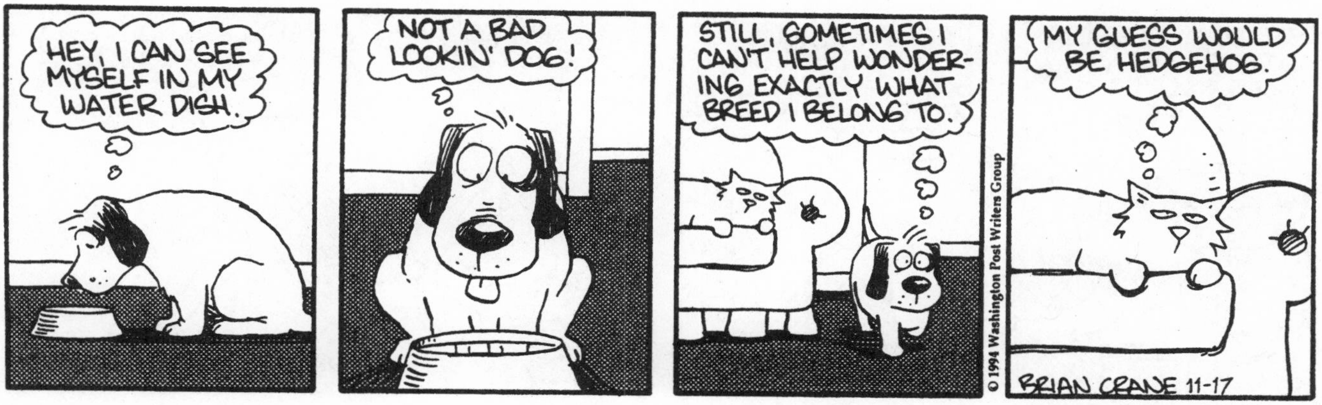

HEY, I CAN SEE MYSELF IN MY WATER DISH.
NOT A BAD LOOKIN' DOG!
STILL, SOMETIMES I CAN'T HELP WONDERING EXACTLY WHAT BREED I BELONG TO.
MY GUESS WOULD BE HEDGEHOG.
© 1994 Washington Post Writers Group
BRIAN CRANE 11-17

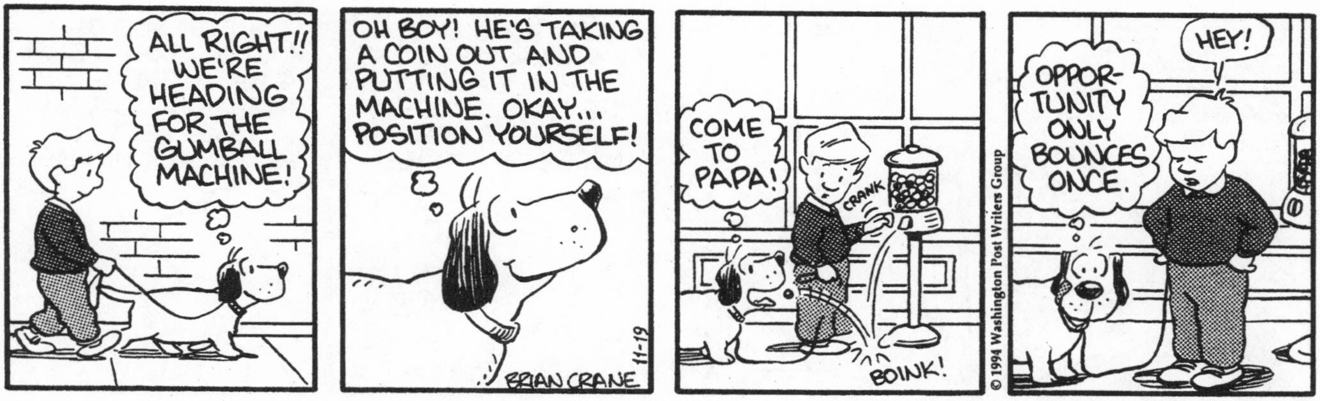

ALL RIGHT!! WE'RE HEADING FOR THE GUMBALL MACHINE!
OH BOY! HE'S TAKING A COIN OUT AND PUTTING IT IN THE MACHINE. OKAY... POSITION YOURSELF!
11-19
BRIAN CRANE
COME TO PAPA!
CRANK
BOINK!
© 1994 Washington Post Writers Group
HEY!
OPPORTUNITY ONLY BOUNCES ONCE.

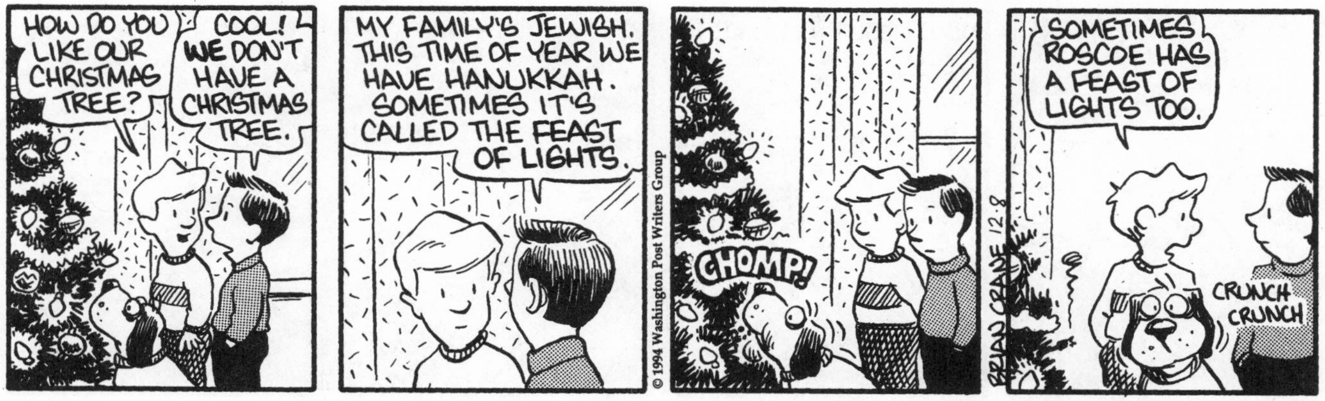

HOW DO YOU LIKE OUR CHRISTMAS TREE?
COOL! WE DON'T HAVE A CHRISTMAS TREE.
MY FAMILY'S JEWISH. THIS TIME OF YEAR WE HAVE HANUKKAH. SOMETIMES IT'S CALLED THE FEAST OF LIGHTS.
© 1994 Washington Post Writers Group
CHOMP!
BRIAN CRANE 12-8
SOMETIMES ROSCOE HAS A FEAST OF LIGHTS TOO.
CRUNCH CRUNCH

116

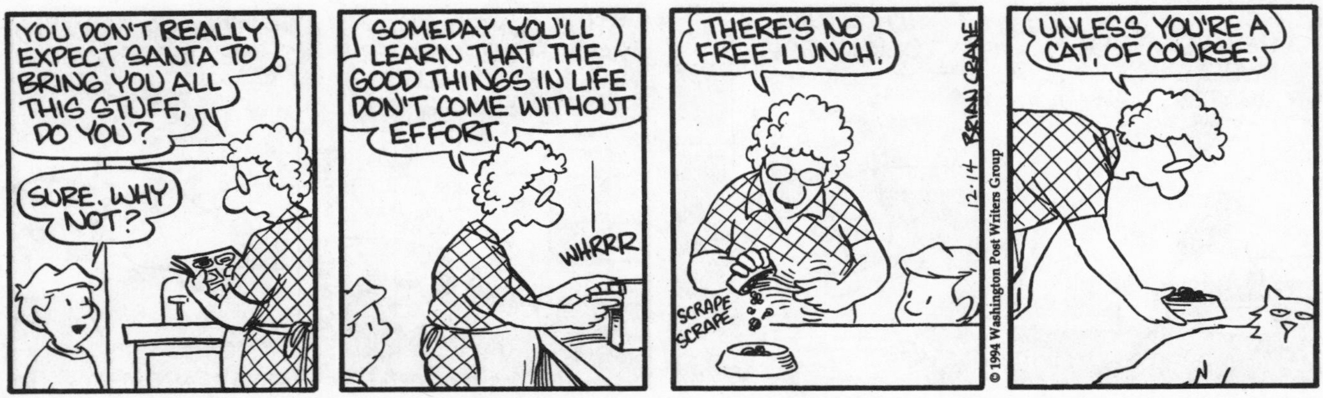
YOU DON'T REALLY EXPECT SANTA TO BRING YOU ALL THIS STUFF, DO YOU?
SURE. WHY NOT?
SOMEDAY YOU'LL LEARN THAT THE GOOD THINGS IN LIFE DON'T COME WITHOUT EFFORT.
WHRRR
THERE'S NO FREE LUNCH.
SCRAPE SCRAPE
12·14 BRIAN CRANE
© 1994 Washington Post Writers Group
UNLESS YOU'RE A CAT, OF COURSE.

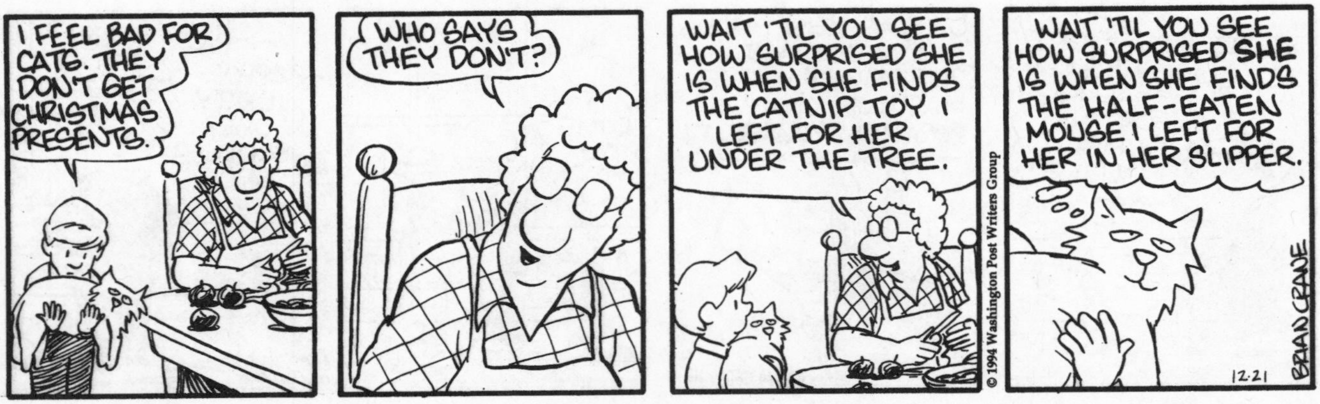
I FEEL BAD FOR CATS. THEY DON'T GET CHRISTMAS PRESENTS.
WHO SAYS THEY DON'T?
WAIT 'TIL YOU SEE HOW SURPRISED SHE IS WHEN SHE FINDS THE CATNIP TOY I LEFT FOR HER UNDER THE TREE.
© 1994 Washington Post Writers Group
WAIT 'TIL YOU SEE HOW SURPRISED SHE IS WHEN SHE FINDS THE HALF-EATEN MOUSE I LEFT FOR HER IN HER SLIPPER.
12·21 BRIAN CRANE

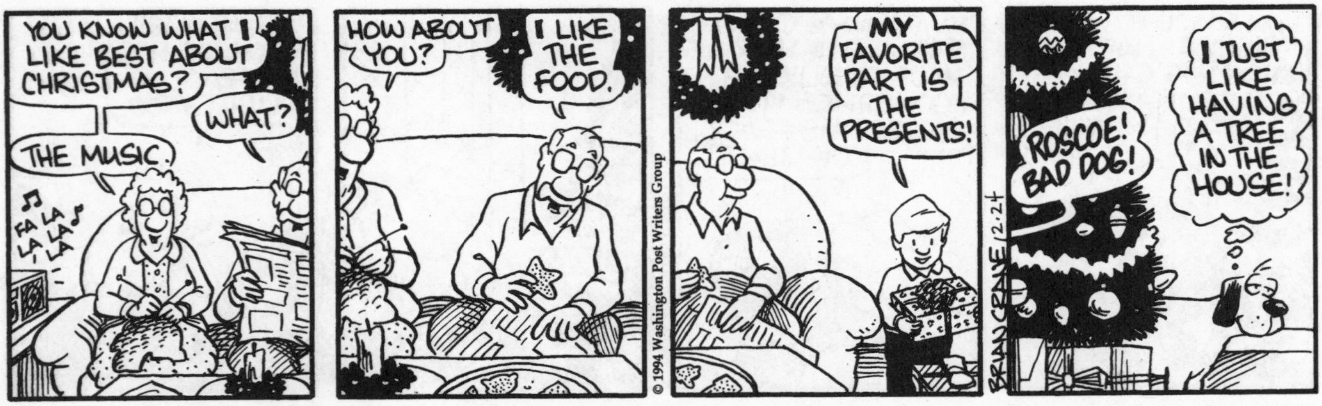
YOU KNOW WHAT I LIKE BEST ABOUT CHRISTMAS?
WHAT?
THE MUSIC.
FA LA LA LA LA
HOW ABOUT YOU?
I LIKE THE FOOD.
© 1994 Washington Post Writers Group
MY FAVORITE PART IS THE PRESENTS!
BRIAN CRANE 12·24
ROSCOE! BAD DOG!
I JUST LIKE HAVING A TREE IN THE HOUSE!

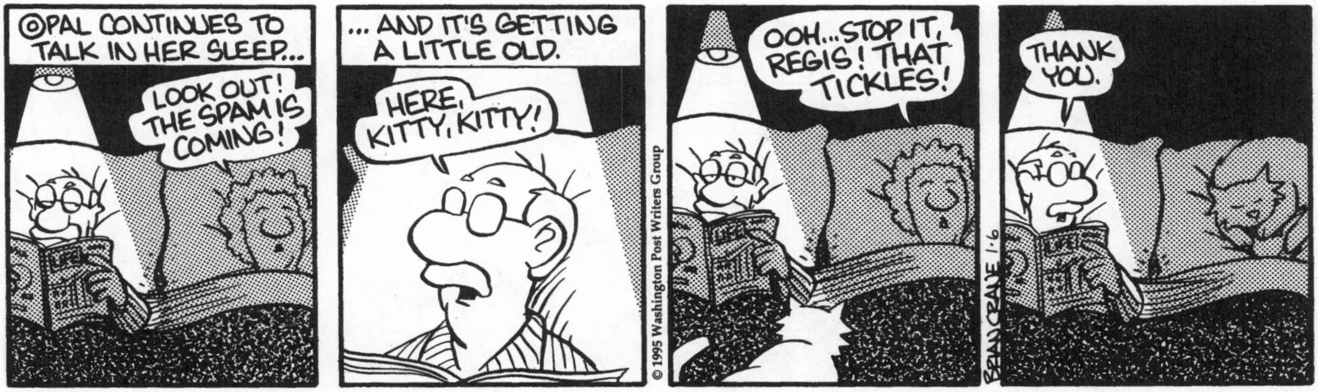
©PAL CONTINUES TO TALK IN HER SLEEP...
LOOK OUT! THE SPAM IS COMING!
... AND IT'S GETTING A LITTLE OLD.
HERE, KITTY, KITTY!
© 1995 Washington Post Writers Group
OOH...STOP IT, REGIS! THAT TICKLES!
THANK YOU.

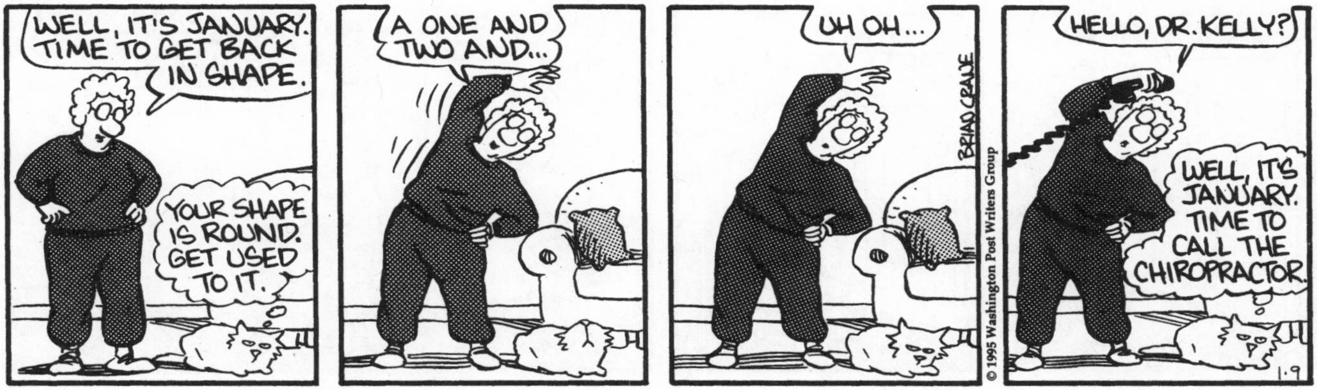
WELL, IT'S JANUARY. TIME TO GET BACK IN SHAPE.
YOUR SHAPE IS ROUND. GET USED TO IT.
A ONE AND TWO AND...
UH OH...
© 1995 Washington Post Writers Group
HELLO, DR. KELLY?
WELL, IT'S JANUARY. TIME TO CALL THE CHIROPRACTOR.

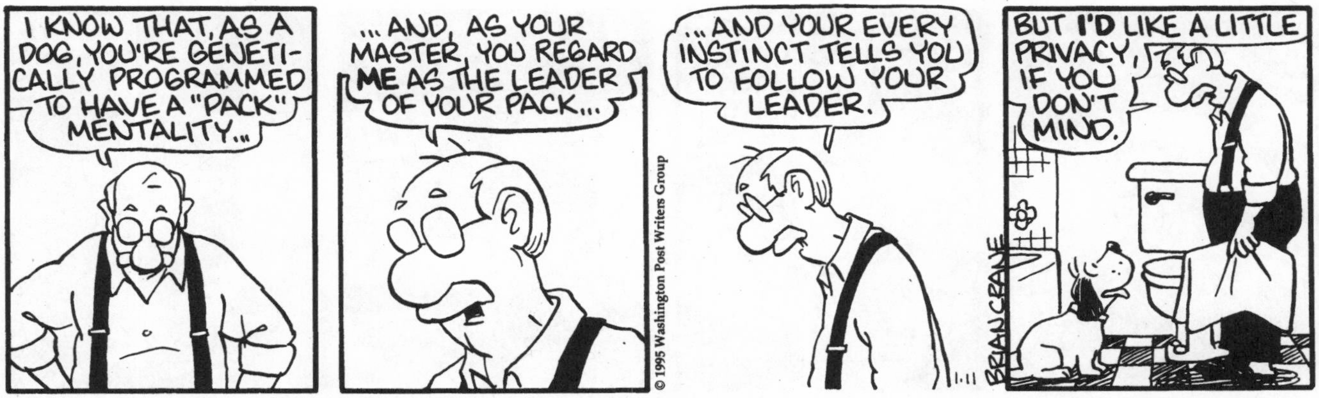
I KNOW THAT, AS A DOG, YOU'RE GENETICALLY PROGRAMMED TO HAVE A "PACK" MENTALITY...
... AND, AS YOUR MASTER, YOU REGARD **ME** AS THE LEADER OF YOUR PACK...
© 1995 Washington Post Writers Group
... AND YOUR EVERY INSTINCT TELLS YOU TO FOLLOW YOUR LEADER.
BUT **I'D** LIKE A LITTLE PRIVACY, IF YOU DON'T MIND.

118

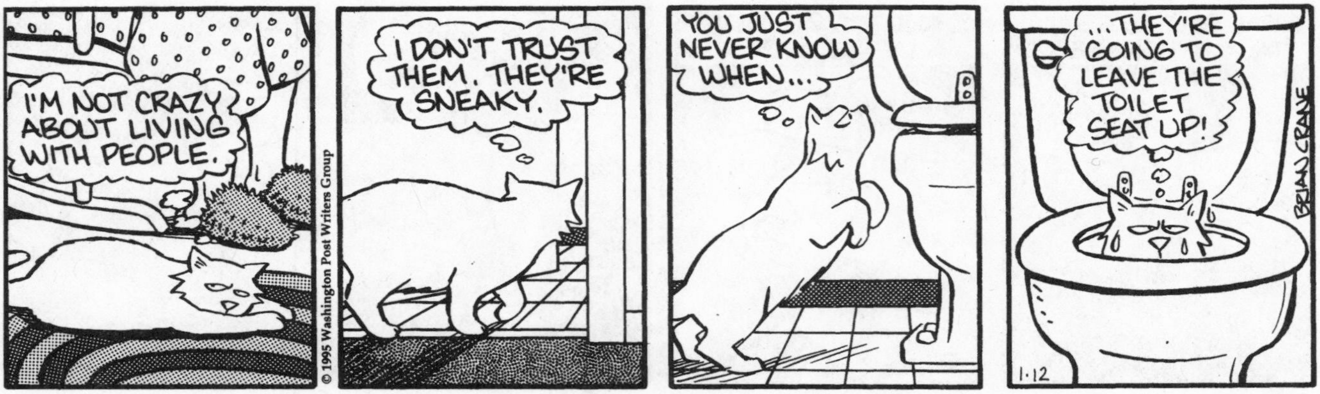
I'M NOT CRAZY ABOUT LIVING WITH PEOPLE.
© 1995 Washington Post Writers Group
I DON'T TRUST THEM. THEY'RE SNEAKY.
YOU JUST NEVER KNOW WHEN...
...THEY'RE GOING TO LEAVE THE TOILET SEAT UP!
BRIAN CRANE
1·12

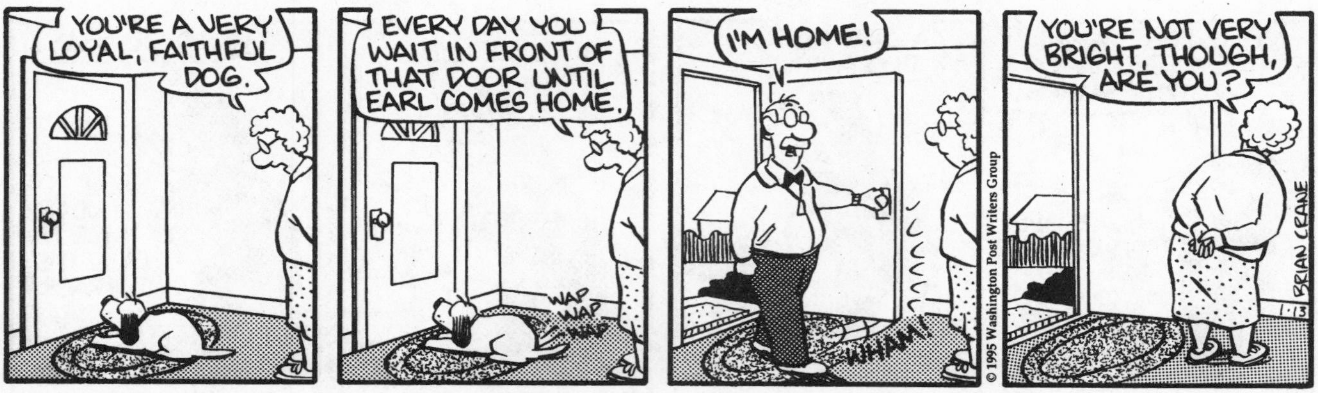
YOU'RE A VERY LOYAL, FAITHFUL DOG.
EVERY DAY YOU WAIT IN FRONT OF THAT DOOR UNTIL EARL COMES HOME.
WAP WAP WAP
I'M HOME!
WHAM!
© 1995 Washington Post Writers Group
YOU'RE NOT VERY BRIGHT, THOUGH, ARE YOU?
BRIAN CRANE
1·13

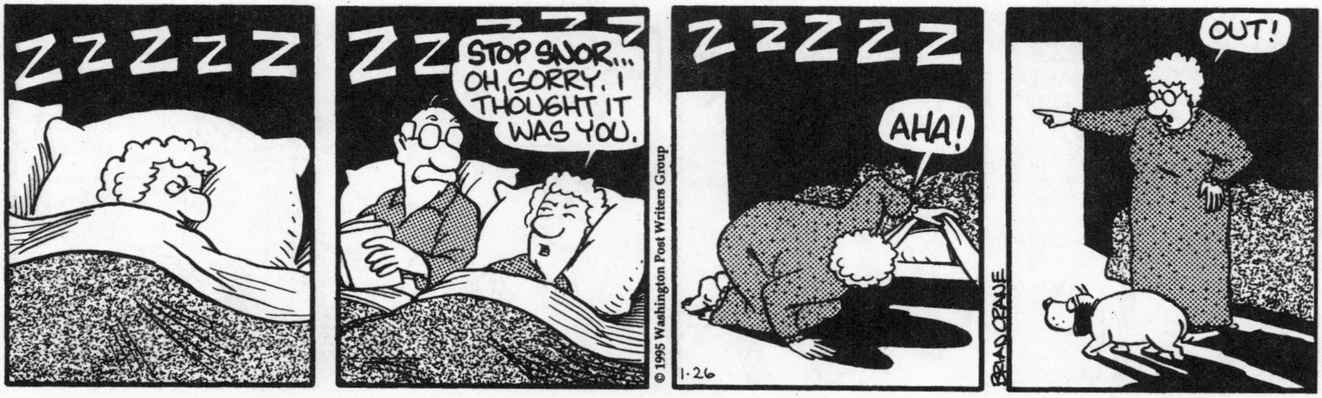
ZZZZZ
ZZ
STOP SNOR... OH, SORRY. I THOUGHT IT WAS YOU.
© 1995 Washington Post Writers Group
ZZZZZZ
AHA!
1·26
BRIAN CRANE
OUT!

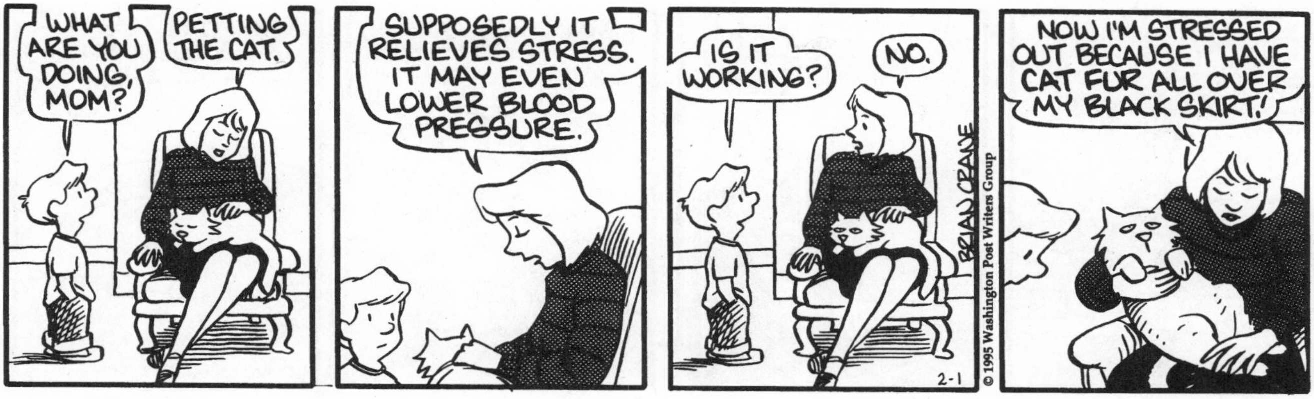
WHAT ARE YOU DOING, MOM?
PETTING THE CAT.
SUPPOSEDLY IT RELIEVES STRESS. IT MAY EVEN LOWER BLOOD PRESSURE.
IS IT WORKING?
NO.
BRIAN CRANE
2-1
© 1995 Washington Post Writers Group
NOW I'M STRESSED OUT BECAUSE I HAVE CAT FUR ALL OVER MY BLACK SKIRT!

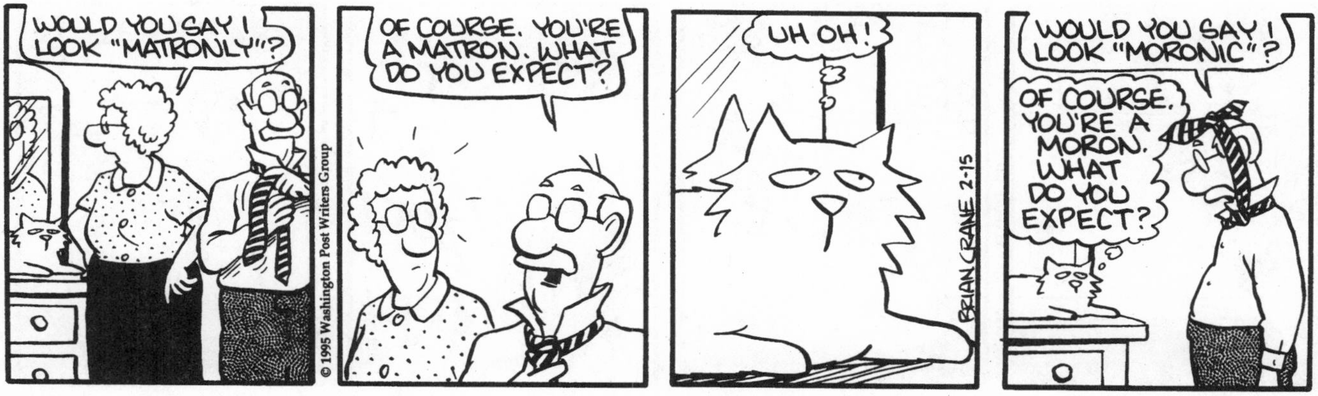
WOULD YOU SAY I LOOK "MATRONLY"?
© 1995 Washington Post Writers Group
OF COURSE. YOU'RE A MATRON. WHAT DO YOU EXPECT?
UH OH!
BRIAN CRANE 2-15
WOULD YOU SAY I LOOK "MORONIC"?
OF COURSE. YOU'RE A MORON. WHAT DO YOU EXPECT?

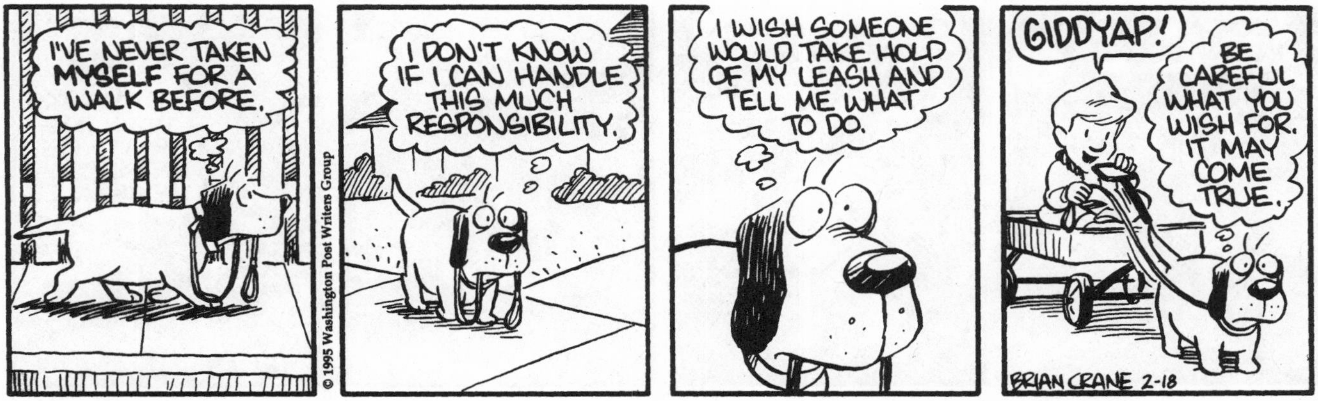
I'VE NEVER TAKEN MYSELF FOR A WALK BEFORE.
© 1995 Washington Post Writers Group
I DON'T KNOW IF I CAN HANDLE THIS MUCH RESPONSIBILITY.
I WISH SOMEONE WOULD TAKE HOLD OF MY LEASH AND TELL ME WHAT TO DO.
GIDDYAP!
BE CAREFUL WHAT YOU WISH FOR. IT MAY COME TRUE.
BRIAN CRANE 2-18

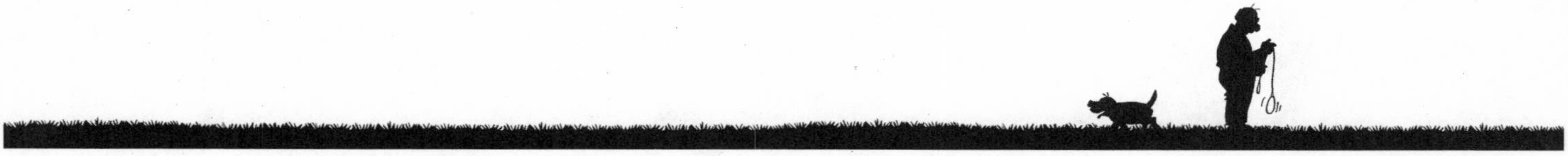

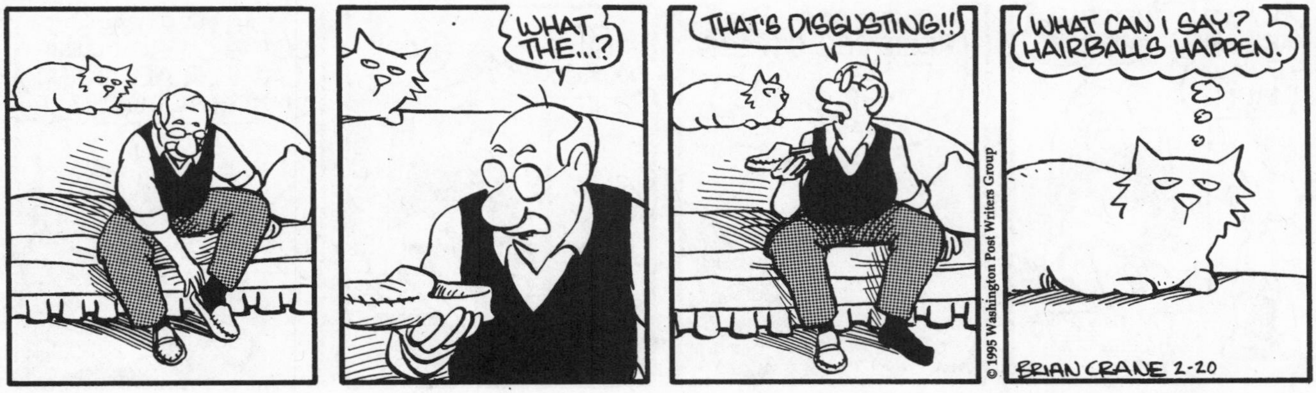
WHAT THE...?
THAT'S DISGUSTING!!
WHAT CAN I SAY? HAIRBALLS HAPPEN.
© 1995 Washington Post Writers Group
BRIAN CRANE 2-20

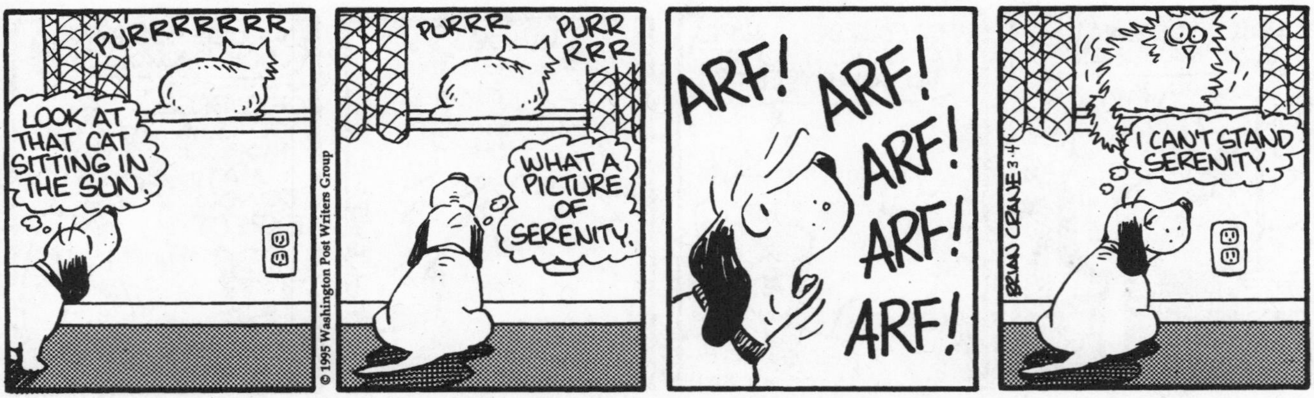
PURRRRRRRR
LOOK AT THAT CAT SITTING IN THE SUN.
PURRR
PURR RRR
WHAT A PICTURE OF SERENITY.
© 1995 Washington Post Writers Group
ARF! ARF! ARF! ARF! ARF!
BRIAN CRANE 3-4
I CAN'T STAND SERENITY.

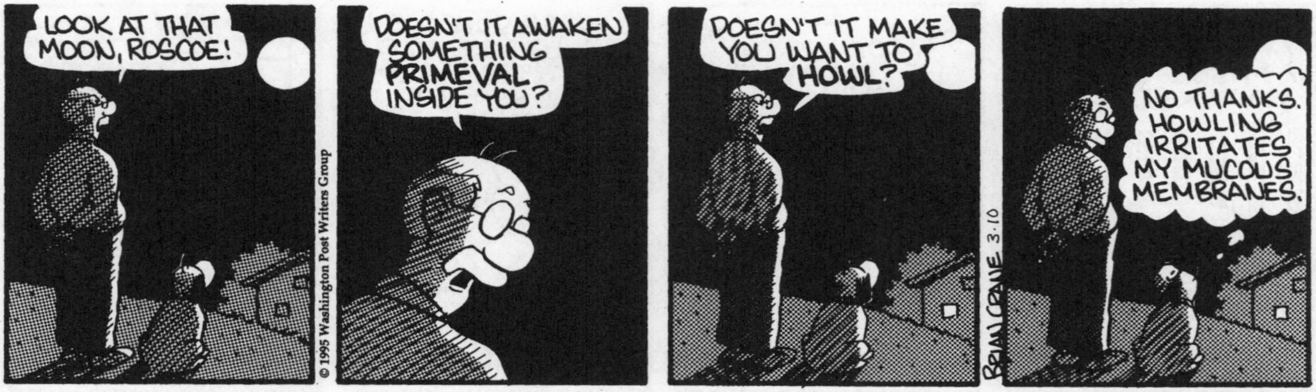
LOOK AT THAT MOON, ROSCOE!
DOESN'T IT AWAKEN SOMETHING PRIMEVAL INSIDE YOU?
© 1995 Washington Post Writers Group
DOESN'T IT MAKE YOU WANT TO HOWL?
BRIAN CRANE 3-10
NO THANKS. HOWLING IRRITATES MY MUCOUS MEMBRANES.

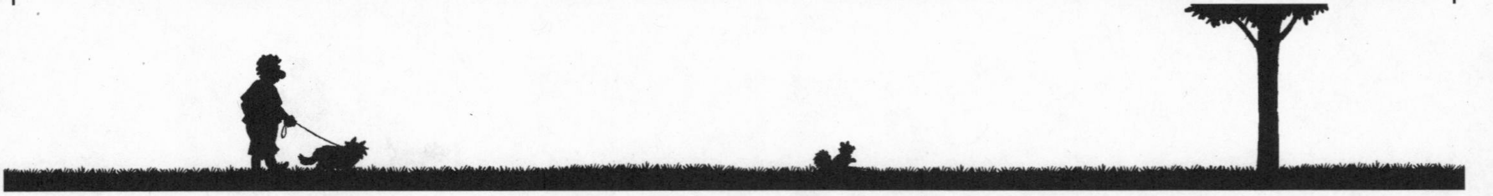

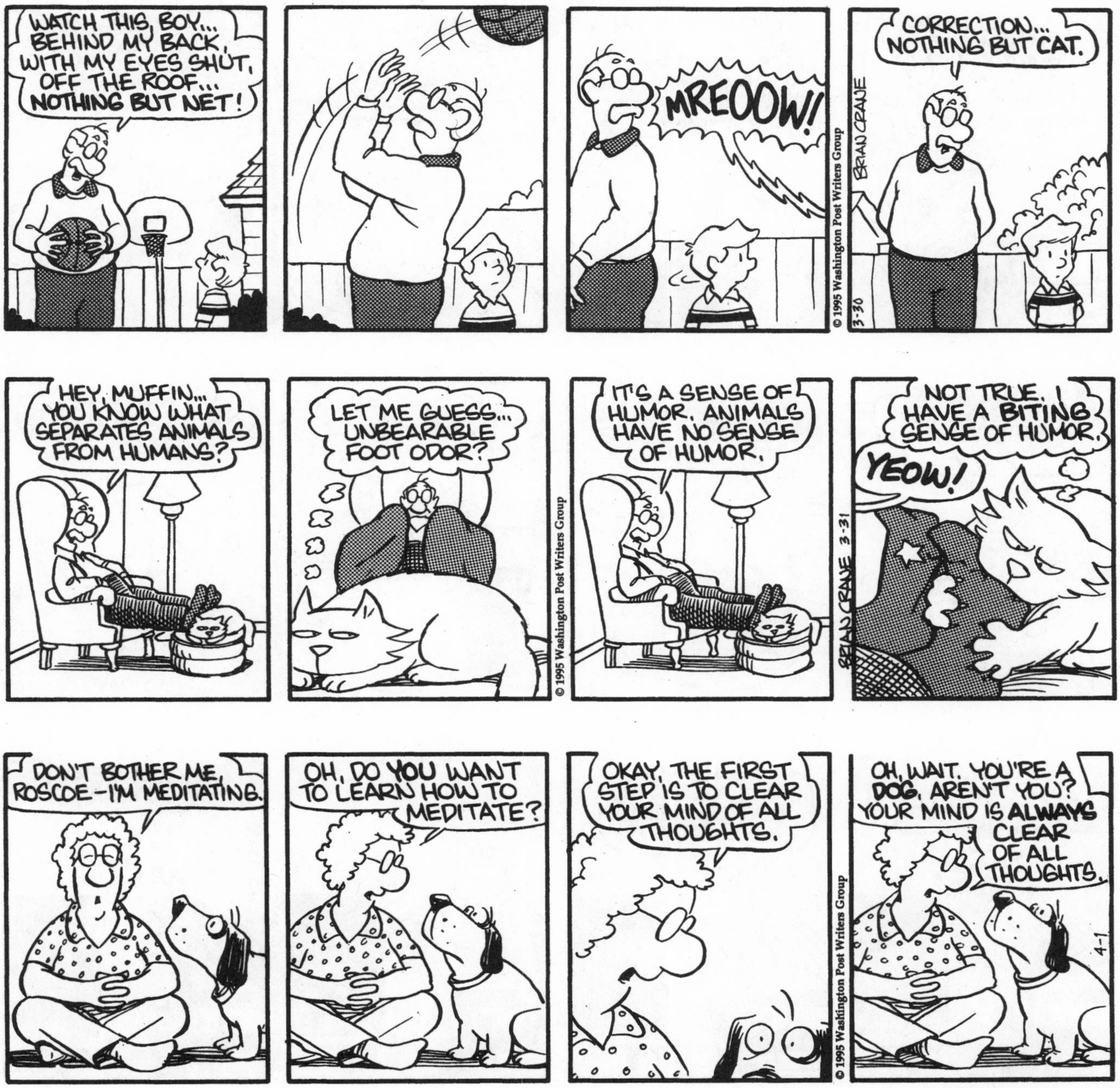
WATCH THIS, BOY... BEHIND MY BACK, WITH MY EYES SHUT, OFF THE ROOF... NOTHING BUT NET!
MREOOW!
CORRECTION... NOTHING BUT CAT.
© 1995 Washington Post Writers Group 3-30
BRIAN CRANE
HEY, MUFFIN... YOU KNOW WHAT SEPARATES ANIMALS FROM HUMANS?
LET ME GUESS... UNBEARABLE FOOT ODOR?
© 1995 Washington Post Writers Group
IT'S A SENSE OF HUMOR. ANIMALS HAVE NO SENSE OF HUMOR.
BRIAN CRANE 3-31
YEOW!
NOT TRUE. I HAVE A BITING SENSE OF HUMOR.
DON'T BOTHER ME, ROSCOE–I'M MEDITATING.
OH, DO YOU WANT TO LEARN HOW TO MEDITATE?
OKAY, THE FIRST STEP IS TO CLEAR YOUR MIND OF ALL THOUGHTS.
© 1995 Washington Post Writers Group
OH, WAIT. YOU'RE A DOG, AREN'T YOU? YOUR MIND IS ALWAYS CLEAR OF ALL THOUGHTS.
4-1

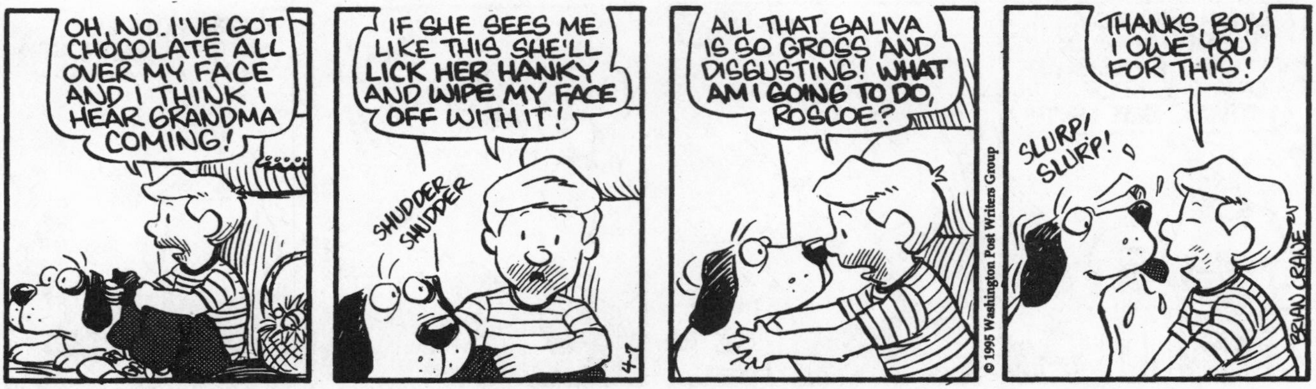

OH, NO. I'VE GOT CHOCOLATE ALL OVER MY FACE AND I THINK I HEAR GRANDMA COMING!
IF SHE SEES ME LIKE THIS SHE'LL LICK HER HANKY AND WIPE MY FACE OFF WITH IT!
SHUDDER SHUDDER
4-7
ALL THAT SALIVA IS SO GROSS AND DISGUSTING! WHAT AM I GOING TO DO, ROSCOE?
© 1995 Washington Post Writers Group
THANKS, BOY. I OWE YOU FOR THIS!
SLURP! SLURP!
BRIAN CRANE

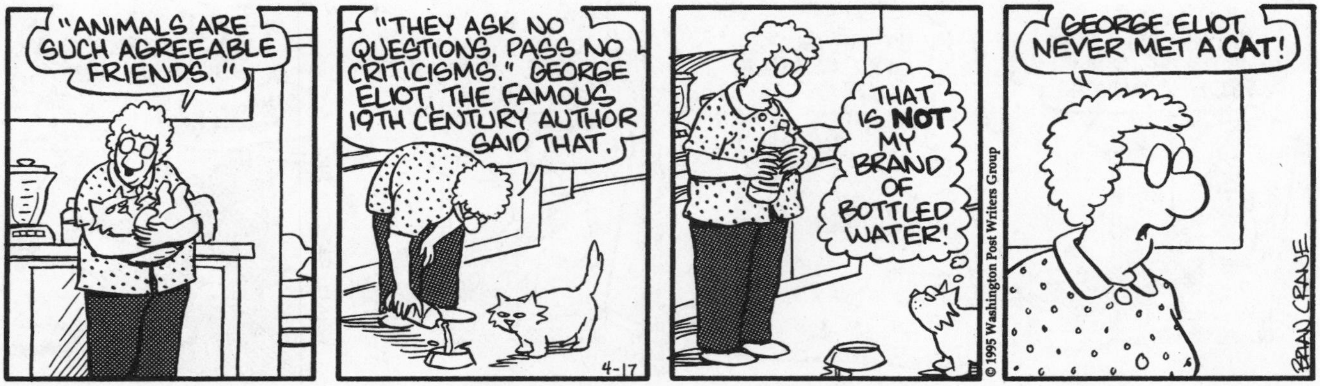

"ANIMALS ARE SUCH AGREEABLE FRIENDS."
"THEY ASK NO QUESTIONS, PASS NO CRITICISMS." GEORGE ELIOT, THE FAMOUS 19TH CENTURY AUTHOR SAID THAT.
4-17
THAT IS NOT MY BRAND OF BOTTLED WATER!
© 1995 Washington Post Writers Group
GEORGE ELIOT NEVER MET A CAT!
BRIAN CRANE

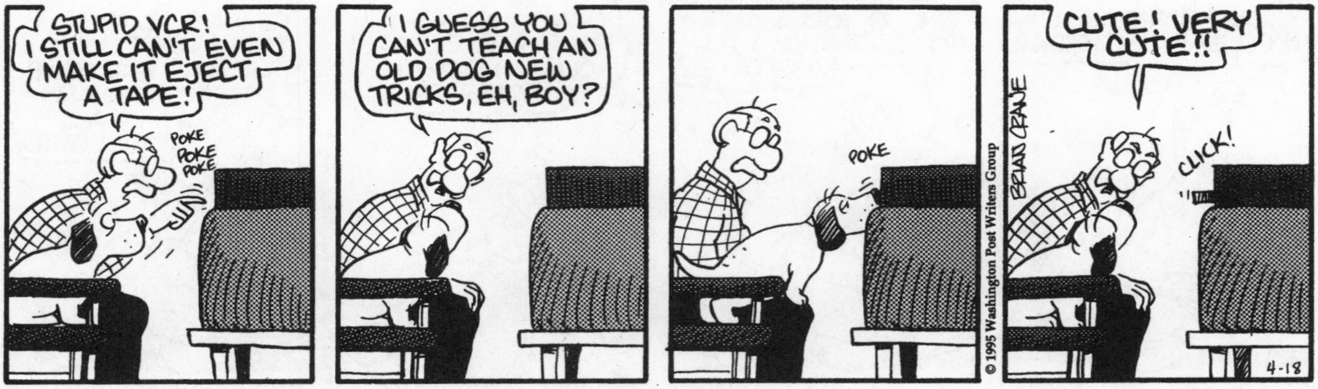

STUPID VCR! I STILL CAN'T EVEN MAKE IT EJECT A TAPE!
POKE POKE POKE
I GUESS YOU CAN'T TEACH AN OLD DOG NEW TRICKS, EH, BOY?
POKE
© 1995 Washington Post Writers Group
BRIAN CRANE
CUTE! VERY CUTE!!
CLICK!
4-18

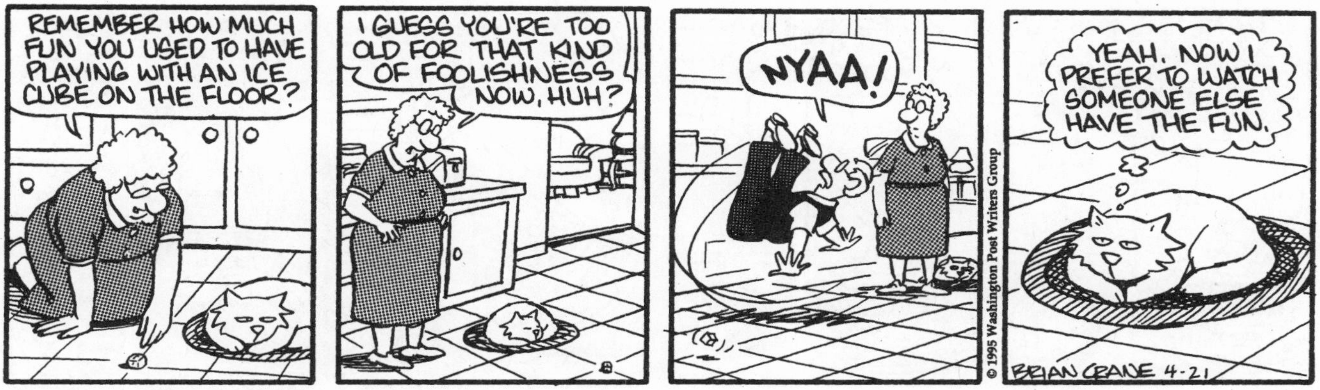
REMEMBER HOW MUCH FUN YOU USED TO HAVE PLAYING WITH AN ICE CUBE ON THE FLOOR?
I GUESS YOU'RE TOO OLD FOR THAT KIND OF FOOLISHNESS NOW, HUH?
NYAA!
© 1995 Washington Post Writers Group
YEAH. NOW I PREFER TO WATCH SOMEONE ELSE HAVE THE FUN.
BRIAN CRANE 4-21

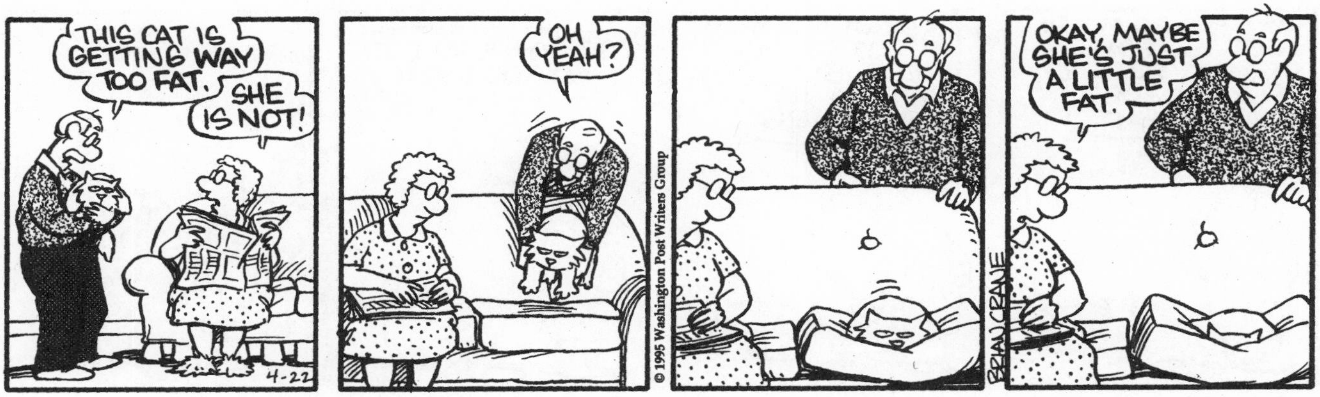
THIS CAT IS GETTING WAY TOO FAT.
SHE IS NOT!
4-22
OH YEAH?
© 1995 Washington Post Writers Group
BRIAN CRANE
OKAY, MAYBE SHE'S JUST A LITTLE FAT.

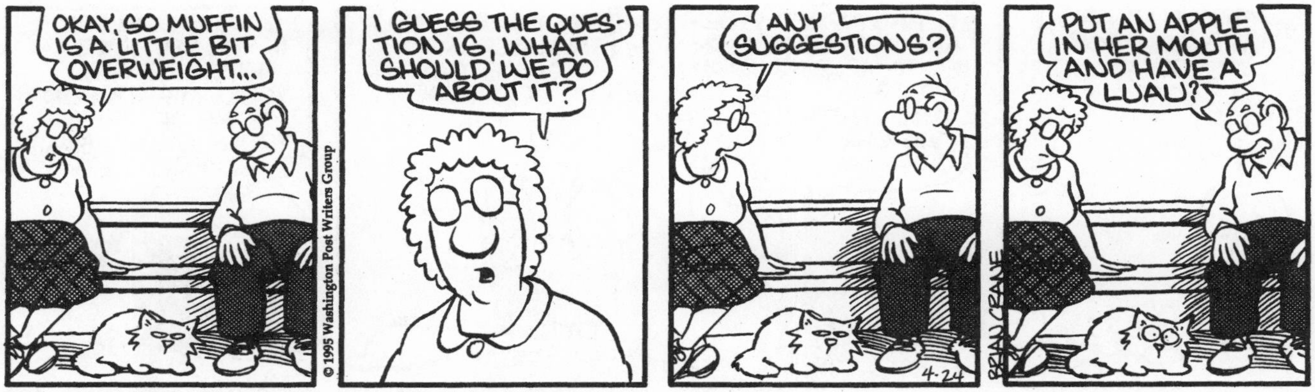
OKAY, SO MUFFIN IS A LITTLE BIT OVERWEIGHT...
© 1995 Washington Post Writers Group
I GUESS THE QUESTION IS, WHAT SHOULD WE DO ABOUT IT?
ANY SUGGESTIONS?
4-24
BRIAN CRANE
PUT AN APPLE IN HER MOUTH AND HAVE A LUAU?

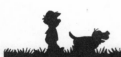

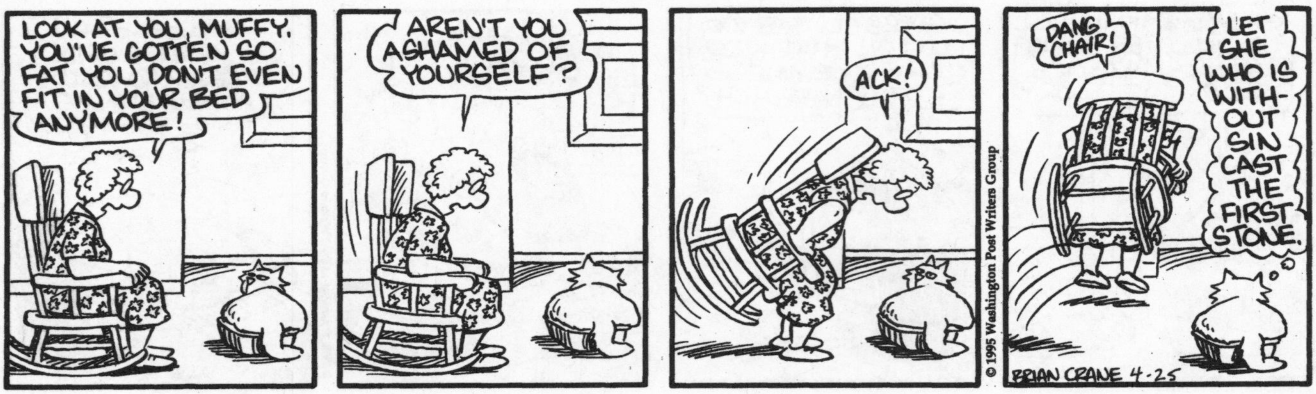
LOOK AT YOU, MUFFY. YOU'VE GOTTEN SO FAT YOU DON'T EVEN FIT IN YOUR BED ANYMORE!
AREN'T YOU ASHAMED OF YOURSELF?
ACK!
DANG CHAIR!
LET SHE WHO IS WITHOUT SIN CAST THE FIRST STONE.
© 1995 Washington Post Writers Group
BRIAN CRANE 4-25

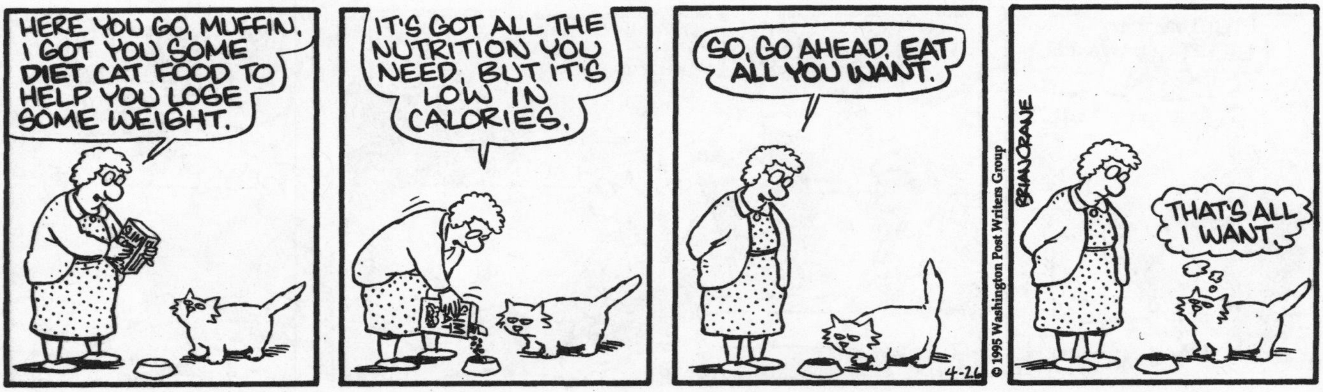
HERE YOU GO, MUFFIN. I GOT YOU SOME DIET CAT FOOD TO HELP YOU LOSE SOME WEIGHT.
IT'S GOT ALL THE NUTRITION YOU NEED, BUT IT'S LOW IN CALORIES.
SO, GO AHEAD, EAT ALL YOU WANT.
4-26
© 1995 Washington Post Writers Group
BRIAN CRANE
THAT'S ALL I WANT.

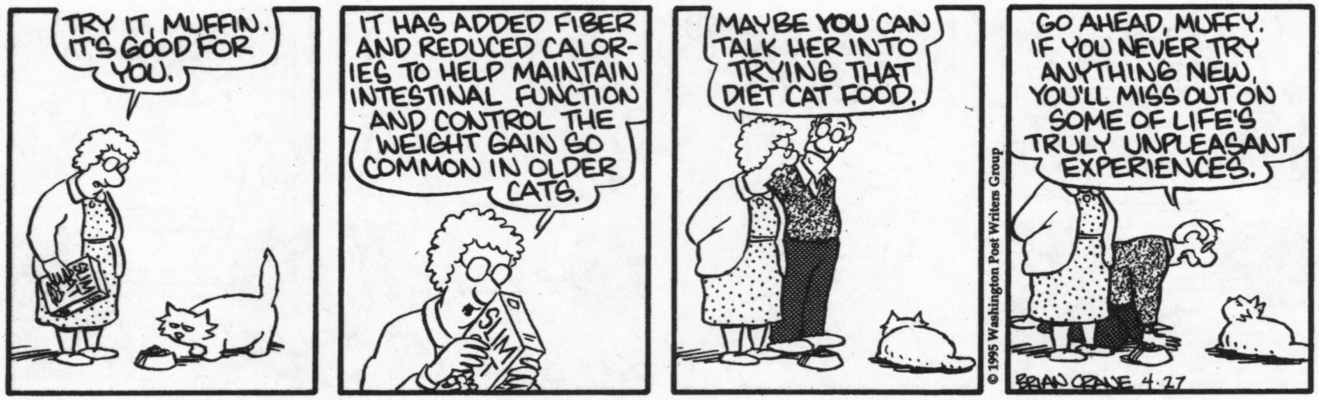
TRY IT, MUFFIN. IT'S GOOD FOR YOU.
IT HAS ADDED FIBER AND REDUCED CALORIES TO HELP MAINTAIN INTESTINAL FUNCTION AND CONTROL THE WEIGHT GAIN SO COMMON IN OLDER CATS.
SLIM
MAYBE YOU CAN TALK HER INTO TRYING THAT DIET CAT FOOD.
GO AHEAD, MUFFY. IF YOU NEVER TRY ANYTHING NEW, YOU'LL MISS OUT ON SOME OF LIFE'S TRULY UNPLEASANT EXPERIENCES.
© 1995 Washington Post Writers Group
BRIAN CRANE 4-27

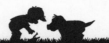

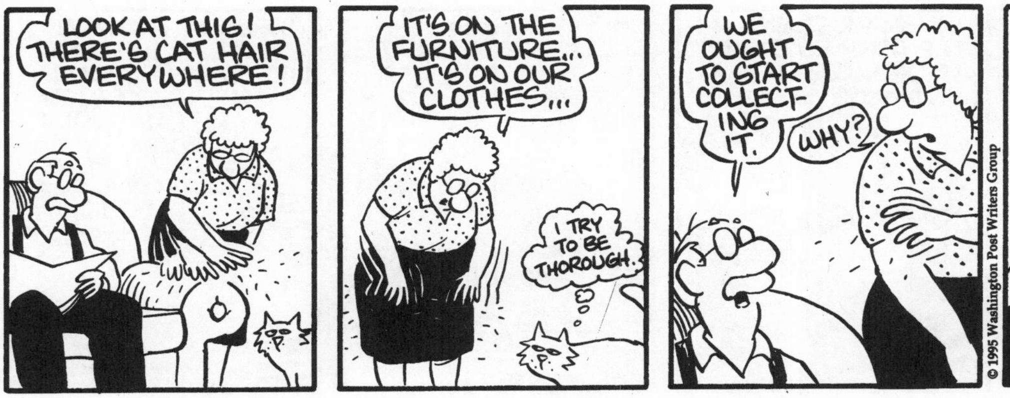
LOOK AT THIS! THERE'S CAT HAIR EVERYWHERE!
IT'S ON THE FURNITURE... IT'S ON OUR CLOTHES...
I TRY TO BE THOROUGH.
WE OUGHT TO START COLLECTING IT.
WHY?
IN A COUPLE OF WEEKS WE'D HAVE ENOUGH TO KNIT A NEW CAT.
BRIAN CRANE 5-6
© 1995 Washington Post Writers Group

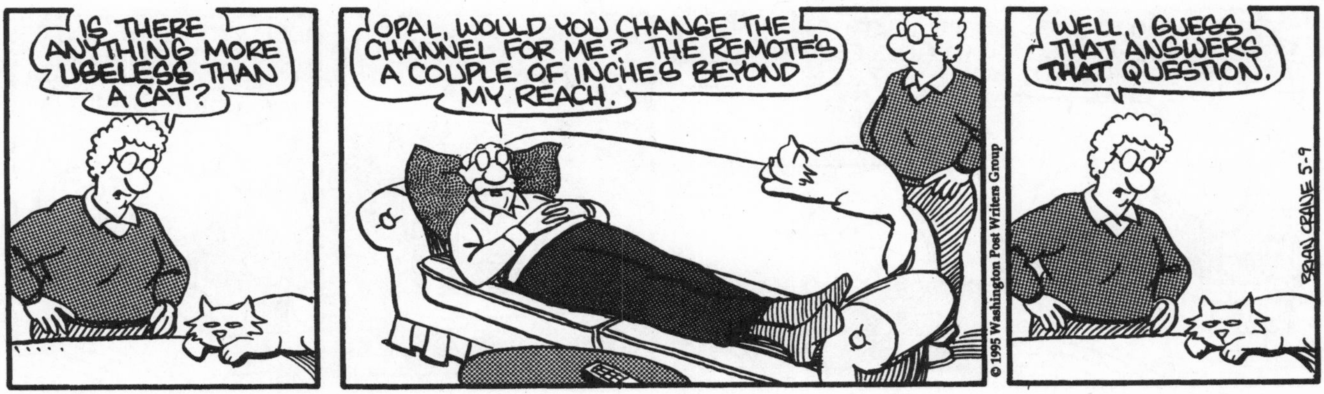
IS THERE ANYTHING MORE USELESS THAN A CAT?
OPAL, WOULD YOU CHANGE THE CHANNEL FOR ME? THE REMOTE'S A COUPLE OF INCHES BEYOND MY REACH.
© 1995 Washington Post Writers Group
WELL, I GUESS THAT ANSWERS THAT QUESTION.
BRIAN CRANE 5-9

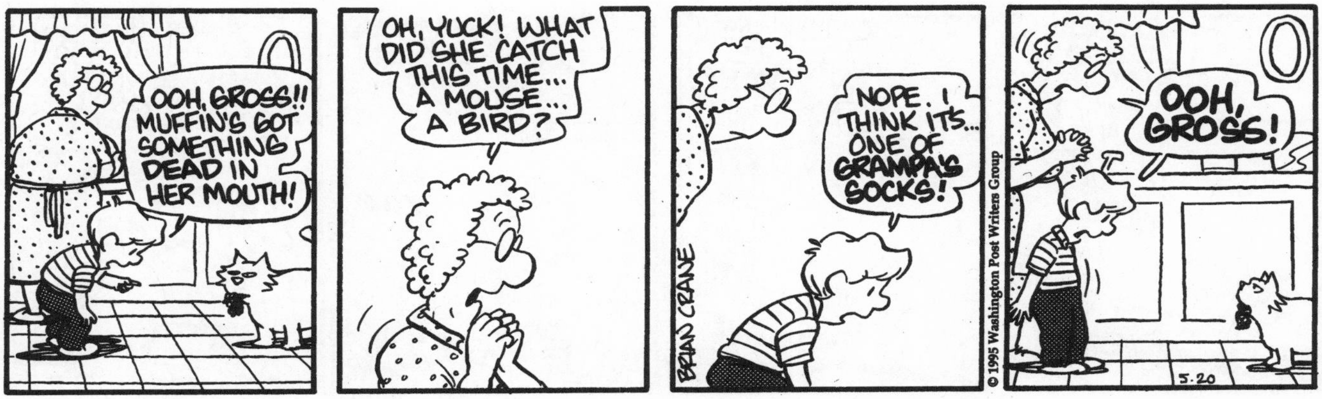
OOH, GROSS!! MUFFIN'S GOT SOMETHING DEAD IN HER MOUTH!
OH, YUCK! WHAT DID SHE CATCH THIS TIME... A MOUSE... A BIRD?
BRIAN CRANE
NOPE. I THINK IT'S... ONE OF GRAMPA'S SOCKS!
© 1995 Washington Post Writers Group
OOH, GROSS!
5.20

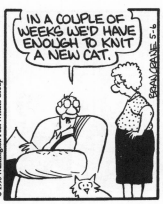

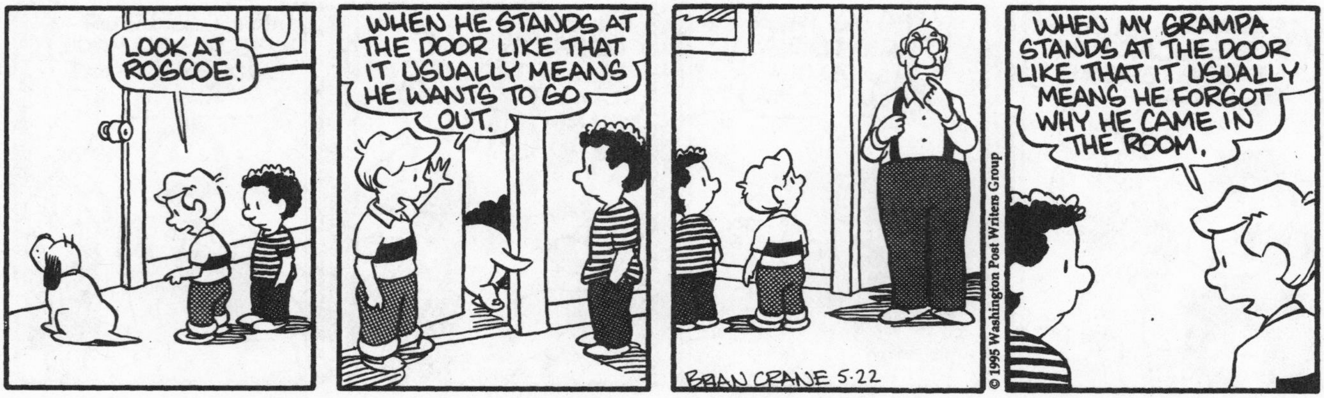

LOOK AT ROSCOE!
WHEN HE STANDS AT THE DOOR LIKE THAT IT USUALLY MEANS HE WANTS TO GO OUT.
BRIAN CRANE 5·22
© 1995 Washington Post Writers Group
WHEN MY GRAMPA STANDS AT THE DOOR LIKE THAT IT USUALLY MEANS HE FORGOT WHY HE CAME IN THE ROOM.

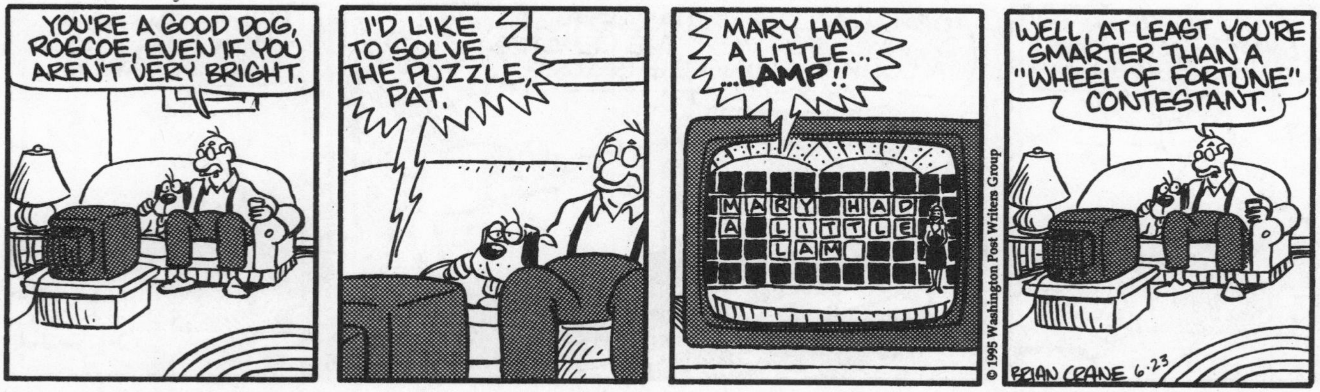

YOU'RE A GOOD DOG, ROSCOE, EVEN IF YOU AREN'T VERY BRIGHT.
I'D LIKE TO SOLVE THE PUZZLE, PAT.
MARY HAD A LITTLE... ...LAMP!!
MARY HAD A LITTLE LAM
© 1995 Washington Post Writers Group
WELL, AT LEAST YOU'RE SMARTER THAN A "WHEEL OF FORTUNE" CONTESTANT.
BRIAN CRANE 6·23

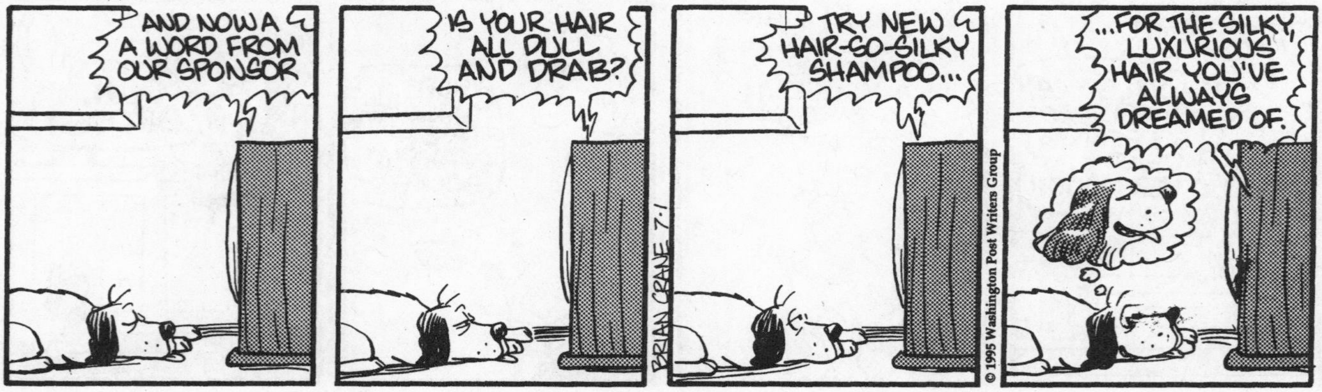

AND NOW A A WORD FROM OUR SPONSOR
IS YOUR HAIR ALL DULL AND DRAB?
BRIAN CRANE 7·1
TRY NEW HAIR-SO-SILKY SHAMPOO...
© 1995 Washington Post Writers Group
...FOR THE SILKY, LUXURIOUS HAIR YOU'VE ALWAYS DREAMED OF.

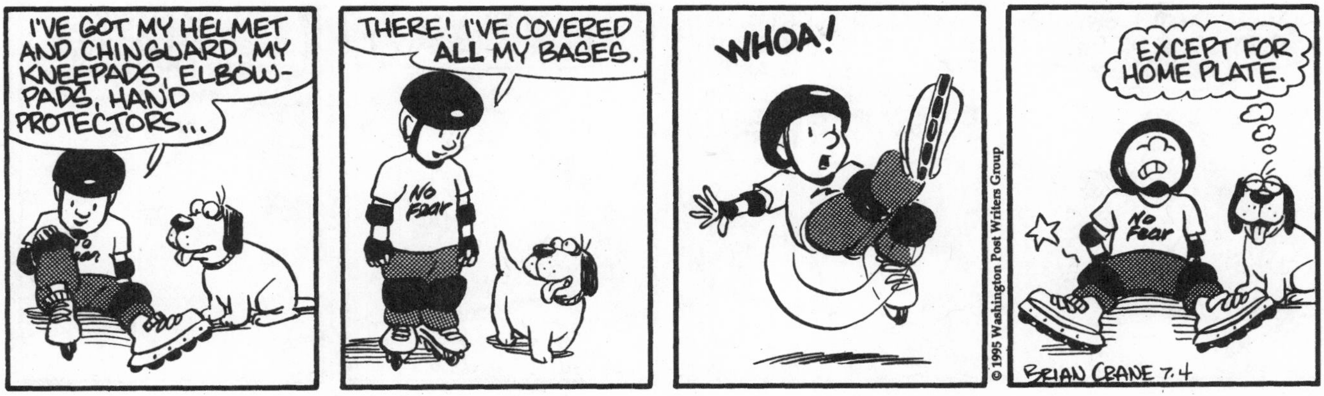
I'VE GOT MY HELMET AND CHINGUARD, MY KNEEPADS, ELBOW-PADS, HAND PROTECTORS...
THERE! I'VE COVERED **ALL** MY BASES.
WHOA!
EXCEPT FOR HOME PLATE.
© 1995 Washington Post Writers Group
BRIAN CRANE 7.4

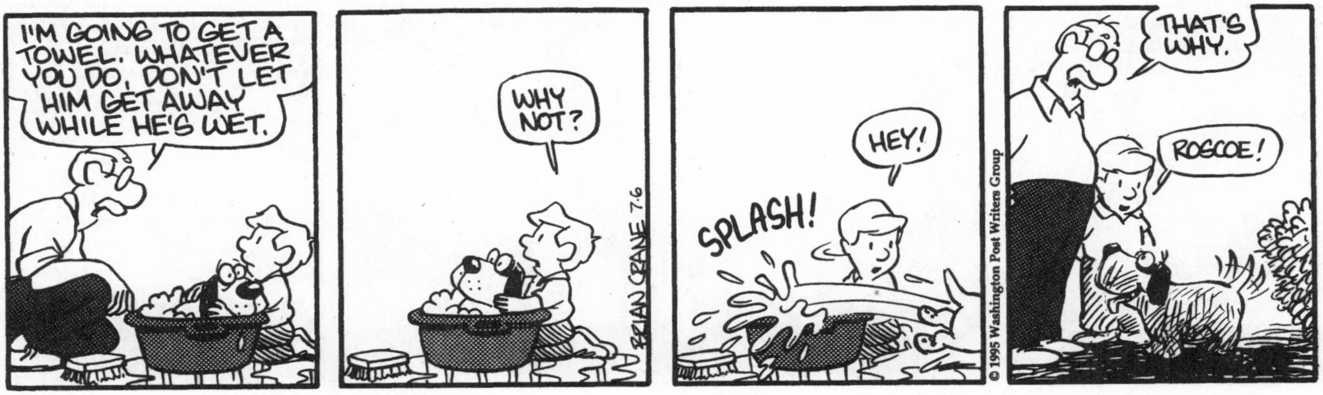
I'M GOING TO GET A TOWEL. WHATEVER YOU DO, DON'T LET HIM GET AWAY WHILE HE'S WET.
WHY NOT?
BRIAN CRANE 7.6
HEY!
SPLASH!
© 1995 Washington Post Writers Group
THAT'S WHY.
ROSCOE!

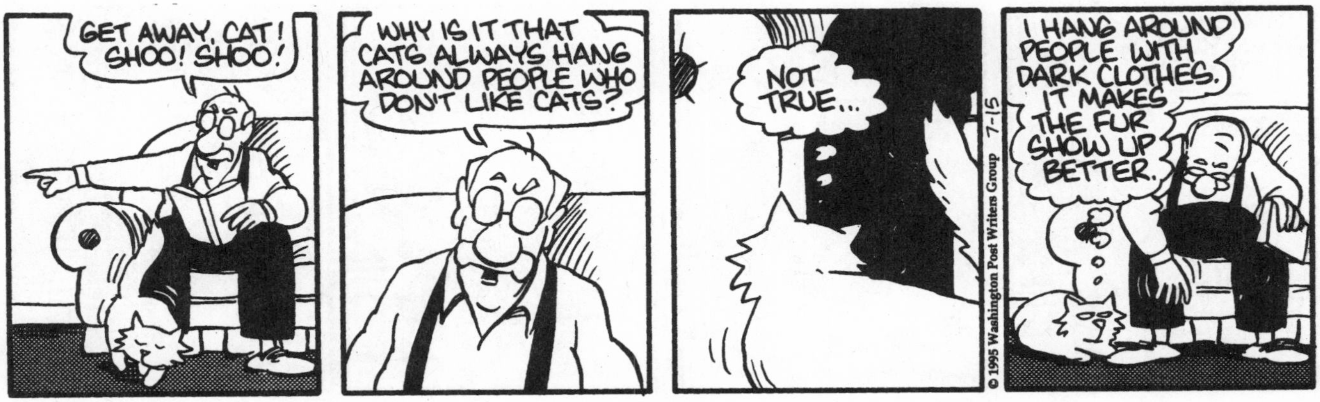
GET AWAY, CAT! SHOO! SHOO!
WHY IS IT THAT CATS ALWAYS HANG AROUND PEOPLE WHO DON'T LIKE CATS?
NOT TRUE...
7-15
© 1995 Washington Post Writers Group
I HANG AROUND PEOPLE WITH DARK CLOTHES. IT MAKES THE FUR SHOW UP BETTER.

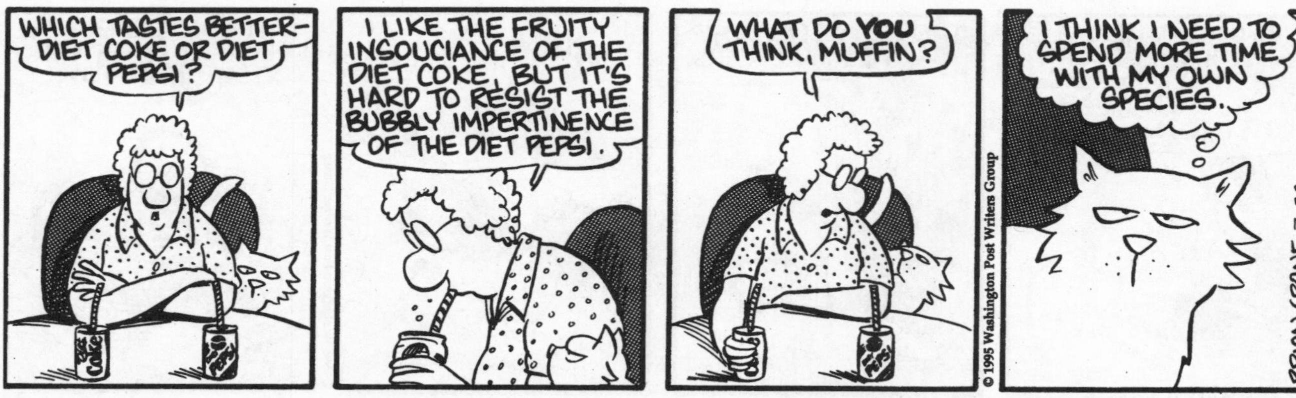
WHICH TASTES BETTER- DIET COKE OR DIET PEPSI?
I LIKE THE FRUITY INSOUCIANCE OF THE DIET COKE, BUT IT'S HARD TO RESIST THE BUBBLY IMPERTINENCE OF THE DIET PEPSI.
WHAT DO **YOU** THINK, MUFFIN?
© 1995 Washington Post Writers Group
I THINK I NEED TO SPEND MORE TIME WITH MY OWN SPECIES.
BRIAN CRANE 7-20

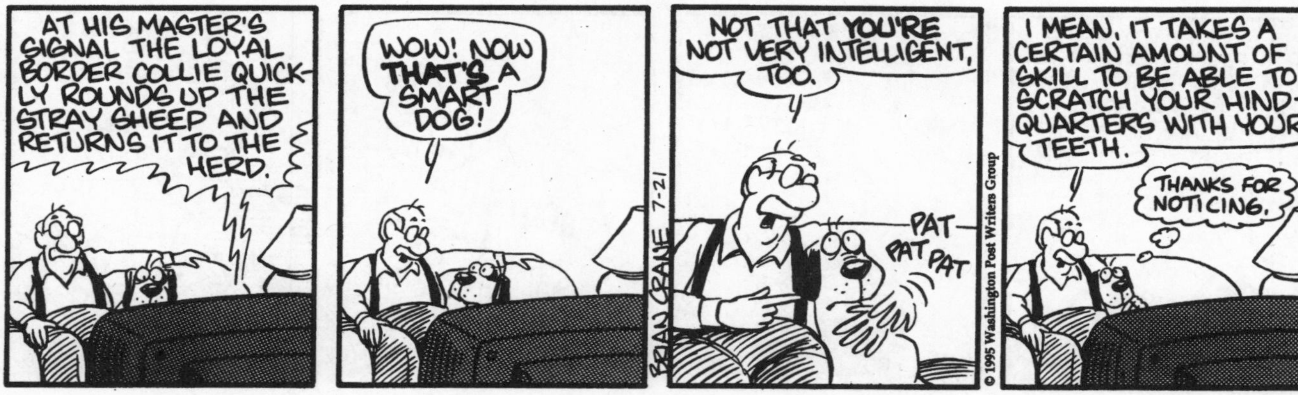
AT HIS MASTER'S SIGNAL THE LOYAL BORDER COLLIE QUICKLY ROUNDS UP THE STRAY SHEEP AND RETURNS IT TO THE HERD.
WOW! NOW **THAT'S** A SMART DOG!
BRIAN CRANE 7-21
NOT THAT **YOU'RE** NOT VERY INTELLIGENT, TOO.
PAT PAT PAT PAT
© 1995 Washington Post Writers Group
I MEAN, IT TAKES A CERTAIN AMOUNT OF SKILL TO BE ABLE TO SCRATCH YOUR HINDQUARTERS WITH YOUR TEETH.
THANKS FOR NOTICING.

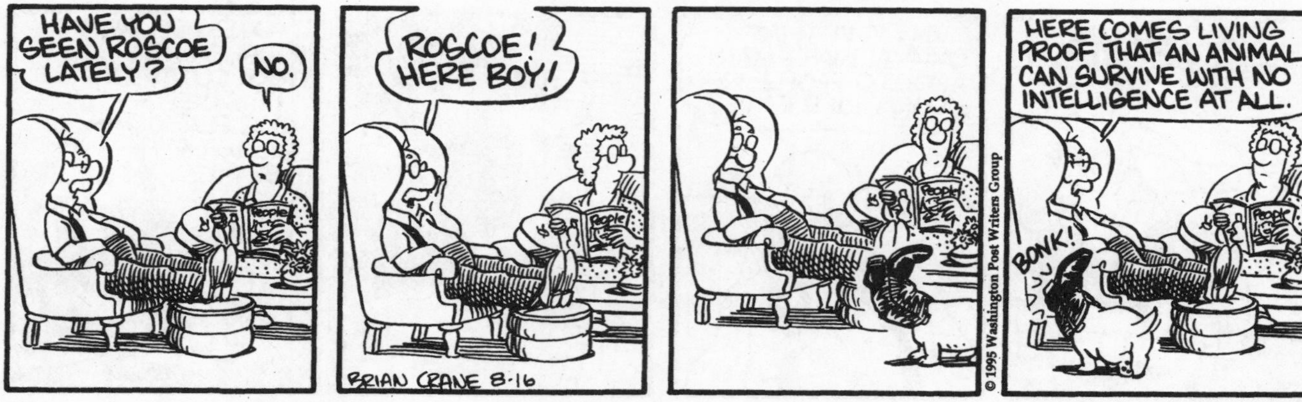
HAVE YOU SEEN ROSCOE LATELY?
NO.
ROSCOE! HERE BOY!
BRIAN CRANE 8-16
© 1995 Washington Post Writers Group
HERE COMES LIVING PROOF THAT AN ANIMAL CAN SURVIVE WITH NO INTELLIGENCE AT ALL.
BONK!

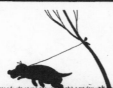

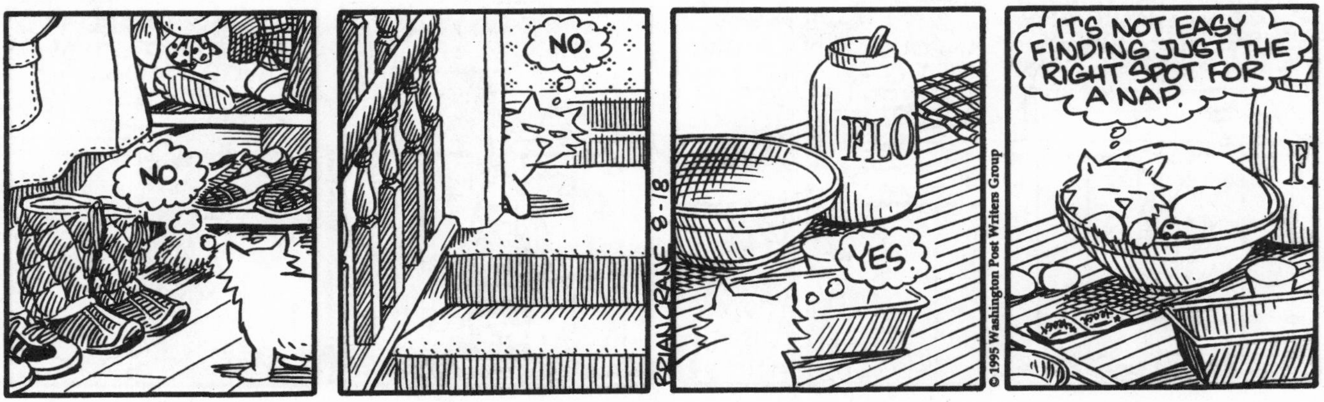
NO.
NO.
BRIAN CRANE 8-18
FLO
YES.
IT'S NOT EASY FINDING JUST THE RIGHT SPOT FOR A NAP.
© 1995 Washington Post Writers Group

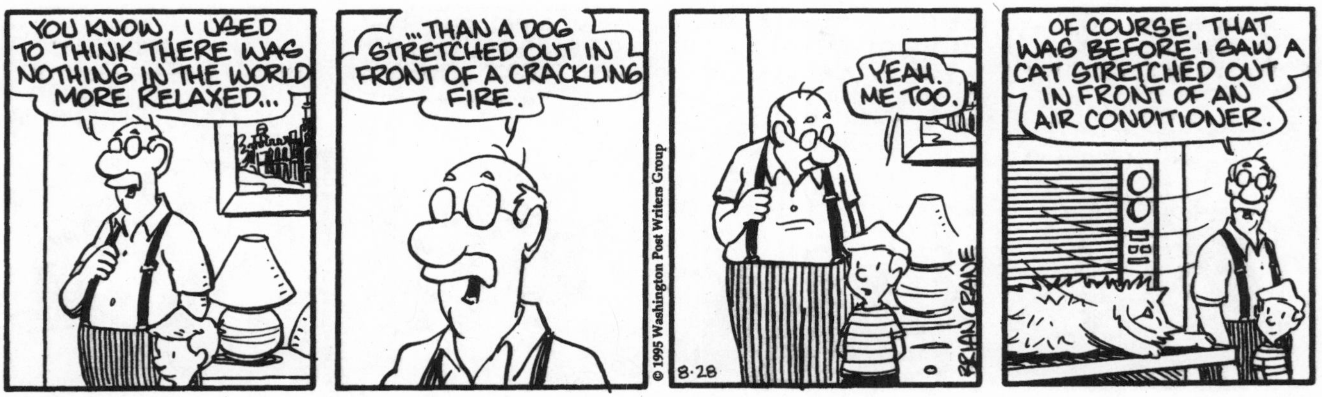
YOU KNOW, I USED TO THINK THERE WAS NOTHING IN THE WORLD MORE RELAXED...
...THAN A DOG STRETCHED OUT IN FRONT OF A CRACKLING FIRE.
© 1995 Washington Post Writers Group
YEAH. ME TOO.
8·28
BRIAN CRANE
OF COURSE, THAT WAS BEFORE I SAW A CAT STRETCHED OUT IN FRONT OF AN AIR CONDITIONER.

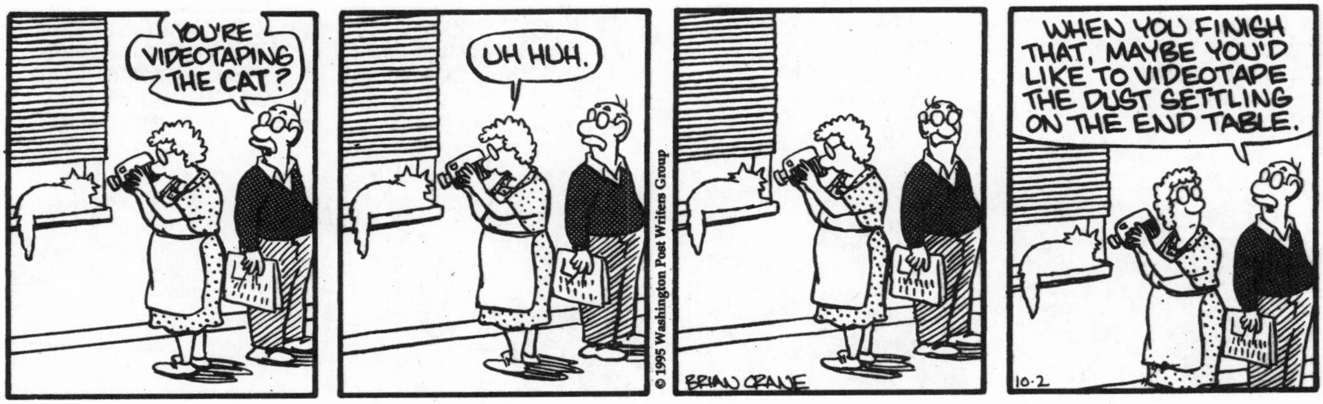
YOU'RE VIDEOTAPING THE CAT?
UH HUH.
© 1995 Washington Post Writers Group
BRIAN CRANE
WHEN YOU FINISH THAT, MAYBE YOU'D LIKE TO VIDEOTAPE THE DUST SETTLING ON THE END TABLE.
10·2

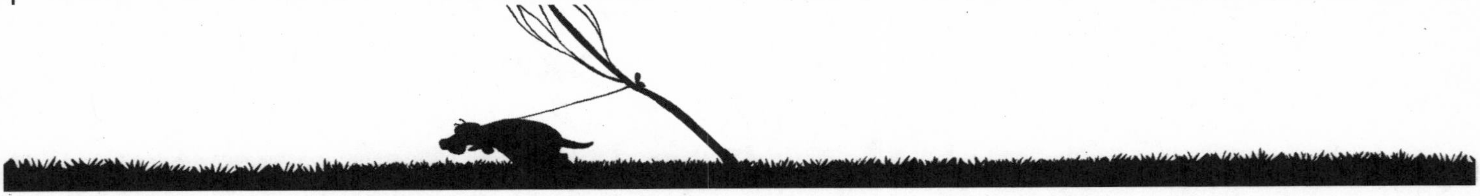

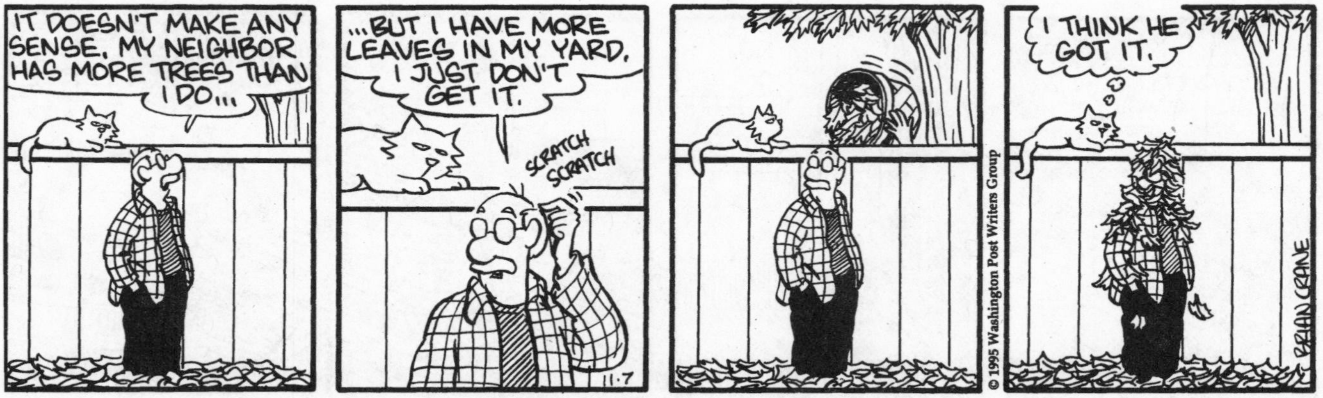
IT DOESN'T MAKE ANY SENSE. MY NEIGHBOR HAS MORE TREES THAN I DO...
...BUT I HAVE MORE LEAVES IN MY YARD. I JUST DON'T GET IT.
SCRATCH SCRATCH
11-7
© 1995 Washington Post Writers Group
I THINK HE GOT IT.
BRIAN CRANE

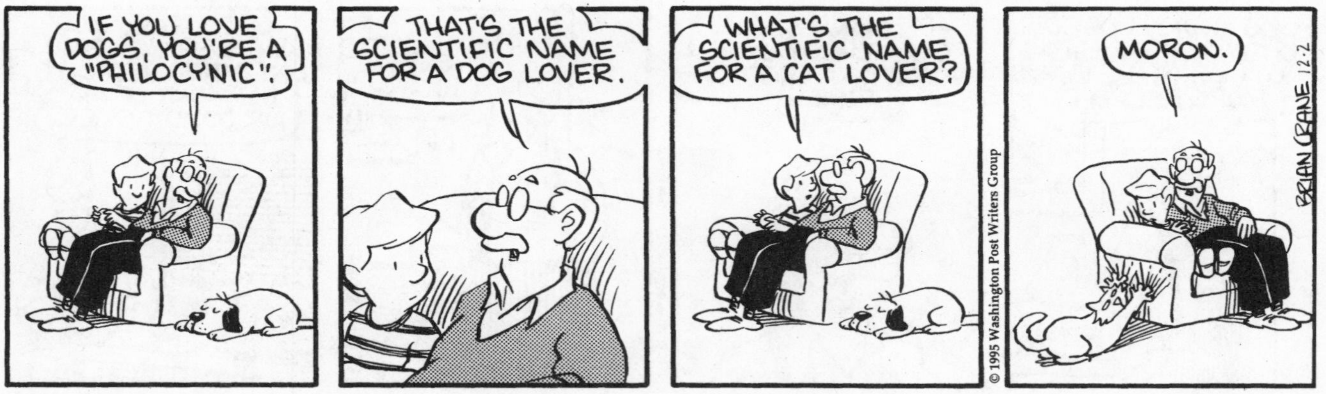
IF YOU LOVE DOGS, YOU'RE A "PHILOCYNIC".
THAT'S THE SCIENTIFIC NAME FOR A DOG LOVER.
WHAT'S THE SCIENTIFIC NAME FOR A CAT LOVER?
© 1995 Washington Post Writers Group
MORON.
BRIAN CRANE 12-2

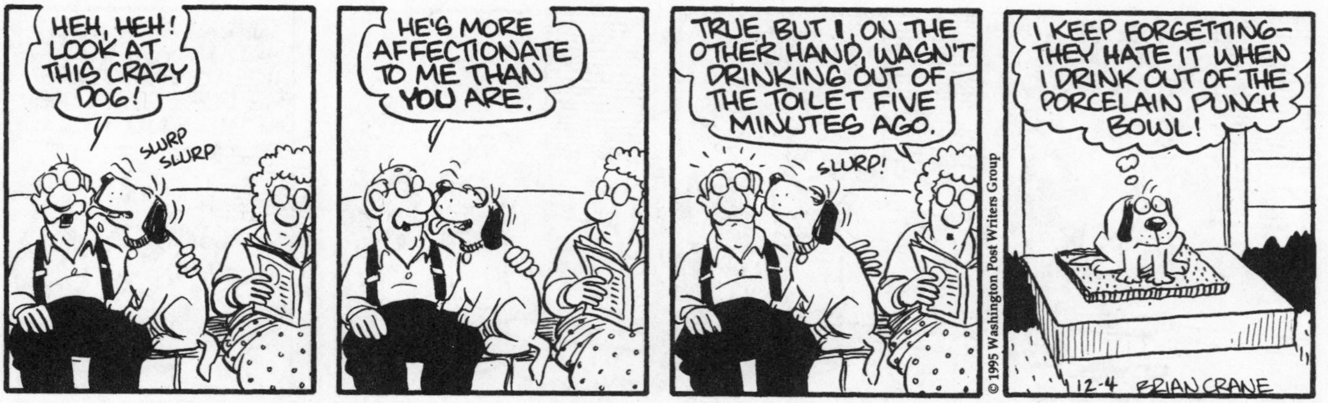
HEH, HEH! LOOK AT THIS CRAZY DOG!
SLURP SLURP
HE'S MORE AFFECTIONATE TO ME THAN YOU ARE.
TRUE, BUT I, ON THE OTHER HAND, WASN'T DRINKING OUT OF THE TOILET FIVE MINUTES AGO.
SLURP!
© 1995 Washington Post Writers Group
I KEEP FORGETTING— THEY HATE IT WHEN I DRINK OUT OF THE PORCELAIN PUNCH BOWL!
12-4 BRIAN CRANE

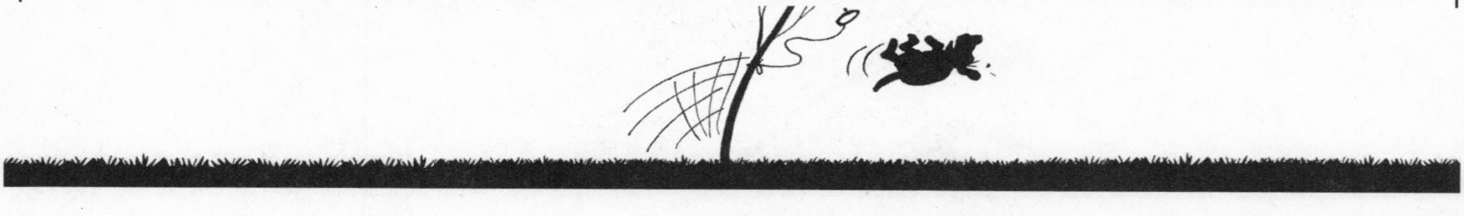

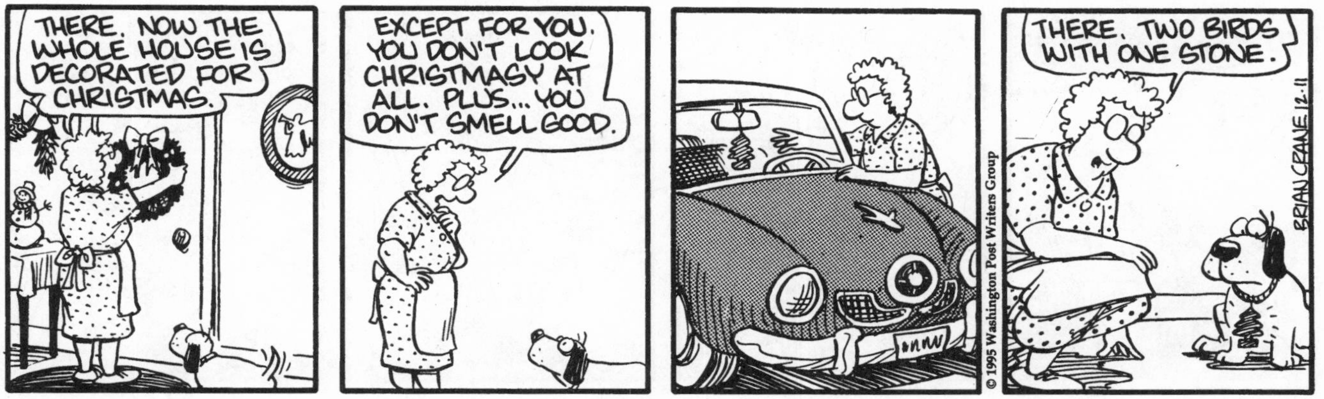
THERE. NOW THE WHOLE HOUSE IS DECORATED FOR CHRISTMAS.
EXCEPT FOR YOU. YOU DON'T LOOK CHRISTMASY AT ALL. PLUS... YOU DON'T SMELL GOOD.
THERE. TWO BIRDS WITH ONE STONE.
BRIAN CRANE 12-11
© 1995 Washington Post Writers Group

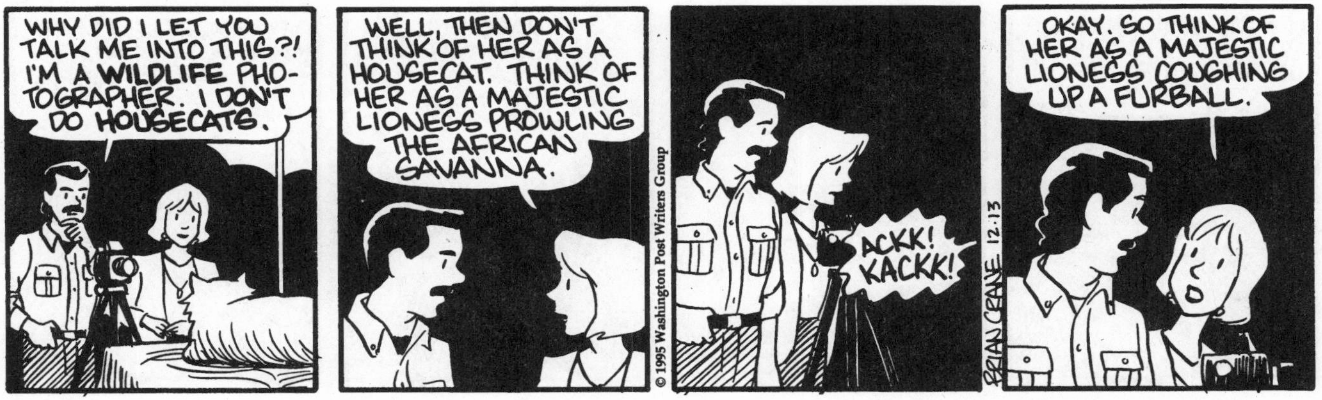
WHY DID I LET YOU TALK ME INTO THIS?! I'M A WILDLIFE PHOTOGRAPHER. I DON'T DO HOUSECATS.
WELL, THEN DON'T THINK OF HER AS A HOUSECAT. THINK OF HER AS A MAJESTIC LIONESS PROWLING THE AFRICAN SAVANNA.
ACKK! KACKK!
OKAY. SO THINK OF HER AS A MAJESTIC LIONESS COUGHING UP A FURBALL.
BRIAN CRANE 12-13
© 1995 Washington Post Writers Group

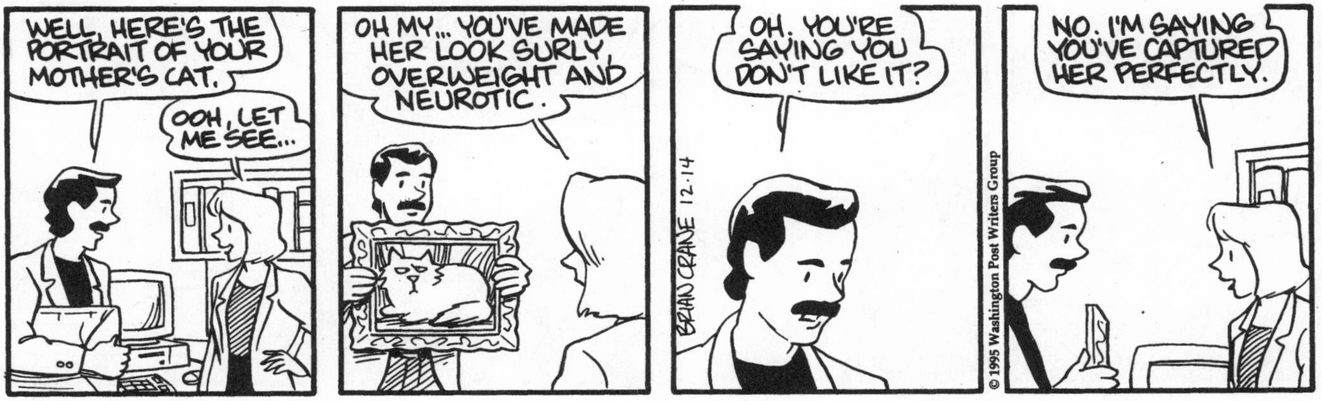
WELL, HERE'S THE PORTRAIT OF YOUR MOTHER'S CAT.
OOH, LET ME SEE...
OH MY... YOU'VE MADE HER LOOK SURLY, OVERWEIGHT AND NEUROTIC.
OH. YOU'RE SAYING YOU DON'T LIKE IT?
NO. I'M SAYING YOU'VE CAPTURED HER PERFECTLY.
BRIAN CRANE 12-14
© 1995 Washington Post Writers Group

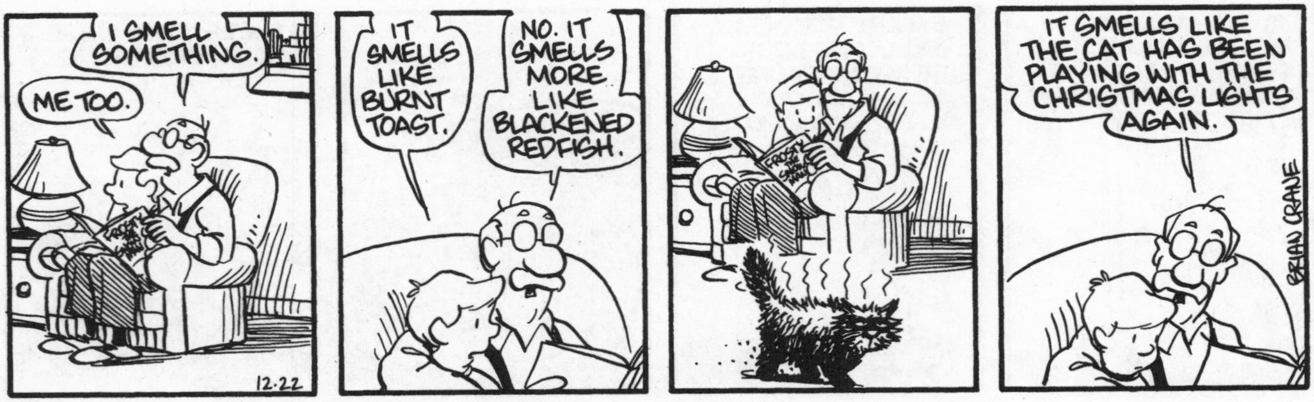
I SMELL SOMETHING.
ME TOO.
12-22
IT SMELLS LIKE BURNT TOAST.
NO. IT SMELLS MORE LIKE BLACKENED REDFISH.
IT SMELLS LIKE THE CAT HAS BEEN PLAYING WITH THE CHRISTMAS LIGHTS AGAIN.
BRIAN CRANE

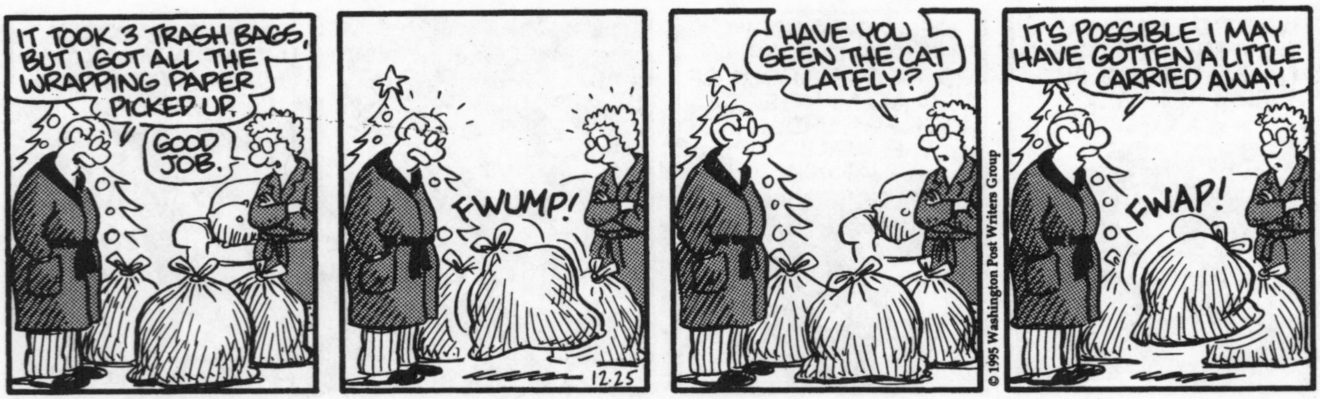
IT TOOK 3 TRASH BAGS, BUT I GOT ALL THE WRAPPING PAPER PICKED UP.
GOOD JOB.
FWUMP!
12-25
HAVE YOU SEEN THE CAT LATELY?
IT'S POSSIBLE I MAY HAVE GOTTEN A LITTLE CARRIED AWAY.
FWAP!

132

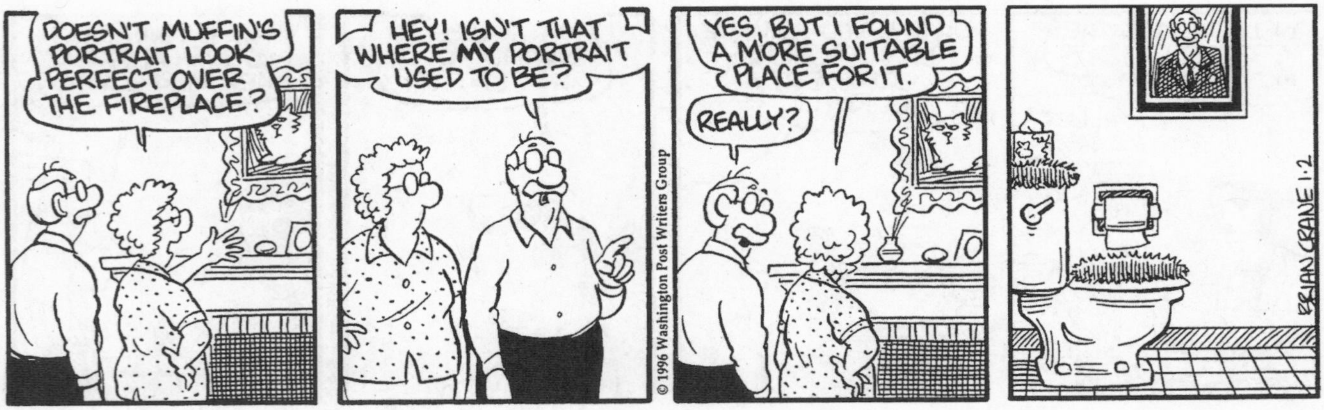
DOESN'T MUFFIN'S PORTRAIT LOOK PERFECT OVER THE FIREPLACE?
HEY! ISN'T THAT WHERE MY PORTRAIT USED TO BE?
YES, BUT I FOUND A MORE SUITABLE PLACE FOR IT.
REALLY?
BRIAN CRANE 1-2

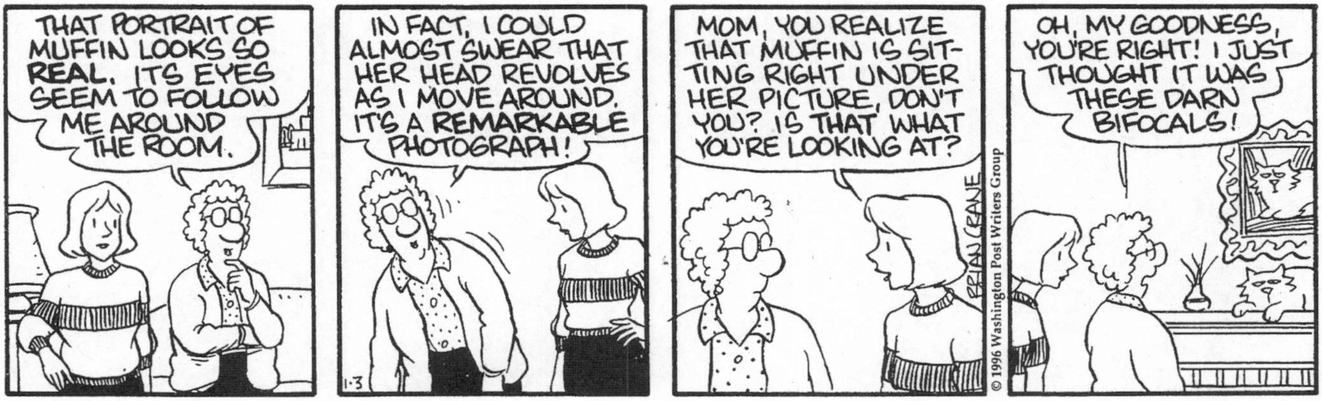
THAT PORTRAIT OF MUFFIN LOOKS SO REAL. ITS EYES SEEM TO FOLLOW ME AROUND THE ROOM.
IN FACT, I COULD ALMOST SWEAR THAT HER HEAD REVOLVES AS I MOVE AROUND. IT'S A REMARKABLE PHOTOGRAPH!
1·3
MOM, YOU REALIZE THAT MUFFIN IS SITTING RIGHT UNDER HER PICTURE, DON'T YOU? IS THAT WHAT YOU'RE LOOKING AT?
BRIAN CRANE
© 1996 Washington Post Writers Group
OH, MY GOODNESS, YOU'RE RIGHT! I JUST THOUGHT IT WAS THESE DARN BIFOCALS!

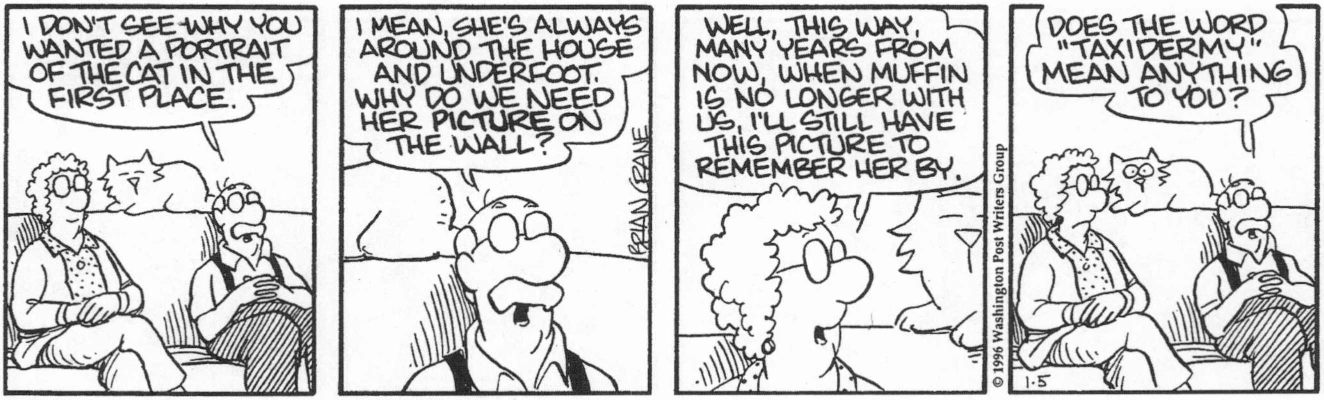
I DON'T SEE WHY YOU WANTED A PORTRAIT OF THE CAT IN THE FIRST PLACE.
I MEAN, SHE'S ALWAYS AROUND THE HOUSE AND UNDERFOOT. WHY DO WE NEED HER PICTURE ON THE WALL?
BRIAN CRANE
WELL, THIS WAY, MANY YEARS FROM NOW, WHEN MUFFIN IS NO LONGER WITH US, I'LL STILL HAVE THIS PICTURE TO REMEMBER HER BY.
© 1996 Washington Post Writers Group
DOES THE WORD "TAXIDERMY" MEAN ANYTHING TO YOU?
1·5

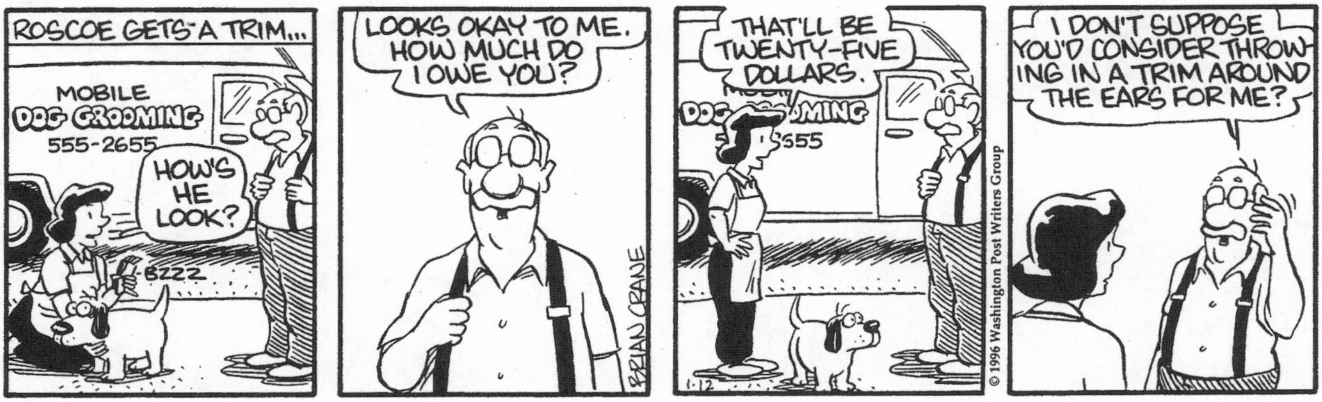
ROSCOE GETS A TRIM...
MOBILE
DOG GROOMING
555-2655
HOW'S HE LOOK?
BZZZ
LOOKS OKAY TO ME. HOW MUCH DO I OWE YOU?
BRIAN CRANE
THAT'LL BE TWENTY-FIVE DOLLARS.
1·12
© 1996 Washington Post Writers Group
I DON'T SUPPOSE YOU'D CONSIDER THROWING IN A TRIM AROUND THE EARS FOR ME?

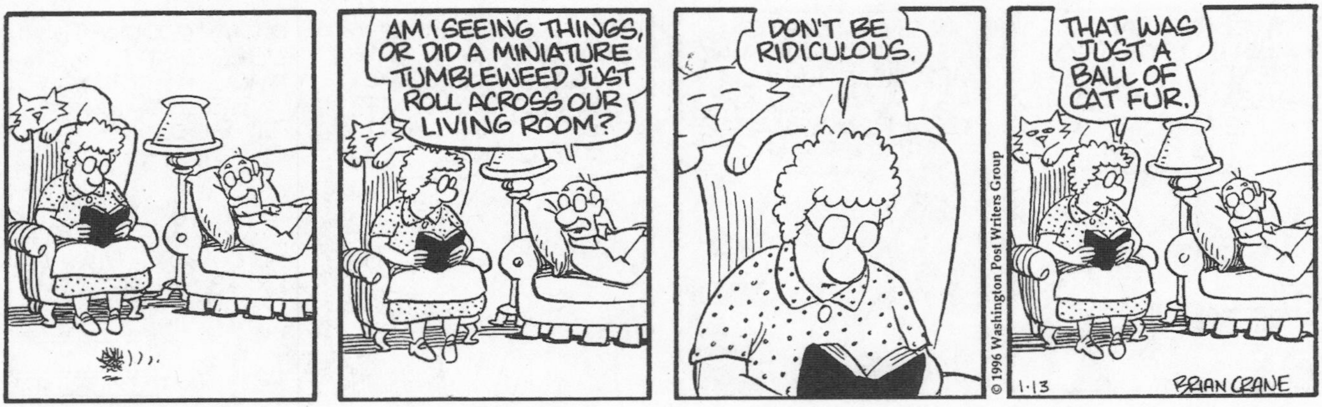
AM I SEEING THINGS, OR DID A MINIATURE TUMBLEWEED JUST ROLL ACROSS OUR LIVING ROOM?
DON'T BE RIDICULOUS.
THAT WAS JUST A BALL OF CAT FUR.
© 1996 Washington Post Writers Group
1·13
BRIAN CRANE

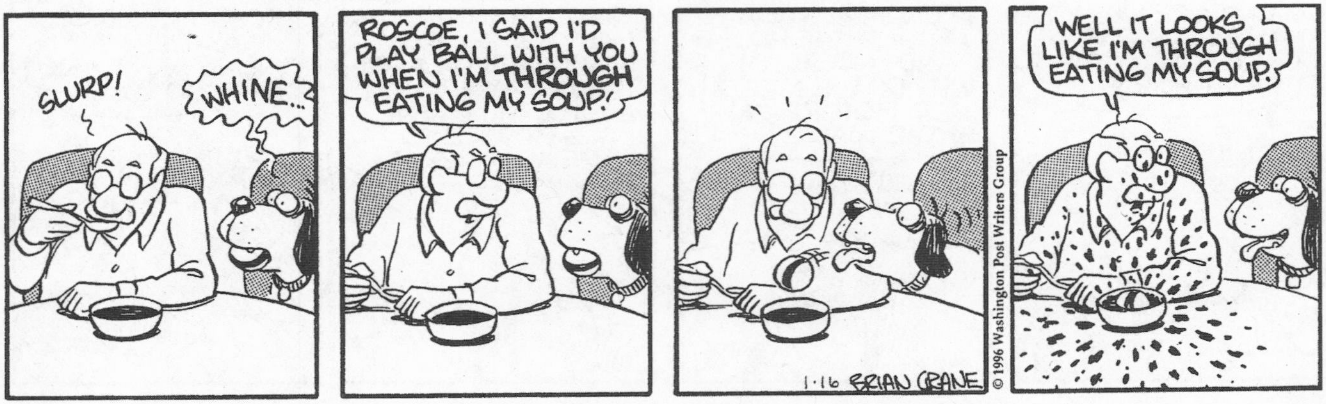
SLURP!
WHINE...
ROSCOE, I SAID I'D PLAY BALL WITH YOU WHEN I'M THROUGH EATING MY SOUP!
1·16 BRIAN CRANE
© 1996 Washington Post Writers Group
WELL IT LOOKS LIKE I'M THROUGH EATING MY SOUP.

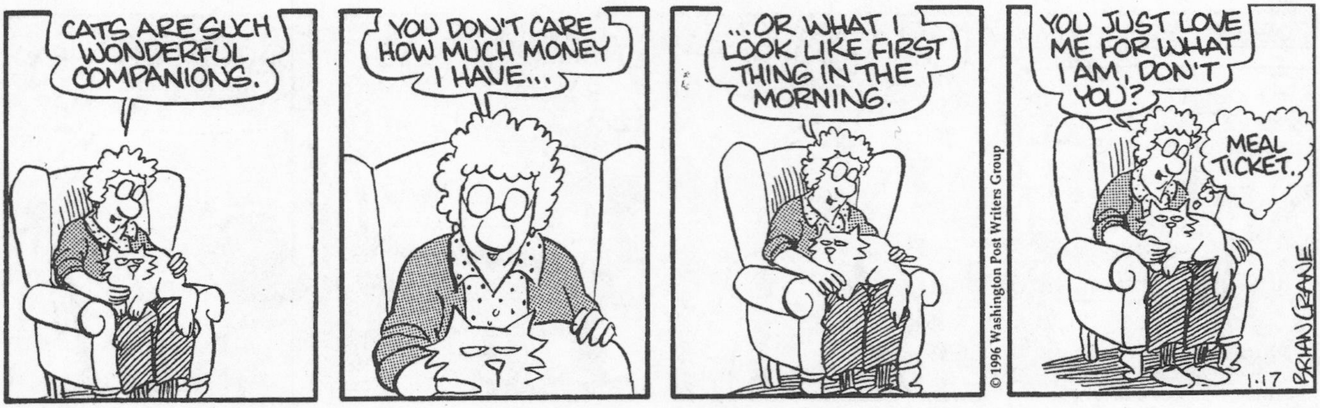
CATS ARE SUCH WONDERFUL COMPANIONS.
YOU DON'T CARE HOW MUCH MONEY I HAVE...
...OR WHAT I LOOK LIKE FIRST THING IN THE MORNING.
© 1996 Washington Post Writers Group
YOU JUST LOVE ME FOR WHAT I AM, DON'T YOU?
MEAL TICKET.
1·17
BRIAN CRANE

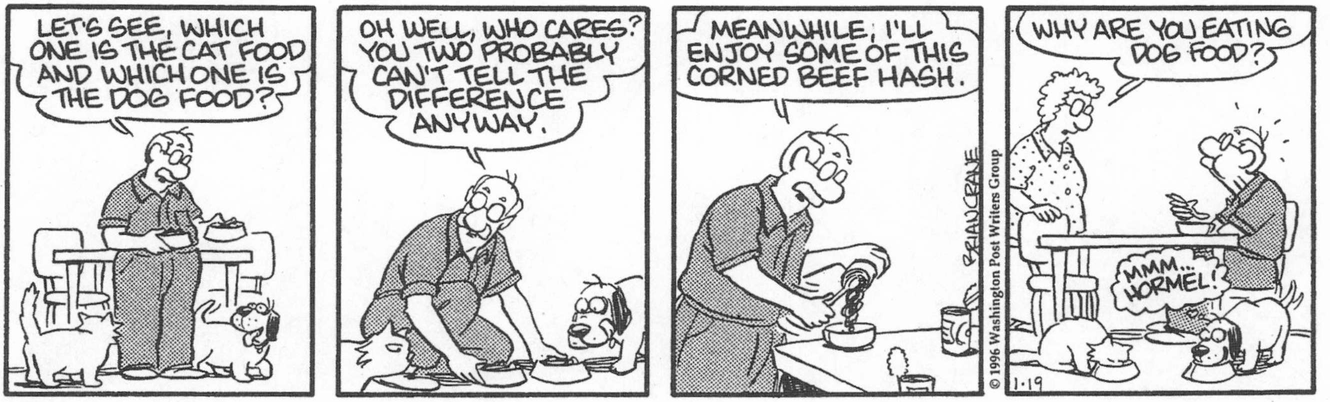
LET'S SEE, WHICH ONE IS THE CAT FOOD AND WHICH ONE IS THE DOG FOOD?
OH WELL, WHO CARES? YOU TWO PROBABLY CAN'T TELL THE DIFFERENCE ANYWAY.
MEANWHILE, I'LL ENJOY SOME OF THIS CORNED BEEF HASH.
BRIAN CRANE
© 1996 Washington Post Writers Group
1·19
WHY ARE YOU EATING DOG FOOD?
MMM... HORMEL!

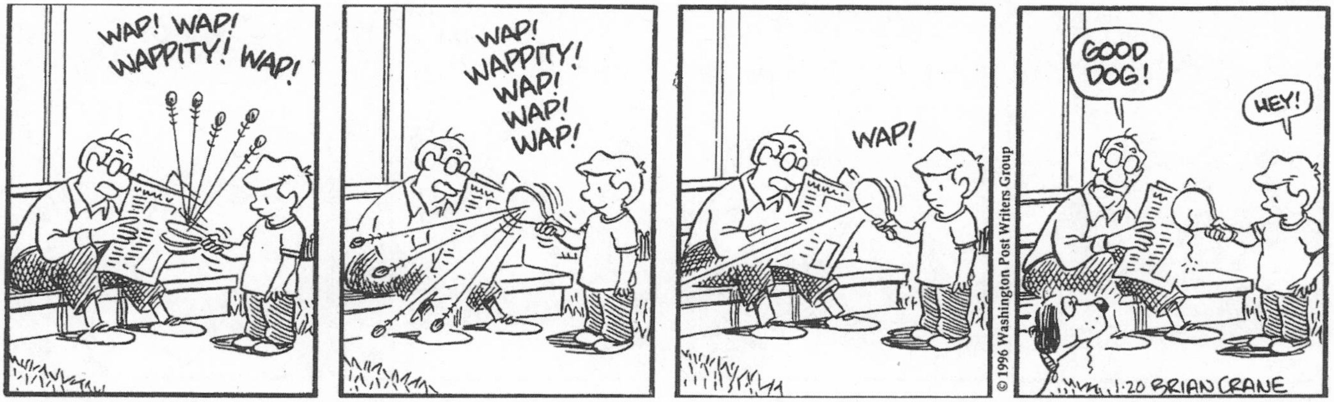
WAP! WAP! WAPPITY! WAP!
WAP! WAPPITY! WAP! WAP! WAP!
WAP!
© 1996 Washington Post Writers Group
GOOD DOG!
HEY!
1·20 BRIAN CRANE

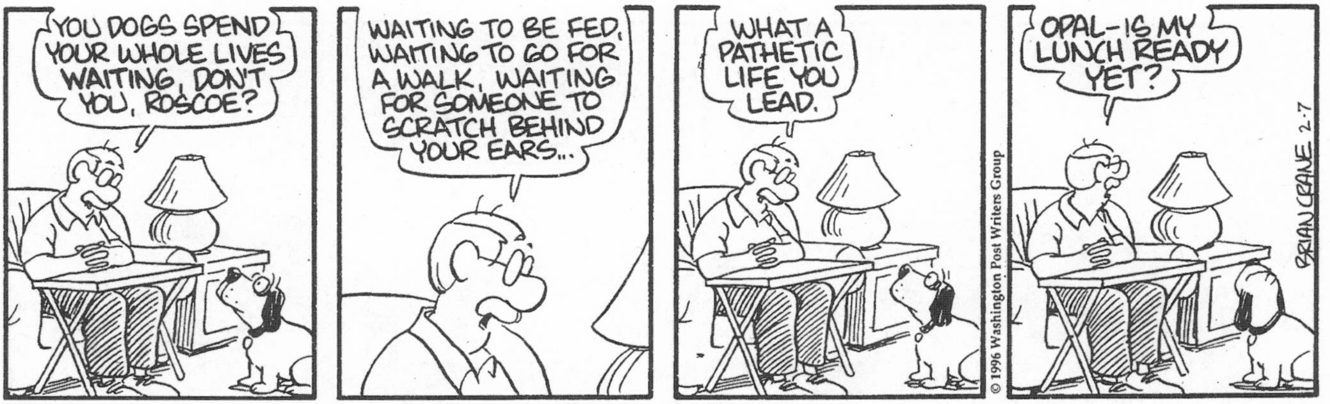
YOU DOGS SPEND YOUR WHOLE LIVES WAITING, DON'T YOU, ROSCOE?
WAITING TO BE FED, WAITING TO GO FOR A WALK, WAITING FOR SOMEONE TO SCRATCH BEHIND YOUR EARS...
WHAT A PATHETIC LIFE YOU LEAD.
© 1996 Washington Post Writers Group
OPAL- IS MY LUNCH READY YET?
BRIAN CRANE 2·7

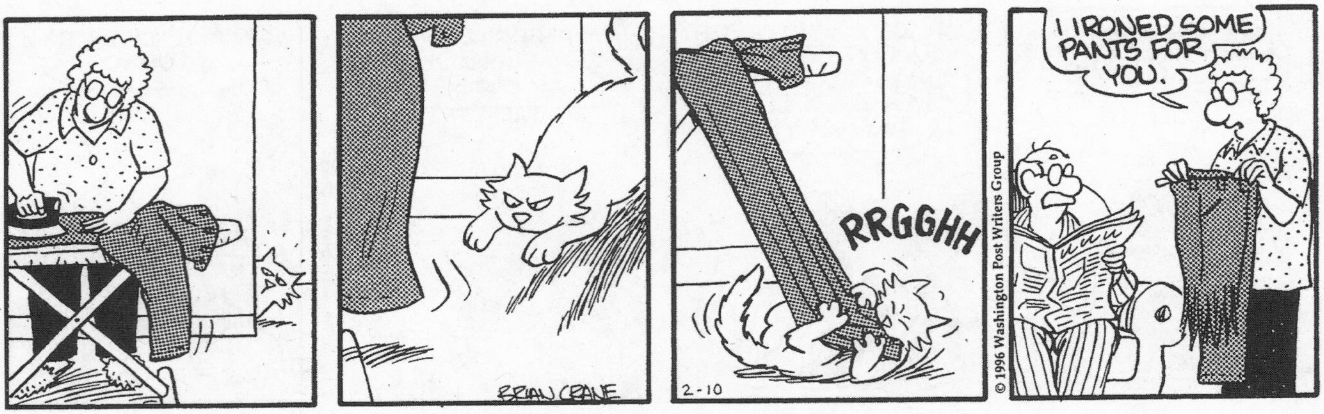

BRIAN CRANE
2-10
RRGGHH
© 1996 Washington Post Writers Group
I IRONED SOME PANTS FOR YOU.

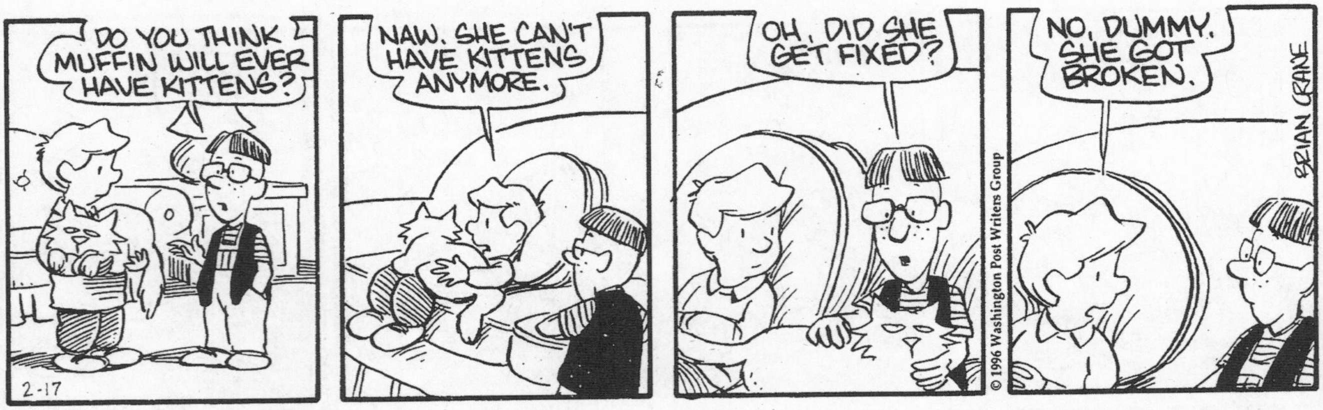

DO YOU THINK MUFFIN WILL EVER HAVE KITTENS?
2-17
NAW. SHE CAN'T HAVE KITTENS ANYMORE.
OH, DID SHE GET FIXED?
© 1996 Washington Post Writers Group
NO, DUMMY. SHE GOT BROKEN.
BRIAN CRANE

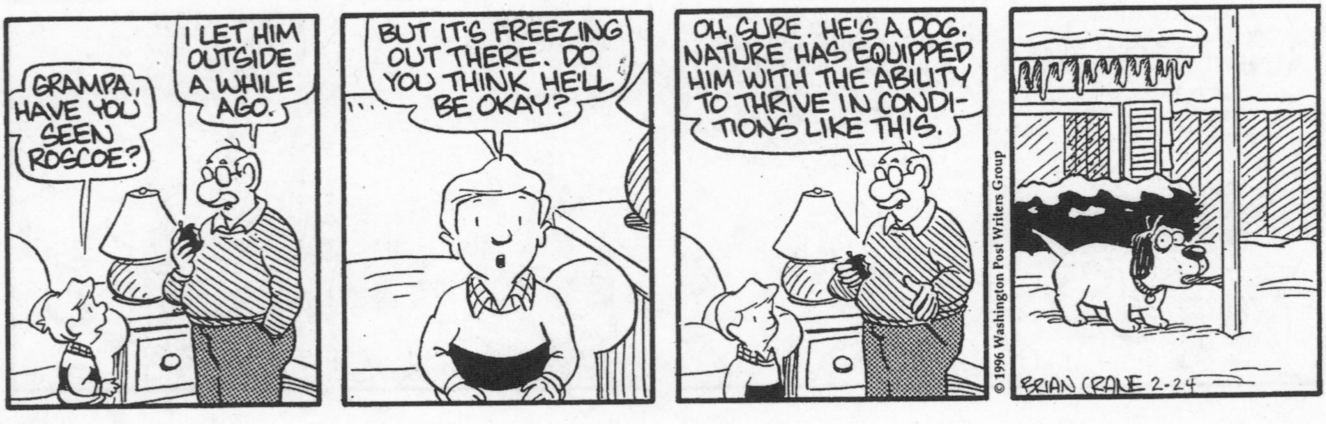

GRAMPA, HAVE YOU SEEN ROSCOE?
I LET HIM OUTSIDE A WHILE AGO.
BUT IT'S FREEZING OUT THERE. DO YOU THINK HE'LL BE OKAY?
OH, SURE. HE'S A DOG. NATURE HAS EQUIPPED HIM WITH THE ABILITY TO THRIVE IN CONDITIONS LIKE THIS.
© 1996 Washington Post Writers Group
BRIAN CRANE 2-24

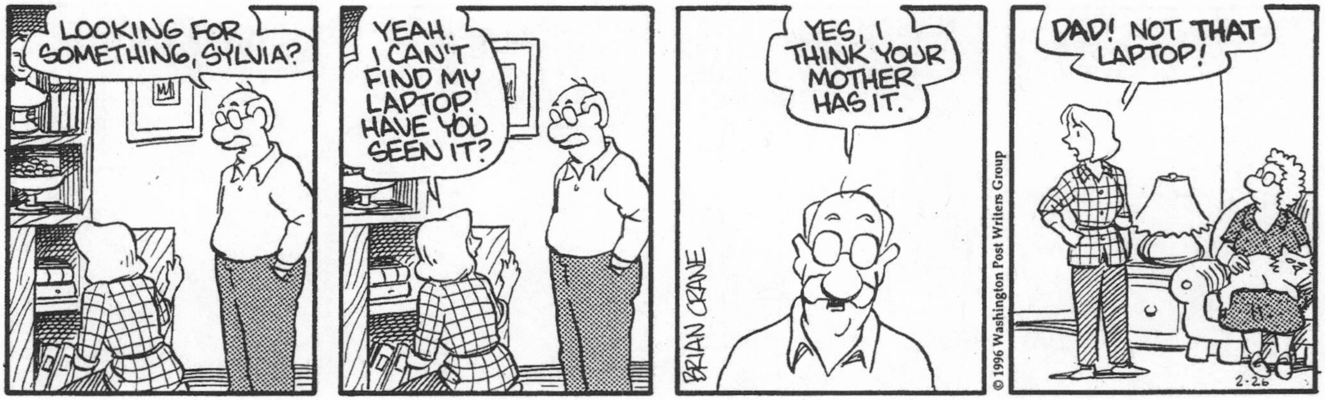
LOOKING FOR SOMETHING, SYLVIA?
YEAH. I CAN'T FIND MY LAPTOP. HAVE YOU SEEN IT?
YES, I THINK YOUR MOTHER HAS IT.
DAD! NOT THAT LAPTOP!
BRIAN CRANE
© 1996 Washington Post Writers Group
2-26

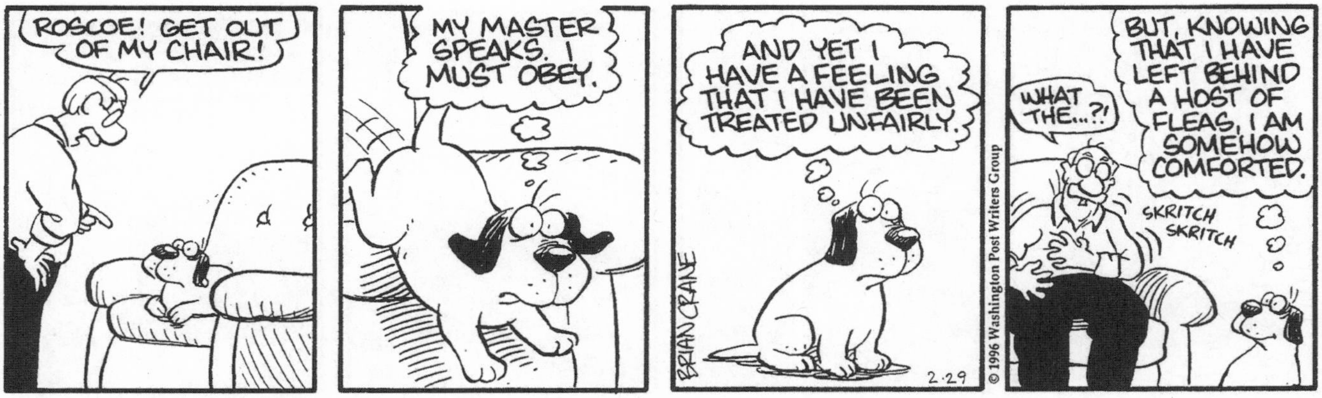
ROSCOE! GET OUT OF MY CHAIR!
MY MASTER SPEAKS. I MUST OBEY.
AND YET I HAVE A FEELING THAT I HAVE BEEN TREATED UNFAIRLY.
WHAT THE...?!
BUT, KNOWING THAT I HAVE LEFT BEHIND A HOST OF FLEAS, I AM SOMEHOW COMFORTED.
SKRITCH SKRITCH
BRIAN CRANE
© 1996 Washington Post Writers Group
2-29

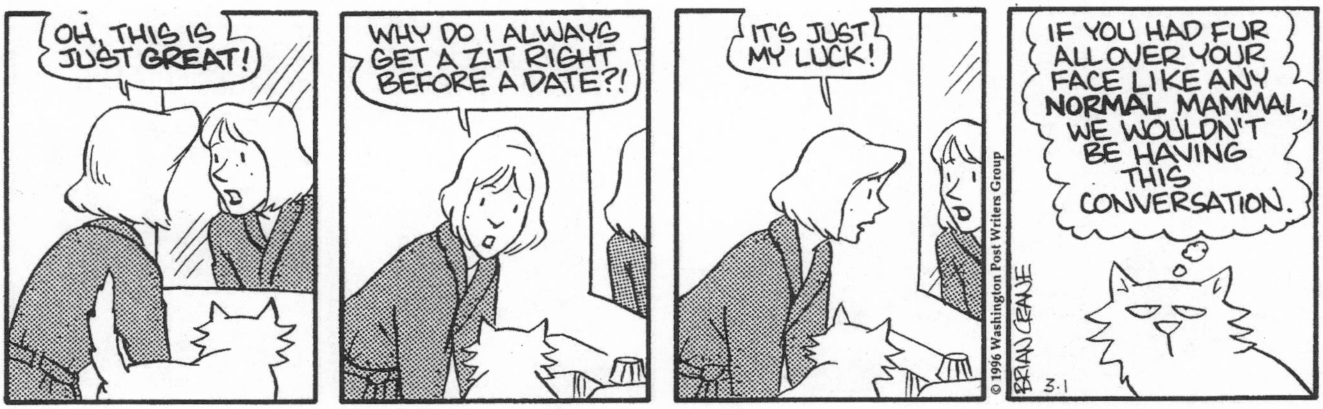
OH, THIS IS JUST GREAT!
WHY DO I ALWAYS GET A ZIT RIGHT BEFORE A DATE?!
IT'S JUST MY LUCK!
IF YOU HAD FUR ALL OVER YOUR FACE LIKE ANY NORMAL MAMMAL, WE WOULDN'T BE HAVING THIS CONVERSATION.
BRIAN CRANE
© 1996 Washington Post Writers Group
3-1

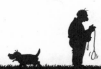

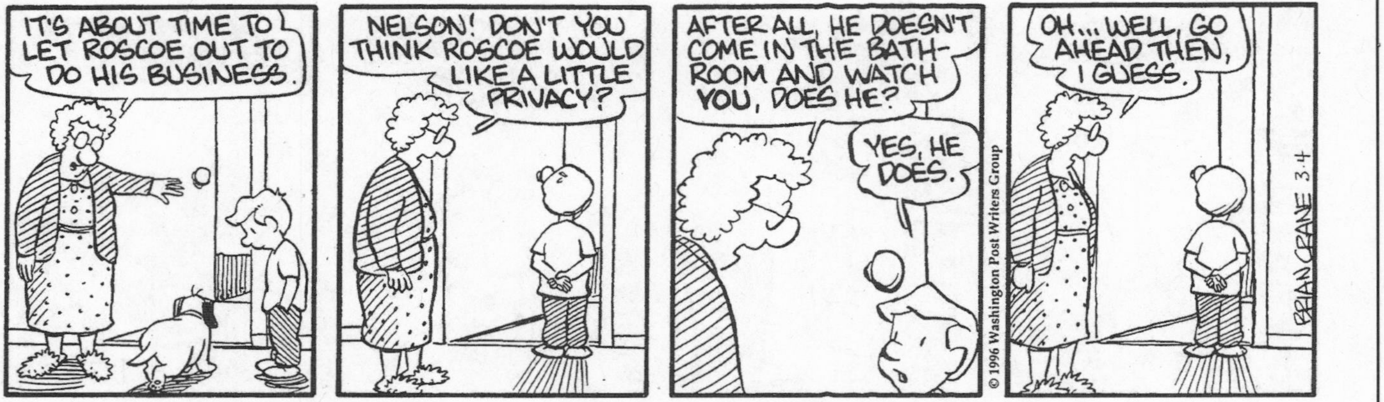
IT'S ABOUT TIME TO LET ROSCOE OUT TO DO HIS BUSINESS.
NELSON! DON'T YOU THINK ROSCOE WOULD LIKE A LITTLE PRIVACY?
AFTER ALL, HE DOESN'T COME IN THE BATH-ROOM AND WATCH YOU, DOES HE?
YES, HE DOES.
© 1996 Washington Post Writers Group
OH... WELL, GO AHEAD THEN, I GUESS.
BRIAN CRANE 3-4

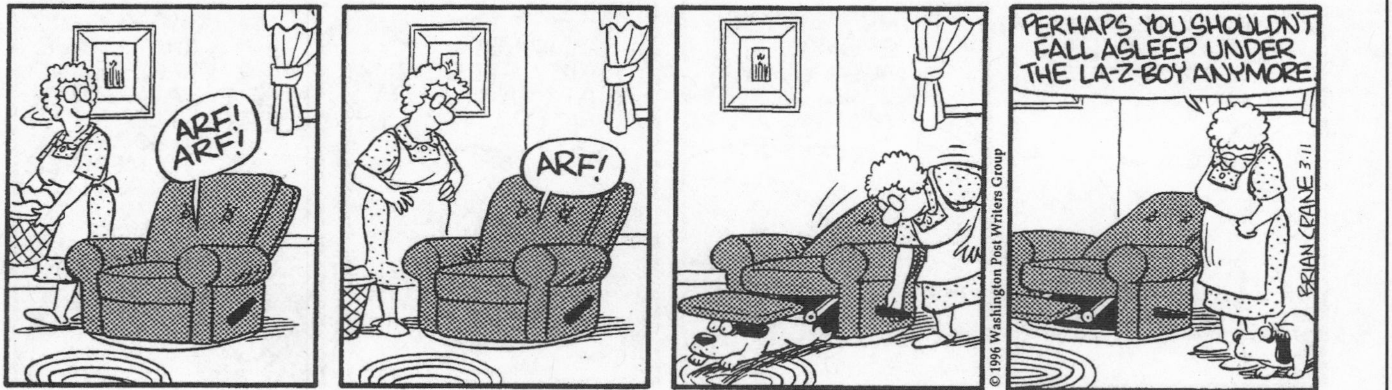
ARF! ARF!
ARF!
© 1996 Washington Post Writers Group
PERHAPS YOU SHOULDN'T FALL ASLEEP UNDER THE LA-Z-BOY ANYMORE.
BRIAN CRANE 3-11

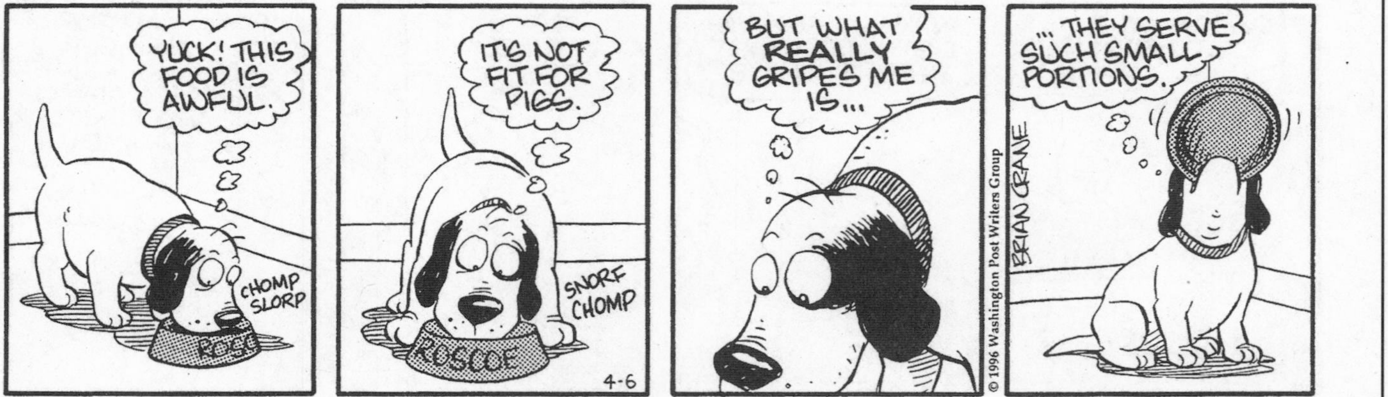
YUCK! THIS FOOD IS AWFUL.
CHOMP SLORP
ROSC
IT'S NOT FIT FOR PIGS.
SNORF CHOMP
ROSCOE
4-6
BUT WHAT REALLY GRIPES ME IS...
© 1996 Washington Post Writers Group
BRIAN CRANE
... THEY SERVE SUCH SMALL PORTIONS.

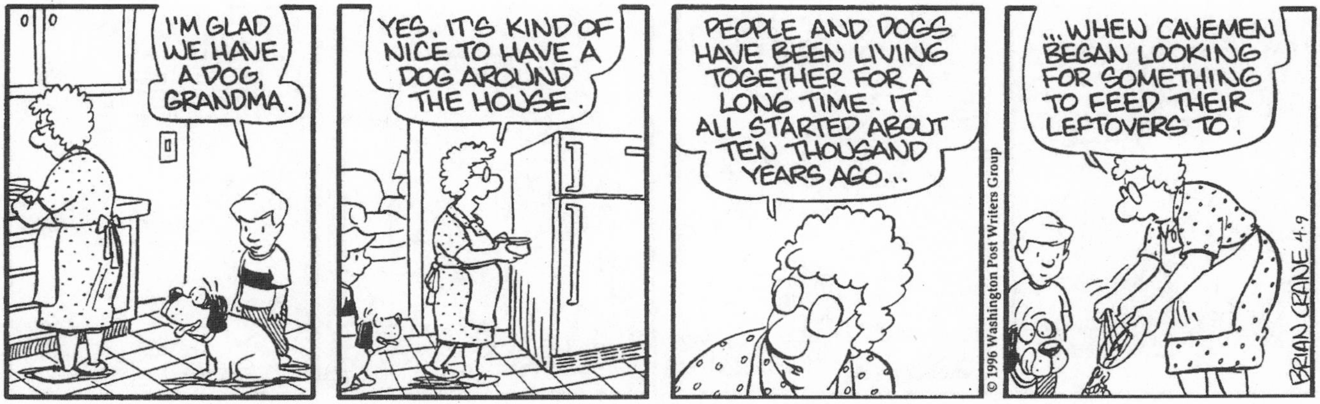

I'M GLAD WE HAVE A DOG, GRANDMA.
YES. IT'S KIND OF NICE TO HAVE A DOG AROUND THE HOUSE.
PEOPLE AND DOGS HAVE BEEN LIVING TOGETHER FOR A LONG TIME. IT ALL STARTED ABOUT TEN THOUSAND YEARS AGO...
...WHEN CAVEMEN BEGAN LOOKING FOR SOMETHING TO FEED THEIR LEFTOVERS TO.
© 1996 Washington Post Writers Group
4·9
BRIAN CRANE

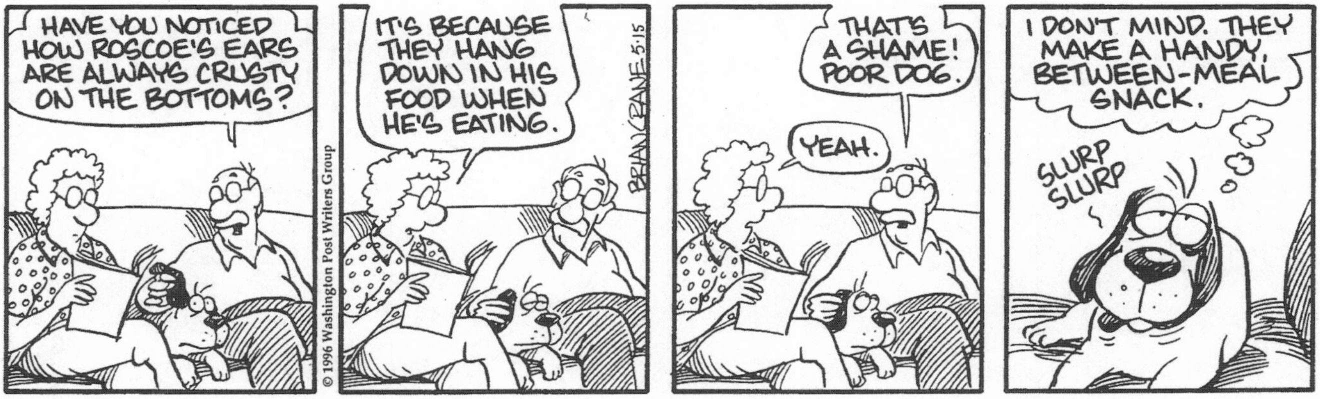

HAVE YOU NOTICED HOW ROSCOE'S EARS ARE ALWAYS CRUSTY ON THE BOTTOMS?
© 1996 Washington Post Writers Group
IT'S BECAUSE THEY HANG DOWN IN HIS FOOD WHEN HE'S EATING.
5·15
BRIAN CRANE
THAT'S A SHAME! POOR DOG.
YEAH.
I DON'T MIND. THEY MAKE A HANDY, BETWEEN-MEAL SNACK.
SLURP SLURP

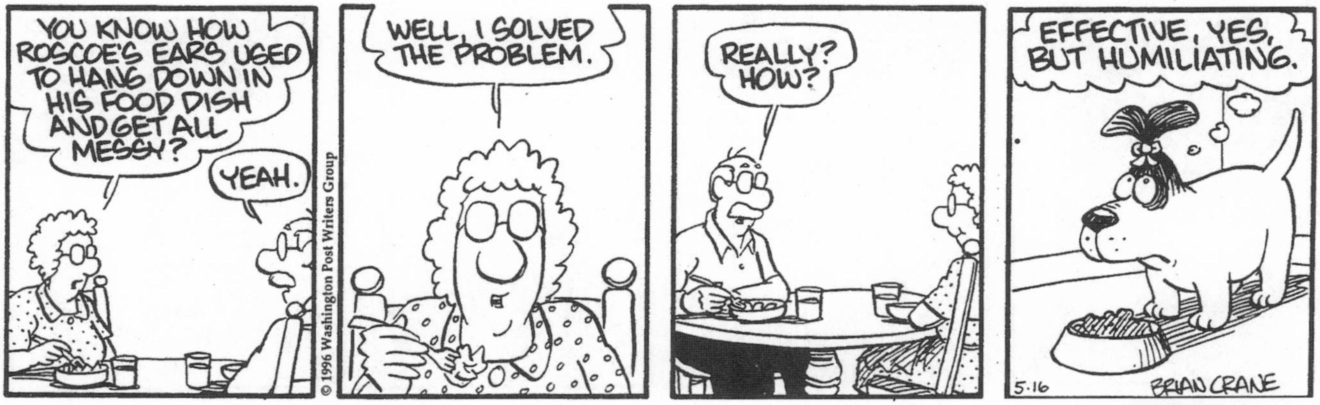

YOU KNOW HOW ROSCOE'S EARS USED TO HANG DOWN IN HIS FOOD DISH AND GET ALL MESSY?
YEAH.
© 1996 Washington Post Writers Group
WELL, I SOLVED THE PROBLEM.
REALLY? HOW?
EFFECTIVE, YES, BUT HUMILIATING.
5·16
BRIAN CRANE

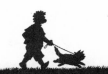

140

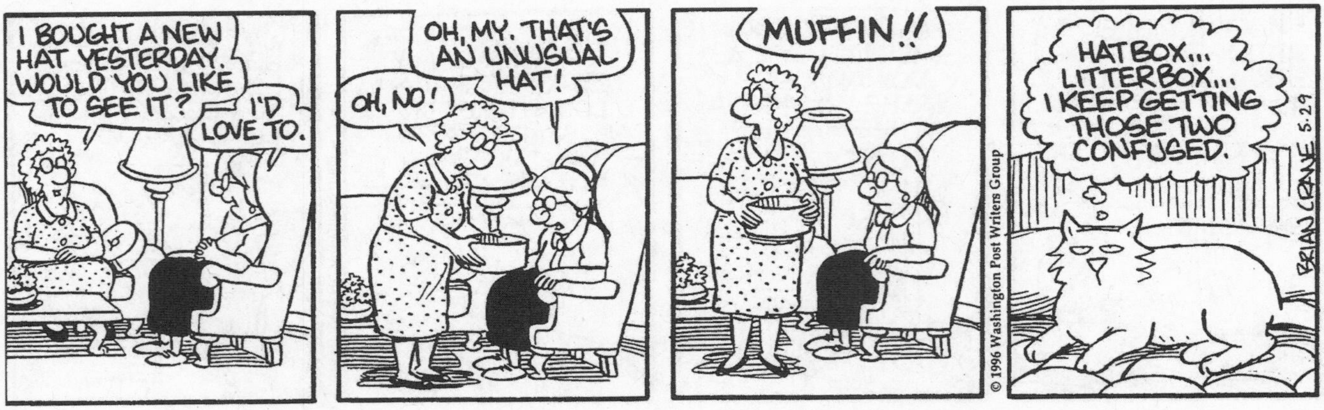

I BOUGHT A NEW HAT YESTERDAY. WOULD YOU LIKE TO SEE IT?
I'D LOVE TO.
OH, MY. THAT'S AN UNUSUAL HAT!
OH, NO!
MUFFIN!!
HATBOX... LITTERBOX... I KEEP GETTING THOSE TWO CONFUSED.
© 1996 Washington Post Writers Group
BRIAN CRANE 5.29

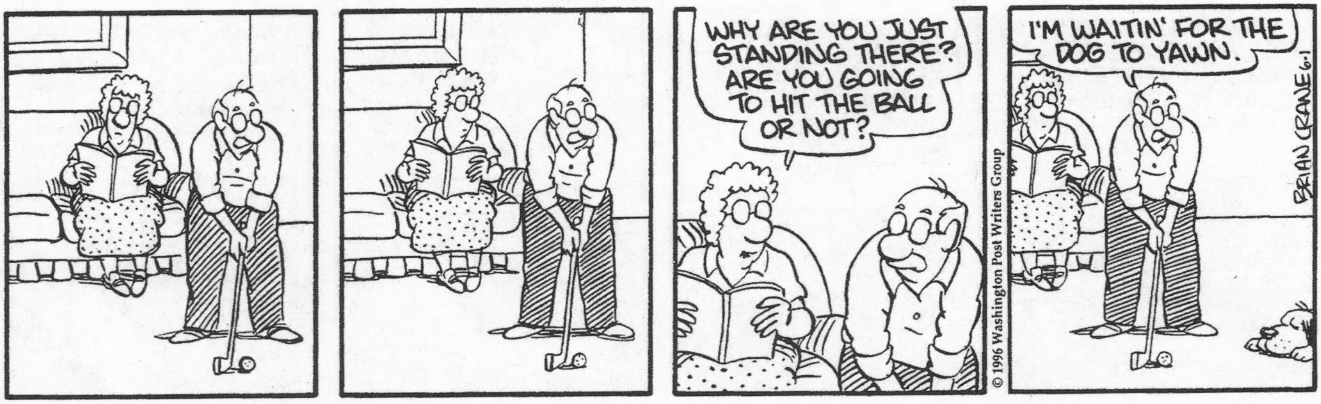

WHY ARE YOU JUST STANDING THERE? ARE YOU GOING TO HIT THE BALL OR NOT?
I'M WAITIN' FOR THE DOG TO YAWN.
© 1996 Washington Post Writers Group
BRIAN CRANE 6.1

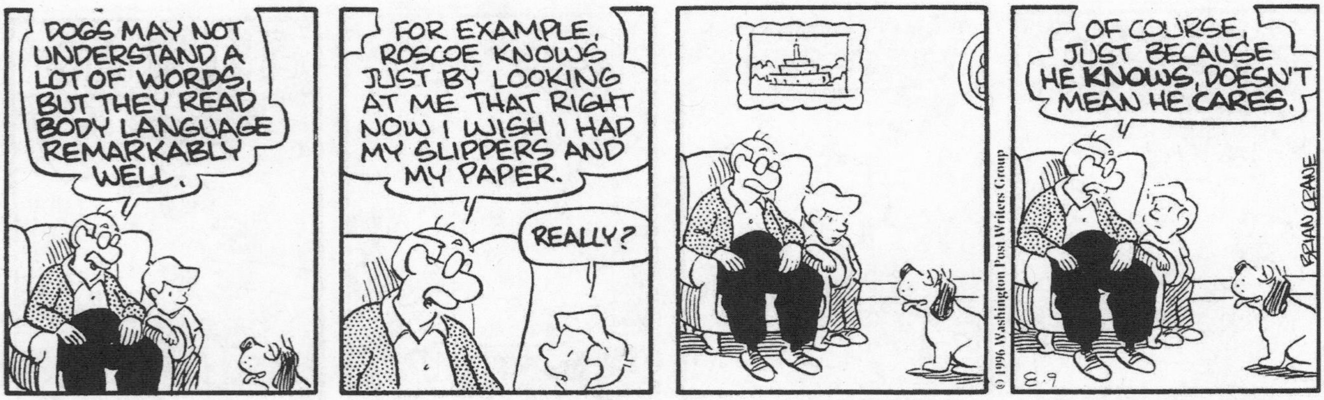

DOGS MAY NOT UNDERSTAND A LOT OF WORDS, BUT THEY READ BODY LANGUAGE REMARKABLY WELL.
FOR EXAMPLE, ROSCOE KNOWS JUST BY LOOKING AT ME THAT RIGHT NOW I WISH I HAD MY SLIPPERS AND MY PAPER.
REALLY?
OF COURSE, JUST BECAUSE HE KNOWS, DOESN'T MEAN HE CARES.
© 1996 Washington Post Writers Group
8.9
BRIAN CRANE

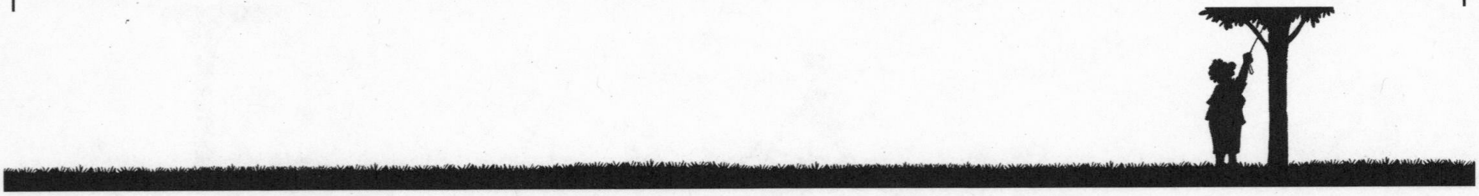

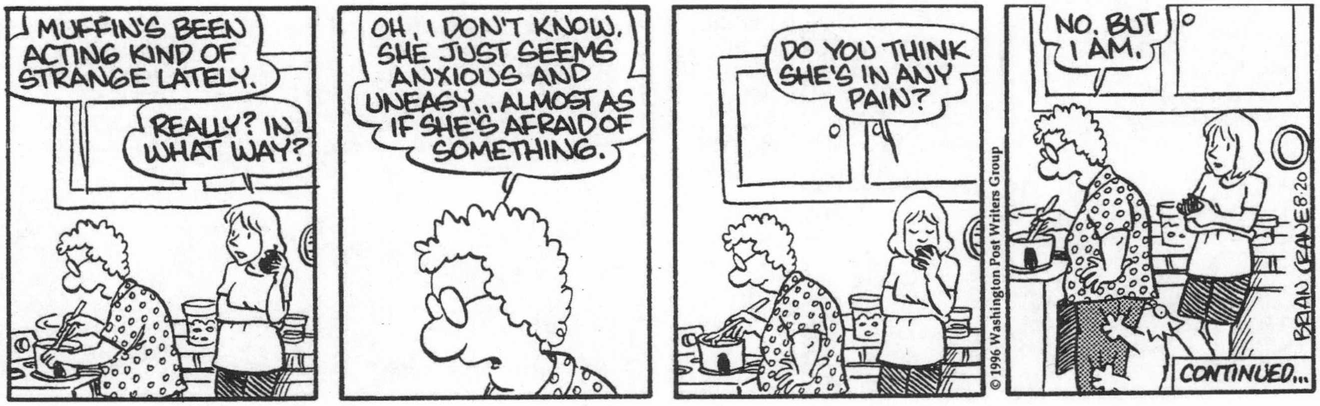
MUFFIN'S BEEN ACTING KIND OF STRANGE LATELY.
REALLY? IN WHAT WAY?
OH, I DON'T KNOW. SHE JUST SEEMS ANXIOUS AND UNEASY... ALMOST AS IF SHE'S AFRAID OF SOMETHING.
DO YOU THINK SHE'S IN ANY PAIN?
© 1996 Washington Post Writers Group
NO. BUT I AM.
BRIAN CRANE 8·20
CONTINUED...

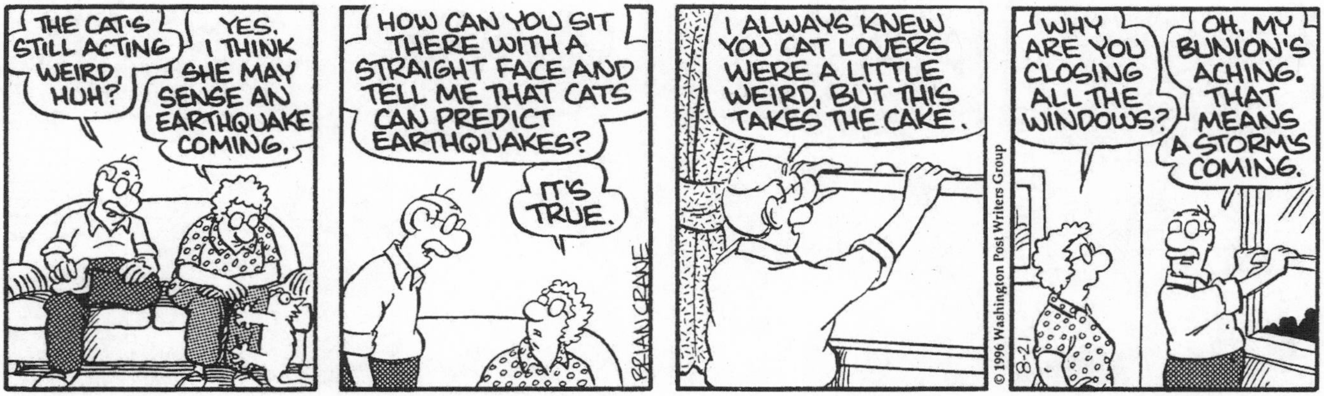
THE CAT'S STILL ACTING WEIRD, HUH?
YES. I THINK SHE MAY SENSE AN EARTHQUAKE COMING.
HOW CAN YOU SIT THERE WITH A STRAIGHT FACE AND TELL ME THAT CATS CAN PREDICT EARTHQUAKES?
IT'S TRUE.
BRIAN CRANE
I ALWAYS KNEW YOU CAT LOVERS WERE A LITTLE WEIRD, BUT THIS TAKES THE CAKE.
© 1996 Washington Post Writers Group
8·21
WHY ARE YOU CLOSING ALL THE WINDOWS?
OH, MY BUNION'S ACHING. THAT MEANS A STORM'S COMING.

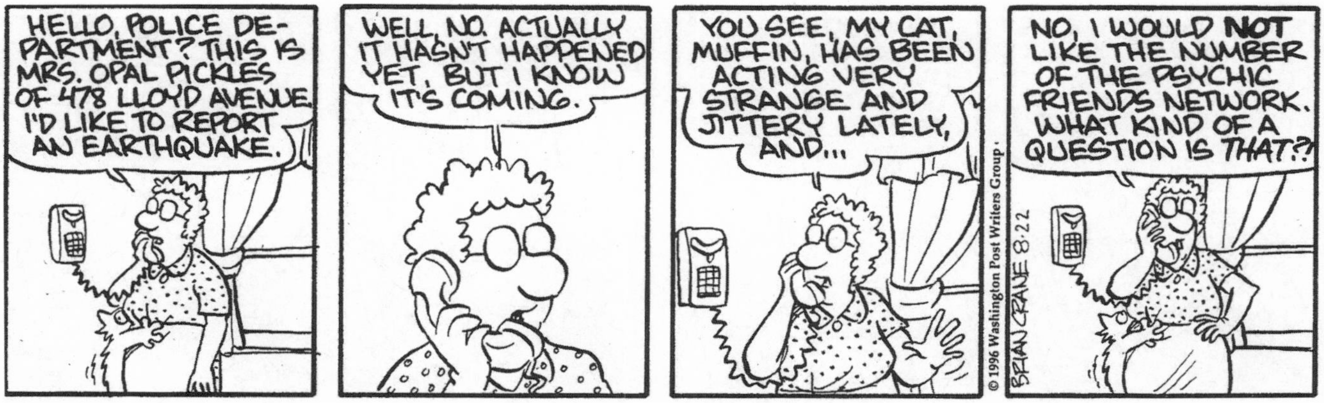
HELLO, POLICE DEPARTMENT? THIS IS MRS. OPAL PICKLES OF 478 LLOYD AVENUE. I'D LIKE TO REPORT AN EARTHQUAKE.
WELL, NO. ACTUALLY IT HASN'T HAPPENED YET, BUT I KNOW IT'S COMING.
YOU SEE, MY CAT, MUFFIN, HAS BEEN ACTING VERY STRANGE AND JITTERY LATELY, AND...
© 1996 Washington Post Writers Group
BRIAN CRANE 8·22
NO, I WOULD **NOT** LIKE THE NUMBER OF THE PSYCHIC FRIENDS NETWORK. WHAT KIND OF A QUESTION IS *THAT*?!

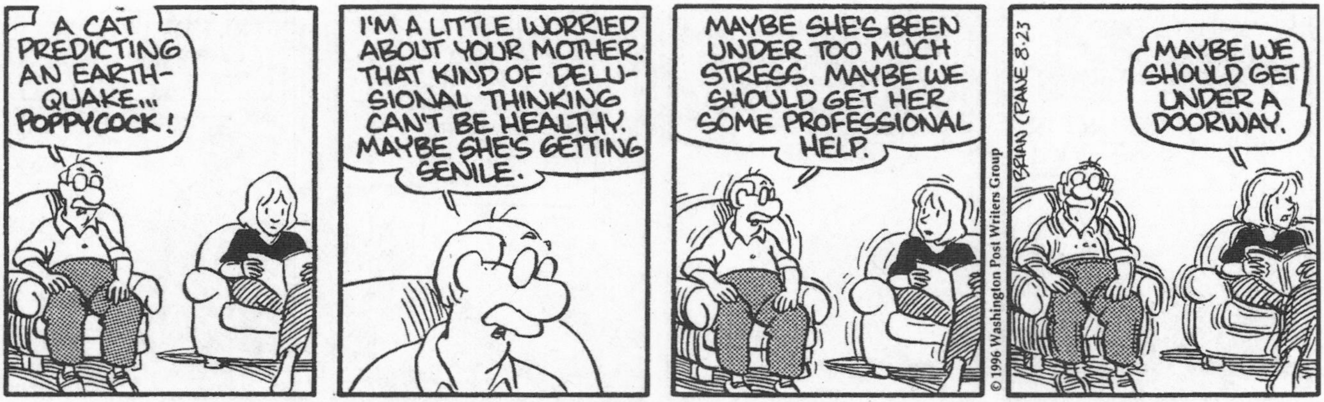
A CAT PREDICTING AN EARTH-QUAKE... POPPYCOCK!
I'M A LITTLE WORRIED ABOUT YOUR MOTHER. THAT KIND OF DELUSIONAL THINKING CAN'T BE HEALTHY. MAYBE SHE'S GETTING SENILE.
MAYBE SHE'S BEEN UNDER TOO MUCH STRESS. MAYBE WE SHOULD GET HER SOME PROFESSIONAL HELP.
BRIAN CRANE 8-23
© 1996 Washington Post Writers Group
MAYBE WE SHOULD GET UNDER A DOORWAY.

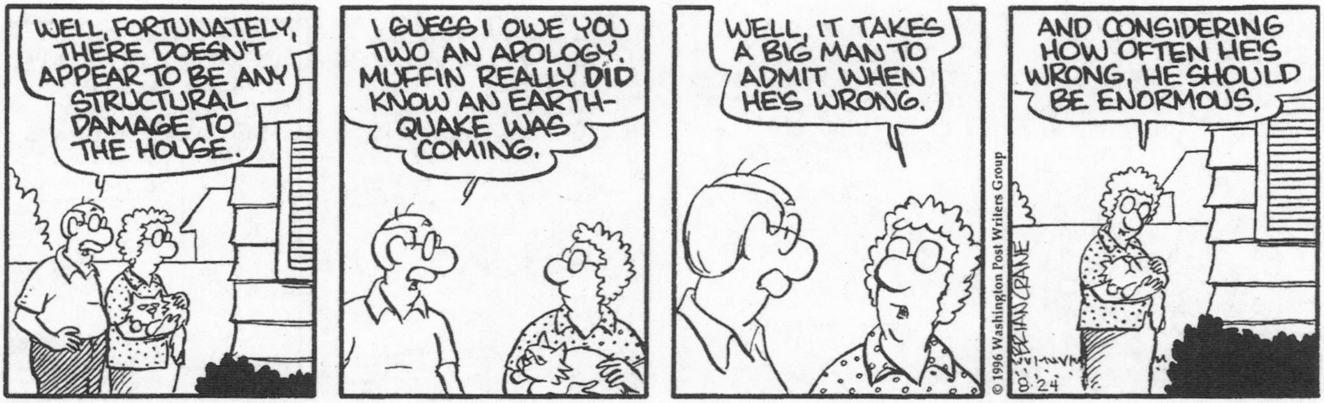
WELL, FORTUNATELY, THERE DOESN'T APPEAR TO BE ANY STRUCTURAL DAMAGE TO THE HOUSE.
I GUESS I OWE YOU TWO AN APOLOGY. MUFFIN REALLY DID KNOW AN EARTH-QUAKE WAS COMING.
WELL, IT TAKES A BIG MAN TO ADMIT WHEN HE'S WRONG.
© 1996 Washington Post Writers Group
BRIAN CRANE 8-24
AND CONSIDERING HOW OFTEN HE'S WRONG, HE SHOULD BE ENORMOUS.

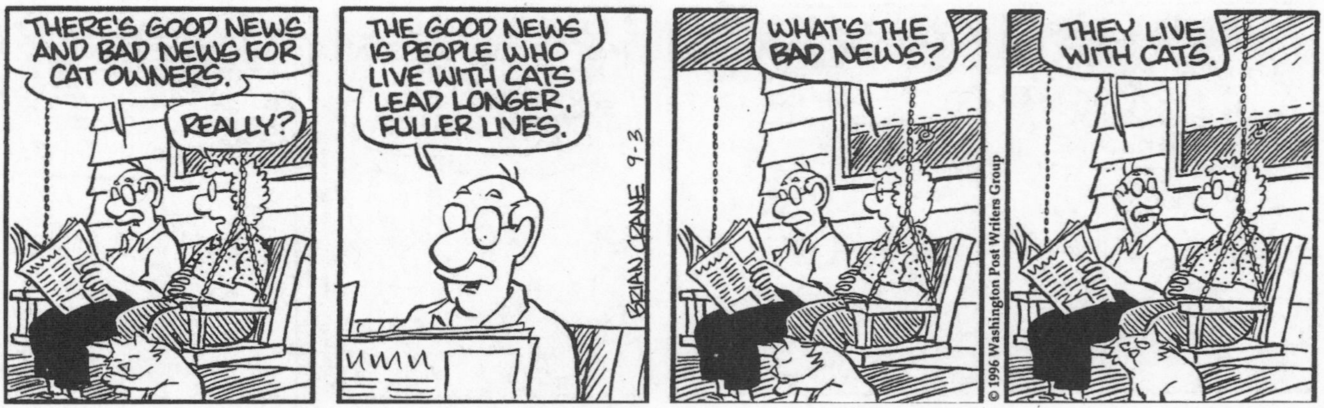
THERE'S GOOD NEWS AND BAD NEWS FOR CAT OWNERS.
REALLY?
THE GOOD NEWS IS PEOPLE WHO LIVE WITH CATS LEAD LONGER, FULLER LIVES.
BRIAN CRANE 9-3
WHAT'S THE BAD NEWS?
© 1996 Washington Post Writers Group
THEY LIVE WITH CATS.

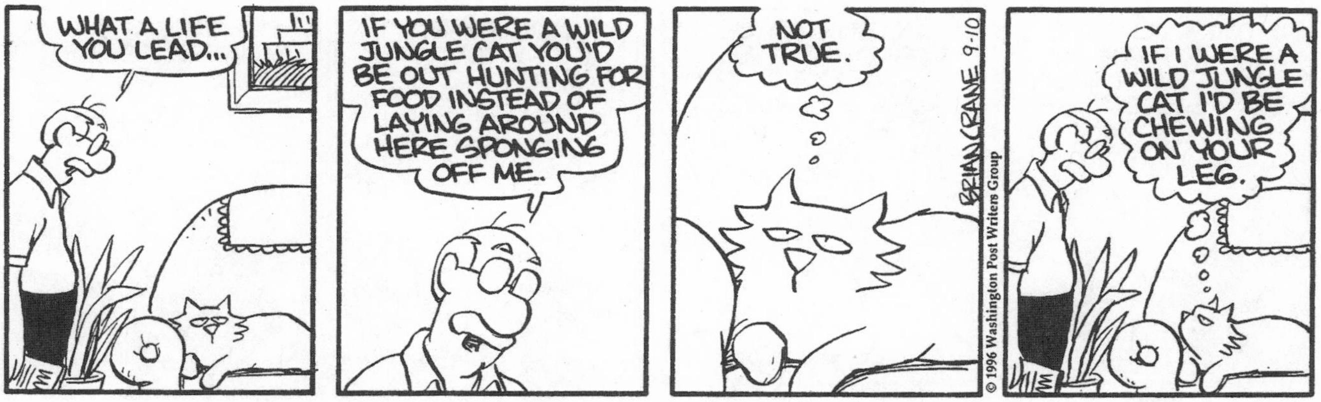
WHAT A LIFE YOU LEAD...
IF YOU WERE A WILD JUNGLE CAT YOU'D BE OUT HUNTING FOR FOOD INSTEAD OF LAYING AROUND HERE SPONGING OFF ME.
NOT TRUE.
BRIAN CRANE 9-10
© 1996 Washington Post Writers Group
IF I WERE A WILD JUNGLE CAT I'D BE CHEWING ON YOUR LEG.

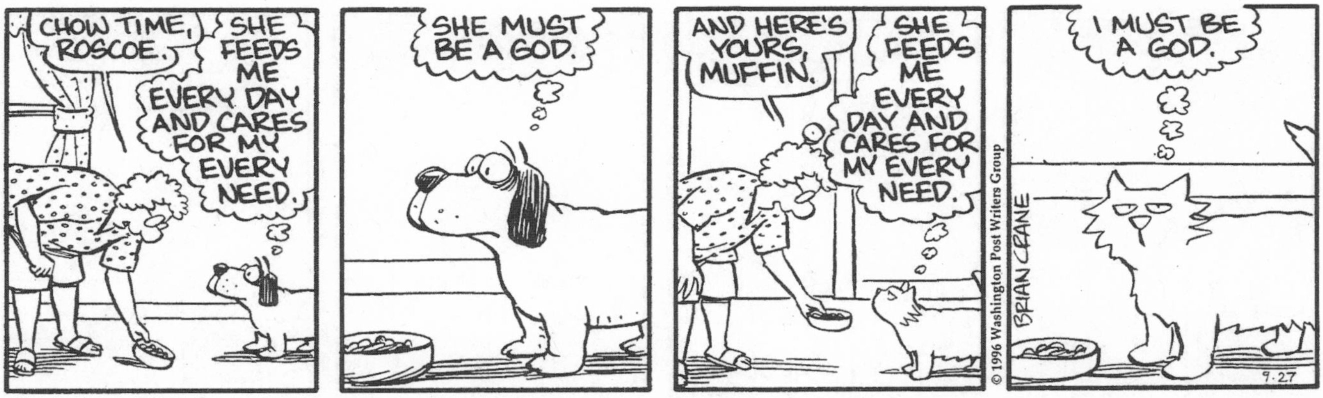
CHOW TIME, ROSCOE.
SHE FEEDS ME EVERY DAY AND CARES FOR MY EVERY NEED.
SHE MUST BE A GOD.
AND HERE'S YOURS, MUFFIN.
SHE FEEDS ME EVERY DAY AND CARES FOR MY EVERY NEED.
© 1996 Washington Post Writers Group
BRIAN CRANE
I MUST BE A GOD.
9·27

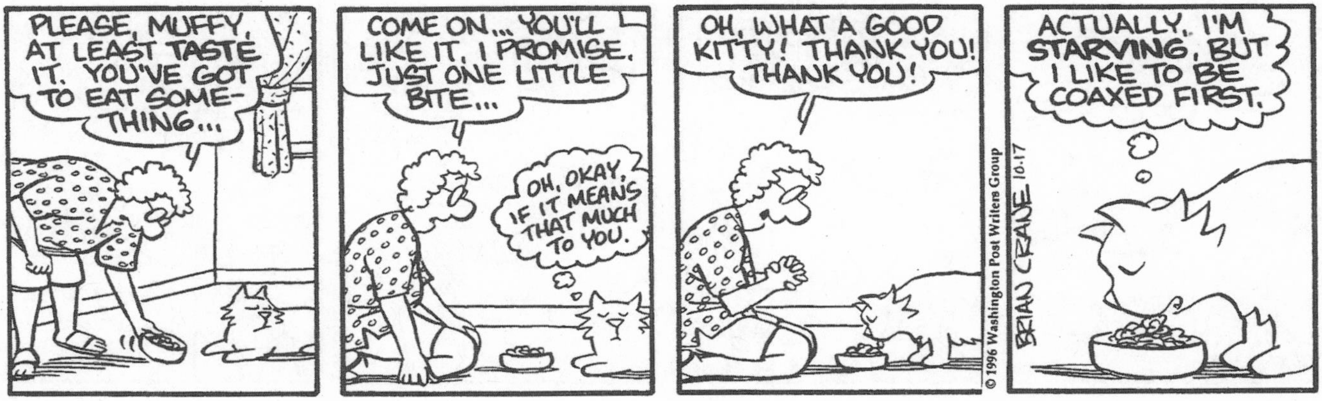
PLEASE, MUFFY, AT LEAST TASTE IT. YOU'VE GOT TO EAT SOME-THING...
COME ON... YOU'LL LIKE IT, I PROMISE. JUST ONE LITTLE BITE...
OH, OKAY, IF IT MEANS THAT MUCH TO YOU.
OH, WHAT A GOOD KITTY! THANK YOU! THANK YOU!
© 1996 Washington Post Writers Group
BRIAN CRANE 10·17
ACTUALLY, I'M STARVING, BUT I LIKE TO BE COAXED FIRST.

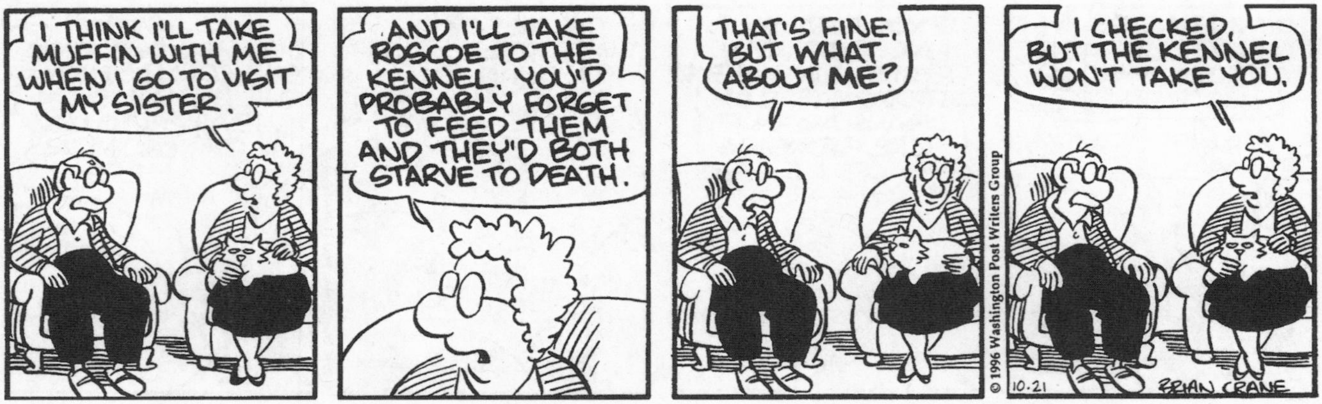
I THINK I'LL TAKE MUFFIN WITH ME WHEN I GO TO VISIT MY SISTER.
AND I'LL TAKE ROSCOE TO THE KENNEL. YOU'D PROBABLY FORGET TO FEED THEM AND THEY'D BOTH STARVE TO DEATH.
THAT'S FINE, BUT WHAT ABOUT ME?
I CHECKED, BUT THE KENNEL WON'T TAKE YOU.
© 1996 Washington Post Writers Group
10-21
BRIAN CRANE

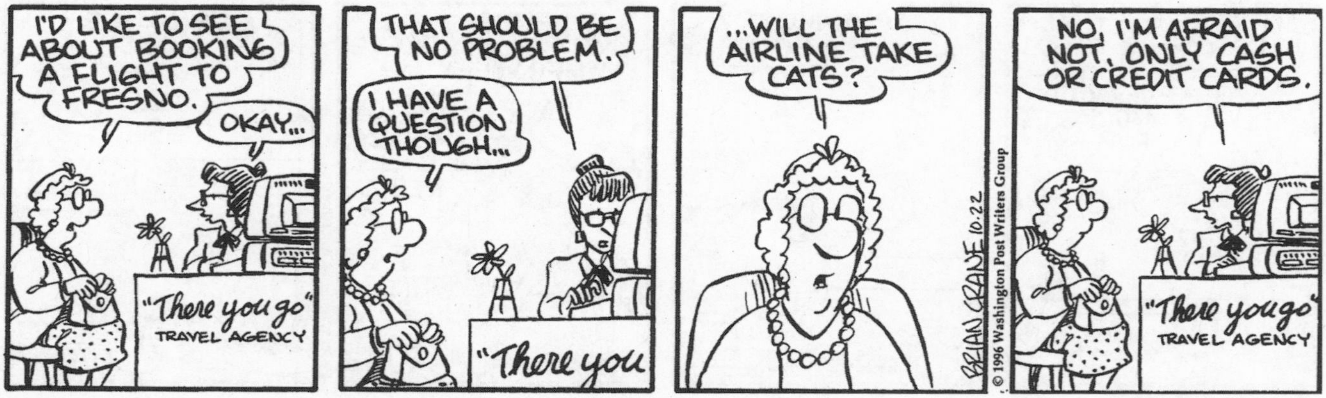
I'D LIKE TO SEE ABOUT BOOKING A FLIGHT TO FRESNO.
OKAY...
"There you go"
TRAVEL AGENCY
THAT SHOULD BE NO PROBLEM.
I HAVE A QUESTION THOUGH...
"There you
...WILL THE AIRLINE TAKE CATS?
BRIAN CRANE 10-22
© 1996 Washington Post Writers Group
NO, I'M AFRAID NOT. ONLY CASH OR CREDIT CARDS.
"There you go"
TRAVEL AGENCY

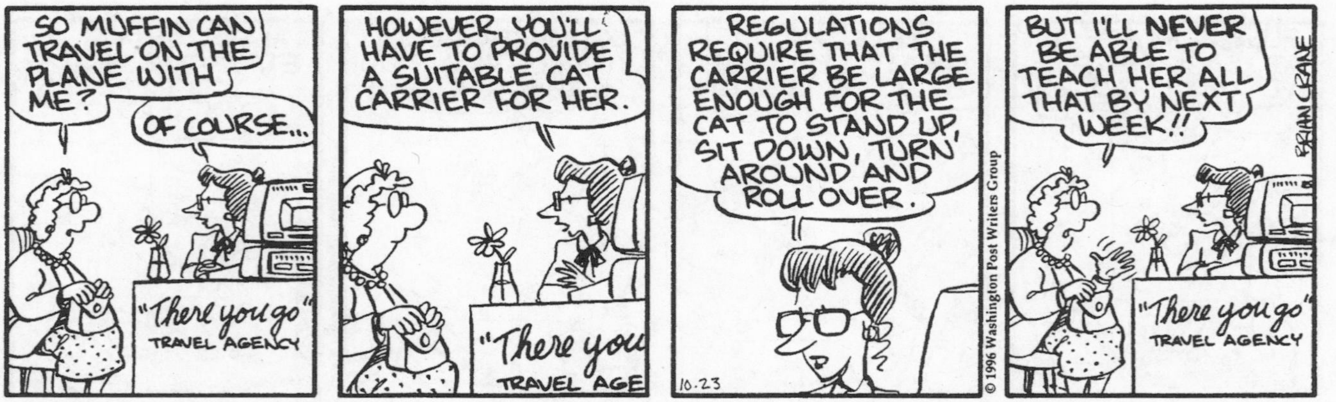
SO MUFFIN CAN TRAVEL ON THE PLANE WITH ME?
OF COURSE...
"There you go"
TRAVEL AGENCY
HOWEVER, YOU'LL HAVE TO PROVIDE A SUITABLE CAT CARRIER FOR HER.
"There you
TRAVEL AGE
REGULATIONS REQUIRE THAT THE CARRIER BE LARGE ENOUGH FOR THE CAT TO STAND UP, SIT DOWN, TURN AROUND AND ROLL OVER.
10-23
© 1996 Washington Post Writers Group
BUT I'LL NEVER BE ABLE TO TEACH HER ALL THAT BY NEXT WEEK!!
BRIAN CRANE
"There you go"
TRAVEL AGENCY

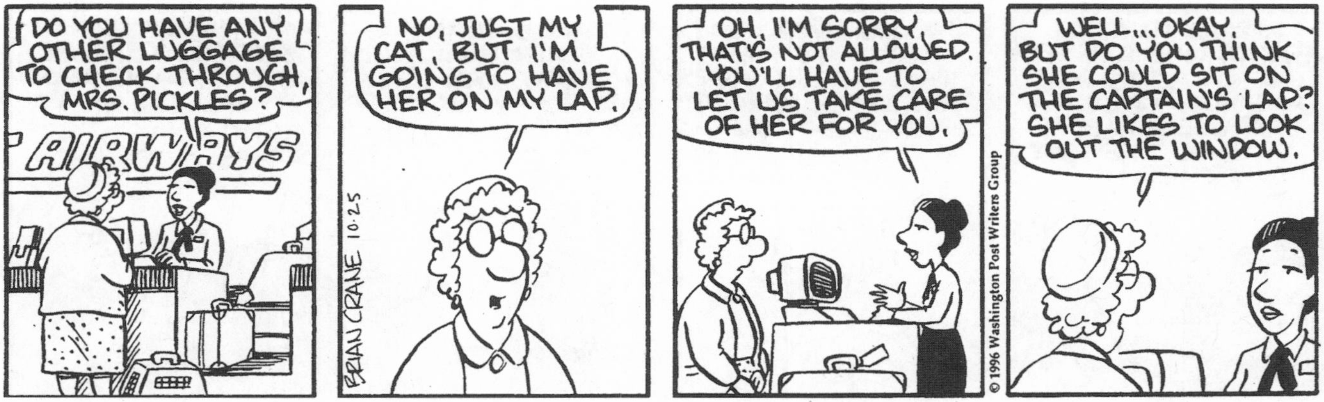
DO YOU HAVE ANY OTHER LUGGAGE TO CHECK THROUGH, MRS. PICKLES?
AIRWAYS
NO, JUST MY CAT, BUT I'M GOING TO HAVE HER ON MY LAP.
BRIAN CRANE 10.25
OH, I'M SORRY, THAT'S NOT ALLOWED. YOU'LL HAVE TO LET US TAKE CARE OF HER FOR YOU.
© 1996 Washington Post Writers Group
WELL... OKAY, BUT DO YOU THINK SHE COULD SIT ON THE CAPTAIN'S LAP? SHE LIKES TO LOOK OUT THE WINDOW.

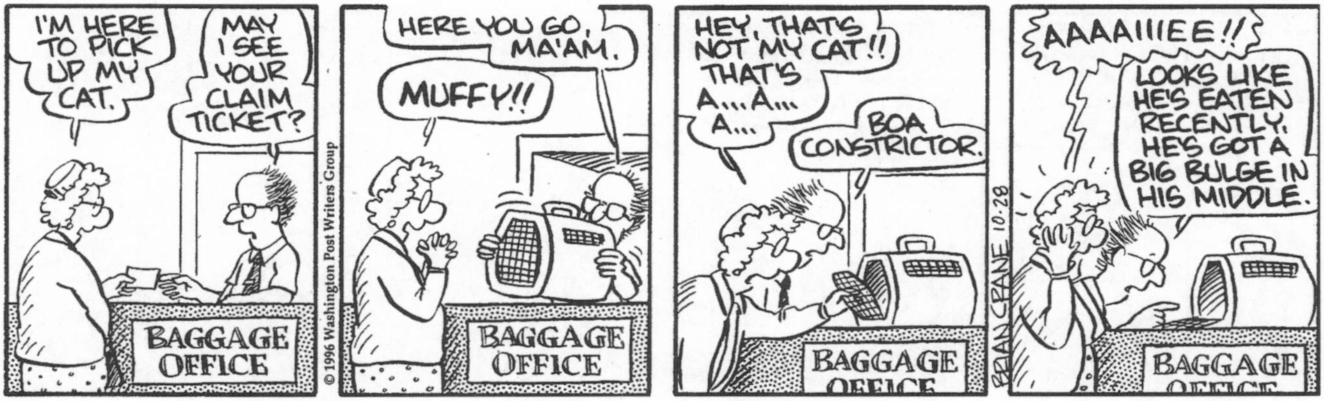
I'M HERE TO PICK UP MY CAT.
MAY I SEE YOUR CLAIM TICKET?
BAGGAGE OFFICE
© 1996 Washington Post Writers Group
HERE YOU GO, MA'AM.
MUFFY!!
BAGGAGE OFFICE
HEY, THAT'S NOT MY CAT!! THAT'S A... A... A...
BOA CONSTRICTOR.
BAGGAGE
BRIAN CRANE 10.28
AAAAIIIEE!!
LOOKS LIKE HE'S EATEN RECENTLY. HE'S GOT A BIG BULGE IN HIS MIDDLE.
BAGGAGE

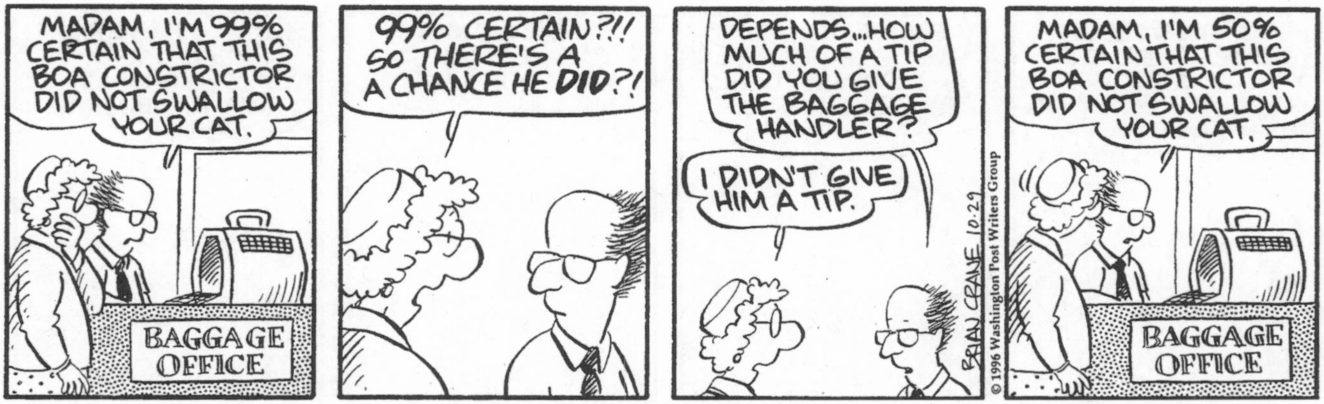
MADAM, I'M 99% CERTAIN THAT THIS BOA CONSTRICTOR DID NOT SWALLOW YOUR CAT.
BAGGAGE OFFICE
99% CERTAIN?!! SO THERE'S A CHANCE HE DID?!
DEPENDS... HOW MUCH OF A TIP DID YOU GIVE THE BAGGAGE HANDLER?
I DIDN'T GIVE HIM A TIP.
BRIAN CRANE 10.29
© 1996 Washington Post Writers Group
MADAM, I'M 50% CERTAIN THAT THIS BOA CONSTRICTOR DID NOT SWALLOW YOUR CAT.
BAGGAGE OFFICE

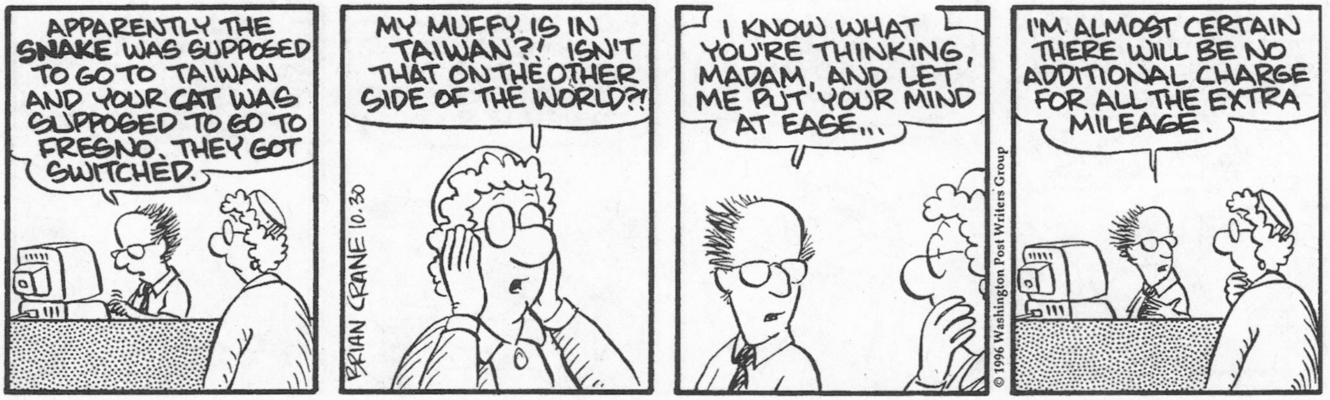
APPARENTLY THE SNAKE WAS SUPPOSED TO GO TO TAIWAN AND YOUR CAT WAS SUPPOSED TO GO TO FRESNO. THEY GOT SWITCHED.
MY MUFFY IS IN TAIWAN?! ISN'T THAT ON THE OTHER SIDE OF THE WORLD?!
BRIAN CRANE 10-30
I KNOW WHAT YOU'RE THINKING, MADAM, AND LET ME PUT YOUR MIND AT EASE...
© 1996 Washington Post Writers Group
I'M ALMOST CERTAIN THERE WILL BE NO ADDITIONAL CHARGE FOR ALL THE EXTRA MILEAGE.

146

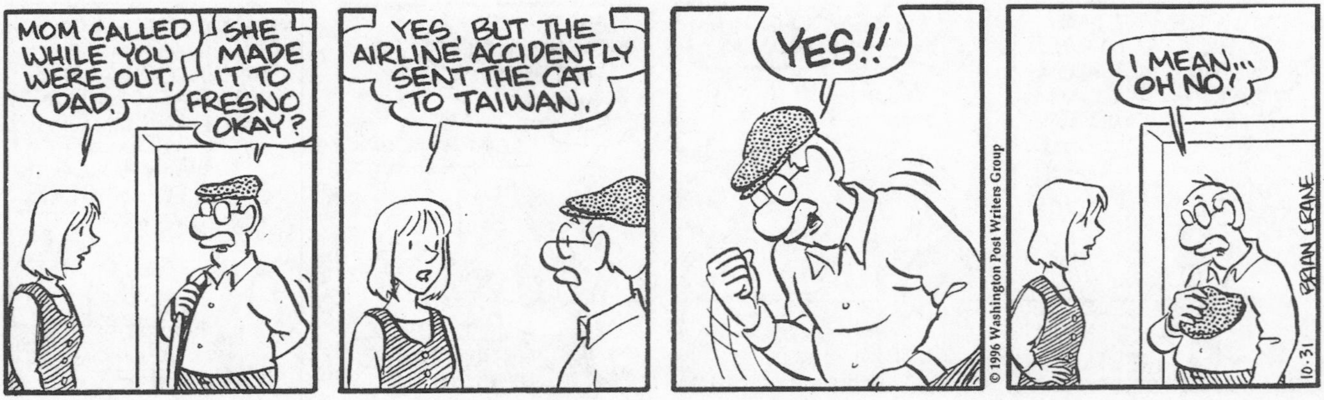
MOM CALLED WHILE YOU WERE OUT, DAD.
SHE MADE IT TO FRESNO OKAY?
YES, BUT THE AIRLINE ACCIDENTLY SENT THE CAT TO TAIWAN.
YES!!
© 1996 Washington Post Writers Group
I MEAN... OH NO!
BRIAN CRANE 10-31

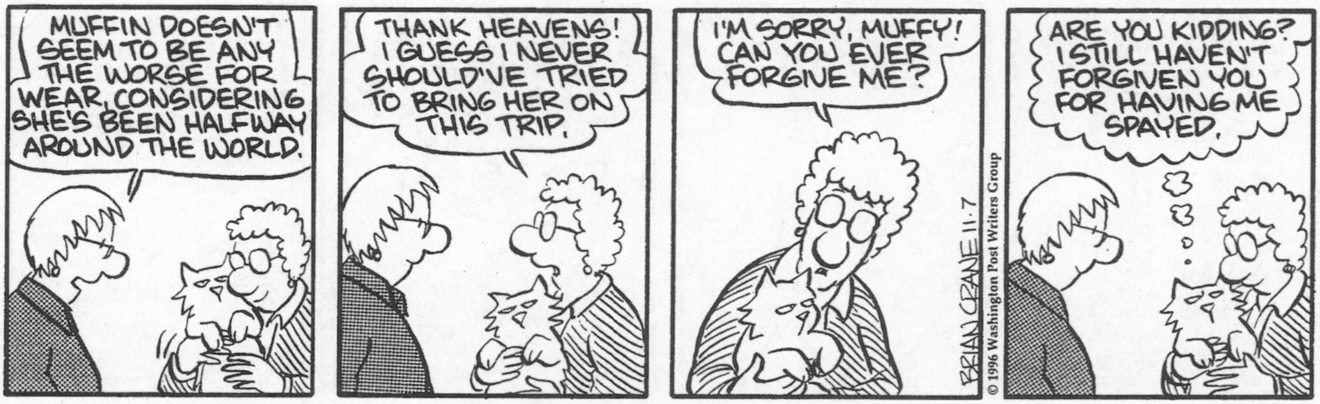
MUFFIN DOESN'T SEEM TO BE ANY THE WORSE FOR WEAR, CONSIDERING SHE'S BEEN HALFWAY AROUND THE WORLD.
THANK HEAVENS! I GUESS I NEVER SHOULD'VE TRIED TO BRING HER ON THIS TRIP.
I'M SORRY, MUFFY! CAN YOU EVER FORGIVE ME?
BRIAN CRANE 11-7
© 1996 Washington Post Writers Group
ARE YOU KIDDING? I STILL HAVEN'T FORGIVEN YOU FOR HAVING ME SPAYED.

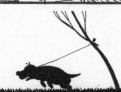

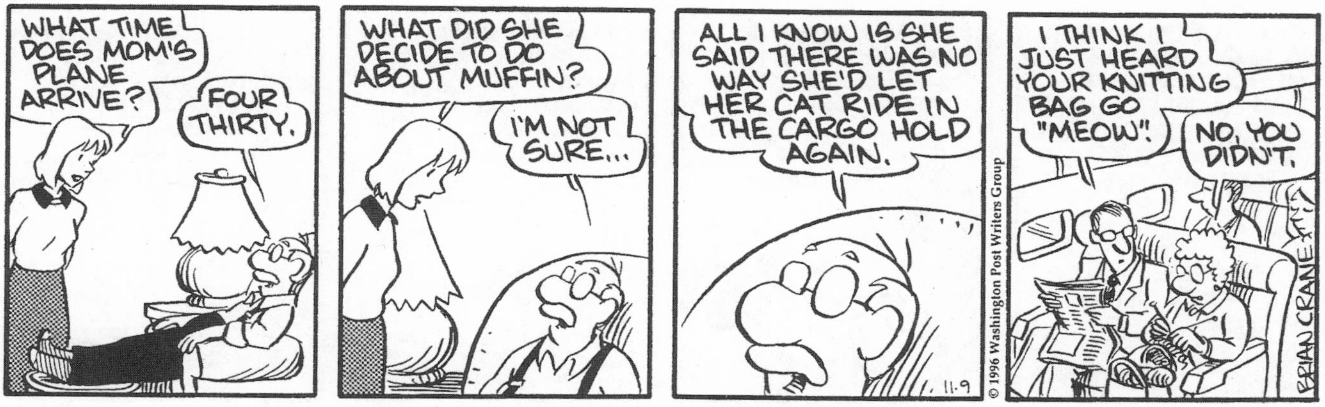
WHAT TIME DOES MOM'S PLANE ARRIVE?
FOUR THIRTY.
WHAT DID SHE DECIDE TO DO ABOUT MUFFIN?
I'M NOT SURE...
ALL I KNOW IS SHE SAID THERE WAS NO WAY SHE'D LET HER CAT RIDE IN THE CARGO HOLD AGAIN.
11-9
© 1996 Washington Post Writers Group
I THINK I JUST HEARD YOUR KNITTING BAG GO "MEOW".
NO, YOU DIDN'T.
BRIAN CRANE

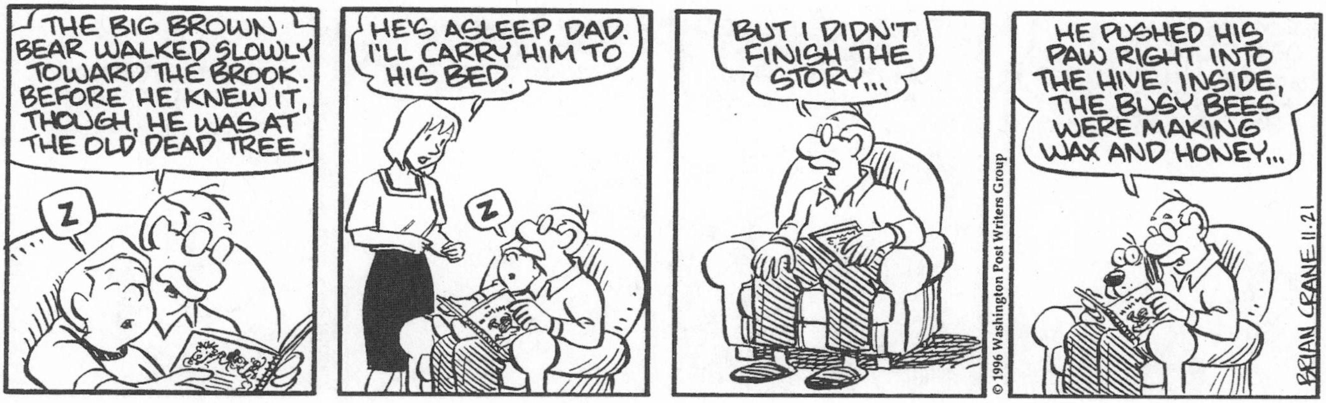
THE BIG BROWN BEAR WALKED SLOWLY TOWARD THE BROOK. BEFORE HE KNEW IT, THOUGH, HE WAS AT THE OLD DEAD TREE.
Z
HE'S ASLEEP, DAD. I'LL CARRY HIM TO HIS BED.
Z
BUT I DIDN'T FINISH THE STORY...
© 1996 Washington Post Writers Group
HE PUSHED HIS PAW RIGHT INTO THE HIVE. INSIDE, THE BUSY BEES WERE MAKING WAX AND HONEY...
BRIAN CRANE 11-21

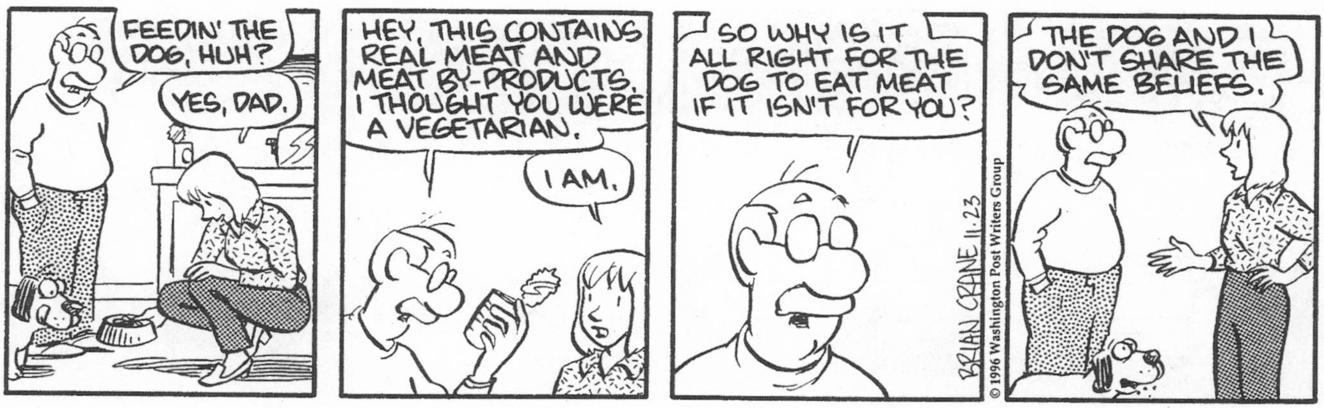
FEEDIN' THE DOG, HUH?
YES, DAD.
HEY, THIS CONTAINS REAL MEAT AND MEAT BY-PRODUCTS. I THOUGHT YOU WERE A VEGETARIAN.
I AM.
SO WHY IS IT ALL RIGHT FOR THE DOG TO EAT MEAT IF IT ISN'T FOR YOU?
BRIAN CRANE 11-23
© 1996 Washington Post Writers Group
THE DOG AND I DON'T SHARE THE SAME BELIEFS.

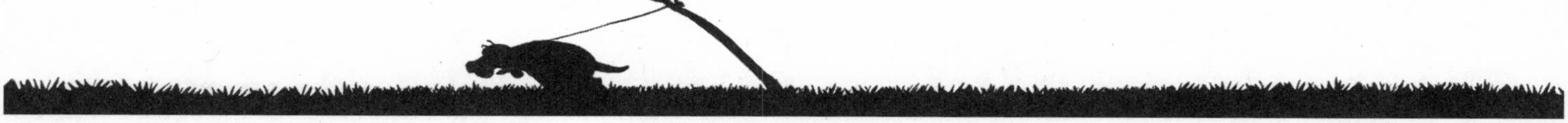

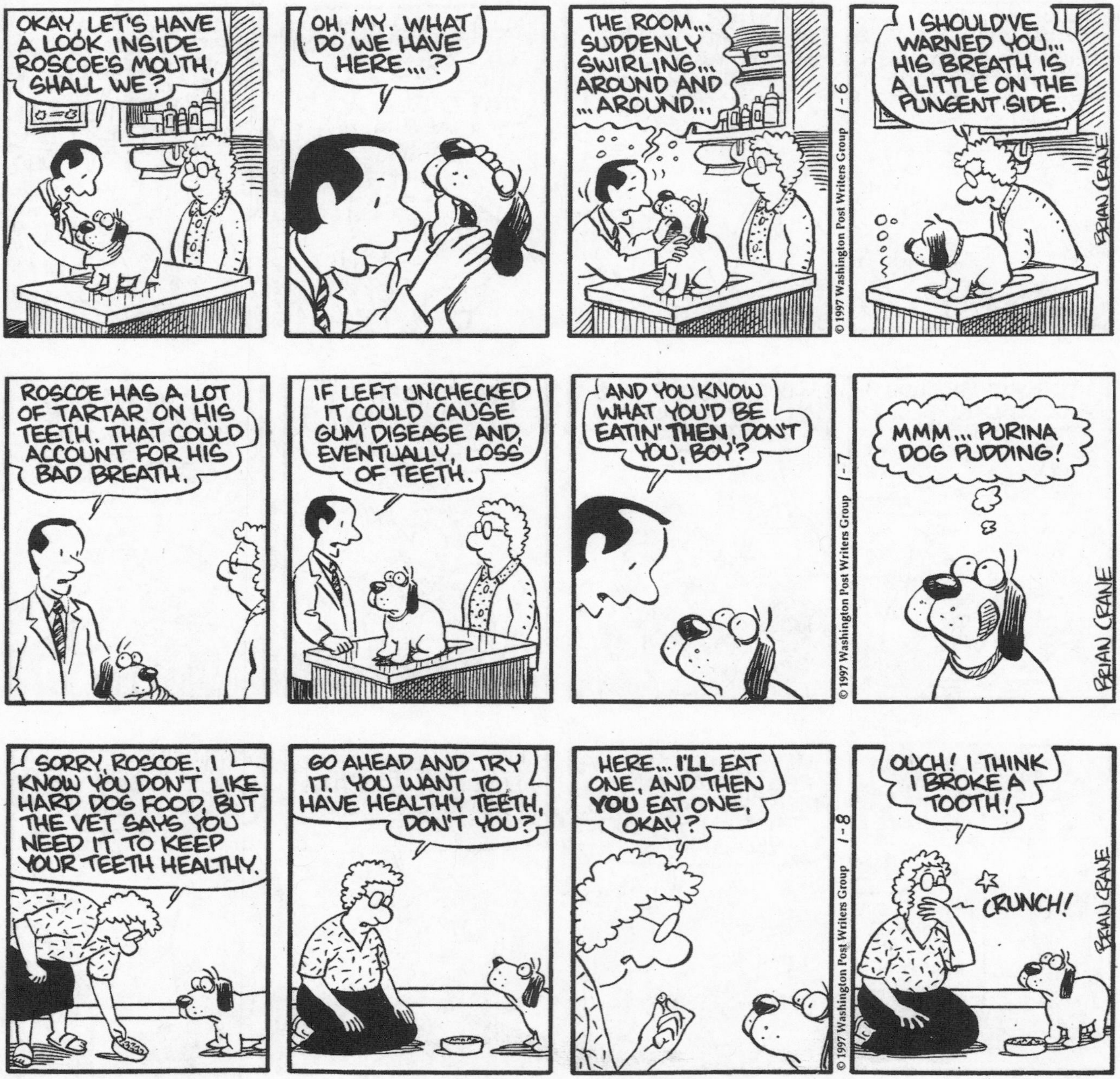
OKAY, LET'S HAVE A LOOK INSIDE ROSCOE'S MOUTH, SHALL WE?
OH, MY. WHAT DO WE HAVE HERE...?
THE ROOM... SUDDENLY SWIRLING... AROUND AND ...AROUND...
© 1997 Washington Post Writers Group 1-6
I SHOULD'VE WARNED YOU... HIS BREATH IS A LITTLE ON THE PUNGENT SIDE.
BRIAN CRANE
ROSCOE HAS A LOT OF TARTAR ON HIS TEETH. THAT COULD ACCOUNT FOR HIS BAD BREATH.
IF LEFT UNCHECKED IT COULD CAUSE GUM DISEASE AND, EVENTUALLY, LOSS OF TEETH.
AND YOU KNOW WHAT YOU'D BE EATIN' THEN, DON'T YOU, BOY?
© 1997 Washington Post Writers Group 1-7
MMM... PURINA DOG PUDDING!
BRIAN CRANE
SORRY, ROSCOE. I KNOW YOU DON'T LIKE HARD DOG FOOD, BUT THE VET SAYS YOU NEED IT TO KEEP YOUR TEETH HEALTHY.
GO AHEAD AND TRY IT. YOU WANT TO HAVE HEALTHY TEETH, DON'T YOU?
HERE... I'LL EAT ONE, AND THEN YOU EAT ONE, OKAY?
© 1997 Washington Post Writers Group 1-8
OUCH! I THINK I BROKE A TOOTH!
CRUNCH!
BRIAN CRANE

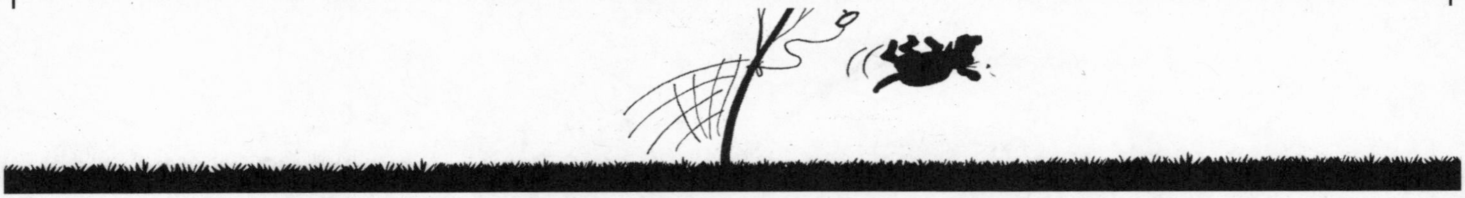

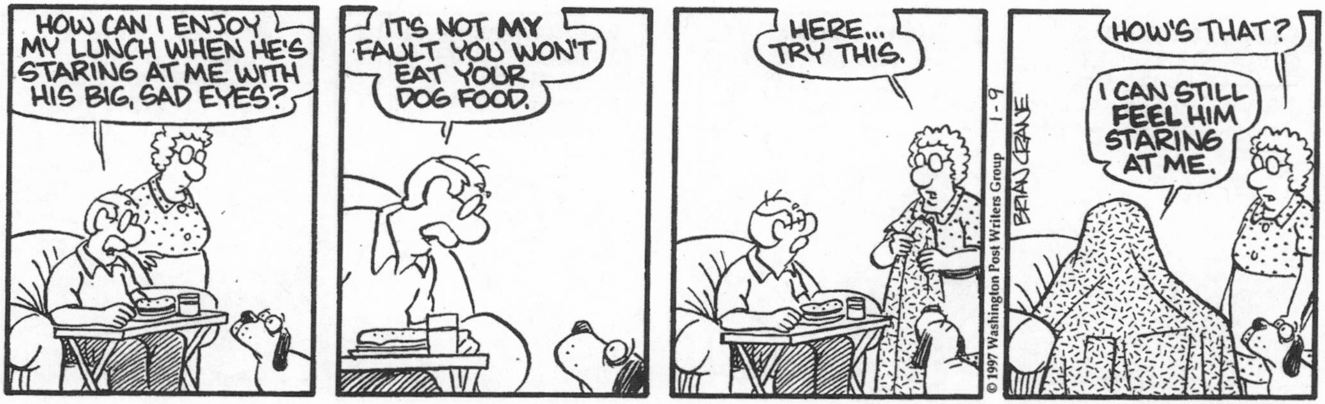
HOW CAN I ENJOY MY LUNCH WHEN HE'S STARING AT ME WITH HIS BIG, SAD EYES?
IT'S NOT MY FAULT YOU WON'T EAT YOUR DOG FOOD.
HERE... TRY THIS.
1-9
© 1997 Washington Post Writers Group
BRIAN CRANE
HOW'S THAT?
I CAN STILL FEEL HIM STARING AT ME.

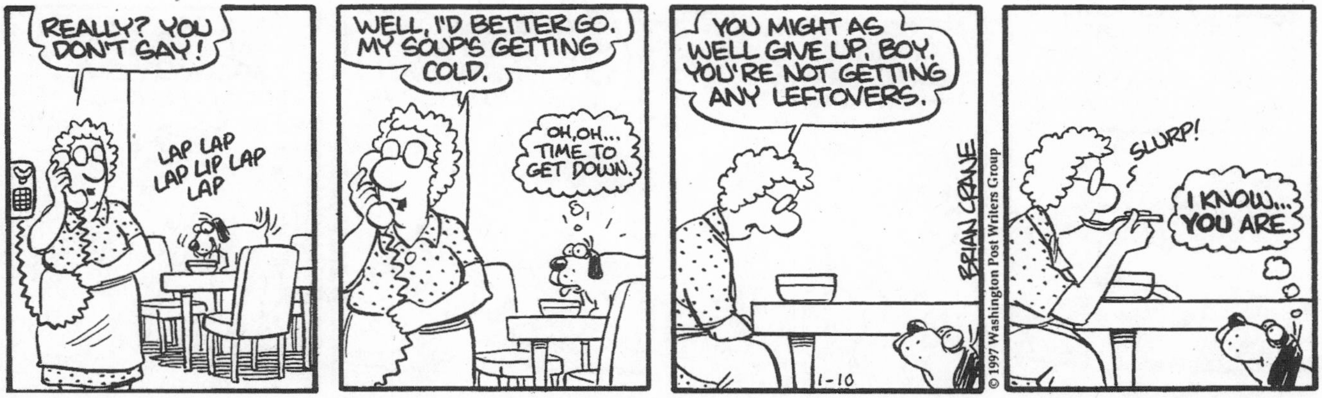
REALLY? YOU DON'T SAY!
LAP LAP LAP LIP LAP LAP
WELL, I'D BETTER GO. MY SOUP'S GETTING COLD.
OH, OH... TIME TO GET DOWN.
YOU MIGHT AS WELL GIVE UP, BOY. YOU'RE NOT GETTING ANY LEFTOVERS.
1-10
BRIAN CRANE
© 1997 Washington Post Writers Group
SLURP!
I KNOW... YOU ARE.

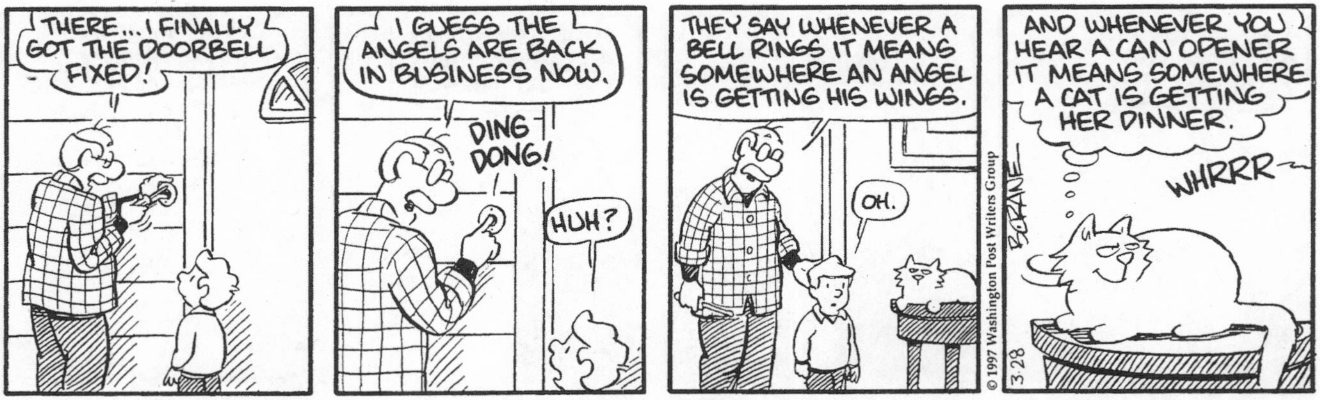
THERE... I FINALLY GOT THE DOORBELL FIXED!
I GUESS THE ANGELS ARE BACK IN BUSINESS NOW.
DING DONG!
HUH?
THEY SAY WHENEVER A BELL RINGS IT MEANS SOMEWHERE AN ANGEL IS GETTING HIS WINGS.
OH.
© 1997 Washington Post Writers Group
3-28
B. CRANE
AND WHENEVER YOU HEAR A CAN OPENER IT MEANS SOMEWHERE A CAT IS GETTING HER DINNER.
WHRRR

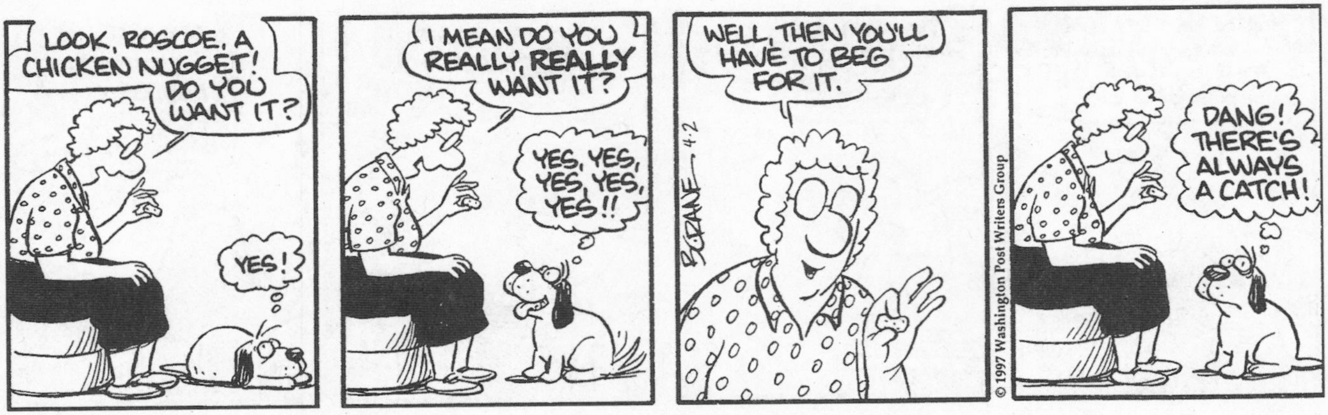
LOOK, ROSCOE, A CHICKEN NUGGET! DO YOU WANT IT?
YES!
I MEAN DO YOU REALLY, REALLY WANT IT?
YES, YES, YES, YES, YES!!
WELL, THEN YOU'LL HAVE TO BEG FOR IT.
DANG! THERE'S ALWAYS A CATCH!
© 1997 Washington Post Writers Group

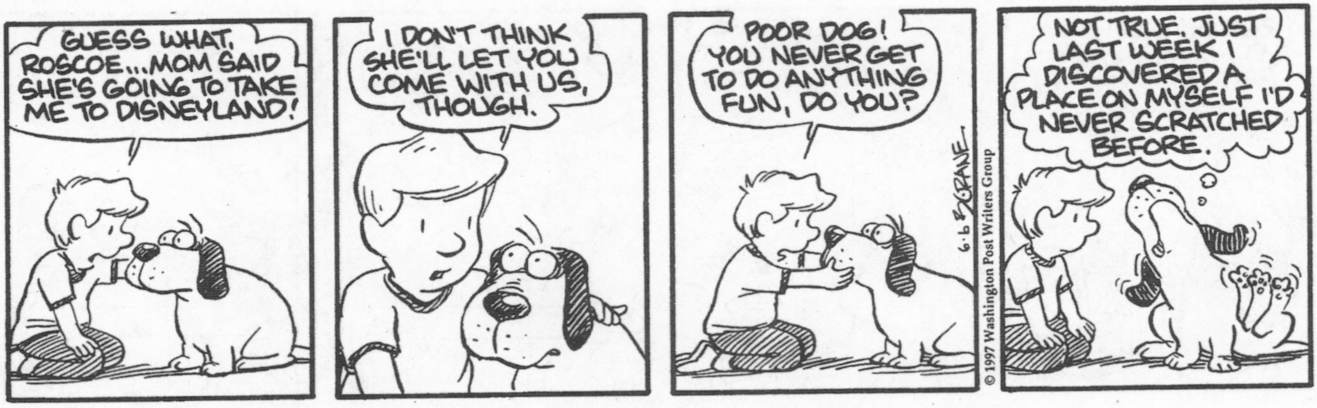
GUESS WHAT, ROSCOE...MOM SAID SHE'S GOING TO TAKE ME TO DISNEYLAND!
I DON'T THINK SHE'LL LET YOU COME WITH US, THOUGH.
POOR DOG! YOU NEVER GET TO DO ANYTHING FUN, DO YOU?
NOT TRUE. JUST LAST WEEK I DISCOVERED A PLACE ON MYSELF I'D NEVER SCRATCHED BEFORE.
© 1997 Washington Post Writers Group

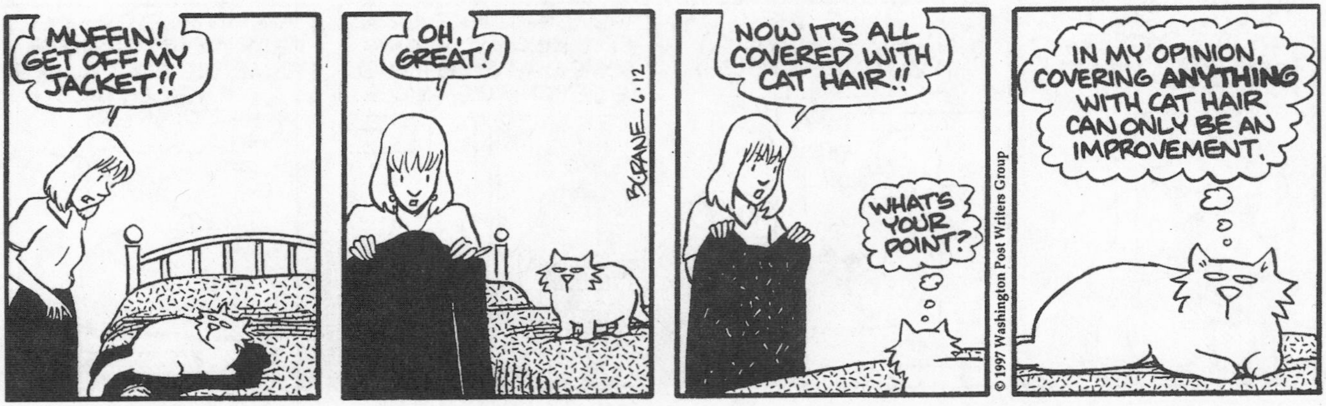
MUFFIN! GET OFF MY JACKET!!
OH, GREAT!
NOW IT'S ALL COVERED WITH CAT HAIR!!
WHAT'S YOUR POINT?
IN MY OPINION, COVERING ANYTHING WITH CAT HAIR CAN ONLY BE AN IMPROVEMENT.
© 1997 Washington Post Writers Group

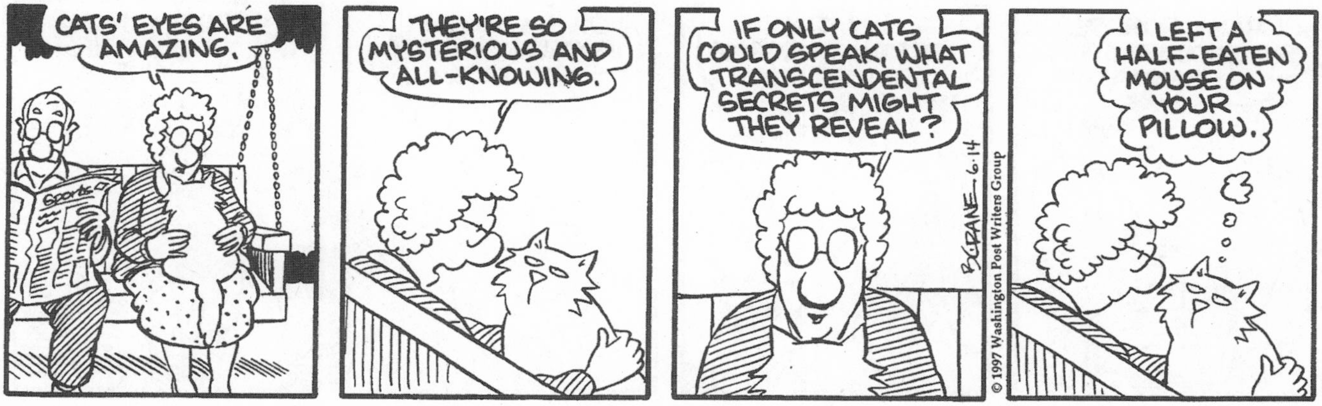
CATS' EYES ARE AMAZING.
THEY'RE SO MYSTERIOUS AND ALL-KNOWING.
IF ONLY CATS COULD SPEAK, WHAT TRANSCENDENTAL SECRETS MIGHT THEY REVEAL?
B.CRANE 6.14
© 1997 Washington Post Writers Group
I LEFT A HALF-EATEN MOUSE ON YOUR PILLOW.

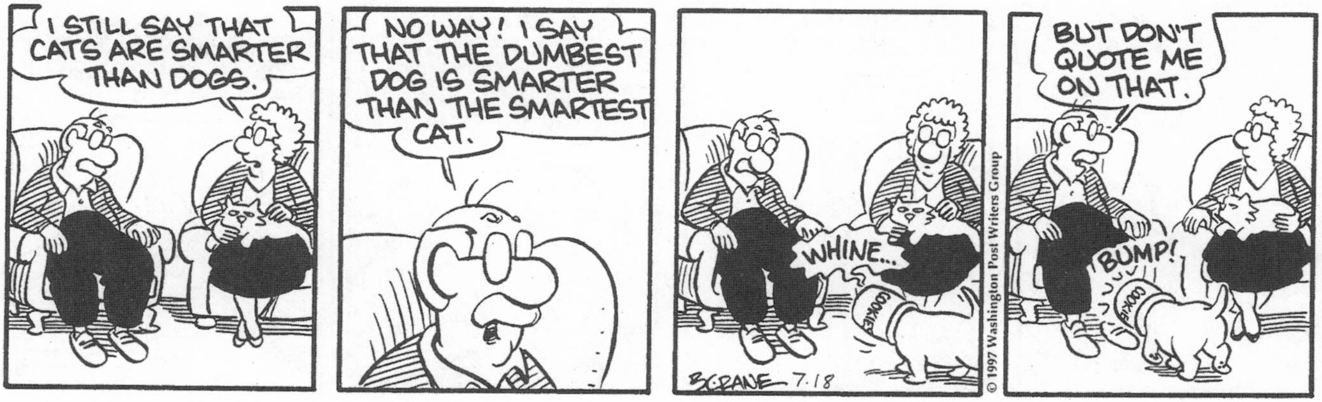
I STILL SAY THAT CATS ARE SMARTER THAN DOGS.
NO WAY! I SAY THAT THE DUMBEST DOG IS SMARTER THAN THE SMARTEST CAT.
WHINE...
COOKIES
B.CRANE 7.18
© 1997 Washington Post Writers Group
BUT DON'T QUOTE ME ON THAT.
BUMP!

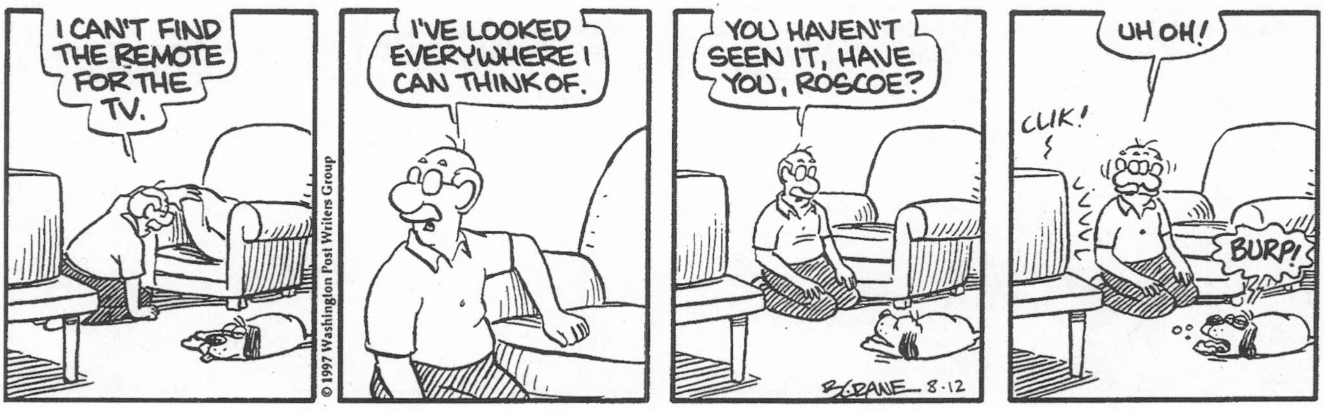
I CAN'T FIND THE REMOTE FOR THE TV.
© 1997 Washington Post Writers Group
I'VE LOOKED EVERYWHERE I CAN THINK OF.
YOU HAVEN'T SEEN IT, HAVE YOU, ROSCOE?
B.CRANE 8.12
UH OH!
CLIK!
BURP!

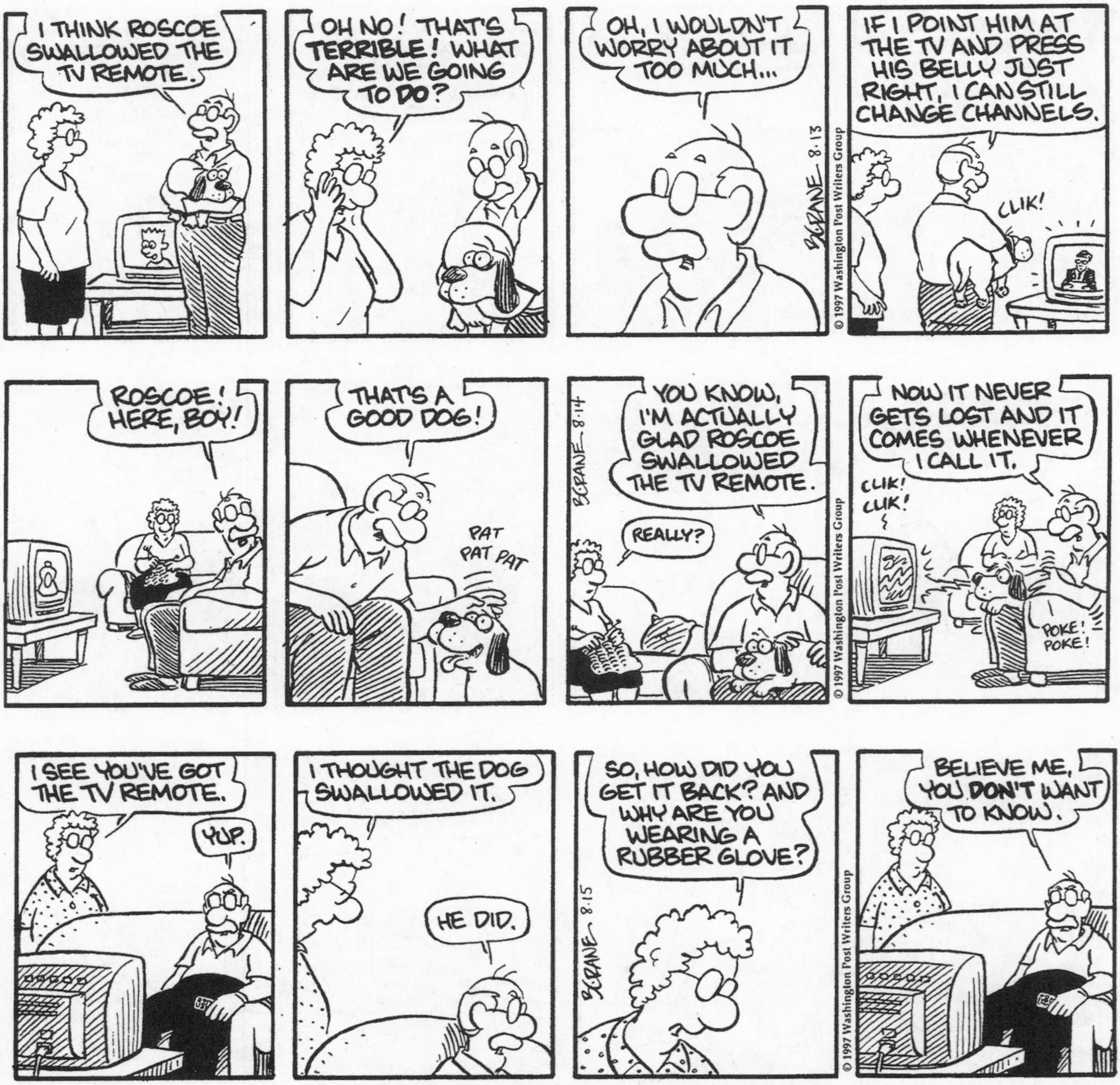
I THINK ROSCOE SWALLOWED THE TV REMOTE.
OH NO! THAT'S TERRIBLE! WHAT ARE WE GOING TO DO?
OH, I WOULDN'T WORRY ABOUT IT TOO MUCH...
B. CRANE 8.13
© 1997 Washington Post Writers Group
IF I POINT HIM AT THE TV AND PRESS HIS BELLY JUST RIGHT, I CAN STILL CHANGE CHANNELS.
CLIK!
ROSCOE! HERE, BOY!
THAT'S A GOOD DOG!
PAT PAT PAT
B. CRANE 8.14
YOU KNOW, I'M ACTUALLY GLAD ROSCOE SWALLOWED THE TV REMOTE.
REALLY?
© 1997 Washington Post Writers Group
NOW IT NEVER GETS LOST AND IT COMES WHENEVER I CALL IT.
CLIK! CLIK!
POKE! POKE!
I SEE YOU'VE GOT THE TV REMOTE.
YUP.
I THOUGHT THE DOG SWALLOWED IT.
HE DID.
B. CRANE 8.15
SO, HOW DID YOU GET IT BACK? AND WHY ARE YOU WEARING A RUBBER GLOVE?
© 1997 Washington Post Writers Group
BELIEVE ME, YOU DON'T WANT TO KNOW.

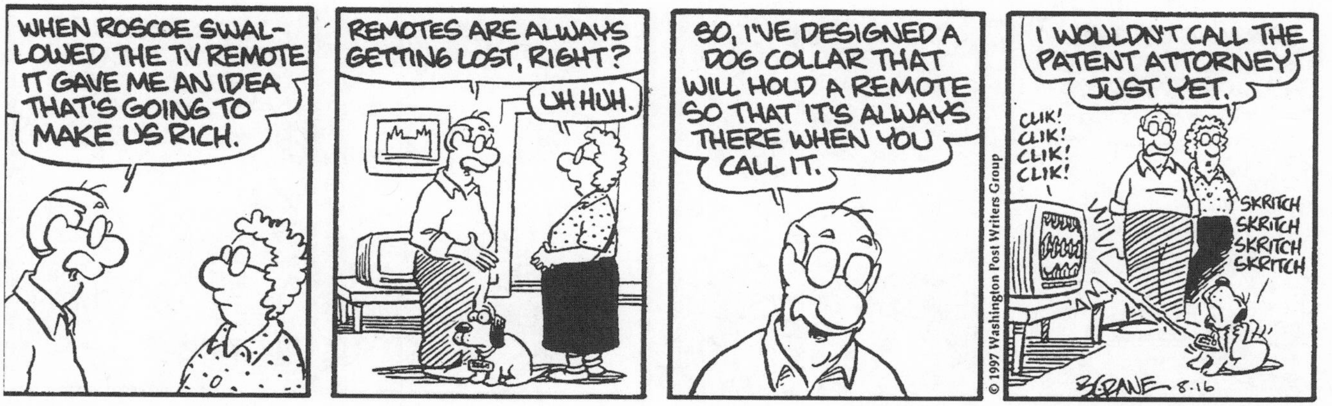
WHEN ROSCOE SWALLOWED THE TV REMOTE IT GAVE ME AN IDEA THAT'S GOING TO MAKE US RICH.
REMOTES ARE ALWAYS GETTING LOST, RIGHT?
UH HUH.
SO, I'VE DESIGNED A DOG COLLAR THAT WILL HOLD A REMOTE SO THAT IT'S ALWAYS THERE WHEN YOU CALL IT.
© 1997 Washington Post Writers Group
I WOULDN'T CALL THE PATENT ATTORNEY JUST YET.
CLIK! CLIK! CLIK! CLIK!
SKRITCH SKRITCH SKRITCH SKRITCH

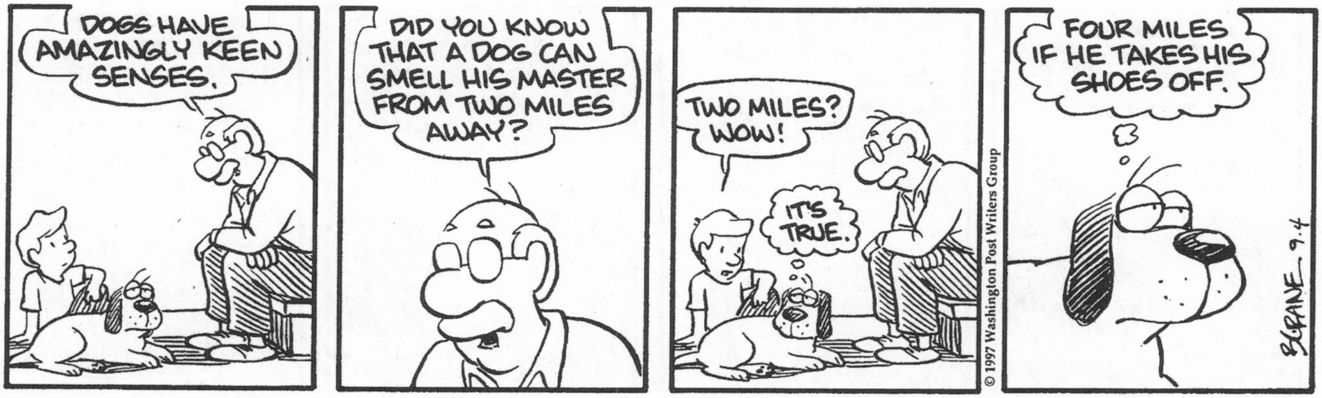
DOGS HAVE AMAZINGLY KEEN SENSES.
DID YOU KNOW THAT A DOG CAN SMELL HIS MASTER FROM TWO MILES AWAY?
TWO MILES? WOW!
IT'S TRUE.
© 1997 Washington Post Writers Group
FOUR MILES IF HE TAKES HIS SHOES OFF.

153

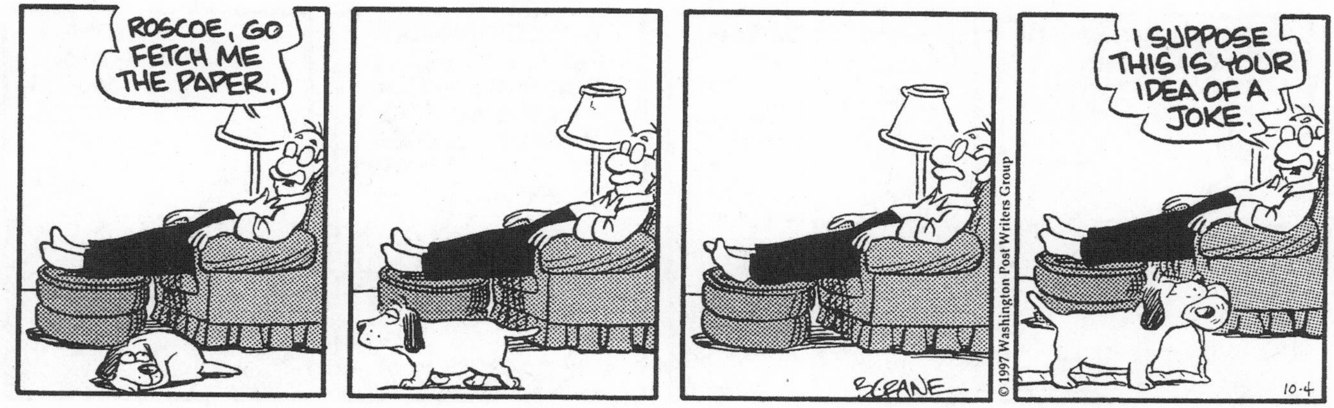
ROSCOE, GO FETCH ME THE PAPER.
© 1997 Washington Post Writers Group
I SUPPOSE THIS IS YOUR IDEA OF A JOKE.

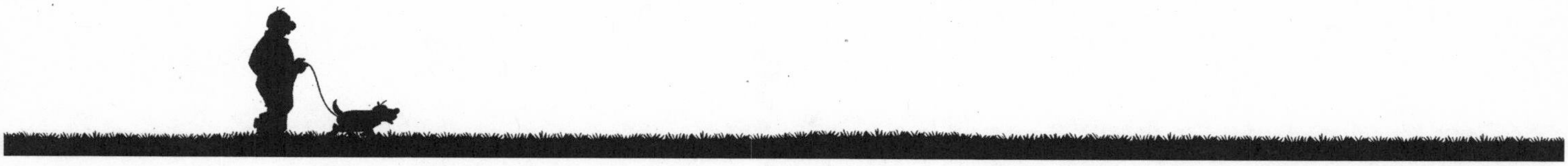

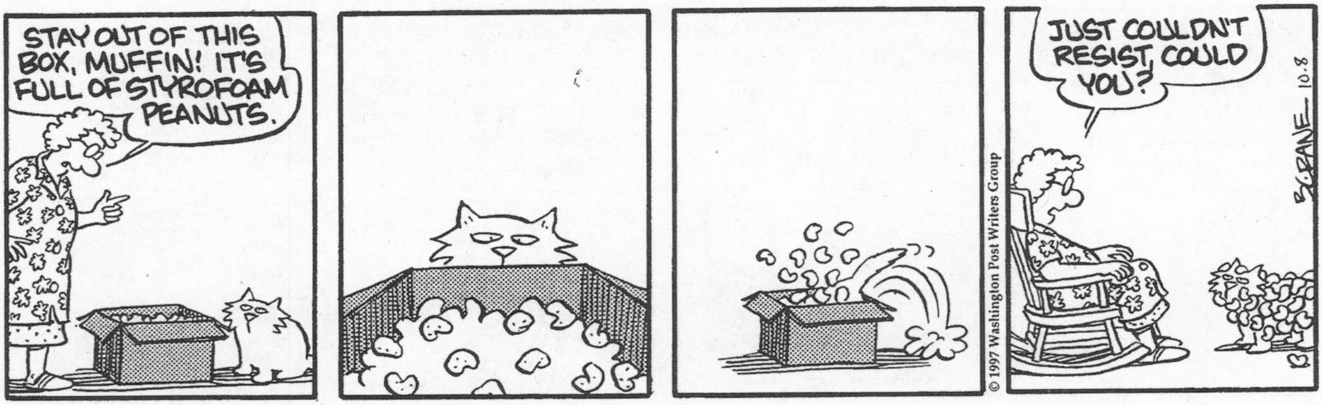
STAY OUT OF THIS BOX, MUFFIN! IT'S FULL OF STYROFOAM PEANUTS.
JUST COULDN'T RESIST, COULD YOU?
© 1997 Washington Post Writers Group

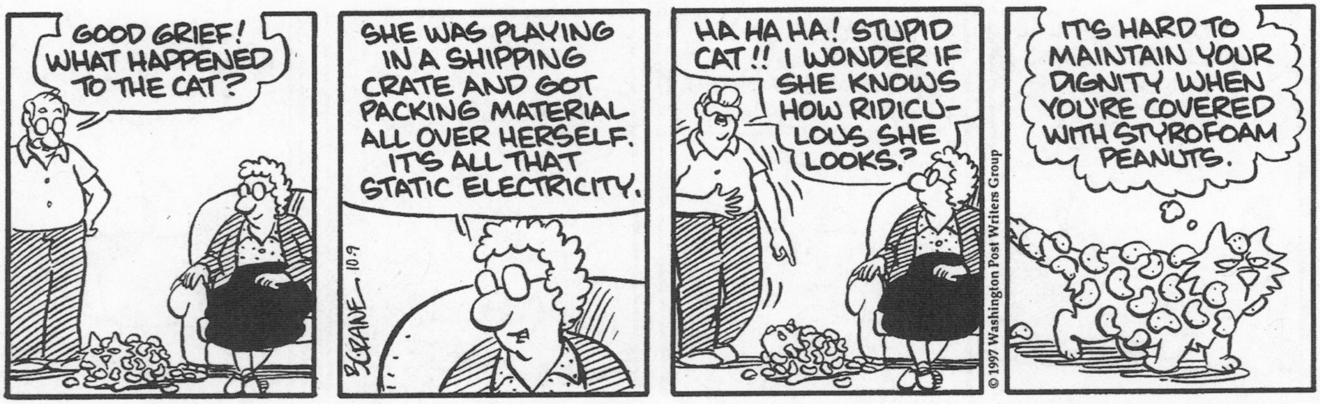
GOOD GRIEF! WHAT HAPPENED TO THE CAT?
SHE WAS PLAYING IN A SHIPPING CRATE AND GOT PACKING MATERIAL ALL OVER HERSELF. IT'S ALL THAT STATIC ELECTRICITY.
HA HA HA! STUPID CAT!! I WONDER IF SHE KNOWS HOW RIDICULOUS SHE LOOKS?
IT'S HARD TO MAINTAIN YOUR DIGNITY WHEN YOU'RE COVERED WITH STYROFOAM PEANUTS.
© 1997 Washington Post Writers Group

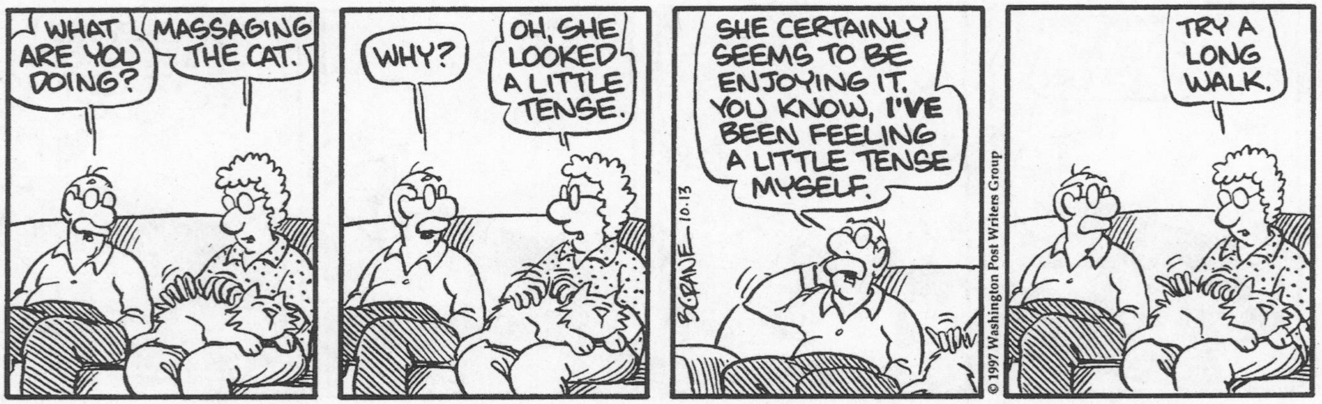
WHAT ARE YOU DOING?
MASSAGING THE CAT.
WHY?
OH, SHE LOOKED A LITTLE TENSE.
SHE CERTAINLY SEEMS TO BE ENJOYING IT. YOU KNOW, I'VE BEEN FEELING A LITTLE TENSE MYSELF.
TRY A LONG WALK.
© 1997 Washington Post Writers Group

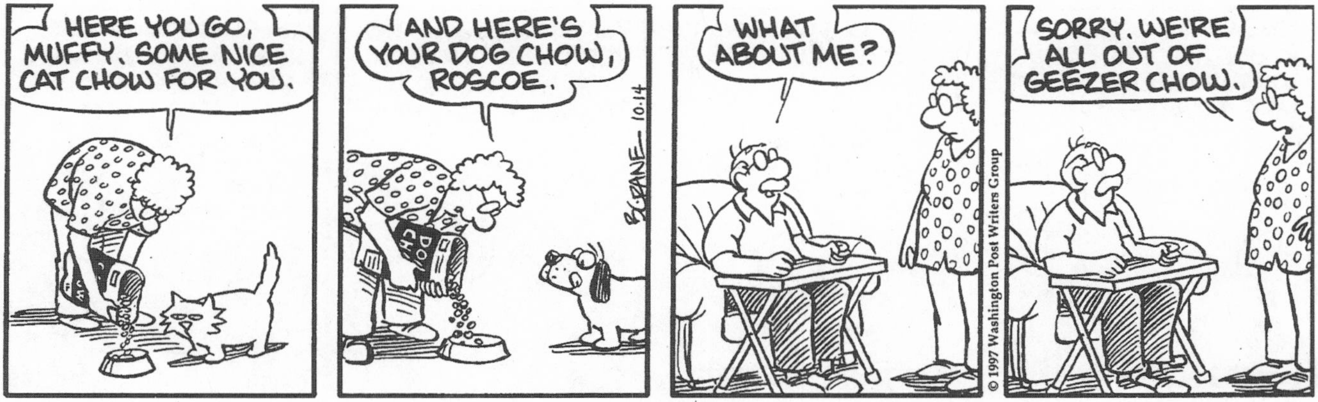
HERE YOU GO, MUFFY. SOME NICE CAT CHOW FOR YOU.
AND HERE'S YOUR DOG CHOW, ROSCOE.
WHAT ABOUT ME?
SORRY. WE'RE ALL OUT OF GEEZER CHOW.
© 1997 Washington Post Writers Group

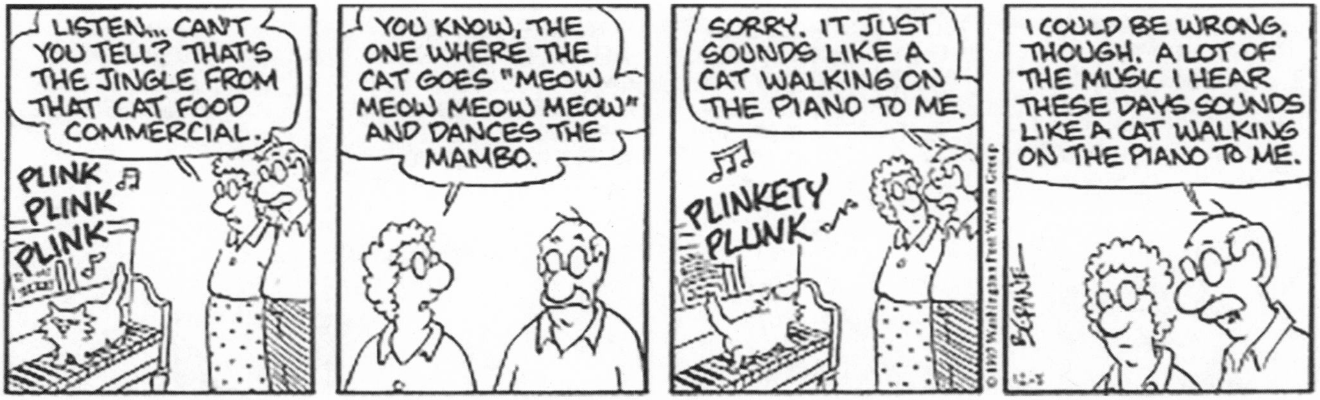
LISTEN... CAN'T YOU TELL? THAT'S THE JINGLE FROM THAT CAT FOOD COMMERCIAL.
PLINK PLINK PLINK
YOU KNOW, THE ONE WHERE THE CAT GOES "MEOW MEOW MEOW MEOW" AND DANCES THE MAMBO.
SORRY. IT JUST SOUNDS LIKE A CAT WALKING ON THE PIANO TO ME.
PLINKETY PLUNK
I COULD BE WRONG, THOUGH. A LOT OF THE MUSIC I HEAR THESE DAYS SOUNDS LIKE A CAT WALKING ON THE PIANO TO ME.

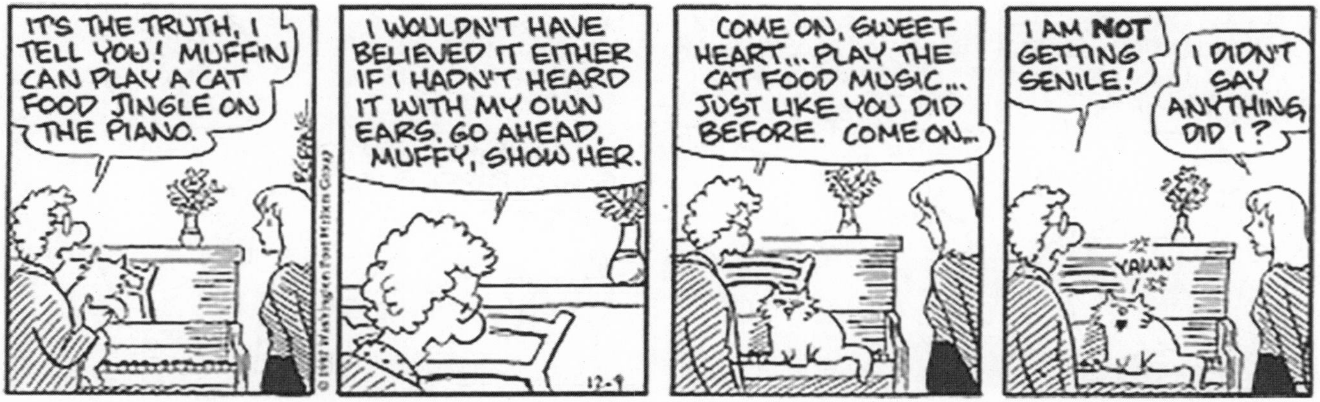
IT'S THE TRUTH, I TELL YOU! MUFFIN CAN PLAY A CAT FOOD JINGLE ON THE PIANO.
I WOULDN'T HAVE BELIEVED IT EITHER IF I HADN'T HEARD IT WITH MY OWN EARS. GO AHEAD, MUFFY, SHOW HER.
COME ON, SWEETHEART... PLAY THE CAT FOOD MUSIC... JUST LIKE YOU DID BEFORE. COME ON...
I AM NOT GETTING SENILE!
I DIDN'T SAY ANYTHING, DID I?
YAWN

SO... WHAT SEEMS TO BE THE PROBLEM WITH MUFFIN, MRS. PICKLES?

DR. J.H. BOOTH PET PSYCHOLOGIST

SHE'S SUDDENLY STARTED PLAYING THE PIANO A LOT LATELY. SHE'S NEVER DONE IT BEFORE.

PLAYING THE PIANO, HUH? AND YOU SAY THIS IS UNUSUAL BEHAVIOR FOR HER?

YES. WHAT DOES IT MEAN, DOCTOR?

I'M GOING TO HAVE TO KEEP HER OVERNIGHT FOR OBSERVATION. WILL YOU NEED A LOANER?

DR. J.H. BOOTH PET PSYCHOLOGIST

I TOOK MUFFIN TO A CAT PSY-CHOLOGIST.

YOU WHAT?!

A CAT PSYCHOLOGIST? I DIDN'T EVEN KNOW THERE WAS SUCH A THING. HOW MUCH IS THAT GOING TO COST?

YOU'RE WORRIED ABOUT COST? YOU CAN'T POSSIBLY PUT A PRICE TAG ON THE MENTAL HEALTH OF OUR CAT, CAN YOU?

PROBABLY NOT.

THEY DON'T MAKE A COIN THAT SMALL.

CAN YOU TELL ME WHAT'S WRONG WITH MY CAT, DOCTOR?

WELL, AFTER MANY HOURS OF PAINSTAKING OBSERVATION AND PSYCHOANALYSIS OF MUFFIN...

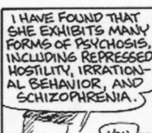

I HAVE FOUND THAT SHE EXHIBITS MANY FORMS OF PSYCHOSIS, INCLUDING REPRESSED HOSTILITY, IRRATION-AL BEHAVIOR, AND SCHIZOPHRENIA.

YOU MEAN...?

YES. SHE'S A VERY NORMAL CAT.

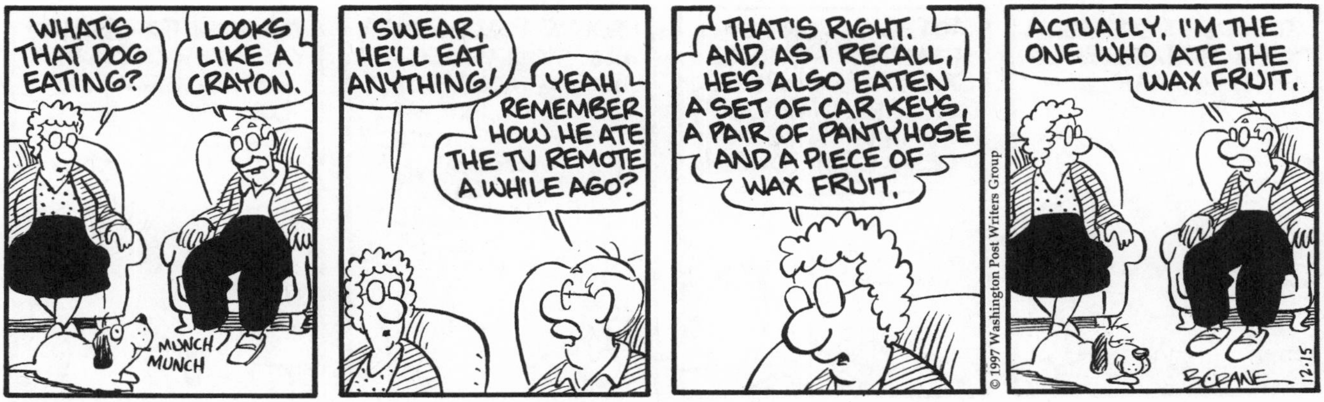
WHAT'S THAT DOG EATING?
LOOKS LIKE A CRAYON.
MUNCH MUNCH
I SWEAR, HE'LL EAT ANYTHING!
YEAH. REMEMBER HOW HE ATE THE TV REMOTE A WHILE AGO?
THAT'S RIGHT. AND, AS I RECALL, HE'S ALSO EATEN A SET OF CAR KEYS, A PAIR OF PANTYHOSE AND A PIECE OF WAX FRUIT.
© 1997 Washington Post Writers Group
ACTUALLY, I'M THE ONE WHO ATE THE WAX FRUIT.
B. CRANE 12-15

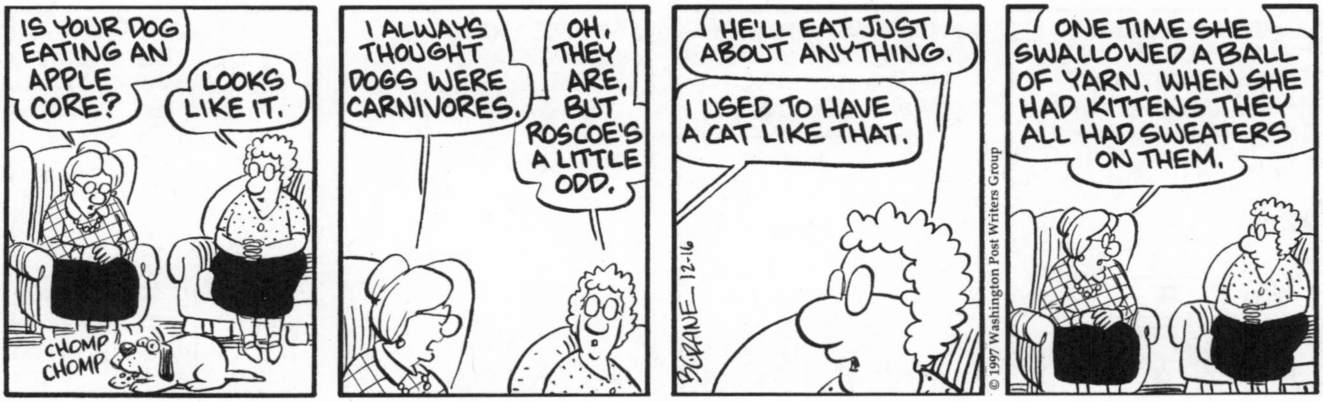
IS YOUR DOG EATING AN APPLE CORE?
LOOKS LIKE IT.
CHOMP CHOMP
I ALWAYS THOUGHT DOGS WERE CARNIVORES.
OH, THEY ARE, BUT ROSCOE'S A LITTLE ODD.
B. CRANE 12-16
HE'LL EAT JUST ABOUT ANYTHING.
I USED TO HAVE A CAT LIKE THAT.
© 1997 Washington Post Writers Group
ONE TIME SHE SWALLOWED A BALL OF YARN. WHEN SHE HAD KITTENS THEY ALL HAD SWEATERS ON THEM.

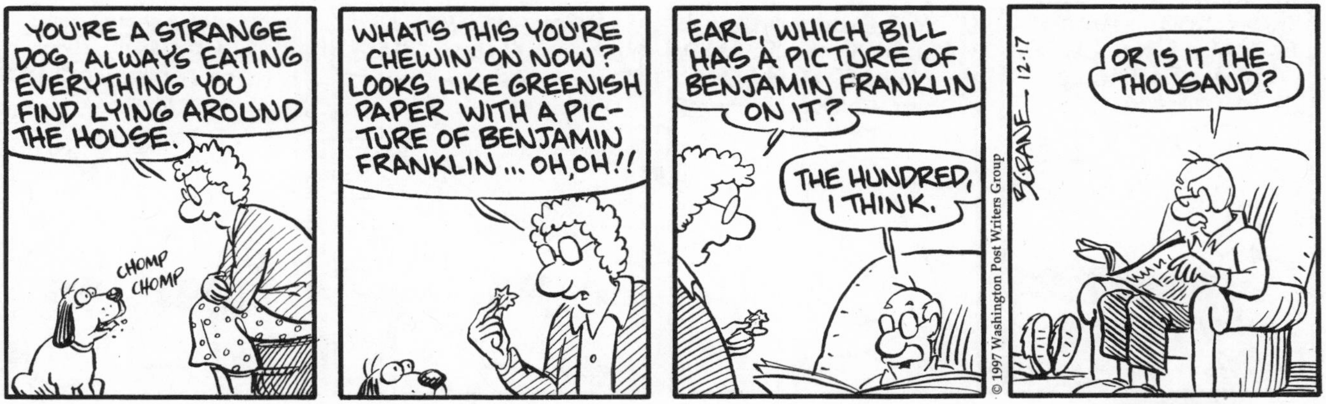
YOU'RE A STRANGE DOG, ALWAYS EATING EVERYTHING YOU FIND LYING AROUND THE HOUSE.
CHOMP CHOMP
WHAT'S THIS YOU'RE CHEWIN' ON NOW? LOOKS LIKE GREENISH PAPER WITH A PICTURE OF BENJAMIN FRANKLIN ... OH, OH!!
EARL, WHICH BILL HAS A PICTURE OF BENJAMIN FRANKLIN ON IT?
THE HUNDRED, I THINK.
© 1997 Washington Post Writers Group
B. CRANE 12-17
OR IS IT THE THOUSAND?

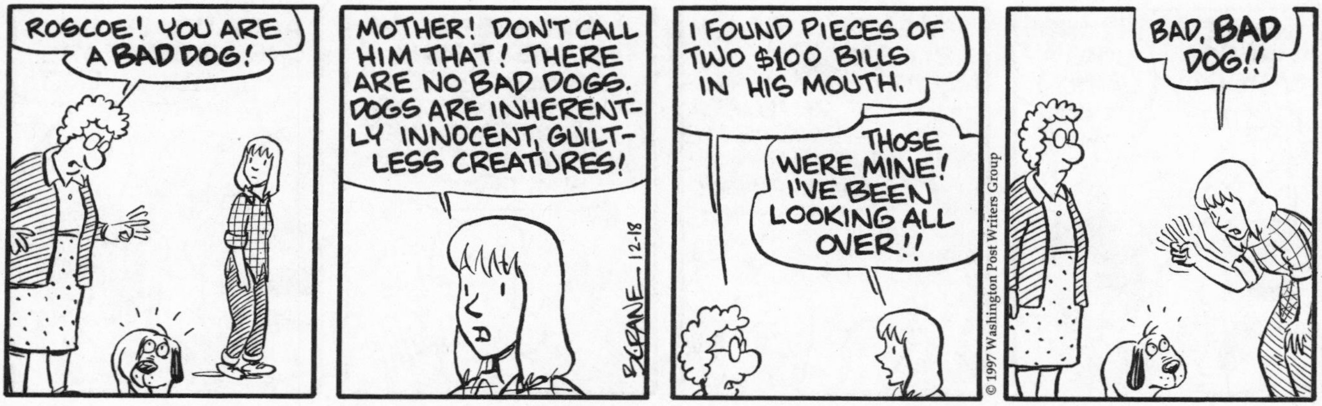
ROSCOE! YOU ARE A BAD DOG!
MOTHER! DON'T CALL HIM THAT! THERE ARE NO BAD DOGS. DOGS ARE INHERENTLY INNOCENT, GUILTLESS CREATURES!
BCRANE 12-18
I FOUND PIECES OF TWO $100 BILLS IN HIS MOUTH.
THOSE WERE MINE! I'VE BEEN LOOKING ALL OVER!!
BAD, BAD DOG!!
© 1997 Washington Post Writers Group

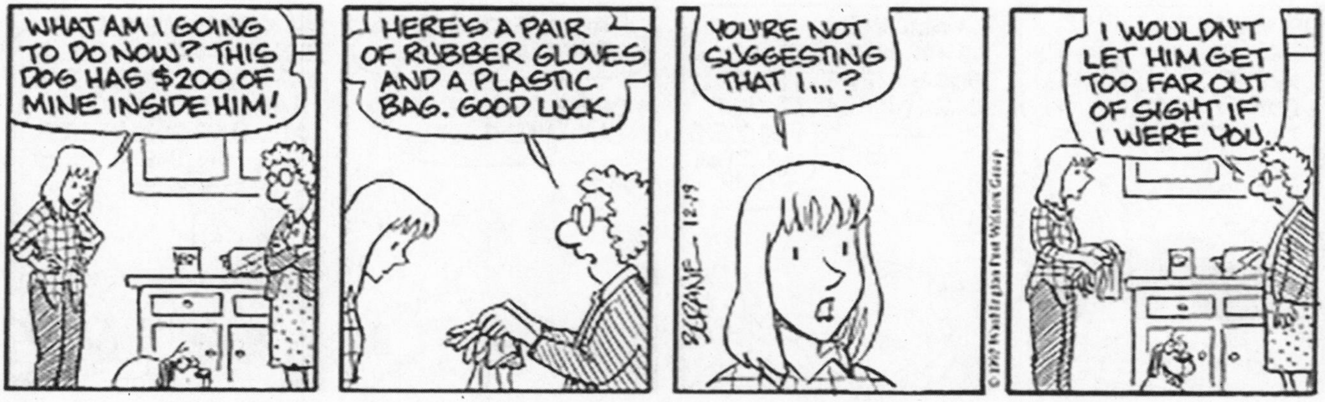
WHAT AM I GOING TO DO NOW? THIS DOG HAS $200 OF MINE INSIDE HIM!
HERE'S A PAIR OF RUBBER GLOVES AND A PLASTIC BAG. GOOD LUCK.
YOU'RE NOT SUGGESTING THAT I...?
BCRANE 12-19
I WOULDN'T LET HIM GET TOO FAR OUT OF SIGHT IF I WERE YOU.

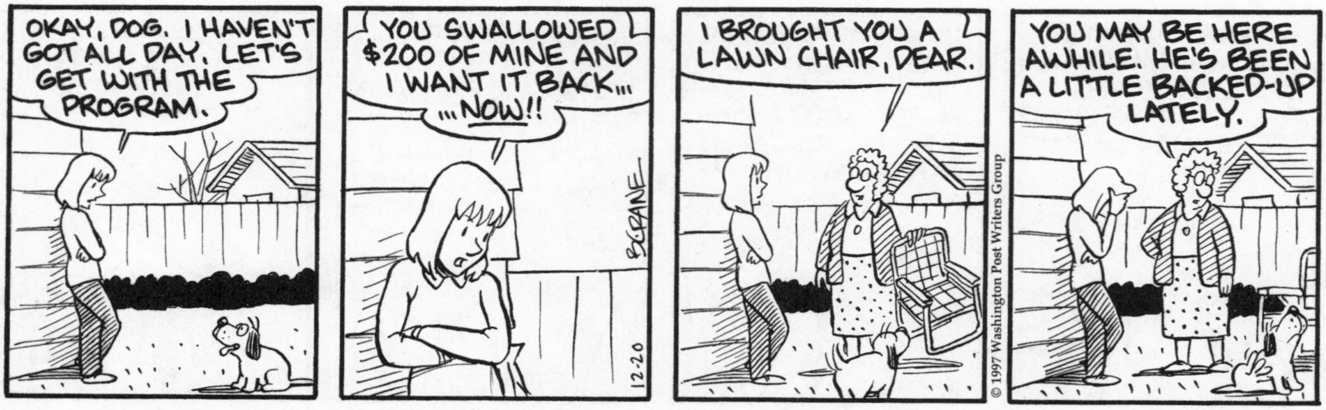
OKAY, DOG. I HAVEN'T GOT ALL DAY. LET'S GET WITH THE PROGRAM.
YOU SWALLOWED $200 OF MINE AND I WANT IT BACK... ...NOW!!
BCRANE 12-20
I BROUGHT YOU A LAWN CHAIR, DEAR.
YOU MAY BE HERE AWHILE. HE'S BEEN A LITTLE BACKED-UP LATELY.
© 1997 Washington Post Writers Group

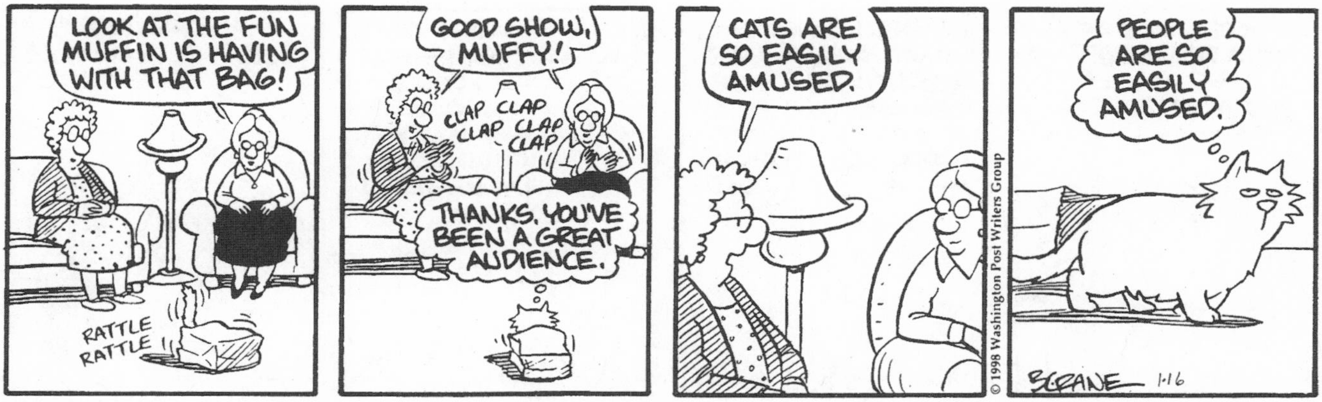
LOOK AT THE FUN MUFFIN IS HAVING WITH THAT BAG!
RATTLE RATTLE
GOOD SHOW, MUFFY!
CLAP CLAP CLAP CLAP CLAP CLAP
THANKS. YOU'VE BEEN A GREAT AUDIENCE.
CATS ARE SO EASILY AMUSED.
© 1998 Washington Post Writers Group
PEOPLE ARE SO EASILY AMUSED.
B.CRANE 1.16

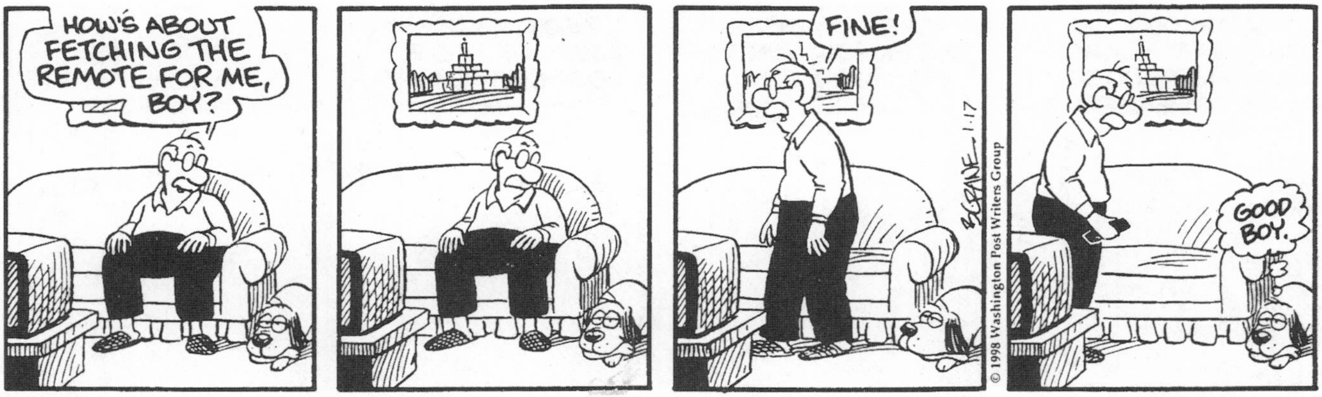
HOW'S ABOUT FETCHING THE REMOTE FOR ME, BOY?
FINE!
B.CRANE 1.17
© 1998 Washington Post Writers Group
GOOD BOY.

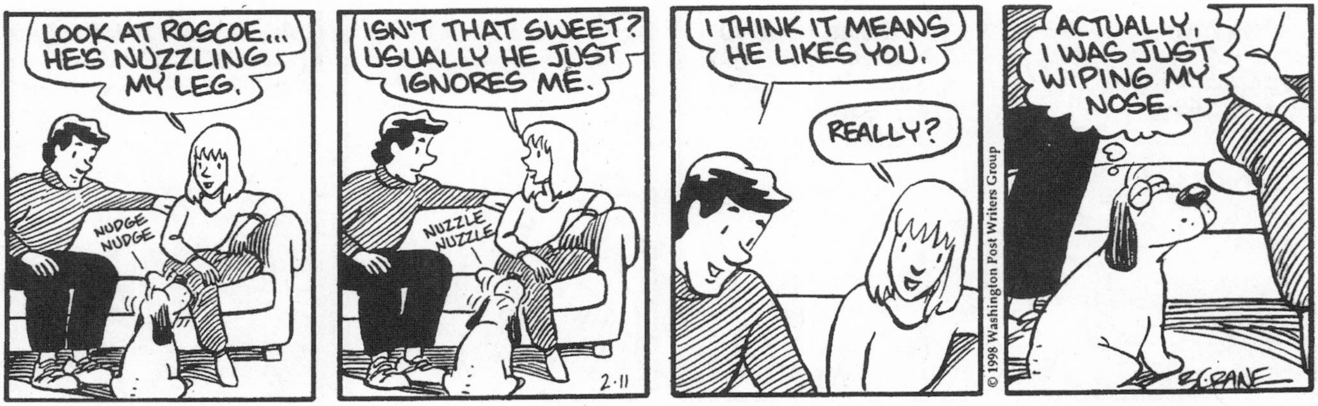
LOOK AT ROSCOE... HE'S NUZZLING MY LEG.
NUDGE NUDGE
ISN'T THAT SWEET? USUALLY HE JUST IGNORES ME.
NUZZLE NUZZLE
2.11
I THINK IT MEANS HE LIKES YOU.
REALLY?
© 1998 Washington Post Writers Group
ACTUALLY, I WAS JUST WIPING MY NOSE.
B.CRANE

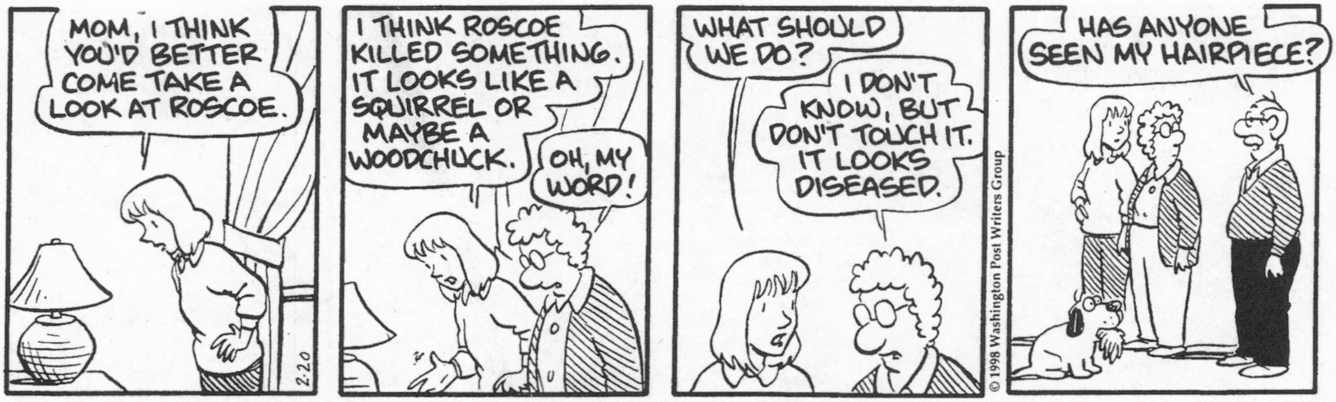
MOM, I THINK YOU'D BETTER COME TAKE A LOOK AT ROSCOE.
2:20
I THINK ROSCOE KILLED SOMETHING. IT LOOKS LIKE A SQUIRREL OR MAYBE A WOODCHUCK.
OH, MY WORD!
WHAT SHOULD WE DO?
I DON'T KNOW, BUT DON'T TOUCH IT. IT LOOKS DISEASED.
© 1998 Washington Post Writers Group
HAS ANYONE SEEN MY HAIRPIECE?

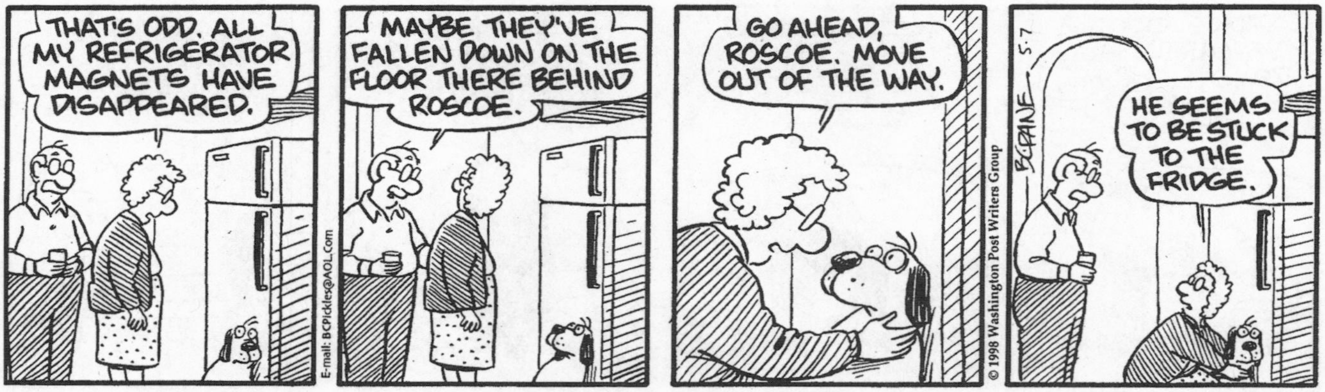
THAT'S ODD. ALL MY REFRIGERATOR MAGNETS HAVE DISAPPEARED.
E-mail: BCPickles@AOL.Com
MAYBE THEY'VE FALLEN DOWN ON THE FLOOR THERE BEHIND ROSCOE.
GO AHEAD, ROSCOE. MOVE OUT OF THE WAY.
© 1998 Washington Post Writers Group
5·7
B.CRANE
HE SEEMS TO BE STUCK TO THE FRIDGE.

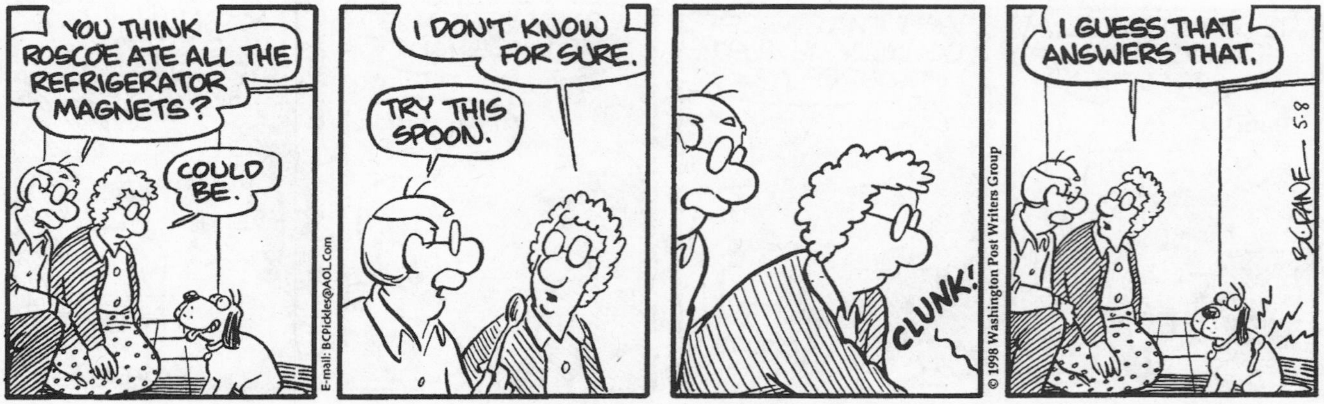
YOU THINK ROSCOE ATE ALL THE REFRIGERATOR MAGNETS?
COULD BE.
E-mail: BCPickles@AOL.Com
I DON'T KNOW FOR SURE.
TRY THIS SPOON.
CLUNK!
© 1998 Washington Post Writers Group
I GUESS THAT ANSWERS THAT.
5·8
B.CRANE

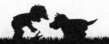

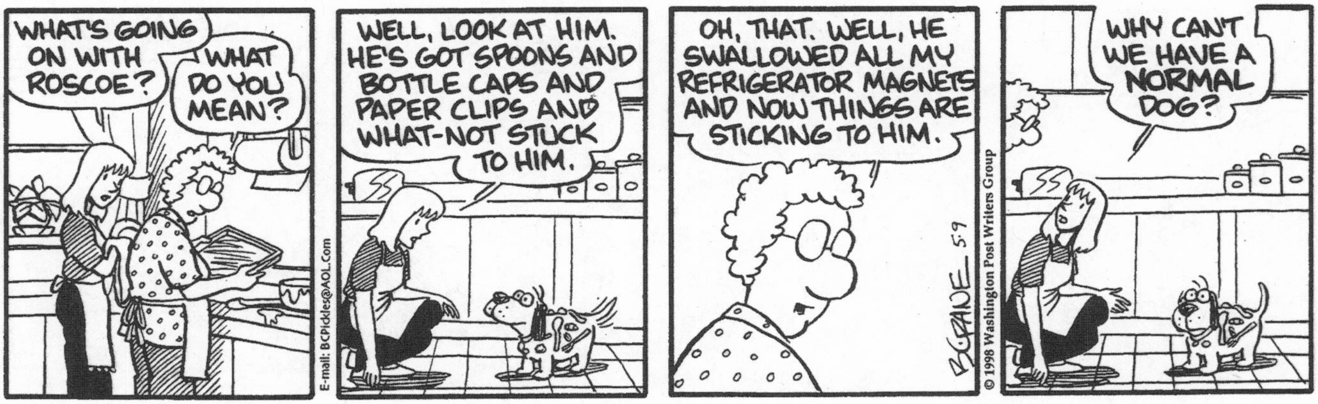
WHAT'S GOING ON WITH ROSCOE?
WHAT DO YOU MEAN?
E-mail: BCPickles@AOL.Com
WELL, LOOK AT HIM. HE'S GOT SPOONS AND BOTTLE CAPS AND PAPER CLIPS AND WHAT-NOT STUCK TO HIM.
OH, THAT. WELL, HE SWALLOWED ALL MY REFRIGERATOR MAGNETS AND NOW THINGS ARE STICKING TO HIM.
B.CRANE 5·9
© 1998 Washington Post Writers Group
WHY CAN'T WE HAVE A NORMAL DOG?

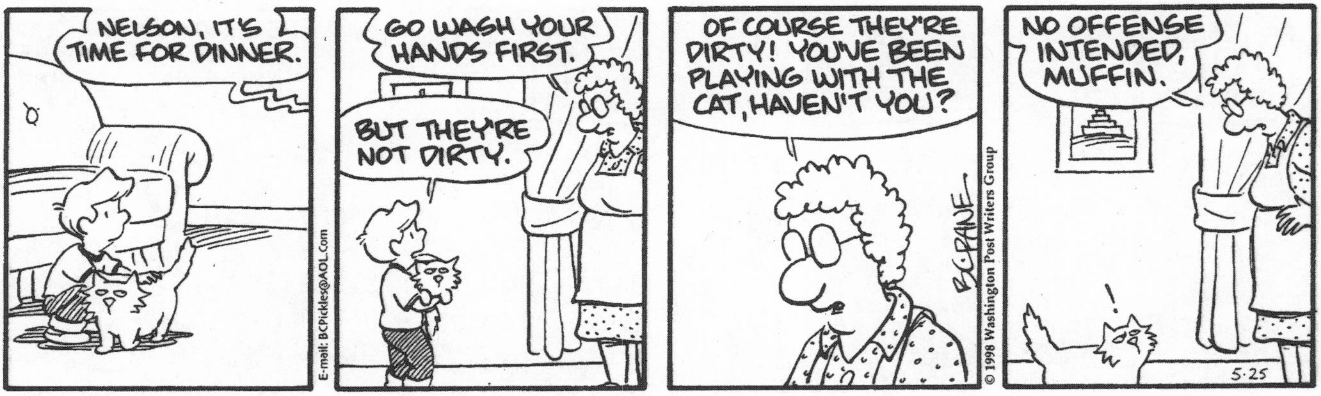
NELSON, IT'S TIME FOR DINNER.
E-mail: BCPickles@AOL.Com
GO WASH YOUR HANDS FIRST.
BUT THEY'RE NOT DIRTY.
OF COURSE THEY'RE DIRTY! YOU'VE BEEN PLAYING WITH THE CAT, HAVEN'T YOU?
B.CRANE
© 1998 Washington Post Writers Group
NO OFFENSE INTENDED, MUFFIN.
5·25

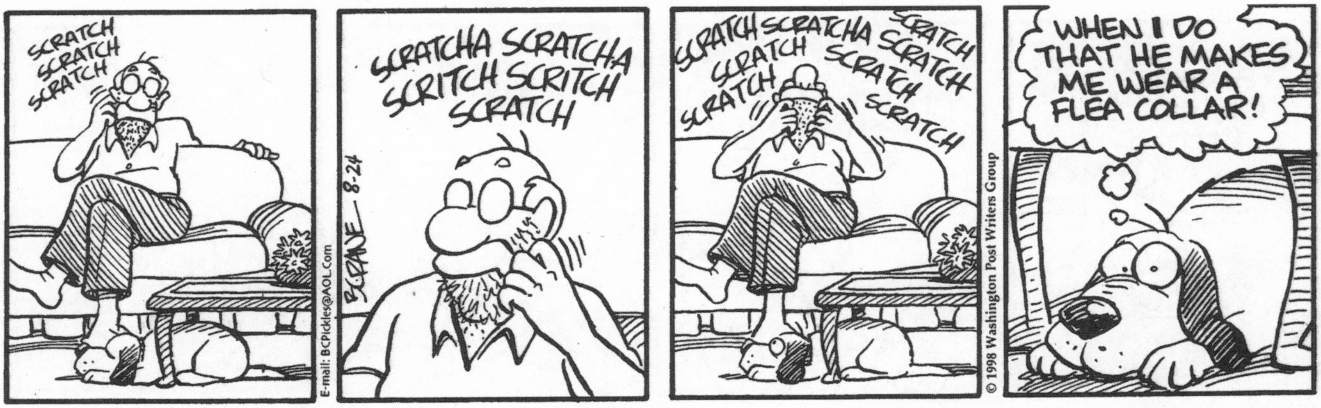
SCRATCH SCRATCH SCRATCH
E-mail: BCPickles@AOL.Com
B.CRANE 8·24
SCRATCHA SCRATCHA SCRITCH SCRITCH SCRATCH
SCRATCH SCRATCHA SCRATCH SCRATCH SCRATCH SCRATCH SCRATCH SCRATCH
© 1998 Washington Post Writers Group
WHEN I DO THAT HE MAKES ME WEAR A FLEA COLLAR!

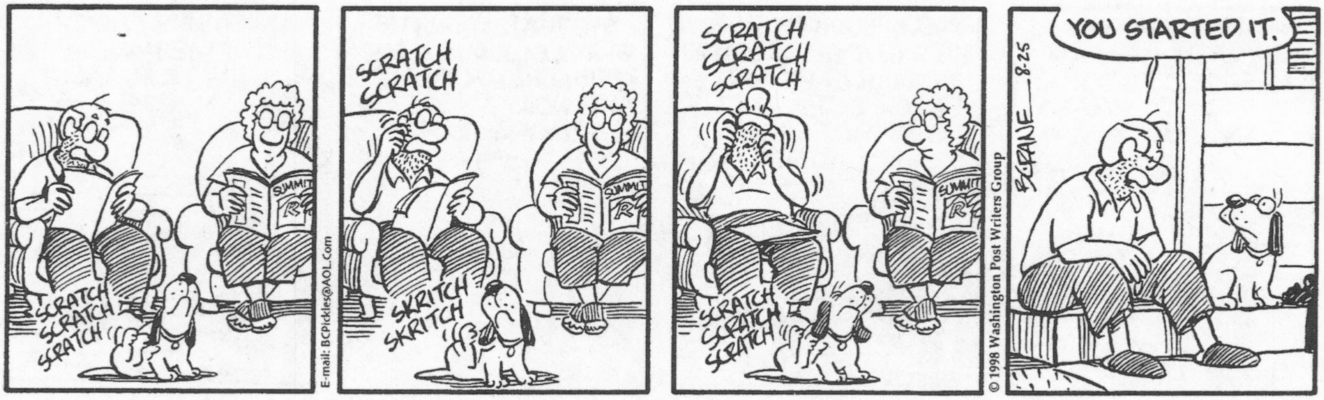
SCRATCH SCRATCH SCRATCH
SUMMIT
E-mail: BCPickles@AOL.Com
SCRATCH SCRATCH
SKRITCH SKRITCH
SUMMIT
SCRATCH SCRATCH SCRATCH
SUMMIT
SCRATCH SCRATCH SCRATCH
© 1998 Washington Post Writers Group
B.CRANE 8-25
YOU STARTED IT.

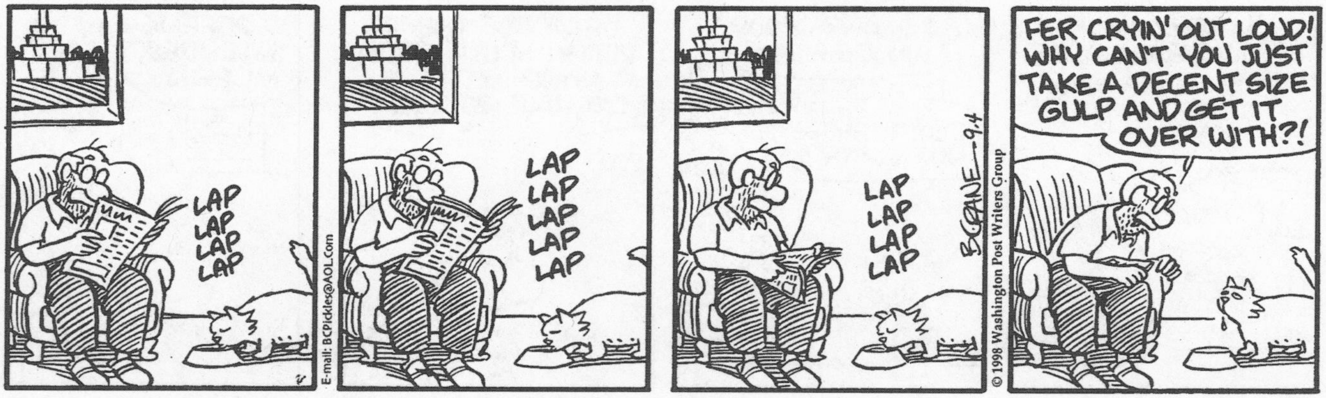
LAP LAP LAP LAP
E-mail: BCPickles@AOL.Com
LAP LAP LAP LAP LAP
LAP LAP LAP LAP
B.CRANE 9-4
© 1998 Washington Post Writers Group
FER CRYIN' OUT LOUD! WHY CAN'T YOU JUST TAKE A DECENT SIZE GULP AND GET IT OVER WITH?!

162

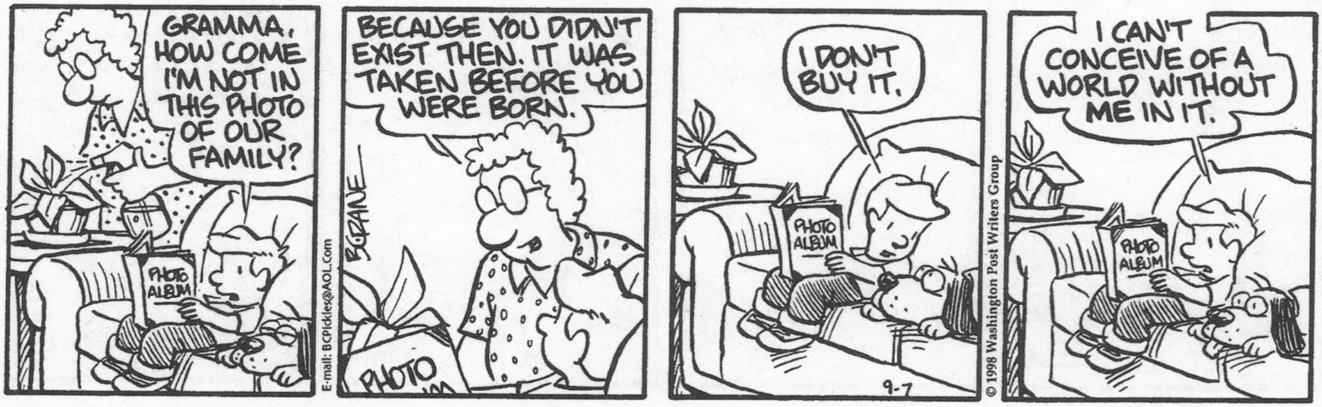
GRAMMA, HOW COME I'M NOT IN THIS PHOTO OF OUR FAMILY?
PHOTO ALBUM
E-mail: BCPickles@AOL.Com
BECAUSE YOU DIDN'T EXIST THEN. IT WAS TAKEN BEFORE YOU WERE BORN.
B.CRANE
PHOTO
I DON'T BUY IT.
PHOTO ALBUM
9-7
© 1998 Washington Post Writers Group
I CAN'T CONCEIVE OF A WORLD WITHOUT ME IN IT.
PHOTO ALBUM

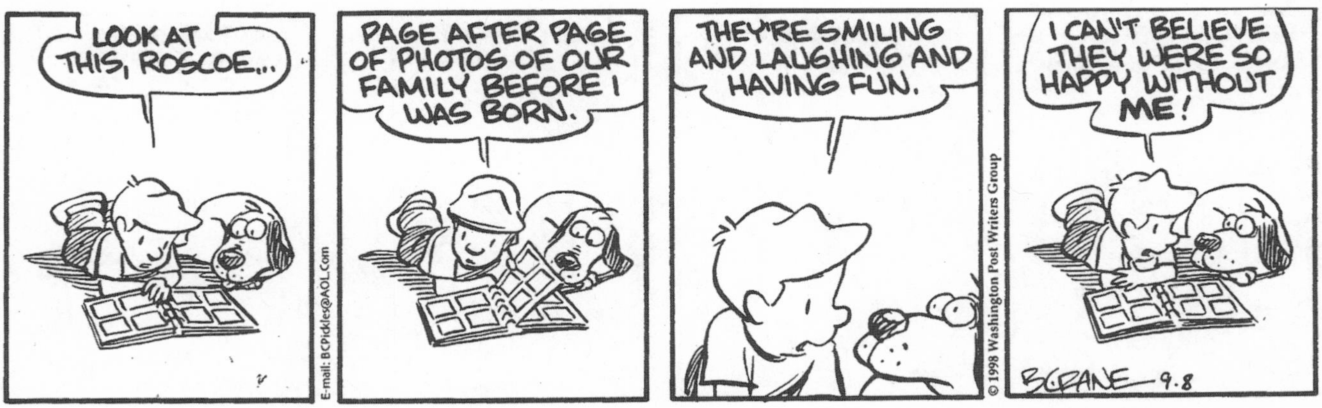
LOOK AT THIS, ROSCOE...
E-mail: BCPickles@AOL.Com
PAGE AFTER PAGE OF PHOTOS OF OUR FAMILY BEFORE I WAS BORN.
THEY'RE SMILING AND LAUGHING AND HAVING FUN.
© 1998 Washington Post Writers Group
I CAN'T BELIEVE THEY WERE SO HAPPY WITHOUT ME!
B.CRANE 9.8

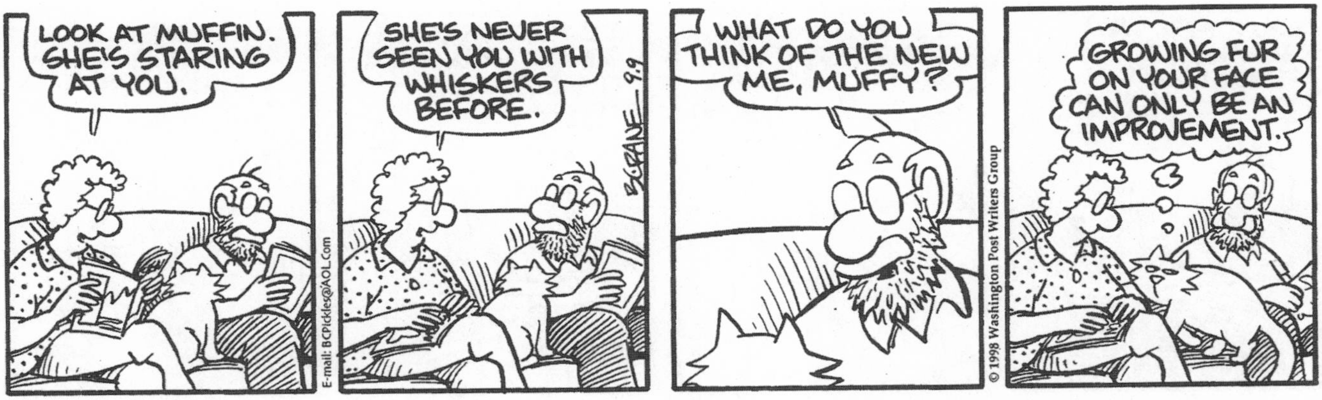
LOOK AT MUFFIN. SHE'S STARING AT YOU.
E-mail: BCPickles@AOL.Com
SHE'S NEVER SEEN YOU WITH WHISKERS BEFORE.
B.CRANE 9.9
WHAT DO YOU THINK OF THE NEW ME, MUFFY?
© 1998 Washington Post Writers Group
GROWING FUR ON YOUR FACE CAN ONLY BE AN IMPROVEMENT.

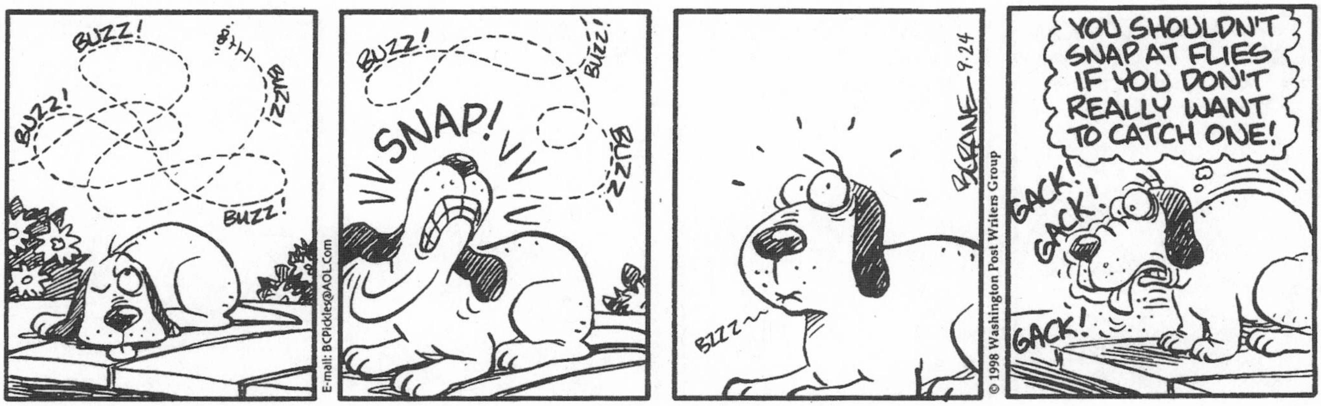
BUZZ!
BUZZ!
BUZZ!
BUZZ!
E-mail: BCPickles@AOL.Com
BUZZ!
BUZZ!
BUZZ!
SNAP!
B.CRANE 9.24
BZZZ~~
© 1998 Washington Post Writers Group
YOU SHOULDN'T SNAP AT FLIES IF YOU DON'T REALLY WANT TO CATCH ONE!
GACK!
GACK!
GACK!

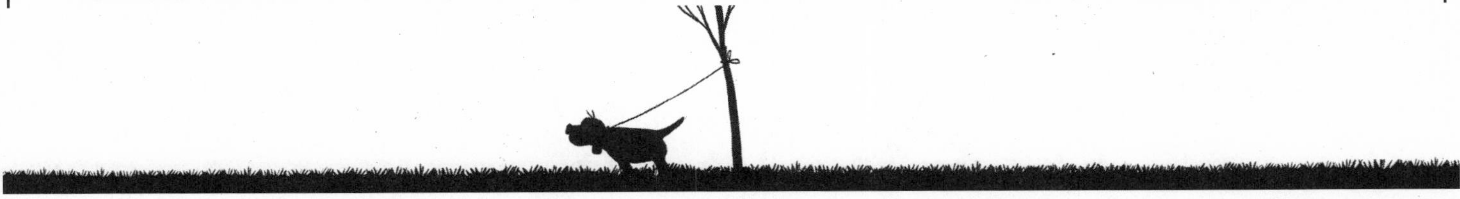

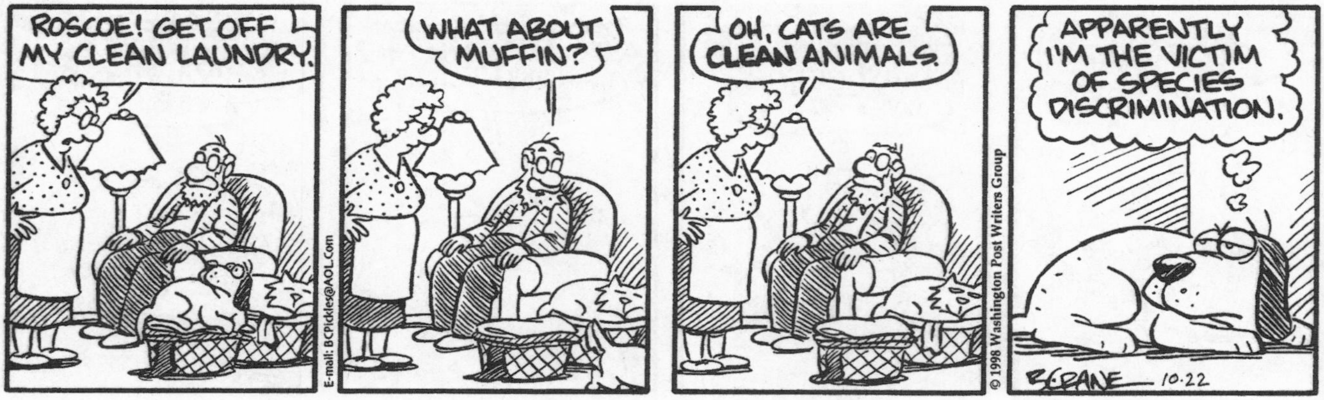
ROSCOE! GET OFF MY CLEAN LAUNDRY.
E-mail: BCPickles@AOL.Com
WHAT ABOUT MUFFIN?
OH, CATS ARE CLEAN ANIMALS.
© 1998 Washington Post Writers Group
APPARENTLY I'M THE VICTIM OF SPECIES DISCRIMINATION.
B. CRANE 10·22

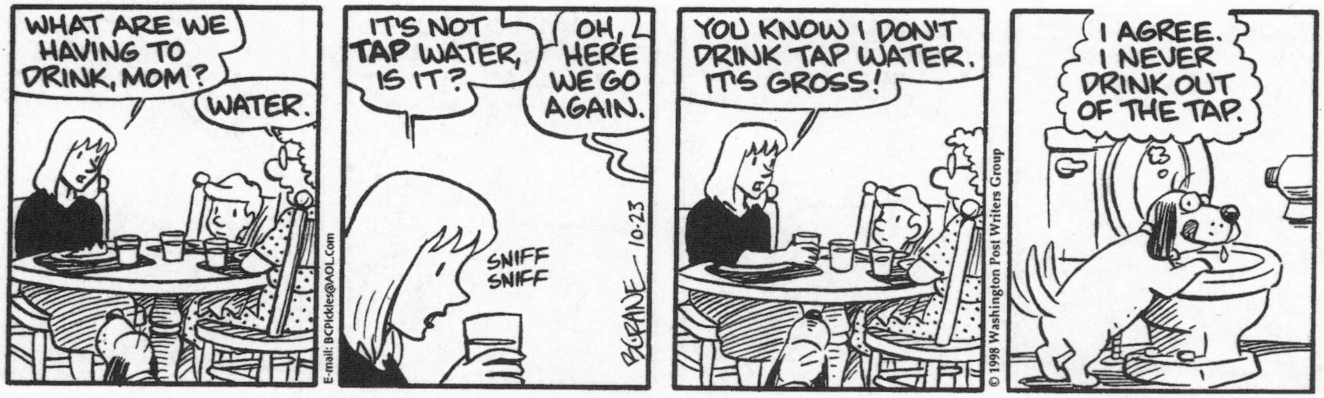
WHAT ARE WE HAVING TO DRINK, MOM?
WATER.
E-mail: BCPickles@AOL.Com
IT'S NOT TAP WATER, IS IT?
OH, HERE WE GO AGAIN.
SNIFF SNIFF
B. CRANE 10·23
YOU KNOW I DON'T DRINK TAP WATER. IT'S GROSS!
© 1998 Washington Post Writers Group
I AGREE. I NEVER DRINK OUT OF THE TAP.

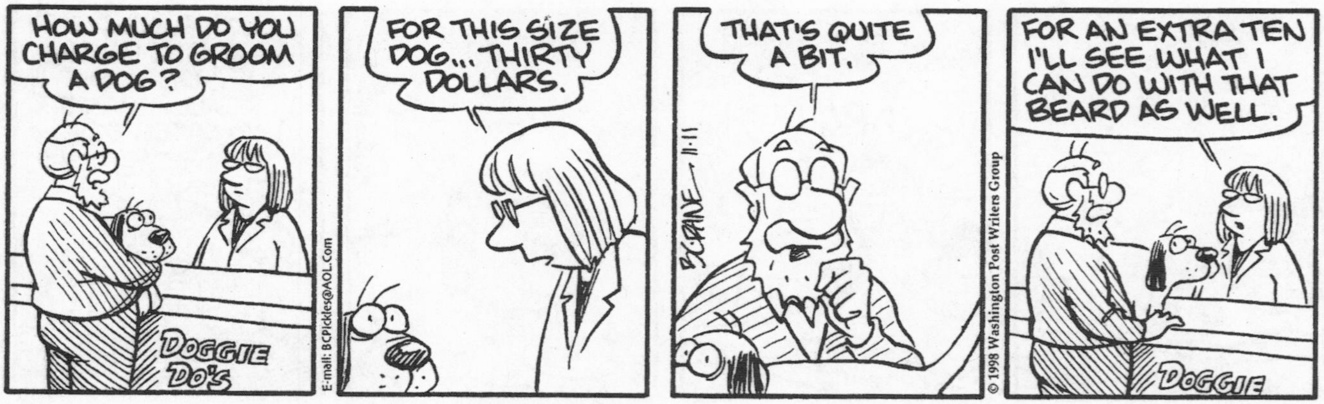
HOW MUCH DO YOU CHARGE TO GROOM A DOG?
DOGGIE DO'S
E-mail: BCPickles@AOL.Com
FOR THIS SIZE DOG... THIRTY DOLLARS.
THAT'S QUITE A BIT.
B. CRANE 11·11
© 1998 Washington Post Writers Group
FOR AN EXTRA TEN I'LL SEE WHAT I CAN DO WITH THAT BEARD AS WELL.
DOGGIE

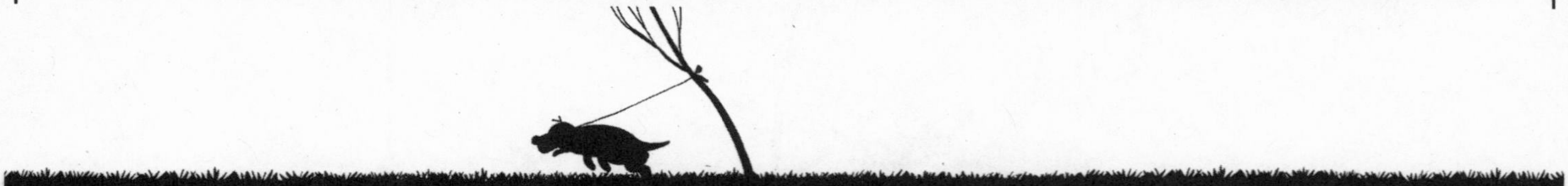

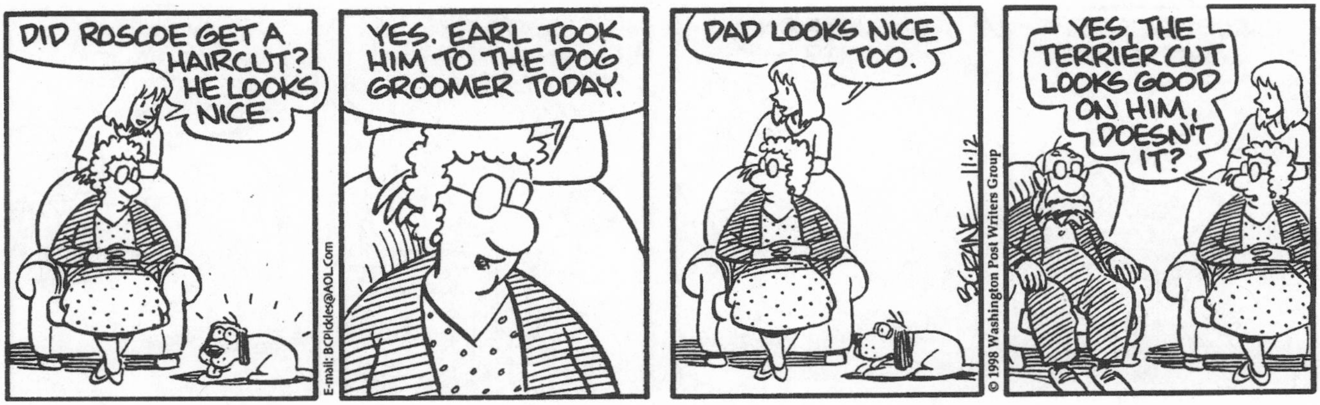
DID ROSCOE GET A HAIRCUT? HE LOOKS NICE.
E-mail: BCPickles@AOL.Com
YES. EARL TOOK HIM TO THE DOG GROOMER TODAY.
DAD LOOKS NICE TOO.
B.CRANE 11·12
© 1998 Washington Post Writers Group
YES, THE TERRIER CUT LOOKS GOOD ON HIM, DOESN'T IT?

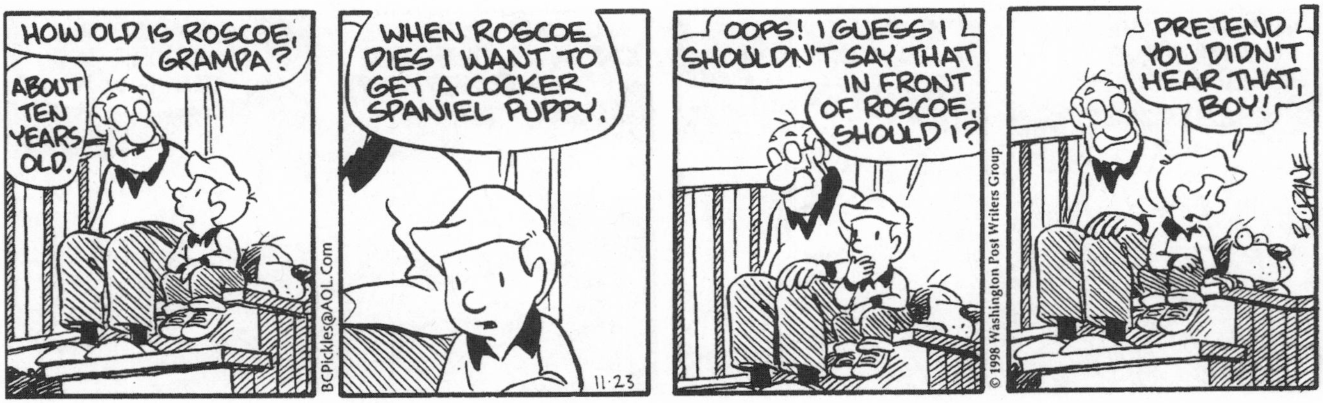
HOW OLD IS ROSCOE, GRAMPA?
ABOUT TEN YEARS OLD.
BCPickles@AOL.Com
WHEN ROSCOE DIES I WANT TO GET A COCKER SPANIEL PUPPY.
11·23
OOPS! I GUESS I SHOULDN'T SAY THAT IN FRONT OF ROSCOE, SHOULD I?
© 1998 Washington Post Writers Group
PRETEND YOU DIDN'T HEAR THAT, BOY!
B.CRANE

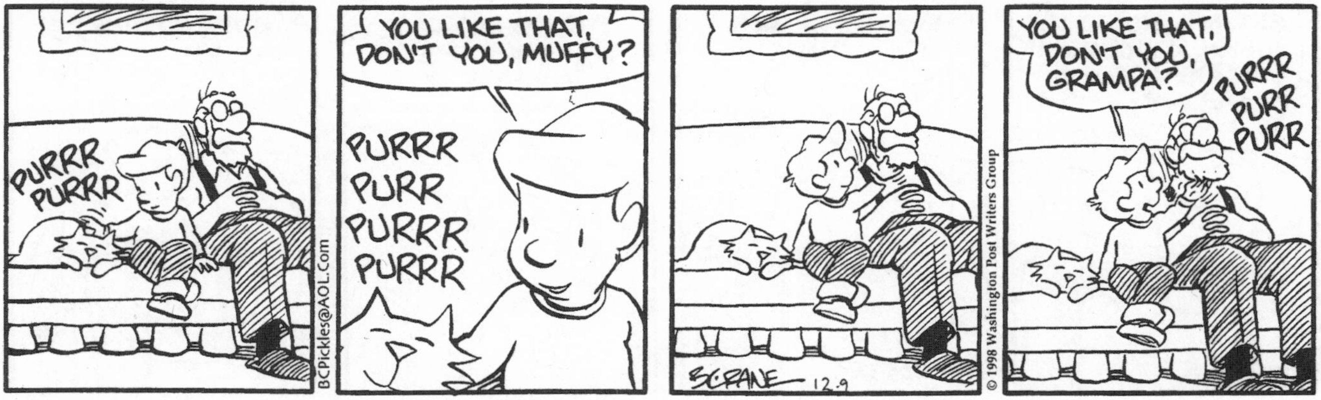
PURRR PURRR
BCPickles@AOL.Com
YOU LIKE THAT, DON'T YOU, MUFFY?
PURRR PURR PURRR PURRR
B.CRANE 12·9
© 1998 Washington Post Writers Group
YOU LIKE THAT, DON'T YOU, GRAMPA?
PURRR PURR PURR

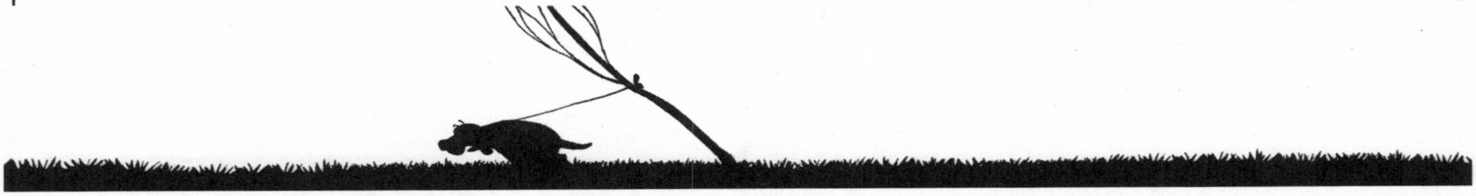

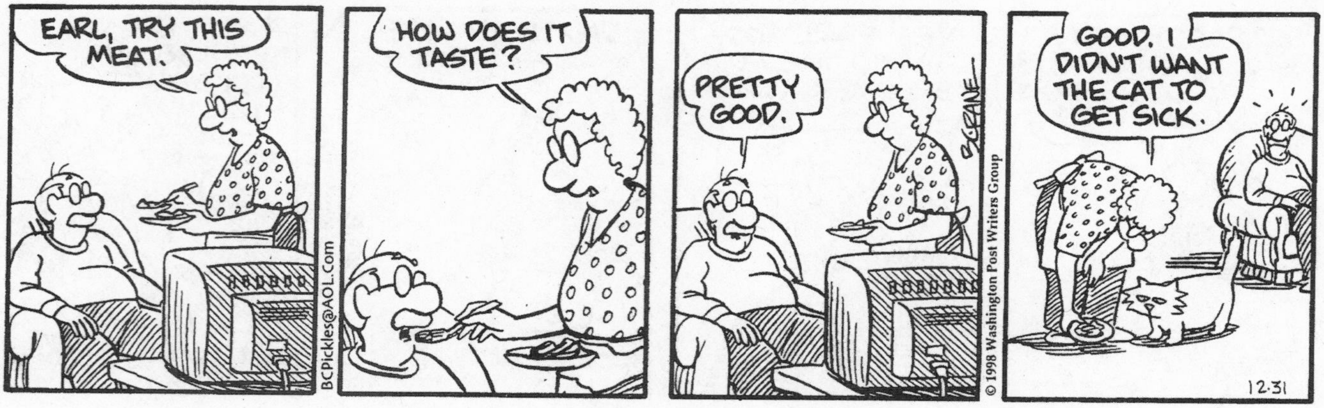
EARL, TRY THIS MEAT.
HOW DOES IT TASTE?
PRETTY GOOD.
GOOD. I DIDN'T WANT THE CAT TO GET SICK.
BCPickles@AOL.Com
© 1998 Washington Post Writers Group
12.31

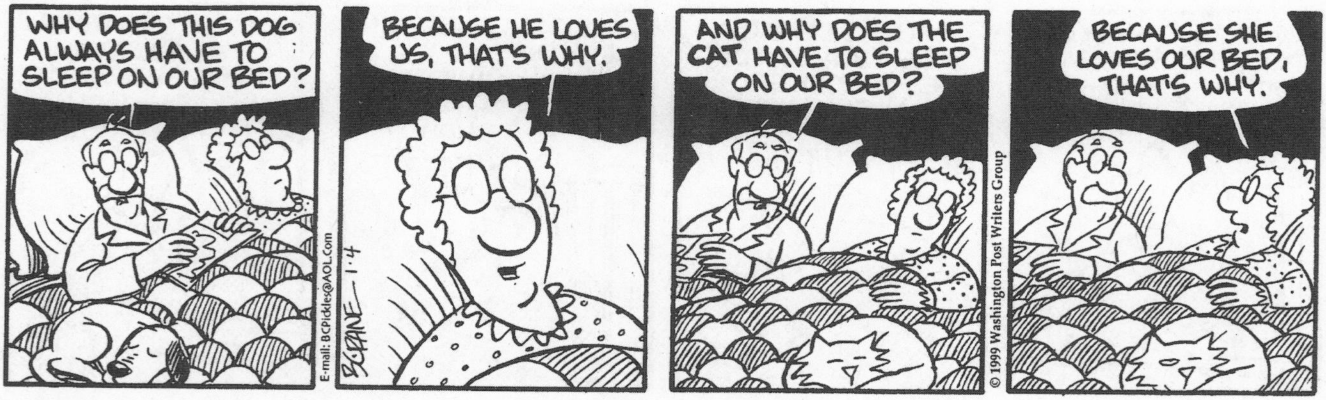
WHY DOES THIS DOG ALWAYS HAVE TO SLEEP ON OUR BED?
BECAUSE HE LOVES US, THAT'S WHY.
AND WHY DOES THE CAT HAVE TO SLEEP ON OUR BED?
BECAUSE SHE LOVES OUR BED, THAT'S WHY.
E-mail: BCPickles@AOL.Com
1.4
© 1999 Washington Post Writers Group

166

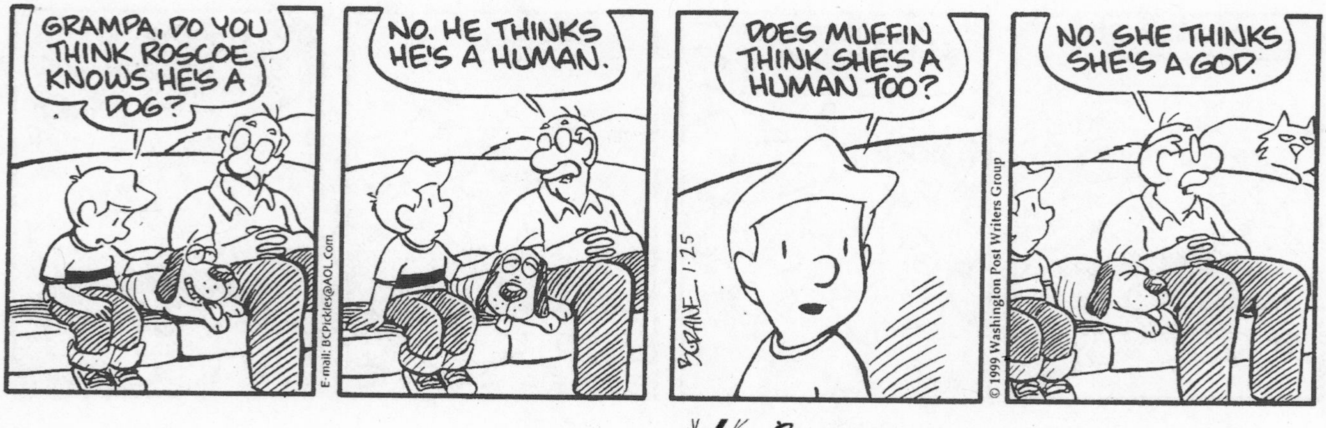
GRAMPA, DO YOU THINK ROSCOE KNOWS HE'S A DOG?
NO. HE THINKS HE'S A HUMAN.
DOES MUFFIN THINK SHE'S A HUMAN TOO?
NO. SHE THINKS SHE'S A GOD.
E-mail: BCPickles@AOL.Com
1.25
© 1999 Washington Post Writers Group

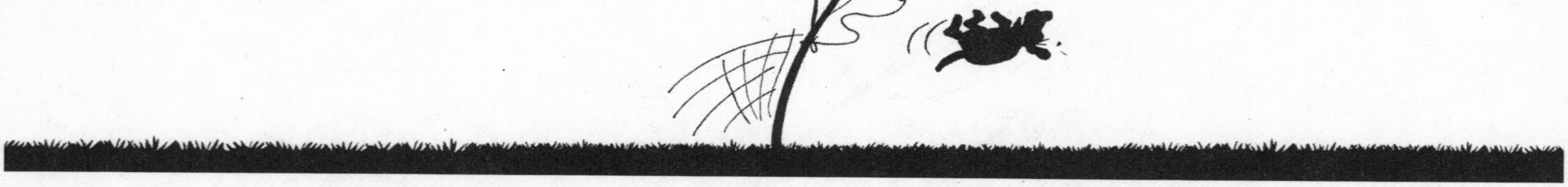

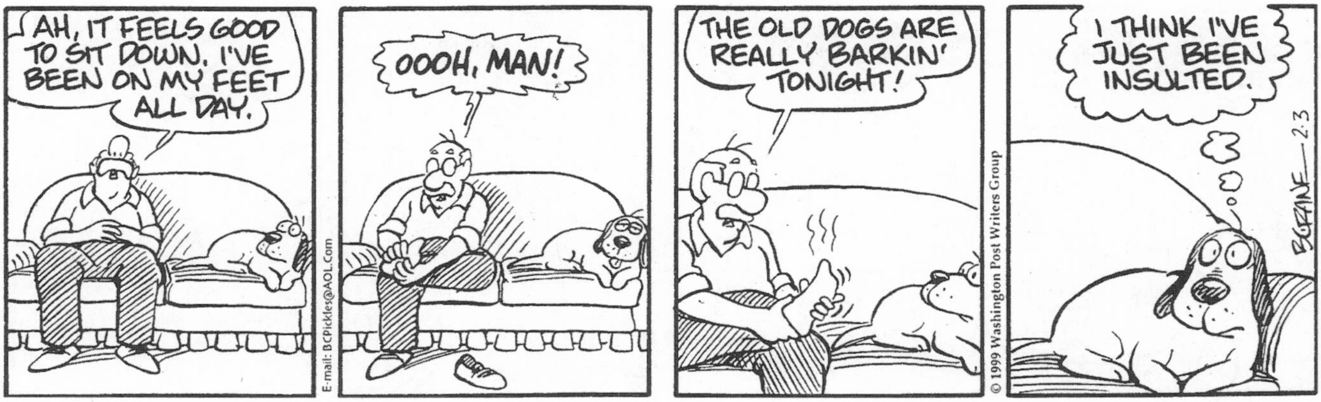
AH, IT FEELS GOOD TO SIT DOWN. I'VE BEEN ON MY FEET ALL DAY.
E-mail: BCPickles@AOL.Com
OOOH, MAN!
THE OLD DOGS ARE REALLY BARKIN' TONIGHT!
© 1999 Washington Post Writers Group
I THINK I'VE JUST BEEN INSULTED.
BCRANE 2.3

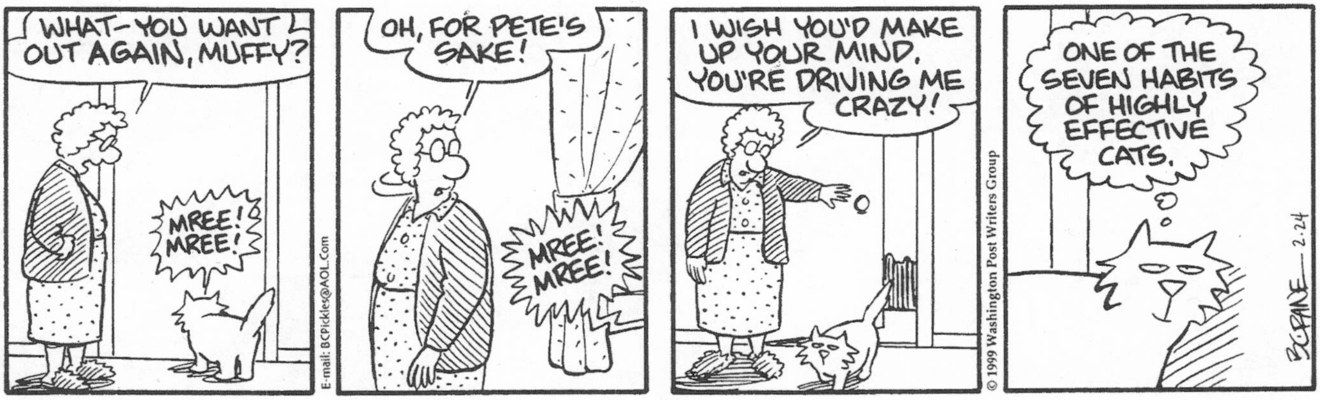
WHAT- YOU WANT OUT AGAIN, MUFFY?
MREE! MREE!
E-mail: BCPickles@AOL.Com
OH, FOR PETE'S SAKE!
MREE! MREE!
I WISH YOU'D MAKE UP YOUR MIND. YOU'RE DRIVING ME CRAZY!
© 1999 Washington Post Writers Group
ONE OF THE SEVEN HABITS OF HIGHLY EFFECTIVE CATS.
BCRANE 2.24

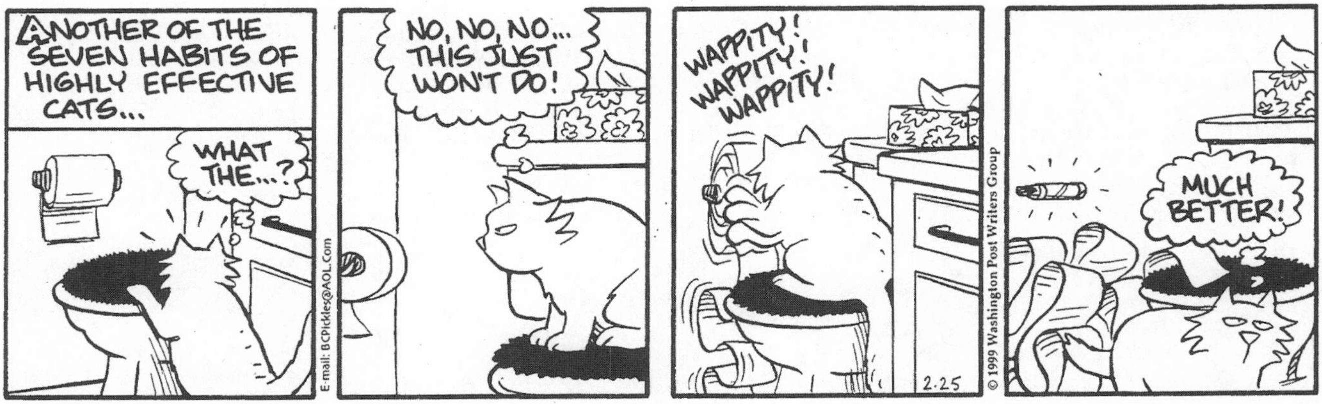
ANOTHER OF THE SEVEN HABITS OF HIGHLY EFFECTIVE CATS...
WHAT THE...?
E-mail: BCPickles@AOL.Com
NO, NO, NO... THIS JUST WON'T DO!
WAPPITY! WAPPITY! WAPPITY!
2.25
© 1999 Washington Post Writers Group
MUCH BETTER!

NUMBER 3 OF THE SEVEN HABITS OF HIGHLY EFFECTIVE CATS...
I CAN'T BELIEVE I PAID THIS MUCH FOR CAT FOOD.
BZZZZ
E-mail: BCPickles@AOL.Com
BUT SINCE IT'S ALL YOU'LL EAT...
B.CRANE 3-1
I CHANGED MY MIND. I DON'T LIKE IT ANYMORE.
© 1999 Washington Post Writers Group
YOU DRIVE ME CRAZY!
GOOD. THEN MY WORK HERE IS DONE.

#4 OF THE SEVEN HABITS OF HIGHLY EFFECTIVE CATS:
NO MATTER WHAT YOU'VE DONE...
© 1999 Washington Post Writers Group
...DO NOT ACKNOWLEDGE GUILT.
MUFFIN! DID YOU DO THIS?
bcpickles@aol.com
!
I SUPPOSE THAT'S SOMETHING THE DNA EXPERTS WILL HAVE TO DETERMINE.
3-8

WHO'S YOUR NEW FRIEND, EMILY?
THIS IS ZELDA. I GOT HER AT THE HUMANE SOCIETY.
E-mail: BCPickles@AOL.Com
SHE'S SO CUTE!
THEY'VE GOT LOTS OF KITTIES THERE THAT NEED HOMES.
B.CRANE 3-9
OH, I COULDN'T ADOPT ANOTHER CAT. MUFFIN GETS SO JEALOUS. IN FACT, IF SHE EVEN KNEW I WAS...
© 1999 Washington Post Writers Group
SAY, WOULD YOU MIND IF I CLOSED THESE CURTAINS?

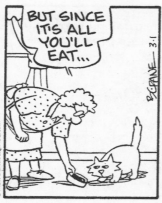

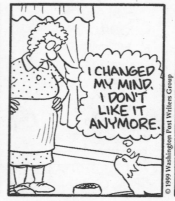

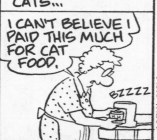

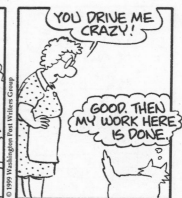

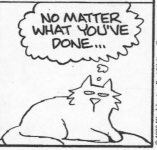

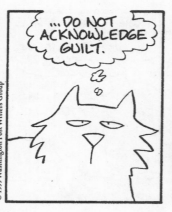

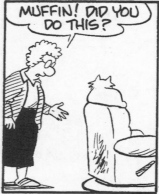

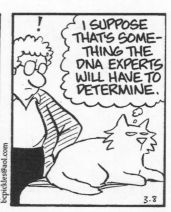

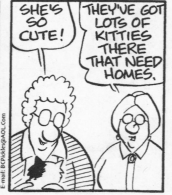

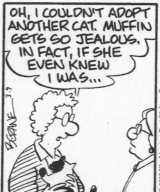

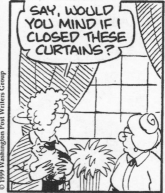

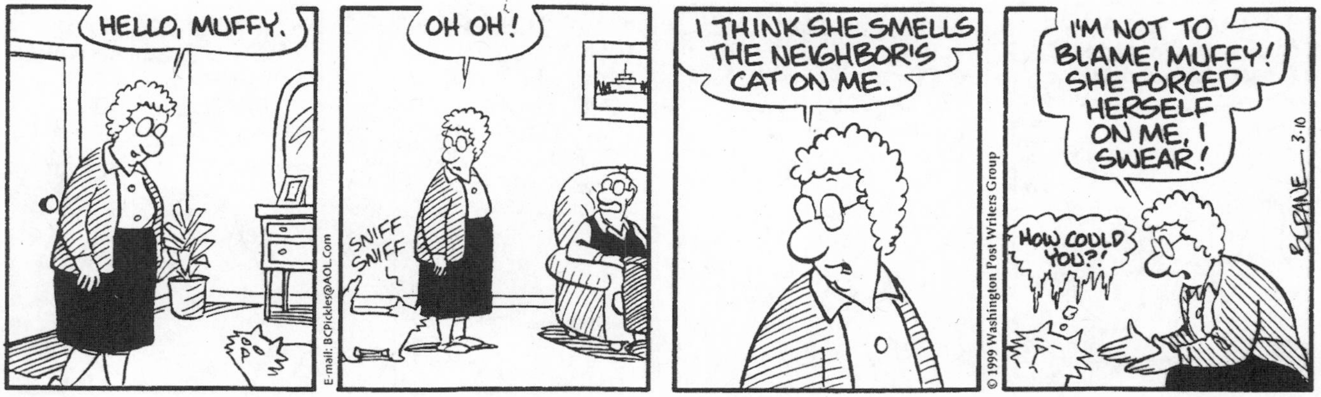
HELLO, MUFFY.
E-mail: BCPickles@AOL.Com
OH OH!
SNIFF SNIFF
I THINK SHE SMELLS THE NEIGHBOR'S CAT ON ME.
© 1999 Washington Post Writers Group
I'M NOT TO BLAME, MUFFY! SHE FORCED HERSELF ON ME, I SWEAR!
HOW COULD YOU?!
B.CRANE 3-10

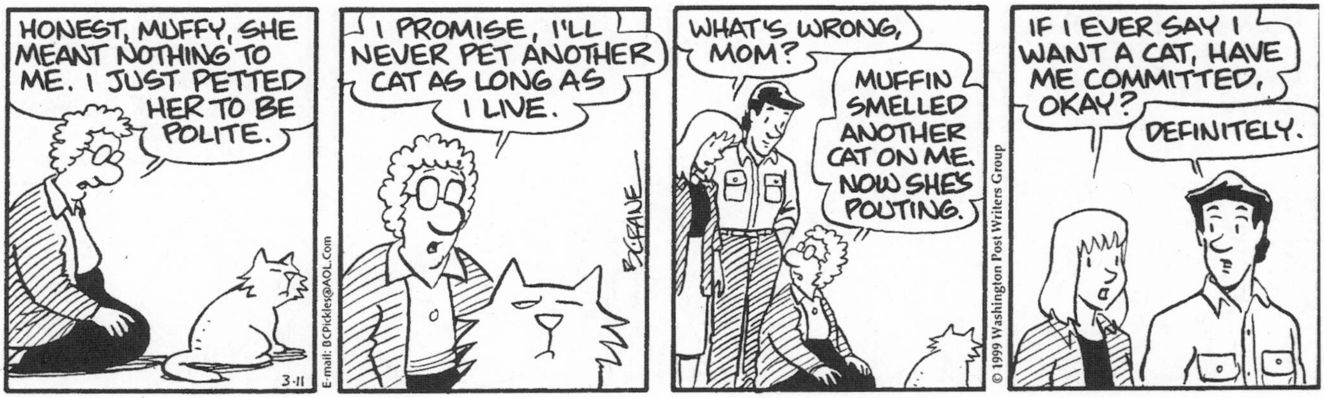
HONEST, MUFFY, SHE MEANT NOTHING TO ME. I JUST PETTED HER TO BE POLITE.
3-11
E-mail: BCPickles@AOL.Com
I PROMISE, I'LL NEVER PET ANOTHER CAT AS LONG AS I LIVE.
B.CRANE
WHAT'S WRONG, MOM?
MUFFIN SMELLED ANOTHER CAT ON ME. NOW SHE'S POUTING.
© 1999 Washington Post Writers Group
IF I EVER SAY I WANT A CAT, HAVE ME COMMITTED, OKAY?
DEFINITELY.

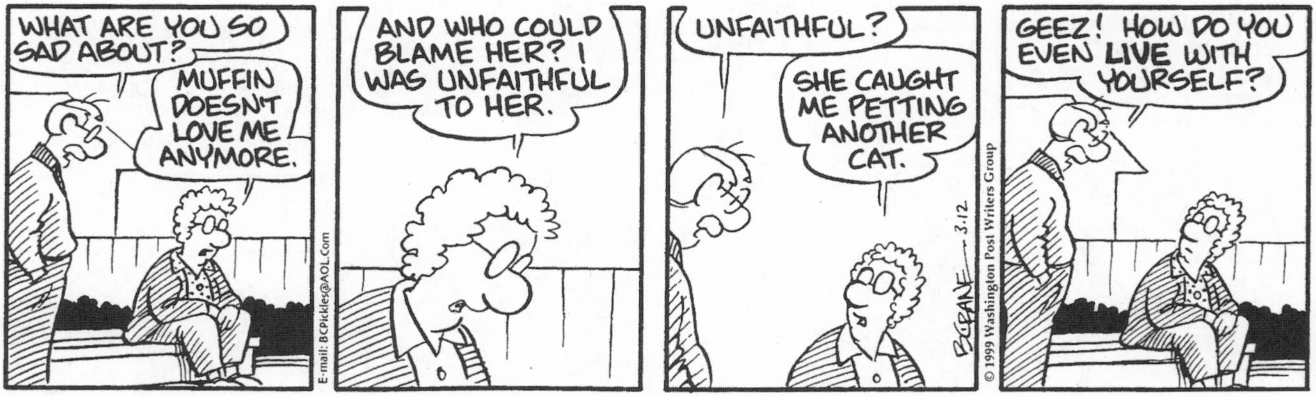
WHAT ARE YOU SO SAD ABOUT?
MUFFIN DOESN'T LOVE ME ANYMORE.
E-mail: BCPickles@AOL.Com
AND WHO COULD BLAME HER? I WAS UNFAITHFUL TO HER.
UNFAITHFUL?
SHE CAUGHT ME PETTING ANOTHER CAT.
B.CRANE 3-12
© 1999 Washington Post Writers Group
GEEZ! HOW DO YOU EVEN LIVE WITH YOURSELF?

169

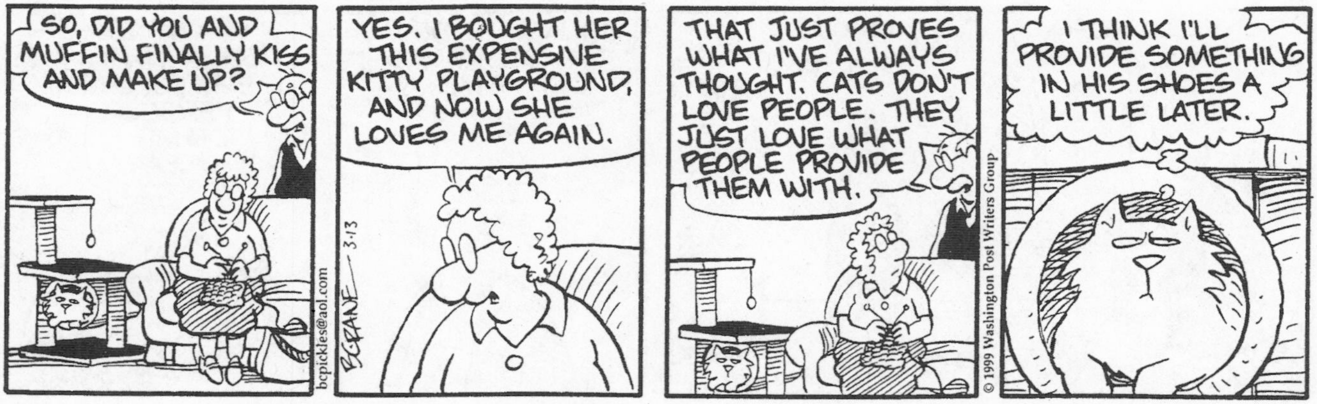
SO, DID YOU AND MUFFIN FINALLY KISS AND MAKE UP?
bcpickles@aol.com
B. CRANE 3-13
YES. I BOUGHT HER THIS EXPENSIVE KITTY PLAYGROUND, AND NOW SHE LOVES ME AGAIN.
THAT JUST PROVES WHAT I'VE ALWAYS THOUGHT. CATS DON'T LOVE PEOPLE. THEY JUST LOVE WHAT PEOPLE PROVIDE THEM WITH.
© 1999 Washington Post Writers Group
I THINK I'LL PROVIDE SOMETHING IN HIS SHOES A LITTLE LATER.

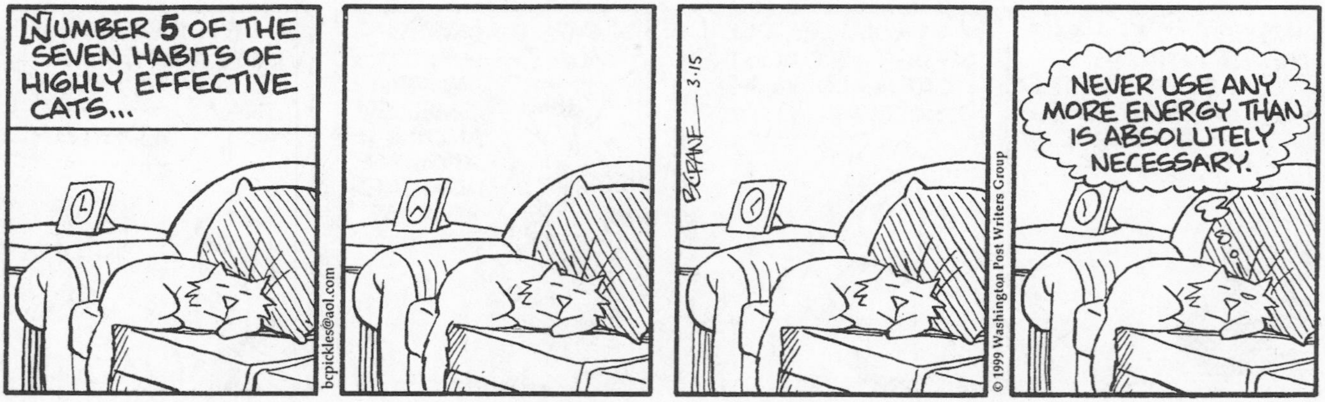
NUMBER 5 OF THE SEVEN HABITS OF HIGHLY EFFECTIVE CATS...
bcpickles@aol.com
B. CRANE 3-15
© 1999 Washington Post Writers Group
NEVER USE ANY MORE ENERGY THAN IS ABSOLUTELY NECESSARY.

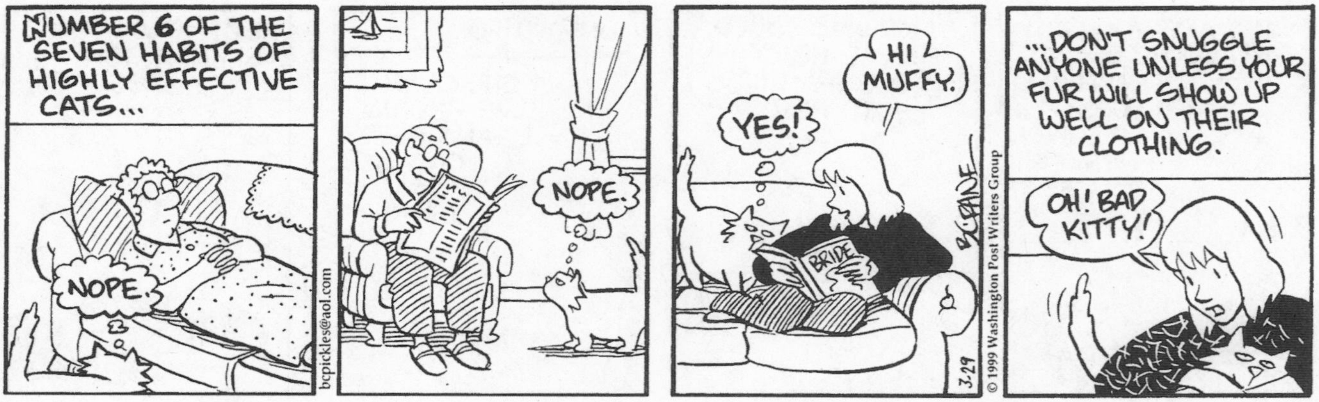
NUMBER 6 OF THE SEVEN HABITS OF HIGHLY EFFECTIVE CATS...
NOPE.
bcpickles@aol.com
NOPE.
HI MUFFY.
YES!
BRIDE
B. CRANE 3-29
© 1999 Washington Post Writers Group
...DON'T SNUGGLE ANYONE UNLESS YOUR FUR WILL SHOW UP WELL ON THEIR CLOTHING.
OH! BAD KITTY!

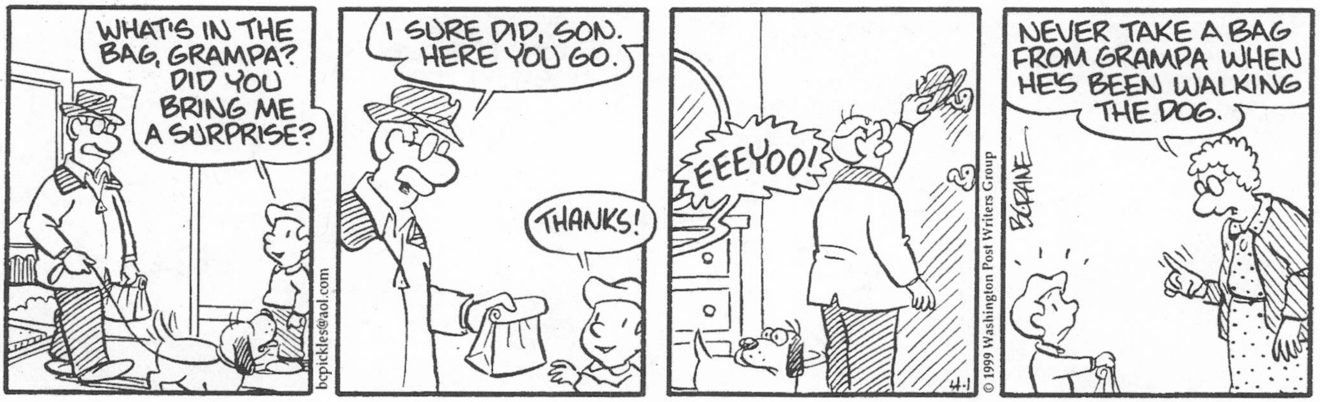
WHAT'S IN THE BAG, GRAMPA? DID YOU BRING ME A SURPRISE?
bcpickles@aol.com
I SURE DID, SON. HERE YOU GO.
THANKS!
EEEYOO!
4-1
© 1999 Washington Post Writers Group
NEVER TAKE A BAG FROM GRAMPA WHEN HE'S BEEN WALKING THE DOG.
BCRANE

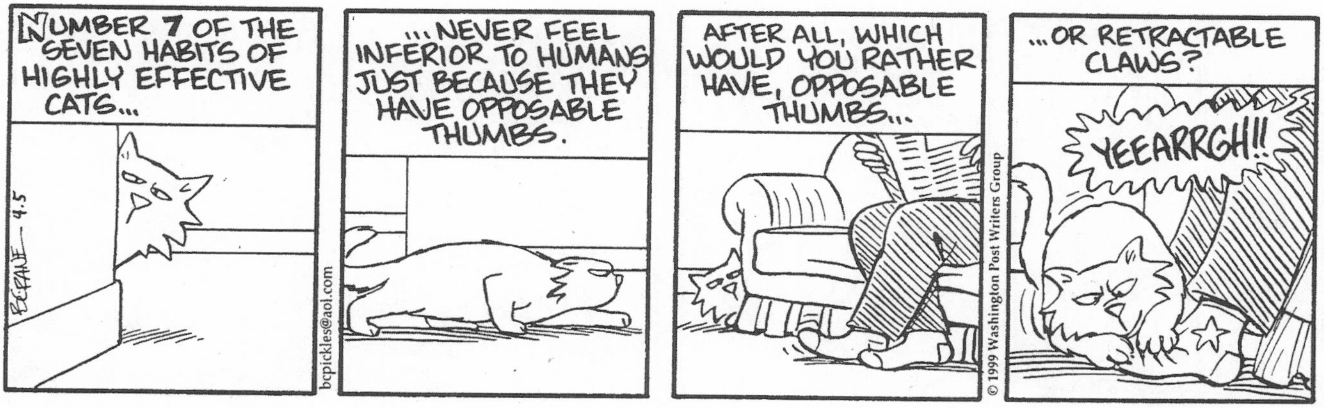
NUMBER 7 OF THE SEVEN HABITS OF HIGHLY EFFECTIVE CATS...
BCRANE 4-5
bcpickles@aol.com
...NEVER FEEL INFERIOR TO HUMANS JUST BECAUSE THEY HAVE OPPOSABLE THUMBS.
AFTER ALL, WHICH WOULD YOU RATHER HAVE, OPPOSABLE THUMBS...
© 1999 Washington Post Writers Group
...OR RETRACTABLE CLAWS?
YEEARRGH!!

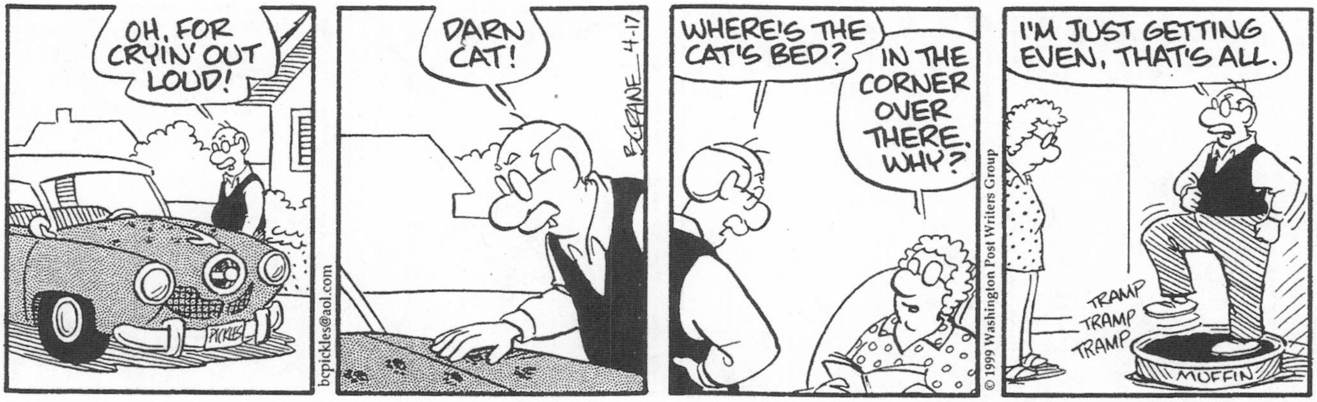
OH, FOR CRYIN' OUT LOUD!
PICKLES
bcpickles@aol.com
DARN CAT!
BCRANE 4-17
WHERE'S THE CAT'S BED?
IN THE CORNER OVER THERE. WHY?
© 1999 Washington Post Writers Group
I'M JUST GETTING EVEN, THAT'S ALL.
TRAMP
TRAMP
TRAMP
MUFFIN

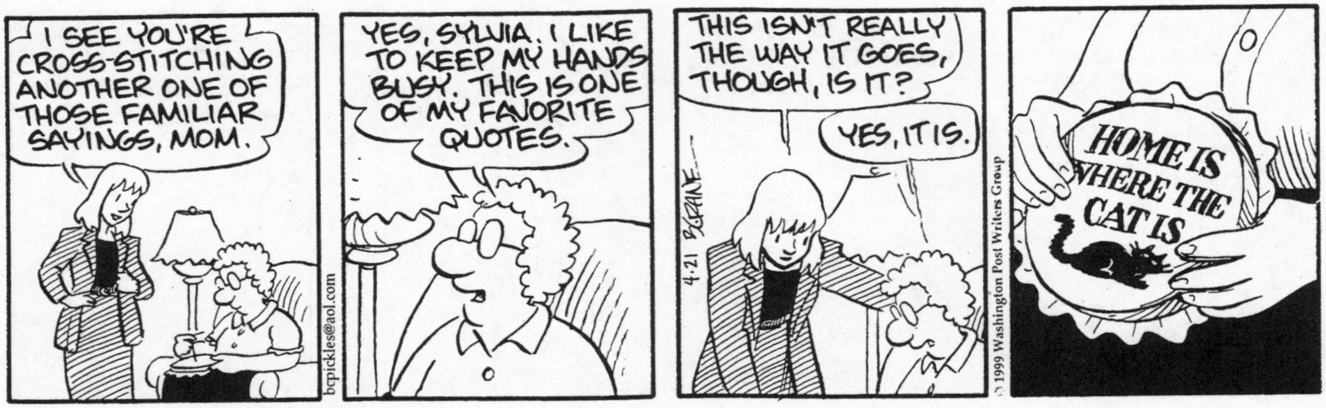
I SEE YOU'RE CROSS-STITCHING ANOTHER ONE OF THOSE FAMILIAR SAYINGS, MOM.
bcpickles@aol.com
YES, SYLVIA. I LIKE TO KEEP MY HANDS BUSY. THIS IS ONE OF MY FAVORITE QUOTES.
THIS ISN'T REALLY THE WAY IT GOES, THOUGH, IS IT?
YES, IT IS.
4.21 B.CRANE
© 1999 Washington Post Writers Group
HOME IS WHERE THE CAT IS

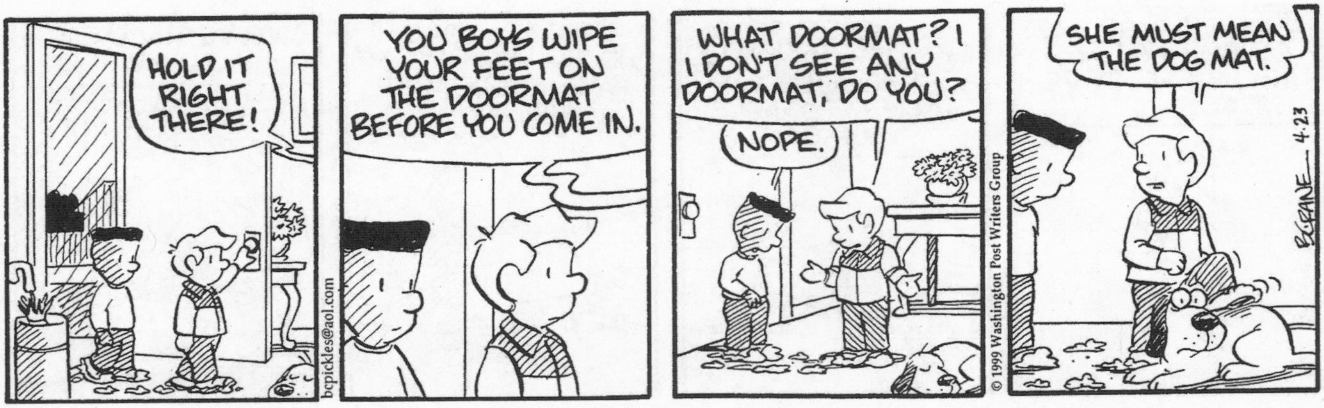
HOLD IT RIGHT THERE!
bcpickles@aol.com
YOU BOYS WIPE YOUR FEET ON THE DOORMAT BEFORE YOU COME IN.
WHAT DOORMAT? I DON'T SEE ANY DOORMAT, DO YOU?
NOPE.
© 1999 Washington Post Writers Group
SHE MUST MEAN THE DOG MAT.
B.CRANE 4.23

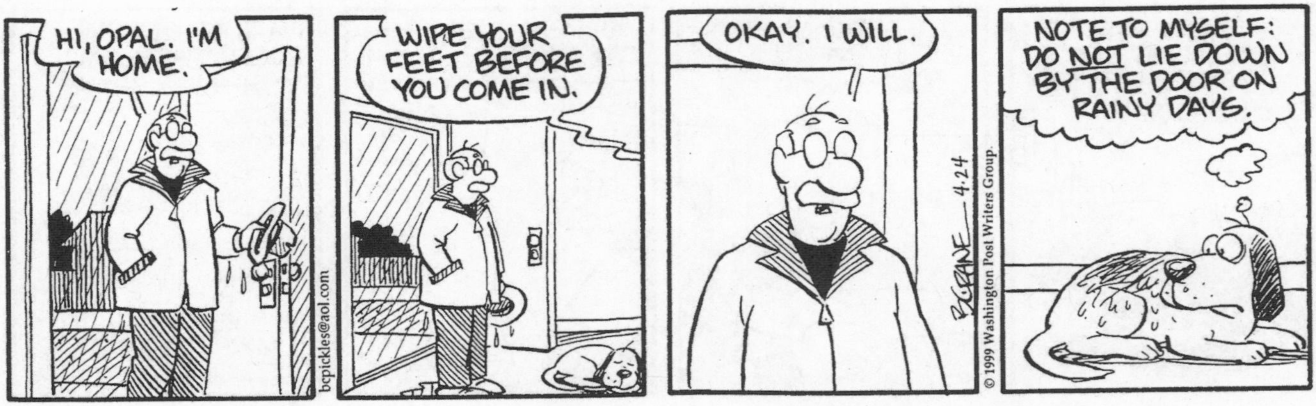
HI, OPAL. I'M HOME.
bcpickles@aol.com
WIPE YOUR FEET BEFORE YOU COME IN.
OKAY. I WILL.
B.CRANE 4.24
© 1999 Washington Post Writers Group
NOTE TO MYSELF: DO NOT LIE DOWN BY THE DOOR ON RAINY DAYS.

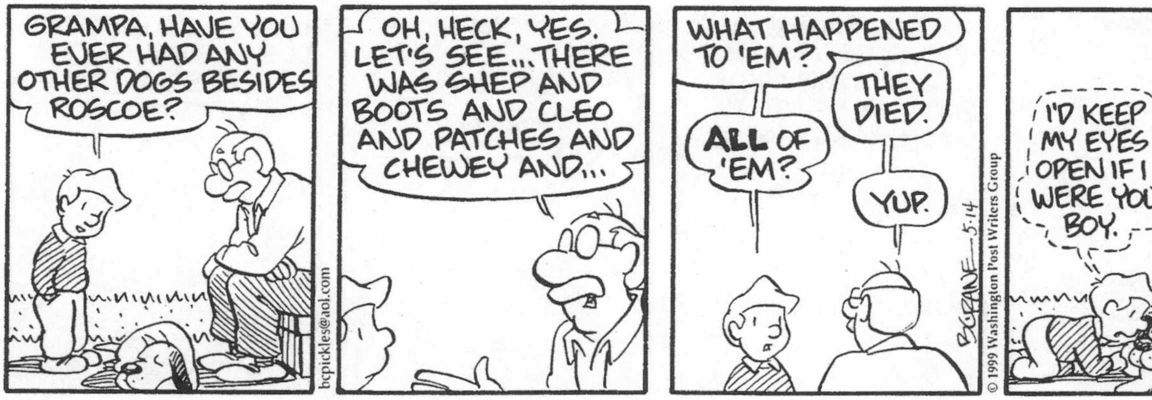
GRAMPA, HAVE YOU EVER HAD ANY OTHER DOGS BESIDES ROSCOE?
bcpickles@aol.com
OH, HECK, YES. LET'S SEE... THERE WAS SHEP AND BOOTS AND CLEO AND PATCHES AND CHEWEY AND...
WHAT HAPPENED TO 'EM?
THEY DIED.
ALL OF 'EM?
YUP.
B.CRANE 5.14
© 1999 Washington Post Writers Group
I'D KEEP MY EYES OPEN IF I WERE YOU, BOY.

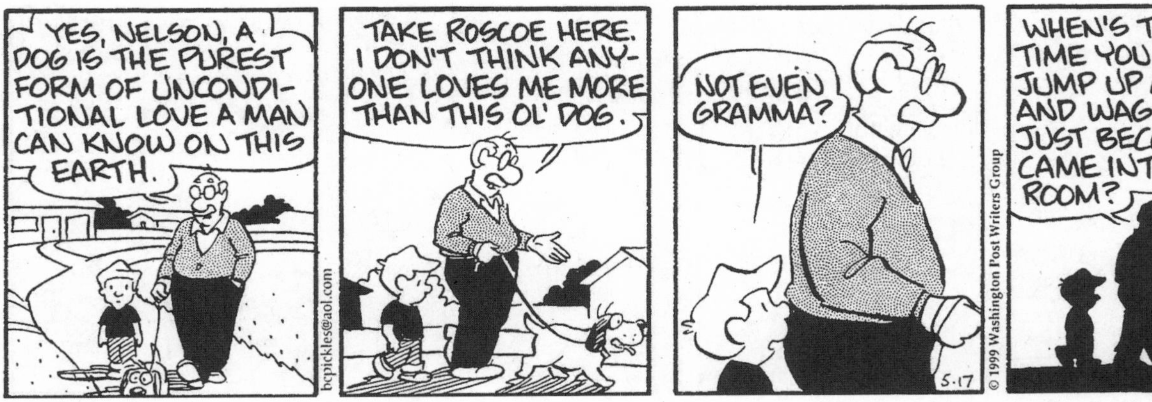
YES, NELSON, A DOG IS THE PUREST FORM OF UNCONDITIONAL LOVE A MAN CAN KNOW ON THIS EARTH.
bcpickles@aol.com
TAKE ROSCOE HERE. I DON'T THINK ANYONE LOVES ME MORE THAN THIS OL' DOG.
NOT EVEN GRAMMA?
5.17
© 1999 Washington Post Writers Group
WHEN'S THE LAST TIME YOU SAW HER JUMP UP AND DOWN AND WAG HER TAIL JUST BECAUSE I CAME INTO THE ROOM?
B.CRANE

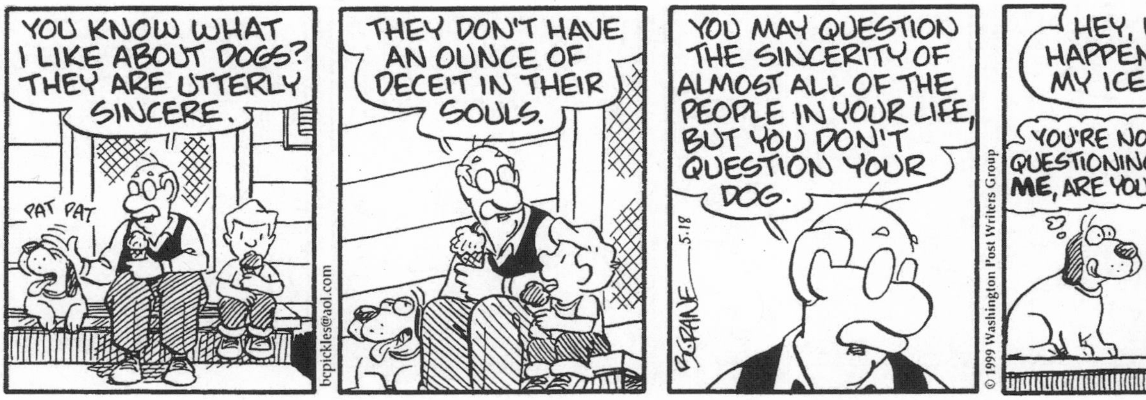
YOU KNOW WHAT I LIKE ABOUT DOGS? THEY ARE UTTERLY SINCERE.
PAT PAT
bcpickles@aol.com
THEY DON'T HAVE AN OUNCE OF DECEIT IN THEIR SOULS.
YOU MAY QUESTION THE SINCERITY OF ALMOST ALL OF THE PEOPLE IN YOUR LIFE, BUT YOU DON'T QUESTION YOUR DOG.
B.CRANE 5.18
© 1999 Washington Post Writers Group
HEY, WHAT HAPPENED TO MY ICE CREAM?
YOU'RE NOT QUESTIONING ME, ARE YOU?

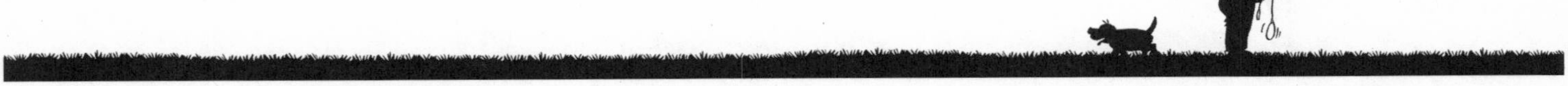

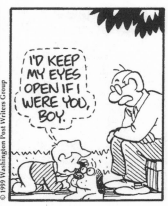

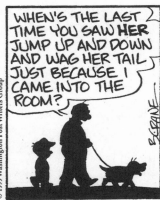

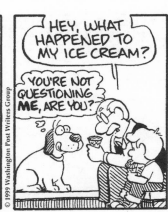

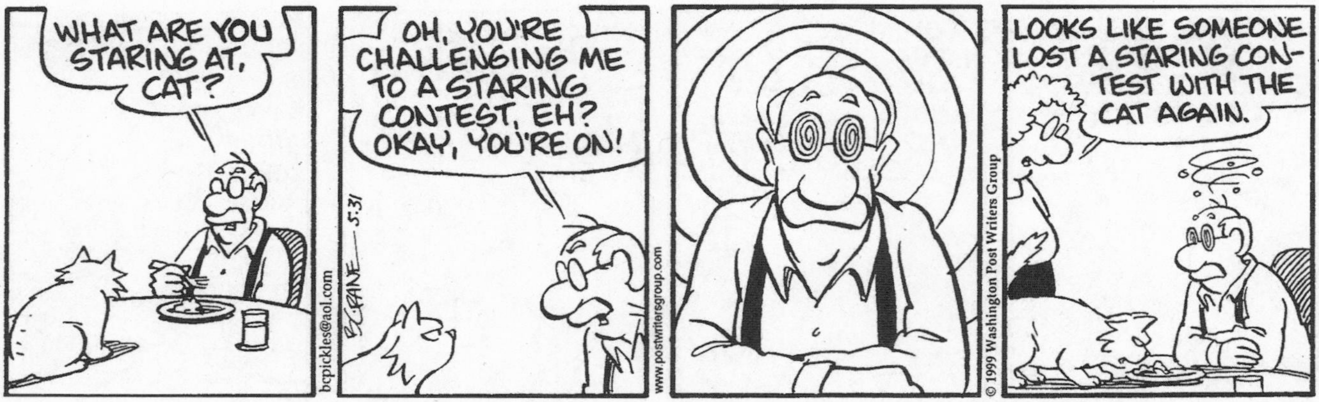
WHAT ARE YOU STARING AT, CAT?
bcpickles@aol.com
OH, YOU'RE CHALLENGING ME TO A STARING CONTEST, EH? OKAY, YOU'RE ON!
5.31
www.postwritersgroup.com
© 1999 Washington Post Writers Group
LOOKS LIKE SOMEONE LOST A STARING CON- TEST WITH THE CAT AGAIN.

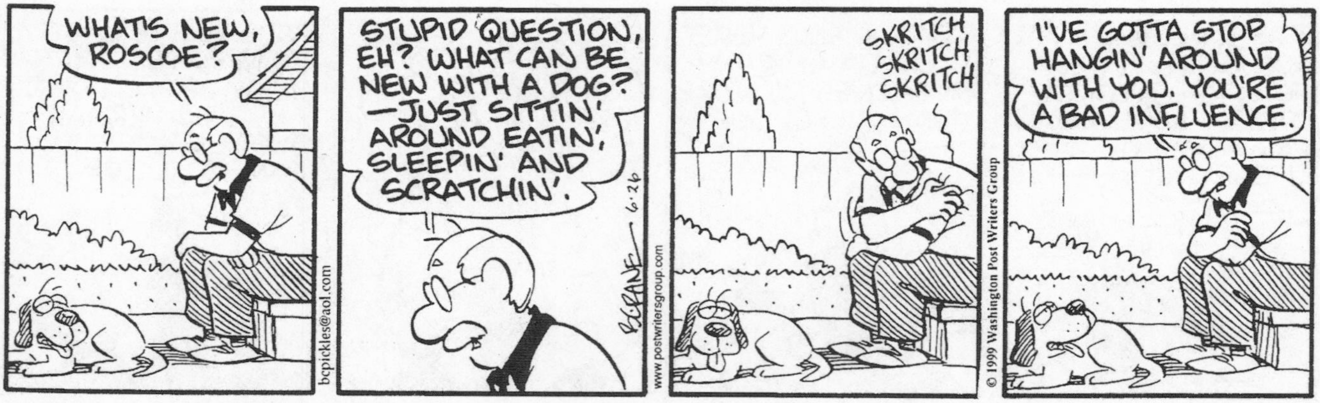
WHAT'S NEW, ROSCOE?
bcpickles@aol.com
STUPID QUESTION, EH? WHAT CAN BE NEW WITH A DOG? —JUST SITTIN' AROUND EATIN', SLEEPIN' AND SCRATCHIN'.
6.26
www.postwritersgroup.com
SKRITCH SKRITCH SKRITCH
© 1999 Washington Post Writers Group
I'VE GOTTA STOP HANGIN' AROUND WITH YOU. YOU'RE A BAD INFLUENCE.

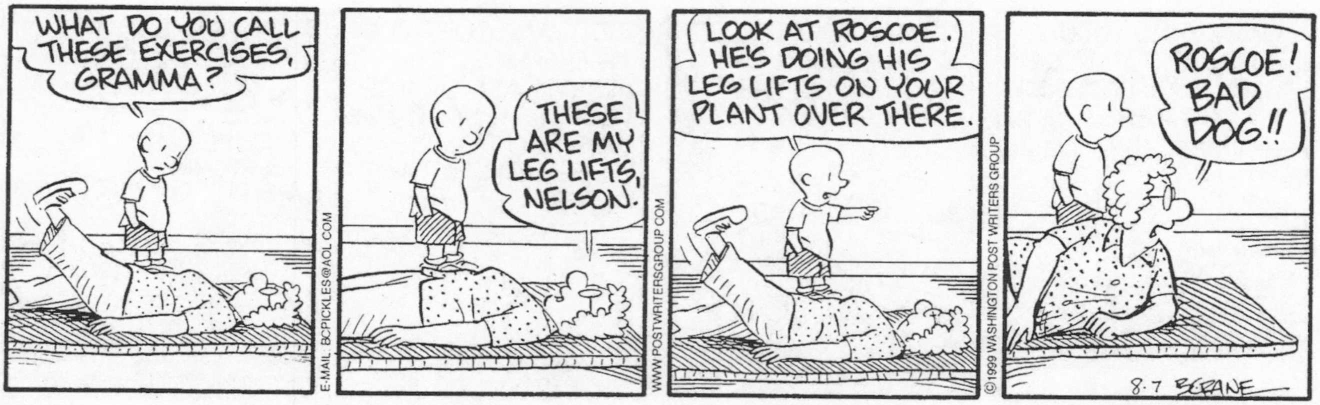
WHAT DO YOU CALL THESE EXERCISES, GRAMMA?
E-MAIL BCPICKLES@AOL.COM
THESE ARE MY LEG LIFTS, NELSON.
WWW.POSTWRITERSGROUP.COM
LOOK AT ROSCOE. HE'S DOING HIS LEG LIFTS ON YOUR PLANT OVER THERE.
©1999 WASHINGTON POST WRITERS GROUP
ROSCOE! BAD DOG!!
8.7

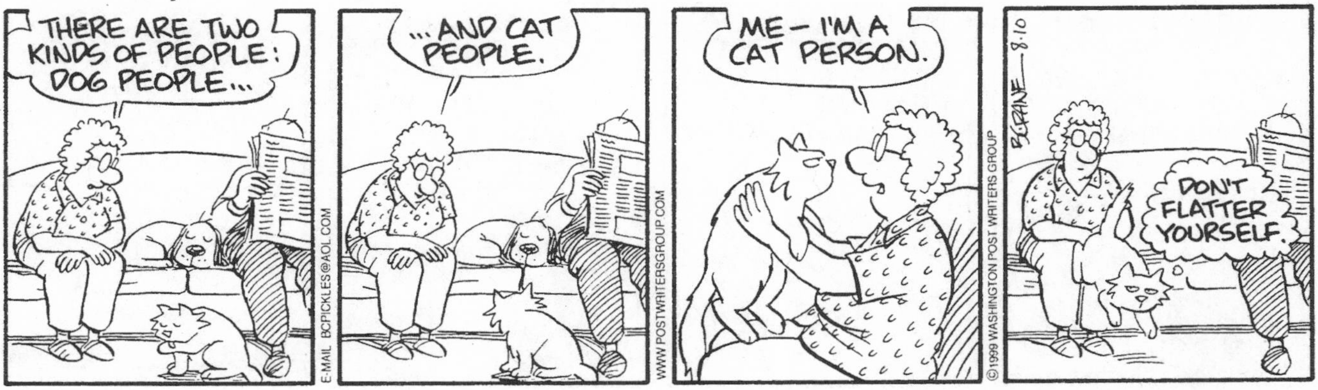
THERE ARE TWO KINDS OF PEOPLE: DOG PEOPLE...
E-MAIL: BCPICKLES@AOL.COM
...AND CAT PEOPLE.
WWW.POSTWRITERSGROUP.COM
ME – I'M A CAT PERSON.
© 1999 WASHINGTON POST WRITERS GROUP
B.C.RANE 8.10
DON'T FLATTER YOURSELF.

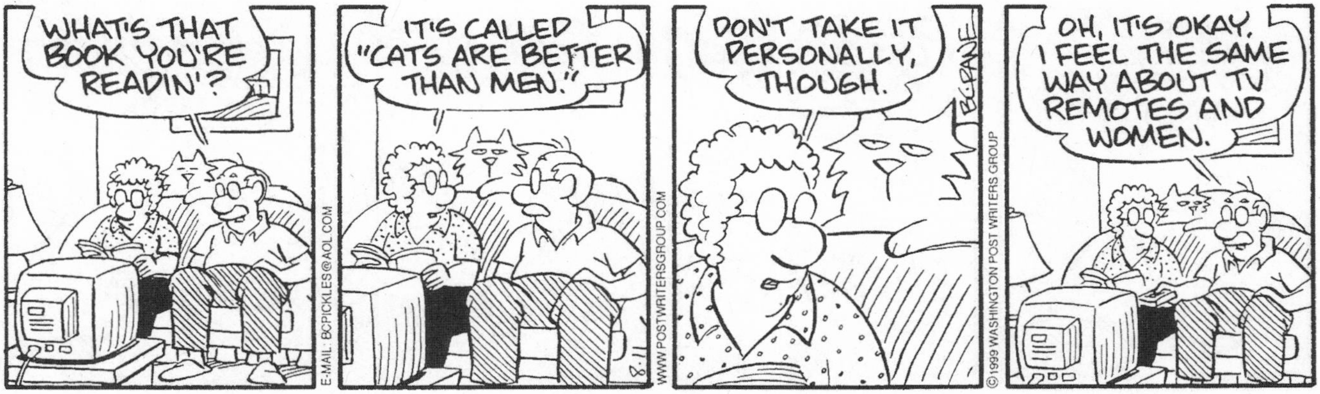
WHAT'S THAT BOOK YOU'RE READIN'?
E-MAIL: BCPICKLES@AOL.COM
IT'S CALLED "CATS ARE BETTER THAN MEN."
8.11
WWW.POSTWRITERSGROUP.COM
DON'T TAKE IT PERSONALLY, THOUGH.
B.C.RANE
© 1999 WASHINGTON POST WRITERS GROUP
OH, IT'S OKAY. I FEEL THE SAME WAY ABOUT TV REMOTES AND WOMEN.

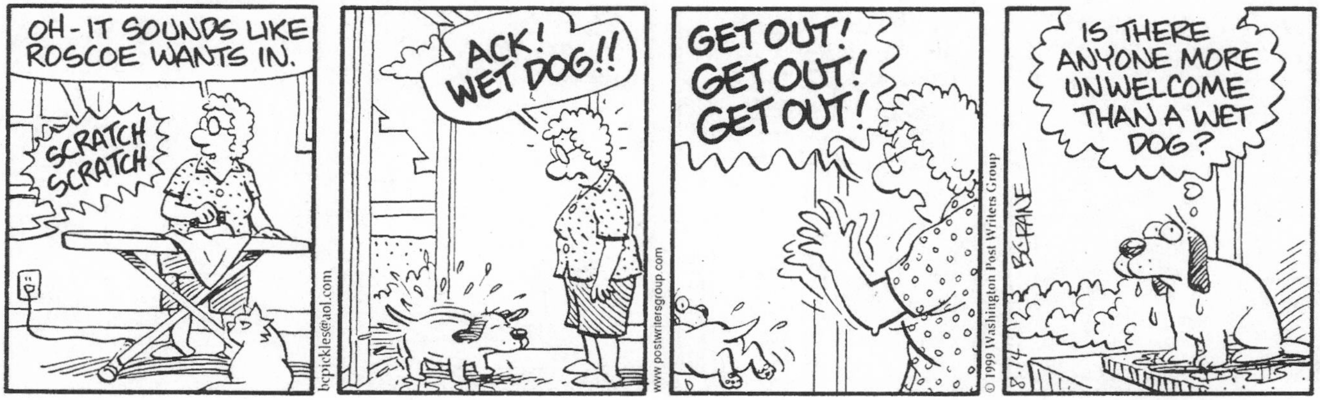
OH – IT SOUNDS LIKE ROSCOE WANTS IN.
SCRATCH SCRATCH
bcpickles@aol.com
ACK! WET DOG!!
www.postwritersgroup.com
GET OUT! GET OUT! GET OUT!
© 1999 Washington Post Writers Group
8.14
B.C.RANE
IS THERE ANYONE MORE UNWELCOME THAN A WET DOG?

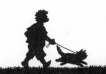

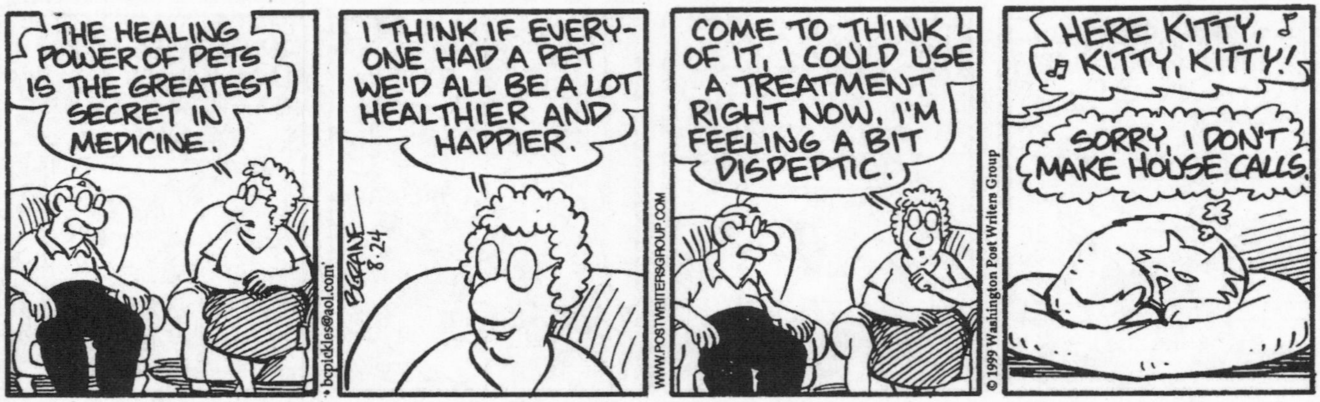
THE HEALING POWER OF PETS IS THE GREATEST SECRET IN MEDICINE.
bcpickles@aol.com
I THINK IF EVERYONE HAD A PET WE'D ALL BE A LOT HEALTHIER AND HAPPIER.
B.CRANE 8-24
WWW.POSTWRITERSGROUP.COM
COME TO THINK OF IT, I COULD USE A TREATMENT RIGHT NOW. I'M FEELING A BIT DISPEPTIC.
© 1999 Washington Post Writers Group
HERE KITTY, KITTY, KITTY!
SORRY, I DON'T MAKE HOUSE CALLS.

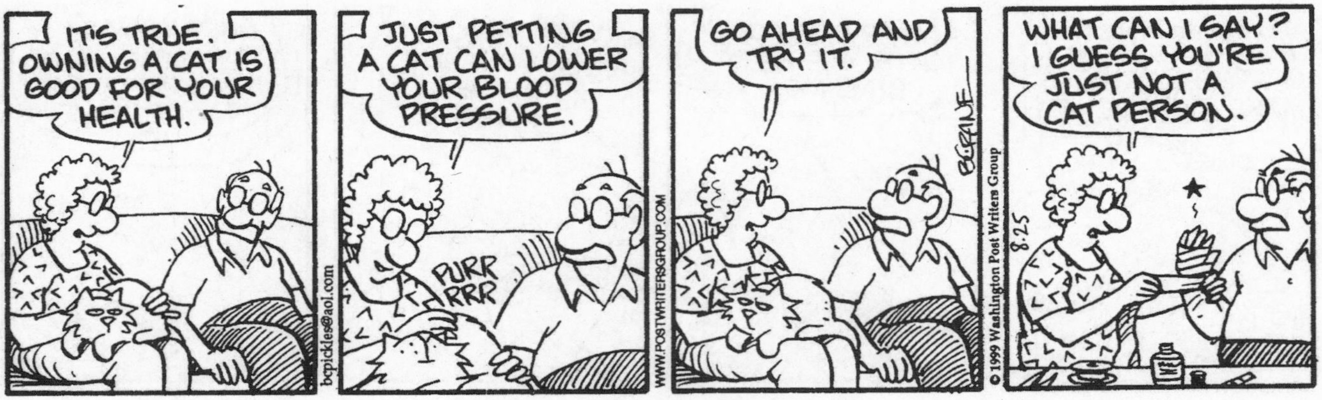
IT'S TRUE. OWNING A CAT IS GOOD FOR YOUR HEALTH.
bcpickles@aol.com
JUST PETTING A CAT CAN LOWER YOUR BLOOD PRESSURE.
PURR RRR
WWW.POSTWRITERSGROUP.COM
GO AHEAD AND TRY IT.
B.CRANE
© 1999 Washington Post Writers Group
8-25
WHAT CAN I SAY? I GUESS YOU'RE JUST NOT A CAT PERSON.

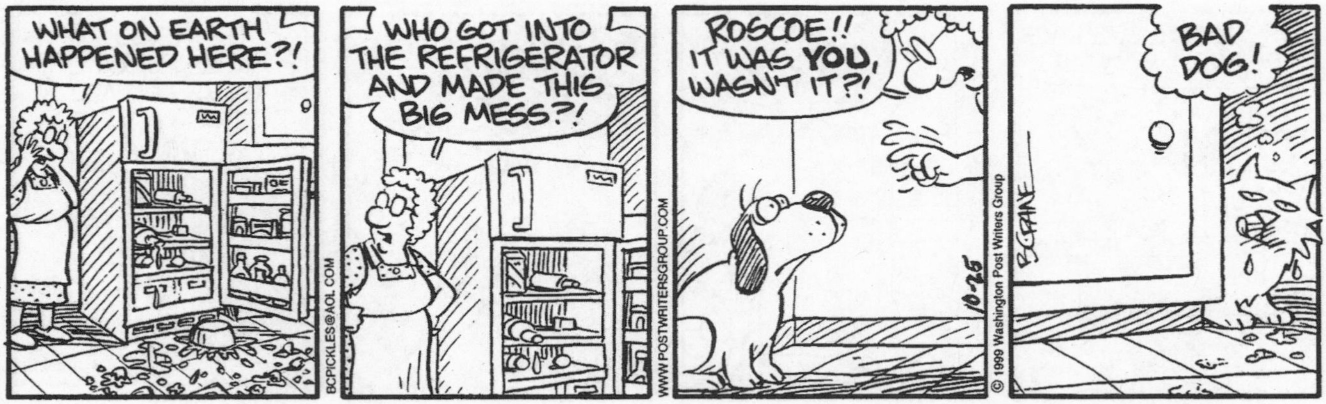
WHAT ON EARTH HAPPENED HERE?!
BCPICKLES@AOL.COM
WHO GOT INTO THE REFRIGERATOR AND MADE THIS BIG MESS?!
WWW.POSTWRITERSGROUP.COM
ROSCOE!! IT WAS **YOU**, WASN'T IT?!
10-25
© 1999 Washington Post Writers Group
B.CRANE
BAD DOG!

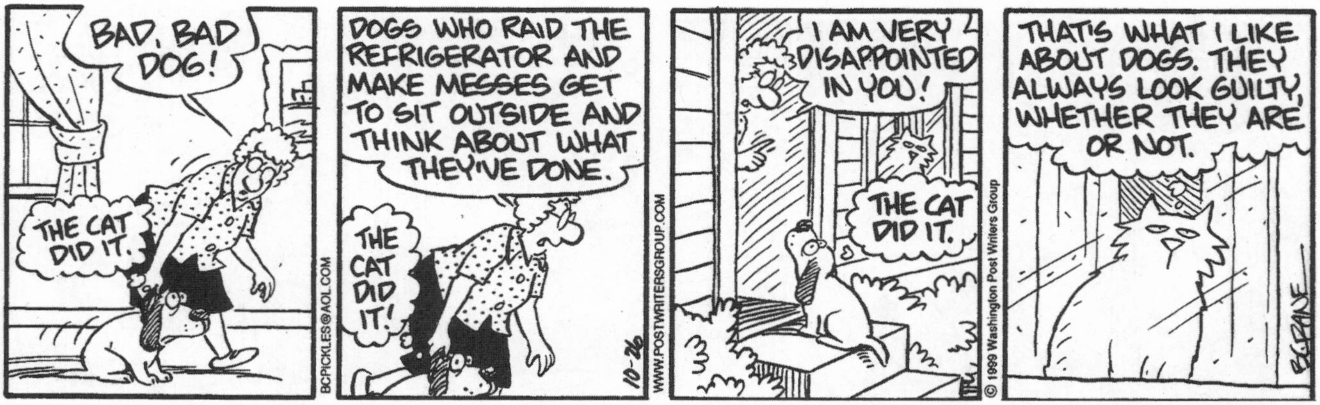

BAD, BAD DOG!
THE CAT DID IT.
BCPICKLES@AOL.COM
DOGS WHO RAID THE REFRIGERATOR AND MAKE MESSES GET TO SIT OUTSIDE AND THINK ABOUT WHAT THEY'VE DONE.
THE CAT DID IT!
10-26
WWW.POSTWRITERSGROUP.COM
I AM VERY DISAPPOINTED IN YOU!
THE CAT DID IT.
© 1999 Washington Post Writers Group
THAT'S WHAT I LIKE ABOUT DOGS. THEY ALWAYS LOOK GUILTY, WHETHER THEY ARE OR NOT.
B.CRANE

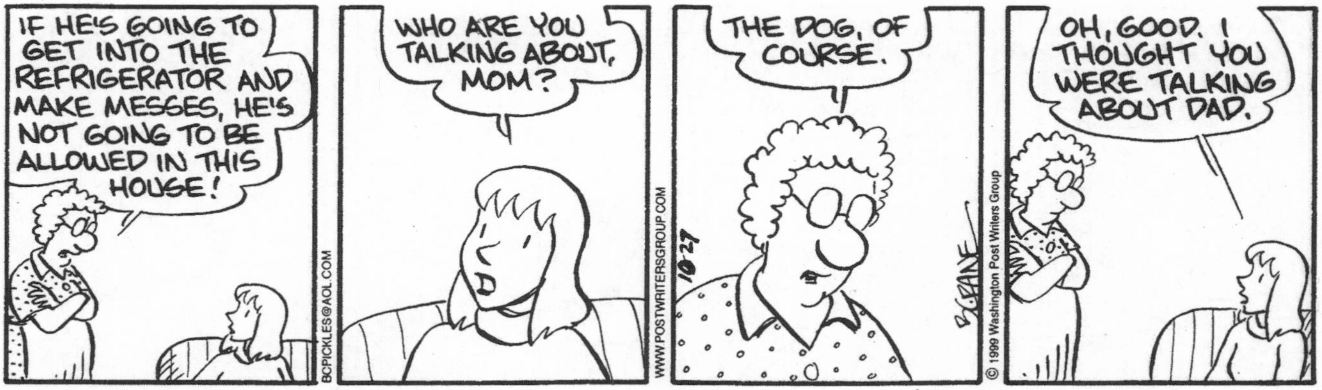

IF HE'S GOING TO GET INTO THE REFRIGERATOR AND MAKE MESSES, HE'S NOT GOING TO BE ALLOWED IN THIS HOUSE!
BCPICKLES@AOL.COM
WHO ARE YOU TALKING ABOUT, MOM?
WWW.POSTWRITERSGROUP.COM
THE DOG, OF COURSE.
10-27
B.CRANE
© 1999 Washington Post Writers Group
OH, GOOD. I THOUGHT YOU WERE TALKING ABOUT DAD.

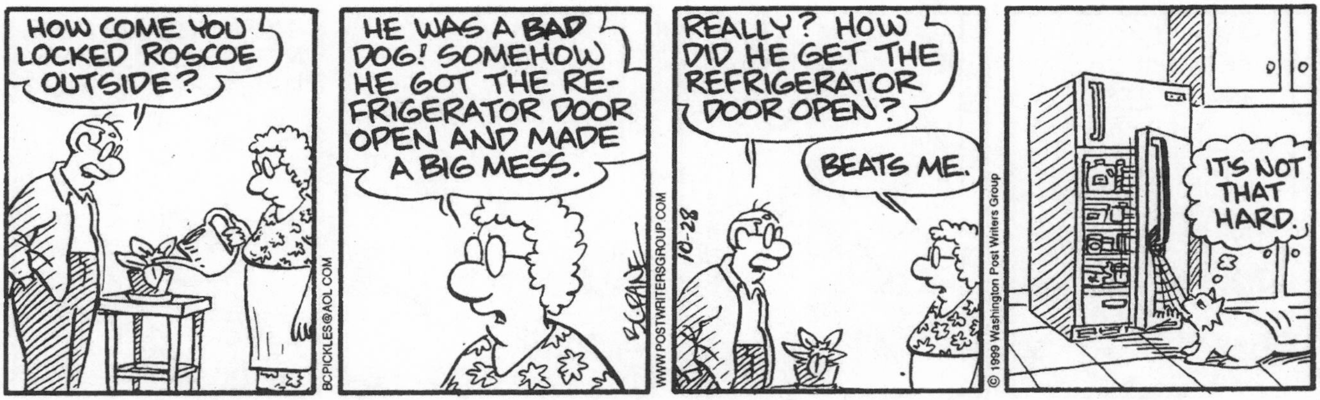

HOW COME YOU LOCKED ROSCOE OUTSIDE?
BCPICKLES@AOL.COM
HE WAS A BAD DOG! SOMEHOW HE GOT THE REFRIGERATOR DOOR OPEN AND MADE A BIG MESS.
B.CRANE
WWW.POSTWRITERSGROUP.COM
REALLY? HOW DID HE GET THE REFRIGERATOR DOOR OPEN?
BEATS ME.
10-28
© 1999 Washington Post Writers Group
IT'S NOT THAT HARD.

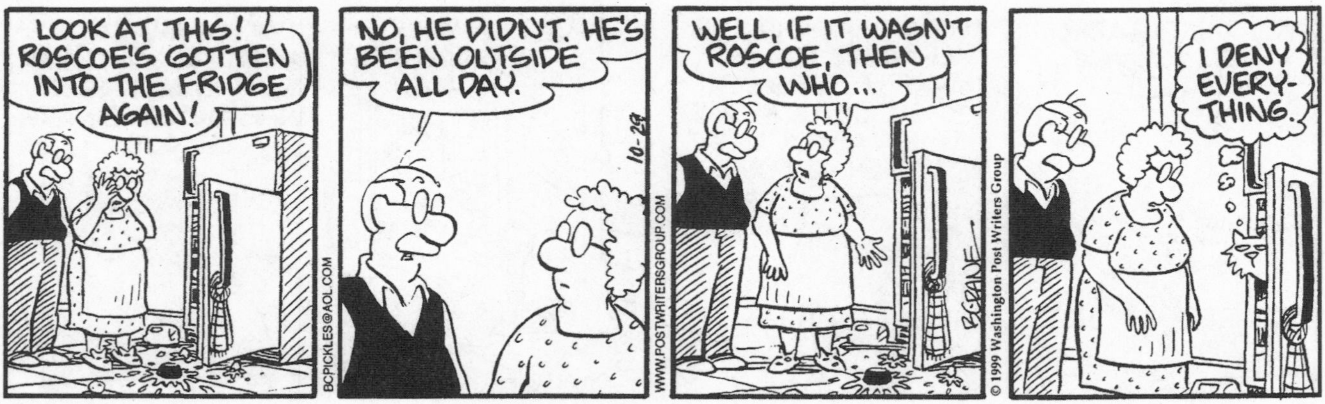
LOOK AT THIS! ROSCOE'S GOTTEN INTO THE FRIDGE AGAIN!
BCPICKLES@AOL.COM
NO, HE DIDN'T. HE'S BEEN OUTSIDE ALL DAY.
10-29
WWW.POSTWRITERSGROUP.COM
WELL, IF IT WASN'T ROSCOE, THEN WHO...
© 1999 Washington Post Writers Group
I DENY EVERY-THING.

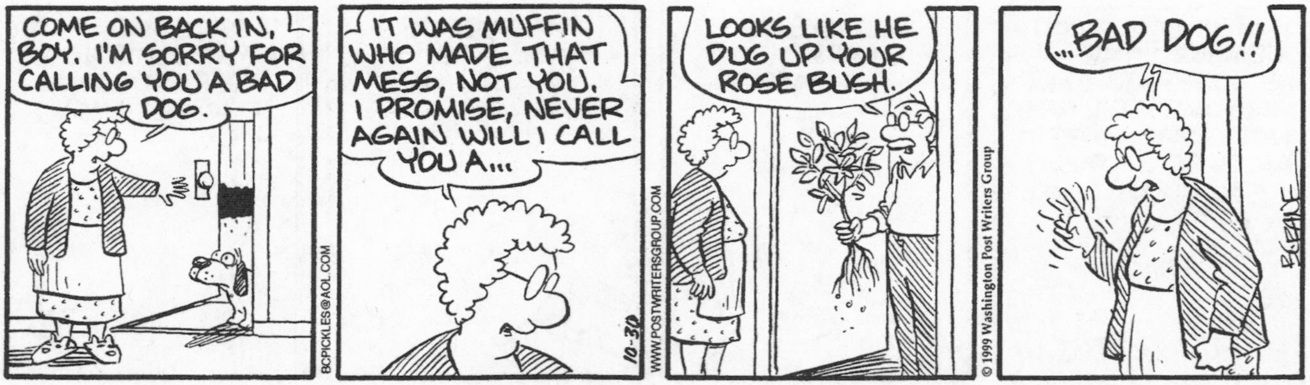
COME ON BACK IN, BOY. I'M SORRY FOR CALLING YOU A BAD DOG.
BCPICKLES@AOL.COM
IT WAS MUFFIN WHO MADE THAT MESS, NOT YOU. I PROMISE, NEVER AGAIN WILL I CALL YOU A...
10-30
WWW.POSTWRITERSGROUP.COM
LOOKS LIKE HE DUG UP YOUR ROSE BUSH.
© 1999 Washington Post Writers Group
...BAD DOG!!

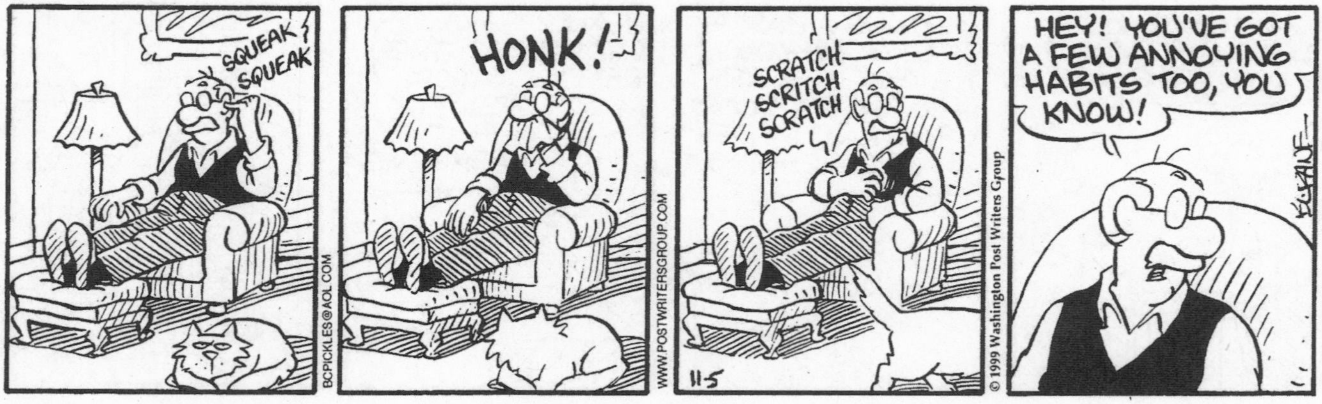
SQUEAK SQUEAK
BCPICKLES@AOL.COM
HONK!
WWW.POSTWRITERSGROUP.COM
SCRATCH SCRITCH SCRATCH
11-5
© 1999 Washington Post Writers Group
HEY! YOU'VE GOT A FEW ANNOYING HABITS TOO, YOU KNOW!

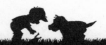

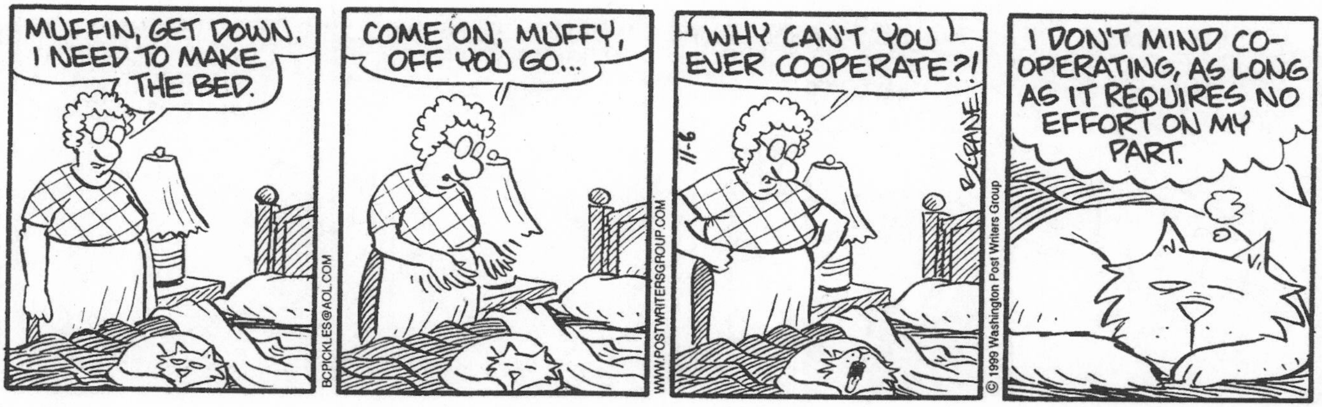
MUFFIN, GET DOWN. I NEED TO MAKE THE BED.
COME ON, MUFFY, OFF YOU GO...
WHY CAN'T YOU EVER COOPERATE?!
I DON'T MIND CO-OPERATING, AS LONG AS IT REQUIRES NO EFFORT ON MY PART.
11-6
BCPICKLES@AOL.COM
WWW.POSTWRITERSGROUP.COM
© 1999 Washington Post Writers Group

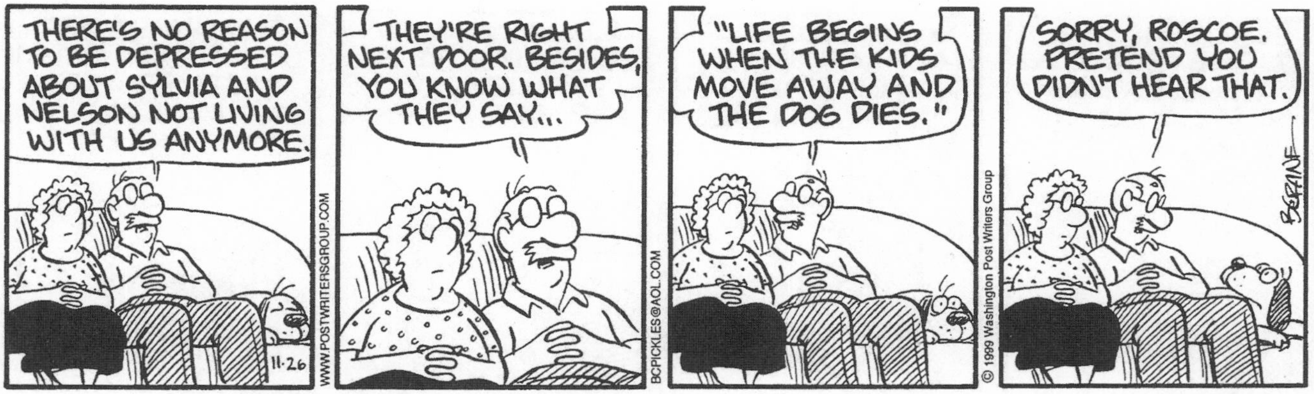
THERE'S NO REASON TO BE DEPRESSED ABOUT SYLVIA AND NELSON NOT LIVING WITH US ANYMORE.
THEY'RE RIGHT NEXT DOOR. BESIDES, YOU KNOW WHAT THEY SAY...
"LIFE BEGINS WHEN THE KIDS MOVE AWAY AND THE DOG DIES."
SORRY, ROSCOE. PRETEND YOU DIDN'T HEAR THAT.
11-26
WWW.POSTWRITERSGROUP.COM
BCPICKLES@AOL.COM
© 1999 Washington Post Writers Group

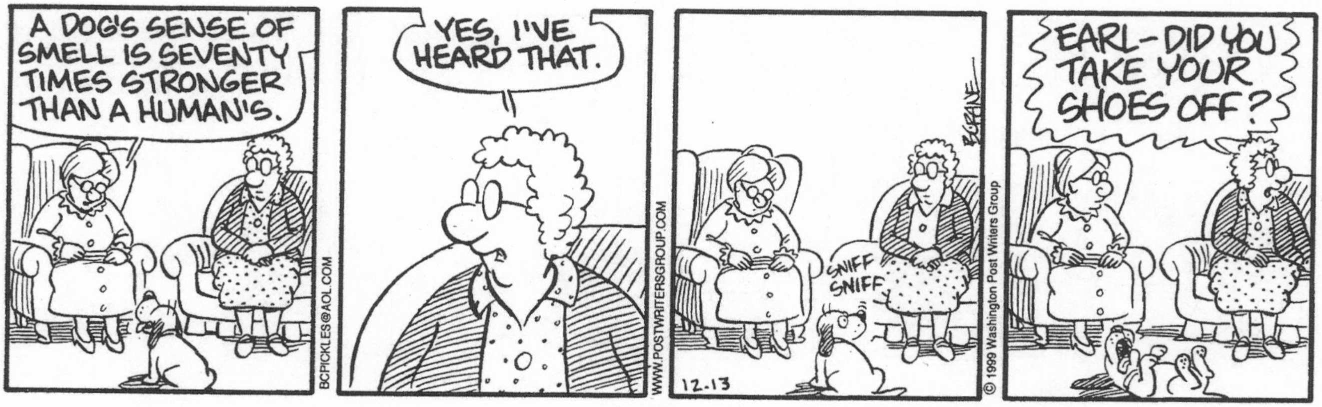
A DOG'S SENSE OF SMELL IS SEVENTY TIMES STRONGER THAN A HUMAN'S.
YES, I'VE HEARD THAT.
SNIFF SNIFF
EARL- DID YOU TAKE YOUR SHOES OFF?
12-13
BCPICKLES@AOL.COM
WWW.POSTWRITERSGROUP.COM
© 1999 Washington Post Writers Group

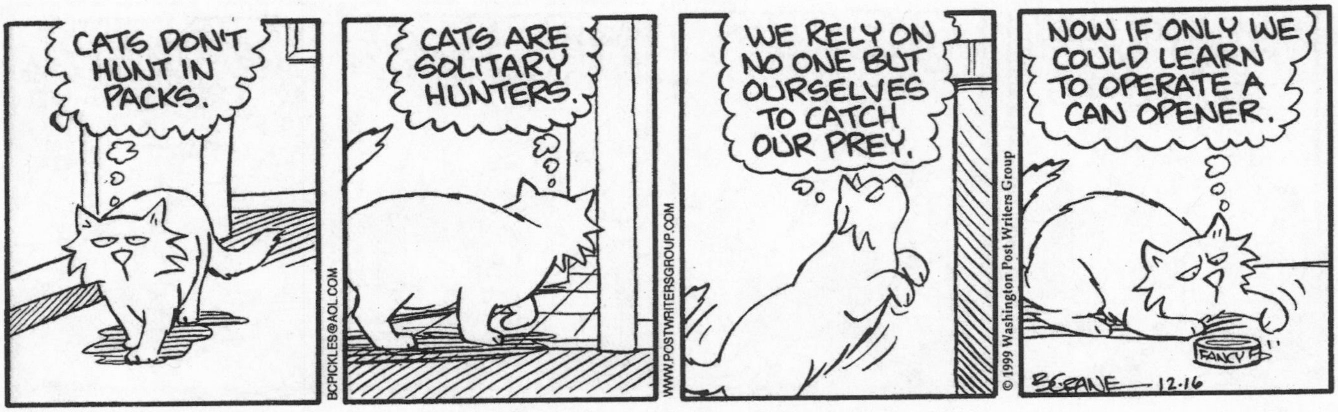
CATS DON'T HUNT IN PACKS.
CATS ARE SOLITARY HUNTERS.
WE RELY ON NO ONE BUT OURSELVES TO CATCH OUR PREY.
NOW IF ONLY WE COULD LEARN TO OPERATE A CAN OPENER.
FANCY
BCPICKLES@AOL.COM
WWW.POSTWRITERSGROUP.COM
© 1999 Washington Post Writers Group
B.CRANE 12-16

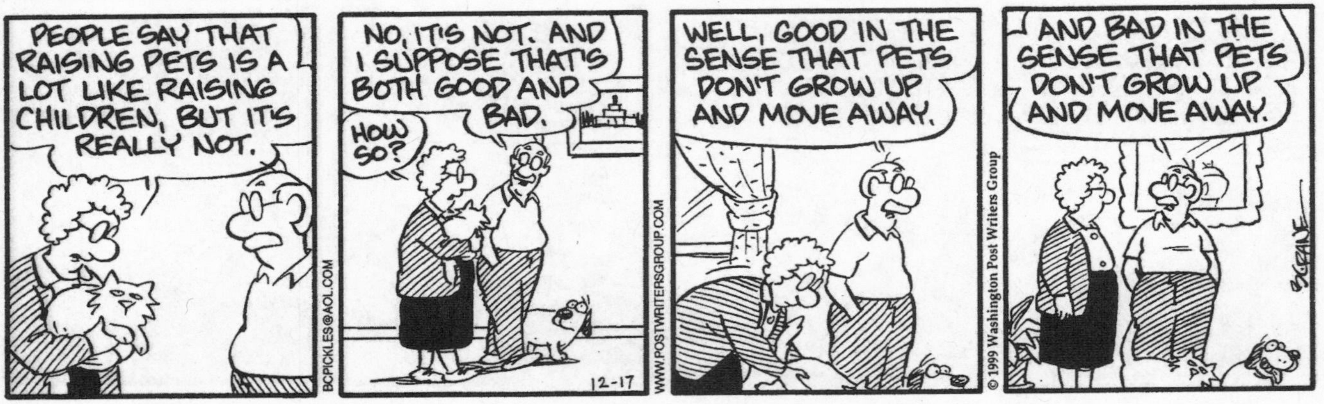
PEOPLE SAY THAT RAISING PETS IS A LOT LIKE RAISING CHILDREN, BUT IT'S REALLY NOT.
NO, IT'S NOT. AND I SUPPOSE THAT'S BOTH GOOD AND BAD.
HOW SO?
WELL, GOOD IN THE SENSE THAT PETS DON'T GROW UP AND MOVE AWAY.
AND BAD IN THE SENSE THAT PETS DON'T GROW UP AND MOVE AWAY.
BCPICKLES@AOL.COM
WWW.POSTWRITERSGROUP.COM
© 1999 Washington Post Writers Group
12-17
B.CRANE

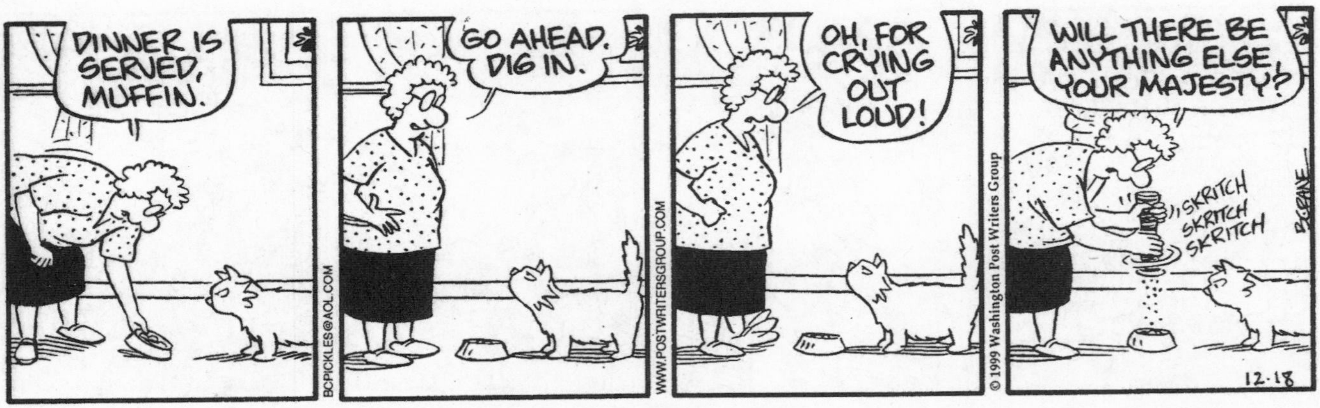
DINNER IS SERVED, MUFFIN.
GO AHEAD. DIG IN.
OH, FOR CRYING OUT LOUD!
WILL THERE BE ANYTHING ELSE, YOUR MAJESTY?
SKRITCH SKRITCH SKRITCH
BCPICKLES@AOL.COM
WWW.POSTWRITERSGROUP.COM
© 1999 Washington Post Writers Group
B.CRANE
12-18

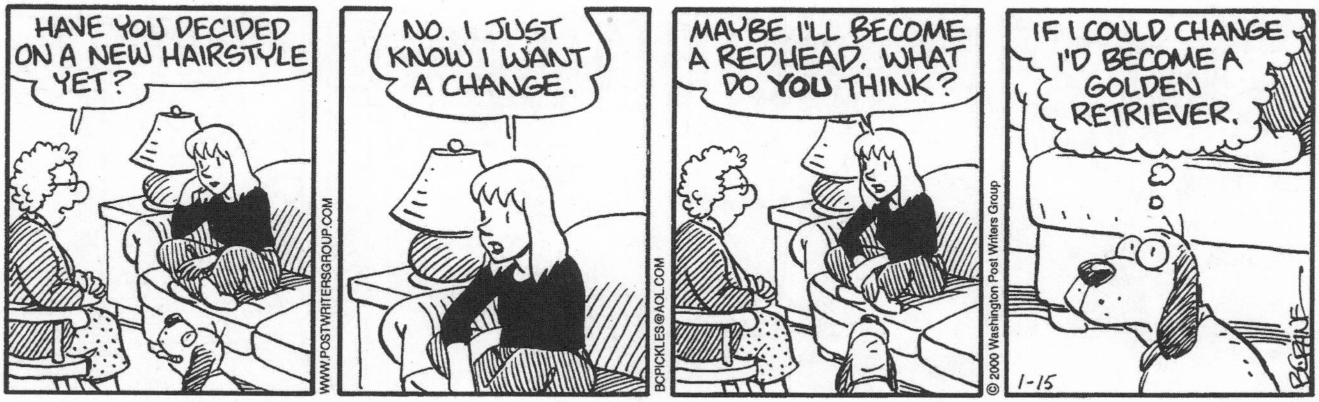
HAVE YOU DECIDED ON A NEW HAIRSTYLE YET?
NO. I JUST KNOW I WANT A CHANGE.
MAYBE I'LL BECOME A REDHEAD. WHAT DO YOU THINK?
IF I COULD CHANGE I'D BECOME A GOLDEN RETRIEVER.
WWW.POSTWRITERSGROUP.COM
BCPICKLES@AOL.COM
© 2000 Washington Post Writers Group
1-15

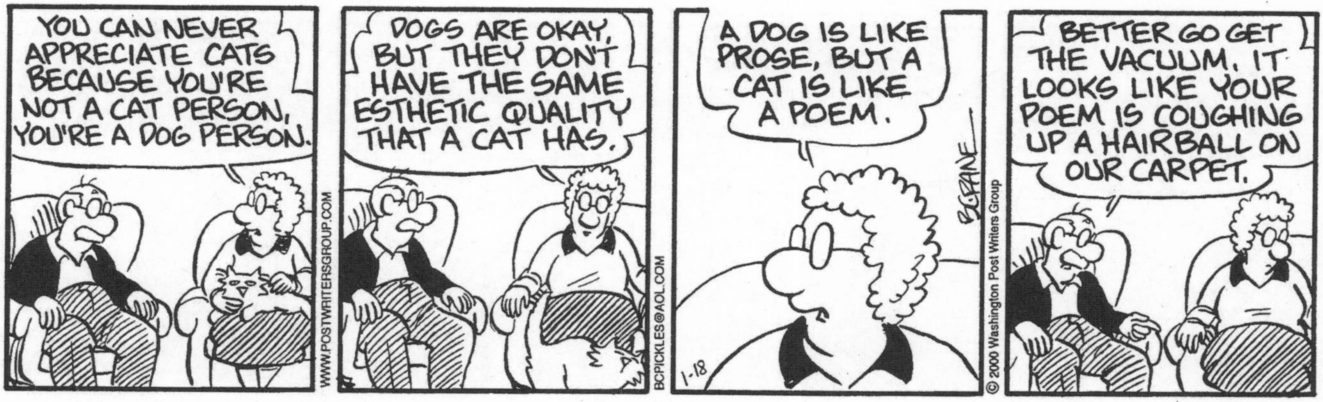
YOU CAN NEVER APPRECIATE CATS BECAUSE YOU'RE NOT A CAT PERSON, YOU'RE A DOG PERSON.
DOGS ARE OKAY, BUT THEY DON'T HAVE THE SAME ESTHETIC QUALITY THAT A CAT HAS.
A DOG IS LIKE PROSE, BUT A CAT IS LIKE A POEM.
BETTER GO GET THE VACUUM. IT LOOKS LIKE YOUR POEM IS COUGHING UP A HAIRBALL ON OUR CARPET.
WWW.POSTWRITERSGROUP.COM
BCPICKLES@AOL.COM
© 2000 Washington Post Writers Group
1-18

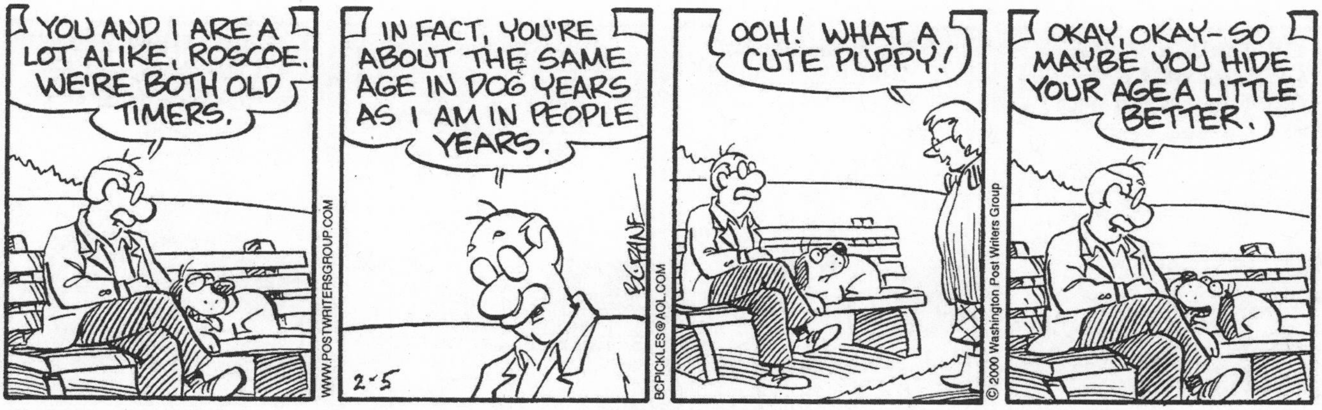
YOU AND I ARE A LOT ALIKE, ROSCOE. WE'RE BOTH OLD TIMERS.
IN FACT, YOU'RE ABOUT THE SAME AGE IN DOG YEARS AS I AM IN PEOPLE YEARS.
OOH! WHAT A CUTE PUPPY!
OKAY, OKAY–SO MAYBE YOU HIDE YOUR AGE A LITTLE BETTER.
WWW.POSTWRITERSGROUP.COM
BCPICKLES@AOL.COM
© 2000 Washington Post Writers Group
2-5

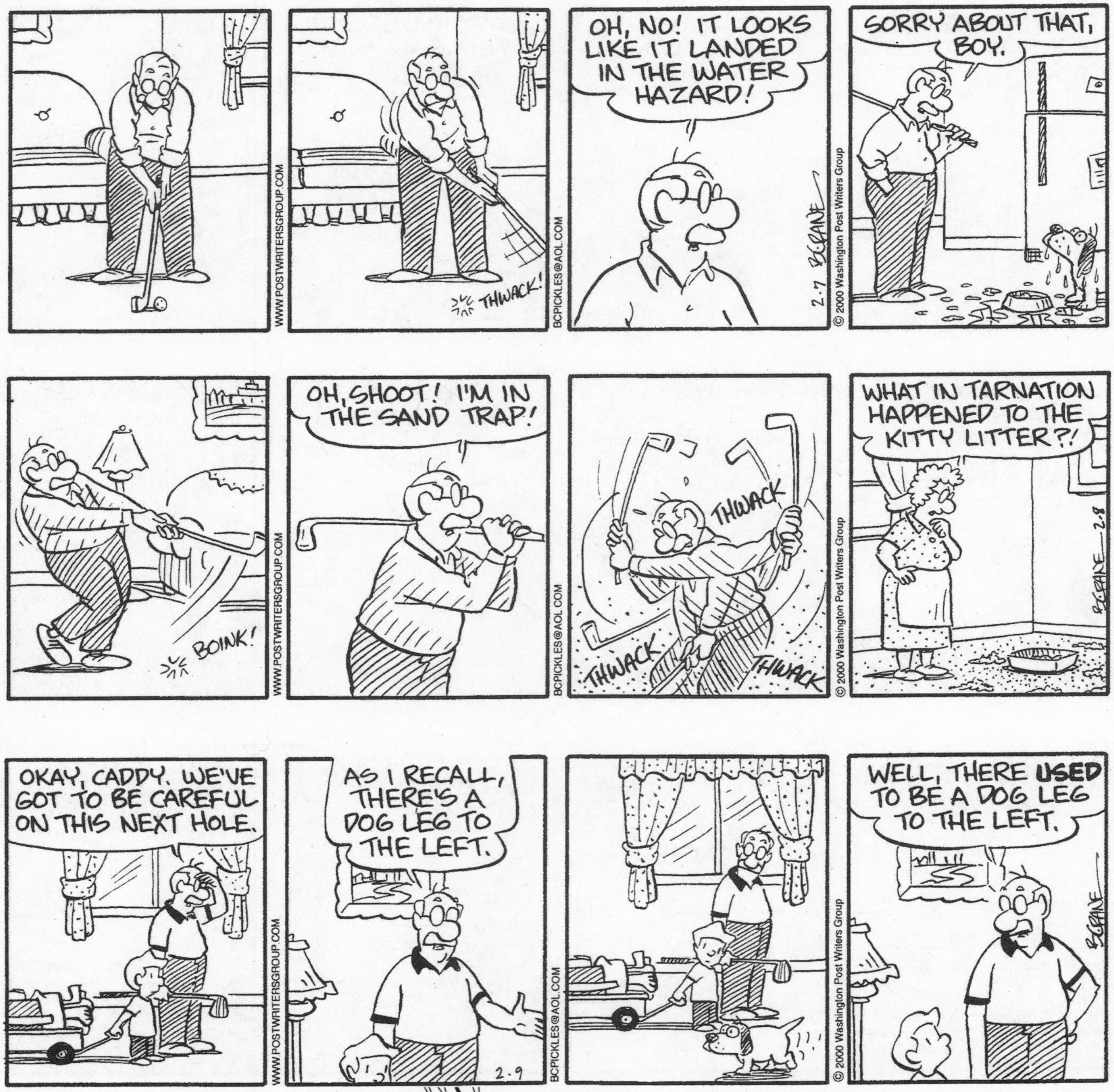
WWW.POSTWRITERSGROUP.COM
THWACK!
BCPICKLES@AOL.COM
OH, NO! IT LOOKS LIKE IT LANDED IN THE WATER HAZARD!
2.7
© 2000 Washington Post Writers Group
SORRY ABOUT THAT, BOY.
BOINK!
WWW.POSTWRITERSGROUP.COM
OH, SHOOT! I'M IN THE SAND TRAP!
BCPICKLES@AOL.COM
THWACK
THWACK
THWACK
© 2000 Washington Post Writers Group
WHAT IN TARNATION HAPPENED TO THE KITTY LITTER?!
2.8
OKAY, CADDY. WE'VE GOT TO BE CAREFUL ON THIS NEXT HOLE.
WWW.POSTWRITERSGROUP.COM
AS I RECALL, THERE'S A DOG LEG TO THE LEFT.
2.9
BCPICKLES@AOL.COM
© 2000 Washington Post Writers Group
WELL, THERE **USED** TO BE A DOG LEG TO THE LEFT.

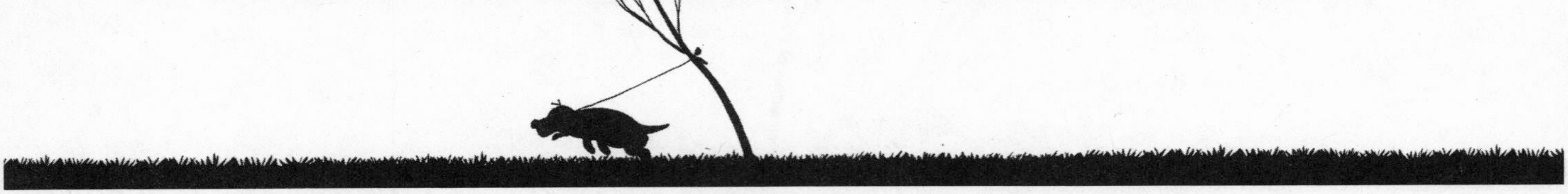

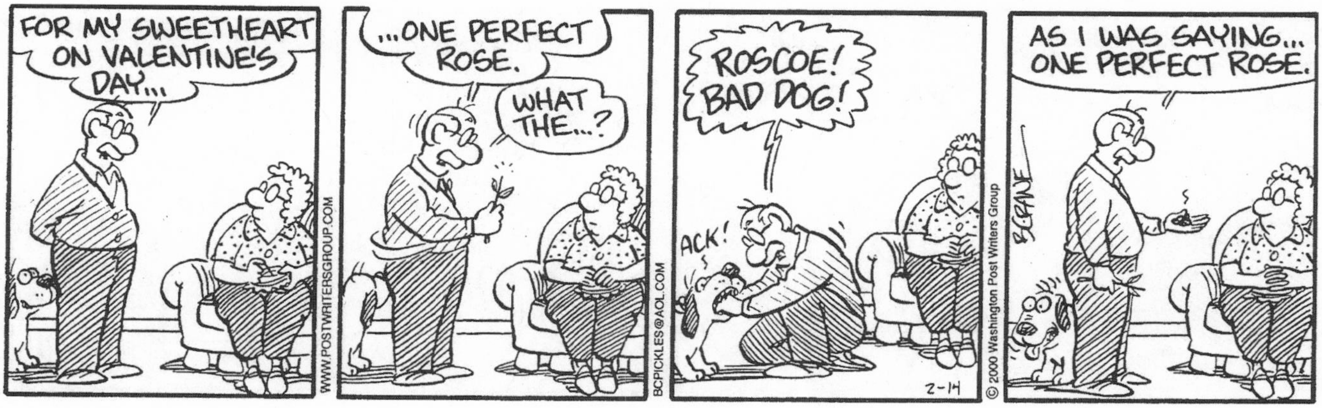
FOR MY SWEETHEART ON VALENTINE'S DAY...
...ONE PERFECT ROSE.
WHAT THE...?
ROSCOE! BAD DOG!
ACK!
AS I WAS SAYING... ONE PERFECT ROSE.
WWW.POSTWRITERSGROUP.COM
BCPICKLES@AOL.COM
2-14
© 2000 Washington Post Writers Group
B.CRANE

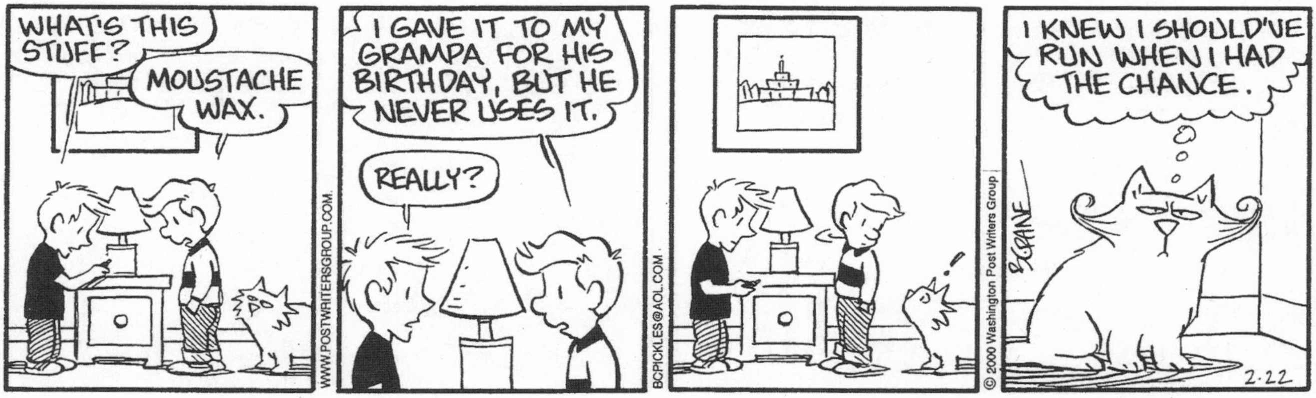
WHAT'S THIS STUFF?
MOUSTACHE WAX.
I GAVE IT TO MY GRAMPA FOR HIS BIRTHDAY, BUT HE NEVER USES IT.
REALLY?
I KNEW I SHOULD'VE RUN WHEN I HAD THE CHANCE.
WWW.POSTWRITERSGROUP.COM.
BCPICKLES@AOL.COM
© 2000 Washington Post Writers Group
B.CRANE
2.22

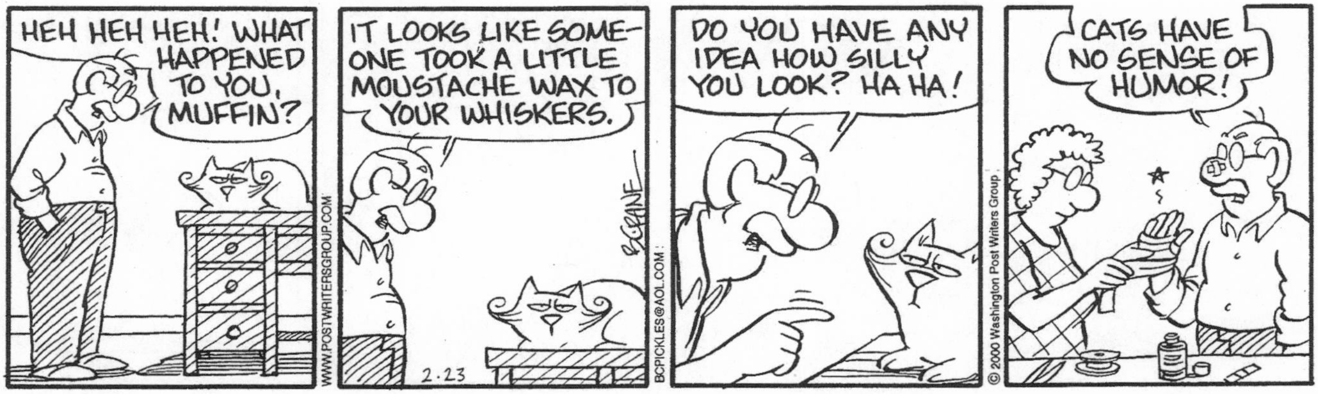
HEH HEH HEH! WHAT HAPPENED TO YOU, MUFFIN?
IT LOOKS LIKE SOMEONE TOOK A LITTLE MOUSTACHE WAX TO YOUR WHISKERS.
DO YOU HAVE ANY IDEA HOW SILLY YOU LOOK? HA HA!
CATS HAVE NO SENSE OF HUMOR!
WWW.POSTWRITERSGROUP.COM
B.CRANE
2.23
BCPICKLES@AOL.COM
© 2000 Washington Post Writers Group

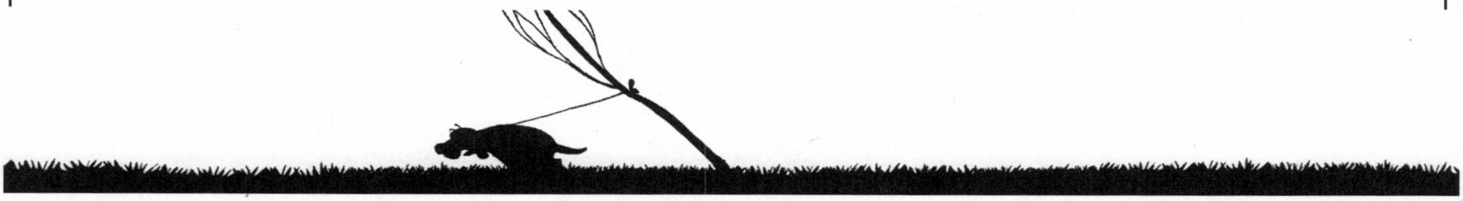

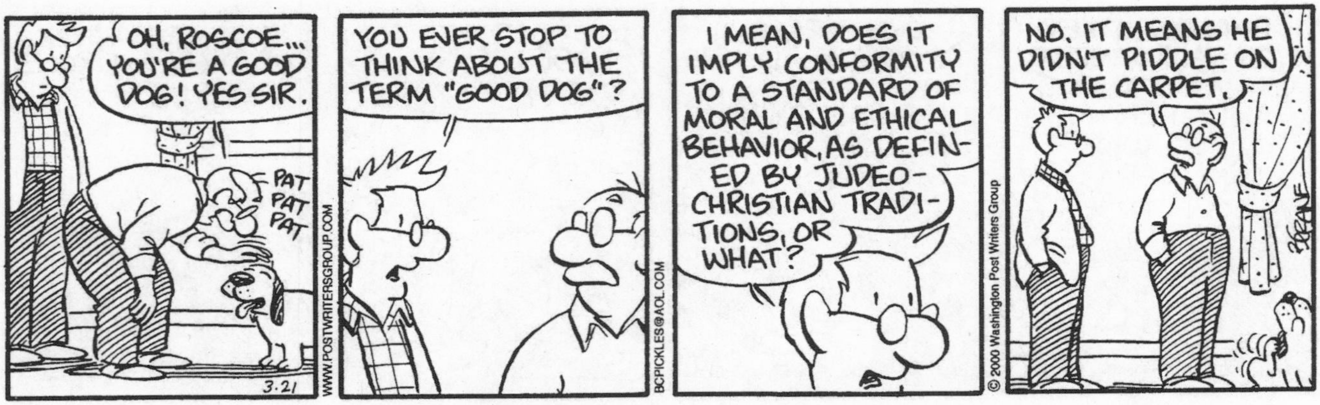
OH, ROSCOE... YOU'RE A GOOD DOG! YES SIR.
PAT PAT PAT
3.21
WWW.POSTWRITERSGROUP.COM
YOU EVER STOP TO THINK ABOUT THE TERM "GOOD DOG"?
BCPICKLES@AOL.COM
I MEAN, DOES IT IMPLY CONFORMITY TO A STANDARD OF MORAL AND ETHICAL BEHAVIOR, AS DEFIN-ED BY JUDEO-CHRISTIAN TRADI-TIONS, OR WHAT?
© 2000 Washington Post Writers Group
NO. IT MEANS HE DIDN'T PIDDLE ON THE CARPET.
B.CRANE

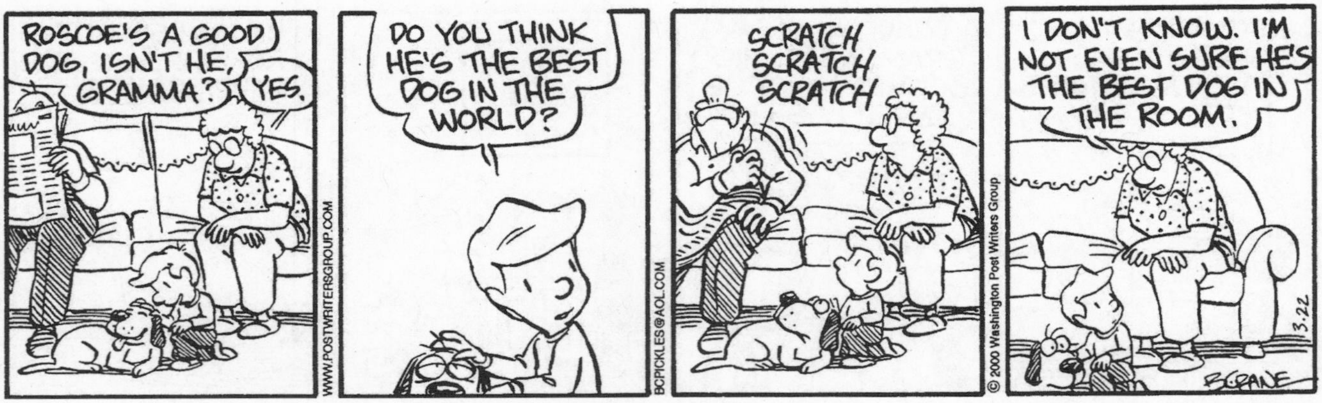
ROSCOE'S A GOOD DOG, ISN'T HE, GRAMMA?
YES.
WWW.POSTWRITERSGROUP.COM
DO YOU THINK HE'S THE BEST DOG IN THE WORLD?
BCPICKLES@AOL.COM
SCRATCH SCRATCH SCRATCH
© 2000 Washington Post Writers Group
I DON'T KNOW. I'M NOT EVEN SURE HE'S THE BEST DOG IN THE ROOM.
3.22
B.CRANE

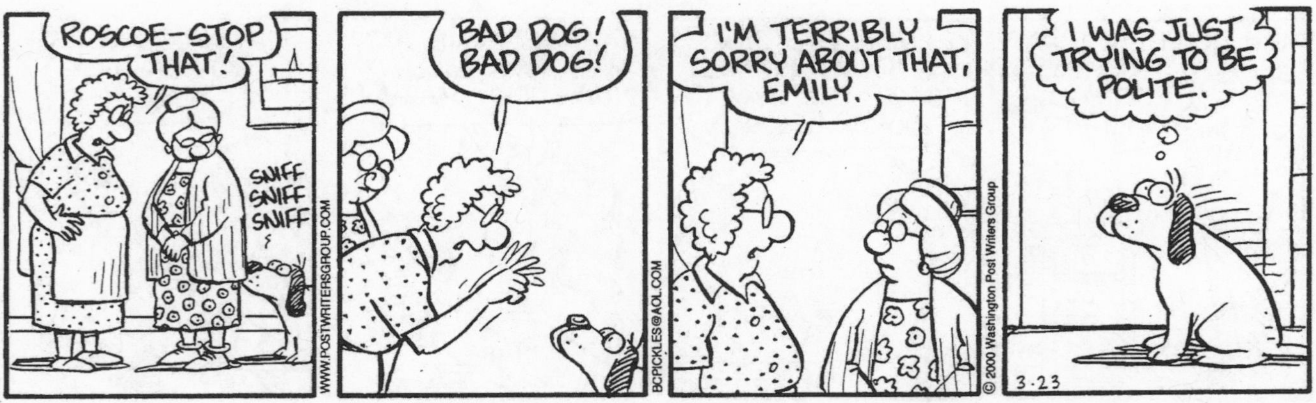
ROSCOE—STOP THAT!
SNIFF SNIFF SNIFF
WWW.POSTWRITERSGROUP.COM
BAD DOG! BAD DOG!
BCPICKLES@AOL.COM
I'M TERRIBLY SORRY ABOUT THAT, EMILY.
© 2000 Washington Post Writers Group
I WAS JUST TRYING TO BE POLITE.
3.23

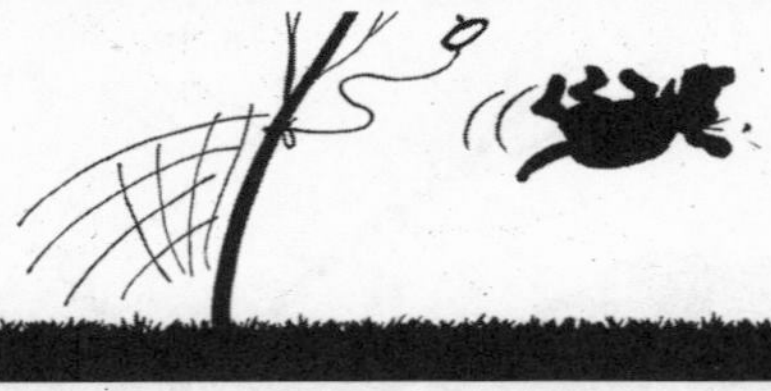

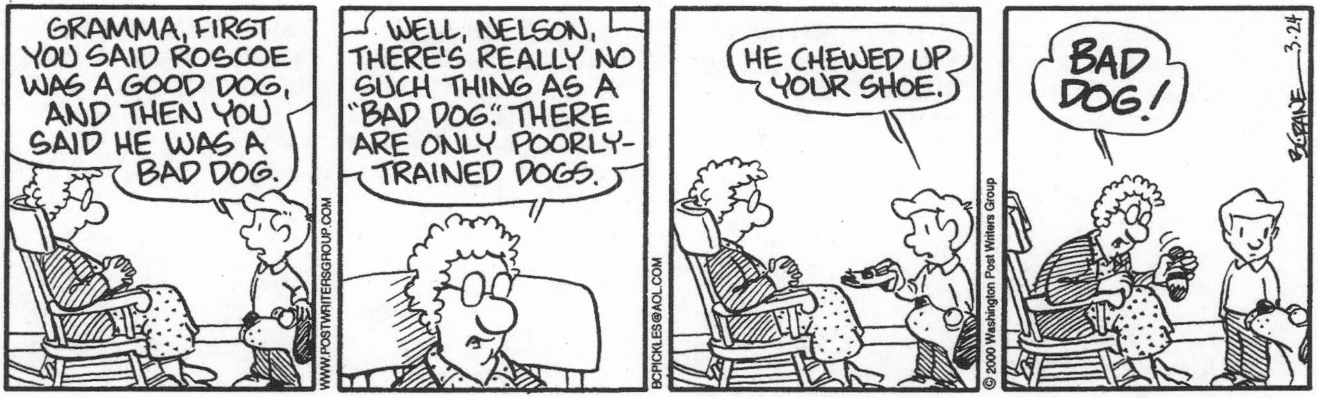
GRAMMA, FIRST YOU SAID ROSCOE WAS A GOOD DOG, AND THEN YOU SAID HE WAS A BAD DOG.
WWW.POSTWRITERSGROUP.COM
WELL, NELSON, THERE'S REALLY NO SUCH THING AS A "BAD DOG." THERE ARE ONLY POORLY-TRAINED DOGS.
BCPICKLES@AOL.COM
HE CHEWED UP YOUR SHOE.
© 2000 Washington Post Writers Group
BAD DOG!
3.24

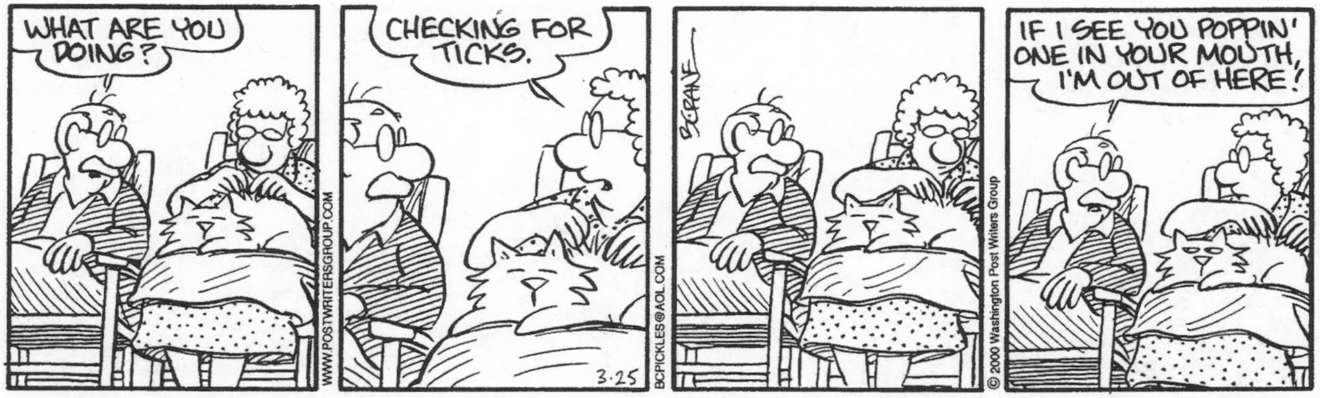
WHAT ARE YOU DOING?
WWW.POSTWRITERSGROUP.COM
CHECKING FOR TICKS.
3.25
BCPICKLES@AOL.COM
© 2000 Washington Post Writers Group
IF I SEE YOU POPPIN' ONE IN YOUR MOUTH, I'M OUT OF HERE!

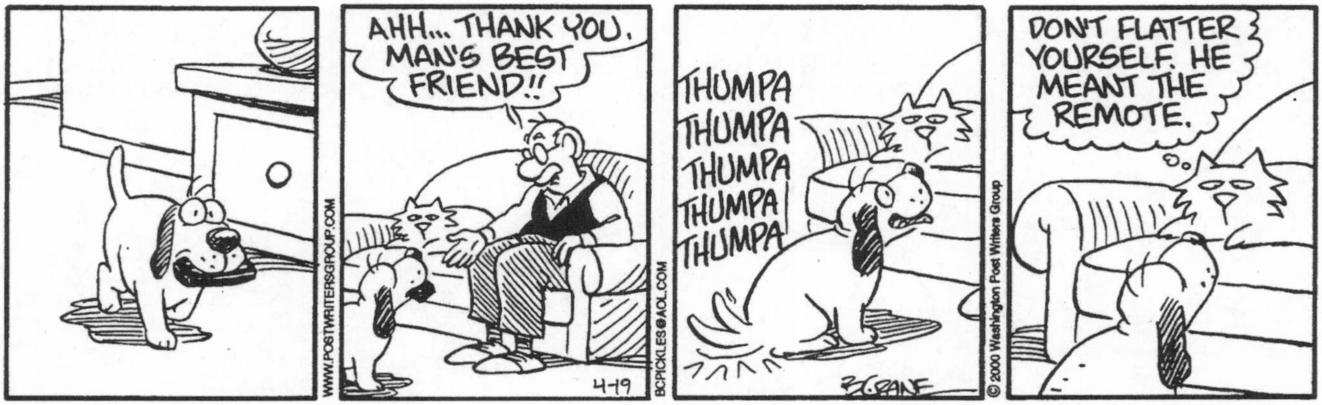
WWW.POSTWRITERSGROUP.COM
AHH... THANK YOU, MAN'S BEST FRIEND!!
4-19
BCPICKLES@AOL.COM
THUMPA
THUMPA
THUMPA
THUMPA
THUMPA
© 2000 Washington Post Writers Group
DON'T FLATTER YOURSELF. HE MEANT THE REMOTE.

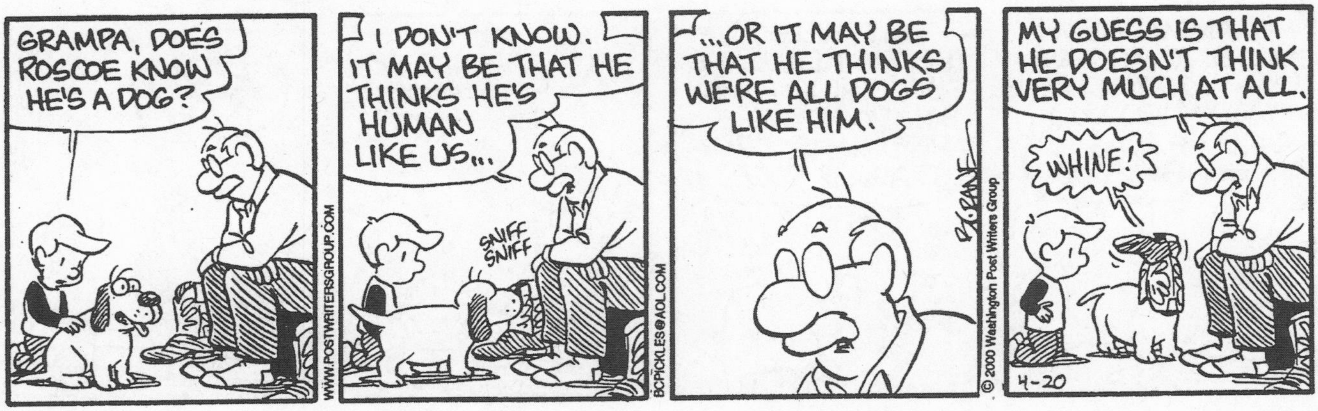
GRAMPA, DOES ROSCOE KNOW HE'S A DOG?
I DON'T KNOW. IT MAY BE THAT HE THINKS HE'S HUMAN LIKE US...
SNIFF SNIFF
WWW.POSTWRITERSGROUP.COM
...OR IT MAY BE THAT HE THINKS WE'RE ALL DOGS LIKE HIM.
BCPICKLES@AOL.COM
MY GUESS IS THAT HE DOESN'T THINK VERY MUCH AT ALL.
WHINE!
© 2000 Washington Post Writers Group
4-20

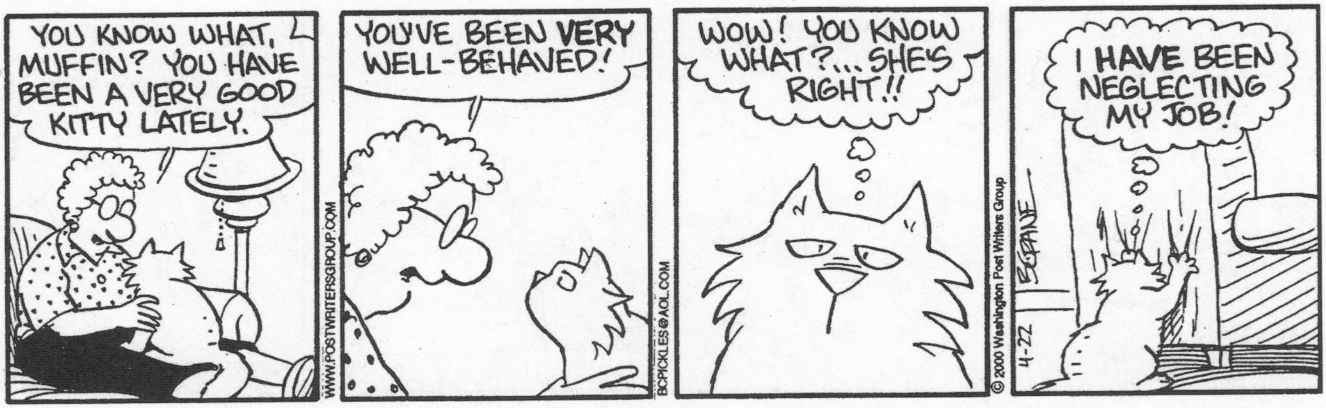
YOU KNOW WHAT, MUFFIN? YOU HAVE BEEN A VERY GOOD KITTY LATELY.
WWW.POSTWRITERSGROUP.COM
YOU'VE BEEN VERY WELL-BEHAVED!
BCPICKLES@AOL.COM
WOW! YOU KNOW WHAT?... SHE'S RIGHT!!
I HAVE BEEN NEGLECTING MY JOB!
© 2000 Washington Post Writers Group
4-22

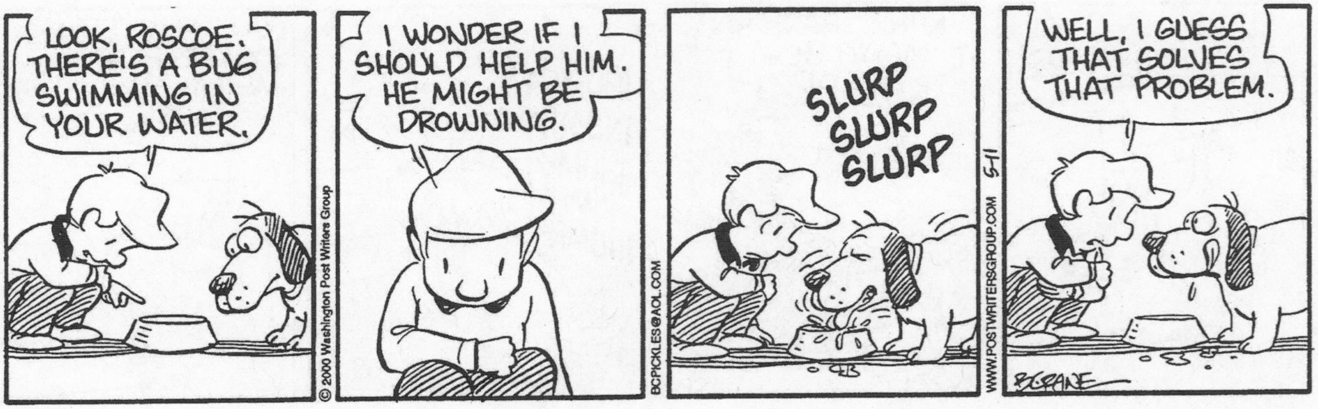
LOOK, ROSCOE. THERE'S A BUG SWIMMING IN YOUR WATER.
© 2000 Washington Post Writers Group
I WONDER IF I SHOULD HELP HIM. HE MIGHT BE DROWNING.
BCPICKLES@AOL.COM
SLURP SLURP SLURP
5-11
WWW.POSTWRITERSGROUP.COM
WELL, I GUESS THAT SOLVES THAT PROBLEM.

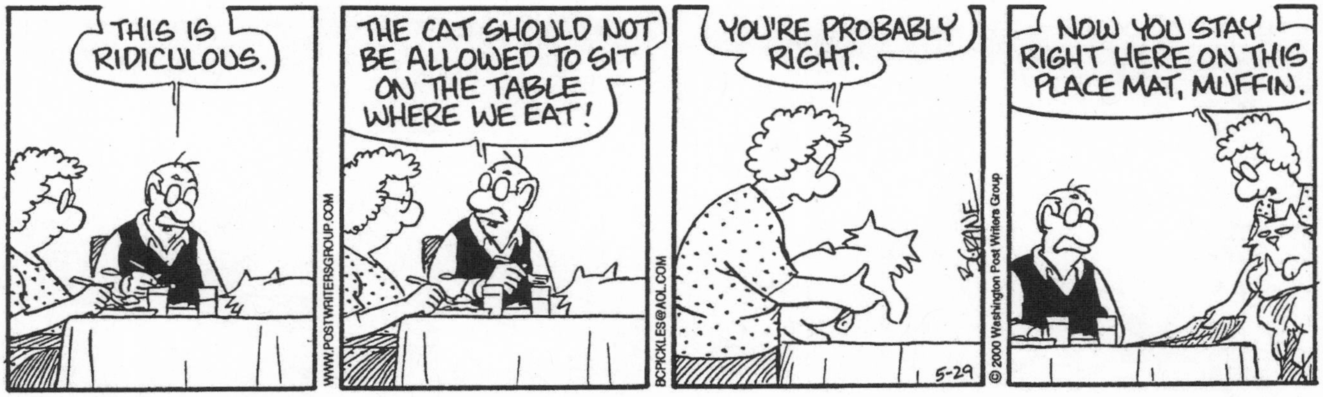
THIS IS RIDICULOUS.
WWW.POSTWRITERSGROUP.COM
THE CAT SHOULD NOT BE ALLOWED TO SIT ON THE TABLE WHERE WE EAT!
BCPICKLES@AOL.COM
YOU'RE PROBABLY RIGHT.
B. CRANE
5-29
© 2000 Washington Post Writers Group
NOW YOU STAY RIGHT HERE ON THIS PLACE MAT, MUFFIN.

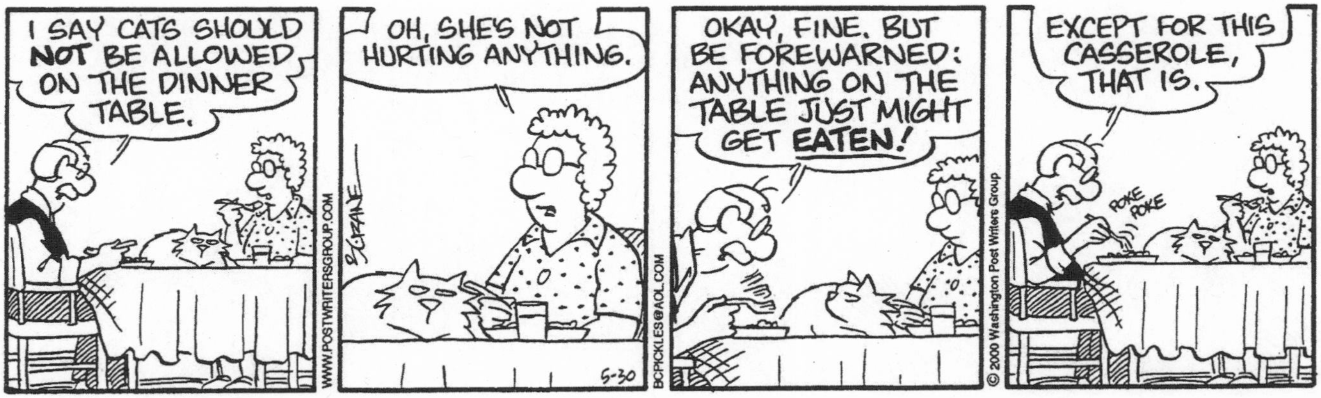
I SAY CATS SHOULD **NOT** BE ALLOWED ON THE DINNER TABLE.
WWW.POSTWRITERSGROUP.COM
OH, SHE'S NOT HURTING ANYTHING.
B. CRANE
5-30
BCPICKLES@AOL.COM
OKAY, FINE. BUT BE FOREWARNED: ANYTHING ON THE TABLE JUST MIGHT GET **EATEN!**
© 2000 Washington Post Writers Group
EXCEPT FOR THIS CASSEROLE, THAT IS.
POKE POKE

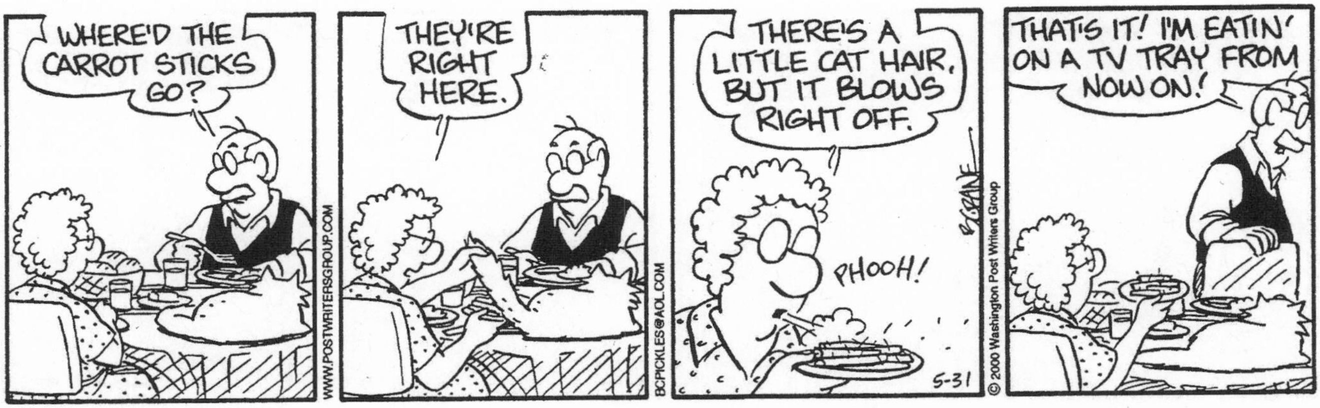
WHERE'D THE CARROT STICKS GO?
WWW.POSTWRITERSGROUP.COM
THEY'RE RIGHT HERE.
BCPICKLES@AOL.COM
THERE'S A LITTLE CAT HAIR, BUT IT BLOWS RIGHT OFF.
PHOOH!
B. CRANE
5-31
© 2000 Washington Post Writers Group
THAT'S IT! I'M EATIN' ON A TV TRAY FROM NOW ON!

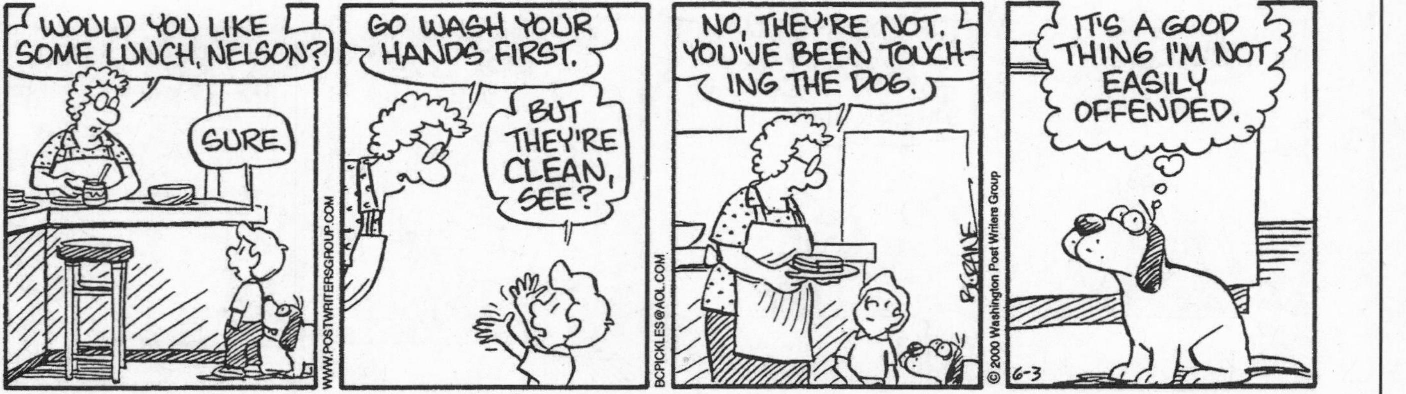
WOULD YOU LIKE SOME LUNCH, NELSON?
SURE.
GO WASH YOUR HANDS FIRST.
BUT THEY'RE CLEAN, SEE?
NO, THEY'RE NOT. YOU'VE BEEN TOUCHING THE DOG.
IT'S A GOOD THING I'M NOT EASILY OFFENDED.
WWW.POSTWRITERSGROUP.COM
BCPICKLES@AOL.COM
© 2000 Washington Post Writers Group
6-3

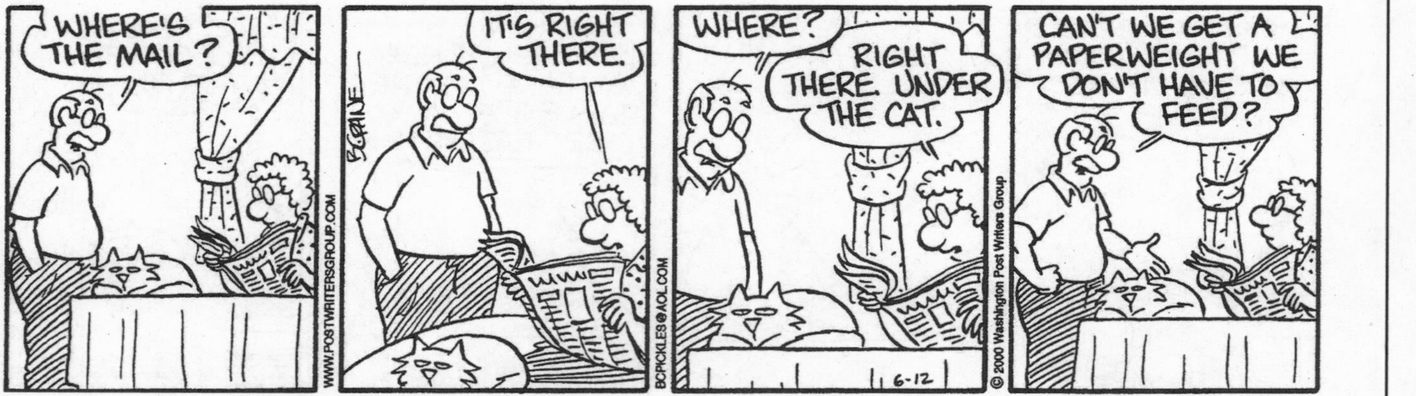
WHERE'S THE MAIL?
IT'S RIGHT THERE.
WHERE?
RIGHT THERE. UNDER THE CAT.
CAN'T WE GET A PAPERWEIGHT WE DON'T HAVE TO FEED?
WWW.POSTWRITERSGROUP.COM
BCPICKLES@AOL.COM
© 2000 Washington Post Writers Group
6-12

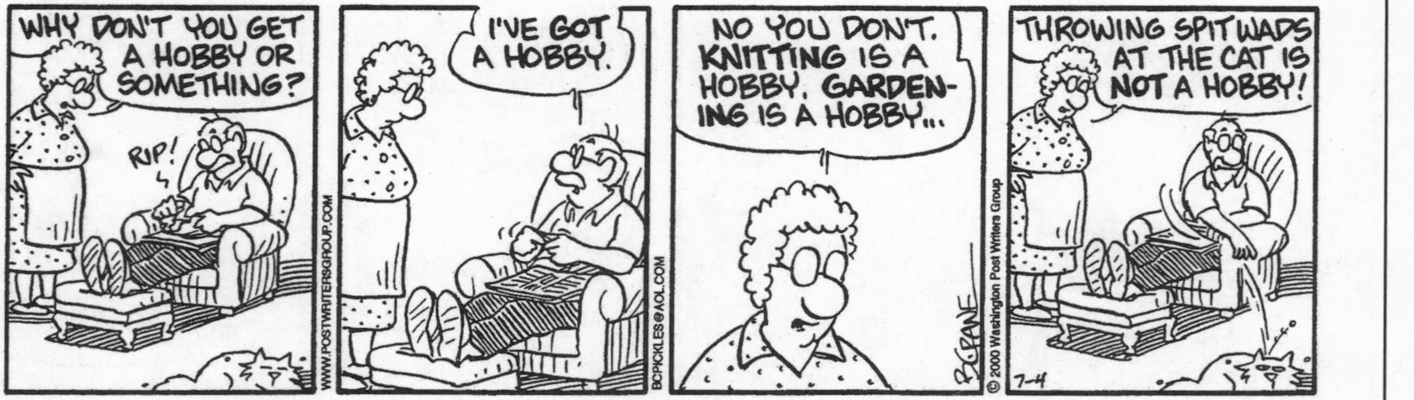
WHY DON'T YOU GET A HOBBY OR SOMETHING?
RIP!
I'VE GOT A HOBBY.
NO YOU DON'T. KNITTING IS A HOBBY. GARDENING IS A HOBBY...
THROWING SPITWADS AT THE CAT IS NOT A HOBBY!
WWW.POSTWRITERSGROUP.COM
BCPICKLES@AOL.COM
© 2000 Washington Post Writers Group
7-4

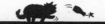

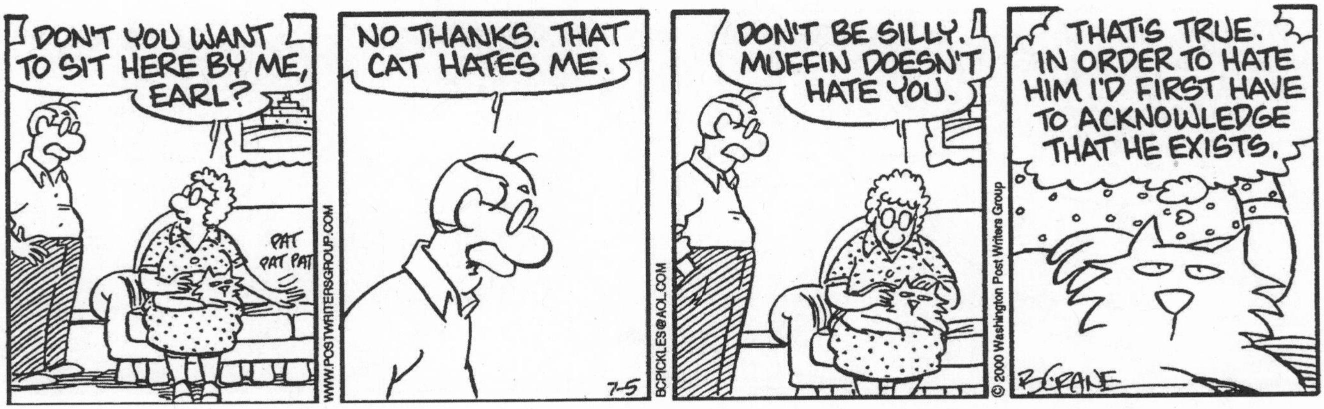
DON'T YOU WANT TO SIT HERE BY ME, EARL?
PAT PAT PAT
WWW.POSTWRITERSGROUP.COM
NO THANKS. THAT CAT HATES ME.
7-5
BCPICKLES@AOL.COM
DON'T BE SILLY. MUFFIN DOESN'T HATE YOU.
© 2000 Washington Post Writers Group
THAT'S TRUE. IN ORDER TO HATE HIM I'D FIRST HAVE TO ACKNOWLEDGE THAT HE EXISTS.
B. CRANE

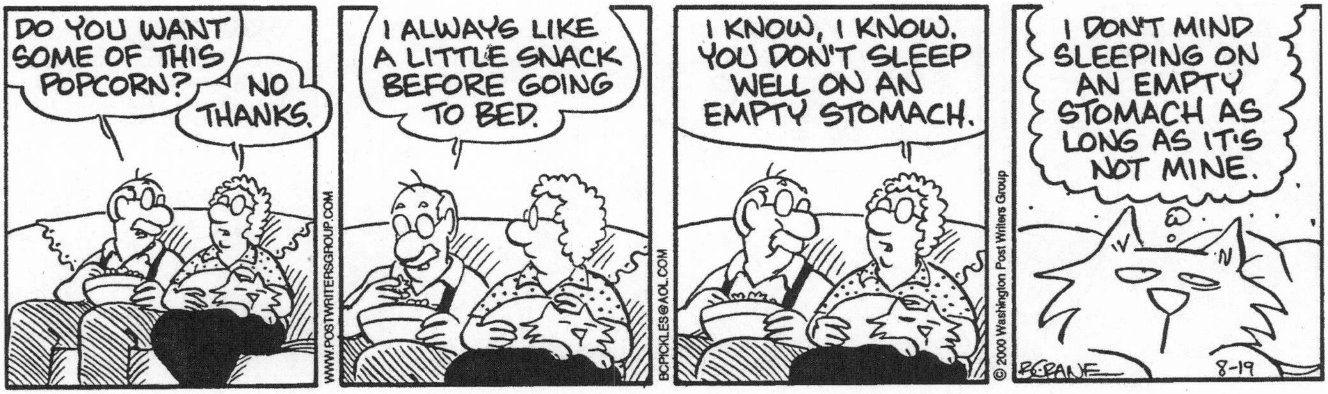
DO YOU WANT SOME OF THIS POPCORN?
NO THANKS.
WWW.POSTWRITERSGROUP.COM
I ALWAYS LIKE A LITTLE SNACK BEFORE GOING TO BED.
BCPICKLES@AOL.COM
I KNOW, I KNOW. YOU DON'T SLEEP WELL ON AN EMPTY STOMACH.
© 2000 Washington Post Writers Group
I DON'T MIND SLEEPING ON AN EMPTY STOMACH AS LONG AS IT'S NOT MINE.
B. CRANE
8-19

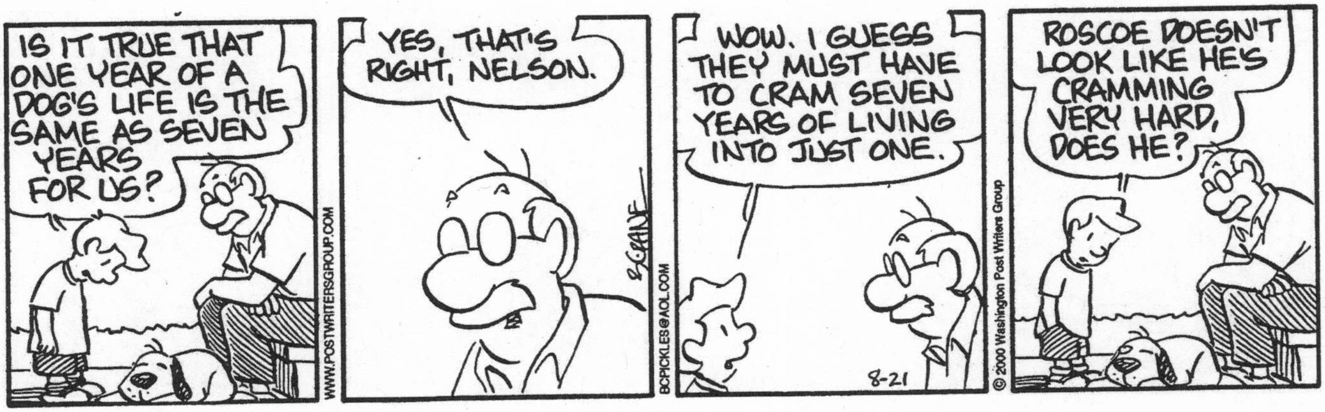
IS IT TRUE THAT ONE YEAR OF A DOG'S LIFE IS THE SAME AS SEVEN YEARS FOR US?
WWW.POSTWRITERSGROUP.COM
YES, THAT'S RIGHT, NELSON.
B. CRANE
BCPICKLES@AOL.COM
WOW. I GUESS THEY MUST HAVE TO CRAM SEVEN YEARS OF LIVING INTO JUST ONE.
8-21
© 2000 Washington Post Writers Group
ROSCOE DOESN'T LOOK LIKE HE'S CRAMMING VERY HARD, DOES HE?

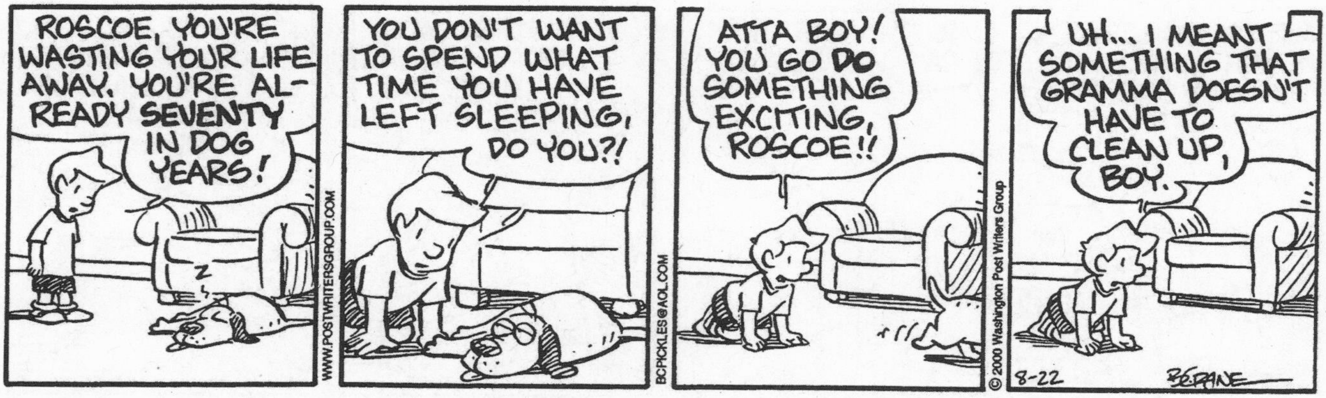
ROSCOE, YOU'RE WASTING YOUR LIFE AWAY. YOU'RE AL-READY SEVENTY IN DOG YEARS!
WWW.POSTWRITERSGROUP.COM
YOU DON'T WANT TO SPEND WHAT TIME YOU HAVE LEFT SLEEPING, DO YOU?!
BCPICKLES@AOL.COM
ATTA BOY! YOU GO DO SOMETHING EXCITING, ROSCOE!!
© 2000 Washington Post Writers Group
UH... I MEANT SOMETHING THAT GRAMMA DOESN'T HAVE TO CLEAN UP, BOY.
8-22

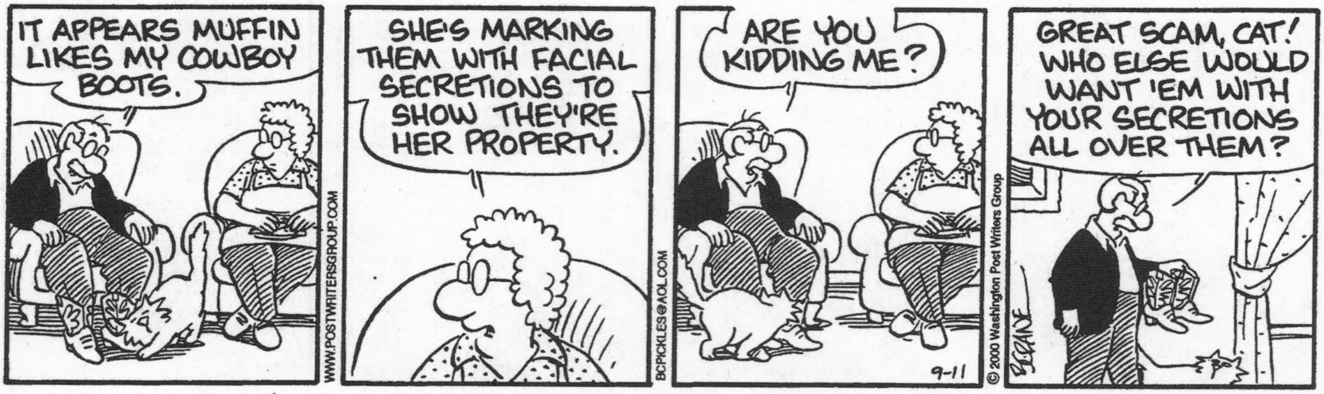
IT APPEARS MUFFIN LIKES MY COWBOY BOOTS.
WWW.POSTWRITERSGROUP.COM
SHE'S MARKING THEM WITH FACIAL SECRETIONS TO SHOW THEY'RE HER PROPERTY.
BCPICKLES@AOL.COM
ARE YOU KIDDING ME?
9-11
© 2000 Washington Post Writers Group
GREAT SCAM, CAT! WHO ELSE WOULD WANT 'EM WITH YOUR SECRETIONS ALL OVER THEM?

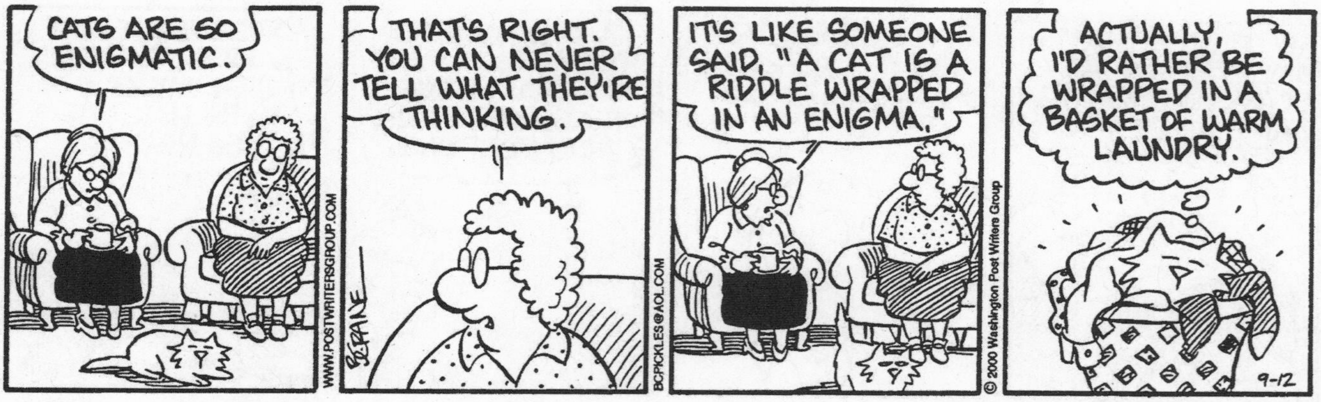
CATS ARE SO ENIGMATIC.
WWW.POSTWRITERSGROUP.COM
THAT'S RIGHT. YOU CAN NEVER TELL WHAT THEY'RE THINKING.
BCPICKLES@AOL.COM
IT'S LIKE SOMEONE SAID, "A CAT IS A RIDDLE WRAPPED IN AN ENIGMA."
© 2000 Washington Post Writers Group
ACTUALLY, I'D RATHER BE WRAPPED IN A BASKET OF WARM LAUNDRY.
9-12

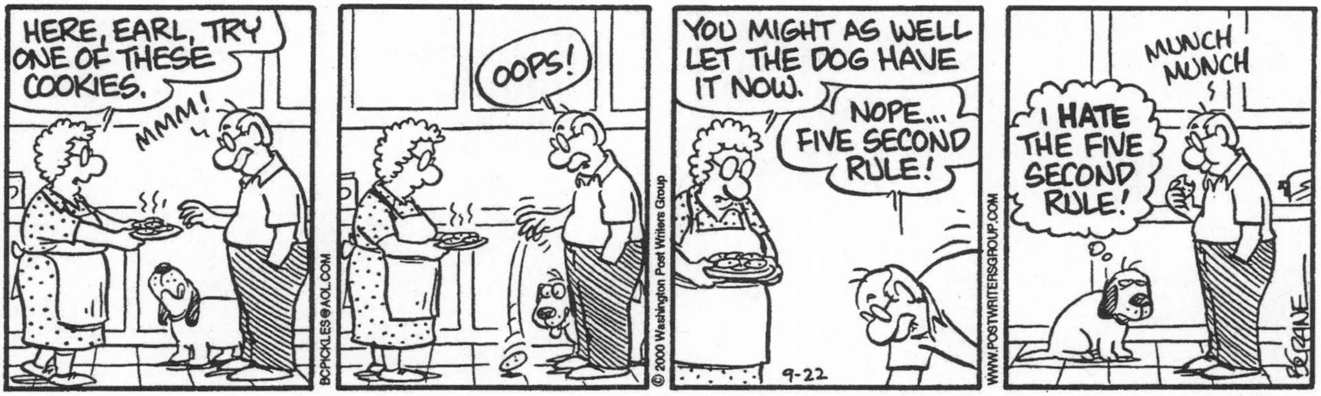
HERE, EARL, TRY ONE OF THESE COOKIES.
MMM!
BCPICKLES@AOL.COM
OOPS!
© 2000 Washington Post Writers Group
YOU MIGHT AS WELL LET THE DOG HAVE IT NOW.
NOPE... FIVE SECOND RULE!
9-22
WWW.POSTWRITERSGROUP.COM
MUNCH MUNCH
I HATE THE FIVE SECOND RULE!

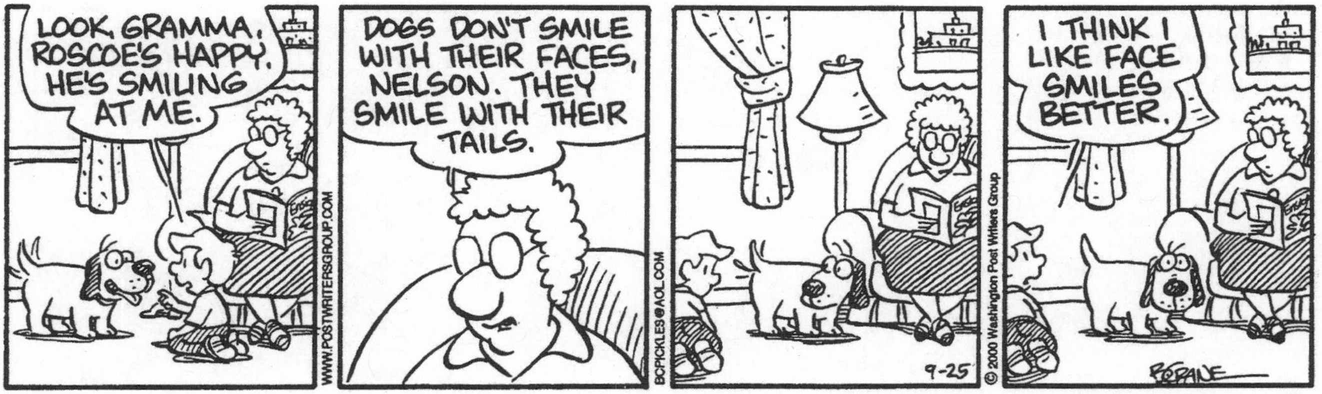
LOOK, GRAMMA, ROSCOE'S HAPPY. HE'S SMILING AT ME.
WWW.POSTWRITERSGROUP.COM
DOGS DON'T SMILE WITH THEIR FACES, NELSON. THEY SMILE WITH THEIR TAILS.
BCPICKLES@AOL.COM
9-25
© 2000 Washington Post Writers Group
I THINK I LIKE FACE SMILES BETTER.

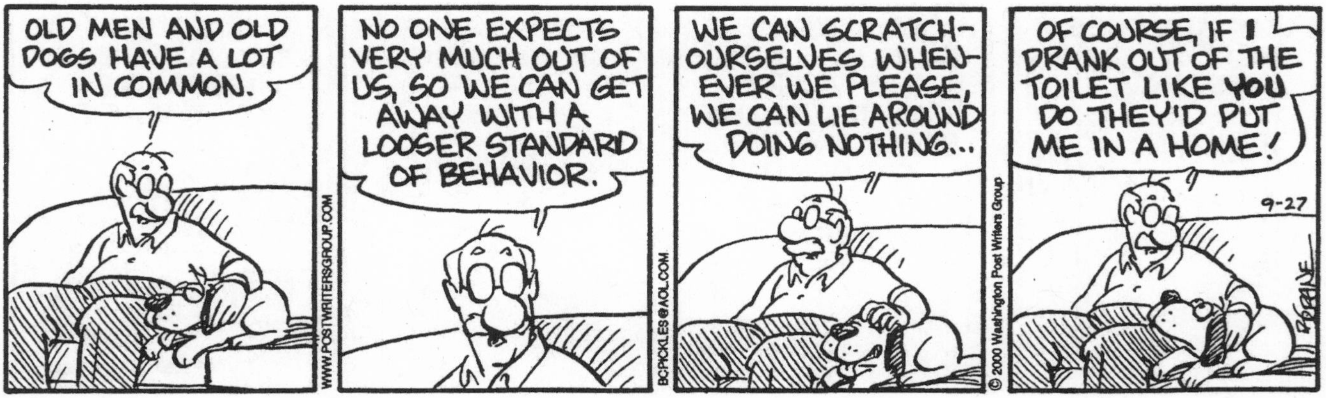
OLD MEN AND OLD DOGS HAVE A LOT IN COMMON.
WWW.POSTWRITERSGROUP.COM
NO ONE EXPECTS VERY MUCH OUT OF US, SO WE CAN GET AWAY WITH A LOOSER STANDARD OF BEHAVIOR.
BCPICKLES@AOL.COM
WE CAN SCRATCH OURSELVES WHENEVER WE PLEASE, WE CAN LIE AROUND DOING NOTHING...
© 2000 Washington Post Writers Group
OF COURSE, IF I DRANK OUT OF THE TOILET LIKE YOU DO THEY'D PUT ME IN A HOME!
9-27

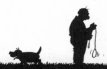

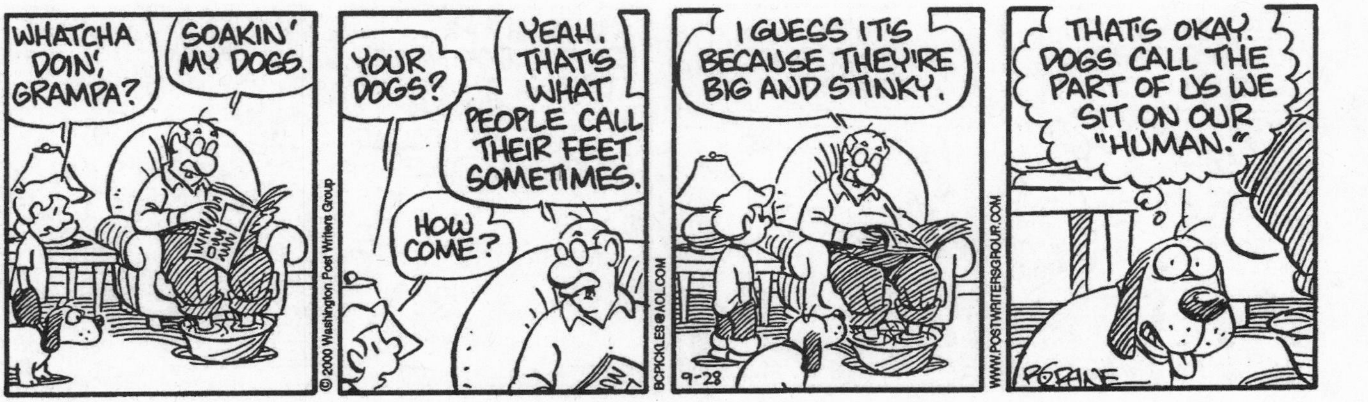
WHATCHA DOIN', GRAMPA?
SOAKIN' MY DOGS.
YOUR DOGS?
YEAH. THAT'S WHAT PEOPLE CALL THEIR FEET SOMETIMES.
HOW COME?
I GUESS IT'S BECAUSE THEY'RE BIG AND STINKY.
THAT'S OKAY. DOGS CALL THE PART OF US WE SIT ON OUR "HUMAN."
© 2000 Washington Post Writers Group
BCPICKLES@AOL.COM
9-28
WWW.POSTWRITERSGROUP.COM
RSRANE

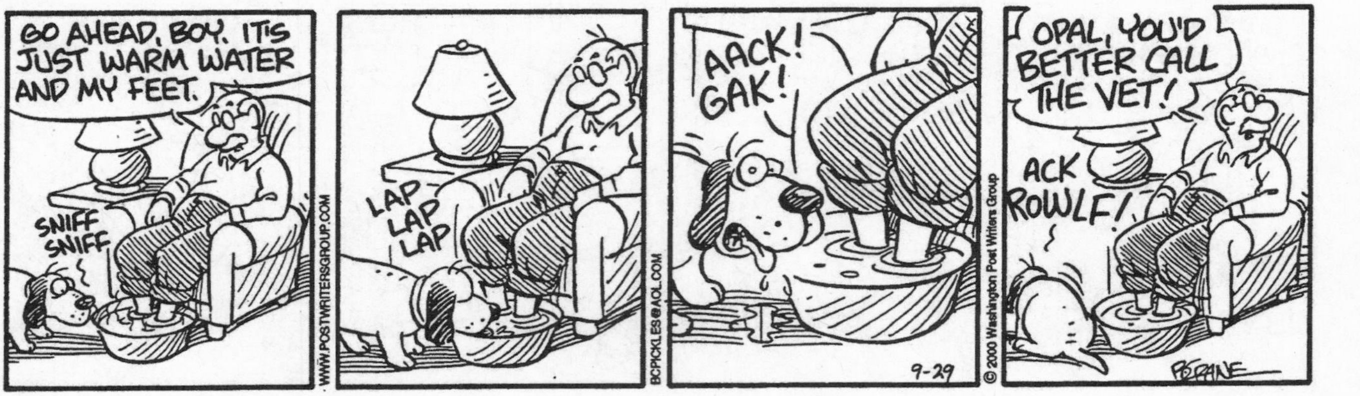
GO AHEAD, BOY. IT'S JUST WARM WATER AND MY FEET.
SNIFF SNIFF
WWW.POSTWRITERSGROUP.COM
LAP LAP LAP
BCPICKLES@AOL.COM
AACK! GAK!
9-29
© 2000 Washington Post Writers Group
OPAL, YOU'D BETTER CALL THE VET!
ACK ROWLF!
RSRANE

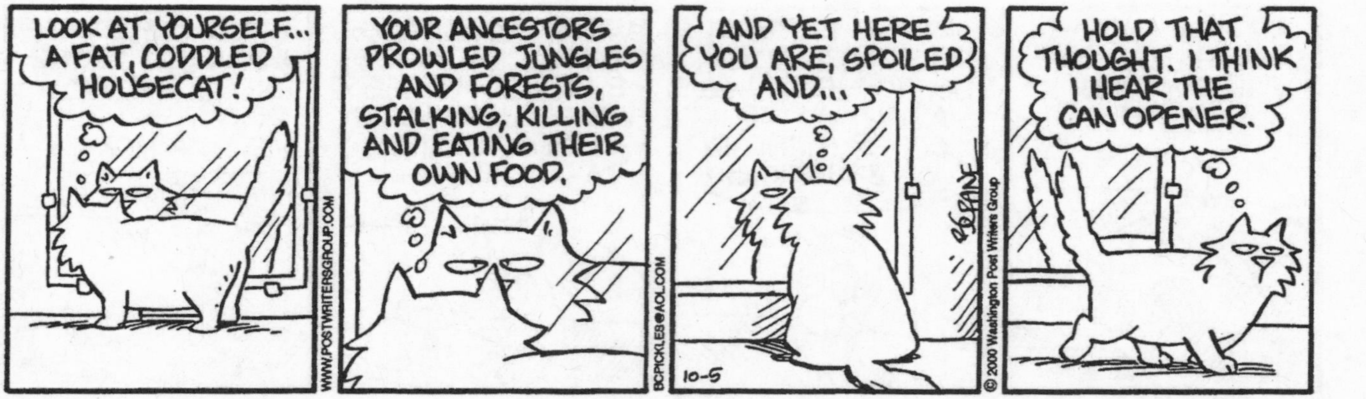
LOOK AT YOURSELF... A FAT, CODDLED HOUSECAT!
WWW.POSTWRITERSGROUP.COM
YOUR ANCESTORS PROWLED JUNGLES AND FORESTS, STALKING, KILLING AND EATING THEIR OWN FOOD.
BCPICKLES@AOL.COM
AND YET HERE YOU ARE, SPOILED AND...
10-5
RSRANE
© 2000 Washington Post Writers Group
HOLD THAT THOUGHT. I THINK I HEAR THE CAN OPENER.

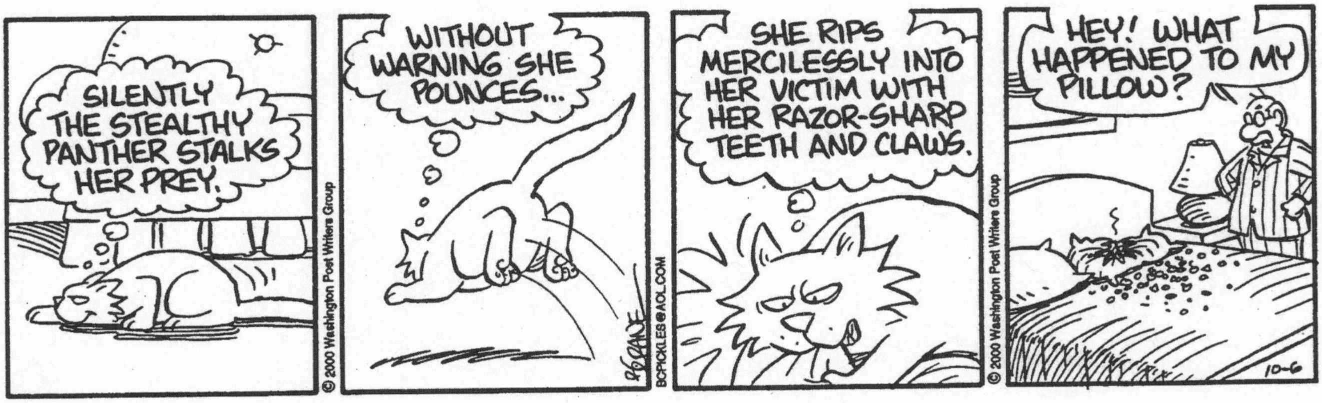
SILENTLY THE STEALTHY PANTHER STALKS HER PREY.
WITHOUT WARNING SHE POUNCES...
SHE RIPS MERCILESSLY INTO HER VICTIM WITH HER RAZOR-SHARP TEETH AND CLAWS.
HEY! WHAT HAPPENED TO MY PILLOW?
© 2000 Washington Post Writers Group
BCPICKLES@AOL.COM
© 2000 Washington Post Writers Group
10-6

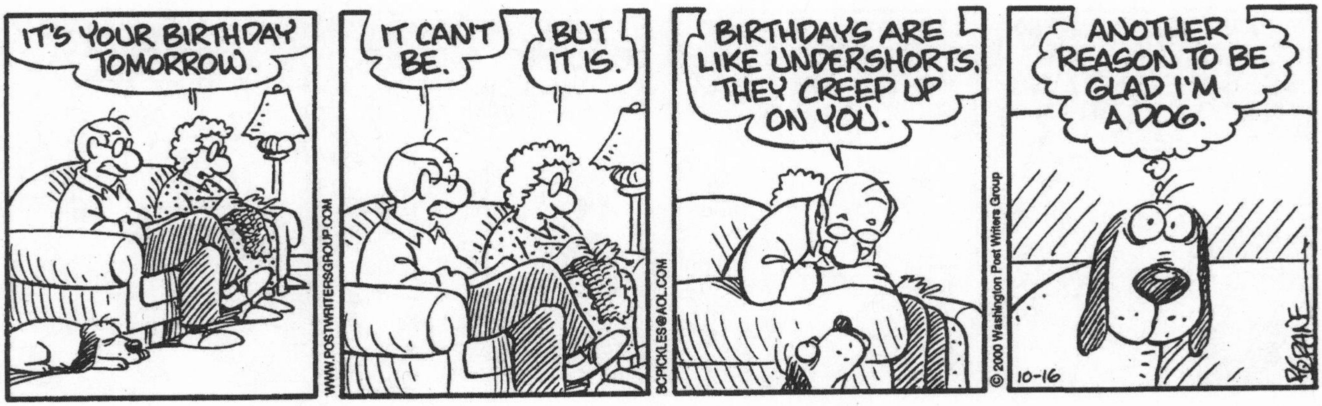
IT'S YOUR BIRTHDAY TOMORROW.
IT CAN'T BE.
BUT IT IS.
BIRTHDAYS ARE LIKE UNDERSHORTS. THEY CREEP UP ON YOU.
ANOTHER REASON TO BE GLAD I'M A DOG.
WWW.POSTWRITERSGROUP.COM
BCPICKLES@AOL.COM
© 2000 Washington Post Writers Group
10-16

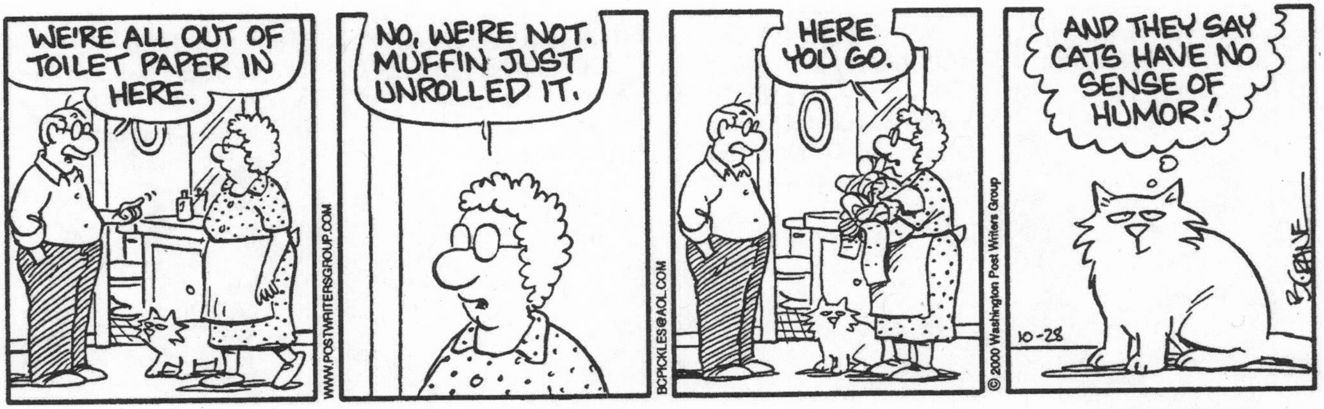
WE'RE ALL OUT OF TOILET PAPER IN HERE.
NO, WE'RE NOT. MUFFIN JUST UNROLLED IT.
HERE YOU GO.
AND THEY SAY CATS HAVE NO SENSE OF HUMOR!
WWW.POSTWRITERSGROUP.COM
BCPICKLES@AOL.COM
© 2000 Washington Post Writers Group
10-28

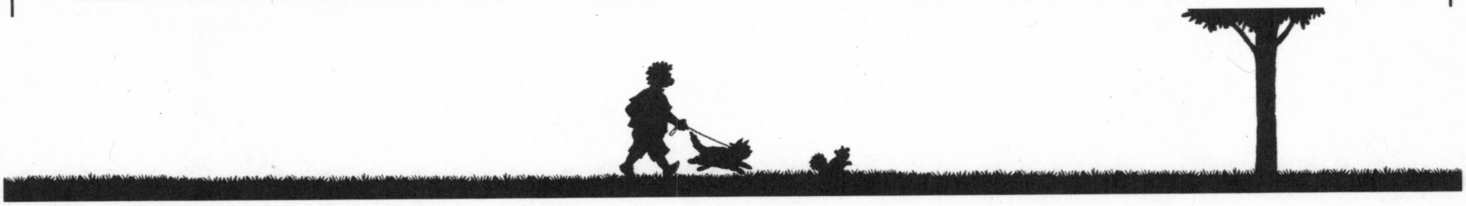

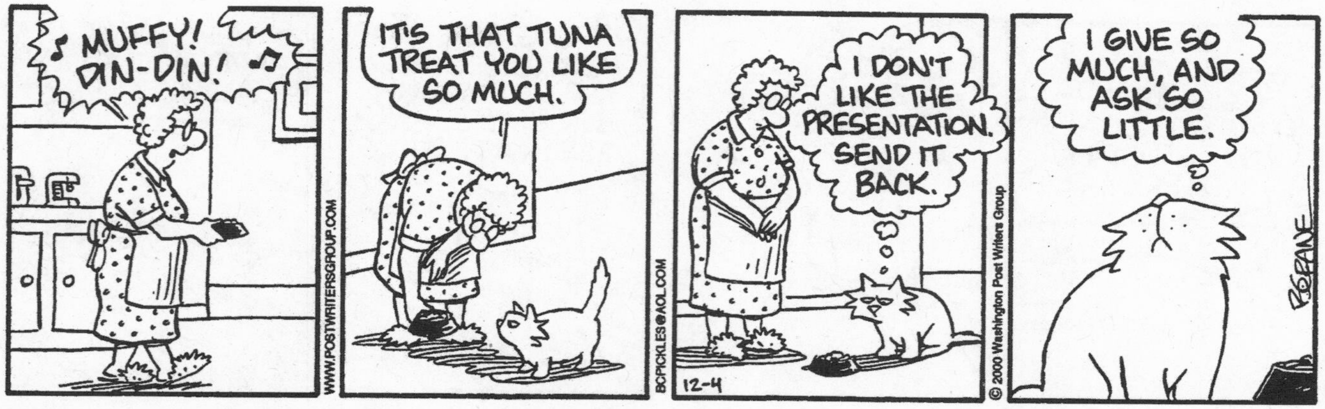
MUFFY! DIN-DIN!
IT'S THAT TUNA TREAT YOU LIKE SO MUCH.
I DON'T LIKE THE PRESENTATION. SEND IT BACK.
I GIVE SO MUCH, AND ASK SO LITTLE.
WWW.POSTWRITERSGROUP.COM
BCPICKLES@AOL.COM
12-4
© 2000 Washington Post Writers Group

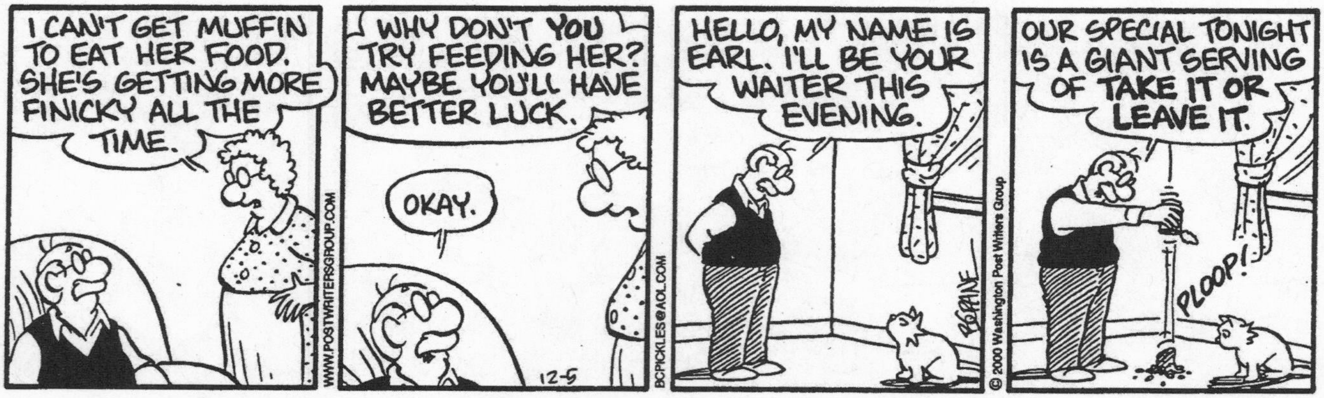
I CAN'T GET MUFFIN TO EAT HER FOOD. SHE'S GETTING MORE FINICKY ALL THE TIME.
WHY DON'T YOU TRY FEEDING HER? MAYBE YOU'LL HAVE BETTER LUCK.
OKAY.
HELLO, MY NAME IS EARL. I'LL BE YOUR WAITER THIS EVENING.
OUR SPECIAL TONIGHT IS A GIANT SERVING OF TAKE IT OR LEAVE IT.
PLOOP!
WWW.POSTWRITERSGROUP.COM
BCPICKLES@AOL.COM
12-5
© 2000 Washington Post Writers Group

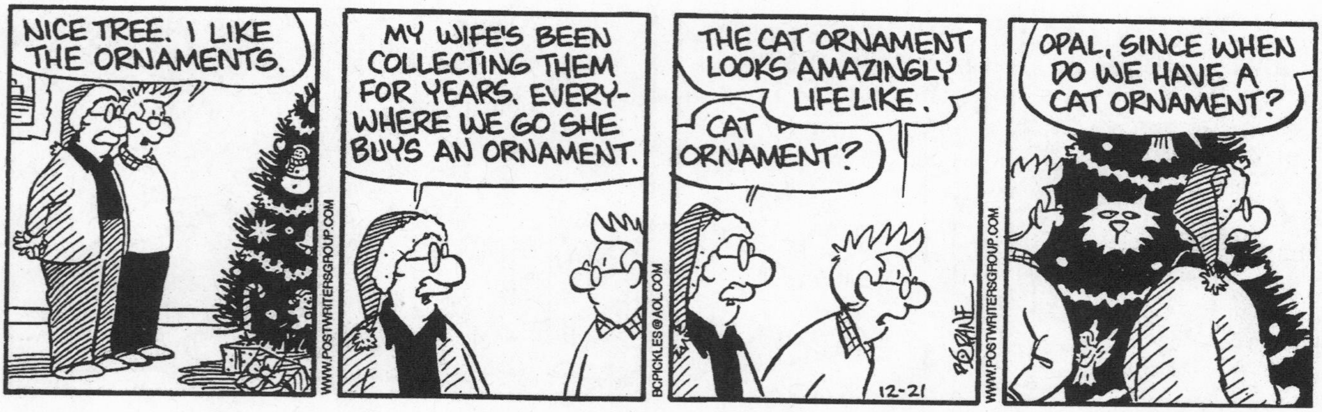
NICE TREE. I LIKE THE ORNAMENTS.
MY WIFE'S BEEN COLLECTING THEM FOR YEARS. EVERYWHERE WE GO SHE BUYS AN ORNAMENT.
THE CAT ORNAMENT LOOKS AMAZINGLY LIFELIKE.
CAT ORNAMENT?
OPAL, SINCE WHEN DO WE HAVE A CAT ORNAMENT?
WWW.POSTWRITERSGROUP.COM
BCPICKLES@AOL.COM
12-21
WWW.POSTWRITERSGROUP.COM

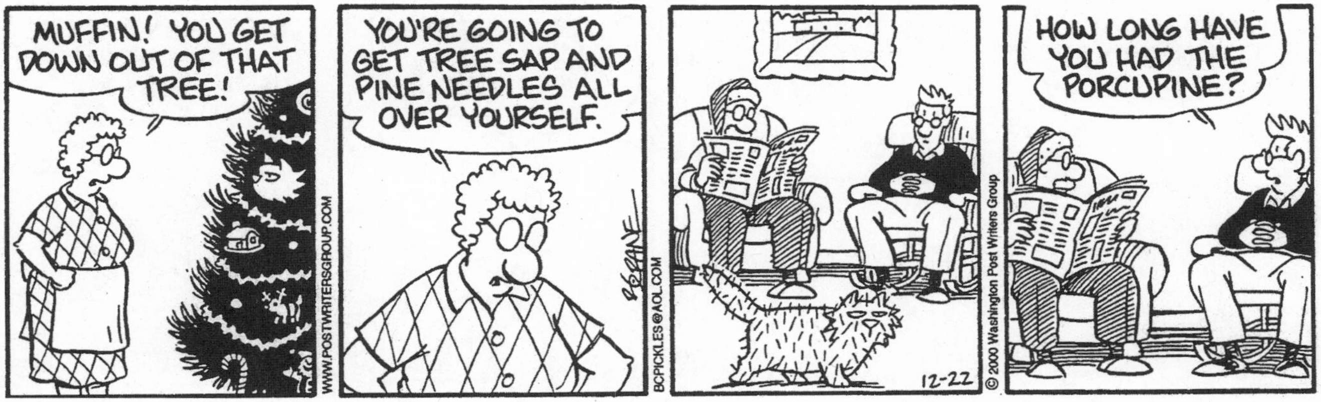
MUFFIN! YOU GET DOWN OUT OF THAT TREE!
WWW.POSTWRITERSGROUP.COM
YOU'RE GOING TO GET TREE SAP AND PINE NEEDLES ALL OVER YOURSELF.
BCPICKLES@AOL.COM
12-22
© 2000 Washington Post Writers Group
HOW LONG HAVE YOU HAD THE PORCUPINE?

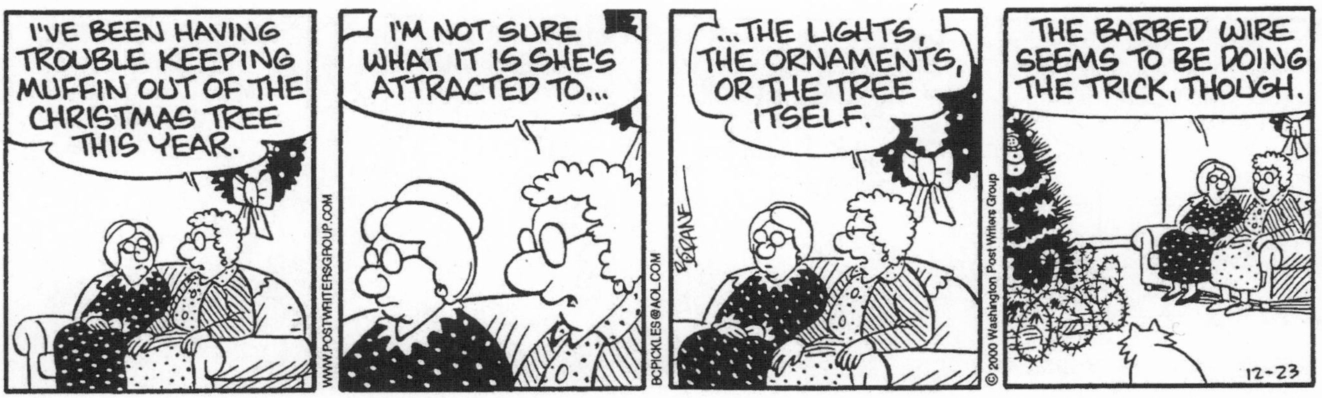
I'VE BEEN HAVING TROUBLE KEEPING MUFFIN OUT OF THE CHRISTMAS TREE THIS YEAR.
WWW.POSTWRITERSGROUP.COM
I'M NOT SURE WHAT IT IS SHE'S ATTRACTED TO...
BCPICKLES@AOL.COM
...THE LIGHTS, THE ORNAMENTS, OR THE TREE ITSELF.
© 2000 Washington Post Writers Group
THE BARBED WIRE SEEMS TO BE DOING THE TRICK, THOUGH.
12-23

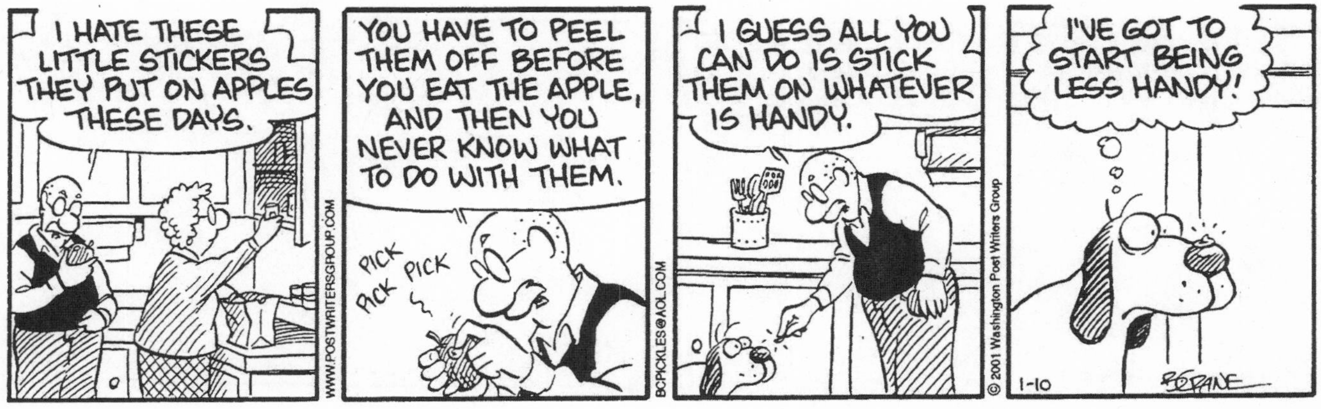
I HATE THESE LITTLE STICKERS THEY PUT ON APPLES THESE DAYS.
WWW.POSTWRITERSGROUP.COM
YOU HAVE TO PEEL THEM OFF BEFORE YOU EAT THE APPLE, AND THEN YOU NEVER KNOW WHAT TO DO WITH THEM.
PICK PICK PICK
BCPICKLES@AOL.COM
I GUESS ALL YOU CAN DO IS STICK THEM ON WHATEVER IS HANDY.
© 2001 Washington Post Writers Group
I'VE GOT TO START BEING LESS HANDY!
1-10

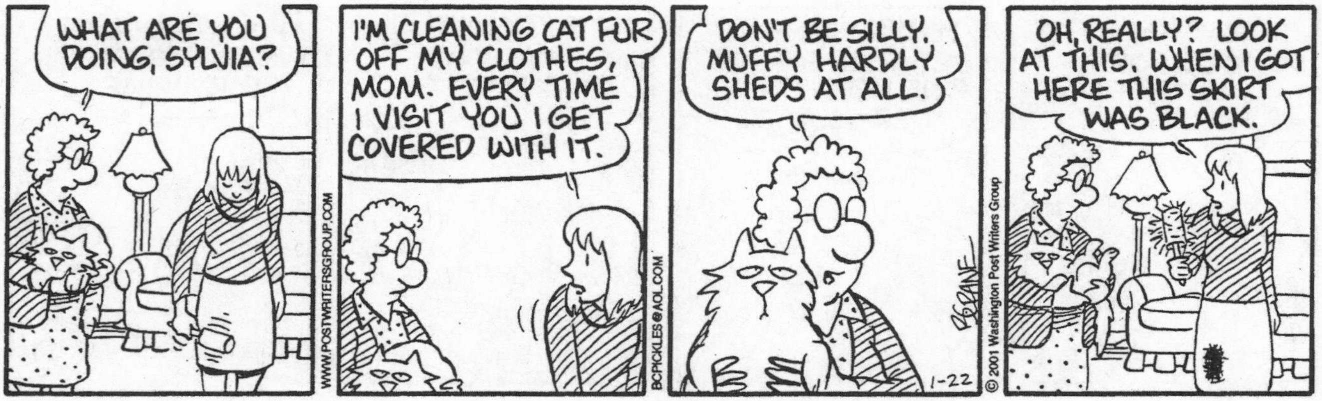
WHAT ARE YOU DOING, SYLVIA?
WWW.POSTWRITERSGROUP.COM
I'M CLEANING CAT FUR OFF MY CLOTHES, MOM. EVERY TIME I VISIT YOU I GET COVERED WITH IT.
BCPICKLES@AOL.COM
DON'T BE SILLY. MUFFY HARDLY SHEDS AT ALL.
1-22
© 2001 Washington Post Writers Group
OH, REALLY? LOOK AT THIS. WHEN I GOT HERE THIS SKIRT WAS BLACK.

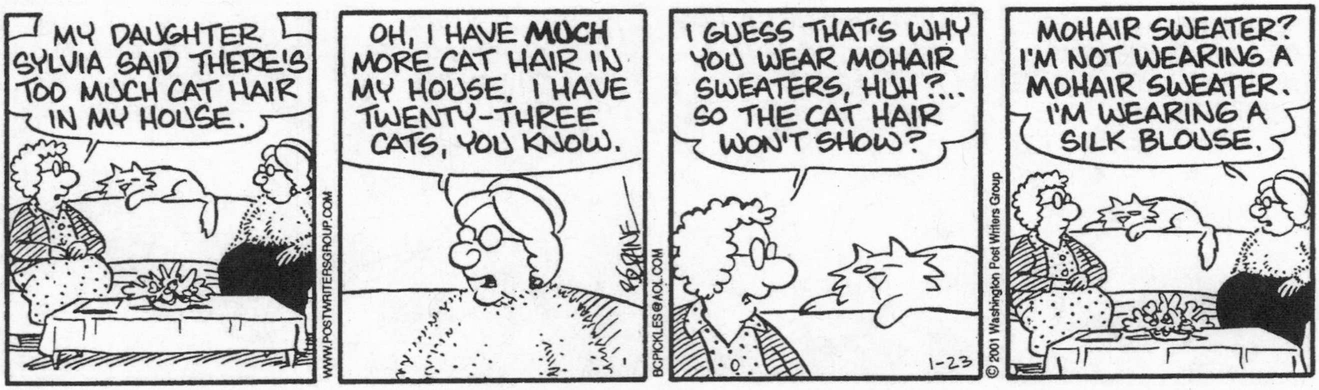
MY DAUGHTER SYLVIA SAID THERE'S TOO MUCH CAT HAIR IN MY HOUSE.
WWW.POSTWRITERSGROUP.COM
OH, I HAVE **MUCH** MORE CAT HAIR IN MY HOUSE. I HAVE TWENTY-THREE CATS, YOU KNOW.
BCPICKLES@AOL.COM
I GUESS THAT'S WHY YOU WEAR MOHAIR SWEATERS, HUH?... SO THE CAT HAIR WON'T SHOW?
1-23
© 2001 Washington Post Writers Group
MOHAIR SWEATER? I'M NOT WEARING A MOHAIR SWEATER. I'M WEARING A SILK BLOUSE.

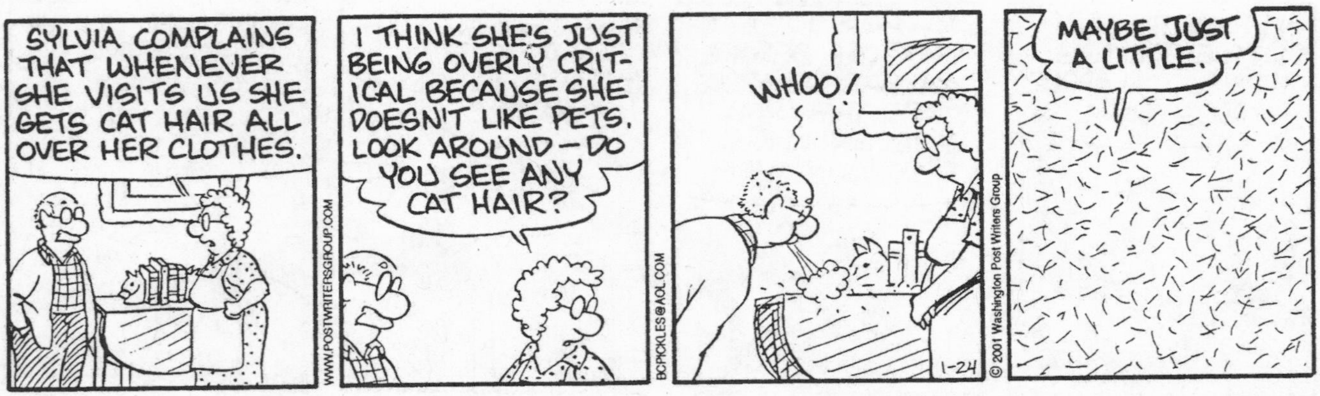
SYLVIA COMPLAINS THAT WHENEVER SHE VISITS US SHE GETS CAT HAIR ALL OVER HER CLOTHES.
WWW.POSTWRITERSGROUP.COM
I THINK SHE'S JUST BEING OVERLY CRIT-ICAL BECAUSE SHE DOESN'T LIKE PETS. LOOK AROUND—DO YOU SEE ANY CAT HAIR?
BCPICKLES@AOL.COM
WHOO!
1-24
© 2001 Washington Post Writers Group
MAYBE JUST A LITTLE.

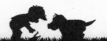

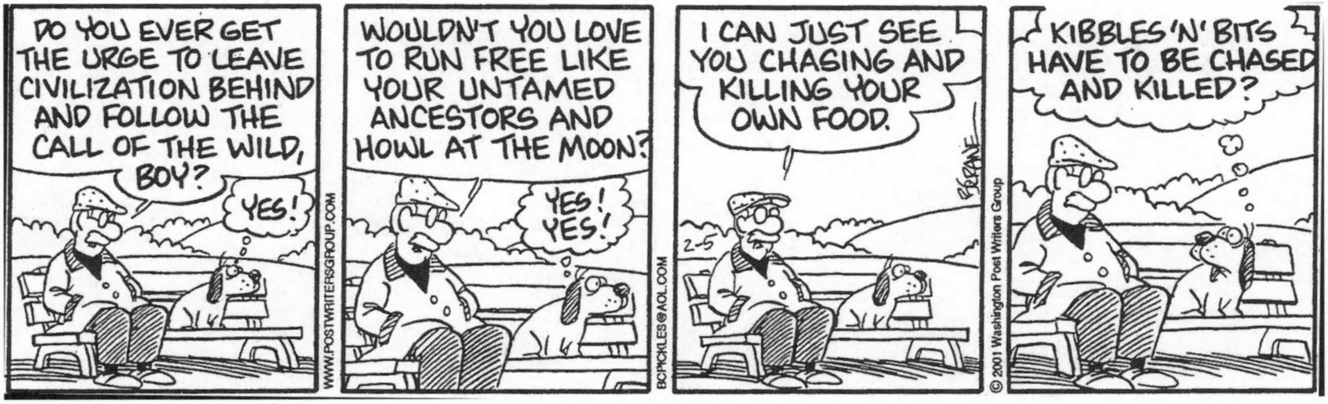
DO YOU EVER GET THE URGE TO LEAVE CIVILIZATION BEHIND AND FOLLOW THE CALL OF THE WILD, BOY?
YES!
WWW.POSTWRITERSGROUP.COM
WOULDN'T YOU LOVE TO RUN FREE LIKE YOUR UNTAMED ANCESTORS AND HOWL AT THE MOON?
YES! YES!
BCPICKLES@AOL.COM
I CAN JUST SEE YOU CHASING AND KILLING YOUR OWN FOOD.
2-5
© 2001 Washington Post Writers Group
KIBBLES 'N' BITS HAVE TO BE CHASED AND KILLED?

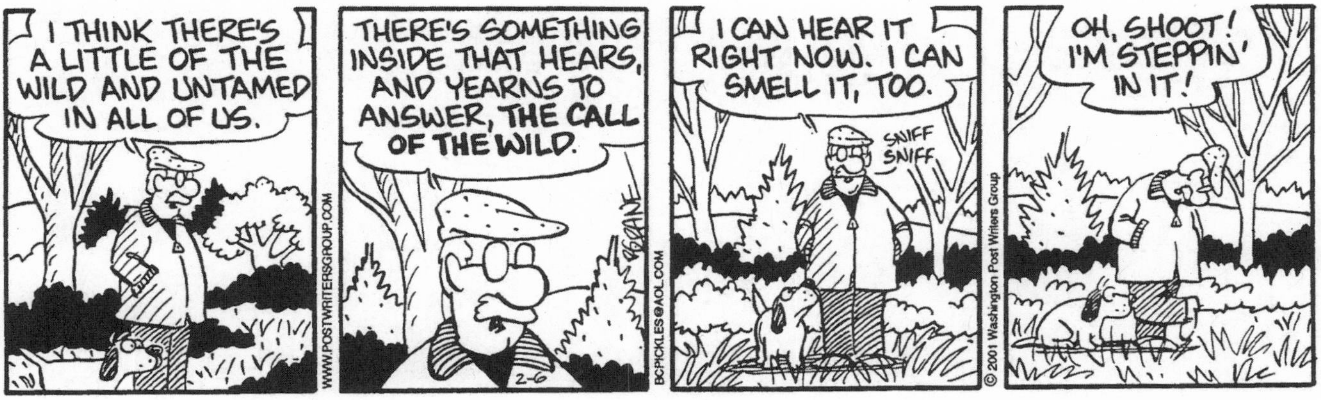
I THINK THERE'S A LITTLE OF THE WILD AND UNTAMED IN ALL OF US.
WWW.POSTWRITERSGROUP.COM
THERE'S SOMETHING INSIDE THAT HEARS, AND YEARNS TO ANSWER, THE CALL OF THE WILD.
2-6
BCPICKLES@AOL.COM
I CAN HEAR IT RIGHT NOW. I CAN SMELL IT, TOO.
SNIFF SNIFF
© 2001 Washington Post Writers Group
OH, SHOOT! I'M STEPPIN' IN IT!

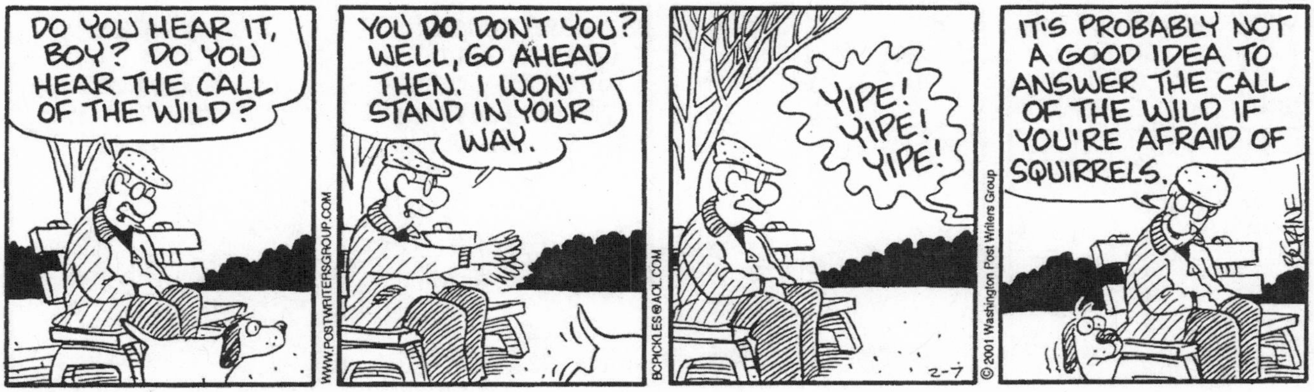
DO YOU HEAR IT, BOY? DO YOU HEAR THE CALL OF THE WILD?
WWW.POSTWRITERSGROUP.COM
YOU DO, DON'T YOU? WELL, GO AHEAD THEN. I WON'T STAND IN YOUR WAY.
BCPICKLES@AOL.COM
YIPE! YIPE! YIPE!
2-7
© 2001 Washington Post Writers Group
IT'S PROBABLY NOT A GOOD IDEA TO ANSWER THE CALL OF THE WILD IF YOU'RE AFRAID OF SQUIRRELS.

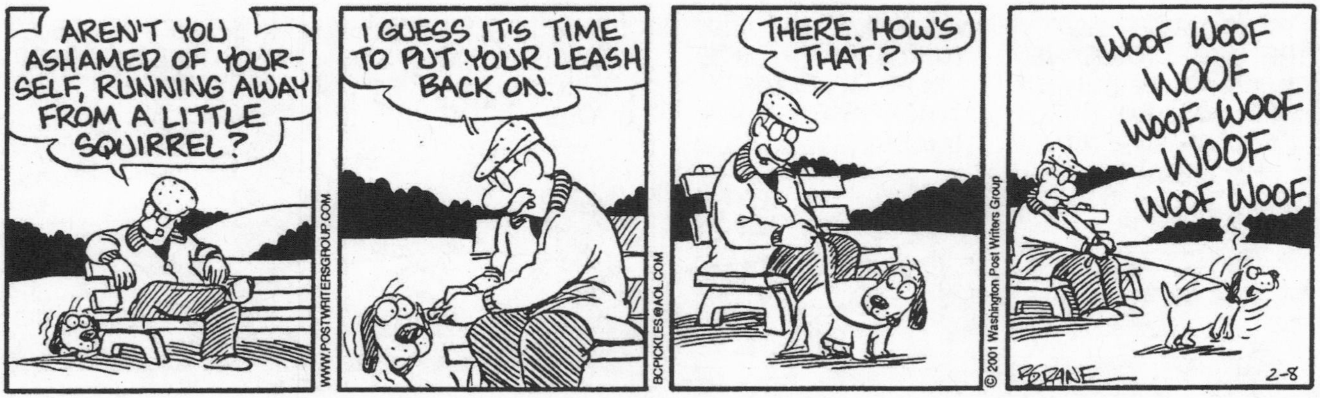
AREN'T YOU ASHAMED OF YOURSELF, RUNNING AWAY FROM A LITTLE SQUIRREL?
WWW.POSTWRITERSGROUP.COM
I GUESS IT'S TIME TO PUT YOUR LEASH BACK ON.
BCPICKLES@AOL.COM
THERE. HOW'S THAT?
© 2001 Washington Post Writers Group
WOOF WOOF
WOOF
WOOF WOOF
WOOF
WOOF WOOF
B. CRANE
2-8

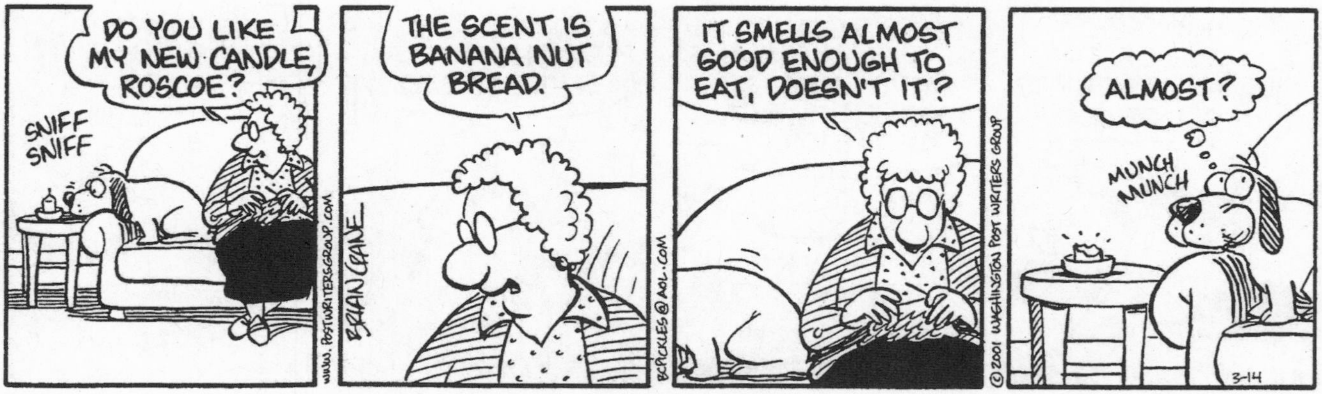
DO YOU LIKE MY NEW CANDLE, ROSCOE?
SNIFF SNIFF
WWW.POSTWRITERSGROUP.COM
THE SCENT IS BANANA NUT BREAD.
BRIAN CRANE
BCPICKLES@AOL.COM
IT SMELLS ALMOST GOOD ENOUGH TO EAT, DOESN'T IT?
© 2001 WASHINGTON POST WRITERS GROUP
ALMOST?
MUNCH MUNCH
3-14

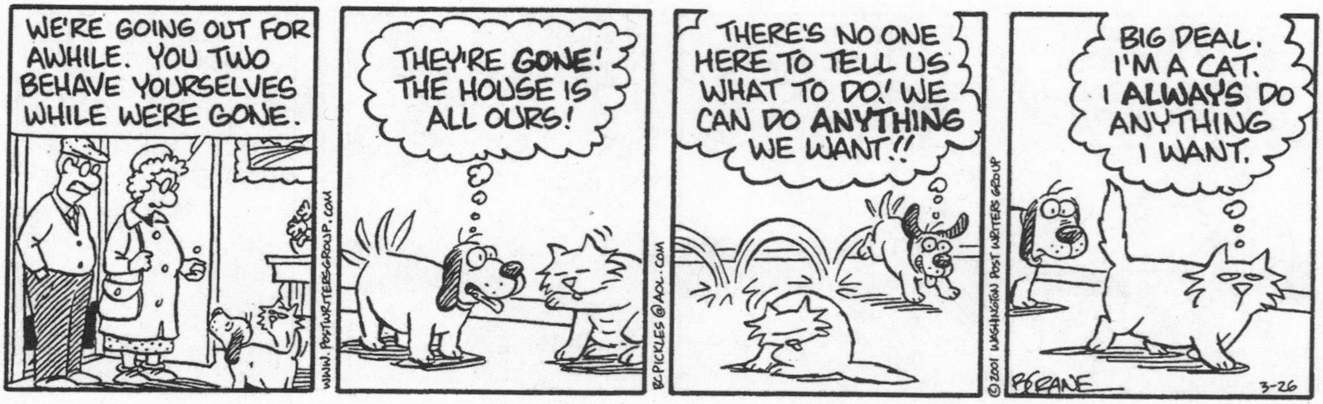
WE'RE GOING OUT FOR AWHILE. YOU TWO BEHAVE YOURSELVES WHILE WE'RE GONE.
WWW.POSTWRITERSGROUP.COM
THEY'RE GONE! THE HOUSE IS ALL OURS!
BCPICKLES@AOL.COM
THERE'S NO ONE HERE TO TELL US WHAT TO DO! WE CAN DO ANYTHING WE WANT!!
© 2001 WASHINGTON POST WRITERS GROUP
BIG DEAL. I'M A CAT. I ALWAYS DO ANYTHING I WANT.
B. CRANE
3-26

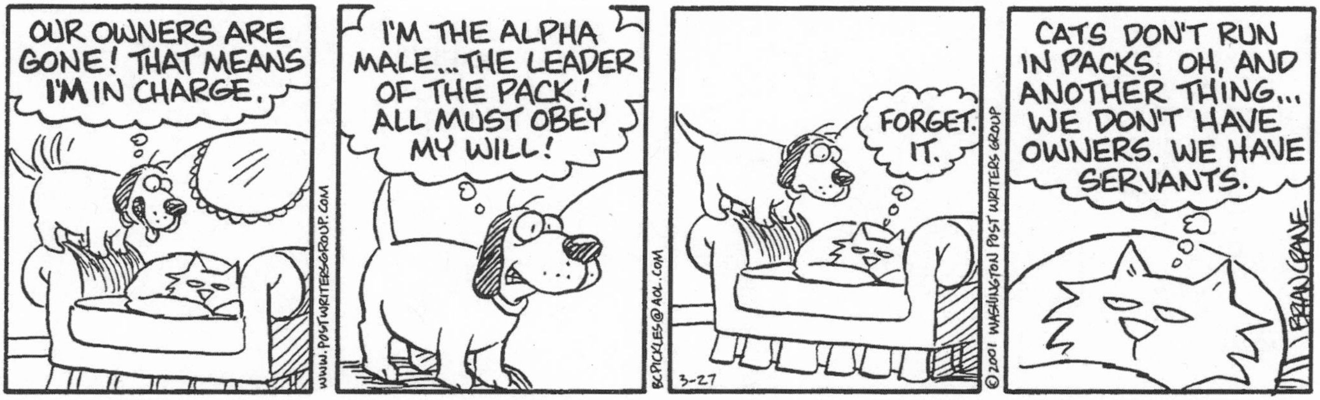
OUR OWNERS ARE GONE! THAT MEANS **I'M** IN CHARGE.
WWW.POSTWRITERSGROUP.COM
I'M THE ALPHA MALE...THE LEADER OF THE PACK! ALL MUST OBEY MY WILL!
BCPICKLES@AOL.COM
FORGET. IT.
3-27
©2001 WASHINGTON POST WRITERS GROUP
CATS DON'T RUN IN PACKS. OH, AND ANOTHER THING... WE DON'T HAVE OWNERS. WE HAVE SERVANTS.
BRIAN CRANE

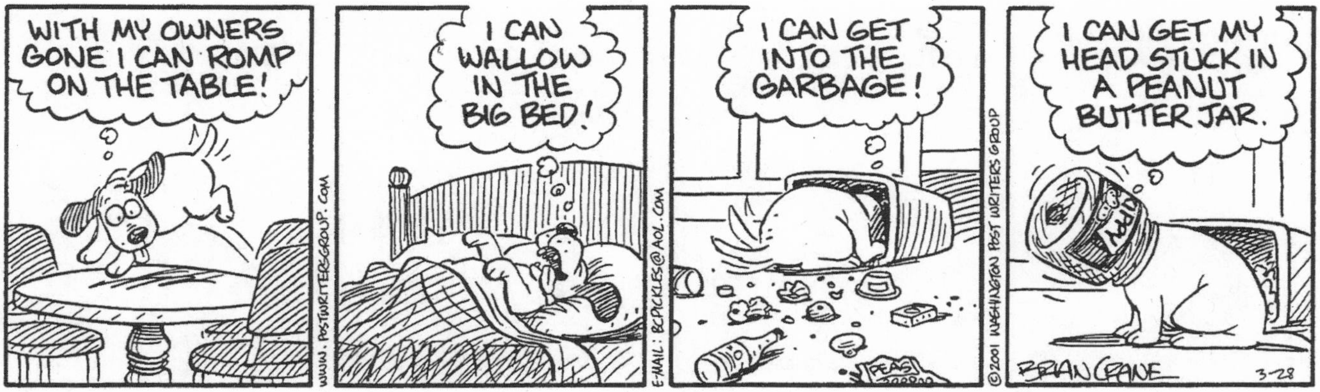
WITH MY OWNERS GONE I CAN ROMP ON THE TABLE!
WWW.POSTWRITERSGROUP.COM
I CAN WALLOW IN THE BIG BED!
E-MAIL: BCPICKLES@AOL.COM
I CAN GET INTO THE GARBAGE!
PEAS
©2001 WASHINGTON POST WRITERS GROUP
I CAN GET MY HEAD STUCK IN A PEANUT BUTTER JAR.
BRIAN CRANE
3-28

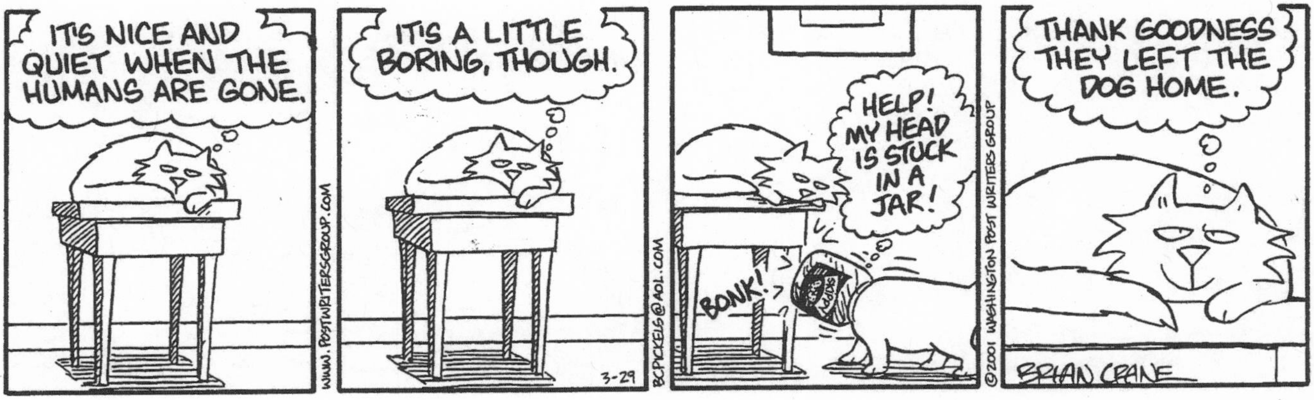
IT'S NICE AND QUIET WHEN THE HUMANS ARE GONE.
WWW.POSTWRITERSGROUP.COM
IT'S A LITTLE BORING, THOUGH.
3-29
BCPICKLES@AOL.COM
HELP! MY HEAD IS STUCK IN A JAR!
BONK!
©2001 WASHINGTON POST WRITERS GROUP
THANK GOODNESS THEY LEFT THE DOG HOME.
BRIAN CRANE

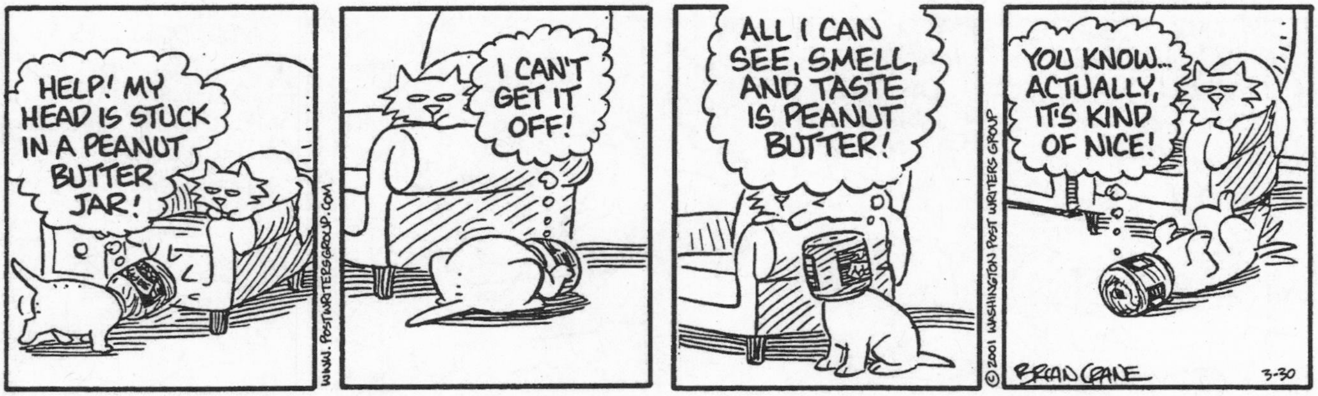
HELP! MY HEAD IS STUCK IN A PEANUT BUTTER JAR!
WWW.POSTWRITERSGROUP.COM
I CAN'T GET IT OFF!
ALL I CAN SEE, SMELL, AND TASTE IS PEANUT BUTTER!
© 2001 WASHINGTON POST WRITERS GROUP
YOU KNOW... ACTUALLY, IT'S KIND OF NICE!
BRIAN CRANE
3-30

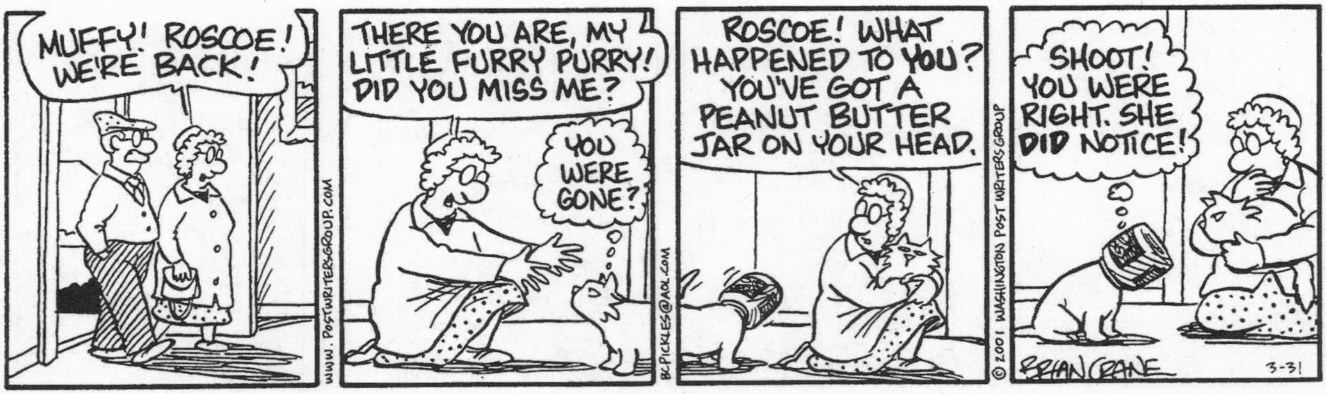
MUFFY! ROSCOE! WE'RE BACK!
WWW.POSTWRITERSGROUP.COM
THERE YOU ARE, MY LITTLE FURRY PURRY! DID YOU MISS ME?
YOU WERE GONE?
BCPICKLES@AOL.COM
ROSCOE! WHAT HAPPENED TO **YOU**? YOU'VE GOT A PEANUT BUTTER JAR ON YOUR HEAD.
© 2001 WASHINGTON POST WRITERS GROUP
SHOOT! YOU WERE RIGHT. SHE **DID** NOTICE!
BRIAN CRANE
3-31

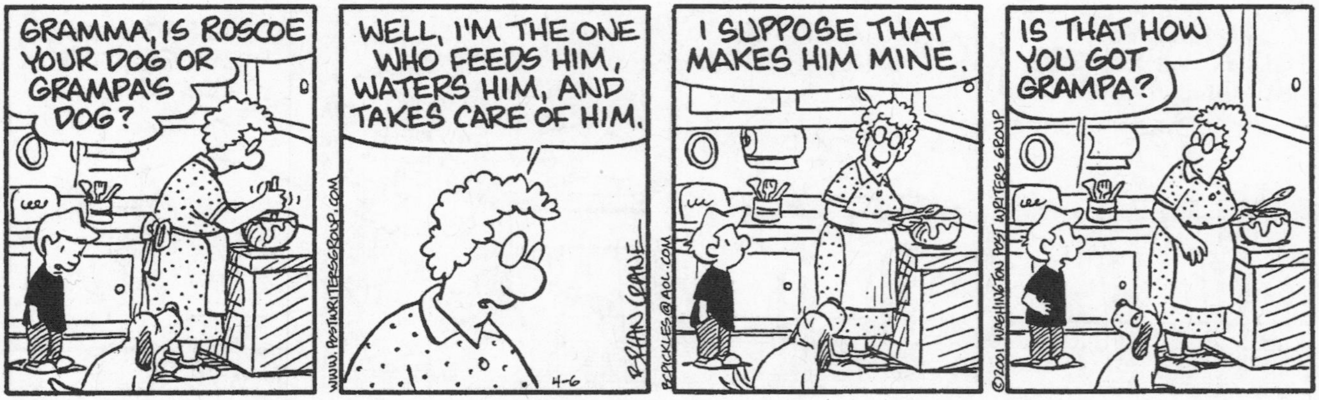
GRAMMA, IS ROSCOE YOUR DOG OR GRAMPA'S DOG?
WWW.POSTWRITERSGROUP.COM
WELL, I'M THE ONE WHO FEEDS HIM, WATERS HIM, AND TAKES CARE OF HIM.
4-6
BRIAN CRANE
BCPICKLES@AOL.COM
I SUPPOSE THAT MAKES HIM MINE.
©2001 WASHINGTON POST WRITERS GROUP
IS THAT HOW YOU GOT GRAMPA?

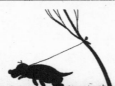

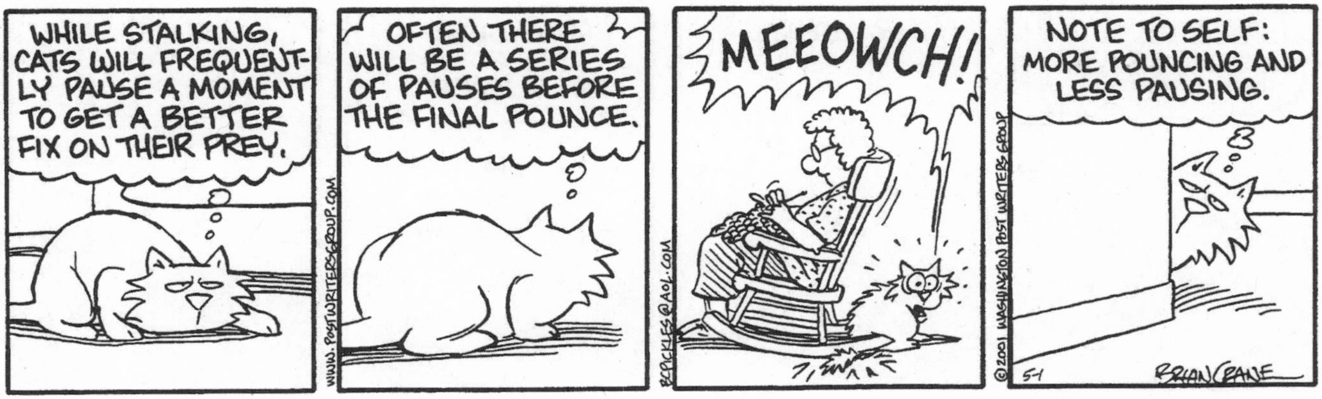
WHILE STALKING, CATS WILL FREQUENTLY PAUSE A MOMENT TO GET A BETTER FIX ON THEIR PREY.
WWW.POSTWRITERSGROUP.COM
OFTEN THERE WILL BE A SERIES OF PAUSES BEFORE THE FINAL POUNCE.
BCPICKLES@AOL.COM
MEEOWCH!
©2001 WASHINGTON POST WRITERS GROUP
NOTE TO SELF: MORE POUNCING AND LESS PAUSING.
5-1
BRIAN CRANE

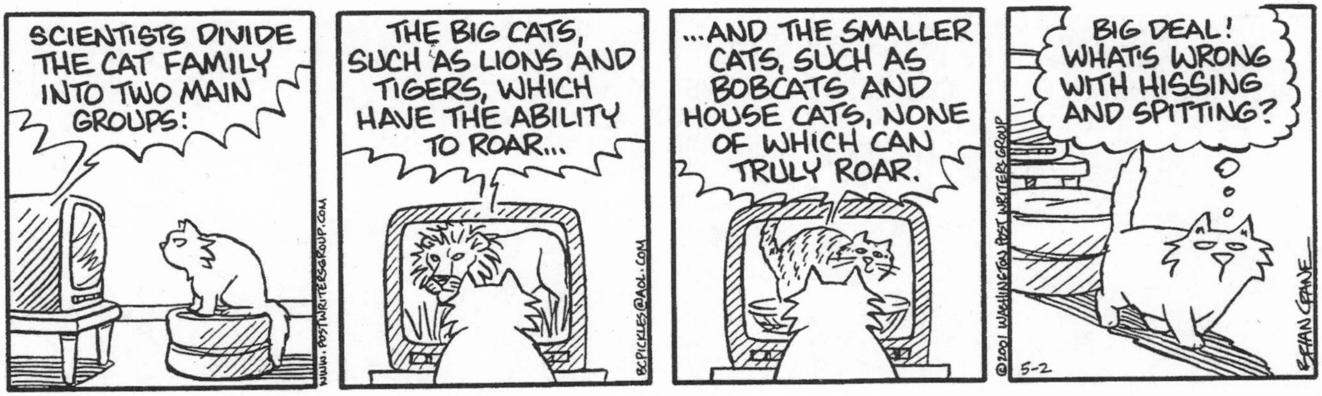
SCIENTISTS DIVIDE THE CAT FAMILY INTO TWO MAIN GROUPS:
WWW.POSTWRITERSGROUP.COM
THE BIG CATS, SUCH AS LIONS AND TIGERS, WHICH HAVE THE ABILITY TO ROAR...
BCPICKLES@AOL.COM
...AND THE SMALLER CATS, SUCH AS BOBCATS AND HOUSE CATS, NONE OF WHICH CAN TRULY ROAR.
©2001 WASHINGTON POST WRITERS GROUP
BIG DEAL! WHAT'S WRONG WITH HISSING AND SPITTING?
5-2
BRIAN CRANE

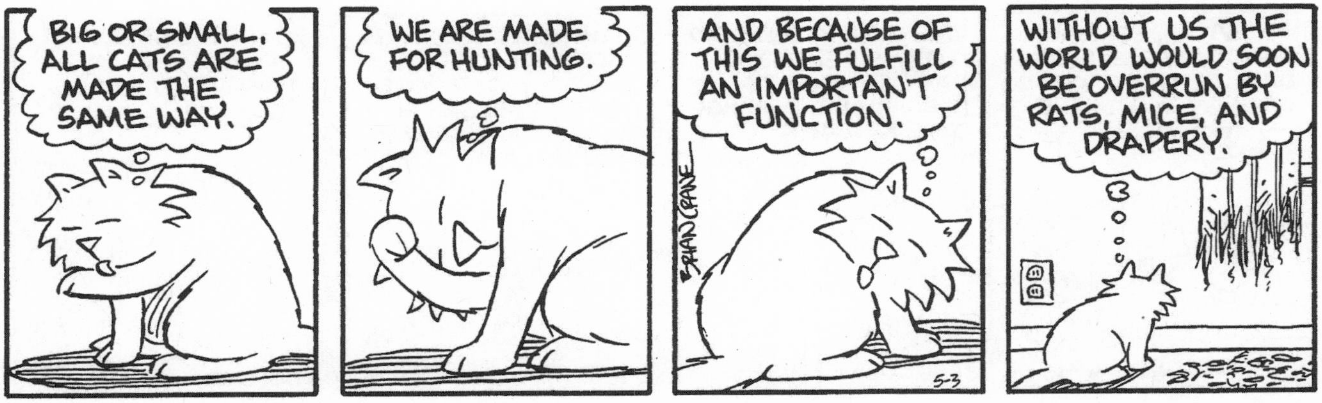
BIG OR SMALL, ALL CATS ARE MADE THE SAME WAY.
WE ARE MADE FOR HUNTING.
AND BECAUSE OF THIS WE FULFILL AN IMPORTANT FUNCTION.
BRIAN CRANE
5-3
WITHOUT US THE WORLD WOULD SOON BE OVERRUN BY RATS, MICE, AND DRAPERY.

201

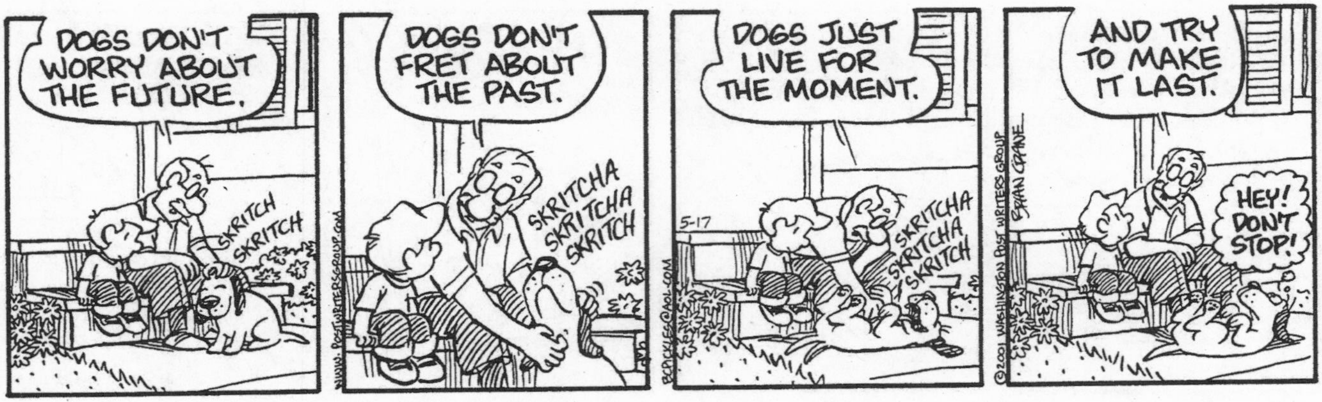
DOGS DON'T WORRY ABOUT THE FUTURE.
SKRITCH SKRITCH
WWW.POSTWRITERSGROUP.COM
DOGS DON'T FRET ABOUT THE PAST.
SKRITCHA SKRITCHA SKRITCH
BCPICKLES@AOL.COM
5-17
DOGS JUST LIVE FOR THE MOMENT.
SKRITCHA SKRITCHA SKRITCH
©2001 WASHINGTON POST WRITERS GROUP
BRIAN CRANE
AND TRY TO MAKE IT LAST.
HEY! DON'T STOP!

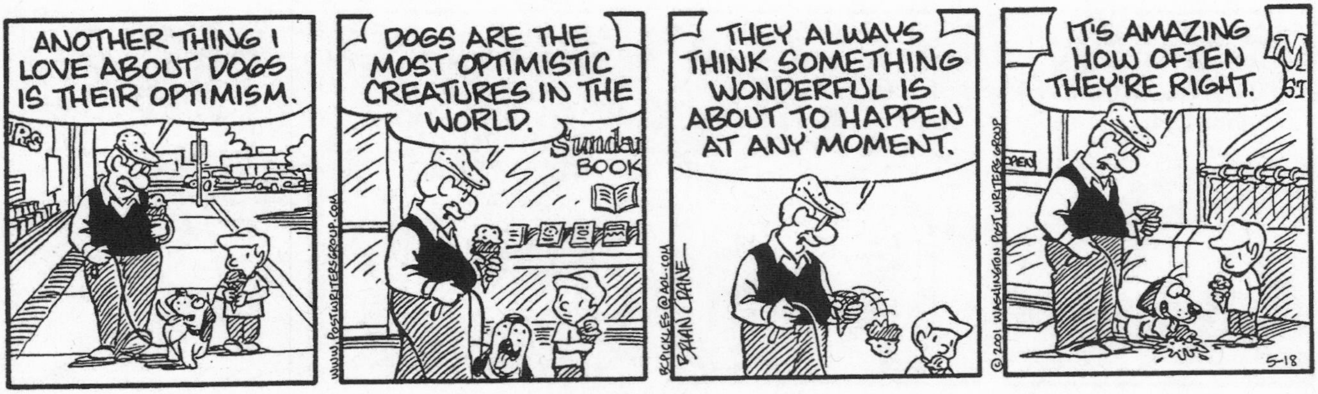
ANOTHER THING I LOVE ABOUT DOGS IS THEIR OPTIMISM.
WWW.POSTWRITERSGROUP.COM
DOGS ARE THE MOST OPTIMISTIC CREATURES IN THE WORLD.
BOOK
BCPICKLES@AOL.COM
BRIAN CRANE
THEY ALWAYS THINK SOMETHING WONDERFUL IS ABOUT TO HAPPEN AT ANY MOMENT.
©2001 WASHINGTON POST WRITERS GROUP
IT'S AMAZING HOW OFTEN THEY'RE RIGHT.
OPEN
5-18

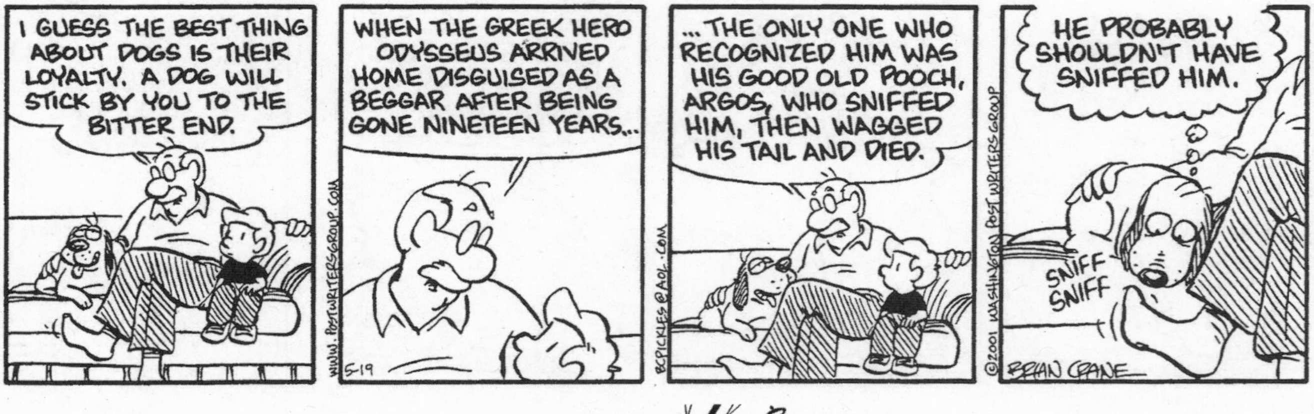
I GUESS THE BEST THING ABOUT DOGS IS THEIR LOYALTY. A DOG WILL STICK BY YOU TO THE BITTER END.
WWW.POSTWRITERSGROUP.COM
5-19
WHEN THE GREEK HERO ODYSSEUS ARRIVED HOME DISGUISED AS A BEGGAR AFTER BEING GONE NINETEEN YEARS...
BCPICKLES@AOL.COM
...THE ONLY ONE WHO RECOGNIZED HIM WAS HIS GOOD OLD POOCH, ARGOS, WHO SNIFFED HIM, THEN WAGGED HIS TAIL AND DIED.
©2001 WASHINGTON POST WRITERS GROUP
HE PROBABLY SHOULDN'T HAVE SNIFFED HIM.
SNIFF SNIFF
BRIAN CRANE

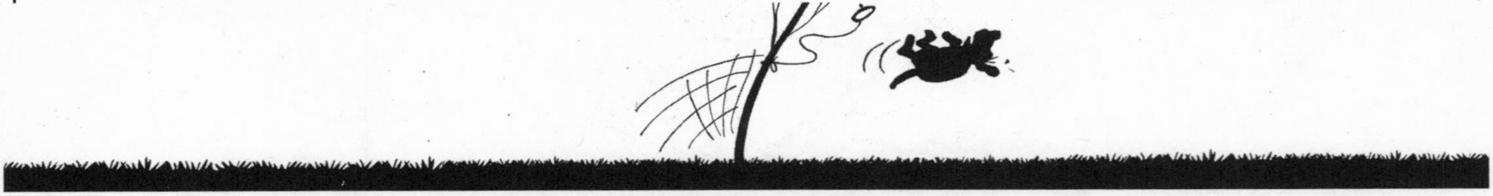

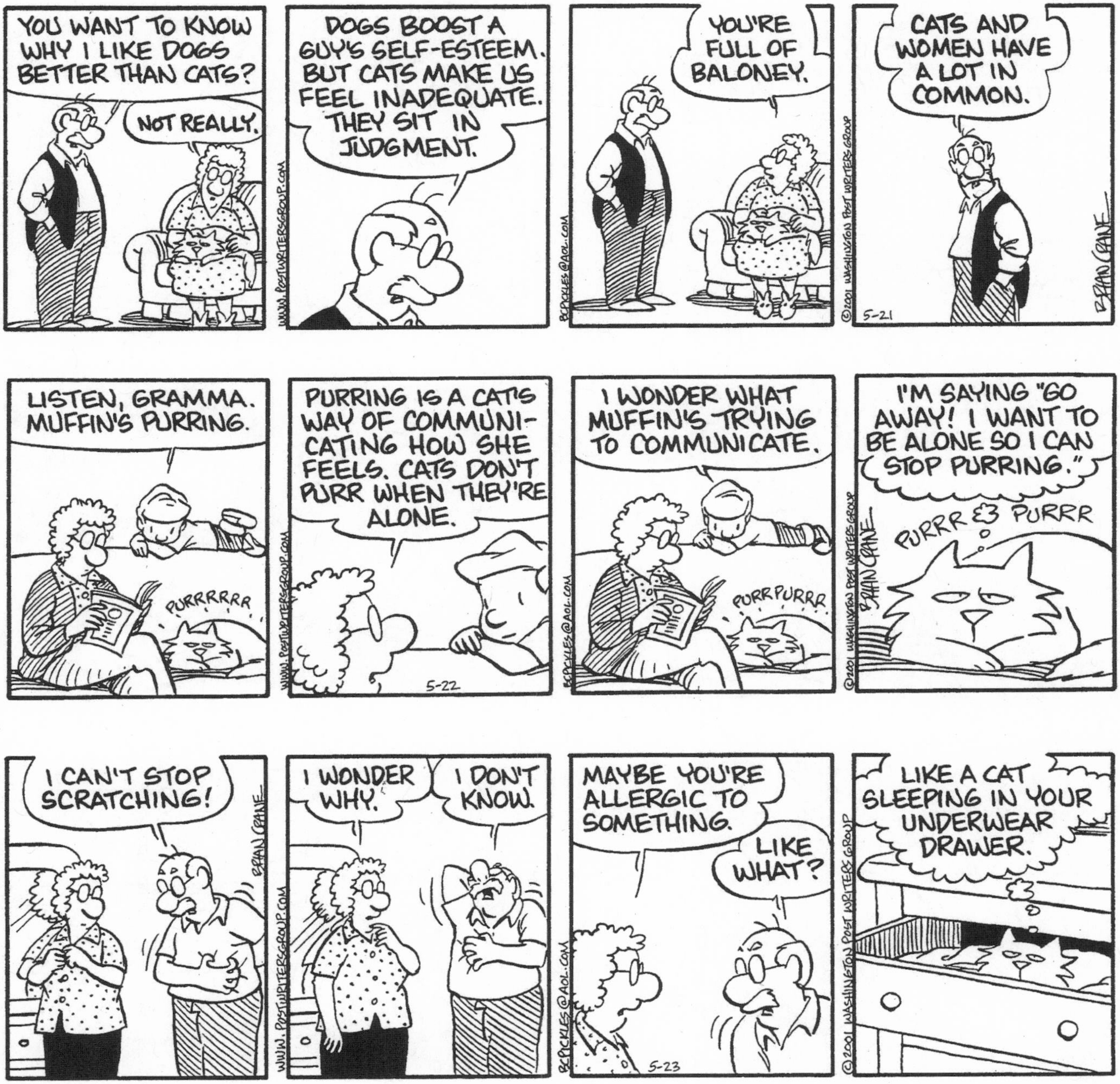
YOU WANT TO KNOW WHY I LIKE DOGS BETTER THAN CATS?
NOT REALLY.
DOGS BOOST A GUY'S SELF-ESTEEM. BUT CATS MAKE US FEEL INADEQUATE. THEY SIT IN JUDGMENT.
WWW.POSTWRITERSGROUP.COM
YOU'RE FULL OF BALONEY.
BCPICKLES@AOL.COM
©2001 WASHINGTON POST WRITERS GROUP
5-21
CATS AND WOMEN HAVE A LOT IN COMMON.
BRIAN CRANE
LISTEN, GRAMMA. MUFFIN'S PURRING.
PURRRRRRR
PURRING IS A CAT'S WAY OF COMMUNICATING HOW SHE FEELS. CATS DON'T PURR WHEN THEY'RE ALONE.
WWW.POSTWRITERSGROUP.COM
5-22
I WONDER WHAT MUFFIN'S TRYING TO COMMUNICATE.
PURR PURRR
BCPICKLES@AOL.COM
©2001 WASHINGTON POST WRITERS GROUP
BRIAN CRANE
I'M SAYING "GO AWAY! I WANT TO BE ALONE SO I CAN STOP PURRING."
PURRR PURRR
I CAN'T STOP SCRATCHING!
BRIAN CRANE
I WONDER WHY.
I DON'T KNOW.
WWW.POSTWRITERSGROUP.COM
MAYBE YOU'RE ALLERGIC TO SOMETHING.
LIKE WHAT?
BCPICKLES@AOL.COM
5-23
LIKE A CAT SLEEPING IN YOUR UNDERWEAR DRAWER.
©2001 WASHINGTON POST WRITERS GROUP

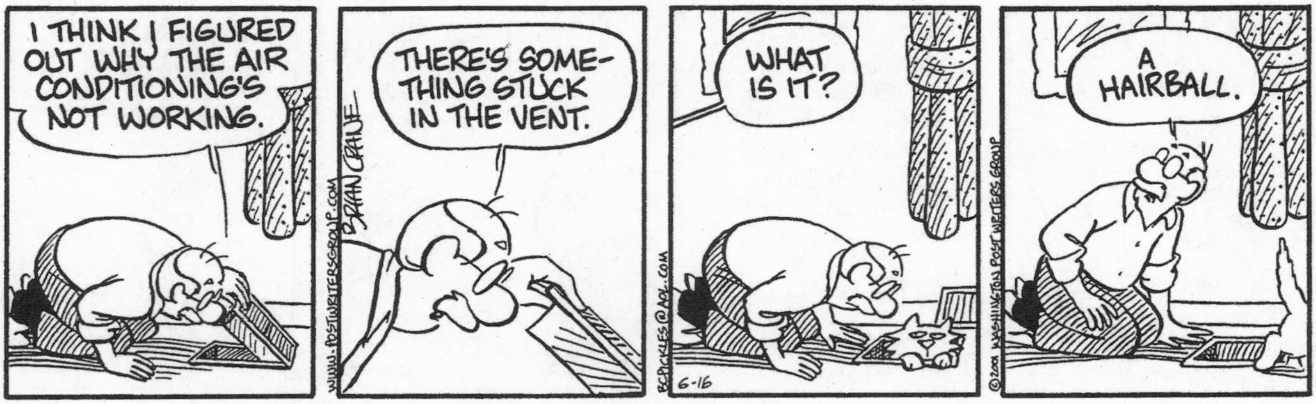
I THINK I FIGURED OUT WHY THE AIR CONDITIONING'S NOT WORKING.
THERE'S SOMETHING STUCK IN THE VENT.
WHAT IS IT?
A HAIRBALL.
WWW.POSTWRITERSGROUP.COM
BRIAN CRANE
BCPICKLES@AOL.COM
6-16
©2001 WASHINGTON POST WRITERS GROUP

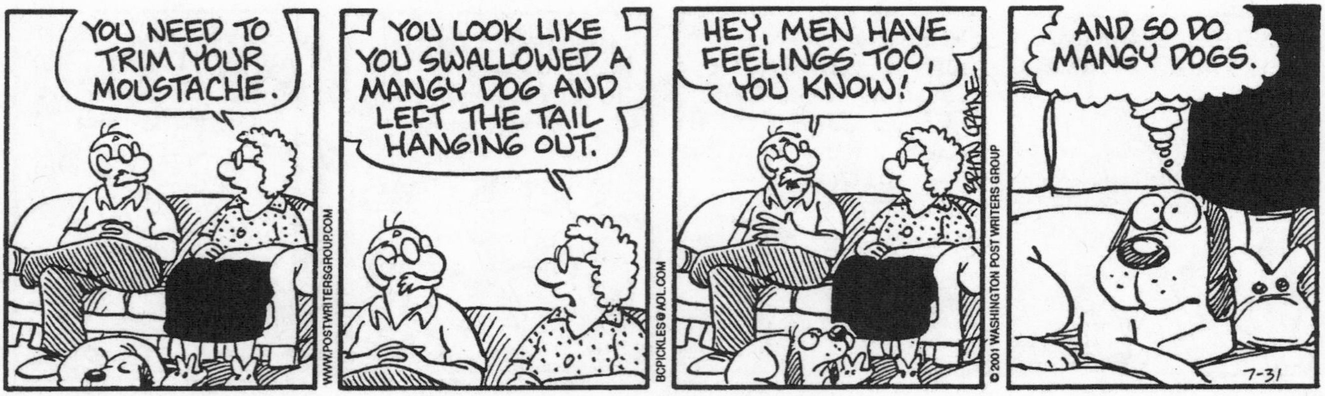
YOU NEED TO TRIM YOUR MOUSTACHE.
YOU LOOK LIKE YOU SWALLOWED A MANGY DOG AND LEFT THE TAIL HANGING OUT.
HEY, MEN HAVE FEELINGS TOO, YOU KNOW!
AND SO DO MANGY DOGS.
WWW.POSTWRITERSGROUP.COM
BCPICKLES@AOL.COM
BRIAN CRANE
© 2001 WASHINGTON POST WRITERS GROUP
7-31

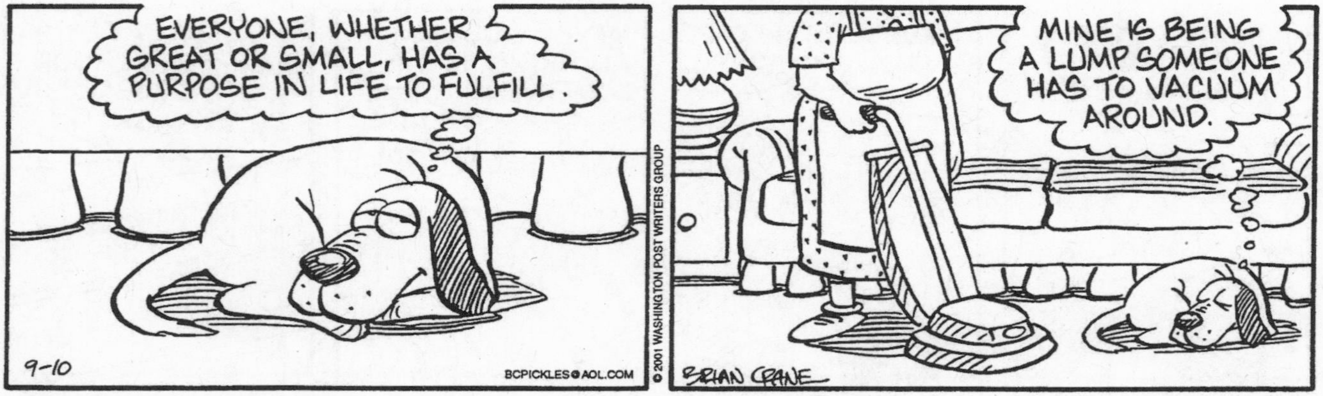
EVERYONE, WHETHER GREAT OR SMALL, HAS A PURPOSE IN LIFE TO FULFILL.
MINE IS BEING A LUMP SOMEONE HAS TO VACUUM AROUND.
9-10
BCPICKLES@AOL.COM
© 2001 WASHINGTON POST WRITERS GROUP
BRIAN CRANE

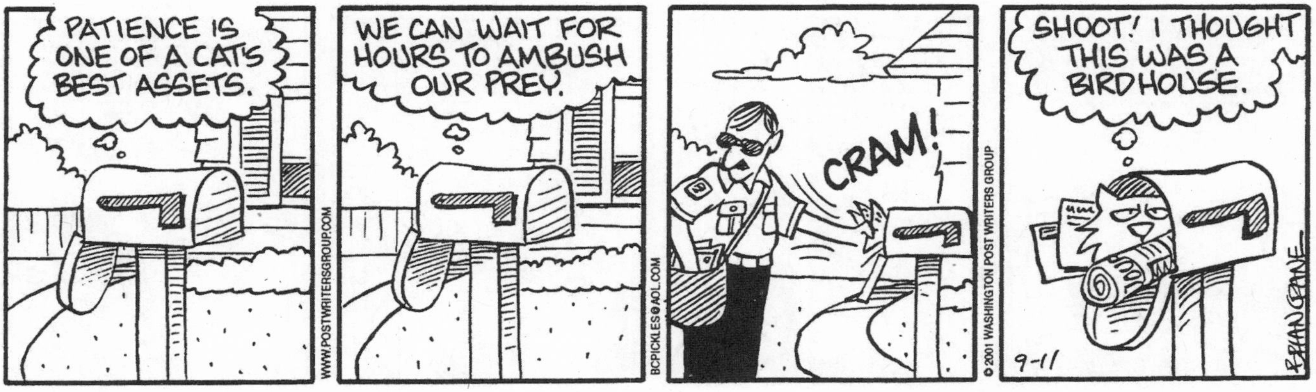
PATIENCE IS ONE OF A CAT'S BEST ASSETS.
WE CAN WAIT FOR HOURS TO AMBUSH OUR PREY.
CRAM!
SHOOT! I THOUGHT THIS WAS A BIRDHOUSE.
WWW.POSTWRITERSGROUP.COM
BCPICKLES@AOL.COM
© 2001 WASHINGTON POST WRITERS GROUP
9-11
BRIAN CRANE

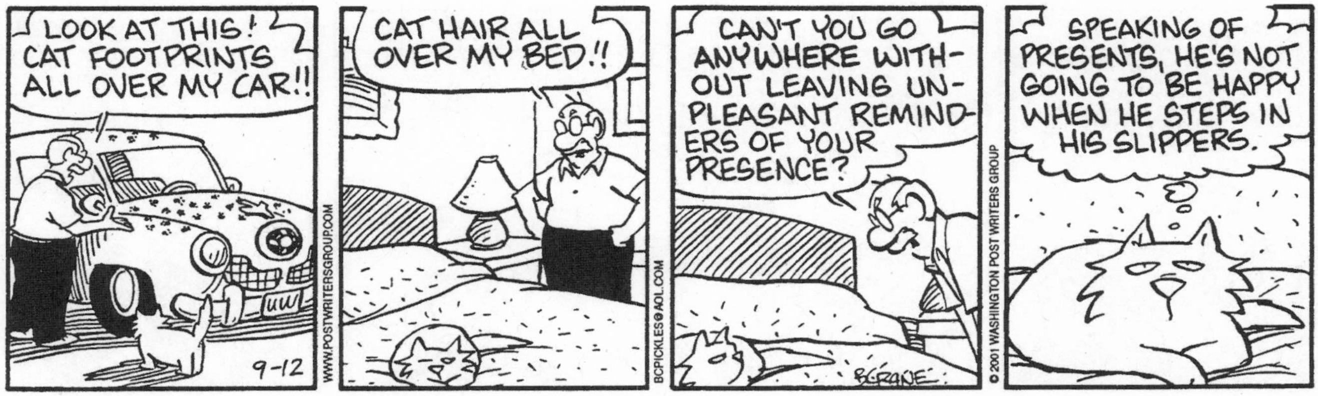
LOOK AT THIS! CAT FOOTPRINTS ALL OVER MY CAR!!
CAT HAIR ALL OVER MY BED!!
CAN'T YOU GO ANYWHERE WITHOUT LEAVING UNPLEASANT REMINDERS OF YOUR PRESENCE?
SPEAKING OF PRESENTS, HE'S NOT GOING TO BE HAPPY WHEN HE STEPS IN HIS SLIPPERS.
9-12
WWW.POSTWRITERSGROUP.COM
BCPICKLES@AOL.COM
B. CRANE
© 2001 WASHINGTON POST WRITERS GROUP

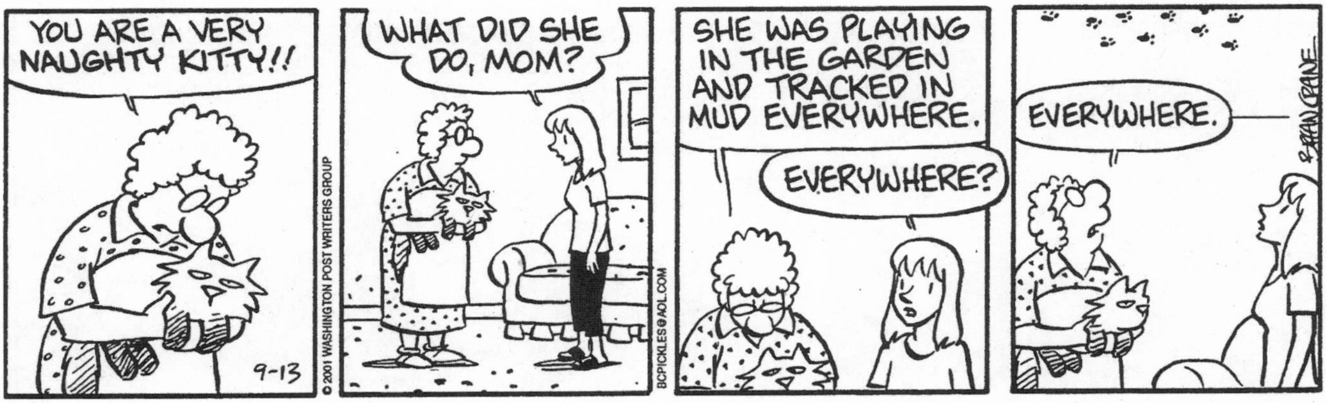
YOU ARE A VERY NAUGHTY KITTY!!
9-13
© 2001 WASHINGTON POST WRITERS GROUP
WHAT DID SHE DO, MOM?
BCPICKLES@AOL.COM
SHE WAS PLAYING IN THE GARDEN AND TRACKED IN MUD EVERYWHERE.
EVERYWHERE?
EVERYWHERE.
BRIAN CRANE

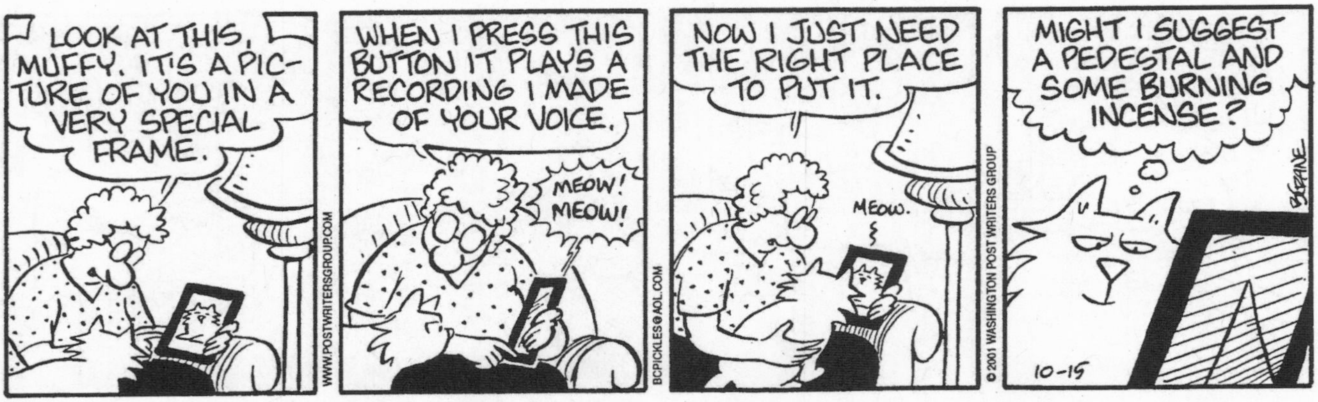
LOOK AT THIS, MUFFY. IT'S A PICTURE OF YOU IN A VERY SPECIAL FRAME.
WWW.POSTWRITERSGROUP.COM
WHEN I PRESS THIS BUTTON IT PLAYS A RECORDING I MADE OF YOUR VOICE.
MEOW! MEOW!
BCPICKLES@AOL.COM
NOW I JUST NEED THE RIGHT PLACE TO PUT IT.
MEOW.
© 2001 WASHINGTON POST WRITERS GROUP
MIGHT I SUGGEST A PEDESTAL AND SOME BURNING INCENSE?
B CRANE
10-15

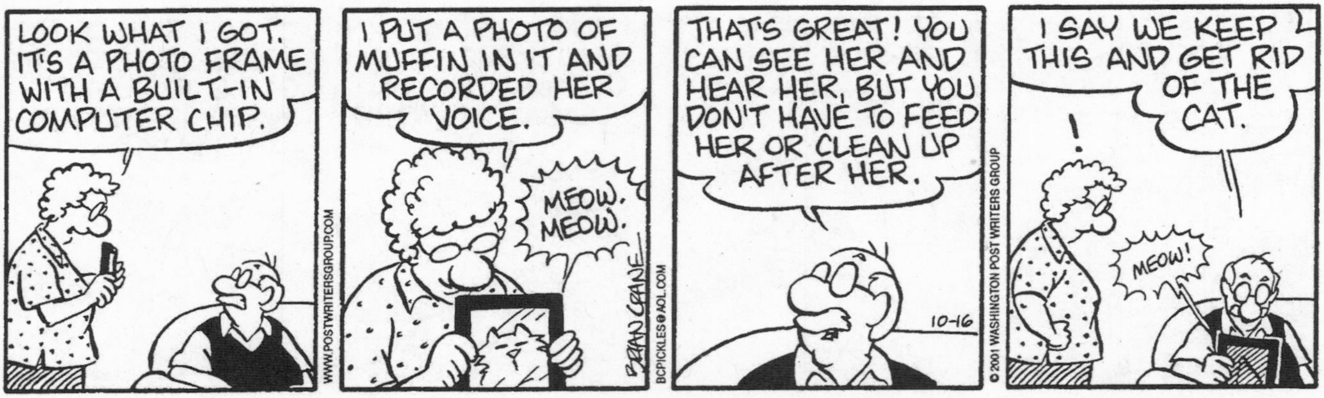
LOOK WHAT I GOT. IT'S A PHOTO FRAME WITH A BUILT-IN COMPUTER CHIP.
WWW.POSTWRITERSGROUP.COM
I PUT A PHOTO OF MUFFIN IN IT AND RECORDED HER VOICE.
MEOW. MEOW.
BRYAN CRANE
BCPICKLES@AOL.COM
THAT'S GREAT! YOU CAN SEE HER AND HEAR HER, BUT YOU DON'T HAVE TO FEED HER OR CLEAN UP AFTER HER.
10-16
© 2001 WASHINGTON POST WRITERS GROUP
I SAY WE KEEP THIS AND GET RID OF THE CAT.
!
MEOW!

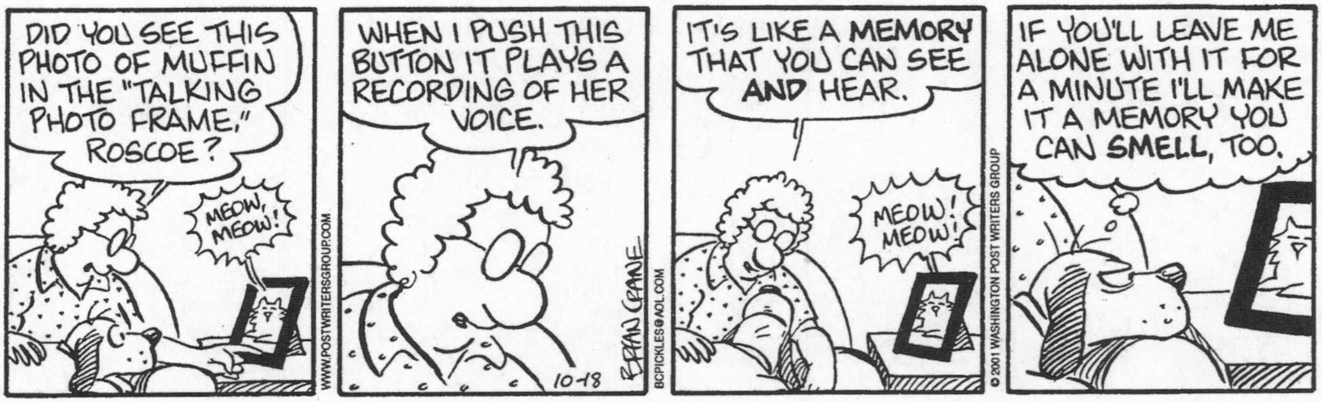
DID YOU SEE THIS PHOTO OF MUFFIN IN THE "TALKING PHOTO FRAME," ROSCOE?
MEOW, MEOW!
WWW.POSTWRITERSGROUP.COM
WHEN I PUSH THIS BUTTON IT PLAYS A RECORDING OF HER VOICE.
10-18
BRYAN CRANE
BCPICKLES@AOL.COM
IT'S LIKE A **MEMORY** THAT YOU CAN SEE **AND** HEAR.
MEOW! MEOW!
© 2001 WASHINGTON POST WRITERS GROUP
IF YOU'LL LEAVE ME ALONE WITH IT FOR A MINUTE I'LL MAKE IT A MEMORY YOU CAN **SMELL**, TOO.

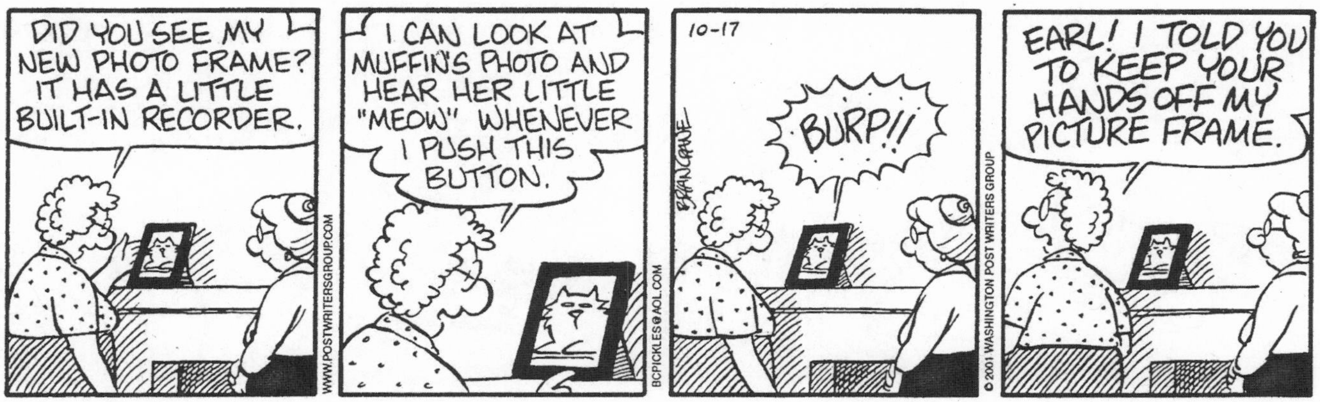
DID YOU SEE MY NEW PHOTO FRAME? IT HAS A LITTLE BUILT-IN RECORDER.
WWW.POSTWRITERSGROUP.COM
I CAN LOOK AT MUFFIN'S PHOTO AND HEAR HER LITTLE "MEOW" WHENEVER I PUSH THIS BUTTON.
BCPICKLES@AOL.COM
10-17
BURP!!
© 2001 WASHINGTON POST WRITERS GROUP
EARL! I TOLD YOU TO KEEP YOUR HANDS OFF MY PICTURE FRAME.

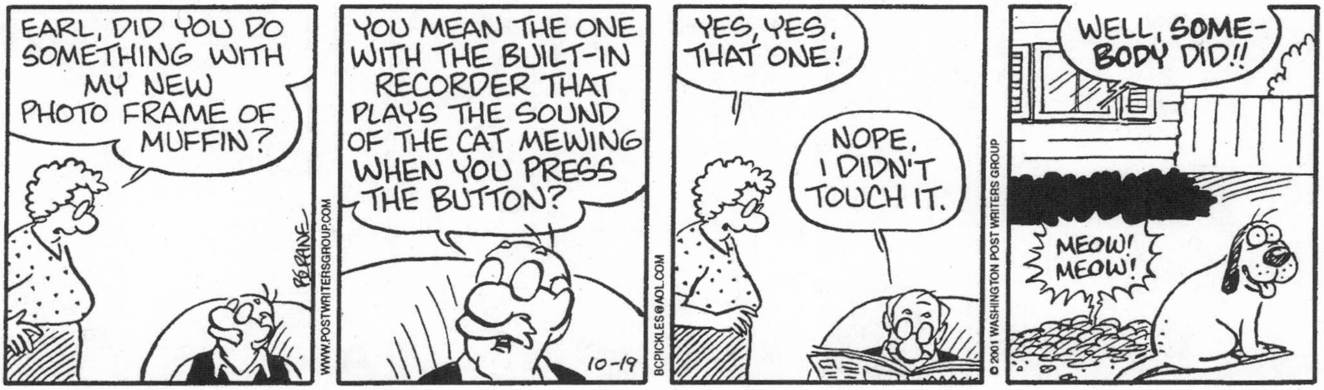
EARL, DID YOU DO SOMETHING WITH MY NEW PHOTO FRAME OF MUFFIN?
WWW.POSTWRITERSGROUP.COM
YOU MEAN THE ONE WITH THE BUILT-IN RECORDER THAT PLAYS THE SOUND OF THE CAT MEWING WHEN YOU PRESS THE BUTTON?
10-19
BCPICKLES@AOL.COM
YES, YES. THAT ONE!
NOPE. I DIDN'T TOUCH IT.
© 2001 WASHINGTON POST WRITERS GROUP
WELL, SOMEBODY DID!!
MEOW! MEOW!

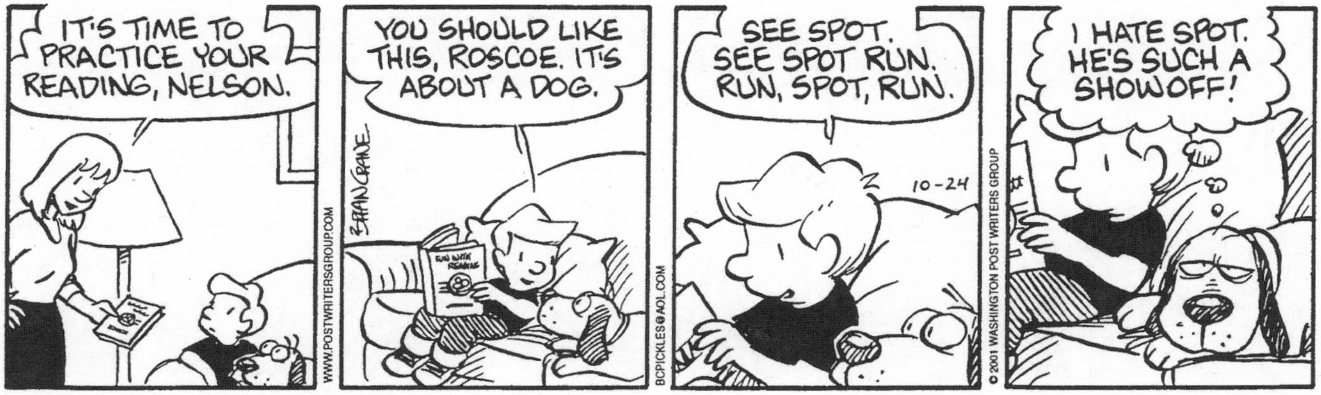
IT'S TIME TO PRACTICE YOUR READING, NELSON.
WWW.POSTWRITERSGROUP.COM
YOU SHOULD LIKE THIS, ROSCOE. IT'S ABOUT A DOG.
BCPICKLES@AOL.COM
SEE SPOT. SEE SPOT RUN. RUN, SPOT, RUN.
10-24
© 2001 WASHINGTON POST WRITERS GROUP
I HATE SPOT. HE'S SUCH A SHOWOFF!

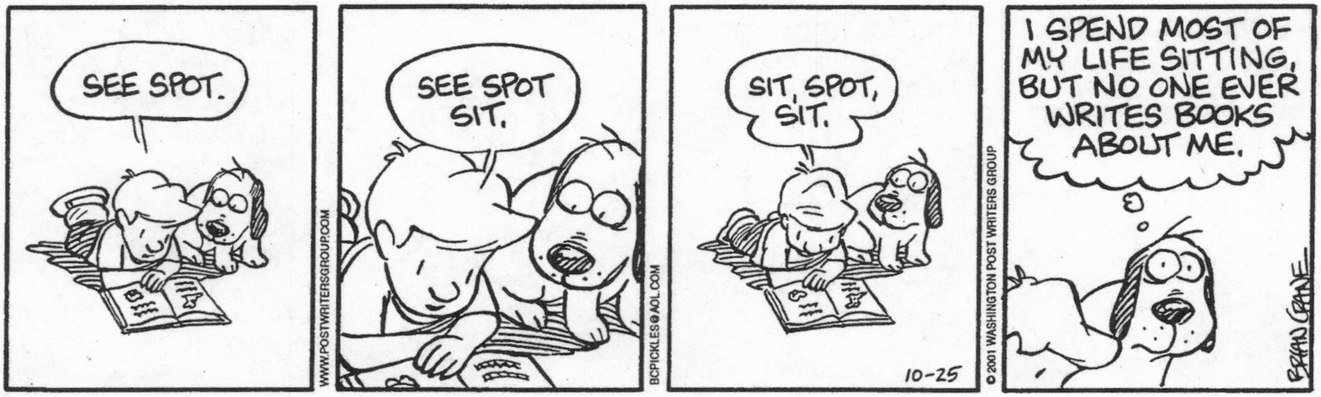
SEE SPOT.
SEE SPOT SIT.
SIT, SPOT, SIT.
I SPEND MOST OF MY LIFE SITTING, BUT NO ONE EVER WRITES BOOKS ABOUT ME.
WWW.POSTWRITERSGROUP.COM
BCPICKLES@AOL.COM
10-25
© 2001 WASHINGTON POST WRITERS GROUP
BRIAN CRANE

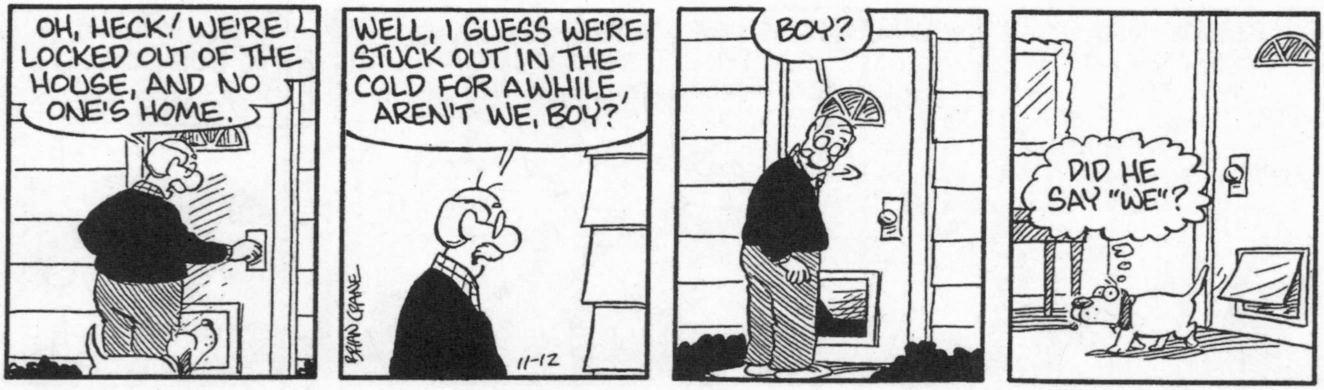
OH, HECK! WE'RE LOCKED OUT OF THE HOUSE, AND NO ONE'S HOME.
WELL, I GUESS WE'RE STUCK OUT IN THE COLD FOR AWHILE, AREN'T WE, BOY?
BRIAN CRANE
11-12
BOY?
DID HE SAY "WE"?

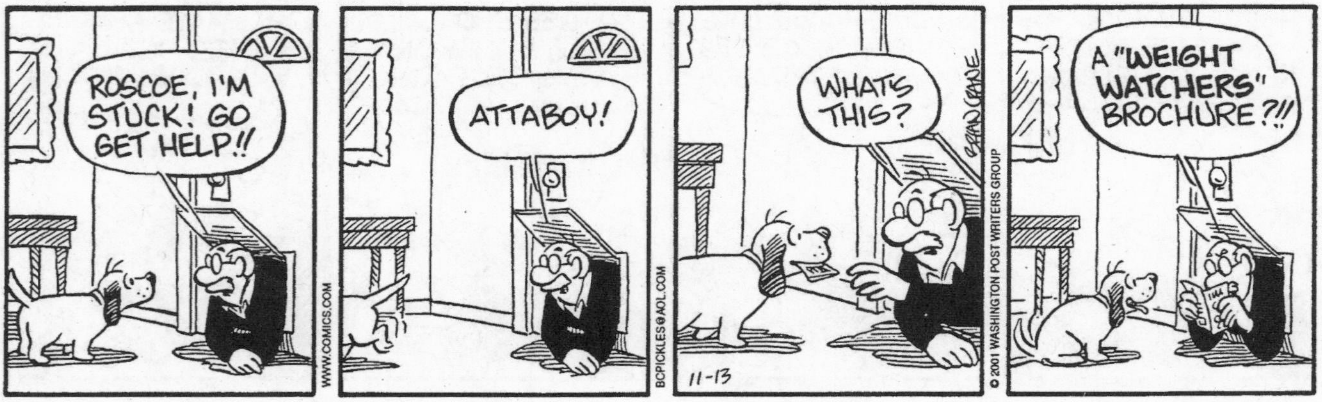
ROSCOE, I'M STUCK! GO GET HELP!!
WWW.COMICS.COM
ATTABOY!
BCPICKLES@AOL.COM
WHAT'S THIS?
BRIAN CRANE
11-13
© 2001 WASHINGTON POST WRITERS GROUP
A "WEIGHT WATCHERS" BROCHURE?!!

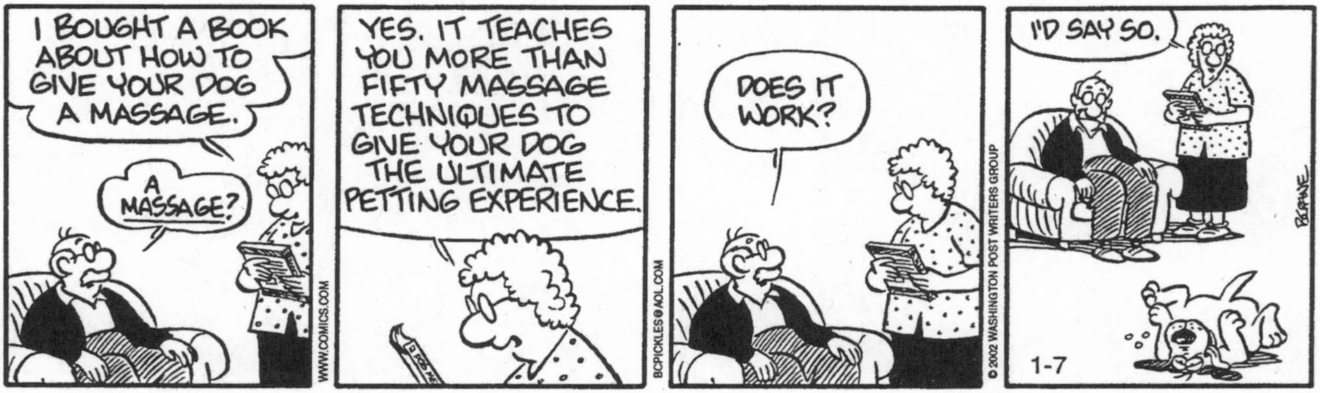
I BOUGHT A BOOK ABOUT HOW TO GIVE YOUR DOG A MASSAGE.
A MASSAGE?
YES. IT TEACHES YOU MORE THAN FIFTY MASSAGE TECHNIQUES TO GIVE YOUR DOG THE ULTIMATE PETTING EXPERIENCE.
DOES IT WORK?
I'D SAY SO.
1-7
WWW.COMICS.COM
BCPICKLES@AOL.COM
© 2002 WASHINGTON POST WRITERS GROUP

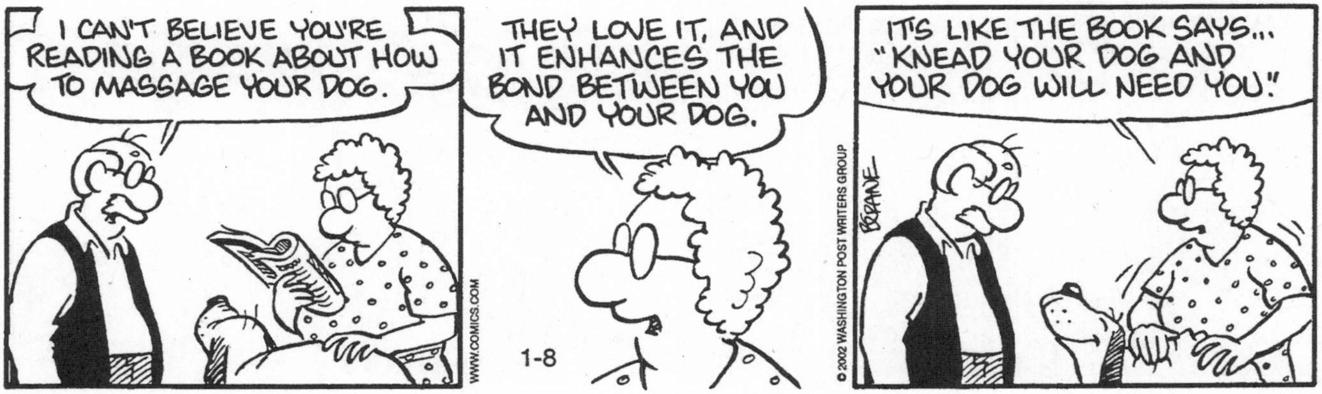
I CAN'T BELIEVE YOU'RE READING A BOOK ABOUT HOW TO MASSAGE YOUR DOG.
THEY LOVE IT, AND IT ENHANCES THE BOND BETWEEN YOU AND YOUR DOG.
IT'S LIKE THE BOOK SAYS... "KNEAD YOUR DOG AND YOUR DOG WILL NEED YOU."
1-8
WWW.COMICS.COM
© 2002 WASHINGTON POST WRITERS GROUP

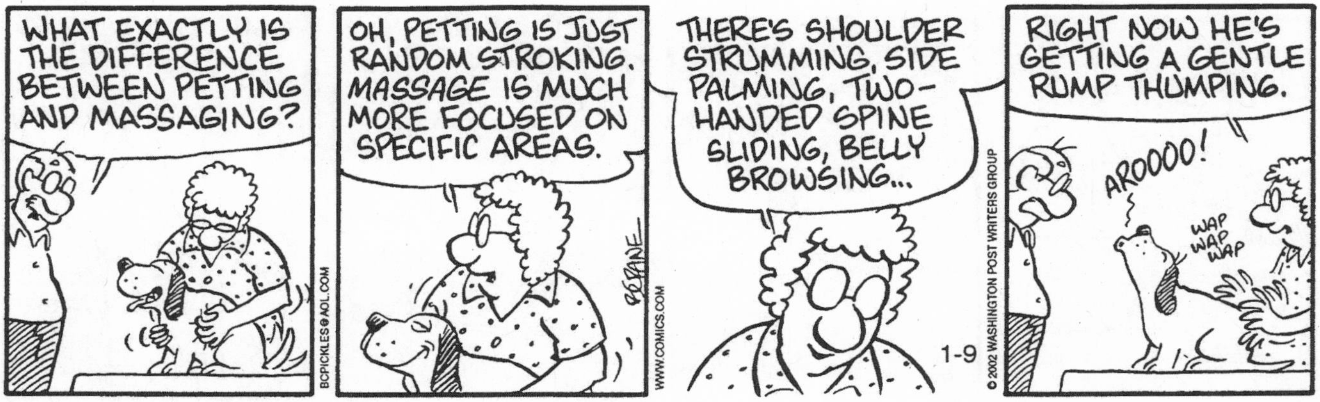
WHAT EXACTLY IS THE DIFFERENCE BETWEEN PETTING AND MASSAGING?
OH, PETTING IS JUST RANDOM STROKING. MASSAGE IS MUCH MORE FOCUSED ON SPECIFIC AREAS.
THERE'S SHOULDER STRUMMING, SIDE PALMING, TWO-HANDED SPINE SLIDING, BELLY BROWSING...
RIGHT NOW HE'S GETTING A GENTLE RUMP THUMPING.
AROOOO!
WAP WAP WAP
1-9
BCPICKLES@AOL.COM
WWW.COMICS.COM
© 2002 WASHINGTON POST WRITERS GROUP

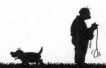

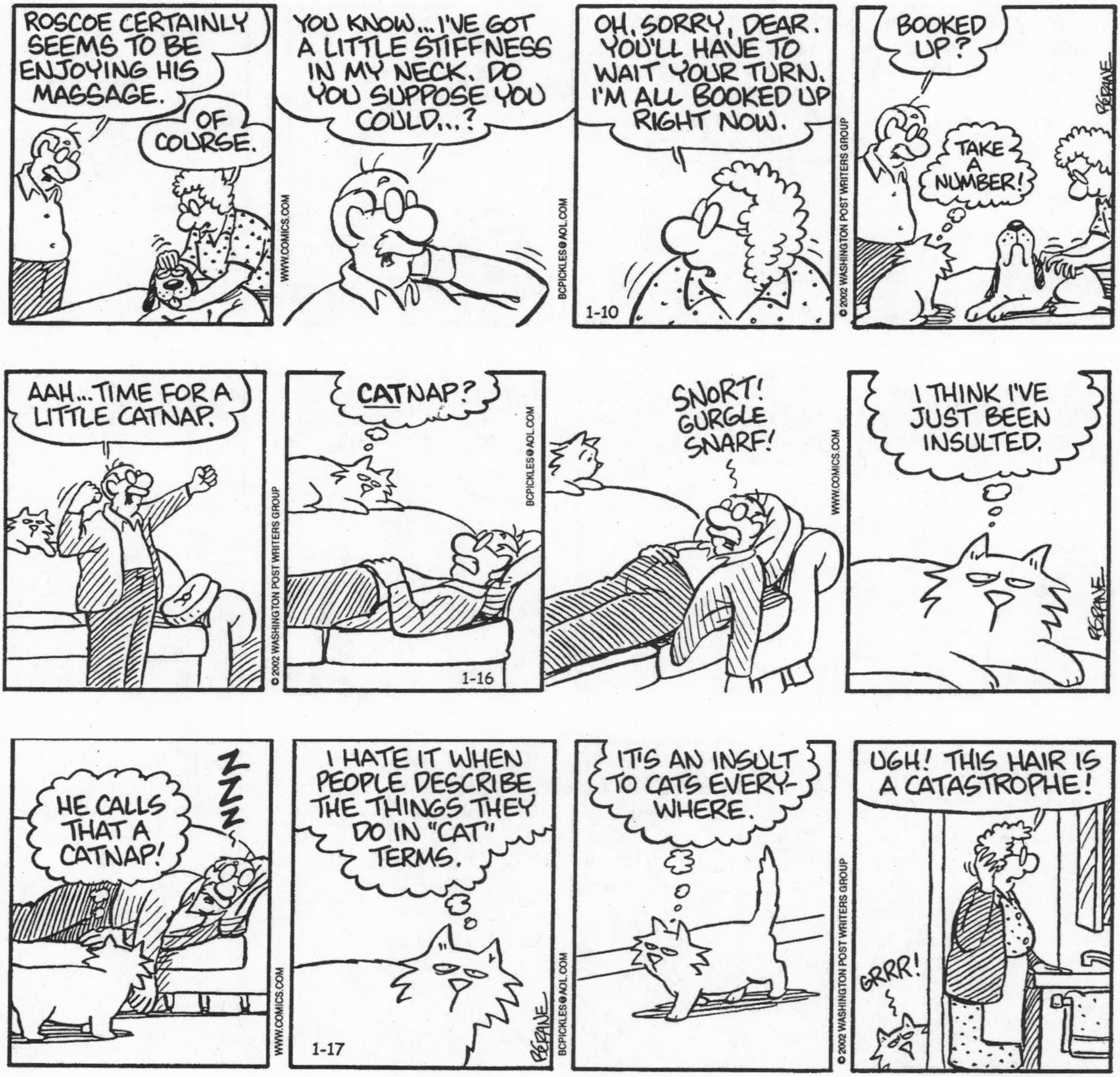
ROSCOE CERTAINLY SEEMS TO BE ENJOYING HIS MASSAGE.
OF COURSE.
WWW.COMICS.COM
YOU KNOW... I'VE GOT A LITTLE STIFFNESS IN MY NECK. DO YOU SUPPOSE YOU COULD...?
BCPICKLES@AOL.COM
1-10
OH, SORRY, DEAR. YOU'LL HAVE TO WAIT YOUR TURN. I'M ALL BOOKED UP RIGHT NOW.
© 2002 WASHINGTON POST WRITERS GROUP
BOOKED UP?
TAKE A NUMBER!
AAH... TIME FOR A LITTLE CATNAP.
© 2002 WASHINGTON POST WRITERS GROUP
CATNAP?
BCPICKLES@AOL.COM
1-16
SNORT! GURGLE SNARF!
WWW.COMICS.COM
I THINK I'VE JUST BEEN INSULTED.
HE CALLS THAT A CATNAP!
ZZZ
WWW.COMICS.COM
I HATE IT WHEN PEOPLE DESCRIBE THE THINGS THEY DO IN "CAT" TERMS.
1-17
BCPICKLES@AOL.COM
IT'S AN INSULT TO CATS EVERYWHERE.
© 2002 WASHINGTON POST WRITERS GROUP
UGH! THIS HAIR IS A CATASTROPHE!
GRRR!

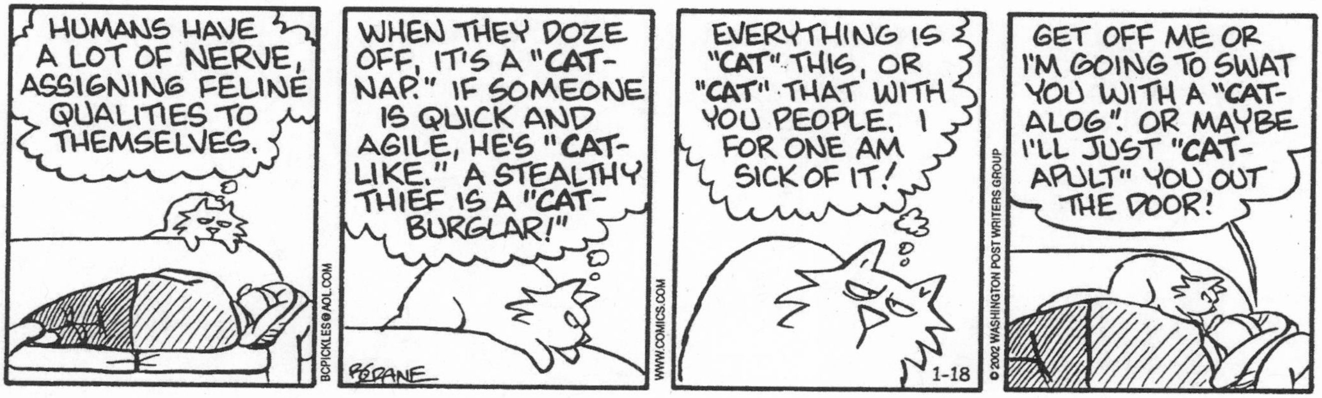
HUMANS HAVE A LOT OF NERVE, ASSIGNING FELINE QUALITIES TO THEMSELVES.
BCPICKLES@AOL.COM
WHEN THEY DOZE OFF, IT'S A "CAT-NAP." IF SOMEONE IS QUICK AND AGILE, HE'S "CAT-LIKE." A STEALTHY THIEF IS A "CAT-BURGLAR!"
WWW.COMICS.COM
EVERYTHING IS "CAT" THIS, OR "CAT" THAT WITH YOU PEOPLE. I FOR ONE AM SICK OF IT!
1-18
© 2002 WASHINGTON POST WRITERS GROUP
GET OFF ME OR I'M GOING TO SWAT YOU WITH A "CAT-ALOG". OR MAYBE I'LL JUST "CAT-APULT" YOU OUT THE DOOR!

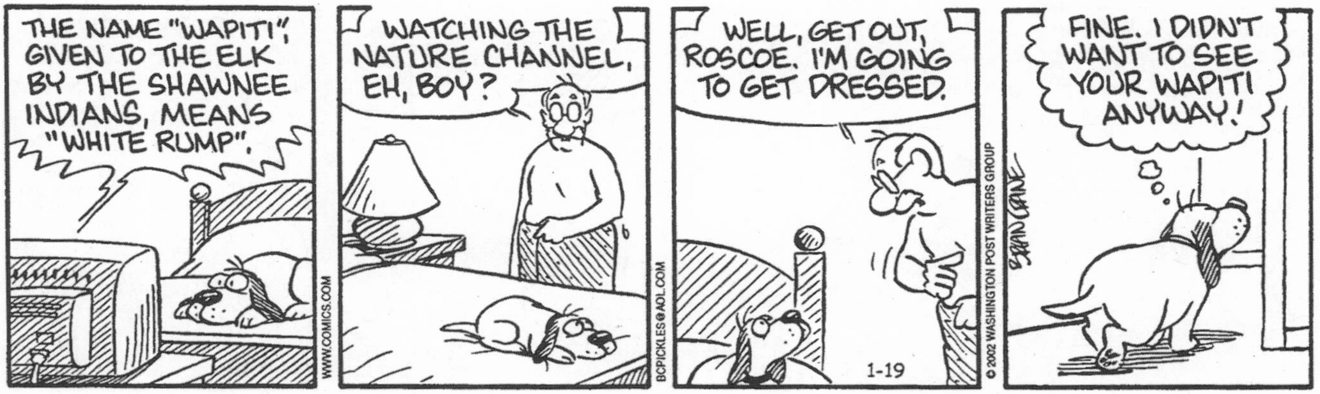
THE NAME "WAPITI", GIVEN TO THE ELK BY THE SHAWNEE INDIANS, MEANS "WHITE RUMP".
WWW.COMICS.COM
WATCHING THE NATURE CHANNEL, EH, BOY?
BCPICKLES@AOL.COM
WELL, GET OUT, ROSCOE. I'M GOING TO GET DRESSED.
1-19
© 2002 WASHINGTON POST WRITERS GROUP
FINE. I DIDN'T WANT TO SEE YOUR WAPITI ANYWAY!

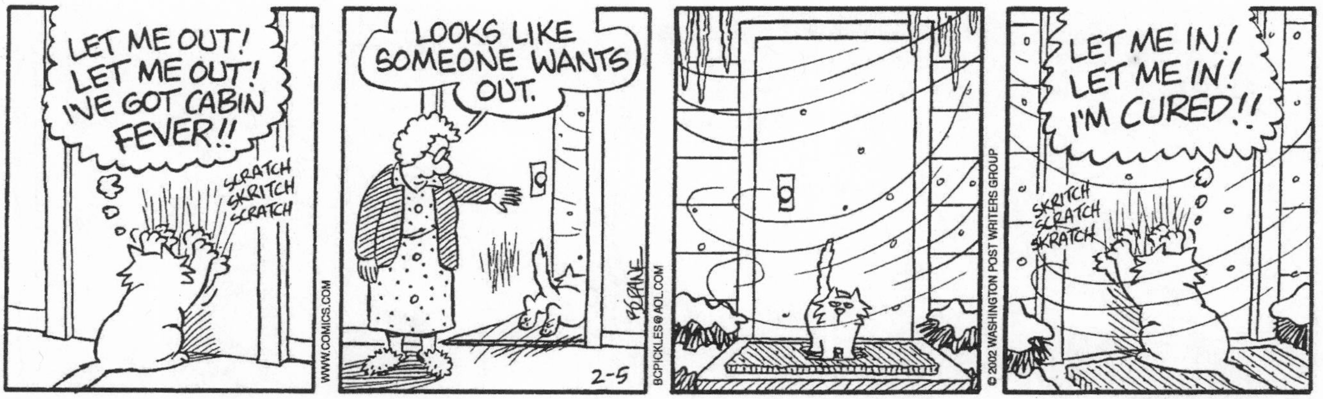
LET ME OUT! LET ME OUT! I'VE GOT CABIN FEVER!!
SCRATCH SKRITCH SCRATCH
WWW.COMICS.COM
LOOKS LIKE SOMEONE WANTS OUT.
2-5
BCPICKLES@AOL.COM
© 2002 WASHINGTON POST WRITERS GROUP
LET ME IN! LET ME IN! I'M CURED!!
SKRITCH SCRATCH SKRATCH

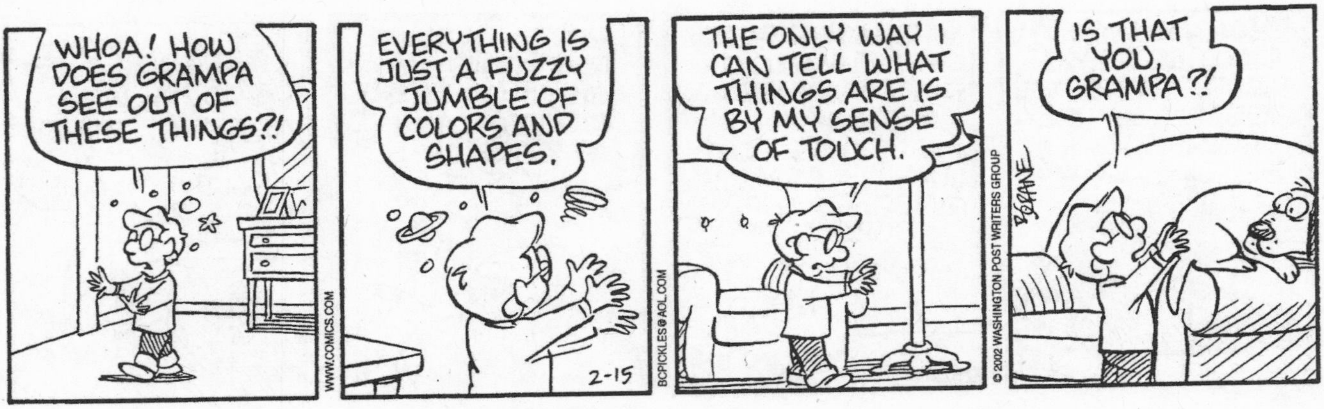
WHOA! HOW DOES GRAMPA SEE OUT OF THESE THINGS?!
WWW.COMICS.COM
EVERYTHING IS JUST A FUZZY JUMBLE OF COLORS AND SHAPES.
2-15
BCPICKLES@AOL.COM
THE ONLY WAY I CAN TELL WHAT THINGS ARE IS BY MY SENSE OF TOUCH.
© 2002 WASHINGTON POST WRITERS GROUP
B.CRANE
IS THAT YOU, GRAMPA?!

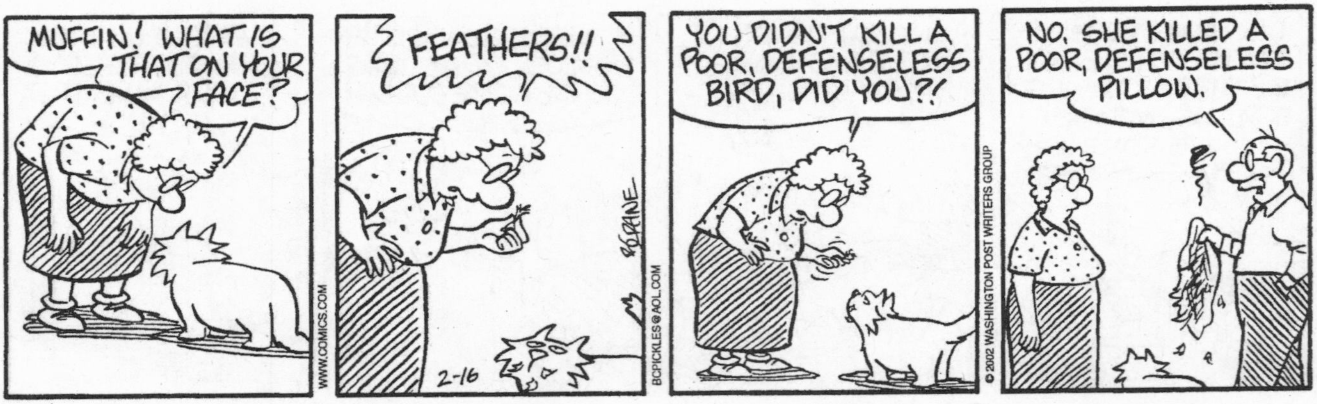
MUFFIN! WHAT IS THAT ON YOUR FACE?
WWW.COMICS.COM
FEATHERS!!
2-16
B.CRANE
BCPICKLES@AOL.COM
YOU DIDN'T KILL A POOR, DEFENSELESS BIRD, DID YOU?!
© 2002 WASHINGTON POST WRITERS GROUP
NO, SHE KILLED A POOR, DEFENSELESS PILLOW.

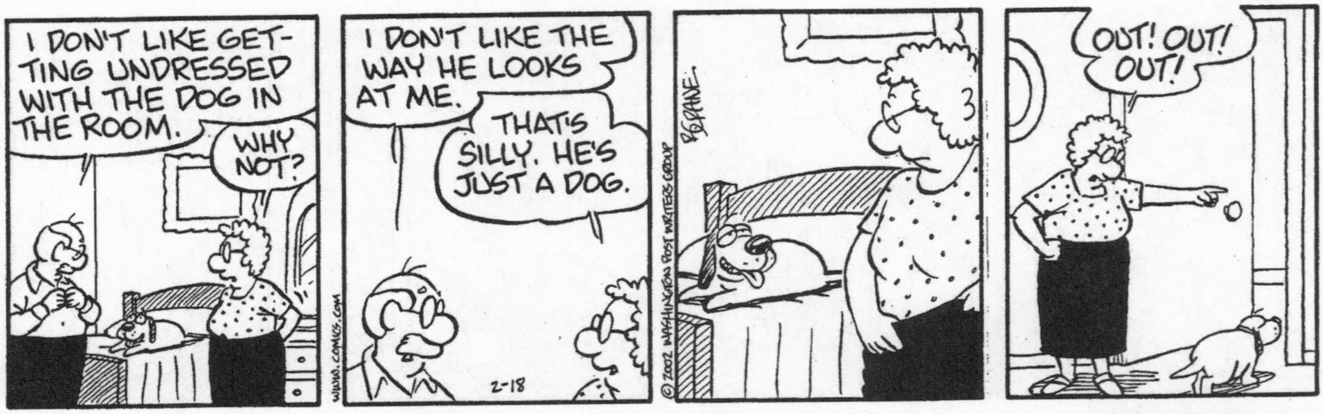
I DON'T LIKE GETTING UNDRESSED WITH THE DOG IN THE ROOM.
WHY NOT?
WWW.COMICS.COM
I DON'T LIKE THE WAY HE LOOKS AT ME.
THAT'S SILLY. HE'S JUST A DOG.
2-18
B.CRANE
© 2002 WASHINGTON POST WRITERS GROUP
OUT! OUT! OUT!

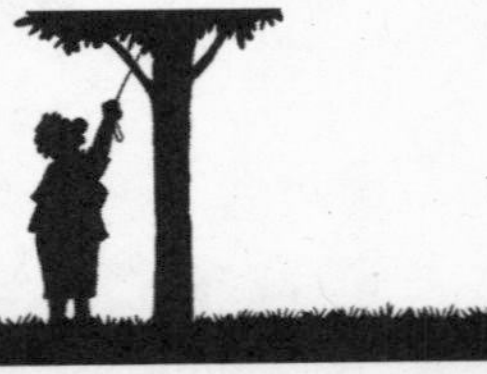

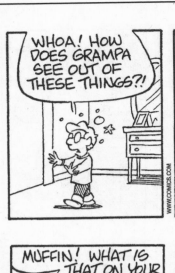

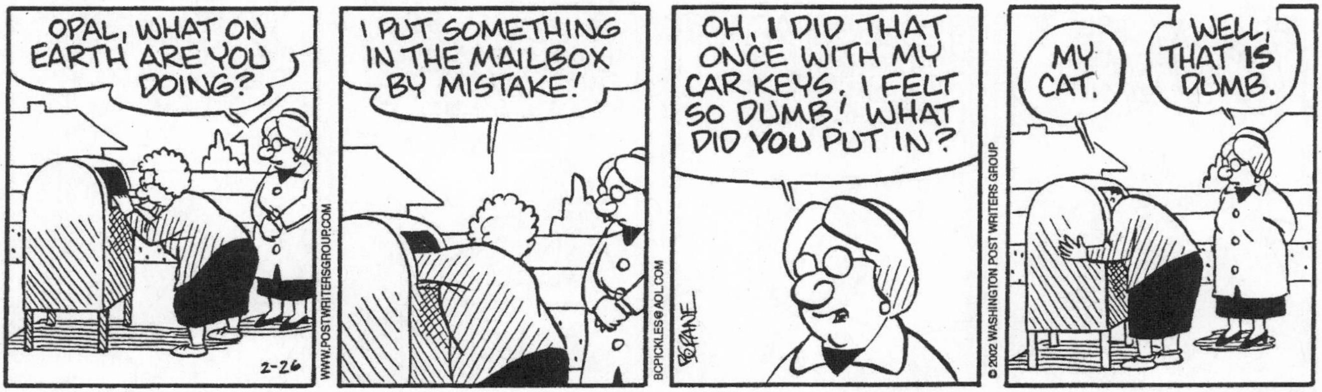
OPAL, WHAT ON EARTH ARE YOU DOING?
2-26
WWW.POSTWRITERSGROUP.COM
I PUT SOMETHING IN THE MAILBOX BY MISTAKE!
BCPICKLES@AOL.COM
OH, I DID THAT ONCE WITH MY CAR KEYS. I FELT SO DUMB! WHAT DID YOU PUT IN?
B.C.PARKER
© 2002 WASHINGTON POST WRITERS GROUP
MY CAT.
WELL, THAT IS DUMB.

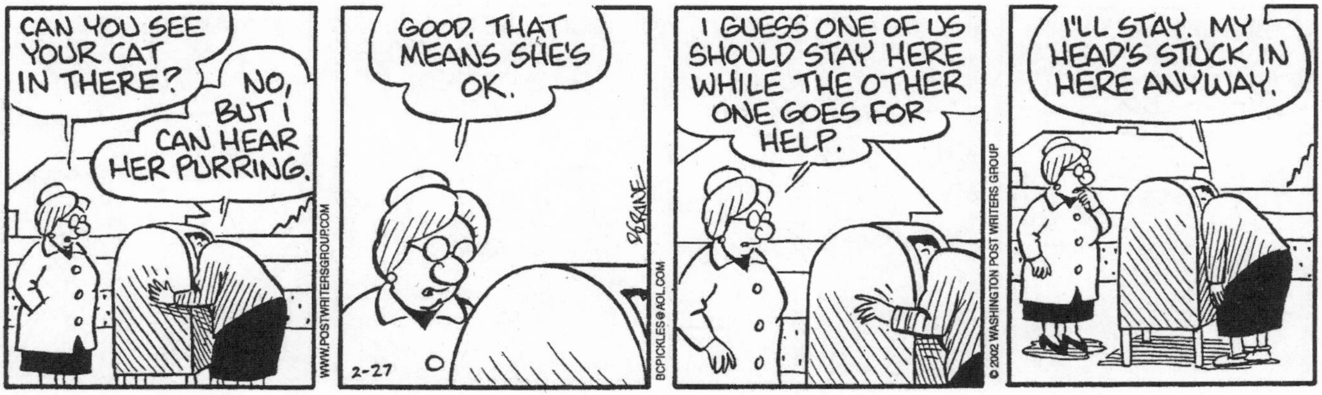
CAN YOU SEE YOUR CAT IN THERE?
NO, BUT I CAN HEAR HER PURRING.
WWW.POSTWRITERSGROUP.COM
GOOD. THAT MEANS SHE'S OK.
2-27
BCPICKLES@AOL.COM
I GUESS ONE OF US SHOULD STAY HERE WHILE THE OTHER ONE GOES FOR HELP.
© 2002 WASHINGTON POST WRITERS GROUP
I'LL STAY. MY HEAD'S STUCK IN HERE ANYWAY.

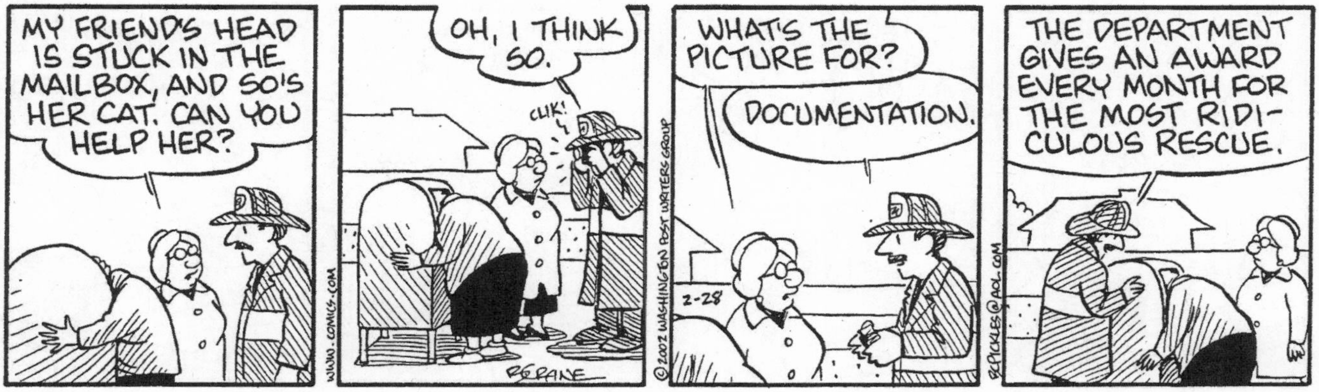
MY FRIEND'S HEAD IS STUCK IN THE MAILBOX, AND SO'S HER CAT. CAN YOU HELP HER?
WWW.COMICS.COM
OH, I THINK SO.
CLIK!
© 2002 WASHINGTON POST WRITERS GROUP
WHAT'S THE PICTURE FOR?
DOCUMENTATION.
2-28
BCPICKLES@AOL.COM
THE DEPARTMENT GIVES AN AWARD EVERY MONTH FOR THE MOST RIDI-CULOUS RESCUE.

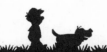

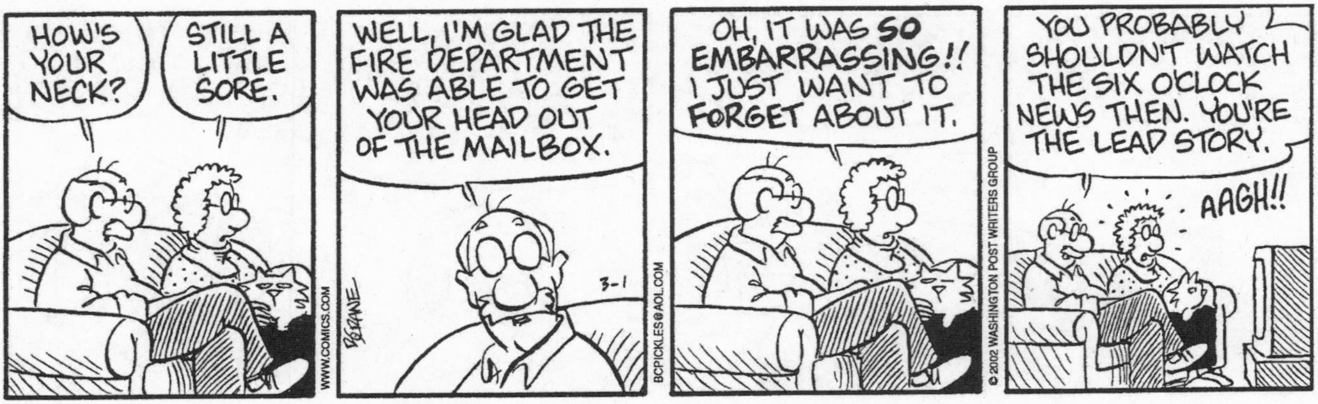
HOW'S YOUR NECK?
STILL A LITTLE SORE.
WWW.COMICS.COM
WELL, I'M GLAD THE FIRE DEPARTMENT WAS ABLE TO GET YOUR HEAD OUT OF THE MAILBOX.
3-1
BCPICKLES@AOL.COM
OH, IT WAS **SO EMBARRASSING!!** I JUST WANT TO **FORGET** ABOUT IT.
© 2002 WASHINGTON POST WRITERS GROUP
YOU PROBABLY SHOULDN'T WATCH THE SIX O'CLOCK NEWS THEN. YOU'RE THE LEAD STORY.
AAGH!!

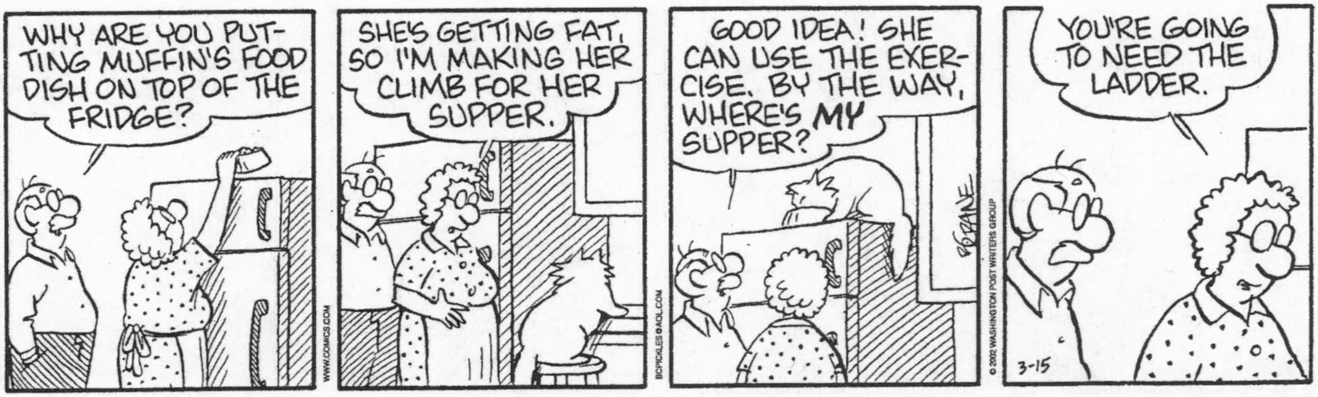
WHY ARE YOU PUTTING MUFFIN'S FOOD DISH ON TOP OF THE FRIDGE?
WWW.COMICS.COM
SHE'S GETTING FAT, SO I'M MAKING HER CLIMB FOR HER SUPPER.
BCPICKLES@AOL.COM
GOOD IDEA! SHE CAN USE THE EXERCISE. BY THE WAY, WHERE'S **MY** SUPPER?
© 2002 WASHINGTON POST WRITERS GROUP
YOU'RE GOING TO NEED THE LADDER.
3-15

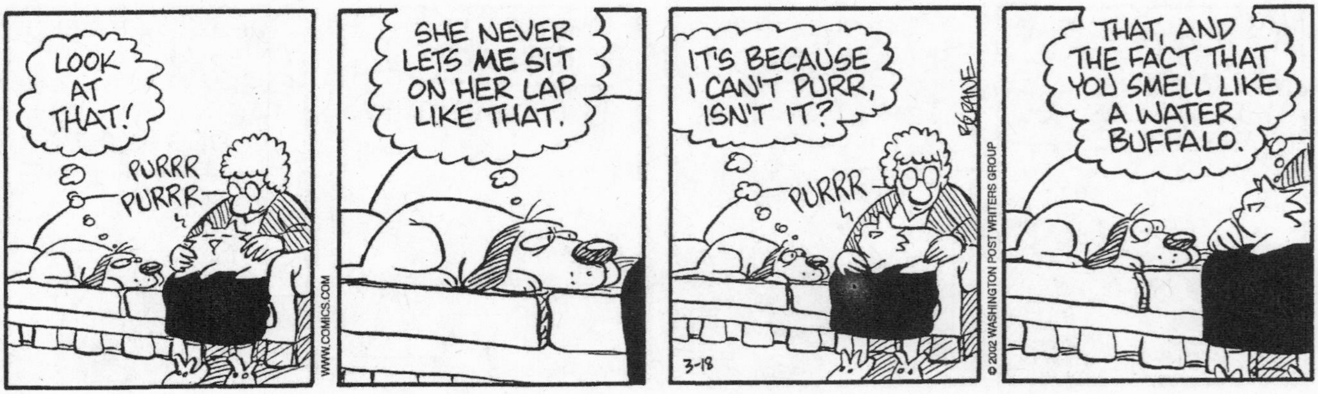
LOOK AT THAT!
PURRR PURRR
WWW.COMICS.COM
SHE NEVER LETS **ME** SIT ON HER LAP LIKE THAT.
IT'S BECAUSE I CAN'T PURR, ISN'T IT?
PURRR
3-18
© 2002 WASHINGTON POST WRITERS GROUP
THAT, AND THE FACT THAT YOU SMELL LIKE A WATER BUFFALO.

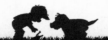

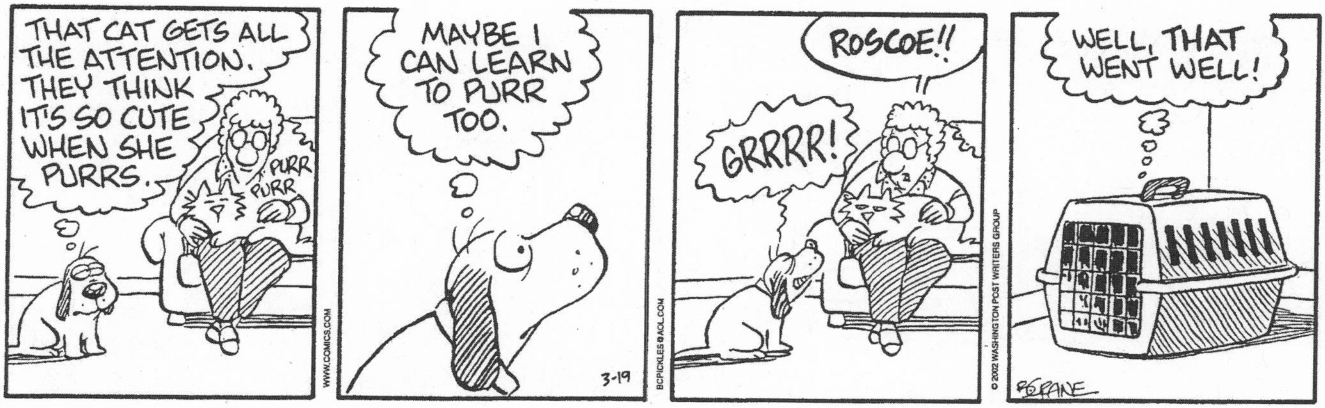
THAT CAT GETS ALL THE ATTENTION. THEY THINK IT'S SO CUTE WHEN SHE PURRS.
PURR PURR
WWW.COMICS.COM
MAYBE I CAN LEARN TO PURR TOO.
3-19
BCPICKLES@AOL.COM
ROSCOE!!
GRRRR!
© 2002 WASHINGTON POST WRITERS GROUP
WELL, THAT WENT WELL!

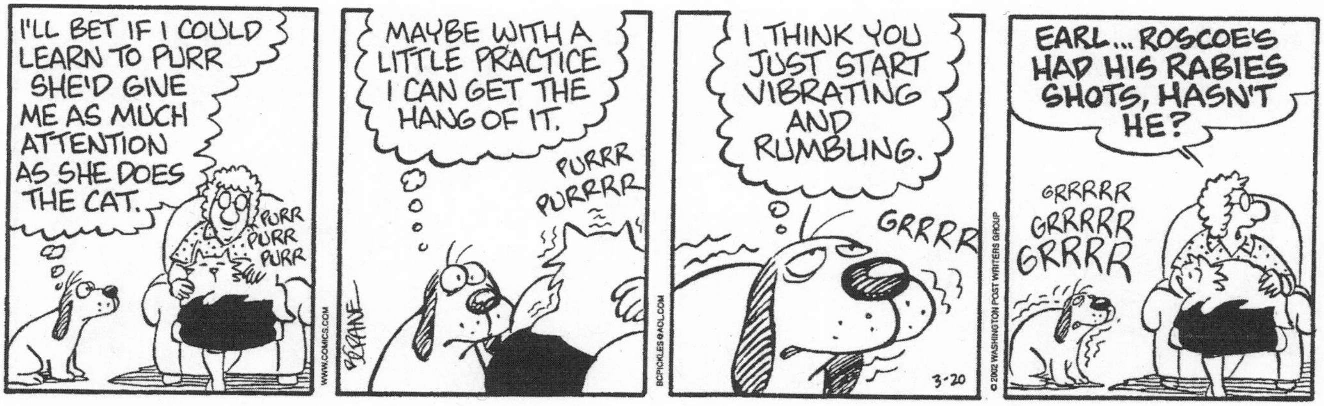
I'LL BET IF I COULD LEARN TO PURR SHE'D GIVE ME AS MUCH ATTENTION AS SHE DOES THE CAT.
PURR PURR PURR
WWW.COMICS.COM
MAYBE WITH A LITTLE PRACTICE I CAN GET THE HANG OF IT.
PURRR PURRRR
BCPICKLES@AOL.COM
I THINK YOU JUST START VIBRATING AND RUMBLING.
GRRRR
3-20
© 2002 WASHINGTON POST WRITERS GROUP
EARL... ROSCOE'S HAD HIS RABIES SHOTS, HASN'T HE?
GRRRRR GRRRRR GRRRR

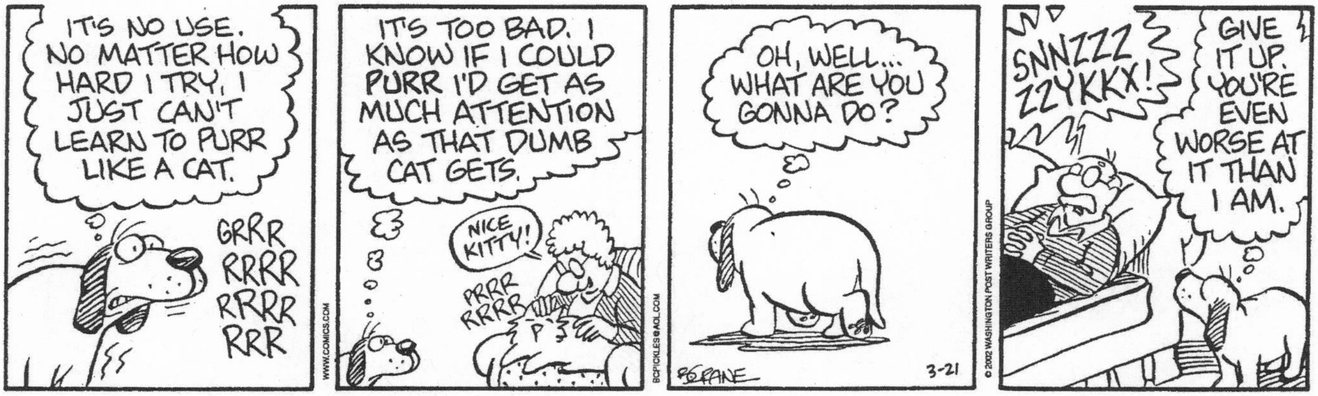
IT'S NO USE. NO MATTER HOW HARD I TRY, I JUST CAN'T LEARN TO PURR LIKE A CAT.
GRRR RRRR RRRR RRR
WWW.COMICS.COM
IT'S TOO BAD. I KNOW IF I COULD PURR I'D GET AS MUCH ATTENTION AS THAT DUMB CAT GETS.
NICE KITTY!
PRRR RRRR
BCPICKLES@AOL.COM
OH, WELL... WHAT ARE YOU GONNA DO?
3-21
© 2002 WASHINGTON POST WRITERS GROUP
SNNZZZ ZZYKKX!
GIVE IT UP. YOU'RE EVEN WORSE AT IT THAN I AM.

215

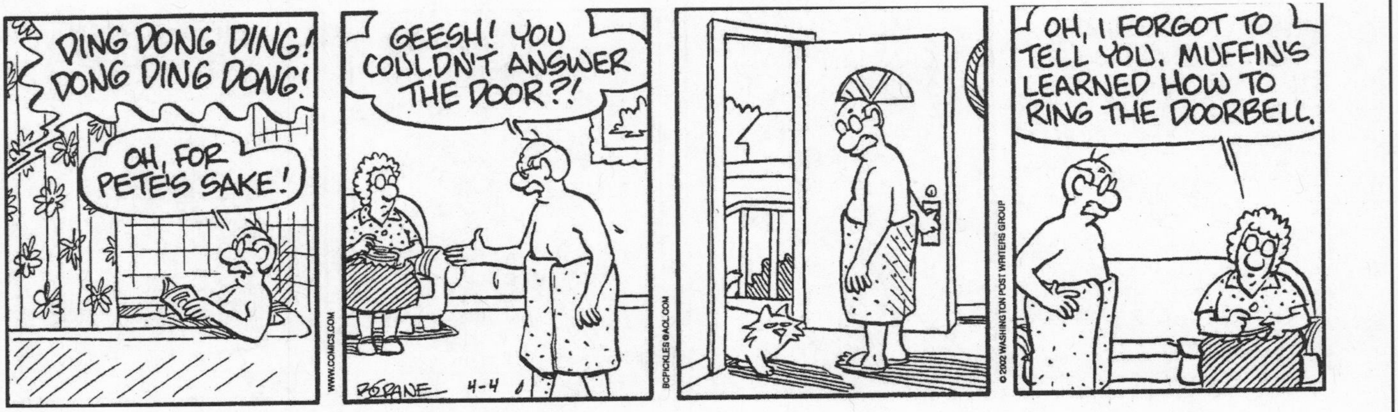
DING DONG DING! DONG DING DONG!
OH, FOR PETE'S SAKE!
GEESH! YOU COULDN'T ANSWER THE DOOR?!
BCRANE 4-4
WWW.COMICS.COM
BCPICKLES@AOL.COM
© 2002 WASHINGTON POST WRITERS GROUP
OH, I FORGOT TO TELL YOU. MUFFIN'S LEARNED HOW TO RING THE DOORBELL.

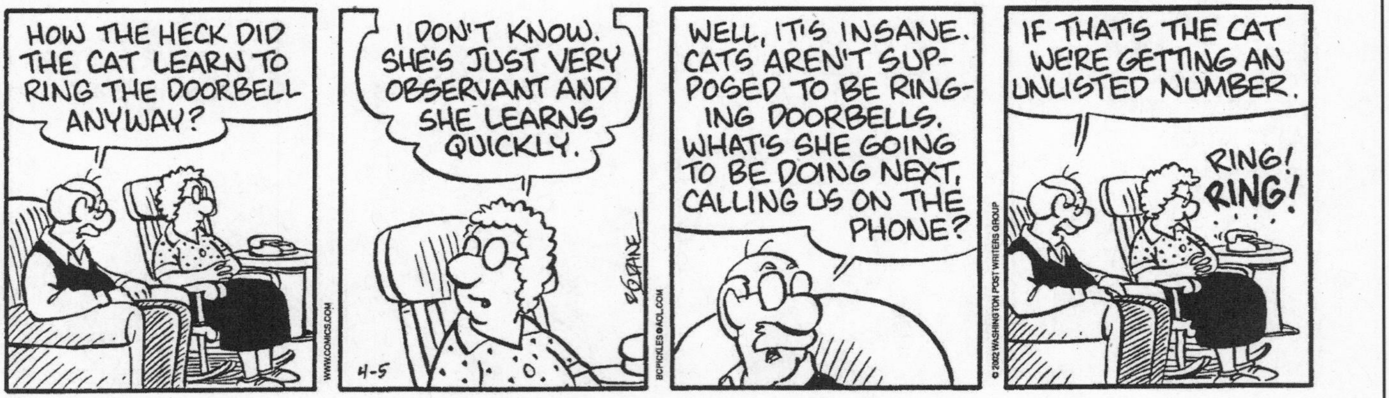
HOW THE HECK DID THE CAT LEARN TO RING THE DOORBELL ANYWAY?
I DON'T KNOW. SHE'S JUST VERY OBSERVANT AND SHE LEARNS QUICKLY.
4-5
BCRANE
WWW.COMICS.COM
BCPICKLES@AOL.COM
WELL, IT'S INSANE. CATS AREN'T SUPPOSED TO BE RINGING DOORBELLS. WHAT'S SHE GOING TO BE DOING NEXT, CALLING US ON THE PHONE?
© 2002 WASHINGTON POST WRITERS GROUP
IF THAT'S THE CAT WE'RE GETTING AN UNLISTED NUMBER.
RING! RING!

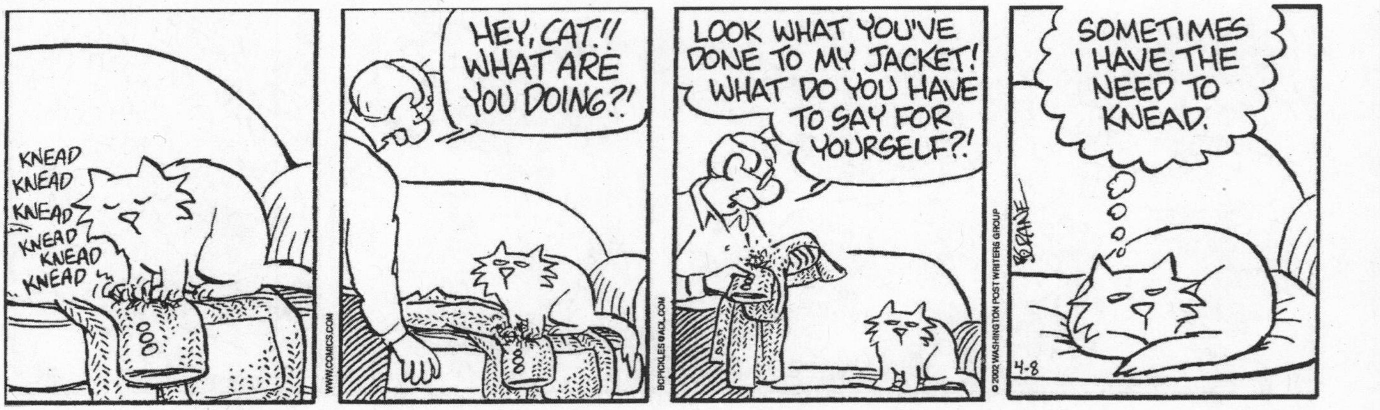
KNEAD KNEAD KNEAD KNEAD KNEAD KNEAD
WWW.COMICS.COM
HEY, CAT!! WHAT ARE YOU DOING?!
BCPICKLES@AOL.COM
LOOK WHAT YOU'VE DONE TO MY JACKET! WHAT DO YOU HAVE TO SAY FOR YOURSELF?!
© 2002 WASHINGTON POST WRITERS GROUP
BCRANE
4-8
SOMETIMES I HAVE THE NEED TO KNEAD.

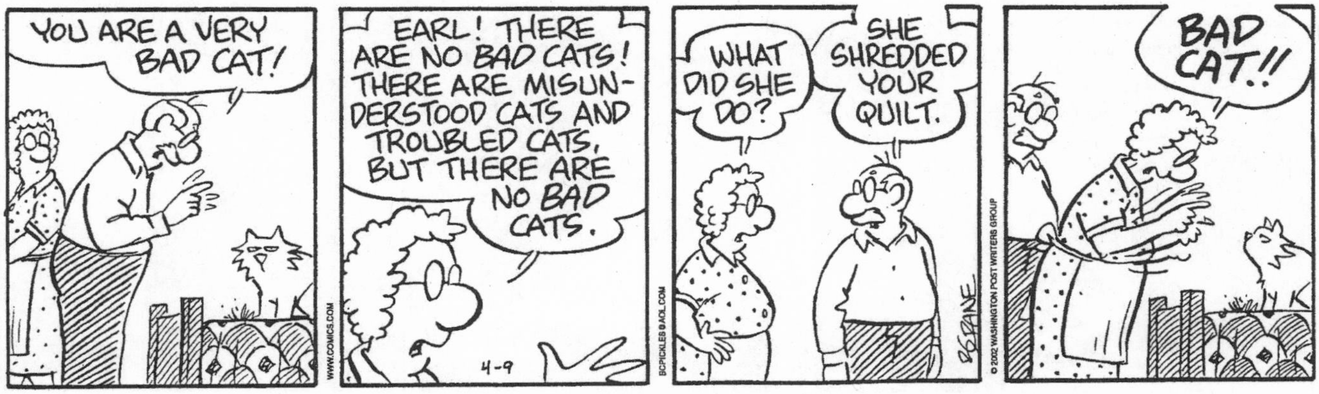
YOU ARE A VERY BAD CAT!
EARL! THERE ARE NO BAD CATS! THERE ARE MISUNDERSTOOD CATS AND TROUBLED CATS, BUT THERE ARE NO BAD CATS.
WHAT DID SHE DO?
SHE SHREDDED YOUR QUILT.
BAD CAT!!
4-9
WWW.COMICS.COM
BCPICKLES@AOL.COM
© 2002 WASHINGTON POST WRITERS GROUP

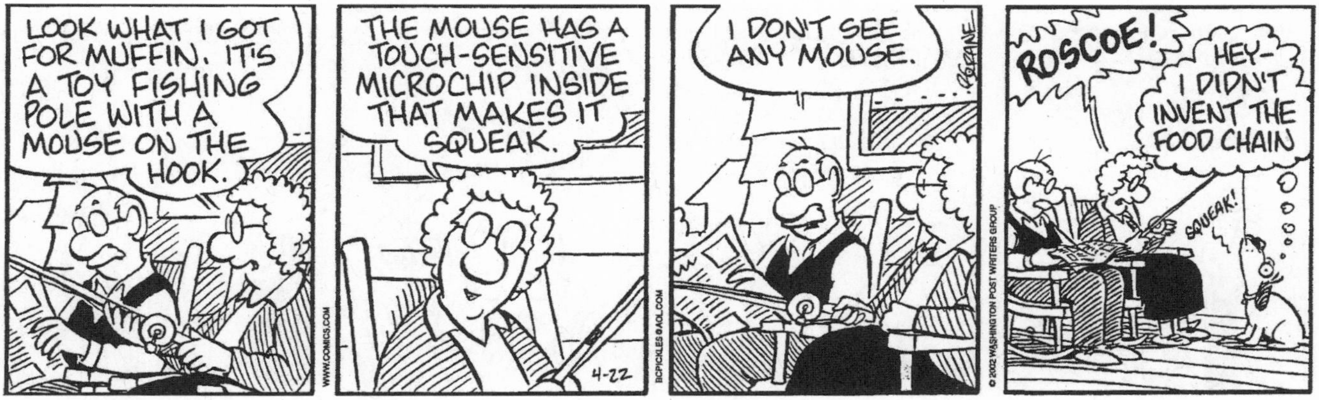
LOOK WHAT I GOT FOR MUFFIN. IT'S A TOY FISHING POLE WITH A MOUSE ON THE HOOK.
THE MOUSE HAS A TOUCH-SENSITIVE MICROCHIP INSIDE THAT MAKES IT SQUEAK.
I DON'T SEE ANY MOUSE.
ROSCOE!
HEY- I DIDN'T INVENT THE FOOD CHAIN
SQUEAK!
4-22
WWW.COMICS.COM
BCPICKLES@AOL.COM
© 2002 WASHINGTON POST WRITERS GROUP

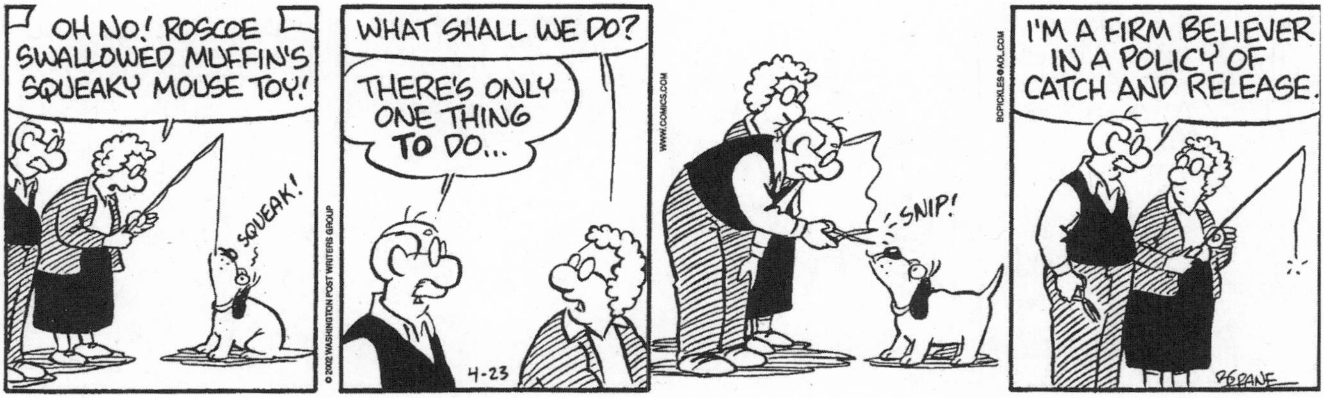
OH NO! ROSCOE SWALLOWED MUFFIN'S SQUEAKY MOUSE TOY!
SQUEAK!
WHAT SHALL WE DO?
THERE'S ONLY ONE THING TO DO...
SNIP!
I'M A FIRM BELIEVER IN A POLICY OF CATCH AND RELEASE.
4-23
WWW.COMICS.COM
BCPICKLES@AOL.COM
© 2002 WASHINGTON POST WRITERS GROUP

218

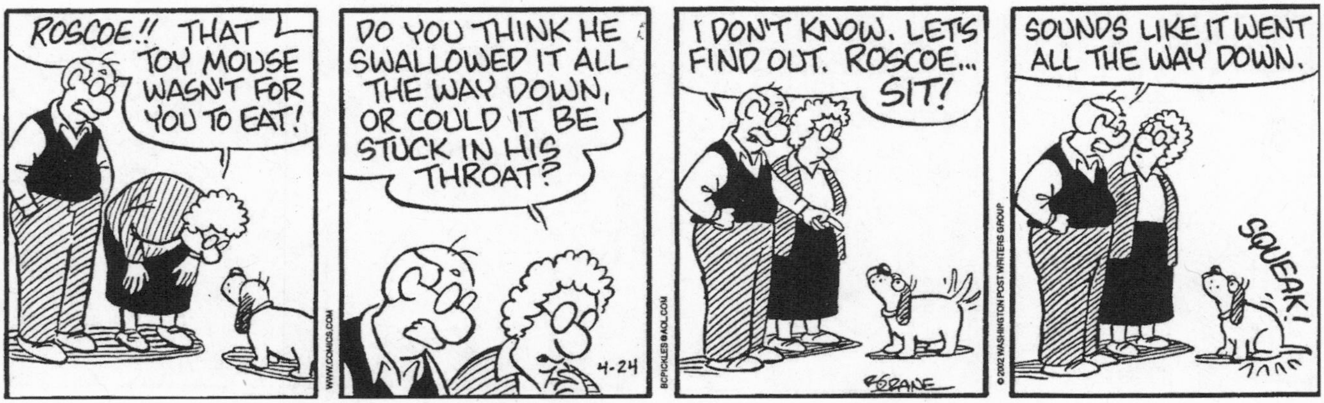
ROSCOE!! THAT TOY MOUSE WASN'T FOR YOU TO EAT!
WWW.COMICS.COM
DO YOU THINK HE SWALLOWED IT ALL THE WAY DOWN, OR COULD IT BE STUCK IN HIS THROAT?
4-24
BCPICKLES@AOL.COM
I DON'T KNOW. LET'S FIND OUT. ROSCOE... SIT!
© 2002 WASHINGTON POST WRITERS GROUP
SOUNDS LIKE IT WENT ALL THE WAY DOWN.
SQUEAK!

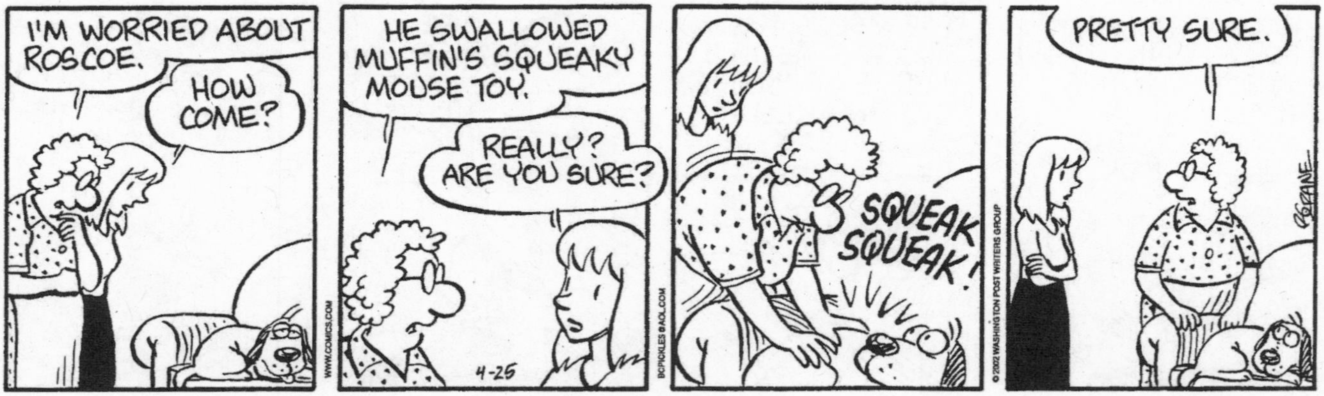
I'M WORRIED ABOUT ROSCOE.
HOW COME?
WWW.COMICS.COM
HE SWALLOWED MUFFIN'S SQUEAKY MOUSE TOY.
REALLY? ARE YOU SURE?
4-25
BCPICKLES@AOL.COM
SQUEAK SQUEAK!
© 2002 WASHINGTON POST WRITERS GROUP
PRETTY SURE.

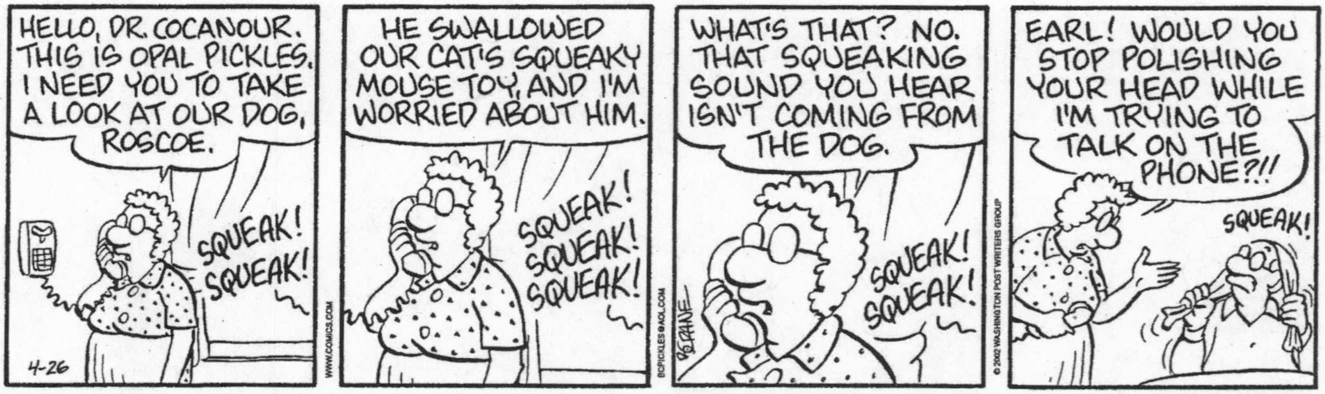
HELLO, DR. COCANOUR. THIS IS OPAL PICKLES. I NEED YOU TO TAKE A LOOK AT OUR DOG, ROSCOE.
SQUEAK! SQUEAK!
4-26
WWW.COMICS.COM
HE SWALLOWED OUR CAT'S SQUEAKY MOUSE TOY, AND I'M WORRIED ABOUT HIM.
SQUEAK! SQUEAK! SQUEAK!
BCPICKLES@AOL.COM
WHAT'S THAT? NO. THAT SQUEAKING SOUND YOU HEAR ISN'T COMING FROM THE DOG.
SQUEAK! SQUEAK!
© 2002 WASHINGTON POST WRITERS GROUP
EARL! WOULD YOU STOP POLISHING YOUR HEAD WHILE I'M TRYING TO TALK ON THE PHONE?!!
SQUEAK!

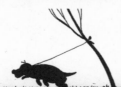

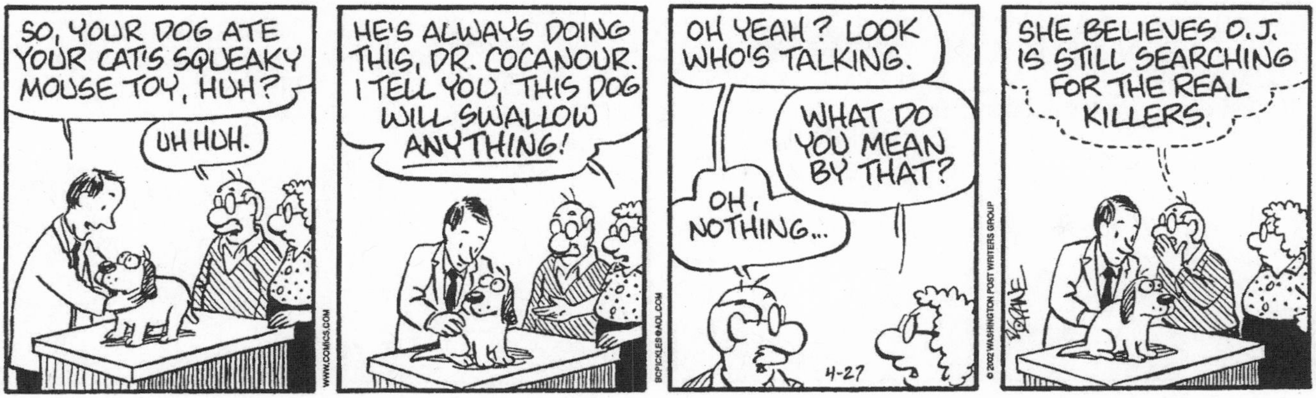
SO, YOUR DOG ATE YOUR CAT'S SQUEAKY MOUSE TOY, HUH?
UH HUH.
HE'S ALWAYS DOING THIS, DR. COCANOUR. I TELL YOU, THIS DOG WILL SWALLOW ANYTHING!
OH YEAH? LOOK WHO'S TALKING.
WHAT DO YOU MEAN BY THAT?
OH, NOTHING...
SHE BELIEVES O.J. IS STILL SEARCHING FOR THE REAL KILLERS.
WWW.COMICS.COM
BCPICKLES@AOL.COM
4-27
© 2002 WASHINGTON POST WRITERS GROUP

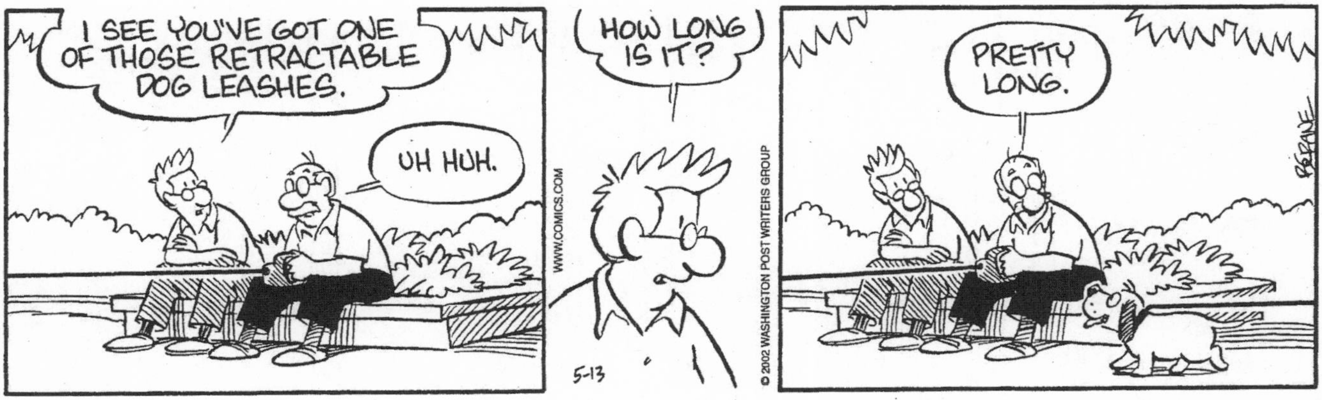
I SEE YOU'VE GOT ONE OF THOSE RETRACTABLE DOG LEASHES.
UH HUH.
HOW LONG IS IT?
PRETTY LONG.
WWW.COMICS.COM
5-13
© 2002 WASHINGTON POST WRITERS GROUP

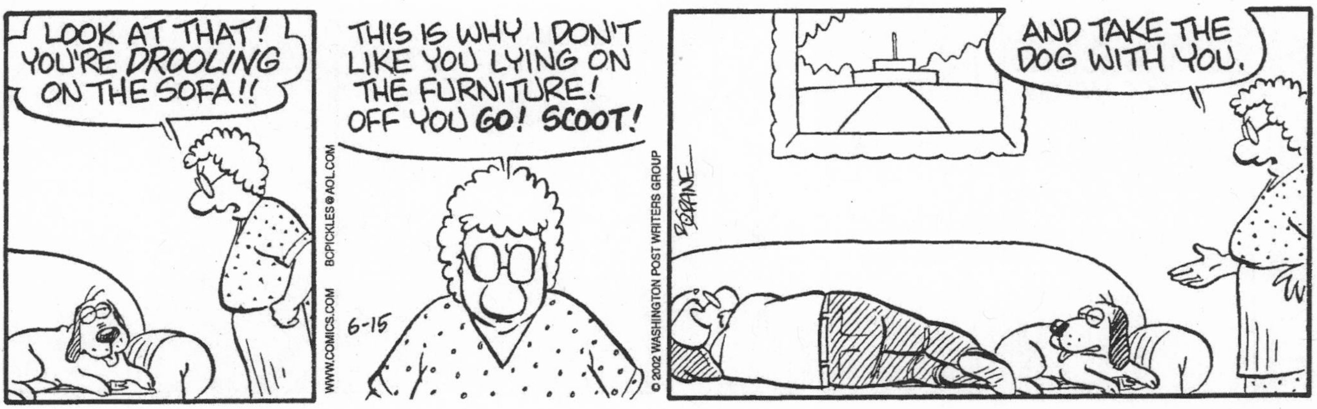
LOOK AT THAT! YOU'RE DROOLING ON THE SOFA!!
THIS IS WHY I DON'T LIKE YOU LYING ON THE FURNITURE! OFF YOU GO! SCOOT!
AND TAKE THE DOG WITH YOU.
WWW.COMICS.COM
BCPICKLES@AOL.COM
6-15
© 2002 WASHINGTON POST WRITERS GROUP

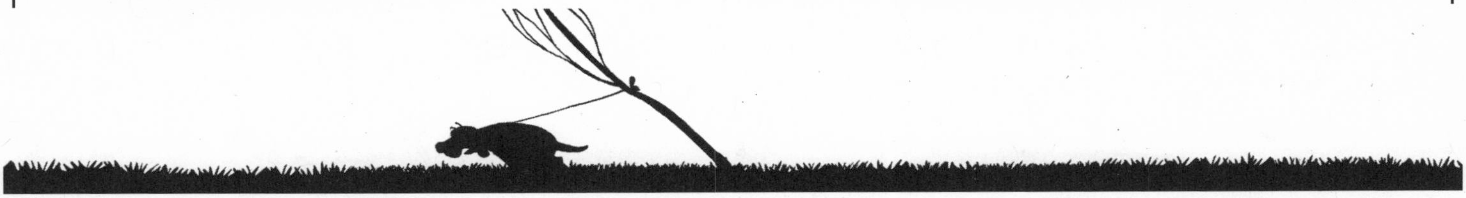

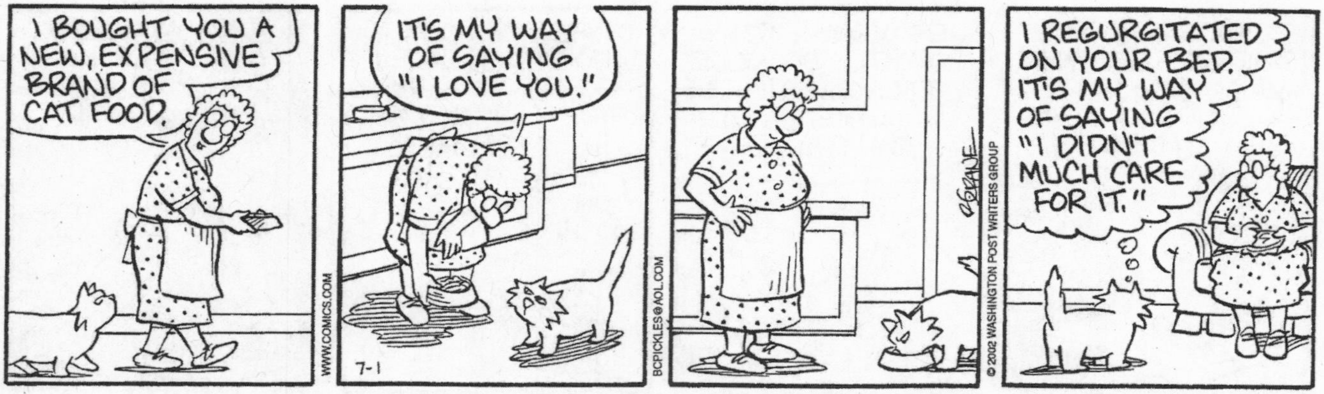
I BOUGHT YOU A NEW, EXPENSIVE BRAND OF CAT FOOD.
IT'S MY WAY OF SAYING "I LOVE YOU."
I REGURGITATED ON YOUR BED. IT'S MY WAY OF SAYING "I DIDN'T MUCH CARE FOR IT."
WWW.COMICS.COM
7-1
BCPICKLES@AOL.COM
© 2002 WASHINGTON POST WRITERS GROUP

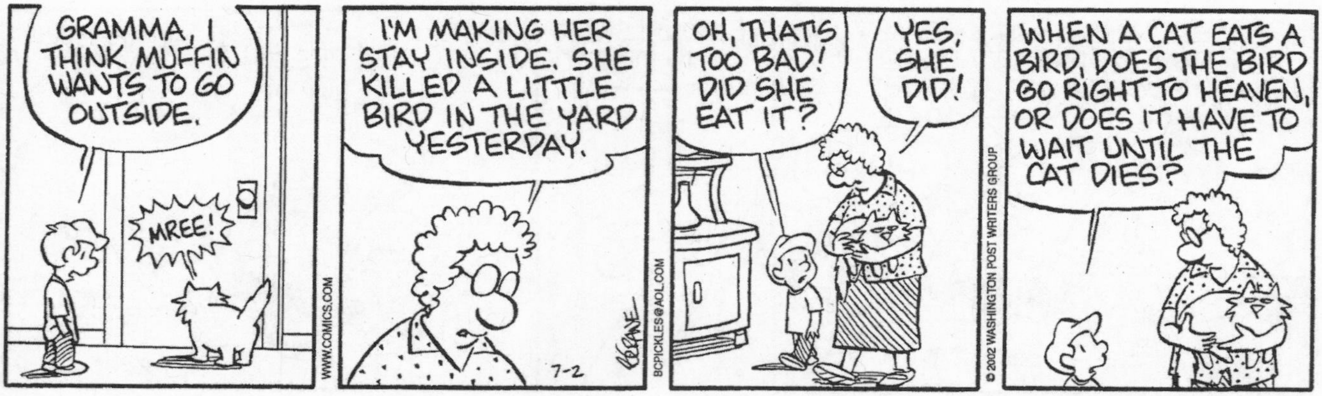
GRAMMA, I THINK MUFFIN WANTS TO GO OUTSIDE.
MREE!
I'M MAKING HER STAY INSIDE. SHE KILLED A LITTLE BIRD IN THE YARD YESTERDAY.
OH, THAT'S TOO BAD! DID SHE EAT IT?
YES, SHE DID!
WHEN A CAT EATS A BIRD, DOES THE BIRD GO RIGHT TO HEAVEN, OR DOES IT HAVE TO WAIT UNTIL THE CAT DIES?
WWW.COMICS.COM
7-2
BCPICKLES@AOL.COM
© 2002 WASHINGTON POST WRITERS GROUP

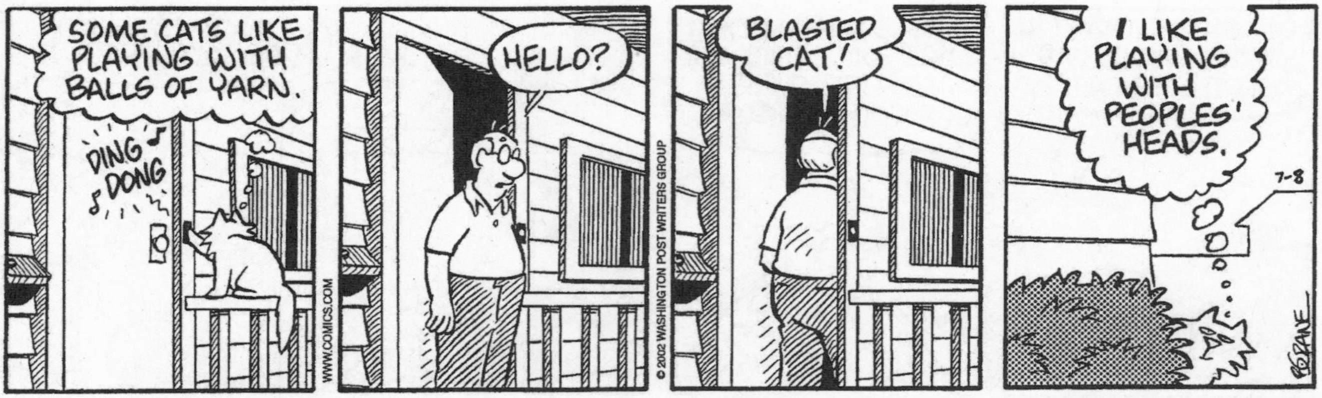
SOME CATS LIKE PLAYING WITH BALLS OF YARN.
DING DONG
HELLO?
BLASTED CAT!
I LIKE PLAYING WITH PEOPLES' HEADS.
7-8
WWW.COMICS.COM
© 2002 WASHINGTON POST WRITERS GROUP

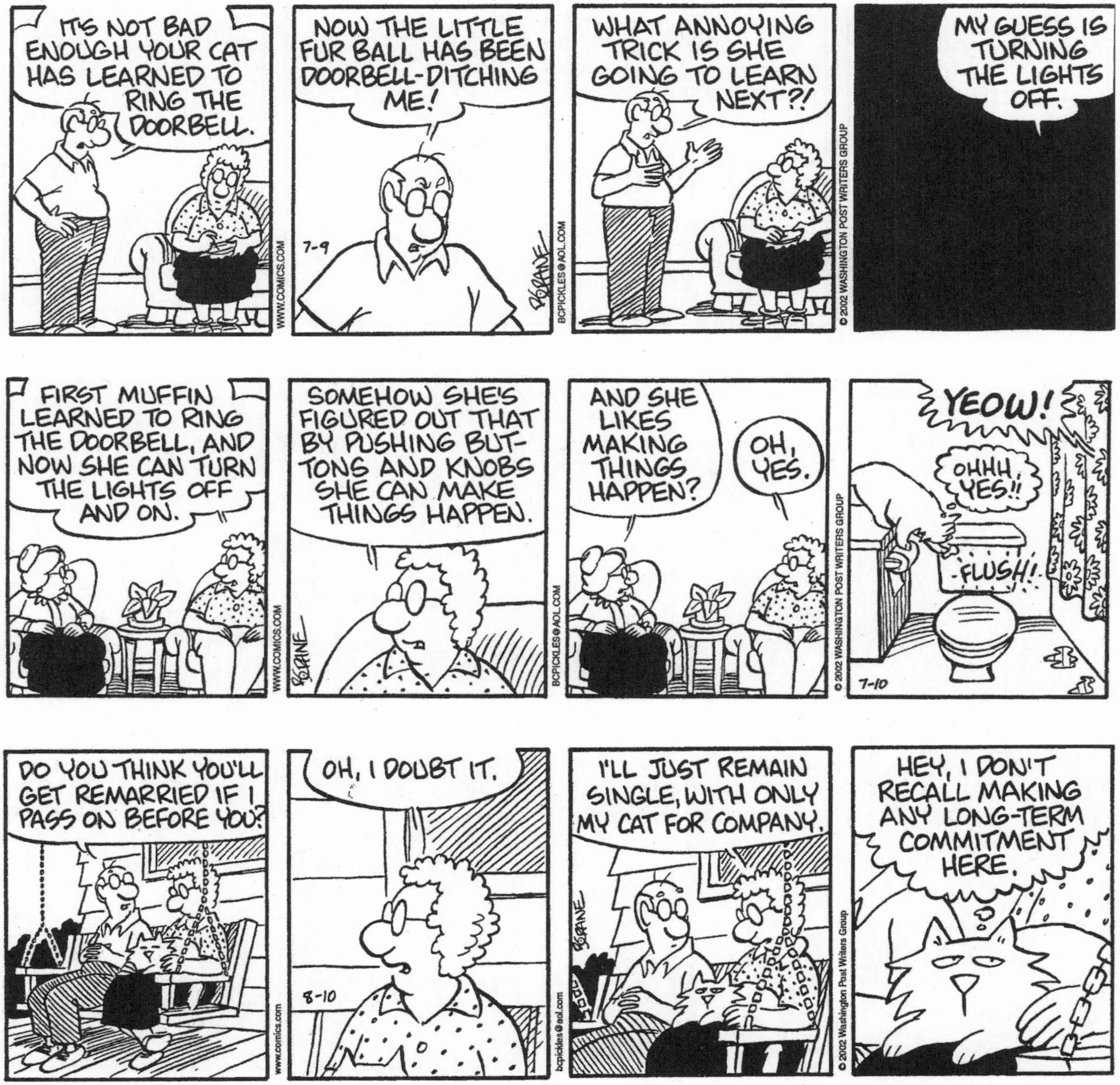
IT'S NOT BAD ENOUGH YOUR CAT HAS LEARNED TO RING THE DOORBELL.
NOW THE LITTLE FUR BALL HAS BEEN DOORBELL-DITCHING ME!
7-9
WHAT ANNOYING TRICK IS SHE GOING TO LEARN NEXT?!
MY GUESS IS TURNING THE LIGHTS OFF.
WWW.COMICS.COM
BCPICKLES@AOL.COM
© 2002 WASHINGTON POST WRITERS GROUP
FIRST MUFFIN LEARNED TO RING THE DOORBELL, AND NOW SHE CAN TURN THE LIGHTS OFF AND ON.
SOMEHOW SHE'S FIGURED OUT THAT BY PUSHING BUTTONS AND KNOBS SHE CAN MAKE THINGS HAPPEN.
AND SHE LIKES MAKING THINGS HAPPEN?
OH, YES.
YEOW!
OHHH, YES!!
FLUSH!
7-10
DO YOU THINK YOU'LL GET REMARRIED IF I PASS ON BEFORE YOU?
OH, I DOUBT IT.
8-10
I'LL JUST REMAIN SINGLE, WITH ONLY MY CAT FOR COMPANY.
HEY, I DON'T RECALL MAKING ANY LONG-TERM COMMITMENT HERE.

I'VE READ THAT SOME DOGS SUFFER FROM SEPARATION ANXIETY.

REALLY?

OH, YES. THEY CAN GET VERY UPSET WHEN THEIR OWNERS LEAVE THEM ALONE.

SOME DOGS REACT TO THE STRESS BY BECOMING DESTRUCTIVE, BARKING CONTINUOUSLY OR MAKING MESSES.

8-13

OTHERS JUST BECOME VERY, VERY CLINGY.

© 2002 Washington Post Writers Group

222

THIS ARTICLE SAYS SOME DOGS WITH SEPARATION ANXIETY BECOME DESTRUCTIVE.

THE STRESS OF BEING ALONE MAKES THEM DIG, CHEW OR SCRATCH AT DOORS.

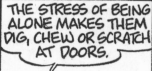

ROSCOE! HOW DID YOU GET OUT?!

PROBABLY OUT OF THAT DOGGIE DOOR.

8-14

WE DON'T HAVE A DOGGIE DOOR THERE.

WE DO NOW.

© 2002 Washington Post Writers Group

SOMETHING HAS TO BE DONE ABOUT ROSCOE'S SEPARATION ANXIETY.

WE CAN'T LET THIS DESTRUCTIVE BEHAVIOR GO ON.

I THINK WE NEED PROFESSIONAL HELP.

YOU MEAN A VETERINARIAN?

8-15

NO. A PET PSYCHIC.

© 2002 Washington Post Writers Group

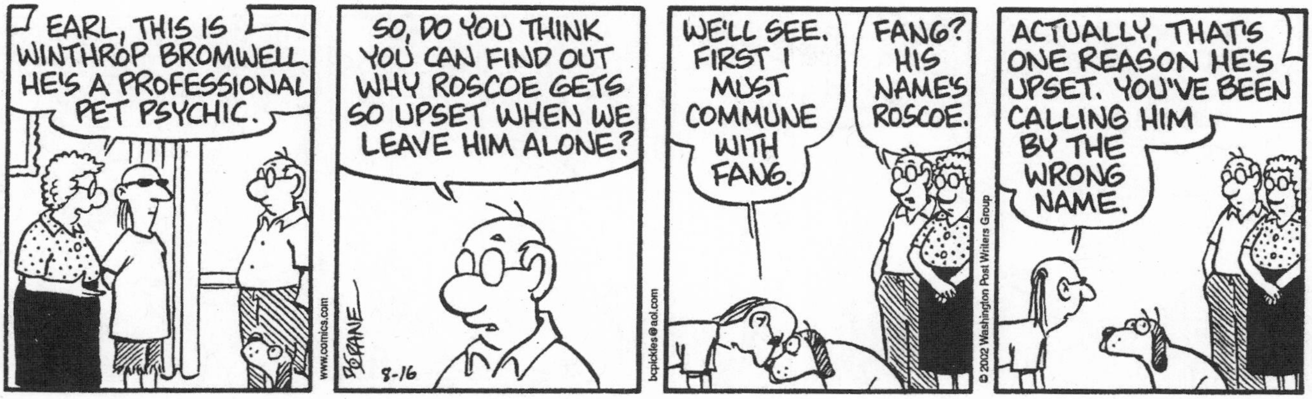
EARL, THIS IS WINTHROP BROMWELL. HE'S A PROFESSIONAL PET PSYCHIC.
www.comics.com
SO, DO YOU THINK YOU CAN FIND OUT WHY ROSCOE GETS SO UPSET WHEN WE LEAVE HIM ALONE?
8-16
bcpickles@aol.com
WE'LL SEE. FIRST I MUST COMMUNE WITH FANG.
FANG? HIS NAME'S ROSCOE.
© 2002 Washington Post Writers Group
ACTUALLY, THAT'S ONE REASON HE'S UPSET. YOU'VE BEEN CALLING HIM BY THE WRONG NAME.

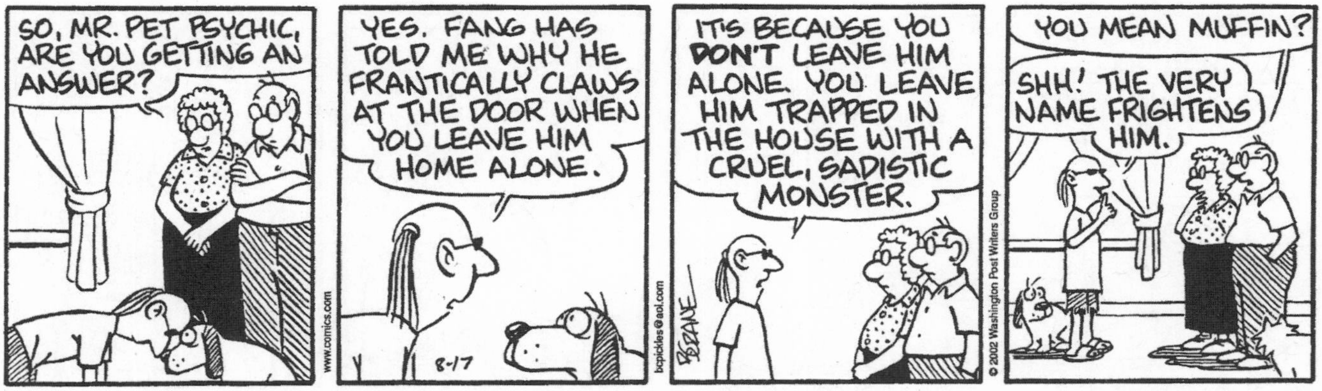
SO, MR. PET PSYCHIC, ARE YOU GETTING AN ANSWER?
www.comics.com
YES. FANG HAS TOLD ME WHY HE FRANTICALLY CLAWS AT THE DOOR WHEN YOU LEAVE HIM HOME ALONE.
8-17
bcpickles@aol.com
IT'S BECAUSE YOU **DON'T** LEAVE HIM ALONE. YOU LEAVE HIM TRAPPED IN THE HOUSE WITH A CRUEL, SADISTIC MONSTER.
© 2002 Washington Post Writers Group
YOU MEAN MUFFIN?
SHH! THE VERY NAME FRIGHTENS HIM.

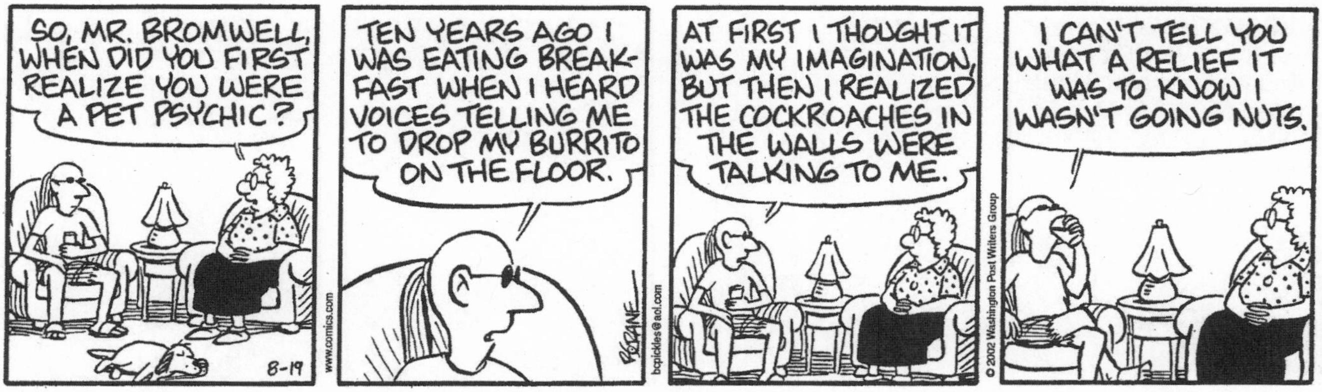
SO, MR. BROMWELL, WHEN DID YOU FIRST REALIZE YOU WERE A PET PSYCHIC?
8-19
www.comics.com
TEN YEARS AGO I WAS EATING BREAKFAST WHEN I HEARD VOICES TELLING ME TO DROP MY BURRITO ON THE FLOOR.
bcpickles@aol.com
AT FIRST I THOUGHT IT WAS MY IMAGINATION, BUT THEN I REALIZED THE COCKROACHES IN THE WALLS WERE TALKING TO ME.
© 2002 Washington Post Writers Group
I CAN'T TELL YOU WHAT A RELIEF IT WAS TO KNOW I WASN'T GOING NUTS.

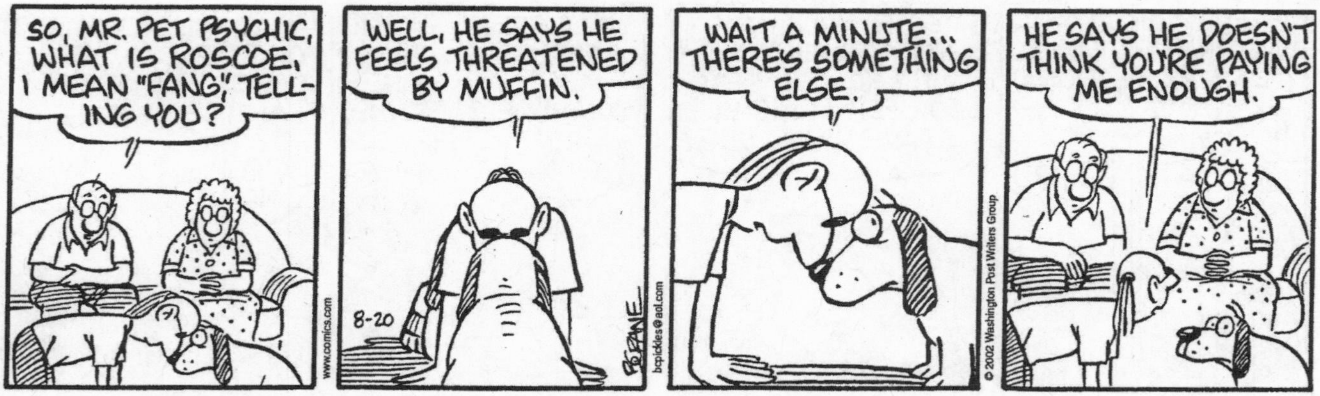
SO, MR. PET PSYCHIC, WHAT IS ROSCOE, I MEAN "FANG," TELLING YOU?
www.comics.com
WELL, HE SAYS HE FEELS THREATENED BY MUFFIN.
8-20
bcpickles@aol.com
WAIT A MINUTE... THERE'S SOMETHING ELSE.
© 2002 Washington Post Writers Group
HE SAYS HE DOESN'T THINK YOU'RE PAYING ME ENOUGH.

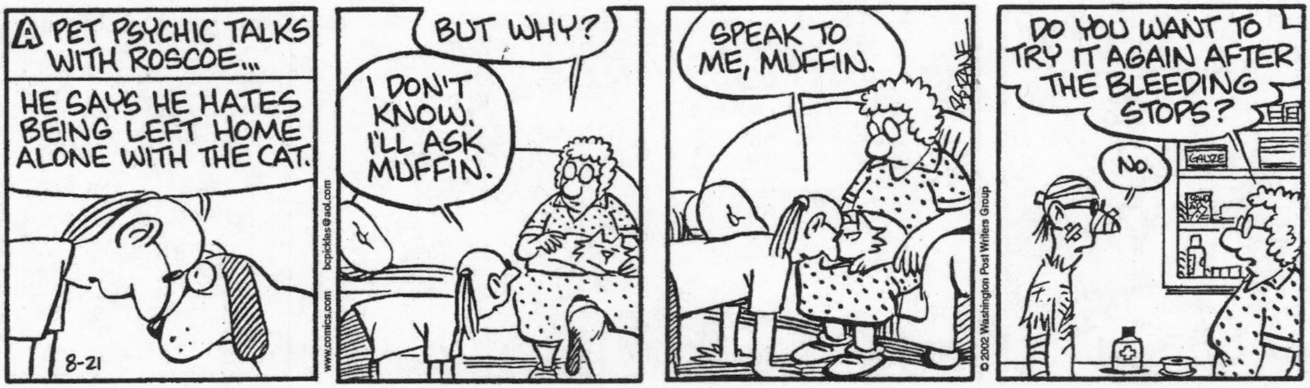
A PET PSYCHIC TALKS WITH ROSCOE...
HE SAYS HE HATES BEING LEFT HOME ALONE WITH THE CAT.
8-21
www.comics.com
bcpickles@aol.com
BUT WHY?
I DON'T KNOW. I'LL ASK MUFFIN.
SPEAK TO ME, MUFFIN.
© 2002 Washington Post Writers Group
DO YOU WANT TO TRY IT AGAIN AFTER THE BLEEDING STOPS?
NO.
GAUZE

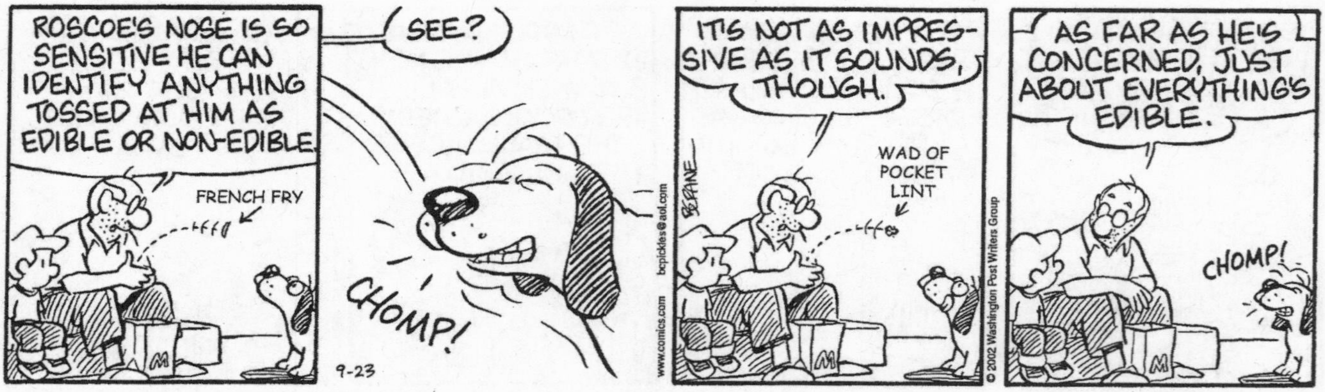
ROSCOE'S NOSE IS SO SENSITIVE HE CAN IDENTIFY ANYTHING TOSSED AT HIM AS EDIBLE OR NON-EDIBLE.
FRENCH FRY
SEE?
CHOMP!
9-23
www.comics.com
bcpickles@aol.com
IT'S NOT AS IMPRESSIVE AS IT SOUNDS, THOUGH.
WAD OF POCKET LINT
© 2002 Washington Post Writers Group
AS FAR AS HE'S CONCERNED, JUST ABOUT EVERYTHING'S EDIBLE.
CHOMP!

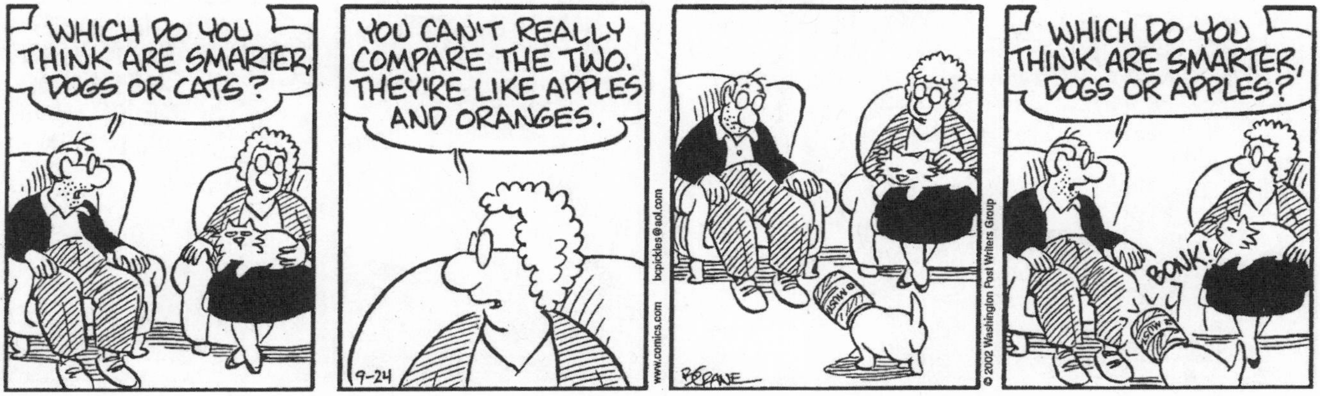
WHICH DO YOU THINK ARE SMARTER, DOGS OR CATS?
YOU CAN'T REALLY COMPARE THE TWO. THEY'RE LIKE APPLES AND ORANGES.
9-24
www.comics.com
bcpickles@aol.com
WHICH DO YOU THINK ARE SMARTER, DOGS OR APPLES?
BONK!
© 2002 Washington Post Writers Group

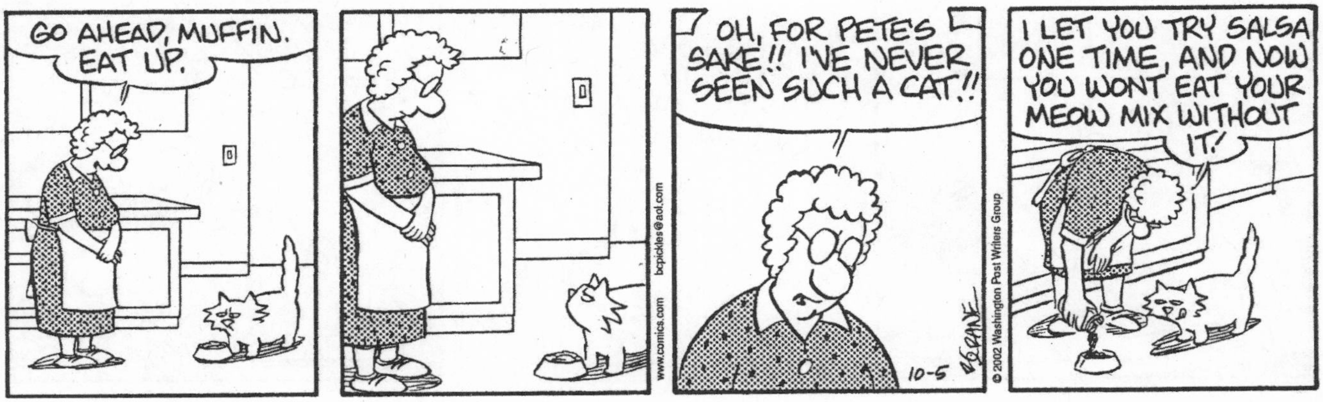
GO AHEAD, MUFFIN. EAT UP.
www.comics.com
bcpickles@aol.com
OH, FOR PETE'S SAKE!! I'VE NEVER SEEN SUCH A CAT!!
10-5
I LET YOU TRY SALSA ONE TIME, AND NOW YOU WONT EAT YOUR MEOW MIX WITHOUT IT!
© 2002 Washington Post Writers Group

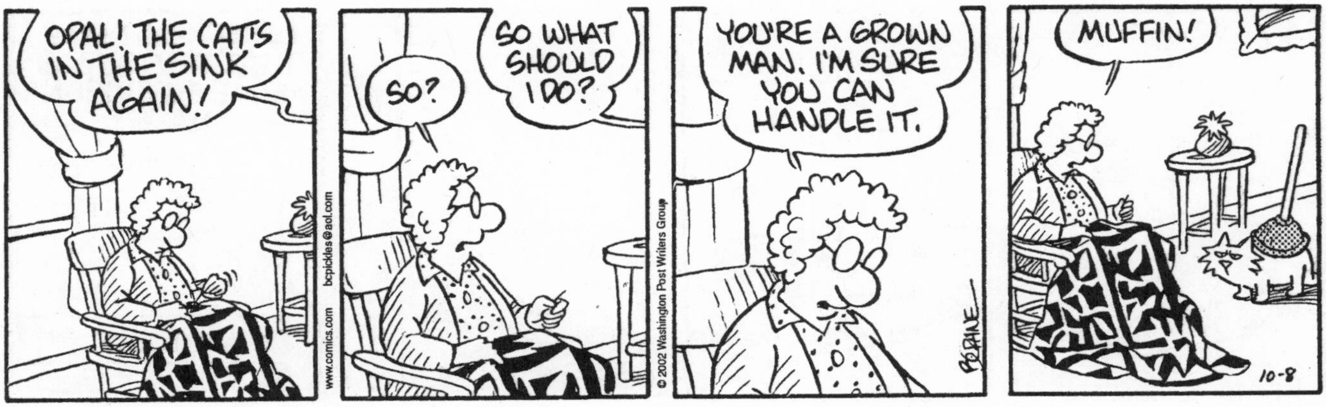
OPAL! THE CAT'S IN THE SINK AGAIN!
www.comics.com
bcpickles@aol.com
SO?
SO WHAT SHOULD I DO?
© 2002 Washington Post Writers Group
YOU'RE A GROWN MAN. I'M SURE YOU CAN HANDLE IT.
MUFFIN!
10-8

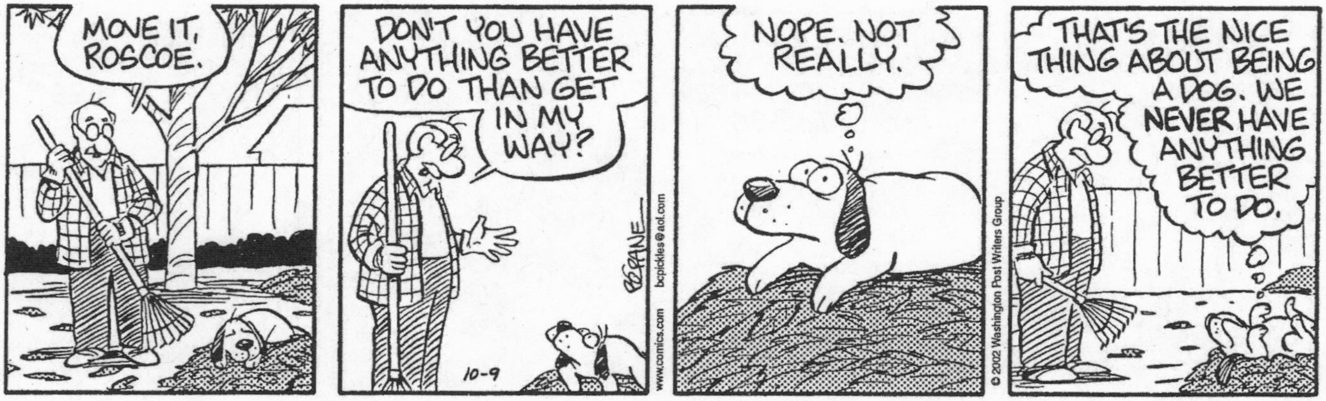
MOVE IT, ROSCOE.
DON'T YOU HAVE ANYTHING BETTER TO DO THAN GET IN MY WAY?
10-9
B.CRANE
www.comics.com bcpickles@aol.com
NOPE. NOT REALLY.
THAT'S THE NICE THING ABOUT BEING A DOG. WE NEVER HAVE ANYTHING BETTER TO DO.
© 2002 Washington Post Writers Group

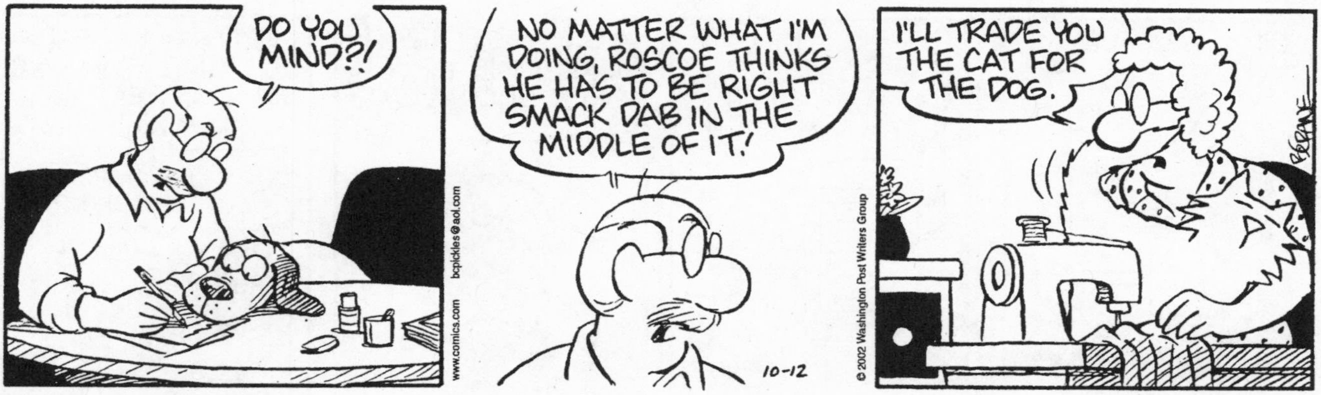
DO YOU MIND?!
www.comics.com bcpickles@aol.com
NO MATTER WHAT I'M DOING, ROSCOE THINKS HE HAS TO BE RIGHT SMACK DAB IN THE MIDDLE OF IT!
10-12
© 2002 Washington Post Writers Group
I'LL TRADE YOU THE CAT FOR THE DOG.
B.CRANE

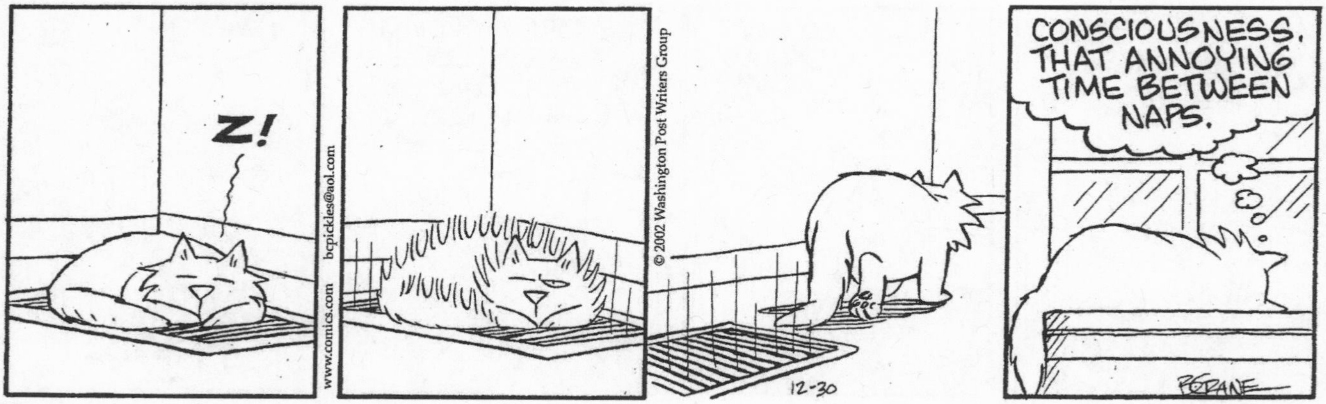
Z!
www.comics.com bcpickles@aol.com
© 2002 Washington Post Writers Group
12-30
CONSCIOUSNESS. THAT ANNOYING TIME BETWEEN NAPS.
B.CRANE

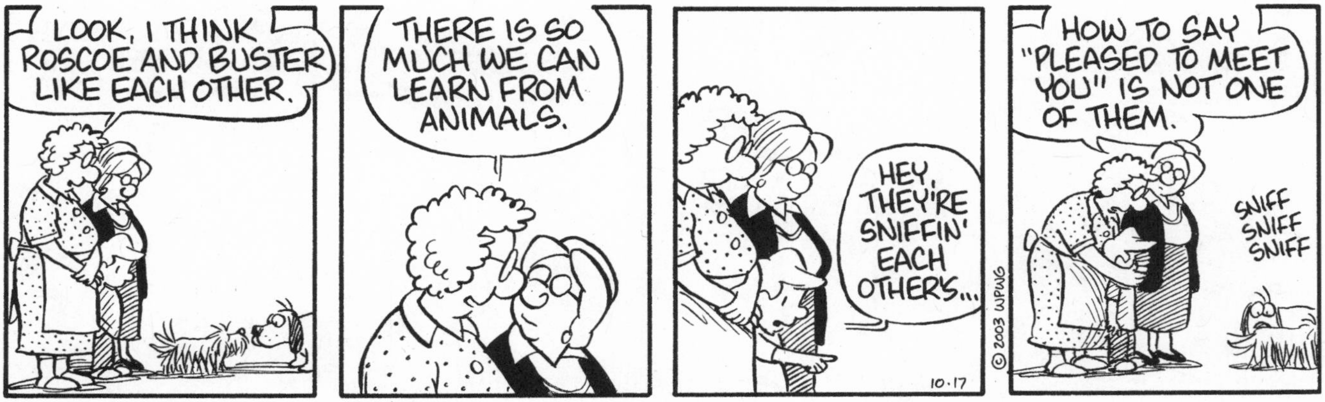
LOOK, I THINK ROSCOE AND BUSTER LIKE EACH OTHER.
THERE IS SO MUCH WE CAN LEARN FROM ANIMALS.
HEY, THEY'RE SNIFFIN' EACH OTHER'S...
10·17
© 2003 WPWG
HOW TO SAY "PLEASED TO MEET YOU" IS NOT ONE OF THEM.
SNIFF SNIFF SNIFF

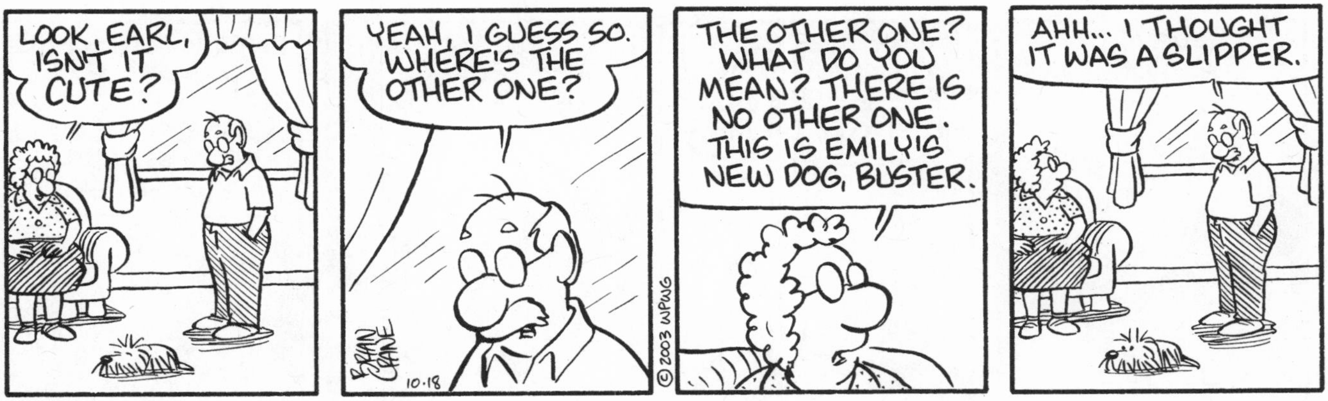
LOOK, EARL, ISN'T IT CUTE?
YEAH, I GUESS SO. WHERE'S THE OTHER ONE?
BRIAN CRANE
10·18
© 2003 WPWG
THE OTHER ONE? WHAT DO YOU MEAN? THERE IS NO OTHER ONE. THIS IS EMILY'S NEW DOG, BUSTER.
AHH... I THOUGHT IT WAS A SLIPPER.

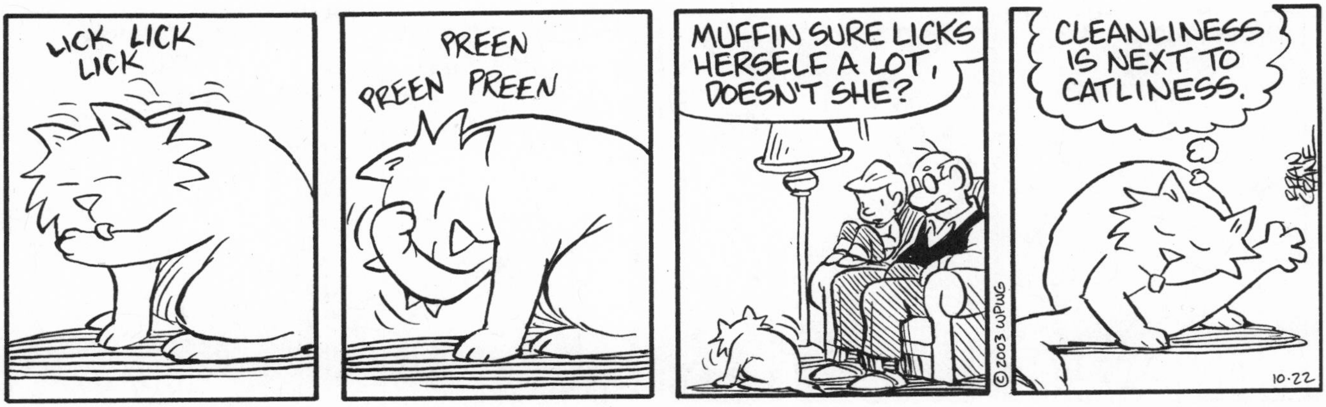
LICK LICK LICK
PREEN PREEN PREEN
MUFFIN SURE LICKS HERSELF A LOT, DOESN'T SHE?
© 2003 WPWG
CLEANLINESS IS NEXT TO CATLINESS.
BRIAN CRANE
10·22

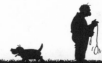

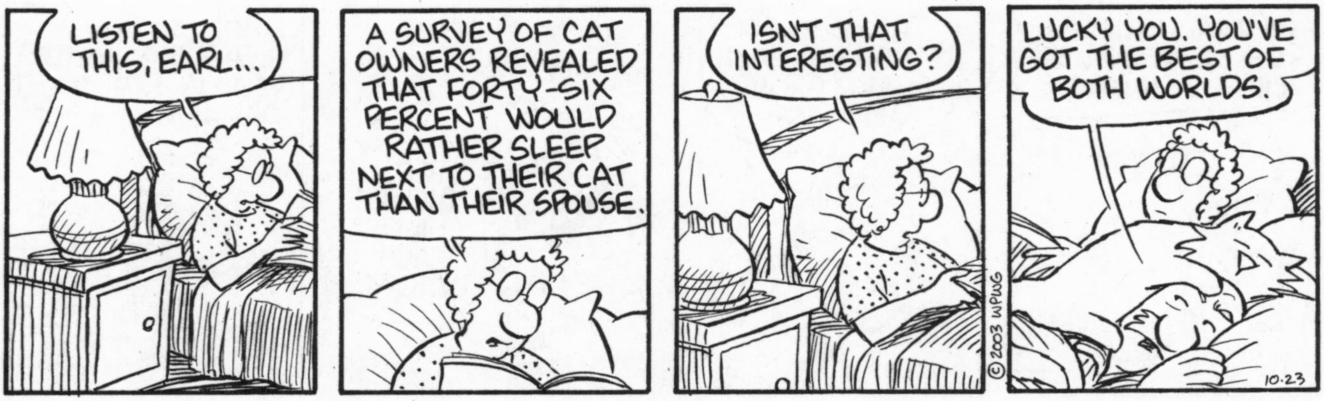
LISTEN TO THIS, EARL...
A SURVEY OF CAT OWNERS REVEALED THAT FORTY-SIX PERCENT WOULD RATHER SLEEP NEXT TO THEIR CAT THAN THEIR SPOUSE.
ISN'T THAT INTERESTING?
© 2003 WPWG
LUCKY YOU. YOU'VE GOT THE BEST OF BOTH WORLDS.
10.23

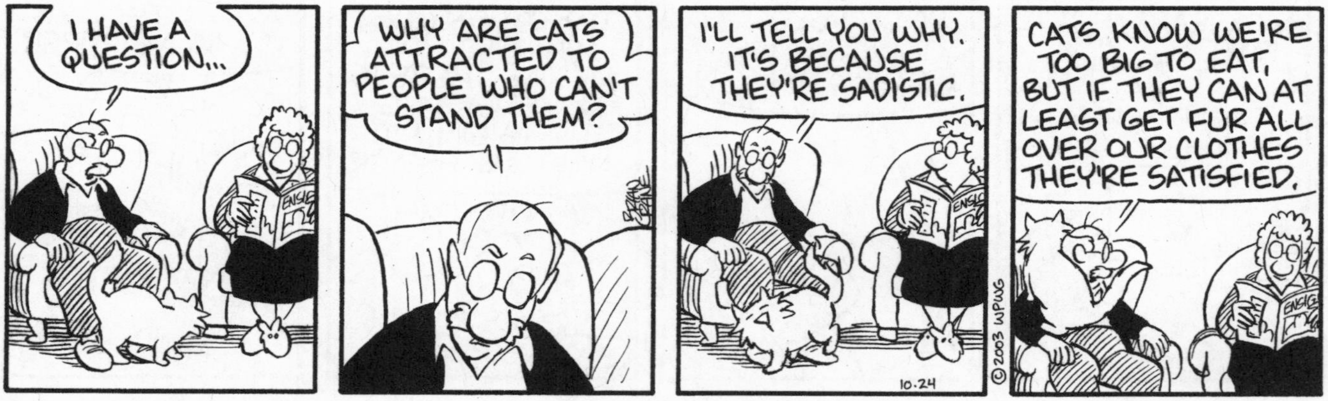
I HAVE A QUESTION...
WHY ARE CATS ATTRACTED TO PEOPLE WHO CAN'T STAND THEM?
I'LL TELL YOU WHY. IT'S BECAUSE THEY'RE SADISTIC.
10.24
© 2003 WPWG
CATS KNOW WE'RE TOO BIG TO EAT, BUT IF THEY CAN AT LEAST GET FUR ALL OVER OUR CLOTHES THEY'RE SATISFIED.

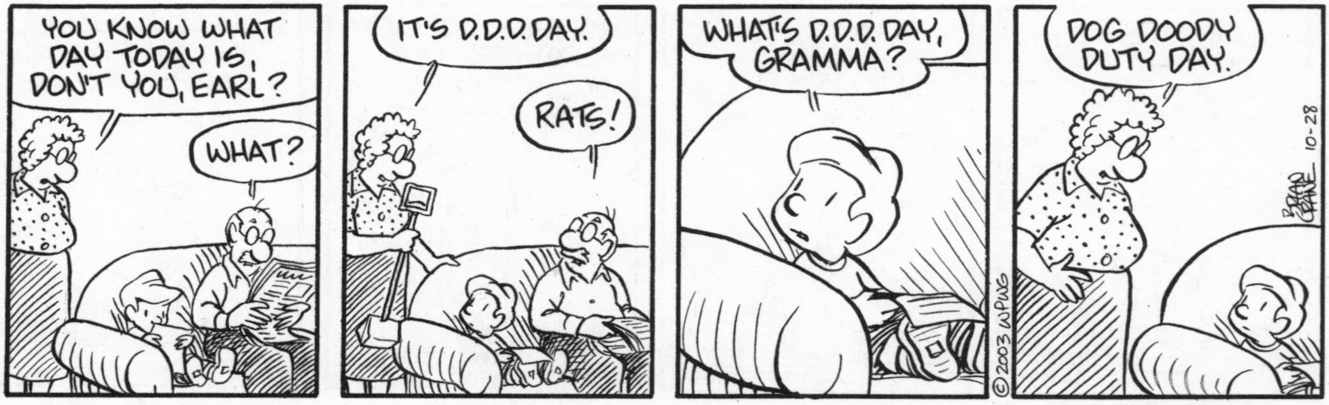
YOU KNOW WHAT DAY TODAY IS, DON'T YOU, EARL?
WHAT?
IT'S D.D.D. DAY.
RATS!
WHAT'S D.D.D. DAY, GRAMMA?
© 2003 WPWG
DOG DOODY DUTY DAY.
10-28

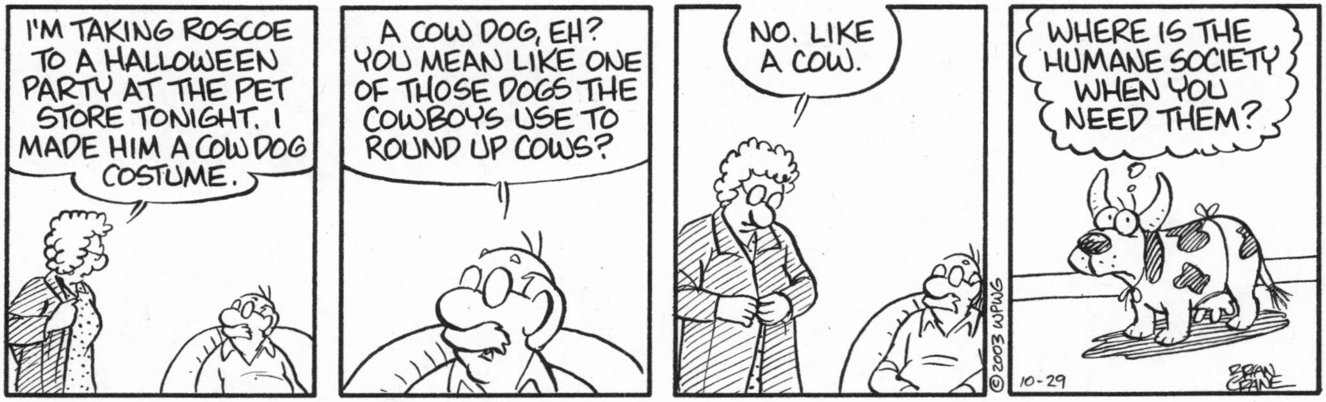
I'M TAKING ROSCOE TO A HALLOWEEN PARTY AT THE PET STORE TONIGHT. I MADE HIM A COW DOG COSTUME.
A COW DOG, EH? YOU MEAN LIKE ONE OF THOSE DOGS THE COWBOYS USE TO ROUND UP COWS?
NO. LIKE A COW.
© 2003 WPWG
WHERE IS THE HUMANE SOCIETY WHEN YOU NEED THEM?
10-29
BRIAN CRANE

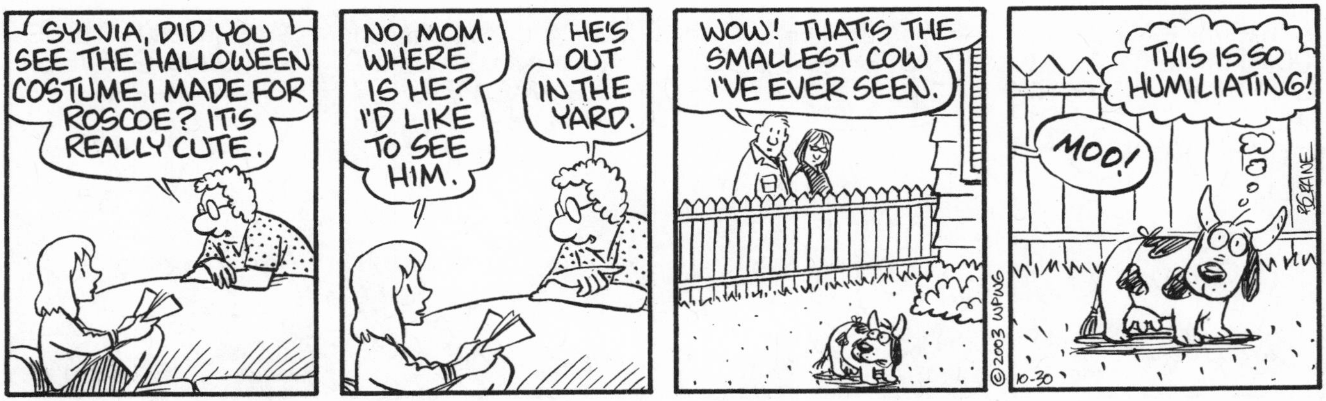
SYLVIA, DID YOU SEE THE HALLOWEEN COSTUME I MADE FOR ROSCOE? IT'S REALLY CUTE.
NO, MOM. WHERE IS HE? I'D LIKE TO SEE HIM.
HE'S OUT IN THE YARD.
WOW! THAT'S THE SMALLEST COW I'VE EVER SEEN.
© 2003 WPWG
THIS IS SO HUMILIATING!
MOO!
BCRANE
10-30

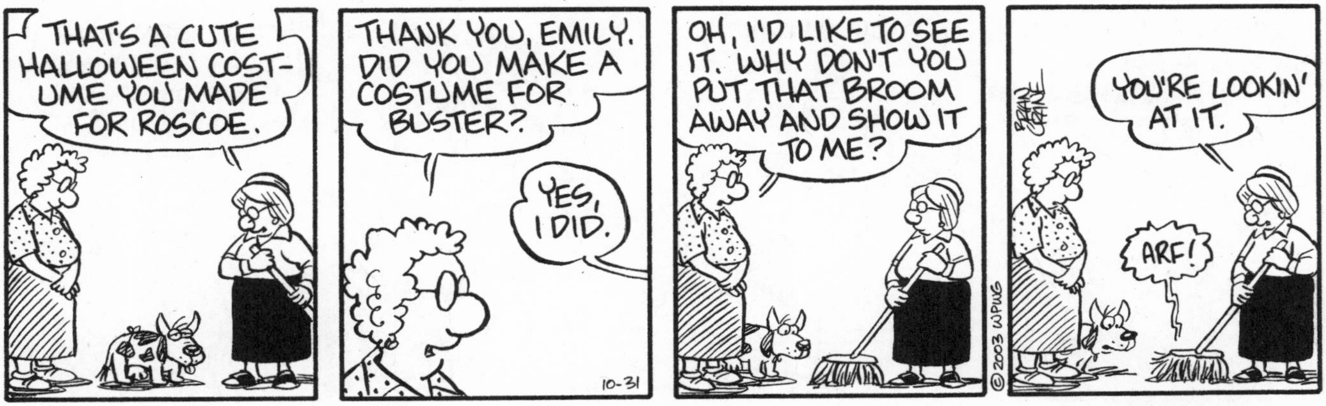
THAT'S A CUTE HALLOWEEN COST-UME YOU MADE FOR ROSCOE.
THANK YOU, EMILY. DID YOU MAKE A COSTUME FOR BUSTER?
YES, I DID.
10-31
OH, I'D LIKE TO SEE IT. WHY DON'T YOU PUT THAT BROOM AWAY AND SHOW IT TO ME?
© 2003 WPWG
BRIAN CRANE
YOU'RE LOOKIN' AT IT.
ARF!

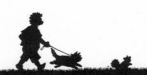

229

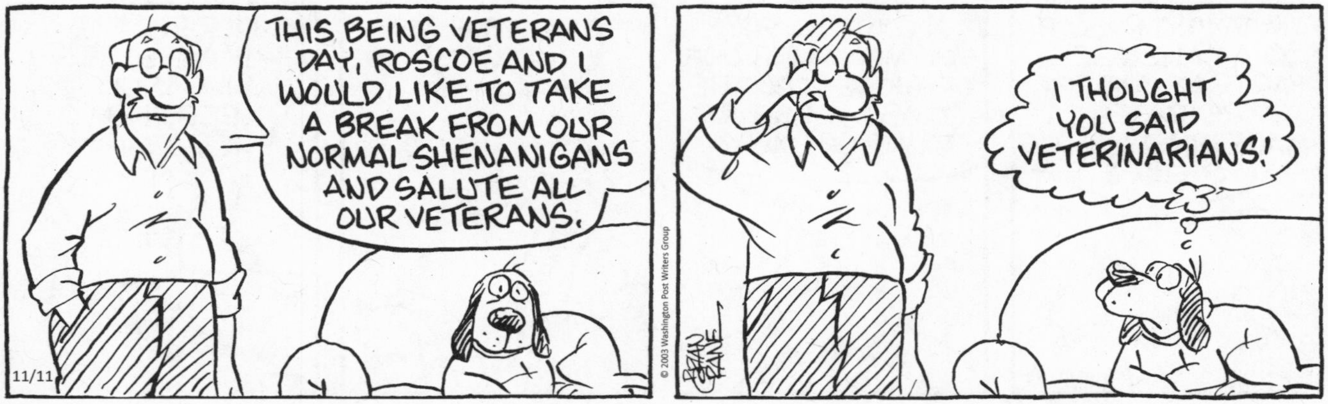

THIS BEING VETERANS DAY, ROSCOE AND I WOULD LIKE TO TAKE A BREAK FROM OUR NORMAL SHENANIGANS AND SALUTE ALL OUR VETERANS.
11/11
© 2003 Washington Post Writers Group
I THOUGHT YOU SAID VETERINARIANS!

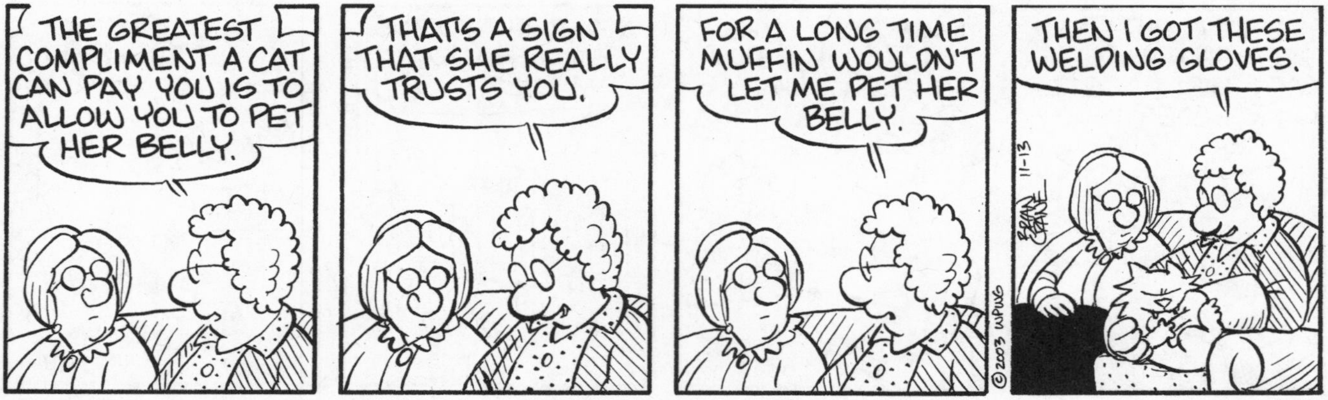

THE GREATEST COMPLIMENT A CAT CAN PAY YOU IS TO ALLOW YOU TO PET HER BELLY.
THAT'S A SIGN THAT SHE REALLY TRUSTS YOU.
FOR A LONG TIME MUFFIN WOULDN'T LET ME PET HER BELLY.
©2003 WPWG
11-13
THEN I GOT THESE WELDING GLOVES.

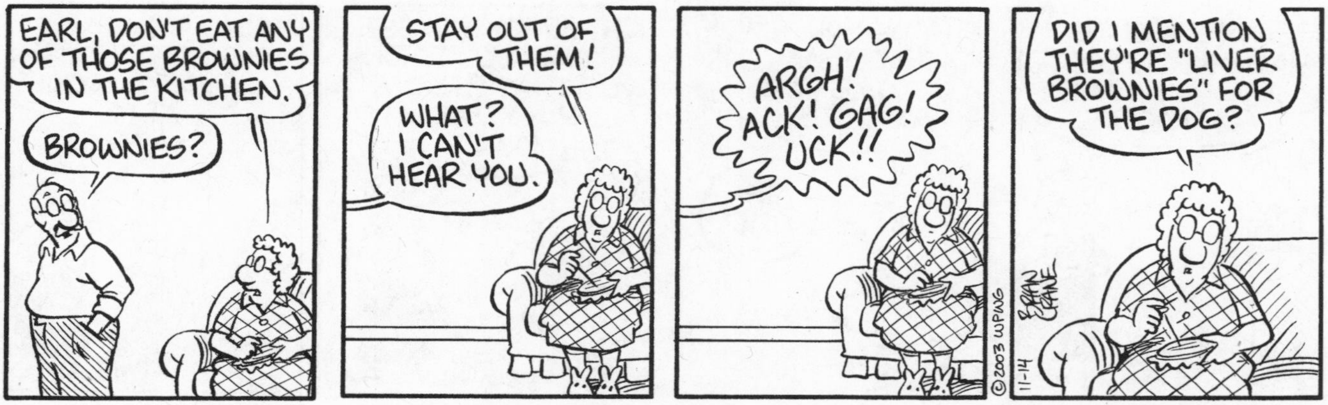

EARL, DON'T EAT ANY OF THOSE BROWNIES IN THE KITCHEN.
BROWNIES?
STAY OUT OF THEM!
WHAT? I CAN'T HEAR YOU.
ARGH! ACK! GAG! UCK!!
©2003 WPWG
11-14
DID I MENTION THEY'RE "LIVER BROWNIES" FOR THE DOG?

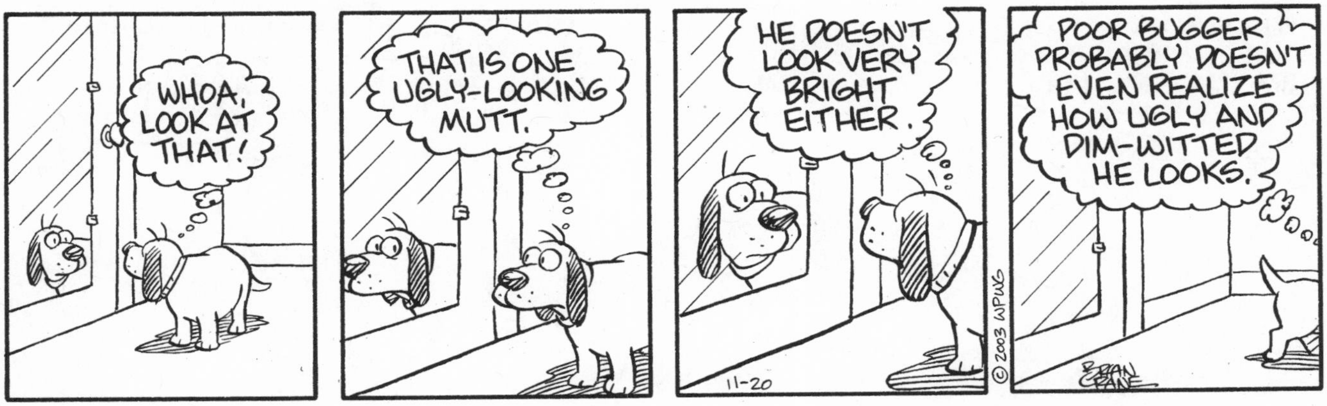
WHOA, LOOK AT THAT!
THAT IS ONE UGLY-LOOKING MUTT.
HE DOESN'T LOOK VERY BRIGHT EITHER.
11-20
© 2003 WPWG
POOR BUGGER PROBABLY DOESN'T EVEN REALIZE HOW UGLY AND DIM-WITTED HE LOOKS.
BRIAN CRANE

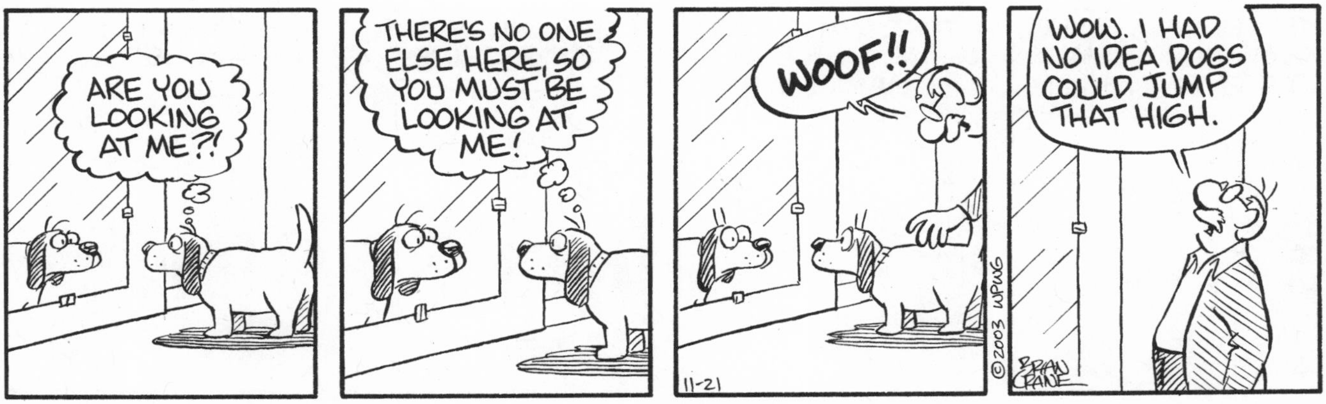
ARE YOU LOOKING AT ME?!
THERE'S NO ONE ELSE HERE, SO YOU MUST BE LOOKING AT ME!
WOOF!!
11-21
© 2003 WPWG
BRIAN CRANE
WOW. I HAD NO IDEA DOGS COULD JUMP THAT HIGH.

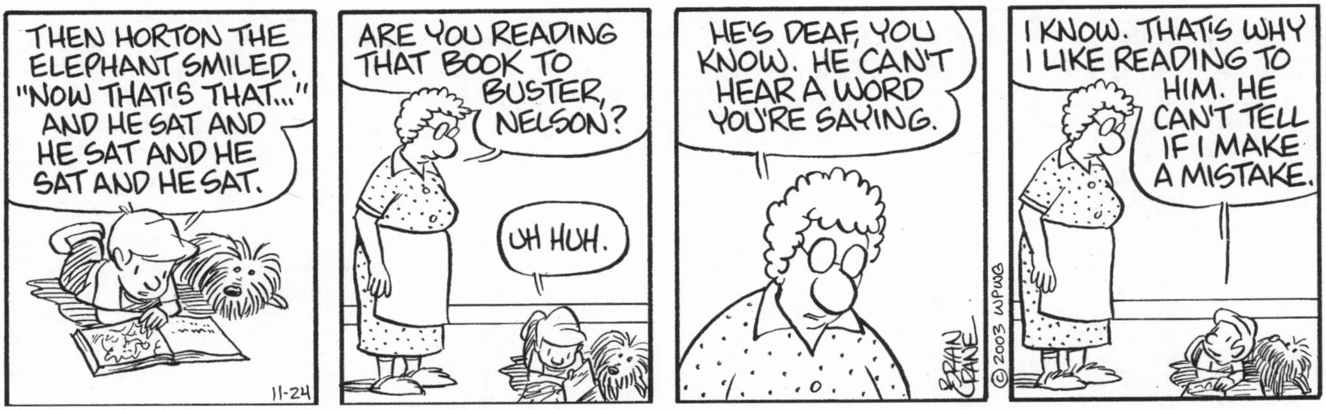
THEN HORTON THE ELEPHANT SMILED. "NOW THAT'S THAT..." AND HE SAT AND HE SAT AND HE SAT AND HE SAT.
11-24
ARE YOU READING THAT BOOK TO BUSTER, NELSON?
UH HUH.
HE'S DEAF, YOU KNOW. HE CAN'T HEAR A WORD YOU'RE SAYING.
BRIAN CRANE
© 2003 WPWG
I KNOW. THAT'S WHY I LIKE READING TO HIM. HE CAN'T TELL IF I MAKE A MISTAKE.

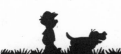

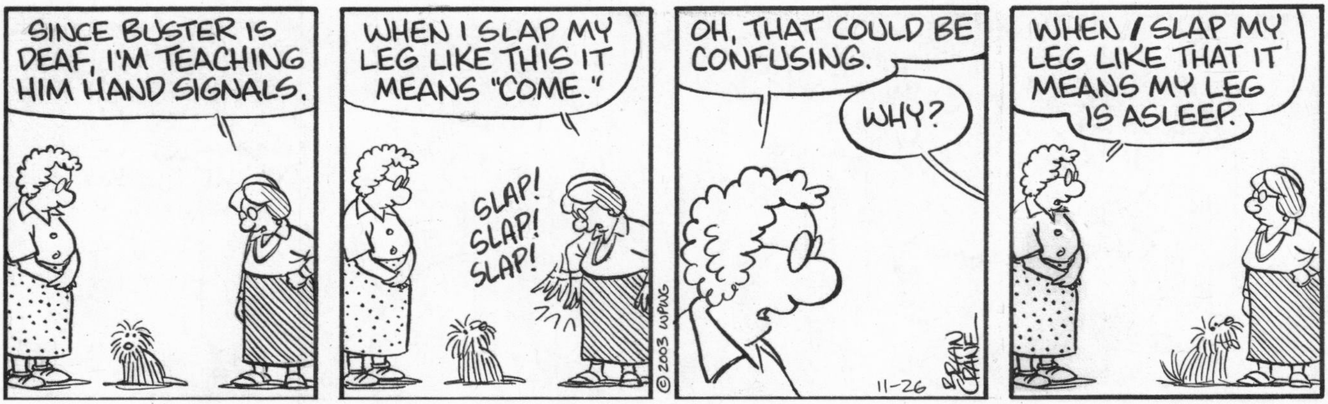

SINCE BUSTER IS DEAF, I'M TEACHING HIM HAND SIGNALS.
WHEN I SLAP MY LEG LIKE THIS IT MEANS "COME."
SLAP! SLAP! SLAP!
© 2003 WPNG
OH, THAT COULD BE CONFUSING.
WHY?
11-26
WHEN I SLAP MY LEG LIKE THAT IT MEANS MY LEG IS ASLEEP.

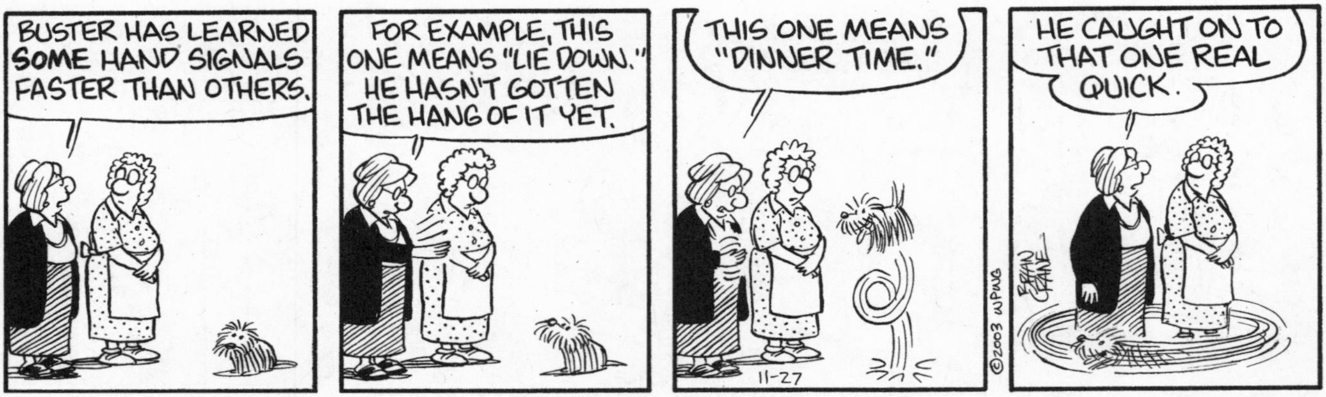

BUSTER HAS LEARNED SOME HAND SIGNALS FASTER THAN OTHERS.
FOR EXAMPLE, THIS ONE MEANS "LIE DOWN." HE HASN'T GOTTEN THE HANG OF IT YET.
THIS ONE MEANS "DINNER TIME."
11-27
©2003 WPNG
HE CAUGHT ON TO THAT ONE REAL QUICK.

232

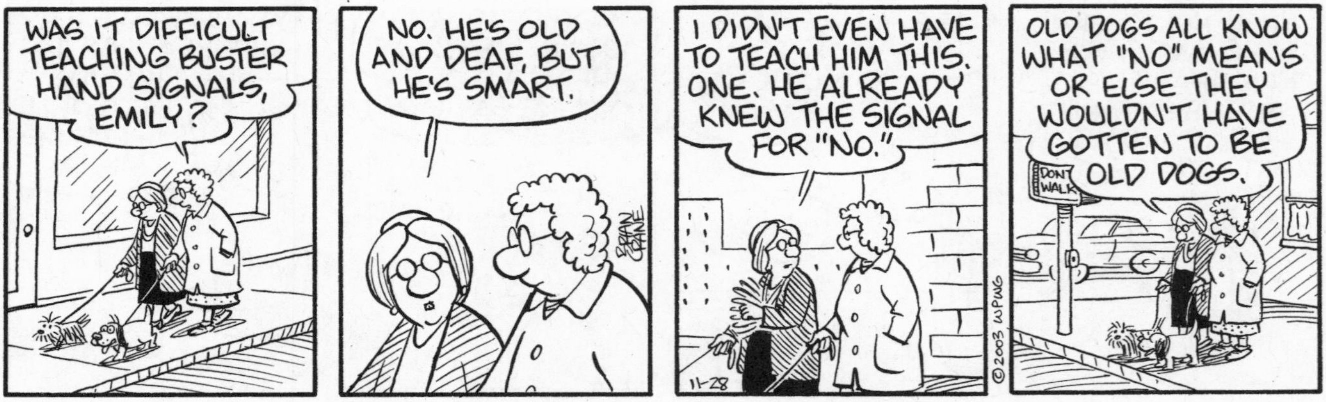

WAS IT DIFFICULT TEACHING BUSTER HAND SIGNALS, EMILY?
NO. HE'S OLD AND DEAF, BUT HE'S SMART.
I DIDN'T EVEN HAVE TO TEACH HIM THIS. ONE. HE ALREADY KNEW THE SIGNAL FOR "NO."
11-28
©2003 WPNG
OLD DOGS ALL KNOW WHAT "NO" MEANS OR ELSE THEY WOULDN'T HAVE GOTTEN TO BE OLD DOGS.
DON'T WALK

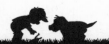

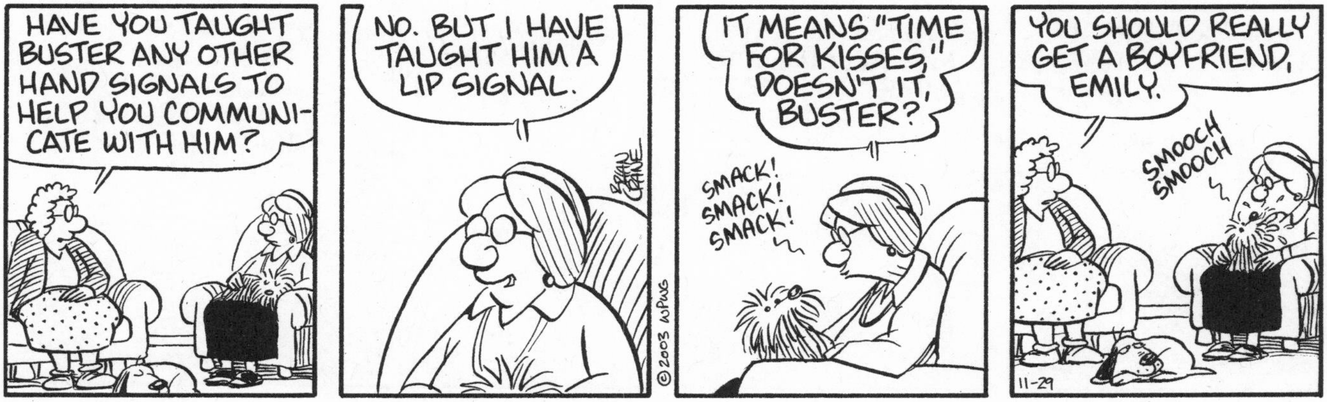
HAVE YOU TAUGHT BUSTER ANY OTHER HAND SIGNALS TO HELP YOU COMMUNICATE WITH HIM?
NO. BUT I HAVE TAUGHT HIM A LIP SIGNAL.
BRIAN CRANE
©2003 WPWG
IT MEANS "TIME FOR KISSES," DOESN'T IT, BUSTER?
SMACK! SMACK! SMACK!
YOU SHOULD REALLY GET A BOYFRIEND, EMILY.
SMOOCH SMOOCH
11-29

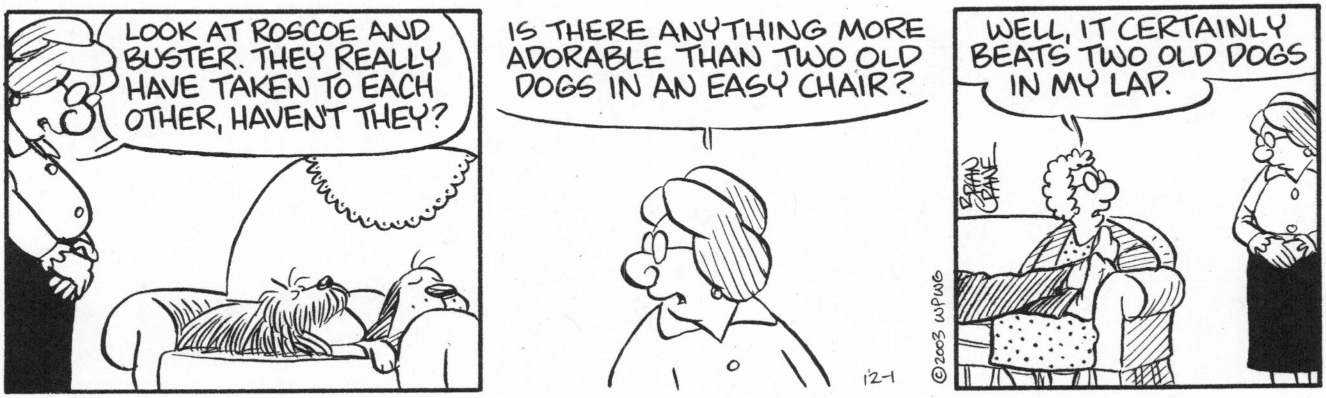
LOOK AT ROSCOE AND BUSTER. THEY REALLY HAVE TAKEN TO EACH OTHER, HAVEN'T THEY?
IS THERE ANYTHING MORE ADORABLE THAN TWO OLD DOGS IN AN EASY CHAIR?
12-1
©2003 WPWG
WELL, IT CERTAINLY BEATS TWO OLD DOGS IN MY LAP.
BRIAN CRANE

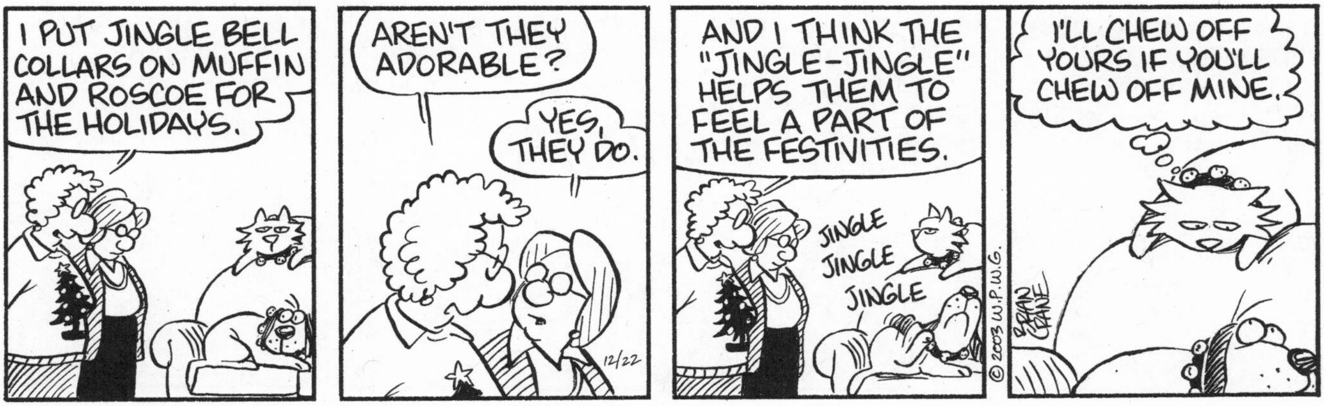
I PUT JINGLE BELL COLLARS ON MUFFIN AND ROSCOE FOR THE HOLIDAYS.
AREN'T THEY ADORABLE?
YES, THEY DO.
12/22
AND I THINK THE "JINGLE-JINGLE" HELPS THEM TO FEEL A PART OF THE FESTIVITIES.
JINGLE
JINGLE
JINGLE
©2003 W.P.W.G.
BRIAN CRANE
I'LL CHEW OFF YOURS IF YOU'LL CHEW OFF MINE.

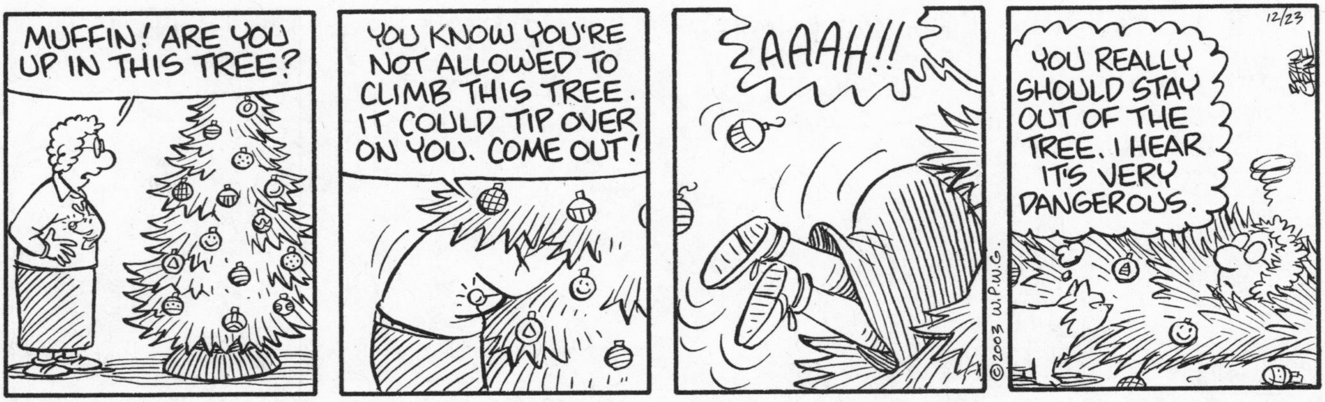
MUFFIN! ARE YOU UP IN THIS TREE?
YOU KNOW YOU'RE NOT ALLOWED TO CLIMB THIS TREE. IT COULD TIP OVER ON YOU. COME OUT!
AAAH!!
©2003 W.P.W.G.
12/23
YOU REALLY SHOULD STAY OUT OF THE TREE. I HEAR IT'S VERY DANGEROUS.

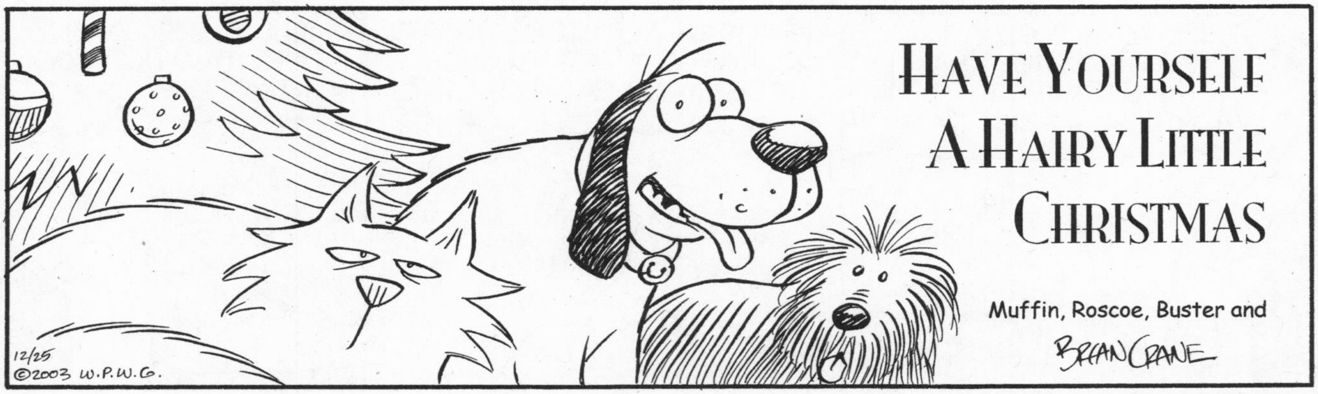
HAVE YOURSELF A HAIRY LITTLE CHRISTMAS
Muffin, Roscoe, Buster and
BRIAN CRANE
12/25
©2003 W.P.W.G.

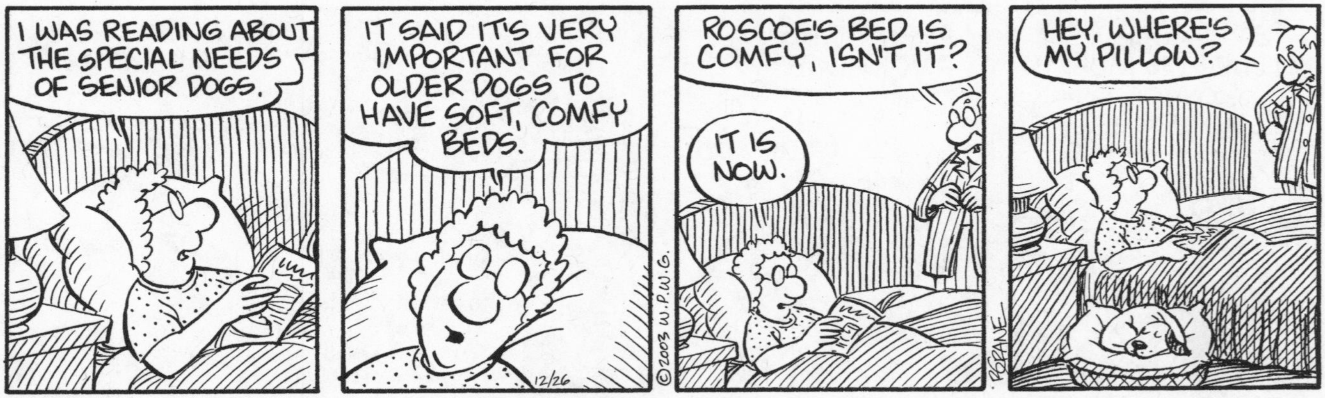
I WAS READING ABOUT THE SPECIAL NEEDS OF SENIOR DOGS.
IT SAID IT'S VERY IMPORTANT FOR OLDER DOGS TO HAVE SOFT, COMFY BEDS.
12/26
©2003 W.P.W.G.
ROSCOE'S BED IS COMFY, ISN'T IT?
IT IS NOW.
HEY, WHERE'S MY PILLOW?

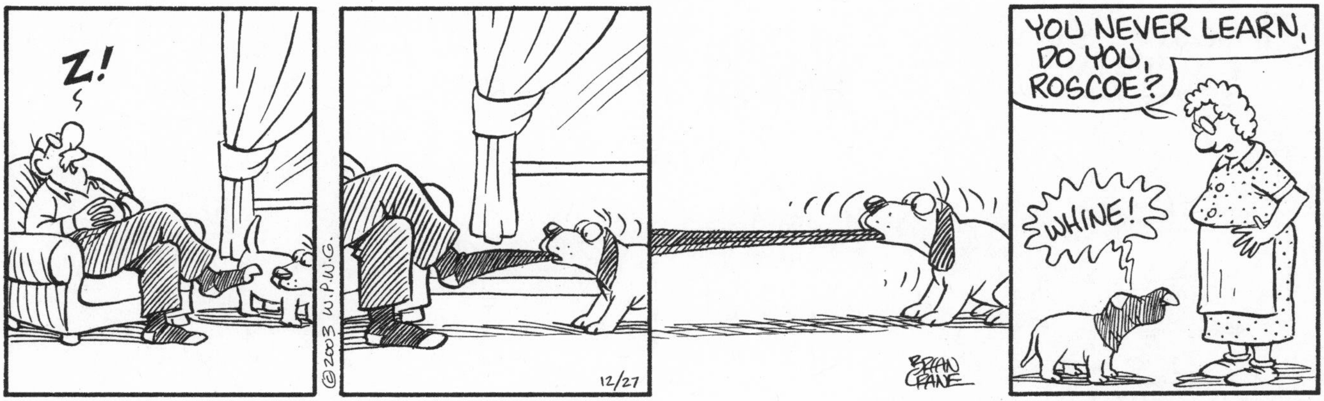
Z!
© 2003 W.P.W.G.
12/27
BRIAN CRANE
YOU NEVER LEARN, DO YOU, ROSCOE?
WHINE!

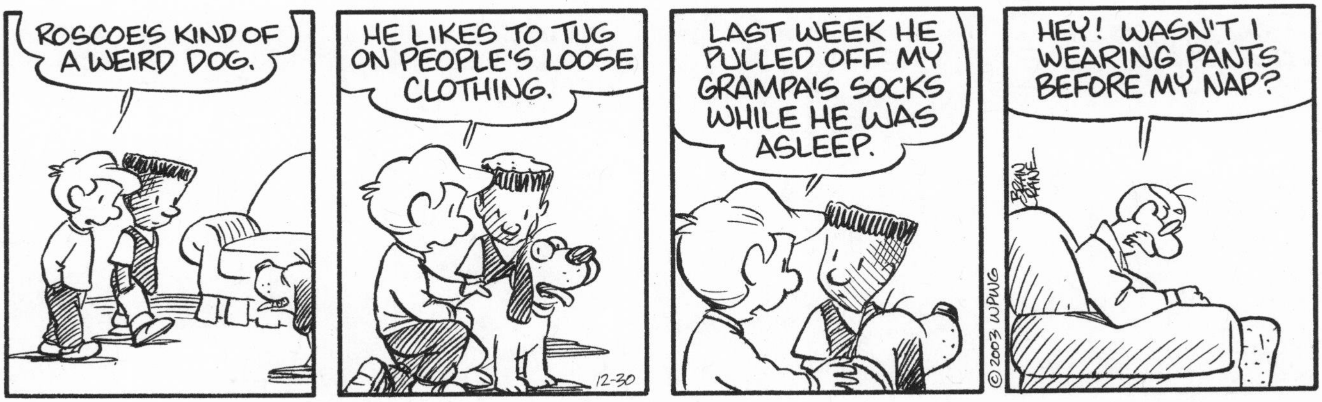
ROSCOE'S KIND OF A WEIRD DOG.
HE LIKES TO TUG ON PEOPLE'S LOOSE CLOTHING.
12-30
LAST WEEK HE PULLED OFF MY GRAMPA'S SOCKS WHILE HE WAS ASLEEP.
© 2003 WPWG
BRIAN CRANE
HEY! WASN'T I WEARING PANTS BEFORE MY NAP?

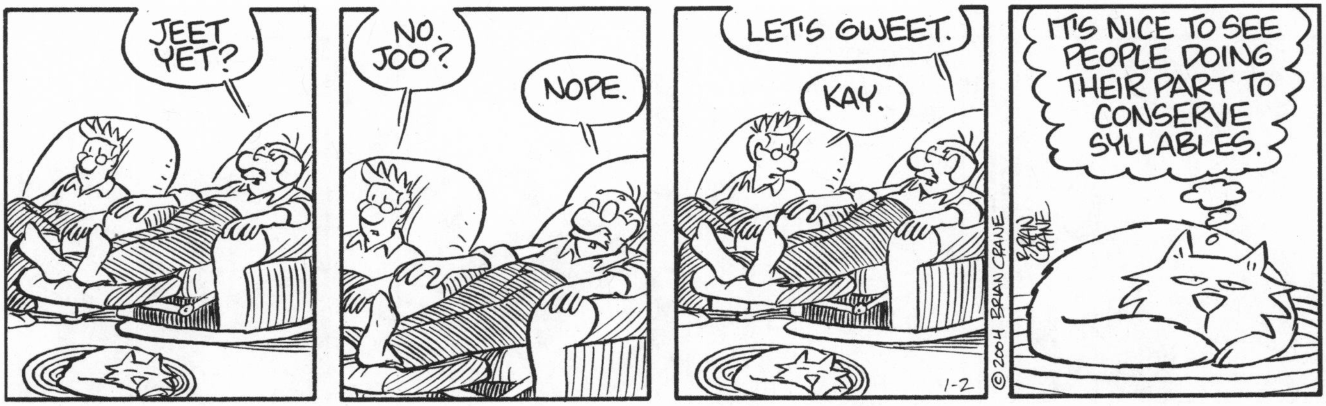
JEET YET?
NO. JOO?
NOPE.
LET'S GWEET.
KAY.
1-2
© 2004 BRIAN CRANE
BRIAN CRANE
IT'S NICE TO SEE PEOPLE DOING THEIR PART TO CONSERVE SYLLABLES.

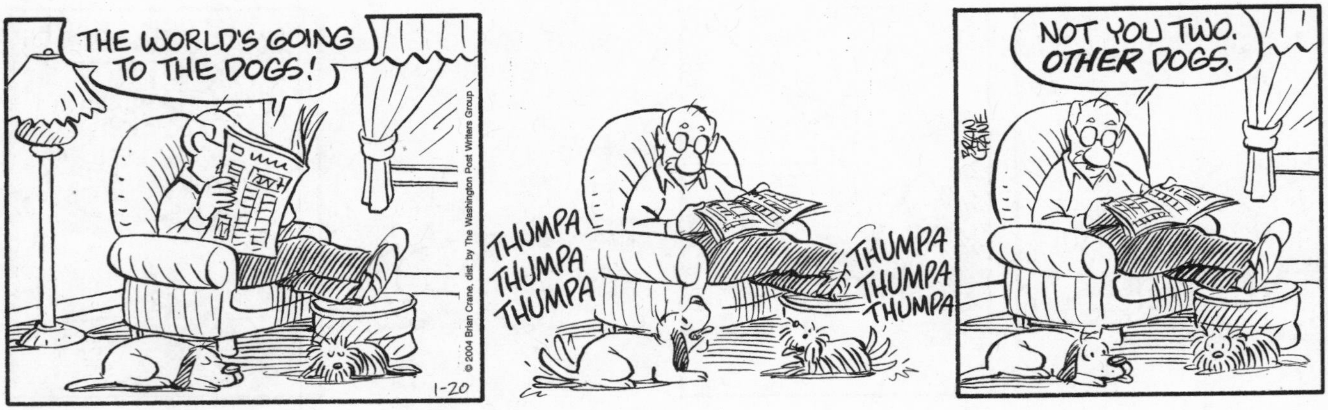
THE WORLD'S GOING TO THE DOGS!
© 2004 Brian Crane, dist. by The Washington Post Writers Group
1-20
THUMPA THUMPA THUMPA
THUMPA THUMPA THUMPA
NOT YOU TWO. OTHER DOGS.
BRIAN CRANE

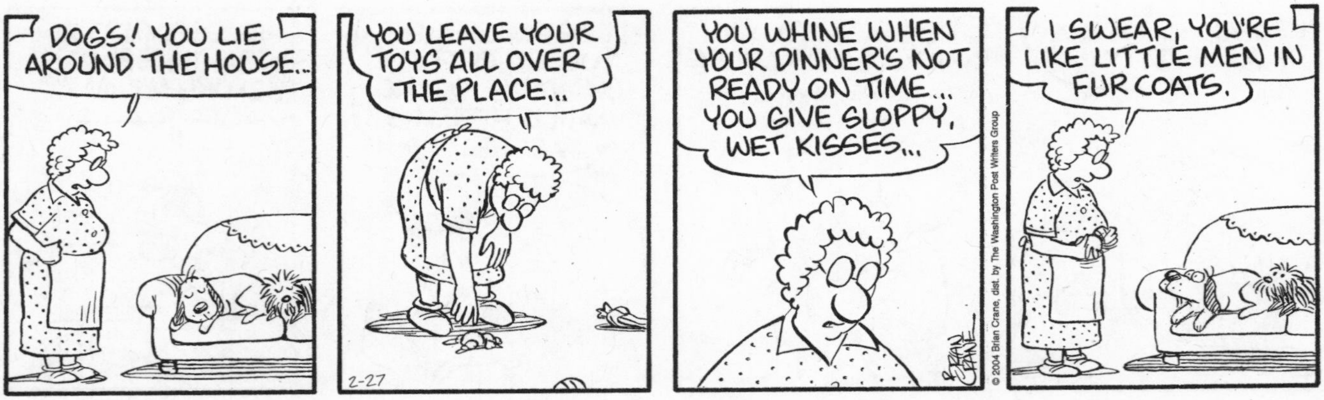
DOGS! YOU LIE AROUND THE HOUSE...
YOU LEAVE YOUR TOYS ALL OVER THE PLACE...
2-27
YOU WHINE WHEN YOUR DINNER'S NOT READY ON TIME... YOU GIVE SLOPPY, WET KISSES...
BRIAN CRANE
© 2004 Brian Crane, dist. by The Washington Post Writers Group
I SWEAR, YOU'RE LIKE LITTLE MEN IN FUR COATS.

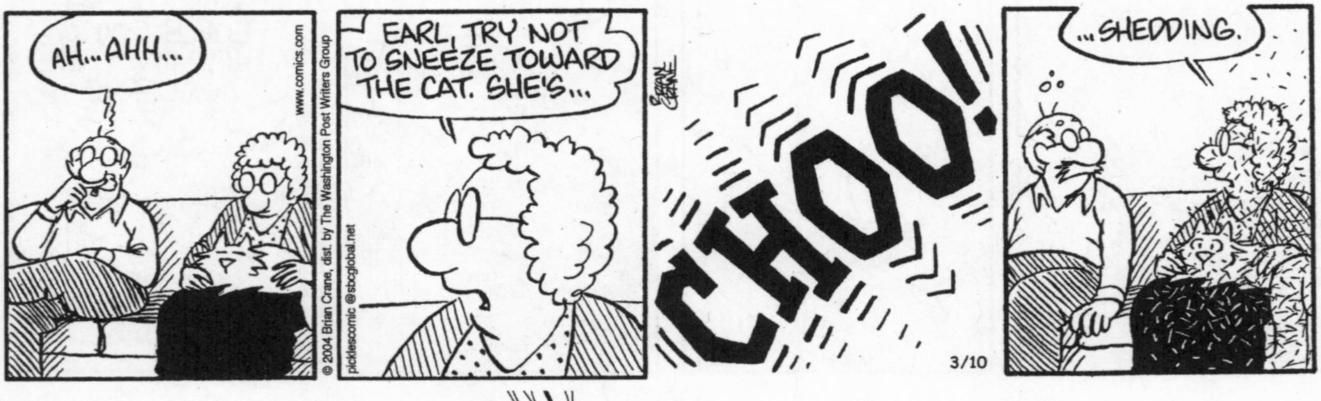
AH...AHH...
www.comics.com
© 2004 Brian Crane, dist. by The Washington Post Writers Group
picklescomic @sbcglobal.net
EARL, TRY NOT TO SNEEZE TOWARD THE CAT. SHE'S...
BRIAN CRANE
CHOO!
3/10
...SHEDDING.

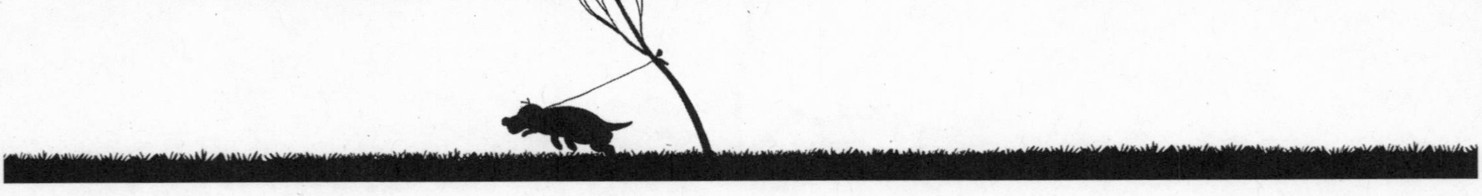

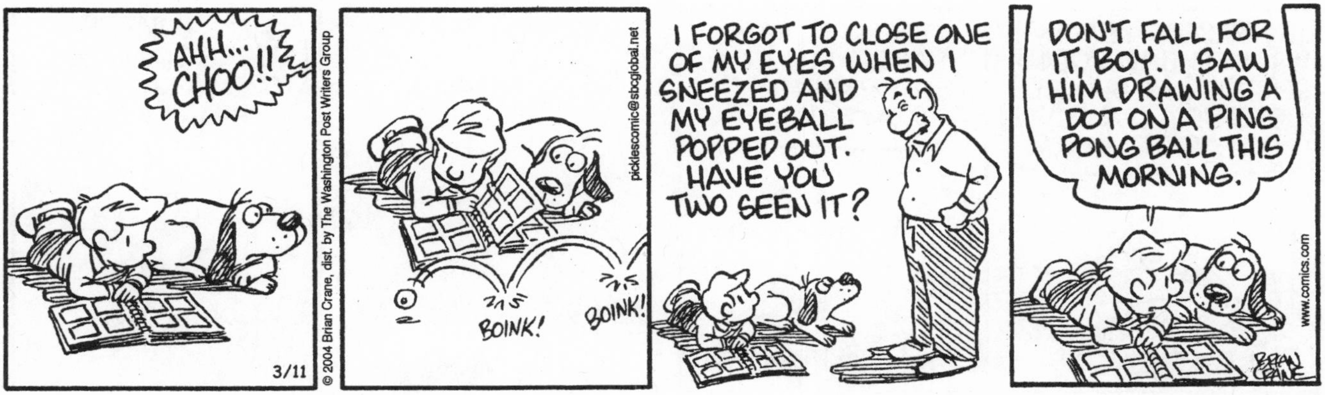
AHH... CHOO!!
3/11
© 2004 Brian Crane, dist. by The Washington Post Writers Group
BOINK!
BOINK!
picklescomic@sbcglobal.net
I FORGOT TO CLOSE ONE OF MY EYES WHEN I SNEEZED AND MY EYEBALL POPPED OUT. HAVE YOU TWO SEEN IT?
DON'T FALL FOR IT, BOY. I SAW HIM DRAWING A DOT ON A PING PONG BALL THIS MORNING.
www.comics.com
BRIAN CRANE

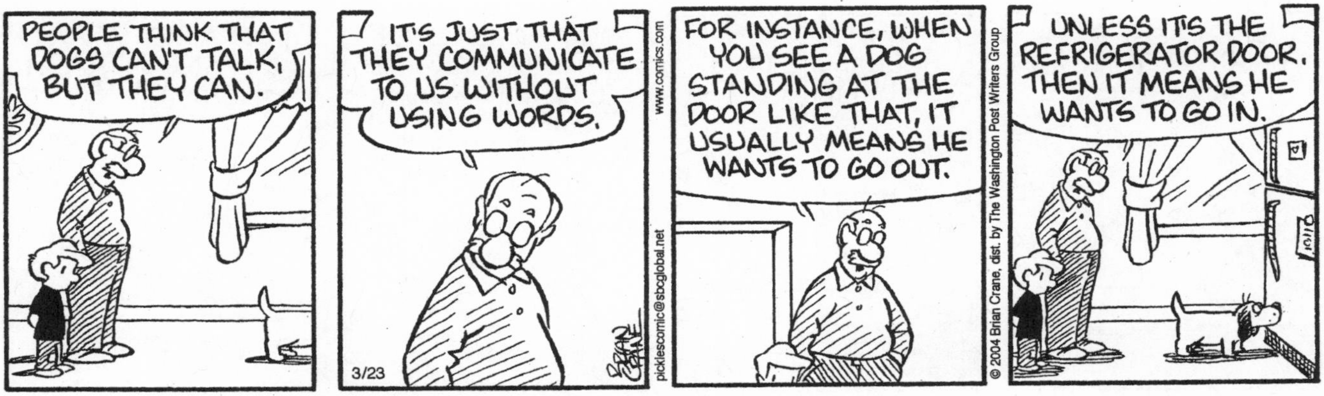
PEOPLE THINK THAT DOGS CAN'T TALK, BUT THEY CAN.
IT'S JUST THAT THEY COMMUNICATE TO US WITHOUT USING WORDS.
3/23
BRIAN CRANE
www.comics.com
picklescomic@sbcglobal.net
FOR INSTANCE, WHEN YOU SEE A DOG STANDING AT THE DOOR LIKE THAT, IT USUALLY MEANS HE WANTS TO GO OUT.
© 2004 Brian Crane, dist. by The Washington Post Writers Group
UNLESS IT'S THE REFRIGERATOR DOOR. THEN IT MEANS HE WANTS TO GO IN.

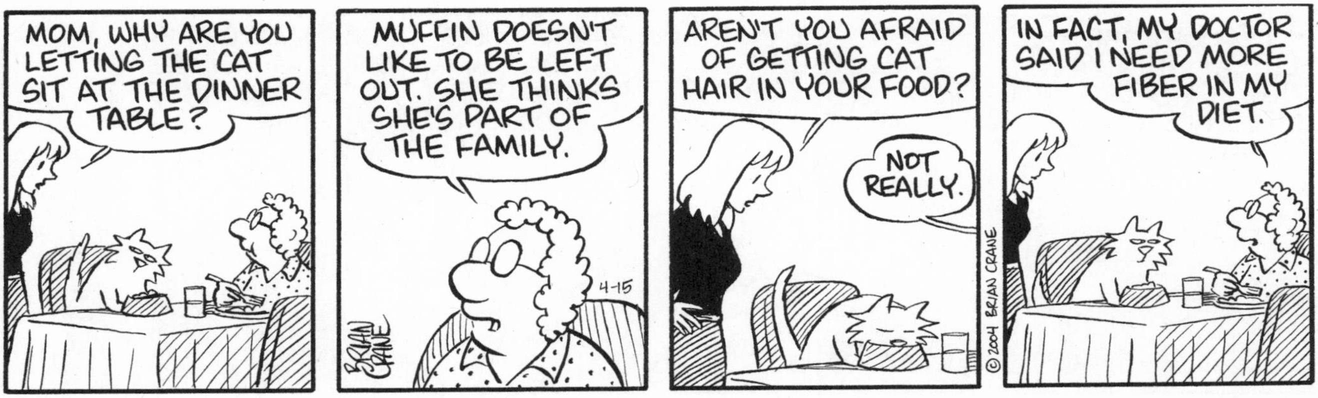
MOM, WHY ARE YOU LETTING THE CAT SIT AT THE DINNER TABLE?
MUFFIN DOESN'T LIKE TO BE LEFT OUT. SHE THINKS SHE'S PART OF THE FAMILY.
4-15
BRIAN CRANE
AREN'T YOU AFRAID OF GETTING CAT HAIR IN YOUR FOOD?
NOT REALLY.
© 2004 BRIAN CRANE
IN FACT, MY DOCTOR SAID I NEED MORE FIBER IN MY DIET.

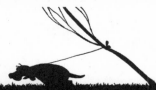

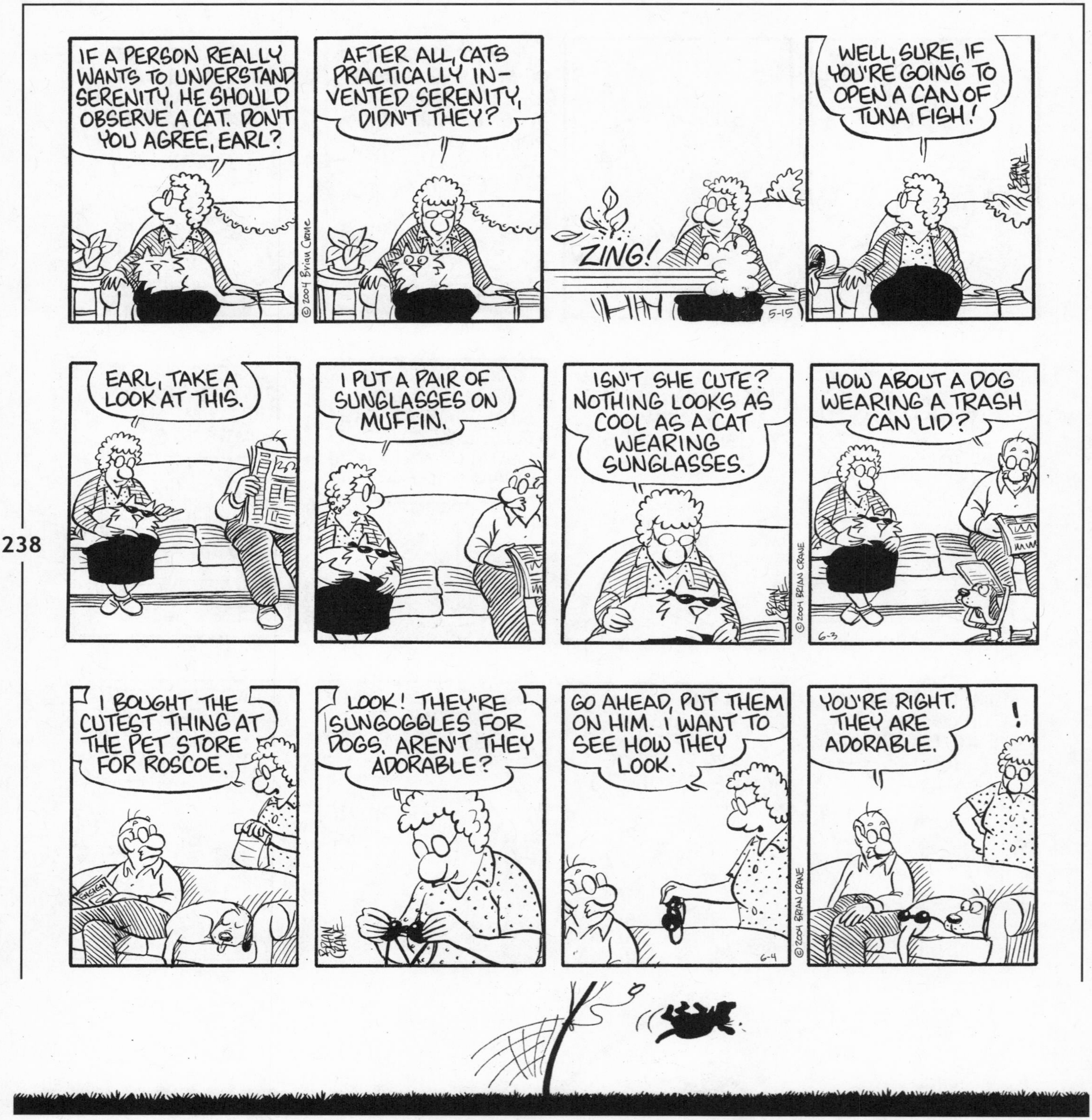

IF A PERSON REALLY WANTS TO UNDERSTAND SERENITY, HE SHOULD OBSERVE A CAT. DON'T YOU AGREE, EARL?
© 2004 Brian Crane
AFTER ALL, CATS PRACTICALLY IN-VENTED SERENITY, DIDN'T THEY?
ZING!
5-15
WELL, SURE, IF YOU'RE GOING TO OPEN A CAN OF TUNA FISH!
BRIAN CRANE
EARL, TAKE A LOOK AT THIS.
I PUT A PAIR OF SUNGLASSES ON MUFFIN.
ISN'T SHE CUTE? NOTHING LOOKS AS COOL AS A CAT WEARING SUNGLASSES.
BRIAN CRANE
© 2004 BRIAN CRANE
HOW ABOUT A DOG WEARING A TRASH CAN LID?
6-3
I BOUGHT THE CUTEST THING AT THE PET STORE FOR ROSCOE.
LOOK! THEY'RE SUNGOGGLES FOR DOGS. AREN'T THEY ADORABLE?
BRIAN CRANE
GO AHEAD, PUT THEM ON HIM. I WANT TO SEE HOW THEY LOOK.
© 2004 BRIAN CRANE
6-4
YOU'RE RIGHT. THEY ARE ADORABLE.
!

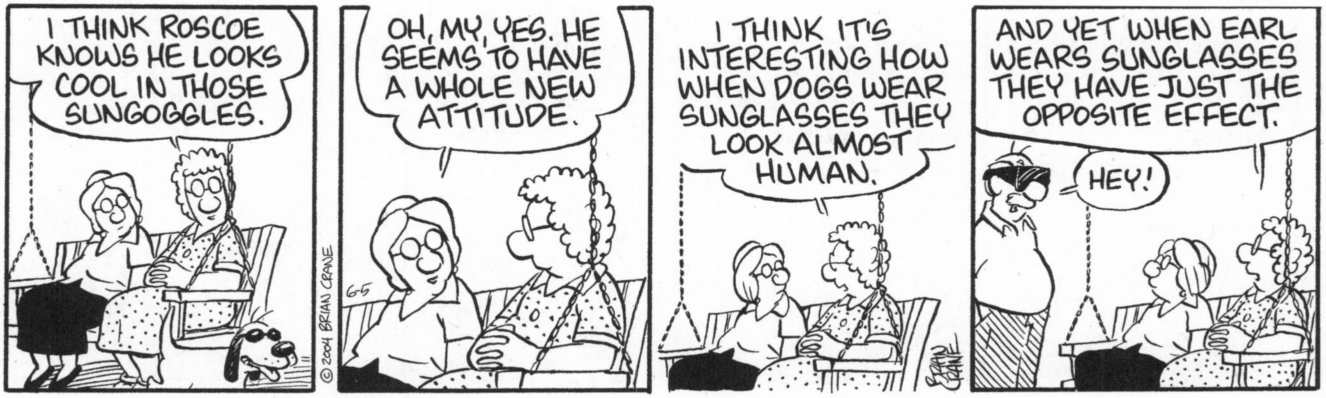
I THINK ROSCOE KNOWS HE LOOKS COOL IN THOSE SUNGOGGLES.
© 2004 BRIAN CRANE
6-5
OH, MY, YES. HE SEEMS TO HAVE A WHOLE NEW ATTITUDE.
I THINK IT'S INTERESTING HOW WHEN DOGS WEAR SUNGLASSES THEY LOOK ALMOST HUMAN.
BRIAN CRANE
AND YET WHEN EARL WEARS SUNGLASSES THEY HAVE JUST THE OPPOSITE EFFECT.
HEY!

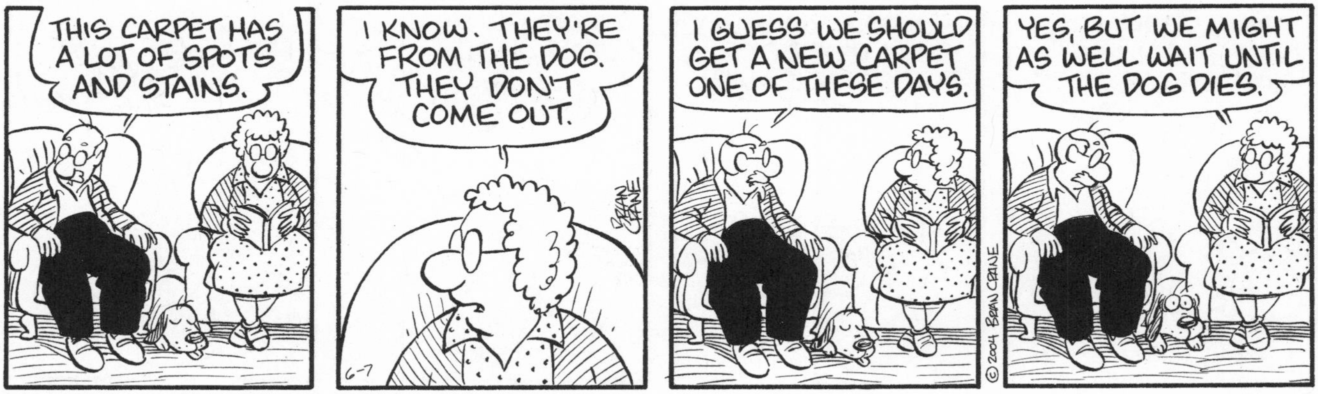
THIS CARPET HAS A LOT OF SPOTS AND STAINS.
I KNOW. THEY'RE FROM THE DOG. THEY DON'T COME OUT.
BRIAN CRANE
6-7
I GUESS WE SHOULD GET A NEW CARPET ONE OF THESE DAYS.
© 2004 BRIAN CRANE
YES, BUT WE MIGHT AS WELL WAIT UNTIL THE DOG DIES.

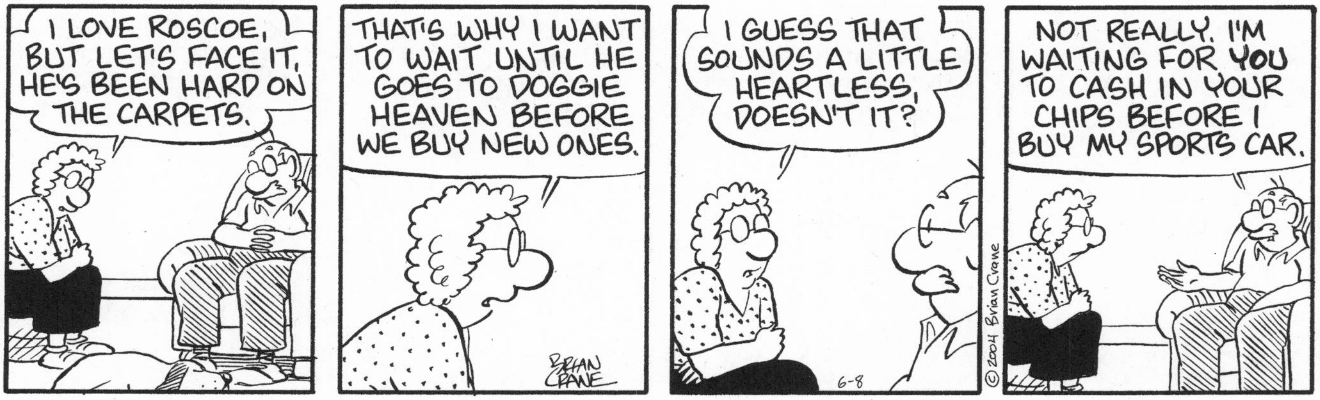
I LOVE ROSCOE, BUT LET'S FACE IT, HE'S BEEN HARD ON THE CARPETS.
THAT'S WHY I WANT TO WAIT UNTIL HE GOES TO DOGGIE HEAVEN BEFORE WE BUY NEW ONES.
BRIAN CRANE
I GUESS THAT SOUNDS A LITTLE HEARTLESS, DOESN'T IT?
6-8
© 2004 Brian Crane
NOT REALLY. I'M WAITING FOR **YOU** TO CASH IN YOUR CHIPS BEFORE I BUY MY SPORTS CAR.

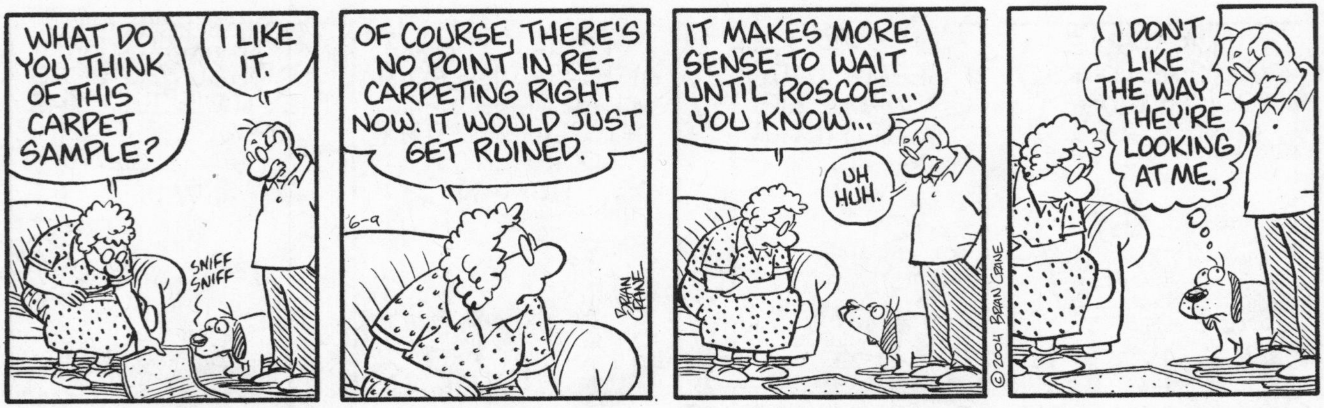
WHAT DO YOU THINK OF THIS CARPET SAMPLE?
I LIKE IT.
SNIFF SNIFF
OF COURSE, THERE'S NO POINT IN RE-CARPETING RIGHT NOW. IT WOULD JUST GET RUINED.
6-9
BRIAN CRANE
IT MAKES MORE SENSE TO WAIT UNTIL ROSCOE... YOU KNOW...
UH HUH.
© 2004 BRIAN CRANE
I DON'T LIKE THE WAY THEY'RE LOOKING AT ME.

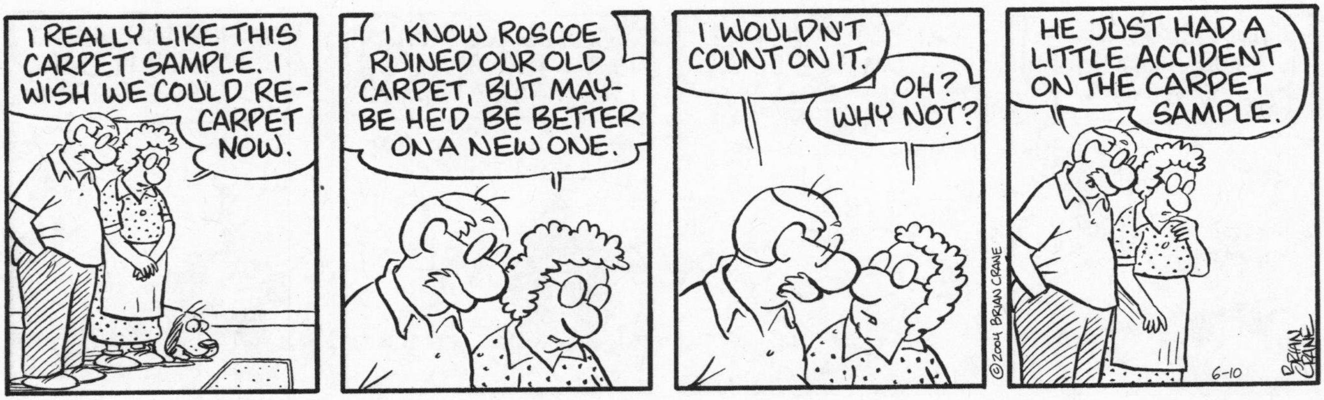
I REALLY LIKE THIS CARPET SAMPLE. I WISH WE COULD RE-CARPET NOW.
I KNOW ROSCOE RUINED OUR OLD CARPET, BUT MAY-BE HE'D BE BETTER ON A NEW ONE.
I WOULDN'T COUNT ON IT.
OH? WHY NOT?
© 2004 BRIAN CRANE
HE JUST HAD A LITTLE ACCIDENT ON THE CARPET SAMPLE.
6-10
BRIAN CRANE

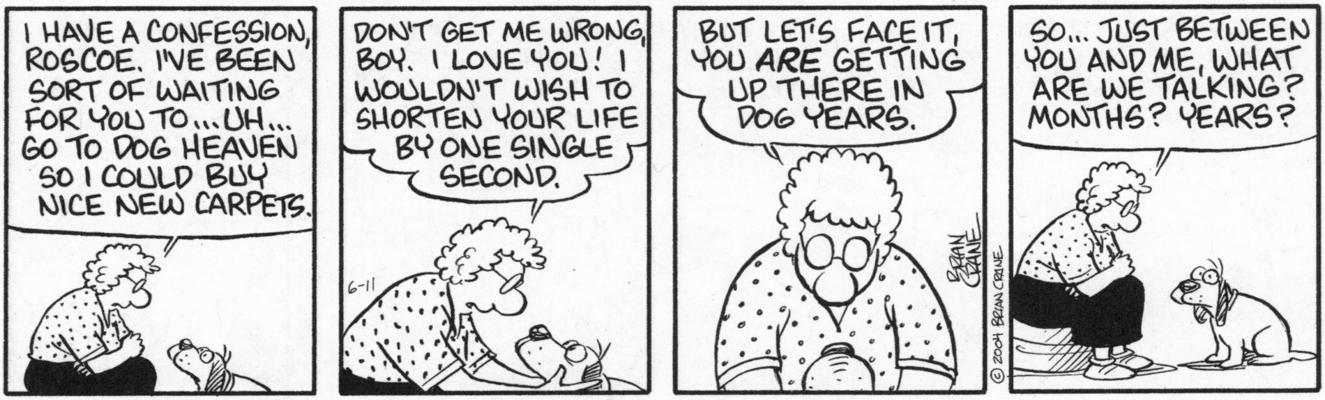
I HAVE A CONFESSION, ROSCOE. I'VE BEEN SORT OF WAITING FOR YOU TO...UH... GO TO DOG HEAVEN SO I COULD BUY NICE NEW CARPETS.
DON'T GET ME WRONG, BOY. I LOVE YOU! I WOULDN'T WISH TO SHORTEN YOUR LIFE BY ONE SINGLE SECOND.
6-11
BUT LET'S FACE IT, YOU ARE GETTING UP THERE IN DOG YEARS.
BRIAN CRANE
© 2004 BRIAN CRANE
SO... JUST BETWEEN YOU AND ME, WHAT ARE WE TALKING? MONTHS? YEARS?

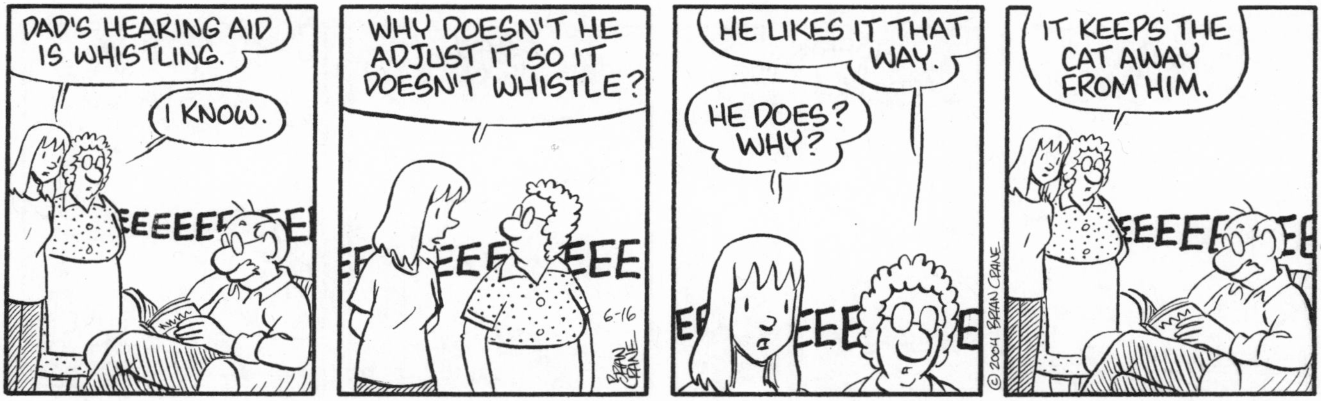
DAD'S HEARING AID IS WHISTLING.
I KNOW.
EEEEEEEEEE
WHY DOESN'T HE ADJUST IT SO IT DOESN'T WHISTLE?
EEEEEEEEEE
6-16
BRIAN CRANE
HE LIKES IT THAT WAY.
HE DOES? WHY?
EEEEEE
© 2004 BRIAN CRANE
IT KEEPS THE CAT AWAY FROM HIM.
EEEEEEEE

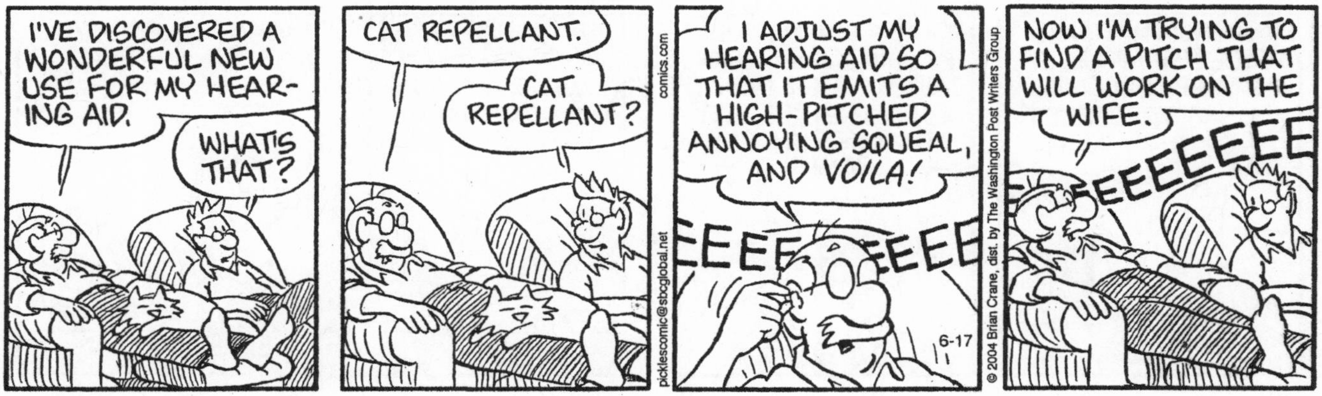
I'VE DISCOVERED A WONDERFUL NEW USE FOR MY HEARING AID.
WHAT'S THAT?
CAT REPELLANT.
CAT REPELLANT?
comics.com
picklescomic@sbcglobal.net
I ADJUST MY HEARING AID SO THAT IT EMITS A HIGH-PITCHED ANNOYING SQUEAL, AND VOILA!
EEEEEEEE
6-17
© 2004 Brian Crane, dist. by The Washington Post Writers Group
NOW I'M TRYING TO FIND A PITCH THAT WILL WORK ON THE WIFE.
EEEEEEEEEE

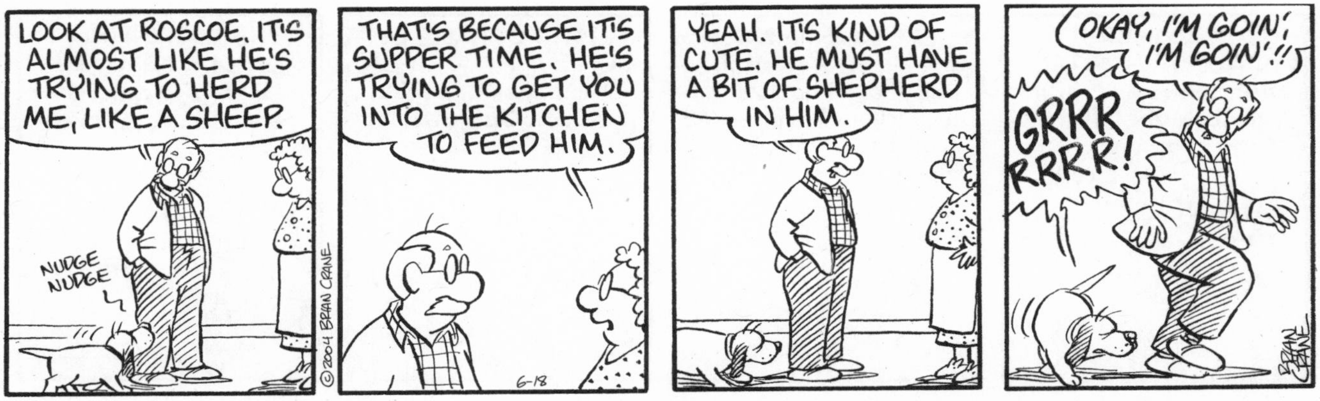
LOOK AT ROSCOE. IT'S ALMOST LIKE HE'S TRYING TO HERD ME, LIKE A SHEEP.
NUDGE NUDGE
© 2004 BRIAN CRANE
THAT'S BECAUSE IT'S SUPPER TIME. HE'S TRYING TO GET YOU INTO THE KITCHEN TO FEED HIM.
6-18
YEAH. IT'S KIND OF CUTE. HE MUST HAVE A BIT OF SHEPHERD IN HIM.
OKAY, I'M GOIN', I'M GOIN'!!
GRRRRRRR!
BRIAN CRANE

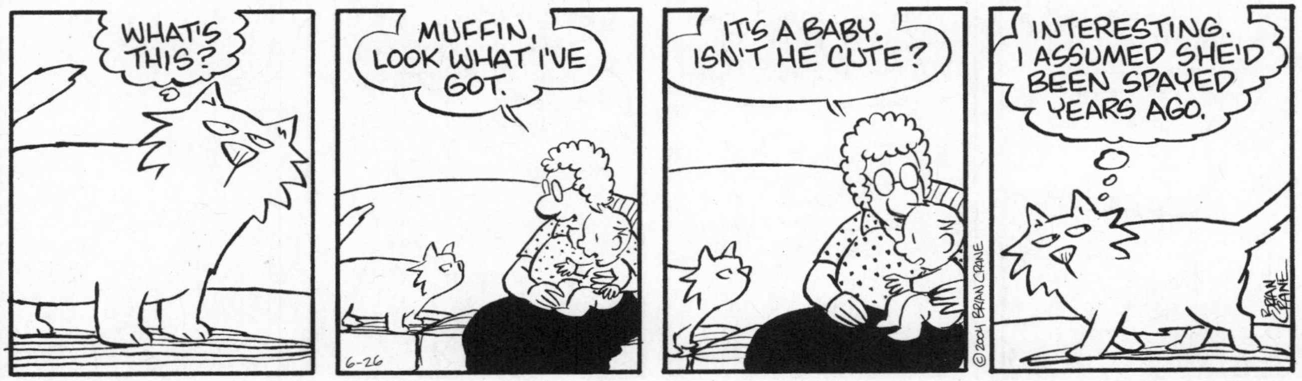
WHAT'S THIS?
MUFFIN, LOOK WHAT I'VE GOT.
6-26
IT'S A BABY. ISN'T HE CUTE?
© 2004 BRIAN CRANE
INTERESTING. I ASSUMED SHE'D BEEN SPAYED YEARS AGO.
BRIAN CRANE

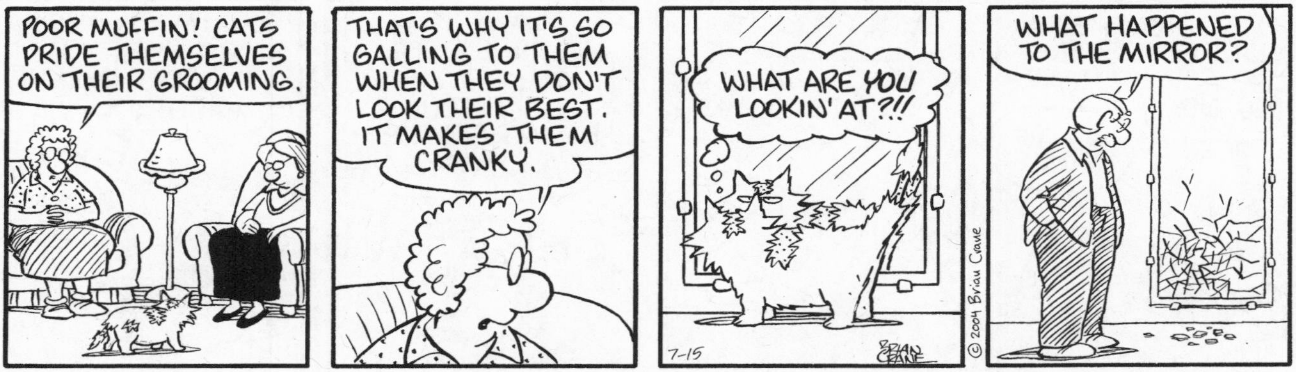
POOR MUFFIN! CATS PRIDE THEMSELVES ON THEIR GROOMING.
THAT'S WHY IT'S SO GALLING TO THEM WHEN THEY DON'T LOOK THEIR BEST. IT MAKES THEM CRANKY.
WHAT ARE YOU LOOKIN' AT?!!
7-15
BRIAN CRANE
© 2004 Brian Crane
WHAT HAPPENED TO THE MIRROR?

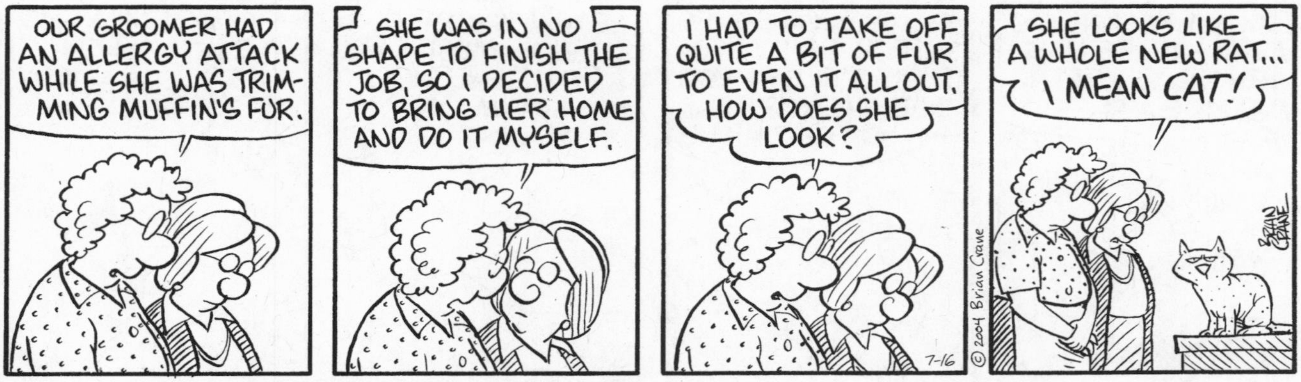
OUR GROOMER HAD AN ALLERGY ATTACK WHILE SHE WAS TRIMMING MUFFIN'S FUR.
SHE WAS IN NO SHAPE TO FINISH THE JOB, SO I DECIDED TO BRING HER HOME AND DO IT MYSELF.
I HAD TO TAKE OFF QUITE A BIT OF FUR TO EVEN IT ALL OUT. HOW DOES SHE LOOK?
7-16
© 2004 Brian Crane
SHE LOOKS LIKE A WHOLE NEW RAT... I MEAN CAT!
BRIAN CRANE

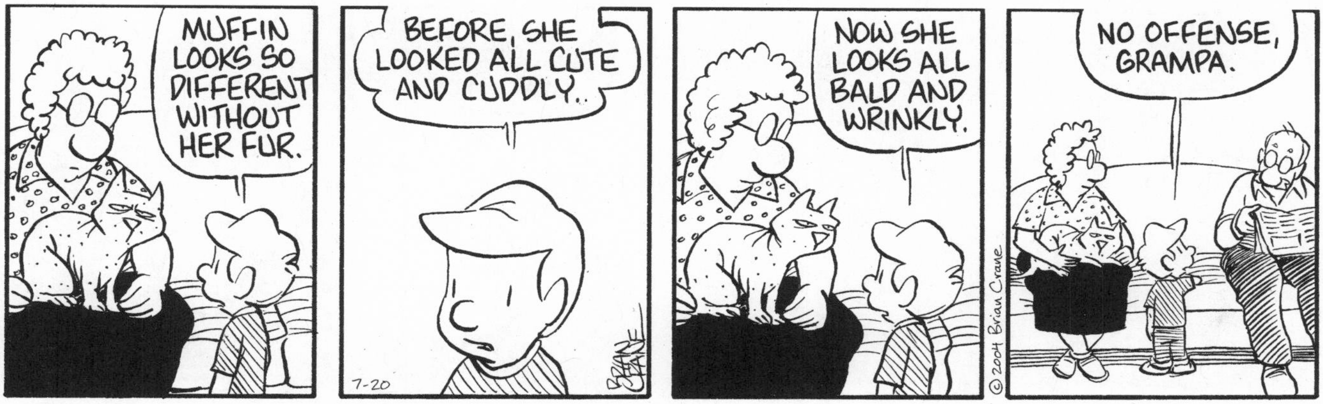
MUFFIN LOOKS SO DIFFERENT WITHOUT HER FUR.
BEFORE, SHE LOOKED ALL CUTE AND CUDDLY...
7-20
BRIAN CRANE
NOW SHE LOOKS ALL BALD AND WRINKLY.
© 2004 Brian Crane
NO OFFENSE, GRAMPA.

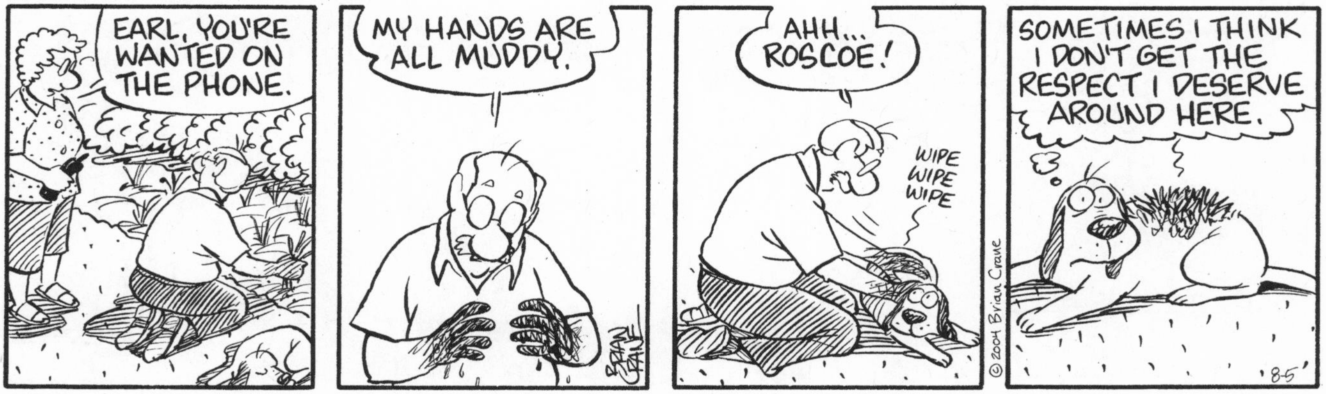
EARL, YOU'RE WANTED ON THE PHONE.
MY HANDS ARE ALL MUDDY.
BRIAN CRANE
AHH... ROSCOE!
WIPE WIPE WIPE
© 2004 Brian Crane
SOMETIMES I THINK I DON'T GET THE RESPECT I DESERVE AROUND HERE.
8-5

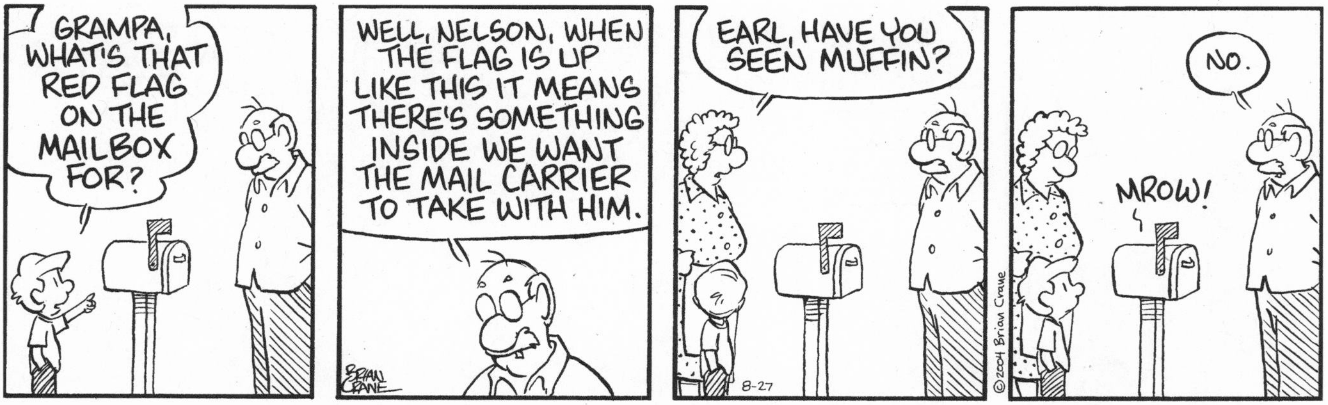
GRAMPA, WHAT'S THAT RED FLAG ON THE MAILBOX FOR?
WELL, NELSON, WHEN THE FLAG IS UP LIKE THIS IT MEANS THERE'S SOMETHING INSIDE WE WANT THE MAIL CARRIER TO TAKE WITH HIM.
BRIAN CRANE
EARL, HAVE YOU SEEN MUFFIN?
8-27
© 2004 Brian Crane
NO.
MROW!

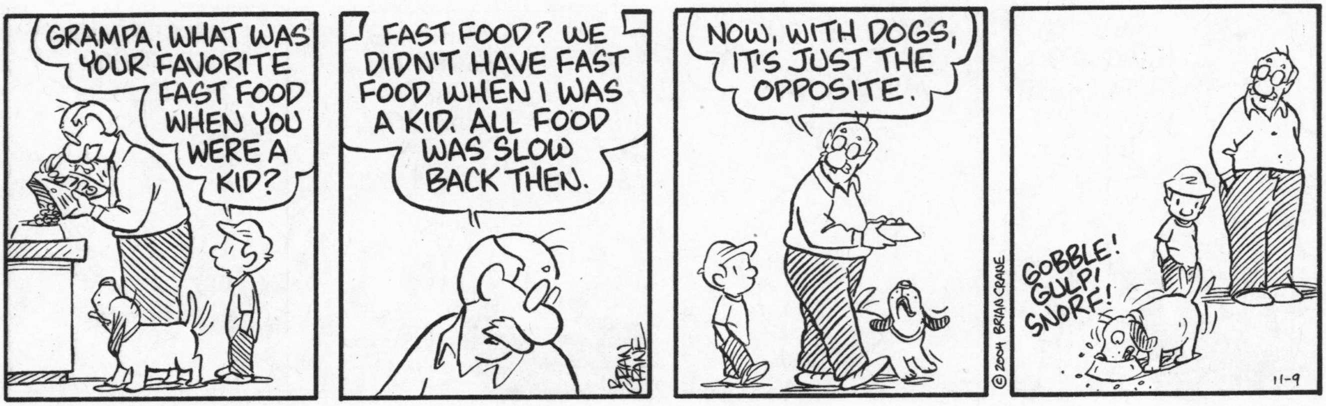
GRAMPA, WHAT WAS YOUR FAVORITE FAST FOOD WHEN YOU WERE A KID?
FAST FOOD? WE DIDN'T HAVE FAST FOOD WHEN I WAS A KID. ALL FOOD WAS SLOW BACK THEN.
BRIAN CRANE
NOW, WITH DOGS, IT'S JUST THE OPPOSITE.
© 2004 BRIAN CRANE
GOBBLE! GULP! SNORF!
11-9

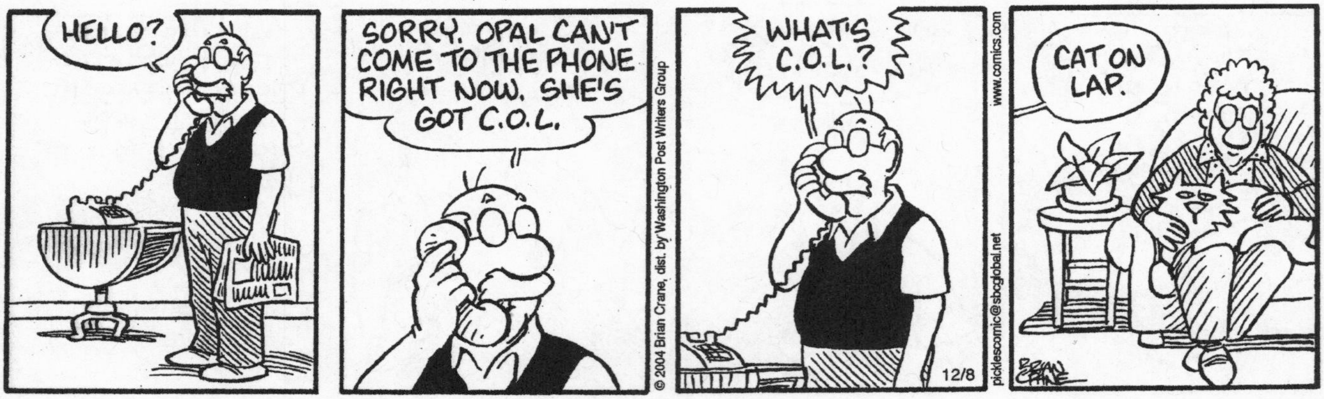
HELLO?
SORRY. OPAL CAN'T COME TO THE PHONE RIGHT NOW. SHE'S GOT C.O.L.
© 2004 Brian Crane, dist. by Washington Post Writers Group
WHAT'S C.O.L.?
12/8
picklescomic@sbcglobal.net
www.comics.com
CAT ON LAP.
BRIAN CRANE

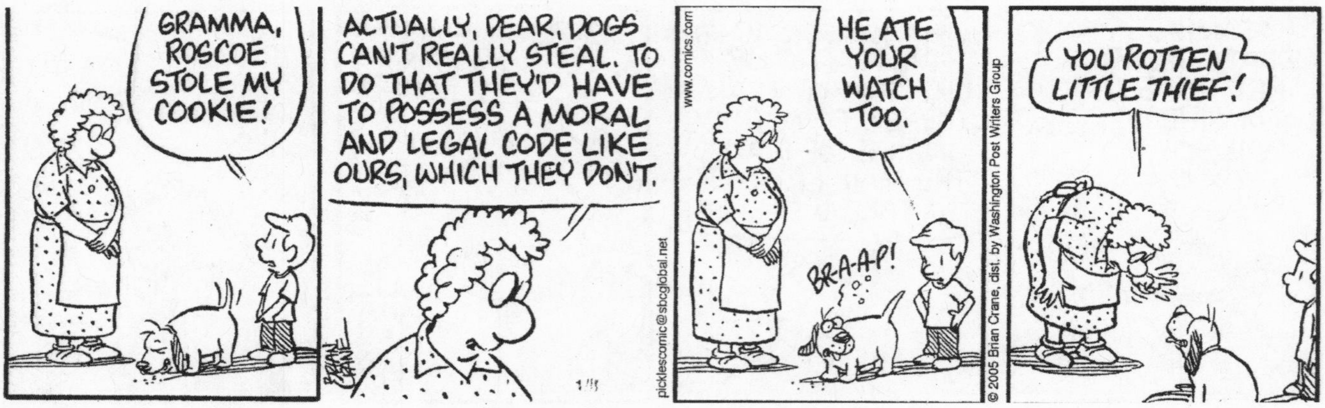
GRAMMA, ROSCOE STOLE MY COOKIE!
ACTUALLY, DEAR, DOGS CAN'T REALLY STEAL. TO DO THAT THEY'D HAVE TO POSSESS A MORAL AND LEGAL CODE LIKE OURS, WHICH THEY DON'T.
BRIAN CRANE
picklescomic@sbcglobal.net
www.comics.com
HE ATE YOUR WATCH TOO.
BR-A-A-P!
© 2005 Brian Crane, dist. by Washington Post Writers Group
YOU ROTTEN LITTLE THIEF!

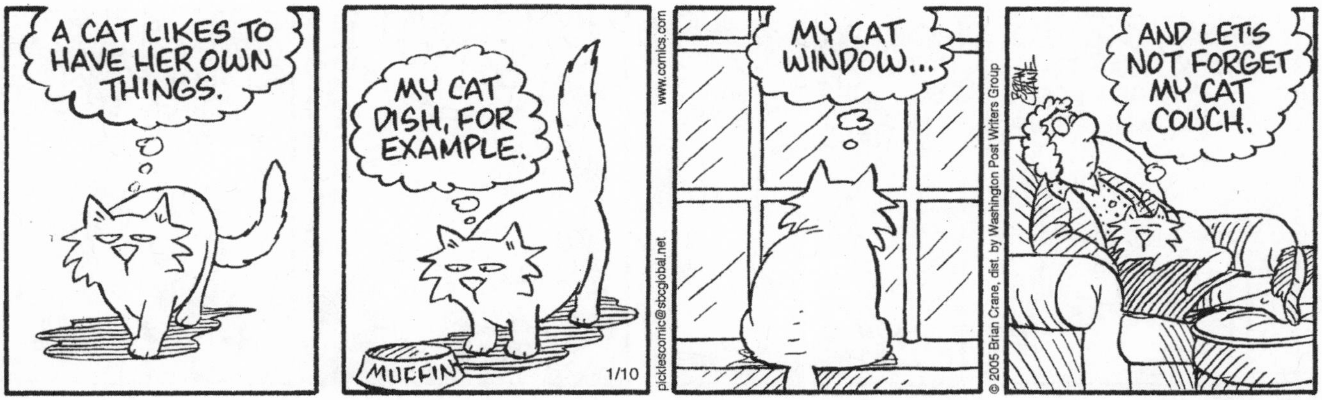
A CAT LIKES TO HAVE HER OWN THINGS.
MY CAT DISH, FOR EXAMPLE.
MUFFIN
1/10
www.comics.com
picklescomic@sbcglobal.net
MY CAT WINDOW...
AND LET'S NOT FORGET MY CAT COUCH.
© 2005 Brian Crane, dist. by Washington Post Writers Group

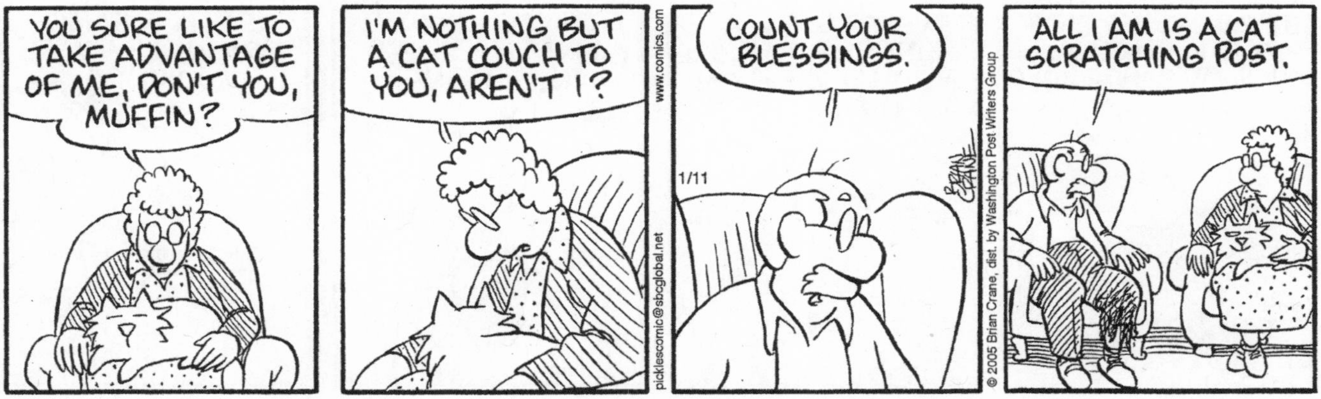
YOU SURE LIKE TO TAKE ADVANTAGE OF ME, DON'T YOU, MUFFIN?
I'M NOTHING BUT A CAT COUCH TO YOU, AREN'T I?
www.comics.com
picklescomic@sbcglobal.net
COUNT YOUR BLESSINGS.
1/11
ALL I AM IS A CAT SCRATCHING POST.
© 2005 Brian Crane, dist. by Washington Post Writers Group

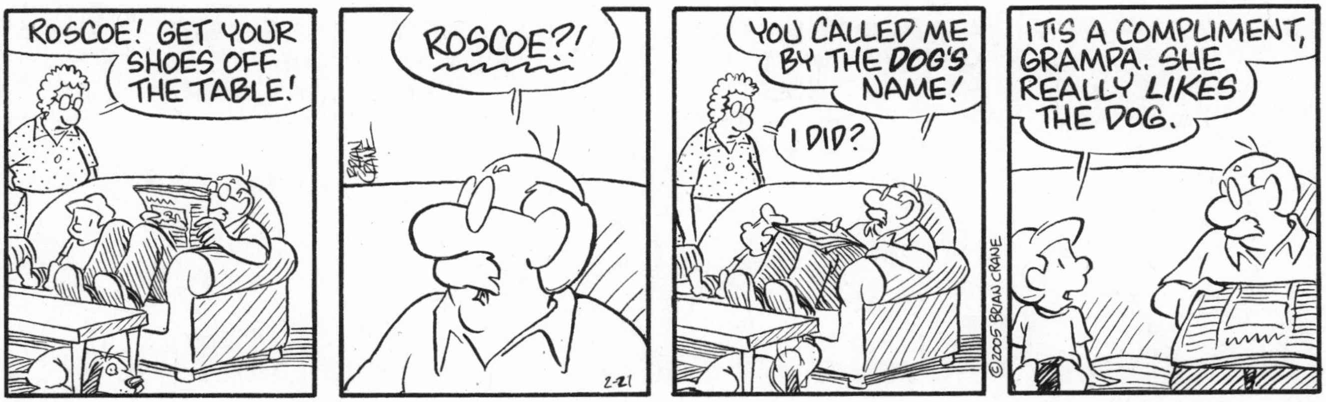
ROSCOE! GET YOUR SHOES OFF THE TABLE!
ROSCOE?!
2-21
YOU CALLED ME BY THE DOG'S NAME!
I DID?
©2005 BRIAN CRANE
IT'S A COMPLIMENT, GRAMPA. SHE REALLY LIKES THE DOG.

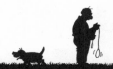

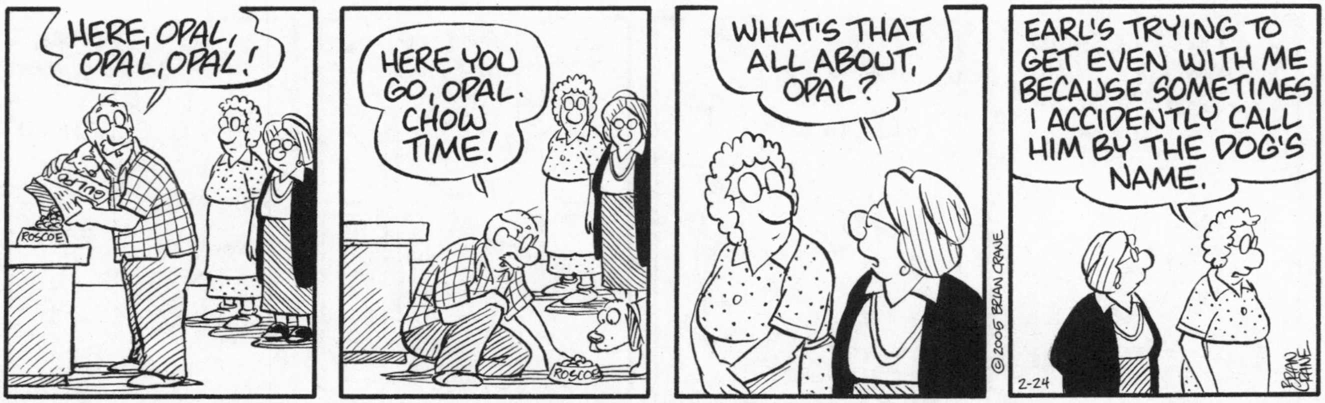
HERE, OPAL, OPAL, OPAL!
HERE YOU GO, OPAL. CHOW TIME!
WHAT'S THAT ALL ABOUT, OPAL?
EARL'S TRYING TO GET EVEN WITH ME BECAUSE SOMETIMES I ACCIDENTLY CALL HIM BY THE DOG'S NAME.
© 2005 BRIAN CRANE
2-24

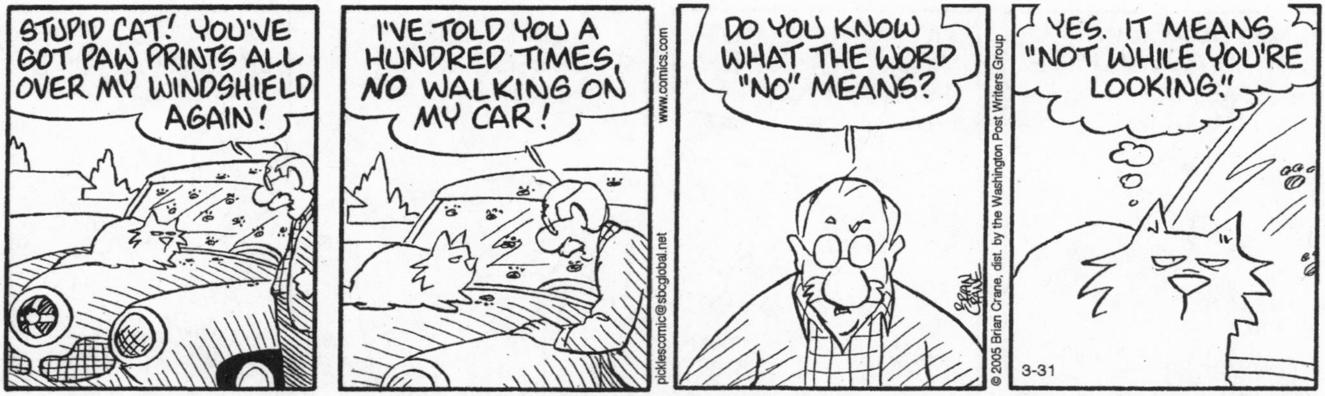
STUPID CAT! YOU'VE GOT PAW PRINTS ALL OVER MY WINDSHIELD AGAIN!
I'VE TOLD YOU A HUNDRED TIMES, NO WALKING ON MY CAR!
DO YOU KNOW WHAT THE WORD "NO" MEANS?
YES. IT MEANS "NOT WHILE YOU'RE LOOKING."
www.comics.com
picklescomic@sbcglobal.net
© 2005 Brian Crane, dist. by the Washington Post Writers Group
3-31

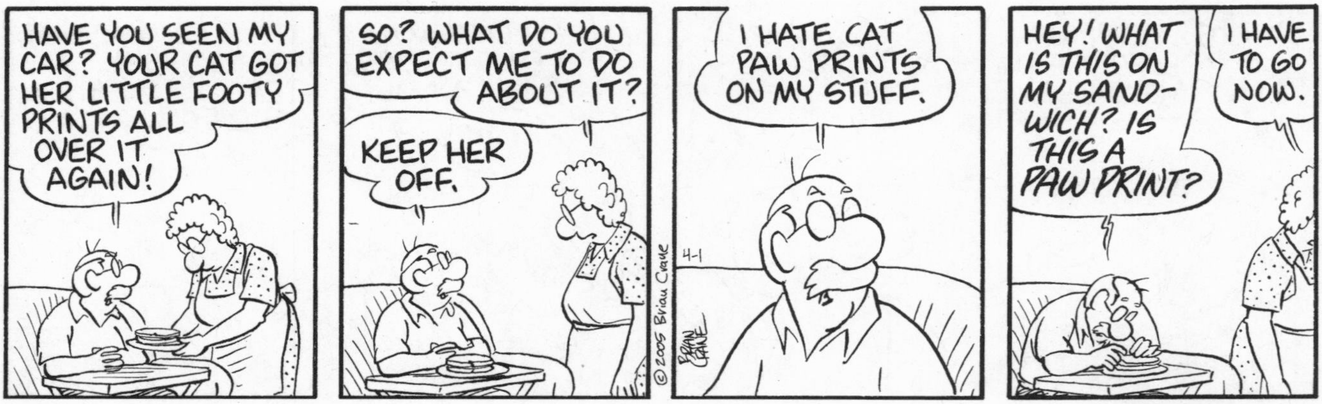
HAVE YOU SEEN MY CAR? YOUR CAT GOT HER LITTLE FOOTY PRINTS ALL OVER IT AGAIN!
SO? WHAT DO YOU EXPECT ME TO DO ABOUT IT?
KEEP HER OFF.
I HATE CAT PAW PRINTS ON MY STUFF.
HEY! WHAT IS THIS ON MY SANDWICH? IS THIS A PAW PRINT?
I HAVE TO GO NOW.
© 2005 Brian Crane
4-1

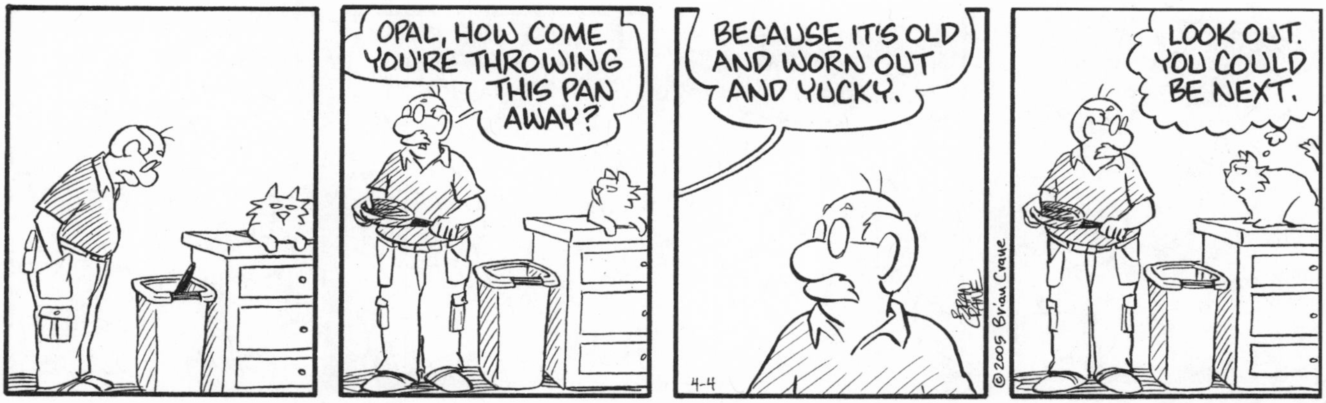
OPAL, HOW COME YOU'RE THROWING THIS PAN AWAY?
BECAUSE IT'S OLD AND WORN OUT AND YUCKY.
4-4
© 2005 Brian Crane
LOOK OUT. YOU COULD BE NEXT.

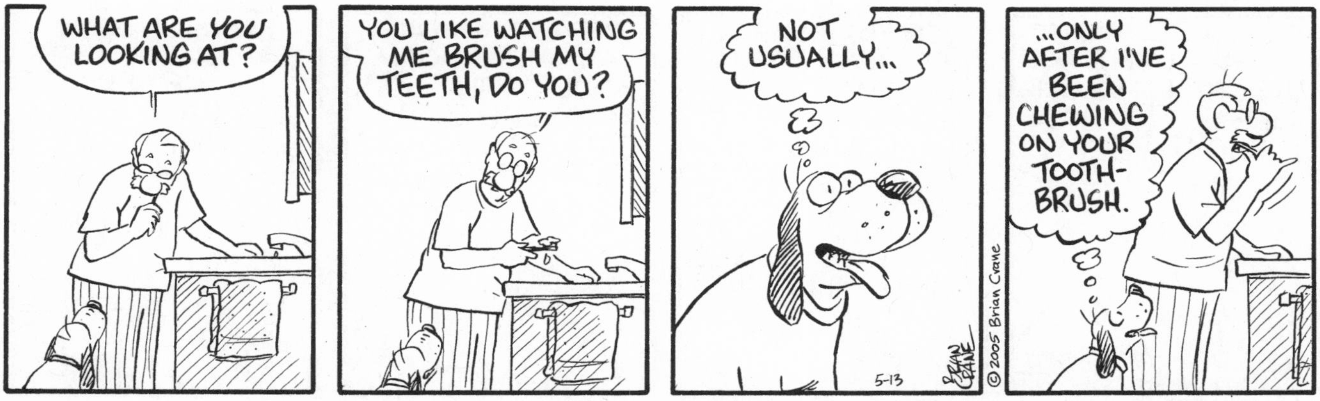
WHAT ARE YOU LOOKING AT?
YOU LIKE WATCHING ME BRUSH MY TEETH, DO YOU?
NOT USUALLY...
5-13
© 2005 Brian Crane
...ONLY AFTER I'VE BEEN CHEWING ON YOUR TOOTH-BRUSH.

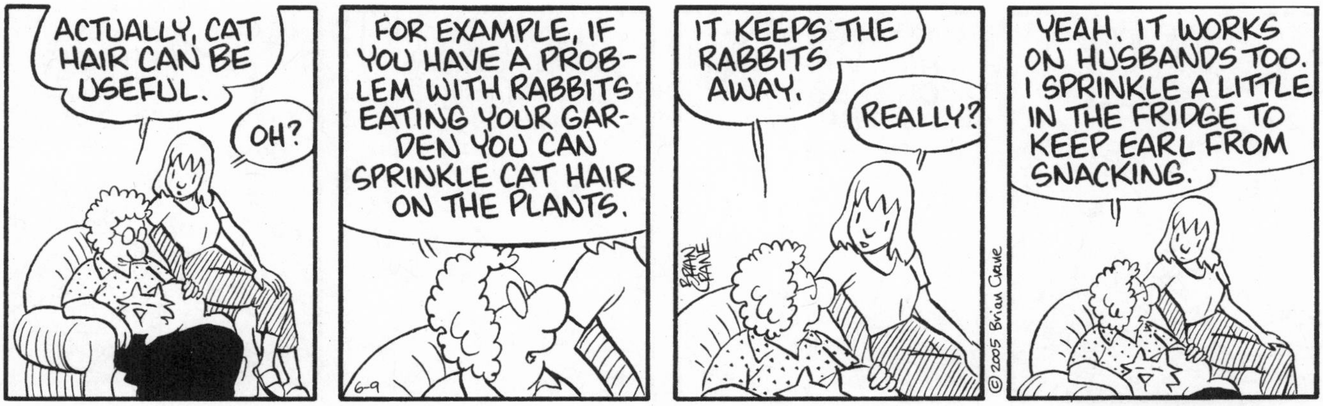
ACTUALLY, CAT HAIR CAN BE USEFUL.
OH?
6-9
FOR EXAMPLE, IF YOU HAVE A PROB-LEM WITH RABBITS EATING YOUR GAR-DEN YOU CAN SPRINKLE CAT HAIR ON THE PLANTS.
IT KEEPS THE RABBITS AWAY.
REALLY?
© 2005 Brian Crane
YEAH. IT WORKS ON HUSBANDS TOO. I SPRINKLE A LITTLE IN THE FRIDGE TO KEEP EARL FROM SNACKING.

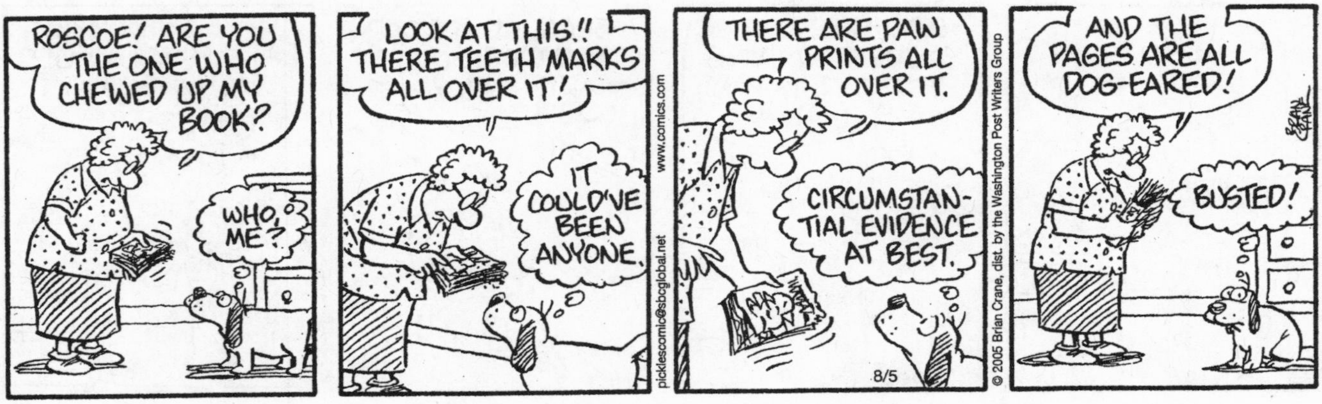
ROSCOE! ARE YOU THE ONE WHO CHEWED UP MY BOOK?
WHO, ME?
LOOK AT THIS!! THERE TEETH MARKS ALL OVER IT!
IT COULD'VE BEEN ANYONE.
www.comics.com
picklescomic@sbcglobal.net
THERE ARE PAW PRINTS ALL OVER IT.
CIRCUMSTANTIAL EVIDENCE AT BEST.
8/5
© 2005 Brian Crane, dist. by the Washington Post Writers Group
AND THE PAGES ARE ALL DOG-EARED!
BUSTED!

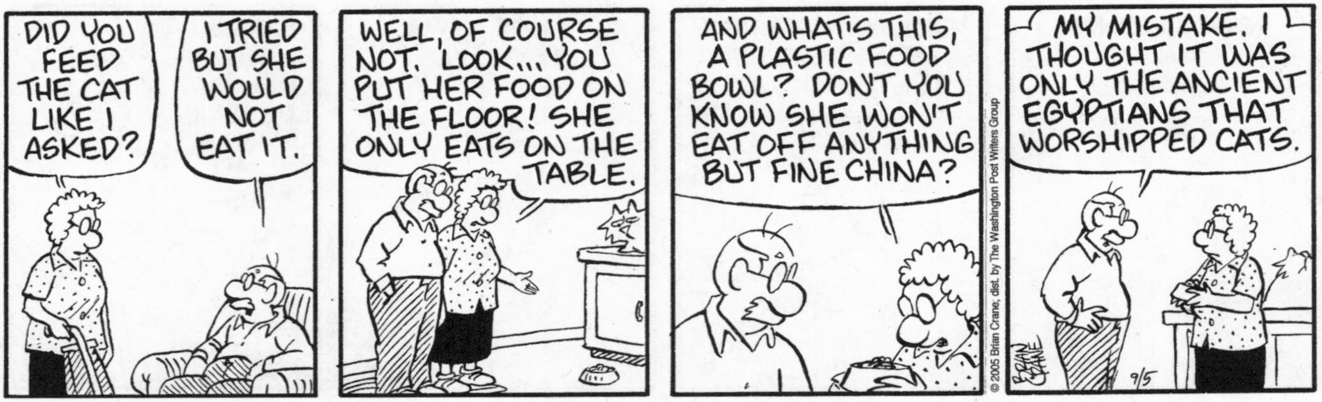
DID YOU FEED THE CAT LIKE I ASKED?
I TRIED BUT SHE WOULD NOT EAT IT.
WELL, OF COURSE NOT. LOOK... YOU PUT HER FOOD ON THE FLOOR! SHE ONLY EATS ON THE TABLE.
AND WHAT'S THIS, A PLASTIC FOOD BOWL? DON'T YOU KNOW SHE WON'T EAT OFF ANYTHING BUT FINE CHINA?
© 2005 Brian Crane, dist. by The Washington Post Writers Group
MY MISTAKE. I THOUGHT IT WAS ONLY THE ANCIENT EGYPTIANS THAT WORSHIPPED CATS.
9/5

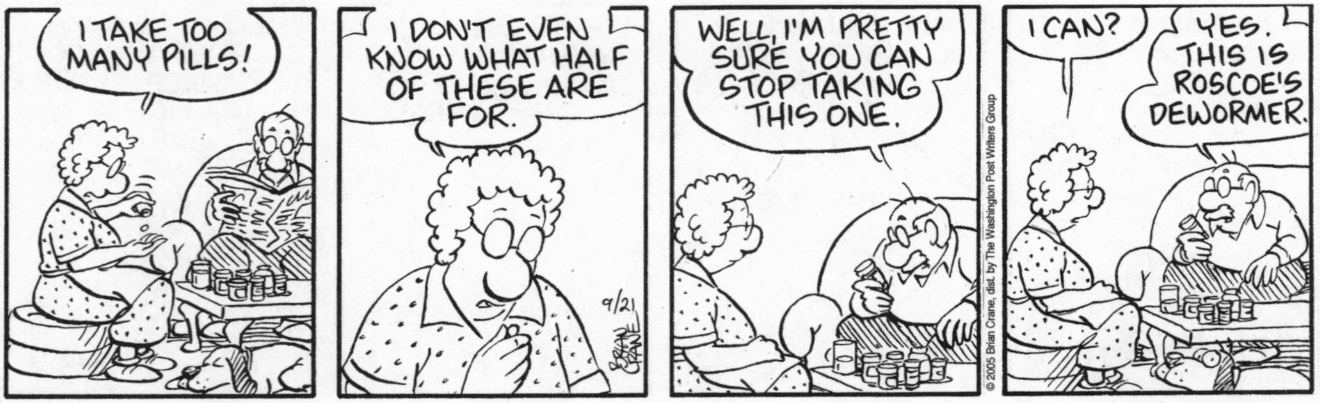
I TAKE TOO MANY PILLS!
I DON'T EVEN KNOW WHAT HALF OF THESE ARE FOR.
9/21
WELL, I'M PRETTY SURE YOU CAN STOP TAKING THIS ONE.
© 2005 Brian Crane, dist. by The Washington Post Writers Group
I CAN?
YES. THIS IS ROSCOE'S DEWORMER.

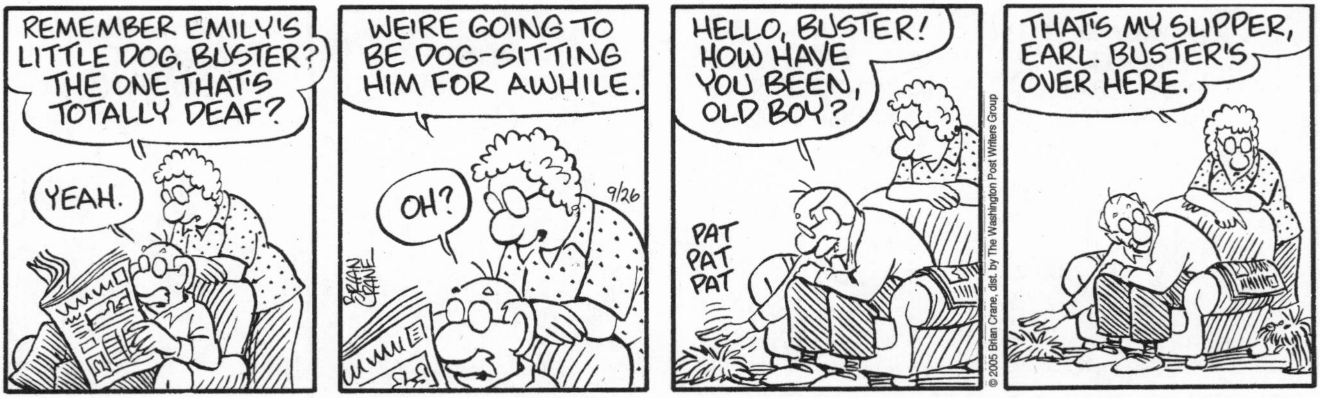
REMEMBER EMILY'S LITTLE DOG, BUSTER? THE ONE THAT'S TOTALLY DEAF?
YEAH.
WE'RE GOING TO BE DOG-SITTING HIM FOR AWHILE.
OH?
9/26
BRIAN CRANE
HELLO, BUSTER! HOW HAVE YOU BEEN, OLD BOY?
PAT PAT PAT
© 2005 Brian Crane, dist. by The Washington Post Writers Group
THAT'S MY SLIPPER, EARL. BUSTER'S OVER HERE.

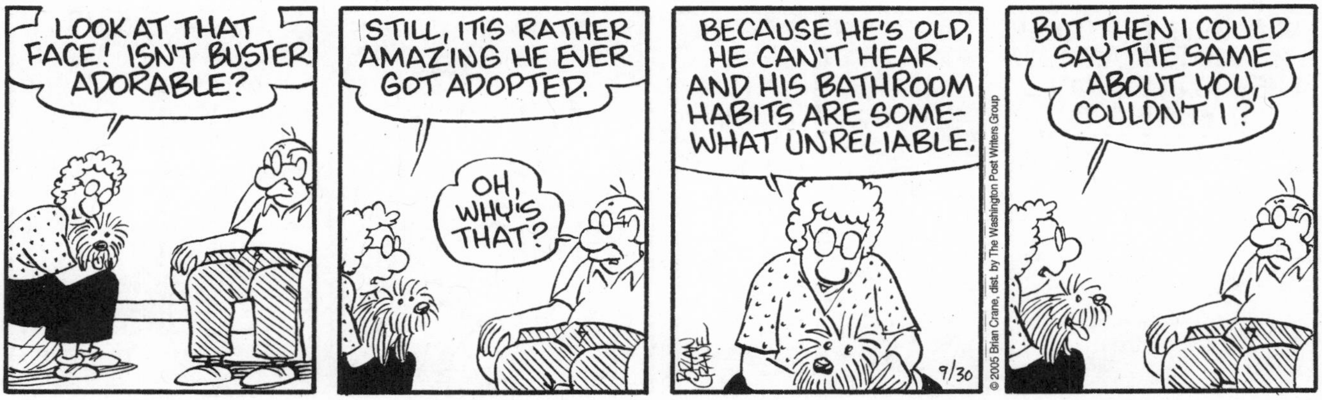
LOOK AT THAT FACE! ISN'T BUSTER ADORABLE?
STILL, IT'S RATHER AMAZING HE EVER GOT ADOPTED.
OH, WHY'S THAT?
BECAUSE HE'S OLD, HE CAN'T HEAR AND HIS BATHROOM HABITS ARE SOME-WHAT UNRELIABLE.
BRIAN CRANE
9/30
© 2005 Brian Crane, dist. by The Washington Post Writers Group
BUT THEN I COULD SAY THE SAME ABOUT YOU, COULDN'T I?

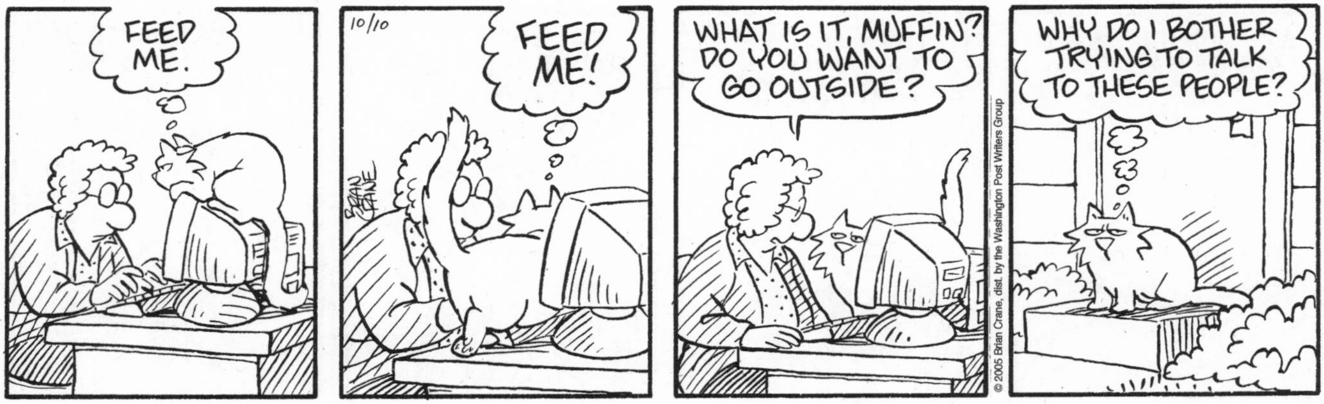
FEED ME.
10/10
FEED ME!
BRIAN CRANE
WHAT IS IT, MUFFIN? DO YOU WANT TO GO OUTSIDE?
© 2005 Brian Crane, dist. by the Washington Post Writers Group
WHY DO I BOTHER TRYING TO TALK TO THESE PEOPLE?

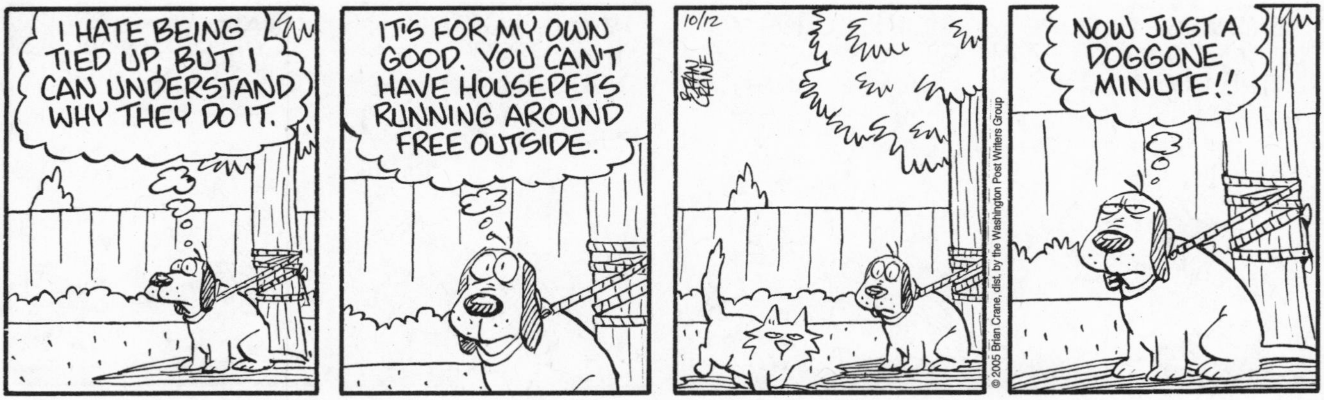
I HATE BEING TIED UP, BUT I CAN UNDERSTAND WHY THEY DO IT.
IT'S FOR MY OWN GOOD. YOU CAN'T HAVE HOUSEPETS RUNNING AROUND FREE OUTSIDE.
10/12
BRIAN CRANE
NOW JUST A DOGGONE MINUTE!!
© 2005 Brian Crane, dist. by the Washington Post Writers Group

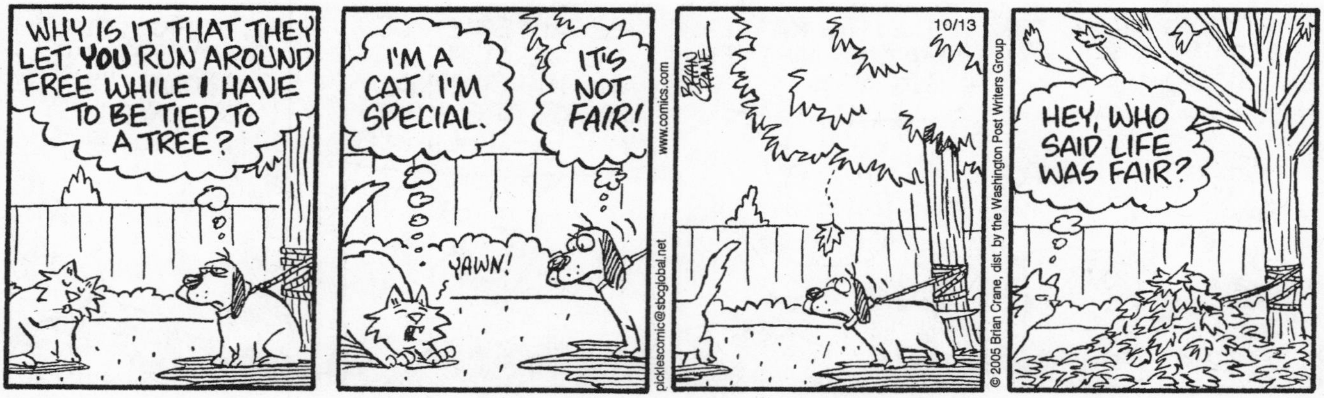
WHY IS IT THAT THEY LET **YOU** RUN AROUND FREE WHILE **I** HAVE TO BE TIED TO A TREE?
I'M A CAT. I'M SPECIAL.
YAWN!
IT'S NOT **FAIR!**
www.comics.com
picklescomic@sbcglobal.net
BRIAN CRANE
10/13
HEY, WHO SAID LIFE WAS FAIR?
© 2005 Brian Crane, dist. by the Washington Post Writers Group

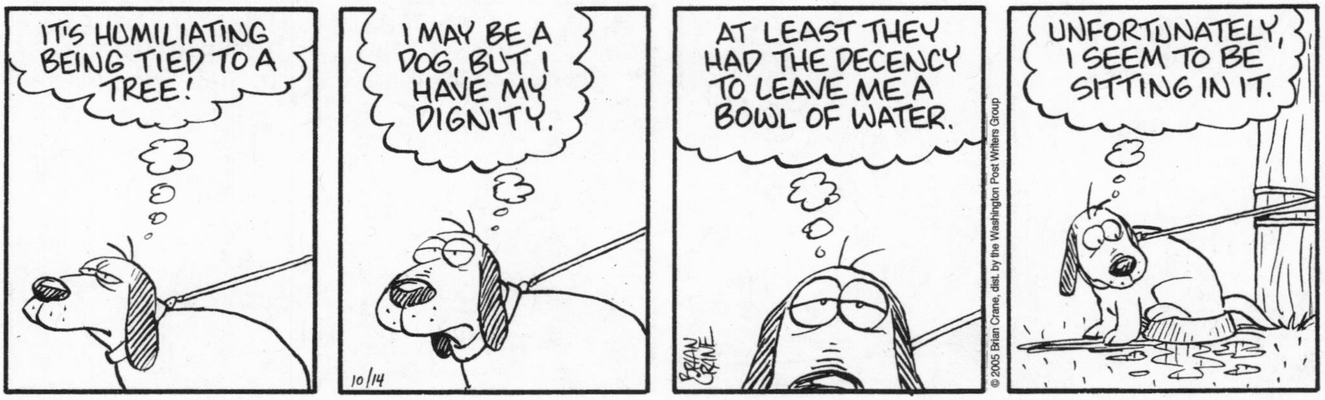
IT'S HUMILIATING BEING TIED TO A TREE!
I MAY BE A DOG, BUT I HAVE MY DIGNITY.
10/14
AT LEAST THEY HAD THE DECENCY TO LEAVE ME A BOWL OF WATER.
BRIAN CRANE
UNFORTUNATELY, I SEEM TO BE SITTING IN IT.
© 2005 Brian Crane, dist. by the Washington Post Writers Group

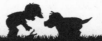

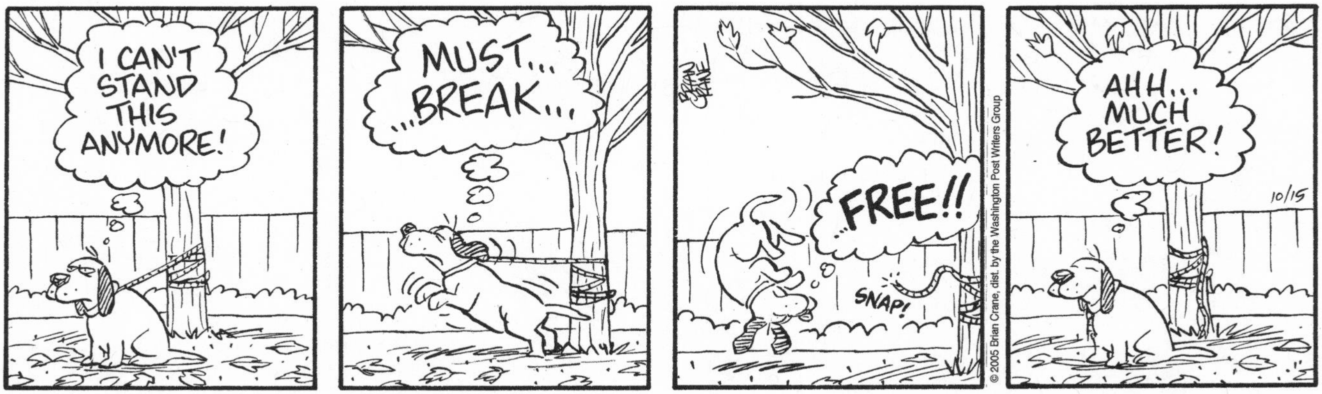
I CAN'T STAND THIS ANYMORE!
MUST... ...BREAK...
BRIAN CRANE
FREE!!
SNAP!
© 2005 Brian Crane, dist. by the Washington Post Writers Group
AHH... MUCH BETTER!
10/15

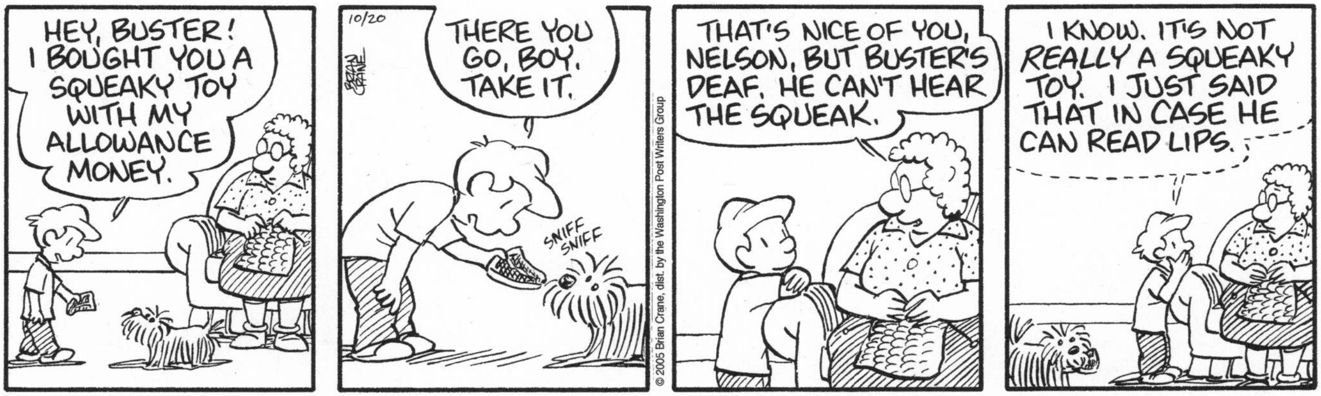
HEY, BUSTER! I BOUGHT YOU A SQUEAKY TOY WITH MY ALLOWANCE MONEY.
10/20
BRIAN CRANE
THERE YOU GO, BOY. TAKE IT.
SNIFF SNIFF
© 2005 Brian Crane, dist. by the Washington Post Writers Group
THAT'S NICE OF YOU, NELSON, BUT BUSTER'S DEAF. HE CAN'T HEAR THE SQUEAK.
I KNOW. IT'S NOT *REALLY* A SQUEAKY TOY. I JUST SAID THAT IN CASE HE CAN READ LIPS.

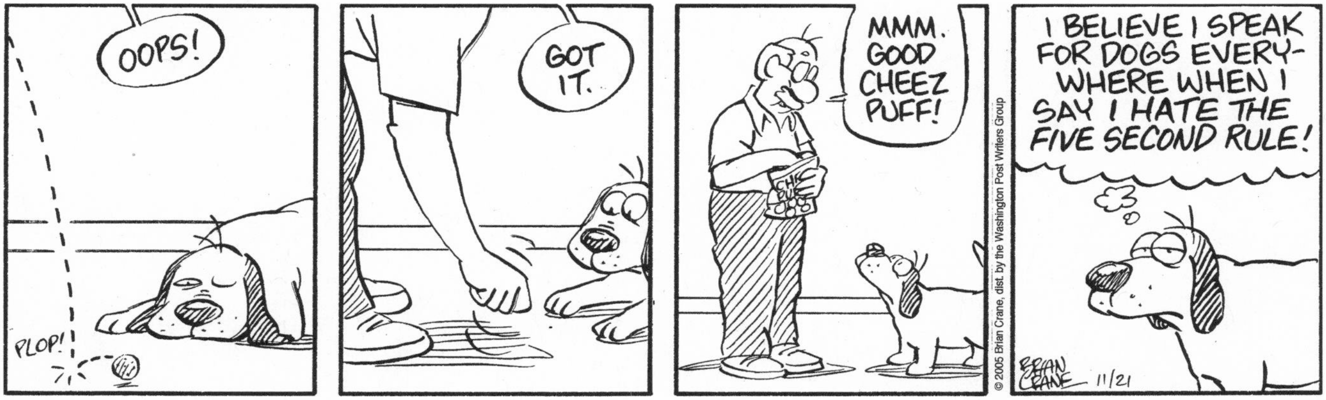
OOPS!
PLOP!
GOT IT.
MMM. GOOD CHEEZ PUFF!
© 2005 Brian Crane, dist. by the Washington Post Writers Group
I BELIEVE I SPEAK FOR DOGS EVERY-WHERE WHEN I SAY I HATE THE *FIVE SECOND RULE!*
BRIAN CRANE
11/21

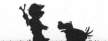

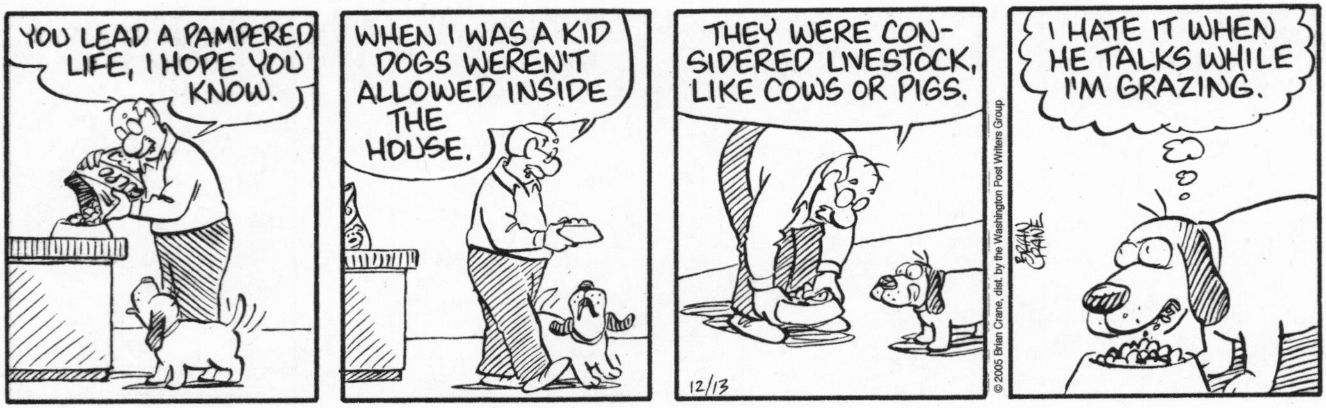
YOU LEAD A PAMPERED LIFE, I HOPE YOU KNOW.
WHEN I WAS A KID DOGS WEREN'T ALLOWED INSIDE THE HOUSE.
THEY WERE CON-SIDERED LIVESTOCK, LIKE COWS OR PIGS.
12/13
© 2005 Brian Crane, dist. by the Washington Post Writers Group
I HATE IT WHEN HE TALKS WHILE I'M GRAZING.
BRIAN CRANE

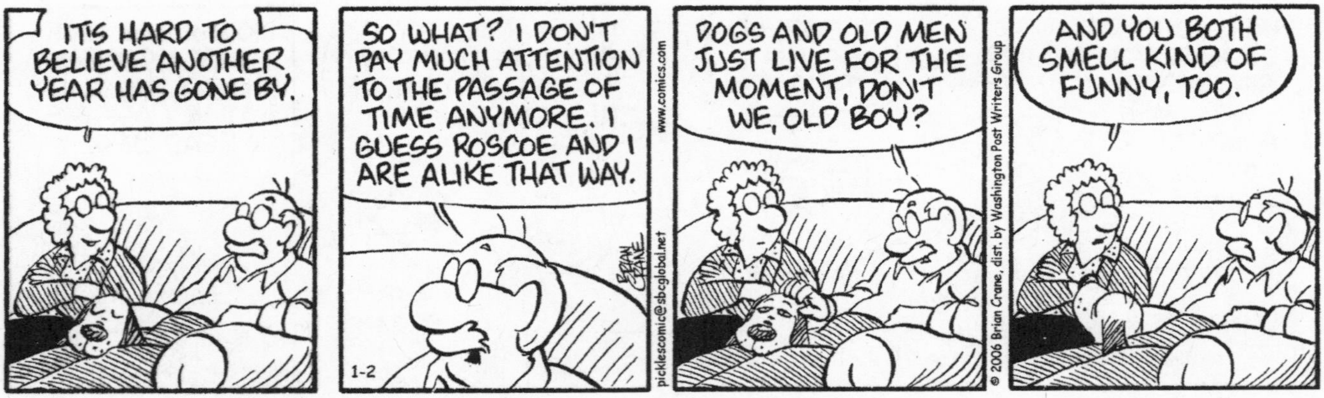
IT'S HARD TO BELIEVE ANOTHER YEAR HAS GONE BY.
SO WHAT? I DON'T PAY MUCH ATTENTION TO THE PASSAGE OF TIME ANYMORE. I GUESS ROSCOE AND I ARE ALIKE THAT WAY.
BRIAN CRANE
1-2
www.comics.com
picklescomic@sbcglobal.net
DOGS AND OLD MEN JUST LIVE FOR THE MOMENT, DON'T WE, OLD BOY?
© 2006 Brian Crane, dist. by Washington Post Writers Group
AND YOU BOTH SMELL KIND OF FUNNY, TOO.

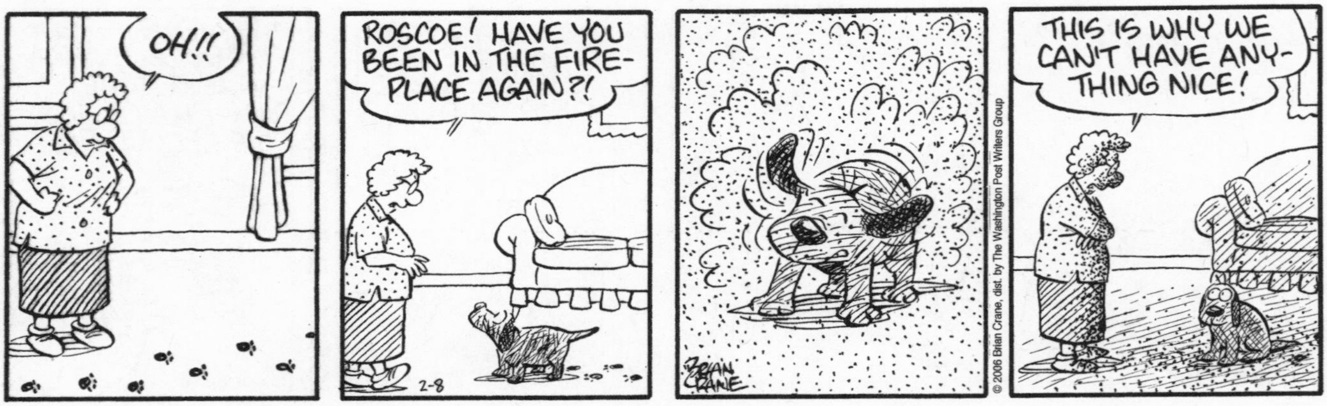
OH!!
ROSCOE! HAVE YOU BEEN IN THE FIRE-PLACE AGAIN?!
2-8
© 2006 Brian Crane, dist. by The Washington Post Writers Group
BRIAN CRANE
THIS IS WHY WE CAN'T HAVE ANY-THING NICE!

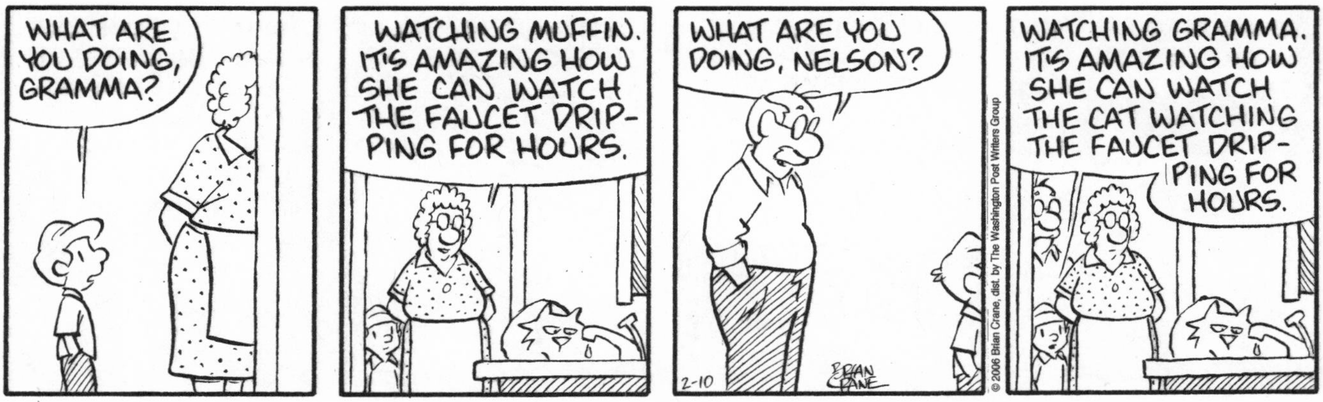
WHAT ARE YOU DOING, GRAMMA?
WATCHING MUFFIN. IT'S AMAZING HOW SHE CAN WATCH THE FAUCET DRIP-PING FOR HOURS.
2-10
WHAT ARE YOU DOING, NELSON?
BRIAN CRANE
© 2006 Brian Crane, dist. by The Washington Post Writers Group
WATCHING GRAMMA. IT'S AMAZING HOW SHE CAN WATCH THE CAT WATCHING THE FAUCET DRIP-PING FOR HOURS.

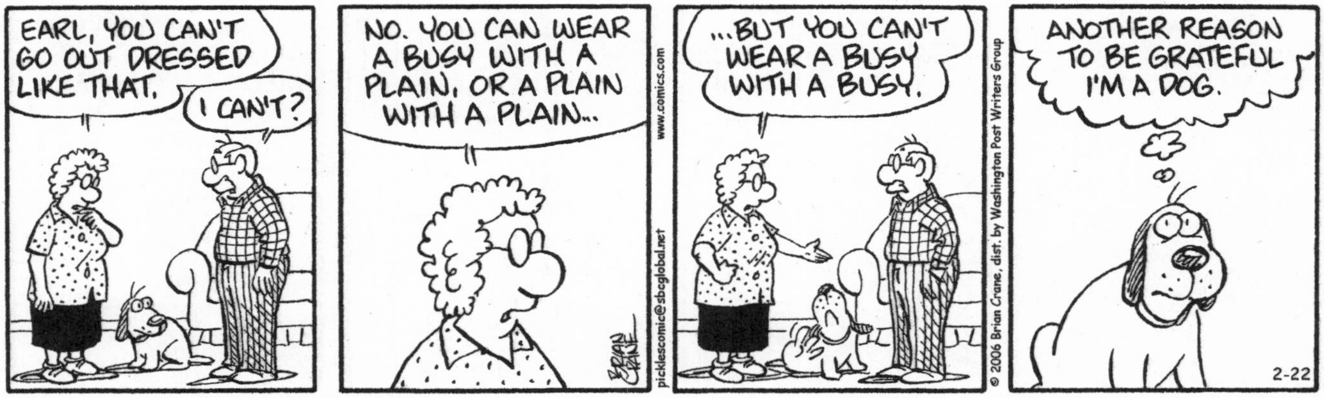
EARL, YOU CAN'T GO OUT DRESSED LIKE THAT.
I CAN'T?
NO. YOU CAN WEAR A BUSY WITH A PLAIN, OR A PLAIN WITH A PLAIN...
BRIAN CRANE
www.comics.com
picklescomic@sbcglobal.net
...BUT YOU CAN'T WEAR A BUSY WITH A BUSY.
© 2006 Brian Crane, dist. by Washington Post Writers Group
ANOTHER REASON TO BE GRATEFUL I'M A DOG.
2-22

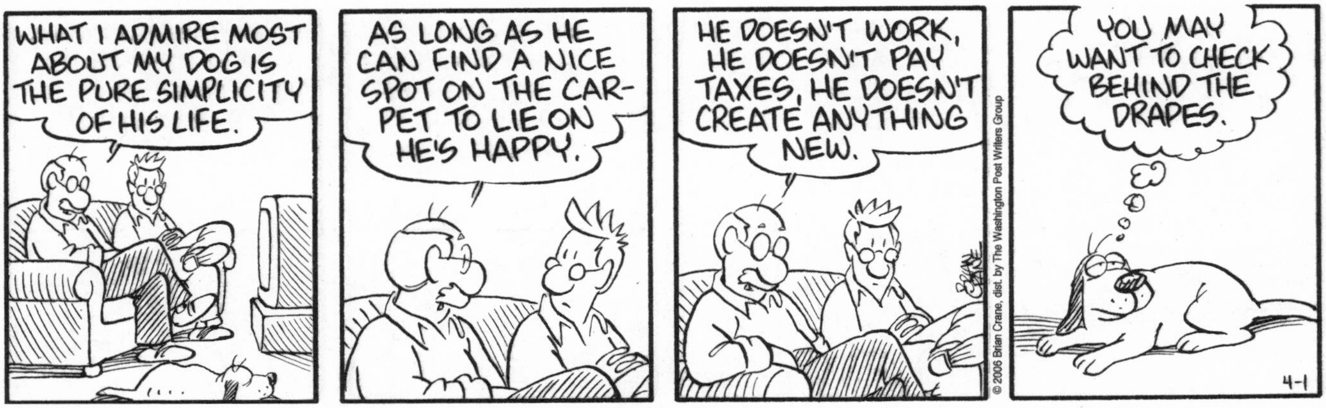
WHAT I ADMIRE MOST ABOUT MY DOG IS THE PURE SIMPLICITY OF HIS LIFE.
AS LONG AS HE CAN FIND A NICE SPOT ON THE CAR-PET TO LIE ON HE'S HAPPY.
HE DOESN'T WORK, HE DOESN'T PAY TAXES, HE DOESN'T CREATE ANYTHING NEW.
BRIAN CRANE
© 2006 Brian Crane, dist. by The Washington Post Writers Group
YOU MAY WANT TO CHECK BEHIND THE DRAPES.
4-1

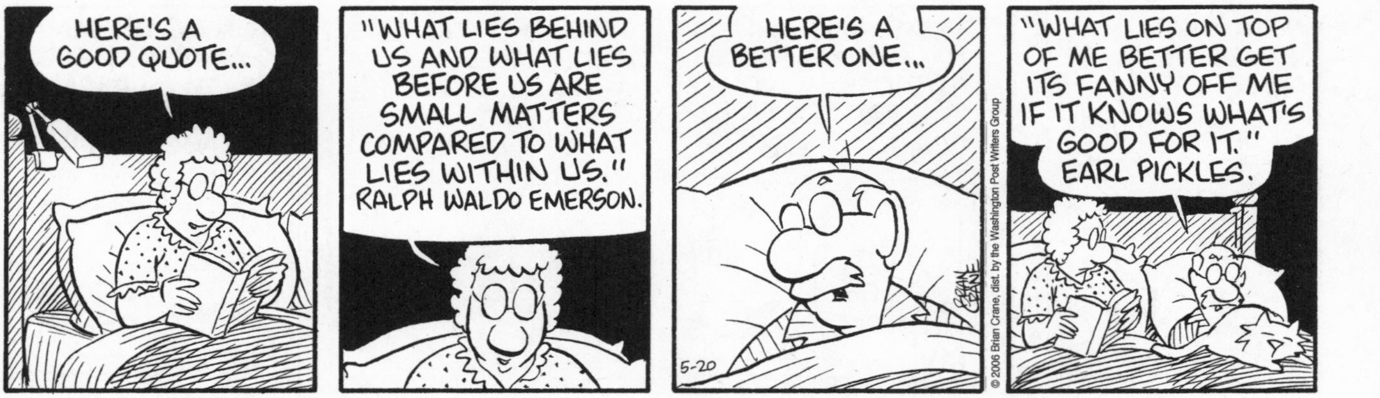
HERE'S A GOOD QUOTE...
"WHAT LIES BEHIND US AND WHAT LIES BEFORE US ARE SMALL MATTERS COMPARED TO WHAT LIES WITHIN US." RALPH WALDO EMERSON.
HERE'S A BETTER ONE...
"WHAT LIES ON TOP OF ME BETTER GET ITS FANNY OFF ME IF IT KNOWS WHAT'S GOOD FOR IT." EARL PICKLES.
5-20
BRIAN CRANE
© 2006 Brian Crane, dist. by the Washington Post Writers Group

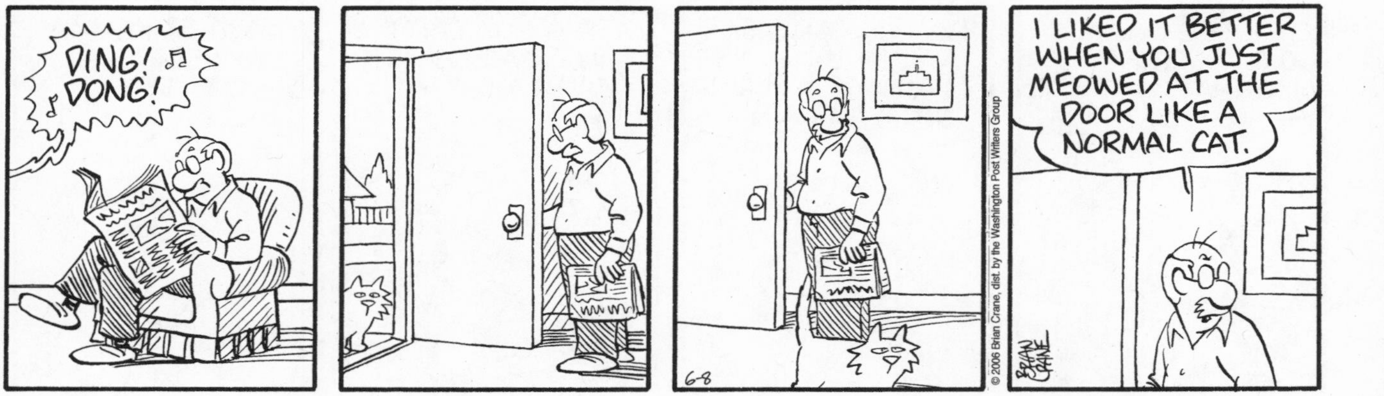
DING! DONG!
I LIKED IT BETTER WHEN YOU JUST MEOWED AT THE DOOR LIKE A NORMAL CAT.
6-8
BRIAN CRANE
© 2006 Brian Crane, dist. by the Washington Post Writers Group

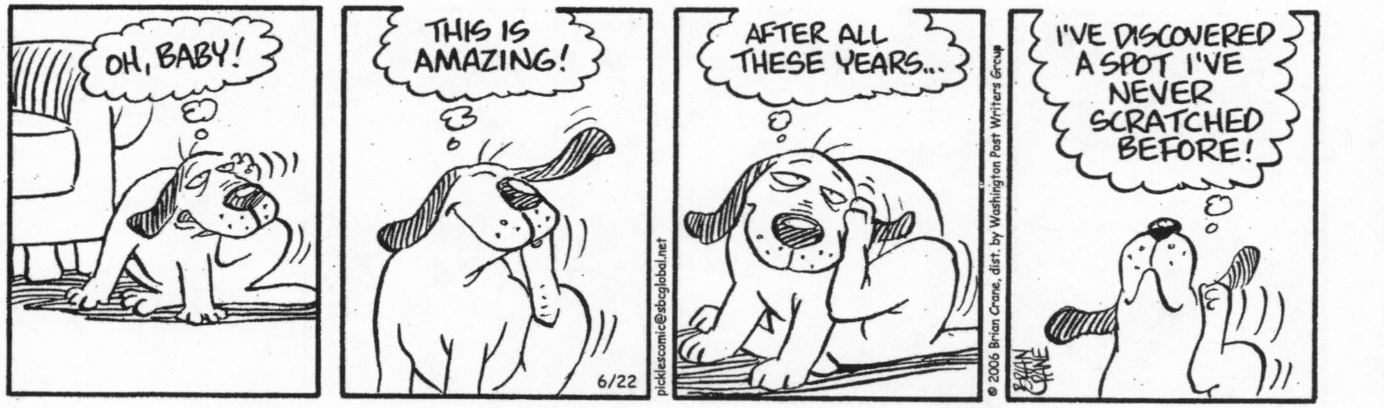
OH, BABY!
THIS IS AMAZING!
AFTER ALL THESE YEARS...
I'VE DISCOVERED A SPOT I'VE NEVER SCRATCHED BEFORE!
6/22
picklescomic@sbcglobal.net
© 2006 Brian Crane, dist. by Washington Post Writers Group
BRIAN CRANE

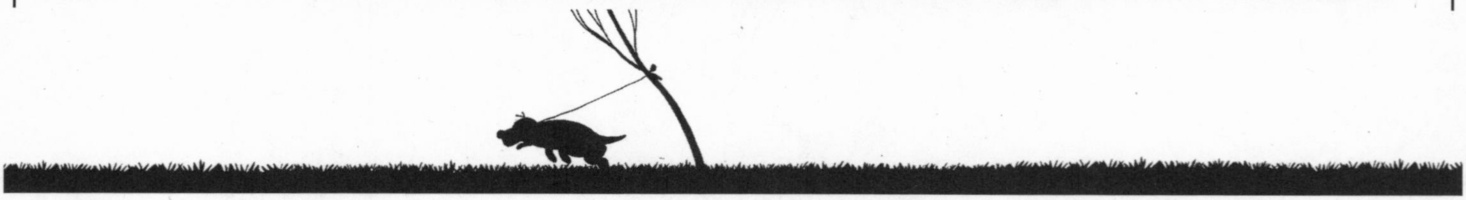

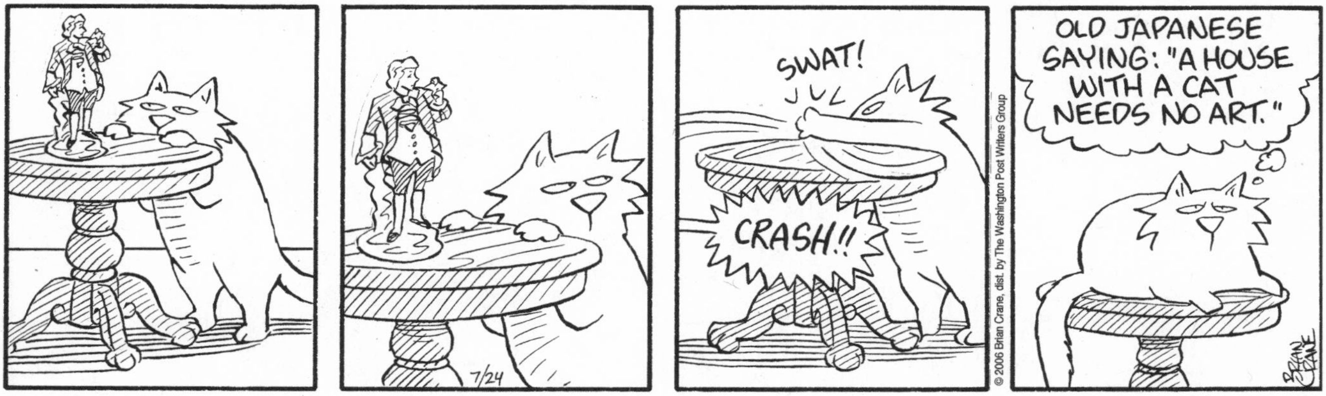
SWAT!
CRASH!!
OLD JAPANESE SAYING: "A HOUSE WITH A CAT NEEDS NO ART."
7/24
© 2006 Brian Crane, dist. by The Washington Post Writers Group

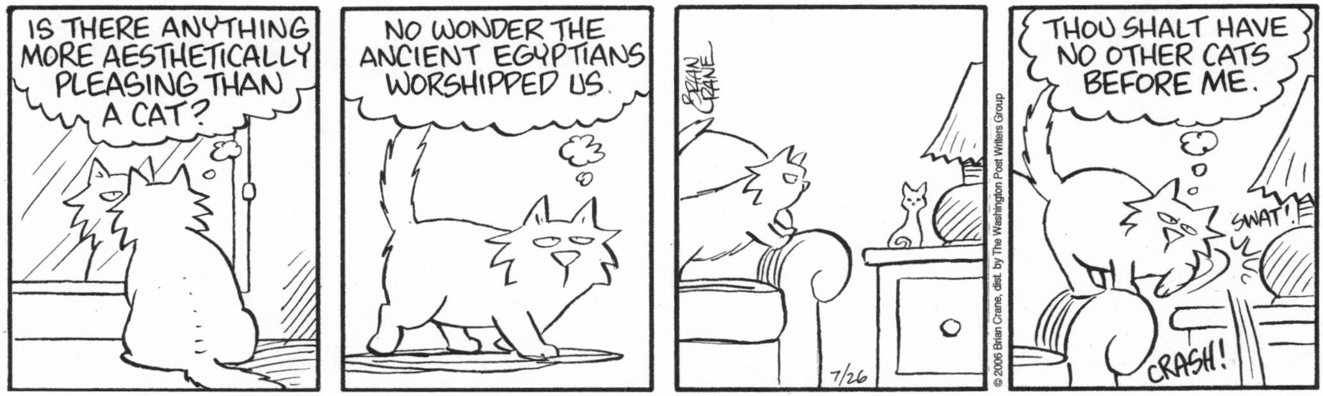
IS THERE ANYTHING MORE AESTHETICALLY PLEASING THAN A CAT?
NO WONDER THE ANCIENT EGYPTIANS WORSHIPPED US.
THOU SHALT HAVE NO OTHER CATS BEFORE ME.
SWAT!
CRASH!
7/26
© 2006 Brian Crane, dist. by The Washington Post Writers Group

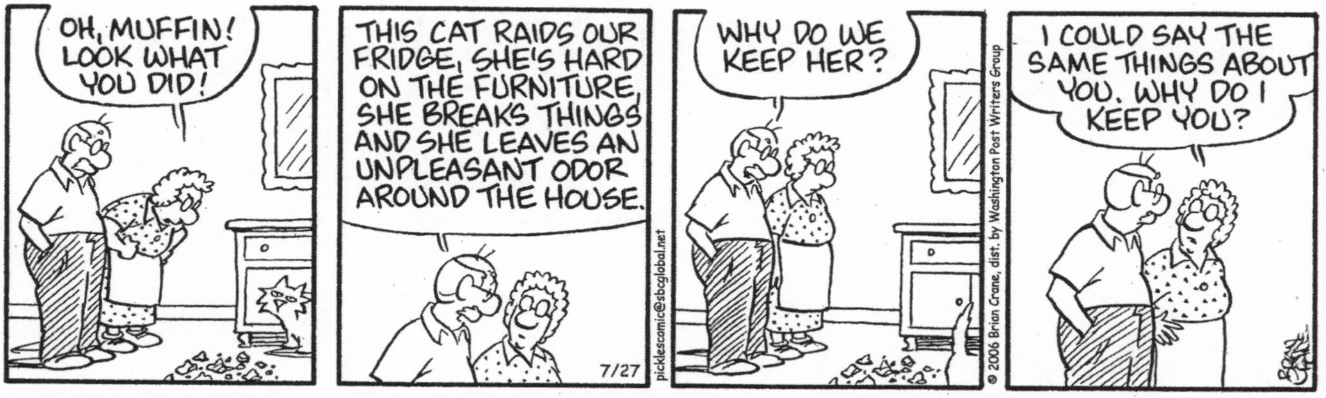
OH, MUFFIN! LOOK WHAT YOU DID!
THIS CAT RAIDS OUR FRIDGE, SHE'S HARD ON THE FURNITURE, SHE BREAKS THINGS AND SHE LEAVES AN UNPLEASANT ODOR AROUND THE HOUSE.
WHY DO WE KEEP HER?
I COULD SAY THE SAME THINGS ABOUT YOU. WHY DO I KEEP YOU?
7/27
picklescomic@sbcglobal.net
© 2006 Brian Crane, dist. by Washington Post Writers Group

256

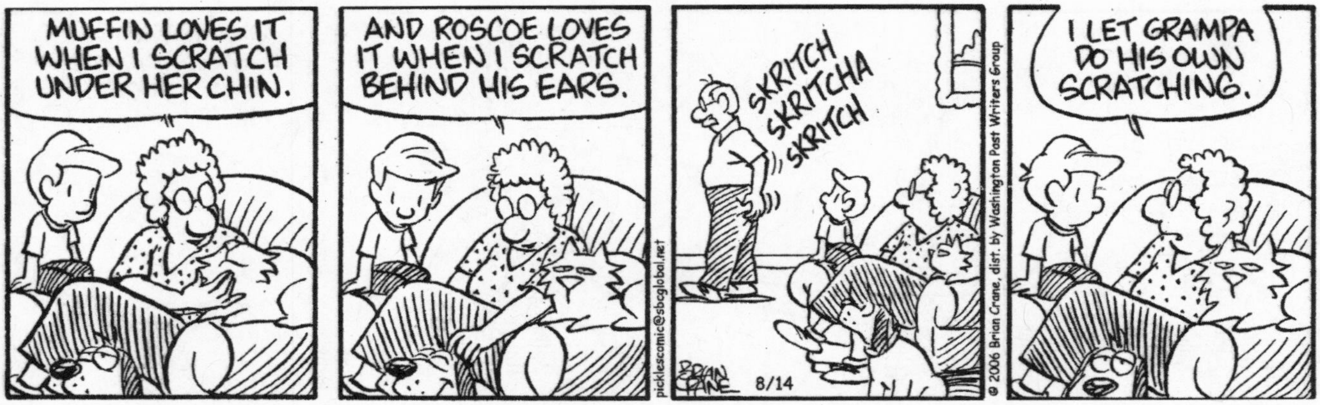
MUFFIN LOVES IT WHEN I SCRATCH UNDER HER CHIN.
AND ROSCOE LOVES IT WHEN I SCRATCH BEHIND HIS EARS.
picklescomic@sbcglobal.net
SKRITCH SKRITCHA SKRITCH
BRIAN CRANE 8/14
© 2006 Brian Crane, dist. by Washington Post Writers Group
I LET GRAMPA DO HIS OWN SCRATCHING.

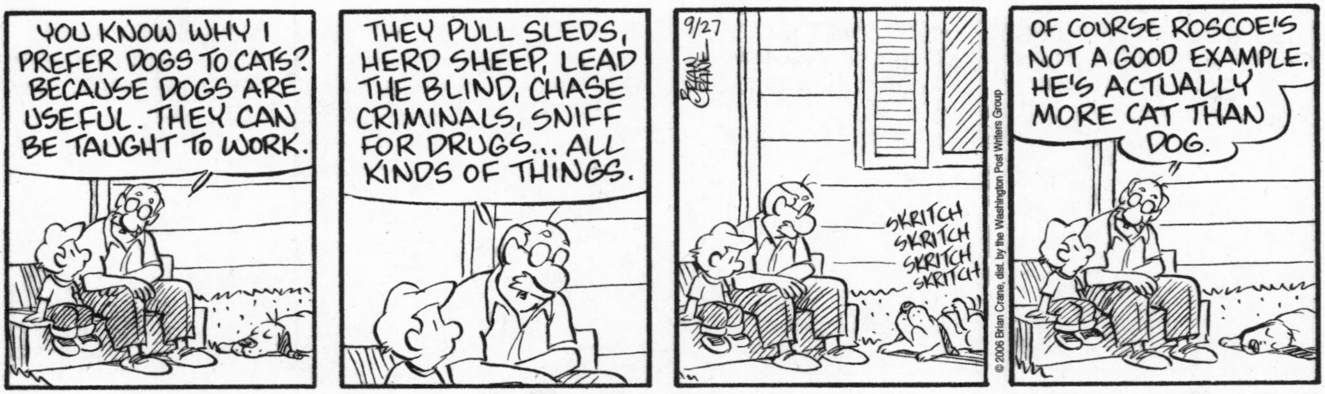
YOU KNOW WHY I PREFER DOGS TO CATS? BECAUSE DOGS ARE USEFUL. THEY CAN BE TAUGHT TO WORK.
THEY PULL SLEDS, HERD SHEEP, LEAD THE BLIND, CHASE CRIMINALS, SNIFF FOR DRUGS... ALL KINDS OF THINGS.
9/27 BRIAN CRANE
SKRITCH SKRITCH SKRITCH SKRITCH
© 2006 Brian Crane, dist. by the Washington Post Writers Group
OF COURSE ROSCOE'S NOT A GOOD EXAMPLE. HE'S ACTUALLY MORE CAT THAN DOG.

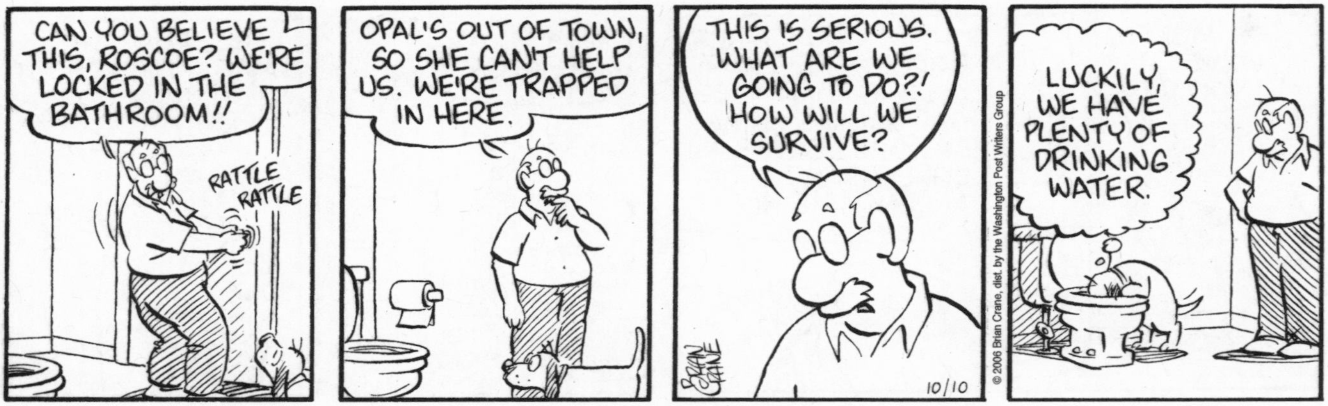
CAN YOU BELIEVE THIS, ROSCOE? WE'RE LOCKED IN THE BATHROOM!!
RATTLE RATTLE
OPAL'S OUT OF TOWN, SO SHE CAN'T HELP US. WE'RE TRAPPED IN HERE.
THIS IS SERIOUS. WHAT ARE WE GOING TO DO?! HOW WILL WE SURVIVE?
BRIAN CRANE 10/10
© 2006 Brian Crane, dist. by the Washington Post Writers Group
LUCKILY, WE HAVE PLENTY OF DRINKING WATER.

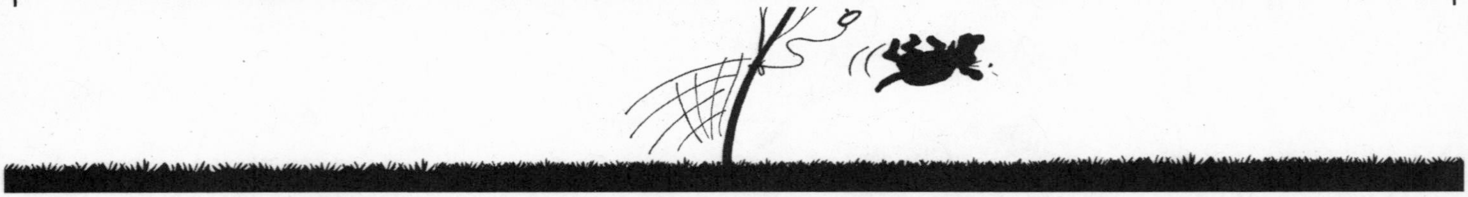

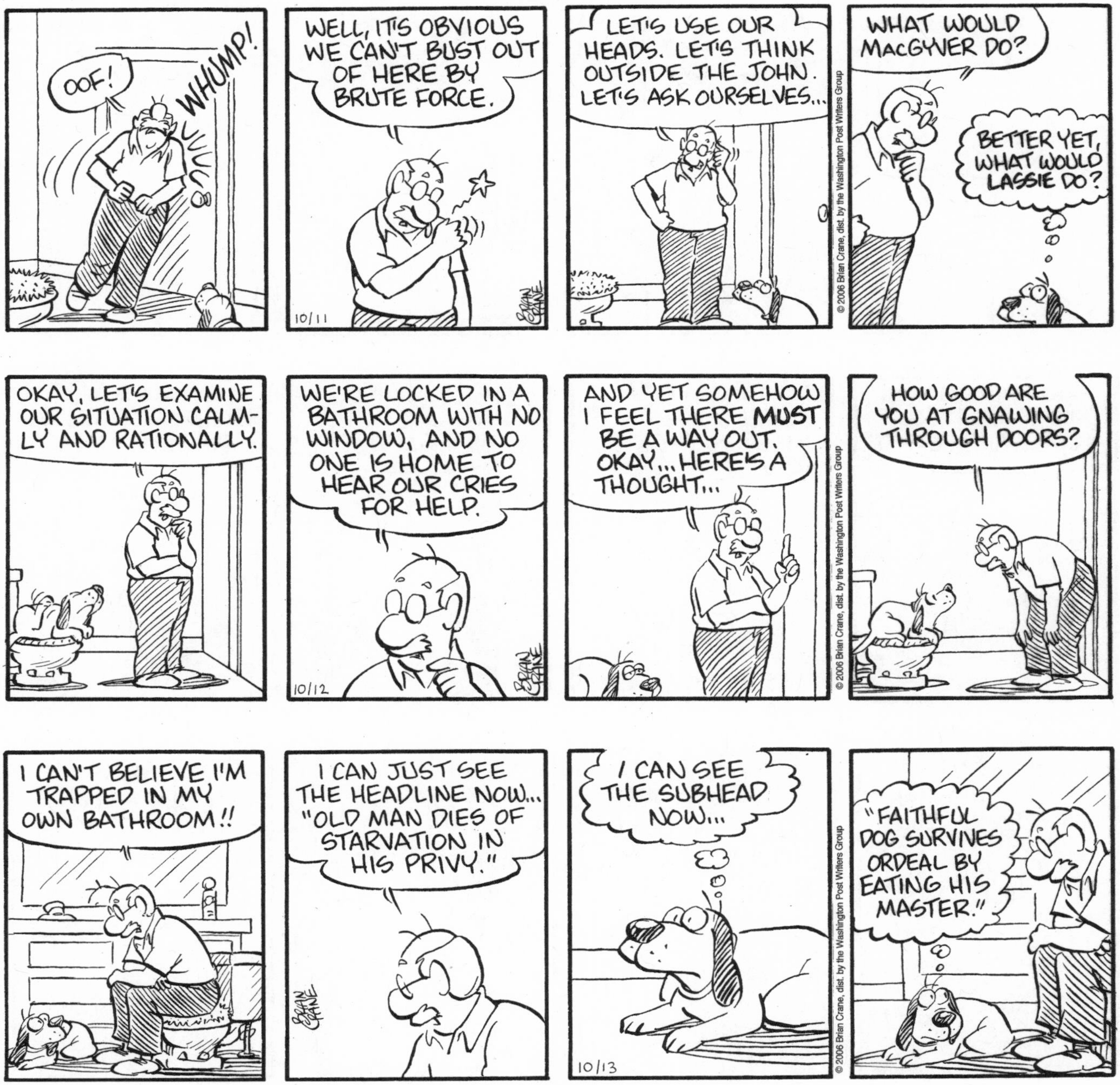
OOF!
WHUMP!
WELL, IT'S OBVIOUS WE CAN'T BUST OUT OF HERE BY BRUTE FORCE.
10/11
BRIAN CRANE
LET'S USE OUR HEADS. LET'S THINK OUTSIDE THE JOHN. LET'S ASK OURSELVES...
© 2006 Brian Crane, dist. by the Washington Post Writers Group
WHAT WOULD MacGYVER DO?
BETTER YET, WHAT WOULD LASSIE DO?
OKAY, LET'S EXAMINE OUR SITUATION CALMLY AND RATIONALLY.
WE'RE LOCKED IN A BATHROOM WITH NO WINDOW, AND NO ONE IS HOME TO HEAR OUR CRIES FOR HELP.
10/12
BRIAN CRANE
AND YET SOMEHOW I FEEL THERE MUST BE A WAY OUT. OKAY... HERE'S A THOUGHT...
© 2006 Brian Crane, dist. by the Washington Post Writers Group
HOW GOOD ARE YOU AT GNAWING THROUGH DOORS?
I CAN'T BELIEVE I'M TRAPPED IN MY OWN BATHROOM!!
I CAN JUST SEE THE HEADLINE NOW... "OLD MAN DIES OF STARVATION IN HIS PRIVY."
BRIAN CRANE
I CAN SEE THE SUBHEAD NOW...
10/13
© 2006 Brian Crane, dist. by the Washington Post Writers Group
"FAITHFUL DOG SURVIVES ORDEAL BY EATING HIS MASTER."

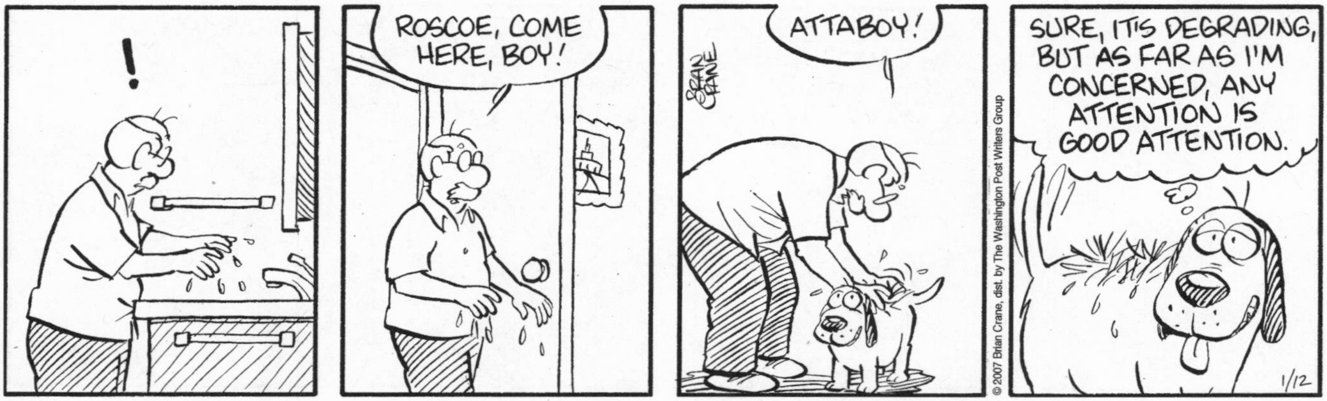
!
ROSCOE, COME HERE, BOY!
ATTABOY!
BRIAN CRANE
© 2007 Brian Crane, dist. by The Washington Post Writers Group
SURE, IT'S DEGRADING, BUT AS FAR AS I'M CONCERNED, ANY ATTENTION IS GOOD ATTENTION.
1/12

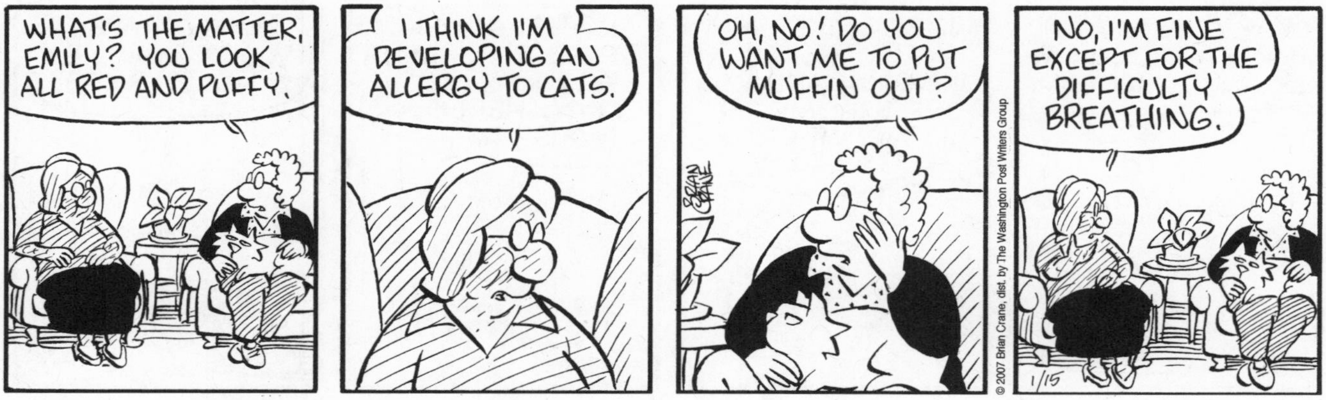
WHAT'S THE MATTER, EMILY? YOU LOOK ALL RED AND PUFFY.
I THINK I'M DEVELOPING AN ALLERGY TO CATS.
OH, NO! DO YOU WANT ME TO PUT MUFFIN OUT?
BRIAN CRANE
© 2007 Brian Crane, dist. by The Washington Post Writers Group
NO, I'M FINE EXCEPT FOR THE DIFFICULTY BREATHING.
1/15

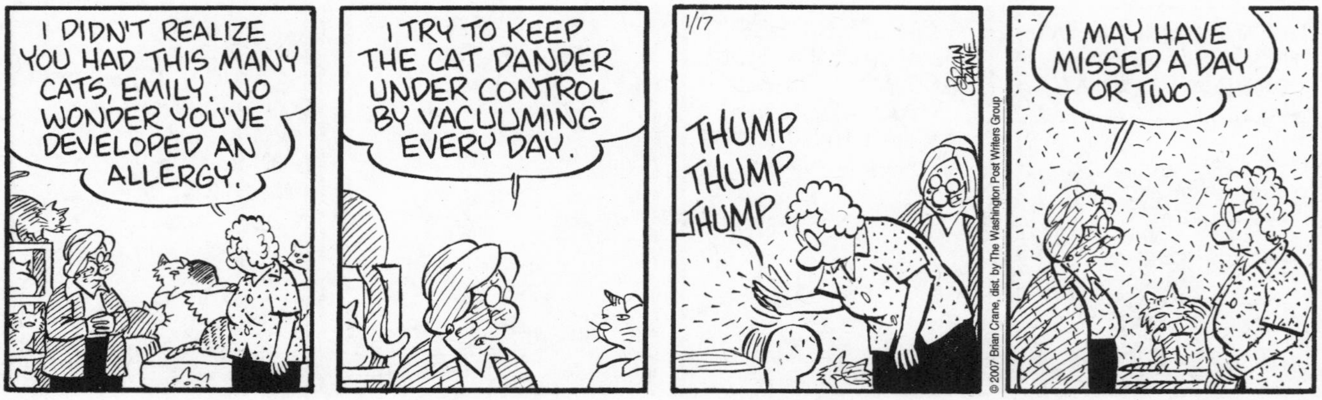
I DIDN'T REALIZE YOU HAD THIS MANY CATS, EMILY. NO WONDER YOU'VE DEVELOPED AN ALLERGY.
I TRY TO KEEP THE CAT DANDER UNDER CONTROL BY VACUUMING EVERY DAY.
1/17
BRIAN CRANE
THUMP
THUMP
THUMP
© 2007 Brian Crane, dist. by The Washington Post Writers Group
I MAY HAVE MISSED A DAY OR TWO.

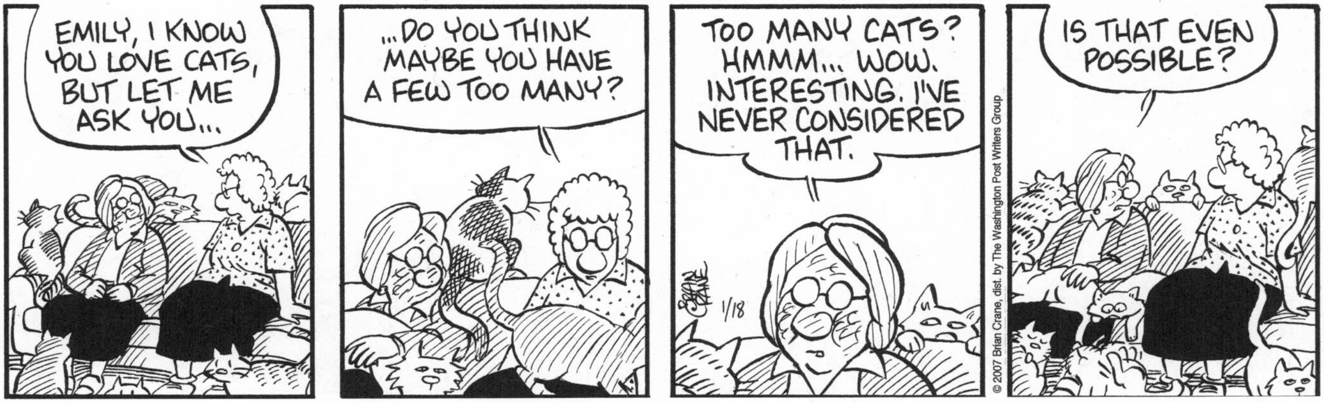
EMILY, I KNOW YOU LOVE CATS, BUT LET ME ASK YOU...
...DO YOU THINK MAYBE YOU HAVE A FEW TOO MANY?
TOO MANY CATS? HMMM... WOW. INTERESTING. I'VE NEVER CONSIDERED THAT.
1/18
IS THAT EVEN POSSIBLE?
© 2007 Brian Crane, dist. by The Washington Post Writers Group

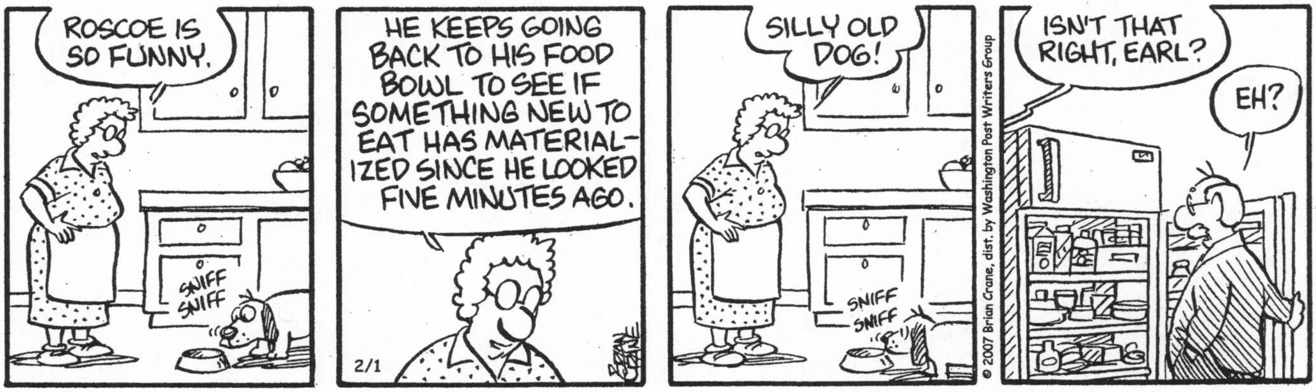
ROSCOE IS SO FUNNY.
SNIFF SNIFF
HE KEEPS GOING BACK TO HIS FOOD BOWL TO SEE IF SOMETHING NEW TO EAT HAS MATERIALIZED SINCE HE LOOKED FIVE MINUTES AGO.
2/1
SILLY OLD DOG!
SNIFF SNIFF
ISN'T THAT RIGHT, EARL?
EH?
© 2007 Brian Crane, dist. by Washington Post Writers Group

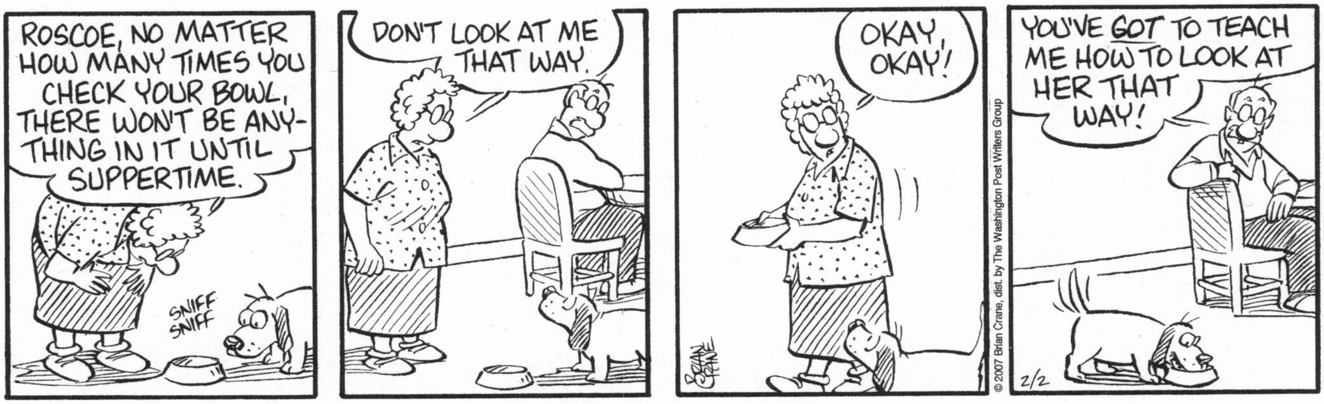
ROSCOE, NO MATTER HOW MANY TIMES YOU CHECK YOUR BOWL, THERE WON'T BE ANYTHING IN IT UNTIL SUPPERTIME.
SNIFF SNIFF
DON'T LOOK AT ME THAT WAY.
OKAY, OKAY!
YOU'VE GOT TO TEACH ME HOW TO LOOK AT HER THAT WAY!
2/2
© 2007 Brian Crane, dist. by The Washington Post Writers Group

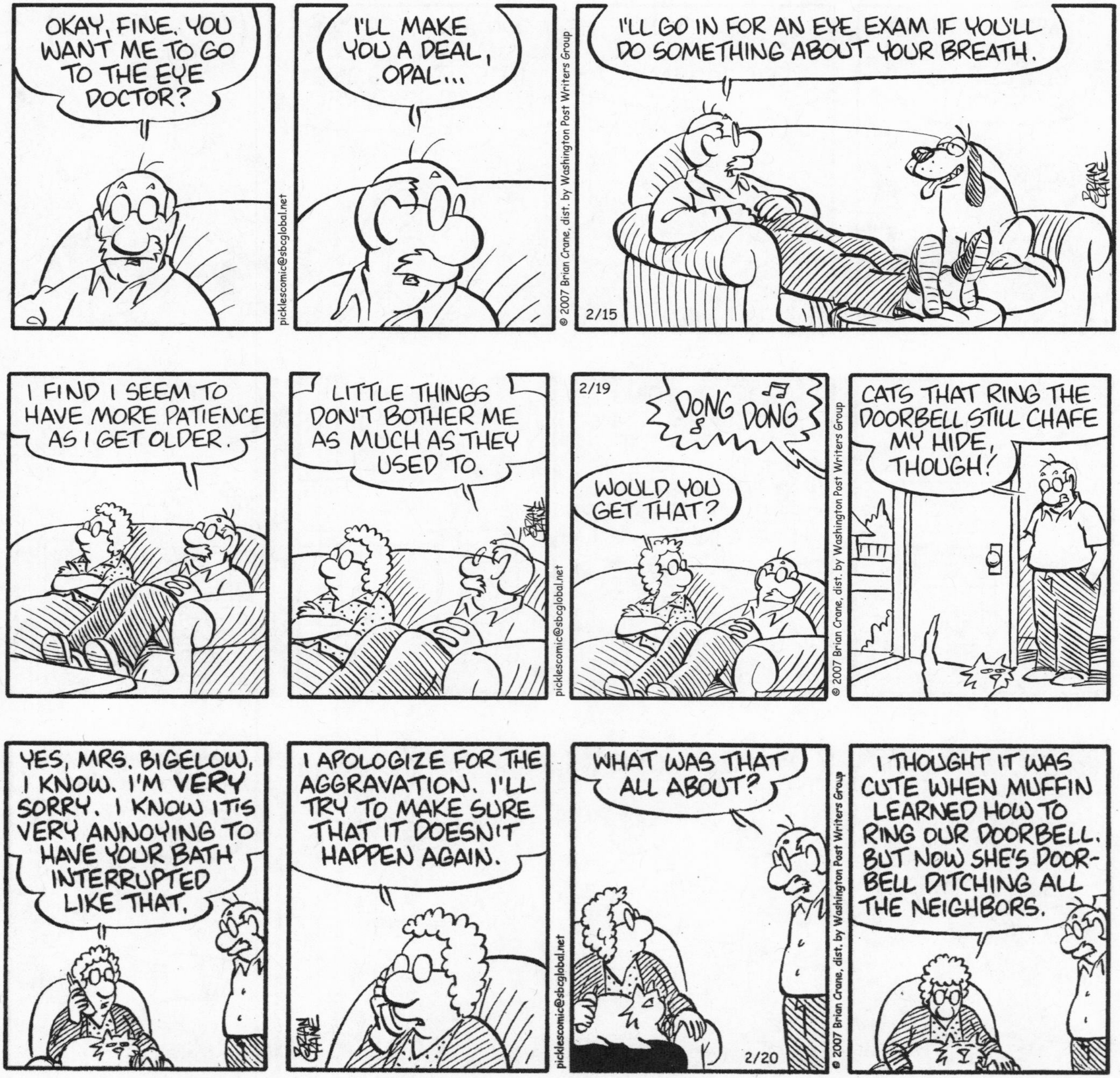
OKAY, FINE. YOU WANT ME TO GO TO THE EYE DOCTOR?
I'LL MAKE YOU A DEAL, OPAL...
I'LL GO IN FOR AN EYE EXAM IF YOU'LL DO SOMETHING ABOUT YOUR BREATH.
picklescomic@sbcglobal.net
© 2007 Brian Crane, dist. by Washington Post Writers Group
2/15
BRIAN CRANE
I FIND I SEEM TO HAVE MORE PATIENCE AS I GET OLDER.
LITTLE THINGS DON'T BOTHER ME AS MUCH AS THEY USED TO.
2/19
DONG DONG
WOULD YOU GET THAT?
CATS THAT RING THE DOORBELL STILL CHAFE MY HIDE, THOUGH!
picklescomic@sbcglobal.net
© 2007 Brian Crane, dist. by Washington Post Writers Group
YES, MRS. BIGELOW, I KNOW. I'M VERY SORRY. I KNOW IT'S VERY ANNOYING TO HAVE YOUR BATH INTERRUPTED LIKE THAT.
I APOLOGIZE FOR THE AGGRAVATION. I'LL TRY TO MAKE SURE THAT IT DOESN'T HAPPEN AGAIN.
WHAT WAS THAT ALL ABOUT?
I THOUGHT IT WAS CUTE WHEN MUFFIN LEARNED HOW TO RING OUR DOORBELL. BUT NOW SHE'S DOOR-BELL DITCHING ALL THE NEIGHBORS.
2/20
picklescomic@sbcglobal.net
© 2007 Brian Crane, dist. by Washington Post Writers Group

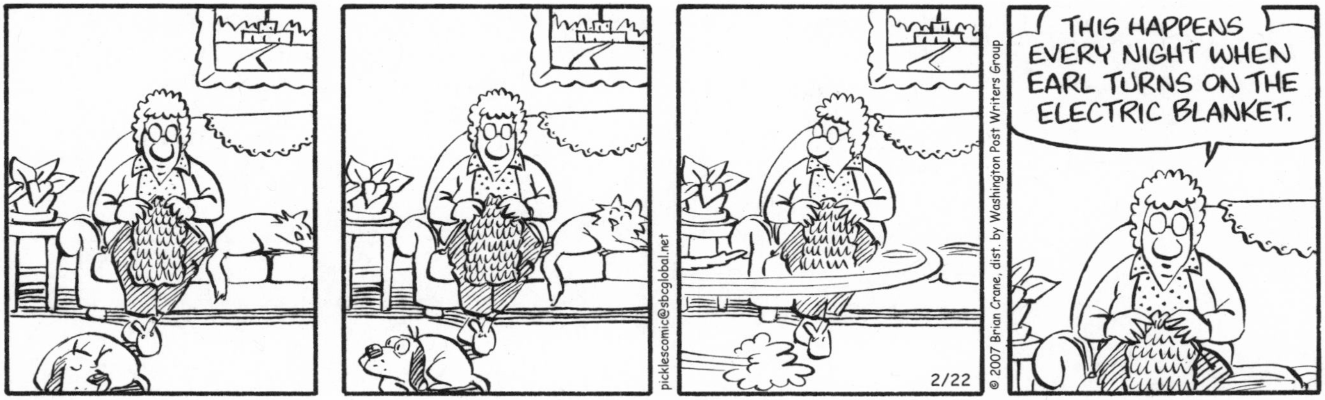

picklescomic@sbcglobal.net
2/22
© 2007 Brian Crane, dist. by Washington Post Writers Group
THIS HAPPENS EVERY NIGHT WHEN EARL TURNS ON THE ELECTRIC BLANKET.

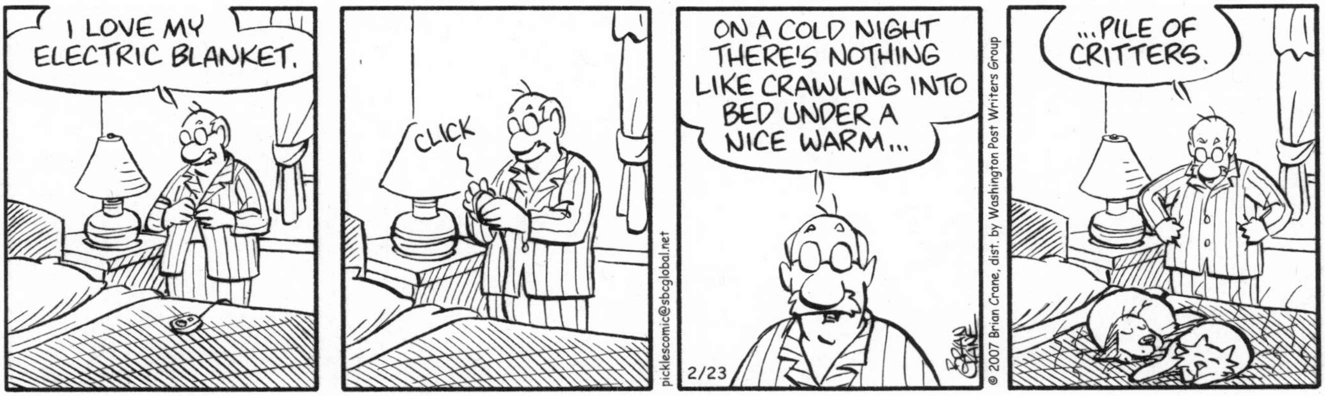

I LOVE MY ELECTRIC BLANKET.
CLICK
picklescomic@sbcglobal.net
ON A COLD NIGHT THERE'S NOTHING LIKE CRAWLING INTO BED UNDER A NICE WARM...
2/23
© 2007 Brian Crane, dist. by Washington Post Writers Group
...PILE OF CRITTERS.

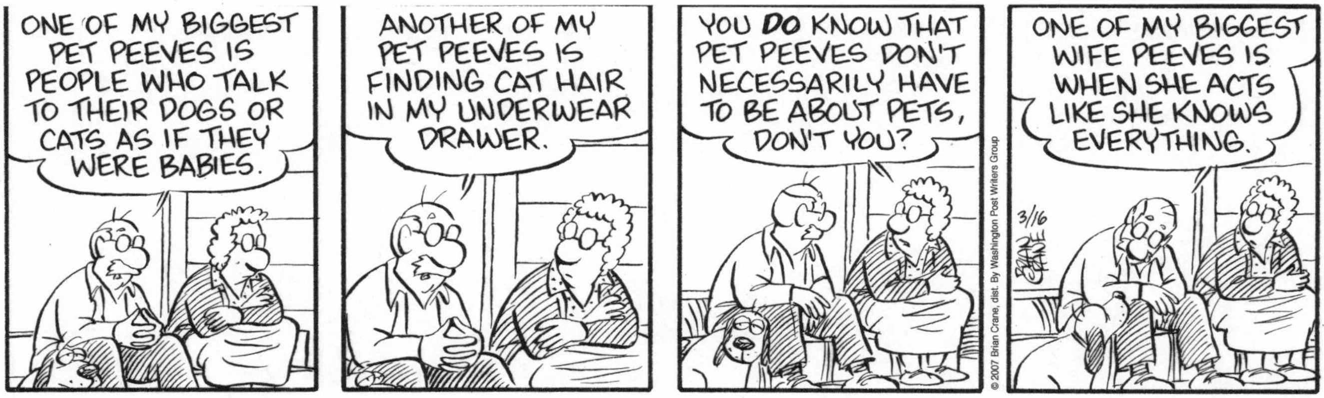

ONE OF MY BIGGEST PET PEEVES IS PEOPLE WHO TALK TO THEIR DOGS OR CATS AS IF THEY WERE BABIES.
ANOTHER OF MY PET PEEVES IS FINDING CAT HAIR IN MY UNDERWEAR DRAWER.
YOU **DO** KNOW THAT PET PEEVES DON'T NECESSARILY HAVE TO BE ABOUT PETS, DON'T YOU?
© 2007 Brian Crane, dist. By Washington Post Writers Group
ONE OF MY BIGGEST WIFE PEEVES IS WHEN SHE ACTS LIKE SHE KNOWS EVERYTHING.
3/16

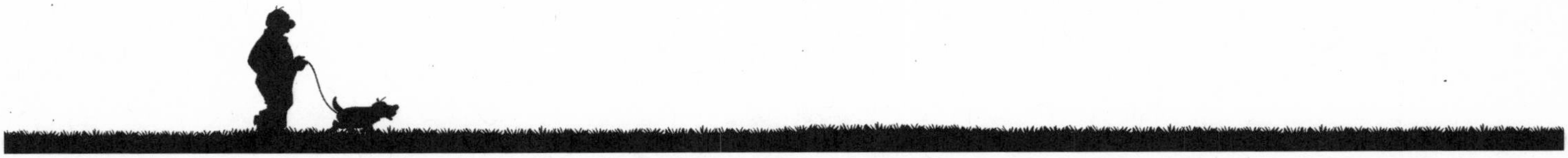

262

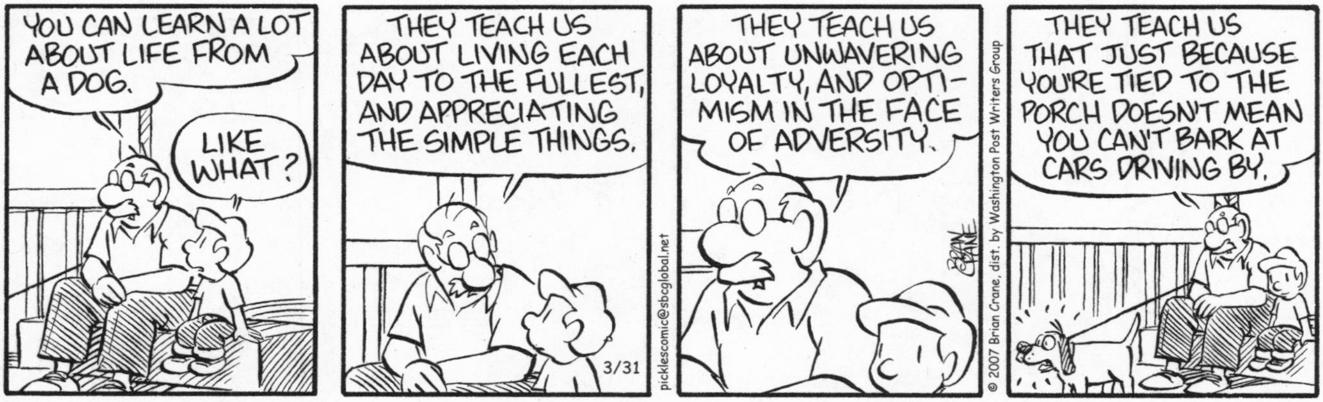
YOU CAN LEARN A LOT ABOUT LIFE FROM A DOG.
LIKE WHAT?
THEY TEACH US ABOUT LIVING EACH DAY TO THE FULLEST, AND APPRECIATING THE SIMPLE THINGS.
3/31
picklescomic@sbcglobal.net
THEY TEACH US ABOUT UNWAVERING LOYALTY, AND OPTI-MISM IN THE FACE OF ADVERSITY.
BRIAN CRANE
© 2007 Brian Crane, dist. by Washington Post Writers Group
THEY TEACH US THAT JUST BECAUSE YOU'RE TIED TO THE PORCH DOESN'T MEAN YOU CAN'T BARK AT CARS DRIVING BY.

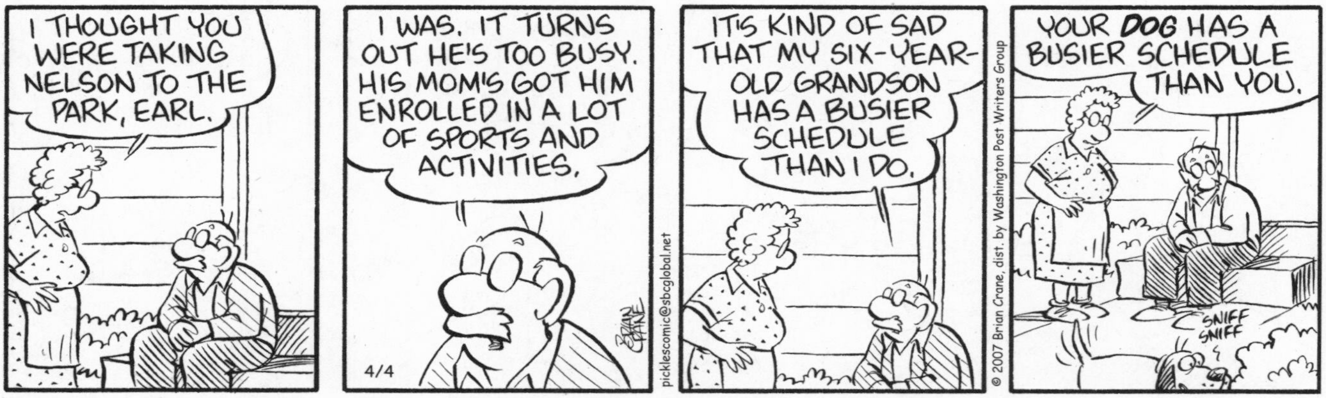
I THOUGHT YOU WERE TAKING NELSON TO THE PARK, EARL.
I WAS. IT TURNS OUT HE'S TOO BUSY. HIS MOM'S GOT HIM ENROLLED IN A LOT OF SPORTS AND ACTIVITIES.
4/4
BRIAN CRANE
picklescomic@sbcglobal.net
IT'S KIND OF SAD THAT MY SIX-YEAR-OLD GRANDSON HAS A BUSIER SCHEDULE THAN I DO.
© 2007 Brian Crane, dist. by Washington Post Writers Group
YOUR DOG HAS A BUSIER SCHEDULE THAN YOU.
SNIFF SNIFF

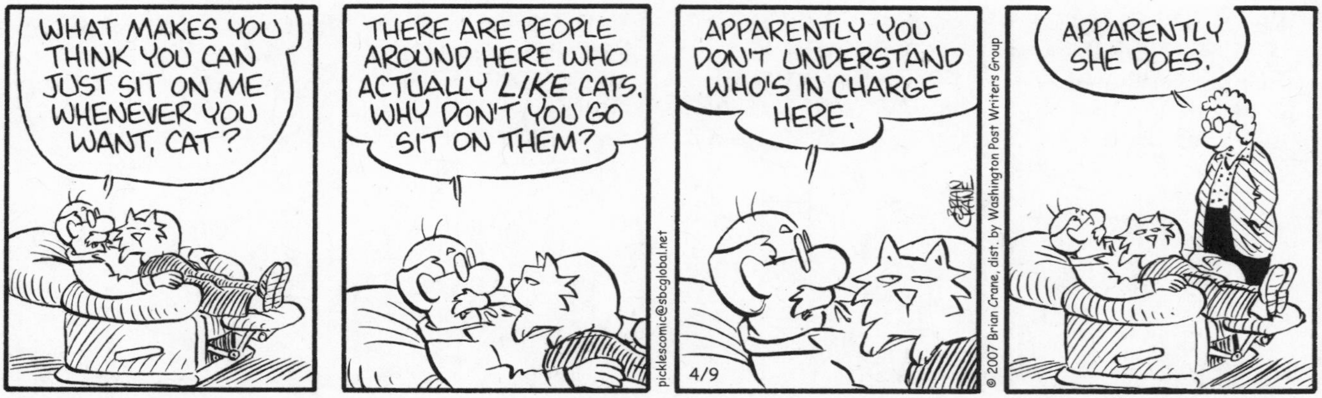
WHAT MAKES YOU THINK YOU CAN JUST SIT ON ME WHENEVER YOU WANT, CAT?
THERE ARE PEOPLE AROUND HERE WHO ACTUALLY LIKE CATS. WHY DON'T YOU GO SIT ON THEM?
picklescomic@sbcglobal.net
APPARENTLY YOU DON'T UNDERSTAND WHO'S IN CHARGE HERE.
BRIAN CRANE
4/9
© 2007 Brian Crane, dist. by Washington Post Writers Group
APPARENTLY SHE DOES.

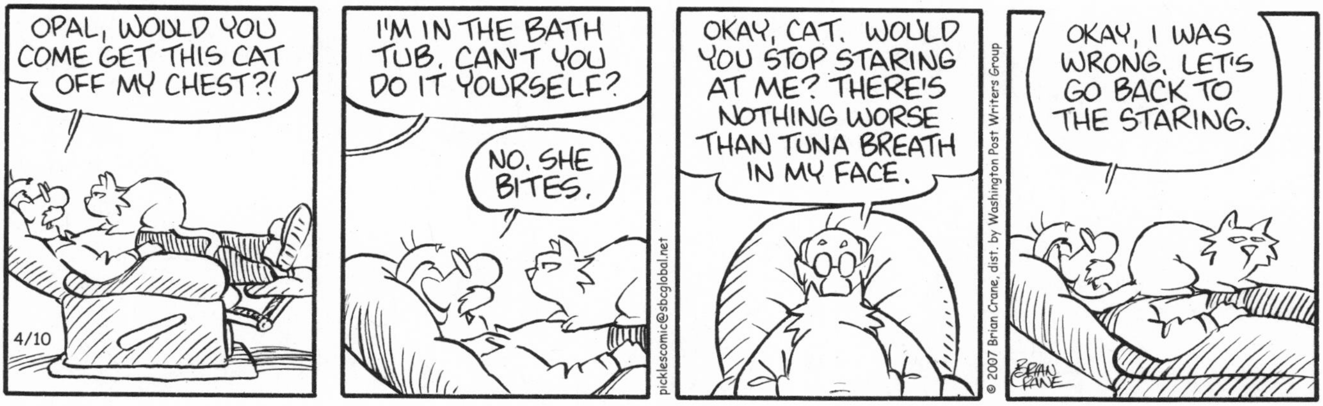
OPAL, WOULD YOU COME GET THIS CAT OFF MY CHEST?!
4/10
I'M IN THE BATH TUB. CAN'T YOU DO IT YOURSELF?
NO. SHE BITES.
picklescomic@sbcglobal.net
OKAY, CAT. WOULD YOU STOP STARING AT ME? THERE'S NOTHING WORSE THAN TUNA BREATH IN MY FACE.
© 2007 Brian Crane, dist. by Washington Post Writers Group
OKAY, I WAS WRONG. LET'S GO BACK TO THE STARING.
BRIAN CRANE

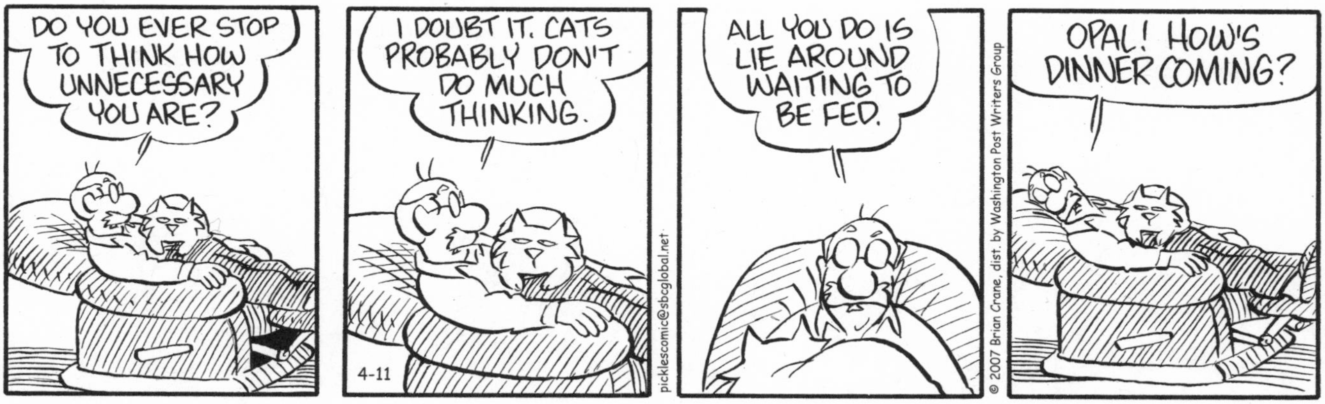
DO YOU EVER STOP TO THINK HOW UNNECESSARY YOU ARE?
I DOUBT IT. CATS PROBABLY DON'T DO MUCH THINKING.
4-11
picklescomic@sbcglobal.net
ALL YOU DO IS LIE AROUND WAITING TO BE FED.
© 2007 Brian Crane, dist. by Washington Post Writers Group
OPAL! HOW'S DINNER COMING?

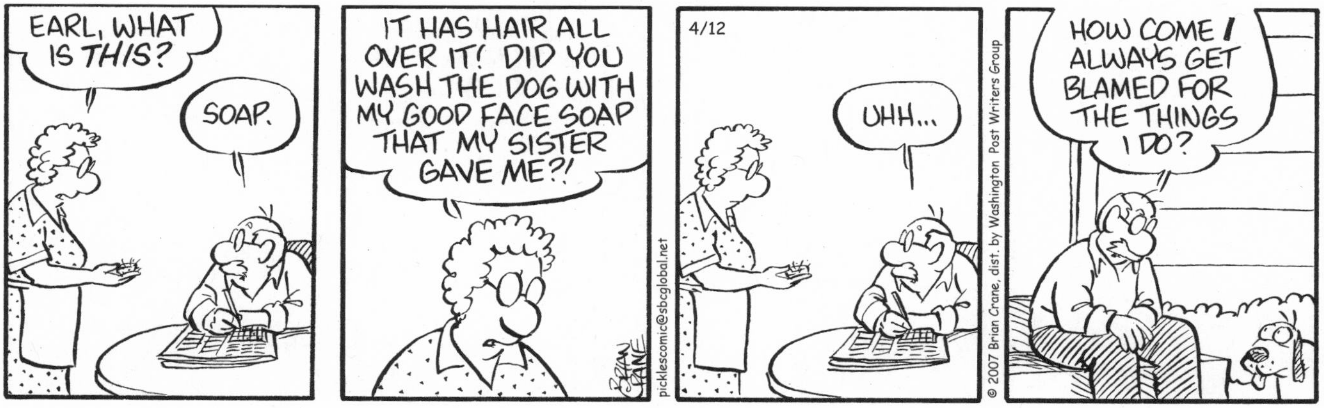
EARL, WHAT IS *THIS*?
SOAP.
IT HAS HAIR ALL OVER IT! DID YOU WASH THE DOG WITH MY GOOD FACE SOAP THAT MY SISTER GAVE ME?!
BRIAN CRANE
picklescomic@sbcglobal.net
4/12
UHH...
© 2007 Brian Crane, dist. by Washington Post Writers Group
HOW COME **I** ALWAYS GET BLAMED FOR THE THINGS I DO?

263

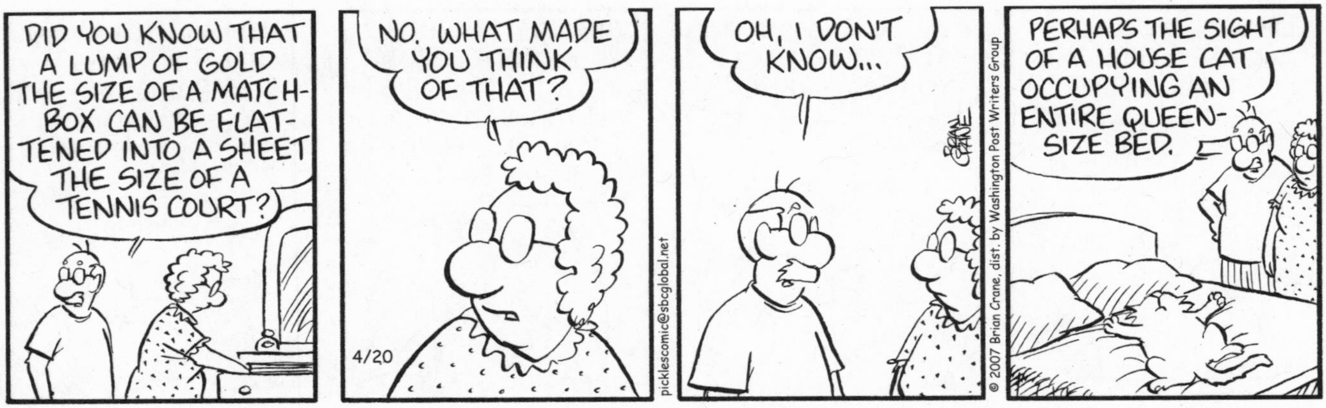
DID YOU KNOW THAT A LUMP OF GOLD THE SIZE OF A MATCH-BOX CAN BE FLAT-TENED INTO A SHEET THE SIZE OF A TENNIS COURT?
NO. WHAT MADE YOU THINK OF THAT?
4/20
picklescomic@sbcglobal.net
OH, I DON'T KNOW...
BRIAN CRANE
© 2007 Brian Crane, dist. by Washington Post Writers Group
PERHAPS THE SIGHT OF A HOUSE CAT OCCUPYING AN ENTIRE QUEEN-SIZE BED.

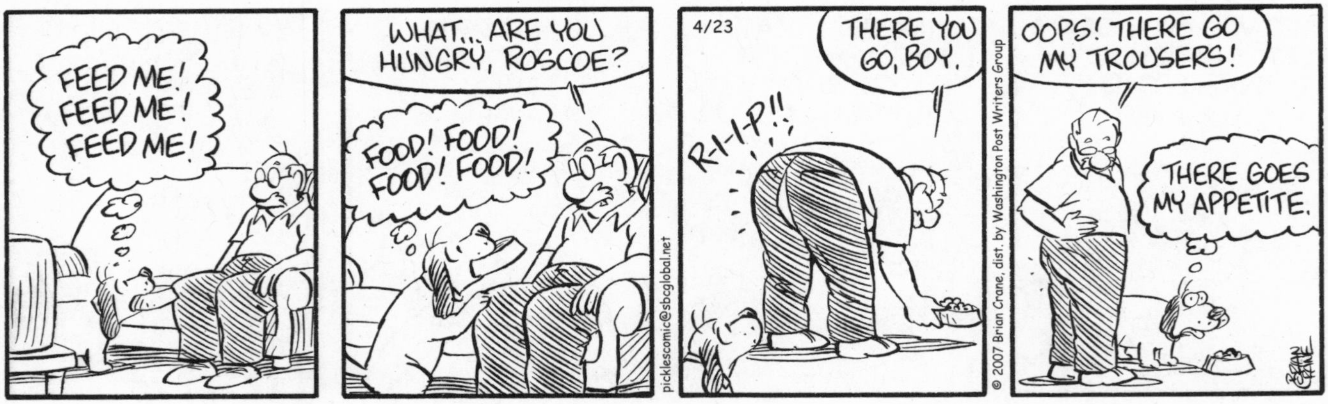
FEED ME! FEED ME! FEED ME!
WHAT... ARE YOU HUNGRY, ROSCOE?
FOOD! FOOD! FOOD! FOOD!
picklescomic@sbcglobal.net
4/23
THERE YOU GO, BOY.
R-I-I-P!!
© 2007 Brian Crane, dist. by Washington Post Writers Group
OOPS! THERE GO MY TROUSERS!
THERE GOES MY APPETITE.
BRIAN CRANE

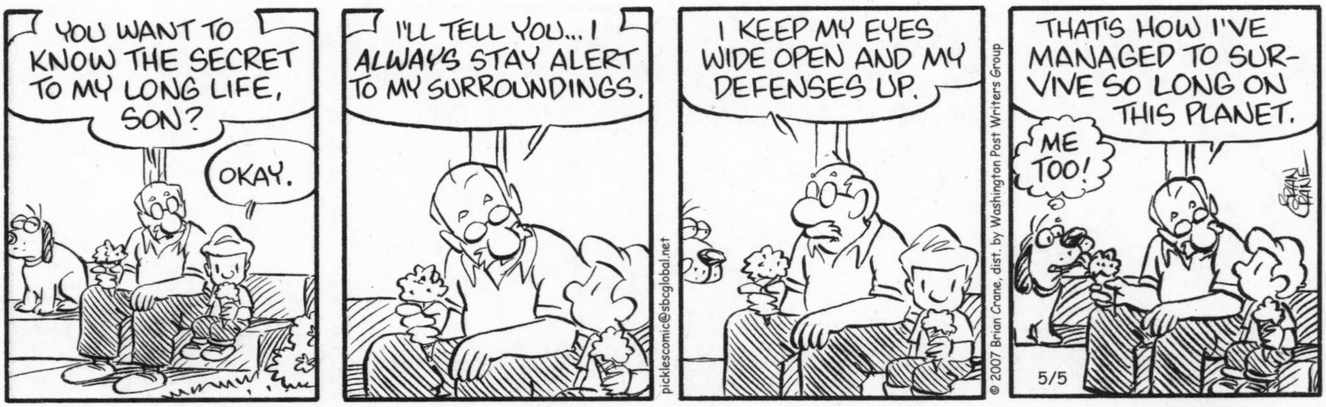
YOU WANT TO KNOW THE SECRET TO MY LONG LIFE, SON?
OKAY.
I'LL TELL YOU... I ALWAYS STAY ALERT TO MY SURROUNDINGS.
picklescomic@sbcglobal.net
I KEEP MY EYES WIDE OPEN AND MY DEFENSES UP.
© 2007 Brian Crane, dist. by Washington Post Writers Group
THAT'S HOW I'VE MANAGED TO SUR-VIVE SO LONG ON THIS PLANET.
ME TOO!
BRIAN CRANE
5/5

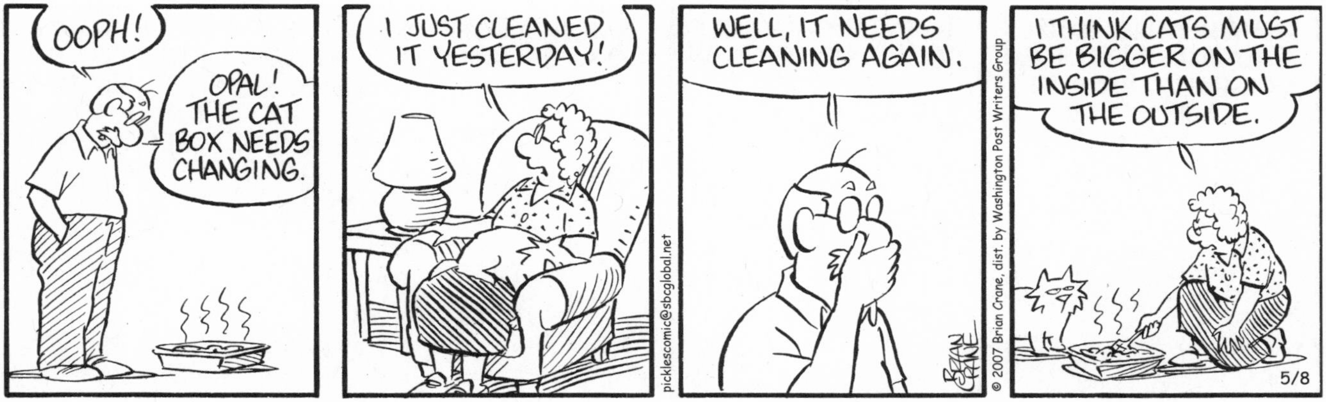
OOPH!
OPAL! THE CAT BOX NEEDS CHANGING.
I JUST CLEANED IT YESTERDAY!
picklescomic@sbcglobal.net
WELL, IT NEEDS CLEANING AGAIN.
BRIAN CRANE
© 2007 Brian Crane, dist. by Washington Post Writers Group
I THINK CATS MUST BE BIGGER ON THE INSIDE THAN ON THE OUTSIDE.
5/8

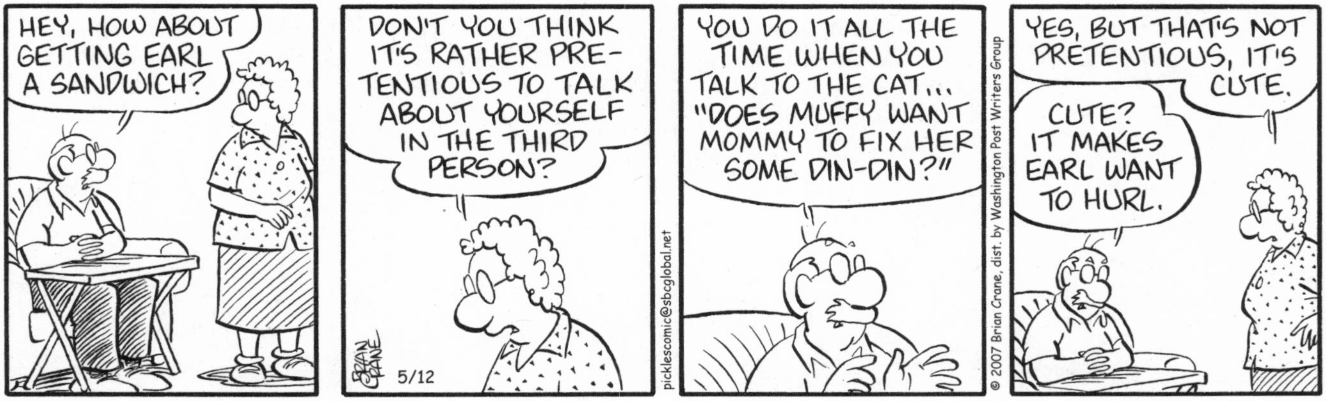
HEY, HOW ABOUT GETTING EARL A SANDWICH?
DON'T YOU THINK IT'S RATHER PRE-TENTIOUS TO TALK ABOUT YOURSELF IN THE THIRD PERSON?
BRIAN CRANE
5/12
picklescomic@sbcglobal.net
YOU DO IT ALL THE TIME WHEN YOU TALK TO THE CAT... "DOES MUFFY WANT MOMMY TO FIX HER SOME DIN-DIN?"
© 2007 Brian Crane, dist. by Washington Post Writers Group
YES, BUT THAT'S NOT PRETENTIOUS, IT'S CUTE.
CUTE? IT MAKES EARL WANT TO HURL.

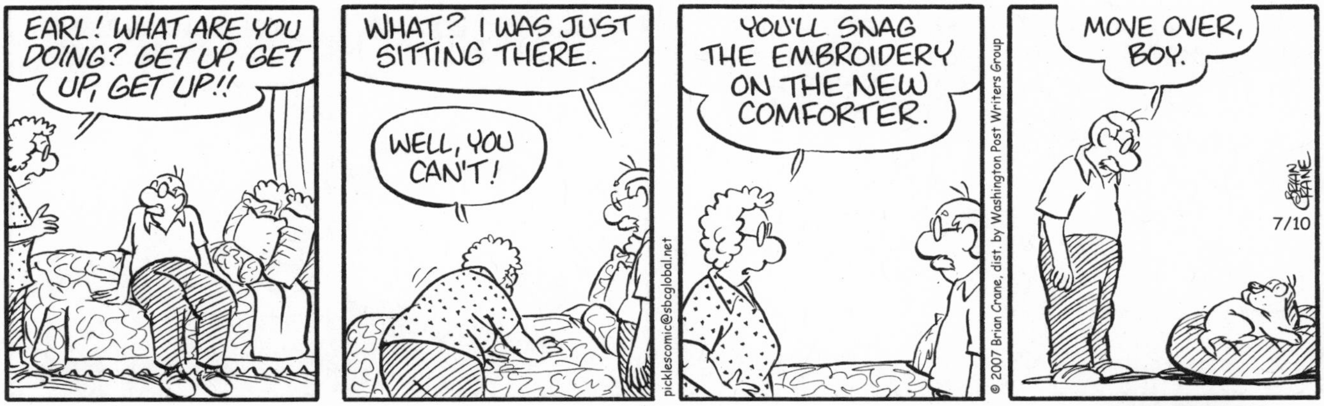
EARL! WHAT ARE YOU DOING? GET UP, GET UP, GET UP!!
WHAT? I WAS JUST SITTING THERE.
WELL, YOU CAN'T!
picklescomic@sbcglobal.net
YOU'LL SNAG THE EMBROIDERY ON THE NEW COMFORTER.
© 2007 Brian Crane, dist. by Washington Post Writers Group
MOVE OVER, BOY.
BRIAN CRANE
7/10

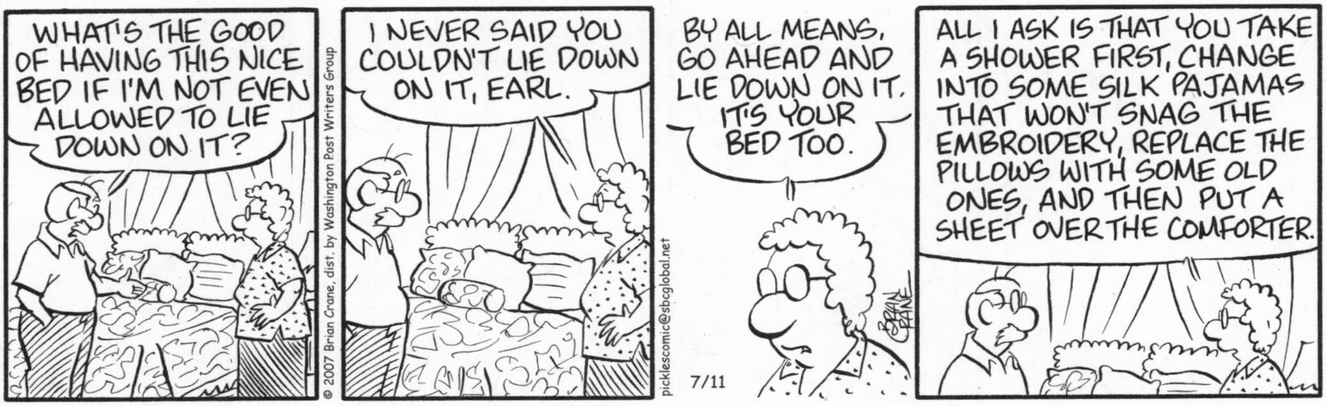
WHAT'S THE GOOD OF HAVING THIS NICE BED IF I'M NOT EVEN ALLOWED TO LIE DOWN ON IT?
© 2007 Brian Crane, dist. by Washington Post Writers Group
I NEVER SAID YOU COULDN'T LIE DOWN ON IT, EARL.
picklescomic@sbcglobal.net
7/11
BY ALL MEANS, GO AHEAD AND LIE DOWN ON IT. IT'S YOUR BED TOO.
ALL I ASK IS THAT YOU TAKE A SHOWER FIRST, CHANGE INTO SOME SILK PAJAMAS THAT WON'T SNAG THE EMBROIDERY, REPLACE THE PILLOWS WITH SOME OLD ONES, AND THEN PUT A SHEET OVER THE COMFORTER.

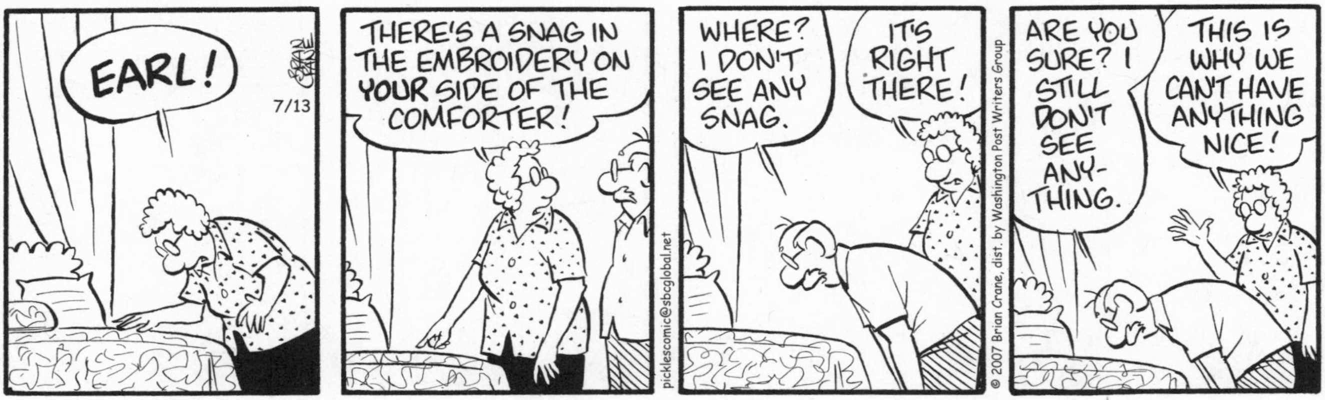
EARL!
7/13
THERE'S A SNAG IN THE EMBROIDERY ON **YOUR** SIDE OF THE COMFORTER!
picklescomic@sbcglobal.net
WHERE? I DON'T SEE ANY SNAG.
IT'S RIGHT THERE!
© 2007 Brian Crane, dist. by Washington Post Writers Group
ARE YOU SURE? I STILL DON'T SEE ANY-THING.
THIS IS WHY WE CAN'T HAVE ANYTHING NICE!

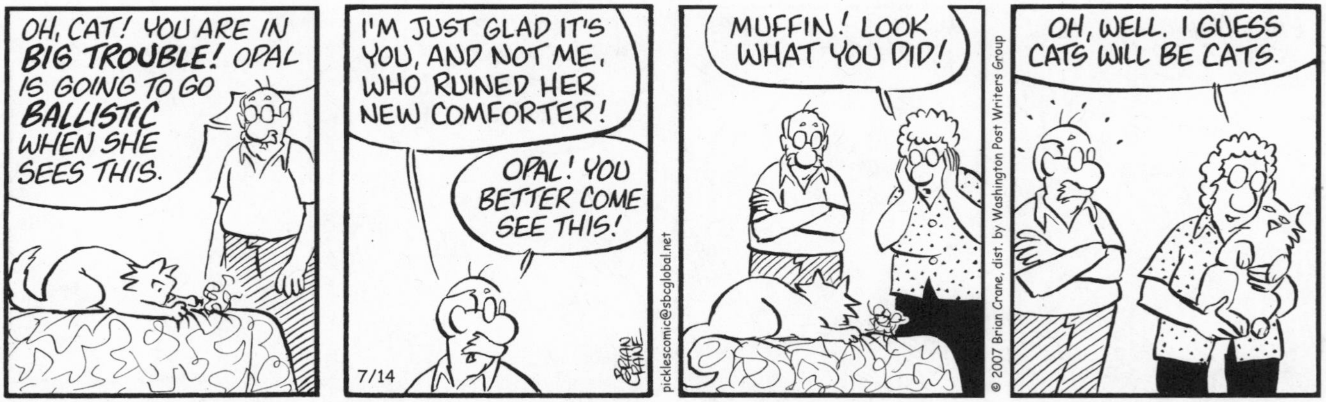
OH, CAT! YOU ARE IN **BIG TROUBLE!** OPAL IS GOING TO GO **BALLISTIC** WHEN SHE SEES THIS.
I'M JUST GLAD IT'S YOU, AND NOT ME, WHO RUINED HER NEW COMFORTER!
OPAL! YOU BETTER COME SEE THIS!
7/14
picklescomic@sbcglobal.net
MUFFIN! LOOK WHAT YOU DID!
© 2007 Brian Crane, dist. by Washington Post Writers Group
OH, WELL. I GUESS CATS WILL BE CATS.

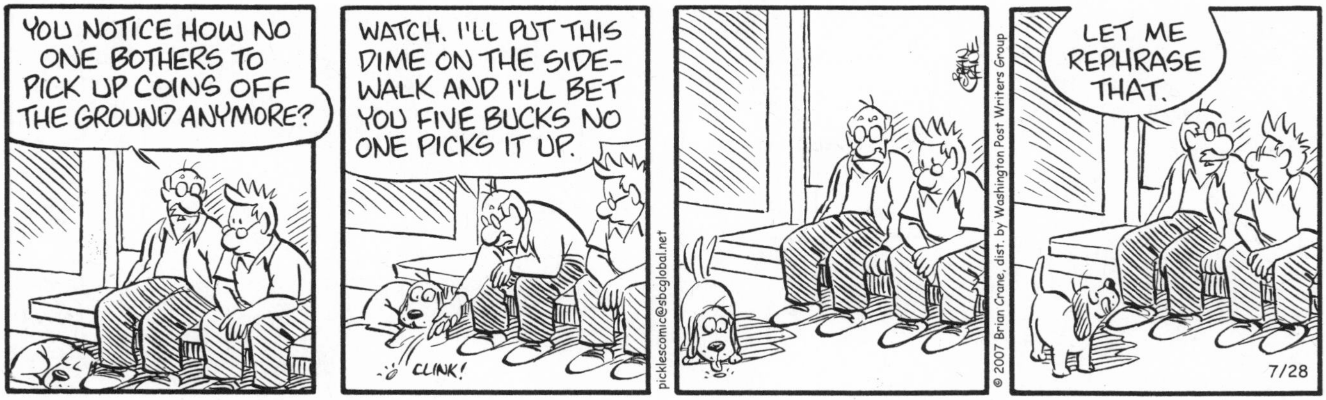
YOU NOTICE HOW NO ONE BOTHERS TO PICK UP COINS OFF THE GROUND ANYMORE?
WATCH. I'LL PUT THIS DIME ON THE SIDE-WALK AND I'LL BET YOU FIVE BUCKS NO ONE PICKS IT UP.
CLINK!
picklescomic@sbcglobal.net
© 2007 Brian Crane, dist. by Washington Post Writers Group
LET ME REPHRASE THAT.
7/28

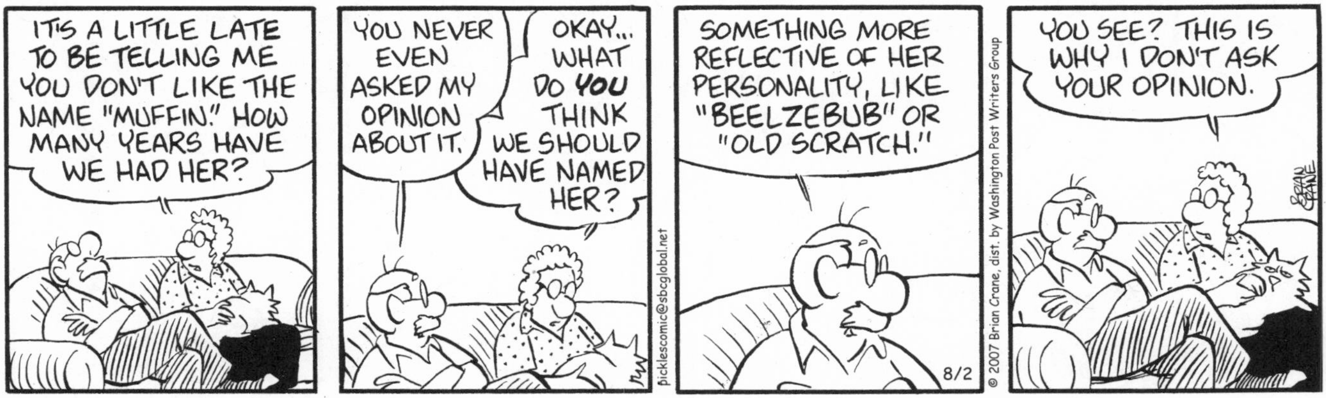
IT'S A LITTLE LATE TO BE TELLING ME YOU DON'T LIKE THE NAME "MUFFIN." HOW MANY YEARS HAVE WE HAD HER?
YOU NEVER EVEN ASKED MY OPINION ABOUT IT.
OKAY... WHAT DO **YOU** THINK WE SHOULD HAVE NAMED HER?
picklescomic@sbcglobal.net
SOMETHING MORE REFLECTIVE OF HER PERSONALITY, LIKE "BEELZEBUB" OR "OLD SCRATCH."
8/2
© 2007 Brian Crane, dist. by Washington Post Writers Group
YOU SEE? THIS IS WHY I DON'T ASK YOUR OPINION.

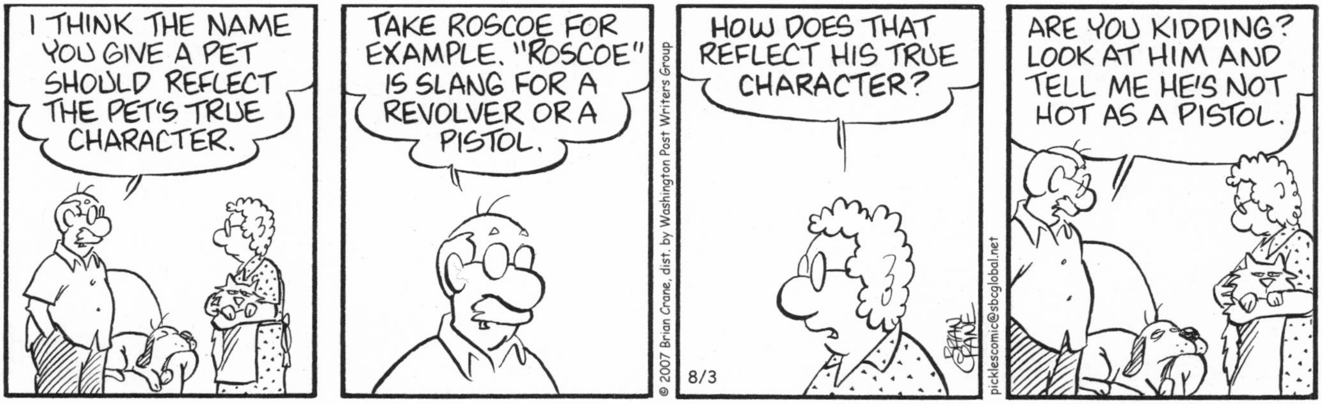
I THINK THE NAME YOU GIVE A PET SHOULD REFLECT THE PET'S TRUE CHARACTER.
TAKE ROSCOE FOR EXAMPLE. "ROSCOE" IS SLANG FOR A REVOLVER OR A PISTOL.
© 2007 Brian Crane, dist. by Washington Post Writers Group
HOW DOES THAT REFLECT HIS TRUE CHARACTER?
8/3
picklescomic@sbcglobal.net
ARE YOU KIDDING? LOOK AT HIM AND TELL ME HE'S NOT HOT AS A PISTOL.

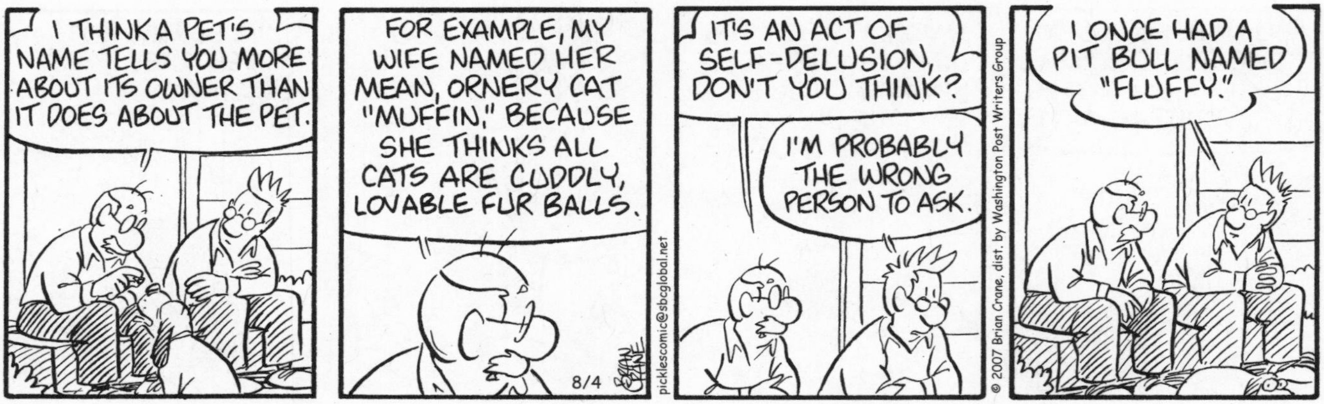
I THINK A PET'S NAME TELLS YOU MORE ABOUT ITS OWNER THAN IT DOES ABOUT THE PET.
FOR EXAMPLE, MY WIFE NAMED HER MEAN, ORNERY CAT "MUFFIN," BECAUSE SHE THINKS ALL CATS ARE CUDDLY, LOVABLE FUR BALLS.
8/4
picklescomic@sbcglobal.net
IT'S AN ACT OF SELF-DELUSION, DON'T YOU THINK?
I'M PROBABLY THE WRONG PERSON TO ASK.
© 2007 Brian Crane, dist. by Washington Post Writers Group
I ONCE HAD A PIT BULL NAMED "FLUFFY."

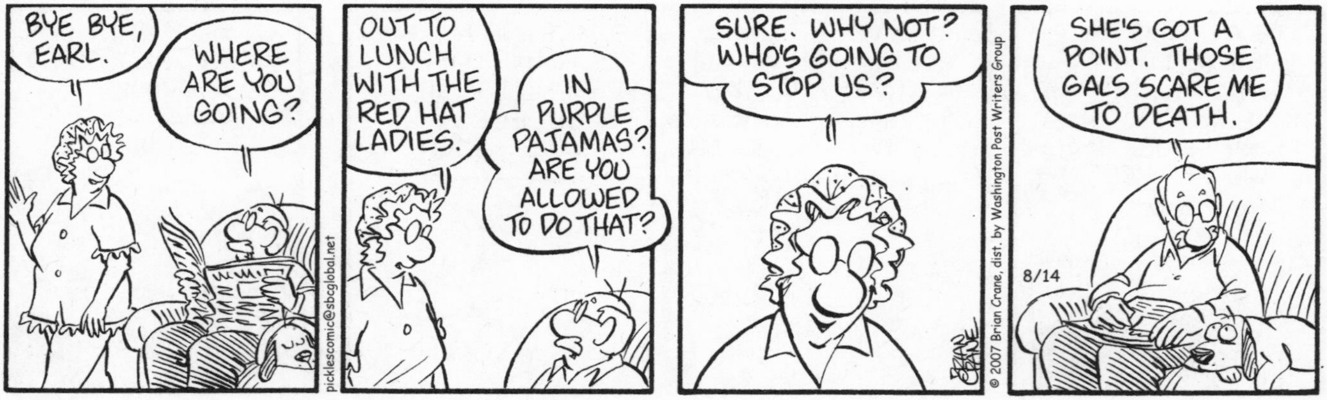
BYE BYE, EARL.
WHERE ARE YOU GOING?
picklescomic@sbcglobal.net
OUT TO LUNCH WITH THE RED HAT LADIES.
IN PURPLE PAJAMAS? ARE YOU ALLOWED TO DO THAT?
SURE. WHY NOT? WHO'S GOING TO STOP US?
© 2007 Brian Crane, dist. by Washington Post Writers Group
SHE'S GOT A POINT. THOSE GALS SCARE ME TO DEATH.
8/14

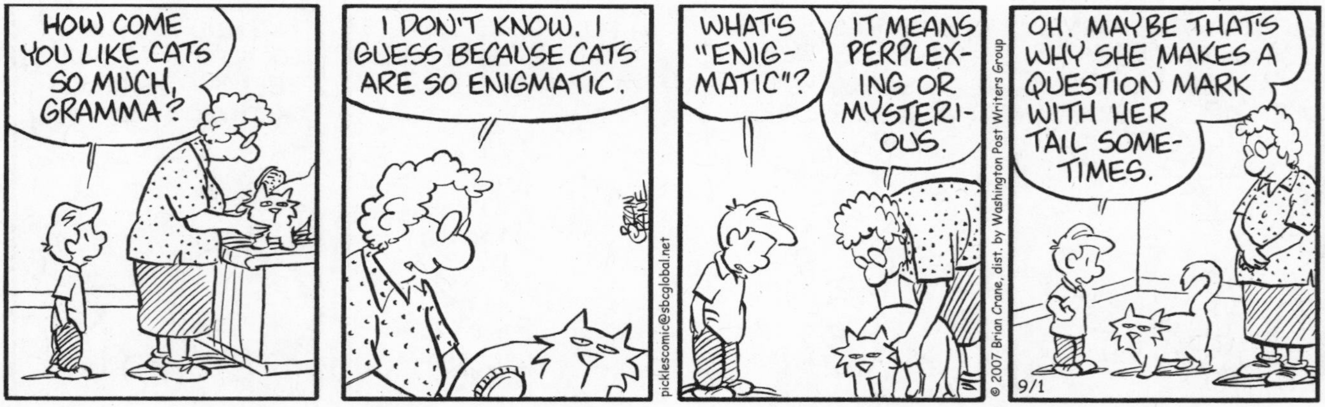
HOW COME YOU LIKE CATS SO MUCH, GRAMMA?
I DON'T KNOW. I GUESS BECAUSE CATS ARE SO ENIGMATIC.
picklescomic@sbcglobal.net
WHAT'S "ENIG-MATIC"?
IT MEANS PERPLEX-ING OR MYSTERI-OUS.
© 2007 Brian Crane, dist. by Washington Post Writers Group
OH. MAYBE THAT'S WHY SHE MAKES A QUESTION MARK WITH HER TAIL SOME-TIMES.
9/1

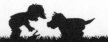

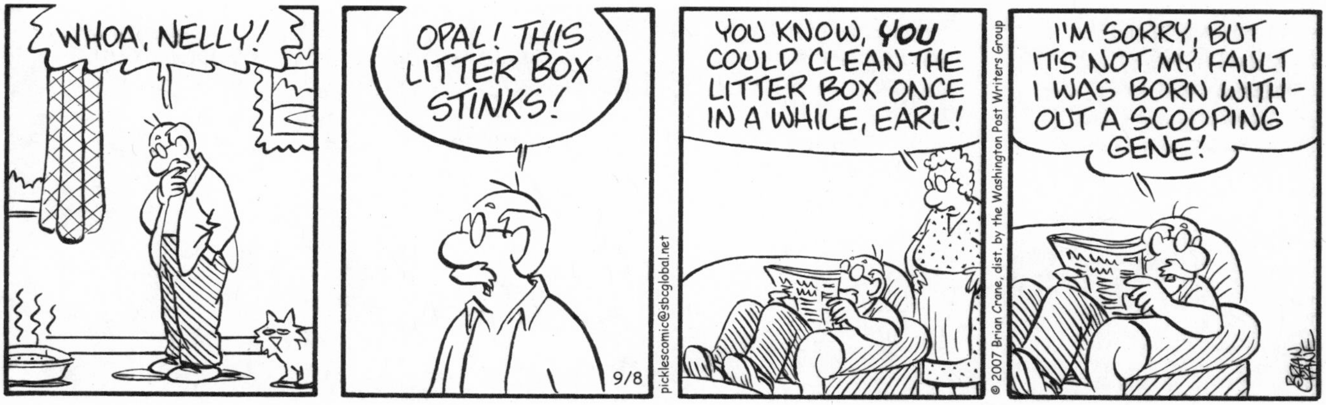
WHOA, NELLY!
OPAL! THIS LITTER BOX STINKS!
9/8
picklescomic@sbcglobal.net
YOU KNOW, **YOU** COULD CLEAN THE LITTER BOX ONCE IN A WHILE, EARL!
© 2007 Brian Crane, dist. by the Washington Post Writers Group
I'M SORRY, BUT IT'S NOT MY FAULT I WAS BORN WITH-OUT A SCOOPING GENE!

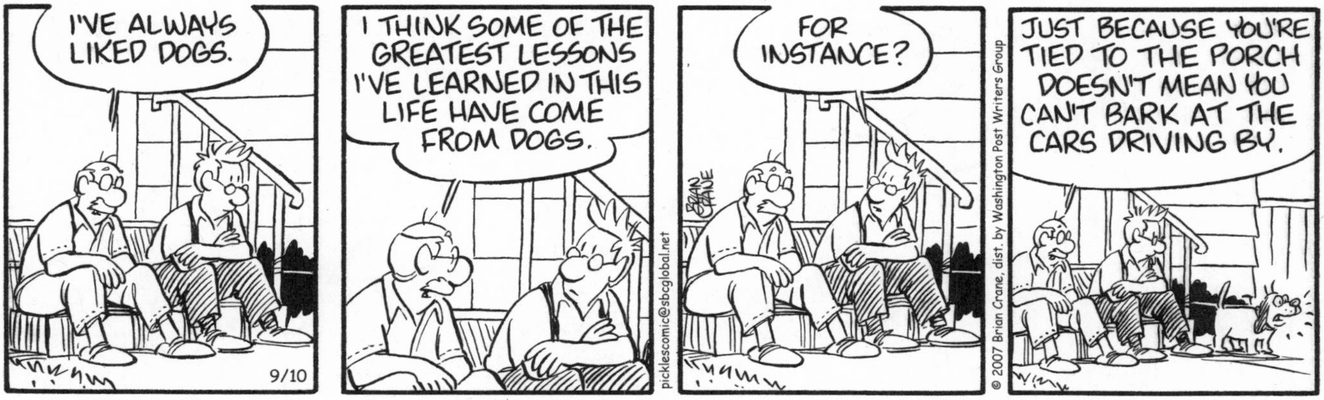
I'VE ALWAYS LIKED DOGS.
9/10
I THINK SOME OF THE GREATEST LESSONS I'VE LEARNED IN THIS LIFE HAVE COME FROM DOGS.
picklescomic@sbcglobal.net
FOR INSTANCE?
© 2007 Brian Crane, dist. by Washington Post Writers Group
JUST BECAUSE YOU'RE TIED TO THE PORCH DOESN'T MEAN YOU CAN'T BARK AT THE CARS DRIVING BY.

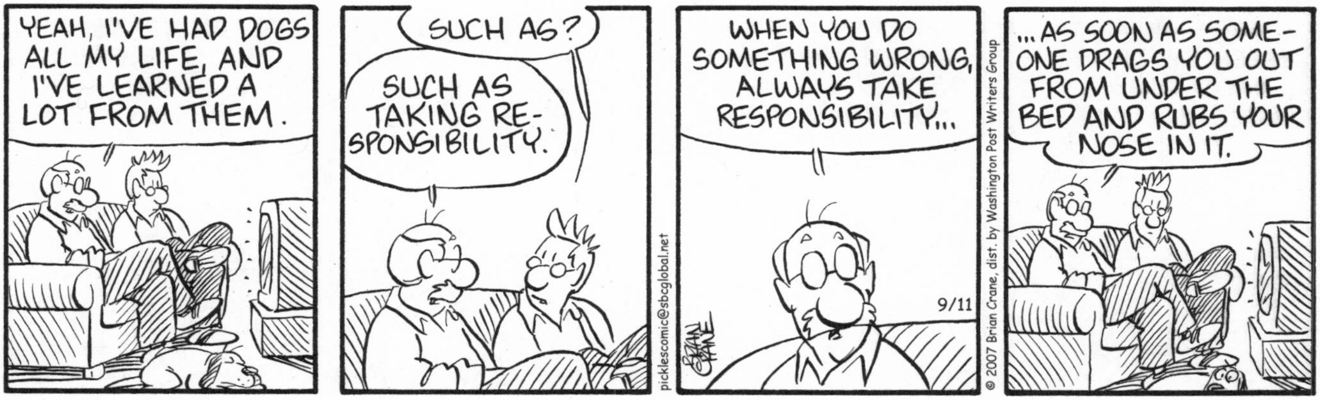
YEAH, I'VE HAD DOGS ALL MY LIFE, AND I'VE LEARNED A LOT FROM THEM.
SUCH AS?
SUCH AS TAKING RE-SPONSIBILITY.
picklescomic@sbcglobal.net
WHEN YOU DO SOMETHING WRONG, ALWAYS TAKE RESPONSIBILITY...
9/11
© 2007 Brian Crane, dist. by Washington Post Writers Group
...AS SOON AS SOME-ONE DRAGS YOU OUT FROM UNDER THE BED AND RUBS YOUR NOSE IN IT.

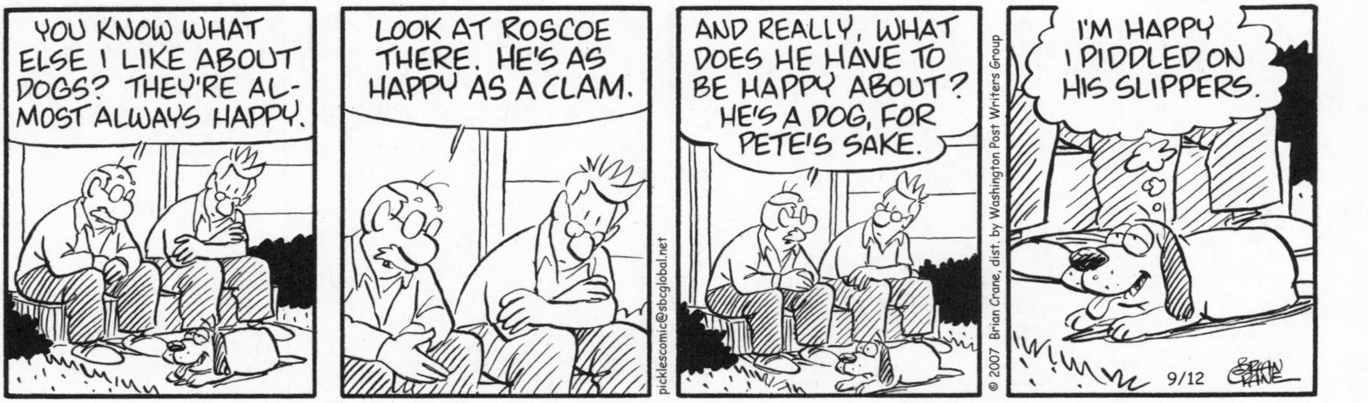
YOU KNOW WHAT ELSE I LIKE ABOUT DOGS? THEY'RE AL-MOST ALWAYS HAPPY.
LOOK AT ROSCOE THERE. HE'S AS HAPPY AS A CLAM.
picklescomic@sbcglobal.net
AND REALLY, WHAT DOES HE HAVE TO BE HAPPY ABOUT? HE'S A DOG, FOR PETE'S SAKE.
© 2007 Brian Crane, dist. by Washington Post Writers Group
I'M HAPPY I PIDDLED ON HIS SLIPPERS.
9/12
BRIAN CRANE

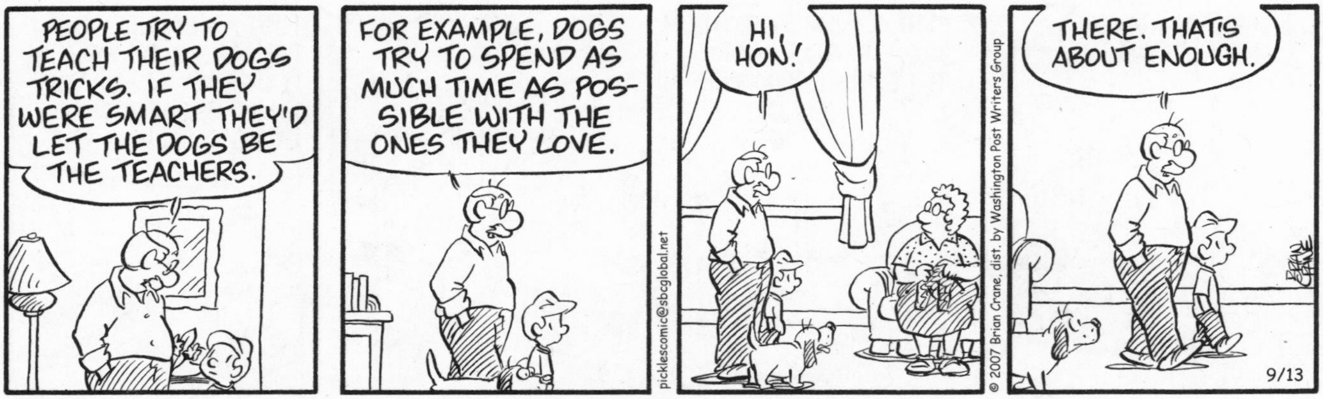
PEOPLE TRY TO TEACH THEIR DOGS TRICKS. IF THEY WERE SMART THEY'D LET THE DOGS BE THE TEACHERS.
FOR EXAMPLE, DOGS TRY TO SPEND AS MUCH TIME AS POS-SIBLE WITH THE ONES THEY LOVE.
picklescomic@sbcglobal.net
HI, HON!
© 2007 Brian Crane, dist. by Washington Post Writers Group
THERE. THAT'S ABOUT ENOUGH.
9/13

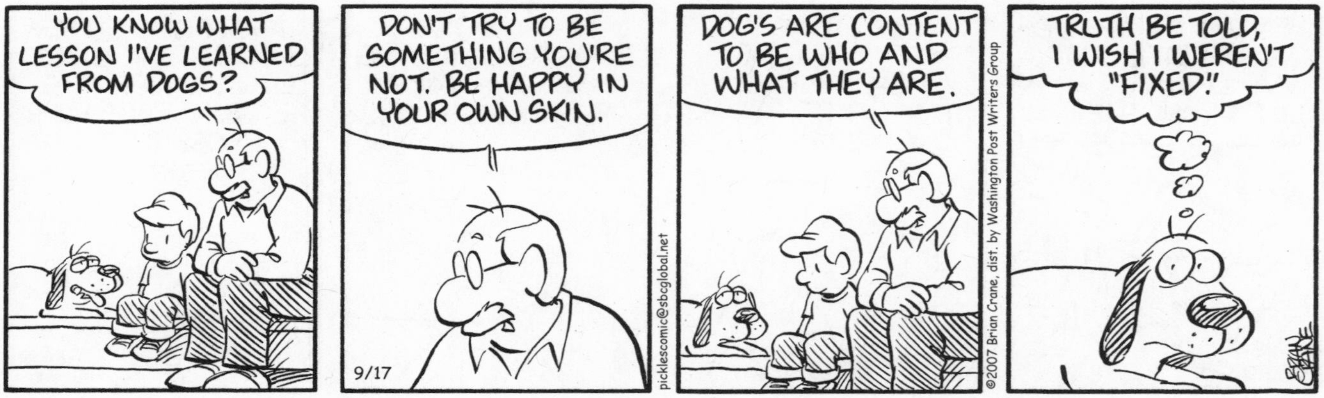
YOU KNOW WHAT LESSON I'VE LEARNED FROM DOGS?
DON'T TRY TO BE SOMETHING YOU'RE NOT. BE HAPPY IN YOUR OWN SKIN.
9/17
picklescomic@sbcglobal.net
DOG'S ARE CONTENT TO BE WHO AND WHAT THEY ARE.
©2007 Brian Crane, dist. by Washington Post Writers Group
TRUTH BE TOLD, I WISH I WEREN'T "FIXED."

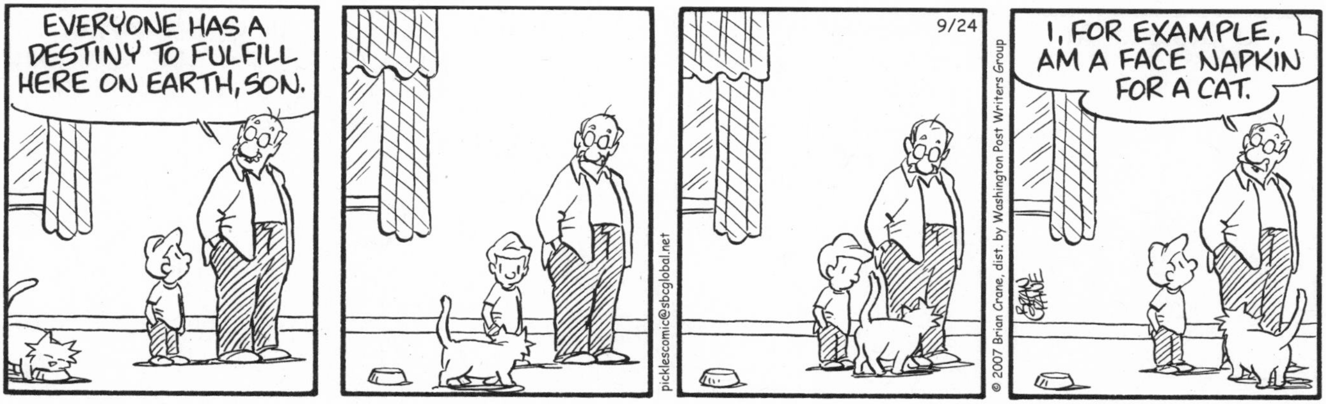
EVERYONE HAS A DESTINY TO FULFILL HERE ON EARTH, SON.
picklescomic@sbcglobal.net
9/24
© 2007 Brian Crane, dist. by Washington Post Writers Group
I, FOR EXAMPLE, AM A FACE NAPKIN FOR A CAT.

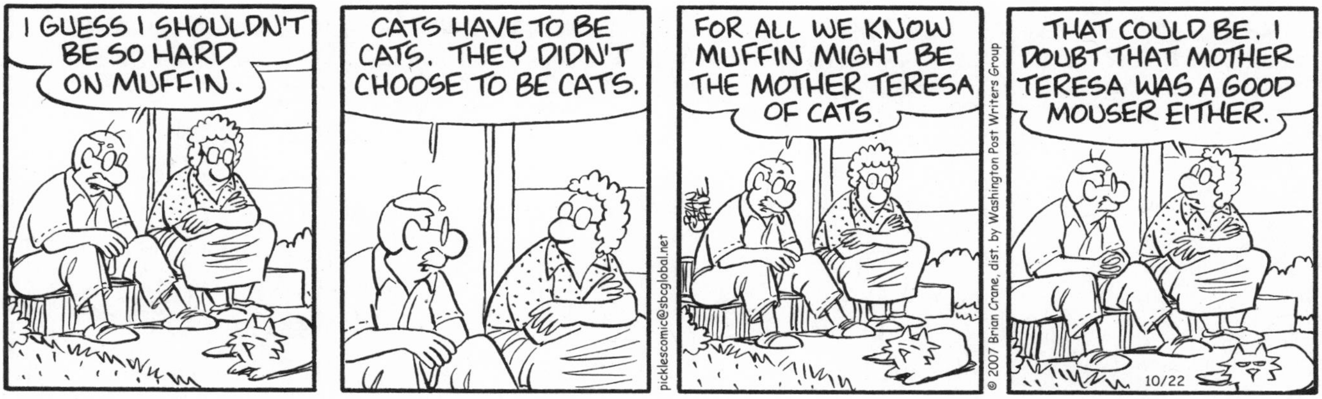
I GUESS I SHOULDN'T BE SO HARD ON MUFFIN.
CATS HAVE TO BE CATS. THEY DIDN'T CHOOSE TO BE CATS.
picklescomic@sbcglobal.net
FOR ALL WE KNOW MUFFIN MIGHT BE THE MOTHER TERESA OF CATS.
© 2007 Brian Crane, dist. by Washington Post Writers Group
THAT COULD BE. I DOUBT THAT MOTHER TERESA WAS A GOOD MOUSER EITHER.
10/22

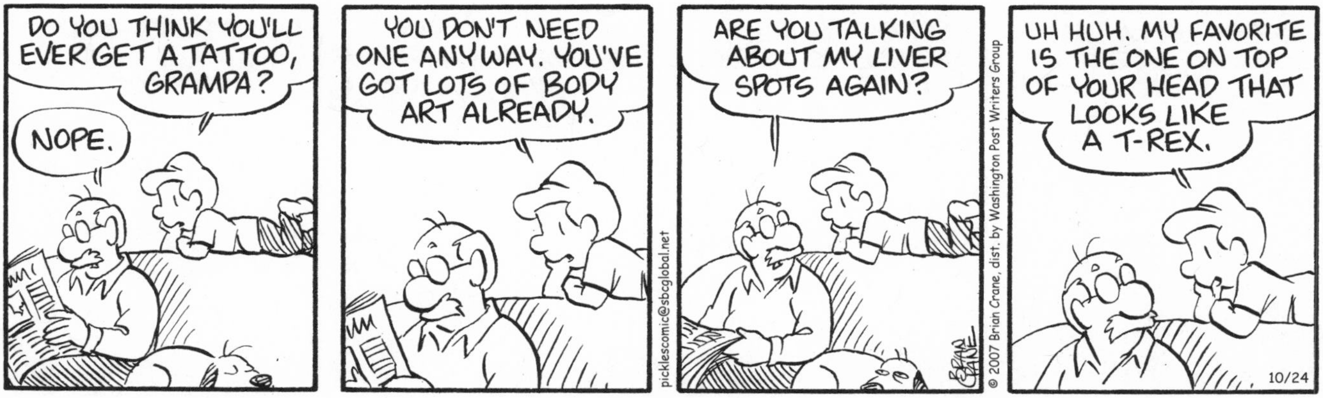
DO YOU THINK YOU'LL EVER GET A TATTOO, GRAMPA?
NOPE.
YOU DON'T NEED ONE ANYWAY. YOU'VE GOT LOTS OF BODY ART ALREADY.
picklescomic@sbcglobal.net
ARE YOU TALKING ABOUT MY LIVER SPOTS AGAIN?
© 2007 Brian Crane, dist. by Washington Post Writers Group
UH HUH. MY FAVORITE IS THE ONE ON TOP OF YOUR HEAD THAT LOOKS LIKE A T-REX.
10/24

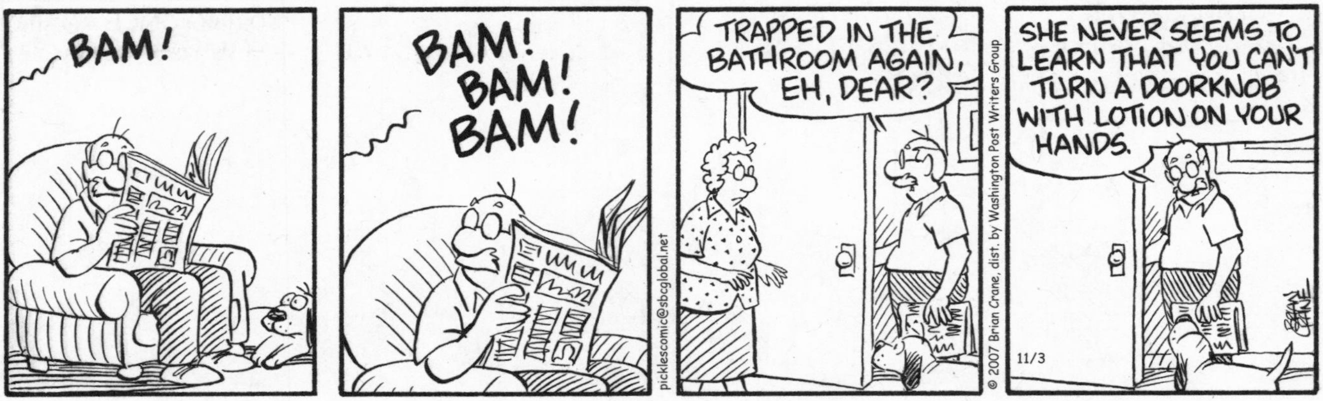
BAM!
BAM! BAM! BAM!
picklescomic@sbcglobal.net
TRAPPED IN THE BATHROOM AGAIN, EH, DEAR?
© 2007 Brian Crane, dist. by Washington Post Writers Group
SHE NEVER SEEMS TO LEARN THAT YOU CAN'T TURN A DOORKNOB WITH LOTION ON YOUR HANDS.
11/3

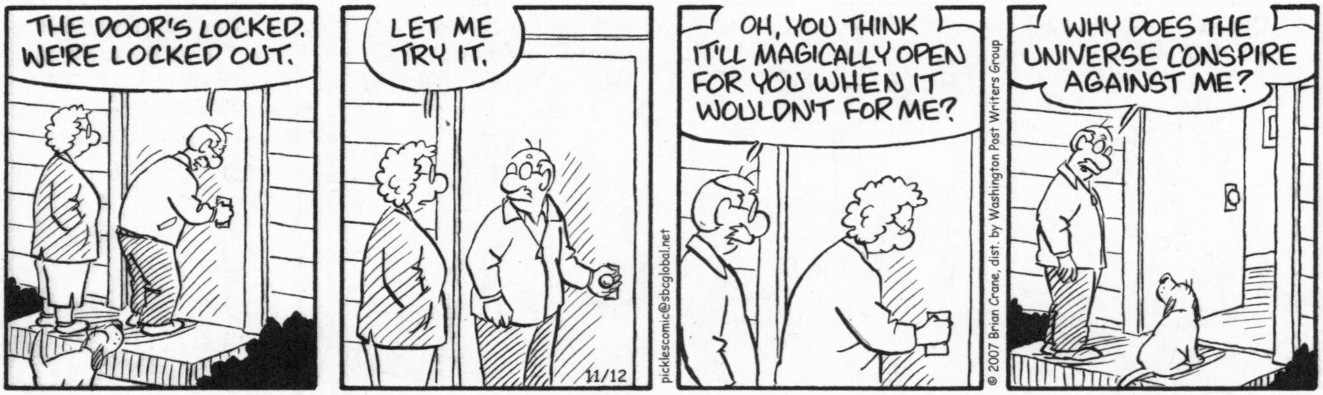
THE DOOR'S LOCKED. WE'RE LOCKED OUT.
LET ME TRY IT.
11/12
picklescomic@sbcglobal.net
OH, YOU THINK IT'LL MAGICALLY OPEN FOR YOU WHEN IT WOULDN'T FOR ME?
© 2007 Brian Crane, dist. by Washington Post Writers Group
WHY DOES THE UNIVERSE CONSPIRE AGAINST ME?

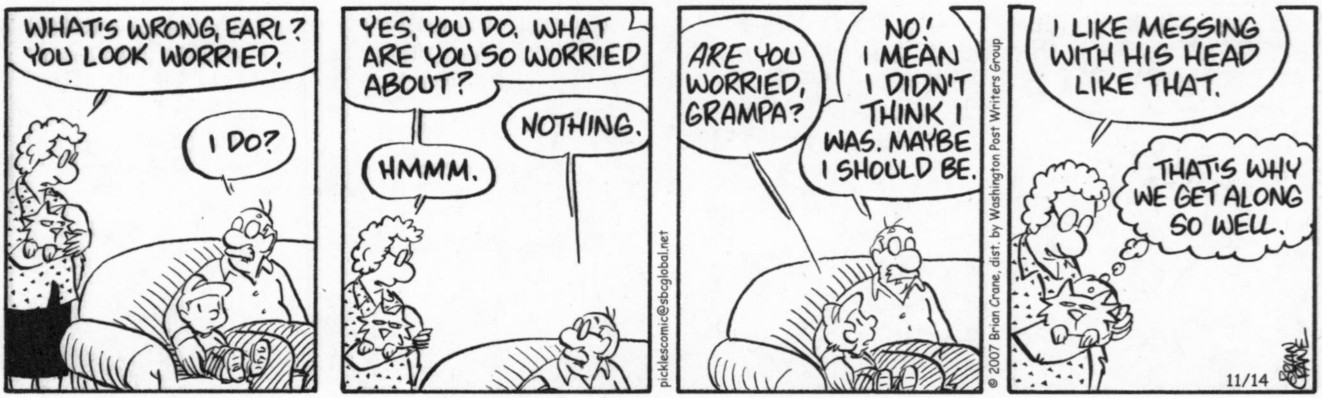
WHAT'S WRONG, EARL? YOU LOOK WORRIED.
I DO?
YES, YOU DO. WHAT ARE YOU SO WORRIED ABOUT?
NOTHING.
HMMM.
picklescomic@sbcglobal.net
ARE YOU WORRIED, GRAMPA?
NO! I MEAN I DIDN'T THINK I WAS. MAYBE I SHOULD BE.
© 2007 Brian Crane, dist. by Washington Post Writers Group
I LIKE MESSING WITH HIS HEAD LIKE THAT.
THAT'S WHY WE GET ALONG SO WELL.
11/14

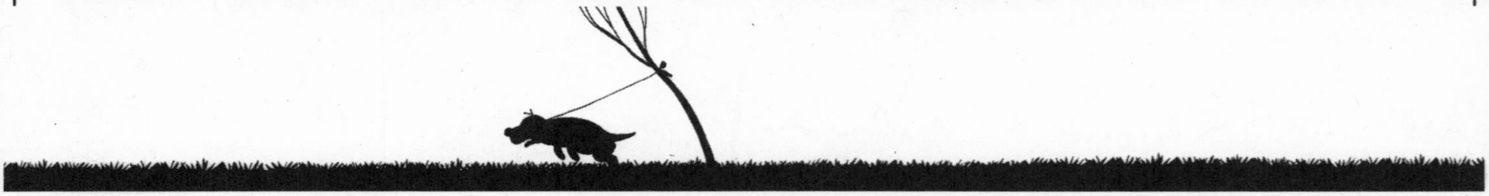

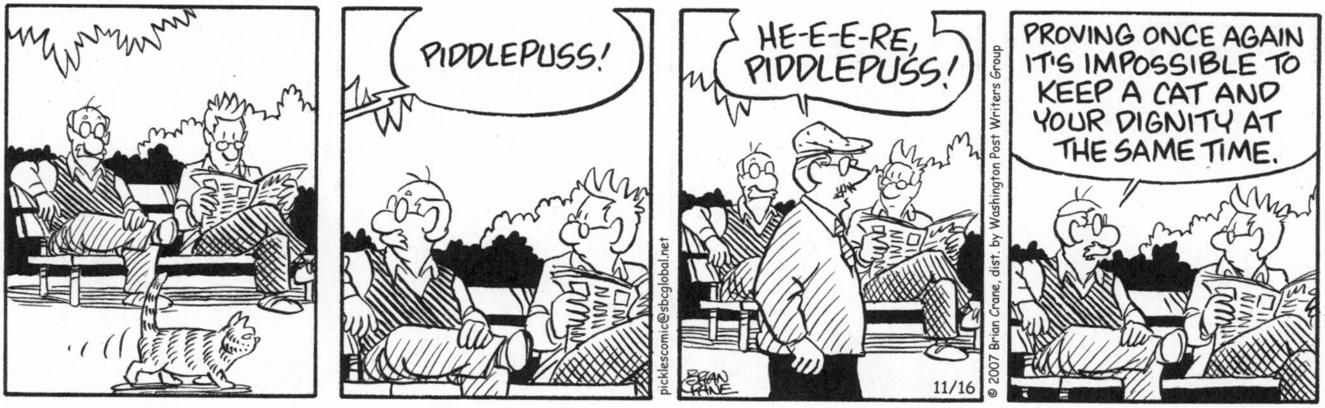
PIDDLEPUSS!
HE-E-E-RE, PIDDLEPUSS!
PROVING ONCE AGAIN IT'S IMPOSSIBLE TO KEEP A CAT AND YOUR DIGNITY AT THE SAME TIME.
picklescomic@sbcglobal.net
BRIAN CRANE
11/16
© 2007 Brian Crane, dist. by Washington Post Writers Group

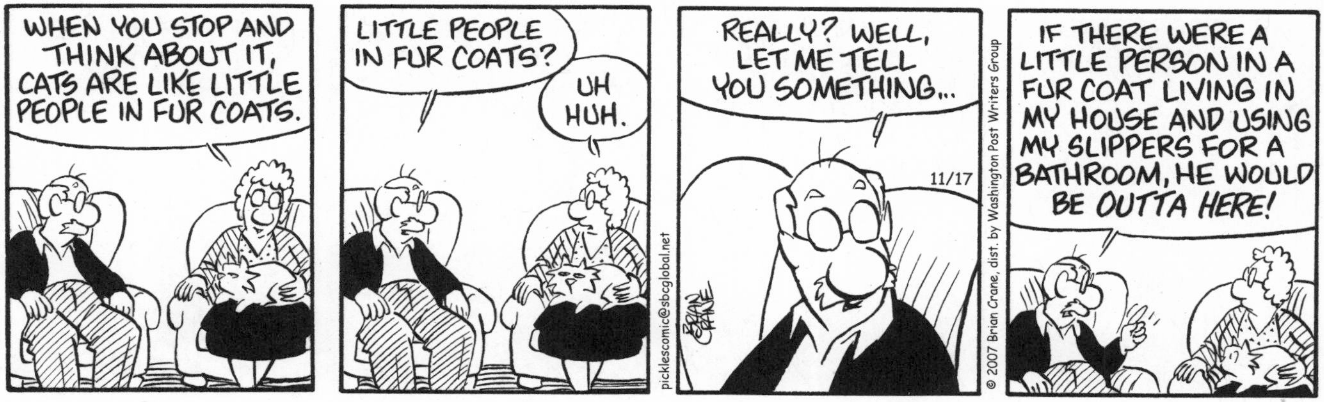
WHEN YOU STOP AND THINK ABOUT IT, CATS ARE LIKE LITTLE PEOPLE IN FUR COATS.
LITTLE PEOPLE IN FUR COATS?
UH HUH.
REALLY? WELL, LET ME TELL YOU SOMETHING...
IF THERE WERE A LITTLE PERSON IN A FUR COAT LIVING IN MY HOUSE AND USING MY SLIPPERS FOR A BATHROOM, HE WOULD BE OUTTA HERE!
picklescomic@sbcglobal.net
BRIAN CRANE
11/17
© 2007 Brian Crane, dist. by Washington Post Writers Group

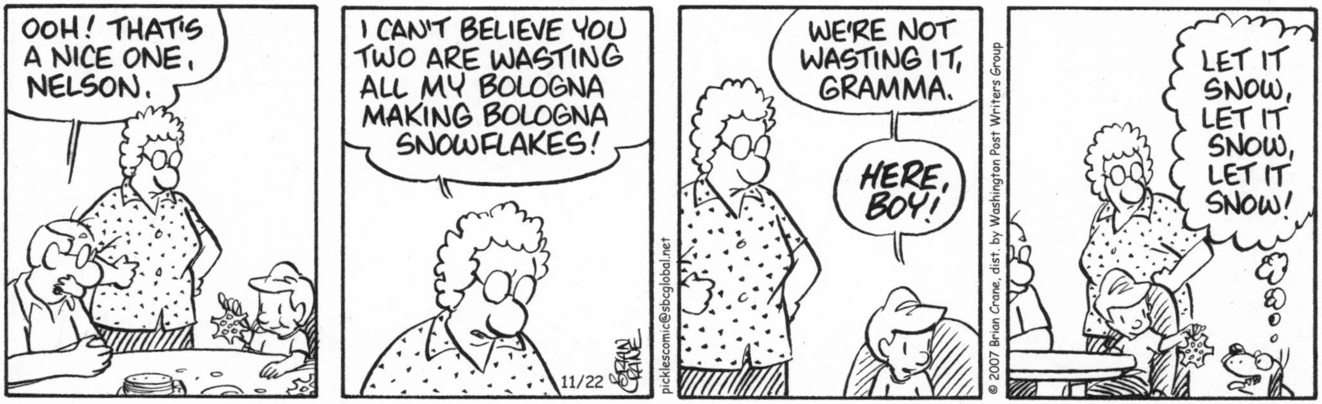
OOH! THAT'S A NICE ONE, NELSON.
I CAN'T BELIEVE YOU TWO ARE WASTING ALL MY BOLOGNA MAKING BOLOGNA SNOWFLAKES!
WE'RE NOT WASTING IT, GRAMMA.
HERE, BOY!
LET IT SNOW, LET IT SNOW, LET IT SNOW!
picklescomic@sbcglobal.net
BRIAN CRANE
11/22
© 2007 Brian Crane, dist. by Washington Post Writers Group

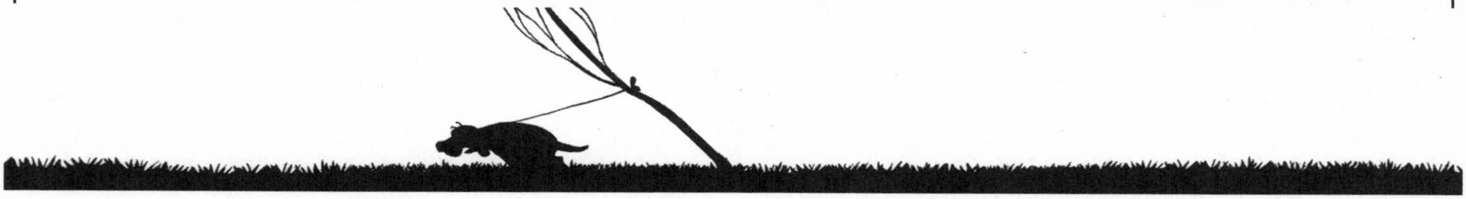

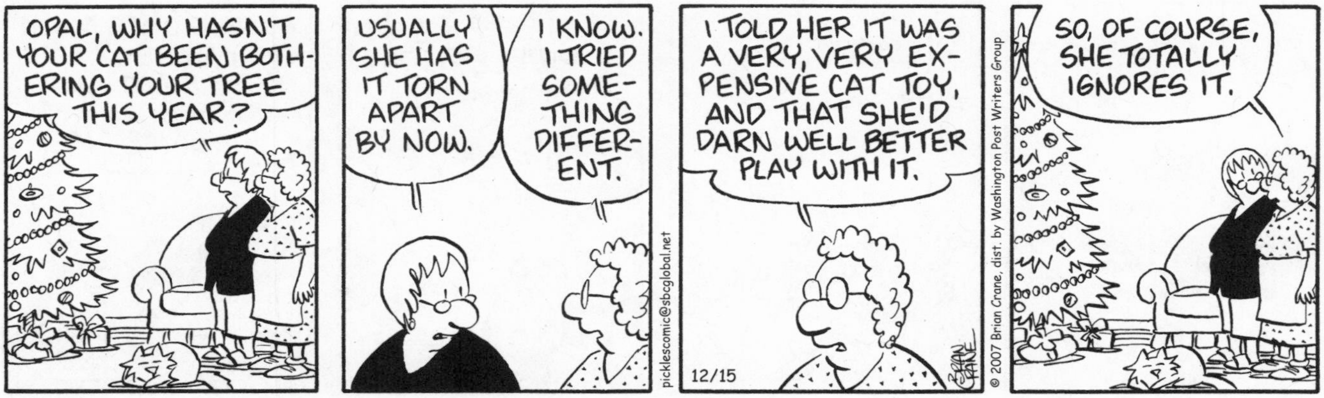
OPAL, WHY HASN'T YOUR CAT BEEN BOTHERING YOUR TREE THIS YEAR?
USUALLY SHE HAS IT TORN APART BY NOW.
I KNOW. I TRIED SOMETHING DIFFERENT.
picklescomic@sbcglobal.net
I TOLD HER IT WAS A VERY, VERY EXPENSIVE CAT TOY, AND THAT SHE'D DARN WELL BETTER PLAY WITH IT.
12/15
© 2007 Brian Crane, dist. by Washington Post Writers Group
SO, OF COURSE, SHE TOTALLY IGNORES IT.

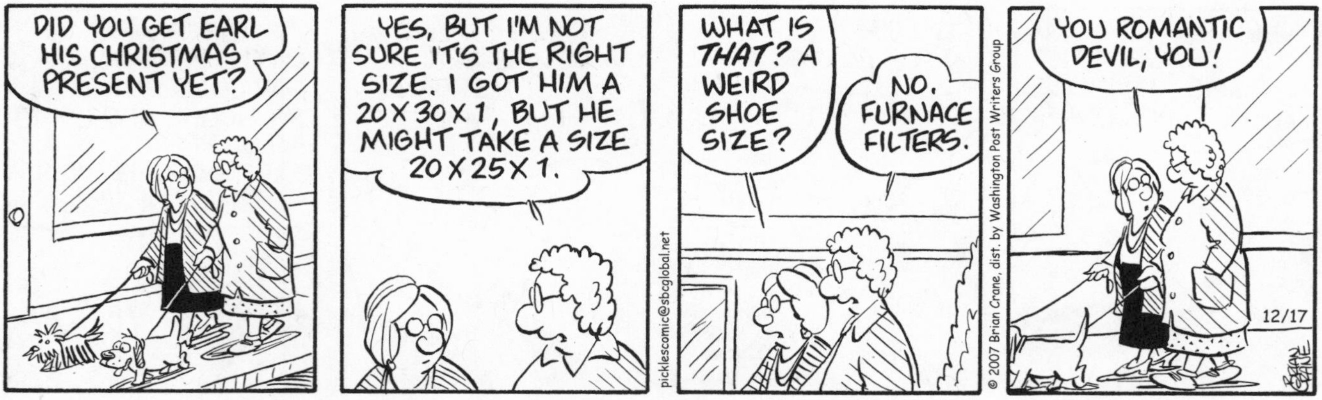
DID YOU GET EARL HIS CHRISTMAS PRESENT YET?
YES, BUT I'M NOT SURE IT'S THE RIGHT SIZE. I GOT HIM A 20 X 30 X 1, BUT HE MIGHT TAKE A SIZE 20 X 25 X 1.
picklescomic@sbcglobal.net
WHAT IS *THAT*? A WEIRD SHOE SIZE?
NO. FURNACE FILTERS.
© 2007 Brian Crane, dist. by Washington Post Writers Group
YOU ROMANTIC DEVIL, YOU!
12/17

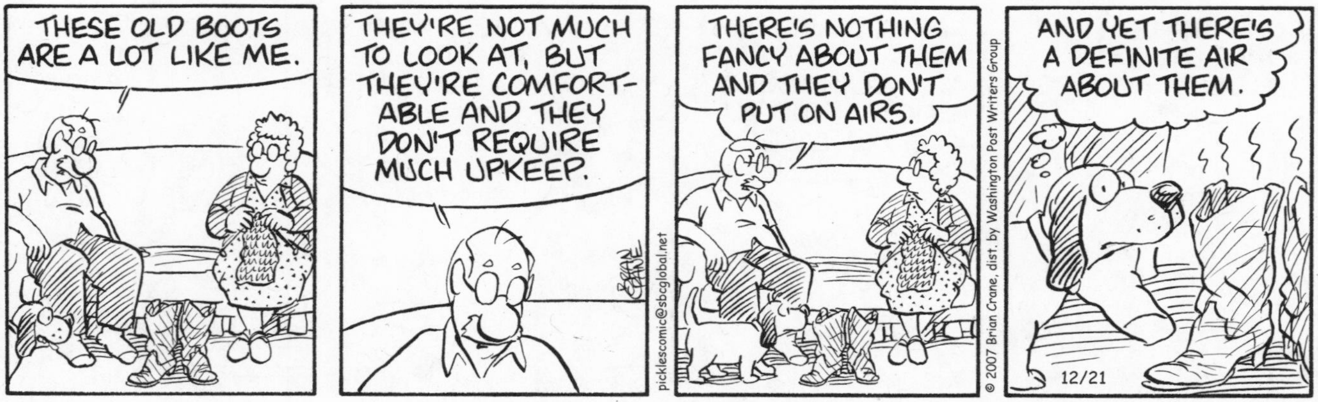
THESE OLD BOOTS ARE A LOT LIKE ME.
THEY'RE NOT MUCH TO LOOK AT, BUT THEY'RE COMFORTABLE AND THEY DON'T REQUIRE MUCH UPKEEP.
picklescomic@sbcglobal.net
THERE'S NOTHING FANCY ABOUT THEM AND THEY DON'T PUT ON AIRS.
© 2007 Brian Crane, dist. by Washington Post Writers Group
AND YET THERE'S A DEFINITE AIR ABOUT THEM.
12/21

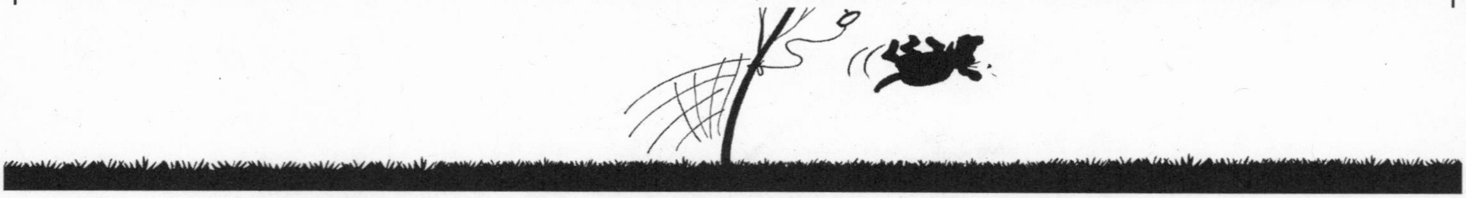

SUNDAYS
(1990 - 2007)

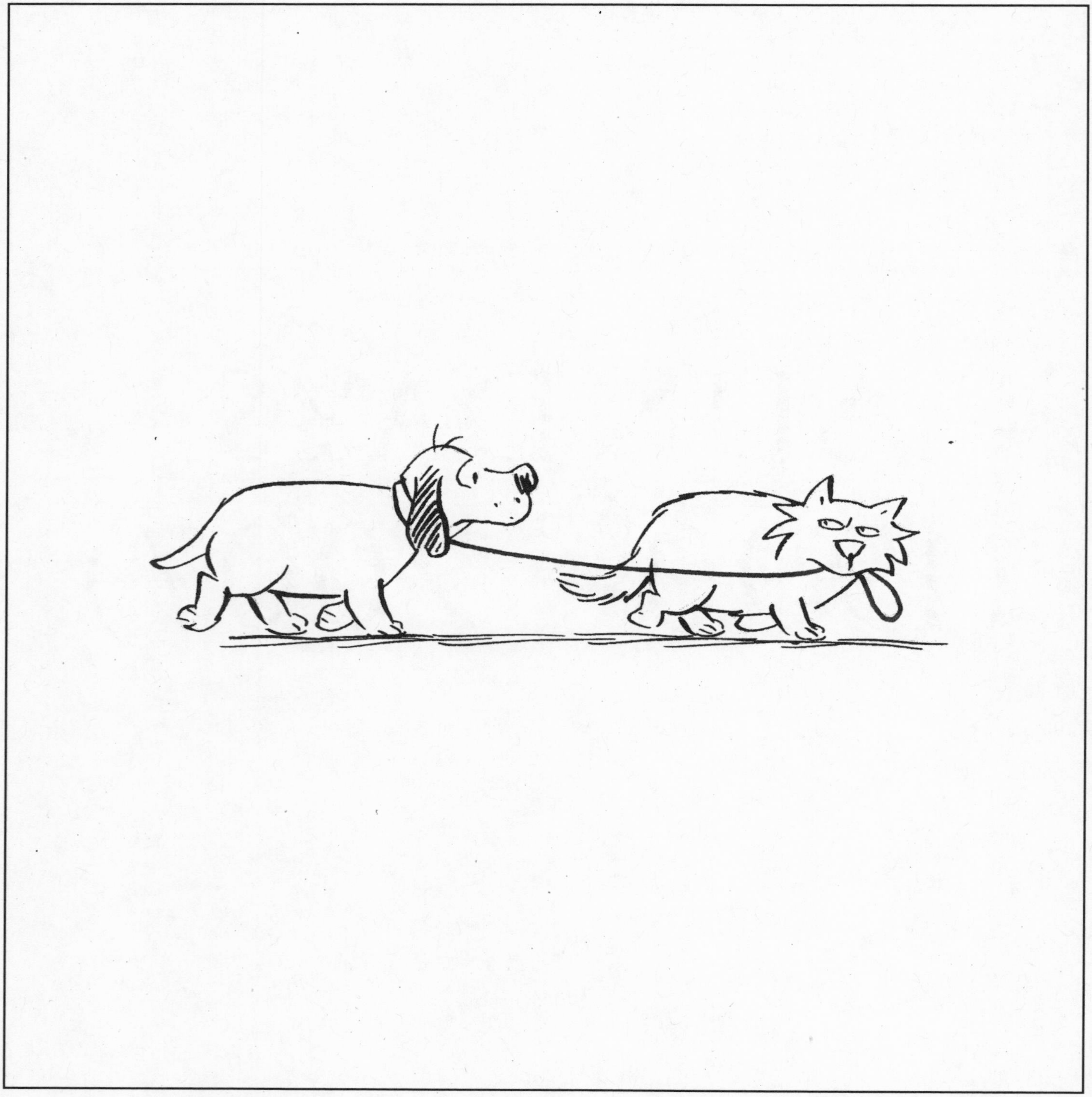

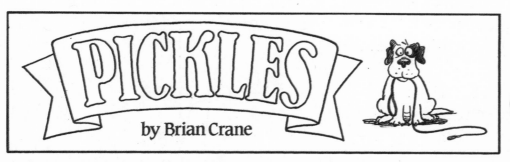

PICKLES
by Brian Crane
AM I TO ASSUME YOU WANT TO TAKE A WALK?
NOTHING GETS BY YOU, DOES IT?
YIP YIP YIP
YIP YIP
YIP YIP YIP
HEY! KNOCK IT OFF!!
GRRRR
GRRR
DON'T JUST STAND THERE, ROSCOE... DO SOMETHING!!
GRRR
GRRR
GRRRR
© 1992 Washington Post Writers Group
3/29
GRRRR
GRRR
GRRRR
GRRRR
GRRRR
BRIAN CRANE

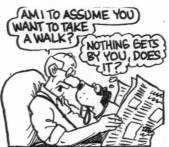

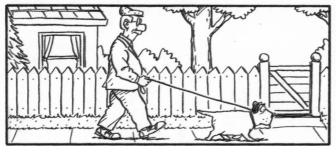

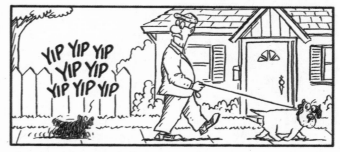

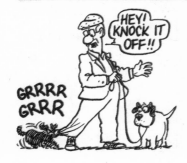

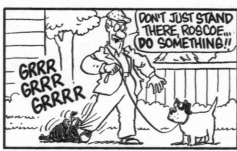

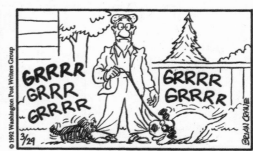

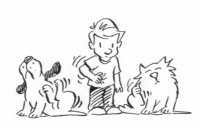

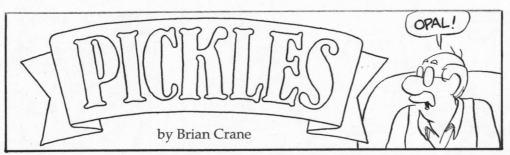

PICKLES

by Brian Crane

OPAL!

WHAT'S THE THERMOSTAT SET AT?

I CAN'T BELIEVE YOU.

HERE IT IS THE MIDDLE OF WINTER AND YOU'VE GOT YOUR FEET STICKIN' OUT OF THE COVERS!

WELL, YOU KNOW ME... MY FEET ARE ALWAYS WARM.

YEAH. AND MINE ARE ALWAYS COLD.

POOR DEAR, HOW COLD ARE THEY?

SCREECH!

© 1996 Washington Post Writers Group 2/4

ASK THE CAT.

BRIAN CRANE

PICKLES
by Brian Crane
CHINKA CHINKA
YOU RANG?
KA-CHINKA
I WANT YOU TO TRY THIS, MUFFIN.
THE ADS SAY IT'LL PUT THE FRISKY BACK IN YOUR CAT.
LET'S SEE IF IT DOES.
ZOOM!
ZING!
© 1998 Washington Post Writers Group
8/30
B.CRANE
ZIP!
ZIP!
HERE, EARL. TRY SOME OF THIS.

279

PICKLES
by Brian Crane
LET'S SEE...IF I WERE AN EASTER EGG, WHERE WOULD I HIDE?
DO YOU HAVE A DEATH WISH, OR WHAT?
AHA! I FOUND ONE!
bcpickles@aol.com
I FOUND ONE TOO!
HERE'S ANOTHER!
!
I HATE EASTER.
4/4
© 1999 Washington Post Writers Group
IT'S THE ONE DAY WHEN OTHER PEOPLE BESIDES ME CAN EAT THINGS THEY FIND UNDER THE FURNITURE.
B. CRANE

PICKLES
by Brian Crane
WHO WANTS TO BE A THOUSANDAIRE?
THEY MUST BE RUNNING OUT OF MONEY.
...AND NOW, A WORD FROM OUR SPONSOR...
BCPICKLES@AOL.COM
HOW YA DOIN', BOY?
SKRITCH SKRITCHA SKRITCH
YOU LIKE THAT, DON'T YOU?
SKRITCHA SKRITCHA
WWW.POSTWRITERSGROUP.COM
FEELS GOOD, DOESN'T IT?
SKRITCHEDY SKRATCH
OOOH YEAH!
SKRITCHY SKRITCH
1-7
© 2000 Washington Post Writers Group
OH, MY SHOW'S BACK ON.
I FEEL SO USED.

PICKLES
by Brian Crane
WHY ARE YOU STARING AT ME LIKE THAT? DO YOU WANT SOMETHING?
WWW.POSTWRITERSGROUP.COM
WHAT IS IT, BOY? DO YOU WANT TO GO FOR A WALK?
YOU THINK IF YOU STARE AT ME LONG ENOUGH WITH THOSE PUPPY-DOG EYES YOU'LL GET YOUR WAY, DON'T YOU?
WELL, IT WON'T WORK. I DON'T WANT TO GO FOR A WALK!
BOPICKLES@AOL.COM
11-19
© 2000 Washington Post Writers Group
OKAY, FINE! YOU WIN! WE'LL GO FOR A WALK!
PUPPY-DOG EYES ALWAYS WORK.
HEY!

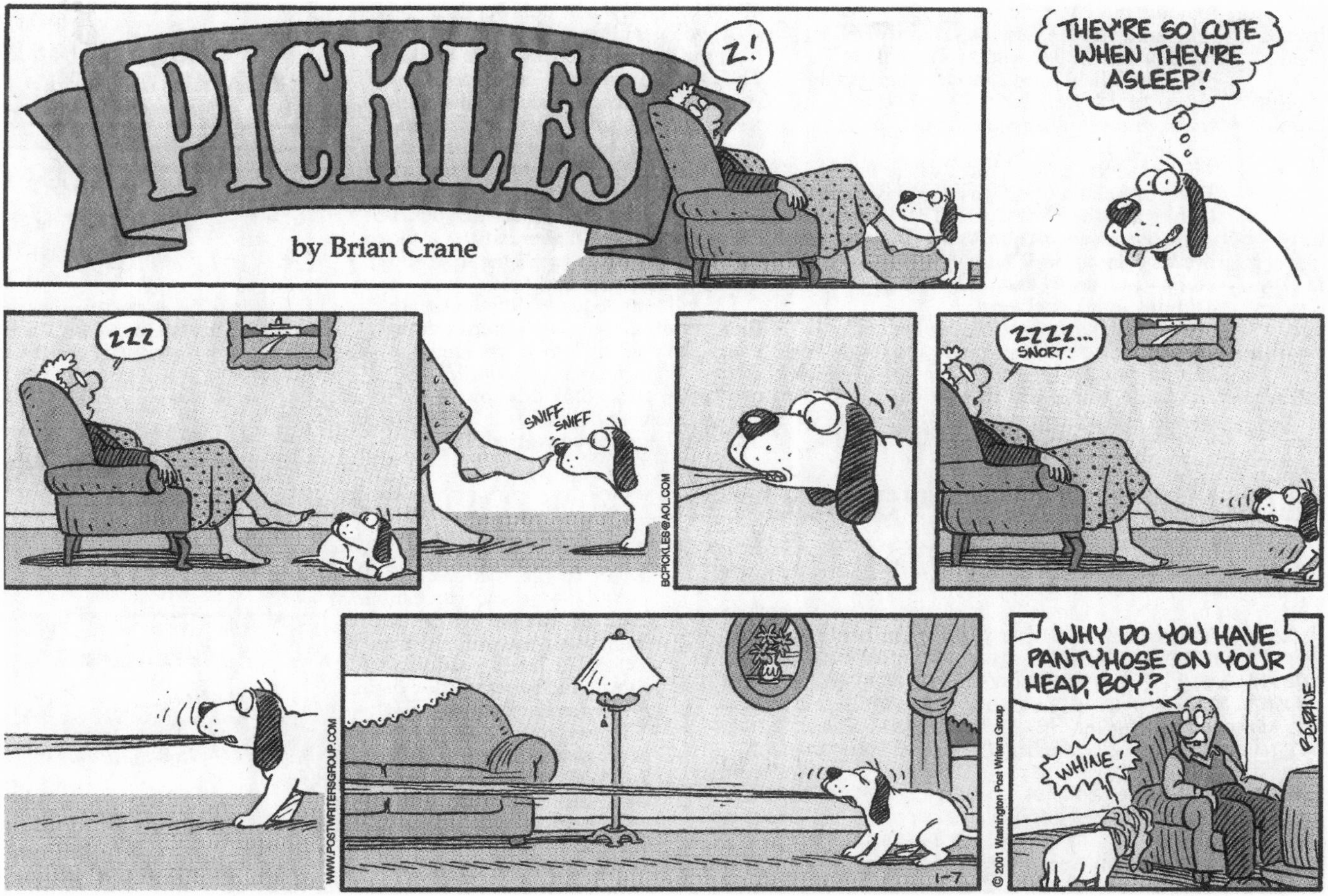
PICKLES
by Brian Crane
Z!
THEY'RE SO CUTE WHEN THEY'RE ASLEEP!
ZZZ
SNIFF SNIFF
BCPICKLES@AOL.COM
ZZZZ... SNORT!
WWW.POSTWRITERSGROUP.COM
1-7
© 2001 Washington Post Writers Group
WHY DO YOU HAVE PANTYHOSE ON YOUR HEAD, BOY?
WHINE!

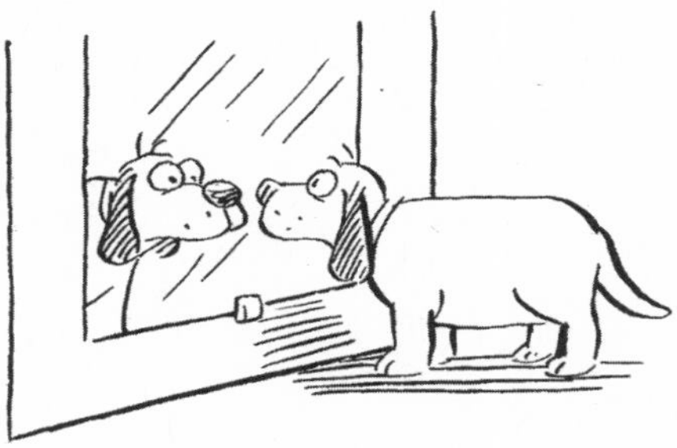

284

PICKLES
by BRIAN CRANE
WHAT DO YOU THINK YOU'RE DOING UP THERE?
YOU'RE BEING VERY CHILDISH.
COME DOWN FROM THERE!
WWW.POSTWRITERSGROUP.COM
OKAY, FINE! STAY THERE. SEE IF I CARE.
IF YOU PREFER SITTING IN A TREE TO BEING WITH ME I SUPPOSE THAT'S UP TO YOU.
I WORK MY FINGERS TO THE BONE FOR YOU AND THIS IS THE THANKS I GET!
I DON'T THINK ASKING YOU TO OBEY A FEW SIMPLE RULES OF BE-HAVIOR IN THE HOUSE IS TOO MUCH TO ASK.
7/22
AND THAT'S ALL I'M GOING TO SAY ABOUT IT.
BCPICKLES@AOL.COM
LET ME KNOW IF YOU CHANGE YOUR MIND AND DECIDE TO COME DOWN.
© 2001 WASHINGTON POST WRITERS GROUP
AND IF YOU DO, BRING THE CAT WITH YOU.

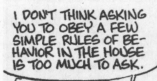

PICKLES
by BRIAN CRANE
WIGGLE WIGGLE WIGGLE
YOU USED TO LIKE TO PLAY FOOTSIE WITH ME!
www.comics.com
!
MGLBLRF...
HMPHF!
11-18 CRANE
LICK! LICK!
FORGET IT! YOU HAD YOUR CHANCE!
?

PICKLES
by BRIAN CRANE
CAN'T YOU FIND SOME-PLACE ELSE TO TAKE CARE OF YOUR PERSONAL HYGIENE?
WHAT ARE YOU LOOKING AT?
I THINK LIVING WITH A MEMBER OF A DIFFERENT SPECIES IS FASCINATING.
REALLY?
OH, YES.
SOMETIMES I ALMOST FEEL LIKE JANE GOODALL, LIVING AMONG THE CHIMPANZEES.
OBSERVING THE STRANGE AND SOMETIMES BIZARRE BEHAVIOR OF OTHER CREATURES IS VERY EYE-OPENING, TO SAY THE LEAST.
IT MAY SEEM ODD OR EVEN REPULSIVE TO ME, BUT I KNOW IT'S ALL PART OF NATURE'S WONDER.
HEY...
YOU **ARE** TALKING ABOUT THE CAT, RIGHT?
www.comics.com
picklescomic@sbcglobal.net
© 2003 Washington Post Writers Group
B. CRANE
10·26

PICKLES
by BRIAN CRANE
AHH... THE HOLIDAYS.
THE HOLIDAYS CAN BE A DANGEROUS TIME TO BE A CAT.
picklescomic@sbcglobal.net
THERE'S THE TINSEL AND RIBBONS, JUST BEGGING US TO NIBBLE ON THEM, AND POSSIBLY LODGING IN OUR INTESTINES.
THE CHRISTMAS TREE IS AN ACCIDENT WAITING TO HAPPEN IF WE SCAMPER TO THE UPPER BRANCHES AND IT TOPPLES OVER.
www.comics.com
AND STAGNANT TREE WATER CAN GIVE US A VERY UPSET STOMACH. GUESS WHO'LL BE DOING THE CLEAN-UP?
AND THOSE POINSETTIA, MISTLETOE AND HOLLY PLANTS — BOY, IF WE MUNCH ON THOSE THERE COULD BE REAL TROUBLE!
OF COURSE, FOR ME THE SCARIEST PART OF THE HOLIDAYS...
OH, THERE YOU ARE, MUFFIN!
12-21
BRIAN CRANE
© 2003 Washington Post Writers Group
...IS THE OLD LADY WHO GETS HER JOLLIES DRESSING ME UP.

287

PICKLES
by BRIAN CRANE
LET'S GO FOR A WALK, BOY!
GOOD MORNING!
www.comics.com
WE'RE HOME, BOY.
...BOY?
© 2004 Brian Crane, dist. by The Washington Post Writers Group
EARL, WHAT ARE YOU DOING?
LOSING MY MIND, APPARENTLY. I COULD'VE SWORN I WAS WALKING THE DOG, BUT...
1-18
picklescomic@sbcglobal.net
GRAMPA, CAN I TAKE YOUR INVISIBLE DOG FOR A WALK NOW?
CRANE

PICKLES
by BRIAN CRANE
WHAT THE...?!
THIS IS NOT WHAT I ORDERED!
I DON'T GET THE RESPECT I DESERVE AROUND HERE.
www.comics.com
picklescomic@sbcglobal.net
THE ANCIENT EGYPTIANS HAD THE RIGHT IDEA.
© 2004 Brian Crane, dist. by The Washington Post Writers Group
THEY WORSHIPPED CATS AS GODS.
I WISH I WERE LIVING BACK THEN.
I'D PROBABLY BE SITTING ON A THRONE RIGHT NOW.
MOVE IT, CAT!
2-29

PICKLES
by Brian Crane
HI, OPAL. I HAVEN'T SEEN YOU FOR A WHILE SO I THOUGHT I'D DROP BY.
COME IN, EMILY.
HAVE YOU BEEN BUSY FOR THE HOLIDAYS, OPAL?
OH, YES!
I'VE BEEN VERY BUSY PET-PROOFING THE HOUSE.
CHRISTMAS CAN BE A DANGEROUS TIME FOR DOGS AND CATS.
OH, I KNOW.
www.comics.com
picklescomic@sbcglobal.net
THERE ARE SO MANY THINGS THEY CAN GET INTO THAT CAN HURT THEM.
LIKE TINSEL.
YES, LIKE TINSEL, AND ORNAMENTS AND LITTLE WIRE HOOKS. THE LIST GOES ON AND ON.
I THINK THE CHRISTMAS TREE ITSELF IS ONE OF THE BIGGEST HAZARDS FOR PETS.
© 2004 Brian Crane, dist. by The Washington Post Writers Group
I AGREE. IT'S IMPORTANT TO KEEP THE TREE AWAY FROM THE PETS.
12/12

PICKLES
by BRIAN CRANE
OH, YOU PUT YOUR ARM AROUND THE DOG BUT NOT YOUR WIFE, HUH?!!
SORRY, DEAR. I WASN'T THINKING.
www.comics.com
picklescomic@sbcglobal.net
SKRITCHA SKRITCHA
SKRITCHA SKRITCH
SKRITCHA SKRITCHA
SKRITCHA SKRITCHA
KNOCK IT OFF!!
2-6
© 2005 Brian Crane, dist. by Washington Post Writers Group
THERE'S JUST NO PLEASING SOME PEOPLE!

PICKLES
BY BRIAN CRANE
THAT DOG SEEMS TO ADORE EARL.
I ♥ 2 KNIT
www.comics.com
picklescomic@sbcglobal.net
WHEREVER EARL GOES, ROSCOE GOES. HE FOLLOWS HIM AROUND LIKE A GROUPIE.
I KNOW. HE'S ALWAYS RIGHT AT EARL'S FEET. HE NEVER LETS HIM OUT OF HIS SIGHT.
IT'S ALMOST LIKE HE WORSHIPS THE GROUND EARL WALKS ON.
ACTUALLY, IT'S NOT THAT HE WORSHIPS THE GROUND EARL WALKS ON.
© 2005 Brian Crane, dist. by Washington Post Writers Group
7-3
IT'S JUST THAT HE KNOWS THAT SOONER OR LATER THERE'S GOING TO BE FOOD FALLING ON THE GROUND HE WALKS ON.
OOPS!
SPLAT!

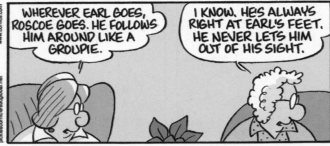

PICKLES
by BRIAN CRANE
WUMPA WUMPA WUMP
THUMPA THUMPA THUMP
WHAT'S THAT AWFUL NOISE?
WUMPA WUMPA WUMPA WUMPA
WUMPA WUMPA WUMP
THE WASHER'S ACTING UP. GO SIT ON IT, WILL YOU?
SIT ON IT?
YES, TO KEEP IT FROM SHAKING ITSELF TO PIECES.
WUMP WUMPA WUMP WUMPA WUMP
OKAY, IF YOU SAY SO.
WUMPA WUMPA WUMPA
WUMPA WUMPA WUMPA
8-21
WUMP WUMPA WUMP
ROSCOE, GO FETCH EARL'S DENTURES.
www.comics.com
picklescomic@sbcglobal.net
© 2005 Brian Crane, dist. by Washington Post Writers Group

PICKLES
by BRIAN CRANE
HEY, ROSCOE, HOW'S IT GOIN'?
SKRITCHA SKRITCHA
NUDGE NUDGE
OH, YOU LIKE THAT, HUH?
SKRITCHA SKRITCH
WHINE!
www.comics.com
picklescomic@sbcglobal.net
FOR CRYIN' OUT LOUD!
WHINE! WHINE! WHINE!
© 2006 Brian Crane, dist. by The Washington Post Writers Group
SCRATCH A DOG ONCE AND YOU'RE BUSY FOR THE REST OF THE DAY.
BRIAN CRANE
2-19

PICKLES
by BRIAN CRANE
YOUR GRANDFATHER IS KIND OF WEIRD.
YEAH. I GUESS.
MY GRAMPA HAS LOTS OF OLD SAYINGS.
ONE THING HE ALWAYS SAYS IS "NEVER ITCH WHERE YOU CAN'T SCRATCH."
WHAT DOES THAT MEAN?
I'M NOT SURE.
SKRITCHA SKRITCHA
picklescomic@sbcglobal.net
8-2
CHOMP CHOMP CHOMP
© 2008 Brian Crane, dist. by The Washington Post Writers Group
I THINK IT JUST APPLIES TO PEOPLE, THOUGH. THERE'S NO PLACE DOGS CAN'T SCRATCH.

PICKLES
by BRIAN CRANE
DING! DONG!
DING! DONG!
MUFFIN!
DING! DONG!
DING! DONG! DING! DONG! DING! DONG!
MUFFIN! IT'S BAD ENOUGH YOU LEARNED HOW TO RING THE DOORBELL. DID YOU HAVE TO TEACH EVERY CAT IN THE NEIGHBORHOOD?!
picklescomic@sbcglobal.net
© 2007 Brian Crane, dist. by The Washington Post Writers Group
BRIAN CRANE 2/4

PICKLES
by BRIAN CRANE
WHY ARE YOU STARING AT ME LIKE THAT?
NO REASON.
YOU EVER NOTICE HOW IF YOU STARE AT SOMEONE'S FACE FOR A WHILE IT STARTS TO LOOK SORT OF WEIRD?
EVEN IF IT'S A TOTALLY FAMILIAR FACE, IT STARTS TO LOOK REALLY GOOFY AND STRANGE.
picklescomic@sbcglobal.net
© 2007 Brian Crane, dist. by The Washington Post Writers Group
2/18
YOU EVER NOTICE IF YOU LOOK AT HIM ON HIS BACK LIKE THAT HE LOOKS LIKE A DEAD BUG?

298

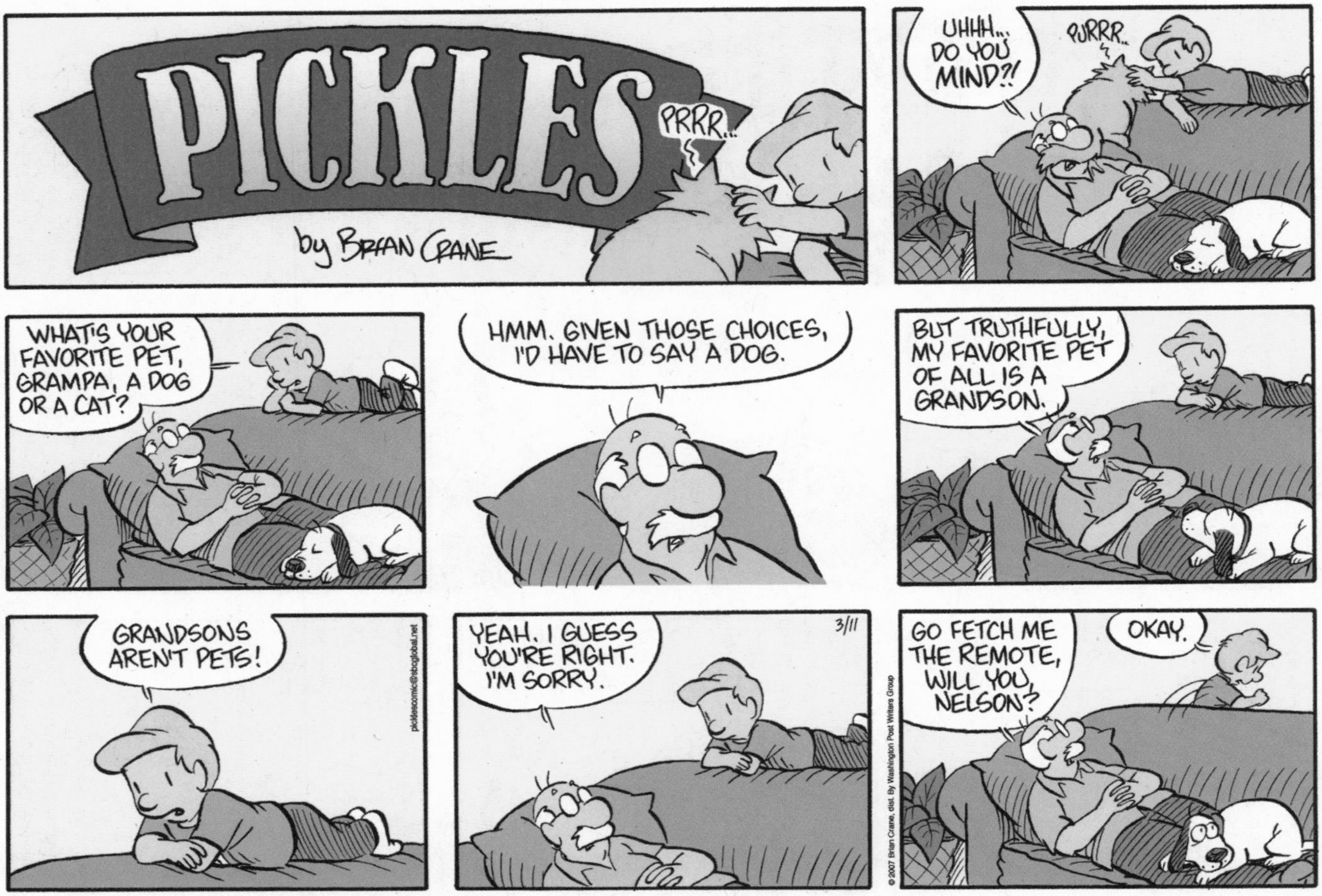
PICKLES
by BRIAN CRANE
PRRR...
UHHH... DO YOU MIND?!
PURRR...
WHAT'S YOUR FAVORITE PET, GRAMPA, A DOG OR A CAT?
HMM. GIVEN THOSE CHOICES, I'D HAVE TO SAY A DOG.
BUT TRUTHFULLY, MY FAVORITE PET OF ALL IS A GRANDSON.
GRANDSONS AREN'T PETS!
picklescomic@sbcglobal.net
YEAH. I GUESS YOU'RE RIGHT. I'M SORRY.
3/11
GO FETCH ME THE REMOTE, WILL YOU, NELSON?
OKAY.
© 2007 Brian Crane, dist. By Washington Post Writers Group

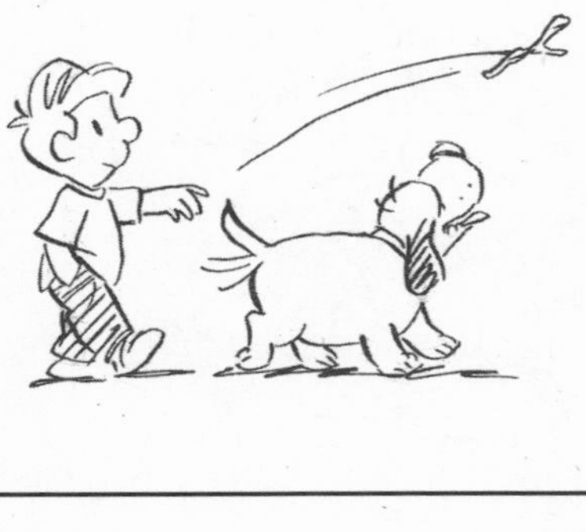

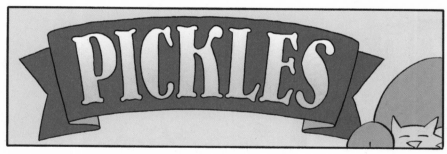

PICKLES
WHERE'VE YOU BEEN, OPAL?
WRAPPING A MOTHER'S DAY PRESENT.
WHO'S THE PRESENT FOR?
IT'S A MOTHER'S DAY GIFT FOR MUFFIN.
A MOTHER'S DAY PRESENT FOR THE CAT?! ISN'T THAT A LITTLE RIDICULOUS?
NO. SHE'S A MOTHER. SHE DID HAVE A LITTER OF KITTENS.
SO WHAT'S NEXT? A FATHER'S DAY GIFT FOR ROSCOE?
OH, WAIT. YOU GOT "FIXED" BEFORE YOU HAD A CHANCE TO...
SORRY ABOUT THAT, BIG GUY.
NICE GOING, MR. SENSITIVE.
picklescomic@sbcglobal.net
5/13
© 2007 Brian Crane, dist. By Washington Post Writers Group

299

PICKLES
by BRIAN CRANE
SNIFF SNAFF
SNIFF SNEEF
SNORF SNARF
DO YOU SMELL THAT?
UH HUH!
OOH! CINNA-MON ROLLS!
THEY'RE FOR THE CHURCH SOCIAL.
DON'T TOUCH THOSE CINNAMON ROLLS! GOD IS WATCHING!
picklescomic@sbcglobal.net
HEY, LOOK... A PIE! SHALL WE HAVE SOME?
WON'T WE GET IN TROUBLE?
DON'T WORRY. GOD'S WATCHING THE CINNAMON ROLLS.
© 2007 Brian Crane, dist. By Washington Post Writers Group
10/14

PICKLES
by BRIAN CRANE
AHH...
AHHCHOO!
WHY ARE YOU REWINDING?
CLICK!
I MISSED SOME OF THE SHOW WHEN I SNEEZED.
picklescomic@sbcglobal.net
LET ME SEE THAT THING.
© 2007 Brian Crane, dist. By Washington Post Writers Group
WHAT ARE YOU DOING?
REWINDING. I BLINKED AND MISSED A MILLISECOND.
CLICK!
GIVE ME THAT REMOTE!
THIS IS WHY I DON'T WATCH TV WITH GRAMMA AND GRAMPA.
10/28
BRIAN CRANE

PICKLES
by BRIAN CRANE
SNIFF SNIFF
PYEW! YOU'VE GOT BAD BREATH, EARL!
REALLY? I BRUSHED MY TEETH.
I DIDN'T WANT TO SAY ANYTHING, BUT YOU SMELL LIKE YOU COULD USE A SHOWER.
picklescomic@sbcglobal.net
I TOOK ONE THIS MORNING!
© 2007 Brian Crane, dist. By Washington Post Writers Group
STUPID DOG!
THEY BOTH SMELL FINE TO ME.
11/18

Brian Crane's *Pickles* is syndicated in over 900 newspapers worldwide. He has been nominated three times for the Outstanding Cartoonist of the Year award by the National Cartoonists Society and won the award in 2013. As of the printing of the first edition of this book, *Pickles* is once again in the running for the National Cartoonist Society's Best Comic Strip of the Year, a prestigious award that the strip has been nominated for twice before, and that it won in 2001, and again in 2019. Crane lives in Sparks, Nevada, with his wife and family, which consists of seven children and twenty-one grandchildren.

ACKNOWLEDGMENTS

I would like to express my gratitude to Baobab Press for their valuable contributions in bringing this collection into publication, and to my editors at the Washington Post Writers Group, Amy Lago and Ann Topor, for making sure all my T's are dotted and my I's are crossed. Or is it the other way around? Thanks also to my sweet wife, Diana, without whose support and encouragement the characters in this tome would still be just scribbles in my sketch book.